SPY BOOK

BOOK

THE ENCYCLOPEDIA OF ESPIONAGE

SPY BOOK

THE ENCYCLOPEDIA OF ESPIONAGE

NORMAN POLMAR & THOMAS B. ALLEN

FOREWORD BY NIGEL WEST

second edition

RANDOM HOUSE
REFERENCE

New York   Toronto   London   Sydney   Aukland

SPY BOOK: The Encyclopedia of Espionage, 2nd Edition

Copyright © 2004, 1998, 1997 by Norman Polmar and Thomas B. Allen

All rights reserved under International and Pan-American Copyright Conventions. No part of this book may be reproduced in any form or by any means, electronic or mechanical, including photocopying, without the written permission of the publisher. All inquiries should be addressed to Random House Reference, Random House, Inc., New York, NY. Published in the United States by Random House, Inc., New York and simultaneously in Canada by Random House of Canada Limited.

Random House is a registered trademark of Random House, Inc.
This work was originally published in hardcover by Random House, Inc. in 1997.

This book is available for special discounts for bulk purchases for sales promotions or premiums. Special editions, including personalized covers, excerpts of existing books, and corporate imprints, can be created in large quantities for special needs. For more information, write to Special Markets/ Premium Sales, 1745 Broadway, MD 6-2, New York, NY, 10019 or e-mail specialmarkets@randomhouse.com.

Please address inquiries about electronic licensing of reference products, for use on a network or in software or on CD-ROM, to the Subsidiary Rights Department, Random House Reference, fax 212-572-6003.

Visit the Random House Reference Web site: www.randomwords.com.

Typeset and printed in the United States of America.

ISBN: 0-375-72025-1

Library of Congress Cataloging-in-Publication data is available.

0 9 8 7 6 5 4 3 2 1

CONTENTS

FOREWORD

Over the years there have been several attempts to produce encyclopedias of espionage, and the authors have encountered three problems. Firstly, there has been the inherent difficulty of the authenticity of the information gleaned in a field notorious for misinformation, deception, and sheer invention. Secondly, there is the obstacle course of writing about topics that at some stage have been classified, leaving some doubt about how much can be revealed about particularly sensitive operations; and finally, there is the challenge of providing the most up-to-date data in a field where there is probably more relevant material being released from official sources, often on intelligence-related subjects, than in any other area of field of research.

I know the pitfalls because in the distant past I have worked for two authors who made good stabs at encapsulating what was then in the public domain in this specialist area into manageable compendiums, but these neither compete nor come anywhere close to achieving the comprehensive nature and intrinsic accuracy of this updated edition of *Spy Book*.

Norman Polmar and Thomas B. Allen are universally acknowledged and respected as leaders in the genre. Polmar and Allen write not just for the *cognoscenti,* but possess the enviable skill of making complex subjects easy to understand for both the professional and the non-*aficionado*. Quite simply, they know the cases, they know the people who ran the cases, and know people who know people! The business of intelligence collection is a veritable minefield of half-truths, spin, mixed-motives, and outright duplicity, with experts often disagreeing over the most fundamental matters. Few publications are reliable, but this is one of them.

Nigel West
London

A PERSPECTIVE ON SPYING

Espionage—long considered the world's second oldest profession—is practiced today with an almost unprecedented fervor. Terrorists who have vowed to bring down the United States—their Great Satan—are spying out U.S. government, military, and industrial targets. American troops entering Afghanistan and Iraq were supported by a host of high-tech spy devices as well as by people on the ground, Americans, British, and Iraqis, who were engaged in spying and intelligence collection. Russian "illegals" under diplomatic cover in Washington are still spying on America. And Israeli is keeping watch on a half-dozen Arab states, using human agents and spy satellites.

When the Soviet Union collapsed at the end of 1991, there was a general assumption that spy activities in the West and East would also collapse. But soon a new enemy emerged for the West: Islamic fundamentalists had declared a *jihad*—a holy war against the West, in particular the United State. To those jihad terrorists, the World Trade Center towers in New York City symbolized the wealth and the power of the West. In Feb. 1993, they attempted to bring it down with a truck laden with explosives in an underground garage; the towers stood, but 10 people died and more than 1,000 were injured. Few Americans in 1993 realized that a new war was already underway. Murderous acts of jihad terrorism would claim American lives in Saudi Arabia; in U.S. embassies in Africa, on the destroyer *Cole*. Still, to most Americans—and to many counter-terrorism authorities in the West, it was not a *real* war. Random terrorist acts were the price of doing business in a violent world.

Then came Sept. 11, 2001. The World Trade Center towers did come down this time, as did a large segment of the Pentagon building in northern Virginia, the headquarters of the U.S. defense establishment. Thousands of Americans died, and at last America realized it was at war.

For this kind of war, the United States mustered warriors and spies as well as a phalanx of intelligence collectors and analysts. At the forefront of this new war is the U.S. Intelligence Community and the intelligence agencies of several other nations, especially Britain, France, and Israel. In the years, months, and weeks before Sept. 11 there had been blunders, failed recognition of enemy plans, and a failure of coordination between U.S. intelligence agencies. To people with long memories, all of this had happened before, when the enemy was Japan and its target was the U.S. Fleet at Pearl Harbor, Hawaii. America had lost the first battle, had learned painful new lessons, and had gone on to win that war.

In the war on terrorism, however, there could be no quick or easy victory. There would be only resolve and frustration, deaths of innocents and deaths of shadowy killers. This would be a war whose history would be almost impossible to write because so much would happen that could not be seen or recorded. And, like the behind-the-scenes intelligence campaigns of World Wars I and II, this new war on terrorism would also have many layers of intelligence, espionage, counter-espionage, and secret activities—to use a cliché, but an accurate one, a "wilderness of mirrors."

The war on terrorism is the latest chapter in the long, often hidden history of spying. And how old is that history? The late Walter L. Pforzheimer, a veteran of the U.S. Central Intelligence Agency and a premier collector of intelligence books and manuscripts, traced espionage to the Garden of Eden. As he told it, the satanic serpent was an enemy agent operating under the cover of a reptile, who enlisted Eve as an intelligence asset to destabilize the relationship between God and the Garden of Eden. Elsewhere in the Bible, Joseph accuses his brothers of being spies when they come into Egypt and fail to recognize the pharaoh's first minister as their sibling. And after the Jews had left Egypt in the Exodus and were wandering in the Sinai Desert, Moses sent princes from each of the 12 tribes to spy out the Promised Land.

Archaeologists have unearthed a sunbaked clay tablet in Syria, written in the 18th century B.C., that shows how old is the idea of using spies as pawns. The inscription, from one ruler of a city-state to another, complains that spies have been released for ransom but that payment has not come. The ultimate fate of those spies is not known.

Since ancient times the rulers of China and Japan have employed espionage as a tool of statecraft. Sometimes in the East spying had a special twist, with deception becoming at least as important as intelligence gathering. Confucius, a fundamental source of Chinese teaching since the 6th century B.C., said, "Confronting a foreign invasion, one should resort to deception, which may suffice in repelling the enemy."

Sun-Tzu, the renowned Chinese general, writing *Ping-fa* (*The Art of War*) in the same century, saw intelligence as a major weapon in war: "If you know the enemy and know yourself, you need not fear a hundred battles. If you know yourself and not the enemy, for every victory you will suffer a defeat. If you know neither yourself nor the enemy, you are a fool and will meet defeat in every battle." (Sun-Tzu's writings were still required reading for Japanese military officers in 1941, when their Navy was planning the sneak attack on the U.S. Fleet at Pearl Harbor.)

Records of the Roman Empire relate that Antonius, a Roman official, defected in A.D. 358 , taking with him troop dispositions. A Roman soldier who deserted to the Persians soon returned to the Roman Army—to spy for the Persians as a double agent. The Byzantine emperor Justin II, given solid intelligence about the defenses of a besieged city, ignored the information, a familiar lament of intelligence officers today.

An Arab official, writing in the 11th century, observed that kings send ambassadors not only for purposes of diplomacy but also for espionage, to try secretly to learn about "the state of the roads, mountain passes, rivers, and grazing grounds . . . what is the size of the king's army and how well it is armed and equipped." They also seek out information about the king: whether he drinks, whether he is "strict in religious matters . . . and does he prefer boys or women."

In Japan's early history, intelligence gatherers included astrologers, practitioners of numerology, and experts in austromancy, divination through study of the winds. By the 12th century A.D., when warlords reigned in Japan, espionage relied less on supernatural or occult means and more on informers. The Japanese empire, wrote a Western historian, "was one network of espionage . . . the fundamental principle of that system of government was suspicion." A spy drawn from the noble samurai class was a ninja, "a samurai who mastered the art of making himself invisible through some artifice and chiefly engaged in espionage."

In England domestic spying evolved into foreign espionage under Sir Francis Walsingham, Secretary of State and adviser to Queen Elizabeth I. Walsingham—whose motto was "Knowledge is never too dear"—built up an extensive intelligence organization in England for activities aimed mainly against Catholics. Although acting with the backing of the Queen, Walsingham financed his espionage operations privately. In 1573 he began developing a foreign intelligence organization that ran agents in France, Germany, Italy, the Low Countries, Spain, and Turkey. He even penetrated some foreign courts. Walsingham, like many of the agents he recruited, was educated at Cambridge University—where, centuries later, Soviet intelligence agencies would also recruit what became known as the Cambridge spy ring.

In the American colonies, Gen. George Washington quickly learned the craft of the spymaster, using espionage and deception to outwit the British. Maj. George Beckwith, the head of British intelligence operations in the Colonies at the end of the Revolutionary War, later wrote: "Washington did not really outfight the British, he simply outspied us!"

By the 1800s the major nations engaged in international commerce began seeing the need for official, permanent state intelligence agencies. In France, Napoléon Bonaparte created a secret police organization whose primary task was the clandestine opening of mail. In Britain, where the government had long opened domestic and foreign mail, the Special Branch of the London Metropolitan Police was set up to investigate internal subversion and crimes committed by domestic and foreign terrorists. In the United States the Office of Naval Intelligence was established in 1882 as the first permanent U.S. agency to collect information on the military affairs of foreign governments.

In 1909, Britain's Committee of Imperial Defence established the Secret Service Bureau, precursor to Britain's Security Service (MI5) and Secret Intelligence Service (MI6). Britain's intelligence apparatus became the model for similar organizations set up by other nations of the West. As Queen Elizabeth I backed Walsingham's intelligence activities when her crown was in danger, so did a later British leader, Winston Churchill, give unstinting support to the country's intelligence and cryptologic agencies when the empire was in danger, declaring in 1940: "The great thing is to get the true picture, whatever it is."

Each nation has its own policies related to the operation of an intelligence system, but certain elements of tradecraft are common to all. Espionage is an old, conservative occupation, handed down through the generations by spies who "come in from the cold" to teach tradecraft at spy schools. Techniques do not change that much from decade to decade.

Most spying is prosaic, not romantic. There have been few glamorous spies, such as the real Mata Hari (who was more naive than dangerous). Even in fiction, the characters who most reflect reality are not Ian Fleming's James Bond but John le Carré's George Smiley and Alec Leamas. As le Carré wrote, "A man who, like Smiley, has lived and worked for years among his country's enemies learns only one prayer: that he may never, never be noticed."

All over the world, most "spies" are merely intelligence agency employees who are looking for very ordinary data. Most of the information that Soviet master spy Rudolf Abel sent to Moscow came from *The New York Times* and *Scientific American*. British historian A. J. P. Taylor once said that 90 percent of the information produced by intelligence agencies can be found in public sources. Sherman Kent, an American historian who became an intelligence officer in the Central Intelligence Agency (CIA), increased that estimate to possibly 95 percent for U.S. information because of the openness of U.S. society.

To prove his point, Kent once commissioned five Yale historians to prepare a report on the U.S. order of battle—military strength and units, down to the division level, along with naval and air strength and descriptions of military aircraft, without using any classified sources. At the end of a summer's work, the scholars gave Kent several hundred pages of information, accompanied by a 30-page summary. Kent estimated that the report was about 90 percent accurate. (The CIA placed in secure files all copies of what became known as the Yale Report.)

Governments seek secret information to eliminate uncertainty in the conducting of foreign affairs or to gain an advantage over other countries. By cracking the Japanese diplomatic code, the United States could deal more certainly with Japan, especially in negotiating the Washington Naval Treaty of 1922. By using a spy under diplomatic cover in Hawaii, the Japanese Navy could learn what U.S. Navy ships were in Pearl Harbor as they developed their plan for a sneak attack.

But codebreaking and spying can never reveal all. The U.S. government, with virtually full access to Japanese diplomatic ciphers, did not know that the Japanese were going to launch the sneak attack on Pearl Harbor, while the Japanese did not know that there were no aircraft carriers—the most important naval targets—in Pearl Harbor on Dec. 7, 1941. Nor did high-level FBI officials pay attention to an alert employee who urged a widespread investigation into why so many young Middle Eastern immigrants were taking flying lessons; only after Sept. 11, 2001, did the FBI discover why those men were taking those lessons. The FBI could take cold comfort in the fact that raw information is never enough, and it is often wrong, especially when taken out of context.

Countries must not only collect information, they must also collate and evaluate it—which makes it intelligence—and then they must know not only how to use it but whether to use it at all. Soviet dictator Josef Stalin believed the report of his master spy Richard Sorge that the Japanese would not attack the Soviet Union in 1941. And this crucial intelligence permitted Stalin to move some divisions from the Far East to fight the German Army when Germany invaded the Soviet Union on June 22, 1941. But when Sorge, and other intelligence sources, warned of that invasion two months before it occurred, Stalin dismissed the warning. Why? Because Stalin believed that warnings from the British were really provocations to force him into a war with Germany. And he distrusted his own intelligence officers (several hundred of whose colleagues he had murdered during the previous few years). National leaders, particularly dictators, usually place ultimate trust in their own judgment and not that of their spies and intelligence chiefs, unless these intelligence evaluations happen to coincide with their own preconceptions.

The Soviet Union collapsed in 1991, unable to continue a transition into the modern, high-tech world without radical and—for the Soviet regime—devastating change. Still, the Soviet intelligence organs, with both domestic and foreign orientation, do continue to exist, albeit with new names. To some degree they also have new "faces"—postage stamps honoring spies are issued, a compact disk is produced with a history of the KGB, and the museum in the Lubyanka "house of horror," long headquarters (and execution place) for Soviet intelligence agencies, is open to tour groups.

Sometimes, too, intelligence does not get to the right place at the right time. U.S. intelligence collected in Bosnia in the summer of 1995 showed that the Bosnian Serbs had recently installed surface-to-air missiles in an area where U.S. aircraft were flying patrols. But that intelligence was not speedily passed on to the U.S. air commanders who were planning those patrols. Thus, when U.S. Air Force Captain Scott O'Grady flew an F-16 fighter over the area, he was not accompanied by specialized aircraft that could detect and jam the missile guidance radars. A totally unexpected missile struck O'Grady's aircraft. He survived. But he had almost been killed because intelligence was not delivered to the right place at the right time.

By 2003, with the U.S.–British campaign against organized terrorism two years old, Western intelligence and counterintelligence officials were adjusting to this new war. Part of that adjustment involved the need to publicly speak about secrets. There are few communiqués in the war on terrorism. But there are many leaks and many attempts by political leaders to place blame for bad news on the intelligence messengers who bring information that does not fit the latest policy or initiative.

Spy Book seeks to describe spies, their tradecraft, the agencies they work for, and the acts of espionage that they have performed. In the almost 4,000 years since the first mention of spies in the Old Testament, many thousands of men and women have spied and worked at breaking into others' communications; many hundreds of spymasters and case officers have directed their efforts; and scores of intelligence agencies have served dozens of nations. From this multitude we have chosen those we believe have had the most influence on world events, as well as those we felt were the most interesting.

Thus, our entries range from the very well known spymasters such as Moses and Gen. George Washington, to the virtually unknown "Cookie Lady" of Saigon and the Dog Skin Report from a French agent. From the short-lived Bureau of Information in the American Civil War to the enduring U.S. Office of Naval Intelligence and the new, untested intelligence staff of the Department of Homeland Security. From the scytale, the secret writing used by the Spartans, to today's spy satellites and Predator drones. From Mata Hari, who is not known to have ever garnered any useful bits of intelligence, to Soviet Colonel Oleg Penkovsky, whose reports had a critical impact on President Kennedy's actions during both the Berlin Crisis of 1961 and the Cuban Missile Crisis of 1962, the two occasions when the United States and Soviet Union came close to nuclear conflict. From the treachery of Benedict Arnold in the Revolution to the treachery of Robert Hanssen, the FBI agent who was 20 years a spy for the Soviets and Russians.

In preparing the manuscript for *Spy Book,* we had to make some difficult decisions about what not to include. We have sought to include what we consider the most important *and* the most interesting people, agencies, operations, terms, and tradecraft. It would have been beyond the realm of possibility to include "everything"—even "everything" that is publicly known about the world of espionage and its related themes.

We began working on this edition of *Spy Book* when the Cold War was fading away and the war on terrorism was still undeclared. In this new war, there were still records and chronicles to pour over, still issues to discuss, off the record, with contemporary practitioners and historians. With the aid of such sources we have produced this new edition, taking the reader into the 21st century and into this new era of the intelligence of terrorism.

This book exists because we were drawn to an art that few historians bother with, even though espionage and counterespionage have been the keys to many historical events. We wrote this book in the belief that a knowledge of how intelligence works makes those who read it better able to understand both history and contemporary events. In undertaking this effort, we decided to use an encyclopedic format because we believe that "looking it up" involves the reader in a personal intelligence collection effort.

Many of the entries in this book describe people and organizations that lie and deceive. We did our best to get to the truth, by interpreting the self-serving claims in the memoirs of spies and spymasters, and by sifting through the exaggerated claims of intelligence services to discern their real accomplishments—and failures. Luckily, we often had access to previously unavailable archival sources, for as the Cold War ebbed, the CIA, the FBI, the National Security Agency (NSA), and the KGB began to open their files. The NSA—the "ears" of U.S. intelligence—released enlightening intercepts of the 1940s, the first of some 60 million NSA documents scheduled for declassification.

Between 1993 and 1997, the CIA made public more than 450 National Intelligence Estimates dealing with the Soviet Union and international communism, considered among the agency's most sensitive documents—not only because they contained secret intelligence but also because they often revealed intelligence failures and blunders. In 1997 the CIA also released 208 documents of equal sensitivity, such as daily and weekly intelligence summaries that went to the President between 1946 and 1950. And in a new outburst of revelations, in 1997 the new Director of Central Intelligence, George J. Tenet, revealed that the total U.S. intelligence budget for 1996 was $26.6 billion. This was the first official disclosure of the budget. "I know now the world has changed,"

Tenet said. Subsequently, he declared budgets secret.

The world changed again in 2001 and many filing drawers slammed shut, many Freedom of Information Act requests went unanswered. But even as intelligence agencies turned away from revelations in the post–Sept. 11, 2001, world, scrutiny of the agencies increased. The Inspector General of the Justice Department, for instance, made public significant portions of its scathing critique of the FBI's failure to spot Hanssen as a long-term spy. Similarly, the White House declassified portions of an intelligence report produced in the weeks leading to the U.S. invasion of Iraq.

The pages made public showed that U.S. intelligence community had a great deal of information and (to quote a phrase often used by commentators), if "the dots had been connected," there would have been sufficient warning. As you can see from reading the Pearl Harbor Attack entry in this book, there are always many "dots" found *after* a catastrophe and it is always possible to "connect" them *afterward*. Investigations and commissions will be looking at the Sept. 11 "dots" for a long time to come, but they will likely find no one to blame.

We know there are still many secrets in the secret world, many intelligence triumphs (and debacles) not yet revealed. For example, the most important Allied intelligence successes of World War II were the codebreaking efforts Ultra and Magic. But from the early 1930s until the early 1970s a veil of secrecy was drawn over these codebreaking activities even though several thousand Americans and Britons—and a few Poles and Frenchmen—knew the secrets. Only after four decades did the keepers of the secrets reveal most—but still not all—of the Ultra and Magic intercepts.

Venona is the code word for the U.S. intercept of Soviet espionage communications that began early in World War II. The intercepts revealed a vast Soviet espionage endeavor to get U.S. military secrets, especially information on the atomic bomb project. In 1996, Venona intercepts unmasked Americans who had spied for the Soviet Union. The Venona messages have still not been fully deciphered or fully revealed. There was still in 2003 a debate on whether President Truman had been "cleared" so he could learn of the Verona disclosures!

When the 21st century replaced the Cold War with the war on terrorism, Western political leaders put new demands on the intelligence agencies that serve them—and sometimes thwart them. Inevitably, there were reorganizations of existing agencies and plans for new ones. People asked, How much intelligence is needed? There was an old answer, which suddenly sounded new. It came from Sun-Tzu: "A hundred ounces of silver spent for information may save ten thousand spent on war."

NORMAN POLMAR
THOMAS B. ALLEN

For updates, go to our website at www.spybook.org

HOW TO USE THIS BOOK

Individuals are listed alphabetically by last names. Similarly, pseudonyms of real people are alphabetized by their last name, followed by [p]. Thus, David Cornwall, who is much better known as John le Carré, is listed as le Carré, John [p]. But fictional characters are listed by their complete fictional names; thus, James Bond is under J, not B, with an [f] for fictional following the name.

U.S. organizations are generally listed by their full names on their first appearance in an entry, followed by their abbreviated form in parentheses. In the case of the CIA (Central Intelligence Agency), FBI (Federal Bureau of Investigation), and NSA (National Security Agency), and certain other intelligence organizations we have judged the abbreviations sufficiently familiar to dispense with the spelled-out version. In the case of foreign organizations, for example the KGB, we have generally used only the abbreviated form, followed when relevant by the spelled-out name in the original language, with the English translation in parentheses.

The abbreviations that are considered "entries" appear in the Glossary that follows this section.

Spy Book: The Encyclopedia of Espionage also has entries on several countries, presenting their history in terms of their intelligence agencies and activities:

China
England-Great Britain-United Kingdom
France
Germany
Israel
Japan
Russia-USSR
United States

Cuba, Iraq, and Vietnam are also entries because these countries became major intelligence targets of other countries. However, as countries are mentioned in numerous entries, they are ordinarily not shown in small capitals, except where we believe that a specific cross-reference would be valuable to the reader.

Because espionage, intelligence, and spies are deeply rooted in most cultures, they are reflected in a variety of aspects of national life. These include literary spies, spies in comics, movies, and television, and a few heroes who appear on postage stamps, all of which topics find a place in this book.

We suggest that readers begin using *Spy Book* by turning to a specific country entry and then to its intelligence agencies, checking cross-references that appear in the master entries. This approach will quickly provide leads to enjoying the book as a chronicle of espionage. To explore espionage further, however, the reader may also have to depend on intuition, which is what spies and their spymasters often must do. "Espionage," as Peter Wright wrote in *Spycatcher*, "is a crime almost devoid of evidence, which is why intuition, for better or worse, always has a large part to play in its successful detection."

Deceit is so much a part of espionage that writing about spies involves a great deal of sorting fact from fiction—or from deliberate disinformation. "The very nature of espionage makes it a difficult subject to research and it is often well nigh impossible to establish exactly what took place during a particular event," according to *A Thread of Deceit*, a book on "espionage myths of World War II" written by Rupert Allason, a former Conservative member of Parliament. A leading authority on

British intelligence, he writes under the pen name Nigel West.

Relatively few accounts of individual spies or intelligence operations stand up to accepted standards of historical research. And relatively few of them had a significant impact on the wars or political decisions in question. This is not to denigrate the importance of such activities as Royal Navy codebreaking in World War I (Room 40) or U.S.–British codebreaking in World War II (Purple-Ultra); or such operations as the dispatch of spies into the Promised Land by Moses, the Soviet atomic spy ring, Red Orchestra, and Double-Cross System; or individuals such as Dusko Popov, Laurance Safford, Richard Sorge, Fritz Kolbe, and the almost legendary members of the Cambridge spy ring.

The importance and effectiveness of specific intelligence agencies have varied (see Abwehr, GRU, CIA, KGB, MI5, MI6, NKVD, NSA, Gestapo, Office of Strategic Services). Some—such as the KGB, NKVD, and Gestapo—were equally or more concerned with internal police-control activities than with foreign intelligence or even counterintelligence operations.

The words *espionage, intelligence,* and *spy* are not listed as entries in the book because of their universal presence. We define these as follows:

ESPIONAGE (1) Intelligence activity directed toward the acquisition of information through clandestine means; (2) clandestine intelligence collection.

INTELLIGENCE Information that has been collected, collated, and analyzed and a body of evidence and the conclusions drawn therefrom, which is acquired and furnished in response to the known or perceived requirements of consumers (as intended recipients of intelligence are known).

SPY A person employed by a government or other entity to obtain secret information or intelligence about another, usually hostile, entity. (The word is rarely used by intelligence professionals, who usually refer to them as agents.)

Enjoy!

GLOSSARY

The following organizations are used as *prime entries* in this book.

BCRA   Central Bureau for Information and Action (France)

BfV   Agency for Constitutional Protection (Germany)

BND   Federal Intelligence Agency (Germany)

BTLC   Technical Bureau for Liaison and Coordination (France)

CIA   Central Intelligence Agency (United States)

CPUSA   Communist Party of the United States of America

DST   Directorate for Surveillance of the Territory (France)

GRU   Military Intelligence (USSR-Russia)

KGB   Committee for State Security (USSR)

MFS   Stasi (East Germany)

MI5   Security Service (Britain)

MI6   Secret Intelligence Service (Britain)

MSS   Ministry of State Security (China)

NKVD   People's Commissariat for Internal Affairs (USSR)

NSA   National Security Agency (United States)

RSHA   Reich Central Security Office (Germany)

SOE   Special Operations Executive (Britain)

ACKNOWLEDGMENTS

Much of what we have written in *Spy Book: The Encyclopedia of Espionage* is based on government records, published books and articles, private correspondence and other papers, court documents (for some of the most recent espionage operations), and lectures and presentations at intelligence conferences. We have also interviewed individuals involved in espionage and intelligence activities. The help provided by some of those individuals cannot be acknowledged in this book. They know who they are, and we thank them.

Those individuals whom we cite with an asterisk in the following list provided material used in an earlier book on espionage that we wrote, *Merchants of Treason* (1988), which was a source for some entries in this book. Several of those individuals kindly provided additional information that is entirely new for *Spy Book*.

FRANCE
    Alexander Sheldon-Duplaix, naval historian

GREAT BRITAIN
    W. J. R. (Jock) Gardner, historian, Naval Historical Branch, Royal Navy
    Lionel Leventhal, publisher, Greenhill Books, Ltd.
    John W. R. Taylor, editor emeritus, *Jane's All the World's Aircraft*
    Nigel West, leading intelligence historian
    Bletchley Park Museum
    Imperial War Museum
    Public Record Office (now part of the British National Archives)

ISRAEL
    Maj. Gen. Meir Amit, former head of the Mossad and Shin Bet
    Maj. Gen. Chaim Herzog, former head of Aman and former President of Israel
    Center for Special Studies
    Israel Defense Forces Spokesman's Office

JAPAN
    Professor Munehiro Miwa, Kyushu Kyoritsu University
    Rear Adm. Tadashi Tajiri, president, Historical Research Institute

NETHERLANDS
    Jurrien Noot, historian

RUSSIA
    Yuri Kobaladze, Russian Intelligence Service
    Conference on the Cuban Missile Crisis sponsored by the Russian Federation Archives, Moscow, September 1994, KGB Museum, Moscow
    Russian Federation Archives

UNITED STATES
    David Battis, industrial security expert*
    Gary Bauer, former domestic counselor to President Reagan*
    Rear Adm. Thomas A. Brooks, USN, Director of Naval Intelligence
    Neill Brown, special agent, Federal Bureau of Investigation*
    Kathleen A. Buck, former general counsel of the Air Force and general counsel of the Department of Defense*

Bernard F. Cavalcante, Naval History Center (U.S. Navy), and his most able assistants Kathy Lloyd and Ella Nargele

Capt. William C. Chapman, USN (Ret.), naval aviator, planner, and analyst

Senator and Secretary of Defense William S. Cohen*

Col. George Connell, USMC, former Deputy Commander Naval Investigative Service*

Judge A. Jay Cristol, Capt. USNR (Ret.), author of *The Liberty Incident*

John Dion, chief of the Espionage Prosecution Unit, Internal Security Section, Department of Justice*

Robert F. Dorr, aviation historian

Dr. Edward Drea, chief, Research and Analysis Division, Center of Military History (U.S. Army)

Stuart Eisen, expert on Col. Thomas E. Lawrence (Lawrence of Arabia)

Capt. C. Dale Everhart, USN (Ret.), former naval intelligence officer*

William (Buck) Farmer, assistant U.S. attorney, principal prosecutor at the Jerry Whitworth trial*

Robert M. Gates, former Director of Central Intelligence*

William W. Geimer, Washington lawyer and founder of the Jamestown Foundation, which provided support for defectors from the Soviet Union and Eastern Europe*

Dr. Jeffrey Greenhut, historian, Naval Security Group

Dr. Richard P. Hallion, chief historian of the Air Force

Joseph Harried, executive vice president, the Atlantic Council*

U.S. District Court judge Alexander Harvey*

David A. Hatch, director, Center for Cryptologic History

Richard Haver, former Deputy Director of Naval Intelligence and senior member of the Intelligence Community Staff

Thomas Henley, former Central Intelligence Agency officer*

Jack Ingram, director, National Cryptologic Museum

David Kahn, historian and the distinguished visiting historian at the Center for Cryptologic History, National Security Agency

Vice Adm. Robert Kirksey, USN (Ret.), former

director, Navy Command, Control, and Communications*

Suzanne Wheeler Klein, public affairs, Central Intelligence Agency

John Lehman, Secretary of the Navy*

Dr. Carolyn Mackenzie, psychiatrist*

Clark Magruder, former Deputy Director of Naval Intelligence"

Robert F. Muse, attorney for Samuel L. Morison*

Ambassador Paul H. Nitze, former Secretary of the Navy and presidential adviser

Alan Plait, electronics maven

Ernest Porter, public affairs office, Federal Bureau of Investigation*

Gary Powers, founder of the Cold War Museum

Dr. Diane Putney, Air Force and Department of Defense historian

J. Stephen Ramey, special agent, Federal Bureau of Investigation*

Dr. Jeffrey Richelson, intelligence historian

Ray Robinson, former analyst with the Central Intelligence Agency and Defense Intelligence Agency

Dr. Frank (Micky) Schubert, historian, Joint Chiefs of Staff

Robert Sinclair, former Central Intelligence Agency officer

Adm. William O. Studeman, former director, National Security Agency and Deputy Director of Central Intelligence

David Szady, special agent, Federal Bureau of Investigation*

John Taylor, historian, National Archives

Capt. Vincent Thomas, USN (Ret.), former Navy public affairs officer involved in a number of intelligence projects, including the USS *Pueblo**

Tina D. Thompson, editor, TRW *Space Log*

Howard J. Varinsky, trial behavior consultant who served in that role for the defense in the Jerry Whitworth trial*

Senator John Warner*

Michael Warner, senior historian, Center for the Study of Intelligence (Central Intelligence Agency)

R. James Woolsey, former Director of Central Intelligence

Jerome Zeifman, former counsel for the House Judiciary Committee who served as a post-trial attorney for Ronald L. Humphrey*

Center for Air Force History (U.S. Air Force)

Center for Cryptologic History (National Security Agency)

Center of Military History (U.S. Army)

Center for the Study of Intelligence (Central Intelligence Agency)

Cold War International History Project, Woodrow Wilson International Center for Scholars, Washington, D.C.

Conference on Cold War Overflights, 1950-1956, sponsored by the Joint Military Intelligence College, Bolling Air Force Base, Washington, D.C., Feb. 2001

Conference on Corona: America's First Reconnaissance Satellite, sponsored by the Central Intelligence Agency and George Washington University, Washington, D.C., May 1995

Conference on Intelligence and National Security in Peace, Crisis, and War, sponsored by the Central Intelligence Agency and Society for Military History, Rosslyn, Va., April 1996

Conference on the Origin and Development of the CIA in the Administration of Harry S. Truman, sponsored by the Central Intelligence Agency and Harry S. Truman Library Institute, Maclean, Va., March 1994

Cryptologic History Symposium, sponsored by the Center for Cryptologic History, National Security Agency, Fort George G. Meade, Md., Oct. 1995

Library of Congress

Museum of the Confederacy (Richmond, Va.)

National Archives

Naval History Center (U.S. Navy)

President's Foreign Intelligence Advisory Board

We also wish to acknowledge general discussions about Soviet intelligence matters with Nicholas Shadron (Nikolai F. Artamonov) and Milan Vego; and general discussions about U.S. intelligence matters with Dr. Ray Cline, former Deputy Director of Central Intelligence; Vice Admiral F. J. (Fritz) Harifinger, USN, Director of Naval Intelligence and later Director of Navy Command, Control, Communications, and Intelligence; Vice Admiral Earl F. (Rex) Rectanus, USN, Director of Naval Intelligence and Deputy Assistant Secretary of Defense for Intelligence; and Vice Admiral E. A. (Al) Burkhalter, USN, former Director of the Intelligence Community Staff.

M'Liz McLendon helped contributed to the project with research, editing, and friendship; Susan March and Maryann Berkowitz undertook research for this project; Constance Allen Witte provided German translations; and our computer gurus and sons, Chris Allen, Roger MacBride Allen, and Michael Polmar, provided technical support, with Roger, a distinguished author in his own right, performing the inevitable last-minute electronic "cutting and pasting."

CHRONOLOGY

c. 1800 b.c.: Joseph's brothers enter Egypt seeking food and are accused of being spies by Joseph, the governor of Egypt, whom they fail to recognize.

c. 1255 b.c.: Led by Moses, the Jews depart Egypt for the Promised Land; Moses and his successor, Joshua, become the first spymasters.

1558 Nov. 17: Elizabeth becomes Queen of England; during her reign (1558–1603) Sir Francis Walsingham will operate a major espionage network on her behalf.

1775 June 15: Continental Congress gives George Washington command of the colonial forces in America. He will serve as his own spymaster.

1776 Dec. 26: Battle of Trenton; Washington, after crossing Delaware River, wins his first major victory over British forces; the victory has great impact on France's decision to help the Americans.

1781 Oct. 19: The British Army at Yorktown, Va., surrenders after American troops and French fleet defeat the British, ending the American Revolutionary War.

1789 July 14: Parisan artisans storm the Bastille prison in Paris, then begin looting and the seizing of aristocratic property throughout France.

1792 Sept. 22: First Republic proclaimed in France.

1793 Jan. 21: King Louis XVI of France is executed as French Revolution reaches a crescendo.

1804 Dec. 2: Monarchy restored in France when Napoléon Bonaparte declares himself Emperor.

1861 April 12: Confederate guns fire on Fort Sumter in Charleston Harbor, S.C., in the first fighting of the American Civil War.

1863 July 1–3: Federal forces win the battle of Gettysburg. This Pennsylvania battle marks the farthest north that Confederate forces reached during the Civil War.

1865 April 2: Union forces capture the Confederate capital of Richmond, Va.; Gen. U.S. Grant and Gen. Robert E. Lee meet a week later to end the war, although the last Confederate forces will not surrender until May 26.

1865 April 14: President Abraham Lincoln shot by Confederate agent John Wilkes Booth; Lincoln dies next morning.

1898 Feb. 15: U.S. battleship *Maine* is sunk in Havana Harbor, Cuba. The unexplained explosion—probably accidental—will lead to war between the United States and Spain.

1898 May 1: Cdre. George Dewey defeats the Spanish Fleet in Manila Bay in a victory that will give the United States control of the Philippines and Guam.

1914 Aug. 1: Germany declares war on Russia and France, beginning World War I. Britain declares war on Germany on Aug. 4.

1915 May 7: A German U-boat sinks the passenger liner *Lusitania* off the coast of Ireland; 1,195 people, including 128 Americans, die.

1917 Feb. 1: Germany begins unrestricted submarine warfare in the Atlantic. U-boat attacks will be a key factor in the decision of the United States to enter the war.

1917 March 15: Czar Nicholas II resigns in Russia, ending the monarchy; a parliamentary government is established.

1917 April 6: The United States declares war on Germany.

1917 June 15: U.S. Congress passes Espionage Act.

1917 Nov. 7: The Bolsheviks seize power in Petrograd (St. Petersburg), overthrowing the parliamentary government and sparking the Russian Revolution and Civil War.

1918 June: U.S. troops land at Murmansk in Russia, ostensibly to protect war supplies; actually, American, British, French, and Japanese troops are in Russia to help the anti-Bolshevik forces.

1918 Nov. 11: World War I ends with an armistice between Germany and the Allies.

1924 Jan. 21: V. I. Lenin dies; Josef Stalin takes control of the Russian government.

1929: Communist Party of the United States founded.

1936 July 29: Troops of Gen. Francisco Franco are flown from Morocco to Spain in German transport planes, over-flying Republican warships that would have intercepted them had they gone by ship. The Spanish Civil War begins with Germany backing the Nationalist (Franco) forces and the Soviet Union supporting the Republican (Loyalist) forces.

1936 Oct.: Japanese begin campaign to conquer China. Japanese troops seize Shanghai in Nov. 1937 and Nanking in Dec. 1937, committing massive numbers of rapes and murders.

1938: Congress enacts the Smith Act. Americans who advocate radical economic or political ideologies are considered subversives under the law. They can now be investigated, fined, or imprisoned.

1938 May: House Un-American Activities Committee formed.

1939 March: Madrid falls to Franco's troops; the Nationalist victory will be complete by April.

1939 Sept. 1: Germany attacks Poland; on Sept. 3 Britain and France declare war on Germany, beginning World War II in Europe.

1940 May 10: Germany invades France, Belgium, and the Netherlands; Winston Churchill becomes Britain's Prime Minister.

1941 June 22: Germany invades the Soviet Union.

1941 Dec. 7: Japanese aircraft carriers and midget submarines make a sneak attack on the U.S. Fleet at Pearl Harbor, Hawaii, bringing the United States into World War II. On Dec. 11 Germany and Italy declare war on the United States.

1942 April 18: U.S. B-25 bombers, led by Lt. Col. James Doolittle, take off from the aircraft carrier *Hornet* on the first bombing raid on Japan.

1942 June 4: After six months of unchecked aggression in the Pacific, the Japanese are defeated for the first time, by smaller U.S. naval forces at the Battle of Midway.

1942 June 25: President Roosevelt and Prime Minister Churchill conclude their second wartime conference in Washington. Among the decisions reached is for a combined effort to develop the atomic bomb. This decision will lead to establishment of the U.S. Manhattan Project, with British participation, headed by Maj. Gen. Leslie Groves.

1942 Aug. 8: U.S. Marines land on Guadalcanal in the Solomon islands in the first U.S. offensive in the Pacific.

1942 Nov. 8: U.S. and British troops invade French-held North Africa in the first Allied offensive in the war.

1942 Nov.: Soviet forces begin offensive along the Don River, leading to the decisive Battle of Stalingrad, which cumulates in the surrender of the German army entrenched there on Jan. 31, 1943. This is the first major military defeat suffered by Germany in the war.

1943 Sept. 3: U.S. and British troops land in Italy; the Italian government's surrender to the Allies will be announced on Sept. 8.

1944 June 6: Allied armies land at Normandy on D-Day.

1944 June 15: U.S. B-29 Superfortress bombers operating from China fly the first heavy bomber strikes against Japan.

1945 April 12: President Roosevelt dies; Harry S. Truman becomes President.

1945 May 2: Berlin surrenders following Adolf Hitler's suicide on April 30. Germany surrenders to the Allies on May 8.

1945 July 16: The first U.S. atomic bomb is detonated at Alamogordo, N. Mex.

1945 Aug. 6: A B-29 drops an atomic bomb on Hiroshima; three days later another B-29 drops an atomic bomb on Nagasaki.

1945 Aug. 15: The Japanese government announces that it will accept Allied terms for ending the war; the formal surrender is signed on the deck of the U.S. battleship *Missouri* in Tokyo Bay on Sept. 2.

1946 Nov.: French troops in Vietnam begin operations again the (communist) Viet Minh, starting a French effort to retain control of Indochina.

1948 April 1: Soviet troops interfere with U.S. and British access to Berlin, beginning the confrontation with the Soviet Union known as the Berlin Blockade. It will continue until Sept. 30, 1949, with U.S. and British aircraft flying 2.3 million tons of food and coal into the city.

1948 May 14: Israeli independence is declared, followed immediately by attacks by five Arab nations.

1949 Jan. 21: Communist troops occupy Peiping (Beijing), China, marking the end of the campaign against the Nationalists and the imminent establishment of the Peoples Republic of China.

1949 Aug. 29: The first Soviet atomic bomb is detonated atop a tower at a test site in the Kazakh desert, between the Caspian and Aral seas. Like the U.S. Trinity test four years earlier, this was a plutonium bomb (as was the U.S. Fat Man).

1950: The Internal Security Act of 1950, sometimes called the McCarran Act or the anticommunist law, is passed over President Truman's veto.

1950 Feb 2: Klaus Fuchs arrested in what will be the first of the arrests leading to the smashing of the Soviet Union's atomic bomb spy ring.

1950 May 22: Harry Gold confesses to the FBI.

1950 June 25: North Korean troops cross the 38th Parallel, invading South Korea, beginning the Korean War. A U.S.-led United Nations force responds.

1950 June 30: United States forces engage in the Korean War.

1950 Nov. 26: Chinese troops began offensive against UN forces in North Korea.

1953 March 5: Soviet dictator Josef Stalin dies.

1953 June 19: Julius and Ethel Rosenberg are executed in the electric chair at Sing Sing Prison.

1953 July 27: A truce brings the Korean War to an end.

1954 May 7: Following a 56-day siege by the Viet Minh, the French garrison at Dien Bien Phu surrenders, with some 10,000 French and allied troops captured and another 10,000 killed. This is the end of the French campaign to retain Indochina.

1954 July 21: The Geneva Conference on Indochina temporarily partitions Vietnam at the 17th parallel. North Vietnam becomes the communist-ruled Democratic Republic of Vietnam. South Vietnam becomes a republic backed by the West, particularly the United States.

1955 Jan. 3: U.S. submarine *Nautilus*—the world's first nuclear-propelled vehicle—gets underway.

1956 Feb. 25: Nikita Khrushchev denounces Stalin at the 20th Communist Party Congress in Moscow.

1956 Oct. 23: Soviet and Hungarian troops begin fighting in Budapest.

1956 Oct. 29: Israeli troops attack Egypt, beginning a conflict that will serve as an excuse for Britain and France to attack Egypt to keep open the Suez Canal.

1957 Oct. 4: The Soviet Union launches the world's first artificial satellite, *Sputnik 1*.

1959 Jan. 1: Fidel Castro takes control of Cuba, ending a three-year guerrilla campaign to oust dictator Fulgencio Batista.

1960 Feb. 13: France successfully tests a nuclear weapon.

1960 May 1: A U.S. U-2 aircraft flown by Francis Gary Powers is shot down over the Soviet Union after four years of flights over the Soviet Union by the spyplanes. Intentional overflights of the Soviet Union by manned aircraft are ended.

1960 Aug. 18: First successful Corona spy satellite photographs the Soviet Union.

1961 April 12: Soviet cosmonaut Yuri Gagarin becomes the first man to orbit Earth.

1961 April 17: Cuban exiles, recruited and trained by the U.S. Central Intelligence Agency, land at the Bay of Pigs in Cuba. Castro's forces repel the invaders.

1961 Aug. 13: East German government erects Berlin Wall to halt the flow of East Germans to the West; more than 3 million had already emigrated.

1962 Oct. 22: President Kennedy announces that the Soviet Union is emplacing ballistic missiles in Cuba. The hard evidence was found by U-2 spyplanes. Cuban Missile crisis ends when the Soviets agree to remove the missiles.

1963 Nov. 22: President Kennedy assassinated. Lyndon B. Johnson becomes President.

1964 Aug. 2: North Vietnamese torpedo boats attack U.S. destroyers on DESOTO patrols in the Gulf of Tonkin. Retaliatory U.S. carrier air strikes on Aug. 4 lead to major U.S. participation in the Vietnam War.

1965 Jan. 1: The Palestine Liberation Organization is established and Palestine "revolution" proclaimed.

1965 March 8: U.S. Marines come ashore at Da Nang, South Vietnam. They are the first U.S. combat troops to enter the ongoing conflict between North Vietnam and South Vietnam.

1967 June 5: Israel wins the Six Day War against Egypt, Jordan, and Syria, leaving Israel in possession of the former Egyptian territories of

Gaza and the Sinai Peninsula; Arab East Jerusalem and the West Bank, formerly part of Jordan; and the Golan Heights, formerly part of Syria. The U.S. intelligence ship *Liberty* is mistakenly attacked by Israeli aircraft and torpedo boats on June 8.

1968 Jan. 30: North Vietnam launches a major assault against South Vietnam on the Vietnamese the lunar new year (Tet), striking in Saigon and other cities. Although the North Vietnamese are thoroughly defeated, U.S. media reports call the Tet offensive a major American defeat, fueling anti-war sentiments.

1969 June 8: President Nixon announces the beginning of U.S. troop withdrawals from Vietnam. The last U.S. combat troops will leave South Vietnam on March 29, 1973.

1972 June 17: "Plumbers" sponsored by the Nixon Administration break into Democratic headquarters at the Watergate building in Washington, D.C. The "Watergate" scandal will lead to the resignation of President Nixon on Aug. 9, 1974.

1972 Sept. 5: During the 20th Olympic Games in Munich, terrorists invade the Israeli dormitory, kill two Israeli athletes and take nine hostage, threatening to kill them unless 200 Arab guerrillas are released. The terrorists—and the hostages—are killed in the crossfire of a failed German police operation.

1973 Oct. 6: On Yom Kippur, holiest day for Jews, Egypt and Syria attack Israel in an attempt to regain territories lost in 1967. Israel hurls back the invaders in a three-week war.

1975 April 29: U.S. personnel are hurriedly evacuated from Saigon as North Vietnamese forces enter the city. North Vietnamese forces take over all of South Vietnam and form the Socialist Republic of Vietnam.

1976 July 3: An Israeli commando unit rescues 103 hostages being held at Entebbe Airport in Uganda, following the hijacking of an Air France airliner. Four of the hostages, seven of the ten hijackers, and about 20 Ugandan soldiers are killed in the raid, as is one Israeli officer. The raid becomes a model for counter-hostage operations.

1979 March 26: Israel Prime Minister Menachem Begin and President Anwar al-Sadat of Egypt sign the Camp David Accord, named after the presidential retreat in Maryland where the agreement was brokered by U.S. President Jimmy Carter.

1979 Dec. 25: Soviet troops invade Afghanistan, beginning a 10-year war. The United States later begins arming the mujahedeen forces fighting the Soviets. Among the fighters is a young Saudi named Osama bin Laden.

1981 Oct. 6: Islamic fundamentalists in Cairo assassinate Egyptian President Mohammed Anwar al-Sadat.

1983 Oct. 23: A suicide truck-bomb attack destroys a U.S. military compound in Beirut, Lebanon, killing 242 Americans, most of them U.S. Marines. Almost simultaneously, another bomb explodes at a French base, killing 58 French troops. Islamic terrorists claim responsibility.

1985 Oct. 7: Palestine Liberation Front terrorists hijack the cruise ship *Achille Lauro* in the Mediterranean, off Egypt. They kill a disabled American tourist. After two days, the terrorists surrender in exchange for a safe passage. But U.S. Navy F-14 fighters intercept the Egyptian aicraft flying the hijackers, forcing it to land in Sicily. Italian authorities take the terrorists into custody.

1987 Dec. 6: The murder of an Israeli in Gaza touches off rioting that spread through the West Bank, Gaza, and Jerusalem, launching what the Palestinian Liberation Organization (PLO) termed the Intifada, or "shaking off."

1988 Dec. 21: Pan Am Flight 103 explodes over Lockerbie, Scotland, killing 259 people on the plane and 11 people on the ground. A multinational investigation leads to the arrest and conviction of a Libyan working for his nation's intelligence service. In Jan. 2001 he is sentenced to life imprisonment.

1989 Nov. 9: Crowds tear down part of the Berlin Wall between East and West Germany, leading to the reunification of Germany on Oct. 3, 1990.

1990 Aug. 2: Iraqi troops invade and occupy Kuwait.

1991 Feb. 27: U.S.-led coalition forces begin 100-hour ground war to liberate Kuwait and destroy Iraq's armies; the ground war followed a month-long air and missile bombardment of Iraq. The war ends in a coalition victory, but Iraqi dictator Saddam Hussein still rules his nation.

1991 Dec.: The Soviet Union collapses, ending the Cold War.

1992 August 26: Bush announces air exclusion zone below 32nd parallel, banning both Iraqi fixed-wing aircraft and helicopters.

1993 Feb. 26: Six people are killed and more than

1,000 injured when a massive explosion rips through the World Trade Center in New York City. In 1994 four men, members of the al Qaeda Islamic terrorist group, are each sentenced to 240 years in prison for masterminding and carrying out the bombing.

1993 June 27: U.S. missile strike is launched against Baghdad on basis of "compelling evidence" that Iraq was involved in the April 1993 assassination attempt on former president Bush in Kuwait.

1995 March 20: Members of Aum Shinrikyo, a religious sect, inject sarin poison gas into the Toyko subway system, killing 10 people and injuring thousands.

1995 July 1: As a result of United Nations inspection (UNSCOM) reports and in the light of irrefutable evidence, Iraq admits for the first time the existence of an offensive biological weapons program but denies the existence of weapons.

1995 Sept. 28: Israeli and Palestine Liberation Organization (PLO) officials in Washington sign the Oslo Agreement, which calls for election of a Palestinian council in the West Bank and Gaza.

1995 Nov. 4: An Israeli right-wing fanatic, infuriated by Prime Minister Yitzhak Rabin's peace efforts, assassinates him.

1996 Jan. 3: PLO chairman Yasser Arafat elected president of the Palestine Authority.

1996 June 25: A tanker truck loaded with at least 5,000 pounds of plastic explosives explodes outside the Khobar Towers, a U.S. military's housing facility in Dhahran, Saudi Arabia, killing 19 American servicemen and wounding 372. Investigators blame terrorists belonging to Saudi Hizballah, or "Party of God."

1998 Aug. 7: Nearly simultaneous bombings destroy U.S. Embassies in Nairobi, Kenya, and Dar es Salaam, Tanzania, killing 231 people, including 12 Americans. The bombings are blamed on Osama bin Laden and his al Qaeda terrorist organization.

1998 November 1: Iraq halts all cooperation with UNSCOM weapons inspectors.

2000 May 24: Last Israel troops leave Lebanon, pulling out of the "southern zone," which Israel had occupied for nearly 20 years.

2000 July 25: Middle East peace talks, brokered by President Bill Clinton at Camp David, collapse after Palestinians refuse an Israeli compromise offer.

2000 Oct. 12: A small boat laden with explosives blows up alongside the U.S. destroyer *Cole* (DDG 67) in Aden, Yemen, blasting a hole in her side, killing 17 sailors and injuring 39. The bombing is blamed on Osama bin Laden's al Qaeda terrorists.

2001 June 13: George Tenet, Director of Central Intelligence, enters truce negotiations with senior Israeli and Palestinian security officials. Israeli foreign minister Shimon Peres and Palestinian president Yasser Arafat later agree to try to achieve a lasting truce. But fighting continues with no peace in sight.

2001 Sept. 11: Al Qaeda terrorists hijack four U.S. airliners. The terrorists crash two of the aircraft into the World Trade Center in New York City; the third strikes the Pentagon in Virginia, across the Potomac River from Washington, D.C. The fourth, which may have had the White House or the U.S. Capitol as its target, crashes in Shanksville, Pa., about 80 miles southeast of Pittsburgh, apparently after a struggle between hijackers and passengers. More than 2,800 persons were killed in New York, including 343 firefighters and 60 police officers, and the 127 passengers and 20 crew members on the two hijacked airliners. At the Pentagon, 125 military and civilian workers were killed, along with the 53 passengers and six crew members on the plane. President George W. Bush confers with his national security advisers and, before the end of the day, orders a war on terrorism, beginning with attacks on the Taliban regime and its al Qaeda allies in Afghanistan.

2001 Oct. 7: U.S. special operations forces and British troops launch military strikes in Afghanistan, beginning a conflict aimed at toppling the ruling Taliban regime, wiping out al Qaeda training camps, and hunting down Osama bin Laden.

2001 Oct. 18: Four al Qaeda terrorists, convicted in the 1998 bombings of U.S. embassies in Africa, are sentenced to life in prison without parole.

2001 Dec. 21: After the collapse of the Taliban, U.S.-backed Hamid Karzai takes over as Afghanistan's new leader, promising democratic elections. U.S. and British forces continue to hunt for Osama bin Laden.

2002 Jan.: First prisoners from Allied operations in Afghanistan arrive at the U.S. naval base at Guantanamo Bay, Cuba. Over time, several hundred suspected Islamic terrorists and enemy combatants will be incarcerated there.

2002 Oct. 7: Bush delivers a speech outlining the case for possible military action against Iraq. Bush stresses that the threat from Iraq stands alone because it gathers the most serious dangers—a tyrant with a history of aggression and weapons of mass destruction (WMD)—in one place.

2002 Oct. 12: As many as seven Americans are among more than 200 killed and over 300 injured by a car bomb at a nightclub on the Indonesian island of Bali on the anniversary of the attack on the U.S. destroyer *Cole* in Yemen in 2000.

2002 Nov. 1: Indonesian authorities arrest a suspect who is a member of the Jemaah Islamiyah, an Islamic militant group linked to al Qaeda.

2003 March 20: U.S. and British forces launch attack on Iraq.

2003 April 9: Baghdad falls to U.S. forces as Iraqi armed resistance ends through most of Iraq. The 24-year rule of Saddam Hussein ends, but he eludes capture. U.S. and British occupation of Iraq begins. National security adviser Condoleeza Rice had said on April 4, "We will leave Iraq completely in the hands of Iraqis as quickly as possible."

2003 May 1: President Bush declares major combat operations over. But, with Saddam Hussein still at large, resistance, including lethal attacks on U.S. and British forces, continues. Allied intelligence officials attribute the resistance to guerrillas still supporting Saddam Hussein and terrorists; Saddam is captured by U.S. troops on Dec. 13.

2003 August 21: United Nations offices bombed in Baghdad. The United Nations envoy to Iraq, Sergio Vieira de Mello of Brazil, is among 20 fatalities in a truck bombing that destroys the offices of the United Nations headquarters in Baghdad. Also among the fatalities is American Richard Hooper of Walnut Creek, California, who was Special Assistant to the U.N. Undersecretary General for Political Affairs.

2004 Feb. 5: George Tenet, Director of Central Intelligence, says no weapons of mass destruction have yet been found in Iraq.

A-2

Intelligence staff of the U.S. Army Air Corps and, subsequently, U.S. Army Air Forces. See AIR FORCE INTELLIGENCE, U.S. and G-2.

A3D Skywarrior (later A-3)

Developed as a long-range, carrier-based nuclear strike aircraft, the Douglas A3D Skywarrior was also flown in large numbers in the specialized photo-RECONNAISSANCE and ELECTRONIC INTELLIGENCE (ELINT) roles. The A3D was the largest aircraft to operate regularly from an aircraft carrier, the tanker version having a takeoff weight of more than 80,000 pounds. It was nicknamed "Whale" because of its size and bulky shape.

The Navy took delivery of 282 Douglas-built Skywarriors of all variants from 1952 to 1961, with squadron service beginning in 1956. Of those, 31 were built as A3D-2P photo planes with up to 12 cameras fitted in the fuselage. Another 24 aircraft were built as

An A3D-2P reconnaissance variant of the U.S. Navy Skywarrior; the plane's 12 cameras and 3 crewmen are arrayed before the aircraft. Note the Skywarrior's camouflage markings, worn by some naval aircraft during the Vietnam War. (U.S. NAVY)

A3D-2Q ELINT collection aircraft, and many "straight" attack aircraft were subsequently modified to ELINT configurations. The A3D-2Q had forward- and side-looking radars and infrared sensors as well as electronic monitoring equipment. The ELINT version was the last flown by the Navy; this variant of the "Whale" was in service until 1991.

The A3D was flown extensively in many roles in the Vietnam War, its tanker variant being especially important for refueling shorter-range planes. The U.S. Air Force flew the B-66 Destroyer derived from the A3D in the bomber, electronic, photo, weather, and research roles; B-66 production totaled 206 aircraft.

The basic A3D had a three-man crew, increasing to seven in the ELINT aircraft and five in the photo planes. In the attack configuration the A3D could carry 12,800 pounds of conventional bombs or an atomic bomb in an internal weapons bay. The twin turbojet aircraft had a maximum speed of 610 mph and a range of 2,000 miles in the attack role.

All A3D aircraft were redesignated in the A-3 series in 1962.

A3J Vigilante (later A-5)

The North American A3J Vigilante was developed as a U.S. Navy carrier-based nuclear strike aircraft, but flew primarily in the supersonic RECONNAISSANCE role. The A3J was intended as a supersonic (Mach 2.1) successor to the A3D SKYWARRIOR to deliver nuclear weapons against targets in the Soviet Union. However, the development of land- and submarine-based ballistic missiles led to the conversion of the existing A3J attack aircraft to the A3J-3P photo role in the early 1960s and the building of additional specialized aircraft.

The A3J was a sleek, swept-wing aircraft with twin turbojet engines. A two-man crew piloted the plane to a maximum speed of 1,385 mph. The single atomic bomb was carried in a tunnel-like weapons bay; the bomb was linked to two fuel tanks that were both ejected from the rear of the aircraft. Conventional bombs or additional fuel tanks could be carried under the wings.

When converted to the photo configuration, the bomb bay was fitted with reconnaissance equipment and side-looking radar as well as cameras, infrared sensors, and ELECTRONIC COUNTERMEASURES equipment.

The first YA3J-1 flew on Aug. 31, 1958, and the bomber version entered Navy service in 1961; the reconnaissance variant became operational in late 1963. About 150 aircraft were built through 1970, most to the reconnaissance configuration. Used extensively in the Vietnam War, they remained in Navy service until 1977. (In 1962 the aircraft was redesignated RA-5C.)

The aircraft carriers that operated A3J reconnaissance aircraft were fitted with an INTEGRATED OPERATIONAL INTELLIGENCE CENTER (IOIC), which could quickly download the sensor data from a returning aircraft and rapidly produce usable intelligence. The first

IOIC became operational on the carrier *Saratoga* in Nov. 1962, before the aircraft were available.

A-11

Lockheed Aircraft Co. designation for the A-12 OXCART spyplane.

A-12 Oxcart

U.S. stealth RECONNAISSANCE aircraft that was the precursor to the SR-71 BLACKBIRD spyplane. The existence of the A-12 aircraft was revealed by President Johnson on Feb. 26, 1964, when, using the Lockheed designation for the plane, he announced:

> The United States has successfully developed an advanced experimental jet aircraft, the A-11, which has been tested in sustained flight at more than 2,000 miles per hour and at altitudes in excess of 70,000 feet. The performance of the A-11 far exceeds that of any other aircraft in the world today.... Several A-11 aircraft are now being flight tested at Edwards Air Force Base in California. The existence of this program is being disclosed today to permit the orderly exploitation of this advanced technology in our military and commercial program.

The President's reference to the A-11 was a deliberate ploy to obfuscate the real designation of the aircraft. Also, the A-12s were flying from a secret air base, not from Edwards.

The A-12 was developed by the CIA and the Lockheed SKUNK WORKS. It had an extremely long, slim fuselage and two enormous jet engines mounted on short, triangular wings. The material selected for the aircraft, a titanium alloy, was scarce, costly, and one for which production was not yet perfected. Of the early deliveries of titanium for the aircraft, some 80 percent had to be rejected. The materials and design required that all A-12s be essentially hand-built. Among the other problems was the need for a special fuel (the aircraft would heat up to about 350°F in flight) and lubricating oil for engines that operated at 600°F.

The A-12 could fly at Mach 3 and, after burning off much of its fuel, could cruise above 90,000 feet. The A-12 became operational in Nov. 1965. The CIA proposed to use the A-12 for OVERFLIGHTS of Cuba, but those missions were not undertaken (see Operation SKYLARK). The first—and only—operational flights of the A-12 took place in 1967 over North Vietnam under the code name BLACK SHIELD. Flying from Kadena Air Force Base on Okinawa, A-12s flew 26 photo missions over North Vietnam between May 31, 1967, and early 1968. Although some A-12 flights were detected and SA-2 surface-to-air missiles were launched against the aircraft, no planes were shot down or damaged. (SA-2 missiles downed the U-2 flown by FRANCIS GARY POWERS over the Soviet Union and the U-2 over Cuba piloted by RUDOLF ANDERSON, JR.)

On Jan. 26, 1968, an A-12 flew a photo mission over North Korea to take photos of the captured U.S. spy ship *PUEBLO*. The flight was detected by radar in China, but no missiles were fired at the aircraft. A second mission over North Korea was flown on May 8, 1968—the last A-12 operational mission.

By March 1968, the U.S. Air Force SR-71 Blackbird aircraft—derived from the A-12—began to arrive on Okinawa to replace the A-12 for North Vietnam overflights. Subsequently, A-12 flights were limited to those essential to maintaining pilot proficiency. During 1968 the surviving A-12 aircraft were placed in storage. (Of the 15 that were built, six were lost in accidents, one crashing while trying to launch a D-21 unmanned reconnaissance vehicle.)

The SR-71 had the advantage of a second crew position to assist in the complex navigation and reconnaissance operations of the aircraft, but the A-12 had more space for cameras and other collection equipment because it carried only a pilot. Two A-12s were modified with a second crew position for the abortive plan to launch D-21s from the aircraft.

The U.S. Air Force YF-12A fighter was derived from the A-12, the principal differences being the addition of a second position for a weapon systems officer and provisions for air-to-air missiles that were to be carried internally. The first flight of the YF-12 variant took place on April 26, 1962; only three fighter aircraft were produced.

SR-71 production consisted of 3 YF-12A and 32 SR-71 aircraft including one SR-71C trainer; the last was created from salvaged a YF-12A and functional mockup components. Just under 20 aircraft were in the inventory in 1990 when the SR-71 was retired, of which only eight or nine were operational at any one time because of the aircraft's high maintenance requirements.

The Pentagon announced the loss of eight SR-71s in accidents through 1970. Unlike the U-2s, none was lost to hostile fire. In his definitive *Lockheed SR-71: The Secret Missions Exposed*, Paul Crickmore lists the operational loss of 5 A-12, 1 MR-12 drone carrier, 13 SR-71, and 1 YF-12A from 1963 to 1989.

The revolutionary A-12 shattered many aviation records. One flight on a circuit over the United States on Dec. 21, 1966, covered 10,198 miles in six hours—an average speed of 1,700 mph. Also see TAGBOARD.

A-54

SEE PAUL THUMMEL

Abakumov, Col. Gen. Viktor Semyonovich

(b. 1894 d. 1954)

Longtime Soviet intelligence apparatchik and protégé of LAVRENTY BERIA. Abakumov was head of SMERSH from 1943 to 1946, and head of the MGB from 1946 to 1951.

Abakumov became a deputy head of the NKVD in 1941 and gained notoriety during World War II as head of Smersh, the armed forces COUNTERINTELLIGENCE agency. As head of Smersh from 1943 to March 1946, Abakumov reported directly to the State Committee of Defense chaired by Josef Stalin. During the war Abakumov held the title of First Deputy Commissar for State Security (Beria being commissar) and held the rank of colonel general after 1943, military rank then being given to officers of state security ORGANS.

He was made Minister of State Security (head of the newly established MGB, the internal police agency) from Oct. 1946 until he was purged by Stalin in Aug. 1951. Stalin had installed him as head of the MGB to reduce Beria's influence, but Abakumov continued his primary loyalty to Beria. (Smersh was merged into the MGB as the Third Chief Directorate [counterintelligence] of that ministry.)

Corruption flourished during Abakumov's tenure as head of the MGB. He was arrested and imprisoned in LUBYANKA in the fall of 1951 in a move by the Soviet dictator to further check the power of Beria. Nikita Khrushchev, then party secretary for Moscow, explained the arrest to MGB officers by citing Abakumov's acts of corruption—such as operating private brothels and importing expensive gifts from the West—and his delay in detecting the so-called Leningrad plot against Stalin.

Beria released Abakumov following Stalin's death in March 1953, but after Beria's execution later that year, Abakumov was rearrested, tried, and executed in early Dec. 1954. The charges brought against him at his trial included fabricating evidence against those convicted in the Leningrad plot against Party officials—which he had largely invented.

In his book *The Time of Stalin* (1981), historian Anton Antonov-Ovseyenko described Abakumov as "that charmingly dull-witted but dependable follower of orders."

Also see KGB.

Abel, Col. Rudolf Ivanovich

(b. 1903 d. 1971)

Soviet master spy who operated in the United States in the 1950s and who, five years after his arrest, was exchanged for U-2 spyplane pilot FRANCIS GARY POWERS.

Abel is believed to have been born with the name Alexander Ivanovich Belov in a town on the Volga River. (Some British sources cite Abel as being born William Fischer, in Britain.)

He claimed that his father, a metalworker, had belonged to liberal groups and that he helped his father distribute Bolshevik literature. Young Abel studied engineering and had a working knowledge of chemistry and nuclear physics. He joined the Young Communist League (*Komsomol*) in 1922.

Fluent in English, German, Polish, and Yiddish as well as Russian, he served in a Red Army communications unit and then worked as a language teacher until 1927, when he joined the OGPU. He was later drafted into the Red Army as a radio specialist. During World War II he served on the German front as an INTELLIGENCE OFFI-CER and is reported to have penetrated the ABWEHR, working as a chauffeur under the name Johann Weiss. (He also appears to have used the name Martin Collins during this period.) Shortly after the Germans invaded the Soviet Union, Abel was promoted to lance corporal in the German Army and given a decoration.

At the end of the war Abel held the rank of major in the NKVD. He illegally entered Canada from France in 1947 using the name Andrew Kayotis. He then crossed the border into the United States in 1948. By 1954 he was working in New York City as a photographer-artist under the name Emil R. Goldfus. He served as resident director or spymaster for the KGB in the New York area, where he controlled the local Soviet spy network as well as operations in North America and Central America. He transmitted information to Moscow and received instructions back by shortwave radio. Abel apparently visited Moscow sometime in 1954–1955 for discussions with senior intelligence officials. While in the United States he was promoted to colonel in the KGB.

Abel was arrested by the FEDERAL BUREAU OF INVESTIGATION in New York City on June 21, 1957, after he had inadvertently given JAMES F. BOZART, a newsboy, a hollow nickel used to transmit secret messages. Abel was tried that fall, convicted, and sentenced to 30 years in prison, as well as being fined $3,000.

He remained in prison until he was exchanged for U-2 pilot Powers on Feb. 10, 1962, on the Glienick Bridge spanning East and West BERLIN, and returned to the Soviet Union. Afterward he "actively participated in the upbringing of young intelligence officers," according to a Soviet statement.

As a young man, according to a Soviet source, Abel "seemed shy and self-conscious. But his shrewd animated eyes, his subtle ironic smile and his neat assured gesture betrayed strong willpower, a keen wit and firm dedication." The Soviet government publicly cited Abel as an intelligence officer in 1965 and he was one of five KGB intelligence officers who were pictured on POSTAGE STAMPS issued by the USSR on Nov. 20, 1990.

ABS

SEE ASSOCIATION FOR BUSINESS SECURITY

Abwehr

German MILITARY INTELLIGENCE organization from 1921 to 1944. Abweh*ren* means "to ward off," signifying COUNTERESPIONAGE. The use of the term Abwehr for the military intelligence agency was a concession to Allied demands that Germany's post–World War I intelligence activities be for "defensive" purposes only.

The Abwehr was created in 1921 as part of the Ministry of Defense when Germany was allowed to establish the Reichswehr (defense force). The first head of the Abwehr was Maj. Friedrich Gempp, a former deputy to Col.

WALTHER NICOLAI, head of German intelligence in World War I. At the time of its establishment the Abwehr consisted of three officers and seven former officers plus a clerical staff. By the mid-1920s it was organized into three sections:

I   Reconnaissance

II   Cipher and Radio Monitoring

III   Counterespionage

The German Navy's intelligence staff was merged with the Abwehr in 1928. In the 1930s, with the rise of the National Socialist (Nazi) movement, the Ministry of Defense was reorganized; surprisingly, on June 7, 1932, a naval officer, Capt. Conrad Patzig, was named chief of the Abwehr. While most of the agency was staffed by Army personnel, the appointment of Patzig perhaps indicated that its small size and limited importance made it unsuitable for an ambitious Army officer. Also, naval officers had more foreign experience than their Army colleagues and understood more of foreign affairs. (Subsequently, each of the three German military services established its own intelligence staff.)

Patzig soon had confrontations with HEINRICH HIMMLER, head of the SS, over Abwehr-sponsored reconnaissance flights across the Polish border; Army leaders feared that the flights would endanger the secret plans for an attack on Poland. Patzig was fired and replaced by WILHELM CANARIS, then also a Navy captain, in Jan. 1935. (Patzig was sent to command the new pocket battleship *Admiral Graf Spee*, a coveted assignment; he later became Chief of Naval Personnel.)

The decision by Adolf Hitler in 1937 to assist Soviet dictator Josef Stalin in the prosecution of the Soviet military leadership exacerbated the antagonism between the SS and the Abwehr. Hitler ordered that the German Army staff should be kept from knowing anything about the planned moves against the Red generals, fearing that their German colleagues might warn them of Stalin's intentions. Accordingly, special SS teams, accompanied by burglary experts from the criminal police, broke into the secret files of the General Staff and the Abwehr and removed documents related to German–Soviet collaboration. To conceal the thefts, fires were started at the break-ins, which included Abwehr headquarters.

In 1938 Hitler replaced the Ministry of War with the *Oberkommando der Wehrmacht*, or OKW (High Command of the Armed Forces); the Abwehr now served as the intelligence agency for OKW, although with considerable independence. Canaris reorganized the Abwehr in 1938, establishing the following major divisions, which existed for the next six years:

I	Espionage	
	G	false documents
	H West	army west (Anglo-American intelligence)
	H Ost	army east (Soviet intelligence)
	Ht	army technical
	i	communications

L	air force
M	naval
T/Lw	technical air force
Wi	economics
II	Sabotage
III	Counterespionage

Both Army and Navy officers headed those sections.

Under Canaris the Abwehr expanded and proved to be relatively efficient during the early stages of World War II, but overall it was ineffective. Much of the intelligence it garnered about Allied intentions was politically unacceptable to the German leadership. Moreover, it was in direct conflict with the SS intelligence activities under REINHARD HEYDRICH and WALTER SCHELLENBERG. Moreover, Abwehr officers became involved with several anti-Hitler plots, even providing explosives for assassination attempts. Canaris employed several Jews in the Abwehr and also used the Abwehr as cover to enable a small number of Jews to escape from Germany into Switzerland.

The SS continually undermined the Abwehr by investigating several Abwehr officers who were believed (correctly) to be helping dissident groups. The SS also accused Canaris of making pessimistic reports to Hitler about the Russian campaign. After one such briefing in early 1944, Hitler reportedly sprang at Canaris, seized him by the lapels, and demanded to know whether the intelligence chief was insinuating that Germany would lose the war.

On Feb. 18, 1944, Hitler signed a decree that set up a unified German intelligence service under the supreme direction of SS chief Himmler. Canaris, by that time a vice admiral, was given a minor position. He was arrested after the generals' abortive attempt to kill Hitler in July 1944 and was executed on April 9, 1945, less than a month before the end of the war.

Abwehr headquarters were located at 76/78 Tirpitzufer in Berlin, adjacent to the OKW offices. In *The Abwehr* (1984), Lauran Paine wrote that the Abwehr building

> was a maze of dim corridors, creaky staircases, a veritable rabbit warren of little rooms served by an antiquated elevator which groaned and swayed in transit and which occasionally did not function at all. Visitors called the place a 'fox-hole'. It was especially unsuitable for an organization as large as the Abwehr had become by 1939, but the Admiral refused to move or to have the building modernized. . . .
>
> The building had some advantages. For example, it was possible to go directly to Wehrmacht Headquarters in the neighboring Bendlerstrasse without crossing the street. It was also strategically located near the Ministries, the various bureaus of civil administrations and the offices of foreign officials.

Following is a list of the Abwehr chiefs:

1921–1927	Col. Friedrich Gernpp
1927–1929	Maj. Günther Schwantes
1930–1932	Lt. Col. Ferdinand von Bredow
1932–1934	Rear Adm. Conrad Patzig
1935–1944	Vice Adm. WILHELM CANARIS

Also see FOREIGN ARMIES EAST, FOREIGN ARMIES WEST, PAUL THÜMMEL.

Access

The ability to obtain classified information through the possession of appropriate SECURITY CLEARANCES.

Accommodation Address

An address where regular mail or sometimes another type of communication is received and then held for pickup, forwarded to or relayed to a member of an intelligence service who does not occupy the premises. Also called a mail drop or live letterbox.

ACINT

SEE ACOUSTIC INTELLIGENCE

Acoustic Intelligence

(ACINT)

Intelligence derived from the collection and processing of acoustic data, especially the noise "signatures" of surface ships, submarines, and underwater weapons detected by sonar.

Action Service

SEE SA

Active Measures

Russian term for intelligence operations that will affect another nation's policies or actions. These can be either covert or overt, and can span a wide variety of activities, including assassination.

Also see DISINFORMATION.

Additive

A series of numbers or letters added to a CIPHER or CODE; the additive is also referred to as the KEY.

ADFGX Cipher

One of the most famous nonmachine CIPHERS ever developed, the ADFGX cipher was developed for German Field Marshal Erich von Ludendorff for his 1918 spring offensive in France. Devised by Col. Fritz Nebel, the cipher was based on a five-by-five square using the letters ADFGX as the axes, as they were easily distinguished in sending Morse code—an important factor for an army using large numbers of radio operators, some poorly trained.

The cipher was based on a checkerboard arrangement that looked like this:

	A	D	F	G	X
A	n	b	x	r	u
D	q	o	k	d	v
F	a	h	s	g	f
G	m	z	c	l	t
X	e	i	p	j	w

Going from the left and then top, the message "attack at dawn" would read:

FA GX GX FA GE DE EA GX DG FA XX AA
a t t a c k a t d a w n

Because of repetition and the frequency of letters in English words, the message was then REENCIPHERED or SUPERENCIPHERED through a transposition system using numbers to break up the frequency of specific letters appearing in messages. The substitution and transposition keys were then changed daily.

French radio intercept operators picked up the first signals in the ADFGX cipher on March 5, 1918. Two weeks later the Germans began their offensive, successfully pushing back the Allies some 40 miles at several points.

Meanwhile the French Cipher Bureau, under the brilliant cryptologist Capt. GEORGES PAINVIN, was able to break the cipher. Painvin found that the opening sections of two intercepted messages had certain similarities and, realizing that the cipher was based on five letters and hence a checkerboard concept, he was able to solve the substitution and transposition keys for one day—April 1, 1918.

Then the French found that the Germans had added a sixth letter—V—to the checkerboard to permit the enciphering of numbers, which previously had to be spelled out. Still, Painvin was again able to break the cipher on June 1. A message from that day enabled the Allies to determine the point of the next German assault, which began on June 9. The Allies were able to counter the Germans in that battle, turning the tide of the campaign on the Western Front.

The story of how Painvin broke into the ADFGX cipher was not revealed until 1966.

Ad Hoc Requirements Committee

U.S. interagency committee established in 1955 by DIRECTOR OF CENTRAL INTELLIGENCE ALLEN W. DULLES to coordinate requirements for the U-2 spyplane program.

AFIO

SEE ASSOCIATION OF FORMER INTELLIGENCE OFFICERS

A Force

SEE LONDON CONTROLLING STATION

AFSA

SEE ARMED FORCES SECURITY AGENCY

Agee, Philip

(b. 1935)

A former AGENT of the CIA and a field officer in Latin America. Although never charged with committing espionage, he is considered a traitor by many of his former colleagues.

Agee joined the CIA in 1957 after graduating from Notre Dame University. He was sent to Uruguay from 1963 to 1966 to support operations against Cuba and to help build up local security forces. In 1967 he was assigned to Mexico City. He resigned from the CIA in 1969.

Agee left the United States in 1971. His book *Inside the Company: CIA Diary* (1975) made good on his earlier threat "to expose CIA officers and agents and to take the measures necessary to drive them out of the countries where they are operating." The book listed the names of 2,500 agents and foreign nationals working for the CIA and effectively crippled agency operations in South America. His 1975 article in the anti-CIA magazine *Counter-Spy* called for the "neutralization" of CIA operatives; the same issue carried the name of RICHARD WELCH, the CIA station chief in Athens. Welch was murdered at the end of the year by a leftist group in Athens.

In response, Congress passed Public Law 97-200, the Intelligence Identities Protection Act of 1982, making it a federal crime to reveal the identity of persons involved in U.S. intelligence activities (see UNITED STATES). In 1979 the State Department revoked Agee's passport because of his activities. On appeal, two lower courts supported his efforts to retain a passport, but in 1981 the Supreme Court upheld the government's right to deny him an American passport by a vote of 7 to 2.

When Iranian terrorists seized the American Embassy in Tehran in 1979, Agee volunteered to analyze the CIA documents that were taken from the embassy. His offer was turned down.

Agee spent time in several countries. At an international conference in Cuba he announced the founding of the Covert Action Information Bulletin that would list CIA operations and agents throughout the world. Agee followed with another book exposing CIA activities, *Dirty Work: The CIA in Western Europe* (1978), later revised under the title *Dirty Work II*. The book listed 841 men and women who Agee alleged were CIA agents and operatives.

In June 1977 he was expelled from Great Britain and subsequently from France, the Netherlands, and West Germany. In 1987 he entered the United States through

Canada using a Nicaraguan passport. The reason for his return after 16 years was to promote his new book, *On the Run*, in which he alleged that the CIA tried to stop him from publishing his first book, *Inside the Company*. There was no Justice Department warrant for his arrest, and he remained at liberty after revealing his identity.

A DEFECTOR from the Cuban intelligence service, Maj. Aspillaga Lombard, said that Cuba had paid Agee $1 million or more, approximately from the time he left the CIA until 1987 (when Lombard came to the United States). Agee denied taking any money from the Cuban government.

Why did Agee do what he did? In a 1975 interview with *Playboy* he declared: "I finally understood after 12 years with the agency, how much suffering it was causing, that millions of people all over the world had been killed or at least had had their lives destroyed by the CIA and the institutions it supports. I just couldn't sit by and do nothing."

Agee resurfaced in Cuba in 2000 as the owner of a travel agency.

Agent

An individual, usually of foreign nationality and not an employee of an intelligence service, who acts under the direction of an intelligence service to obtain or assist in obtaining information for intelligence or COUNTERINTELLIGENCE purposes, or who performs other intelligence functions. A secret agent is sometimes referred to as an undercover agent.

Within the U.S. INTELLIGENCE COMMUNITY the FBI uses the term "agent" for its officers, as does the U.S. Secret Service, regardless of whether or not they are involved in intelligence or espionage activities.

Also see CONFUSION AGENT, CONTROLLED FOREIGN AGENT, COOPTED AGENT, DOUBLE AGENT, HONORARY AGENT, ILLEGAL AGENT, NOTIONAL AGENT, POTENTIAL AGENT, PRINCIPAL AGENT, PROVOCATION AGENT, REDOUBLED AGENT, SECRET AGENT, TRIPLE AGENT, UNWITTING AGENT.

Agent 007

CODE NAME for the fictional JAMES BOND [F] created by IAN FLEMING. The prefix 00, according to Fleming's writings, indicated that Bond had a "license to kill" from Her Majesty's government.

Agent 711

CODE NAME for GEORGE WASHINGTON in a code developed by his Revolutionary War spy chief, Maj. BENJAMIN TALLMADGE.

Agent 86

SEE MAXWELL SMART [F]

Agent-in-Place

An individual who offers his or her services to another country while continuing to remain in position so that information that is passed is current. These can be MOLES.

Among the more important agents-in-place have been Soviet GRU Col. OLEG PENKOVSKY and CIA official ALDRICH H. AMES. Also see CAMBRIDGE SPY RING.

Agent Net

An intelligence-gathering unit of AGENTS supervised by a PRINCIPAL AGENT who is operating under the direction of an INTELLIGENCE OFFICER.

Agent of Influence

An individual who can be used to exert covert influence on foreign officials, the news media, or pressure groups to advance the objectives of a foreign government.

Agent Provocateur

AGENT who instigates incriminating overt acts by individuals or groups whom the police, for example, already have under suspicion, to help discredit them.

Agent School

SEE A-SCHULE, CAMP PEARY, NAKANO, SPY SCHOOL

Agent Tom

Soviet intelligence CODE NAME for HAROLD (KIM) PHILBY.

AGER

U.S. Navy designation for passive INTELLIGENCE COLLECTION SHIPS. The letters AGER indicated miscellaneous auxiliary (AG)—environmental research (ER).

Three small converted cargo ships were assigned this classification in the late 1960s: the *Banner* (AGER 1), *PUEBLO* (AGER 2), and *Palm Beach* (AGER 3). Converted for the collection of SIGNALS INTELLIGENCE, the ships were manned by Navy personnel but operated under the aegis of the NSA with some civilian specialists on board. Their COVER was the collection of oceanographic and other environmental information, although their real role was readily apparent from their operations and electronic antennas. The ships carried a minimal armament of machine guns and small arms.

Additional conversions were planned, but the entire AGER program was abandoned after the Israeli attack on the *LIBERTY* in 1967 and the capture of the *Pueblo* by North Korea in 1968.

AGI

U.S.–NORTH ATLANTIC TREATY ORGANIZATION designation for foreign INTELLIGENCE COLLECTION SHIPS, especially Soviet units during the Cold War.

Agnes

Name given to the first BOMBE installed at BLETCHLEY PARK in 1940. Because of the fear of German air attack on Bletchley Park, subsequent Bombes were also installed in nearby estates and villages.

Agranat Commission

Israeli commission established in Nov. 1973 in the wake of the Yom Kippur War to establish "blame" for the surprise assault by Egyptian forces that crossed the Suez Canal. The commission was named for its chairman, Shimon Agranat, president of Israel's supreme court.

The commission issued a scathing preliminary report on April 2, 1974, focusing on the assessment of warnings of possible Egyptian moves by AMAN (Israeli MILITARY INTELLIGENCE). The report recommended the removal of the chief of military intelligence, Maj. Gen. Ehahu Zeira, and three other INTELLIGENCE OFFICERS. Aman was taken to task, not only for the surprise aspects of the assault, but also for the initial unsuccessful Israeli counterattack against Egypt on Oct. 8.

In their book *Israel's Secret Wars* (1991), Ian Black and Benny Morris wrote:

> Israel's grand intelligence failure in 1973 offered two main lessons: that preconceptions and prejudices will often prevail over hard facts, especially when those facts point towards a bleak future; and that intelligence agencies, however well led and organized and however sophisticated their equipment, will invariably encounter difficulties in separating the wheat (good intelligence) from chaff (misleading or irrelevant intelligence), significant signals from meaningless 'noise.' In the end it will always be up to the assessors and evaluators, and the political masters they serve, to interpret correctly the available intelligence.

Zeira, who had received high praise for his role as deputy chief of Aman in the Six Day War in 1967, was forced to retire. The commission also laid blame on the chief of staff of the Israeli armed forces and the commander of the Southern Command. It cleared Prime Minister Golda Meir and Minister of Defense Moshe Dayan of "direct responsibility" for the disaster. Still, Meir and Dayan resigned after the report was issued.

The commission also recommended changes in the organization of the Israeli intelligence community. The MOSSAD and small research department of the Foreign Ministry would have an increased role in intelligence assessments, thus ending Aman's control of intelligence evaluation.

The commission's final report was published on Jan. 30, 1975.

AGTR

U.S. Navy designation for passive INTELLIGENCE COLLECTION SHIPS. The letters AGTR indicated miscellaneous auxiliary (AG)—technical research (TR).

Five ships were converted for the collection of SIGNALS INTELLIGENCE and assigned this classification in the 1960s: *Oxford* (AGTR 1), *Georgetown* (AGTR 2), *Jamestown* (AGTR 3), *Belmont* (AGTR 4), and *LIBERTY* (AGTR 5). The ships were manned by Navy personnel but operated under the aegis of the NSA with some civilian specialists on board. Like their AGER counterparts, the ships were easily recognized as intelligence ships because of their operations and antennas. The ships carried a minimal armament of machine guns and small arms.

The AGTR program was abandoned after the Israeli air and torpedo boat attacks on the *Liberty* in 1967 and the capture of the *PUEBLO* (AGER 2) by North Korea in 1968.

The *Oxford* was engaged in intercepting Soviet communications off the coast of Cuba during the CUBAN MISSILE CRISIS of Oct. 1962.

Ahadi [p]

(b. 1918?)

Born in the United States of Syrian parents, Ahadi married a naturalized Egyptian worker and subsequently spied against the United States for Egypt. She was an ideological spy and may not have received any payment for her efforts.

She married in 1948. After a 25-year career as an intelligence analyst for the U.S. Air Force, Ahadi began her espionage activities in 1967. At the time she was head of an intelligence division at 21st Air Force Headquarters. According to Ahadi, her spying started as a result of the Israeli victory over Egypt, Jordan, and Syria in the Six Day War of 1967.

Ahadi claimed that she had passed only three classified documents (one SECRET and two CONFIDENTIAL) plus unclassified material to Egypt. Caught a short time after she began spying, she was not prosecuted but was allowed to retire for medical (psychiatric) reasons.

AIB

SEE ALLIED INTELLIGENCE BUREAU

Air America

An AIR PROPRIETARY operated by the CIA. The airline was based on the CIVIL AIR TRANSPORT (CAT) airline, already operated under the aegis of the CIA since the early

1950s. The airline was given the corporate name Air America in 1959.

Air America operated with commercial success, in part through contracts with the U.S. Air Force. The airline was very active in Southeast Asia during the Vietnam War, being involved in a variety of both political and military support operations in addition to flying cargo for various governments, intelligence services, and private customers. Air America pilots also performed combat rescues of downed pilots in Laos, and flew forward air control missions over Laos, guiding U.S., Laotian, and Thai aircraft in ground attacks. Some U.S. Air Force pilots were SHEEP DIPPED to Air America during that period.

Air America pilots flew various transport and utility aircraft, including H-34 helicopters on loan from the U.S. Marine Corps. Armed T-28 Trojan trainers were apparently flown in on strikes in Laos.

Air America was disbanded in 1981.

The airline was the subject of the 1990 film *Air America*, starring Mel Gibson and Robert Downey, Jr. The film was based on a book by Richard Rush.

Also see CIVIL AIR TRANSPORT, CONTINENTAL AIR SERVICES, and STEVE CANYON.

Aircraft

Aircraft have been used as spy platforms since the eve of World War I. The first known use of an aircraft for military operations was a RECONNAISSANCE flight on Oct. 23, 1911, in North Africa, where Italy and Turkey were fighting for possession of Tripolitania and Cyrenaica (now parts of Libya). The Italians possessed a few primitive aircraft, and on that date Capt. Piazza, flying a Blériot XI monoplane, reported on Turkish troops and positions that he sighted between Tripoli and Azizia on his one-hour flight. (Nine days later Italian planes carried out the first-ever bombing raid on an enemy.)

In the same campaign, on Feb. 24–25, 1912, Capt. Piazza again made history by taking the first aerial photographs of enemy forces from an aircraft. And on April 19 his colleague Commandant Sulsi, flying the airship *P.3*, took the first aerial motion picture films of an enemy encampment.

WORLD WAR I

During the war of 1914–1918 the initial means of aerial intelligence collection was the pilot's own visual observations. Subsequently, hand-held cameras were fitted and used by a second crewman. Larger cameras were later mounted on the rear machine-gun ring. Still later, a camera hole was cut in the bottom of the fuselage.

The airplanes of the Allies (Britain, France, Italy, Russia, United States) and the Central Powers (Germany and Austria) carried out extensive aerial photography during the war, as well as general aerial reconnaissance. One efficient reconnaissance aircraft could provide more intelligence for a field commander than could several hundred, or even several thousand, cavalry. Aircraft went

aloft throughout daylight hours, often escorted by fighter planes to protect them from enemy attack. They took photos of enemy troops on the move, the extensive trench system of the Western Front, and important towns and cities. Specialists in PHOTOGRAPHIC INTERPRETATION examined the photos in detail to discover even minute changes in the landscape that could indicate an enemy's movements or even intentions.

By the end of the war the Germans alone were taking about 4,000 aerial photographs a day. As DAVID KAHN, expert on German intelligence, observed in *Hitler's Spies* (1978), "After 1917, both Allied and Central Powers so feared [aerial reconnaissance] that neither dared move troops in daylight hours."

One of the most popular reconnaissance aircraft of the World War I period was the British de Havilland D.H.4; many of the de Havillands were modified specifically for photo reconnaissance. The most impressive reconnaissance aircraft were the Russian Il'ya Murometz bombers, the world's first four-engine military aircraft. Some 40 of these planes, designed by Igor Sikorsky, made about 440 bombing raids over enemy territory from 1915 to 1917. On all of their missions—bombing as well as reconnaissance—the planes carried a still-frame camera that provided the Russian Army a total of some 7,000 aerial photographs.

The long-range Il'ya Mourometz bombers could be considered the world's first strategic reconnaissance aircraft, seeking STRATEGIC INTELLIGENCE on German activities far behind the front lines. Those aircraft that sought information on front-line defenses, supply dumps, and troop and ship movements collected TACTICAL INTELLIGENCE.

When the United States entered the war, in April 1917, its army already had experience in aerial photography. Extensive photo-reconnaissance missions had been flown in 1916 when General John J. (Blackjack) Pershing led a punitive expedition into Mexico. About 15 Curtis-built Jenny biplanes were used for visual and photo-reconnaissance in the campaign.

Between World Wars I and II, several nations made extensive progress in the development of aerial photography. As war approached in Europe again, the French Air Force began photo-reconnaissance flights over western Germany in 1936. Beginning in Feb. 1939, Australian pilot SIDNEY COTTON made several photographic flights over Germany, Italy, and North Africa in secretly modified Lockheed 12-A Super Electra aircraft on behalf of French and British intelligence agencies. After the outbreak of the war he continued his flights over German ports in his modified civilian aircraft because British military photo planes were relatively ineffective.

On the eve of World War II, the German airship *GRAF ZEPPELIN* carried out electronic reconnaissance of new British radar installations. It was employed by the Luftwaffe in the spring of 1939 to measure the wavelengths of British radars and to pinpoint the location of the radar sites, an ELECTRONIC INTELLIGENCE (ELINT) or FERRET operation. The airship was used because airplanes at the time lacked the endurance and space for electronic equipment necessary for such work.

WORLD WAR II

During this conflict, from 1939 to 1945, all belligerent countries used aircraft for reconnaissance and intelligence collection. Initially, standard aircraft were fitted with cameras, usually at the expense of their guns. Particularly successful in the reconnaissance role in British service were the SPITFIRE fighter and the twin-engine MOSQUITO aircraft; they were designated PR for Photo-Reconnaissance and FR for Fighter-Reconnaissance. The latter, a multirole aircraft made of plywood, was noted for its long range and high speed, which enabled it to easily evade hostile fighters.

The principal German tactical reconnaissance aircraft were variants of the Me (Bf) 109, the top-performing fighter at the start of the European war, and the twin-engine Me (Bf) 110 and Me 210 fighters. Several German bomber-type aircraft were employed in the "recce" role; the Ju 86P and Ju 86R were successful high-altitude photo planes adapted from an unsuccessful bomber, and the Ju 88 flew throughout the war and on every front. The AR 234 BLITZ (lightning), world's first jet bomber, was widely employed as a long-range reconnaissance aircraft during the last year of the war.

Britain entered the war with little aerial reconnaissance capability, being forced to rely on civilian pilot Sidney Cotton and his aircraft for early photography of German targets. But soon this role was taken over by the reconnaissance variants of the high-performance Spitfire and Mosquito recce aircraft.

The U.S. Army Air Forces (AAF) modified a variety of aircraft for reconnaissance and intelligence collection (usually given the designation prefix F for "Foto"):

F-5	P-38 Lightning
F-6	P-51 Mustang
F-7	B-24 Liberator
F-8	Mosquito
F-9	B-17 Flying Fortress
F-10	B-25 Mitchell
F-13	B-29 SUPER FORTRESS
F-14	P-80 Shooting Star
F-16	P-61 Black Widow
FA-26	A-26 Intruder

Major U.S. Navy reconnaissance aircraft included the PB4Y-1P Liberator bomber and the F6F-5P Hellcat carrier-based fighter.

Only a few specialized photo-reconnaissance aircraft were developed during the war, principally the F-11 and F-12, the former a twin-engine aircraft designed by aviation pioneer-industrialist Howard Hughes. (With Hughes at the controls, one of the two XF-11 prototypes crashed during a test flight. Seriously injured, Hughes was given codeine, to which he became addicted. He grew a mustache to hide a scar from the crash.) The F-12 Rainbow was a long-range, four-engine aircraft; only one prototype was built.

Photo-reconnaissance became a part of virtually every military operation in the war. The U.S. Ninth Air Force, operating from bases in Britain and then northwestern Europe, flew more than 600 photo missions a month in support of ground and air forces during the last year of the war. British planes also provided photo coverage of the region.

Throughout World War II, Allied and German aircraft were used to fly AGENTS into enemy territory. Agents were usually parachuted into the hostile area at night, as were supplies for agents previously dropped and guerrillas. Periodically, aircraft would land in the enemy territory to take out agents or special DEFECTORS from the enemy side. A variety of aircraft were used in these missions, with the Luftwaffe employing several captured aircraft to make their penetration of hostile air space easier, among them a captured Soviet four-engine TB-7 (ANT-42) and several American B-17 Flying Fortress and B-24 Liberator bombers. In addition to parachuting agents, the Luftwaffe also employed a three-man container that was carried under the aircraft and parachuted to the ground carrying the agents and their equipment (see PAG). *Kampfgeschwader* (Bomber Wing) KG 200 was established specially to carry out those clandestine flights behind enemy lines.

The Allied air forces also used aircraft for electronic ferret missions. The first U.S. effort came in the fall of 1942 when a Navy team with the CODE NAME Cast Mike Project No. 1 began using a modified B-17 Flying Fortress bomber on ELINT missions over the Solomon Islands. Based on Espiritu Santo in the New Hebrides Islands, the team carried out eight long-range missions with both American and New Zealand flight crews. Subsequently, the Cast Mike team flew PBY-5A Catalina flying boats in the ELINT role during the Solomons–New Britain campaigns and by mid-1944 was flying up to the Philippines to detect Japanese radar emissions. The Navy also employed modified carrier-based TBM Avengers in the ELINT role.

The AAF commenced ELINT operations when a modified B-24D Liberator searched out Japanese radars on the Aleutian Islands of Attu and Kiska. The plane flew three long-range missions from Adak, Alaska, in March 1943. Extensively modified AAF B-17F Flying Fortresses also carried out ELINT missions in the Mediterranean area from bases in North Africa beginning in May 1943. (In that role they worked alongside modified British Wellington bombers.)

The importance of detecting and classifying enemy radar emissions was not universally understood, however, and when the first ELINT-configured B-24s reached the Southwest Pacific in late 1943, the local commanders ripped out their "black boxes" and used the aircraft as standard bombers. Additional ELINT-configured B-24s sent out in Oct. 1943 were "protected" from misuse and employed for their intended purpose. Those planes flew through 1945 against Japanese forces in the Pacific, including the home islands.

By the end of World War II, electronic intelligence collection had joined photo-reconnaissance as a needed intelligence tool of successful commanders.

COLD WAR ERA

In the post–World War II period, aircraft were used extensively in strategic and tactical reconnaissance roles. U.S. and British aerial spying efforts were driven mainly by the continued failure of Western agents on the ground to survive their spy missions, due in large part to the traitors DONALD MACLEAN and HAROLD (KIM) PHILBY.

The first major ELINT or ferret mission of the post-war era came in Sept. 1946, when an obsolete B-17 was fitted with electronic analyzers and recorders and sent to overfly a Soviet ice station in the Arctic. U.S. military leaders were concerned that the facility might have a military purpose, but the B-17 detected no signs of radar emissions. The following year a U.S. C-47 Dakota flying over Austria and Soviet-occupied East Germany was fired on by highly accurate antiaircraft guns despite a heavily overcast sky. Concerned that Soviet forces might have advanced gun-control radars, the AAF outfitted a pair of B-17s that flew ferret missions in the area. The flights determined that the Soviets were using captured German radars.

After these incidents ELINT missions became a regular activity of U.S. military forces. The U.S. Air Force (established as a separate service in 1947) next employed modified B-29 Superfortress bombers, while the Navy initially flew PBM Mariner flying boats and (mostly) modified PB4Y-2 PRIVATEERS, the single-tail variant of the Liberator bomber.

When the Korean War began, in June 1950, the United States used RB-29s for photo-reconnaissance of North Korea. Later, RB-45C (B-45 TORNADO) turbojet aircraft were used. From the fall of 1950 both aircraft required fighter escorts to protect them from the Chinese MiG-15 interceptors that inundated the North Korean skies. Although U.S. recce aircraft were attacked and some damaged, none was lost.

The number of photo sorties by USAF planes reached 2,400 in May 1952 and averaged 1,792 per month from April 1952 through March 1953. These sorties provided U.S. ground forces with 64,657 photographic negatives in March 1953. This effort was in addition to Navy and Marine photo missions, most flown by F2H-lP Banshee aircraft, which could operate from carriers as well as land bases. Some U.S. photo planes streaked across the Yalu River, separating North Korea from Manchuria, to photograph MiGs at their bases in the sanctuary of Manchuria. These flights penetrating Chinese territory included RF-80 Shooting Stars at the beginning of the conflict and later RF-86 Sabres.

Farther south, between May 11 and June 12, 1955, F2H-2P Banshees from a Marine land-based photo squadron overflew the Fukien Province of China. The unarmed photo planes, some escorted by Marine-piloted F2H-2 fighters, flew from Tainan airfield on Taiwan, seeking out evidence that China was planning an amphibious assault against Taiwan. A total of 27 overflight sorties were flown by the Marines, whose F2H-2P aircraft normally were based in South Korea.

Early in the Cold War the United States also began an extensive BALLOON program—sending balloons carrying cameras (Project MOBY DICK) and a few with ferret equipment (Project GRAND UNION) over the Soviet Union. The balloons, usually carried by winds from west to east, were intended to be recovered in the western Pacific and Alaska. The balloon effort was less than successful. Intelligence equipment failed, balloon control devices malfunctioned, and recovery was difficult, with many landing in the Soviet Union or Soviet-controlled Eastern Europe.

Manned aircraft were sent over the Soviet Union and along the periphery of the Soviet and Chinese empires in large numbers. U.S. Air Force planes flew into the Soviet Arctic areas, mainly from Alaska. These flights were halted by President Harry S. Truman when the Korean War began, in June 1950. Intelligence on interior Soviet targets was needed, however, for strategic analysis and for planning strategic bombing missions.

The British were asked to help, and apparently the first deep penetration flights over the Soviet Union were made by U.S. Air Force RB-45 Tornado photo planes with British markings flown by British crews. Those were night missions, the first on April 19–20, 1952, when three RB-45 aircraft sought to record radar targets for U.S. bombers. These flights were detected by the Soviets, who tried to intercept them but without success. A second British-piloted, three-plane RB-45 mission was flown on the night of April 29–30, 1954.

The British were also asked to use their new CANBERRA bomber aircraft to undertake a long-range photo mission over the missile test facility at Kapustan Yar on the Volga River. The British flew this mssion in 1952 and a second mission in July 1953. The latter Canberra was damaged by anti-aircraft gunfire, although the plane landed safely in Iran.

Long-range, high-altitude photo missions to garner intelligence were also flown by the "recce" variants of the massive B-36 PEACEMAKER strategic bomber. Camera-equipped B-36s overflew Soviet territory in the early 1950s. The threat from Soviet jet fighters led to a "featherweight" modification of the 10-engine bombers, removing their defensive guns and other equipment to reduce weight and permit them to fly at higher altitudes on spy missions. But such planes—carrying more than 20 crewmen—were still relatively vulnerable.

In response to the requirement for such overflights to spy out Soviet bomber and missile developments, the United States produced the highly effective U-2 spyplane, which successfully overflew the USSR from 1956 until one was shot down by Soviet air defense missiles during the 24th overflight mission on May 1, 1960. Those flights were flown in a joint CIA–Air Force project. From 1976 all U-2s were operated by the Air Force. The U-2 was essentially a powered glider, carrying both cameras and ELINT sensors. The U-2 was extremely successful for several years, until overtaken by Soviet surface-to-air missile technology.

The so-called SKUNK WORKS of the Lockheed Corp. produced the A-12 OXCART and the derivative SR-71 BLACKBIRD as successors to the firm's U-2. Those aircraft, in contrast to the U-2, relied on speed as well as altitude and a smaller radar cross-section for survival. Both the A-12 and SR-71 were capable of speeds above 2,000 mph (Mach 3) and altitudes above 85,000 feet and were used extensively for strategic reconnaissance, although never over their intended target, the Soviet Union. CIA-operated A-12s overflew North Vietnam and North Korea in 1967–1968, apparently the plane's only operational use; the Air Force SR-71 overflew North Vietnam and China in the 1960s, as well as targets in the Middle East. The A-12 and SR-71 were rated as the world's fastest aircraft, although by the late 1980s there were reports of an even faster spyplane given the code-name AURORA.

The retirement of the SR-71 in Feb. 1990 came just a year before the Gulf War of 1991, with the U-2 and SATELLITES providing strategic reconnaissance of the Middle East in the 1990s and into the 21st century. SR-71s were briefly reactivated for research by the National Aeronautics and Space Administration (NASA). Several U-2s and advanced ER-1 variants were also flown by NASA.

The U-2 continues to fly as an Air Force strategic reconnaissance aircraft, long after its intended successor, the A-12/SR-71, has been retired. In an attempt to save the giant B-70 Valkyrie strategic bomber from cancellation, the Air Force had proposed a reconnaissance-strike configuration for that aircraft—the RS-70 VALKYRIE. However, the B-70 was stillborn, and neither the bomber nor reconnaissance variants entered production.

From the 1960s onward, photo-reconnaissance and then ELINT surveillance of the Soviet Union was carried out by satellites. Aircraft continued to provide superior imagery and could often give more timely coverage than satellites (because of the time needed to retrieve films) through the 1970s. The U.S. KH-11 satellite, first launched in Dec. 1976, became the first U.S. spy satellite to have a direct downlink for photographic transmission, providing national leaders with ground imagery within a few hours after the satellite passed over its target.

Also used for long-range spy missions were the "bigwing" RB-57s, American-produced variants of the British Canberra bomber. Interestingly, in the early '60s, the United States gave the Nationalist Chinese government of Taiwan several U-2, RB-57, and RF-101 aircraft to fly over mainland China, their intelligence products being shared by both governments.

The British later employed Valiant and then Victor long-range bombers configured for photo-reconnaissance, although none is believed to have overflown the Soviet Union.

Massive aircraft ELINT efforts were mounted along the periphery of the Soviet Union and China, the planes flying from friendly bases in western Europe, North Africa, and the Far East. Sometimes the planes would fly directly toward the Soviet or Chinese border and pull away at the last minute or—on occasion—intentionally penetrate the border to force activation of specific defensive radars so that their location and characteristics could be recorded. More than 1,000 ELINT flights were made almost every year of the Cold War by the USAF RB-47 Stratojet, the RB-50 Superfortress (an improved B-29), and later the RC-135

C-135 STRATOTANKER aircraft, with the Navy flying P4M-1Q MERCATOR, P2V NEPTUNE, P3V ORION, EC-121 (EC-121 SUPER CONSTELLATION), and carrier-based A3D-2Q SKYWARRIOR aircraft in the ferret role. Several of those aircraft were attacked by enemy fighters, and some were shot down (see AIRCRAFT SHOT DOWN).

A large number of tactical reconnaissance aircraft (photo and ELINT) were also developed by the U.S. armed forces. Sometimes the tactical and strategic-intelligence-collection roles overlapped, as happened during the CUBAN MISSILE CRISIS of Oct. 1962. The initial intelligence on the Soviet deployment of strategic missiles to Cuba came from U-2 high-flying aircraft. The CIA flew U-2 Cuban overflight missions from Aug. 5 to Oct. 7, 1962; the USAF Strategic Air Command flew the subsequent Cuban U-2 flights, beginning on Oct. 14 (one of which was shot down by a Soviet surface-to-air missile). Details of the buildup came from low-flying Navy F8U-1P CRUSADER photo planes, later supplemented by Air Force RF-101 Voodoo aircraft.

The ubiquitous A3D Skywarrior, which was normally flown from aircraft carriers despite its 35-ton takeoff weight, was employed in photo- and electronic-reconnaissance variants. The slightly smaller carrier-based A3J VIGILANTE, capable of 1,385 mph (Mach 2.1), provided a long-range photo capability for the fleet. The USAF flew a greatly modified variant of the A3D in the electronic surveillance role with the designation EB-66 and in the photo-reconnaissance role as the RB-66.

In Oct. 1962 the U.S. military aircraft designation scheme was changed to combine Army, Air Force, and Navy aircraft into a single system. The P2V Neptune was changed to P-2, P3V Orion to P-3, WV Warning Star to EC-121, A3D Skywarrior to A-3, A3J-lP Vigilante to RA-5C, and F8U-1P Crusader to RF-8A.

Most of those aircraft were employed in the Vietnam War, as was the RF-4, the unarmed photo-reconnaissance variant of the F4H PHANTOM, one of the top-performing fighters flown by the Air Force, Navy, and Marine Corps. The venerable Air Force EC-47 Dakota, or "Gooney Bird," was employed over the jungles of South Vietnam as a radio direction-finding platform. Those planes were used to direct U.S. air strikes and artillery fire against communist command posts. The only other transport to achieve anything near the success of the C-47, the C-130 Hercules, also flew in an ELINT role for the United States as the EC-130.

Unmanned aircraft were long used by the U.S. military services as aerial targets for anti-aircraft gunnery and missile training. By the 1960s the USAF had adopted the Teledyne Ryan–produced aerial target to produce the AQM-34 BUFFALO HUNTER reconnaissance drone.

From Aug. 1964 through June 1975 the Air Force flew 3,435 photographic and electronic reconnaissance sorties over North and South Vietnam with those drones. Improved reconnaissance drones have been produced, usually as BLACK projects, shrouded in secrecy. The unusual D-21 unmanned reconnaissance vehicle was intended to be carried aloft and launched by A-12 and SR-21 aircraft. Instead it became operational with

B-52H strategic bombers, which carried the D-21 aloft to be flown over mainland China. More than a dozen such flights were made.

The Israelis developed the highly publicized Scout reconnaissance drone, which was used in large numbers for reconnaissance as well as for other missions during the Israeli assault into Lebanon in 1982. The drones, resembling model aircraft, used television cameras with telephoto lenses in the spy role. During the 1982 invasion, the Israelis used them to seek out Syrian anti-aircraft installations in Lebanon; the Scout drones also overflew U.S. naval ships in Beirut's harbor—once while Secretary of Defense Caspar Weinberger was on a pier—without being detected by American forces, because of the drone's "stealth" characteristics. Several follow-on variants of these Israeli-developed drones have been produced, including the Pioneer model that was used effectively by the U.S. Army, Navy, and Marine Corps in the Gulf War of 1991.

The CIA and Air Force subsequently developed several long-range reconnaissance drones, notably the GLOBAL HAWK and PREDATOR. The latter has also been fitted with air-to-surface missiles, providing a "look-and-shoot" capability. (See UNMANNED AERIAL VEHICLES.)

The brief but violent Gulf War of Jan.–Feb. 1991 saw the extensive use of manned aircraft as well as the Pioneer drone for reconnaissance/intelligence collection. The high-flying U-2 saw service, as did outdated USAF RF-4C Phantoms and Navy F-14 Tomcat fighters fitted with the TARPS reconnaissance pod, which suffered, however, from a lack of specially trained pilots and other factors. More significant for keeping track of Iraqi ground and air activities were the two experimental E-8 JSTARS aircraft and E-2C Hawkeye, E-3 Sentry, EA-3B Skywarrior, and EP-3 Orion electronic aircraft (the E-2 was carrier-based, the others land-based). High marks for photo-reconnaissance in the Gulf War also went to the British Tornado and Saudi Arabian RF-5E Tiger.

SOVIET EFFORTS

The Soviet Union, which lacked overseas bases from which to fly reconnaissance aircraft against the United States, was limited in intelligence collection during the Cold War prior to the development of satellites. Like the United States, the Soviet Union also adopted bomber-type aircraft for the long-range reconnaissance role, principally the Tu-16 BADGER and Tu-22 BLINDER medium-range bombers, and the Mya-4 BISON and Tu-20 BEAR long-range bombers. The Badger, Blinder, and Bison were turbojet aircraft; the large Bear, however, was the only turboprop aircraft to achieve operational status as a bomber with any air force. This large, graceful aircraft, with four engines fitted with contra-rotating propellers, has been used for both strategic reconnaissance (Bear-E) and naval reconnaissance (Bear-D and -F), the Bear-D being fitted with a video datalink for guiding anti-ship missiles in attacks on allied warships. The Bears have a range in excess of 7,500 miles, which can be extended through in-flight refueling.

Soviet naval Badgers and then Bears began extensive overflights of U.S. naval ships on the high seas beginning in March 1963. Operating from bases in Soviet Siberia, these flights ranged as far as the outer Hawaiian Islands, serving as training flights as well as spying on U.S. naval forces. The Soviet flights, often escorted by U.S. fighters, soon extended to the Atlantic and Mediterranean areas. The latter flights sometimes originated from bases in Egypt, where some Soviet aircraft flew with Egyptian markings.

The first major overseas reconnaissance flights by Soviet aircraft occurred during the Soviet Okean multi-ocean exercises of April 1970, when a pair of Bear-D reconnaissance planes took off from the Kola Peninsula, flew around North Cape and down the Norwegian Sea, over Soviet ships operating in the Iceland–Faeroes gap, and then continued south to land in Cuba. This nonstop flight of more than 5,000 miles marked the first time that Bear aircraft had landed outside a Soviet-bloc country. After remaining in Cuba for a few days, the Bears returned to their home base. In late April another pair of Bear-D aircraft flew into Cuba, and a third pair made the flight in May 1970, establishing a regular pattern for such operations. There were several such flights every year through the 1980s, with two Bears in each flight. Bear-F aircraft joined the Bear-D flights to Cuba in 1983.

Until the end of the Cold War the Bears conducted general surveillance and ELINT collection along the coast of North America, generally flying 200 to 250 miles offshore.

In 1973 pairs of Bear aircraft began flying into Conakry, Guinea. On several occasions Bears in Cuba and Bears in Conakry appear to have carried out coordinated reconnaissance flights over the south and central Atlantic. Soviet aircraft ceased flying out of Conakry in 1977, and the pattern changed as Bear-D flights began to use the airfield at Luanda, Angola. Those flights crossed the Atlantic between Cuba and Angola.

Several specialized strategic reconnaissance aircraft were developed by the Soviets in the Cold War era. The most impressive Soviet spy aircraft was the RSR strategic reconnaissance jet, which never became operational. That effort began in 1953, the same year that American U-2 development began. The Soviet program was far more ambitious: a plane able to fly 1,850 mph (Mach 2.8) at an altitude of about 100,000 feet (the subsonic U-2 operated at about 70,000 feet). The advance-design RSR was so radical a development that the NM-1, a slower technology demonstration aircraft, was built first, flying in 1959 or 1960. The NM-1 revealed a number of problems, as was to be expected with such an advanced aircraft, and by the end of 1960 the program was canceled.

More akin to the American U-2 in concept was the M-17 MYSTIC, essentially a powered glider developed by the Myasishchev design bureau. First flown in the early 1980s, the aircraft has operated above 70,000 feet, but like the U-2 it is slow, flying at 466 mph. And like the U-2, the Russian aircraft also flies scientific research missions.

The Soviets have also modified several fighter-type aircraft for tactical reconnaissance. Two were particularly significant in the East-West confrontation, the YAK-

25R MANDRAKE and Yak-28 Flashfight-D, both products of the Yakovlev design bureau. The Mandrake was a strategic reconnaissance aircraft, adapted from a twin-jet, swept-wing fighter for all-weather and night operations. It was provided with a straight wing (to increase range and lift) and a variety of sensors. The plane's ceiling may have approached 70,000 feet. The Yak-25R reconnaissance aircraft—most or all believed to have been converted from Yak-25 fighters—entered service in about 1959. Those aircraft made several overflights of China. The Yak-28 was a tactical bomber and tactical reconnaissance aircraft derived from the Yak-25 design; the widely used Yak-28R Brewer-D was a multi-sensor aircraft that entered service in about 1969, with several electronic sensors fitted in the former weapons bay and several cameras fitted in the nose. According to several criteria, the most advanced reconnaissance aircraft developed in the Soviet Union were variants of the Su-24 Fencer strike aircraft, which is still in wide use.

MIDDLE EAST SPY MISSIONS

Beyond strategic reconnaissance flights by U.S. and British aircraft over the Soviet Union and Soviet spy flights over Britain and the periphery of the United States, all three countries flew reconnaissance missions over Israel and the Arab states during the Cold War period. In the Israeli War of Independence (1948–1949), British and Egyptian aircraft flying from Egypt flew reconnaissance flights over Israeli territory. During the summer and fall of 1948, Mosquito aircraft made several overflights of Israeli territory at about 30,000 feet. They flew with immunity, as available Israeli fighters could not reach that altitude in time to engage the aircraft. The fledgling Israeli Air Force shot down a Mosquito on Nov. 20, 1948, and several Spitfires on spy flights in 1949. (See AIRCRAFT SHOT DOWN.)

During subsequent years U.S. and Soviet reconnaissance aircraft would overfly Israel. The former included U-2s and the latter advanced MiGs flying from Egypt; several MiGs piloted by Russians were shot down by Israeli pilots. On July 19, 1963, a pair of Israeli Mirage fighters fired warning shots to force a U.S. RB-57A Canberra to land at Lod (later Ben-Gurion) Airport.

The Israelis in turn used camera-equipped Meteors, then Mirages, and later RF-4 Phantoms to spy out targets in the surrounding Arab countries.

TACTICAL AND BATTLEFIELD RECONNAISSANCE

Several armies operate tactical and battlefield reconnaissance aircraft for collecting visual, photographic, and electronic intelligence. These include both fixed-wing aircraft and helicopters. All of the aircraft used for reconnaissance have been adapted from other primary roles, except those that are specifically mentioned in this entry.

The U.S. ARMY SECURITY AGENCY developed its first aircraft for electronic collection efforts in 1962. These included COMMUNICATIONS INTELLIGENCE against enemy radio transmissions, and SIGNALS INTELLIGENCE against tactical radars. Current U.S. Army aircraft employed in these roles are the RC-7, derived from the commercial DASH-7, and RC-12 Super King Air as well as the EH-60 Blackhawk helicopter. (See GUARDRAIL.)

A variety of Unmanned Aerial Vehicles (UAV) are available for tactical reconnaissance. These resemble model aircraft, and come in a variety of sizes and with different sensors. The smallest UAV in large-scale service is the Dragon Eye flown by the U.S. Marine Corps, which is carried in a backpack and "launched" by being thrown into the air by hand. The GLOBAL HAWK UAV has trans-ocean range, while the PREDATOR UAV has been armed for attacking aircraft and targets on the ground.

Aircraft Shot Down

During the U.S. invasion of Afghanistan in Oct. 2001 and the Anglo-American invasion of Iraq in March–April 2003, extensive use was made of UAVs for SURVEILLANCE and for targeting hostile forces. Some UAVs were able to transmit targeting images directly to attacking manned aircraft.

Numerous U.S. RECONNAISSANCE and intelligence collection aircraft were fired on during the Cold War by Soviet and Chinese fighter aircraft and surface-to-air missiles. The first known attack on a U.S. aircraft by Soviet forces after World War II occurred when Yak fighters fired on and forced down a B-29 SUPERFORTRESS dropping supplies to prisoners of war near Hamhung, Korea, on Aug. 29, 1945. The first attack on a RECONNAISSANCE AIRCRAFT occurred near Soviet-occupied Port Arthur when a U.S. Navy PBM Mariner, a twin-engine patrol aircraft on a routine missions to monitor Japanese ships evacuating troops from North China, was "buzzed" by a Soviet fighter on Oct. 15, 1945; the PBM had flown within about two miles of the Chinese coast, but the fighter did not open fire on the PBM until the American aircraft was some 40 miles south of Port Arthur. The PBM came down to wave-top level to escape its attacker.

The known U.S. aircraft losses are listed below, as is one CIA COURIER flight forced down in the Soviet Union in 1958. Additional reconnaissance aircraft lost during the Korean and Vietnam Wars are not listed here. There are reports—not confirmed by U.S. officials—that a reconnaissance version of the B-36 PEACEMAKER crashed in or near the Soviet Union while on an overflight in the 1950s.

Approximately 150 American fliers were killed in these incidents. In 1992 Russian President Boris Yeltsin said that 12 downed American fliers had been taken prisoner and held in secret by the Soviets; none was believed to be alive when the Soviet Union broke apart in late 1991. (In 1997 NSA revealed that 64 cryptologists were among those who lost their lives while on aerial reconnaissance missions.)

Several U.S. intelligence collection aircraft were attacked by hostile fighters but not lost, although some suffered damage. Most attackers were Soviet or Chinese,

A British photographer adjusts his camera on a World War I aircraft prior to a mission. Aerial photography has been an invaluable intelligence tool for almost a century, and continues in importance despite the advance of satellite photography. (IMPERIAL WAR MUSEUM)

but an EC-130 Hercules and RC-135 (C-135 STRA-TOTANKER) aircraft were intercepted by Libyan fighters. In addition to the U.S. aircraft listed below, it is believed that five U-2, three RB-57 CANBERRA, and two RF-101 (F-101 VOODOO) aircraft flown by Taiwanese pilots were shot down over China.

April 8, 1950: U.S. Navy PB4Y-2 PRIVATEER ELINT aircraft shot down by Soviet fighters over the Baltic Sea; none of the crew of 10 survived, although there were reports of some being captured by the Soviets. The plane was unarmed.

Nov. 6, 1951: U.S. Navy P2V-3 NEPTUNE patrol aircraft on a weather reconnaissance disappeared off the coast of Siberia after being fired on by Soviet fighters. All 10 crewmen were lost.

June 13, 1952: U.S. Air Force RB-29 Superfortress and its 12 crewmen disappeared on a reconnaissance mission over the Sea of Japan without a trace; a Soviet fighter attack was reported by some sources.

Oct. 7, 1952: U.S. Air Force RB-29A Superfortress on a routine flight off the coast of Japan disappeared, probably shot down by Soviet fighters. Eight crewmen were lost.

Nov. 29, 1952: CIA cargo plane shot down over northeast China; captured crew members JOHN DOWNEY and RICHARD FECTAU were returned to the United States in 1973 and 1971, respectively. Two other men on board the plane were killed when it crashed and were buried near the crash site. (See BOOK OF HONOR)

Jan. 18, 1953: U.S. Navy P2V-5 Neptune forced to ditch in the Formosa Strait off Swatow, China, after being fired on by Chinese anti-aircraft guns. Seven crewmen were missing, two of whom were possibly taken prisoner by the Chinese. A U.S. Coast Guard flying boat crashed on takeoff during the search for the missing aircraft, raising the total fatalities in the incident to 11.

July 29, 1953: U.S. Air Force RB-50 Superfortress shot down by Soviet fighters over the Sea of Japan. The copilot was rescued, but the other 16 crewmen were lost, although seven parachuted out and some may have been captured by the Soviets.

Sept. 4, 1954: U.S. Navy P2V-5 Neptune shot down by

Soviet fighters some 40 miles off the Siberian coast; one crewman was killed, and nine survivors were rescued the following day.

Nov. 7, 1954: U.S. Air Force RB-29 Superfortress shot down near Hokkaido, Japan, by Soviet fighters. Of the 11 crewmen who bailed out, one died and the others were rescued.

June 22, 1955: U.S. Navy P2V-5 Neptune attacked by Soviet fighters near St. Lawrence Island in the Bering Sea. The plane crash-landed on the island. Seven of the 10 crew members were injured, but there were no fatalities.

Aug. 22, 1956: U.S. Navy P4M-1Q MERCATOR ELINT aircraft shot down over the Shengszu Islands, 37 miles off the coast of China, while on a night mission. All of the 16 men were killed; several bodies were found by U.S. search aircraft.

June 27, 1958: U.S. Air Force C-118 transport on a CIA courier mission with six crewmen and three CIA personnel was damaged by Soviet fighters and forced down 100 miles inside Soviet Armenia. Of the five men who parachuted from the aircraft before it landed, two were injured; all were questioned and released after 10 days. The flight had taken off from an airfield in Adana, Turkey, and was headed east toward Tehran when it crossed into Soviet air space during bad weather and was attacked by fighters. The plane was not configured for a spy mission.

Sept. 2, 1958: U.S. Air Force EC-130 Hercules on an ELINT mission with 17 men on board was shot down by Soviet fighters and crashed in Soviet Armenia. Six bodies were returned by the Soviet government; no mention was made of the other 11 crewmen. All 17 apparently died in the crash.

June 16, 1959: U.S. Navy P4M-1Q Mercator was attacked by Soviet fighters over the Sea of Japan, 85 miles east of Wonsan, North Korea. The damaged plane returned to Niho Air Base in Japan with its tail gunner seriously wounded.

May 1, 1960: CIA-operated U-2 spyplane shot down by a Soviet surface-to-air missile near Sverdlovsk; the pilot, FRANCIS GARY POWERS, was captured and subsequently tried for espionage by the Soviets, found guilty, and imprisoned.

July 1, 1960: U.S. Air Force RB-47 ELINT version of the B-47 STRATOJET aircraft flying from a base in England shot down by Soviet MiG-19 fighters over the Barents Sea. Of the six crewmen, four were reported killed when the plane crashed; the two survivors were released by the Soviet government on Jan. 25, 1961, after incarceration in the LUBYANKA PRISON.

Oct. 27, 1962: U.S. Air Force U-2 shot down by a Soviet SA-2 surface-to-air missile while overflying Cuba; the pilot, Air Force Maj. RUDOLF ANDERSON, JR., was killed.

March 10, 1964: U.S. Air Force RB-66 Destroyer shot down over East Germany by a Soviet fighter. The three-man crew parachuted from the plane; one was injured. All three men were returned to U.S. custody.

April 15, 1969: U.S. Navy EC-121M Warning Star on an ELINT mission off the coast of North Korea was shot down by Korean fighters. All 31 crew on board were killed; two bodies were recovered at sea. (See C-121 CONSTELLATION.)

Feb. 5, 1973: U.S. Air Force EC-47Q Skytrain on an intelligence mission over Laos was shot down by ground fire. Four crewmen were on board; according to some reports, two crewmen were captured and may have been taken to the Soviet Union for interrogation. (The loss occurred one week after the Paris peace agreement ending the Vietnam War.)

April 1, 2001: U.S. Navy EP-3E Orion ELINT aircraft flying over international waters off the coast of China was harassed by and collided with a Chinese J-8 fighter aircraft. The latter crashed into the sea, killing its pilot. The damaged U.S. aircaft, with a crew of 24 men and women, made a forced landing on Hainan Island. The crew and aircraft were seized by Chinese officials; the crew was released on April 12. The aircraft was taken apart by American technicians, flown out in a Russian Antonov An-124 cargo aircraft in July 2001, and returned to the United States.

There are no known instances of Soviet reconnaissance aircraft being shot down by U.S. forces. A Soviet BADGER did crash at sea within sight of the U.S. carrier *Essex* on May 25, 1968, during a series of Soviet overflights of the U.S. ship. There were no survivors from the aircraft.

Several Soviet planes with Egyptian markings, however, have been downed by Israeli fighters in the Middle East. The Israelis have also shot down several British reconnaissance aircraft: On Nov. 20, 1948, a newly arrived Israeli P-51D Mustang took off and intercepted a MOSQUITO PR.34 on a spy flight. Although the Mustang's guns jammed after firing a few rounds, the Mosquito was hit and crashed into the Mediterranean, killing both crewmen. (The Mustang pilot was Wayne Peake, an American ex–Army Air Forces volunteer pilot fighting with the Israelis.)

On Jan. 7, 1949, the morning that a cease-fire between Israel and Egypt went into effect, several British armed reconnaissance aircraft overflew Israeli-held territory in the Negev Desert. Four SPITFIRE FR.18 aircraft on a low-level mission were fired on by Israeli anti-aircraft guns; one was shot down, its pilot bailing out and being captured by the Israelis. As the three other Spitfire pilots watched the parachute descending to earth, two Israeli Spitfire Mk.IX fighters arrived on the scene and shot down the other three armed photo aircraft; one pilot was killed and two bailed out safely. (Four British Tempest fighters sent to look for the missing "Spits" were also jumped by Israeli fighters; one was shot down, and the survivors returned fire before fleeing into Egyptian air space.)

Also see NATIONAL VIGILANCE PARK.

Air Force Intelligence, U.S.

Intelligence collection has been the primary purpose of military aviation since its beginning in the early 1900s. When Gen. John J. Pershing led a punitive U.S. Army expedition into Mexico in 1916 he had under his command the 1st Aero Squadron. With about 15 Curtiss Jenny biplanes, the squadron provided Pershing's troops with detailed photo and visual RECONNAISSANCE of the operating area.

Aircraft and manned BALLOONS were used to collect battlefield intelligence during World War I. This was primarily TACTICAL INTELLIGENCE to assist battlefield commanders in making decisions. Under the aegis of the U.S. Army Signal Corps, these aircraft and balloons made a major contribution to Allied reconnaissance efforts in France during 1917–1918.

When World War I ended in Nov. 1918 the Army Air Service (established that year) included several observation squadrons and 23 balloon companies. Between the world wars the Army Air Corps (from 1926) concentrated mainly on aerial reconnaissance with respect to intelligence. The Army's General Staff and MILITARY INTELLIGENCE Division carried out other intelligence activities for the Air Corps.

A pioneer in aerial photography was George W. Goddard, a commercial artist who enlisted as a private in the Signal Corps in 1917. After attending the first officers' class in aerial photography (at Cornell University), he was commissioned and assigned to France to direct Army aerial photography. Those orders were canceled when the war ended; instead he underwent flight training, subsequently becoming a world pioneer in aerial photography. (Goddard retired in 1953 as a brigadier general.)

The Army's air arm was reorganized as the Army Air Forces (AAF) in June 1941. An air staff was established, with the assistant chief of air staff (intelligence), or A-2, being the senior INTELLIGENCE OFFICER of the AAF. The intelligence officers at the command and wing level were also designated A-2, while those at group and squadron levels were designated S-2.

When large numbers of U.S. heavy bombers began to deploy to England in 1942 there was a rapid buildup of AAF intelligence activities, as targets had to be selected and target folders compiled for bomber crews. These intelligence officers were soon debriefing returning bomber crews on target conditions, enemy flak and fighters, and other factors. PHOTOGRAPHIC INTERPRETATION became a vital AAF activity, both for target selection and, after a strike, for bomb damage assessment. A variety of specialized reconnaissance aircraft were employed. (See AIRCRAFT.)

In the European theater AAF intelligence officers were aided by the highly capable Royal Air Force, with services and the sharing intelligence. But in the Pacific the AAF was largely on its own in seeking intelligence on Japanese targets. Because the distances between home bases and targets were greater in the Pacific than in the European theater, less was known about Japan and the Japanese than about the Germans and Italians. These and other factors made intelligence collection in the Pacific problematic.

The bombing of Japan, for example, was a major challenge for U.S. intelligence officers. After a few, ineffective B-29 SUPERFORTRESS raids against the Japanese home islands flown from China, the first strikes against Japan by B-29s flying from the Mariana Islands came on Oct. 13, 1944. Before that raid, a single F-13 aircraft—the photo-reconnaissance version of the B-29—took off from Saipan to overfly Japan. Piloted by Capt. Ralph D. Steakley, this was the first American plane to fly over Tokyo since the Doolittle raid of April 1942. The photo plane, named *Tokyo Rose*, overflew several urban areas, spending 35 minutes over Tokyo. The plane's cameras took thousands of photographs: "We got the best pictures we could have hoped for. There wasn't really another chance like that for the rest of the war. Those photographs were a godsend," wrote Gen. Curtis LeMay, the B-29 commander in the Marianas.

POSTWAR AIR INTELLIGENCE

The U.S. Air Force, established in 1947, took over the intelligence resources of the AAF. Intelligence collection became more sophisticated, with high-performance aircraft that carried not only cameras but also ELECTRONIC INTELLIGENCE (ELINT) collection and other sensors. Air Force pilots, on "leave" from the service, flew U-2 spyplanes over the Soviet Union in the late 1950s—until ex-Air Force pilot FRANCIS GARY POWERS was shot down on May 1, 1960. Air Force U-2s were again fired upon during the CUBAN MISSILE CRISIS with a U-2 flown by Maj. RUDOLPH ANDERSON, JR. being shot down. Anderson was the only combat casualty of the crisis. (There were several other U.S. AIRCRAFT SHOT DOWN by the USSR and China in the 1950s and 1960s.)

The U-2 was but one of several specialized reconnaissance aircraft flown by the U.S. Air Force: The B-57 CANBERRA and SR-71 BLACKBIRD provided high-altitude capabilities, while the ELINT variants of the C-135 STRATOTANKER provided one of the most important spy platforms of the Cold War. (See also RIVET JOINT.)

By the mid-1960s and the Vietnam War the Air Force also employed unmanned UNMANNED AERIAL VEHICLES that overflew targets without exposing pilots to hostile fire. From 1969 to 1971, Air Force B-52H strategic bombers launched four D-21 supersonic reconnaissance drones over China; all failed to return with film of their TARGETS. In this period the Air Force also went into space for reconnaissance, profiting from U.S. spy SATELLITES while planning to operate the MANNED ORBITAL LABORATORY to collect intelligence. (That project had a brief existence.)

The senior intelligence officer of the Air Staff—the headquarters staff of the U.S. Air Force—is the Assistant Chief of Staff Intelligence (code AF/IN). On June 27, 1972, the Air Force Intelligence Service was established to provide specialized intelligence support to Air Force headquarters and major commanders around the world. This name was changed to the Air Intelligence Agency (AIA) on Oct. 1, 1993. It was subordinated to the Air Combat Command during the Air Force realignment of Feb. 1, 2001.

The AIA, with headquarters at Lackland Air Force Base, San Antonio, Texas, has responsibility for intelligence collection, security, electronic combat, and treaty-monitoring support within the Air Force. The agency directs the activities of the NATIONAL AIR INTELLIGENCE CENTER, the Air Force Information Warfare Center, 67th Information Operations Wing, and 70th Intelligence Wing. It also operates the Joint Information Operations Center at Lackland, which is subordinate to the U.S. Space Command. The center was established in Sept. 1999.

Air Proprietary

Airlines established or sponsored by an intelligence agency that are ostensibly private, commercial entities. They are employed by the agency to carry out clandestine operations, usually in addition to aboveboard operations. The affiliation with the intelligence organization is usually secret. See AIR AMERICA, CIVIL AIR TRANSPORT, CONTINENTAL AIR SERVICES.

Air Spy

World War II slang for a PHOTOGRAPHIC INTERPRETATION specialist; also called a photo interpreter.

Ajax

U.S. CODE NAME for joint British and CIA operation in 1953 to remove Dr. Mohammed Mossadegh as prime minister of Iran. The British code name for the operation was Boot.

Akashi, Baron Motojiro

(b. 1860? d. 1919)

Japanese Army colonel sent to Europe in 1900 as a roving military ATTACHÉ. His principal mission was to set up contacts with Russian revolutionaries living in France, Sweden, Germany, and Switzerland; he also sought out intelligence on Russia's military forces.

Akashi was already considered a knowledgeable military adviser and tactical expert at the time that he was sent to Russia. He knew SIDNEY REILLY and persuaded him to do some intelligence work for the Japanese.

Highly popular in European circles because of his paintings and poems as well as his military reputation, he was successful in seeking out information for his government. Akashi was promoted to full general and was en route to Formosa (Taiwan) to become governor general when he died.

Also see BLACK DRAGON SOCIETY.

Akhmerov, Isskhak Abdulovich

Soviet INTELLIGENCE OFFICER who did two U.S. tours of duty as an ILLEGAL and was a HANDLER of many AGENTS who appear in the VENONA decrypts.

Akhmerov entered the United States in 1934 and im-mediately began recruiting students at Columbia University while learning English and slipping into a new identity. This included finding a wife, Helen Lowry, niece of EARL BROWDER, American Communist Party leader. (See CPUSA). She worked alongside him and became an NKVD agent. Her CRYPTONYM was Nelly, his was Bill.

Akhmerov sometimes used the cover of a clothier and used many aliases. When he was handling MICHAEL, STRAIGHT, he used the alias Michael Green. ELIZABETH BENTLEY knew him as Bill. For a time he also ran MARTHA DODD. He served as a highly successful operative during what historian Allen Weinstein and former KGB officer Alexander Vassiliev, authors of *The Haunted Wood: Soviet Espionage in America—The Stalin Era* (1999), call the "golden age" of communist spying.

Albani, Alessandro

(b. 1692 d. 1779)

Italian cardinal, art collector, and spy who operated in Rome for the British government against the Jacobites, supporters of the Stuart claimants to the British throne.

Alberti, Leon Battista

(b. 1404 d. 1472)

The illegitimate son of a wealthy Florentine merchant, Alberti was a star of the Italian Renaissance—architect, painter, writer, and composer. His *De Re Aedificatoria*, the first printed book on architecture, apparently influenced the building of St. Peter's Basilica in Rome and other churches. His own architectural accomplishments included the Rucellai Palace, the facade of the Santa Maria Novella Church in Florence, and the Church of San Francesco in Rimini.

He applied his genius to helping the Pope's retinue decipher secret communications that came into their possession. He wrote an essay on the subject in 1466 or 1467 that earned him, according to codebreaking historian DAVID KAHN, the appellation "Father of Western Cryptology." This 25-page document remains the oldest known Western text on CRYPTANALYSIS. The essay told not only how to solve CIPHERS, but also how to prevent their solution by using his CIPHER DISK, which had two concentric, rotating circles that provided for letter and number substitutions. (The essay was published in 1568 in a collection of Alberti's works.)

Aliyev, Geidar A.

(b. 1923?)

Soviet KGB official and member of the Politburo. Aliyev began his career in 1941 as a member of the security police in his native Soviet republic of Azerbaijan. He rose through the ranks of the secret police to become chief of the KGB in Azerbaijan in 1967; two years after that he became head of the Communist Party in Azerbaijan. He was successful in improving the economic and general situation in Azerbaijan.

While head of the Azerbaijan party he was named a candidate member of the (USSR) Politburo in 1976. Upon the death of Leonid Brezhnev in Nov. 1982 he moved to Moscow to become a First Deputy Prime Minister of the USSR and a full (voting) member of the Politburo.

In his biography *Gorbachev* (1986), Russian political historian Zhores A. Medvedev called Aliyev a "bright, ambitious KGB professional."

All-Source Intelligence

Intelligence based on all available information, including OPEN SOURCE data.

Allason, Rupert

SEE NIGEL WEST [P]

Allen, E.J.

SEE ALLAN PINKERTON

Allen, Gen. Lew, Jr.

(b. 1925)

Air Force officer and one of the most notable directors of the NSA, holding that position from Aug. 1973 to July 1977.

A graduate of the U.S. Military Academy, he later earned his master's and doctorate degrees from the University of Illinois. During his career as a junior Air Force officer he had several assignments involving nuclear weapons. A rated pilot, he flew more than 4,000 hours.

In 1961 he was assigned to the Office of the Director of Research and Engineering within the Defense Department, from which time he worked with the NATIONAL RECONNAISSANCE OFFICE (NRO), which is responsible for U.S. spy SATELLITE operations. From 1965 to 1968 Allen held the post of deputy director of the Air Force's Special Projects Office (part of the NRO structure) in Los Angeles, followed by other positions in the Air Force's satellite organizations. He became director of the Special Projects Office in 1971.

In March 1973 the newly appointed DIRECTOR OF CENTRAL INTELLIGENCE, JAMES SCHLESINGER, named Allen head of the INTELLIGENCE COMMUNITY staff. After little more than five months in that assignment, in Aug. 1973 he became director of the NSA.

As head of the NSA, Allen was immediately embroiled in the storm over the agency's domestic eavesdropping (see MINARET and SHAMROCK). The Congress, courts, and news media all demanded to know the role of the NSA in the extensive wiretapping of American citizens that was being revealed by a number of sources. On Aug. 8, 1975, Allen became the first head of the NSA

ever to testify before a congressional committee when he appeared before the House Select Committee on Intelligence (the PIKE COMMITTEE).

The four-hour, closed (classified) session before the committee was followed by an equally arduous session on Oct. 29, 1975, before the Senate Intelligence Committee, then known as the CHURCH COMMITTEE.

Allen revealed that the NSA "watch list"—names that would trigger NSA attention when intercepted in overseas telephone or cable communications—contained about 1,700 Americans and almost 6,000 foreign individuals. Because several agencies provided their "watch lists" to the NSA, there was some duplication; still, the numbers were impressive.

Most significant, Allen and two of his deputies stated, as JAMES BAMFORD wrote in *The Puzzle Palace* (1982),

> that NSA exists somewhere in an extralegal limbo, unrestrained by the same laws and statutes that govern the rest of the nation, and was made all the more significant when weighed alongside an earlier question by Pennsylvania senator Richard Schweiker. Asked whether it would be possible to use NSA's watch list and massive technological capability "to monitor domestic conversations within the United States if some person with malintent desired to do it." Allen replied, "I suppose that such a thing is technically possible."

The battle was then joined between the executive branch and Congress over access to records related to intercepts from the NSA and other government intelligence agencies, as well as cable companies. Although Allen did not appear in the subsequent hearings, knowledgeable witnesses did, and the NSA was stung by a report of the House Government Operations Committee which, after examining NSA eavesdropping activities, declared that the enormous secrecy surrounding the agency was "obsessive and unfounded."

Allen survived the ordeal, leaving the NSA in July 1977.

He subsequently served, briefly, as Commander of Air Force Systems Command, from Aug. 1977 to Mar. 1978. On July 1, 1978, he was sworn in as Chief of Staff of the U.S. Air Force. He held the No. 1 military position in that service until retiring from active duty in June 1982.

Allen, Chief Radioman Michael H.

A retired Navy senior chief radioman convicted of espionage for selling classified digests of U.S. intelligence on Philippine internal affairs to Philippine military police. Allen was arrested in Dec. 1986. The Navy had investigated Allen for five months after coworkers reported that he was acting suspiciously.

Allen served in the Navy from 1950 to 1972. After retiring from the Navy, Allen worked as a civilian clerk at the station's telecommunications center. He also ran an automobile dealership, and passed along the classified information to build up good relations with the police, officials said.

The documents, which included information on rebel force movements, were passed to the Philippine Constabulary, a branch of the Armed Forces of the Philippines that was notorious for cracking down on dissidents. Most of the information was prepared by the NAVAL INVESTIGATIVE SERVICE (NIS), which was a primary collector of U.S. intelligence in the Philippines. At least one NIS UNDERCOVER AGENT was BLOWN by Allen's disclosures.

He was sentenced to eight years in prison, fined $10,000, and ordered to forfeit additional Navy retirement pay. (He was tried by a Navy court because he was technically a naval reservist.)

Allen's arrest, less than two years after that of JOHN A. WALKER and JERRY A. WHITWORTH, demonstrated the vulnerability of communications personnel to recruitment by foreign intelligence agencies.

Alley, Maj. Stephen

British INTELLIGENCE OFFICER in Russia during the Russian Revolution of 1917. Alley was born and brought up in Russia.

He was head of Britain's Secret Intelligence Service (MI6) operations in Russia during World War I and the Russian Revolution. Reportedly, when told to assassinate Josef Stalin (who became ruler of the Soviet Union in the 1920s), Alley refused. He later told a friend: "I didn't always obey orders. Once I was asked to rub out Stalin. Never did like the chap much, but he regarded me as a friend, and the idea of walking into his office and killing him offended me." Alley also remarked that he was not happy with the escape plan for him after the assassination.

Alley and most of the British Embassy were evacuated from St. Petersburg in Feb. 1918, departing Archangel by ship for Britain.

In 1919 he joined Britain's Security Service (MI5), where he worked for several years. After retiring from MI5 he ran a commodities business in Paris. He subsequently returned to England, being recalled to intelligence service in World War II. ROBERT BRUCE LOCKHART, who was in Russia during the revolution, later wrote of Alley in *Reilly: The First Man* (1987): "I had occasion to meet him from time to time during World War II, when, like many intelligence officers, he was in uniform. He seemed to have as many medal ribbons on his chest as General [Douglas] MacArthur but I never learned what they were all for." (Ironically, MacArthur invariably appeared in undress khaki uniform, with no ribbons on his shirt.)

Allied Intelligence Bureau
(AIB)

Combined U.S.-Australian intelligence organization for Gen. Douglas MacArthur's Southwest Pacific Area command during World War II. The AIB was established in Australia on July 6, 1942—four months after MacArthur fled from the Japanese armies engulfing the Philippines.

The AIB served as an umbrella organization for a number of sabotage and other clandestine units already in existence. Its charter called for these activities to "obtain and report information on the Southwest Pacific Area.... Weaken the enemy by sabotage and destruction of morale.... Render aid and assistance to local [guerrilla] efforts in enemy-occupied territories."

The AIB operated under the direction of MacArthur's chief INTELLIGENCE OFFICER, Col. CHARLES WILLOUGHBY, with Col. G.C. Roberts, the Director of Intelligence of the Australian Army, serving as controller of the AIB. (Most of MacArthur's troops at the time were Australians.) Capt. Allison Ind, an officer from Willoughby's staff, was named as Roberts's deputy.

In addition to planning and carrying out intelligence collection, sabotage, and guerrilla support missions in New Guinea, the Solomon Islands, and the Philippines, the AIB operated the chain of COAST WATCHERS who kept track of Japanese movements in the region. AIB teams were sent into islands behind Japanese lines to collect intelligence or undertake sabotage missions. They were carried to their destinations in small craft and U.S. SUBMARINES.

AIB operations produced numerous successes—and some failures. For example, an Australian–Portuguese team of 34 men was landed on the Japanese-held island of Timor, east of Java. They were captured by the Japanese in Sept. 1943. The Japanese used the group's radio to transmit false information to the AIB, which accepted it as valid. Two more AIB parties subsequently landed on Timor and were easily captured by the Japanese. The AIB did not learn of the deception until the war was over.

The existence of the AIB and its activities caused MacArthur to reject the use of the OFFICE OF STRATEGIC SERVICES in his theater. The bureau was abolished at the end of the war in the Pacific.

Alphabetical Typewriter 97

SEE PURPLE

Alsos Mission

General name for intelligence collection missions that followed U.S. combat troops in Europe to examine newly occupied areas for signs of German or Italian progress on the atomic bomb. Alsos was a cooperative effort of the Manhattan Project under Maj. Gen. Leslie Groves, the Office of Scientific Research, the Army intelligence staff (G-2), and the Navy. The Navy subsequently left the Alsos project, having established its own intelligence mission in Europe.

The Alsos mission was headed by Lt. Col. Boris T. Pash, an Army INTELLIGENCE OFFICER, and consisted of scientific and military personnel. Pash led his group to Italy in 1943 to examine institutes and university laboratories, and to France, Belgium, and Germany in 1944–1945. The mission performed poorly in Italy, but it did obtain considerable information on German nuclear weapon efforts and helped to capture several German atomic scientists who subsequently worked in the West. (Soviet troops had stripped the Kaiser-Wilhelm Institute in Berlin, the center of German atomic research, before U.S. troops reached the city. The Alsos mission found that a U.S. intelligence unit was using the building as its headquarters and had dumped the few remaining pieces of equipment and material in the backyard, unaware of their importance.)

The CODE NAME Alsos was chosen by Gen. Groves because *alsos* is the Greek word for "grove."

Alternate Meet

A prearranged location for a clandestine meeting to take place in the event that a regularly scheduled meet is missed for any reason.

Aman

The Intelligence Corps of the Israel Defense Forces (IDF). MILITARY INTELLIGENCE was established as a department of the operations branch of the Army's General Staff shortly after the State of ISRAEL came into being on May 14, 1948. Military intelligence was virtually nonexistent for the struggling Israeli Army at the start of Israel's War of Independence (1948–1949) despite the prior existence of the SHAI organization. During the summer of 1948, military intelligence underwent several reorganizations and increased its effectiveness, in part due to an influx of cryptanalysts, radio operators, and other technicians, many of whom had served in the U.S. and British armies. Both intelligence collection—including SIGNALS INTELLIGENCE against Arab radio transmissions—and intelligence analysis were improved, and special operations for both intelligence collection and sabotage were undertaken in neighboring Arab states.

In 1953 military intelligence was elevated to the Intelligence Branch of the armed forces, generally called Aman, the Hebrew acronym for *Agaf Modi'in* (information wing).

Aman specializes in intelligence about Arab countries with a secondary emphasis on African states, which are potentially both enemies and allies of Israel, and the Soviet Union/Russia. The last has been an intelligence TARGET because of the large-scale arms transfers from the Soviet Union and Eastern Bloc states to Arab and African countries beginning in 1955, as well as training provided to officers from those countries. In the 1970s the activities of Aman expanded (as did those of other Israeli intelligence agencies) to counter the increase in worldwide terrorist activities against Israeli interests.

Estimates and warnings of Israeli military intelligence have generally been highly accurate, with few exceptions. However, those warnings have not always been heeded by Israeli military and political leaders.

The image of Israeli military intelligence has been hurt by some major scandals. The first chief, ISSER BE'ERI, was removed in Jan. 1949 after the execution of MEIR TUBIANSKY, a Jew suspected of having given information to the Arabs and the British. Be'eri had tried him with a kangaroo court. Subsequently, Binyamin Gibli was forced to quit in 1955 over the LAVON AFFAIR, a sabotage operation in Egypt. In addition, Yehoshafat Harkabi was discharged after his 1958 mishandling of a national mobilization exercise for Army reservists. Thus, three of the IDF's first four intelligence chiefs were fired.

Among the more successful heads of military intelligence were the multifaceted CHAIM HERZOG, who twice held the post and later became President of Israel, and MEIR AMIT, who also was head of the MOSSAD from 1963 to 1967 and brought modern management practices to Israeli intelligence. Aharon Yariv and his deputy and successor, Eliahu Zeira, were among the military leaders who shared in the praise for Israel's overwhelming success in the Six Day War (1967). But Zeira's career was destroyed by the intelligence failures on the eve of the Yom Kippur War (1973).

A decade later Yehoshua Saguy was replaced as head of Aman after an inquiry into the massacre of refugee camps in Beirut by Lebanese Phalangists, to whom Israeli forces allowed access to the camps. Saguy did not trust the Phalangists and did not want to cooperate with them, but he was overruled by the Israeli military commander, who took the advice of Mossad officials. The Israeli commission into the massacres concluded that Saguy had displayed "indifference and conspicuous lack of concern" about the affair and recommended his removal; he resigned on March 1, 1983. (No action was recommended against the head of the Mossad, Nahum Admoni, who had taken the post only four days before the massacres.)

Three chiefs of Aman have become Chief of Staff of the IDF: Ehud Barak (1991–1995), Amon Lipkin (1995–1998), and Moshe Ya'alon (2002–).

In the early 1950s, COUNTERINTELLIGENCE functions were removed from Israeli military intelligence. Accordingly, except for field security of military forces, all security functions are now preformed in Israel by the civilian police (Special Branch) and the (civilian) SHIN BET (Security Service).

Aman serves as the intelligence agency for both the IDF command structure and the Israeli Army; the Israeli Air Force and Navy additionally have small intelligence staffs that specialize in acquiring and analyzing information in their respective areas of interest. Aman is the largest of the Israeli intelligence organizations; according to Dan Raviv and Yossi Melman in *Every Spy a Prince* (1990), in the late 1980s it had a strength of some 7,000 men and women.

Heads of Israeli military intelligence:

(1947)–1949	Isser Be'eri (civilian)
1949–1950	Col. Chaim Herzog
1950–1955	Col. Binyarnin Gibli
1955–1959	Maj. Gen. Yehoshafat Harkabi
1959–1962	Maj. Gen. Chaim Herzog

1962–1963	Maj. Gen. Meir Armit
1964–1972	Maj. Gen. Aharon Yariv
1972–1974	Maj. Gen. Ehahu Zeira
1974–1978	Maj. Gen. Shlomo Gazit
1979–1983	Maj. Gen. Yehoshua Saguy
1983–1985	Maj. Gen. Ehud Barak
1986–1991	Maj. Gen. Amnon Shahak (formerly Lipkin)
1991–1995	Maj. Gen. Uri Saguy
1995–1998	Maj. Gen. Moshe Ya'alon
1998–2001	Maj. Gen. Eli Zeira
2001–	Maj. Gen. Aharon Ze'evi-Farkash

Ambler, Eric

(b. 1909 d. 1998)

English author of realistic spy novels. Unlike IAN FLEMING'S JAMES BOND [F], an Ambler hero is a character who survives not through gadgets but through his own intellectual skill and stamina.

Ambler's earliest spy novels anticipated a Europe at war: *The Dark Frontier* (1936), *The Uncommon Danger* (1937), *Epitaph for a Spy* (1938), *Cause for Alarm* (1938), and *The Mask of Dimitrios* (1939) (published in America as *A Coffin for Dimitrios*). *Epitaph for a Spy* was made into the film *Hotel Reserve* (1944).

He wrote the screenplay for *Topkapi*, involving jewel theft and intrigue, which was released in 1964; it was based on his 1963 novel *The Light of Day*.

Like many intellectuals, in the 1930s Ambler displayed leftist sympathies and strongly opposed fascism. Although two of his novels, *Uncommon Danger* and *Cause for Alarm*, featured a heroic Soviet agent, Andreas Zaleshoff, Ambler was not a communist. Most of his other spy novels featured ordinary Englishmen drawn into a world of espionage and intrigue.

During World War II he served in the Royal Artillery as a private and, subsequently, was assigned to a combat photographic unit and then to the film unit at the War Office. He wrote and produced nearly 100 training and propaganda films. At the end of the war he was a lieutenant colonel.

Also see LITERARY SPIES and MOVIES.

Amerasia Case

Investigation into the use of classified U.S. government documents by a magazine accused of following the communist line on China. *Amerasia*, which focused on U.S.–Asian affairs, had among its contributors officials of the State Department. The *Amerasia* affair was a sensation at the beginning of the congressional spies-in-government investigations of the late 1940s and 1950s.

In 1945 the magazine published an OFFICE OF STRATEGIC SERVICES (OSS) report on Thailand. OSS agents, in a BLACK BAG JOB, broke into the offices of the magazine and found classified documents. Then came an investigation by the FBI.

The FBI arrested Philip Jaffe, the editor of the magazine, and two contributors—Emmanuel Larsen of the State Department and Lt. Andrew Roth of the OFFICE OF NAVAL INTELLIGENCE (ONI)—for violating security regulations. (An ONI officer told a congressional committee that there were thousands of "fellow travelers" in the U.S. Navy at that time. The committee was investigating the loyalty of government employees. "Fellow travelers" allegedly followed the communist line but were not communists.)

Jaffe pleaded guilty to possession of classified documents. Larsen pleaded nolo contendere (no contest). Both were fined. Charges were dropped against Roth.

Among the *Amerasia* documents was a carbon copy of a memorandum traced to John Stewart Service, a career State Department officer. The memorandum contained the substance of a message from President Roosevelt to Generalissimo Chiang Kai-shek, the Chinese leader fighting a civil war against Chinese communists. Service, highly critical of Chiang, was dismissed in 1951, but reinstated in 1957.

Ames, Aldrich H.

(b. 1941)

A CIA COUNTERINTELLIGENCE officer who spied for the Soviets and, after the fall of the Soviet Union, for Russia. When Ames was arrested in 1994, federal officials said that he had perpetrated the costliest breach of security in CIA history. During his nine years as a spy he revealed more than 100 covert operations and betrayed more than 30 operatives spying for the CIA and other Western intelligence services. At least 10 betrayed Russians and East Europeans were executed. Among them was Maj. Gen. DIMITRI POLYAKOV, a Soviet GRU officer who spied for the United States for nearly 20 years and provided invaluable information.

Ames claimed that he began his spying by providing the Soviets with relatively useless information in a scam to make money. But a retired KGB officer, Viktor Cherkashin, said in 1997 that the first secrets Ames sold were the identities of two KGB officers who were DOUBLE AGENTS for the United States then stationed at the Soviet Embassy in Washington. The officers, Valery Martynov and Sergey Motorin, had been recruited by the FBI. Both were later executed.

Ames also provided the Soviets with information about two technical espionage operations run by the CIA: TUNNELS to tap Soviet communications to a space facility outside Moscow and Project Absorb, a device used to count the number of nuclear warheads carried by Soviet intercontinental missiles.

Another damaging effect of Ames's treachery was the incredible malfeasance of CIA officers who, aware that many of their AGENTS were being compromised, sent the White House and Pentagon tainted reports between 1986 and 1994. Dozens of reports on Soviet and Russian weapons developments and arms control efforts were known to be based on information from Moscow-controlled agents. But the CIA officials who knew this did not acknowledge the information in their reports. According to a Senate Select Intelligence Committee report, 11 reports sent to Presidents Ronald Reagan, GEORGE H. W. BUSH, and Bill Clinton did not reveal CIA reservations about the sources. But reports to the Pentagon during the same time included "some indication of some concern as to source"—without indicating that the "concern" was based on the suspicion that the source was Moscow-controlled.

Ames began spying in 1985, when he was the head of the CIA's Soviet Counterintelligence Division. Although he had been under suspicion as a Soviet MOLE for some time, not until 1992 did investigators begin to close in on him. His arrest rocked the CIA, touched off congressional demands for a housecleaning, brought down R. JAMES WOOLSEY, DIRECTOR OF CENTRAL INTELLIGENCE (DCI), and led to the early retirement of several high-ranking CIA officers.

In what a congressional critic called an "almost unbelievable" series of blunders, CIA investigators failed to link Ames's lavish lifestyle with the possibility that he was earning extra money as a spy. Soviet and Russian HANDLERS paid him at least $2.7 million during his career as a mole. He bought a $540,000 home for cash and drove a $40,000 red XJ6 Jaguar on his $69,843 annual salary. He had a lackluster record and was often drunk and accused of breaches of routine security.

The CIA's failure to ferret out Ames, said a report of the SENATE SELECT COMMITTEE ON INTELLIGENCE, "led to the loss of virtually all of C.I.A.'s intelligence assets targeted at the Soviet Union at the height of the cold war."

The mole hunt began in 1986 after the execution of two Soviet intelligence officers who had been recruited by the FBI. At first investigators believed that the agents had been betrayed by EDWARD LEE HOWARD, a CIA officer who had defected in 1985, or even CLAYTON LONETREE, a U.S. Marine guard convicted of espionage at the American Embassy in Moscow.

However, after the disappearance of three more agents, investigators reluctantly accepted the overwhelming probability that the information was coming from inside the CIA. Not until 1991, however, did the CIA confer with the FBI about the spy fears. The FBI launched an investigation CODE NAMED Nightmover. (A later probe was code-named Operation Anlace; an anlace is a short two-edged dagger.)

Ames was one of 20 suspects. Although he had passed POLYGRAPH tests in 1986 and 1991, Ames was transferred to the relatively insensitive CIA counternarcotics division. But he managed to keep on spying, obtaining highly classified documents that had nothing to do with his new assignment. In June 1992 the FBI successfully petitioned the secret FOREIGN INTELLIGENCE SURVEILLANCE COURT for permission to tap Ames's phone and covertly enter his home to install cameras and electronic BUGS and to tap his home computer. In Oct. 1992, when he said he was going to Colombia to visit his in-laws, his superiors learned that he was planning to go to Caracas, Venezuela. Under clandestine FBI surveillance, he was seen making contact with a Russian agent.

Hoping to catch Ames getting or receiving material

Aldrich H. Ames and his red Jaguar XJ6 at the moment of his arrest in 1994. Ames protested his innocence, which was ignored. He had betrayed more than 30 Western agents to Soviet intelligence services. (FEDERAL BUREAU OF INVESTIGATION)

from a DROP, the FBI initially delayed arresting him. Then, concerned that his Russian handlers were growing suspicious, the FBI began to close in. He was arrested on Feb. 21, 1994, the day before he was to leave for Moscow for an official CIA business meeting with Russian intelligence specialists on narcotics. Also arrested was his wife, Rosario, 41. The couple had a five-year-old son, Paul.

The son of a CIA officer, Ames met his first wife, Nan, in the CIA. When he was assigned to the Mexico City station in 1981, however, his wife did not accompany him; and his marriage, already failing, soon ended in divorce. In Mexico he met and later married Colombian-born Rosario, a low-level CIA source.

As a Soviet expert in the CIA, he had debriefed Soviet DEFECTOR VITALY YURCHENKO in 1985 and had been the key handler of ARKADY SHEVCHENKO, Under Secretary for Political Affairs at the UNITED NATIONS and the highest-ranking Soviet official to defect to the United States.

Under a plea bargain with federal prosecutors, Ames pleaded guilty to espionage and accepted a life sentence without parole. He was to cooperate with the CIA and FBI in exchange for mercy toward Rosario, who was given a 63-month sentence that, with good behavior, could be shortened to 42 months. But even in prison Ames continued to negotiate, trying to trade further cooperation for more inmate privileges.

In 1996 the U.S. Congress passed legislation providing American citizenship to the widows and children of Russians killed after Ames betrayed them.

Amit, Maj. Gen. Meir

(b. 1921)

Head of AMAN, the Israeli MILITARY INTELLIGENCE corps, from 1962 to 1963, and head of the MOSSAD from 1963 to 1968. Born in Palestine as Meir Slutzki, Amit grew up on a kibbutz (agricultural settlement).

He joined the Haganah, the underground Jewish

army, and in the Israeli War of Independence (1948–1949) he was a company commander and battalion commander, and then deputy commander of the famed Golani Brigade. He remained in the Israeli Army after the war, serving in infantry and tank units. In the Suez campaign (1956) he was second in command to Israeli military chief Moshe Dayan. While in military service, during 1961 Amit received a master's degree in business from Columbia University in New York City.

When Amit became head of the Aman in 1962, three of his four predecessors had been fired. Still, without prior intelligence experience, Amit took charge and brought modern management techniques to the service. This was accomplished despite intense rivalry and disagreements with ISSER HAREL, the head of the MOSSAD and Israel's MEMUNEH—the de facto head of all intelligence activities.

Then, without warning, on March 26, 1963, Prime Minister David Ben-Gurion called Amit into his office, having sent a plane to fetch him back from an inspection of military units near the Dead Sea. Armit was to take over the Mossad immediately. Harel had held that position for almost 12 years. (Amit's deputy, Maj. Aharon Yariv, succeeded him as head of the Aman.)

In *Every Spy a Prince* (1990), journalists Dan Raviv and Yossi Melman describe Amit's style:

> The new chief aimed to transform the Mossad into a serious and modern intelligence organization focusing on what Amit considered to be its major task: the collection of military and political data on the Arab states. He regarded the Mossad as an information-gathering body that would henceforth eschew show-off operations, which he viewed as a waste of resources. Influenced by the economic and business courses he took in the United States, Amit wished to imitate the American corporate mentality and style of management.

Amit's tenure as head of the Mossad lasted until Sept. 1968, and encompassed the highly successful Six Day War (1967). Intelligence collected by the Mossad and, especially, by the Aman (led by Yariv) was a key factor in providing Israel with an overwhelming victory against its Arab antagonists. A few days before the war, Amit secretly flew to the United States to tell President Johnson and RICHARD HELMS (the DIRECTOR OF CENTRAL INTELLIGENCE), and Secretary of Defense Robert McNamara, that the situation in the Middle East was extremely serious and that Israel had to go to war because of the Egyptian blockade that cut off Israeli access to the Red Sea and the Indian Ocean.

After retiring from the Mossad, Amit became president of Koors Industries, the largest industrial complex in Israel. After nine years at Koors he entered politics, becoming a member of the *Knesset* (parliament) and Minister of Transport and Communications.

Returning to business in 1982, he initiated project Amos, the first Israeli communications SATELLITE.

Amit, Maj. Yossi

(b. 1945)

Israeli Army INTELLIGENCE OFFICER who spied for the United States.

Amit had served in the Israeli Army, including the elite paratroopers, before being assigned to AMAN, the MILITARY INTELLIGENCE service. He was shot in the chest during a secret operation and was classified as partially disabled.

He was arrested on March 14, 1986, tried, and in 1987 convicted by a three-judge court of spying for the United States. He was sentenced to a 12-year prison term.

The case was tried in camera and kept secret by the Israeli government until 1993.

Amtorg

Soviet COVER organization for a spy operation run in the United States during the 1920s and 1930s. Amtorg was an abbreviation for *Amerikanskaya Torgovlya*—Trade Company USA.

Amtorg traces its beginnings to 1921, when Dr. ARMAND HAMMER, who had just graduated from Columbia University's College of Physicians and Surgeons, traveled to Moscow with a letter of introduction to V. I. Lenin. Armand was the son of Dr. Julius Hammer, a Russian-American socialist and friend of Lenin. A physician, Julius also owned a pharmaceutical company. Armand hoped to collect on a $150,000 debt the Russian government owed his father for drugs smuggled into the country during an Allied blockade of Russia.

Lenin eased Armand Hammer into what was to be a long and profitable business arrangement with the Soviet Union. In 1924 this led to the setting up of a Hammer-Soviet joint venture: the American Trading Organization. One of the officials helping Hammer was FELIKS EDMUNDOVICH DZERZHINSKY, founding director of the CHEKA, who operated under the guise of chairman of the Concessions Committee, which had helped to set up the joint venture. Thus, the Soviet intelligence apparatus was built into Amtorg from the beginning. To Hammer, Amtorg was a business deal; to the Soviets it was a way to juggle three missions: lobbying for diplomatic recognition of the Soviet Union; carrying on legitimate trade and purchasing; and espionage.

Many Amtorg officials were Soviet INTELLIGENCE OFFICERS seeking to steal industrial and military secrets and to recruit Americans, especially members of the Communist Party of the United States, as AGENTS. Amtorg remained active for many years after the United States recognized the Soviet regime in 1933. In 1948 the FBI raided a Soviet freighter and seized contraband illegal for export: Amtorg-acquired scientific instruments used for atomic research. Amtorg was disestablished a short time later.

Anadyr

Soviet CODE WORD for the massive, secret effort to emplace strategic missiles and protective air, naval, and ground forces in Cuba in 1962. The name Anadyr was itself a COVER, being the name of a Siberian port, far from the Caribbean.

Also see CUBAN MISSILE CRISIS.

Anderson, Maj. Rudolph, Jr.

(b. 1927 d. 1962)

U.S. U-2 RECONNAISSANCE aircraft pilot shot down over Cuba on Oct. 27, 1962, during the CUBAN MISSILE CRISIS. He was one of the two U.S. Air Force pilots who carried out the initial Air Force U-2 flights over Cuba that revealed the presence of Soviet ballistic missiles on the island.

The CIA had flown U-2 flights over Cuba since Oct. 1960; flights by Air Force–piloted U-2s over Cuba began on the night of Oct. 13–14, 1962, flown initially by two pilots from the Air Force's 4080th Strategic Reconnaissance Wing. Anderson flew one of two Air Force U-2 missions over Cuba on the following day, Oct. 15. He flew additional missions and again took off from McCoy Air Force Base in Florida on the morning of Oct. 27 for a flight over Cuba. Over the eastern end of the island, his U-2C aircraft was hit by an SA-2 surface-to-air missile launched by a Soviet missile battery. Anderson was killed when his plane crashed on an island in the Banes–Antilla area.

Robert Kennedy wrote in *Thirteen Days* (1969) of the following reaction when news of Anderson's loss reached the White House:

> "How can we send any more U-2 pilots into this area tomorrow unless we take out all of the SAM [Surface-to-Air Missile] sites?" the President asked. "We are now in an entirely new ball game." At first, there was almost unanimous agreement that we had to attack early the next morning with bombers and fighters and destroy the SAM sites. But again the President pulled everyone back. "It isn't the first step that concerns me," he said, "but both sides excalating to the fourth and fifth step—and we don't go to the sixth because there is no one around to do so. We must remind ourselves we are embarking on a very hazardous course."

No U.S. military action was taken in response to the Anderson shootdown; and both the U-2 flights and low-level reconnaissance continued. Anderson was the only U.S. combat casualty of the Cuban missile crisis. (At least one other U-2 was fired on by an SA-2 missile.)

Maj. Anderson's body was returned to the United States by the Cuban government on May 4, 1963.

André, Maj. John

(b. 1751 d. 1780)

British Army officer of the 54th Foot, serving as adjutant general to the British commander in New York, Gen. Sir Henry Clinton, during the American Revolution. André was also in charge of spy operations in the area.

André had been a suitor of 17-year-old Peggy Shippen before her marriage to BENEDICT ARNOLD, a leading continental officer. André entered into correspondence with Arnold in 1779 and in Sept. 1780 arranged for him to surrender the West Point territory and its important fortifications to the British. Gustavus was the CODE NAME used by André while dealing with Arnold.

André was captured on Sept. 24, 1780, after meeting with Arnold and trying to return to British lines. Following his capture, Gen. Clinton attempted to bargain for his release, but Gen. GEORGE WASHINGTON would accept only one person in exchange: Arnold.

The British major was tried as a spy and hanged at Tappan, New York, on Oct. 2, 1780. Calm and collected, André placed the noose around his own neck and tied his own handkerchief as a blindfold. His remains were reinterred in Westminster Abbey in London on Nov. 28, 1821. (He is one of only two acknowledged spies to be interred at Westminster; the other is APHRA BEHN.)

The three Americans who helped to capture André were awarded specially struck medals and a cash award by the Continental Congress.

André used the code name John Anderson when dealing with Arnold.

The execution of Maj. John André, a British officer caught behind American lines during the American Revolutionary War. He had been the handler of the American traitor Benedict Arnold, who had agreed to surrender West Point, a key military post on the Hudson River, to the British. (NATIONAL ARCHIVES)

Andrew, Christopher

Leading academic expert on national intelligence issues. In Dec. 2002 he was named historian of the British Security Service (MI5) with the specific task of writing a history to mark the centenary of MI5 in 2009. He has written or coauthored several significant books in the intelligence field.

Previously Andrew was professor of modern and contemporary history and chair of the History Department at Cambridge University. A former visiting professor of national security at Harvard University, he has been a guest lecturer at several other American universities, and has appeared frequently on American and British television programs.

His major works in the intelligence field include *KGB: The Inside Story* (1990), with OLEG GORDIEVSKY; *For the President's Eyes Only: Secret Intelligence and the American Presidency from Washington to Bush* (1995), and *The Sword and the Shield: The Mitrokhin Archive and the Secret History of the KGB* (1999), with VASILI MITROKHIN.

Antheil, Henry W., Jr.

SEE TYLER G. KENT

Andropov, Yuri Vladimirovich

(b. 1914 d. 1984)

Head of the Soviet KGB from 1967 to 1982 and, subsequently, president of the USSR and General Secretary of the Communist Party—the senior positions in the Soviet regime.

Born in the northern Caucasus, the son of a railway employee, Andropov studied at the university in Petrozarodsk and the Technical School of Water Transportation in Rybinsk, from which he graduated in 1936. At that time he began his political career as a *Komsomol* (youth) organizer. During World War II he served as a political commissar on the Finnish front and then served in a series of Communist Party positions, gaining a reputation as an expert on Eastern Europe. Some sources indicate that Andropov began working for the state security services in 1939.

He became head of the Political Department of the Central Committee in 1951. Subsequently, as Soviet ambassador to Hungary from 1954, he was instrumental in calling for Soviet military intervention during the ill-fated Hungarian revolt of 1956. From 1957 to 1967 Andropov was chief of the Central Committee department in charge of relations with foreign Communist Party organizations. He was promoted to Party secretariat in 1962.

In May 1967 Andropov was elevated to candidate membership in the decision-making Politburo and became chairman of the Committee for State Security—the head of the KGB—with the rank of General of the Army.

Yuri Andropov was the only head of the Soviet secret police apparatus to become the head of the government. Lavrenty Beria had expected to succeed Josef Stalin when the Soviet dictator died in March 1953, but he was arrested and executed by his colleagues. (WORLD WIDE)

In 1968 Andropov warned the Soviet leadership of a major Western plot to undermine Communist Party control of Czechoslovakia, helping to precipitate the Soviet assault against the Dubcek government. Under Andropov's directions some 30 KGB ILLEGALS posing as Western tourists on the eve of the invasion put up inflammatory posters and painted slogans calling for the overthrow of communist leaders.

In April 1973 Andropov became the first state security chief since LAVRENTY BERIA to have full membership in the Politburo. The KGB made major improvements in both image and effectiveness as Andropov brought a new level of discipline, decision, and intellectual skills to the security organ. Foreign intelligence collection became more sophisticated and, like the West, the Soviets increasingly employed high-tech methods of intelligence collection. At the same time he intensified the use of AGENTS "on the ground."

In May 1982 Andropov left the security apparatus to become a secretary of the Central Committee of the Communist Party. When Soviet leader Leonid Brezhnev died in late 1982, Andropov succeeded him. The Western press labeled the new Soviet leader a "relatively open-minded man," a strange description for a longtime CHEK-

IST. The 68-year-old Andropov was described by *The Washington Post* as "an urbane man who can speak English." Hungarian officials, the report continued,

recall Andropov's stay in Budapest as Soviet ambassador during the military intervention by Moscow in 1956 and the suppression of the uprising. Despite his role in the Soviet suppression of the Hungarian revolt, he is remembered as a diplomat who took the trouble to learn Hungarian and understand the country's distinctive culture.

Part of Andropov's appeal to Western journalists stemmed from his being the first Russian leader since Czar Nicholas II to be fluent in English. Several Soviet sources suggested that Andropov had a special ability to put people at ease, although he was not a "hugger" like Khrushchev and Brezhnev. Also, Andropov's totally urbane personality stood in sharp contrast to the rustic character of his predecessors.

Andropov's tenure as head of the Soviet Union was brief. Three months after he became General Secretary on Nov. 12, 1982, his diabetic kidneys ceased to function and he was placed on an artificial kidney machine. He made his last public appearance in Aug. 1983, nearly six months before his death on Feb. 9, 1984.

With the American GEORGE H. W. BUSH and Israeli CHAIM HERZOG, Andropov was the only head of a major inelligence service to become chief of state.

Angel

Slang used by INTELLIGENCE OFFICERS and AGENTS for a member of an opposing intelligence service.

Angleton, James Jesus

(b. 1917 d. 1987)

Leading COUNTERINTELLIGENCE specialist of the U.S. CIA at the height of the Cold War. A CIA "hard-liner," Angleton believed strongly that the Soviet intelligence apparatus was continually trying to infiltrate the CIA.

Born in Boise, Idaho, he was 16 when his father, a business executive, was transferred to Italy. He was educated in an English preparatory school as well as college prior to entering Yale University in 1937. There he helped to establish a poetry magazine, *Furioso*, reflecting his interest in literature and poetry.

In 1943, two years after graduating from Yale, he entered the Army and joined the OFFICE OF STRATEGIC SERVICES (OSS). In London, where he sometimes visited T. S. Eliot in off hours, he was assigned to X-2, the counterintelligence branch of the OSS, which also handled ULTRA material. He got to know officers in the British intelligence services MI5 and MI6, including HAROLD (KIM) PHILBY. In 1944 Angleton was sent to Rome to head the X-2 Italian branch, working against Italian fascist intelligence activities. One of the Vatican contacts Angleton developed was a priest who later became Pope Paul VI. The Angleton legend was already established: Maj. Gen. WILLIAM DONOVAN called him the "most professional counterintelligence officer" in the OSS.

Angleton prepared detailed studies of German intelligence units and photographs of German officers wanted for interrogation or possible war crimes trial. He got the photographs by canvassing Rome's photo studios for negatives, knowing that German officers often posed there for portraits to be sent home.

After the war, assigned to the Strategic Services Unit in War Department, Angleton worked with Italian counterintelligence against Soviet intelligence activities. During this period he made connections with the Jewish underground in Europe, which later developed into a close and long-term relationship with the Israeli MOSSAD.

Angleton joined the CIA at its inception in 1947 and in 1954 established the first CIA counterintelligence office. One of his earliest assignments involved COVERT ACTION: the CIA involvement in the 1948 Italian general election, which, thanks to CIA funds, ended in the Communists' defeat.

He served more than 20 years as head of counterintelligence at CIA, where he was variously known as Mother, the Gray Ghost, and Virginia Thin—a reference to his cadaverous frame. Angleton was forced to resign in Dec. 1974 when WILLIAM COLBY, the DIRECTOR OF CENTRAL INTELLIGENCE, became convinced that Angleton's frenzied hunt for a Soviet MOLE was hurting the CIA. At the time he retired, Angleton headed an office of some 300 men and women. (Under Colby the office was reportedly reduced to about 80.)

One of Angleton's most notorious cases was the prolonged investigation of KGB defector YURI NOSENKO, who claimed to have been the CASE OFFICER for Lee Harvey Oswald when the American was in the Soviet Union. Nosenko insisted that the KGB was not involved with the assassination of President John F. Kennedy.

After retiring to his hobbies of fly-fishing and orchid growing, in 1975 Angleton was awarded the Distinguished Intelligence Medal, the highest CIA decoration.

Also see WILDERNESS OF MIRRORS.

Anlace

SEE ALDRICH H. AMES

Anthropoid

British CODE NAME for the operation to assassinate German official REINHARD HEYDRICH in 1941.

Antietam

The Battle of Antietam Creek was the scene of the failure of the most significant intelligence coup of the American Civil War. On Sept. 12, 1862, as Confederate forces under Gen. Robert E. Lee thrust northward into Maryland, two Union soldiers of the 27th Indiana Regiment, resting in an open field near Frederick, Maryland, found an envelope containing three cigars. The cigars were wrapped in paper—a copy of Gen. Lee's Special Orders No. 191, his plan for the invasion of Maryland. In *Mr. Lincoln's Army* (1951), distinguished Civil War historian Bruce Catton called the soldiers' find "... the greatest security leak in American military history—the only one that ever finally affected the outcome of a great war."

The plan promptly reached the Union field commander, Maj. Gen. George B. McClellan. Young (age 34) and charismatic, he was the commander of the Army of the Potomac and the second-ranking officer in the Union Army. Although McClellan took immediate actions to exploit the intelligence coup, he failed to destroy Lee's army upon bringing it to battle on Sept. 17. McClellan had a two-to-one superiority of troops over Lee but suffered from his own timidity, a poor battle plan, and critical shortcomings in his subordinate Maj. Gen. Ambrose E. Burnside. McClellan was also hampered by faulty intelligence provided by ALLAN PINKERTON.

The Battle of Antietam Creek (called Sharpsburg by the Confederates) marked the bloodiest day in American military history: 11,657 Union soldiers were killed or wounded, and the Confederates suffered 9,300 casualties.

Apparat

An espionage ring or CELL.

Aquacade

SEE RHYOLITE

Aquarium

Slang for the headquarters of Soviet-Russian MILITARY INTELLIGENCE (GRU). Located on Khoroshevskiy Highway in the Moscow suburb of Khodynke, the main building is a nine-story structure whose largely glass external walls account for its nickname. (Many GRU officers refer to the building as *steklyashka*, "piece of glass.")

GRU DEFECTOR Vladimir Rezun, writing under the pen name VIKTOR SUVOROV, called his 1987 book about the GRU *Aquarium.*

Ar 234 Blitz (Lightning)

The world's first jet-propelled bomber, employed on long-range RECONNAISSANCE missions over Europe in 1944–1945. Like several other German jet-propelled aircraft, this high-performance plane arrived on the scene too late to have an impact on the war.

The Ar 234V7 reconnaissance version, carrying various combinations of cameras, was first flown operationally over France on Aug. 2, 1944; reconnaissance flights were later flown over Britain. The Ar 234B-2

bomber version became operational in late 1944 and could carry up to 4,410 pounds of bombs. The first bombing raids were made during the Battle of the Bulge in Dec. 1944. Limited by fuel shortages, these sporadic missions continued until the end of the war in early May 1945.

Built by the Arado firm, the bomber was developed in response to a German Air Ministry requirement for a high-speed reconnaissance aircraft. It first flew on July 30, 1943, and entered production in Sept. 1944. Originally a twin-jet aircraft, the eighth prototype (Ar 234V8), which flew on Feb. 4, 1944, had four turbojet engines. There were continued problems with the jet engines, which had a normal service life of only 25 flight hours. Several night-fighter variants of the Ar 234 were also developed, and a planned but never built Ar 234 variant was to carry a V-1 guided missile, or "buzz bomb."

The twin-engine At 234B-2 production variant had a top speed of 461 mph, an operational ceiling of 36,000 feet, and a range of more than 950 miles (while carrying a 2,205-pound bomb to half that distance). The four-engine At 234 could reach 546 mph. The few Ar 234C aircraft that were completed had pressurized cockpits.

Aralov, Gen. Simon Ivanovich

(b. 1880 d. 1969)

First chief of Soviet MILITARY INTELLIGENCE (GRU), in 1918–1919, and subsequently a senior official in military intelligence although twice arrested in Stalinist purges.

Born to a wealthy merchant family, Aralov entered the Russian Army in 1905 and was an early member of the Bolshevik Party. He served in World War I as a major in military intelligence. After taking part in the October Revolution of 1917 on the Bolshevik side, he helped to establish the CHEKA. Rapidly promoted, in Oct. 1918 Aralov became the first chief of the GRU. In July 1920 he moved to the post of chief of intelligence of the 12th Red Army, then to that of the 14th Red Army. He subsequently became head of intelligence for the Southwest Front during the Russian Civil War. Beginning in 1921 Aralov was a deputy chief of military intelligence, working under diplomatic COVER in Turkey, Latvia, and Lithuania. He was later responsible for setting up RESIDENT offices in the United States, Germany, and Japan.

In Stalin's anti-military purges beginning in 1937, Aralov was dismissed from all military posts and made a deputy director of the Literature Museum. He was arrested in 1938 and spent three years in prison, after which he served as a private in a penal battalion. By the end of World War II, however, he had been promoted to colonel, and when the war was over he was reassigned to the GRU.

Arrested again in 1946, he spent 10 years in a concentration camp. Upon his liberation in 1956 he was immediately appointed deputy to the chief of the GRU. A year later he was again dismissed as part of Nikita Khrushchev's purge of Marshal of the Soviet Union Georgi Zhukov and his clique. Aralov then lived quietly, writing about the Civil War, until his death.

Arcos Affair

Diplomatic uproar over a Soviet spy ring that operated in England in the 1920s. The Soviet Trade Delegation, which was riddled with spies, had offices in London with the All Russia Cooperative Society, Ltd. (ARCOS). The British Security Service (MI5) suspected that Arcos personnel were INTELLIGENCE OFFICERS. At the request of MI5, some 150 police officers staged raids on the offices and warehouses in May 1927.

After sifting through the 250,000 confiscated documents, British officials said that they had found evidence of espionage and broke off diplomatic relations with the Soviet Union. Britain had severed relations three years previously after an incident known as the ZINOVIEV letter.

In the wake of this episode, called the Arcos affair, the Soviets shifted from using LEGAL agents, such as diplomats and trade representatives, to using ILLEGALS, many of them not Russian. The Soviets ran a similar spy operation in the United States under an organization known as AMTORG.

Argon

U.S. mapping SATELLITE developed in parallel with the CORONA spy satellite. Project Argon grew out of a U.S. military requirement for precise geodetic data on the Soviet Union for targeting U.S. strategic missiles.

The project, approved by the White House in 1959, was managed within the CIA's Corona project to avoid competing for satellite launch resources and to simplify security. The early Argon missions with the KH-5 camera were flown independently, but later flights "piggybacked" on Corona satellites. (See KEYHOLE.)

The Argon system flew 12 missions between Feb. 17, 1961, and Aug. 21, 1964, and the satellite's camera was operational from May 1962 to Aug. 1964. Six of the 12 were considered successful; six did not produce useful film.

The KH-5 camera had a ground resolution of 460 feet, that is, it could map objects 460 feet in size. Argon orbited at an average altitude of 200 miles.

Argus

Proposed U.S. spy SATELLITE for SIGNALS INTELLIGENCE collection. Its development to replace the RHYOLITE satellite was formally approved by DIRECTOR OF CENTRAL INTELLIGENCE WILLIAM COLBY, in 1971.

However, Secretary of Defense JAMES SCHLESINGER ruled that the system was not necessary. Colby appealed the cancellation to President Gerald Ford, who directed the NATIONAL SECURITY COUNCIL to examine the issue. Based on the council's recommendation, Ford backed Colby. But Congress refused to fund the satellite and the project died.

Arisue, Lt. Gen. Seizo

Head of Japanese MILITARY INTELLIGENCE during most of World War II.

Arisue was Japan's military ATTACHÉ in Rome during the 1930s. In the late 1930s he served in North China. Describing a meeting with the Army Chief of Staff when Arisue returned to Japan, British writers Meirion and Susie Harries in their *Soldiers of the Sun* (1991) relate a story that may be apocryphal: One of the Chief of Staff's aides joined them, saying that he had just been to the Meiji Shrine to pray for success on Guadalcanal, where U.S. and Japanese troops were locked in brutal combat. Reportedly, Arisue asked, "Where's Guadalcanal?"

The authors use the story to make the point that the Army's main preoccupation was not with the Pacific theater, but with the Asian mainland. This was the situation facing Arisue when he became Chief of the Army General Staff's Second Bureau (intelligence) in Aug. 1942. He served until the end of the war in Aug. 1945.

A day after the atomic bombing of Hiroshima on Aug. 6, 1945, he flew to the devastated city to meet with surviving officers to gain first-hand information on the catastrophe. Subsequently, Arisue was selected by the prime minister to officially greet Gen. Douglas MacArthur's advance party when it landed at Atsugi airfield on Aug. 28, 1945. Meeting the U.S. Army officers, he escorted them to a tent and offered orange punch. When the Americans hesitated, Arisue picked up a glass of the punch and drained it.

After the war Arisue used his knowledge of the Far East and Soviet Union as a bargaining chip to ingratiate himself with Gen. MacArthur's intelligence staff. Working closely with Maj. Gen. CHARLES A. WILLOUGHBY, they formed a "historical research team" of former Japanese intelligence officers to support MacArthur's staff.

Arlington Hall

This former girls' school in Arlington, Va., a suburb of Washington, D.C., became the site of the U.S. Army's SIGNAL INTELLIGENCE SERVICE (SIS) in World War II.

From its formation in 1930 until 1942, SIS was housed in the Munitions Building on the Washington Mall, part of a complex of "temporary" buildings erected for World War I. The spaces immediately became overcrowded at the start of World War II. At first it was expected that SIS would be housed in the almost completed Pentagon building across the Potomac River. Before that move could be made, however, the decision was made to locate SIS at a site of its own, preferably outside Washington, where there would be room for expansion and where security could be maintained.

The site ultimately chosen, after several alternatives were considered, was the Arlington Hall Junior College on Route 50. This location was a few miles from the Pentagon and relatively close to the primary East Coast SIS radio intercept station being planned at Vint Hill Farms, near Warrenton, Va. The location was also close to housing in the Washington area for the rapidly growing SIS staff.

The property was purchased for $650,000 plus $40,000 for additional furnishings. The War Department took possession on June 14, 1942, and SIS immediately began moving personnel, files, and machinery to the school. The move was completed on Aug. 24.

Almost immediately construction began on additional buildings as well as security for the TOP SECRET facility.

Simultaneously, the Navy's CRYPTANALYSIS staff relocated from the Washington Mall complex to another former school at Nebraska and Massachusetts Avenues in northwest Washington. (See NAVAL SECURITY STATION.)

The successor agencies to SIS remained at Arlington Hall until the late 1980s.

Armed Forces Security Agency (AFSA)

Established on May 20, 1949, to consolidate the activities of the U.S. Army, Navy, and Air Force in the area of CRYPTOLOGY in a single agency, under the direction and control of the Joint Chiefs of Staff. The agency thus had responsibility for all COMMUNICATIONS INTELLIGENCE (COMINT) and COMMUNICATIONS SECURITY (COMSEC) activities of the armed forces. The existence of the agency was secret at the time that it was set up.

By Jan. 1950 the military services had transferred sufficient personnel—uniformed and civilian—to AFSA for it to begin operations. But when the outbreak of the Korean War in June 1950 required a rapid expansion of U.S. COMINT and COMSEC activities, the new agency was not capable of meeting those requirements. According to an official history, during the war "the quality of strategic intelligence derived from COMINT fell below that which had been provided in World War II." There were clashes between AFSA and the services, COMINT CONSUMERS, and the State Department.

In reality, AFSA had simply become a fourth cryptologic service, competing with the activities of the Army, Navy, and Air Force. As a result of a special panel established by President Truman in late 1951, in Oct. 1952, the NSA was established to overcome the problems experienced with AFSA.

There were two directors of AFSA:

July 1949–July 1951	Rear Adm. Earl E. Stone, USN
July 1951–Nov. 1952	Maj. Gen. Ralph J. Canine, USA

Also see FORT MEADE.

Army Intelligence, U.S.

The birth of U.S. Army intelligence dates to 1776 when a young officer, NATHAN HALE, volunteered to go behind British lines and spy for Gen. GEORGE WASHINGTON, who had a profound belief in the need for TACTICAL INTELLIGENCE. Hale, wearing civilian clothes, was caught and hanged as a spy. Hale was a lone operative, a volunteer who had no intelligence organization behind him. That was to be the condition of Army intelligence for many years.

As the young United States of America expanded westward, exploratory expeditions—Lewis and Clark to the Northwest, Pike to Colorado—were partly intelligence-collecting missions. Capt. Benjamin L. E. Bonneville, heading out on an expedition beyond the Rocky Mountains in 1832, was ordered to gather intelligence on the "warriors that may be in each tribe or nation that you meet with. . . ." Through the rest of the 19th century, the only organization for intelligence-gathering for clashes between the Army and Indians were units known as Indian Scouts.

In the new republic's first international conflict, the War of 1812 with Britain, there was no intelligence organization. During the Mexican War in 1845, the Army established the Mexican Spy Scout Company, a gang of Mexican bandits who spied for the United States.

Both sides had intelligence-gathering agencies during the Civil War, the Union for a time depending upon a civilian, ALLAN PINKERTON, and the Confederacy using volunteer AGENTS, many of them women (see EMMA EDMONDS, BELLE BOYD). Later in the war, the Union established the BUREAU OF MILITARY INFORMATION, commanded by Col. GEORGE H. SHARPE. Although limited to the Army of the Potomac, it was the first official U.S. Army intelligence organization.

The Civil War also saw the first use of aerial RECONNAISSANCE (see BALLOONS). Intelligence figured prominently in the Battle of ANTIETAM, but as ALLEN W. DULLES wrote in *The Craft of Intelligence* (1963), "No great battles were won or lost or evaded because of superior intelligence. Intelligence operations were limited for the most part to more or less localized and temporary targets."

INFORMATION AND ATTACHÉS

An official MILITARY INTELLIGENCE organization was finally established in the U.S. Army in 1885, when, according to tradition, the Secretary of War asked a simple question about a foreign army and was told that the War Department did not have the answer to that question or any like it. In anticipation of more questions, the War Department established what was grandly called the Military Information Division (MID), under the Miscellaneous Branch of the Adjutant General's Office. The division had one officer and one clerk assigned to the task of searching newspapers, State Department reports, and other sources. (Three years before, the U.S. Navy had started gathering its own information through the OFFICE OF NAVAL INTELLIGENCE.)

In 1889 the Army began its first permanent military ATTACHÉ system, sending officers to BERLIN, VIENNA, Paris, London, and St. Petersburg. Because the Army did not have money to support its attachés beyond their regular pay, only wealthy officers could be given the assignment. Untrained and often mere dilettantes dabbling in intelligence, most of those early attachés produced little information of value.

The MID, however, was growing in value. By the time of the Spanish-American War in 1898, the MID was a fully functioning intelligence agency—preparing maps, analyzing information from the attachés, and responding to requests from CONSUMERS. The military attaché's reports on the movement of troops and matériel were analyzed to produce accurate estimates for the War Department. An MID study on the weather and terrain of Cuba, prepared at the request of the White House, recommended that troops not be sent there until winter because of the potentially debilitating effects of tropical weather on U.S. soldiers. Displeased by what he saw as a negative report, the Secretary of War told the chief of MID that he would not be promoted.

The famous "message to Garcia"—the subject of a widely published inspirational essay by Elbert Hubbard—was carried by an MID officer, Lt. Andrew S. Rowan, to Gen. Calixto García y Iñigues, the commander of the Cuban rebel army. Capt. RALPH H. VAN DEMAN, another MID officer in Cuba during the war, was to become one of the most important figures in Army intelligence.

In the Philippines after the 1898 war, Van Deman gathered intelligence against native rebels and Japanese, precursors of a war to come, already seeking their own intelligence there. He discovered that the rebels were planning to assassinate Gen. Arthur MacArthur (father of Gen. Douglas MacArthur of World War II fame).

When the Army organized a general staff system, the MID became the second division of the General Staff, a rise in status (see G-2). But due to bureaucratic infighting, the MID was subsumed under the Army War College, and effective intelligence work entered a hiatus.

WORLD WAR I

When the United States entered World War I, the MID became the Military Intelligence Division under Maj. Van Deman, who established the Army's first extensive DOMESTIC INTELLIGENCE program to oversee the American Protective League, the brainchild of a Chicago advertising man, to track down spies and draft dodgers. Van Deman later stiffened control over league members. Although league members had no legal law enforcement power, they tapped telephones and searched suspects' offices. He also sent black agents into black communities to investigate reports of German attempts to exploit racial tensions. MID itself had a Negative Division that undertook COUNTERINTELLIGENCE, and a Positive Division, which handled intelligence. A Cipher Bureau was set up under Lt. HERBERT O. YARDLEY, who would become the foremost cryptographer of the era. MID's search for spies produced one major German agent, LOTHAR WITZKE, who was captured in Mexico.

In France, the U.S. Army's Corps of Intelligence Police (CIP), a motley group that included French draft dodgers and American criminals—all of whom could speak French—patrolled forward areas, hunting spies and saboteurs. The Radio Intelligence Section monitored German transmissions and listened to U.S. traffic for security violations.

After the war, a pared-down MID concentrated on making maps, doing research on aerial photography, and adapting to the shortages and frustrations of the peacetime Army. One of the intelligence innovations of this time was a horse-carried radio receiver for mounted cavalry units. When the "Bonus Army" (veterans seeking immediate payment of a promised bonus) marched on Washington in 1932, CIP agents mingled with the marchers to gather intelligence.

In 1930 the Army Signal Corps set up a new codebreaking unit under WILLIAM F. FRIEDMAN, who had been in front-line radio intelligence during the war; he headed the newly formed SIGNAL INTELLIGENCE SERVICE (SIS), developing electromechanical encryption and decryption devices. SIS interception stations were established in Texas, California, the Panama Canal Zone, Hawaii, and the Philippines. In 1940 Friedman and his staff broke the principal Japanese diplomatic code, called PURPLE.

WORLD WAR II

Army codebreakers had triumphed over Japanese code makers. But the triumph was short-lived, for the PEARL HARBOR ATTACK of Dec. 7, 1941, was immediately viewed as an intelligence failure. It was not. The failure lay in the inability of the fledgling INTELLIGENCE COMMUNITY (a term not yet in use) to recognize the need to get its PRODUCT and evaluations to the highest levels of the military and the White House.

Behind the codebreakers there was little. "Prior to World War II," Gen. George C. Marshall later said, "our foreign intelligence was little more than what a military attaché could learn at dinner, more or less over the coffee cups." Between the wars, Gen. Dwight D. Eisenhower said, "no funds were provided with which to establish the basic requirements of an intelligence system—a far-flung organization of fact finders."

What did quickly develop—first the COORDINATOR OF INFORMATION and then the OFFICE OF STRATEGIC SERVICES (OSS)—emerged not from the Army but from the efforts of then-Col. WILLIAM J. DONOVAN. Although the OSS was placed under theoretical military control, it was essentially a wartime Army-Navy-civilian organization that reported to the Joint Chiefs of Staff.

MID remained the intelligence arm of the Army, but its duties were more administrative than operational. Most of its effort was concentrated in the Military District of Washington, investigating the loyalty of civilian and military personnel of the War Department and aiding in the protection of government buildings, bridges, and utilities in the city.

The G-2 branch of the Army's General Staff had responsibility for disseminating intelligence about the enemy and specific warnings about the danger of subversive activities. The major Army intelligence activities with respect to the collection of information about the enemy and preparation of intelligence estimates were undertaken by theater commanders; for the Army these were Gen. MacArthur in the Southwest Pacific Area and Gen. Eisenhower in the North African–Mediterranean–European areas.

In the field, as the Army increased in size—from five active divisions in 1939 to 89 divisions at the end of the war—so too did the number and size of Army intelligence units. Officers with the assignment of G-2 were found at every level of the Army down to battalions (some 800 men). RECONNAISSANCE units gathered TACTI-CAL INTELLIGENCE for commanders. Every infantry division had a 155-man reconnaissance troop; the armored divisions had a 900-man cavalry reconnaissance squadron, which rode jeeps and tanks rather than horses. There were also specialized Signal Corps units that intercepted enemy communications, while the 2ND SIGNAL BATTALION operated the higher-level Army intercepts for the Signals Intelligence Service and its successors.

The CIP changed its name to the COUNTER INTELLIGENCE CORPS (CIC). In the United States, CIC agents worked with the FBI in raids on known Nazi sympathizers. Overseas, CIC agents were attached to combat divisions to play a variety of roles, from getting the maps of enemy minefields and analyzing captured enemy documents, to ferreting out collaborators and enemy agents. CIC men were among the first Allied solders to enter Rome in June 1944.

In the southwest Pacific, intelligence was sparse to begin with and was tightly controlled by Gen. Douglas MacArthur (see AUNT MINNIES). He barred the OSS from his command, having already set up his own organizations, the ALLIED INTELLIGENCE BUREAU and the Allied Translator and Interpreter Section, which used American NISEI soldiers to interrogate Japanese prisoners, read captured enemy documents, and conduct psychological warfare. CIC units often worked with the Nisei in security investigations in combat and occupied areas.

In the field, officers from combat arms served as the G-2 down to the battalion level. At the level of the field army there was an intelligence battalion and an ARMY SECURITY AGENCY group, while there were intelligence companies at the corps and division levels. COMBAT INTELLIGENCE became more complex, as enemy capabilities and intentions in such diverse fields as chemical and nuclear weapons, electronic intercept, and electronic countermeasures had to be added to the traditional need for intelligence about such matters as topography, the enemy's ORDER OF BATTLE, leadership, equipment, intentions, and communications.

COLD WAR INTELLIGENCE

CIC personnel became key members of occupation forces in Germany and in Japan. In Germany they helped investigate war crimes and assess who was and was not a Nazi. In Japan, the CIC arrested war crimes defendants, including former Prime Minister Hideki Tojo. In both countries, the CIC soon was investigating communists and looking for Soviet-sponsored espionage. The Cold War had begun.

The rapid demobilization of the Army, the loss of highly skilled reserve officers, and the 1947 establishment of the CIA all conspired to lessen the importance of Army intelligence outside the Army itself. And the creation of the U.S. Air Force took away the Army's aerial reconnaissance assets. Out of the ashes came the ARMY SECURITY AGENCY (ASA), set up in Sept. 1945 to take over "all signals intelligence and communications security establishments, units, and personnel." The ASA operated under the Army's Assistant Chief of Staff (Intelligence). A

particular part of its charter was CRYPTOLOGY. In barely three years the ASA was disbanded and replaced by the ARMED FORCES SECURITY AGENCY, which secretly evolved into the National Security Agency (NSA).

The CIC, like Army intelligence itself, played a minor role in the Korean War. A small network of U.S.-controlled Korean agents, in place when the war began, was quickly BLOWN. Army intelligence was so ill prepared that there were no parachutes for potential agents; they were trained to jump by parachute by stepping out of the back of a speeding jeep. Nearly every Korean sent behind the lines, sometimes by parachute, sometimes by rubber boat, was killed or captured.

The creation of the DEFENSE INTELLIGENCE AGENCY (DIA) in 1961 further diluted Army intelligence activities, since the DIA was given the responsibility of supplying intelligence support for General Staff studies. In the same year the CIC became the Intelligence Corps (the name was changed again in 1965 to become the Intelligence Corps Command); its principal task was counterintelligence within the United States and in Army units at home and abroad.

VIETNAM AND BEYOND

Intelligence units were part of the general buildup of U.S. forces in Vietnam. By 1965 the largest concentration of Army intelligence personnel was in the Military Assistance Command, Vietnam (MACV). Other military intelligence groups were spread around the country with both intelligence-gathering and counterintelligence functions. Besides an intelligence center in Saigon, there were also centers for interrogation and the analysis of enemy documents and matériel. Long-range reconnaissance patrols provided tactical intelligence, often at the cost of high casualties.

Military intelligence officers worked with South Vietnamese and CIA officers in the PHOENIX program, which became controversial because its stated purpose of pacifying areas often led to the assassination of real and suspected Viet Cong. Many HUMAN INTELLIGENCE operations were under the control of the STUDIES AND OBSERVATION GROUP, which inserted intelligence teams into enemy-controlled territory.

On the home front, Army counterintelligence agents joined the FBI in gathering information on antiwar groups. At demonstrations in Washington, D.C., clean-cut young men with close-cropped hair, often in suits and ties, stood out in the crowds of protesters clad in jeans and T-shirts. They were Army agents, theoretically gathering intelligence under Army Intelligence Command guidelines requiring the Army to be ready to respond to civil disturbances. In reality, they were part of the campaigns of the Johnson and Nixon administrations against the antiwar movement.

The collection of domestic intelligence triggered lawsuits that charged the Army with illegally spying on civilians, as well as criticism from civil liberties groups. In May 1970, panicky Army National Guardsmen fired on students and outside agitators at Ohio's Kent State University who were at a rally protesting the widening of the war in Southeast Asia. They killed four people and wounded eight. Although the guardsmen had nothing to do with the Army's domestic intelligence program, the shooting stunned Army officials, and the program was quietly ended.

Like the rest of the Army, intelligence officers were anxious to get Vietnam behind them. As the Army settled down to another era of peace, it reorganized. In 1984 all Army intelligence production was centralized under the Army Intelligence Agency. At the tactical level, the Army created Combat Electronic Warfare and Intelligence units to bring ELECTRONIC INTELLIGENCE closer to the battlefield. The units got their first taste of combat during the Persian Gulf War in 1991, the most electronic and computerized conflict yet fought.

Army intelligence units had an important role in the Gulf War of 1991 as well as in the invasion of Iraq in 2003. Following the latter conflict, analysts in the 104th Military Intelligence Battalion were able to locate deposed Iraqi dictator Saddam Hussein, enabling troops to capture him (see IRAQ). Also see TASK FORCE 20.

Army Intelligence and Security Command

(INSCOM)

U.S. Army command established on Jan. 1, 1977, combining the ARMY SECURITY AGENCY and other field activities of ARMY INTELLIGENCE, INSCOM was the result of an Army study conducted in 1974 that recommended a new command structure for intelligence activities above the corps level and the provision of direct support to intelligence operations at the corps, division, and unit levels.

The functional merger and restructuring of INSCOM were completed on Oct. 1, 1977. Initially headquartered at ARLINGTON HALL in Arlington, Va., INSCOM moved to FORT MEADE, Md., in 1981; again to the Arlington Hall site in 1986; and to Fort Belvoir, Va., in 1989.

Beginning in 1986, the five multidiscipline intelligence groups within INSCOM were redesignated as brigades. In wartime, reserve personnel were to be called up to bring the brigades to full strength. The end of the Cold War in 1991 saw a broadening of INSCOM activities and areas of interest. During the Gulf War of 1991, INSCOM's 513th Military Intelligence Brigade was deployed to Saudi Arabia to support U.S. ground forces in that conflict.

Further realignment of component units followed: the 115th Military Intelligence Group in Hawaii provides support for Pacific operations; the 116th Group at Fort Gordon, Ga., provides support for European, American, and Middle Eastern operations; the 300th Military Intelligence Brigade in Draper, Utah, supports Army linguist requirements ariund the world, and contains several Army National Guard battalions; the 501st Brigdae is at Yongsan, South Korea; the 513rd Brigade is at Fort Gordon, Ga.; and the 704th Brigade at Fort Belvoir, Va., supports Army SIGNALS INTLLIGENCE activities. Also, the 111th Military Intelligence Brigade operates the U.S.

Army Intelligence Center at Fort Huachucha, Ariz., to provide training and support for INSCOM.

Army Security Agency

(ASA)

U.S. Army agency responsible for all SIGNALS INTELLIGENCE (SIGINT) and COMMUNICATIONS SECURITY (COMSEC) activities, establishments, units, and personnel from 1945 to 1977.

Previously, the Army's Signal Security Agency (SSA), and before that the SIGNAL INTELLIGENCE SERVICE (SIS), had those responsibilities. SSA was renamed the Army Security Agency on Sept. 15, 1945. At that time administrative responsibility for the Army's SIGINT efforts was removed from the chief signal officer and placed under ARMY INTELLIGENCE (G-2).

The ASA inherited not only the mission and functions performed by the wartime agencies but also the 2ND SIGNAL SERVICE BATTALION and the SIGINT and COMSEC activities previously controlled by theater and Army and Army Air Forces commanders in the field.

In 1948–1949 there was some dismantling of the ASA as aviation-related components were transferred to the Air Force Security Service following the establishment of an independent U.S. Air Force in 1947. Subsequently, in 1949 most ASA functions were transferred to the ARMED FORCES SECURITY AGENCY, a new joint-service organization that later evolved into the National Security Agency (NSA).

From late 1945 until 1975, the ASA carried out one of the largest DOMESTIC INTELLIGENCE projects ever undertaken in the United States, Operation SHAMROCK, which gave Army Intelligence access to all sent and received foreign cables of private American citizens and commercial firms, as well as foreign embassies and consulates. This was an illegal continuation of the wartime practice of intercepting overseas cable traffic.

The ASA also had a major role in the development of advance computers for use in cryptologic operations, a project that was taken over by the NSA after its establishment.

The ASA's remaining activities and components were merged with Army Intelligence in 1977 to form the ARMY INTELLIGENCE AND SECURITY COMMAND.

Arnika

British CODE WORD for intelligence material provided by Soviet Col. OLEG PENKOVSKY.
Also see RUPEE.

Arnold, Maj. Gen. Benedict

(b. 1741 d. 1801)

American pharmacist and businessman, and the foremost colonial combat commander of the American Revolution until he became the country's most infamous traitor.

Maj. Gen. Benedict Arnold. (NATIONAL ARCHIVES)

Born in Norwich, Conn., Arnold ran away from home at the age of 14 to fight in the French and Indian War (1755–1763). Afterward he managed a bookstore and drugstore. He joined the Continental Army as a colonel on April 9, 1775, and shared command of the successful assault on Fort Ticonderoga later that year. He was severely wounded during the unsuccessful assault on Quebec at the end of the year.

Despite his loyal service and a personal tribute from Gen. GEORGE WASHINGTON, Arnold was given a public reprimand for some of his actions while military governor of Philadelphia. While at Philadelphia he married Peggy Shippen, almost 20 years his junior. Her family was very pro-British and during the earlier British occupation of Philadelphia she had befriended JOHN ANDRÉ, a young British officer.

Arnold was passed over for promotion to major general by Congress in Feb. 1777, but was belatedly promoted to that rank three months later. He was cited as the victor in the Battle of Saratoga in Oct. 1777, where he was again wounded.

Gen. Washington considered Arnold to be his finest field commander. Yet Arnold was court-martialed—and cleared—in 1779 for violations while raising funds. Believing that he was being unjustly treated, in May 1779 he began conspiring with the British through Maj. John André, who used the CODE NAME Gustavus. The following year, while in command of the fort at West Point,

Arnold negotiated with the British to surrender West Point territory and forts—and possibly George Washington—for £20,000 and equivalent rank in the British Army. The plot was foiled when Revolutionary sympathizers captured André after finding incriminating documents on him. At the time Washington was on his way to West Point.

As soon as he learned of André's capture, Arnold fled to the British lines, where he received £6,315 for his efforts and was made a general officer in the British Army. He formed a regiment of Tories and American deserters, called the "American Legion," and led raids in the south, burning Richmond, and the north, where, rampaging in his native state, he torched New London, Conn.

He went to England in Dec. 1781, then moved briefly to Canada for an ill-fated business venture. Arnold was unable to obtain a military commission during the wars of the French Revolution, although he served as volunteer quartermaster for the British force that fought the French in the West Indies in 1794–1795. He lived mainly in England until he died as a pensioner on June 14, 1801.

American historian Nathan Miller has written that as a military commander Arnold closely resembled Gen. George S. Patton (1885–1945) in his military style and attitudes.

Art Barn

Small building in Rock Creek Park, Washington, D.C., used for displaying the works of local artists and also during the Cold War as an observation post for the FBI. FBI agents could keep selected Eastern Bloc embassies under SURVEILLANCE from a tiny room with a locked door on the second floor of the two-story building.

Artamonov, Nikolai Fedrovich

SEE NICHOLAS SHADRIN

Artuzov, Artur Khristianovich

(b. 1891 d. 1939?)

Senior Soviet intelligence official. Born A. K. Frauchi, Artuzov was the son of an Italian-Swiss cheese maker who had settled in Russia. Russian historian Anton Antonov-Ovseyenko described Artuzov in *The Time of Stalin* (1981) as "[a] quiet, unassuming man, [who] did not wear any badges of distinction and looked like a kindly village schoolteacher."

Artuzov was chief of COUNTERINTELLIGENCE in the CHEKA and succeeding organs of Soviet state security, and then head of the First Directorate (foreign intelligence) of the OGPU from 1929 to 1934. He specialized in developing methods of penetrating foreign embassies and compromising diplomats in Soviet Russia, and was one of the founders of the TRUST. During the 1930s Artuzov was assigned to MILITARY INTELLIGENCE (GRU) for a short period.

As an NKVD official, Artuzov disagreed with Soviet dictator Josef Stalin over matters related to Germany and Poland, and he tried to conform to some standards of conduct during the purges of the 1930s, alienating Stalin, who ordered him arrested and shot. Before his execution in the LUBYANKA prison—probably in 1939—Artuzov reportedly scrawled on the wall of his cell: "It is an honest man's duty to kill Stalin."

ASA

SEE ARMY SECURITY AGENCY

Asché

SEE HANS-THILO SCHMIDT

A-Schule

The Nazi SS operated two major SPY SCHOOLS during World War II—the A-Schule West near The Hague in the Netherlands and A-Schule Ost in Belgrade, Yugoslavia. Those "agent schools" taught men and women the TRADECRAFT of espionage, such as Morse code, radio operation, placement of explosives, how to ride a motorcycle, and use of guns, including firing various types of pistols with both the right and left hand (in the event one was injured). The technical classes would correspond to the agent's intended assignment and were small, five or six students seeming to be the maximum.

Physical training was also stressed and there was some Nazi political indoctrination, as required in most educational activities of the Third Reich. The students' stay at A-Schule also varied, being measured in weeks and months. They could leave the school at night only if accompanied by a member of the staff.

There were several lesser German spy schools that operated during the war.

ASIO

SEE AUSTRALIAN SECURITY AND INTELLIGENCE ORGANIZATION

Assessment

Analysis of the reliability or validity of information or intelligence, or a statement resulting from this process.

Asset

Any resources—human, technical, or other—available to an intelligence or security service for operational use. In U.S. usage, usually a person.

Assistant Chief of Staff (Intelligence)

SEE DEPUTY CHIEF OF STAFF (INTELLIGENCE)

Association for Business Security (ABS)

Security organization formed by former Soviet INTELLIGENCE OFFICERS. The formation of ABS was announced in early 1993, with its head identified as Victor Budanov, a retired major general and former chief of COUNTERINTELLIGENCE for the external spy services of the KGB. Gerald P. Burke, a former assistant director of the NSA, said that his consulting firm had formed "a business agreement" with ABS.

ABS services include security protection for business executives visiting the former Soviet Union; investigations of possible business partners who are residents of Russia and other former Soviet republics; and security measures to guard against INDUSTRIAL ESPIONAGE.

Association of Former Intelligence Officers (AFIO)

Formed in 1975 to promote "public understanding of, and support for, a strong and responsible national intelligence establishment," the organization believes that effective intelligence is the first line of defense for the United States against surprise from abroad, subversion at home, and possibly dangerous miscalculation by national leaders in the conduct of foreign and defense policy. The group publishes a monthly newsletter called *Periscope*. In 2003 its membership was some 3,000.

Astor, Capt. William Vincent

(b. 1891 d. 1959)

Longtime friend and financial supporter of President Roosevelt, who appointed him in 1941 to coordinate U.S. intelligence activities overseas. During World War I Astor had served in the Navy in the European theater as an ensign.

In 1927 Astor had founded, with KERMIT ROOSEVELT, a secret society known simply as the ROOM. Other powerful men in the Room included banker Winthrop W. Aldrich and Foreign Service officer David K. E. Bruce. Several members, including a former MI6 officer, had intelligence experience.

In the 1930s Astor regularly entertained Roosevelt aboard his yacht *Nourmahal* and is known to have discussed intelligence-related subjects with the President, Kermit Roosevelt, and major banking and literary figures while on board. As a naval reserve INTELLIGENCE OFFICER, Astor was already active in low-level intelligence activities, and he regularly gave President Roosevelt information picked up during yacht cruises in the Caribbean and the Panama Canal Zone.

In *Conflict of Duty* (1983), historian Jeffery M. Dorwart describes Astor's reputation among intelligence officers during the 1930s as that of "a slightly naive but enthusiastic and valuable volunteer informant." In particular, during 1938 Astor cruised to islands in the central Pacific area, gathering data on ports, airfields, and other features of that future battleground. "The information gathering side of our cruise has proved interesting, instructive, and, I hope, will be helpful," Astor cabled to the president.

When World War II began in Europe in Sept. 1939, the Room changed its name to the Club and took a more active role in providing intelligence directly to Roosevelt. Aldrich provided information on Japanese commercial transactions and on the Soviet Union's financial dealings through its intelligence COVER organization AMTORG. Astor, who was on the board of directors of Western Union, supplied intercepts of foreign cables. The banker members of the Club were particularly useful because, as Astor told the President, "Espionage and sabotage need money, and that has to pass through banks at one stage or another."

Astor was involved in so many quasi-intelligence activities that, at his request, on June 26, 1940, Roosevelt advised the Chief of Naval Operations, Adm. Harold R. Stark:

> I simply wanted to let you know that I requested [Astor] to coordinate the Intelligence work in the New York area, and, of course, want him given every assistance. Among other things, I would like . . . great weight given his recommendation on the selection of candidates because of his wide knowledge of men and affairs in connection with general Intelligence work.

Early the following year Astor lunched with Roosevelt and the newly appointed DIRECTOR OF NAVAL INTELLIGENCE (DNI), Capt. Alan G. Kirk. The discussion centered on Astor's forthcoming appointment as coordinator of intelligence for the New York area with oversight for the activities of Army and Navy intelligence as well as the FBI.

For several months Astor followed his charter, a letter from the DNI, which had been approved by Roosevelt on March 19, 1941. Astor pursued clandestine and illegal activities while attempting to coordinate U.S. intelligence in the metropolitan area.

Astor's position was strongly opposed, however, by the military service chiefs and by FBI director J. EDGAR HOOVER. Moreover, Roosevelt had another favorite spy coming on center stage: war veteran and lawyer WILLIAM DONOVAN. Roosevelt was sending Donovan on far-ranging assignments in a Europe already at war, and he was rapidly gaining support from the British for Donovan's appointment as the U.S. intelligence chief. Finally, on July 11, 1941, Roosevelt appointed Donovan director of a new foreign intelligence collection agency, giving him the title COORDINATOR OF INFORMATION.

Faced with Donovan's appointment, lack of support from the intelligence services, and the general difficulties of attempting to operate an espionage operation in those circumstances, Astor became sickly. In Oct. 1941 he entered a hospital for stomach surgery. From his hospital bed he attempted to carry on his duties.

Although he remained the New York area controller until 1944, Astor had few real duties, mostly in support of the area naval command. He was all but ignored by Donovan and the intelligence agencies.

Atkins, Vera

(b. 1908 d. 2000)

Principal assistant to Maj. Maurice Buckmaster, director of the French section of the Special Operations Executive (SOE) during World War II.

Atkins, the daughter of an English mother and Rumanian father, was brought up in Bucharest. The family moved to England in 1933. Soon after the war began she joined the SOE and took on responsibility for the AGENTS sent into France, their selection and training. She went to extraordinary lengths to establish LEGENDS for her agents, making certain that they and their clothing could pass inspection by German soldiers or the GESTAPO, should they be detained. She sent one of her agents to a dentist to have his fillings redone in the French manner.

She also displayed formidable skills as an interrogator, questioning a number of high-profile prisoners of war, including Rudolf Hess, Adolf Hitler's deputy who flew to England and was captured on May 10, 1941.

After the war Atkins sought to learn the fate of 118 British agents who never returned from behind enemy lines. Through exhaustive investigation and interrogation of witnesses, she managed to uncover the fate of all but one. The 118th, a compulsive gambler, was last seen in Monte Carlo carrying 3 million francs of British funds. She had sent 39 female agents to France; 13 of them never returned.

Atkins was demobilized in 1947.

ATOMAL

CLASSIFICATION used by the NORTH ATLANTIC TREATY ORGANIZATION (NATO) to identify RESTRICTED DATA (i.e., atomic energy material) provided by the United States to NATO.

Atomic Spy Ring

During World War II the Soviet government operated a large spy ring that sought atomic secrets in Great Britain, Canada, and—primarily—the United States. The Soviet effort continued, albeit at a lesser level of intensity, during the Cold War.

The atomic bomb project was undoubtedly the most closely held Anglo-American war secret; the details of the program were known to far fewer people than those who had knowledge of Allied codebreaking efforts. Indeed, an important factor in the decision in early 1942 to have the U.S. Army manage the atomic bomb project (Manhattan District) was the conviction that the army was the agency best prepared in wartime to enforce security.

The Manhattan District's security officer could call

upon the resources of G-2 and the War Department's MILITARY INTELLIGENCE DIVISION, which shared responsibility for matters of espionage, COUNTERESPIONAGE, and sabotage in the United States with the FBI and the OFFICE OF NAVAL INTELLIGENCE. But security for the Manhattan District was a dismal failure.

The head of the atomic bomb project, Brig. Gen. Leslie R. Groves, decided to allow some scientists with communist connections to be employed. The most notable example was J. Robert Oppenheimer, whom Groves made head of the LOS ALAMOS nuclear laboratory in New Mexico. In the 1930s Oppenheimer had been attracted to a number of communist-front organizations and had made regular contributions to communist-supported causes. His friends, wife, and brother had earlier been Communist Party members. He had not.

Still, Groves selected Oppenheimer to direct development of the atomic bomb. There is no indication that he ever knowingly betrayed that trust, although he continued—against Groves's orders—to associate with known communists. (Oppenheimer and Enrico Fermi, a leading nuclear physicist, were assigned the Soviet CODE NAMES Star and Editor, respectively, as sources of information provided by Soviet spies.)

By the end of 1941 the Soviet NKVD had knowledge of U.S. and British interest in the development of an atomic bomb. The primary source was JOHN CAIRNCROSS, a member of the CAMBRIDGE SPY RING. Cairncross was secretary to Lord MAURICE HANKEY, who in the summer of 1941 was made chairman of the British government committee looking into the potential of atomic energy.

Cairncross's London HANDLER, YURI MODIN, wrote in My Five Cambridge Friends (1994): "Without fear of exaggeration, I can confirm that we in the USSR knew absolutely everything about the technical and political aspects of atomic bomb development."

Soviet intelligence succeeded in placing several spies in addition to Cairncross in positions where they could learn secrets of the atomic bomb. The principal spies were KLAUS FUCHS and DAVID GREENGLASS, who worked on technical aspects of the bomb at the Los Alamos lab; ALAN NUNN MAY and BRUNO PONTECORVO, scientists working in Canada; and DONALD MACLEAN, from 1944 the first secretary at the British Embassy in Washington, D.C., and from the summer of 1945 the coordinator of Anglo-American atomic bomb efforts, the Manhattan Project and Tube Alloys Project, respectively. (May was run by the GRU, Soviet MILITARY INTELLIGENCE.)

To support these spies the Soviets established networks of couriers and handlers in the United States. Their reports and—from May—uranium samples were sent directly to LAVRENTY BERIA, head of the Commissariat for Internal Affairs (NKVD). Beria was able to provide Soviet dictator Josef Stalin and Soviet scientists with details of the atomic bomb project—including the test schedule.

At the conference of Allied leaders in the BERLIN suburb of Potsdam in July 1945, President Truman told Stalin that the United States possessed a new bomb of tremendous power. Stalin seemed uninterested. After hearing of the "new weapon of unusual destructive force" from President Truman on July 24, 1945, Stalin returned to his residence on Potsdam's Kaiserstrasse and telephoned Beria. An officer in Beria's office at the time of the call, Vladimir Chikov, recalled the telephone conversation in his book From Moscow to Los Alamos (1992):

> *Stalin*: Hello, Lavrenty. Do you know anything about tests of the American atomic bomb?
>
> *Beria*: Yes, Comrade Stalin. According to our information it should have been tested two weeks ago, but we still do not have the results of the experimental detonation.
>
> *Stalin*: You have been misinformed, Lavrenty. A test of an atomic bomb took place two days ago. Truman is trying to exert pressure, dominate.... His attitude is particularly aggressive toward the Soviet Union. Of course, the factor of the atom bomb was working for Truman. We understand that. But a policy of blackmail and intimidation is unacceptable for us. We therefore gave no grounds for thinking that anything could intimidate us. Lavrenty, we should not allow any other country to have a decisive military superiority over us. Tell Comrade [Igor Vasilyevich] Kurchatov that he has to hurry with his "parcel," and ask him what our scientists need to accelerate the work. [Kurchatov was head of the Soviet atomic bomb project.]

Beria's spies had predicted that the first atomic bomb test would be held on July 4; their report was correct, but the test was delayed until July 16. The Soviet atomic bomb effort was accelerated. Beria took personal and direct interest in the project, encouraging and threatening participants in the efforts, and making extensive use of the intelligence provided by the atomic spy ring.

"Atomic espionage was almost as valuable to us in the political and diplomatic spheres as it was in the military," wrote NKVD Lt. Gen. PAVEL SUDOPLATOV in Special Tasks (1994). Sudoplatov was in charge of Department S, organized to supervise the atomic intelligence activities of the NKVD and GRU. According to his memoirs,

> When Fuchs reported . . . he also provided key data on the production of uranium 235. Fuchs revealed American production. . . . This was of highest importance, because from this information we could calculate the number of atomic bombs possessed by the Americans. Thus, we were able to determine that the United States was not prepared for a nuclear war with us at the end of the 1940s or even the early 1950s. . . . Only by 1955 did we estimate that the stockpile of American and British nuclear weapons would be sufficient to destroy the Soviet Union.

Fuchs—the most important atomic spy—also provided technical information on the plutonium bomb (Fat Man), including its assembly and detonation. This information helped accelerate Soviet bomb development.

No Soviet spy was caught red-handed. But the atomic spy ring began to unravel in 1946. Radio messages sent from the Soviet spy handlers in the United States to Moscow were intercepted by the U.S. Army SIGNAL INTELLIGENCE SERVICE, but decoding did not start until the summer of 1946. At that time MEREDITH GARDNER, a U.S. Army cryptologist, was able to break into one of the messages and discovered that it contained a list of scientists working for the Manhattan District. The messages and their decryption, undertaken in collaboration with the British GOVERNMENT CODE AND CYPHER SCHOOL, was given the U.S. code name VENONA.

Slow, careful cryptanalysis efforts followed. Not until 1949 was there conclusive evidence from Venona that led to Fuchs, who was then investigated by Scotland Yard's SPECIAL BRANCH. On Jan. 27, 1950, he confessed that from 1942 to 1949 he had been working for the Soviets. Evidence provided by Fuchs led the FBI to HARRY GOLD, who had been his courier. Gold, arrested on May 22, 1950, on espionage charges, confessed to U.S. officials and revealed another Los Alamos spy, Greenglass, as well as MORTON SOBELL, and JULIUS ROSENBERG and his wife, Ethel. Greenglass was Ethel Rosenberg's brother, and Sobell was a longtime friend of Julius Rosenberg. All were involved in stealing atomic secrets. (Prior to his involvement with atomic secrets, Rosenberg had funneled other U.S. defense secrets to the Soviets.)

Stalin "mentioned the Rosenbergs with warmth. . . . I heard from Stalin and [Commissar of Foreign Affairs V. M.] Molotov that the Rosenbergs had provided very significant help in accelerating the production of our atomic bomb," recalled Nikita Khrushchev in *Khrushchev Remembers: The Glasnost Tapes* (1990). All of these members of the ring were tried and convicted of espionage or conspiracy to commit wartime espionage. The Rosenbergs were executed on June 19, 1953; the others were sent to prison.

There were other physicists and scientists at Los Alamos with whom the Soviets had contact, according to Sudoplatov. But they "were not formally recruited as agents."

After the arrest of Fuchs, British and U.S. counterespionage services investigated other scientists who had communist links. Pontecorvo had worked on atomic energy in both Canada and Britain, but had a home in the United States. The FBI searched his home and found evidence linking him with the Communist Party. The FBI sent the information to the MI6 representative in Washington, D.C., HAROLD (KIM) PHILBY, a Soviet MOLE. He was able to suppress the information until Pontecorvo could flee to the Soviet Union in Oct. 1950.

Another aspect of the atomic spy ring was revealed in 1946 following the defection of IGOR S. GOUZENKO, a CIPHER clerk at the Soviet Embassy in Ottawa, Ontario, Canada. His revelations led to the exposure of Col. NIKOLAI ZABOTIN, the GRU RESIDENT in Ottawa, and scientist May, as well as others involved in stealing atomic secrets. May and nine others involved in atomic espionage in Canada were sent to prison. (Zabotin escaped back to the Soviet Union.)

Maclean, who provided the Soviets with valuable intelligence on U.S. nuclear policies, fled from Britain to Moscow in 1951 when he was about to be arrested.

On Feb. 4, 1944, the Military Policy Committee of the U.S. atomic bomb program reported that "no espionage activities by the Axis nations with respect to his project have been discovered, although there have been suspicious indications." The committee was correct. Rather, it was the wartime ally of the United States, the Soviet Union, that successfully spied out the atomic bomb secrets.

During the Cold War era, Soviet espionage efforts against the U.S. atomic bomb and subsequent hydrogen bomb programs continued, but apparently at a lower level of interest than against other Western weapons and technologies. After the establishment of communist China in 1949, that country also sought American nuclear secrets.

Also see ALEXANDER FEKLISOV.

Attaché

Military and naval attachés are officers assigned to foreign capitals to provide liaison to foreign military forces, overtly to collect information and, if appropriate, to gather intelligence. Those officers may be intelligence specialists or general service officers. For example, virtually all Soviet-Russian attachés are GRU officers; U.S. attachés may be either type of officer.

Describing the requirements for an attaché, Rear Adm. Roger Welles, the U.S. DIRECTOR OF NAVAL INTELLIGENCE during World War I, wrote:

> The mere fact that an officer knew a foreign language was not positive proof that he would make a good attaché. . . . He should be a man with keen imagination, able to draw correct conclusions from very scanty evidence, courteous in manner, a man of the world (but not too worldly) and, in general, with sufficient intelligence to be a good mixer in all classes of society. . . .

In general, as a courtesy, military attachés are considered members of their country's diplomatic corps and accorded diplomatic immunity and other privileges, although they are not diplomats.

The first military officers attached to diplomatic staffs to report on foreign military activities were probably French officers sent to various European capitals in the 18th century. Napoléon Bonaparte adopted this practice in the early 19th century.

In 1889 the U.S. Congress approved the first U.S. Army attaché assignments, with officers subsequently being sent to five major European capitals: BERLIN, VIENNA, Paris, London, and St. Petersburg. Public funds were limited for these assignments; in his *Crusade in Europe* (1948), Gen. Dwight D. Eisenhower wrote:

> since public funds were not available to meet the unusual expenses of this type of duty, only officers

with independent means could normally be detailed to these posts. Usually they were estimable, socially acceptable gentlemen; few knew the essentials of intelligence work.

The first official naval attaché was sent by France to London in 1860. Several European naval attachés were assigned to the United States after the American Civil War at a time of significant developments in warship design, armament, and propulsion. The first U.S. naval officer officially assigned as an attaché was Comdr. Francis M. Ramsey, who was sent to Europe in 1872 to study foreign ordnance developments. A decade later, Capt. Robert W. Shulfeldt was assigned to the U.S. legation in Peking at the request of the State Department.

The first U.S. naval attaché assigned by the OFFICE OF NAVAL INTELLIGENCE was Lt. Comdr. French Chadwick, noted for his ability to recall facts and details; he was sent to London in 1882.

In the United States, the FBI began to send legal attachés to South America during World War II to counter Nazi efforts to influence local governments, although the term did not come into vogue until the Cold War era. Subsequently FBI legal attachés (called "legats") were sent to several countries to coordinate anti-terrorist, anti-drug smuggling, and other law-enforcement activities.

The FBI's 46th Legal Attaché office in a foreign capital was established in Beijing in 2002.

Aunt Minnies

Photographs taken by commercial photographers, journalists, and tourists that show an area of interest or intelligence TARGET. Often these are the only ground-level photos available to an intelligence agency of a location of particular interest.

These are called Aunt Minnies because someone's aunt (or wife or husband) was often in the photos along with the location of interest.

During World War II the U.S. OFFICE OF STRATEGIC SERVICES scoured antiques shops for Aunt Minnie postcards, while magazine publishers' files, especially those of the *National Geographic Magazine*, were searched for photographs of target areas.

Aurora

Hypersonic spyplane reportedly under development by the United States to replace the SR-71 BLACKBIRD. The existence of the aircraft has been steadfastly denied by U.S. Air Force and Defense Department officials. Speculation on the existence or at least development of such a spyplane increased on the eve of the SR-71's withdrawal from service in 1991.

Contemporary SATELLITES, complemented by the updated U-2 spyplane and UNMANNED AERIAL VEHICLES, apparently can provide the required OVERHEAD RECONNAISSANCE capabilities.

Journalists and aviation writers, however, have reported a delta-wing, low-observable stealth aircraft that has flown at speeds of up to Mach 5. The aircraft is said to have a delta shape with twin tail fins (no horizontal tail surfaces). British aviation writer Bill Sweetman reported that there have been eyewitness reports of such a plane, including a sighting over the North Sea in Aug. 1989. He also said that such an aircraft could have speeds up to Mach 8 (some 5,300 mph).

Furthermore, there has been press speculation that the proposed National Aero-Space Plane (NASP), with a shape similar to that attributed to the Aurora, could have been a COVER program for the Aurora. The rarely publicized NASP program—subsequently cancelled—was established to develop a commercial aircraft that could fly at Mach 6 for two hours (8,635 miles). Interestingly, the NASP was given a military designation, X-30, and was jointly sponsored by the U.S. Air Force and the National Aeronautics and Space Administration.

The name Aurora is based on a CODE NAME inadvertently published in a 1985 Pentagon budget request. The Department of Defense would say only that it was a classified program.

Ausland/Abwehr

SEE ABWEHR

Australian Security and Intelligence Organization (ASIO)

Internal security agency whose principal misson is COUNTERINTELLIGENCE. It also engages in intelligence collection.

The ASIO evolved from the ALLIED INTELLIGENCE BUREAU (AIB) of World War II. After the war Australian officials, wanting an independent intelligence service, turned to Col. C. G. Roberts, who had been the director of AIB. The Australians were also helped by ROGER HOLLIS prior to his elevation to head of MI5, the British counterintelligence agency.

The ASIO was founded in 1949, with Sir Charles Spry as its first director. Formerly the director of MILITARY INTELLIGENCE in Australia, he remained the director of ASIO for 19 years.

Fears of Soviet penetration of the ASIO persisted for years. CHARLES (DICKIE) ELLIS, an MI6 officer suspected of communist leanings (see Capt. S. PAYNE BEST) and a friend of traitor HAROLD (KIM) PHILBY, left MI6 in the wake of Philby's resignation in 1951. Ellis took early retirement and became a consultant to the ASIO.

Some MI6 intelligence that would have been of interest to Australia was withheld or altered so that if there were a MOLE in ASIO, he or she would not be able to track the information to sources or methods. Confirmation that a mole existed came in April 1954 when VLADIMIR M. PETROV, an INTELLIGENCE OFFICER at the Soviet Embassy in Canberra, defected. He reported that the U.S. interception and decryption of Soviet intelligence information known as VENONA indeed been compromised.

Petrov named two officials in the Australian Department of External Affairs as Soviet moles and revealed a widespread Soviet spy network in Australia that was attempting to get information on uranium mines in Australia. Because Australian officials aided in the subsequent defection of Petrov's wife, the Soviets broke off diplomatic relations with Australia.

Australia's next major espionage incident came in April 1983 when ASIO discovered that an intelligence officer in the Soviet Embassy had attempted to recruit AGENTS OF INFLUENCE. One of them, Labor Party official David Combe, was a friend of Prime Minister Bob Hawke. Information gleaned from an ASIO tap on Combe's phone led Hawke to order his ministers not to have any contact with Combe. When the opposition heard of this, speculation grew about Soviet penetration of the Australian government.

After a high-level Australian commission looked into the matter, restrictions were placed on ASIO, requiring the intelligence agency to notify the Prime Minister and Attorney General when a major espionage case was beginning. A cabinet-level security committee was given oversight of ASIO.

The agency has strong ties with both British and U.S. intelligence agencies. A joint British-Australian unit, for example, operated a radio-intercept station in Hong Kong to monitor Chinese communications until Hong Kong was returned to China in 1997.

The huge Chinese Embassy building that opened in Canberra in 1990 was reportedly laced with fiberoptic wiring for listening devices installed by U.S. and Australian intelligence technicians.

At the peak of the operation, 30 employees from the U.S. NSA worked with ASIO to install the high-tech BUGS. The signals from the devices went to the British Embassy in Canberra and then to Washington, D.C. When the Australia media planned to reveal the bugging, ASIO attempted to stop the revelations through legal action. But the report was revealed.

Automedon

British merchant ship of 7,528 deadweight tons whose capture by the German raider *Atlantis* just west of Singapore on Nov. 11, 1940, yielded valuable intelligence to the Germans.

The *Atlantis* was one of several German heavily armed merchant-type ships employed to attack Allied merchant ships. The raiders generally sought their prey in remote areas, not in the major shipping lanes where escorted convoys would be encountered.

Upon being ordered to stop by the German raider, the *Automedon* sent an emergency radio signal. The *Atlantis* immediately began shelling the helpless *Automedon*. German sailors then boarded the British ship and seized classified mail pouches.

One packet was intended for the new British commander-in-chief in the Far East, Sir Robert Brooke-Popham, whose headquarters were in Singapore. The secret documents included minutes of the British War Cabinet meeting on Aug. 8, 1940, which delineated British weaknesses and the vulnerability of the fortress at Singapore.

The packet reached the German naval ATTACHÉ in Tokyo, Rear Adm. Paul Wenneker, on Dec. 5, 1940. He radioed a summary to BERLIN and, on direct orders from Adolf Hitler, passed the documents to the Japanese Navy on Dec. 12. Significantly, the lack of coordination between the Japanese War and Navy ministries may have limited the usefulness of the *Automedon* papers to the Japanese Army's campaign against Singapore in early 1942.

The *Automedon* was one of 22 merchant ships, totaling 145,697 gross registered tons, that were sunk or captured by the *Atlantis* from March 1940, when she left Germany, to Nov. 22, 1941, when she was lost in the south Atlantic. The most successful of the German merchant raiders, *Atlantis* was sunk because British codebreakers succeeded in breaking into the U-boat operational CIPHER. The signals to the submarine *U-126* to rendezvous with the *Atlantis* were deciphered at BLETCHLEY PARK, and a British warship was directed to the location of their planned meeting.

The *Atlantis* was refueling the U-boat when she was attacked by the British cruiser *Devonshire*. The captain of the *Atlantis* scuttled his ship when escape from the more heavily gunned *Devonshire* became impossible. Later the submarine *U-126*, which the *Atlantis* had been refueling when attacked, took aboard 55 *Atlantis* crewmen; another 200 men "camped" on the surfaced U-boat's deck, wearing life jackets; and 200 more were in six small boats that the U-boat towed. Other submarines and a German surface ship took off some of the survivors. The latter was sunk by the British. After a lengthy odyssey, all but eight of the crew of the *Atlantis* reached Germany.

Ayalon, Rear Adm. Ami

(b. 1945)

The first head of SHIN BET, the Israeli COUNTERINTELLIGENCE service, to be publicly named upon his appointment, and the first naval officer to head the service. He held that position from Jan. 1996 to 2000.

Ayalon took up the position following the resignation of Karmi Gilon, who took full responsibility for Shin Bet's failure to prevent the assassination of Prime Minister Yitzhak Rabin on Nov. 4, 1995. (Rabin had previously asked Ayalon to take the post.)

He entered the Navy in 1963 and served as a commando (frogman) before attending the naval officer course in 1970–1973. He subsequently held several small craft and shore commands prior to serving as deputy commander of the Navy from 1988 to 1991. After studying at the U.S. Naval War College and earning a master's degree at Harvard University, he became commander of the Israeli Navy in 1993, a post he held through Dec. 1995.

Ayalon won the Medal of Supreme Bravery, Israel's highest combat award, during a commando raid on heavily fortified Green Island, at the southern entrance to the Suez Canal, on July 19, 1969.

Azeff, Ievno (Eugene)

(b. 1869 d. 1918)

Russian DOUBLE AGENT in early years of the 20th century who worked for the czarist secret police while also a secret member of the Russian Socialist Revolutionary Party. He betrayed fellow party members and plans to the secret police while helping to kill government officials.

The son of a poor Jewish tailor, in 1892 Azeff stole some money from his employer and ran away to Karlsruhe, Germany. He enrolled in the Karlsruhe Polytechnic, which several other Russian revolutionary students attended. In 1893 he wrote to the OKHRANA (Russian secret police), offering to spy on his Russian fellow students. The Okhrana considered him a good candidate for an agent and took him on in June 1893.

In 1894 in Switzerland Azeff met the leaders of one of the Russian revolutionary groups. He was chosen to make contact with the leaders of the movement in other European locations as well as in Russia itself. Azeff passed all of the information he gathered to Okhrana as well as to the revolutionaries. By the early 1900s he was being paid 500 roubles a month by the Okhrana, an extraordinary sum for a spy.

From 1904 to 1908, Azeff was head of a revolutionary group's "battle organization," which planned bombings and assassinations. He planned the murder by bombing of W. K. Plehve, Minister of Interior and head of the police in Russia, and the assassination of the Grand Duke Serge, the Czar's uncle. Both plots succeeded. He also planned an attempt on the Czar's life, which failed.

Although Azeff was accused of being a double agent in 1905 and in 1906, he always managed to outwit his opponents. In 1908, however, he was tried in Paris by a revolutionary tribunal. He disappeared from Paris at this time and wandered around Europe. In 1915 he was arrested by German officials and jailed. He died in Berlin on April 24, 1918.

Graham Stephenson, in his *History of Russia: 1812–1945*, wrote of Azeff that "so skillfully did he conceal his tracks that it is still impossible to say which side he mainly betrayed."

Azeff's CODE NAME among revolutionaries was Valentine.

Azorian

Overall CODE NAME of the CIA operation to employ the heavy-lift ship *HUGHES GLOMAR EXPLORER* to lift a sunken Soviet missile submarine from the ocean floor in the Pacific.

Also see Project JENNIFER.

B Team

An outside group, given unprecedented access to classified material, that reviewed estimates of the Soviet military by the CIA.

The idea of an external review was rooted in a controversy that erupted inside the INTELLIGENCE COMMUNITY following circulation of the CIA's 1975 estimate of Soviet military expenditures. Retired Adm. George W. Anderson, Jr., the head of the PRESIDENT'S FOREIGN INTELLIGENCE ADVISORY BOARD, said that the study had underestimated Soviet capabilities. President Ford reacted by deciding that the CIA's estimates should be reviewed by impartial outsiders, a group that became known as Team B, or the B Team.

The B Team was headed by Dr. Richard E. Pipes, a Harvard University professor and frequent critic of the CIA's Soviet estimates (he became an Assistant Secretary of Defense in the Reagan administration). The CIA's own group, Team A (or A Team), was headed by Howard Stoertz, the agency's top INTELLIGENCE OFFICER on the Soviet Union. JOHN A. PAISLEY, a CIA intelligence officer fluent in Russian and an agency specialist on the Soviet Union, acted as liaison between the agency and the B Team, supplying its members with the highly classified information they requested. (When Paisley mysteriously died in Sept. 1978, there was speculation about his allegiances to the agency and the B Team.)

The other members of the B Team included Paul H. Nitze, a Strategic Arms Limitation Talks (SALT) negotiator and a high-level government insider since World War II; Air Force generals John Vogt and Jasper A. Welch, Jr.; William R. Van Cleave, another SALT negotiator; Col. Thomas Wolfe of the RAND Corp.; Paul Wolfowitz of the Arms Control and Disarmament Agency (who later became Deputy Secretary of Defense in the George W.

Bush administration); and Army Lt. Gen. Daniel O. Graham, who had been director of the DEFENSE INTELLIGENCE AGENCY (DIA) when the Soviet estimate controversy began.

Graham was an outspoken critic of the CIA and a passionate defender of the DIA, claiming that its knowledge of MILITARY INTELLIGENCE made it a more reliable assessor of Soviet military might. Other members, a later declassified description of the B Team said, were "deliberately selected from among experienced political and military analysts of Soviet affairs known to take a more somber view of the Soviet strategic threat than that accepted as the intelligence community's consensus."

The DIRECTOR OF CENTRAL INTELLIGENCE (DCI) when the review process began was WILLIAM E. COLBY, who accepted the evaluation as another act of penance for the CIA's involvement in the WATERGATE scandal. When GEORGE H. W. BUSH succeeded Colby as DCI, there was hope inside the agency that he would quietly end what had become A Team versus B Team competition. But Bush decided to let the review continue.

Existence of the B Team review became known through a news leak in 1976, touching off a congressional investigation. The B Team's findings did not become publicly known until Oct. 1992, when the CIA declassified the B report as well as the A report, in the form of the agency's own 1976 NATIONAL INTELLIGENCE ESTIMATE (NIE) of Soviet strategic forces.

The B Team foresaw "a relatively short-term threat cresting, say, in 1980 to 1983," as Soviet military power grew faster than the West's. The A Team foresaw no major threat. But in the A report were dissents from the Department of State—because the CIA analysts were too alarmed—and from service intelligence agencies, which chastised the CIA for not taking the Soviets seriously enough.

The B Team report said that U.S. intelligence estimates through 1975 "substantially misperceived the motivations behind Soviet strategic programs, and thereby tended consistently to underestimate their intensity, scope and implicit threat." The critics maintained that the CIA had relied excessively on "hard data" from SATELLITES and ELECTRONIC INTELLIGENCE and did not give enough weight to "soft data," such as the public and private statements of Soviet intentions about a "commitment to what is euphemistically called 'the worldwide triumph of socialism,' but in fact connotes global Soviet hegemony."

Soviet strategy, the B Team members said, called for "peaceful coexistence (better known in the West as détente)," although "both détente and SALT are seen by Soviet leaders not as cooperative efforts to ensure global peace but as means more effectively to compete with the United States."

The idea of having an outside review was widely criticized, and it reverberated for years inside the CIA. The agency's Directorate of Intelligence (DI) in particular saw the move as an attempt to politicize the PRODUCT that the directorate was most proud of, its NIEs. Former DI director RAY CLINE, quoted by Mark Perry in *Eclipse* (1992), was still indignant about the review years later. "The incident was a purposeful attempt to cast doubt on the agency's expertise," he said. "It was a challenge to an institution and it was clearly political, and it was antiintellectual."

B-2

Intelligence organization of a U.S. brigade or battalion in the World War II era. See G-2.

B-29 Superfortress

The U.S. B-29 Superfortress was the most effective bomber of any nation to see combat in World War II. Photo-RECONNAISSANCE variants were flown in large numbers in the war against Japan and on reconnaissance missions against North Korea during the Korean conflict (1950–1953).

The first B-29 bombing mission was flown against Japanese-held Bangkok from airfields in India on June 5, 1944 (using landing fields in China as staging bases). B-29s subsequently bombed the Japanese home islands from bases in China and, from Oct. 1944, bases in the Mariana Islands. The latter included massive incendiary bombings against Japanese cities and the atomic bombings of Hiroshima and Nagasaki in Aug. 1945.

Reconnaissance variants of the B-29—initially designated F-13—followed many bombing strikes to obtain bomb-damage assessment photos. The standard photo-reconnaissance aircraft arrangement was six cameras plus racks for additional units.

On Sept. 3, 1949, a U.S. Air Force WB-29 weather reconnaissance aircraft flying from Japan to Alaska, fitted to detect radioactivity in the atmosphere, detected the first signs of a Soviet nuclear test. (A high-level panel of U.S. experts, looking at the aircraft's findings, concluded that the Soviets had exploded an atomic bomb.)

RB-29 aircraft (as the F-13s were redesignated in 1948) were used extensively in the Korean War. Several RB-29s were attacked by MiG-15 fighters during the Korean War; some were damaged, but none shot down. However, three B-29s were shot down by Soviet fighter aircraft over international waters while on reconnaissance missions (see AIRCRAFT SHOT DOWN).

All RB-29s were discarded by the end of 1953.

The first XB-29 flew on Sept. 21, 1942. Production of the Boeing-designed B-29 totaled 3,996, with all but 230 delivered by August 1945 (another 5,000 B-29s were cancelled at the end of the war). Maximum speed was 358 mph and maximum bomb load was 20,000 pounds. Defensive armament was 8 or 10 .50-caliber machine guns in four remote-control turrets, plus a tail turret mounting two machine guns and one 20-mm cannon. The normal bomber crew was 11 men; the F-13 photo aircraft had a crew of nine (with some guns removed).

The B-50 Superfortress, an improved variant of the B-29, was flown after World War II in both bomber and reconnaissance roles.

B-36 Peacemaker

Controversial U.S. Air Force strategic bomber of the early nuclear era that was also employed as a long-range, high-altitude STRATEGIC RECONNAISSANCE aircraft.

Although development of the B-36 began before American entry into World War II—to provide a bomber that could strike Europe from bases in the United States in the event that Britain fell to the Germans—the bomber did not become operational until 1951. It served in bombing and strategic reconnaissance roles with the U.S. Strategic Air Command through 1959. Little information has been released about RB-36 reconnaissance operations and there is no official U.S. confirmation of any B-36 overflights of the Soviet Union. However, the authors of *Spy Book* were told of two such missions:

The first flight by B-36 bombers beyond the continental United States occurred on Jan. 16, 1951, when six of the 10-engine B-36D bombers flew into the RAF base at Lakenheath, England. Three planes were fitted with a battery of hidden cameras. From Lakenheath the three camera planes each flew a reconnaissance mission over the Soviet base complex at Murmansk on the Kola Peninsula. The planes returned safely to Lakenheath, although two MiG fighters are said to have tried to intercept them. The six B-36D aircraft flew back to their continental U.S. base on Jan. 20.

Reportedly, there were also two overflights of the Soviet base complex at Vladivostok by camera-equipped B-36D aircraft. Those overflights are said to have occurred during Aug.–Sept. 1953, when a flight of 23 B-36s temporarily operated from bases in Japan, Okinawa, and Guam. As part of this deployment two B-36D photo missions are reported to have been flown over the major So-

A giant, ten-engine RB-36D reconnaissance aircraft retracts a YRF-84F "parasite" reconnaissance fighter after the smaller aircraft has hooked on in flight. In the 1930s the U.S. Navy similarly operated small planes from two large, aircraft-carrying airships. (U.S. AIR FORCE)

viet base complex at Vladivostok from the U.S. air base at Kadena, Japan. It is not clear from available records whether those were the same modified B-36Ds that had earlier overflown Murmansk or were specialized RB-36D aircraft. Regardless, on both operations the camera-carrying aircraft were "hidden" among "straight" B-36s during overseas deployments.

The specialized RB-36 variant entered service with the Strategic Air Command in June 1951. In the RB-36D configuration the aircraft was fitted with 14 high-altitude cameras (weighing 3,300 pounds) in the forward bomb bay, 80 flash bombs could be carried in the second bomb bay, 3,000-gallon fuel tanks were provided in the third bomb bay, and ELECTRONIC COUNTERMEASURES (ECM) equipment was installed in the fourth bomb bay. The largest of the cameras had a 47-inch focal length. The RB-36D endurance was 30 hours, originally with a crew of 22 men.

Eight remote-control power turrets, each with two 20-mm cannon, were fitted in the initial RB-36D configuration; subsequently, all guns except the tail turret were removed from those aircraft and the crew was reduced to 19.

The RB-36 was the largest reconnaissance aircraft flown by any nation. With the turbojet engines it could reach 348 mph at near maximum altitude. While USAF documents credited the aircraft with a maximum altitude of 40,000 feet, there are reports that the aircraft could climb considerably higher, with 60,000 feet cited by some sources.

The USAF took delivery of 385 Convair B-36s, including 24 RB-36D, 24 RB-36F, and 73 RB-36H reconnaissance variants (31 percent of the total procurement). In addition, 22 B-36A aircraft were converted to the RB-36E configuration and 29 B-36B aircraft were temporarily modified as RB-36B photo planes. In June 1954 the primary role of the RB-36 fleet was changed to heavy bombardment. The aftermost bomb bay was converted

to a functional bomb bay with the ECM equipment being moved to the crew compartment.

The B-36 was the largest combat aircraft to enter service. It was 162 feet long and had a 230-foot wingspan. Maximum bomb load was 43 tons, with a gross aircraft weight reaching 410,000 pounds in the B-36J. The aircraft was propelled by six large piston-pusher engines, supplemented in later models by four turbojets in underwing pods. A prototype, all-jet variant of the B-36 with swept wings designated YB-60 was developed in an unsuccessful attempt to compete with the B-52 Stratofortress. Another B-36 was employed to test the effects of an airborne nuclear reactor (it was not powered by the reactor).

As Soviet air defenses improved in the 1950s, an effort was made to increase the altitude of the RB-36 through the "featherweight" program, in which most of the aircraft guns and some other gear were removed to reduce weight; the crew of featherweight RB-36s numbered only 19. The featherweight aircraft could reach an altitude of just over 45,000 feet, some 5,000 to 8,000 feet more than a standard aircraft. To extend the RB-36 reconnaissance capabilities further, RF-84 Thunderflash tactical photo aircraft were evaluated in a "parasite" role: The RF-84 would be carried by the RB-36D partially recessed in the bomber's fuselage and released to overfly the target at high speed, and return to be recovered in flight by the "mother" aircraft. Seven GRB-36D featherweight bombers and 23 RF-84K fighters were modified (each bomber was to carry one RF-84), but after flight trials this scheme was discarded in 1956 as impractical. In another project, a B-36 evaluated "carrying" two RF-84 aircraft attached to the bomber's wingtips.

The first flight of the XB-36 took place on Aug. 8, 1946, and the first reconnaissance aircraft, an RB-36D, flew on Dec. 18, 1949. At its peak strength, the operational B-36 force in 1953 numbered 209 bombers and

133 reconnaissance aircraft. None ever dropped a bomb in anger.

B-45 Tornado

The first post–World War II jet-propelled bomber to enter production, the RB-45C flew important photo-RECONNAISSANCE missions over North Korea and the Soviet Union, the latter among the first OVERFLIGHTS of the Cold War.

The B-45 became operational in Nov. 1948. (The world's first jet-propelled bomber had been the German AR 234 BLITZ.) Although a four-engine aircraft, the B-45 was a tactical bomber, intended to carry either atomic or conventional bombs. B-45 aircraft began to arrive in Britain in 1952 for the nuclear strike role.

Only RB-45C reconnaissance aircraft saw action in the Korean War (1950–1953), with three being flown in an effort to continue photo coverage of communist-held areas in the face of the threat of MiG-15 fighter aircraft. Beginning in Feb. 1951, for several months the RB-45s were able to outrun MiGs where piston-engine photo aircraft could not survive. However, by the end of the year, after several attempted intercepts by MiG-15s, the RB-45 flights were restricted to "safe" areas during daylight.

After the Korean War started, President Truman restricted reconnaissance flights that might be considered provocative by the Soviet Union. However, the U.S. Strategic Air Command badly needed radar images of potential Soviet targets. The British were asked to help, and apparently the first deep penetration flights over the Soviet Union were undertaken by U.S. Air Force RB-45C Tornado photo planes with British markings, flown by British crews.

These were night flights, the first on April 19–20, 1952, when three RB-45 aircraft sought to record radar targets for U.S. bombers. The Soviets detected the flights and tried to intercept them, but without success. A second British-piloted, three-plane RB-45 mission was flown on the night of April 29–30, 1954.

Subsequently, from 1954 RB-45s were flown by the U.S. 19th Reconnaissance Wing, based at the Royal Air Force (RAF) base Sculthorpe. Several wore RAF markings and at least two British crews were assigned to the wing, although no further missions are known to have been flown over the Soviet Union.

The B-45 evolved from a 1944 Army Air Forces requirement for a series of jet-propelled bombers. Developed by North American, the first XB-45 flew in 1947. It was a straight-wing aircraft with four turbojet engines, paired in nacelles mounted in each wing. An internal bomb bay could carry 11 tons of bombs. The defensive guns were two .50-caliber machine guns in a manned tail turret. B-45s began entering squadron service in 1948. Only 106 B-45s were delivered, of which 33 were RB-45C reconnaissance variants, in addition to three XB-45 aircraft.

The first RB-45C flew on May 3, 1949. It had five camera positions and (like the bombers) was flown by a crew of four. The bomb bay was used to carry additional fuel and, for night flights, photo-flash bombs. The RB-45C entered service in 1950, and the first planes went overseas that same year. All B-45s were phased out of service by 1959.

B-47 Stratojet

The first swept-wing, jet-propelled bomber produced in large numbers by any nation. The RB-47 variant of this was flown extensively for photographic and electronic RECONNAISSANCE. The B-47 Stratojet was produced in larger numbers than any other Western bomber of the Cold War era.

Bill Gunston, a leading aviation writer, has observed that the B-47 was "a design so advanced technically as to appear genuinely futuristic." In addition to its high speed and sleek configuration, the B-47 was highly automated, permitting a reduction in the number of crew from the 11 in a B-29 SUPERFORTRESS—of roughly the same gross weight—to only three: pilot, copilot, and bombardier/navigator. All defensive guns were deleted except for a remote-control tail turret with two 20-mm cannon. The six-jet B-47 relied on speed (maximum 660 mph for the B-47E) and electronic JAMMING to avoid enemy fighters. The bombers could deliver an atomic bomb or 18,000 pounds of conventional bombs.

Beginning in 1953 the Air Force converted 24 bomber aircraft to the RB-47B photo-reconnaissance configuration, fitting eight cameras in the aircraft's bomb bay. Subsequently, 240 specialized RB-47E photo planes and 32 RB-47H and 15 RB-47K electronic reconnaissance aircraft were built. The photo planes had 11 cameras fitted and a crew of three; the electronic planes had five or six crewmen.

In 1952 a modified B-47B fitted with special cameras flew one of the first OVERFLIGHTS of the Soviet Union. On Oct. 15, 1952, the B-47B took off from Fairbanks, Alaska, was refueled in flight by tanker aircraft, and proceeded to fly over the northeastern portion of Siberia at an altitude above 40,000 feet. The TARGETS were suspected Soviet bomber bases. Although Soviet fighters attempted to intercept the photo plane, none did.

That B-47B mission took almost eight hours and covered a 3,500-mile route, of which some 800 miles were over Soviet territory. Although some of the area was covered by clouds, valuable photographs were obtained.

Subsequently RB-47s flew innumerable reconnaissance missions along the Soviet periphery. An RB-47H was shot down by Soviet fighters over the Barents Sea on July 1, 1960. Of the six crewmen, four were reported killed when the plane crashed; the two survivors were released by the Soviet government on Jan. 25, 1961, the day after President Kennedy's inauguration. (The delay by Nikita Khrushchev in releasing the fliers was part of his effort to defeat and discredit candidate Nixon. Khrushchev later boasted that he had cast the "deciding ballot" in Kennedy's election "over that son of a bitch Richard Nixon.")

Another RB-47H was seriously damaged by North Korean fighters in April 1965 but returned safely to base.

The first flight of an XB-47 took place on Dec. 17, 1947, with the RB-47B being the first production model. A total of 2,258 B-47s were produced through 1957. The U.S. Air Force achieved peak operational strength in early 1957 with 1,260 bombers and some 300 reconnaissance aircraft plus another 300 used for training and specialized duties.

In the early 1960s, Secretary of Defense Robert S. McNamara accelerated retirement of the B-47s as part of his emphasis on intercontinental ballistic missiles in place of manned bombers. The last bomb-carrying B-47 was retired in Feb. 1966, although RB-47s remained in service until Dec. 1967. (The U.S. Navy later reactivated three EB-47E aircraft to support missile and electronic warfare projects.)

B-57

SEE CANBERRA

B-70

SEE RS-70 VALKYRIE

Baba, Ens. Stephen A.

U.S. Navy officer who mailed classified material on electronic warfare to the South African embassy in Washington, D.C., in Sept. 1981. Embassy officials turned the documents over to the U.S. government and Baba, assigned to a missile ship whose home port was San Diego, Calif., was promptly arrested.

During Baba's court-martial it was learned that he wanted money to bring his Filipina girlfriend to the United States. In Jan. 1982 he was sentenced to eight years' hard labor, later reduced to two years.

Babington, Anthony

(b. 1561 d. 1586)

English Catholic undercover AGENT who operated against the Protestant Elizabethan monarchy. Babington, a zealous supporter of Mary, Queen of Scots, in 1586 was one of the leaders in a plot to assassinate Queen Elizabeth I and place Mary, then Elizabeth's prisoner, on the English throne. Spies working for Sir FRANCIS WALSINGHAM learned of the plot and arrested Babington. He was tried and executed.

Although Mary denied knowledge of the plot, she was later tried before the Star Chamber and found guilty on questionable evidence produced by Walsingham. Elizabeth signed her death warrant and Mary was beheaded on Feb. 8, 1587.

Also see THOMAS PHELIPPES.

Babington-Smith, Constance

(b. 1912 d. 2000)

British aviation writer who served as one of the leading Allied PHOTOGRAPHIC INTERPRETATION specialists during World War II.

An aviation enthusiast, she wrote for *The Aeroplane* magazine before the war. Babington-Smith served in the Women's Auxiliary Air Force in World War II, attaining the rank of flight officer. She became an expert in aerial photographic interpretation and is credited with being the first analyst to identify the German V-1 "buzz bombs" at the German missile test site of Peeneüminde in May 1943. In 1945 she was assigned to the U.S. Army Air Forces' intelligence staff in Washington, D.C., working on photographic interpretation for the Pacific theater. She was awarded the U.S. Legion of Merit for her work, as well as an MBE in Britain.

From 1946 to 1950 she was a researcher for *Life* magazine, her principal assignment being to assemble illustrations for the memoirs of Winston Churchill. She wrote books, among them *Air Spy: The Story of Photo Intelligence in World War II* (1957) and *Testing Time* (1961).

Babysitter

Intelligence slang for a bodyguard.

Background Investigation

(BI)

A detailed inquiry to determine an individual's reliability and honesty. Background investigations are usually required to provide an individual with a security clearance. Records of birth, citizenship, education, and employment are verified. Credit and travel information are also usually requested, as well as the individual's possible friends and relations who live in other countries. Investigators usually get additional information from neighbors, friends, and employers.

U.S. background investigations also include a review of all federal agencies for derogatory information (NATIONAL AGENCY CHECK) and a check of police and court records.

Special background investigations conducted by FBI agents establish security clearances for high-ranking political officials, such as potential cabinet members. No background investigations for security clearance are carried out for elected officials, including members of Congress serving on INTELLIGENCE OVERSIGHT committees.

Also see DEFENSE SECURITY SERVICE (D&S).

Backstopping

Verification and support of COVER arrangements for an AGENT in anticipation of inquiries or other actions that might test the credibility of his or her cover.

Baden-Powell, Maj. Gen. Sir Robert

(b. 1857 d. 1941)

British Army officer who fostered innovative intelligence techniques. He was also the founder of the Boy Scout movement.

Baden-Powell joined the 13th Hussars in 1876 and served in India, Afghanistan, and South Africa. While serving in India as a junior officer, he developed small-unit patrolling and RECONNAISSANCE procedures that later became basic Army tactics. A decade later, in Bechuanaland and in the Sudan, he pioneered the use of observation BALLOONS for reconnaissance.

He led the 217-day defense of besieged Mafeking (from Oct. 1899 to May 1900) in the Boer War and became a national hero. After the war he recruited and trained the South African constabulary. Baden-Powell is credited with carrying out official and unofficial intelligence missions into hostile territory, often in disguise, from 1880 to 1902.

Official records, which did not disclose his espionage work, listed him as inspector general of the South African constabulary in 1900 and head of the South African cavalry from 1903 to 1907. He retired from the army in 1910 with the rank of major general.

When he learned that his military textbook *Aids to Scouting* (1899) was being used to train boys in woodcraft, he became interested in camping for boys. He set up an experimental camp in 1907 and, after retiring, devoted his energies to organizing the movement that became the Boy Scouts. His sister Agnes inaugurated the Girl Guides in 1910.

Baden-Powell was knighted in 1909 and raised to the peerage in 1929, becoming Baron Baden-Powell of Gilwell.

Badger (Tu-16)

A highly versatile Soviet turbojet-powered medium bomber that has been widely used by the Soviet-Russian Air Forces and Navy for more than five decades. It has flown in the ELECTRONIC INTELLIGENCE (ELINT) role as well as bomber, anti-ship missile, photo-RECONNAISSANCE, ELECTRONIC COUNTERMEASURES, and tanker roles.

Badgers have ranged far and wide over the oceans adjacent to the Soviet Union, seeking out Western ships. From 1967 to 1972, Badger reconnaissance aircraft were based in Egypt to support Soviet naval activities in the eastern Mediterranean. Some of these planes had Egyptian markings but appear to have been flown only by Soviet crews. Badgers also flew from the former U.S. airfield at Cam Ranh Bay in Vietnam from about 1980 until the demise of the Soviet Union in 1991. Badgers regularly searched out U.S. ships at sea. During a series of Soviet OVERFLIGHTS of the U.S. carrier *Essex* on May 25, 1968, a Badger crashed at sea within sight of the ship after making a tight turn. There were no survivors.

The Tupolev-designed Badger has a swept-wing configuration with two large turbojet engines housed in nacelles faired into the fuselage at the wing roots. Maximum speed of early bombers was 650 mph. Bomber variants have a large internal bomb bay that can accommodate about 20,000 pounds of bombs. The later Badger-G strike aircraft carry one or two large air-to-surface missiles under the fuselage or on wing pylons. Most aircraft have two 23-mm cannon in dorsal, ventral, and tail mounts; and bombers not having a large nose radome can mount a seventh cannon fixed on the starboard side of the nose. Photo-reconnaissance variants have cameras mounted in the bomb bay. Bomber versions are flown by crews of six or seven.

Tu-16 is the military designation for the aircraft; Badger is the U.S. designation. (The Tupolev design bureau's designation for the Badger was Tu-88.) The Badger-D and K were configured for ELINT/maritime reconnaissance, the E for photo-reconnaissance, and the F for both ELINT and photo-reconnaissance. (The other variants were primarily bombers or missile carriers.)

The Badger's first flight took place in 1952 with squadron delivery to the Air Forces starting in 1954; deliveries to the Navy began in the late 1950s, with many Air Forces aircraft being transferred to the Navy. Approximately 2,000 Badgers were built in the Soviet Union through the mid-1960s, and another 100 were produced in China (those aircraft being designated H-6). Badgers continue to fly in Russian and Chinese military service. Soviet-built Badgers have been transferred to China, Egypt, Indonesia, Iraq, and Libya.

Baillie-Stewart, Norman

(b. 1909 d. 1966)

British Army officer who spied for Germany in the 1930s. The son of a British officer who served in the Indian Army, Baillie-Stewart spent some time in the Royal Naval College, but left because of illness. In 1925 entered Sandhurst Military Academy, graduating in 1928 and being commissioned in the Seaforth Highlanders.

On a visit to Nazi Germany in 1932 he was recruited as an AGENT, and when he returned to Britain he sent information about the British armed forces to Germany. He was well paid for his efforts, and it was his sudden wealth that caused suspicion of his clandestine activities.

Arrested, court-martialed, and convicted of espionage, he was sentenced to five years and imprisoned in the Tower of London, becoming known as "the officer in the Tower." When he was released in 1936, he moved to Germany, where he spent the war.

In early 1945, U.S. Army INTELLIGENCE OFFICERS in Ault Aussee, Austria, were using Baillie-Stewart as an interpreter. When the war in Europe ended in May 1945, British MI5 investigators revealed his identity, and the Americans arrested him. He was flown to England in 1945 to be tried for treason. But MI5 investigators determined that he was a German national because he had worked for Germany and could be tried only for lesser violations of wartime regulations prohibiting pro-

German activities. On Jan. 10, 1946, he was convicted of those charges and sentenced to five years in prison. When he was released in 1949 he moved to Dublin. With John Murdoch he wrote *The Officer in the Tower* (1967).

Bakatin, Vadim Viktorovich

(b. 1937)

Head of the KGB after the failure of the Aug. 1991 coup against the Soviet government of Mikhail Gorbachev. Bakatin was an opponent of the KGB's secret police powers; upon taking office he called the KGB a "vicious state within a state."

An ethnic Russian, Bakatin came from a well-off Siberian family. He was educated at the Novosibirsk Construction Engineering Institute and joined the Communist Party in 1964. He rose through the ranks, being appointed Minister of the Interior in 1988. In accordance with Gorbachev's policy of "openness," or glasnost, Bakatin fired senior KGB officials—including his own son, a KGB officer. He scaled back the Communist Party influence in the national police force (militia), declared that he would eliminate domestic spying, and give citizens access to their KGB files.

But in Dec. 1990, Gorbachev's opponents forced him to fire Bakatin. Bakatin found refuge as a national security adviser to Gorbachev as well as a member of the Russian parliament. When Boris Yeltsin offered to make Bakatin his candidate for vice president in the 1991 Russian presidential election, he turned Yeltsin down and ran against him.

A member of the Russian parliament and of Gorbachev's National Security Council at the time of the 1991 coup, he immediately resigned his position in protest but rescinded his decision the following day. He then joined YEVGENY PRIMAKOV and others in urging that troops be ordered out of Moscow to avoid the possibility of bloodshed. On Aug. 21, he joined Primakov and others who flew to the Crimea in an effort to prevent the possible assassination of Gorbachev by the plotters.

Gorbachev appointed him as chairman of the KGB in Aug. 1991 to replace coup participant VLADIMIR KRYUCHKOV. Under Bakatin's direction the KGB began to change its composition and mission; the ground and maritime border troops became a separate agency, the KGB combat forces were transferred to the Soviet Army (ground forces), and the Kremlin guard and communications troops were made directly responsible to the Soviet government.

Bakatin's tenure was again brief, as Gorbachev was forced to fire him again, in Nov. 1991, on the eve of the demise of the Soviet regime. The former KGB official once declared, "Making capitalism out of socialism is like making eggs from an omelet."

Baker, Josephine

(b. 1906 d. 1975)

American who spied against the Germans in France in World War II. Born in St. Louis, she was one of the most famous black stars of the Broadway stage in the 1920s. After a sensational debut in Paris in 1925, she remained in France, becoming a French citizen in 1937.

When France declared war on Germany in Sept. 1939, Jacques Abtey, chief of COUNTERINTELLIGENCE in Paris for the French military intelligence agency, the DEUXIÉME BUREAU, recruited her as a secret informer. (Like the Germans, the French referred to such an unpaid informer as an HONORARY AGENT.) Abtey had to be persuaded to recruit Baker, for he felt that she might turn out to be a DOUBLE AGENT like MATA HARI. But Baker convinced him that if necessary she would give her life for France.

She had supported Italian dictator Mussolini's invasion of Abyssinia (Ethiopia), and so she had many contacts in the Italian Embassy in Paris. From them, and from friends in the Japanese Embassy, she obtained information about German troop movements. After Germany conquered France in 1940, as a black French citizen she could have been sent to a concentration camp. She left Paris, vowing never to perform there while the Germans occupied the city.

Under the 1940 armistice between Germany and France, much of the south and the French colonies in North Africa and elsewhere came under the administration of a collaborationist government with its capital in Vichy. In Nov. 1940 Baker made her way out of Vichy France into Spain and then to Lisbon, Portugal. She was accompanied by Abtey, who was using a fake passport identifying him as her ballet master. With them went important Deuxiéme Bureau intelligence information, written in INVISIBLE INK on Baker's sheet music; photographs were hidden in her clothing. The information was passed to British intelligence officers in neutral Portugal.

Later in the war, she carried information from Morocco to Lisbon, often working directly for Col. Paul Paillole, a legendary French intelligence officer. (See FRANCE.) For her work in the war she was awarded the Croix de Guerre and the Medal of Resistance. Her wartime activities were reported in Abtey's book *The Secret War of Josephine Baker* (1949).

Baker, Lafayette C.

(b. 1826 d. 1868)

Union spymaster in Washington during the American Civil War. Born in New York state, Baker grew up in Michigan and wandered as a youth. In San Francisco during the Gold Rush of 1849 he became a vigilante—an experience in rough justice that he would carry over to his Civil War career.

When the war began he became a spy for the Union under the COVER name Sam Munson. Arrested behind Confederate lines, he was questioned by Jefferson Davis, President of the Confederacy, who ordered his arrest. Baker escaped and managed to get back to Union forces.

His next post was director of COUNTERINTELLIGENCE for Secretary of State William Seward, who soon turned Baker and his detectives over to the War Department. Baker became an AGENT for Secretary of War Edwin

Stanton, who was greatly concerned about the infiltration of Confederate agents into Washington. Baker caught one famous spy, BELLE BOYD, and rounded up dozens of suspected Southern sympathizers. He also drove war profiteers and bribe-taking government employees out of the city.

Officially, Baker was provost marshal of the War Department, but he sometimes called his organization the National Detective Bureau. (In his postwar memoirs he styled it the U.S. SECRET SERVICE, which was in fact founded after the war.) Although Baker is often called the successor to ALLAN PINKERTON as the Union's intelligence expert, the two spymasters had overlapping tenures. Neither actually held the post of chief of Union intelligence—which was nonexistent.

Baker showed himself to be a brutal spy hunter. Ignoring the law and holding suspects with little or no evidence, Baker did reduce the Confederate presence in Washington. But he failed to find the agents who conspired to assassinate President Abraham Lincoln. He led the manhunt for assassin JOHN WILKES BOOTH, but he failed to capture Booth alive.

Lincoln's successor, President Andrew Johnson, fired Baker as an untrustworthy man still loyal to Johnson's enemy, Secretary Stanton. When Johnson fired Stanton without seeking the permission of the Senate, impeachment proceedings began. Baker testified at the impeachment hearings, lying about documents that he thought would hurt Johnson, if they had existed. Baker's performance at the Johnson hearings ended his career. He later wrote of his spying in a memoir grandly titled *The History of the United States Secret Service* (1867).

Bald Eagle

U.S. Air Force CODE NAME for the modification of B-57 CANBERRA aircraft for the high-altitude RECONNAISSANCE role. The principal modifications were the provision of wide wings and high-altitude cameras.

Ball, Sir Joseph

Politician who ran an intelligence operation within Britain's Conservative Party. Ball, who had been in MI5 during World War I, set up what he called "a little intelligence service of our own" in 1927. He targeted the Labour Party, placing his own SECRET AGENTS in it, hoping to expose communists and discredit the party.

Ball's group was one of several privately funded amateur agencies founded during the "red scare" that gripped Britain in the 1920s. The OFFICIAL SECRETS ACT was tightened with an eye to getting the "enemy within," and the ARCOS AFFAIR of 1927 proved that the Soviet Union was conspiring to overthrow the British government. Ball's spying was particularly inspired by the election in 1924 of Britain's first Labour government, which many Conservatives incorrectly linked to communism.

In Oct. 1937 Ball and his group, seeking better ties with fascist Italy, established a direct link between Italian dictator Benito Mussolini and Prime Minister Neville Chamberlain, bypassing Foreign Secretary Anthony Eden and the Foreign Office. In Feb. 1938 Eden resigned over such intervention.

In 1940, another scare—this time fears of a German FIFTH COLUMN—led to the setting up of a "Security Executive" to oversee intelligence agencies. Ball was cochairman of the executive.

Balloons

Long before the U-2 spyplane or SATELLITES performed OVERHEAD RECONNAISSANCE, intelligence gatherers used balloons for spying. BENJAMIN FRANKLIN was one of the first intelligence operatives to see the potential use of balloons for espionage. Soon after the first flights of the hot-air balloons of Jacques and Joseph Montgolfier in 1783, Franklin wrote that balloons "may be sufficient for certain purposes, such as elevating an Engineer to take a View of an Enemy's Army, Works, Etc., conveying Intelligence into, or out of a besieged Town, giving Signals to distant Places, or the like."

Intelligence-gathering balloons, manned and tethered to the ground, were in use by the end of the 18th century. During the American Civil War, hydrogen-filled balloons raised Union observers some 300 feet above the ground, giving them a 15-mile view for gathering TACTICAL INTELLIGENCE. Thaddeus S. C. Lowe, developer of the Union balloon force, was credited with providing timely INDICATIONS AND WARNING in the Virginia battles of Fair Oaks and Gaines' Mill. Observation balloons were also sent aloft from barges.

Lowe developed a horse-drawn hydrogen generator that could inflate a balloon in less than three hours. He also installed telegraph lines to the balloon, allowing the observer to flash instant messages about what he saw. Fifty seamstresses stitched together the seven balloons that made up the initial Union observation squadron.

The Confederacy had three balloons: one hot-air model, which crash-landed, and two gas-filled types called "silk dress" balloons because they were reputedly sewn from Southern belles' gowns. None was effectively used in the field.

In France the use of balloons continued into the 19th century. During the German siege of Paris in 1870–1871, balloons carried mail and carrier pigeons, which returned with dispatches.

Early in the 20th century, observation balloons seemed to be destined to rise no more; in 1911 the French Army officially declared them obsolete, to be replaced by dirigibles. But balloons came back in World War I, when both Germany and the Allies made use of them for gathering tactical intelligence.

French balloons, able to rise to 6,000 feet and withstand 70-mph winds, topped the German balloons in altitude and performance. But by the end of the war it was evident that balloons could not prevail against the airplane, and again balloons faded away as observation platforms.

The Cold War saw the brief renaissance of the balloon. In 1952 an Air Force–sponsored study group

Two observers in a British balloon prepare to search out targets in German-held territory. Note their telephone microphones, large map board, and two parachute canisters—for hasty evacuation if their balloon is attacked by German fighters. (IMPERIAL WAR MUSEUM)

known as Beacon Hill addressed new approaches to aerial reconnaissance, such as photography from high-flying aircraft and camera-carrying balloons. One of the more unusual proposals examined by the panel was an "invisible" dirigible: This was to be a giant, almost flat airship with a blue-tinted, nonreflective coating that would cruise at an altitude of 90,000 feet along the borders of the Soviet Union at very slow speeds, using a large lens to photograph targets of interest. That project was not pursued, although Beacon Hill was one of the origins of the U-2 program.

Based on a 1951 study by the RAND Corp., in Jan. 1956 the United States began launching several hundred camera-equipped balloons over Soviet territory as part of a secret program with the CODE NAME GENETRIX. The camera-carrying balloons, launched by U.S. intelligence teams in Western Europe, were intended to photograph areas of the Soviet Union and Eastern Bloc countries and were to be recovered in the western Pacific. At its destination, a ground control station would send a radio signal causing the camera and exposed film to be parachuted to the ground. If the equipment landed in the water, it would float, and a transmitter would emit a homing signal to guide searchers. The balloons could be maintained at a constant altitude and were launched to follow known air currents. The camera could record the map coordinates of every photograph taken and held sufficient film for 450 to 500 photographs, according to a Soviet source.

The program was cancelled within months because of Soviet protests, and few made successful flights. By the end of Feb. 1956 the Air Force had launched a total of 516 balloons. Only 46 payloads were eventually recovered—the last not until 1958. And of those, only 34 flights provided useful photography.

In its Feb. 1956 protest the Soviet government claimed that the United States was inundating its air space with aerial photographic balloons. The Soviets offered a reward for anyone finding a balloon and turning it over to authorities. A display in Moscow exhibited 250 balloons and instrument containers, which the Soviets offered as proof of their charges. They claimed that the radio-controlled balloons were "able to traverse the entire breadth of the Soviet Union in seven to ten days and then release their [obcamera] apparatus by parachute into friendly hands." A Soviet spokesperson claimed that each balloon carried nearly 1,500 pounds of equipment and contained a transmitter that gave a location signal at regular intervals.

(By sheer chance the steel bar on the Genetrix balloons that held the camera payload and ballasting system resonated when struck by radar pulses from the principal Soviet air search radar. This made it possible for radar operators at U.S. and NATO radar sites along the periphery of the Soviet Union to locate a number of previously unknown radar installations.)

In 1958 President Eisenhower approved Project WS-461L (code name Melting Pot), based on assurances that a new camera would allow the balloons to fly high enough to be undetectable. These launches took place from a U.S. Navy carrier in the Bering Sea, taking advantage of unusual air currents that could carry the balloons as high as 110,000 feet on a west-to-east flight path. When the Soviets protested the new flights within a month of the first launches, Eisenhower angrily cancelled that program. No payloads were recovered.

Subsequently, U.S. intelligence agencies employed tethered, unmanned balloons—sometimes referred to as aerostats—to carry sensors aloft. These were used with varying degrees of success in the Vietnam War and against drug traffickers in the Caribbean area. In 1995 the NATIONAL RECONNAISSANCE OFFICE proposed a new reconnaissance balloon program to employ stratospheric balloons using advanced technology equipment to serve as low-cost, stationary SATELLITES. The proposed design called for the balloons to be one to two times the size of a Boeing 747 aircraft and to be tethered at altitudes of about 65,000 feet, carrying radar and optical systems. So far as is known, the program was not being pursued when this book went to press.

Baltch, Robert

SEE ALEXANDR SOKOLOV

Bamford, James

Author and investigative reporter. Bamford wrote *The Puzzle Palace* (1982), subtitled "A Report on America's Most Secret Agency," the first detailed and authoritative report on the NSA.

Bamford is one of the few experts on the NSA who is

completely independent of the agency. He was an investigative producer for ABC News, responsible for stories that ranged from Cold War espionage to war crimes in Bosnia.

The Puzzle Palace emerged from what Bamford called "a torrent of FREEDOM OF INFORMATION ACT requests," interviews, and an exhaustive hunt for information through not only the documents requested but also from congressional hearings. The highly secretive NSA was not happy with the book, although it has become a textbook in courses on intelligence and foreign policy at the Defense Intelligence College, the National War College, Yale University, and many other universities. (The release of VENONA materials, beginning in 1995, inspired the publication of books that gave new coverage to the NSA. Also finding their way into new books were more than 32,000 pages of NSA information either released directly by the agency or obtained through Freedom of Information requests). In 1995 the Library of Congress catalog listed only 12 books on the NSA, of which four were editions of *The Puzzle Palace*. By comparison, there were 522 books listed on the CIA.

Curious about the NSA's hostile reaction to the book, Bamford, a lawyer, filed a Freedom of Information Act request for any files the NSA might have on him. He was told that there were none.

He had seen the CODE NAME Esquire on documents and he filed another Freedom of Information for "Esquire" documents. This time the NSA responded with hundreds of SANITIZED documents showing that Bamford and his book had been discussed not only by NSA officials but also by the U.S. Attorney General and the White House and that unsuccessful attempts had been made to get galley proofs of the book prior to publication.

Bamford's follow-up book about the NSA was *Body of Secrets* (2001), discussing NSA activities from the Cold War to the "dawn of a new century." This book contains an extensive discussion of the Israeli attack on the U.S. intelligence ship *LIBERTY*, in which Bamford declared that the attack was premeditated. He based that conclusion in part on statements by a U.S. Navy chief petty officer, Marvin E. Nowicki, who was a Hebrew linguist and intercept supervisor in the U.S. Navy ELECTRONIC INTELLIGENCE aircraft that was over the area of the attack (see C-121 CONSTELLATION).

But Bamford misrepresented Nowicki's view, according to a letter that the Navy linguist wrote to *The Wall Street Journal*. He said that there were clear, recorded intercepts. "My position, which is opposite of Mr. Bamford's," he wrote, "is that the attack, though terrible and tragic especially to the crew members and their families on that ill-fated day in June 1967, was a gross error."

Bancroft, Edward

(b. 1744 d. 1821)

American DOUBLE AGENT, serving both sides during the American Revolutionary War. A native of Massachusetts, Bancroft as a youth traveled to Guiana, South America,

living on an American's plantation while working on a book about Guiana.

In 1766, at age 22, he went to London and became a member of the Royal College of Physicians and the Royal Society. In London he befriended BENJAMIN FRANKLIN, then the London agent, or lobbyist, for Pennsylvania. Bancroft assisted Franklin, who was gathering information on British attitudes toward the American colonies.

Back in America, Franklin reestablished contact with Bancroft through Silas Deane, a young American whom Franklin had sent to Europe as an intelligence AGENT. Bancroft, meanwhile, had been recruited by the British SECRET SERVICE to spy on Deane and other Americans working in Paris to obtain French aid for the coming American Revolution. Deane, believing that Bancroft was a key agent in Franklin's European spy operations, confided in him.

In Sept. 1776 the American Continental Congress created a diplomatic commission to represent the American Colonies in the French court. The members were Franklin, Deane, and Arthur Lee, a London lawyer who had also been an agent for Franklin. Bancroft, at the suggestion of his British HANDLERS, succeeded in penetrating the commission when Franklin hired him as its secretary.

Bancroft kept contact with his handlers through a DEAD DROP: a bottle in a hole in the root of a tree in the Tuileries gardens. He made frequent trips to London as an undercover agent for Franklin. Fearing that Franklin might suspect the ease with which Bancroft traveled to England, Bancroft engineered an "arrest" and was held briefly.

Arthur Lee heard from a sea captain that Bancroft had been seen meeting with British officials, but Franklin paid no heed. Besides, Lee's own private secretary had been exposed as a spy, and Lee had not spotted him. Lee returned to America. Franklin refused to believe claims about Bancroft's duplicity.

Bancroft gave extremely valuable and accurate information to London, reporting, for example, that France and the Colonies had formed a military alliance. But, as so often happens in espionage, Bancroft's reports were not wholly believed. King George III suspected that Bancroft, a stock speculator, might be trying to use the information to affect the market.

After the Revolutionary War, Bancroft continued to work for both sides. In 1789 he went on a mission to Ireland to learn whether the Irish, with French and American aid, would rise against the British.

Judging from his papers, Bancroft's descendants viewed him as a scientist who knew Franklin and published several well-regarded scientific papers. He was not revealed as a spy until the 1880s, when an American researcher, reading newly opened British archives, discovered Bancroft's other life.

Bancroft, Mary

(b. 1903 d. 1997)

American AGENT in Switzerland during World War II and lover of ALLEN W. DULLES, who was the U.S. spymaster there and, later, DIRECTOR OF CENTRAL INTELLIGENCE.

Bancroft, the wife of a Swiss accountant who traveled frequently, was spotted as a potential agent by Gerald Mayer, a former NBC radio technician who, like Dulles, was with the OFFICE OF STRATEGIC SERVICES (OSS). Dulles, ordered to Switzerland by OSS, had assigned Mayer to find agents. Bancroft, a Boston debutante and Smith College graduate, had lived in Switzerland since 1934. She spoke fluent German and French and knew her way around Zurich and Bern.

Bancroft was introduced to Dulles over drinks in the Hotel Baur am Lac in Zurich in Dec. 1942. Dulles was under diplomatic COVER at the American Embassy in Bern. Dulles took her on as an agent, saying, "We can let the work cover the romance and let the romance cover the work." She agreed, simultaneously serving Dulles as lover and spy. Once a week she would take the train from Zurich to Bern to help Dulles prepare his telephoned report to OSS chief WILLIAM DONOVAN. "Spy master and spy mistress," as Godfrey Hodgson wrote, "would then retire to bed together."

Dulles assigned her to translate the writings of Hans Bernd Gisevius, a German INTELLIGENCE OFFICER for the ABWEHR and a member of the anti-Nazi underground. Bancroft became romantically involved with Gisevius as her affair with Dulles cooled. When Dulles's wife, Clover, arrived in Bern, she told Bancroft that she knew what was going on. The two women became close friends.

Bancroft's *Autobiography of a Spy* was published in 1983.

Barannikov, Lt. Gen. Viktor Pavlovich

(b. 1940 d. 1995)

Russian official who held key positions during the period of breakup of the Soviet Union. His career with agencies of the Ministry of Internal Affairs (MVD) began in 1961.

Barannikov was the Russian Minister of Internal Affairs at the end of the Soviet regime (Sept. 1990–Aug. 1991), becoming the Soviet Minister of Internal Affairs after the failure of the coup against Mikhail Gorbachev (Aug. 1991–Jan. 1992). With the end of the Soviet regime, he also became the Director General of the Federal Security Agency of the Russian Federation (Jan. 1992), and then Minister of Security of the Russian Federation (Jan. 1992–July 1993).

In these latter positions Barannikov began the transfer of the Interior Ministry's power to the republics and ordered the national police (militia) to remain apart from the political chaos engulfing the capital.

But in Oct. 1993 he was arrested as one of the leaders of the abortive revolution in Moscow and was incarcerated. He was freed in Feb. 1994 by a resolution of the Russian parliament.

Barannikov died of a heart attack the following year.

Barbarossa

CODE NAME for the German offensive against the Soviet Union in June 1941. The plan was originally called Fritz and then Directive 21. On Dec. 18, 1940, Adolf Hitler renamed the operation Barbarossa, the surname of Frederick I (1121–1190). Legend had it that Frederick would rise from his deathlike sleep and restore Germany to power again.

The U.S. and British governments had ample warning of the planned German invasion of the Soviet Union through their codebreaking effort ENIGMA-ULTRA; they also had a British spy in the ABWEHR (German MILITARY INTELLIGENCE). By mid-1940 British intelligence agencies were seeing increasing indications that Germany was planning an assault on the Soviet Union.

In July 1940 the British Secret Intelligence Service (MI6) reported that the Soviet military ATTACHÉ in BERLIN had warned Moscow that Germany was preparing to attack Russia. (This warning occurred as German–Soviet trade was increasing, with the Soviets providing mostly raw materials and the Germans supplying arms and machinery.)

The litany of warnings continued to increase. On Aug. 22, 1940, PAUL THUMMEL, Britain's DOUBLE AGENT in German intelligence, reported that the German Army's intelligence branch responsible for the Soviet Union, FOREIGN ARMIES EAST, had been expanding since June, and that the COUNTERINTELLIGENCE activities against the Soviet Union were also to be increased as a matter of urgency. Further, the German intelligence staff in Rumania had been reinforced by specialists on the southern Ukraine, the Crimea, and Caucasus.

In the official history *British Intelligence in the Second World War* (1979), F. HARRY HINSLEY and his colleagues observed that by late March 1941 Enigma revealed details of German troop movements: "For the Prime Minister, for some of the intelligence bodies . . . and after some hesitation, the Foreign Office. . . . this intelligence provided the first confirmation that Germany's main preparations were directed against Russia." On March 30 the British codebreaking staff at BLETCHLEY PARK "concluded that the Enigma evidence pointed to the possibility of some large-scale operation against Russia, 'either for intimidation or for actual attack'."

On April 3, Prime Minister Winston Churchill sent his only direct message to Soviet dictator Josef Stalin before the German assault. Referring to "a trusted agent," Churchill told of German troop movements and concluded, "Your Excellency will readily appreciate the significance of these facts." (To Churchill's anger, the British ambassador in Moscow delayed delivery of the message, fearing that Stalin would consider it provocative.)

The crescendo of reports was building. Hinsley wrote that by this time

> The Swedes had pieced together a fairly accurate estimate of Germany's intentions; they gave their information to the United States Ambassador to Moscow on 24 March. By 1 April, it appears, the Yugoslav Military Attaché in Berlin had got wind of the German plan, and his government had passed his information to Moscow via London. It has been claimed that since the beginning of 1941

the Vichy authorities had been giving the Soviet embassy their intelligence about the eastward movement of German divisions. And it is beyond doubt that from 20 March the United States government had renewed its warnings to the Soviet Ambassador in Washington, advising him on the basis of decrypted Japanese diplomatic messages that Germany would attack Russia within 2 months.

The information in Washington was based mainly on MAGIC intercepts of Japanese diplomatic communications. On May 22 they revealed a message from the Japanese ambassador in Moscow that it was "not mere rumor that Germany may attack Russia shortly." Magic later revealed that on June 6, 1941, Gen. HIROSHI OSHIMA, the Japanese ambassador in Berlin, advised Tokyo that Germany would invade the Soviet Union on June 22.

During this period Stalin also had access to the British codebreaking efforts through the spies of the CAMBRIDGE SPY RING.

The Soviet dictator chose to ignore the alarms from the West. He was certainly distrustful of the "capitalist" regimes, and he especially disliked Churchill, who had tried to strangle the Bolshevik revolution in its infancy some 20 years earlier. Stalin's own MILITARY INTELLIGENCE organization, the GRU, provided warning of the impending attack, which he ignored (see FILIPP GOLIKOV). While Stalin himself ignored these warnings and forbade the Red Army to make preparations to meet an assault, which he feared would be provocative to the Germans, the Soviet Navy did make all possible preparations to meet the Barbarossa assault on the morning of June 22.

Barbie, Klaus

(b. 1914 d. 1991)

German SD chief in Lyon, France, during World War II. Barbie had been shielded by the U.S. Army's Counter Intelligence Corps (CIC) whose officers wanted his help in getting information about other Nazis and Soviet AGENTS.

Barbie was called "the Butcher of Lyon" for the torture and murder of 4,000 Jews and Resistance fighters during World War II. He was twice given the death sentence in absentia by French courts.

But while war crimes investigators hunted for him, he was in a SAFE HOUSE in Augsburg, being debriefed by CIC officers on his knowledge of German and Soviet intelligence. In 1951 he escaped to South America and lived in Peru and then in Bolivia, where he kept in touch with pro-Nazi Bolivian officials. One of them testified at Barbie's 1987 trial that Barbie founded a rightist death squad, consorted with drug traffickers, and helped right-wing leaders get intelligence and arms while in Bolivia.

Nazi hunters found Barbie in the 1970s, but the Bolivian military government protected him until 1983, when a civilian government turned him over to France.

Barbie, who had been quoted by a German magazine in 1979 as saying, "I regret each Jew I did not kill," was accused of both executing more than 4,000 people and deporting 7,000 French Jews to concentration camps. Because of a 20-year statute of limitations, his earlier sentences had become void. But he was tried under a French law stating that Nazis responsible for abominable crimes "should be pursued to the ends of the earth. . . ."

Eyewitnesses at Barbie's trial told of seeing him savagely beat Jean Moulin, the leader of the French Resistance selected by Charles de Gaulle to unite anti-German groups. Moulin died on a prison train. Others said that Barbie personally tortured and beheaded prisoners.

The 1987 trial ended with Barbie sentenced to life imprisonment for crimes against humanity. He died of cancer in prison in 1991.

Barclay, Cecil

British MI6 officer stationed in Moscow during World War II to provide selected ULTRA material to F. F. KUZNETSOV, the head of Soviet MILITARY INTELLIGENCE (GRU).

British and U.S. intelligence officials had decided not to tell their Soviet allies about the source of the Ultra material. But the Soviets knew a great deal about Ultra, primarily through JOHN CAIRNCROSS, a DOUBLE AGENT of the CAMBRIDGE SPY RING who worked at BLETCHLEY PARK, the codebreaking source of Ultra.

Kuznetsov seems to have wanted Barclay to know that the Soviets were not entirely ignorant of Ultra. One day he handed Barclay a captured Luftwaffe code book and told him to make certain that it got to the "right place."

Also see ENIGMA.

Barium

Russian term for false information that is provided to a source suspected of leaking classified material. After the "barium dose" is fed to the suspect, the intelligence ORGANS will attempt to locate where the information is found in foreign intelligence agencies and determine who could have provided it.

Barnett, David

(b. 1933)

The first CIA officer ever to be charged with espionage. A 1955 graduate of the University of Michigan, Barnett joined the CIA in 1958, serving as an analyst with U.S. ARMY INTELLIGENCE in South Korea and Washington, D.C. After two years as a staff officer in the Directorate of Operations at CIA headquarters in Langley, Va., in 1967 he was assigned, under diplomatic COVER, to Surabaya, Indonesia, where he was responsible for recruiting local Soviet officials to spy for the United States.

In the 1960s Indonesia received billions of dollars worth of Soviet military equipment, especially warships and aircraft. The CIA's Operation Habrink provided the United States with a large amount of intelligence on Soviet weapons systems being transferred to Indonesia, along with some hardware.

Barnett gave the Soviets Habrink information between Oct. 31, 1976, and Feb. 27, 1977, meeting with KGB operatives in VIENNA and Jakarta. He resigned from the agency in 1970 but continued to perform work for the CIA on a contract basis. Following his resignation, he returned to Indonesia, where he managed a shrimp factory before setting up a furniture-exporting business. His firm faltered, and by 1976 he owed $100,000. At that time he approached the KGB in Jakarta. After telling what he knew of CIA operations against the Soviets, he betrayed the identities of 30 CIA employees working under cover and the names of seven Soviet consular officials whom the CIA had hoped to recruit in Surabaya.

In 1977 the KGB persuaded him to apply for staff positions in the U.S. Congress, on the Senate or House intelligence committees, or with the INTELLIGENCE OVERSIGHT BOARD. Although he was unable to obtain positions with those groups, he did provide the KGB with classified material.

He was arrested by the FBI and indicted in Oct. 1980.

Barnett's work for the Soviets represented the deepest proven penetration of the CIA by the KGB at the time of his arrest. For $92,000 he had sold the KGB details of one of the most successful undercover operations the CIA ever conducted against the Soviet Union. He was convicted of espionage, and on Jan. 8, 1981, he was sentenced to 18 years' imprisonment. He was paroled after serving 10 years.

Barron, John D.

A *Reader's Digest* editor who played an important role in efforts by the FBI to publicize the official story about U.S. Navy spy JOHN WALKER. Barron, a former Navy INTELLIGENCE OFFICER and an expert on the KGB, testified at both of the trials of FBI agent RICHARD MILLER and at the trial of JERRY WHITWORTH, a colleague of John Walker.

Barron was so much a part of the prosecution team at the Whitworth trial that Assistant U.S. Attorney William Farmer asked that he be allowed to sit with the team during the trial. The judge turned down the request.

FBI officials said that they sought Barron out as an expert witness because, as a writer not connected with the bureau, he did not have to worry about whether he would inadvertently divulge a secret while on the stand. Testifying under oath in the Whitworth trial, Barron admitted that he did hold a SECURITY CLEARANCE, implying that it gave him access to SATELLITE intelligence. While testifying about how a CIA satellite manual was sold to the Soviets (see WILLIAM P. KAMPILES), he referred to OVERHEAD photography as so sensitive "that we can see the color of a man's beard," a detail not generally known. Barron did not receive any compensation for his services to the FBI. But he has received a great deal of help that translates into commercial successes for his books. In his *Breaking the Ring* (1987), Barron laid out the official account of the FBI's capture of Walker and the other members of his ring. His books include *KGB: The Secret*

Work of Soviet Secret Agents (1974) and *KGB Today: The Hidden Hand* (1983), both published by Reader's Digest Press; and *Operation Solo* (1996).

Also see SOLO.

Barstow, Mrs. Montagu

SEE BARONESS EMMUSKA ORCZY

Basic Intelligence

Fundamental, factual, and generally permanent information about a nation's characteristics, such as its physical, social, economic, political, and cultural properties. Such intelligence, attained through the examination and analysis of OPEN SOURCES, is the foundation for intelligence obtained by covert means.

Bates, Ann

Loyalist American who spied for the British during the Revolutionary War. A Philadelphia schoolteacher, she was married to a man assigned to a British Army unit as an artillery repairman. Her husband joined the British troops evacuating Philadelphia and marching to New York City in 1778. Claiming to be a Patriot, she managed to get through the American lines at Philadelphia and traveled to New York, where she became an AGENT in the spy ring directed by Maj. JOHN ANDRÉ.

Under the COVER name "Mrs. Barnes" she spied on American troops. She carried a token (description still unknown) that would identify her as a British spy to an American officer who was spying for the British. But by the time she reached American headquarters at White Plains, N.Y., the officer had left the Army.

Posing as a peddler, she listened in on conversations, located gun emplacements, and even walked into the headquarters of Gen. GEORGE WASHINGTON. "I had the Opportunity of going through their whole Army Remarking at the same time the strength & Situation of each Brigade, & the Number of Cannon with their Situation and Weight of Ball each Cannon was Charged with," she later wrote. She also helped other spies (never identified) get through the American lines and stay at SAFE HOUSES as they made their way back to British-held territory.

On another mission to an American encampment near Dobbs Ferry, N.Y., she counted men and guns and inventoried provisions. Her "timly information" about American troop movements led to British decisions to strengthen the garrison in Rhode Island.

Her husband accompanied British artillery to South Carolina in 1780, and there her espionage career ended, for she was given no more missions. The couple sailed to England in 1781. Later deserted by her husband, she successfully petitioned for a small pension for her work in America.

Bay of Pigs

SEE CIA and CUBA

Bazna, Elyeza

SEE CICERO

Bazoft, Farzad

(b. 1959 d. 1990)

Journalist executed as a spy by Iraq. Bazoft, an Iranian-born exile in England, was hanged in Baghdad on March 15, 1990, after a revolutionary court found him guilty of spying for Israel and Britain. Although he made a confession on Iraqi television, he denied the charges in court.

Bazoft, who had lived in Britain since 1975, had served a year in prison in 1981 for robbing a savings and loan office north of London. Later he became a police informer. This shady background led to speculation that, like *Observer* correspondent HAROLD (KIM) PHILBY in the 1950s, Bazoft may have been using his journalism as a COVER for espionage.

The execution took place despite pleas for clemency from Britain, UNITED NATIONS Secretary-General Javier Perez de Cuellar, Amnesty International, the European Community, and international press groups. Prime Minister Margaret Thatcher called the execution barbaric. President Saddam Hussein, rejecting the mercy pleas, denounced Bazoft as "a British and Israeli agent."

Bazoft's arrest followed his attempt in Sept. 1989 to check reports of a massive explosion at a weapons facility 30 miles south of Baghdad. Bazoft was reporting for *The Observer*. A British nurse, Daphne Parish, 53, who drove Bazoft to the secret Iskandaria military complex, was jailed for 15 years.

In 2003, Kadem Askar, a former colonel in the Iraqi intelligence service, was quoted in the *Observer* as saying that Bazoft was innocent. Askar had arrested and interrogated Bazoft. The *Observer* said that Bazoft had been investigating reports that 700 people had been killed by the explosion.

BCRA

Bureau Central de Renseignements et d'Action (Central Bureau for Information and Action), the COVERT ACTION and sabotage agency established by Gen. Charles de Gaulle during World War II. With headquarters in London as part of the Free French forces, the BCRA handled some AGENTS sent to France, but worked with Resistance groups through cooperation with the British SOE (Special Operations Executive).

The organization was at first called the BCRAM (Central Bureau for Information and Military Action). The military <u>M</u> was dropped after a French politician in London complained that it implied military participation in political matters.

Rival British and French agencies often battled over jurisdictional and operational questions, reflecting the animosity between Prime Minister Churchill and de Gaulle. Moreover, BCRA officials often had their eye on postwar France rather than current operations. One of the first BCRA projects was to compile a card file on some 100,000 French men and women, classifying them as hostile, favorable, or indifferent to de Gaulle's Free France.

"Col. Passy"—Col. ANDRÉ DEWAVRIN used the name of a Paris Métro stop as a COVER—set up the BCRA primarily to send agents into German-occupied France and to assess reports of French fugitives from there. Assessments of BCRA's effectiveness were mixed. The British gave its work low marks, seeing it as a weak link in the French Resistance; the Americans rated it a bit higher. Many French observers felt that its interests were more political than military and accurately predicted that it would not survive the war. It was disbanded and its duties were taken over in 1944 by GSS.

Also see FRANCE.

B-Dienst

German Navy CRYPTANALYSIS service in World War II. *B-Dienst*—the abbreviation for *Beobachtungdienst*, or Observation Service—was highly effective in decoding Allied radio traffic for use in guiding of U-boats to convoy positions. B-Dienst was particularly useful because Germany lacked other intelligence sources on Allied convoy movements. The service was a major contribution to the German successes in the Battle of the Atlantic, providing U-boats with timely information on Allied convoy movements.

The service traced its origins to 1919, when members of the Imperial German Navy's World War I code-breaking organization were recalled to active service. B-Dienst had several successes against British naval CODES in the 1920s and 1930s, and by the eve of World War II was succeeding in breaking other foreign codes. B-Dienst received a bonanza when the British destroyer *Sikh* was sunk in shallow water off Tobruk in Sept. 1942 and her code books were recovered. Some British naval codes were read through the critical Atlantic convoy battles of March 1943. But U.S. Navy codes could not be read consistently. In April 1942, even this meager code-breaking success stopped because the U.S. Navy began to use a new machine CIPHER system.

B-Dienst's importance began to decline in April 1943, when the British code broken in Sept. 1942 went out of use.

Many of the service's files—and hence its effectiveness—were destroyed in an Allied air raid on BERLIN in Nov. 1943. As the war progressed, improved Allied coding expertise also continued to reduce the ability of B-Dienst to read codes. Still, according to intelligence historian DAVID KAHN, B-Dienst compiled "a record unmatched by any other intelligence agency of the Third Reich."

During the war the B-Dienst staff grew to some 5,000 men and women, of whom about 1,100 were stationed in Berlin. After the Nov. 1943 bombing, B-Dienst headquarters were moved from Berlin to Eberswaide, some 25 miles northeast of the capital.

During 1943 the organization was intercepting about 8,500 Allied messages per day, although some were duplicates and certainly not all could be deciphered.

Beach, Thomas

(b. 1841 d. 1894)

British SECRET AGENT who spied on Irish-Americans suspected of plotting to return to Ireland and lead a rebellion. The Americans, who called themselves the Fenians, also planned to invade Canada.

Beach, born in England, immigrated to America and fought on the Union side in the Civil War. After the war, he heard reports about the Fenians, who took their name from the warriors who had guarded the legendary Irish leader Finn MacCool in the 3rd century. The Fenian movement began in Ireland and America in the 1850s, although in Ireland it was usually called the Irish Republican Brotherhood. Members took an oath to devote their lives to making Ireland a republic, independent of Britain.

Beach wrote to relatives in England about the American Fenians, and the relatives passed the information to British officials. The British had already infiltrated the Irish revolutionaries but, having no ASSETS among the American Fenian ranks, asked Beach to become a DOUBLE AGENT.

Beach got word of the planned Fenian invasion of Canada in 1866 and reported it to England before the Fenians crossed the border. They were quickly repulsed. Beach later joined the Fenians and was so trusted that he accompanied a Fenian leader to Washington to appeal to President Andrew Johnson for American support of Irish freedom. He also made a trip to Canada as a Fenian secret agent on a RECONNAISSANCE mission for another invasion in 1870. He tipped off Canadian officials, who easily stopped the invaders.

When the Fenian movement faded away in 1877, Beach returned to England and continued his anti-Irish work. He helped to hatch a British intelligence plot to ruin Charles Stewart Parnell by forging and then publishing letters supposedly written by Parnell that urged the assassination of British politicians. The plot was exposed and so was Beach.

Beall, John

(b. 1835 d. 1865)

Confederate spy during the American Civil War. Wounded while fighting under Gen. Stonewall Jackson, Beall became a privateer for the Confederacy. He was captured after seizing several Union ships in Chesapeake Bay.

After being freed in a prisoner exchange, Beall hatched sabotage plots, none of which succeeded. He was captured again, this time in northern New York, where he hoped to wreck trains by tearing up rails. After being tried and convicted of espionage and sabotage, he was hanged.

Bear (Tu-20/Tu-95)

A large, graceful aircraft, the Bear was the world's only operational strategic bomber to be propelled by turbo-prop engines—combination turbojet and reciprocating power plants. The Bear remains in the Russian Air Force as a missile-carrying strike aircraft and in Navy service as an important long-range SURVEILLANCE and missile guidance aircraft as well as in other naval roles.

The Bear was produced by the Andrei N. Tupolev design bureau to provide an aircraft capable of reaching targets in the United States from Soviet bases with a nuclear weapon. The Bear is believed to have made the first air drop of a Soviet nuclear weapon, on Nov. 6, 1955.

The Bear entered service in 1955 as a strategic bomber. Subsequently the Bear-D surveillance variant entered naval service in the mid-1960s for ocean surveillance and missile targeting. That aircraft carries no offensive weapons; rather, it has the large Big Bulge surface-search radar and a Video Data Link (VDL) (called Drambuie by Western intelligence) for transmitting target data to missile-launching ships and submarines.

Soon after it entered naval service, the Bear-D began overflying U.S. warships on the high seas. Starting in April 1970, pairs of Bear-D aircraft took off from the Kola Peninsula, flew around North Cape and down the Norwegian Sea and North Atlantic to land in Cuba; after a few days in Cuba the Bears returned to their home base. During those nonstop flights of more than 5,000 miles, the Bears conducted surveillance and collected ELECTRONIC INTELLIGENCE along the coast of North America, generally flying 200 to 250 miles offshore.

In 1973 pairs of Bear aircraft began flying into Conakry, Guinea. On several occasions Bears in Cuba and Bears in Conakry appear to have carried out coordinated RECONNAISSANCE over the south and central Atlantic. Soviet aircraft ceased flying out of Conakry in 1977, and the pattern changed as Bear-D flights began to use the airfield at Luanda, Angola. From 1981 until the demise of the Soviet Union in 1991 the presence of Bears in Cuba was virtually continuous. (Bear-F antisubmarine aircraft joined the Bear-D flights to Cuba in 1983.)

From 1974 long-range flights by Bear-D aircraft from Soviet Far Eastern bases in the Pacific were supplemented by operations from the former U.S. air bases at Da Nang and Cam Ranh Bay in Vietnam. From 1979 to 1991 Bear-D/F aircraft operations from Vietnam were continuous.

Although ocean surveillance and targeting for naval missiles has been largely taken over by SATELLITES, Bear-D aircraft continue in these roles for the Russian Navy. (See SOVIET OCEAN SURVEILLANCE SYSTEM.)

The Bear-E model was produced as a photo-reconnaissance aircraft for the Air Force. The Bear-F was a Navy anti-submarine aircraft. The Bear-G was a remake of earlier bombers to carry guided missiles. The Bear-H was a new-production missile aircraft that entered service in 1984, and the Bear-J was a naval communications relay aircraft. Earlier Bear bombers have been rebuilt to a missile-launching configuration, and production at a slow rate continued into the 1990s. Thus, the Bear has been in continuous production longer than any aircraft in history: more than 45 years! More than 350 aircraft have been produced.

The Bear is a large, swept-wing aircraft with four turboprop engines fitted in streamlined nacelles faired into the wings. Each turboprop engine has two contra-rotating, variable-pitch, four-blade propellers, which can produce a speed of almost Mach 1. The aircraft's long range—more than 7,000 miles for the Bear-D—can be further extended through in-flight refueling via a fixed receiving probe fitted in the nose. The normal crew is 7 or 8 men.

Tu-95 is the Tupolev design bureau's designation, which is sometimes used (incorrectly) in the West to indicate military versions of the aircraft. The initial military designation was Tu-20, with Bear-F and later production aircraft having the military designation Tu-142.

Beaumarchais, Pierre

(b. 1733 d. 1799)

French playwright and a SECRET AGENT who did undercover work for King Louis XVI during the American Revolutionary War. Beaumarchais, who wrote the plays

A Soviet Tu-20 Bear-D reconnaissance aircraft reveals its graceful lines as it flies toward U.S. warships over the North Pacific in 1971. A U.S. Navy F-4 Phantom fighter from the aircraft carrier Midway *keeps careful watch on the large aircraft.* (U.S. NAVY)

on which *The Marriage of Figaro* and *The Barber of Seville* were based, was a close adviser to the king. Both were firm believers in COVERT ACTION as a way to advance France's anti-British policy.

The king authorized funds to draw eight shiploads of military stores from royal arsenals. Beaumarchais, using his own funds, government contributions from Spain, and money from others in France and Spain, set up a purported import-export firm, Hortalez et Compagnie. In modern espionage terms this was a PROPRIETARY COMPANY.

Beaumarchais ran a fleet of up to 50 ships to carry the guns, ammunition, and other matériel, ostensibly to the French West Indies. From there, they continued to American ports. Many scholars believe that the American victory at Saratoga in Oct. 1777 was possible only because of the timely arrival of French supplies. The Saratoga victory in turn showed that the Americans could win the Revolution and thus played a role in establishing the American-French alliance in Feb. 1778.

Earlier, Beaumarchais had run another undercover mission. He went to London under an assumed name and quashed a plot aimed at embarrassing the king by revealing that France had a contingency plan to invade England.

Beauregard, Brig. Gen. Pierre G. T.

(b. 1818 d. 1893)

Confederate officer who developed an extensive spy NETWORK during the American Civil War. An 1838 graduate of the U.S. Military Academy, Beauregard fought in the Mexican War. The Louisiana-born Beauregard was superintendent of the Military Academy at West Point, N.Y., for five days in 1861 before being removed because he said he would join the South if war began.

On April 12, 1861, artillery under his command fired the first shots of the Civil War—a barrage whose target was Fort Sumter in Charleston, S.C., harbor. He served with distinction throughout the war both on the battlefield and as a spymaster. He ordered one of his officers, Capt. Thomas Jordan, to set up an intelligence network headed by Rose Greenhow, a wealthy Washington, D.C., society matron who collected POLITICAL and MILITARY INTELLIGENCE, especially at dinner parties.

The most important information Jordan and Greenhow obtained involved the Battle of Bull Run (called First Manassas by the South). On July 10, 1861, Greenhow used a woman as a COURIER, hiding a message in her hair. The woman, Betty Duvall, got through the Union lines and had the information passed to Beauregard: The Union was planning to march south in six days. Subsequent messages gave the site: Bull Run, near Manassas, Va.

Beauregard added the Jordan-Greenhow information to other intelligence, including the results of prisoner interrogation, and prepared the strategy that turned the Battle of Bull Run into a rout of Union forces.

Beauregard shared command of the Confederate Army in the Battle of Shiloh in 1862. He then commanded defenses at Charleston against Union attacks,

and in 1864 fought at Petersburg, Va. He was a full general at the end of the war (one of eight in the Confederate Army).

He later became president of the New Orleans, Jacksonville, and Mississippi Railroad, and served as Adjutant General of Louisiana.

Bruce Catton, in *Mr. Lincoln's Army* (1951), called Beauregard "flamboyant . . . something of a young Napoleon . . . in ardent southern Esteem. . . ." He was a highly capable commander, but his continued questioning of orders at times bordered on insubordination.

Becker, Johann

(b. 1912 d. 1971)

Chief of German SD espionage in Latin America during World War II.

Born in Leipzig, Becker joined the Nazi Party in 1930 and was accepted into the SS and later commissioned as a lieutenant. His espionage career began in 1937 when he arrived in Buenos Aires as a businessman. Early in the war he returned to Germany and then reappeared in Argentina as a diplomatic courier.

Becker, charged with gathering POLITICAL INTELLIGENCE, organized a spy ring. (The ABWEHR was charged with collecting MILITARY INTELLIGENCE.) He maintained radio contact with Germany through operatives who transmitted at various frequencies from isolated farms to evade detection. He also set up a shop to produce MICRODOTS, which he applied to publications sent to Germany by COURIER or mail.

Becker analyzed American publications and radio broadcasts and sought out sympathizers among anti-American diplomats, government officials, and military officers. One of his sources was Col. Juan Perón, the future dictator. "Becker's spying flourished in the benign pro-Axis political climate," according to David Kahn in *Hitler's Spies* (1978). But the climate drastically changed in 1944 when Argentina, seeking German arms, was rebuffed by German diplomats and turned to WALTER SCHELLENBERG, director of the SD's foreign intelligence bureau.

Schellenberg tried to set up negotiations in Spain with an Argentinian. But at Trinidad, en route to Spain, he was stopped by British intelligence. The incident increased U.S. pressure on Argentina to drop its pro-Axis stance. Argentina broke off diplomatic relations with Germany on Jan. 26, 1944, and Argentinian security forces began arresting suspected German spies.

Becker managed to keep the ring going, but another wave of arrests in the summer all but smashed it. Spy hunters seized dozens of radios, new microdot machinery, and three ENIGMA CIPHER machines. Becker went into hiding but continued making reports. He passed them, along with cash, to a confederate who supposedly gave the packets to Spanish seamen, who would send them to ACCOMMODATION ADDRESSES in Germany.

Instead, the confederate kept the money and the messages; they were found in his closet when he was arrested.

Becker himself was arrested and imprisoned in April 1945, just before Germany surrendered. He was later released and returned to Germany, where he disappeared.

Allied assessors of Becker's labors concluded that he had sent little timely information to Germany. U-boats sank five ships whose sailing times he had reported, but, as Kahn noted, the U-boats had not received any messages about those ships.

Beer, Col. Israel

(b. 1912 d. 1968)

Israeli Army officer who spied for the Soviet Union. Beer's involvement with Israel began when he fled from VIENNA to Palestine in 1938, after the Nazi takeover of his native Austria. When he joined the Haganah, the Jewish underground army, he said he was an an experienced guerrilla who had fought against pro-Nazi forces in Austria in 1934 and against the fascists in Spain as a member of the International Brigade in the Spanish Civil War. He also said he had a doctorate in history.

After serving in the Israeli War of Independence in 1948–1949, he was a prime candidate to become the Army's deputy chief of staff. Apparently frustrated by not being appointed, Beer resigned his commission and became military correspondent for an Israeli newspaper. In 1953 he became a supporter of David Ben-Gurion's Mapai party and befriended leading defense figures, including Shimon Peres, a future prime minister, as well as Ben-Gurion. He wrote for the Mapai party newspaper, *Davar*, and in 1955 Ben-Gurion commissioned Beer to write the official history of the 1948–1949 war. This gave him access to Ben-Gurion as well as to the classified military archives. Moshe Dayan, the Army chief of staff, and ISSER HAREL, head of the MOSSAD, opposed his appointment. Neither trusted Beer.

Such access was extremely valuable for a Soviet AGENT. Beer had apparently been recruited by the Soviets during the Spanish Civil War.

Beer's tendency to overextend himself—by showing up at high-level meetings without invitation, for example—put him under suspicion. The Mossad also discovered that he had begun an unsanctioned relationship with REINHARD GEHLEN, head of West Germany's intelligence service (BND), after approval for such meetings had been denied. Gehlen was particularly eager to establish ties with Israeli intelligence after the 1956 Sinai campaign, and Beer offered to be the go-between, which would give his Soviet spymasters another source of West German intelligence.

According to Dan Raviv and Yossi Melman's *Every Spy a Prince* (1990), "The West Germans, brimming with their postwar willingness to please the Israelis, granted Beer a surprising degree of access to the German army, NORTH ATLANTIC TREATY ORGANIZATION installations, and American and other bases. Beer even obtained, for his Soviet handlers, details of the construction contracts for U.S. nuclear missile sites in Europe."

Harel had heard tales about Beer as far back as the British-French invasion of Suez in 1956. (Harel may also have been tipped by the British intelligence.) Because of Beer's connections to men of power, Harel at first held back. But he finally placed him under surveillance, and on March 30, 1961, Beer was seen handing over documents to Victor Sokolow, a KGB officer serving under diplomatic COVER in Tel Aviv. The documents included extracts from Ben-Gurion's diary. Beer was arrested the next morning.

On trial for espionage, Beer admitted that he had not fought in Spain and did not have a doctorate. Later, he repudiated his confession, claimed that he had spoken the truth originally, and insisted that whatever he did, his motive was patriotism, for he feared that Israel was being hurt by its pro-West diplomacy. He was sentenced to 15 years in prison, where he died in 1968.

Be'eri, Isser

(b. 1901 d. 1958)

First chief of AMAN, Israeli MILITARY INTELLIGENCE, with rank of colonel, when the Israeli Army was established in 1948. Previously, Be'eri had been head of SHAI, the intelligence arm of the Haganah, the Jewish defense force that predated the founding of the state of Israel.

Shai was dissolved six weeks after the birth of Israel on May 14, 1948. Be'eri formed and took charge of *Aman*, the key agency that emerged from Shai. On June 30, the day he became director of Aman, he accused Capt. Meir Toubianski, an Israeli Army officer, of treason, convicted him in what Be'eri called a "field court-martial," and immediately ordered the captain executed by an Army firing squad. The evidence against Toubianski was entirely circumstantial, and years later he was posthumously found to be innocent.

That same day Be'eri's operatives tortured an Arab aide to the mayor of Haifa. According to *Every Spy a Prince* (1990), an authoritative history of Israeli intelligence, Be'eri's men "beat him, dripped water on his head, pulled his teeth out, burned the soles of his feet, and injected drugs into his bloodstream," before releasing him without having made any charges against him. (In 1964 the government, revealing the 1948 torture, paid compensation to the Arab.)

Several weeks after these incidents, Be'eri's men abducted a DOUBLE AGENT who was supposedly working for the Arabs but was employed by the Israelis on suspicion that he was a TRIPLE AGENT (really working for the Arabs). The agent was summarily shot.

Prime Minister David Ben-Gurion, who was also Minister of Defense, learned of the shooting and ordered an investigation, which revealed the torture case described above. A military court in Dec. 1948 found Be'eri guilty of manslaughter. He was demoted to private, removed from his position, and dismissed from military service. On July 19, 1949, Be'eri was arrested again and charged with the execution of Toubianski. He was tried and found guilty in Nov. 1949 and sentenced to a token one day in prison "in consideration of . . . loyal service . . . [he] has rendered to Israel."

Be'eri, a tall, balding man, was nicknamed "Isser the Big." He dropped his original name, Isser Birentzweig, adopting a Hebrew name, as did many of his contemporaries during the campaign to establish the state of Israel.

Beesley, Patrick

(b. 1913 d. 1986)

Senior intelligence analyst from 1939 to 1945 in the British Admiralty's OPERATIONAL INTELLIGENCE CENTRE. He was particularly concerned with application of ULTRA decryptions to the naval war. He was a graduate of Trinity College, Cambridge, and held a commission in the Royal Navy Volunteer Reserve from 1939 to 1959.

In *Very Special Intelligence: The Story of the Admiralty's Operational Intelligence Centre 1939–1945* (1977), Beesly told of the incredible breadth of information provided to the Admiralty by Ultra (the Very Special Intelligence). The tracking room of the center could eventually read verbatim communications between U-boat command in Germany and the U-boats in the Atlantic as they took place, through the efforts of the codebreakers at BLETCHLEY PARK.

Beesly was also proud of the working relationship between the Operational Intelligence Center and its U.S. Navy counterpart in Washington, D.C. The cooperation between the two naval activities, he wrote, "was probably closer than between any other British and American organizations in any Service and in any theatre."

Behn, Aphra

(b. 1640 d. 1689)

British novelist and spy. Sent to Holland to persuade William Scot, a dubious DOUBLE AGENT, to return to England's side, she went beyond her brief. The information she sent back to England, using her own CODE, included a warning that a Dutch fleet was going to attempt to blockade the Thames. Her warning was ignored, and the fleet came.

She had to pawn her own jewelry to finance her espionage and borrowed money to pay for her return to England. Jailed for failing to repay the loan, she was later freed by the government, which paid her debts. She gave up spying and became a novelist. She is best known for the anti-slavery novel *Oroonoko, or the Royal Slave* (1688). She is one of two known spies interred in London's Westminster Abbey, the other being Maj. JOHN ANDRÉ.

Belfrage, Cedric

(b. 1904 d. 1990)

British INTELLIGENCE OFFICER who spied for the Soviet Union.

Belfrage was a member of the Communist Party of Great Britain when he came to America some time in 1940 to work for BRITISH SECURITY COORDINATION (BSC).

The secret agency—subordinate to MI6—operated out of Rockefeller Center, in New York City, during World War II. The BSC established a British intelligence presence in the United States before U.S. entry into the war. It then continued to work with the OFFICE OF STRATEGIC SERVICES.

A writer, Belfrage was believed to have supervised BLACK PROPAGANDA, which was extensively used by the BSC to spread information about the British war effort and DISINFORMATION about the Nazis.

The BSC was a highly secret, sensitive organization whose existence did not become publicly known until the 1960s. Belfrage was accused of revealing information about the BSC to his Soviet HANDLER while he was working there.

ELIZABETH BENTLEY, a COURIER for a Soviet spy ring in New York City and Washington, D.C., named Belfrage as a man who worked for the Soviets when she began publicly confessing in 1948 before U.S. congressional committees. He was deported from the United States as an undesirable alien.

Later, U.S. codebreakers discovered that both Bentley and Belfrage, among others, were mentioned in Soviet intelligence messages from the United States to Moscow.

Also see VENONA.

Bell

CODE NAME for U.S. Navy CRYPTANALYSIS station Belconnen established in the spring of 1942 in Melbourne, Australia. The station—colocated with the intelligence division of the Royal Australian Navy—was manned by Australians, U.S. Navy personnel evacuated from the Philippines (see CAST), and some British specialists who had escaped from Singapore. Japanese messages were being intercepted and decrypted at Bell by mid-May 1942.

The Bell station worked closely with the CENTRAL BUREAU of Gen. Douglas MacArthur's Southwest Pacific command, but from an operational viewpoint it was closely linked with HYPO (FRUPAC) at Pearl Harbor and the NEGAT (Op-20-G) staff in Washington, D.C.

The code name Bell was derived from Belconnen.

Bell, William H.

(b. 1921)

An employee of the Hughes Aircraft Corp. arrested for selling secrets about several projects to MARIAN ZACHARSKI, a representative of a Polish intelligence service. Bell received about $110,000 in cash and gold coins worth about $60,000. The material that Bell sold to Zacharski included documents on a type of "quiet radar" that would enable a tank to aim radar at an enemy target without alerting the enemy.

Bell was arrested for espionage by the FBI in 1981, after a Pole assigned to the UNITED NATIONS defected and informed the FBI about Polish intelligence activities in the United States. Zacharski was a stand-in for the KGB.

Bell, who agreed to cooperate with the FBI, engaged Zacharski in an incriminating conversation while wearing an FBI listening device strapped under his shirt. Zacharski was arrested for espionage and sentenced to life imprisonment. Bell received an eight-year sentence for espionage.

Bentley, Elizabeth

(b. 1908 d. 1963)

American secretary who was a COURIER for a Soviet intelligence network operating in the United States. From 1938 to 1944, she said, she carried information, including copies of U.S. government documents, for her lover, who was a key figure in the network.

Bentley joined the American Communist Party while she was a student at Columbia University, having earlier attended Vassar College. While in Italy to study Italian, she became anti-fascist and in 1935 joined the American League against War and Fascism, a communist underground organization.

In 1938 she became a secretary at the Italian Library of Information in New York. There she discovered that the library was also a front for the Italian government's Propaganda Ministry. Bentley used her position to gather information on Benito Mussolini's government and passed it on to the Italian Communist Party.

Those activities brought her into contact with JACOB GOLOS, a Russian émigré and an American citizen, who worked for the Society for Technical Aid to Soviet Russia, a front for Soviet INDUSTRIAL ESPIONAGE. Golos, who was a member of the American Communist Party, also worked for the Soviet NKVD.

The couple became lovers and Bentley became involved in the Soviet ATOMIC SPY RING, in particular with KLAUS FUCHS, HARRY GOLD, and DAVID GREENGLASS.

In 1945 Bentley, at the time employed in a bookstore, revealed her espionage activities to the FBI and later to a federal grand jury. Reportedly, an FBI agent she was dating was unable to convince her to reveal her communist involvement. She told of an underground that involved people in New York City, including WHITTAKER CHAMBERS, and in Washington, D.C., where many federal government officials were among the members.

Bentley later went public with her story, testifying in July 1948 before a subcommittee of the Senate Investigating Committee and the House Un-American Activities Committee. The press described the plump, middle-aged woman as the "blonde spy queen." In testimony, which launched an era of communists-in-government charges, she talked of Washington "communist cells," implicating Harry Dexter White, who had been an Assistant Secretary of the Treasury, and William Remington, a Department of Commerce official. White vigorously denied her charges in testimony. Remington, later jailed for perjury before a congressional committee, was killed in prison by a fellow inmate.

Later decryption of Soviet intelligence communications showed Bentley appearing in messages under the COVER name Good Girl. She died in 1963 from heart disease.

Also see VENONA.

Berg, Igor

SEE ALEXANDR ORLOV

Berg, Morris (Moe)

(b. 1902 d. 1972)

American baseball player and SECRET AGENT.

The son of Russian immigrants, Berg played high school baseball in Newark, N.J., and at Princeton University, where he majored in languages. After he graduated, the Brooklyn Dodgers signed him as a catcher, launching his 16-year professional baseball career. In 1934, under COVER of a touring baseball player, he made films of Tokyo Harbor and Japanese military installations at the request of U.S. intelligence.

After leaving baseball, in 1941 Berg went on a fact-finding mission to Latin America for Nelson Rockefeller, coordinator of Inter-American Affairs for President Roosevelt. At that time the FBI had jurisdiction over U.S. COUNTERINTELLIGENCE in Latin America, and it is probable that Berg gathered intelligence for the FBI.

In 1943 Berg joined the OFFICE OF STRATEGIC SERVICES (OSS). He parachuted into Yugoslavia to assess the anti-German efforts of Josip Broz Tito's partisans. He also entered German-occupied Norway as part of the Allied effort to find and destroy a heavy-water plant that was part of the unsuccessful German effort to build an atomic bomb.

Berg's OSS work took him to Bern, Switzerland, where he met with ALLEN W. DULLES, then the chief of OSS intelligence there, and later the DIRECTOR OF CENTRAL INTELLIGENCE. Berg later worked for the NORTH ATLANTIC TREATY ORGANIZATION and is believed to have continued to accept intelligence assignments during the 1950s and 1960s.

Beria, Lavrenty Pavlovich

(b. 1899 d. 1953)

Head of the NKVD (Commissariat for Internal Affairs) and other intelligence and security ORGANS under Josef Stalin from 1938 until his execution in 1953.

Beria ran the vast Soviet internal police apparatus, the prison camp system, and a global espionage network. He was also tasked with supervising the Soviet atomic bomb project during the war.

Long a close associate of Stalin, Beria had been head of the secret police in the dictator's native Georgia, where he was a ruthless policeman and a methodical collector of intelligence. Soon after his appointment to head the NKVD in Dec. 1938, Beria was made a candidate (nonvoting) member of the ruling Politburo, the first chief of the secret police to join that powerful body. (At the time there were 10 full voting members, including Stalin and the newly appointed Nikita Khrushchev.)

Beria's predecessor, NIKOLAY IVANOVICH YEZHOV—who had at one point intended to arrest Beria—was himself arrested on Beria's orders, taken to a psychiatric institute, and a short time later reportedly was found hanging from a window bar. The survivors of the era of GENVIKH GREGOREVICH YAGODA, as well as many of the Yezhov period, were also executed by Beria's NKVD executioners.

To Stalin, Beria was the acme of the secret police officer. To many others in the Soviet Union he was a monster, already infamous as a lecher. He regularly picked up young girls on the street and took them to his office, where he forced them to commit sodomy and then raped them. The threat of the arrest of their families was usually a sufficient inducement for them to suffer in silence, although some are reported to have committed suicide in shame. One of his victims, a young girl who had voluntarily come to Beria's office to plead for her arrested brother, was held for several days and raped repeatedly. Beria then decided to "keep her" by marrying her. The change in his marital status did not end his perversions with young girls and with women employed by the NKVD, sometimes in his own home as well as in his LUBYANKA office.

After taking over the NKVD, he stepped up the SUR-VEILLANCE in foreign countries of the few remaining old Bolsheviks, among them Leon Trotsky, who had been Stalin's rival to succeed V. I. Lenin. A Beria assassin killed Trotsky in Mexico in 1940. (See UTKA.) Many thousands more fell to the pistols of Beria's executioners as Stalin's purges continued until the Soviet Union and Germany went to war in June 1941.

With the outbreak of war, Beria became one of Stalin's most important lieutenants. A deputy premier since Feb. 1941, he became a member of the State Defense Committee during the war. He was promoted to Marshal of the Soviet Union in 1945 and made a full member of the Politburo in 1946.

During the war the secret police took on the added tasks of protecting the Kremlin leadership and watching for disloyalty in the armies fighting the Germans. The latter role included the establishment of NKVD fighting formations and military COUNTERINTELLIGENCE units. (See SMERSH.)

Beria's NKVD also undertook foreign intelligence. Soviet diplomatic delegations to Britain, Canada, and the United States were assigned NKVD operatives to seek out military information that could be of value to the Kremlin. (See ATOMIC SPY RING.) A Soviet purchasing commission under Beria was established in the United States to speed the transfer of arms to the Soviet Union. With more than 1,000 employees, the commission also became a collection point for secrets.

Stalin also put Beria in charge of atomic bomb development and gave him responsibility for copying the three B-29 SUPERFORTRESS bombers that had come down in Siberia during the war. Stalin envisioned their use as Soviet atomic bomb carriers.

After the war Beria continued in his various roles and made the fatal error of imagining himself as Stalin's successor. In 1949, when Stalin made Khrushchev the Secretary of the Moscow City and Regional Party Committees, Khrushchev sensed that he was being brought to Moscow "to influence the balance of power." Stalin, Khrushchev observed, seemed "afraid of Beria and would have been glad to get rid of him but didn't know how to do it."

Beria had handpicked trusted Georgians for Stalin's household staff, including the kitchen workers. As Stalin's suspicions of Beria grew, he replaced Beria's Georgians with Russians. He also tried to play Col. Gen. VIKTOR SEMYONOVICH ABAKUMOV—head of the newly established MGB, the internal security agency—against Beria. But Abakumov remained cautiously loyal to Beria and was purged by Stalin in Aug. 1951. Abakumov's successor, SEMYON IGNATIEV, brought in military-political veterans of the war (including future leader Leonid Brezhnev) to infuse party strength into the MGB, a move that undermined Beria's hold on the security apparatus.

But Beria remained as strong and depraved as ever. A story told at this time by a Georgian party official, recounted by Amy Knight in *Beria* (1993) captures a few chilling moments in Beria's life. Beria had taken the official for a high-speed ride in his German-made speedboat when they passed a young woman who was training for a swimming competition.

Lavrenty Beria. (WORLD WIDE)

Beria stopped the boat and insisted that she come aboard. Almost immediately he began making lewd suggestions and indicating his desire to seduce her, despite her obvious terror of him. He then turned to [his companion] and, saying he wanted to be alone with the woman, ordered him to jump off the boat and swim back. When the latter replied that he could not swim, Beria pushed him overboard.

Beria's bodyguards, watching from shore, rushed out in a boat and saved the man. Beria's actions were no surprise to henchmen who knew that he had a special fondness for women athletes and always demanded to be given the right to select for his pleasure the women sent from Georgia to Moscow each year for the annual Day of Physical Culture.

In 1951 Stalin began a purge of officials in Georgia, a clear warning of his displeasure with Beria, as was Stalin's paranoid concoction of the "Doctors' Plot," an anti-Semitic campaign, begun in Jan. 1953, which labeled the officially sanctioned Jewish Anti-fascist Committee a U.S. intelligence COVER organization. The doctors, most of them Jewish, were charged with planning to "cut short the lives of active public figures in the Soviet Union." Beria was implicitly criticized because his security forces should have nipped the alleged plot in the bud and because he had been associated with the group, formed during the war to reach out to Jews worldwide.

By early 1953 Beria's days were numbered. On the night of March 1, 1953, Beria apparently walked the short distance from his own villa to Stalin's dacha at Kuntsevo, a Moscow suburb. According to a popular story, Beria met with Stalin alone in the dictator's study. A short time later Stalin was found lying on the floor of the room, having suffered a stroke. He regained consciousness briefly but was unable to speak. He died late on March 5.

Racing back to his headquarters in Moscow, Beria set in motion carefully calculated plans to take over the government. He named Georgi Malenkov, a weak colleague, as premier, and assigned others to a collective leadership, designating himself a vice chairman of the Council of Ministers with continued control of state security. (Among his first acts were the closing of Stalin's villa and the transportation of all of the late dictator's belongings to warehouses; purges were begun of the physicians who had examined Stalin's body.)

Beria strengthened the security troops in Moscow and, in a series of moves designed to install himself as a liberal successor to iron-fisted Stalin, eased prison regulations, ordered the release of some 1 million prisoners not considered dangerous to state security, repudiated the Doctors' Plot, and planned a reform of laws allowing arbitrary arrest. He also signaled a change in foreign policy with a story in *Pravda* praising President Eisenhower and declaring Soviet interest in ending the Cold War. In June 1953, Beria's liberal policies spread to East Germany, touching off rioting. Moscow responded by crushing the incipient revolt with tanks (see GERMANY).

Meanwhile, opposition to Beria was growing within the Soviet leadership. On June 26 he went to the Kremlin for a meeting of the leadership. In a carefully planned coup spearheaded by Khrushchev and Marshal Georgi Zhukov, Beria was arrested.

He was tried by the Soviet Supreme Court on a series of treason charges in Dec. 1953, condemned to death, and executed on the day a verdict was reached, Dec. 23. But there are other, conflicting versions of how Beria died. Khrushchev claimed that "Beria came into the conference room one day without his bodyguard and I shot him." Another, more likely account, by Col. OLEG PENKOVSKY, a Western spy in the Kremlin, claims that after his arrest "Beria was shot in the basement of the Moscow Military District Headquarters building. . . . General [Frol] Kozlov shot him in the presence of other generals. . . . After the execution, Beria's corpse was soaked with gasoline and burned there in the cellar." Still another account attributes the execution to Lt. Gen. P. F. Batitisky after the colonel deputed to shoot him could not do so. In 2000, Russia's Supreme Court rejected an appeal from Beria's relatives, who claimed that his sentence and execution were illegal.

Berlin

Capital of the German Reich from 1871 to 1945 and of the unified, modern Germany since 1999.

The city symbolized the dream of a unified Germany during the Cold War. There East and West were split in a battleground of espionage. And here was a stage for espionage MOVIES and LITERARY SPIES, a city of grim reality made into a city of spy fiction.

In the Middle Ages Berlin was an independent city, incorporated into the kingdom of Frederick the Great in the 15th century. The prosperous city knew the intrigues of spymaster Cardinal DE ARMAND JEAN RICHELIEU during the Thirty Years War (1618–1648); and in the next two centuries it was occupied by Austrian, Russian, and French forces, each with its own set of spies.

After the fall of Napoléon in 1814 and the rise of Prussia, Berlin became the center of Prussian power. It would retain its importance as the 19th century ended, becoming also a city of avant-garde art and decadent night life and a rendezvous for INTELLIGENCE OFFICERS and their AGENTS. The British Secret Intelligence Service (MI6) had a station there early in the 20th century to keep watch on the Bolsheviks, who were themselves using the city as an espionage hub. Military ATTACHÉS of the major powers did their duty as gentlemen spies.

Berlin, a communications and rail center, was spared damage in World War I. Its main role came in 1918 when communist agents inspired riots in its streets, contributing to the collapse of imperial Germany. The Versailles Treaty of 1919 established a German republic, with its capital in quiet Weimar rather than riotous Berlin. But the republic died under the onslaught of hyperinflation, mass unemployment, and the exploitation of unrest by both the communists and the new fascists of the National Socialist Party, the Nazis.

JOHN W. DULLES, a future U.S. DIRECTOR OF CENTRAL INTELLIGENCE, was posted to Berlin in 1920, midway through his 10-year diplomatic career. In Berlin Dulles saw the Nazi swastika for the first time. This sight and conversations with Germans under watch by Nazi agents, he later wrote, left him with a "sinister impression" of the city.

The ABWEHR, the German MILITARY INTELLIGENCE agency, was part of the German War Ministry. In its early days the Abwehr used Jewish and Swiss agents for the gathering of ECONOMIC INTELLIGENCE that had possible military implications. At another Abwehr building in Berlin was a SPY SCHOOL.

Berlin was the scene of several Nazi intrigues in the 1930s. On the night of June 30, 1934—the Night of the Long Knives—Chancellor Adolf Hitler ordered the massacre of the brownshirted SA, Nazi storm troopers whose leader, Ernst Roehm, was a rival for power. More than 150 SA leaders were rounded up and taken to a coal cellar at a barracks at the Lichterfelde Cadet School in Berlin. In groups of eight they were taken out and shot by SS firing squads. Roehm was later killed elsewhere, as were an unknown number of his followers.

For years GESTAPO agents had been persecuting Jews and other Germans designated as enemies of the state. In 1936 the Gestapo ceased its open terrorism so that visitors to Berlin for the Olympics would gain a better impression of Hitler's Germany. Anti-Jewish signs were taken down as visitors streamed to the huge, swastika-adorned Olympic stadium. (RICHARD HELMS, a future U.S. Director of Central Intelligence, was in Germany at the time and interviewed Hitler for United Press.)

On Nov. 21, 1937, Hitler, who was trying to win the German Army over to his side, confided his plans of aggression—because Germany needed *Lebensraum* ("living room")—to a meeting in the Reichstag (Parliament) of high-ranking military officers. (Hitler's military adjutant, Friedrich Hossbach, took notes, and the meeting became known as the Hossbach Conference.)

Hitler ran into opposition from the most senior officers at the conference, Field Marshal Werner von Blomberg, Minister of Defense and supreme commander of the Wehrmacht (German Army); and Col. Gen. Werner Freiherr von Fritsch, commander in chief of the Wehrmacht. Both men lived in Berlin, whose chief of police, Wolf Heinrich Graf von Helldorf, had agents gathering intelligence on both of them. The SS was also involved in a plot to get rid of Blomberg and Fritsch.

On Jan. 12, 1938, Blomberg, a widower, married his secretary, Eva Gruhn. Helldorf produced evidence that Blomberg had married a prostitute, disgracing the officer corps and insulting Hitler, who had attended the wedding. Blomberg resigned from the Army. The next month, HEINRICH HIMMLER, chief of the SS, produced evidence that Fritsch was a HOMOSEXUAL, committing offenses prohibited by the German criminal code. The evidence primarily consisted of the word of a young Berlin homosexual prostitute known as "Bavarian Joe." Fritsch was forced to resign from the Army, although he was subsequently cleared by a military court of honor.

Later recalled, he was killed on a Polish battlefield a few days into the war he had opposed.

WORLD WAR II

The Third Reich, with its capital in Berlin, Hitler said, would last 1,000 years. His Air Force chief, Hermann Göring, vowed that Berlin would never be bombed. But British and American bombers blasted the city to rubble, and it became the last battlefield of the European War. From an intelligence viewpoint, the worst raids came in Nov. 1943, when the records of the B-DIENST, the German Navy's highly effective CRYPTANALYSIS service, were destroyed. The armed forces intelligence service, the Abwehr, fearing such a fate, had moved in April 1943 to Zossen, about 20 miles south of Berlin.

As the Red Army neared the city in March 1945, German COUNTERINTELLIGENCE officers continued to work in a frenzied effort to round up and execute suspected subversives. In the underground bunker where he spent his last days, Hitler raved about *das Leck* ("the Leak"). Someone was leaking information, which Hitler could sometimes pick up on British radio programs beamed to Germany.

"Hitler on this matter was not just imagining things. I, too, am still convinced there was such a penetration. . . ." wrote Albert Speer, Minister of Armament and War Production—and Hitler's personal architect. Speer planned to kill Hitler by introducing poison gas into the Führerbunker. But, Speer later claimed, the air-intake system had been changed and he could not find a way to use the gas.

The RSHA, the secret service under HEINRICH HIMMLER, functioned until the final hours of the Third Reich. On April 26, with Red Army troops in Berlin, the investigation into *das Leck* went on. An SS officer in the bunker asked for a trace on a telephone number. Incredibly, amidst shelling from Soviet artillery, the Berlin central telephone exchange responded with the trace, and the SS found the suspected culprit and executed him.

Hitler and his just-married mistress, Eva Braun, committed suicide in the bunker on April 30. In the last great espionage coup of wartime Berlin, a Soviet military intelligence unit collected Hitler's remains and for decades kept his fate secret. British officials, determined to find out what happened, commissioned HUGH TREVOR-ROPER, an intelligence officer and historian, to investigate. Using reports of prisoners, eyewitnesses in the bunker, and U.S. Army counterintelligence sources, Trevor-Roper submitted a secret report in Nov. 1945 to the British government and the Quadripartite Intelligence Committee in Berlin (Berlin was by then under four-power control, with British, U.S., French, and Soviet zones). Trevor-Roper suggested asking the Soviets for certain information in their hands from captured people and seized documents.

But the answers did not come until the 1970s. The report evolved into Trevor-Roper's most famous book, *The Last Days of Hitler* (seven editions through 1995). Both Allen Dulles and Richard Helms, who served in the OFFICE OF STRATEGIC SERVICES during the war, went to Berlin to learn what their estwhile allies, the Soviets, were going to do in occupied Germany.

THE TWO BERLINS

Under the four-power zone system, Berlin was also divided and was host to four intelligence systems, with the United States, Britain, and France aligned against the Soviet Union. VIENNA, the longtime spy nest of Europe, surrendered the role of espionage capital to Berlin. The Allies feigned unity, establishing a four-power council to govern the city while East and West spied on each other.

At times during the Cold War there were an estimated 8,000 spies operating in the two Germanys, with most of them in Berlin. But all the West's spying failed to produce advance warning of the crises that made Berlin a flashpoint where World War III might begin.

The first crisis came in 1948. After weeks of harass-ing Western road and rail movement into Berlin, on June 24 the Soviet Union cut off all rail, road, and river traffic, besieging more than 2 million residents of Berlin. The Soviets hoped to force the Western powers to abandon the city and cancel plans to make the Western zones of Germany into an independent republic.

President Truman reacted by ordering a massive expansion of an airlift of military planes established during the earlier harassment. The Berlin Airlift went on for 321 days, with more than 277,000 flights bringing in some 2.5 million tons of food and fuel.

As a counter to the aggressive Soviet blockade, the United States dispatched a formation of B-29 SUPER-FORTRESS bombers to bases in England. Ostensibly they were capable of carrying nuclear weapons; the planes were not, but the Soviets knew that immediately through the efforts of members of Soviet CAMBRIDGE SPY RING. During the airlift the U.S. Joint Chiefs of Staff did have on hand a war plan, code-named Trojan, for bombing 30

Berlin, a hotbed of espionage since the 17th century, continues its role during the Cold War. The "Berlin Wall" separated east (communism) from west (democracy). Here, Checkpoint Charlie is seen from the western side, with U.S. troops mounting guard while East German troops observe from a blockhouse. (U.S. ARMY)

Soviet cities with nuclear bombs. By the time the Soviet blockade ended in May 1949, the West had formed the NORTH ATLANTIC TREATY ORGANIZATION as a bulwark against Soviet aggression in Western Europe.

The contining cold warfare between the Soviet Union and the West also led to the formation in 1949 of the Bundesrepublik (Federal Republic of Germany, or West Germany) from the U.S., French, and British zones, followed by the German Democratic Republic (East Germany) from the Soviet zone. This divided the city into East Berlin and West Berlin, with the latter considered by West Germany to be a *Land*, or state. Berlin was the capital of East Germany.

In June 1953, after the death of Soviet dictator Josef Stalin and during the short reign of former secret police chief LAVRENTY BERIA, East Germans briefly rose in revolt. As the insurrection was being crushed by Soviet tanks, Henry Heckscher, the CIA chief of station in Berlin, cabled Washington, asking for permission to arm the rioters. At that time, U.S. foreign policy called for the liberation of "captive nations" but not, as it turned out, with American-supplied rifles. Heckscher's request was rejected.

Early in June 1961 President Kennedy met in Vienna with Soviet leader Nikita Khrushchev, who stunned Kennedy with his cold response to suggestions of an accord. On June 15, Khrushchev chose Berlin as a place to stoke new tension, declaring that he would turn the entire city over to East Germany unless the West recognized that territory as a sovereign nation.

Kennedy reacted by calling up 250,000 military reservists and activating several mothballed U.S. Navy ships. Contingency plans were drawn up. In U.S. war games played by high-level civilian and military officials, strategists considered—and abandoned—firing an aerial nuclear "warning shot" over the Atlantic to convince the Soviets that military action in Berlin could trigger a nuclear war.

Thousands of East Germans had been fleeing to the West since the end of the war. With the crisis continuing through the summer, the flow increased, draining skilled workers, technicians, and scientists from East Germany. Then, with Western leaders getting no advance warning from their intelligence sources, in August 1962 the Soviets and East Germans began swiftly erecting a wall and other barriers along the length of the East–West border. Kennedy, once more fuming at a U.S. intelligence failure, ignored the outcries of a few members of Congress who wanted a U.S. military response.

The East–West border soon bristled with high fences, barbed wire barriers, and guard towers, and was seeded with land mines. All of it, focused on Berlin, became known as the Berlin Wall. Hundreds of East Berliners would risk their lives, and sometimes lose their lives, trying to get across the wall. Spies by the thousands got through the wall, sometimes by sheer courage and sometimes by treachery. West Germany's intelligence agency, the BND, and its counterintelligence agency, the BFV, were frequently penetrated by agents for the Stasi (MFS), East Germany's intelligence agency and secret police, or by the KGB.

Nothing made the Berlin Wall more of an emblem of espionage than *The Spy Who Came in from the Cold* (1963) by JOHN LE CARRÉ, a classic novel of the Cold War that became a classic film starring British actor Richard Burton. The Berlin Wall looms over the story, which ends with the British intelligence officer Leamas and Liz, his naive young lover, dead in its shadow.

In the real world of espionage, the BERLIN TUNNEL, a British-American operation to tap Soviet–East German communications, was itself a saga of treachery. Betrayed by a British turncoat before it was even built, the tunnel supplied a steady stream of DISINFORMATION to the West.

BERLIN REUNITED

In 1988 Mikhail Gorbachev, a reform-minded leader who had become head of the Soviet government three years before, announced a policy of nonintervention in Eastern Europe and a reduction in Soviet troops based in those countries. This set the stage for the end of communist control in East Germany and the other Eastern Bloc nations.

When Hungary opened its border with Austria, throngs of East Germans headed for Hungary, ostensibly on vacation. While Stasi agents tried to fathom what was going on, the vacationers kept on moving, fleeing into West Germany via Austria. In Oct. 1989, East German dictator Erich Honecker was purged, and on Nov. 9, as demonstrations flared in East Berlin, East Germany opened its border with West Germany. In Dec. 1990 the East German leadership resigned, promising free elections in May. The Berlin Wall was crumbling. The last section of the wall fell at midnight on Oct. 3–4, 1990, marking the reunification of Germany.

Berlin's history as a spy center did not end with its reunification. In what had been East Berlin, West German intelligence officials pored over the files of the Stasi, trying to re-create the dealings of spies and counterspies during the Cold War. At the same time, former East German citizens sought to get their Stasi dossiers. Many of them learned that their Berlin neighbors, friends, and even family members had spied on them for years.

In 1999 the capital of the reunited Germany was moved back to Berlin, the capital of West Gemrany having been in the city of Bonn.

Berlin Tunnel

British-American intelligence project that involved digging a tunnel from West BERLIN into East Berlin to reach underground cables and tap Soviet–East German communications.

The idea of the tunnel was inspired by a similar one dug in postwar VIENNA while that city was under joint U.S., French, British, and Soviet control. The Berlin Tunnel was planned by the British Secret Intelligence Service (MI6) and the CIA, but it was CIA money and manpower that carried it out. Many details of the project are still classified, and authoritative information on it is scant.

ALLEN W. DULLES, then DIRECTOR OF CENTRAL INTELLIGENCE, authorized the project in 1954 and ordered that "as little as possible" be "reduced to writing."

The Vienna wiretap operation had been given the CODE NAME Silver; Dulles code-named the Berlin tunnel Operation Gold. By one account, REINHARD GEHLEN, the West German intelligence chief, first alerted Dulles to the location of a crucial telephone junction, six feet underground, where three cables came together close to the border of the American sector of West Berlin. British and U.S. intelligence officials met in London to plan the tunnel. Among those at the early meetings was GEORGE BLAKE, an MI6 INTELLIGENCE OFFICER who was a spy for the KGB.

In Dec. 1953 the operation was put under the direction of WILLIAM K. HARVEY, a former FBI official who transferred to the CIA. Harvey used a U.S. Army supply depot as the West German terminus of the tunnel. U.S. Army engineers spent a year digging a tunnel and secretly carrying off the dirt. The tunnel was 300 yards long and 15 feet below the surface with a headroom of 6½ feet (higher in the equipment rooms). It ended at an electronic box for the tapping of the cables. There West Germans and Americans listened to and recorded messages flowing to and from Soviet military headquarters in Zossen, near Berlin; conversations between Moscow and the Soviet Embassy in East Berlin; and communications between East German and Soviet officials.

In Washington, D.C., a team of CIA translators and analysts worked constantly on the vast amount of intercepts, which included both high-level talk and barracks gossip. There were so many intercepts to sift through that the work of mining Operation Gold continued until Sept. 1958.

The KGB decided to let Operation Gold go on, seeing it as a potential tool for DISINFORMATION. Apparently, the KGB did not inform the Soviet military command in Berlin of the tunnel, at least not initially, hence there was useful information coming from the Soviet military communications through cable.

On April 21, 1956, about a year after the tapping began, Soviet and East German soldiers broke into the eastern end of the tunnel. The Soviets made a propaganda coup of the tunnel, calling it a "breach of the norms of international law" and a "gangster act." (Coincidentally, three Dulles siblings felt the impact of the tunnel raid: Allen Dulles, his brother John Foster Dulles, who was Secretary of State, and their sister Eleanore Dulles, the State Department's Berlin desk officer. "It's all Allen's fault," she told Foster.)

After Allen Dulles retired he wrote gleefully about the tunnel in his book *The Craft of Intelligence* (1963). Although Dulles must have known about Blake's betrayal, he did not mention it. He said that during the first snowfall of the winter of 1954–1955, "the snow just above the tunnel was melting because of the heat coming up from underneath. In no time at all a beautiful path was going to appear in the snow, going from West to East Berlin, which any watchful policeman couldn't help but notice." Tunnel technicians quickly turned off the heat and the crisis passed.

Not until Blake's arrest, trial, and conviction in 1961 did Western officials realize that the tunnel had been betrayed before even the first shovelful of dirt was carted away. However, neither Dulles nor the CIA revealed the deception, and for years, while publicly celebrating the value of the tunnel, CIA analysts secretly argued over the worth of what they had obtained. By one assessment, the Soviets allowed ordinary military communications to flow through the cables so that the West would realize that no aggressive Soviet move was being planned against ever-tense West Berlin.

In a secret report, declassified in 1999, CIA analysts said, "Throughout the life of the source (11 May 1955–22 April 1956) we were kept currently informed of Soviet intentions in Berlin; the tunnel provided the inside story of every 'incident' occurring in Berlin during the period."

Bernhard

German CODE NAME for the secret World War II operation that produced more than £100 million in counterfeit English banknotes in an effort to undermine the British economy. The effort was unsuccessful; most of the notes were produced in 1945 and hidden when Germany was about to capitulate.

However, some of the notes were given to the German spy CICERO, who was paid £300,000 for photographing documents in the residence of the British ambassador to Turkey. Most of his payments were in forged £5 bank notes. Counterfeit money was apparently used for other German intelligence operations as well.

Berryer, Nicolas-René

(b. 1703 d. 1762)

French spymaster. During the reign of King Louis XV, Berryer, a Paris police official, used espionage principally to protect Jeanne Antoinette Aetioles, the Marquise de Pompadour, the king's mistress. Berryer set up a *cabinet noir* ("black chamber") in which his agents opened letters sent through the French postal system, read and noted the contents when pertinent, and resealed the envelopes, sending them on to their intended recipients.

Bertrand, Brig. Gen. Gustave

Leading French cryptologist of the World War II era, whose efforts helped to break into the CIPHERS of the German ENIGMA.

Bertrand enlisted in 1914 as a private. The following year he was wounded during the ill-fated Allied attempt to open a passage through the Turkish Straits. After the war he was assigned to the French Army's cipher activities.

As a captain in the French Army's radio intelligence section in 1926, he realized that the Germans had introduced an electrical cipher machine. He began the herculean task of breaking into Enigma ciphers. In 1930 he became head of the scientific, technical, and decoding staff of French intelligence—the SR (Service de Renseignements). The following year he began dealing with HANS-THILO SCHMIDT, a French AGENT with the CODE NAME Asché, who worked in the German military cipher bureau. From the fall of 1931 until June 1939, Bertrand held 19 meetings in several European countries with Asché, who supplied invaluable Enigma documents and manuals.

On Dec. 7, 1931, Bertrand visited Warsaw to meet with the BIURO SZFROW, the Polish cryptanalysis service. He brought with him documents provided by Asché, which enabled the Biuro Szfrow to break into Enigma keys to read German military communications. Bertrand provided the Poles with additional documents from Asché in 1932, and by the end of that year the Poles achieved the first deciphering of a complete German radio message.

Also in 1931, Bertrand provided documents to the British GOVERNMENT CODE AND CYPHER SCHOOL. The British codebreakers then showed little interest in working with Bertrand, but they contacted him in 1936, beginning a promising exchange of information between the two agencies, although the British were not able to break into Enigma ciphers.

French–Polish coordination also continued, but by mid-Dec. 1938 the Polish cryptologists needed major assistance because of the costs involved in building electrical-mechanical machines to break the Enigma ciphers. On Jan. 9 and 10, 1939, Bertrand hosted a conference in Paris of the top cryptologists from France, Poland, and Great Britain. Thus Britain, the only country that would survive the coming German onslaught, would have the basis for breaking into German ciphers during the war. Bertrand attended another three-country cryptology conference in Poland in July 1939. The Poles agreed to provide the British and French with one of their Enigma machines.

After the fall of Poland in Sept. 1939, the surviving Polish cryptographers escaped to France, where Bertrand merged them into his own cipher bureau at Gretz-Armainvillers, northeast of Paris—a facility code-named BRUNO. When the Germans overran northern France in May 1940, Bertrand flew most of his cryptologists to North Africa, first to Oran and later to Algiers, where they remained for several months. Subsequently, he brought them by ship to a location near Nimes in Vichy France, where they worked at station CADIX until Oct. 1942. A month later, with German troops occupying Vichy territory, his cryptologists fled once more.

Bertrand was captured in 1943 by the ABWEHR, the German military intelligence service. Possibly with the collusion of Abwehr officials, he was able to escape in 1944 and managed to reach Britain.

After the war, Bertrand remained in French intelligence activities, rising to the rank of general. When he retired he wrote an account of the Enigma effort, *Enigma ou la plus Grande Enigme de la Guerre 1939–1945* (1973). The book created considerable controversy and led to counterclaims within intelligence circles, although it gained surprisingly little public attention.

Berzin, Yan Karlovich

(b. 1889 d. 1939)

Chief of the GRU, Soviet MILITARY INTELLIGENCE, from 1924 to 1938 and commander of Soviet forces in the Spanish Civil War.

Born in Latvia as Peter Kyuzis, he was conscripted into the Russian Army in World War I but deserted. As a revolutionary he was wounded and arrested, imprisoned, and exiled to Siberia. He returned to participate in the October Revolution of 1917. Afterwards he worked in the central apparatus of the CHEKA in Russia and then Latvia. He was a fervent supporter of the establishment of a communist dictatorship in Latvia and one of the organizers and leaders of the Latvian Red Army (subsequently the 15th Red Army).

Berzin formally entered the Red Army in 1919 and played a part in the suppression of the Russian sailors' mutiny at Kronstadt in 1921. He particularly distinguished himself during the pursuit and liquidation of the sailors who had rebeled against Lenin's dictatorship.

In April 1921 Berzin became deputy chief of the GRU, but from his first days in military intelligence he was its de facto head. In March 1924 he was officially designated chief of the GRU. As a result of his energy and talents, the GRU became an outstanding intelligence organization, and Berzin gained a reputation as a superb intelligence officer.

When the Stalinist purges were being planned in 1935, Berzin traveled to the Far East with several trusted assistants to kill several NKVD officials. In 1936, while retaining nominal command of the GRU, Berzin went to Madrid, where he carried out his most notable spy recruitments while working under cover, officially as chief military adviser to the Republican government during the Spanish Civil War. However, he was effectively the commander of the Republican forces during the war. To sustain this cover story, his deputies, ISOF UNSHILIKHT and then SOLOMON URITSKI, carried out his duties in Moscow.

Upon returning to the Soviet Union, Berzin continued to head the GRU until May 13, 1939, when he was arrested. On July 29 he was shot in the basement of the Metropole Hotel in Moscow.

Best, Capt. S. Payne

(b. 1885 d. ?)

British INTELLIGENCE OFFICER captured by the Germans early in World War II.

Payne, an accountant who had graduated from the London School of Economics, served in British Army intelligence during World War I. After the war, when he moved to The Hague, he remained in the Army reserve and continued in intelligence work. In The Hague he was well known at the court of Queen Wilhelmina, while in northern Germany he cut a monocled figure among the noble German families. Although he earned his living as an advertising agent and a manufacturer of pharmaceutical products, he was accepted as a well-connected, upper-class Englishman.

Best was also working for the British Secret Intelligence Service (MI6). In 1938 he probably set up a meeting between Sir STEWART MENZIES, who was later to become "C," the head of MI6, and an emissary of Gen. Ludwig Beck, chief of the German General Staff and a leader of a military-political plot against Adolf Hitler. The emissary proposed negotiations that would topple Hitler in exchange for British retraction of certain provisions of the Versailles Treaty. The suggestion was not accepted, but the military plotting against Hitler continued, as did British interest in anti-Hitler plots.

Best, under his businessman COVER, was working with Maj. H. R. STEVENS, who was under a typical MI6 cover of passport officer in The Hague. They did not get along. But together they attempted to make contact with representatives of the Beck plotters, whom British Foreign Office officials referred to as "the German opposition." One of the contacts was in reality a DOUBLE AGENT working for the SD, the espionage section of the Nazi SS. To prove high-level official British backing of the meeting, Menzies arranged for the British Broadcasting Corp. to make a slight change in the introduction to its regular news broadcast to Germany. (This was a frequently used gambit to prove the bona fides of Allied intelligence AGENTS dealing with suspicious accomplices in other countries.)

Best was empowered to tell the Germans that Britain would accept an end to the war and grant Germany its territorial claims up to 1938 if the German Army overthrew Hitler. On Oct. 20, 1939, not quite six weeks after Britain had declared war on Germany, the German double agent, posing as a dissident leader, led Best, Stevens, and a Dutch intelligence officer to a Dutch village on the German-Dutch border. There they met two German Army officers who claimed to represent a general in the anti-Hitler plot. Best, who spoke excellent German and was well acquainted with Germans of the Prussian officer mold, suspected that the officers were Nazis.

At a second meeting on Oct. 30, in The Hague, another German, calling himself "Schaemmel," appeared. He was WALTER SCHELLENBERG, deputy leader of the SD. Schaernmel told the British officers that the Army would arrest Hitler. At a subsequent meeting Schaernmel said that the leaders of the plot wanted to speak directly with British government officials.

The British agents said that a plane would pick up the Germans at Venlo, near the Dutch–German border. On Nov. 8, while Best and Stevens awaited the German delegation, a car smashed through the border checkpoint, gunmen firing at the Dutch guards. Germans leaped from the car, grabbed the two Britons, and sped back across the border into Germany.

In SD custody, Best and Stevens were interrogated relentlessly by the GESTAPO and gave up MI6 secrets. This was confirmed after the war when British intelligence officers discovered a German document that cited Stevens as a source of detailed information about MI6. The document, for use by the Gestapo after Hitler invaded England, contained a detailed description of the structure of MI6 and information about many officers. Best also gave information, but in debriefing after the war, he said he bemused his interrogators by telling them about the SEX practices of his colleagues.

Best and Stevens remained prisoners for the rest of the war. In April 1945 Allied troops found them, along with some German-held hostages, in Niederorf, a small village in Bavaria.

A postwar investigation into German knowledge of MI6 showed that while Stevens gave up more information than Best, a third MI6 officer, CHARLES (DICKIE) ELLIS, who remained in the secret service until the 1950s, had also acted as a source of information before the war. One of Ellis's four wives was Russian. While Ellis was stationed in Paris before the war, his brother-in-law, who also worked for the ABWEHR, was one of his agents. To earn extra money, Ellis sold information about MI6 to the Abwehr through his brother-in-law.

Also see BLACK BOOK, VENLO INCIDENT.

Beurton, Mrs. Sonia

SEE URSULA KUCZYNSKI

BfV

Bundesamt für Verfassungsschutz (Agency for Constitutional Protection) is GERMANY's COUNTERINTELIGENCE agency.

Early in the Cold War British and American INTELLIGENCE OFFICERS helped to establish the BfV, modeling it on Britain's counterintelligence service MI5. Like MI5, BfV did not have the power of arrest as the British and Americans did not want West Germany to create an institution resembling the GESTAPO or SS.

From 1950 to 1990 the BfV's work was overshadowed by the large presence of British and U.S. intelligence activities in West Germany. In 1990, with the reunification of East and West Germany, the BfV became an agency of the reunited Germany.

Like the BND, the West German foreign intelligence agency, the BfV had two phases: the Cold War and postreunification. During the era of divided Germanys (1945–1990), West Germany and, especially, BERLIN were major operating areas for AGENTS of all major U.S., British, and Soviet intelligence agencies as well as East Germany's notorious Soviet-controlled security agency, the Stasi (see MFS). For many of the border-crossing spies the BfV was a TARGET. The fact that the two Germanys shared a common language and culture made the discovery of these agents and MOLES extremely difficult.

The BfV was ravaged by moles and defectors. In July 1954 Dr. OTTO JOHN, the director of BfV, went into East Berlin and did not return until Dec. 1955. He had been in the Soviet Union and had joined the Stasi, but he claimed he had been kidnapped. His bizarre actions devastated the BfV.

Two of the most serious BfV defections were long-time moles: In 1960 Alfred Frenzel, a member of the West German parliament's defense committee, and in 1974, GÜNTHER GUILLAUME, a protégé of Chancellor Willy Brandt and a key member of his staff, were revealed. The Guillaume scandal, coming in the wake of other security breakdowns, led to Brandt's resignation.

Another shocking betrayal was that of Gabriele Gast, who worked for six years on the weekly intelligence summary submitted to Helmut Kohl during his 1982–1990 tenure as Chancellor of West Germany. Gast sometimes passed copies of the summary to the Stasi before Kohl saw them.

Ironically, the erection of the Berlin Wall in 1961 aided the BfV because it introduced checkpoints and scrutiny of the identification papers of border crossers. By the early 1980s the agency seemed to have regained its effectiveness. But that illusion was shattered in 1985 when HANS JOACHIM TIEDGE, who had directed counterintelligence operations against East Germany, defected to East Germany. Both the BfV and the BND were reorganized after the unmasking of Tiedge.

In 1990—after German reunification—the BfV got the opportunity to examine the files of the Stasi. The files revealed that the penetration of the BfV had been far worse than had been assumed. "The people in the West were foolish enough to believe that these files contained the story of only this [Eastern] side of the country. But there is plenty in there about the other side as well," said Werner Fischer, the head of the German citizens' committee that administered the files. In them were videotapes of people engaged in sexual acts—obviously for SEX blackmail purposes—and transcripts of phone taps.

Using the files as evidence, police initially arrested more than a dozen espionage suspects, including Klaus Kuron, a West German counterintelligence officer whose task was to TURN some of the estimated 8,000 East German spies working in West Germany. Kuron admitted that he had been a DOUBLE AGENT for more than eight years, receiving $2,500 a month from the Stasi for the information he passed, such as the names of agents he had turned. Herbert Hellenbroich, who had been the head of Bfv when Tiedge defected, called the Stasi operation "the highest goal there is—to put an agent exactly where Kuron was."

When Britain and the United States helped West Germany create its intelligence agencies, Nazis formed the cadre of the new organizations. Similarly, after reunification, the BfV had to assume that ex-Stasi double agents would hide their status and try to remain in the BfV. One of the largest operations in BfV history involved its ferreting out Stasi members.

The BfV described itself in 2003 as having a mission to "monitor the activities directed against the free democratic order (so-called 'left-wing' and 'right-wing' extremist activities). It is also responsible for counter-espionage and also collects information on the activities of foreigners, where these pose a threat to security."

BI

SEE BACKGROUND INVESTIGATION

Biblical Spies

There are several references to spies in the Bible. In Genesis, the first book in the Old Testament—one of the books that Jews call the Five Books of Moses or Torah—are the first references to spies; in Exodus, both Moses and Joshua are portrayed as spymasters. And in the New Testament, the Romans use Judas as a MOLE to betray Christ.

The first biblical reference to spying is found in Genesis 42:9, when Joseph, who is then governor of Egypt, ranking second only to the Pharaoh, confronts his brothers, who do not recognize him. "Whence come ye?" he asks. "From the land of Canaan to buy food," they respond. "Ye are spies," he says, "to see the nakedness of the land ye are come." By nakedness he meant the weak spots along Egypt's northeastern border, the nation's most vulnerable area. Any stranger in that area would naturally be accused of spying.

The earliest recorded spy mission is reported in Numbers 13, which begins: "And the Lord spake unto Moses, saying: 'Send thou men, that they may search the land of Canaan, which I give unto the children of Israel; of every tribe of their fathers shall ye send a man, every one a prince among them'."

Moses picks one man from each of the 12 tribes—their names and tribes are given—and sends them into the Promised Land on a 40-day mission, giving them specific orders:

> Get you up this way southward, and go up into the mountain: And see the land, what it is; and the people that dwelleth therein, whether they be strong or weak, few or many; And what the land is that they dwell in, whether it be good or bad; and what cities they be that they dwell in, whether in tents, or in strong holds; and what the land is, whether it be fat or lean, whether there be wood therein, or not. . . . (Numbers 13:17–20)

Moses's espionage activities produce a problem familiar to modern spymasters: His AGENTS return with varying reports. Some say there are giants in the land and strongly advise against invasion. Only two of the 12 spies advise an invasion. Frightened by the horrendous reports of the strength of the inhabitants, the Jewish people panic. To punish them, God holds them back from the Promised Land for 40 years, "after the number of the days in which ye searched the land." (Numbers 14:34)

Of the two men who supported an invasion, God calls Caleb "My servant," and he alone of the spies will survive the 40 years to enter the Promised Land. Caleb would be given Hebron and the neighboring hill country. (Numbers 14:24)

Another biblical spy mission is compromised. Arad,

king of the Canaanites, captures some of Moses's spies, and, as often happens with spies, they are kept prisoner and presumably interrogated. They are apparently freed when the Israelites seize Canaanite cities. (Numbers 21:1-3)

After the death of Moses, Joshua becomes leader of the Jews and also assumes charge of espionage operations. He sends two spies out "to spy secretly, saying, Go view the land, even Jericho." (Joshua 1:2) Those participants in the second oldest profession hide in the home of a woman of the oldest profession, the harlot Rahab. An informer tells the king of Jericho, who orders Rahab to betray the spies. She says that Israelite spies did stay at her house but insists that they have left, going out of the city gates just before they closed. The king's men rush off while she takes the spies to the roof of her house and covers them with stalks of flax.

Later, after receiving an assurance that she and her family will be spared if the Israelites take the city, she "lets them down by a cord through the window: for her house [is] upon the town wall. . . ." (Joshua 1:15) Before they leave, the Israelite spies tell her to bind a scarlet thread in that window as a sign to invaders not to destroy the house. The spies escape, reconnoiter, and return to Joshua, who, on the basis of their secret report, attacks Jericho, sparing the house with the scarlet thread. (During the American Civil War, a secret society that supplied information to the Union used a scarlet thread as a badge. The society was also called the Red Strings.)

The U.S. CIA once took a droll look at Biblical spying. In the initially classified CIA journal STUDIES IN INTELLIGENCE, an analyst noted that the major difference between the operations of Moses and Joshua was in how the spies made their respective reports. Moses's spies made public reports, setting off a panic; Joshua's spies reported privately. The analyst said that the situation Moses encountered was similar to the one the U.S. INTELLIGENCE COMMUNITY faces under oversight scrutiny:

> Moses' operation, conducted by amateurs more or less in the public domain resulted in a weakening of Moses' position of authority, led to a loss of the people's confidence in themselves, and precipitated an extended period of severe national punishment. Joshua's operation, conducted in private by professionals, led to an achievement of national destiny.

And, the article added, Joshua "did not have an oversight problem, nor did he worry about defining a politically acceptable mission scenario."

Another Bible story touching on espionage features betrayal by a women using SEX to garner secrets. When Samson goes to Gaza and visits a harlot, she tells Philistine officials, who then lie in wait for him at the gates of the city. But Samson swaggers up and rips out the gates. He meets his fate, however, at the hands of another woman, Delilah, who is hired to seduce the strong man. (She is playing a role that the KGB called a SWALLOW.)

The lords of the Philistines pay her 1,100 pieces of silver to betray Samson. When, intoxicated with love, Samson tells her that his hair is the secret of his strength, she waits until he is asleep and has a confederate shave his head. The Philistines blind and imprison him. After his hair has grown back sufficiently to restore his strength, Samson ends his own life by pulling down a building with thousands of his enemies in it. (Judges 16)

In the New Testament, the use of Judas as a mole provides a typical example of an espionage operation in a Roman colony: The rulers employ natives because only they have the language and social skills needed to melt into the population. Another New Testament espionage activity is mentioned by Paul, who mysteriously mentions that "false brethren" who "came in privily to spy out our liberty which we have in Christ Jesus, that they might bring us into bondage." (Galatians 2:4)

Big Bird

Popular name for the U.S. low-altitude spy SATELLITE that combined infrared, photo, and SIGNALS INTELLIGENCE (SIGINT) capabilities.

First launched on June 15, 1971, by a Titan 3D booster, the Big Bird satellite weighed 15 tons, was 55 feet long, and housed two KH-9 series cameras that were able to distinguish objects as small as eight inches from an altitude of 90 miles. This was the first U.S. RECONNAISSANCE satellite that could photograph such small objects. Each camera had two film canisters to be parachuted to earth for aerial recovery.

Five of the Big Bird missions carried a third, aerial mapping camera with one film canister. Experiments were conducted in transmitting photos by radio signal, but that effort failed.

A FERRET SIGINT capability was added to the basic camera satellite as a "hitchhiker."

The Big Bird satellites were launched at the rate of about two per year from 1971 to 1984; 19 successful launches were followed by one failure, on April 18, 1986, in which the booster exploded after takeoff. The Big Bird's major limitation was its relatively short life span, which started out at some 52 days; by 1978 it was extended to 179 days (the average orbital life was 138 days with a maximum of 275 days achieved in 1983).

The satellite was developed under the project designation Code 467. Its BYEMAN name was Hexagon.

Bigot List

Names of people who have ACCESS to a highly COMPARTMENTED project or activity. During World War II, for example, there was a Bigot List of the names of U.S. and British officers who knew the date and locations of the Allied invasion of Normandy in June 1944 (Operation Overlord). "Bigot" officers could enter Bigot offices and read Bigot documents, a privilege denied to uncleared officers, regardless of their rank. British intelligence officials chose the odd codeword Bigot by reversing the letters of two words—*To Gib*—that had been stamped on the papers of officers going to Gibraltar for the invasion of North Africa in Nov. 1942.

Another Bigot List contained the names of members of the secret Interagency Committee on Intelligence (Ad Hoc), which met in 1969 to consider ways to monitor "U.S. revolutionary leaders and organizations" involved in anti-Vietnam War protests. Out of this committee came the HUSTON PLAN.

Also see DECEPTION and FORTITUDE.

Big Safari

U.S. Air Force program office responsible for the development of special reconnaissance equipment and apparently for some reconnaissance AIRCRAFT. The office, which manages highly classified or BLACK programs, was established in the 1950s.

Big Safari uses highly streamlined and innovative management and acquisition procedures. Many of these are outside of the normal Department of Defense practices, but are considered acceptable for the highly classified reconnaissance programs.

Among the Big Safari aircraft projects have been the SR-71 BLACKBIRD and RC-135 RIVET JOINT (see C-135). To accelerate the addition of a laser seeker and guided missiles to the PREDATOR program, that UNMANNED AERIAL VEHICLE was transferred to Big Safari during the Kosovo air campaign of 1999.

Biographic Leverage

Use of secret background information to induce or blackmail a person to work in the intelligence or espionage field. The person need not be a spy, but could, for example, be a SPOTTER or COURIER.

Birch, John

(b. 1918 d. 1945)

U.S. INTELLIGENCE OFFICER who served in China. The son of American missionaries, Georgia-born John Birch went to China as a missionary in 1940 and stayed there after the PEARL HARBOR ATTACK made Americans in China the hunted enemies of the Japanese. In April 1942, a Chinese peasant in Shangjao took him to a sampan where Lt. Col. James (Jimmie) Doolittle and his crew were hiding. Doolittle had led the first U.S. bombing raid on Japan on April 18.

Birch led Doolittle and his men to safety. As they were parting on the way to Chungking, Birch asked Doolittle to request Maj. Gen. Claire L. Chennault, the U.S. aviation commander in China, to take him on as a chaplain. Chennault got Birch a U.S. Army commission, but used him as an intelligence officer. As Chennault later wrote, "Birch passed through the Japanese lines to contact Chinese guerrillas on the Yangtze, and spent months with them, setting up radio stations overlooking the main river ports to give us accurate information on enemy ship movements." He became known as "the eyes of the Fourteenth Air Force."

Later in the war Birch worked as an intelligence liaison officer to the Nationalist Chinese Army in Shangtung Province, in northern China. In the spring of 1945 the OFFICE OF STRATEGIC SERVICES (OSS) took charge of intelligence work in China and recruited Birch. After the Japanese surrender on Aug. 15, 1945, the OSS stayed on in China, looking for Allied prisoners of war, disarming the Japanese, and searching for useful intelligence material while the Chinese civil war raged around them.

On Aug. 25, 1945, near Qingdao, Chinese communists killed Birch for no apparent reason. In 1958, Robert Welch, a well-known anti-communist, hailed Birch as the "first casualty" of the Cold War and founded the ultra-conservative John Birch Society.

Bird, The

SEE FORT HOLABIRD

Bird Watcher

Slang used by British INTELLIGENCE OFFICERS for a spy.

Bison (Mya-4)

Developed by the Myasischev design bureau as a strategic bomber, the Bison was also employed in large numbers by the Soviet Air Forces in the long-range RECONNAISSANCE role. The Bison was considered unsuccessful as a strategic bomber because of its relatively slow speed and limited range, which were caused by the limitations of available jet engines.

The Bison was a swept-wing aircraft with four turbojet engines fitted in the wing roots and a maximum speed of 621 mph. It had two internal weapon bays for carrying up to 10,000 pounds of nuclear or conventional bombs. Some aircraft were fitted with a fixed 23-mm cannon in the nose and six to 10 23-mm cannon in twin turrets above and below the forward fuselage and in the tail. All were eventually fitted with in-flight refueling equipment.

Slightly smaller than the contemporary U.S. B-52 Stratofortress, the Soviet aircraft first flew in late 1953 and became operational in early 1956. It was thus a contemporary of the Tupolev turboprop BEAR strategic bomber and reconnaissance aircraft.

An estimated 200 to 300 aircraft were built. The Bison-B variant was a specialized strategic reconnaissance aircraft fitted with both cameras and ELECTRONIC INTELLIGENCE systems.

Code-named Bison by Western intelligence, the aircraft was known by the Russians as *Molot* ("hammer"). The aircraft had the design bureau designations M-4 and 201-M, and bore the Soviet military designation Mya-4.

Bissell, Maj. Gen. Clayton L.

(b. 1896 d. 1972)

Head of the U.S. Army's MILITARY INTELLIGENCE Division (G-2) during the latter part of World War II. His efforts placed both Army CRYPTANALYSIS and communications intercept activities under the Military Intelligence Division; previously those efforts had been controlled by the Signal Corps.

Bissell joined the U.S. Army Air Service in 1917 and while a fighter pilot in France he shot down five German aircraft, becoming an aerial ace. He remained in the Air Service after the war, pioneering night-flying techniques.

When the United States entered World War II, he went to China to serve as air officer to Maj. Gen. Joseph W. Stilwell, commander of U.S. forces in Burma and China and chief of staff to Chiang Kai-shek, the Nationalist Chinese leader. In Aug. 1942 Bissell, as a major general, became commander of the Tenth Air Force in the China-Burma-India theater. However, as a supporter of Stilwell he had difficulties with Chiang, who favored another American air officer, Maj. Gen. Claire L. Chennault. At Chiang's insistence, Chennault was given command of all air operations in China in March 1943.

In July 1943 Bissell was ordered back to the United States to become the assistant chief of intelligence (A-2) of the Army Air Forces. Seven months later, in Feb. 1944, he was made head of Army intelligence. There his efforts spurred better cooperation with the Navy in SIGNALS INTELLIGENCE, and on Sept. 15, 1945—13 days after the end of the war—the establishment of the ARMY SECURITY AGENCY to control "all signals intelligence and security establishments, units, and personnel" and to function directly under the Military Intelligence Division.

Bissell served as G-2 until Jan. 1946. He subsequently served as air ATTACHÉ at the U.S. Embassy in London.

Bissell, Richard M., Jr.

(b. 1910 d. 1994)

Senior U.S. INTELLIGENCE OFFICER who was head of clandestine operations for the CIA, including the disastrous Bay of Pigs invasion. He also managed the CIA's development of the U-2 spyplane and spy SATELLITES.

A graduate of Yale University who went on to study at the London School of Economics and then returned to Yale, Bissell became a member of the Yale economics faculty while still a graduate student. Poor eyesight kept him out of uniform in World War II, but he served in the Department of Commerce and the War Shipping Administration.

When the war ended, he moved on to the Economic Cooperation Administration, working on the creation of the Marshall Plan for European recovery. In 1954 he joined the CIA under ALLEN W. DULLES, then DIRECTOR OF CENTRAL INTELLIGENCE (DCI). Dulles took a special interest in this fellow member of the Eastern establishment and made him a special assistant. Bissell had a hand in an early CIA COVERT ACTION, the overthrow of the leftist government of Guatemala in 1954. The operation involved the raising and training of a small band of right-wing Guatemalan exiles and using propaganda to magnify the band into an army.

Promoted to deputy director of plans, he managed the development of the U-2 spyplane and advanced camera systems. He managed development of the CORONA SATELLITE and the SR-71 BLACKBIRD spyplane. He acted with extraordinary independence; when Dulles indicated that President Eisenhower wanted to keep U-2 flights to a minimum, Bissell, without consulting Dulles, arranged for British pilots to make the spy flights. Pilots said they worked for the "RBAF"—the Richard Bissell Air Force.

In 1959, as Bissell was moving up to become director of plans, Fidel Castro was taking over Cuba and imposing a communist regime. At that time, when Bissell was looked upon as a potential successor to Dulles, the DCI handed Bissell an assignment that could have made that succession a reality: Dulles gave Bissell the task of toppling Castro by means similar to those the CIA had used in Guatemala.

In March 1960 President Eisenhower approved a plan to train about 25 Cuban exiles who would train others in what the CIA hoped would be a revolt against Castro. Bissell had a bigger plan: a secret radio station broadcasting propaganda to Cuba, rebel aircraft based in Nicaragua, an invasion force of 1,400 troops, and a government in exile poised to take over after the invasion.

At the same time he plotted ways to embarrass Castro, for example, by putting hallucinogenic drugs in his cigars and making his beard fall off. Bissell also hoped to induce Mafia hit men to assassinate Castro. Further, Bissell made the Congolese leader Patrice Lumumba a candidate for assassination.

The Cuban invasion force kept expanding, despite Eisenhower's insistence that it be small and not traceable to the United States. CIA operatives, including future WATERGATE plotter E. HOWARD HUNT, recruited and trained the exiles at secret bases in Guatemala. As indications grew that Castro expected an invasion, Bissell continued to expand the invasion force.

Meanwhile, in Jan. 1961 President Eisenhower's term ended and John F. Kennedy became President. Some time before the 1960 election, Dulles had briefed Kennedy on the planned invasion of Cuba, describing it as an action that would trigger a revolt within Cuba. As President, Kennedy authorized the invasion without being aware of the extent and riskiness of Bissell's plan. At a briefing in March 1961, Kennedy told Bissell to "reduce the noise level." Bissell responded by moving the landing site from the city of Trinidad to a desolate area known as Bahia de los Cochinos, the Bay of Pigs. His request for direct support by U.S. warplanes was rejected by the White House.

The invasion, on April 17, was a disaster: Ships were sunk, landing craft were hung up on reefs, planes were shot down, some invaders were massacred as they came ashore, and 1,189 men were taken prisoner. Nine months later Bissell resigned. Dulles also was forced to resign.

Bissell went on to become the vice president and later president of the Institute for Defense Analysis, a nonprofit research organization. He subsequently became director of marketing and economic planning for United Aircraft, a major defense contractor.

Biuro Szfrow

The Polish CIPHER bureau, established in 1931 to combine radio intelligence and CRYPTOLOGY within the Second Bureau (intelligence) of the Polish General Staff.

In 1920, two years after the establishment of the Polish state, the nation was at war with Russia, which was itself still in the throes of a civil war. The Polish cryptologists had several successes against Russian communications during the conflict. Subsequently, as Germany emerged as Poland's enemy, Polish cryptologists turned their attention to the West. Thus, in 1931 the Biuro Szfrow was organized into four branches under the direction of Maj. Gwido Langer:

BS.1   Polish ciphers
BS.2   radio intelligence
BS.3   Russian ciphers
BS.4   German ciphers

The latter two branches were also responsible for COUNTERINTELLIGENCE and radio intercepts in their TARGET countries.

The German armed forces began using the ENIGMA cipher machine in 1926. As the German use of the machine was realized, it became the focus of Biuro Szfrow's efforts. The Polish agency purchased a commercial Enigma and made contact with the French cipher bureau. On Dec. 7, 1931, Capt. GUSTAVE BERTRAND arrived in Warsaw to meet with the Polish cryptologists; he brought with him documents provided by HANS-THILO SCHMIDT, a French AGENT with the CODE NAME Asché who had access to German Enigma secrets. These documents enabled the *Biuro Szfrow* to break into Enigma keys to read German military communications. (Bertrand provided the Poles with additional documents from Asché in 1932.)

The Polish agency achieved the first deciphering of a complete German radio message in the last week of Dec. 1932. Steady progress on reading secret German communications continued, peaking in 1938 when Biuro Szfrow was reading German Army and Air Force radio traffic enciphered with Enigma almost daily. The German naval ciphers were more difficult to read, as the Navy used a five-ROTOR Enigma, while the other services employed four-rotor machines.

But Polish success ended in Sept. 1938, when the Germans changed the operating procedures for their Enigma machines. Although the keys had always been changed periodically, message after message had been sent with the rotors in the same position. Now the settings changed with each message.

The Polish cryptologists were stymied. Marian Rejewski set about solving the new challenge. He designed a machine—essentially six interconnected Enigmas—that

he called a BOMBA, after a popular Polish ice cream dish. His theory was that the machine, an electrical-mechanical calculating device, could test every possible rotor position within two hours. When the Bomba found the proper solution, its motor would stop, and a light would come on. Multiple Bombas would be employed to test each possible rotor setting. It was an expensive project—each Bomba cost 100,000 zlotys—but by Nov. 1938 the Bombas were ready, and the Biuro Szfrow was again reading German signals.

Another Polish cryptographic development at this time was the PERFORATED SHEET. Conceived by Henryk Zygalski, this was a manual means of determining rotor positions. Each sheet of paper would have about 1,000 holes cut into it in a predetermined pattern. Twenty-six sheets were needed, one for each rotor position (26 letters of the alphabet). When the sheets were laid one on top of another, at some point holes would be aligned, revealing a rotor setting.

But the Germans again changed their procedure, and by mid-Dec. 1938 the Polish cryptologists were again stumped. Langer, now a lieutenant colonel, met again with the French and this time also with the British. Cryptologists from the three nations met in Paris, in great secrecy, on Jan. 9 and 10, 1939. But they had no solution to the now impenetrable German ciphers.

Polish agents determined that the Germans were now using four and five rotors in their Enigmas. Some progress was being made with existing Bombas and perforated sheets, but more would be needed to regain virtually immediate deciphering: 60 Bombas and 60 sets of perforated sheets.

This was too great a burden for the Poles, so the General Staff made the decision to share the problem—and the costs—with Britain and France. A second conference was held from July 24 to 27, 1939, in Warsaw and the town of Pyry, a few miles south of the capital, where the Biuro Szfrow was located, in buildings completed two years earlier. Bertrand again represented the French; the British cryptologists were ALASTAIR DENNISTON, who had been at the Paris meeting, and Dillwyn Knox, both of the GOVERNMENT CODE AND CYPHER SCHOOL.

The Poles explained their innermost Enigma secrets to the foreigners; an Enigma machine, Bomba, and perforated sheets would be forthcoming in the interests of stopping Nazi Germany, the common enemy, from further expansion. The following month—the last month of peace in Europe—the Poles delivered the Enigmas to their allies. On Sept. 1, 1939, German aircraft and Panzers struck Poland; 16 days later Soviet armies smashed into Poland from the east.

After the German invasion the Biuro Szfrow was ordered to leave Pyry and move to Brześć, on the Bug River, where the Polish High Command was to move its headquarters. But the advance of the Red Army rendered those plans meaningless. The Polish cryptologists were ordered to destroy their equipment. Meanwhile, the French Embassy quickly provided them with passports, train tickets, and money to make their escape to Paris. A Polish team of 15, led by Langer, escaped the Germans and began working with the French cryptologists at Gretz-Armainvillers, northeast of Paris—a facility given the code name Bruno. The Polish team was known by the code name Ekipa Z. (Other Polish cryptologists were captured by the Germans, but they never revealed their profession or secrets of their success against Enigma.)

When the Germans overran northern France in May 1940, Bertrand flew most of his cryptologists—including the Poles—to Oran and later to Algiers in North Africa, where they remained for several months. Subsequently, he brought them by ship to a location near Nimes in Vichy France, where they worked at station CADIX until Nov. 1942, when the Poles and other cryptologists fled once more. Several of the survivors of the Biuro Szfrow reached England via Spain and Portugal. (For security reasons they were not allowed to go to BLETCHLEY PARK.) Langer and several of his compatriots were captured by the Germans and spent the remainder of the war in prison camps.

In England the Poles were sent to Boxmoor, near London, where they formed the cryptanalysis section of the signal battalion of the Polish General Staff. They did work on some assignments from Bletchley Park as well as supporting Polish requirements.

After the war, when the Soviets occupied Poland, they installed their own regime, with Soviet-trained army, general staff, and intelligence agency. The Biuro Szfrow ceased to exist.

BJs

British intelligence term for highly secret diplomatic intercepts from several nations, including the United States, from 1919 to about 1939. The seemingly secure cables, sent in diplomatic CODES, were routinely intercepted and decrypted by British SIGNAL INTELLIGENCE facilities. The documents were so secret that no direct reference to their source was ever disclosed by British officials. Their existence was acknowledged at a history conference at the NSA in 1997.

The term comes from the blue jackets in which the documents were filed by the Foreign Office.

Black

(1) Term connoting secrecy, including secrecy of the existence or purpose of a specific program or hardware (i.e., black box, black program).

(2) Term used to indicate reliance on concealment of an activity rather than reliance on a COVER. In some cases, "black" also denotes illegal concealment.

Black Bag Job

Slang for surreptitious entry into an office or home to obtain files or materials illegally. Such break-ins dot the history of U.S. intelligence agencies, especially the FBI. The FBI break-ins were often requested by NSA codebreakers who wanted photographs of code books or diagrams of

CODE and CIPHER machines. Break-ins were also staged to install BUGS and wiretaps.

Possibly the earliest intelligence-related break-ins occurred as early as 1920, as the U.S. Navy financed a series of break-ins of Japanese consular and other offices in New York City by the OFFICE OF NAVAL INTELLIGENCE, the FBI, and local police to steal codes. Those break-ins—all made without detection—may have continued until as late as 1939. (See NAVY COMMUNICATIONS INTELLIGENCE.)

Black bag jobs ended officially for the FBI on July 19, 1966, when FBI director J. EDGAR HOOVER signed a memorandum saying that the practice "which includes also surreptitious entrances upon premises of any kind, will not meet with my approval in the future." Hoover later relented, saying he would order a surreptitious entry only under direct orders from the President or Attorney General.

A 1976 study by the congressional Select Committee to Study Governmental Operations said that before 1966 the FBI conducted more than 200 "black bag jobs." Between 1960 and 1976, the committee said that the FBI had conducted more than 500 warrantless, surreptitious microphone installations against intelligence and internal security targets.

Under the short-lived HUSTON PLAN during the Nixon administration, black bag jobs would have been resumed. But Hoover prevailed, insisting that he would not authorize a break-in without the written authorization of the President. The Huston Plan died, but the Nixon administration continued to demand improved DOMESTIC INTELLIGENCE. The Interagency Committee on Intelligence (Ad Hoc) was established and, ultimately, led to the PLUMBERS' illegal break-ins, including WATERGATE.

In 1981 the Justice Department sought authorization for surreptitious entries in the FOREIGN INTELLIGENCE SURVEILLANCE COURT. The court ruled that such acts needed presidential approval, not court authorization. In Dec. 1981 President Reagan gave the Attorney General the power to order black bag jobs, provided that they were conducted against a "foreign power or an agent of a foreign power."

Blackbird

General term used for high-performance RECONNAISSANCE aircraft developed by the United States as successors to the U-2 spyplane. Those were the A-12 OXCART and its derivative, the YF-12 fighter aircraft, and the SR-71 BLACKBIRD.

Black Book

Name given by the British to *Sonderfahndungsliste G.B.* (Special Search List Great Britain), compiled by the German RSHA as part of the German preparations to invade Britain. The 2,820 people on the list were British subjects and European exiles who were to be arrested and "taken into protective custody" by the GESTAPO following the invasion. The list was alphabetical, and when the existence of the Black Book became known after the war, people on the list proudly proclaimed their "ranking" as an indication of their importance to the Nazis as enemies of the Third Reich.

On the list were leading politicians, such as Winston Churchill and Anthony Eden, along with authors H. G. Wells, Noel Coward, Virginia Woolf, E. M. Forster, Rebecca West, C. P. Snow, and Aldous Huxley (who had immigrated to the United States in 1936). Sigmund Freud was also on the list, although he had died on Sept. 23, 1939.

Others included Lord BADEN-POWELL, founder of the Boy Scouts, who had been involved in British intelligence; cartoonist David Low; and Lady Astor. Among the Americans inexplicably on the list were Bernard Baruch and Paul Robeson. Absent from it was George Bernard Shaw, whom the Germans apparently saw as a potential friend because he had written a pro-peace essay a month after the war began.

The man who was to head the roundup of the enemies was an SS officer, Frank Six, a former dean of the economics faculty at the University of BERLIN. Documents named him as commander of proposed action groups—the designation for SS units that committed mass murders in Europe. Six was eventually convicted of war crimes and sentenced to 20 years in 1948, but he was released in 1952.

Another RSHA "invasion plan" publication found by the British Secret Intelligence Service (MI6) after the war gave a detailed description of MI6 and MI5, the British COUNTERINTELLIGENCE service. Subsequent investigation by the intelligence agencies established that two captured MI6 INTELLIGENCE OFFICERS and a third suspect had given the Germans the facts for the publication. Also see Capt. S. PAYNE BEST, Col. CHARLES H. ELLIS.

Black Box

Classified equipment or device, generally for electronic SURVEILLANCE; often military equipment fitted in a spyplane (see AIRCRAFT), INTELLIGENCE COLLECTION SHIP, or SUBMARINE.

Black Chamber

(1) Site of American codebreaking also known as the Cryptographic Bureau, or Section 8 of MILITARY INTELLIGENCE. HERBERT O. YARDLEY set up the Black Chamber in 1912. Secretary of State Henry L. Stimson ordered it shut down, reputedly saying, "Gentlemen do not read each other's mail." Yardley used the site's name as a title for his book, *The American Black Chamber* (1931). (See CRYPTOGRAPHY.)

(2) Name for the 16th-century French secret office set up to tamper with the mail. When King Henry IV established the *Poste aux Lettres* in 1590, his government officials began the long French tradition of the *cabinet noir*—the secret "black chamber" where letters were opened, read, and resealed. The work inspired the recruitment of experts in the art of restoring broken seals. The letter-opening practice spawned the development of CRYPTOSYSTEMS for encrypting and decrypting letters. Although the French revolutionaries of 1789 protested against tampering with the mails, they set up *comités de surveillance*, whose duties included opening the mail of suspected and avowed royalists.

Black chambers continued through the Napoleonic era and on into the 20th century. Once, to prove interception, a French woman sent her foreign husband a letter saying that three violets were enclosed. "When the letter arrived," wrote Douglas Porch in *The French Secret Services* (1995), "it actually contained three violets—the *cabinet noir*, fearing that they had lost the flowers, actually placed three violets into the envelope which had contained none."

The British established a similar secret system for tampering with the mails. (See BODE FAMILY.)

Black Dragon Society

Powerful Japanese secret society formed in 1901 to expel the Russians from Manchuria. The society, which gathered intelligence and aided the government against Russia, continued to influence Japanese foreign policy until World War II.

The northern Manchurian border with Russia was the Amur River, known to the Chinese as the Black Dragon River and to the Japanese as Kokuryu. Ryohei Uchida, a leading member of another intelligence organization, the BLACK OCEAN SOCIETY, founded the Black Dragon Society primarily because the earlier society had become known to the outside world. Uchida, who had often visited Russia, also believed that only Russia seriously threatened Japan, and thus he wanted intelligence that focused on Russia.

Black Dragon became the most powerful and aggressive secret society in Japan. Its members, recruited among young patriots, called themselves "brave knights." Its existence and its rapidly growing size remained secret for many years, even though cabinet ministers and high-ranking military officers were members. The first reference to it in Japanese publications occurs in the 1930s.

Soon after its founding, the society showed its power by insisting on the right to approve all military ATTACHÉS posted abroad. The first test came when the War Office named as attaché to Russia Col. MOTOJIRO AKASHI, a baron who had been on the Imperial Headquarters Staff during the Sino-Japanese War of 1894–1895. While enthusiastically accepting Akashi, the society also successfully demanded that he be made a "roving attaché" to enable him to get information from Russian exiles, many of them revolutionaries in other European countries. Under instructions from the society, Akashi paid the exiles for information on Russian intelligence services.

Initially the society sought information only about Russia and Manchuria, but by the late 1930s it was also seeking intelligence on Korea, China, the Philippines,

Malaya, Hong Kong, Singapore, India, Afghanistan, Ethiopia, Turkey, Morocco, the Caribbean, South American countries, and the United States. The society also developed strong ties with Sun Yat-sen, the Nationalist Party leader who would usher China into the modern age.

In the 1930s Western journalists often mentioned the Black Dragon Society, sometimes identifying it as a force behind the throne, at other times making it sound like a criminal organization. Aspects of it were criminal, and its leader was sometimes called the "Darkside Emperor." It remained shadowy and political, developing vague ties with Nazis before fading from sight in the late 1930s.

In Sept. 1945, in restructuring Japanese society, Gen. Douglas MacArthur formally abolished the society and ordered the arrest of seven of its alleged leaders. U.S. intelligence, however, was out of date. Two of the leaders were not actual members, one had died in 1938, another had killed himself in 1943, and the others had formally renounced their membership years before.

Black Hand

Balkan terrorist organization run by Serbian separatists against the Austro-Hungarian Empire. The Black Hand was founded in Belgrade in 1911 with the goal of uniting Serbia with Bosnia and Herzegovina. Its name, stamped on walls or threatening letters, was a terrifying symbol throughout the Balkans. The Black Hand struck at anyone deemed an enemy of the Serbs. Its motto was "Union or Death."

The secret society's founder, Col. Dragutin Dimitrijevic, was chief of intelligence of the Serbian Army's General Staff. He used the Black Hand to demonstrate Serbia's power during the Balkan Wars of 1912–1913, striking terror through assassinations and sabotage. It was Dimitrijevic who ordered the assassination of Archduke Franz Ferdinand, heir to the Austrian throne, at Sarajevo in June 1914. The Austrian government used the incident as an excuse to declare war on Serbia, triggering the outbreak of World War I a few weeks later.

In Dec. 1916, after an investigation into an alleged assassination attempt on the regent Alexander in Salonika, Dimitrijevic was arrested as a plotter. In a trial that Serbians said was rigged, he and two supporters were sentenced to death. They were executed in June 1917. At a staged retrial in Belgrade in 1953, the Supreme People's Court found the defendants not guilty and declared them rehabilitated.

Black Intelligence

Common term used among Union military officers during the American Civil War for intelligence on Confederate forces provided by Negroes. "This source represented the single most prolific and productive category of intelligence obtained and acted on by Union forces throughout the Civil War," wrote P. K. Rose, a CIA officer, in the Winter 1998–1999 issue of *Studies in Intelligence*.

Black List

COUNTERINTELLIGENCE listing of hostile collaborators, sympathizers, intelligence suspects, or other persons viewed as threatening to the security of friendly military forces.

Black Ocean Society

Secret society founded in 1881 to expand Japanese influence and to obtain intelligence from China, Korea, Manchuria, and Russia. The society was the first organization to provide Japan with foreign intelligence from undercover ASSETS.

The society's Japanese name, *Genyosha*, comes from *Genkai nada*, the black ocean, or strait, that separates Kyushu, Japan's southernmost island, from Korea. Kotaro Hiraoka, member of a wealthy samurai family on Kyushu, founded the society in 1881. But the best known leader of the society was Mitsuru Toyama, a low-born, self-made man of Kyushu. Toyama, with two swords hanging from his waist, was the boss of masterless samurai, the *ronin*, the "enforcers" of the society.

A nationalist group with the slogan "Honor the Imperial Family," Black Ocean was in reality "a terrorist organization and a school for spies," wrote G. R. Storry in *The Double Patriots* (1957), a study of Japanese societies. Before the end of the 19th century such organizations banded together as the East Asia One Culture Society and set up an espionage training school in Shanghai.

China was a special TARGET of Black Ocean intelligence efforts. Serving as an unacknowledged branch of government, the society provided the Japanese Army with intelligence. Toyama also set up spy operations for the Army in China, with Black Ocean Society headquarters at Hankow.

The society consistently used SEX for its intelligence collection, establishing bordellos in Japan, China, and Korea to attract the paymasters of other Chinese secret societies and officials whose pillow talk provided important information. Through prostitution and blackmail, the Black Ocean Society was thus able to obtain not only intelligence but also money to finance itself.

A Black Ocean subsidiary group, the *Tenyukyo*, spied in Korea and sought out subversives in a program aimed at weakening the local government for an eventual Japanese takeover.

Also see BLACK DRAGON SOCIETY.

Black Propaganda

Propaganda that purports to emanate from a source other than the true one. During World War II, for example, British black propaganda specialists in England produced radio broadcasts that seemed to come from Germany or German-occupied areas. The propaganda was designed to undermine morale or to create tensions that would hurt the German war effort. "Radio Deutschland," on the German radio dial near the signal of a real

German station, was directed at Germany and won from German propaganda chief Joseph Goebbels the begrudging note in his diary: "The station does a clever job of propaganda. . . ."

Most German soldiers who heard the broadcasts believed that they were German. Some German prisoners of war boasted that they worked for Radio Deutschland, hoping to prove their anti-Hitler feelings to Allied interrogators. So secret was the British hoax that the interrogators, aware of the radio station but not its true producers, believed the prisoners.

Black Shield

Overflights by U.S. A-12 OXCART spyplanes over North Vietnam in 1967–1968. The flights operated from Kadena Air Force Base on Okinawa.

Planning for use of the CIA A-12s over North Vietnam had begun in 1965, but because of the need for intelligence about the possible introduction of Soviet Surface-to-Air Missiles (SAM) into North Vietnam, A-12 missions were not flown over the war area until 1967. After extensive discussions, on May 16, 1967, President Johnson approved the use of the A-12 based on the superiority of the aircraft's cameras and survivability in comparison with the U-2 spyplane.

Two weeks later, three A-12 aircraft and 260 officers and airmen were deployed to Okinawa. On May 31 an A-12 took off from Okinawa on the aircraft's first operational mission. The plane made two reconnaissance passes, one over North Vietnam and one over the so-called Demilitarized Zone. The flight lasted three hours, 39 minutes, with the cruise legs flown at Mach 3.1 (more than 2,000 mph).

The aircraft photographed 70 of the 190 existing SAM sites and nine other priority targets. The A-12 did not detect radar signals over the targets, indicating that this first mission had gone completely unnoticed by North Vietnamese. Additional SAM detection missions flown by the A-12 determined that through mid-July there were no actual missiles in North Vietnam, although launch sites were being prepared for them.

On a typical Black Shield mission over North Vietnam, an Air Force tanker would refuel the A-12 shortly after takeoff and carry out a second refueling near Thailand after the photographic runs. The A-12 would then return to Okinawa. The aircraft spent only 12½ minutes over North Vietnam during a "low-speed" photo pass. At Okinawa the film was quickly removed from the cameras, packaged, and dispatched by special plane to a processing facility at the Air Force photo center in Japan. The A-12's photos could be in the hands of American commanders in the Pacific within 24 hours of the plane's touchdown on Okinawa.

Between May 31 and Dec. 31, 1967, the A-12s flew 22 missions over North Vietnam. On Sept. 17 a North Vietnamese radar detected an A-12 and on Oct. 28 a SAM site launched an SA-2 missile against an A-12. Two days later at least six missiles were fired against an A-12 on its second pass over North Vietnam (confirmed by missile vapor trails on mission photography). The aircraft was hit by a missile fragment but was not seriously damaged.

The high-performance reconnaissance missions over North Vietnam were taken over by Air Force SR-71 BLACKBIRD aircraft in 1968.

Blake, Al

Former U.S. Navy yeoman who helped the OFFICE OF NAVAL INTELLIGENCE (ONI) and FBI capture two major Japanese spies in California before the PEARL HARBOR ATTACK.

Japanese NAVAL INTELLIGENCE was concentrating on Hawaii at the time Blake was contacted by Toraichi Kono, who had been actor Charlie Chaplin's valet. Using that connection as a conversational ploy, Kono became friendly with Blake and suggested that if Blake reenlisted in the Navy he could earn a great deal of money. In March 1941, Kono introduced Blake to Comdr. Itaru Tachibana, who ran a spy NETWORK as "Mr. Yamamoto," the owner of several California nightclubs. He had already begun working on plans to blow up bridges and power stations when Japan went to war against the United States. He offered Blake $2,500 to go to Hawaii to obtain classified information and an additional $5,000 when he brought it back.

Blake told the story to the ONI, which tapped his telephone and recorded his conversations with the Japanese. The ONI, working with the FBI, discovered Tachibana's double life. Blake was told to continue his dealings with the Japanese and agree to travel to Hawaii. There, under ONI directions, he contacted an officer on the battleship *Pennsylvania* who had been briefed by the ONI. The officer gave Blake documents that would please the Japanese but would not betray any real U.S. secrets.

In June 1941 the FBI arrested Kono and Tachibana, who were charged with conspiracy against the United States on behalf of a foreign power.

Blake, George

(b. 1922)

A senior British Secret Intelligence Service (MI6) officer who spied for the KGB. Through his betrayal of AGENTS and Western intelligence operations, he was one of the most valuable British spies ever recruited by the Soviets.

He was born in Rotterdam as George Behne. His mother was a Dutch Lutheran and his father an Egyptian Jew who had served in the British Army in World War I. His father held a British passport and patriotically named his son after King George V. When World War II began he was in Holland, finishing high school. Blake briefly worked for the Dutch resistance after the German invasion in 1940 before making his way to England via Vichy France and Spain. He enlisted in the Royal Navy and, because of his language skills, was assigned to the Dutch section of MI6 in London. In 1944 he was commissioned as a sub-lieutenant.

After the war he was sent to Hamburg, where he recruited former German naval and army officers for MI6 intelligence NETWORKS in East Germany. He was next ordered to Cambridge University to take a Russian-language course for officers of the armed services.

In Oct. 1948 Blake was sent to Seoul, South Korea, to head the new MI6 station there. When North Korean troops poured across the border in June 1950, he was captured. While a prisoner he told his captors that he wished to contact the Soviet Embassy in Pyongyang, North Korea. This was the first step on the long road of his betrayal. In his autobiography, *No Other Choice* (1990), Blake said that neither then nor at any other time was he paid for his spying. "I did what I did for ideological reasons, never for money," he wrote.

When he was released in 1953, Blake traveled back to England on the Trans-Siberian railway. At Otpor, on the China-Soviet border, he met his Soviet HANDLER, who later appeared in London to run Blake. There Blake was placed in MI6's new Y Section, which handled telephone taps of Soviets in Austria and BUGS in buildings occupied by Soviet missions in Britain and countries in Western Europe. (The "Y" may have derived from Y SERVICE, a World War II signals-intercept agency.)

By his account, in Oct. 1953 he made his first delivery, "a list of top secret technical operations carried out by MI6 against Soviet targets with a precise indication of their nature and location. They were divided into two parts: telephone tapping operations and microphone operations." One of Blake's most momentous disclosures was the building of the BERLIN TUNNEL (Operation GOLD), which he revealed to the Soviets while it was still in the planning stage.

Blake married an MI6 secretary who was the daughter of an MI6 officer, and in 1955 he was sent to BERLIN. Working there, in London, and in Lebanon, he had what on the surface appeared to be a relatively routine MI6 career. All the while he also worked for the KGB.

In 1961 he was in Lebanon, studying Arabic in a school used by Western intelligence agencies, when he was abruptly summoned to London and accused of being a longtime Soviet spy. Lt. Col. MICHAL GOLENIEWSKI, a DEFECTOR from the Polish Intelligence Service, had given the CIA information that there was a spy in MI6, and British investigators had tracked down the tip to Blake.

He confessed, was arrested for violating the OFFICIAL SECRETS ACT, and was swiftly tried at the Old Bailey, where he was convicted and sentenced to 42 years in prison, "a year for each agent betrayed," according to accounts that he named—and thus doomed—all 42 British agents in the Soviet Union. It was the longest such sentence in modern British legal history. Blake himself claimed he had turned in some 400 agents and that none of them had been killed.

In Wormwood Scrubs Prison he was put on special watch as a potential escapee, as was another inmate, GORDON LONSDALE. While walking in the yard one day, Lonsdale predicted that he and Blake would be together in Moscow in 1967 to celebrate the 50th anniversary of the October Revolution. After Lonsdale was transferred to another prison, Blake was taken off special watch and given a job sewing diplomatic mail pouches.

On Oct. 22, 1966, according to Blake, he knocked out a loosened iron bar on his cell window, slid down a roof, and dropped to the ground; then he climbed up a nylon rope ladder with knitting-needle rungs, and dropped down a wall into the waiting arms of a confederate who had a car and a hideout flat. Blake said that the elaborate escape was a friendly gesture engineered by Sean Bourke, a member of the Irish Republican Army (IRA) who had met Blake in jail. Also aiding in the escape were a doctor, who treated Blake's broken wrist, and two former inmates, who had served 18 months for organizing anti-nuclear demonstrations at a U.S. Air Force base.

Bourke, the demonstrators, and still another helper all managed to get Blake out of England in a van. They crossed the channel from Dover and drove to East Germany, where Blake left them. (Bourke soon departed for Ireland, where he wrote a book about the escape and successfully fought extradition to England. He died in 1982.) Rumors persisted for years that the KGB had financed the escape, enlisting the IRA but not using any Soviet agents.

In the Soviet Union Blake got a job translating in a publishing house. Divorced while he was in prison in England, he remarried in Moscow and had a son. Although he was in Beirut when HAROLD (KIM) PHILBY was there, the two men later said they had never met until they became friends in Moscow. There Blake introduced Philby to the woman he later married. Blake formed a closer friendship with DONALD MACLEAN. Like Blake—and unlike Philby—Maclean tried to make a life as a communist in Moscow.

In a television interview on his 80th birthday in Nov. 2002, Blake said the years he had spent in Russia were "the happiest of my life." Russian sources said he spent some of those recent years conducting a master class at a SPY SCHOOL run by the FSB, the Russian successor to the KGB.

Bletchley Park

Site of the British codebreaking GOVERNMENT CODE AND CYPHER SCHOOL (GC&CS) and World War II headquarters for the CRYPTANALYSIS that produced ULTRA, the deciphers of German CIPHERS.

Located some 50 miles north of London, "B.P.," as it was called, was the site of one of the most important events of World War II: the cracking of the German ENIGMA machine ciphers. Bletchley Park was also called Station X, originally the designated evacuation headquarters for the Secret Intelligence Service, MI6. But it became instead a warren of mathematicians, chess players, linguists, and eccentrics with no particular specialty other than a keen mind. (One highly valuable man was seen one day carrying his hat in his hand and his briefcase on his head.) Together with military officers they would decipher, translate, and analyze an incredible amount of enemy communications. German U-boat traffic during one period was averaging 3,000 messages a day.

Sir Herbert Leon, a Victorian businessman, built Bletchley Park in the 1860s and named it after a scruffy industrial town about halfway between Oxford and Cambridge. To an architect's eye it was "a maudlin and monstrous pile" reflecting "the architectural gaucherie of the mid-Victorian era." GC&CS moved to B.P. in Aug. 1939.

The 55-acre site was chosen because it was linked to London by a major road and rail line, and because of its proximity to both Oxford and Cambridge, the universities that would provide B.P. with much of its brain-power.

The main building was a solid redbrick edifice in what one observer called "would-be Tudor-Gothic style." New electrical and telephone lines were installed. The billiard room became a telephone exchange, the tower room a wireless room. Antennas were strung between chimneys and onto trees. Riggers from the Royal Navy cut the tops off tall trees and strapped antennas to them, linking them to one of the dozens of Nissen huts near the mansion. The huts were attached together by hallways, forming a series of H-shaped structures. Later B.P. got a standby electrical system powered by two marine diesel engines. There were air raid shelters, and blast walls were installed in buildings where the most important codebreaking equipment was operating.

By April 1940 codebreakers could read a great deal of German traffic, and a site was needed for the mammoth effort of turning this traffic into timely, useful intelligence. By the time full-scale operations started, the U.S.-British partnership in Enigma codebreaking continued at B.P. The first delegation of U.S. Army and Navy specialists arrived early in 1941. They delivered a PURPLE machine being used to crack Japanese diplomatic ciphers. (See BRUSA AGREEMENT.)

Among the Americans who passed through B.P. were Col. TELFORD TAYLOR, a future war crimes prosecutor; Capt. ALFRED FRIENDLY, a future managing editor of *The Washington Post*; William Bundy, a future assistant secretary of state; Lewis F. Powell, Jr., a future U.S. Supreme Court justice; and John B. Oakes, an editorial writer for *The New York Times*.

Several hundred men and women worked at B.P. when operations began there. As the work force grew, so did the number of small, one-story huts. Because of security, once someone was assigned to B.P., he or she could expect to remain there until the war was over. Civilians had to live nearby, many in cramped boarding houses. Most military personnel bunked at two nearby Royal Air Force bases.

"There was an amazing spirit at the place," Friendly later wrote in *The Washington Post*. "Morale was high because everyone knew the fantastically successful results of our daily-and-nightly endeavors. It was one place in the military where there was no sense of futility, of useless work or of nonsense."

The Ultra chain began at one hut, where German radio traffic intercepts were processed. In a second hut the intercepts were decrypted and translated. A Z PRIORITIES system was set up to establish the messages' priority ratings—from Z for the lowest to five Zs for the highest—and sent to INTELLIGENCE OFFICERS in a third hut. There the Ultra material was encrypted and readied for routing to designated recipients. (See SPECIAL LIAISON UNIT.)

Snippets of information noted in an intercept—designations of German units, names, even ball-bearing serial numbers—were filed in the Index, which began as cards in a shoe box and grew to fill a room staffed by nine women working three shifts. A copy of the Index was maintained, for safekeeping, at the majestic Bodleian Library in Oxford.

Many men and women tended the BOMBE and COLOSSUS machines, which needed constant attention. In his *Very Special Intelligence* (1977), Patrick Beesley, of the Admiralty's OPERATIONAL INTELLIGENCE CENTRE, especially cited the 1,200 Wrens (members of the WRNS, the Women's Royal Naval Service) at Bletchley Park:

> Why only W.R.N.S. were chosen for this monotonous work is not clear. It was a soul-destroying job and very like being in prison, except there was no remission for good conduct. Quite the reverse: once detailed, that remained the lot of these devoted and highly intelligent girls for the duration. There were few chances of promotion, no contact with the rest of the Navy, and, due to the very necessary security restrictions, little social life when off duty. Mechanical servicing of the 'Bombes', as they were known, was the responsibility of a small band of R.A.F. [Royal Air Force] technicians, whose life was no more glamorous or interesting than that of the W.R.N.S. Almost the only recognition that this dedicated band of men and women received was a typical message, greatly appreciated, from Winston Churchill, commending them for the fact that, 'The chickens were laying so well without clucking!'

Prime Minister Churchill's remark about the chickens was accurate. The secrets of B.P. were well kept. The only known serious breach of security was the espionage of JOHN CAIRNCROSS, a British intelligence officer who spied for Soviet Union. While at Bletchley Park he passed intercepted and decrypted Ultra material to the Soviets.

Intelligence professionals, muttering about amateurs taking over Bletchley Park, sometimes called the place "Little King's" because Cambridge's King's College produced so many B.P. workers. British scholars included Alan Ming, a brilliant King's College mathematician who led the effort to solve Enigma by building a primitive computer; Leonard Palmer, who deciphered Minoan and Mycenean inscriptions; novelist Angus Wilson, an eccentric who reputedly once ran around the B.P. swan pool stark naked. Others were professors of Greek, Italian, German, Russian, classics, linguistics, and history.

Royal Navy Comdr. ALASTAIR DENNISTON was in charge of B.P. until 1942, when he was succeeded by Comdr. EDWARD TRAVIS, a "great table-thumper" who ruled a crew unlike any he would find in the Royal Navy. Many of the dons and the other academicians were so odd and incorrigible that security officers despaired at ever teaching them to follow the rules. Four of them one day managed to get a letter to Churchill complaining that their work "is being held up, and in some cases is not being done at all" because of a lack of personnel.

Churchill responded with a demand for action by the officer ultimately in charge of Bletchley Park, the intelligence chief, Sir STEWART MENZIES. Although angered by the academicians' breach of the chain of command, Menzies did add personnel. By the end of the war, there were some 12,000 men and women, uniformed and civilian, working at B.P.

Churchill, who took a keen interest in Bletchley Park, once visited there with Menzies. In seeing the great variety of personalities who served there, Churchill remarked to Menzies, "I know I told you to leave no stone unturned to find the necessary staff, but I didn't mean you to take me so literally."

The codebreakers departed soon after the war. In 1991 a campaign was begun to save Bletchley Park from demolition by property developers. Shortly thereater an effort was begun to rebuild one of the Colossus machines. In July 1994 His Royal Highness the Duke of Kent opened the codebreaking MUSEUM at Bletchley Park and formally inaugurated the Colossus Rebuild Project. Today much of the facility has been restored and is open to the public.

The Soviet CODE NAME for Bletchley Park was "resort."

Blind Date

A meeting by an INTELLIGENCE OFFICER and another person, especially an AGENT, at the time and place of the other person's choosing. There is always the danger that the officer is being set up for capture or an attempt to TURN him.

Bloch, David

One of the first spies to enter enemy territory by parachute. Bloch joined the French 152nd Infantry Regiment in World War I and subsequently volunteered to be a French AGENT behind German lines.

On the night of June 22–23, 1916, he was parachuted into German-held Alsace, about 12 miles from his hometown of Gübwiller. He was parachuted in his military uniform and changed into civilian clothes after he landed. He was to be picked up by an airplane one week later. During the next six days he collected intelligence on German troop dispositions and sent back messages to

French lines with carrier pigeons that had dropped with him in a basket. (See PIGEON POST.)

On his last day he decided to visit Gübwiller, hoping to get a glimpse of his home and possibly his family. He wore a small beard as a means of disguise. Upon leaving the town he was detained by a German patrol, which took him to the local commander. After he was denounced by someone in the town who recognized him, he was confronted with his father and his true identity was revealed.

He was executed by firing squad on Aug. 1, 1916.

Bloch, Felix S.

(b. 1935)

U.S. diplomat dismissed in 1990 from the State Department after a highly publicized, inconclusive espionage investigation. Bloch was the highest-ranking State Department official to be publicly involved in an espionage case since World War II. FBI agent ROBERT HANSSEN, who was charged with espionage in 2001, was accused of disclosing to the Russians that the FBI was building a spy case against Bloch. Hanssen's betrayal, the FBI said, "led the KGB to warn Bloch that he was under investigation, and completely compromised the investigation."

The FBI revealed that Hanssen had told his Russian HANDLERS in Nov. 2000: "Bloch was such a schnook . . . I almost hated protecting him, but then he was your friend . . . If our [FBI] guy sent to Paris had balls or brains, both [Bloch and Gikman] would have been dead meat. Fortunately for you he had neither . . . The French said, 'Should we take them down?' He went all wet. He'd never made a decision before, why start then. It was that close."

Bloch, who was born in Austria, attended the University of Pennsylvania, and joined the State Department in 1958. He initially served as an intelligence researcher. In 1960 he was assigned to the U.S. Consulate in Düsseldorf, West Germany, as a commercial officer. From 1963 to 1965, he served in the U.S. Consulate in Caracas, Venezuela. After receiving a master's degree from the University of California at Berkeley in 1966, he went to BERLIN, where he served as a U.S. trade official. In the mid-1970s, after the United States established diplomatic relations with East Germany, Bloch was posted there as an economic officer.

It was at that time, U.S. officials believe, that KGB officers first approached him. From 1983 to 1987 Bloch was deputy chief of the U.S. mission in the VIENNA embassy, which in Dec. 1986 was the scene of the espionage confession of Marine Sgt. CLAYTON J. LONETREE. Bloch was the second-ranking diplomat at the U.S. Embassy in Vienna when U.S. security officers linked him to a known KGB INTELLIGENCE OFFICER. The CIA maintains a large and active station in Vienna, a city long notorious as a center for espionage activities by many nations. While serving under inexperienced, politically appointed ambassadors, Bloch often acted as the man in charge and thus had extensive access to CIA material.

Bloch was first publicly linked to espionage activities

in July 1989, when the State Department announced that the FBI was investigating "illegal activities" involving Bloch, including "the extent of the compromise which has occurred." The accusations against Bloch stemmed from an alleged incident that was widely reported, although not officially confirmed: French COUNTERINTELLI-GENCE officers were said to have videotaped Bloch as he handed a briefcase to a known KGB AGENT in Paris. According to the leaked official account, the French were following a UNITED NATIONS employee stationed in Paris, who operated under diplomatic immunity in France and could not be arrested.

U.S. and Austrian counterintelligence officials had the KGB agent under SURVEILLANCE when he was in Austria, where he traveled with a Finnish passport issued to "Reino Gikman," an executive of a computer firm. In Austria, which he had been visiting since 1979, he had to work as an ILLEGAL and could be arrested if he were caught. It is probably for that reason that he arranged the meeting with Bloch in Paris. U.S. NSA phone-tappers picked up a transatlantic phone call that "Gikman" made to Bloch, then in Washington, in which they set up a meeting in Paris a few days later.

In a classic example of cooperation, the NSA alerted the CIA, which passed the information to the FBI. The FBI asked French counterintelligence to videotape the meeting.

Shortly after the rendezvous, an FBI wiretap on Bloch picked up a call in which someone told Bloch, "There is a virus about, and you may be infected with it." The call was believed to have come from a KGB agent. Although the warning call certainly implied KGB knowledge of the overt investigation, no U.S. official acknowledged a leak. The warning undoubtedly came through Hanssen.

Back in Washington, Bloch was kept under such obvious surveillance that reporters joined federal agents trailing the diplomat, making the surveillance a media circus. Reports about Bloch leaked from official sources, who claimed he took large sums of money from the KGB.

When the first accusations were made in 1989, Bloch was suspended with pay from his duties as director of the State Department's Bureau of European and Canadian Affairs and his SECURITY CLEARANCES were revoked. On Feb. 7, 1990, the State Department dismissed Bloch as a SECURITY RISK. His dismissal came under a rarely invoked law that allows the firing of federal employees "in the interests of national security." Officials said that the State Department had never before used the law. Officials apparently used the law on this occasion because the government did not have enough evidence to indict and try Bloch for espionage.

Bloch left Washington soon after his dismissal and moved to Chapel Hill, N.C., where he worked as a part-time bus driver and a bagger at a supermarket. In Jan. 1993 he was arrested for stealing $100.59 worth of groceries from the store. He was fined $60, ordered to perform 48 hours of community service, and told to donate $100 to a charity.

Blowback

DECEPTION planted abroad by an intelligence agency to mislead people in other countries, then returning to the originating nation, where it misleads that people or even the government itself. When WILLIAM COLBY, the U.S. DIRECTOR OF CENTRAL INTELLIGENCE, testified before the CHURCH COMMITTEE in 1977, he admitted that the CIA disseminated information that blew back to the United States and was picked up by the media as true. (See DISINFORMATION.)

Blown

Exposure of personnel, an installation (such as a SAFE HOUSE), or other elements of a clandestine activity or organization. A blown AGENT is one whose identity is known to the opposition.

Blue, Rear Adm. Victor

(b. 1865 d. 1928)

U.S. naval officer who served as a spy during the Spanish-American War. Blue, a graduate of the Naval Academy, was a lieutenant on board the gunboat *Suwanee*, which was blockading Cuba in June 1898 when a need arose for TACTICAL INTELLIGENCE ashore.

Blue went ashore in a small boat and made contact with Cuban revolutionaries fighting against Spanish control of the island. On another mission he gained knowledge about Spanish coastal defenses. Later, with the aid of the guerrillas, he made his way through the Spanish defense perimeter around Santiago to get a view of the harbor. To bottle up the Spanish fleet in Santiago, blockaders had sunk a ship in the channel. They needed to know whether they had successfully kept the Spaniards from going to sea. From a hilltop he could see that all the ships were still in port.

Blue, on still another RECONNAISSANCE mission ashore, prepared plans for storming the harbor. But that proved unnecessary because the Spanish ships, attempting to break through the blockade, were run aground under ferocious gunfire from U.S. warships during a running battle along the coast.

Blue, who commanded the battleship *Texas* in World War I, retired in 1919 as a rear admiral.

Bluebell

Operation of the U.S. CIA to infiltrate AGENTS into North Korea shortly after the Korean War began in June 1950. Those agents sought intelligence about North Korean plans and movements. Most of them were refugees from South Korea, caught behind the front lines as North Korean forces advanced southward.

Although many of the agents were caught, others were able to provide useful information to U.S. INTELLI-

GENCE OFFICERS. Children among the refugees proved the most observant and were able to provide the most worthwhile information.

Blue Code

Japanese Navy CODE and CIPHER system adopted at the end of 1930, the successor to the Red code. The codes were given their color names by the U.S. NAVY COMMUNICATIONS INTELLIGENCE staff (OP-20-G), based on the color of the book bindings in which they were recorded.

"It had taken more than three years of incredible mind-boggling work to break a complex code and cipher system by pure cryptanalysis—the hard way. No other code breakers had ever achieved such a breakthrough," wrote Rear Adm. EDWIN T. LAYTON, a senior U.S. INTELLIGENCE OFFICER in his autobiography, *"And I Was There"* (1985).

Beginning in the fall of 1931, a U.S. Navy team led by Mrs. Agnes Meyer Driscoll undertook the effort, stripping away a two-tier layer of protective encipherment and then working out the meanings of some 85,000 basic code groups. The introduction of IBM tabulating machines to do some of the work marked one of the first uses of electrical-mechanical devices to break into a code.

The Blue code was superseded on Nov. 1, 1938, when the Japanese Navy adopted a new code series, replaced a year later by the JN-SERIES CIPHERS. Even after the Blue code was dropped, the U.S. Navy continued to work on intercepted messages that had not previously been decoded. One of these revealed that the battleship *Haruna*, completed in 1915, had achieved a speed of 32 knots after her rebuilding. Publicly, the Japanese government as well as the reference book *Jane's Fighting Ships* had credited the ship with only 26 knots. This difference was significant, as the fastest U.S. battleships in the 1930s could reach only 21 knots, while U.S. battleships under construction were to be 27-knot ships.

Blue Cradle

U.S. Air Force slang for the RB-47 RECONNAISSANCE version of the B-47 STRATOJET aircraft.

Blue Gemini

U.S. Air Force proposal to undertake two-man Gemini capsule flights as training and support for the proposed MANNED ORBITING LABORATORY (MOL), a space SURVEILLANCE platform. As proposed in June 1962, the Air Force wanted at least six Blue Gemini missions to be flown by Air Force pilots in support of the MOL program.

The Blue Gemini plan was canceled by Jan. 1963. It lacked support from both the Air Force and the National Aeronautics and Space Administration, both of which feared competition with other programs.

Blue Moon

CODE NAME for U.S. high-level RECONNAISSANCE flights over Cuba in Oct. 1962. The flights were flown by the U.S. Air Force U-2 spyplane.

Blumberg, Binyamin

(b. 1930 d. 1992)

Head of the highly secret Israeli intelligence agency founded to guard Israeli efforts to build nuclear weapons. Blumberg set up the agency in 1957; initially called the Office of Special Assignments, operating secretly out of the Defense Ministry, it later became the Lishka leKishrei Mada (Science Liaison Bureau), secretly known as *LAKAM*, an acronym of its Hebrew name.

A member of a kibbutz (collective agricultural settlement), Blumberg joined the Haganah, the secret Jewish defense force that operated prior to the establishment of the state of Israel on May 14, 1948. He fought in the War of Independence (1948–1949) and then joined the SHIN BET, the security service of the new state. He was assigned to be chief of security for the Ministry of Defense—inside the ministry itself as well as in the design bureaus and factories producing weapons.

In the mid-1950s, when France assisted Israel in constructing its first atomic reactor, Blumberg's office was given the assignment of ensuring security at the top-secret facility at Dimona in the Negev Desert. In the mid-1960s, when President Charles de Gaulle ended French support for the Israeli nuclear program, Blumberg sought nuclear material from other sources. His first success was the acquisition of 21 tons of heavy water from Norway. Subsequently, he obtained uranium—illegally—from the United States; the U.S. Atomic Energy Commission reported that 587 pounds of uranium was missing from a U.S. firm that Blumberg dealt with. Blumberg's AGENTS also worked with the Israeli MOSSAD to snatch 200 tons of uranium oxide that disappeared from a ship (see Operation PLUMBAT).

Ever expanding his activities, Blumberg used his operatives to steal other technology and equipment, especially in the missile field. But Blumberg's successes earned him criticism. In *Every Spy a Prince* (1990) Dan Raviv and Yossi Melman wrote:

> Among the few Israelis who knew of Lakam there were some who complained that Blumberg was far too partial to his friends, giving them information and freelance assignments that helped make them rich. There were even nasty rumors that the Lakam chief was profiting personally, although few people doubted his ascetic probity and modest lifestyle.

After Menachem Begin and his right-wing Likud Party took office in May 1977, efforts increased to dismiss Blumberg, who was linked to the Labor Party establishment. He was subjected to tighter controls but he survived for the time being. Ariel Sharon, Begin's Minister of Defense, decided that Blumberg must go because of the increasing criticism—including allegations of money laundering—and because he wanted his own man as head of the Lakam. Accordingly, in 1981 Blumberg was succeeded by RAFAEL EITAN.

Blunt, Sir Anthony Frederick

(b. 1907 d. 1983)

The FOURTH MAN in the CAMBRIDGE SPY RING, Great Britain's most notorious espionage case. The first two were GUY BURGESS and DONALD MACLEAN. HAROLD (KIM) PHILBY was often referred to as the "third man."

The son of an Anglican clergyman, Blunt first studied mathematics and philosophy at Cambridge, but then switched to art history and edited *The Venture*, a literary magazine. He invited Burgess into the Apostles, a Cambridge society, many of whose members harbored two secrets: They espoused Marxism and were HOMOSEXUALS. He claimed that it was Burgess who recruited him as a spy, but the truth about his recruitment is lost in a KGB-inspired fog of claims.

Blunt became an officer in MI5 during World War II, representing the agency at weekly meetings of the wartime JOINT INTELLIGENCE COMMITTEE. The extent of Blunt's work for the Soviets will probably never be known. Some of his actions, however, have been disclosed by both British and Soviet writers.

Working for MI5, he kept the neutral missions in London under SURVEILLANCE and was able to open their diplomatic bags and photograph the contents. He passed on to his Soviet HANDLERS what he was able to learn about the attitude of neutrals to the war, their assessment of the British war effort, and any intelligence that neutrals had received from their own sources. He betrayed the name and job of every MI5 officer. According to Tom Driberg, an MI5 AGENT who penetrated the Communist Party of Great Britain early in World War II, Blunt managed to get him expelled from the Party because Driberg was getting close to discovering communist penetration of MI5.

For a few months Blunt was the officer in charge of the Watcher Service—the women and men who carried out surveillance of foreign agents and spy suspects. Blunt gave all of them their individual weekly tasks and knew the details of each case. He reportedly analyzed surveillance techniques, recommended changes—and then passed everything about British surveillance on to the Soviets. As a result, Soviet agents could elude British WATCHERS. Blunt stopped working full-time for MI5, becoming Surveyor (curator) of the King's Pictures in April 1945, but continued to work one or two days a week for the agency.

In Aug. 1945, under the auspices of MI5, he went to Germany to select pieces of art from the home of the Duke of Brunswick that were related to British history; and, although officially discharged from MI5 in Sept. 1945, that month he flew to Rome on a three-week as-

signment to comb the Italian intelligence files. He did find items of interest to his Soviet masters on that mission. Indeed, according to KGB files described in *The Crown Jewels* by NIGEL WEST and Oleg Tsarev, Blunt delivered 1,771 documents to his Soviet handlers between 1941 and 1945, the most active period of his espionage.

After the war Blunt became an internationally renowned art expert and for many years was professor of art history at the University of London. As a friend said of him, Blunt was "profoundly English." He was deputy director of the Courtauld Institute and taught art history at Oxford, Cambridge, and London universities. He was knighted in 1956. In 1963 he spent some months in America as a visiting professor for the summer term at Pennsylvania State University.

After the defection of Maclean and Burgess, YURI MODIN, the Soviet handler who helped to engineer their escape, told Blunt that he should also defect. According to Modin, Blunt refused, saying he did not like the "living conditions" in Moscow. He also said there would be suspicions about him, but "I have decided that they have no direct evidence. I will withstand it."

Following the revelation of the espionage activities of

Sir Anthony Blunt. (UPI/BETTMAN)

Burgess, Maclean, and Philby, British COUNTERINTELLI-GENCE officers began to believe that Blunt was a MOLE. He was finally exposed by the American MICHAEL STRAIGHT, who told the FBI in 1963 that Blunt had recruited him for the Soviets at Cambridge University in the 1930s.

Blunt was repeatedly questioned by MI5's Arthur Martin and PETER WRIGHT, the latter writing in *Spycatcher* (1987) that he feared Blunt was giving only DISINFORMATION and bits of information that the Soviets wanted him to give. Wright met with Blunt almost every month for six years, slowly extracting bits of information from him. "Blunt," Wright wrote, "was one of the most elegant, charming and cultivated men I have met. He could speak five languages, and the range and depth of his knowledge was profoundly impressive."

After being given immunity from prosecution, Blunt confessed in 1964. He said he had recruited others, including JOHN CAIRNCROSS, who had worked at the GOVERNMENT CODE AND CYPHER SCHOOL as well as for the Secret Intelligence Service (MI6). Not until 1979, when Prime Minister Margaret Thatcher admitted Blunt's espionage in a statement to Parliament, was Blunt's treachery officially confirmed. He admitted, Thatcher said, that "he had been recruited by and had acted as a talent spotter for Russian intelligence before the war when he was a don at Cambridge. . . . He was stripped of his knighthood, Trinity College revoked his fellowship, and he was expelled from the British Academy."

Shunned by the class he had served and betrayed, Blunt lived a lonely, empty life until he died in March 1983 of a heart ailment.

The Soviets had assigned Blunt the CODE NAMES "Fred," "Tony," and "Van."

BND

Bundesnachrichtendienst (Federal Intelligence Agency). Formed by West Germany in 1956, the BND at first was essentially the intelligence network that had been run for Nazi Germany against the Soviet Union by Lt. Gen. REINHARD GEHLEN.

During the 1950s the U.S. CIA controlled West German intelligence through Gehlen. Gradually, he assumed control. Like the COUNTERINTELLIGENCE agency BFV, the BND had two lives: the first as an agency serving West Germany and the second serving a united Germany after 1990. During its West German period the perception of the BND was tied to Gehlen, whose acquisition by U.S. intelligence officials was ranked as a major Cold War coup. But the many critics of Gehlen questioned his effectiveness.

HEINZ FELFE, an ex-Nazi who was chief of counterintelligence against the Soviets under Gehlen, was arrested in 1961 on charges of having been a spy for the Soviets for a decade. The information came from an East German DEFECTOR in what became a numbingly frequent event: The West Germans would catch an East German AGENT working for the Soviets or for the East German secret police agency, the STASI.

Despite frequent penetrations of the BND, Helmut Kohl protected it and the BfV during his 1982–1990 tenure as Chancellor of West Germany. But Kohl reacted swiftly in 1985, when HANS JOACHIM TIEDGE, a senior counterintelligence officer in the BfV, defected to East Germany. In an attempt to stem the rivalry between the BND and the BfV, Kohl had appointed Herbert Hellenbroich, who had headed the BfV, to take over the BND. But an investigation showed that Tiedge was a chronic alcoholic and Hellenbroich knew it. Accordingly, after a month as head of the BND, Hellenbroich went into early retirement. He was replaced by Hans-Georg Wieck, a diplomat who had been the West German ambassador to the Soviet Union and to the NORTH ATLANTIC TREATY ORGANIZATION.

The suspicions and hemorrhaging of West German secrets through the BND and BfV finally ended with the reunification of Germany.

BNE

SEE BOARD OF NATIONAL ESTIMATES

Board of National Estimates

(BNE)

Group within the CIA established in 1950 to provide independent intelligence analysis, not subject to political pressure or institutional bias. The board produced overall assessments of world problems for the U.S. INTELLIGENCE COMMUNITY in the form of NATIONAL INTELLIGENCE ESTIMATES.

The DIRECTOR OF CENTRAL INTELLIGENCE appointed the board's 12 members from the retired military community, the State Department, the academic community, and the CIA. The board was abolished in 1973 with the appointment of 12 National Intelligence Officers within the CIA who were to provide specialized areas of expertise. The UNITED STATES INTELLIGENCE BOARD largely continues the functions of the BNE.

Bode Family

The Bode Family was brought from Hanover to England in 1732 to staff the SECRET OFFICE of the Post Office, which intercepted and read mail, both domestic and foreign. The understanding was that the family's children would enjoy government patronage.

Bode remained chief of the Secret Office for 52 years, until 1784. (He died two years later, at age 91.) When he retired he was succeeded by Mr. Todd, with the principal staff being Bode's three sons and Todd's nephew, Mr. Madison. Todd was employed by the Secret Office from 1751 or 1752 until 1792, and when he retired, he was succeeded by his nephew. William Bode, one of the elder Bode's sons, became chief of the Secret Office in 1799.

During the parliamentary debates into mail opening in 1844, William Bode, still head of the Secret Office, gave testimony to both the House of Commons and the House of Lords. Following the publicity, the office was abolished by Lord Palmerston, the Secretary of State for Foreign Affairs, on Jan. 1, 1847. After the staff was pensioned off, there were numerous appeals against the injustice done to the Bode Family.

Bodyguard

CODE NAME for the overall DECEPTION plan for the Allied invasion of Europe in World War II. The plan was developed to help hide the real date, time, and details of D-DAY, the June 6, 1944, Normandy landings. The code name may have been inspired by a remark made by Prime Minister Winston Churchill: "In wartime, truth is so precious that she should always be attended by a bodyguard of lies."

The complex deception plan was developed by the TWENTY COMMITTEE and coordinated by the LONDON CONTROLLING SECTION. The Twenty Committee turned German AGENTS in Britain into DOUBLE AGENTS, who transmitted more than 250 false messages about the invasion. The portion of the plan specifically related to the landings was FORTITUDE, which included a nonexistent army—the FIRST U.S. ARMY GROUP or FUSAG.

To restrict information about D-Day, beginning in April 1944 military leaves were prohibited outside the United Kingdom, civilian travel along the coast was curtailed, and all outgoing mail—including diplomatic mail—was censored. To deceive the Germans about the location of the landing, separate deception operations were carried out. In Scotland, the British arranged for radio transmissions from nonexistent divisions seemingly poised for an assault on Norway. A British actor who closely resembled Gen. Bernard L. Montgomery was sent to Gibraltar to spotlight the Mediterranean area as a possible invasion site.

The only known leak occurred in Turkey, where a German spy who was the British ambassador's valet learned the Allied code name for D-Day (Overlord) but nothing else about the invasion. (See CICERO.)

Boeckenhaupt, Staff Sgt. Herbert

U.S. Air Force sergeant assigned to the Air Force Headquarters Command in the Pentagon. In 1967 Boeckenhaupt was arrested for selling secrets to the Soviet Union, tried, convicted, and sentenced to 30 years.

Compared with those given to other servicemen spies, Boeckenhaupt's sentence was harsh, indicating that he had had a long, or at least successful, career as a spy. But little about the case was revealed at the time because the CIA was tightly guarding what is believed now to have been the source who exposed Boeckenhaupt: Maj. Gen. DIMITRI POLYAKOV, a Soviet GRU officer who spied for the United States for nearly 20 years as an AGENT-IN-PLACE.

Bokhane, Sergei

Deputy head of the GRU, Soviet MILITARY INTELLIGENCE, in Athens, Greece, who defected to the West in 1985. At the time of his defection his COVER was first secretary of the Soviet Embassy in Athens. Soon after he defected, Greek authorities arrested three Greek citizens and charged them with spying for the Soviet Union.

The Greek government handed over Bokhane's wife and daughter to Soviet officials in response to Soviet demands.

Bolo

SEE BOLSHEVIK LIQUIDATION CLUB

Bolshakov, Georgi Nikotovich

Editor of the English-language Soviet magazine *USSR* and a senior Soviet KGB officer in the United States during the early 1960s. He was a principal in the exchange of private correspondence between Premier Nikita Khrushchev and President Kennedy that began in Sept. 1961. Bolshakov was also an intermediary between White House and Soviet officials during the CUBAN MISSILE CRISIS in 1962.

On Oct. 6, 1962, Bolshakov personally delivered a verbal message from Khrushchev to Robert Kennedy, the U.S. Attorney General, the President's brother, and close adviser:

> Premier Khrushchev is concerned about the situation being built up by the United States around Cuba, and we repeat that the Soviet Union is supplying Cuba exclusively defensive weapons intended for protecting the interests of the Cuban revolution. . . .

Kennedy asked Bolshakov to repeat the verbal message and carefully wrote it down. The next day Bolshakov was invited to lunch by journalist Charles Bartlett, a close friend of President Kennedy. He told the Soviet editor that the President wanted the message from Khrushchev in writing. Bolshakov repeated the message, word for word, as he had told it to Robert Kennedy and then wrote the message down and passed it across the table to Bartlett.

Nine days later President Kennedy was shown the U-2 spyplane photos of Soviet offensive missiles in Cuba. On Oct. 24, Bartlett showed Bolshakov 20 of the U-2 photos that revealed missile sites. The photos were marked "For the President's Eyes Only."

Asked what he thought the photos showed, Bolshakov replied: "Baseball fields, perhaps?"

The next day the photos were released to the press. Bolshakov still denied that the Soviets had offensive weapons in Cuba although—unknown to him—Khrushchev had communicated to Kennedy by other means that the weapons were in fact in Cuba. That ended

Bolshakov's credibility with the Kennedys. His successor as go-between with the President was the KGB RESIDENT in Washington, ALEKSANDR FEKLISOV.

He "seemed to us all an honest fellow," Arthur M. Schlesinger, Jr., wrote of Bolshakov in *A Thousand Days* (1965).

Bolshevik Liquidation Club

Purported anti-Bolshevik dining club at the time of the Russian Revolution and Civil War. The club, also known as Bolo, was supposedly founded by master spy SIDNEY REILLY and members of MI6, the British Secret Intelligence Service, who were working to bring down the Bolshevik regime.

Bomba

High-speed calculating machine developed by Polish military intelligence before World War II to perform the calculations necessary for using a German ENIGMA encryption machine without knowledge of the specific ROTOR settings. The Bomba had portions of six Enigma machines wired into its circuits.

In July 1939 British and French code specialists met with their Polish counterparts in the Pyry Forest near Warsaw, Poland. Along with other material, the technical drawings of the Bomba were turned over to the Allies. Subsequently, in 1940 the Bomba concept was transformed into the British-built BOMBE supercalculating machines. (The term *Bombe* was also applied, apparently retroactively, to the original Polish machine.)

The Bomba was primarily the product of Polish mathematician-cryptanalyst Marian Rejewski.

Bombe

High-speed calculating machine used by the British at BLETCHLEY PARK and by the Americans in Washington, D.C., to determine German ENIGMA machine ROTOR settings. The Bombe series was developed from the Polish BOMBA.

There were several versions of these electro-mechanical (not electronic) devices, which could rapidly test the possible daily rotor settings for Enigma machines. As RONALD LEWIN explained in *Ultra Goes to War* (1978),

the order of placing the wheels [rotors] in the Enigma could be varied in sixty different ways, and for each order 17,576 possible settings for the individual wheels [rotors] had to be checked, no human brain could conceivably compete with the electro-magnetic bombe in reaching, and very consistently reaching, an answer to questions of such magnitude.

The first Bombe was assembled at Bletchley Park in early 1940. The device, 6½ feet high and 7¼ feet deep,

was a mass of lights, plugs, and wires. Additional Bombes were constructed to permit simultaneous attacks on the various CODES used by the German armed forces and the GESTAPO. From mid-1943 the U.S. MILITARY INTELLIGENCE services were operating Bombes in the United States to help break Axis codes.

The British Bombes were operated and serviced (they were continually spewing forth printed paper) by Wrens—members of the WRNS (Women's Royal Naval Service)—while U.S. Army and Navy Bombes were operated mostly by WACs (Women's Army Corps) and WAVES (Women Accepted for Volunteer Emergency Service in the Navy).

Also see COLOSSUS.

Boniface

CODE NAME used by Prime Minister Winston Churchill for ULTRA intelligence. He used it on the theory that should the enemy learn the code name they would assume that he was relying on a secret AGENT.

Book Cipher or Book Code

A book, letter, or other document that is used as a CIPHER or CODE by references to specific pages, lines, or words. Both the sender and recipient of the message must have the same document at hand.

Numbers can indicate pages, lines, words, or letters to spell out the message. Biblical texts are also used in this manner.

Book of Honor

Memorial book in the foyer of the main building of CIA headquarters in LANGLEY, Va. The book contains 86 stars, and carved into the marble facade of the foyer are 86 stars and the dedication: "in honor of those members of the Central Intelligence Agency who gave their lives in the service of their country." However, only 45 names are provided in the book. The others are unnamed because they, like their deeds and deaths, remain classified. The stars are presented in chronological order.

The memorial was sculpted by Harold Vogel in 1974.

Multiple deaths occurred in 1961 (five) and 1965 (seven), most undoubtedly related to the Vietnam War. The eight in 1983 probably related to bombings of U.S. installations in Beirut. The only large-scale U.S. military action that occurred in 1989 was the American invasion of Panama; but it is not known whether any or all of the seven stars are involved with action in Panama.

New names were unofficially revealed in 1997 when *The Washington Post* published the identities and backgrounds of five men and a woman who had been anonymous stars on the wall. The author of the article, Ted Gup, followed up with *Book of Honor* (2000), which added more details to otherwise anonymous lives. The following information comes from Gup's book and other sources. Names in boldface appear in the Book of Honor.

Douglas S. Mackiernan, the unnamed man honored by the first star. He was shot to death in China on April 29, 1950. He had been a U.S. Army meteorologist working in China during World War II. In 1947, at the age of 35, he joined the CIA, under diplomatic COVER as a State Department officer in what was then known as Tihwa, a remote town (now the city of Urumqi, Xinjiang) in northwestern China. When the State Department closed the consulate at Tihwa on Aug. 16, 1949, he was ordered to stay behind, possibly to monitor the fallout of the first Soviet atomic bomb, which would be exploded on Aug. 29. He then left the area, making a perilous trek by horse and camel to Tibet. Near the border he was shot, apparently by tense border guards on the frontier. His death was later revealed as that of a State Department "vice consul" fleeing China as the communists took power.

Robert C. Snoddy and **Norman A. Schwartz,** pilots for CIVIL AIR TRANSPORT, a CIA PROPRIETARY COMPANY. On Nov. 29, 1952, they were about to pick up a Chinese AGENT somewhere in northern China when their C-47 Dakota was shot down. They were killed and buried at the crash site. Two other CIA operatives, JOHN DOWNEY and ROBERT FECTEAU, were captured alive and remained imprisoned for two decades.

Barbara Annette Robbins, a 21-year-old CIA secretary under diplomatic cover at the U.S. Embassy in Saigon, South Vietnam. She was killed on March 30, 1965, when a car filled with explosives blew up near the embassy. Twenty-one others were killed and 186 wounded. Although Barbara Robbins' name does not appear in the Book of Honor, it does appear on Department of State plaque honoring employees killed on duty. Thus her cover lives on.

Mike Maloney, son of a covert CIA INTELLIGENCE OFFICER. Maloney, a CIA intelligence officer under cover as an employee of the U.S. Agency for International Development, was killed on Oct. 12, 1965, in the crash of an AIR AMERICA helicopter in Laos. He was assigned to the training of Laotians to secretly aid Americans trying to stop supplies from reaching the Viet Cong via the Ho Chi Minh Trail.

Richard Spicer, killed on Oct. 18, 1984, in a plane crash on a mission in support of Nicaragua contras. Also killed were two others on the flight over El Salvador. Their names—**Scott J. Vanlieshout** and **Curtis R. Wood**—appear in the Book of Honor. Spicer was not acknowledged as a CIA employee, apparently because his cover was even deeper than that of his comrades. An Air Force veteran, he became a CIA pilot who flew planes equipped with infrared sensors to detect the movement of guerrillas.

Lawrence N. Freedman, a former Green Beret in Vietnam, a trained sniper, and a Delta Force survivor of the abortive Desert One operation to rescue U.S. hostages in Iran in 1980. He apparently joined the CIA in 1990. On Dec. 23, 1992, at the age of 51, he was in Somalia as part of Operation Restore Hope—a mission to deliver food to starving Somalians—when the jeep he was driving was destroyed by a land mine. His actual paramilitary assignment was never disclosed. He was identified publicly as a civilian employee of the Department of Defense. He posthumously received the Intelligence Star for exceptional service. A letter accompanying the citation for the medal asked his wife not to "disclose the details on which the awards were based."

Thomas Willard Ray, shot to death on April 19, 1961, in Cuba. He was a casualty of the CIA–sponsored Bay of Pigs invasion. (See CUBA.) The 30-year-old pilot was killed on the ground in a firefight after his aircraft was shot down. In 1973 he was posthumously—and secretly—awarded the CIA's Distinguished Intelligence Cross for "exceptional heroism" on an "extremely hazardous mission of the highest national priority." Six years later, Cuban authorities shipped his body to the United States. The CIA never publicly acknowledged his death.

Information on the other memorialized CIA names came from Gup and other sources, but never officially from the CIA:

Leo F. Baker, Wade C. Gray, and **Riley W. Shamburger, Jr.** were, like Thomas Ray, killed during the Bay of Pigs invasion. Baker was the flight engineer in the plane piloted by Ray. Baker's body was buried in the Cristobal Colón cemetery in Havana; in his wallet was a false Social Security card identifying him under another name. Shamburger and Gray are believed to have died when their aircraft crashed off Giron Beach, Cuba. Their bodies were never found. All four men had belonged to the Alabama National Guard.

Michael M. Deuel, son of a career CIA officer, was under cover as an employee of the Agency for International Development (AID) in Laos when he was killed in the same Oct. 1966 helicopter crash that killed Mike Maloney (above). Also killed in the crash were a pilot and mechanic, both employees of Air America. **Wayne J. McNulty** is also a casualty of the "secret war" in Laos; details of his 1969 death are still not publicly known. Nor are any details available on **John W. Kearns** or **Richard M. Sisk,** whose deaths coincide with the CIA's large presence in Laos, which fell soon after Vietnam and became the Lao People's Republic in 1975; it still is one of the world's few communist nations.

Tucker Gougelmann, a paramilitary officer, was publicly acknowledged in 2001 when the CIA said he had died in Vietnam in 1976 after being interrogated and tortured for nearly a year. He had joined the CIA after retirement from the U.S. Marine Corps as a colonel. He inserted agents into Korea during the Korean War and went to Vietnam in 1962, running a covert maritime operation that included U.S. Navy Seals. He also served in Europe and Afghanistan during his 23-year CIA career. He retired from the CIA in 1972 but returned to Saigon in 1975 to try to aid a group of orphans he had supported. He missed the last flight out of Saigon, was captured, and disappeared. His name had not been added to the Wall of Honor because of a policy that only CIA employees who died in the line of duty could be so honored. This policy was changed for him because the CIA decided that he died in his torturers' hands because he had worked for the CIA.

JOHNNY MICHAEL SPANN and **Helge Boes** were killed in Afghanistan. Boes, 32, was killed on Feb. 5, 2003, during a live-fire training exercise, when a grenade detonated prematurely. Boes, a CASE OFFICER, was preparing a group for an intelligence-collection operation.

1950 ★
1951 ★ Jerome P. Ginley
1952 ★ Robert C. Snoddy
     ★ Norman A. Schwartz
1956 ★ William P. Boteler
     ★ Howard Carey
     ★ Frank G. Grace Jr.
     ★ Wilburn S. Rose
1960 ★ Chiyoki Ikeda
1961 ★ Nels L. Benson
     ★ Thomas W. Ray
     ★ Leo F. Baker
     ★ Wade C. Gray
     ★ Riley W. Shamburger, Jr.
1964 ★ John G. Merriman
1965 ★
     ★
     ★ Buster Edens
     ★ Edward Johnson
     ★ Michael M. Deuel
     ★ Mike Maloney
     ★ John W. Waltz
1966 ★ Louis A. O'Jibway
1967 ★ Walter L. Ray
1968 ★ Billy Jack Johnson
     ★ Jack W. Weeks
     ★ Wayne J. McNulty
     ★ Richard M. Sisk
1970 ★
1971 ★ Paul C. Davis
     ★ David L. Konzelman
1972 ★ John Peterson
     ★ Wilbur Murray Greene
1973 ★ Raymond L. Seaborg
     ★ John W. Kearns
1974 ★
1975 ★ William E. Bennett
     ★ RICHARD S. WELCH
1976 ★ James A. Rawlings
1977 ★ Tucker Gougelmann
1978 ★
     ★
     ★
1983 ★
     ★ Robert C. Ames
     ★
     ★
     ★
     ★
     ★
     ★
1984 ★ Scott J. Vanlieshout
     ★ Curtis R. Wood

     ★
     ★
1985 ★ WILLIAM F. BUCKLEY
1987 ★ Richard D. Krobock
1988 ★
1989 ★
     ★
     ★
     ★
     ★
     ★
     ★
1992 ★
     ★
1993 ★ Lansing H. Bennett, M.D.
     ★ Frank A. Darling
     ★
1995 ★
1996 ★ James M. Lewek
     ★ John A. Celli
     ★
1998 ★
     ★
2001 ★ JOHNNY MICHAEL SPANN
2003 ★ Helge Boes
     ★ William Francis Carlson
     ★ Christopher Glenn Mueller
     ★

Boot

British CODE NAME for joint British and U.S. CIA operation in 1953 to remove Dr. Mohammed Mossadegh as Prime Minister of Iran. The U.S. code name was AJAX.

Booth, John Wilkes

(b. 1838 d. 1865)

The assassin of President Abraham Lincoln. Booth had previously served during the American Civil War as a COURIER for the Confederate Secret Service. John Wilkes was the son of actor Junius Brutus Booth and brother of Edwin Booth, one of history's great performers of Shakespeare's *Hamlet*.

Booth originally planned to kidnap Lincoln, but after the Confederate forces surrendered on April 9, 1865, he committed himself to killing the President. After shooting Lincoln at Ford's Theater in Washington on April 14, he fled the city. Federal troops trapped him at Port Royal, Va., and he was shot and killed. His associates had planned other government assassinations, including Gen. Ulysses S. Grant, but Lincoln was their only victim slain.

Born Classified

Term applied to U.S. atomic energy information, which is automatically classified unless positive action is taken to declassify it. See RESTRICTED DATA.

Bossard, Frank

(b. 1912 d. ?)

A British spy who is believed to have been unmasked by a controversial Soviet DEFECTOR known as TOP HAT. When Top Hat told interrogators in 1965 that the Soviets were getting information on guided missiles from an AGENT in the British government, several suspects were put under surveillance.

One of the suspects was Frank Bossard, who worked in the Guided Weapons Research and Development Division of the Air Ministry. He was seen regularly retrieving a suitcase checked from the left luggage office in London's Waterloo Station. He would then check into a hotel under an assumed name, spend an hour, and return the suitcase. British Secret Intelligence Service (MI6) officers seized the suitcase and found it contained a document-copying camera and a record of Russian songs.

The GOVERNMENT COMMUNICATIONS HEADQUARTERS, which monitored Soviet radio transmissions, identified the songs as having been transmitted from a GRU transmitter in Moscow. The songs, which were broadcast over Radio Moscow at certain times, indicated what DEAD DROPS Bossard was to use to deposit film and retrieve money. "The Volga Boat Song" had a special meaning: "Cease operations immediately." But Bossard apparently did not get such a warning. He was arrested on March 15, 1965, while photographing top-secret documents. Investigators said that he had been selling secrets since 1961. On May 10, 1965, he was sentenced to 21 years in prison.

Boston Series

SEE FRITZ KOLBE

Boursicot, Bernard

French Foreign Service employee lured into spying by a male Chinese opera singer posing as a woman. Boursicot met Shi Pei Pu in 1965, soon after arriving in Beijing as a 20-year-old accountant to work in the French Embassy. Shi Pei Pu, who appeared to be an effeminate man in masculine clothing, told Boursicot that "she" was a woman brought up as a male and played both male and female roles in the Beijing Opera. They became lovers.

Boursicot left Beijing and quit the Foreign Service a few months later. In 1969, having rejoined the Foreign Service, he was reassigned to the Beijing Embassy as an archivist. Boursicot began as an unpaid volunteer spy, slipping papers from the embassy to Chinese who met him at Shi Pei Pu's apartment. Shi Pei Pu told Boursicot that his son had been born after he left. The baby, Shi Pei Pu said, had been sent to a relative near the Soviet border because in Beijing his foreign features would get him in trouble during the Cultural Revolution that was convulsing China at that time. Boursicot remained in the embassy until 1972. During that time he continued to be a spy and a lover but never saw the child.

In 1973 he returned to China for a visit and met a seven-year-old presented to him as his son, Bertrand. He again rejoined the Foreign Service in 1975, serving for a time at the French Consulate in New Orleans, La. Then he was sent to the French Embassy in Ulan Bator, Mongolia. He resumed spying, taking documents to the Chinese during his official (French) courier runs from Ulan Bator to Beijing. The romance had cooled somewhat—Boursicot, a bisexual, had had several other lovers by then. But he began making arrangements for Shi Pei Pu and the boy to come to France, where he hoped to adopt the boy.

Shi Pei Pu finally came to Paris in 1983 as an opera singer. By then officers of DST, the French agency responsible for internal security, had discovered Boursicot's spying. They arrested him, charging him with delivering information to AGENTS of a foreign power. When they arrested Shi Pei Pu as an accomplice, they did not know whether to treat the prisoner as a male or a female. A judge ordered a physical examination, which determined that he was a man. By some genital contortions, Shi Pei Pu explained, he could convince a casual viewer that he was a woman. "Of course, one could not look too closely," Joyce Wadler wrote in *Liaison* (1993). "It was only illusion."

Shi Pei Pu had bought Bertrand as a baby from a family of Uighurs (Turkic-speaking, Caucasian Muslims who inhabit northwest China).

At their trial in May 1986, Boursicot's lawyer scoffed at the results of his feeble espionage. "This case," the lawyer said, "is absolutely at the bottom of the ladder in the spying world."

Each defendant was sentenced to six years in prison. Shi Pei Pu was pardoned in April 1987, Boursicot the following August. The story became famous through the play *M. Butterfly*, by David Henry Hwang.

Bowie, Walter

(b. 1831 d. 1864)

Confederate spy during the American Civil War. A Maryland lawyer drawn to the Confederacy by strong southern sympathies, he spied as "Wat Bowie." After he made several successful spying trips to Washington, D.C., an informer unmasked him in 1862. Arrested, convicted, and facing execution, he escaped from a Washington prison and continued spying. Cornered sometime later in a house, he slipped away in the guise of a slave girl.

Bowie next became one of Mosby's Rangers, guerrillas who marauded behind federal lines under the command of John Singleton Mosby. Federal troops sometimes treated Mosby's men as spies, hanging seven of them without trial. Bowie escaped that fate, but he was killed in 1864 during a futile attempt to kidnap the Governor of Maryland.

Boxers

Western name for members of a secret Chinese organization called *Yi He Tuan* (the Society of Harmonious Fists), which gathered intelligence on Westerners in China. The inspiration for such secret societies—distrust of foreigners—has endured into modern times, influencing the intelligence agencies of both the Chinese Nationalists and the People's Republic of China.

Boxers were rebels who promised to fight with "fists of justice" to overthrow the Manchu Dynasty and drive out the "long-nosed devils" (Westerners), who, according to the Boxers, were taking over China with the acquiescence of the Manchus. Only an anti-foreign organization, the Boxers believed, could safely provide China with the secret service the nation needed.

Under the slogan "protect the country, destroy the foreigner," in 1899 the Boxers began persecuting Chinese Christians and using spies and assassins to spread terror through much of China. In June 1900 the dowager empress submitted to Boxer power and ordered all foreigners killed. An international military force seized Peking, the Chinese capital, driving out the court and defeating the Boxers.

Boyce, Christopher

(b. 1953)

American who, with ANDREW D. LEE, sold SATELLITE secrets to the Soviets. Boyce was released from prison in March 2003 after serving more than 25 years. He was placed on parole until 2046, which would have been his release date had he not been set free.

Sen. Daniel P. Moynihan, assessing the damage that Boyce and Lee had done, said in 1981 that the Soviets had learned enough to make U.S. satellites "temporarily, at least, useless" because "the Soviets could block them." The "fear that that would happen, had happened, permeated the Senate and, as much as any one thing, was responsible for the failure of the SALT [Strategic Arms Limitation Talks] treaty."

Boyce, a college dropout, was hired in 1975 by TRW of Redondo Beach, Calif., a high-technology contractor working on U.S. spy satellites, then one of the most secret U.S. defense programs. Boyce, as the son and nephew of former FBI agents, got his job through his father, who knew a former FBI colleague at TRW. Boyce worked at a sensitive post. Despite his youth and lack of experience, he was given TOP SECRET clearances that allowed him to handle highly classified documents. He had access to TRW's "black vault," the seemingly secure communications facility for the transmitting of coded satellite information from TRW to the headquarters of the CIA in LANGLEY, Va.

Soon after Boyce joined TRW he began plotting with Lee, a longtime friend, to sell the satellite and CRYPTOLOGY secrets that he worked with to the Soviet Union. Boyce sent Lee to Mexico City to make contact with the KGB in the Soviet Embassy. For two years Boyce photographed documents and gave the films to Lee, who passed them on to KGB INTELLIGENCE OFFICERS in Mexico City and VIENNA. Boyce so impressed his KGB HANDLER that he urged him to return to college and enter either the

CIA or the State Department and become a career spy. He was promised Soviet citizenship at the end of his career.

Lee's espionage was revealed by a fluke. Mexican police saw him throw something onto the grounds of the Soviet Embassy in Mexico City. While police were questioning him, Lee hailed a U.S. diplomat, who had been to the embassy on business, and asked him for help. That U.S. diplomat called another, who accompanied Lee to police headquarters, where authorities found that he was carrying an envelope full of film strips. The police gave prints of the film to U.S. officials because the photos were of U.S. documents marked "Top Secret." (Lee was paroled in 1998.)

When FBI agents questioned Lee, he implicated Boyce. The FBI arrested Boyce on the campus of the University of California at Riverside, where he was enrolled in a Chinese studies program. At first the pair claimed that they were only fooling the Soviets by peddling worthless documents. Then Boyce claimed that he had acted out of his disenchantment with the United States because of the Vietnam War and WATERGATE. He also said he was shocked at what he learned about CIA operations.

But at their trials the government proved that they had been motivated by greed, selling government secrets for more than $70,000. Lee spent much of his share to support his drug habit. Both men were convicted of espionage. Boyce was sentenced to 40 years and Lee to life imprisonment. "What he did," a CIA intelligence officer said of Boyce, "amounted to a national calamity." Among the secrets he revealed was information about how the United States monitored Soviet missile tests. Knowing this, the Soviets changed their telemetry, thwarting the U.S. monitors.

The two young men became celebrity spies, made famous by the best-selling book *The Falcon and the Snowman* (1979), by Robert Lindsey. *Falcon* referred to Boyce's hawking hobby and *Snowman* referred to Lee's drug use. The book was later made into a movie of the same title.

In Feb. 1980 Boyce escaped from the federal prison at Lompoc, Calif. by cutting through a 10-foot chain-link fence with a pair of wire cutters. He moved about the Northwest, robbing banks and planning to escape to the Soviet Union. While U.S. marshals followed tips that he was in Costa Rica, Australia, Mexico, and South Africa, Boyce bought a 29-foot salmon trawler in Port Angeles, Wash., and hoped to sail to the Bering Strait and reach Soviet territory, Big Diomede Island. Learning how dangerous that voyage would be, he decided to fly. He was taking flying lessons and had learned to solo when U.S. marshals and FBI agents found him in Port Angeles in Aug. 1981.

For his escape, a judge added three years to his 40-year sentence. For robbing 17 banks in Idaho, Montana, and Washington, he received 25 more years.

Testifying in April 1985 before a Senate committee investigating security among defense contractors, Boyce told of drinking schnapps and banana daiquiris in the black vault with other TRW employees. One of them pasted the photo of a monkey on his security badge and still got into top-secret TRW offices.

Boyd, Belle

(b. 1844 d. 1900)

One of several female Confederate AGENTS of the American Civil War. Isabelle Boyd, born in Martinsburg, W. Va., was a beautiful young woman known as Belle. She graduated from Mount Washington Female College in Baltimore, Md., in 1860.

When Virginia seceded from the Union in 1861, Belle's father joined the Confederate Army, serving under Maj. Gen. Thomas (Stonewall) Jackson. She later claimed that when Union solders invaded her home, she fatally shot one. At the urging of a Confederate INTELLIGENCE OFFICER, she began to spy for the South.

Arrested twice and interrogated once by ALLAN PINKERTON, the Union's COUNTERINTELLIGENCE expert, beautiful Belle Boyd talked her way out of formal charges and was released both times.

Boyd continued her espionage even though she was now a marked woman. While staying in a hotel in Front Royal, Va., she overheard Union officers quartered there discussing military plans. She slipped out of the hotel and made her way through Union lines to tell Jackson's intelligence officer that Front Royal, a vital crossroads in the Shenandoah Valley, was undergarrisoned. Jackson wrote her a personal note of thanks.

Arrested in 1863 by LAFAYETTE BAKER, Pinkerton's successor, she was held for a month in a Washington, D.C., prison. After being released in an exchange of prisoners, she sailed for England on board a Confederate ship in the spring of 1864. When the blockade runner was captured by a Union ship, she was again taken prisoner, and this time condemned to death. But a Union officer, Samuel Hardinge, fell in love with her, helped her gain her freedom, and married her. He died a few months later.

After the war, she went on stage in London and New York, dramatizing her life as a spy. She wrote *Belle Boyd in Camp and Prison* (1865), a romanticized version of her adventures.

Bozart, James F.

Newspaper boy for *The Brooklyn Eagle*, a New York newspaper, who found among his coins a hollowed-out 1948 Jefferson nickel containing microfilm. The coin, inadvertently given to Bozart by RUDOLF ABEL on June 22, 1953, helped the FBI to track down and arrest Abel.

B.P.

SEE BLETCHLEY PARK

Bracy, Cpl. Arnold

U.S. Marine arrested and later exonerated in the frenzied NAVAL INVESTIGATIVE SERVICE (NIS) probe of the 1987 "SEX-for-secrets" scandal at the U.S. Embassy in Moscow. Bracy was one of 18 Marine embassy guards to face disciplinary charges following claims that some Marines had helped Soviets gain entry to secret facilities in the embassy. Bracy was accused of having sex with a Soviet woman who served as a cook for a U.S. diplomat. Bracy's lawyer blamed his arrest on "shabby and unethical" work by NIS investigators.

Also see CLAYTON LONETREE.

Brandon

CODE NAME for British Special Operations Executive (SOE) activities in North Africa in support of Operation Torch, the Anglo-American landings in Nov. 1942.

Brass Knob

CODE NAME for U.S. low-level RECONNAISSANCE flights over Cuba in Oct. 1962. They were flown by photo variants of the Navy-Marine Corps F8U CRUSADER and Air Force RF-101 VOODOO aircraft.

Also see CUBAN MISSILE CRISIS.

Brewster, Caleb

(b. 1747 d. 1827)

Patriot SECRET AGENT during the American Revolution. Brewster, sailing a small boat, attacked British shipping in Long Island Sound at the beginning of the war. Maj. BENJAMIN TALLMADGE, the chief spy HANDLER for Gen. GEORGE WASHINGTON, asked Brewster to become a member of what became the CULPER RING.

The ring collected intelligence about the British forces occupying New York City and passed it on to Tallmadge in Connecticut. A coded message went from ROBERT TOWNSEND in New York City to Austin Roe, a tavern keeper from Setauket, Long Island, who used his travels to New York for supplies as a COVER for his role of COURIER. Roe put the message in a DEAD DROP, such as a hollow tree trunk, on the Setauket farm of ABRAHAM WOODHULL.

Brewster plucked the message from the dead drop and sailed across Long Island Sound to Fairfield, Conn., where Tallmadge or another INTELLIGENCE OFFICER would get the message and take it to Washington's headquarters. Brewster's boats were known in Fairfield as the "spy boats." This open secret, however, never reached British agents.

There was one close call. One night in Oct. 1781, Brewster was having supper in Fairfield when a man who called himself Patrick Walker chatted with him. Walker, a

British spy posing as a Patriot, got Brewster talking about American plans. But, possibly suspecting the stranger, Brewster did not reveal anything about the Culper Ring.

Bride

Early British CODE NAME for the VENONA codebreaking project. It was succeeded by Drug and then Venona.

Brigade 2056

Cuban exile unit trained by the CIA for the ill-fated Bay of Pigs invasion in 1961. (See CUBA.) The brigade was trained mainly in Guatemala by CIA officers and paramilitary experts.

The invasion force was designated Brigade 2056, from the number of a soldier—56—who was killed during training; the prefix 20 was added to confuse Cuban intelligence about the size and number of invading units.

Britain

SEE ENGLAND-GREAT BRITAIN-UNITED KINGDOM

British Security Co-ordination

(BSC)

COVER organization set up in New York City by the British Secret Intelligence Service (MI6) in May 1940. The office, established for intelligence and propaganda purposes, was headed by WILLIAM STEPHENSON, a Canadian working for MI6. Although the British and Americans were cooperating at the Prime Minister–President level at that time, the arrival of "British spies" in the United States infuriated J. EDGAR HOOVER, director of the FBI, and the U.S. State Department.

The British agency was registered with the State Department as a foreign entity. It was openly known as the British Passport Control Office and operated out of offices in Rockefeller Center.

Stephenson, responding to FBI hostility toward the organization, once asked, "Does J. Edgar think he's fighting on Bunker Hill against us Redcoats?" Stephenson and Hoover agreed that the British would not hire Americans, but they did. The Americans were given British identification numbers in a series beginning with 48, presumably for the 48 states.

Broadway

Slang for the headquarters of the British Secret Intelligence Service (MI6) from 1924 to 1966. The GOVERNMENT CODE AND CYPHER SCHOOL was also located there in the 1920s and 1930s.

The term originated from the headquarters' location at No. 54 Broadway, opposite St. James's Park and adjacent to QUEEN ANNE'S GATE in London. The MI6 office had the COVER of the Passport Control Office.

HAROLD (KIM) PHILBY, a MOLE in British intelligence, described the Broadway office as "a dingy building, a warren of wooden partitions and frosted glass windows," served by an "ancient lift."

Bronson, Staff Sgt. [P]

Pseudonym of a U.S. Air Force sergeant, formerly assigned to the 6950th Electronics Security Squadron in England. He had been spying for the GRU for several years when he became the subject of an investigation in 1978. To protect sensitive sources, Bronson was not prosecuted but instead administratively discharged from the service.

Bronze Godess

Slang for British copies of German ENIGMA CIPHER machines.

Brossolete, Pierre

(b. 1903 d. 1944)

French AGENT who spied against the Germans in World War II. A Parisian journalist, he refused to write when the Germans conquered France in May 1940 and took control of the press and radio. He worked with the French Resistance from 1940 to 1942 and then made his way to London, where he worked for Gen. Charles de Gaulle's BCRA and Britain's SOE (Special Operations Executive).

He twice made a dangerous passage to Paris. An avowed socialist, he was respected by both left and right and gave valuable counsel in uniting Resistance groups. On his second mission he was caught by the GESTAPO. Rather than risk giving Resistance secrets under interrogation, he leaped to his death while in custody.

Browder, Earl R.

(b. 1891 d. 1973)

An American communist and CPUSA leader who was an AGENT for Soviet intelligence. His work for the NKVD and the GRU, long suspected, was publicly confirmed with the release of the VENONA intercepts of Soviet intelligence traffic.

In a 1938 message to the NKVD, for example, Browder asked that his sister, Marguerite (also known as Margaret), be transferred to the United States from Germany, where she was a radio operator and a member of an extensive Soviet spy apparatus. Because of his "increasing involvement in national political affairs and growing connections in Washington political circles," his message said, "it might become dangerous to this political work if hostile circles in America should by any means obtain knowledge of my sister's work." The NKVD accepted Browder's request and returned Marguerite to the United States. Browder's brother Bill also worked for the NKVD.

Browder, whose family traced its American roots to the mid-18th century, was general secretary of the CPUSA. He was the party's candidate for President in 1936 and 1940.

Browder, who opposed U.S. entry into World War I, was tried and convicted of violating federal law by refusing to register for the draft. He served a short prison sentence. An indication of Browder's political power came in 1933 when he was pardoned by newly elected President Franklin D. Roosevelt. By then he was head of the CPUSA, a post he held from 1929 to 1944. (Browder broke with Roosevelt in 1939 after the President condemned the Nazi-Soviet Nonaggression Pact.)

In 1926 he married a Russian, Raissa Berkman, and went to China three years later as the general secretary of the Pan-Pacific Trade Union Secretariat. When he returned to the United States in 1929 he began his public leadership of the CPUSA while carrying on his clandestine work for Soviet intelligence.

Browder's work as a spymaster was demonstrated in a July 1944 message sent to Moscow by the NKVD. It said that he had met with an agent who worked as the secretary to a prominent journalist. Browder warned that she should be withdrawn from espionage work because she was nervous and ill.

Browder was expelled from the CPUSA as a deviationist in 1946 after he urged Soviet cooperation with the West.

His CRYPTONYM was "Joseph Dixon," and in Venona messages he was referred to as "Helmsman."

Brown, Joseph G.

Former U.S. airman who pleaded guilty in April 1993 to conspiring to commit espionage by delivering secret CIA documents to a Philippine government official. He was sentenced to almost six years in prison.

The arrest of Brown by the FBI ended an investigation that had begun in April 1991 after an internal CIA inquiry determined that Virginia Jean Baynes, a CIA employee in the U.S. Embassy in Manila, had passed classified documents to Brown. Baynes had met Brown at a karate class that he had taught.

The FBI said that the documents included CIA documents on TERRORIST INTELLIGENCE in Iraq during the Persian Gulf War of 1991 and assassination plots by a Philippine insurgent group. Baynes pleaded guilty to espionage in May 1992, and served a 41-month prison term.

Brown, Petty Officer 3rd Class Russell P.

An electronics warfare technician on board the U.S. aircraft carrier *Midway*, Brown conspired with a fellow crewman, Navy airman recruit James R. Wilmoth, by passing him material about U.S. electronic warfare equipment and tactics. Brown was arrested for conspiracy to commit espionage and sentenced by court-martial to 10 years' hard labor. Wilmoth, who tried to sell classified materials obtained from Brown to a Soviet agent in Japan, was court-martialed and in Oct. 1989 was sentenced to 35 years in prison.

Bruno

CODE NAME for the French Cinquième Bureau, the pre-World War II CRYPTANALYSIS center in the Château de Vignobles in Gretz. When the Poles gave copies of the German ENIGMA machine to the French, it was taken to Bruno, which was also sometimes known as PC Bruno.

About 70 people, including 48 Frenchmen, 15 Poles, and 7 Spaniards, worked at Bruno. The Spaniards, codenamed Team D, were left-wingers and probably communists who had fled Spain after the Spanish Civil War. Although the Poles distrusted them, the Spaniards were particularly valuable in cracking Spanish and Italian codes.

Through a teletype system run by a British liaison officer, Bruno was connected with the British Expeditionary Force and BLETCHLEY PARK, the codebreaking facility in Britain.

Also see GUSTAVE BERTRAND.

BRUSA Agreement

British–United States Agreement signed on May 17, 1943, as a formal pact for the exchange of COMMUNICATIONS INTELLIGENCE (COMINT) information between the two countries, at the time at war with Germany and Japan. "The significance of the pact was monumental. It established for the first time intimate cooperation on COMINT of the highest level. It provided for exchange of personnel, joint regulations for the handling of the supersensitive material, and methods of distribution," wrote JAMES BAMFORD in *The Puzzle Palace* (1982).

Codebreakers of the U.S. Army, U.S. Navy, and the British GOVERNMENT CODE AND CYPHER SCHOOL had exchanged COMINT information and CIPHER machines since late 1941. BRUSA imposed complete collaboration at every level of codebreaking activities, as well as forcing both nations to adopt similar CODE WORDS, codebreaking priorities, and procedures for handling ULTRA and PURPLE material.

The codebreaking agencies of Australia and Canada were quickly integrated into the BRUSA protocols. (See CENTRAL BUREAU.)

The success of BRUSA led to the follow-on UKUSA AGREEMENT of 1947.

Brush Contact

A brief, public, but discreet meeting of an AGENT and his HANDLER or another INTELLIGENCE OFFICER in which information, documents, or funds are exchanged. There is no conversation between the two.

To the untrained observer, such a meeting (also called a brief encounter or meeting) would appear accidental, between two persons who are unknown to each other.

BSC

SEE BRITISH SECURITY CO-ORDINATION

BTLC

Bureau Technique de Liaison et de Coordination (Technical Bureau for Liaison and Coordination). The BTLC was created in 1948 when thousands of Indochinese emigrated to France. The BTLC operated under the Colonial Ministry, which had a security service both in France and in French colonies.

The ministry's largest agency was *Service de Liaison avec les Originaires des Territoires Français d'Outre-mer* (SLOTFOM), the service for liaison between France and its overseas territories. BTLC was formed to coordinate primarily with SLOTFOM in response to French officials' fears of espionage, sabotage, and subversion by communist AGENTS infiltrated into France from Indochina and French North Africa.

Adding another agency to the welter of French intelligence services increased confusion about the conduct of COUNTERINTELLIGENCE among French citizens and noncitizens in cities in France (known as "metropolitan France," since all colonies were considered parts of France). The émigrés were already under scrutiny by the SÛRETÉ GÉNÉRALE, the DEUXIÈME BUREAU, and the SDECE.

As the agencies fought for turf in France and in the colonies, in 1949 the BTLC even tried to investigate the French government itself for "leaks" to communists. (The communist Vietminh radio had broadcast excerpts from a secret French Army report on policy in Indochina.)

By 1951 SLOTFORM had virtually disappeared under the bureaucratic pressure of the new agency, BTLC, which became the paramount security service of the Colonial Ministry. The power of the ministry and BTLC drastically declined after French withdrawal from Indochina and the creation of Algeria and Morocco as independent states.

Buchan, John

(b. 1875 d. 1940)

Scots author and INTELLIGENCE OFFICER. Buchan wrote extensively on subjects ranging from travel to religion, but he is remembered most for his novels of adventure and espionage.

In his 1915 spy thriller, *The Thirty-Nine Steps*, Richard Hannay saves Britain by keeping secrets from the Germans, which were to be carried out by a stage performer with an incredible memory. The character of Hannay, who stumbles into a career as a secret agent and thwarts the Germans in *Greenmantle* (1916) and *Mr. Standfast* (1919), was based on a British Army officer, Gen. Sir Edmund Ironside, a hero in both the Boer War and World War I, and later Chief of the Imperial General Staff.

Soon after *The Thirty-Nine Steps* was published, Buchan went to France, first as a war correspondent and then as an officer in the Intelligence Corps. Later, as director of British wartime propaganda, he covertly worked with MI6 and British NAVAL INTELLIGENCE to smuggle propaganda publications into Europe.

Buchan drew much of the atmosphere in *Greenmantle* from his knowledge of a secret mission conducted by Capt. THOMAS E. LAWRENCE ("Lawrence of Arabia") and Aubrey Herbert, a friend from Buchan's Oxford days. Herbert became Sandy Arbuthnot in *Greenmantle* and in *The Three Hostages* (1924).

Raised to the peerage in 1935 as the first Baron Tweedsmuir of Elsfield, Buchan was later appointed Governor General of Canada.

Buchmann, Airman Edward O.

A putative spy who in 1985, while a student at the 3463rd Munitions and Weapons Maintenance Training Squadron at Lowry Air Force Base, Colo., contacted East Germans, and subsequently Soviets, and offered to spy. Agents of the Air Force's Office of Special Investigation and FBI agents teamed up to run a sting operation against Buchmann. Arrested and court-martialed, he was sentenced to 30 months' confinement and a dishonorable discharge.

Bucher, Comdr. Lloyd M.

(b. 1928 d. 2004)

Commanding officer of U.S. intelligence ship PUEBLO when she was captured by North Korean forces in international waters off the coast of North Korea on Jan. 23, 1968. Bucher, a submarine officer who had commanded the *Pueblo* since her commissioning in May 1967, was imprisoned with the *Pueblo* crew from the day of the ship's capture until Dec. 23, 1968.

Bucher lived in Boys Town, Neb., as a youth and enlisted in the Navy in 1945 at the age of 17. After being released from active duty, he obtained a commission through the Navy's college reserve officer program and was recalled to active duty after graduation in 1953. He served on a surface ship, submarines, and on fleet staffs prior to being given command of the *Pueblo*.

The first U.S. Navy officer to surrender a U.S. naval ship in more than 160 years, Bucher was recommended for court-martial by a naval court of inquiry. But Secretary of the Navy John H. Chafee overruled the recommendation, saying that the ship's crew "have suffered enough." From 1969 to 1971 Bucher was on the staff of the Naval Postgraduate School. He then served as chief staff officer to Commander Mine Flotilla 1 until his retirement in 1973.

He was sharply criticized not only for giving up his ship but also for allowing CRYPTOMATERIAL to fall into North Korean and, ultimately, Soviet hands. In his defense he claimed that his request for a modern emergency destruction system had been turned down; he said he spent $1,300 from the captain's fund for crew comfort on a commercial incinerator that was inadequate.

Bucher also questioned the failure of the Navy to respond to his distress calls. "I never styled myself a hero," he wrote in 1989. "The story of the *Pueblo* in a nutshell is one of a naval officer, his crew, and his ship, sent to do a job; things went bad, and the Navy abandoned them." With Mark Rosovich he wrote *Bucher: My Story* (1970).

Buckley, William

(b. 1928 d. 1985)

CIA station chief in Beirut and the CIA's top counterterrorism expert. He was kidnapped in Beirut by the Islamic Jihad on March 16, 1984. Interrogated and tortured for more than a year, he was finally murdered in June 1985. His kidnappers said his death was in revenge for an Israeli attack on PLO facilities in Beirut.

Buckley twice enlisted in the U.S. Army—in June 1945, just before World War II ended, and in June 1951, when he was commissioned a second lieutenant and fought in the Korean War. Twice wounded, he won a Silver Star for his singlehanded capture of a North Korean machine gun nest.

His CIA career began in 1954, while he was still in the Army. At CIA headquarters in LANGLEY, Va., he was given physical and psychological tests then used for recruiting AGENTS for COVERT ACTIONS and the Army became his CIA COVER. He entered the Army's new special warfare school at Fort Bragg, N.C., and later learned wiretap skills at FORT MEADE, Md., where the CIA often used an Army reserve unit that specialized in intercept operations.

He finally began openly working for the CIA at Langley, analyzing the BERLIN TUNNEL, a CIA-British intelligence project that was not producing the expected intelligence. Frustrated by the office work, Buckley asked for a transfer to the field.

He was sent to Florida to train Cuban exiles who were to invade their homeland in the 1961 debacle known as the Bay of Pigs. Next came a return to Fort Bragg, where he became one of the few CIA men to undergo Green Beret training. Shipped off to Vietnam, he worked with South Vietnamese INTELLIGENCE OFFICERS to plan attacks against the Vietcong in the central highlands and to thwart North Vietnamese and Soviet intelligence operations in Laos. He led dozens of dangerous missions into Laos and North Vietnam and was an operative in the STUDIES AND OBSERVATION GROUP (SOG), which sent patrols deep into enemy territory. Veterans of SOG also link him to Operation PHOENIX, the CIA program for assassinating Vietcong leaders. (See VIETNAM.)

By 1973, Buckley was back in Langley. He was later sent to Bonn, West Germany, and then to Syria under diplomatic cover. But he was BURNED by the Syrian government and had to be recalled as an identified intelligence officer. He also served briefly in Egypt and Pakistan.

After working as a CIA adviser on the ill-fated 1979 attempt to rescue U.S. hostages in Iran, Buckley trained Army anti-terrorist teams and set up a CIA counterterrorism office. Around that time, when he was apparently in official retirement, he was called back to Langley full time by WILLIAM J. CASEY, who had heard enough about Buckley to want him at hand. After a while Casey reluctantly sent Buckley back into the field, this time to Egypt, where he trained Egyptian security forces, including President Anwar Sadat's bodyguards. On Oct. 6, 1981, Sadat was assassinated, and 60 days later Buckley, highly critical of the lack of protection given Sadat, was back in Langley.

Casey, alarmed about the lack of seasoned officers available for Middle East duty, personally asked Buckley to return to Lebanon, even though he would be known there. Buckley stayed in Lebanon until PLO forces evacuated Beirut in Aug. 1982. Casey next asked Buckley to establish an anti-terrorist policy for the Reagan administration.

In March 1983 a terrorist detonated a bomb outside the U.S. Embassy in Beirut, killing 16 Americans, including Robert Ames, chief of the CIA Near East Division. Casey ordered Buckley back to Beirut as CIA station chief to replace Ames, his thin cover being a political analyst for the U.S. State Department.

Buckley worked desperately to try to infiltrate terrorist organizations in Lebanon. After a terrorist blew up the U.S. Marine barracks in Beirut on Oct. 23, killing 241 servicemen, Buckley worked even harder. Then, on March 16, 1984, as he drove the half mile from his apartment to the British compound that also served as headquarters for American interests in Lebanon, he was kidnapped. His kidnappers stopped his car, swiftly dragged him into their vehicle, and sped off.

Casey demanded that Buckley be found. Agents of Army Intelligence and the FBI were sent to Beirut. SATELLITES were used to get high-resolution photographs of possible terrorist hideouts. But he was not found. U.S. intelligence officials believe that he was taken from Beirut to the Bekaa Valley and then into Syria. Tortured and questioned incessantly, he was in failing health when, fearing he would die in their hands, his abductors took him to Tehran for medical treatment. He died there in June 1985. (See IRAN-CONTRA AFFAIR.)

His skeletal remains, found in a plastic bag near Beirut Airport in Dec. 1991, were buried in Arlington Cemetery with full military honors.

Buffalo Hunter

Name given to U.S. unmanned RECONNAISSANCE aircraft or drones flown over North Vietnam during the 1960s and early 1970s to collect TACTICAL INTELLIGENCE and STRATEGIC INTELLIGENCE. These unmanned aircraft were launched from airborne DC-130 Hercules cargo aircraft that remained over friendly territory; after their photo flight, the drones few back to a location where they could be landed and their film recovered; the drones were reusable.

At the peak of the Buffalo Hunter operations, the drones made 30 to 40 flights per month over North Vietnam and adjacent areas of Indochina controlled by communist forces.

Also see UNMANNED AERIAL VEHICLES.

Buffalo Slaughter

CODE WORD assigned by the FBI to the investigation of a U.S. government scientist who revealed U.S. submarine quieting secrets to the Soviet Union. Not publicly identified, the scientist worked at the National Engineering Laboratory at Arco, Idaho, where Navy nuclear propulsion systems are tested and reactor operators are trained.

In Dec. 1978 the scientist walked into the Soviet Embassy in Ottawa, Canada, and handed over secrets related to U.S. quieting technology. His espionage followed the revelations almost a decade earlier to the Soviets by JOHN WALKER that it was relatively easy for the United States to detect Soviet submarines because of their high noise levels (see SOUND SURVEILLANCE SYSTEM).

While details of the Buffalo Slaughter investigation are still highly classified—even the name of the scientist—it appears likely that the U.S. technologies he sold included how reactor noises are suppressed through natural convection of steam, isolating machinery on internal "rafts," and other features.

As a result of those spy efforts and their normal submarine development efforts, about 1990 the Soviets began putting to sea submarines of the improved Akula (Project 971) class, which were as quiet as the latest U.S. submarines.

The scientist was not prosecuted in return for revealing precisely what he told the Soviets.

Bug

(1) Concealed listening device or other equipment used in audio SURVEILLANCE. Modern technology permits some communications and electronic equipment to be monitored from remote sites (such as outside of a building), although usually line-of-sight is required for the monitoring device. TEMPEST is one term for protective equipment and procedures against such external monitoring.

(2) To install such a device; the term *bugged* refers to a room or object that contains a concealed listening device.

Bundesnachrichtendienst

SEE BND

Bunke, Haidee Tamara

(b. ? d. 1967)

Soviet AGENT who was the mistress of Cuban revolutionary Che Guevara.

"Tania" Bunke is believed to have betrayed Guevara to his killers by leaking a map showing his jungle headquarters. Guevara, who helped Fidel Castro take over CUBA, was organizing guerrilla movements in several Latin American countries. Although the Soviets supported Castro and anti-American guerrilla warfare, they did not trust Guevara. Bunke, who became his mistress, was assigned by the Soviets to spy on him.

In April 1967, U.S.-trained Bolivian rangers ambushed Bunke, Guevara, and other guerrillas in a Bolivian jungle. She was pregnant when she was killed.

Guevara had been marked for death by the CIA in 1960, at the time of the planning of the U.S.-backed Bay of Pigs invasion. But the CIA was not involved in Guevara's death in 1967, for analysts correctly believed that his death would make a martyr of him. Intelligence specialists agree that the killing of Guevara was ordered by the President of Bolivia, René Barrientos. Whether Bunke was also to be killed is not known. Analysts point out that Bunke, initially hailed as a revolutionary heroine, was suddenly dropped by Castro propagandists.

Burchett, Wilfred

(b. 1911 d. 1983)

Australian journalist accused of spying for the Soviet Union.

On Sept. 3, 1945, Burchett managed to get into Hiroshima and write, for *The London Daily Express*, the first story describing the radiation that followed the explosion of the world's first atomic bomb. He was denounced by U.S. occupation authorities as "falling victim to Japanese propaganda" and was nearly expelled from Japan. The incident began Burchett's long history of confrontation with U.S. authorities.

In 1951, Burchett went to China and then to Korea, writing Asian news for *Ce Soir*, a left-wing Paris newspaper. An admitted communist sympathizer, Burchett covered the Korean War from North Korea and was considered an anti-American correspondent. One of his dispatches asserted that the United States was using germ warfare in Korea; the story was denounced by U.S. spokesmen. When the peace talks began, many Western journalists used him as a source because of his close connection with the North Korean-Chinese delegation. U.S. authorities warned correspondents not to accept information from Burchett, but to no avail.

Claims that Burchett had Soviet connections began after the Korean War, when former U.S. prisoners of war said he had taken part in the "brainwashing" that forced them to make anti-American confessions or sign petitions urging the United States to end the war.

Many Americans believed that North Korean and

Chinese interrogators somehow used diabolical brain-washing techniques; that seemed the only possible explanation for the fact that about 70 percent of U.S. prisoners confessed or signed petitions. In 1953 ALLEN W. DULLES, the DIRECTOR OF CENTRAL INTELLIGENCE, ordered a study of communist brainwashing.

In 1963 Burchett began reporting on Vietnam for the British Communist Party's *Morning Star*, the U.S. left-wing *National Guardian*, and Japanese publications. He worked out of Hanoi, writing pro-Vietcong dispatches and living as an honored guest of the communist regime. His anti-American reporting, he said, inspired U.S. air strikes on the camps he stayed in as he traveled with the Vietcong.

In 1972, when President Nixon visited China, he was introduced to Burchett by Premier Zhou Enlai. "Ah, yes," Nixon said, shaking hands with Burchett, "You're an Australian correspondent. I've heard of you."

Burchett once said that the CIA had offered him $100,000 to spy for the United States during the Korean War. A DEFECTOR from the KGB reportedly named him as a Soviet spy, but no espionage case was ever made against him.

Bureau Central de Renseignments et d'Action

SEE BCRA

Bureau of Military Information

Intelligence organization of the Union Army during the U.S. Civil War. Maj. Gen. Joseph Hooker, as commander of the Army of the Potomac, early in 1863 ordered Col. GEORGE H. SHARPE, his deputy provost marshal, to create a "secret service" to gather TACTICAL INTELLIGENCE. Sharpe set up what he called the Bureau of Military Information, which soon had AGENTS—sometimes called scouts—working behind Confederate lines.

The bureau developed extremely accurate ORDER OF BATTLE information on Confederate forces and regularly produced intelligence reports based on information collected not only from agents but also from prisoners of war, refugees, Southern newspapers, and BALLOON observations.

Bureau agents discovered a planned Confederate thrust across the Potomac River into Maryland. Intelligence provided by the agents enabled Union forces to maneuver and force a change in Confederate plans, setting up what became the battle of Gettysburg, the turning point in the Civil War.

In March 1864, when Gen. Ulysses S. Grant became commander of the Union Army, he promoted Sharpe to brevet brigadier general and made the bureau an integral part of his headquarters. It was dissolved when the Civil War ended. Although the bureau gave intelligence a new, professional status during the war, not until the 20th century would there be another U.S. Army organization comparable to the bureau.

Bureau of Intelligence and Research

(INR)

U.S. Department of State organization that develops policy research and analysis. Established in Sept. 1945 by President Truman, it was initially staffed by INTELLIGENCE OFFICERS and analysts from the OFFICE OF STRATEGIC SERVICES (OSS).

For a short time the INR seemed destined to become the primary U.S. intelligence agency. But when Truman began organizing a national security apparatus to combat the Soviet Union, he saw the need for an intelligence agency independent of the existing federal bureaucracy and in 1947 created the CIA, which eclipsed the INR.

The INR charter called for it to coordinate research for the State Department, not the President. The INR's work was confined to the gathering of "positive foreign intelligence pertinent to the formulation and execution of foreign policy." The NATIONAL SECURITY COUNCIL, created at the same time as the CIA, was linked directly to the President, while the INR remained inside the State Department, headed by a director with a rank equivalent to an Assistant Secretary of State.

The INR's PRODUCT typically was not intelligence but an appraisal, for State Department use, of a current event from the viewpoint of U.S. interests. But the bureau, which also analyzes geographical and international boundary issues, surfaced as an INTELLIGENCE COMMUNITY player in 2003 when its analysts disputed Bush administration assertions that Iraq was acquiring nuclear weapons.

Bureau Technique de Liaison et de Coordination

SEE BTLC

Burgess, Guy de Moncey

(b. 1911 d. 1963)

Member of the CAMBRIDGE SPY RING who spied for the Soviet Union during his entire career as a British official.

Along with HAROLD (KIM) PHILBY, DONALD MACLEAN, and ANTHONY BLUNT, he was recruited to work for the Soviet Union while at Cambridge University in the 1930s. According to YURI MODIN, the Soviet HANDLER of the Cambridge spies, Burgess "was the man who recruited Blunt, and so on down the line; the real leader was Burgess."

The son of a Royal Navy officer, Burgess entered the Royal Naval College at Dartmouth. He abruptly left Dartmouth—later claiming he had eye problems—and entered Eton, where he won a scholarship to Cambridge. Blunt and Burgess were members of the Apostles, a secret society at Cambridge notorious for its anti-establishment ways.

A brilliant undergraduate in history, he espoused communism at Cambridge but was ordered by his Soviet recruiters to cease any open sympathy for communism. He gave himself a new ideological identity by ostensibly converting to fascism. He joined the Anglo-German Fellowship, visited Germany, attended the 1936 Olympics in BERLIN, and became friendly with a HOMOSEXUAL German diplomat. (Burgess and Blunt were homosexual; Maclean was bisexual.)

After graduation Burgess unsuccessfully tried to get a job with the Conservative Party and *The Times* of London. He finally became a broadcaster for the British Broadcasting Corp. Around this time, he later claimed, he began receiving payment from British intelligence for small jobs he was asked to do. For instance, he informed his British handlers about secret deliberations of the French cabinet, his source being a French homosexual friend who was also a communist and a diplomat.

In Jan. 1939, Burgess went to work for MI6 in a new department that handled propaganda and subversion. Told by his Soviet handlers to keep watch on White Russian émigrés, he was able simultaneously to please both his Soviet and British spymasters by working on the investigation that led to the arrest of ANNA WOLKOFF. During World War II he also worked in the office of the Special Operations Executive (SOE).

Burgess maintained a large London flat, and Anthony Blunt, who worked for MI5, often visited there, fueling gossip about the homosexuality of both men. According to Blunt, Burgess at one point was told by his Soviet handlers to court Clarissa Churchill, Prime Minister Winston Churchill's niece. Burgess made a feeble try.

In 1944 Burgess was offered a temporary job with the Foreign Office's Press Department, allowing him access to some diplomatic intelligence. After examining Soviet-era files, NIGEL WEST and Oleg Tsarev wrote in *The Crown Jewels* (1998), "Burgess's arrival in the Press Department marked a turning-point in his clandestine career and the CENTRE was overwhelmed by the breadth and abundance of papers now available" [to him]. He soon received permission to take official papers home with him to review—there to easily photograph them for the Soviets!

Indeed, Burgess was so prolific as a spy that at times the Centre questioned the RESIDENT in London about his being a possible DOUBLE AGENT. A Soviet evaluation cited in *The Crown Jewels* of his role as a spy reads: "[He] is a very peculiar person and to apply ordinary standards to him would be the roughest mistake."

As the war in Europe was ending, Burgess became secretary and personal assistant to Hector McNeil, Minister of State at the Foreign Office and Foreign Secretary Ernest Bevin's right-hand man. Sometimes he stood in for McNeil at important meetings when the latter was absent or sick. One major secret Burgess passed on to the Soviets was Prime Minister Clement Attlee's decision that Britain should produce nuclear weapons.

Near the end of 1947, Burgess, often drunk and disheveled, was wearing out his welcome in McNeil's office. A post was found for him in the new Information Research Department, a propaganda agency set up to counter Soviet propaganda. His alcoholic life continued,

prompting a friend to note in his diary, "Oh my dear, what a sad, sad thing this constant drinking is! Guy used to have one of the most rapid and acute minds I knew."

Reprimanded by the Foreign Office for, among other misdeeds, a wild vacation spree in Tangier, Burgess was given one more chance: In the fall of 1950 he was posted as second secretary—with vaguely defined duties—to the British Embassy in Washington.

In the embassy, he thrust himself into matters concerning the Korean War, which had started in June 1950. Also in the embassy was Philby, as the liaison between the British MI6 and the U.S. CIA and FBI. Thus, during the Korean War, the Soviets were receiving highly secret information from two major sources in the United States as well as from Maclean, who was in charge of the American Desk at the Foreign Office in London.

When Burgess arrived in Washington in the summer of 1950, he lived with the Philbys and their five children, to the chagrin of Aileen Philby. One night, during a party at Philby's home, Burgess came in drunk and uninvited, disgusting all of the guests, most of whom were FBI and CIA officials—including JAMES JESUS ANGLETON of the CIA and WILLIAM K. HARVEY of the FBI. Burgess insulted Harvey's wife, Libby, adding a new enemy to a growing list. Harvey began checking into the backgrounds of Burgess and Philby but was not able to obtain enough evidence to prove his increasing suspicions that they might be Soviet MOLES.

In Jan. 1951 Philby learned that VENONA codebreakers had evidence that could expose Maclean as a Soviet mole. He wanted to warn Maclean, then in London, but could not risk cabling or telephoning him. Burgess decided to get himself expelled from the embassy so that he could return to London and personally warn Maclean. For Burgess, outlandish behavior came naturally, and so he continued to insult and disgust British and American hosts and guests. His downfall finally came in April after a wild drive in his Lincoln convertible to Charleston, S.C., where he was to represent Britain at a military conference at the Citadel, a private military academy. In Virginia he got three speeding tickets and insulted several state police officers. An outraged Governor of Virginia, through the U.S. State Department, complained to the British ambassador, who sent Burgess back to London— for what would be his last spy mission.

After Burgess arrived in London, he contacted Blunt, who relayed the news about Maclean to his then Soviet handler, Yuri Modin. Modin in turn urgently asked for instructions from THE CENTER, as NKVD headquarters in Moscow was known. The Center authorized Maclean's flight from England.

Maclean, who was under government SURVEILLANCE, met with Burgess at the Reform Club. Philby, despite the risk, sent Burgess a cable, ostensibly about Burgess's car, which was still in Washington. "It's getting very hot over here," the message concluded. On Friday, May 25, 1951, Burgess fled with Maclean. Although Philby later said that Burgess had vowed not to flee all the way with Maclean, he continued on to the Soviet Union. When MI5 investigators decided to search Burgess's flat, they asked Blunt to get a key, which he obtained from one of Burgess's lovers. But before he gave it to MI5, he gave it to NKVD operatives. "This breathtaking, almost comical stroke of luck," Modin wrote, "gave us several hours to tidy up after Burgess and destroy anything there that might possibly compromise us or one of our agents."

Burgess and Maclean were kept for months in widely separated apartments in Kuibyshev (now Samara), about 550 miles southeast of Moscow, before being allowed to live in the capital. Burgess languished in Moscow, never giving up the hope that someday he would return to England. Unlike Maclean, Burgess did not plunge into his new life. Homosexuality was a problem for him in Moscow but according to Modin, Burgess "had an official lover and a number of unofficial ones."

Burgess met an English actress on tour in Moscow and persuaded her to take his measurements for a suit to be made by his London tailor. The incident later became the basis for the MOVIE *An Englishman Abroad*.

Burgess died of arteriosclerosis in 1963. Philby, who had arrived in Moscow shortly before, refused to attend the funeral. (According to NIGEL WEST in *A Matter of Trust* [1982], Burgess, "on his death-bed, had denounced Philby as a British agent." Burgess may have believed this, but most intelligence authorities give it little credence.) Maclean gave the elegy. Burgess's ashes were later buried in a churchyard cemetery in England.

Cautiously evaluating Burgess decades after he con-

trolled him, Yuri Modin wrote in his memoir, *My Five Cambridge Friends* (1994), that Burgess "was extraordinarily cultured, and his mind was subtle enough to grasp the most difficult concepts. His views were invariably pertinent, original and interesting."

Burgess's Soviet CODE NAMES were "Hicks," "Jim," "Madchen," and "Paul."

Burn

Slang for the deliberate sacrifice of an intelligence AGENT in order to protect a more important spy or MOLE or possibly a NETWORK. Frequently an agent will be burned when there are indications that he has already been compromised or BLOWN, often in such a manner as to reinforce the credibility of a mole.

Also see Col. MICHAL GOLIENEWSKI.

Burrows, William E.

(b. 1937)

Journalism professor and investigative reporter whose book *Deep Black: Space Espionage and National Security* (1986) revealed many previously unreported facts about space SURVEILLANCE. Also of note is his *By Any Means Necessary: America's Secret Air War in the Cold War* (2001).

Burrows, who holds degrees in international relations from Columbia University, has written articles for several papers as well as a number of important books about space exploration.

Burton, Sir Richard

(b. 1821 d. 1890)

British explorer and writer who spied for his country.

The son of a retired British Army officer, Burton was a linguist even before he entered Oxford, where he spent two years studying ancient Greek, Latin, and Arabic. He was already fluent in modern Greek, German, French, Portuguese, Spanish, and Italian. He is reputed to have eventually learned 35 languages.

When he left Oxford he joined the East India Company's mercenary army and served as a commissioned officer in Sind (now Pakistan). There he began a lifelong career of spying for the British while simultaneously exploring exotic places. Traveling in disguise, he could pose as a native to get intelligence on dissidents plotting against the British.

When British Army authorities suspected that some of their troops were patronizing HOMOSEXUAL brothels in Karachi, Burton was asked to investigate. He turned in a report so graphic that it shocked his superiors, who forced him to leave the Army. The British closed the brothels.

Burton then left India to explore the Arabian Peninsula and Somaliland. In 1855 and again in 1857 he was commissioned by the British Foreign Office to find the source of the Nile. He did not succeed, but his expedition

Guy Burgess, 1957. (ARCHIVES PHOTOS)

cleared the way for the next wave of British explorers. In 1858, posing as a Muslim pilgrim, he entered the forbidden Arabian cities of Mecca and Medina. During all of his explorations he collected intelligence for the British government. He also served as a consul, officially collecting intelligence in Brazil, Damascus, and Trieste.

His numerous books included translations of Oriental erotica—the *Kama Sutra of Vatsyayana* and *The Perfumed Garden*—and a monumental translation of the *Arabian Nights*. After his death his wife destroyed his diaries and unpublished manuscripts. Although he was made a knight commander of St. Michael and St. George in 1887, he was never formally knighted by Queen Victoria.

Bush, George H. W.

(b. 1924)

DIRECTOR OF CENTRAL INTELLIGENCE (DCI) from Nov. 1975 to Jan. 1977 and President of the United States from Jan. 1989 to Jan. 1993.

A graduate of Yale and the son of U.S. Senator Prescott Bush, George Bush entered in the U.S. Navy early in World War II and was reportedly the youngest pilot in the Navy when he received his wings. On Sept. 2, 1944 his aircraft, a TBM Avenger, was shot down by Japanese ground fire near Okinawa. He was rescued by a U.S. submarine.

After the war he left his Connecticut roots and settled in Texas, where he went into the oil business. He got to know the Arab world particularly well; his Zapata Oil firm won the contract to build Kuwait's first offshore oil rig. From 1967 to 1971 he was a member of Congress from Texas. After serving for less than a year as the U.S. ambassador to the UNITED NATIONS, in 1971 he became chairman of the Republican National Committee. After President Nixon's historic trip to China in 1972, Bush became chief of the U.S. liaison office in Beijing, the establishment of which was a prelude to full diplomatic recognition.

Appointed DCI in 1975, he increased the use of ELECTRONIC INTELLIGENCE and SATELLITES, putting money and talent into the development of the KEYHOLE satellites. His interest in high-technology espionage caused some dissension on the HUMAN INTELLIGENCE side of the CIA. He was also criticized inside the CIA for allowing the B TEAM to conduct an outside evaluation of the agency.

While Bush was DCI the DEFENSE INTELLIGENCE AGENCY (DIA) discovered that Panama dictator Manuel Antonio Noriega, a key CIA informant, had bought intelligence information from three U.S. soldiers in Panama—the "Singing Sergeants," as the DIA called them. Conservative Republican members of Congress were criticizing President Ford for "giving away" the Panama Canal in negotiations then going on. Bush decided not to move against Noriega or the Singing Sergeants because of the political uproar that would ensue.

After the victory of Democrat Jimmy Carter over President Ford, Bush was replaced at DCI by Adm. STANSFIELD TURNER. Bush again plunged into Republican politics, unsuccessfully running for the GOP presidential nomination in 1980, then becoming Ronald Reagan's vice-presidential running mate. As Vice President, Bush gained more intelligence experience chairing the Special Situations Group, the Reagan administration's crisis management team. He played a key role in the setting of policy for the invasion of Grenada. His name often came up in the myriad of investigations into the IRAN-CONTRA AFFAIR, but he remained out of the scandal.

In 1988 he was the Republican candidate for President, defeating Democrat Michael Dukakis. When he was inaugurated in Jan. 1989, Bush became one of three modern heads of state who had previously directed a major intelligence agency. The others were Soviet leader YURI ANDROPOV and Israeli President CHAIM HERZOG. As President, Bush continued the tenure of DCI WILLIAM H. WEBSTER, but, during important meetings on the war with Iraq, Webster was excluded from administration strategy sessions, and his relationship with Bush cooled. Webster was succeeded in May 1991 by ROBERT M. GATES, whom

George H.W. Bush, 1989. (U.S. DEPARTMENT OF DEFENSE/R.D. WARD)

Bush knew and admired when he was Vice President and Gates was Deputy DCI.

Questions about the Iran-Contra matter were still being asked as Bush's term ended. Much of the information centered on e-mail messages at the Reagan White House preserved on backup tapes. On Bush's last day as President, Jan. 19, 1993, he signed a secret agreement with Don Wilson, head of the National Archives. An archives team removed the tapes from White House offices, preventing incoming Clinton appointees from gaining access to them. Bush intended to keep the tapes. President Clinton later essentially upheld Bush's move by trying to prevent the tapes from becoming public. But court action by the private NATIONAL SECURITY ARCHIVE kept the tapes in the public domain, like paper archives, and got them declassified. Nothing in them implicated Bush in the Iran-Contra affair.

In 1998 the CIA Headquarters at LANGLEY, Va., was renamed the George Bush Center for Intelligence.

Butenko, John

American civilian electronics engineer convicted in 1964 of conspiring to give information on the U.S. Strategic Air Command's communication system to the Soviet Union. He received a 30-year sentence.

Igor Ivanov, a Soviet AGENT tried with Butenko, was given a similar sentence but stayed out of jail through legal maneuvers and was eventually allowed to return to the Soviet Union.

Byeman

U.S. CODE NAME established in 1962 as a general term for electronic- and photo-reconnaissance SATELLITES. It was later expanded to include the SR-71 BLACKBIRD and U-2 spyplanes.

According to historian JEFFREY T. RICHELSON in *America's Secret Eyes in Space* (1990), "Individuals might be granted access to the product of a reconnaissance satellite but still would not be given access to information about the satellite itself—its code name, orbital parameters, or capabilities—unless they had the appropriate Byeman clearance."

Bywater, Hector C.

(b. 1884 d. 1940)

British journalist who served as a SECRET AGENT for British intelligence and in the 1920s predicted Japanese naval strategies for World War II.

Born in England, Bywater spent several years as a youth in Brooklyn, N.Y., and at the age of 19 became a reporter for the *New York Herald*. Bywater began his career as a naval correspondent by writing sidebars to the main *Herald* stories about the Russo-Japanese War of 1904–1905. His writing was based on his knowledge of warships, which had fascinated him since childhood.

Bywater returned to England and, while working as a journalist specializing in naval affairs, examined German naval facilities for British intelligence. Fluent in German, he collected a great deal of intelligence. Once, in 1901, he was picked up for questioning by German authorities who suspected that he was a spy. He talked his way out, and later went to work on an English-language newspaper in Dresden. He was also a freelance writer for naval publications in Britain.

Bywater later wrote that he had been recruited personally by a man known to him only as "C" (Sir MANSFIELD CUMMINGS), the first head of MI6, the British Secret Intelligence Service. Bywater was secretly given the pay and allowances of a lieutenant commander in the Royal Navy. As part of his COVER, Bywater certified himself as an American citizen, which was easy to do because of his years in the United States. His brother Ulysses, the U.S. consul in Dresden, had already made the same U.S. claim to citizenship.

After World War I began in Aug. 1914, Bywater was transferred to NAVAL INTELLIGENCE, and in 1915 he was sent to the United States to work his way into the German-American community in Hoboken, N.J., where MI6 suspected that there were saboteurs who had been putting time bombs in ships leaving the United States for Britain. Bywater later claimed to have found the saboteurs, but in U.S. accounts of the case, he is not mentioned. (See HORST VON DER GOLTZ.)

Bywater quit working in intelligence after the war, turning full time to journalism. He was the unacknowledged coauthor of *The Fleets at War* (1914) and several other books. *Sea-Power in the Pacific: A Study of the American-Japanese Naval Problem* (1921) brought him international recognition as an expert on navies. On the basis of his experience, he covered the Washington Naval Conference of 1922 for *The Baltimore Sun*.

His next book, *The Great Pacific War* (1925), was an account of an imaginary sea war between Japan and the United States from 1931 to 1933, in which the Japanese plan a surprise attack on the American fleet. The decisive clash between the fleets of the two nations takes place off the Philippines. In the battle, the U.S. fleet is wiped out and 2,500 men are killed. The Japanese take Guam and the Philippines. Air power plays no important role. (In this somewhat prophetic novel, however, he did not foresee that the Japanese would undertake the PEARL HARBOR ATTACK.

Both of Bywater's books were translated and widely read by officers of the Imperial Japanese Navy, among them Adm. ISOROKU YAMAMOTO. While naval ATTACHÉ at the Japanese Embassy in Washington, D.C., he became intrigued with Bywater's books. According to William H. Honan in *Visions of Infamy* (1991), Bywater and Yamamoto met at least once, in Dec. 1934, "and whiled away an evening discussion on the prospects for peace and war over a bottle of Scotch." Honan speculated that Yamamoto was so influenced by Bywater's imaginary war that the Japanese admiral derived some of his strategy from it.

"C"

(1) Traditional CODE NAME for the head of the British Secret Intelligence Service (MI6). The letter "C" was originally used because the first director of MI6 was Capt. Sir MANSFIELD CUMMING.

(2) CONFIDENTIAL.

C-121 Constellation

The Constellation was a futuristic airliner and the most advanced transport of the World War II era. After the war the enlarged Model 749 Constellation was acquired in large numbers by the U.S. Air Force and U.S. Navy as transports and as specialized electronic SURVEILLANCE aircraft.

Given the Air Force designation C-121 and, prior to 1962, a variety of Navy designations, the "Super Connies" were employed mostly as radar picket aircraft, carrying large air-search radars to detect Soviet bombers approaching the United States. From the mid-1950s until 1965 the Air Force and Navy kept those aircraft aloft day and night as part of radar barrier across North America and parts of the Atlantic and Pacific Oceans.

During the Vietnam War the U.S. Air Force operated EC-121s over Southeast Asia to warn of airborne North Vietnamese fighters and to guide U.S. aircraft. The Navy employed EC-121M radar aircraft for ELECTRONIC INTELLIGENCE (ELINT) collection, operating under the direction of the NSA. Those planes in part replaced Navy spy ships that had been withdrawn from ELINT operations after the Israeli attack on the LIBERTY and the North Korean capture of the PUEBLO.

A Navy EC-121 from Navy squadron VQ-2 was in the vicinity of the Liberty when she was attacked by Israeli aircraft and torpedo boats on June 8, 1967. There were Hebrew linguists on board the aircraft (there were none on the Liberty). The senior linguist contends that the aircraft's intercepts of Israeli communications proves that the Israeli attack was a tragic mistake. (See JAMES BAMFORD, VQ SQUADRONS.)

Another Navy EC-121 aircraft, operating off the coast of North Korea over international waters, was shot down by North Korean fighters on April 15, 1969. All 31 crewmembers on board were killed. Searchers later recovered two bodies at sea. That plane belonged to Navy squadron VQ-1. American reaction to the shootdown was, like the response to the Pueblo's capture by North Koreans, very limited because of U.S. involvement in the Vietnam War.

The EC-121 was replaced in the ELINT role by the RC-135 (see below).

Conceived in 1939 by Howard Hughes, then owner of TWA airlines, the Constellation was a four-engine transport, distinguished by its streamlined fuselage and triple tail fins. The postwar radar versions had massive dorsal and ventral radar "humps." (One Navy plane was fitted with a "saucer"-type radome.) The radar aircraft, carrying six tons of electronic gear, could search an area of 40,000 square miles with every radar sweep. The EC-121 was flown by a crew of five plus about 12 electronic technicians and operators; relief crewmen were also carried for missions up to 10 hours—a total crew of 24 to 31 men.

The first military versions of the Constellation were taken over from the Lockheed production line in 1943 for use as transports; they were designated C-69 by the Army Air Forces and R7O by the Navy.

The first of 142 radar-equipped Constellations for the Navy—named Warning Star—was delivered in 1955, originally designated PO and then WV. Air Force procurement of 82 RC-121/EC-121 aircraft followed (with the Navy planes being given the EC-121 designation in 1962). The nation's last electronic/radar EC-121 was retired by the Navy in 1982.

C-135 Stratotanker

The U.S. military version of the Boeing 707 airliner, the C-135 was employed in large numbers by the U.S. Air Force as an aerial tanker, transport, airborne command post, and ELECTRONIC INTELLIGENCE (ELINT) collection aircraft. In the ELINT role the RC-135 was one of the most effective spyplanes of the Cold War.

Easily identified by their plethora of electronic antennas and bulges on their fuselage, some of the aircraft also have distinctive "slab" antennas for Side-Looking Aircraft Radar (SLAR) mounted on the forward fuselage. The RC-135s operated along the periphery of the Soviet Union-Russia, as well as in other crisis areas.

For example, on Sept. 21, 1980, U.S. Navy F-14 Tomcat fighters from the carrier *John F. Kennedy* chased off a flight of eight Libyan fighters—flown by Syrian pilots—that were harassing an RC-135 flying some 200 miles off the coast of Libya. That encounter followed an incident on Sept. 16 in which two Libyan fighters approached an RC-135. Intercepts of radio communications from Libyan ground controllers indicated that the pilots were told to fire on the RC-135, which observed each fighter firing one missile. There was no damage to the U.S. plane.

On Sept. 1, 1983, Soviet fighters shot down a Korean Airlines 747 airliner (flight KAL 007) that had strayed over the Kamchatka Peninsula and Sakhalin Island in the Soviet Far East. All 269 persons on board the 747 were killed in the predawn intercept, among them 61 American citizens, including Congressman Lawrence P. McDonald. The Soviets may have confused the civilian 747 with a U.S. Air Force RC-135 that had earlier been flying to the east of Kamchatka. (The aircraft have a superficial resemblance, but the 747 is much larger.)

The RC-135 aircraft were flown by the Air Force's Strategic Air Command (SAC), and were based at Offutt Air Force Base in Nebraska. The overall RC-135 program was known by the CODE NAME RIVET JOINT. (With the demise of SAC in 1992 the Rivet Joint aircraft were transferred to the Air Combat Command and are still based at Offutt.)

There are several variants of the RC-135 with different types of electronic intercept equipment. These include the Combat Sent aircraft, which fly missions designated Have Terra and Have Sent, seeking out special types of radar emitters. The Burning Star program tracks Soviet-Russian and Chinese strategic missile tests in the Pacific.

The C-135 was the world's first jet-propelled tanker. Derived from the Boeing 707, it is a swept-wing aircraft with four turbojet engine pods under the wings; the RC-135 aircraft have turbofan engines to increase their range (those engines being later refitted to tanker aircraft). In the KC-135 tanker version more than 30,000 gallons of jet fuel can be transferred in flight to other aircraft. Maximum speed is 600 mph. Normal mission time is 11 hours; in-flight refueling can increase this to 23 hours.

The RC-135C variant has a flight crew of five plus eight electronic technicians and operators; five relief crewmen bring the total to 18.

The first KC-135 tanker was flown in 1956 and delivered to the Air Force in Jan. 1957; 820 KC-135s were produced (including 12 for the French Air Force). The first flight of an ELINT aircraft, the RC-135C, took place in 1966. Reportedly, 21 existing C-135 transports and KC-13S tankers were rebuilt to RC-135 configurations. In early 1993 the Air Force modified a weather observation WC-135B as the first U.S. OPEN SKIES aircraft for OVERFLIGHTS of former Warsaw Pact countries.

Other variants of the 707 in Air Force service include C-135 transports, the E-3 Sentry AWACS radar aircraft, EC-135 airborne command posts, WC-135 weather aircraft, VC-137 special transports, EC-18 electronic aircraft, and the E-8 J-STARs radar SURVEILLANCE aircraft.

The U.S. Navy took over two KC-135A tankers in 1977–1978 for use as ELECTRONIC COUNTERMEASURES exercise aircraft, designated NKC-135. The Navy subsequently procured 16 E-6 Mercury aircraft for communications relay to strategic missile submarines. Those aircraft subsequently were configured to also fulfill the Air Force Looking Glass role, providing airborne control of land-based strategic missiles and manned strategic bombers.

In 2003 the U.S. Air Force had an inventory of 21 RC-135, two EC-135, and two OC-135 aircraft, the last configured for the OPEN SKIES mission.

Cabinet Noir

SEE BLACK CHAMBER

Cadix

French CODE NAME for radio intercept and CRYPTANALYSIS center near Nîmes in Vichy France from late 1940, after northern France was occupied by the Germans, until Oct. 1942. It was the successor to BRUNO.

Col. GUSTAVE BERTRAND, head of the French cryptanalysis activities, had fled the advancing Germans with his team of French and Polish cryptologists to French North Africa. (See BIURO SZFROW.) After conditions in France stabilized and the Vichy government was installed in southern (unoccupied) France, Bertrand brought his cryptologists by ship to Marseilles; they were established in the castle of Les Fouzes, near Uzès, not far from Nîmes.

Given the designation Cadix, Bertrand's staff of cryptologists numbered 10 Frenchmen, 15 Poles, and 7 Spaniards; the Poles had the code name GROUP 300. All had French documents to enable them to survive periodic German searches.

Cadix was fitted with radio intercept equipment, CIPHER machines, and other equipment. A radio link to Britain was established as the cryptologists began to intercept and read German signals. Intercepts were also provided by Vichy French listening stations at Marseilles, Montpellier, and Pau. The French post office also intercepted German calls and apparently forwarded recordings to Cadix.

The center was in operation until Oct. 1942, when, with German troops seeking their location, Bertrand and his cryptologists fled. (In early Nov. 1942, immediately following the American-British landings in French North Africa, German troops occupied Vichy France.)

Caesar

The Caesar alphabet, or CIPHER, was a substitution cipher named for one of its most famous practitioners and possibly its inventor, the Roman general and statesman Julius Caesar (100 B.C.–44 B.C.).

The cipher substitutes a letter from a scrambled alphabet for each letter in the standard alphabet. The method of scrambling can change, but both the sender and receiver must know the one being employed. Today any substitution cipher that employs one alphabet in proper order is termed Caesar.

Cairncross, John

(b. 1913 d. 1995)

British spy for the Soviet Union who was recruited into the Soviet-created CAMBRIDGE SPY RING. He was sometimes referred to as the "FIFTH MAN," the others being ANTHONY BLUNT, GUY BURGESS, DONALD MACLEAN, and HAROLD (KIM) PHILBY.

Cairncross, a dedicated Marxist and openly a member of the British Communist Party while at Cambridge, was ordered by his Soviet HANDLER to drop out of the party and apply for a post in the Foreign Office. During his government career he worked at the GOVERNMENT CODE AND CYPHER SCHOOL (GC&CS) at BLETCHLEY PARK, MI6, and the Treasury.

Cairncross was a Scot, one of eight children of an ironmonger and a teacher. Later evaluations by his fellow spies, according to NIGEL WEST and Oleg Tsarev in *The Crown Jewels* (1998), included: "He is pedantic, industrious, zealous and thrifty. He knows the value of money and how to handle it. He is modest and simple." And, "He is simple, sometimes naive and rather provincial. He is very trusting and fnds it difficult to hide his views." But also, "He is disciplined and cautious. He trusts us absolutely and we carry great authority with him."

He was not of the privileged class that spawned other Cambridge spies. But he had a broader formal education than any of them. After attending Glasgow University, he completed degrees in German and French at the Sorbonne; he then went to Cambridge on a scholarship, taking a first in modern languages. He was fluent in French, German, Italian, and Spanish, and could read and understand several others.

In 1936 he achieved the highest scores in both the Home Office and Foreign Office examinations, an unprecedented accomplishment. He joined the Foreign Office, for a time working with Maclean in the Central Department (responsible for Belgium, Germany, and France).

His spying went back to 1939 at least, when he passed on information to Burgess about British politicians, particularly regarding their attitudes toward Nazi Germany. This information was of great interest to the Soviet Union, which signed a nonaggression pact with Germany on Aug. 23, 1939. In 1940 Cairncross became private secretary to Lord MAURICE HANKEY, the minister responsible for overseeing INTELLIGENCE SERVICES.

After Hankey left the government, in Aug. 1942 Cairncross was assigned to GC&CS, where he passed intercepted and decrypted ULTRA material to his NKVD handler; especially valuable were the ENIGMA keys that he obtained. In June 1943, because of eye strain, he was posted to MI6, initially working in the same COUNTERINTELLIGENCE branch as Philby; a short time later he was transferred to the political branch. He was a prolific MOLE, providing the Soviets with copies or originals of 3,449 documents in 1941, 1,452 in 1942, 94 in 1943, and 794 in 1944.

One of his handlers, YURI MODIN, wrote that while at Bletchley Park he had learned details about the German Tiger tank, German Air Force bases in the Soviet Union, and the order for the spring 1943 German offensive, which British codebreakers had intercepted. These in-

John Cairncross, 1947. (FRANCE-SOIR)

cluded decrypted *Luftwaffe* signals that were important to the Soviet victory in the battle of Kursk in 1943. The Soviet government awarded him the Order of the Red Banner for that work and in late 1944 he was given a gift of £250 by his handler for his "long and useful" work.

Cairncross went to work at the Treasury in June 1945, just after the war in Europe had ended. His work for the Soviets was suddenly broken off on Oct. 22, 1945, when IGOR GOUZENKO defected in Canada. He continued to rise to more significant posts in Treasury and he was again contacted by the KGB RESIDENT in June 1948 and immediately began passing valuable information to the Soviets.

When Burgess and Maclean fled to the Soviet Union in 1951, Treasury papers in Cairncross's handwriting were found in Burgess's apartment. At about the same tme in 1951, Cairncross was transferred to the Ministry of Supply (because of a personality conflict), where he still had access to numerous classified documents.

Subsequently, in Sept. 1951 he was questioned by MI5 MOLE hunters. Cairncross denied being a spy, but he was fired from the government without a pension and left Britain under a cloud. He then worked on economic development projects for the UNITED NATIONS in Africa and the Far East. He also lectured for a time at American universities. A French scholar, he translated several classic French works into English and was considered an authority on Molière.

Blunt, questioned after being given immunity in 1964, named Cairncross as a Soviet spy, and Cairncross made a full confession to MI5. He was not prosecuted, however, because officials believed that he had not done much damage as a spy; also, his espionage had taken place many years earlier.

He claimed that he had aided the Soviet Union as an ally denied vital information during World War II. But he insisted that he had not spied during the subsequent Cold War.

After more than 40 years in exile, Cairncross returned to Britain in 1995 and married his companion of recent years, American opera singer Gayle Brinkerhoff. He was finishing his memoirs when he suffered two strokes and died that same year.

His Soviet CODE NAMES were, appropriately, "Liszt" and "Molière," the composer and writer whom he most admired, as well as "Karel."

His autobiography, *Enigma Spy,* was published in Britain in 1997.

Cambodia

SEE VIETNAM

Cambridge Spy Ring

Popular term for the spies recruited by the Soviet NKVD at Cambridge University in the 1930s. Those known spies were GUY BURGESS, DONALD MACLEAN, and HAROLD (KIM) PHILBY. ANTHONY BLUNT was a TALENT SPOTTER at Cam-

bridge. Although JOHN CAIRNCROSS attended Cambridge and was a member of the spy ring, he was not recruited at the school. They were among history's most successful spies, penetrating both British and American secrets at the highest levels of government.

Most accounts consider the first recruit to have been Blunt, who in turn won over Cairncross and at least one other Cambridge student, Leo Long. But according to YURI MODIN, a Soviet HANDLER of the Cambridge spies, Burgess "was the man who recruited Blunt, and so on down the line; the real leader was Burgess." Modin, in his memoir, *My Five Cambridge Friends* (1994), wrote that the internal Soviet intelligence name for Philby, Maclean, Burgess, Cairncross, and Blunt was the "Cambridge Five." Modin recalled that the five "were by no means a tightly knit group; each was radically different in character." All, according to Modin, refused to accept any money for their spying. (But after Maclean's defection, the KGB deposited £2,000 in a Swiss bank account in his wife's name.)

Soviet spy recruiters targeted upper-class Cambridge students at a time of widespread disillusionment for British young people, a time when many British intellectuals questioned the West's political and economic systems. Contemporaries referred to a "Cambridge Comintern," noting that students who succumbed to communism believed they were working for international communism rather than for Soviet dictator Josef Stalin and the Kremlin. (The Comintern, or Communist International, had been established in 1919, ostensibly as a way for communist parties throughout the world to pursue common objectives. In reality it was a mechanism of Soviet communism.)

A secret Cambridge society, the Apostles, attracted Burgess, Blunt, and Long, the last a minor figure who said most of his spying was in Germany during and immediately after the war. The Apostles sequestered themselves from fellow students, not only because they believed in their own intellectual superiority but also because so many of them harbored two secrets: they espoused Marxism and were HOMOSEXUAL.

Economist John Maynard Keynes said of his fellow Apostles, "We repudiated entirely customary morals, conventions, and traditional wisdom. . . . [W]e recognized no moral obligation on us, no inner sanction, to conform or obey." Another Apostle, novelist E. M. Forster, said that if an Apostle were forced to chose between betraying his friend and betraying his country, he "hoped he would betray his country." The quotation, which reverberated when the Cambridge spies were unmasked, was only partially fulfilled. Philby, Burgess, Maclean, and Blunt protected one another. But Blunt, when promised immunity if he helped British intelligence officers, named Cairncross and Long.

Inquiries initiated by the unmasking of the Cambridge spies led British COUNTERINTELLIGENCE officers to identify almost 40 probable spies, living or dead, according to British MOLE hunter PETER WRIGHT. For Americans, however, interest focused on what U.S. secrets were revealed by the Cambridge spies. Philby, Burgess, and

Maclean all had access to highly secret American materials, especially information about U.S. COUNTERESPIONAGE efforts, plans for atomic bomb production, and, during the Korean War (1950–1953), American strategic planning. All three passed this sensitive information on to their Soviet controllers, along with vast amounts of secret British material.

For years after the exposure of Philby, Burgess, and Maclean there were suspicions and rumors that "the fourth man" in the Cambridge spy ring was Anthony Blunt, a friend of the others, a fellow of Cambridge's Trinity College, and an officer in MI5 during World War II. Blunt was finally exposed when an American, MICHAEL STRAIGHT, told the FBI in 1963 that Blunt had recruited him for the Soviets while he was at Cambridge University in the 1930s. The Joint Services Language School at Cambridge, used for teaching Russian to British intelligence specialists, was also a recruiting center for the Soviets.

Camp Peary

SPY SCHOOL for the CIA near Williamsburg, Va. Officially, Camp Peary does not exist. The 10,000-acre site—also known as "The Farm"—is supposedly a Department of Defense facility called the Armed Forces Experimental Training Activity.

Students, called Career Trainees, take an 18-week course in "operational intelligence" or TRADECRAFT. If they get through the course, they begin working as INTELLIGENCE OFFICERS and CASE OFFICERS for the Directorate of Operations—the CIA's clandestine service, or, as some CIA people call it, "the spy shop."

Courses include "Flaps and Seals" (surreptitiously opening and resealing letters), "Picks and Locks," clandestine photography, and the use of disguises. CIA officers receive additional paramilitary training at Harvey Point, N.C., and in isolated areas of the United States.

Camp Peary was established early in World War II as a Naval Construction Training Center for Navy construction battalions ("Seabees").

Camp X

British SPY SCHOOL located at Whitby in Ontario, Canada. It was established in Dec. 1941 as a collaborative effort of BRITISH SECURITY CO-ORDINATION (BSC) and the Canadian government. The facility was intended from the outset to train American as well as British AGENTS, the former from the OFFICE OF STRATEGIC SERVICES and the FBI. This included a weekend course for OSS executives.

Courses at Camp X covered most of the agent activities—such as hand-to-hand combat, sabotage, intelligence collection, escape and evasion, radio operation, map reading, and hand weapons. A nearby military airfield at Oshawa facilitated aircraft participation in the training.

IAN FLEMING was among the more notable trainees at the camp.

Camp X was known as Camp J within the Canadian armed forces, while the Royal Canadian Mounted Police used the less fanciful "S25-1-1" and MI6, the parent organization of BSC, referred to it as "STS-103" for Special Training School 103.

The facility was turned over to the Canadian Army in 1945.

Canaris, Vice Adm. Wilhelm Franz

(b. 1887 d. 1945)

Chief of the ABWEHR (German MILITARY INTELLIGENCE) from 1935 to 1944. Canaris was one of the most enigmatic German officials of the war, holding a high position in the Nazi regime while generally opposing the policies of Adolf Hitler.

The son of an industrialist of Greek origin, Canaris enlisted in the German Navy as a midshipman in 1905 and attended the Kiel Naval College in 1907. As a professional naval officer, he carried out shore assignments as well as serving on several ships, including the cruiser *Dresden* in the South Pacific at the start of World War I. When the cruiser was scuttled in March 1915 (after being cornered by superior British warships), Canaris was able to return to Germany aboard a merchant ship, in disguise, via England! He was engaged in intelligence work in Spain and Italy from 1916 to 1918, when he took command of a submarine. After the war Canaris remained in the Navy, rising to command the old battleship *Schlesien* in 1932–1933.

Canaris became chief of military intelligence on Jan. 1, 1935, with the rank of rear admiral. During the Spanish Civil War he organized German naval assistance to the Nationalist side, developing close relationships with several Spanish officials. Intelligence historian DAVID KAHN describes Canaris in *Hitler's Spies* (1978):

> His hair was prematurely white, and so they called him "old Whitehead." His manner was unmilitary. He moved softly and inconspicuously. In his office, the "Fox's Lair," he would suddenly appear: no one had heard him come. He preferred mufti to his uniforms, and when he did wear one, it was usually his shabbiest. He placed little value on appearances. He threw his decorations into a drawer with other odds and ends. . . . [His subordinates] learned of his promotions to rear and vice admiral from other sources. . . . He never seemed warm enough. Even in the summer he sometimes wore an overcoat.

Canaris enjoyed tennis and horseback riding. When he was in BERLIN, his riding partner was often WALTER SCHELLENBERG, his professional enemy, who was personally to place him under arrest in July 1944.

Initially Canaris was a strong supporter of Hitler because of his stand against the Versailles Treaty and communism. But he soon turned against Hitler's ruthless rule and supported Hitler's opponents within the armed forces (although Canaris was initially against proposals to kill Hitler).

During World War II he maintained tight control over the Abwehr, which was not a particularly effective intelligence service, perhaps because of Canaris's ineptitude or his anti-Hitler attitude. He enlisted some anti-Hitler conspirators and some Jews into the Abwehr to help protect them. Canaris was in constant conflict with the SS, which regularly investigated Abwehr officials and AGENTS.

In Feb. 1944, after efforts by the SS to engineer Canaris's removal, Hitler dismissed the admiral from the Abwehr and abolished the agency. Briefly retired, Canaris was soon appointed chief of the Office for Commercial and Economic Warfare. He was arrested on July 23, 1944, following the abortive July 20 plot against Hitler—although he was not specifically identified by any of the plotters. Shackled day and night, Canaris was held at the Flossenbürg concentration camp, north of Munich. He was continually interrogated by the SS, and eventually tortured.

On April 5, with Soviet troops encircling his underground bunker in Berlin, Hitler ordered Canaris's execution. Late on April 8, 1945, Canaris was given another brutal interrogation. When he was returned to his cell about midnight, he tapped a final message to a prisoner in the adjacent cell:

I am dying for my country. I have a clear conscience. As an officer you will understand that I did no more than my patriotic duty in trying to oppose the criminal madness of Hitler, who was leading Germany to its ruin. It was in vain, as I know now that my country will go under, as I knew already in 1942.

Shortly after 5:30 A.M. on April 9, 1945, SS guards placed a noose of piano wire around his neck and hanged him—slowly. He was presumed dead and taken down, but was then found to be still alive and was hanged a second time. His body was incinerated. (HANS OSTER, former chief of staff of the Abwehr, was hanged a few moments before Canaris.)

There are stories that Canaris met during World War I with MATA HARI in Spain, and possibly with WILLIAM DONOVAN, head of the U.S. OFFICE OF STRATEGIC SERVICES (OSS), in Switzerland during World War II. Canaris and Hari, however, were in Madrid at the same time only once, and it is unlikely that they did meet; similarly, the possibility of Canaris having met the head of the OSS is extremely remote.

Canberra (B-57)

British-developed, turbojet bomber that overflew the Soviet Union for intelligence collection on behalf of the United States. Effective bomber aircraft, British- and American-built Canberras were configured for tactical as well as high-altitude strategic RECONNAISSANCE, the latter to supplement U.S. U-2 spy plane operations.

The British were asked in 1952 by the CIA to use their new Canberra aircraft to undertake a long-range photo mission over the missile test facility at Kapustan Yar, on the Volga River. The British flew this mission, probably in 1952, and apparently also flew a second in July 1953. The latter Canberra was damaged by anti-aircraft gunfire, although the plane landed safely in Iran.

The English Electric–built Canberra was the first jet-propelled bomber to enter British service. The de facto successor to the highly effective MOSQUITO aircraft of World War II fame, the prototype Canberra first flew on May 13, 1949, with the first bomber aircraft becoming operational in 1951. The Canberra could carry conventional or nuclear bombs or multiple 20-mm cannon in an internal bomb bay.

The first specialized PR.3 aircraft entered squadron service in 1953, with the wide-wing PR.9 becoming operational in 1960, that plane having an operational altitude of more than 60,000 feet. By the mid-1950s five Royal Air Force strategic reconnaissance squadrons had Canberras in addition to Canberra bomber formations. In both bomber and photo-reconnaissance variants the Canberra was unarmed, relying on speed, altitude, and maneuverability to escape enemy fighters.

The first specialized photo aircraft, the PR.3 variant, and its successors had a lengthened fuselage to accommodate up to seven cameras in the bomb bay; the later PR.9 had improved engines and extended wings for high-altitude operations. The Canberra PR.7 had a maximum speed of 580 mph at 40,000 feet; the aircraft's service ceiling was 48,000 feet, and its range was 4,300 miles. The standard Canberra was flown by a crew of two or three: a pilot and navigator and, in the bomber variants, a bombardier. In 1955 a modified Canberra established an official world altitude record of 65,890 feet (which was promptly and secretly broken by a U-2 aircraft).

British firms built 1,055 Canberras of all types, including 155 PR variants; another 57 aircraft were built in Australia, and in the United States the aircraft was built by the Glenn L. Martin Co. Designated B-57, the first of these planes flew on June 28, 1954. The U.S. Air Force procured 403 B-57s including 20 specialized RB-57D and 16 RB-57F variants for strategic reconnaissance.

The RB-57D and RB-57F were "wide-wing" aircraft for high-altitude flight. The standard B-57 wingspan was 64 feet, increased to 105 feet in the RB-57D and 122½ feet in the RB-57F. The RB-57F could reach 68,500 feet and had a range of 4,250 miles. The RB-57D had a crew of only one, while the RB-57F had a more effective two-man crew. Several wide-wing B-57s were supplied to Taiwan for spy flights over China. (There were also RB-57A, RB-57C, and RB-57E variants for tactical reconnaissance.)

The Royal Air Force still flew the Canberra PR.9 reconnaissance aircraft in first-line service at the start of the 21st century.

Carbons

Paper that produces SECRET WRITING through the use of chemicals.

Cardano, Gerolamo

(b. 1501 d. 1576)

Sixteenth-century Milanese physician, mathematician, and author of books on a variety of subjects. He produced a revolutionary CIPHER system that bears his name—the Cardano grille. In its basic form, the grille is a piece of cloth or paper placed over a sheet of paper containing a "normal" letter. The cloth or paper placed over the letter has holes or small windows cut into it, each of which is numbered. When placed over the letter, the windows cut in the cloth or sheet reveal letters that, read in the order indicated, display a secret message. This was the first recorded transposition cipher.

Cardano developed other CODE schemes, few if any of which were practical. More significantly, he developed a scheme for secretly opening mail in such a way that a letter could be read without the recipient's knowing it had been intercepted. A thin rod was inserted into the envelope and the letter carefully wound around the rod, which was then withdrawn through the fold. After the letter was read, it could be reinserted in the envelope in the reverse manner.

He was considered the outstanding mathematician of his time, and lectured and published on that subject. His *Liber de ludo aleae* (Book on Games of Chance) was the first systematic computations of probabilities.

In 1570, while a professor in Bologna, he was arrested and accused of heresy. After several months of incarceration he was allowed to privately abjure, but lost his position and the right to publish books.

Caribbean Marine Aero Corporation

A PROPRIETARY COMPANY of the CIA that used Cuban exile pilots to fly B-26 Invader bombers to suppress the pro-communist Congo revolt of 1964.

Carney, Sgt. Jeffrey M.

U.S. Air Force intelligence specialist who spied for East Germany while assigned to a highly secret NSA facility. Carney was a linguist and communications specialist at Tempelhof Central Airport in BERLIN from April 1982 to April 1984. He was assigned to an electronics security group that worked for the NSA. The unit eavesdropped on communications of Eastern Bloc countries.

From Berlin, Carney was posted to Goodfellow Air Force Base in Texas, where he was an instructor. In 1985, probably fearing he was under suspicion for espionage, Carney deserted the Air Force and defected to East Germany.

Air Force investigators said that he had helped East German AGENTS spy on U.S. diplomats and military officers in Berlin, continuing his espionage at the Goodfellow base. Investigators said he copied classified documents and passed them to East German agents. The Air Force did not say how he transferred the documents, how he left the United States, or how he was tracked down. Nor was Carney's NSA connection officially acknowledged.

Carney was arrested in April 1991 in what had been communist East Berlin. Investigators probably learned of his espionage from the files of the Stasi, the East German intelligence agency (see MFS). Western investigators gained access to the files in Oct. 1990 following the reunification of East and West Germany. After being extensively debriefed by U.S. COUNTERINTELLIGENCE officers, Carney pleaded guilty to charges of espionage, conspiracy, and desertion during a court-martial at Andrews Air Force Base, near Washington, D.C., in Dec. 1991. He was sentenced to 38 years in prison.

Caroz, Ya'akov

AGENT in the Israeli SHAI and, subsequently, MOSSAD intelligence services.

Hungarian-born, Caroz served with the British in Syria and then with the Shai, the intelligence service of the Haganah, the Jewish underground army in Palestine. He also worked in North Africa, bringing Jews to the newly established state of Israel.

In July 1949 he joined the Israeli COUNTERINTELLIGENCE service, the SHIN BET. Immediately appointed head of the Tel Aviv region, he had responsibilities for watching the numerous foreign embassies in the city as well as their AGENTS. He subsequently served briefly as head of the Jerusalem region before becoming chief of the important Arab department of Shin Bet in 1952.

Caroz transferred to the Mossad, Israel's foreign intelligence service, in 1954 and was assigned as its representative in Paris. There he built up close relations with the DST, France's internal security service. This link was mutually beneficial, as the French had a great need for intelligence about Arab activities following the Algerian revolt that began in 1954. (The relationship facilitated the immigration of Moroccan Jews to Israel at a difficult time in French-Arab relations, and French-Israeli military collaboration was vital to the Israeli success in the Suez campaign of 1956.)

In 1954 Caroz became the first head of the foreign relations division of the Mossad. In that position he was able to establish links with several countries that did not wish overt relations with Israel.

Caroz was serving as the deputy director of the Mossad when, following a bout of governmental infighting, he retired from government service in 1966.

Caroz subsequently served on the editorial board of the Israeli newspaper *Yediot Aharonot* and is the author of *The Arab Secret Services* (1978).

Carpetbagger

U.S. air operation in Europe in support of the OFFICE OF STRATEGIC SERVICES (OSS). The missions were mostly parachuting and picking up OSS AGENTS in German-occupied territory and parachuting supplies to various resistance groups.

Britain's Royal Air Force (RAF) had begun air operations in support of the Special Operations Executive (SOE) in July 1940, shortly after German troops occupied Norway, Denmark, France, and the Low Countries. RAF aircraft subsequently supported U.S. OSS operations on the European continent when they began in 1943. But it soon became evident that the RAF was unable to devote all of the resources wanted to support the OSS, and Operation Carpetbagger began.

In July 1943—in the midst of a controversy between the U.S. Army Air Forces (AAF) and the U.S. Navy—the AAF's 479th Anti-Submarine Group began operations against German U-boats in the eastern Atlantic from bases in Britain. Trained for low-level night flying, and operating under the control of the RAF Coastal Command, the 479th was the obvious choice to fly support operations for the OSS.

Several four-engine B-24 Liberator bombers of the group's 4th and 22nd Squadrons were withdrawn from service to be modified for OSS operations: Their "belly" ball gun turrets were removed and replaced with a cargo hatch for agents, or "Joes," to parachute from the planes; the noses were modified with a plexiglass "greenhouse" to permit the bombardier a good view of the drop zone; the single .50-caliber machine guns in the waist and oxygen equipment were removed; directional navigation gear and air-to-ground radios were fitted; and flame suppressors were installed in the engines to suppress the blue exhaust flames. A crew of eight normally flew the modified B-24s.

Meanwhile, the AAF withdrew from the anti-submarine role in Aug. 1943 and the Carpetbagger units were redesignated the 36th and 406th Bombardment Squadrons, subsequently assigned to the 801st Bombardment Group, set up in March 1944. In May 1944 the 788th and 850th Bombardment Squadrons were also assigned to the Carpetbagger role.

The first Carpetbagger mission to support OSS and French underground activities was flown on the night of Jan. 4–5, 1944. The seven-hour B-24 flight was a success, although several aircraft and fliers had been lost in training flights over England. The first combat loss came on the night of March 2–3, when a B-24 was brought down over France by flak; another was similarly lost the following night.

In preparation for the D-DAY landings in France on June 6, 1944, the Carpetbaggers flew 17 successful B-24 sorties on the night of June 3–4, the largest number flown to date. They made more sorties on the next two nights, carrying arms and equipment for the French underground, as well as 100 of the three-person OSS JEDBURGH teams.

During July 1944—the peak month of the war for Carpetbagger operations—the four B-24 squadrons dropped almost 4,700 supply containers, 2,900 smaller packages, 1,378 bundles of propaganda leaflets, and 62 "Joes." That month the squadrons began flying four C-47 Dakotas, twin-engine transport planes that could land and pick up agents in enemy territory. The B-24s also ranged farther afield, flying one mission to drop agents

and supplies in German-held Norway and two to Denmark. Periodically, the B-24s were returned to standard bombing missions, having retained their bomb racks.

On April 16, 1945, when the last Carpetbagger mission was flown, the low-flying aircraft had delivered more than 1,000 "Joes" as well as tons of arms and other supplies. Twenty-five B-24s had been lost, or one for every 74.4 successful sorties—a much better survival rate than that of four-engine bombers in bombing missions over Europe. The squadrons lost 208 men. The official history *The Army Air Forces in World War II* (1951) describes the night missions by the large B-24s:

The [Carpetbagger] aircraft, whether fires were lighted or not, circled over the pinpoint [drop zone] flashing the letter of the day. Upon receiving the proper response by Aldis lamp or flashlight, the crew prepared for the drop. The pilot let down to 700 feet or less, reduced his air speed to about 130 miles per hour, and flashed the drop signal to the dispatcher. Several runs over the target were required to drop the entire load, and some accidents were unavoidable while flying on the deck at near-stalling speeds.

Separate from the Carpetbagger squadrons, B-24 Liberators and B-17 Flying Fortress bombers of bombardment groups based in England flew large-scale drop missions to the Marquis underground units in France during June–Aug. 1944.

Carr, Sam

(b. 1906 d. ?)

Secretary of the Canadian Communist Party from 1937. Active in Soviet espionage activities in Canada, Carr's role in espionage was revealed when IGOR GOUZENKO, a Soviet MILITARY INTELLIGENCE (GRU) officer, defected to Canadian officials in Sept. 1945.

Born Schmil Kogan in the Ukraine, Carr anglicized his name when he immigrated to Canada in Aug. 1924. Initially he worked on a farm, and in 1925 he became a member of the Communist Youth league. From about 1929 to 1931 he attended the Lenin Institute in the Soviet Union and undoubtedly received espionage training at that time. Carr served as a TALENT SPOTTER and HANDLER for AGENTS working under Col. NIKOLAI ZABOTIN, the GRU RESIDENT in Ottawa. In June 1940 he was ordered to be detained but went underground. (Canada had gone to war on Sept. 10, 1939.)

He was convicted in Nov. 1941 of three charges related to espionage in Canada and sentenced to 10 years in prison. Carr surrendered to Canadian authorities on Sept. 25, 1942, and was placed in jail. Two weeks later, on Oct. 6, he declared himself a Soviet citizen.

Released in 1945 with the end of the war, Carr was not arrested on Gouzenko's evidence until Jan. 1949. After being tried and convicted, he was given a six-year prison sentence.

He also used the name Sam Cohen; he was given the CODE NAME "Frank" by the GRU.

Carranza, Lt. Ramon

Spanish naval ATTACHÉ in Washington, D.C., who engaged in espionage—which was completely bungled—during the Spanish-American War (1898).

After the U.S. battleship *Maine* was sunk in Havana Harbor on Feb. 15, 1898, Congress established a committee to inquire into the disaster. After the American consul general in Havana and Capt. Charles D. Sigsbee, captain of the *Maine*, testified that they were convinced that Spanish authorities were responsible for the explosion, Carranza challenged them to duels.

War followed soon after, and the Spanish minister in Washington and his staff, including Carranza, were told to depart. Carranza traveled only as far as Montreal, Quebec, Canada, where he rented a house and began espionage activities against the United States. His extravagant lifestyle led U.S. Secret Service officials—the Treasury Department's branch responsible for stopping counterfeiters and forgers—to put Carranza under SURVEILLANCE. A Treasury agent rented a room next to Carranza's suite in a Toronto hotel and observed him dealing with an American, identified as George Downing, who had served on the U.S. armored cruiser *Brooklyn*. Carranza wanted him to go to Washington and attempt to determine U.S. warship movements.

Using an ACCOMMODATION ADDRESS in Canada, Downing wrote a letter to Carranza that was intercepted by the U.S. post office. The letter revealed details of naval operations in the western Pacific, where Commo. George Dewey was preparing for operations against Spanish forces in the Philippines. Downing was arrested; he reportedly hanged himself before being brought to trial.

Carranza continued to recruit AGENTS, offering considerable money to Canadians and other neutrals to spy against the United States. He even hired a private detective to help him find spies. Every recruit Carranza engaged was tracked by U.S. officials, and correspondence from Carranza to some of his would-be agents was intercepted, revealing his violation of Canadian neutrality. He was sent back to Spain, having gained no intelligence.

Carré, Mathilde

(b. 1908 d. 1970?)

French TRIPLE AGENT in World War II. The daughter of a decorated French Army officer, Carré was recruited in the fall of 1940 by the French underground in German-occupied Paris. She was very active in the underground, mostly preparing reports on German forces and activities for the Allied headquarters in London.

After her NETWORK was betrayed, Carré was arrested by the Germans on Nov. 17, 1941. An ABWEHR officer offered to save her from a firing squad if she would work for the Germans and reveal the identities of her colleagues in the underground. She was also offered a salary of 60,000 francs per month. She agreed.

More members of the underground were quickly arrested because of Carré. Along with these people, the Germans seized four radio transmitters. Carré knew the CODES and schedules used to communicate with London and agreed to keep up the radio contacts, the arrests to be kept secret as long as possible.

The ruse went far enough for Carré to assist a British SOE operative in occupied France, Pierre de Vomecourt, in making contact with London and arranging for an aircraft to pick him up at a secret rendezvous. The Germans even considered having Carré fly back to England with him to obtain more information about SOE operations. However, the British officer became suspicious of her and, when confronted, she broke down in tears and confessed all.

Vomecourt decided to trust her. After the aircraft failed to pick them up, Carré made arrangements for a British motor torpedo boat to take them from the coast of Brittany on the night of Feb. 26–27, 1942.

In Britain, Vomecourt revealed Carré's treachery. The SOE decided to "trust" Carré, who became a triple agent, revealing names of Abwehr officers, details of their COUNTERESPIONAGE activities, and other information to the British.

Vomecourt soon returned to France and in April 1942 was captured by the Germans. Fearing that he might be forced to reveal Carré's triple-crossing activities, the British imprisoned her for the remainder of the war. She was then handed over to French authorities and in 1949 was tried, convicted, and sentenced to death. Her sentence was commuted to life imprisonment, but she was released in 1954.

Her book *J'ai été chatte* (I was the cat) was published in 1959. Her underground CODE NAMES were "Lily" and, subsequently, "Cat."

Cartwright, Col. Henry

British INTELLIGENCE OFFICER in Switzerland during World War II.

Cartwright, who had escaped from German captivity—some reports say 12 times—during World War I, was the British military ATTACHÉ in Bern and also served as the local representative of MI9, a British office that handled escaped Allied prisoners.

Fearing a provocation from the ABWEHR, the German MILITARY INTELLIGENCE agency, he refused to set up a meeting with Dr. FRITZ KOLBE, who said he had documents that provided insight into the intentions of the German Foreign Ministry. The German appeared on Aug. 16, 1943, a friend having made the appointment. Kolbe's possession of a score of classified telegrams and an offer to spy for Britain were ignored.

Kolbe then took his offer to the Bern representative of the U.S. OFFICE OF STRATEGIC SERVICES, the highly receptive ALLEN W. DULLES.

CAS

SEE CONTINENTAL AIR SERVICES

Casanova, Giovanni

(b. 1725 d. 1798)

Venetian adventurer, soldier, writer, and SECRET AGENT in the service of King Louis XV of France. He is remembered chiefly as a libertine, and his name is synonymous with sexual exploits.

Denounced in Venice as a magician in 1755, Casanova was sentenced to five years in prison. He engineered a spectacular escape in 1756 and made his way to Paris, where he introduced the lottery and made a fortune. In this period he traveled extensively and spied for the king of France. He later returned to Venice, where he gathered DOMESTIC INTELLIGENCE from 1774 to 1782.

Casanova was a versatile writer, and his extensive autobiographies demonstrate his powers of observation as well as providing excellent descriptions of 18th-century society in European cities.

Cascio, Staff Sgt. Giuseppe

U.S. Air Force photographic laboratory technician stationed at an air base in South Korea. The 34-year-old Cascio was arrested in 1952 after trying to sell flight-test data on the F-86E Sabre aircraft to the North Koreans.

During World War II Cascio had been a bombardier, earning two Distinguished Flying Crosses. A reserve officer, he was released from the Air Force in late 1948 and enlisted as a staff sergeant in 1949.

In Korea, he received classified information from Staff Sgt. JOHN P. JONES and, using military payment certificates for payment, passed the material to a Korean civilian who was employed by the North Korean intelligence service.

He was apprehended by Air Force security agents. On June 8, 1953, he was convicted of conspiracy to pass secrets to the enemy as well as on 16 charges of having used military payment certificates illegally; he was sentenced to 20 years at hard labor and received a dishonorable discharge.

Case

An intelligence operation in its entirety, or the record of an intelligence operation.

Casement, Sir Roger (David)

(b. 1864 d. 1916)

The only Briton to be executed for espionage during World War I. His was the first execution in Britain for treason in more than a century.

A diplomat, Casement was British consul in Portuguese East Africa (1895–98), Angola (1898–1900), Congo Free State (1901–04), and Brazil (1906–11). He gained international fame for exposing atrocities in the exploitation of native labor by white traders in parts of Africa, and he was knighted in 1911.

Ill health forced Casement to retire to Ireland in 1912. Late the following year he became involved with the anti-British movement in Ireland and in July 1914 traveled to New York City to seek American support for that effort. When World War I began in Aug. 1914, he came to believe that Germany might help Ireland gain independence from British rule. In Nov. 1914 he went to BERLIN, hoping to convince the Germans to send an expedition to Ireland and to encourage Irish prisoners of war to form an anti-British force. Neither proposal was successful.

In April 1916 a German U-boat put him ashore in Ireland. He was arrested on April 21 and taken to England, where he was tried and, on June 29, convicted of treason. Many prominent persons appealed for leniency, but he was hanged on Aug. 3. The legal proceedings against Casement continue to evoke controversy, in part because of the belief that British authorities were prejudiced against him over evidence that he was a HOMOSEXUAL.

Case Officer

A professional member of an intelligence organization who is responsible for providing direction to an AGENT and recruiting and controlling agents on a specific case.

Also see HANDLER.

Casey, William J.

(b. 1913 d. 1987)

Officer in the U.S. OFFICE OF STRATEGIC SERVICES (OSS) during World War II and the DIRECTOR OF CENTRAL INTELLIGENCE (DCI) from 1981 to 1987. While DCI, he was heavily involved in the major scandal of the Reagan administration: the trading of arms to Iran for the attempted release of Americans held hostage in Lebanon, and the illegal transfer of arms to anti-communist forces in Nicaragua (see IRAN-CONTRA AFFAIR).

After attending Fordham University, Casey graduated from law school at St. John's University in 1937. He joined the Navy in 1943 and was transferred to the OSS in 1944 as aide to the chief of the OSS London headquarters. Of his arrival in London, Casey later wrote, that he "surely contributed to the impression" that moved MALCOLM MUGGERIDGE to comment: "Ah, those first OSS arrivals in London. How well I remember them, arriving like *jeunes filles en fleur* straight from a finishing school, all fresh and innocent, to start work in our frowsy old intelligence brothel."

But Casey and his OSS colleagues quickly broke from their British tutors and began operations in their own style. As chief of OSS secret intelligence in Europe, he sent JEDBURGH agents into German-controlled areas of France to work with the French resistance. Casey infiltrated other AGENTS, many of them recruited from German prisoners of war, into Germany on intelligence-gathering missions during the latter phases of the European war.

After the war, Casey returned to the world of law and finance. In 1966 he unsuccessfully ran for the Republican nomination in a hotly contested congressional race in Long Island, N.Y. President Nixon appointed him chairman of the Securities and Exchange Commission, where he served from 1971 to 1973, and he was president of the Export-Import Bank from 1974 to 1976 and a member of the PRESIDENT'S FOREIGN INTELLIGENCE ADVISORY BOARD from 1976 to 1977. After serving as the manager of Ronald Reagan's successful presidential campaign in 1980, he was appointed DCI in Jan. 1981.

The Iran-Contra affair, which rocked the Reagan administration, came about because of a desire to free Western hostages held by terrorists in Lebanon and support anti-communist forces in Central America. A complex scheme, developed in part by Lt. Col. Oliver North, a Marine officer on the staff of the NATIONAL SECURITY COUNCIL, involved the transfer of U.S.-supplied arms to Iran by Israelis, and the use of the proceeds from those sales to buy arms for the Contras in Nicaragua. Congress had outlawed such sales, and Casey's staff lied to congressional investigating committees (see CLAIR E. GEORGE). Other illicit activities of the CIA at the time included the mining of Nicaraguan harbors in an effort to stop Soviet ships from supplying communist forces.

Casey's tenure also covered the period during which the Reagan administration sought to create the conditions that finally led to the fall of the Soviet regime. Reagan's "Star Wars" and arms limitations initiatives demanded extensive intelligence on Soviet arms programs as well as political intelligence.

Casey served as DCI until he suffered a stroke and stepped down in Jan. 1987, shortly before his death. His book *The Secret War Against Hitler*, an account of intelligence operations in Europe during World War II, was published posthumously in 1988.

Also see BOB WOODWARD.

Cast

CODE NAME for U.S. Navy CRYPTANALYSIS station located in an underground tunnel on the island of Corregidor in Manila Bay, the Philippine Islands, from the late 1930s through April 1942. The station decrypted Japanese radio transmissions intercepted by a nearby U.S. Army radio intercept center.

When Corregidor was under Japanese assault in April 1942, the head of Cast, Comdr. RUDOLPH J. FABIAN, and 75 of his cryptanalysts and communications technicians were evacuated by U.S. submarine to Australia. There the Cast team was reconstituted as the Belcormen station (see BELL).

Cast was the phonetic word indicating the letter C in military communications at the time, indicating Corregidor.

(See PURPLE.)

CAT

SEE CIVIL AIR TRANSPORT

Cavanagh, Thomas P.

(b. 1944)

U.S. aerospace engineer who tried to sell secrets related to the B-2 stealth bomber to Soviet AGENTS.

Cavanagh became interested in electronics while in the U.S. Navy, where he served as a communications specialist for four years. After being discharged from the Navy, he went to work at Hughes Aircraft Corp. In 1981 he became an engineer at Northrop. By 1984 he was a senior engineer in Northrop's advanced systems division.

Sometime in 1984, desperate for money, Cavanagh called a Soviet diplomatic office—probably the consulate in San Francisco—and attempted to offer classified documents to a Soviet INTELLIGENCE OFFICER. He had 25 credit accounts and many debts, including a $17,000 bill from Club Med.

The FBI, using unexplained methods (undoubtedly electronic intercept of the phone call), detected Cavanagh's attempt and showed more interest than the Soviets did. An FBI undercover agent, posing as a Soviet, called Cavanagh and set up a meeting for Dec. 10, 1984, at the Cockatoo Motel near Los Angeles, Calif.

Cavanagh appeared at the motel with a sample of the kind of documents he could provide. At a second meeting he provided more documents, including secrets about the highly classified stealth bomber. "I'm in debt up to my ears," he told the FBI agents. "I'm after big money." He was promised $25,000 in cash each month for 10 years if he kept supplying a steady stream of Northrop secrets. He agreed.

A third meeting was arranged, and when he passed more documents to the bogus Soviet operatives he was arrested. On March 14, 1985, he pleaded guilty to two counts of espionage and was sentenced to life in prison.

Cavell, Edith Louisa

(b. 1865 d. 1915)

British nurse, often mistakenly labeled a spy, who was executed by the Germans in World War I. Cavell was working at the Berkendael Medical Institute, a Red Cross hospital, in Brussels when Germany occupied Belgium in Aug. 1914. She joined an Allied underground that helped British, Belgian, and French troops make their way into neutral Holland, but she did not engage in espionage.

In Aug. 1915, when about 200 Allied soldiers were hidden in the hospital, German officers arrested her and several others on the hospital staff. She confessed her underground activities and, after a court-martial, on Oct. 9 she was sentenced to death.

American and Spanish diplomats representing neutral nations, tried to get her sentence reprieved, but on Oct. 12 she was brought before a firing squad and executed. Although often classified as a spy, she was condemned not for espionage but for harboring Allied soldiers and helping them to escape. Her last words were, "Patriotism is not enough; I must have no hatred or bitterness towards anyone."

Cell

The lowest and most expendable group in an espionage network.

Cellar, The

Term used by officials of Soviet intelligence and security agencies to refer to execution or incarceration at the LUBYANKA state security complex in Moscow. In fact, the cellar was used for executions only; it contained no cells. The principal internal prison is located on the sixth floor of the building.
Also see NKVD.

Centre, The

Russian slang for Moscow headquarters of the Soviet espionage establishment (see KGB, MVD).

Center for Special Studies

Studies center and memorial to slain Israeli INTELLIGENCE OFFICERS, dedicated on June 6, 1985. Located at G'lilot, just north of Tel Aviv, the memorial portion of the center consists of a stone labyrinth, with each of several courtyards representing a period in the history of Arab-Israeli conflict. Engraved on the walls are the names of more than 400 fallen male and female intelligence officers and AGENTS who died while on active duty. The first name engraved is that of Jacob Bokai, a Syrian-born Jew who was assigned to enter Jordan with a group of refugees on May 4, 1949, one year after Israel was established. He was arrested by the Jordanians and hanged as a spy on Aug. 3, 1949. A special corner of the memorial is without names, dedicated to those fallen men and women whose role in Israeli intelligence activities cannot yet be revealed.

The center's design is also based on a maze. The first director of the center, Yeshayahu Daliot, a former intelligence officer, told *The New York Times*: "The idea of the labyrinthine maze was to create an impression of interminable search, of changing direction, of complexity and infinity, which is what intelligence-gathering is all about."

The studies portion of the center contains a museum, meeting rooms, library, amphitheater, and offices. It is used for conferences, professional training courses, and

The murder of Nurse Edith Cavell as a spy by the "Huns" in 1915 became a cause célèbre *in the Allied camp, with articles, editorials, drawings, recruiting posters, and even post cards depicting her execution by a German firing squad.* (COURTESY OF INTERNATIONAL SPY MUSEUM)

ceremonies for the Israeli armed forces and intelligence community.

Center for the Study of Intelligence

Established in 1975 within the CIA as a focal point for internal research and study. In 1992, under the direction of ROBERT M. GATES, the DIRECTOR OF CENTRAL INTELLIGENCE, the center was reorganized to include the CIA's history staff (first formed in 1951).

Subsequently, the center began publishing previously classified documents related to the Cold War, the first being *CIA Documents on the Cuban Missile Crisis, 1962*, published 30 years after that historic event (see CUBAN MISSILE CRISIS). Additional volumes of historic CIA documents followed. The second volume was *Selected Estimates on the Soviet Union, 1950–1959*, published in 1993.

The third volume in the series, *The CIA under Harry Truman*, was produced in conjunction with a CIA conference that took place in March 1994, near Washington, D.C., held jointly with the Harry S. Truman Presidential Library. This and later conferences were unclassified, being intended for historians and scholars in the intelligence field.

The Center has also become responsable for the journal *Studies in Intelligence*, an excellent (now unclassified) collection of "articles on the historical, operational, doctrinal, and theoretical aspects of intelligence."

Central Bureau

Combined U.S.-Australian codebreaking organization for Gen. Douglas MacArthur's Southwest Pacific Area during World War II. The bureau had four assignments: to provide MacArthur with SIGNALS INTELLIGENCE derived from Japanese radio communications; to be responsible for COMMUNICATIONS SECURITY; to work with the SIGNAL INTELLIGENCE SERVICE (SIS) in Washington, D.C., to solve Japanese Army CODES; and to exchange intelligence with U.S. Navy and British forces. The Navy was particularly important, as Navy ULTRA intercepts of Japanese naval communications were a key factor in MacArthur's planning and operations. (Japanese Army codes were not "read" on a continuous basis until the spring of 1944.)

After fleeing from the Philippines to Australia in March 1942, on April 1, MacArthur asked the War Department to send trained cryptologists to Australia to supplement the few men he had brought out from Corregidor in Manila Harbor. The unit in the Philippines, known as Station 6, had identified Japanese communication systems in use and had provided some early warning of air raids. With the help of a captured code book, Station 6 had gained insight into Japanese tactical codes. In late March 1942, when it became evident that the Japanese would overrun the Philippines, most of the Army codebreakers were flown to Australia. But when the Japanese captured the island of Corregidor, the last stronghold of regular U.S. forces in the Philippines, they were able to capture six enlisted men from Station 6.

(Only one survived the brutality and privation of Japanese prison camps.)

The Central Bureau was formally established in Melbourne on April 15 by survivors of the codebreaking unit in the Philippines and cryptologists dispatched from the U.S. 837th Signal Service Detachment. The soldiers were commanded by Maj. ABRAHAM SINKOV, who had worked with WILLIAM FRIEDMAN when he was breaking into the Japanese PURPLE code in the 1930s.

Brig. Gen. Spencer B. Akin, who was MacArthur's chief signal officer in the Philippines and a former chief of SIS, became head of the Central Bureau, with Sinkov serving as head of the U.S. Army component. From the outset, NISEI soldiers were integrated into the Central Bureau to provide vital Japanese-language expertise.

Working with the Americans was a large contingent of Australian Army and Royal Australian Air Force specialists, among them veterans of the efforts to break into the tactical communications of Gen. Erwin Rommel's Afrika Korps. British codebreakers evacuated from Singapore were also assigned. The Central Bureau was supported by the U.S. Navy's codebreaking station at Belcommen in Melbourne, which was under MacArthur's operational command although it was not integrated into the bureau. (See BELL.)

Significantly, Akin outranked MacArthur's chief INTELLIGENCE OFFICER, Col. CHARLES WILLOUGHBY, who had also been in the Philippines when the war began. Army historian Edward Drea, in his outstanding *MacArthur's Ultra* (1992), observed:

> As Central Bureau's chief, Akin enjoyed the prerogative of passing important raw (unanalyzed) decryptions directly to MacArthur, although he was bureaucratically shrewd enough to inform MacArthur's alter ego, [Chief of Staff Richard] Sutherland, first. With Sutherland's approval, Akin transmitted pertinent intelligence from the decryptions directly to field commands over the Southwest Pacific Headquarters' signal channel. Akin's unique, unscheduled, direct access to MacArthur continued throughout the war.

Willoughby's staff analyzed the decryptions and provided the intelligence to MacArthur's planning staff. His use of intelligence, especially that provided by codebreaking, varied. During the two-year campaign for New Guinea, Willoughby constantly underestimated Japanese strength despite often being given accurate data by the codebreakers. MacArthur—and to a lesser degree his air commander, Lt. Gen. George C. Kenney—often refused to accept codebreakers' intelligence, especially when it conflicted with their preconceived views. This attitude was due in part to the fact that Navy Ultra was the principal source of communications intelligence in the Pacific. (MacArthur himself constantly exaggerated Japanese casualties in his battles. And he always underestimated his own combat casualties, never mentioning the thousands of his troops put out of action because of disease and exhaustion from jungle fighting.)

Although unable to read Japanese Army communications until early 1944, the Central Bureau could scrutinize radio call signs, message priorities, and addresses. Coupled with HIGH-FREQUENCY DIRECTION FINDING, which located Japanese transmitters, such TRAFFIC ANALYSIS could reveal the disposition of Japanese troops, relationships between units and forces, and other valuable intelligence. Moreover, the bureau's cryptologists, working with SIS specialists at ARLINGTON HALL, played a major role in the breakthrough of Jan. 1944 that provided access to the Japanese Army's communications. (See CRYPTANALYSIS.)

Drea also wrote that the breakthrough

> transformed Central Bureau overnight into a first-rate cryptanalytic center capable of reading thousands of enemy radio messages. By imaginative use of state-of-the-art technology, such as early IBM equipment, and the application of ingenuity and creativity, Allied cryptanalysts were able to keep pace with subsequent Japanese changes to these army codes and to read hidden messages with regularity.... Central Bureau's contributions to code-breaking during the Pacific war were as significant as they were extensive.

During the war the Central Bureau accompanied MacArthur's headquarters as it was moved from Australia (originally Melbourne, then Brisbane) first to New Guinea, then to Leyte, and finally to Luzon in the Philippines. By the end of the Pacific War the bureau had a staff numbering some 4,000 men and women. It was disestablished at the end of the war.

Central Bureau of Investigation and Statistics

Intelligence arm of the National Military Council of Nationalist China from 1932 to 1946.

TAI LI was the organizer and chief of the bureau under Chiang Kai-shek's Nationalist Chinese government during World War II. The bureau became a dreaded secret police agency. Its officers were known as the Blueshirts, even though they usually wore plain clothes.

The "statistics" function of the bureau gave Tai Li a legal reason for having his operatives study the records of all government units that produced statistics, including colleges and hospitals.

Central Intelligence Agency

SEE CIA

Central Intelligence Group

The direct forerunner of the CIA, the CIG was established by President Truman's executive order on Jan. 22, 1946. The CIG became the CIA on Sept. 18, 1947.

The following were directors of the CIG:

Jan. 1946–June 1946	Rear Adm. SIDNEY SOUERS, USN
June 1946–May 1947	Gen. HOYT S. VANDENBERG, USAF
May 1947–Sept. 1947	Rear Adm. ROSCOE H. HILLENKOETTER, USN

Central Research Agency

North Vietnamese agency responsible for MILITARY INTELLIGENCE during the 1960s and 1970s (that is, the period of the Vietnam War). Civilian intelligence was the responsibility of the Public Security Ministry.

The agency was believed to have six staff divisions: (1) administration, (2) technical, (3) communications, (4) training, (5) security, and (6) collection.

Century House

Headquarters for the British Secret Intelligence Service (MI6), located adjacent to London's Lambeth North Underground (subway) station, south of the Thames River. MI6 moved there from its BROADWAY offices in 1966. Three decades later, in 1993, MI6 moved again, to a spectacular, modern building complex at Vauxhall Cross, on the south bank of the Thames, across the river from the Tate Gallery.

CEWI

SEE COMBAT ELECTRONIC WARFARE AND INTELLIGENCE

CFI

SEE COMMITTEE ON FOREIGN INTELLIGENCE

Chalet

The second major U.S. SATELLITE for the collection of COMMUNICATIONS INTELLIGENCE and TELEMETRY INTELLIGENCE. The successor to the RHYOLITE system, the first Chalet satellite achieved orbit on June 10, 1978.

The satellite was placed in a geosynchronous orbit some 22,300 miles above the earth to monitor Soviet and Chinese microwave communications as well as telemetry data transmitted during the two nations' intercontinental ballistic missile tests.

Additional Chalet launches took place in 1979 and 1981.

After the CODE NAME Chalet was mentioned in *The New York Times* the name was changed to Vortex. This system was apparently succeeded by the MAGNUM satellite.

Chambers, Whittaker

(b. 1901 d. 1961)

Time magazine editor who, in confessing to having been a Soviet spy, charged that State Department official ALGER HISS was also a spy for the Soviets.

Born in Philadelphia, Chambers attended Columbia University but was forced to leave after two years because a play he had written was deemed blasphemous. In 1925 he joined the CPUSA and married a party member. About 1931 he became a member of an underground CELL of the party that was being used by the Soviet Union as a breeding ground for spies.

Chambers moved to Baltimore in 1934 and began acting as a COURIER, delivering to a Soviet HANDLER government documents stolen or photographed by government employees. He gradually became disillusioned. In Aug. 1939, two days after Germany and the Soviet Union signed a nonaggression pact, he told authorities what he knew about Americans spying for the Soviet Union. The signing of the pact had been an act of heresy for Chambers and for many other Americans who had espoused communism as the ideological antithesis of Hitler's hated Nazism.

He went to U.S. Assistant Secretary of State Adolf Berle and told him that Berle's valuable aide, Alger Hiss, was a spy. Berle scoffed at the charge.

In July 1948 Chambers, by then a senior editor for *Time* magazine, told the House Un-American Activities Committee that Hiss had been a fellow communist in the 1930s and had given Chambers State Department documents that he had passed to a Soviet handler. Chambers described his attraction to communism in words that made it sound like the political equivalent of a religious conversion. Like many other Americans who embraced communism in the 1930s, he saw himself as choosing the only path that a peace-loving, globally minded American intellectual could take.

As he explained,

I had joined the Communist Party in 1924. No one recruited me. I had become convinced that the society in which we live, western civilization, had reached a crisis, of which the First World War was the military expression, and that it was doomed to collapse or revert to barbarism. I did not understand the causes of the crisis or know what to do about it. But I felt that, as an intelligent man, I must do something. In the writings of Karl Marx I thought I had found the explanation of the historical and economic causes. In the writings of Lenin I thought I had found the answer to the question, what to do?

What he did was serve in a Moscow-directed underground organization centered in Washington, D.C. "The purpose of this group at that time," Chambers said, "was not primarily espionage. Its original purpose was the Communist infiltration of the American Government. But espionage was certainly one of its eventual objectives."

Chaos

U.S. domestic SURVEILLANCE operation conducted by the FBI during the Vietnam War to determine whether anti-war protest movements in the United States were communist-inspired. (For details, see FBI.)

Chebrikov, Gen. of the Army Viktor Mikhailovich

(b. 1923 d. 1999)

Head of the KGB from 1983 to 1988 and member of the ruling *Politburo*. A protégé of long-serving Soviet leader Leonid Brezhnev, Chebrikov served as head of the KGB during the transition period from Brezhnev to Mikhail Gorbachev.

Chebrikov was a KGB officer in his native Dnepropetrovsk in the late 1950s and early 1960s. He was brought to KGB headquarters in 1967 by Brezhnev to become chief of the Personnel Directorate. He served as a deputy chairman of the KGB from 1968 to April 1982, and as first deputy chairman from April to Dec. 1982.

At the end of the year, in a surprise move, he was promoted by YURI ANDROPOV to chair the KGB. A year later, in Nov. 1983, he was given the rank of general of the Army in the KGB, the first security officer to hold that rank. (With the retirement of Marshal of the Soviet Union Viktor Kulikov in 1988, Chebrikov became the senior Soviet "military" officer on active duty.)

He was a candidate member of the *Politburo* from Dec. 1983 and became a full voting member in April 1985; this advancement attests to the high regard Gorbachev had for him at the time.

This period marked major changes in Eastern Europe, and the desire of Eastern bloc countries to seek independence from Moscow's control soon spread to Cuba. In 1987 Chebrikov flew to Cuba in an attempt to restore intelligence cooperation between the KGB and Cuba's *Direccion General de la Inteligencia*.

But while Gorbachev sought stronger economic ties with the West, in 1987 Chebrikov attacked the West for "the subversive activity of the imperial states' special services. . . ." He could not survive with such an attitude, and on Oct. 1, 1988, Gorbachev removed him from the KGB and appointed him to head a new Central Committee commission on legal policy.

Cheka

The Cheka—derived from the Russian *Chrezvychainaya Komissiya po Borbe s Kontr-revolutisiei i Sabotazhem* (the Extraordinary Commission for Combating Counter-revolution and Sabotage)—was the Bolshevik ORGAN responsible for state security from 1917 to 1922. During that period it was changed to VCheka (Central Cheka). It was renamed GPU in 1922–1923 and OGPU from 1923 to 1934 (see below).

On Dec. 20, 1917, a few weeks after the Bolsheviks took control of Russia, V. I. Lenin directed the establishment of the Cheka as a police-intelligence force to protect the Bolshevik revolution. The Cheka initially comprised largely Baltic Fleet sailors, who had been in the forefront of the revolution. Lenin chose FELIKS DZERZHINSKY, a political agitator of noble Polish heritage, to establish and head the Cheka. Dzerzhinsky, the commandant of the Bolshevik headquarters and the man personally responsible for safeguarding Lenin and other party leaders during the Bolshevik takeover of Oct. 1917, was considered to be Lenin's closest personal friend.

Three specific tasks were assigned to the Cheka:

1. To investigate and liquidate all attempts or actions connected with counterrevolution or sabotage, no matter where they came from, throughout Russia.
2. To hand over for trial by revolutionary tribunal all saboteurs and counterrevolutionaries, and to elaborate measures to fight them.
3. To carry out only preliminary investigations in so far as necessary for preventive purposes.

Significantly, the Cheka had no legal authority to carry out executions. Still, the expediencies of the Russian Civil War (1917–1920) led to executions by the Cheka. After the first such actions against leftist socialist revolutionaries on Feb. 24, 1918, the Cheka established three-man courts called troikas. These soon became notorious as an extralegal means of sanctioning Cheka executions. The first Cheka executions occurred in Petrograd (later Leningrad and now, again, St. Petersburg), in the Petropavlovsk Fortress. That structure, dating from 1703, became known as the "center of butchery."

The ferocity of the Civil War led to the infamous decree "On the Red Terror" issued on Sept. 5, 1918. That decree inspired large numbers of Bolshevik Party members to strengthen the Cheka, established concentration camps, approved the shooting of all those found to be in contact with counterrevolutionary organizations, and provided for publication of their names and the reasons for such executions. Twelve days later the Cheka was formally empowered to sentence and execute people without reference to revolutionary tribunals. Dzerzhinsky took pride in observing that in the majority of cases only 24 hours elapsed from arrest to sentence—and execution took little additional time.

Execution by pistol and rifle could not keep pace with the number of "counterrevolutionaries" sentenced to death. Soon Dzerzhinsky ordered machine guns used in executions. In Petrograd there were so many death sentences that the condemned were tied in pairs, back-to-back, loaded on wooden barges at night, and taken out into the Gulf of Finland, past the Tolbukhin lighthouse, and drowned. When a westerly wind blew, the bodies floated into Kronstadt Harbor on Kotlin Island.

The brutality of the Cheka in the revolutionary period is vividly described in the memoirs of ace spy SIDNEY REILLY, a virulent anti-Bolshevik agent and organizer of counterrevolutionary activities in Russia:

The *Chekia* raids were conducted with a degree of callousness and brutality which to a civilized mind is inconceivable. On one occasion, when the inhabitants of one apartment failed to remove the chain from the door through the extremity of terror, a Red soldier threw a bomb [grenade] through the opening. In another place they had no response to their knocking. The victim this time was an old lady, confined to her bed through a stroke, which had resulted from the murder of her husband before her eyes during the massacres of the previous year. Nobody else was in the flat and one of the Red soldiers, impatient at the delay, threw a grenade at the door. The bomb exploded, killing or wounding five soldiers. The soldiers returned that night and butchered the old lady in her bed as a "reprisal" for the damage.

A month after its establishment, the Cheka had a staff of 23; two years later it had at least 37,000 officials and employees; and by mid-1921 it numbered 31,000 civilians, 137,000 internal security troops, and 94,000 frontier troops—a total of more than a 250,000 men and women. (Some estimates list higher numbers.)

The Cheka's powers were further extended when, in March 1920, it was authorized to send *suspects* to forced labor camps for up to five years by administrative decision if the investigation did not "reveal sufficient evidence" for judicial proceedings.

The Cheka also operated "press gangs" that rounded up thousands of men and women to work on fortifications and other projects during the fighting against the Germans before the Bolshevik capitulation in 1918. Later the Cheka impressed workers for other labor projects, some for use against the White Russian and Allied forces during the Civil War.

On Dec. 20, 1920, the Foreign Department of the Cheka (*Inostranny Otdel*, or INO) was established under Mikhail Trilisser, formalizing efforts to seek out counterrevolutionaries who were beyond Russian borders. By that time it was feared that the large numbers of both former White officers and officials abroad, and active political émigrés, especially in BERLIN and Paris, could eventually bring down the Bolshevik regime. The INO dispatched AGENTS and assassins to infiltrate, discredit, and destroy counterrevolutionary movements. Thus, foreign activities of the security organ—including intelligence collection—evolved from this defensive role. Among its several successes against counterrevolutionary efforts was the TRUST operation. (The Cheka had dispatched agents abroad prior to setting up the INO, but essentially on an ad hoc basis.)

Trilisser also encouraged the use of advanced technologies—such as radio—in Cheka intelligence work and the deployment of Cheka agents to collect scientific and technical intelligence from the West. The latter effort involved placing potential agents in long-term technical and language-training programs. Also, Dzerzhinsky established Special Departments (*Osobye Otdely*, or OO) within the Cheka to provide for COUNTERINTELLIGENCE and Party control within the armed forces.

The excesses of the Cheka led to its being renamed. It became the General Political Administration (*Gosu-*

darstvennoye Politicheskoye Upravleniye, or GPU) on Feb. 6, 1922. The GPU was technically subordinate to the People's Commissariat for Internal Affairs (NKVD), also established in Feb. 1922; Dzerzhinsky served as head of both the NKVD and the GPU. In July 1923 the GPU became an independent commissariat, the Unified State Political Administration (*Ob'edinyonnoye Gosudarstvennoye Politicheskoye Upravleniye*, or OGPU). Dzerzhinsky continued as head of the OGPU until his death in 1926, giving up the lesser NKVD position. His principal deputies were VYACHESLAV MENZHINSKY and GENRIKH YAGODA.

Dzerzhinsky was succeeded as head of the OGPU by Menzhinsky, also of Polish noble heritage, who also served until his death in 1934. Yagoda in turn became his principal deputy. (The initials GPU and OGPU were used interchangeably until 1934.)

While the size of the Cheka and its successor organizations was highly classified, by the early 1920s there were indications that it had a strength of some 30,000.

By 1925 the Cheka-GPU-OGPU organs were believed to have executed more than 250,000 enemies of the Bolshevik leadership as well as some members of their families. The Cheka had responsibility for an estimated 1,300,000 prisoners in the Soviet Union's approximately 6,000 jails. In addition, hundreds of thousands of other Russians were being exiled to the first Soviet prison communities in remote areas, the start of the Gulag Archipelago—the constellation of prison-concentration camps for political and criminal prisoners that soon studded the desolate Soviet landscape. The OGPU's Main Administration of Corrective Labor Camps (*Glavnoye Uprovlenye Lagerey*, or Gulag) was formally established in 1930 under Yagoda, although a network of concentration camps had been established in 1919.

During the 1920s Stalin used the OGPU as his principal tool to crush opposition from the country's peasants. With assistance from the Red Army, the OGPU forced the movement of millions of peasants and the collectivization of farms.

The OGPU was assimilated into the reorganized NKVD on July 10, 1934.

Chiefs of the Cheka-GPU-OGPU were F. E. Dzerzhinsky, from 1917 to 1926, and V. R. Menzhinsky, from 1926 to 1934.

Chekist

Originally, a member of the CHEKA. Subsequently used as slang to identify any member of a Russian-Soviet state security ORGAN.

Chicken Feed

Intelligence knowingly provided to an enemy intelligence agency through an AGENT or a DOUBLE AGENT. Such intelligence must be of sufficient quality to convince the enemy agency of its authenticity and, therefore, of the usefulness of continuing to operate the agent. By the same token, however, it must not divulge intelligence that can hurt one's own side.

Chiffrierabteilung

The Cipher Office—generally referred to as Chi—of the German armed forces during World War II. The agency was responsible for intercepts, CRYPTANALYSIS, and developing and distributing CIPHERS to German forces. In addition, the German Army, Air Force, and Navy had their own intercept/cryptanalysis agencies (see B-DIENST). Of these four services, those of the Air Force and Navy had the most success during the war.

The Germans were able to learn about British operations in North Africa by deciphering the communications of the U.S. military ATTACHÉ in Cairo, Col. BONNER FELLERS and, after U.S. troops landed in western (French) North Africa in Nov. 1942, by solving the U.S. M-209 CIPHER MACHINE. Italian military intelligence had broken into the U.S. Embassy in Rome and stolen the attaché CODE, which was passed on to the Germans. Also, since U.S. Army codebreakers in North Africa had also broken into the code, the Germans had access to top British tactical plans and operations.

Breaking the M-209 gave the Germans access to U.S. Army communications at the division and lower levels.

The Germans also had codebreaking successes against British tactical communications. However, the Germans felt that higher-level Allied communications were invulnerable to codebreaking; the war diary of Germany's Army Group C stated that it was not even worthwhile intercepting higher-level communications.

Childers, Erskine

(b. 1870 d. 1922)

Anglo-Irish soldier, sailor, adventurer, and author of the first modern spy novel.

Childers, a skilled yachtsman, frequently sailed the German coast and threaded his way through the Frisian Islands. He became convinced that Germany planned to invade England via those islands. He turned that belief into his only novel—*The Riddle of the Sands*, first published in 1903 (and made into a film in 1984, starring Michael York). The novel was not published in the United States until 1915, although Childers had traveled to the United States in 1903 and met and married an American.

In the novel two British yachtsmen stumble on German plans to launch an invasion of England from the Frisians. Childers' invasion theory was so realistic that the first edition of the novel carried a note from the First Sea Lord, Adm. Sir John Fisher, who wrote: "It so happens that, while this book was in the press, a number of measures have been taken by the Government to counteract some of the very weaknesses and dangers which are alluded to above." It achieved the author's purpose of awakening the British government to the threat of an invasion from Germany.

The Royal Navy quickly created a North Sea Fleet and announced that a new North Sea naval base would be established in partial reaction to the fear of such an invasion. In May 1910 two Royal Navy officers, following in Childers' fictional wake along the German coast and the Frisian Islands, were arrested by the Germans for espionage. After serving three years in prison, they were pardoned in a German gesture of goodwill toward England.

Childers was a clerk in the House of Commons from 1895 until 1910, except when he served in the British Army in the South African (Boer) War (1899–1902). He resigned from the House to work for the Irish cause. However, during World War I he served as an INTELLIGENCE OFFICER in the Royal Navy and was decorated for participating in North Sea operations.

Childers was brought up in Ireland and educated at Cambridge. Although a Protestant, he began to support Irish home rule in 1908 and lent his considerable prestige as an author to that cause as well as his abilities as a yachtsman for gun running. According to some reports, guns that he and his wife brought to Ireland in their yacht in 1914 were vital to the Easter uprising of 1916.

As a member of the Irish Republican Army he served as secretary in the negotiation of the treaty with Britain that established the Irish Free State in 1921. However, he opposed the treaty and took De Valera's side in the civil war that followed. He was arrested for carrying a revolver—given to him by IRA commander Michael Collins; he never used the diminutive weapon, but was sentenced to death and executed by a Free State firing squad on Nov. 24, 1922. Many in Britain and Ireland considered him a DOUBLE AGENT, although there is no firm evidence to support that theory.

In Nov. 1940, when a German invasion of England was again feared, *The Riddle of the Sands* was republished.

His son Erskine Hamilton Childers was President of Ireland in 1973–1974.

Chin, Larry Wu-Tai (also Chin Wu-Tai)

(b. 1923 d. 1986)

Chinese-born analyst employed by the CIA who spied for the People's Republic of China for more than 30 years.

From 1948 to 1952 Chin was employed by the U.S. Army mission in Shanghai and then in Hong Kong. He then became an employee of the FOREIGN BROADCAST INFORMATION SERVICE (FBIS), a division of the CIA, until he retired in 1981. At the FBIS he translated and analyzed classified documents from covert sources.

Beginning in about 1952, Chin provided classified information to China. The first information that he gave was on the location of Chinese prisoners of war in Korea. Subsequently, Chin was able to provide the Chinese government with U.S. government appraisals of foreign issues. He was paid more than $180,000 for his services by China.

Chin was arrested in Washington, D.C., in 1985, tried, and in Feb. 1986 convicted of 17 counts of espionage, conspiracy, and tax fraud. On Feb. 21, 1986, he committed suicide while in jail by tying a plastic bag over his head. It is likely that he would have been sentenced to life imprisonment.

China

In its ancient history China was the Middle Kingdom, the center of the world, with little interest in the barbarians beyond its borders. Intelligence activities were internal, devoted to preventing plots against the emperor, through spies in court and in the best brothels. As for espionage against external enemies of the state, there was the wisdom of SUN TZU, who in the 6th century B.C. wrote *Ping-fa* (The Art of War). Sun Tzu's dicta on the "use of spies" are still respected by Eastern and Western INTELLIGENCE OFFICERS. His work is required reading for U.S. Marine Corps officers, and Mao Zedong read it to learn how to fight a successful civil war and win control of China.

For centuries Sun Tzu's writings inspired the thinking of Chinese officials planning plots and counterplots. Not until 625 A.D., however, did China have an imperial secret service built into the state bureaucracy. Empress Wu Chao established that organization to keep watch over anyone who would dare challenge her. Secret policemen who were specialists in torture were taught their trade in a school, complete with a grisly textbook.

China's xenophobia severely restricted the development of an efficient external espionage agency. The Manchu court, the last Chinese monarchy, had an imperial espionage organization, but it was as corrupt as the other arms of the bureaucracy, more adept at gathering bribes than intelligence. In contrast, dissidents plotting rebellion against the Manchus in the late 19th century did have effective spies. The most efficient of these rebels were the BOXERS—the Western name for the members of the secret Chinese organization *Yi He Tuan* (the Society of Harmonious Fists). They vowed to overthrow the Manchu dynasty and drive out the "long-nosed devils," the Westerners who were taking over China. Slipping in and out of Western conclaves in Peking (Beijing), they learned about the area's military defenses, finding weak points.

In June 1900 the Boxers struck. Foreign troops eventually put down the rebellion, and in the anarchy that followed, Russia seized southern Manchuria. The ubiquitous SIDNEY REILLY in 1902 reported to the British Secret Service (MI6) that "the Manchus are finished. It is only a matter of time before China becomes the playground of the great powers. Their intelligence service, such as it is, for all practical purposes simply does not exist."

UNOFFICIAL ESPIONAGE

What did exist was another kind of intelligence service, a network of merchants and prominent, anti-monarchist Chinese, loosely linked in secret societies called Triads. Knowing that the imperial intelligence service had few

ASSETS outside of China, revolutionaries—led by Sun Yat-sen—did much of their plotting in Hong Kong. His espionage organization reached out to wealthy and democratically minded Chinese scattered around the Western world.

Both Japan and China had secret societies made up of influential men who formed shadowy backstage governments. Seeing Sun Yat-sen as a stabilizing force in China, a powerful Japanese secret group, the BLACK OCEAN SOCIETY, gave him substantial financial support. He himself used China's Triad societies as the foundation of his personal intelligence service, the *Hsing Chung-hui* (Revive China) Society. He allied himself with merchants who wanted trade with the West as much as he wanted democracy for China.

When Sun's followers tried to take over the Canton provincial government in 1895, some of them were seized and executed. Sun escaped to Japan, where he won the support of the new and powerful BLACK DRAGON SOCIETY and secretly obtained funds from Japan's Foreign Ministry. Later, while he was in England, Chinese secret police kidnapped him, only to be forced by the British government to give him up.

Another sanctuary for Chinese revolutionaries was France. The SÛRETÉ GÉNÉRALE, the French internal security agency, kept close watch over the Chinese revolutionaries who gathered in the "Chinatown" of the 13th arrondissement. Among the young rebels were Zhou Enlai, a future leader of China, and KANG SHENG (then known as Zhang Shuping), who became the director of Chinese intelligence operations under Mao Zedong.

THE COMMUNIST TE WU

Both Zhou Enlai and Kang Sheng returned to China in the early 1920s to rebuild the Chinese Communist Party. A directive published in 1928, and probably written by Soviet-trained Kang, established a party security apparatus: "Detectives must be attached to all branches of our organization to keep watch on suspect persons. The Party must rid itself secretly of all traitors or agents of the opposing party. . . ." Not set down on paper was another objective: the infiltration of government organizations.

Zhou Enlai became head of the Te Wu, the Chinese Secret Service, sometimes translated as the Department for Special Affairs. Chinese today still refer to the various security agencies as Te Wu, or "secret agency," much as those people in German-occupied Europe during World War II called all Nazi security agencies the GESTAPO.

Sun Yat-sen proclaimed himself President of China in 1921, maintaining power through his strong secret service, the hidden side of his National People's Party, the Kuomintang. By cooperating with Zhou Enlai's Communist Party, Sun got financial help from the Soviet Union, which also provided itself with intelligence through military advisers and a growing espionage network. In 1924, Sun founded the Whampoa Military Academy and appointed a rising army officer, Chiang Kai-shek, as its director. His faculty included several Soviet officers.

As the power of the Chinese Communist Party grew,

Chiang Kai-shek relied more on his own secret service to counter the communist secret service. One of the architects of the Nationalists' intelligence was MORRIS COHEN, who had been an adviser and arms merchant for Sun. Nicknamed "Two-Gun" for his normal means of self protection, Cohen later went to work for Chiang, becoming his bodyguard and a pioneer in setting up what was to become known as the "China Lobby" in the United States.

Chiang's intelligence arm was officially named the CENTRAL BUREAU OF INVESTIGATION AND STATISTICS. The head of the bureau was TAI LI, a sadistic military policeman called the "Butcher." Directing a dreaded secret police force known as the Blueshirts, he rose to the rank of lieutenant general and became one of the most powerful men in China. He planted AGENTS in newspaper offices, banks, cultural organizations, and throughout the government. And so did the communist Te Wu.

By Oct. 1928 Chiang's Kuomintang forces were in control of much of China. The urban-based, banker-backed Kuomintang did little to help the peasants. Exploited by landowners and subject to frequent famines, the peasants turned increasingly to the promises of the Communist Party.

WORLD WAR II

Although most of the world did not realize it, World War II began along a stretch of railroad track near the northeastern Chinese city of Mukden (now Shenyang) on Sept. 18, 1931. Japanese troops, claiming that Chinese had sabotaged the Japanese-owned South Manchuria Railway, seized Mukden. This bogus "Mukden incident" initiated a swift conquest of northeastern China by the Japanese, who set up the state of Manchukuo and installed a puppet emperor, Henry Pu Yi, China's last emperor, who was deposed in 1912.

Chiang, more interested in fighting communists than Japanese, did little to stop the invaders. But after the Japanese PEARL HARBOR ATTACK on Dec. 7, 1941, and America's entry into World War II, Chiang's representatives stepped up lobbying efforts in Washington, D.C. The China Lobby, made up of pro-Chiang Americans and abetted by Chiang's charming wife, had two missions: to get aid for Chiang and to denounce Mao's communists.

American money poured into China. Tai Li, Chiang's secret police chief, became director of the Sino-American Cooperative Organization (SACO), which had up to 3,000 U.S. military personnel in China for weather reporting, combat operations, and intelligence activities. Through SACO, Tai Li learned the names of Chinese agents working for the U.S. OFFICE OF STRATEGIC SERVICES (OSS). Tai Li reputedly confronted Brig. Gen. WILLIAM DONOVAN, head of the OSS. "If the OSS tries to operate outside SACO," Tai Li warned, "I will kill your agents." Donovan then threatened to kill one of Tai Li's generals for every agent killed. The alleged incident did not result in any deaths, but it does illustrate the tension between U.S. and Chinese intelligence agencies during the war.

The Chinese cooperated with the OSS in parachuting agents behind Japanese lines. And the OSS sent Ilya (Bill) Tolstoy (grandson of Leo Tolstoy) and another officer into Tibet on a mission to tell the Dalai Lama that Tibet could count on U.S. help. But no one knew which country—Japan or China—Tibet should fear more, for either country could be an invader.

The OSS bewilderment about China's intentions toward Tibet epitomized the U.S. wartime experience in China: lack of trust and lack of knowledge. As World War II ended with China torn apart by civil war, some U.S. diplomats predicted that the communists would defeat Chiang Kai-shek. Those Americans were called communist sympathizers by congressional critics of the Truman administration's China policy. "Who lost China?" the critics asked, after Mao proclaimed the People's Republic of China in Sept. 1949. The question became part of the rhetoric during the hunt for communist agents in the U.S. government in the 1940s and 1950s. (See AMERASIA case, JOHN BIRCH, UNITED STATES.)

Chiang Kai-shek moved his Kuomintang government to the island of Formosa (now Taiwan), 90 miles off mainland China. The United States recognized Formosa as the "true China" and continued to do so until 1972, when President Nixon took the first steps toward recognition of the People's Republic.

Much of the intelligence and internal security in China today is the legacy of Wang Dongxing. An illiterate peasant when he met Mao in the 1930s, Wang became Mao's most trusted bodyguard. In 1949 he guarded Mao on the only trip the Chinese leader ever made out of China—a visit to Soviet dictator Josef Stalin in Moscow. In that same year Wang became director of the Security Department of the Central Committee of the Communist Party and assistant director of the Ministry of Public Security's Eighth Bureau, which ran the *Laogai*, the notorious "reform through labor" camps. He later headed Detachment 8341, a division of about 15,000 men whose specific mission was to guard members of the Central Committee. Wang's duties included the procurement of young women for Mao, who believed that sexual activity slowed down aging, according to Mao's personal physician.

SPYING ON CHINA

Taiwan became a base for U.S. effort to spy on "Red" China. Taiwanese agents were sent in by boat or parachute. Near Taiwan's capital, Taipei, a U.S. listening post, known as Shu Lin Kou, monitored military communications. The CIA set up radio stations to beam Western news to China and floated leaflets and publications into China via BALLOONS. U.S.-supplied B-57 CANBERRA and U-2 spyplanes overflew China from Taiwan; some of the Taiwanese-piloted aircraft were shot down. (See AIR-CRAFT SHOT DOWN.) Several unmanned D-21 spyplanes were sent over China by the United States but failed to provide useful intelligence.

In 1962, following another Chinese-Indian clash, the New Delhi government turned to the West for military assistance (although continuing to procure arms from the Soviet Union). As part of this relationship, in early 1964 the Indian government agreed to the CIA's use of the Charbatia air base near Cuttack, on the eastern coast of India. A CIA team and a U-2 were flown into Charbatia. Two or three U-2 overflights of China and Tibet were undertaken, the first in May 1964 and probably the last one in Dec. 1964, shortly after the first Chinese nuclear test at Lop Nor. The flights were successful and intelligence about Chinese military forces in the border region was shared with the Indian government in this highly secret operation.

The most notorious spyplane incident occurred in Nov. 1952, when two CIA INTELLIGENCE OFFICERS were captured after their aircraft was shot down. China jailed the two men—JOHN DOWNEY and RICHARD FECTEAU—as spies.

With the development of U.S. spy SATELLITES, the need for risky manned aircraft flights lessened. U.S. recognition of China in 1972 reduced the importance of Taiwan as a spy base. Because Taiwan could no longer have U.S. diplomatic representation, the United States set up a federally funded private organization, the American Institute on Taiwan. The director was James Lilley, who had been the CIA's national intelligence officer for China. The CIA, of course, continued to work from Taiwan. So did the NSA, electronically monitoring the mainland.

The Soviet Union had been gathering intelligence in China since the rise of the Chinese Communist Party. After Mao took control, the NKVD and then the KGB played a dual role, spying for the Soviet Union and helping China to spy. The Soviet advisers helped China by sharing intelligence information and allowing China access to some of the intelligence gathered by East Germany and other Warsaw Pact nations supported by the KGB and Soviet MILITARY INTELLIGENCE (GRU).

China's principal spy station in Europe was in The Hague, the Netherlands, because of its large population of Indonesians of Chinese descent. In July 1966, Liao Ho-Shu, chargé d'affaires at the Chinese Embassy in The Hague, arranged the kidnapping of a potential Chinese DEFECTOR from a Dutch hospital.

The man, an engineer at an international conference, died after the kidnapping. He had been savagely beaten. The incident was widely publicized in the West and exposed Liao Ho-Shu as a wily operative.

In Jan. 1969 Liao Ho-Shu appealed to the Dutch for political asylum, and the following month he was handed over to the CIA as the West's highest-ranking Chinese defector. But suspicions quickly grew that he was in reality a DOUBLE AGENT—a *Te Wu* operative assigned to penetrate the CIA. He was given routine translation assignments and some work at Georgetown University in Washington, D.C. Around the time the United States was reestablishing relations with China, Liao Ho-Shu is believed to have been offered to China in a SPY SWAP for John Downey, the CIA officer imprisoned in China when his spyplane was shot down in 1952. Sometime around March 1973, coinciding with Downey's release, Liao was allowed to return to China.

China's intelligence exploits sometimes amaze Western intelligence officers. BERNARD BOURSICOT, a remarkably naïve French Foreign Service employee, was lured into spying by a male Chinese opera singer posing as a woman. From Chinese sources, Westerners were given another story of an identity switch. A young Chinese-American woman, visiting China in the 1950s, was drowned in a shipwreck. Chinese security officers found her body and her passport. They disguised a trained English-speaking agent to look like the dead woman and sent her back to America with the CODE NAME "Lily Petal," before news of the passport holder's death reached the United States. Once in the United States she assumed a new identity in the Chinatown of a U.S. city and worked for many years as a recruiter and agent.

LOSING ELDER BROTHER

China's break with the Soviet Union in the 1960s was a setback for Chinese intelligence agencies. They were so modeled on Soviet secret police organizations that a portrait of FELIKS DZERZHINSKY, founder of the CHEKA, hung in Chinese intelligence offices in homage to their mentors. In intelligence, as in the building of factories and high rises, the Chinese referred to the Soviets as "our elder brothers."

Following the break, U.S. and Chinese intelligence agencies worked together for a time against the common Soviet enemy. Sino-U.S. operations supplied arms to Afghanistan rebels after the Soviet invasion of Afghanistan in 1978. Agencies of the two countries also worked together to thwart the Soviets in Angola, getting arms to the forces opposing the Soviet-backed Popular Movement for the Liberation of Angola. The Chinese also allowed U.S. SIGNALS INTELLIGENCE listening posts to operate in Xinjiang to monitor Soviet missile and nuclear testing. The data was shared with the Chinese.

Relations between the Chinese and the Soviets remained cool until the end of the Soviet regime. In Jan. 1974 China expelled five Soviet diplomats for espionage after Chinese security agents caught them in the act of spying as KGB officers. The agents filmed a meeting between the KGB HANDLERS meeting with an agent under the Paho River Bridge outside Beijing. The state-controlled media reported that the Soviets handed over and received intelligence, counterrevolutionary documents, a radio transmitter and receiver, means of SECRET WRITING, forged border passes, and other materials and money for espionage activities. They were caught on the spot by Chinese public security personnel and militiamen.

With the radio transmitter were frequencies and times for receiving instructions and sending information to Moscow. The spy was identified as Li Hung-shu. The Chinese said he had been recruited in 1967, sent secretly to a Soviet SPY SCHOOL, and returned to China in 1971. The Chinese knew so much about Li that Western intelligence officials speculated that he had been TURNED and may have been a DOUBLE AGENT when the KGB set up the meeting under the bridge.

In May 1983 Chinese officials announced that about 200 Chinese citizens had been arrested in 1982 for spying for the Soviet Union. The only details of any of these alleged spies concerned Hanson Huang. A native of Hong Kong and a graduate of Harvard Law School, he was convicted of spying in Feb. 1984. He had taught law at Beijing University and worked as a legal adviser to a Chinese government organization seeking foreign capital. The Chinese did not say who Huang was spying for, but the presumption was the United States. He was sentenced to 10 years in prison.

The first concrete move toward U.S. recognition of China came with the establishment of a U.S. liaison office in Beijing headed by GEORGE H. W. BUSH, who would later become DIRECTOR OF CENTRAL INTELLIGENCE. CIA officers worked in the liaison office and have been in Beijing ever since. When the two countries opened embassies in each other's capitals, both also sent military ATTACHÉS along with their ambassadors. Traditionally, attachés are "gentlemen spies" and are treated as diplomats when they are caught in some mild form of spying—say, photographing a new military aircraft from a public area. But China does not act traditionally, and when the U.S. air attaché was expelled in Jan. 1996, there were no diplomatic niceties.

Even relatively routine information is difficult to get in China. Names of intelligence agencies—but not responsibilities—are changed frequently for security reasons. Western knowledge about the structure of Chinese intelligence was scant until disclosures in 1985 by a rare defector, Yu Zhensan, the former director of the Foreign Affairs Bureau of the MSS (Ministry of State Security), the principal Chinese intelligence agency.

The MSS was a bureau under the Ministry of Public Security (MPS) until it was given ministry status in 1983. Officials said they also hoped that MSS agents would "improve their social standing" and become "liked by the people."

The MSS took over many of the duties of the MPS, including domestic surveillance. MSS maintains bureaus devoted to Taiwan, Hong Kong, and Macao, along with a Foreign Affairs Bureau that oversees MSS operations elsewhere in the world. Two Beijing-based MSS agencies have innocent-sounding names. The Beijing College of International Relations is an espionage school that trains MSS employees; the Institute for Contemporary International Relations is an analysis center that publishes a classified journal, *Contemporary International Relations*, for senior officials. The institute also trains agents being sent abroad by MSS, the Foreign Affairs Ministry's Intelligence Department, and the Defense Ministry's External Relations Bureau.

Routine police work is left to the MPS and the People's Armed Police—1.2 million police officers, border guards, and guards at government buildings and foreign embassies. The Political Security Bureau monitors Chinese who have contact with foreigners. The Communist Party also maintains a watch over people by keeping workers together day and night in "work units," concentrating colleagues in specified living areas. Thus, for example, all low- and middle-level Foreign Ministry employees live in the same blocks of apartments. A stranger entering the apartments is quickly spotted and reported, through the party hierarchy, to security officials.

SPYING ON EVERYONE

Writing of China before its "discovery" by the West in the 17th century, Etienne Balaz in *Chinese Civilization and Bureaucracy* (1964) describes a land of peasants ruled by a bureaucracy whose "tentacles reached everywhere. It marked every member of society and every sphere of life with its stamp. Nothing escaped it; for the least deviation from prescribed paths had to be kept in check lest it should lead to rebellion, and any dislocation, however slight, was a threat to the system as a whole."

In the early years of the 21st century little has changed, even though China is embracing its own form of capitalism. Now as ever, China's secret service bureaucracy focuses primarily inward, alert more for subversion than for espionage by outsiders. The circulation of city and provincial maps is restricted. The government limits the use of fax machines, controls all computer networks, and strictly limits access to the INTERNET. Anyone attempting to use the Internet or log onto a computer network must have a security check and connect through the Ministry of Post and Telecommunications or another approved ministry. Hong Kong, which became the Hong Kong Special Administrative Region of China in 1997 under a Chinese-British agreement, escapes some surveillance because of its relative autonomy. A massive demonstration in 2003, protesting security legislation, for example, could not have occurred elsewhere in China.

The government agency *Xinhua* (New China News Agency) filters foreign news agency dispatches before they reach the state-controlled media. After examining all news entering the country, *Xinhua* sends a realistic view of world news to party and political leaders; information considered safe to distribute goes to the state-controlled media. In 1996, claiming that national security demanded tighter controls, *Xinhua* restricted the flow of electronic economic news—the information about stocks, bonds, and commodities distributed to Chinese banks and financial firms.

Xinhua is one of several COVER organizations used by Chinese intelligence. Another is the Chinese People's Friendship Association. Students, especially graduate students, have also been used as spies overseas. The Ministry of Foreign Affairs has a Diplomatic Services Bureau that supplies embassies and consulates in China with clerks, maids, chauffeurs, maids, and even nannies. All report to intelligence handlers.

China's Foreign Affairs Office, which has branches throughout the country, is fundamentally an intelligence service and only secondarily a diplomatic organization. The office's interpreters are assigned to foreign visitors, especially journalists, not only to translate but also to observe who talks to the journalists and what the conversations are about.

Foreign residents in Beijing are assigned apartments in compounds guarded by People's Armed Police, who report the arrivals and departures of visitors, particularly Chinese nationals. Journalists and diplomats are kept under surveillance by plain-clothes police, hidden video cameras, phone taps, and BUGS in offices and apartments. Hotels catering to foreign visitors are bugged.

China's intelligence TARGETS, in order of importance, appear to be Russia, India, Vietnam, and the United States. As a regional power, China focuses its assets on its neighbors. High priority also is given to spying on Tibetans and on the Turkic-speaking Muslims who make up the majority population in China's far northwest province of Xinjiang.

China invaded Tibet in 1950 and made it a province. Tibetans who resisted were jailed or killed, and attempts to rebel were crushed. To counter Tibetan resistance, the Chinese recruited local agents, trained them in espionage, and infiltrated them into all levels of Tibetan society. The informers and their secret police masters have not stopped the anti-Chinese demonstrations but have snuffed out rebellion. (Chinese officials have tried to weaken the binding force in Tibet—its form of Buddhism known as Lamaism—but the principal religious leader, the Dalai Lama, self-exiled to India, has remained a defiant figure for decades.)

In Xinjiang native peoples, mainly Uighurs and Khazaks, refer to Chinese by their ancient name, Han Chinese. Beijing keeps down revolt by giving Communist Party posts and political jobs to Beijing-trained native people or to Han Chinese. Xinjiang is a daunting problem for Chinese intelligence agencies because of language, cultural, and religious barriers between Han Chinese and the Muslims.

Security forces are chiefly concerned with keeping dissidents in check. When prodemocracy students rallied in Beijing's Tiananmen Square in June 1989, they were labeled counter-revolutionaries, and all internal security forces, including those of the People's Liberation Army, cracked down on anyone considered a dissident. The Army may have massacred hundreds of students in the square while other arms of the security apparatus moved swiftly to quell any real or imagined threat against the government. Thousands were jailed.

From surveillance to harassment to arrest and inevitable conviction, the MSS is the leading agency in the silencing of dissidents. Authorized to "exercise powers granted to public security institutions," the MSS jails or places under close surveillance prodemocracy dissidents, especially those known in the West. Typical of its operations was the handling of Wei Jingsheng, who was arrested in 1979 for scrawling a demand for democracy on a wall in Beijing. Wei, then 29, was sentenced to 15 years for "providing foreigners with important military information" and "engaging in activities that jeopardized state security." Left unexplained was how Wei, an electrician in the Beijing Zoo, could have obtained secret military information. Released in Sept. 1993, he continued his dissent, was rearrested in April 1994, and in Dec. 1995 was tried for "conspiring to subvert the government" and sentenced to 14 more years in prison. In 1997 he was released on medical parole and deported to the United States, where he continued his human-rights crusade.

AGAINST THE UNITED STATES

The arrest in 1986 of LARRY CHIN, a longtime CIA employee, on charges of espionage, did not awaken American officials to the level of Chinese espionage against the United States. He was not looked upon as a master spy, and his suicide ended the case. (Yu Zhensan probably exposed Chin; see above.) But new allegations about Chinese intelligence activities in the 1990s shocked many Americans. Chinese funds mysteriously appeared as contributions to the 1996 Democratic presidential campaign of Bill Clinton.

The scope of Chinese espionage in the United States was outlined in a 1998 congressional report that targeted Chinese students, scientists, and "other visitors to the United States" as responding to MSS information requests by mining OPEN SOURCE outlets, such as "university libraries, research institutions, the Internet, and unclassified databases." The report also singled out national laboratories, such as LOS ALAMOS, as sites for science and technology information gathering by Chinese scientists on exchange programs. Such programs, the report said, are "creating vulnerabilities in safeguarding U.S. technical intelligence."

As for ECONOMIC INTELLIGENCE, the report said, "China's official collectors of economic intelligence prefer to use collection methods that are low-key and non-threatening. For example, the MSS, operating both in the United States and in China, . . . is particularly active against U.S. businessmen and other Westerners inside China."

The FBI did target WEN HO LEE as a spy at the LOS ALAMOS nuclear laboratory, but the case against him was not strong enough for an espionage trial. He went free in Sept. 2000. Then, in 2003, came the arrest of KATRINA M. LEUNG, who may have been a DOUBLE AGENT while supposedly providing intelligence to her FBI handler, who was also her lover.

Leung's arrest in California came as other Chinese in that state were being charged with INDUSTRIAL ESPIONAGE. Between Oct. 2002 and Jan. 2003 five Chinese businessmen were accused of illegally shipping equipment or trade secrets from Silicon Valley to China. In one case, a Chinese man bought a high-speed computer from Sandia National Laboratories. The computer had been used on classified projects, including the development of nuclear weapons. Officials learned of the purchase in time to keep it from leaving the United States.

On a diplomatic level, relations are often strained by incidents involving intelligence operations. China angrily denounced the United States and the CIA in 1999, following the bombing of its embassy in Belgrade. On May 7, 1999, in the midst of the NORTH ATLANTIC TREATY ORGANIZATION (NATO) campaign to end genocide in Serbia, an American B-2 stealth bomber bombed the embassy. The CIA, publicly acknowledging the "unintended attack," said that it had happened "because a number of systems and procedures that are used to identify and verify potential targets did not work." The Chinese refused to accept the U.S. explanation, charging that the attack was a deliberate "NATO conspiracy."

In April 2001, two Chinese fighters intercepted a U.S. Navy RECONNAISSANCE aircraft gathering ELECTRONIC INTELLIGENCE in international airspace along the Chinese coast. (See P3V ORION.) One of the fighters collided with the Navy aircraft, badly damaging it and forcing it to make an emergency landing at a Chinese air base on Hainan Island. The Chinese held the 24 crew members for 11 days, until the United States apologized for the death of the Chinese pilot and the landing. But the Chinese would not allow the EP-3 to be repaired and flown out. It was dismantled and flown out in a cargo plane.

In 2002, Chinese technicians found BUGS in a new Boeing 767-300ER, China's presidential aircraft. *The Washington Post* reported that the Chinese believed U.S. intelligence agencies had planted 27 listening devices, "including devices in the presidential bathroom and in the headboard of the presidential bed."

Besides the MSS and the military intelligence department of the People's Liberation Army, China maintains at least four other intelligence-gathering agencies:

Political Legal Leading Group. A Communist Party agency that oversees intelligence and law enforcement relating to internal affairs. It operates under the party's Military Commission, whose concerns include internal order.

Investigations Department. A Communist Party agency that carries out political investigations of party members.

United Front Works Department. Another Communist Party agency that handles "overseas Chinese," who are usually citizens of other nations. (China considers all Chinese to be subjects of China, no matter where they live.) Works Department agents, many of them stationed in Chinese embassies and consulates as LEGALS, try to get influential people of Chinese ancestry to follow the party line. The agents also watch over Chinese scientists and academicians working overseas, making sure they come home.

The Commission of Science, Technology, and Industry for National Defense. Sends agents to the United States and Western nations as employees of cover organizations such as the New Era Corp., the Chinese International Trust and Investment Corp. (CITI), and Poly Technologies, to purchase defense equipment and technologies restricted for export. SEE ECONOMIC INTELLIGENCE.

Chi Pao k'o

Organizational Security Section of China's intelligence apparatus. Chi Pao k'o is concerned primarily with internal security as applied to government workers, students, and other Chinese who, for various reasons, come under scrutiny. Another section, Cheng pao k'o, focuses on COUNTERINTELLIGENCE and operations involving what

Chinese officials call "overseas Chinese"—people of Chinese descent who do not live in China and may be citizens of another country.

Choir

British Security Service (MI5) attempt in 1955 to plant a microphone in the Soviet Consulate in the Bayswater area of London. When the building next door was being renovated, MI5 operatives, under the COVER of decorators, drilled through the 18 inches of wall between the two buildings to push a pinhole into a consulate conference room and install a highly sensitive microphone.

The BUG was successful for about six months and then suddenly ceased to operate. The pinhole opening had apparently been detected and filled in. A British AGENT was later able to determine that a soundproof second wall had also been installed over the wall where the bug had been planted, destroying its value.

Church, Dr. Benjamin

(b. 1734 d. 1777 ?)

American who spied for the British during the American Revolution.

Born in Newport, R.I., Church studied medicine in Boston after graduating from Harvard University in 1754. He was a member of both the Provincial Congress of Massachusetts and a member of the Sons of Liberty rebel organization, along with patriot leaders John and Samuel Adams, John Hancock, and Paul Revere.

But when talk of independence began in 1765, Church became a Loyalist AGENT while acting the part of an American patriot. When war erupted in 1775 Church was ordered to report to Gen. Thomas Gage, the British military governor of Massachusetts.

In May 1775 he consulted to the Continental Congress meeting in Philadelphia about the defense of the colony. There he was unanimously elected director and chief physician of the first army hospital, at Cambridge, and, shortly thereafter, a surgeon with the American colonial forces. He was finally unmasked when a COURIER who was caught by Colonial troops exposed him. She carried a message in CODE, but cryptographers working for Gen. GEORGE WASHINGTON deciphered it. They were able to see how effective Church's spying had been.

Gen. Washington discharged Church from his army positions, but did not bring charges against him. The Congress, however, was not as lenient. He was arrested, tried for treason, and imprisoned until 1777. In one of America's first SPY SWAPS, he was exchanged to the British for a captured Colonial physician. Church then sailed for the West Indies but his ship was never heard from again.

Church Committee

U.S. Senate investigating committee that looked into intelligence operations in 1975–1976. Generally known by the name of its chairperson, Democrat Frank Church from Idaho, its official name was the Senate Select Committee to Study Governmental Operations with Respect to Intelligence Activities.

The Church Committee was particularly concerned about domestic spying, especially Operation SHAMROCK, carried out by the NSA. Listening to NSA witnesses, the senators were shocked to hear that the government had been intercepting overseas cables since 1940.

While the hearings were being conducted, President Ford personally telephoned Senator Church in an effort to halt the revelations, explaining the dangers of public disclosures of NSA operations. But the public hearings continued. Also discussed in the hearings was the Nixon administration's consideration of the HUSTON PLAN.

Senator Church summed up his views on NSA activities: "The technological capacity that the intelligence community has given the government could enable it to impose total tyranny, and there would be no way to fight back. . . . Such is the capability of this technology. . . ." The committee issued its final report on April 26, 1976.

During the hearings—but not before the committee—JAMES JESUS ANGLETON, the COUNTERESPIONAGE chief of the CIA, was quoted as saying, in what he believed to be an off-the-record comment, "It is inconceivable that a secret intelligence arm of the government has to comply with all the overt orders of the government."

Church had served in ARMY INTELLIGENCE during World War II, being assigned to the China-Burma-India theater. He passed the bar in 1950 and served in the Senate from 1956 until Jan. 1981, having failed to win re-election for a fifth term.

Also see PIKE COMMITTEE.

Chuzhoi

Slang in Soviet-Russian intelligence agencies for someone who serves as an AGENT for other than ideological or political reasons—usually for payment or to gain advancement within a commercial or government organization. Chuzhoi is Russian for "alien."

CI

SEE COUNTER INTELLIGENCE

CIA

(CENTRAL INTELLIGENCE AGENCY)

Established by President Truman to coordinate U.S. intelligence, the CIA has become a global agency for collecting and evaluating intelligence and for extending U.S. influence through COVERT ACTION.

The CIA was conceived by Maj. Gen. WILLIAM DONOVAN, director of the OFFICE OF STRATEGIC SERVICES (OSS). In 1944 Donovan suggested to President Roosevelt that after World War II the United States should create a peacetime, worldwide intelligence service. Roosevelt died before the war ended, however, and nothing was done to carry out "Wild Bill" Donovan's suggestion. Donovan's plan won few friends in Washington, D.C. The idea of an independent intelligence agency came under attack from the armed forces, which had their own intelligence arms; the State Department, which wanted no competitors in foreign affairs; and the FBI, whose director, J. EDGAR HOOVER, had not liked the OSS and did not want it perpetuated in peacetime.

President Truman, who himself feared that an intelligence agency might be used against Americans, abolished the OSS in Oct. 1945. Over Donovan's objections, he transferred the OSS research and analysis branch to the State Department and the OSS clandestine intelligence collection and COUNTERINTELLIGENCE branches to the War Department, which combined them as the short-lived Strategic Services Unit.

Bureaucratic arguing over intelligence turf continued, and in Jan. 1946 Truman responded by establishing the CENTRAL INTELLIGENCE GROUP (CIG), which was to coordinate U.S. intelligence under the direction of a NATIONAL INTELLIGENCE AUTHORITY, composed of a presidential representative and the Secretaries of State, War, and the Navy. Truman appointed Rear Adm. SIDNEY W. SOUERS, the deputy director of NAVAL INTELLIGENCE, to a post that Truman called DIRECTOR OF CENTRAL INTELLIGENCE (DCI). The principal activity of the CIG was producing for Truman a daily and weekly summary of intelligence and operational cables.

Pressure continued for a centralized intelligence agency along the lines that Donovan had laid out. The Cold War was beginning and the idea of a major intelligence agency was incorporated into the National Security Act of 1947, which created the Department of Defense to unify the armed forces and the NATIONAL SECURITY COUNCIL (NSC) to coordinate defense and foreign policy. This agency would advise the NSC "in matters concerning such intelligence activities . . . as relate to national security." As Donovan had urged, the new agency would have no police powers.

With the passage of the act in Sept. 1947 the Central Intelligence Agency was born. Truman's naval aide, then-Comdr. William C. Mott, recalled that while walking with President Truman on Oahu in Oct. 1950, the President gave the following reason for having established the CIA:

I am a creature of Congress, and when I suddenly became President I had little or no knowledge how policies had been arrived at before my accession. I had information coming at me from 200 different sources and no one to boil it down for me. I am a creature of the Congress and I wanted them to pass a law setting up the NSC and putting the [vice president] in business for the first time in our history. And then I wanted to set up an organization to boil down intelligence and make presentations to me.

There would be no director of the CIA per se. Rather, the DCI would simultaneously head the CIA and have responsibility for all U.S. intelligence collection. Truman would later say that he used the CIA only for intelligence collection, but he was the first president to allow the agency to engage in covert actions, which were called "psychological operations" under a secret NSC directive issued in Dec. 1947. Covert operations—aiding anti-communist parties in Italian elections and arming anti-communists in the Greek Civil War—were the secret underpinnings of the publicly proclaimed Truman Doctrine to halt the spread of communism.

The operations, said the NSC directive, were to "counteract Soviet and Soviet-inspired activities which constitute a threat to world peace and security or are designed to discredit and defeat the aims and activities of the United States. . . ." Only three copies of the directive were made: one for the White House, one for the State Department, and one for Rear Adm. ROSCOE H. HILLENKOETTER, DCI when the CIA was established.

A mechanism for covert action soon developed: The NSC would recommend such action when it decided that some U.S. foreign policy objective could not be fulfilled by diplomatic means and when military action was judged to be too extreme or too dangerous. The DCI would be asked to direct the action in such a way that the administration could give a PLAUSIBLE DENIAL of U.S. involvement.

A 1949 amendment to the 1947 act permitted the CIA to keep its official titles and salaries secret, hide its budget, and award contracts to private firms without bids. The agency was also allowed to award permanent residency to aliens and their families. (This usually meant giving sanctuary to DEFECTORS and foreign AGENTS.)

The CIA set up an Office of Special Operations (OSO) to handle covert action. In June 1948 another NSC directive authorized "preventive direct action, including sabotage, anti-sabotage, demolition and evacuation measures, subversion against hostile states, including assistance to underground resistance groups. . . ." Because Hillenkoetter did not feel comfortable ordering covert actions, the task was given to a new organization, the Office of Policy Coordination (OPC), to be supervised by the State Department. Frank Wisner, an OSS veteran who was Assistant Secretary of State, ran the OPC, which would share quarters with the CIA—a row of "temporary" World War I buildings on the Mall in Washington, D.C.

The OPC's first major covert operation was a series of joint British-U.S. attempts to infiltrate guerrillas into Albania to incite revolt against the communist government of Enver Hoxha. Betrayed by HAROLD (KIM) PHILBY, a Soviet MOLE in the British Secret Intelligence Service (MI6), the operation was a disaster, with every agent being captured.

After the Soviet Union exploded its first atomic bomb in Aug. 1949, Wisner parachuted CIA-trained Ukrainian émigrés into the Soviet Union. The agents carried radios and were to transmit reports to CIA HANDLERS in West Germany. For five years Wisner dropped agents or sent them in by boat along the Baltic coast.

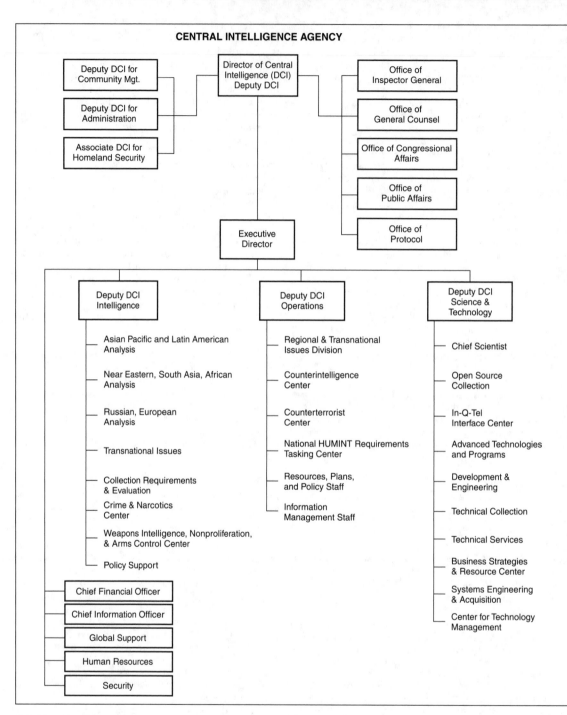

CENTRAL INTELLIGENCE AGENCY

Deputy DCI for Community Mgt.

Deputy DCI for Administration

Associate DCI for Homeland Security

Director of Central Intelligence (DCI) Deputy DCI

Office of Inspector General

Office of General Counsel

Office of Congressional Affairs

Office of Public Affairs

Office of Protocol

Executive Director

Deputy DCI Intelligence

- Asian Pacific and Latin American Analysis
- Near Eastern, South Asia, African Analysis
- Russian, European Analysis
- Transnational Issues
- Collection Requirements & Evaluation
- Crime & Narcotics Center
- Weapons Intelligence, Nonproliferation, & Arms Control Center
- Policy Support

Chief Financial Officer

Chief Information Officer

Global Support

Human Resources

Security

Deputy DCI Operations

- Regional & Transnational Issues Division
- Counterintelligence Center
- Counterterrorist Center
- National HUMINT Requirements Tasking Center
- Resources, Plans, and Policy Staff
- Information Management Staff

Deputy DCI Science & Technology

- Chief Scientist
- Open Source Collection
- In-Q-Tel Interface Center
- Advanced Technologies and Programs
- Development & Engineering
- Technical Collection
- Technical Services
- Business Strategies & Resource Center
- Systems Engineering & Acquisition
- Center for Technology Management

U.S. Central Intelligence Agency.

None of the agents sent anything more than a signal warning that they were in Soviet hands.

A bureaucratic turf battle quietly raged between the OSO and the OPC (whose employees usually had higher salaries than their OSO counterparts). The conflict crystallized when the OSO tried to recruit an agent in Thailand not knowing that he was already working for the OPC. In April 1950 the NSC heated up the rhetoric of its directives, asserting that "a defeat of free institutions anywhere is a defeat everywhere" and calling for "a vigorous political offensive against the Soviet Union."

When the Korean War began two months later, the OPC was on the rise and the OSO, the intelligence collection branch of the CIA, was faltering. Although it had noted the growth of North Korean forces along the border with South Korea, the OSO had not foreseen the invasion of South Korea.

After the North did invade on June 25, 1950, the next intelligence failure in Korea came when the CIA repeatedly told the President that Chinese intervention was unlikely. (The U.S. commander-in-chief in the Far East, General Douglas MacArthur, also believed that the Chinese would not directly intervene in the Korean conflict.)

Hillenkoetter infuriated Truman by claiming publicly that the CIA had adequately warned the President about the North Korean assault. Continuing the tradition of naming someone of military background as DCI, in Oct. 1950 Truman replaced Hillenkoetter with Lt. Gen. WALTER BEDELL SMITH, who had been Gen. Dwight D. Eisenhower's chief of staff during World War II. Inside the CIA, officials knew that the OSO-OPC rivalry was ruining the agency and that it needed drastic reorganization. Smith pulled the OPC away from the State Department and made it an office of the CIA. He also created the OFFICE OF NATIONAL ESTIMATES (ONE) to focus on producing first-rate analyses of intelligence issues.

With the OSO and OPC now together under one CIA roof, Smith gave the two offices one boss, creating the post of deputy director for plans and naming experienced spymaster and OSS veteran ALLEN W. DULLES to head it. Wisner's OPC continued to dominate the activities of the CIA, conducting paramilitary operations in Korea and China, developing resistance movements in Eastern Europe, and hiding arms caches in Western Europe for use by the "liberation" groups that Wisner was trying to create should the Soviets overrun Western Europe. In an operation given the CODE NAME Red Sox-Red Cap, Wisner trained a cadre of Polish, Romanian, Hungarian, and Czech émigrés to lead the future liberation movement in Eastern Europe.

In 1952 Smith ended the OSO-OPC problem by creating the Directorate of Plans, the CIA's clandestine service, and appointing Dulles as its head. When Eisenhower succeeded Truman as President in January 1953, he selected Dulles as the first civilian DCI. During Dulles's nine years as DCI, he made the CIA America's principal force for fighting the Cold War. Leaving the administration of the agency to others, Dulles again became the spymaster. His nickname inside the CIA was the Great White Case Officer.

THE ELITE AGENCY

Jokesters claimed that "OSS" meant "Oh, So Social!" because such a great number of OSS operatives came from aristocratic backgrounds and Ivy League universities. Many were Yale graduates, steered into the OSS by Arnold Wolfers, master of Pierson College and professor of international relations. As the OSS evolved into the CIA, it "came to outclass our once legendary Secret Service as a sleek Cadillac does an ancient hansom cab," said British writer MALCOLM MUGGERIDGE.

Dulles was a Princeton man. Yale graduate RICHARD M. BISSELL, JR., who later became one of the CIA's most daring executives, was an early recruit under Dulles. Sherman Kent, a history professor who left Yale for the OSS, joined the CIA and became director of the ONE. Among his bright young CIA recruits was Yale graduate William Bundy (later to become Assistant Secretary of Defense and a key player in the Vietnam War). As Yale historian Robin W. Winks wrote in *Cloak & Gown* (1987):

> The laying on of hands, quietly and effectively, in the college, at the master's tea and in the seminar, over a cup at Mory's and during a break in crew practice, had by the 1950s become so accepted, as John Downey, a graduate of 1951 remarked, that it was taken for granted that one would serve the nation in some way. . . .

(JOHN DOWNEY joined the CIA after graduating. Shot down on a spy mission over China in Nov. 1952, he then spent more than 20 years in a Chinese prison.)

Dulles created the culture that would sustain the CIA for the next 20 years: We have the power to do anything the President asks us to do. We can use any means to gain our objectives. This might mean using a Nazi spy chief (see REINHARD GEHLEN), setting up COVER organizations (see RADIO FREE EUROPE), or planning assassinations (see CUBA). Dulles did have limits. When he heard of a plan to use a ballerina to compromise a Soviet officer, he was shocked and said that SEX would never be used in an operation while he was DCI.

Dulles sounded the call for a worldwide crusade against the Soviet Union. "We believe that all Kremlin policies and courses of action are directed toward the attainment of the Kremlin's long-range objective of a communist world dominated by Moscow," said a CIA estimate written soon after Eisenhower became President.

Although Dulles paid little heed to day-to-day management of the agency, during his tenure the structure of the CIA began to evolve into what it is today. Under Dulles a NATIONAL INTELLIGENCE COUNCIL produced the NATIONAL INTELLIGENCE ESTIMATES (NIEs). The CIA still publishes NIEs on specific countries, areas, and subjects of importance.

Added to the DCI's senior staff since Dulles's era have been an Inspector General (IG) and staff, an associate director for military support, and an arms control intelligence staff. The IG, nominated by the President and confirmed by the Senate, acts independently of any agency component and reports directly to the DCI. The IG independently conducts inspections and investigations, as well as auditing and overseeing the grievance-handling system.

The rest of the agency is organized into directorates under deputy directors, who are referred to by the initials of their directorates. The Deputy Director for Intelligence (DDI) manages the evaluation, analysis, production, and dissemination of intelligence. The DDI is responsible to CONSUMERS for the timeliness, accuracy, and relevance of the intelligence they receive.

The Deputy Director for Operations (DDO) is responsible for the clandestine collection of foreign intelligence, including HUMAN INTELLIGENCE (HUMINT) as well as the management of the clandestine collection of foreign SIGNALS INTELLIGENCE. Although by law the CIA cannot operate in the United States, the DDO can collect foreign intelligence volunteered by people and organizations in the United States. (This directorate had been named the Directorate of Plans until its name was changed to Directorate of Operations by DCI JAMES R. SCHLESINGER in 1972.)

Since 1992 the DDO has been assisted by an associate deputy director for military affairs and by the chairperson of the National HUMINT Requirements Tasking Center, who coordinates HUMINT collection among all U.S. intelligence agencies. There is also a Counterterrorism Center that coordinates INTELLIGENCE COMMUNITY information on terrorists. The DDO, often referred to as the "spy shop," was once so secret that its director's photograph could not be published. The DDO still is not officially identified.

The Deputy Director for Administration (DDA) supports CIA and Intelligence Community activities under the jurisdiction of the DCI. Functions include finance, medical services, communications, logistics, human resources, training, and security.

The Deputy Director for Science and Technology (DDS&T) collects and processes information gathered by technical collection systems. DDS&T responsibilities include the NATIONAL PHOTOGRAPHIC INTERPRETATION CENTER and the Foreign Broadcast Information Service (FBIS). (The NATIONAL RECONNAISSANCE OFFICE, although a collection system, is an independent arm of the intelligence community under the aegis of the Department of Defense.) The DDS&T, established in the early 1960s, also develops equipment to improve the collection and processing of information.

One of the DDS&T's little-known creations, not revealed until 1997, was an eavesdropping cat, wired with a tiny microphone and fur-covered antenna. The cat was run over by a taxi before it had a chance to become a feline spy.

ANTONIO J. MENDEZ, honored in 1997 as the agency's master of disguise, revealed that the CIA created a nonexistent movie, complete with advertisements in Hollywood trade papers, as part of the background for fabricating a LEGEND to get six Americans out of Tehran during the hostage crisis in 1980. The Americans, disguised as actors and film crew members for the fake movie, managed to convince the Iranians that they were innocent filmmakers and not escaped hostages.

THE COVERT ACTION ERA

From 1950 to 1961, CIA covert operations ranged the globe. CIA talent and funds supported Chinese Nationalist guerrillas in Burma in the hope that they would establish an anti-communist foothold in mainland China. In 1950 U.S. Army Lt. Col. EDWARD G. LANSDALE, working for Wisner's OPC, ended the Huk insurgency in the Philippines by funding and running the campaign that got Ramón Magsaysay appointed Secretary of Defense and later elected president. CIA operatives overthrew Egyptian King Farouk in 1952 and brought in Gamal Abdel Nasser.

In 1953 CIA Middle East expert KERMIT ROOSEVELT led the action that overthrew Iranian Premier MOHAMMED MOSSADEGH and restored Shah Muhammad Reza Pahlavi to his peacock throne. In 1954 the CIA set up a paramilitary operation to overthrow Guatemala's leftist president, Jacobo Arbenz Guzmán, who had made the mistake of attacking the United Fruit Co. The CIA coup was directed by C. Tracy Barnes, another Yale graduate, assisted by E. HOWARD HUNT, an OSS veteran.

After talking to Allen Dulles, Arthur Hays Sulzberger, the publisher of *The New York Times*, aided the coup by agreeing to keep correspondent Sydney Gruson out of Guatemala because, Dulles said, the CIA did not consider him politically sound. In reality, Gruson said, "I had a reputation with the CIA. I got in their hair." The involvement of Sulzberger was not revealed until 1997.

The CIA was largely unknown to the American public at that time. But some information about the secret operations leaked out. Concerned about potential American reaction to the covert Cold War, President Eisenhower asked for an evaluation from a commission, headed by retired Gen. James Doolittle, a World War II hero for his daring bombing raid on Tokyo from the carrier *Hornet*. "If the United States is to survive," the Doolittle report said, "long standing American concepts of 'fair play' must be reconsidered. We must develop effective espionage and counterespionage services and must learn to subvert, sabotage, and destroy our enemies by more clever, more sophisticated and more effective methods than those used against us."

If Eisenhower was wondering what would happen when his nation discovered the SECRET WORLD, he found out in May 1960. Since July 1956, U-2 spyplanes, developed under the CIA's Richard Bissell, had been flying over the Soviet Union. On May 1, 1960, a U-2 piloted by FRANCIS GARY POWERS was shot down over Sverdlovsk by a Soviet surface-to-air missile. The United States at first tried to cover up the incident by claiming it was a weather plane that had flown off course. But the U-2 wreckage was recovered, revealing its true purpose, and Powers, who survived the crash, admitted that he had been hired by the CIA. "The downing of the U-2 was the

CIA's first massive public failure, the first time many Americans discovered that their government practiced espionage," wrote historian Michael R. Beschloss in *Mayday* (1986). "May 1960 was the first time many learned that their leaders did not always tell them the truth."

The shooting down of the U-2 did more than expose a secret CIA operation. Around the incident swirled the first whiff of public distrust of the U.S. government. Another covert action was brewing: a plan to overthrow Fidel Castro, the communist leader of Cuba. That operation was to be inherited by Eisenhower's successor, John F. Kennedy.

THE ERA OF DISASTERS

In April 1961 came the debacle of the Bay of Pigs, named for the landing area of a disastrous CIA-sponsored attempt to invade Cuba. Some 1,400 Cuban exiles, recruited and trained by the CIA, attempted to invade CUBA and trigger a revolution against Castro. Richard Bissell and E. Howard Hunt were again involved in this operation. This one, however, failed catastrophically.

President Kennedy reportedly said he wanted to smash the CIA into a thousand pieces after the debacle of the Bay of Pigs. But he merely accepted the resignation of Dulles and Bissell, replaced Dulles with JOHN A. MCCONE, former chairman of the Atomic Energy Commission, and authorized Operation MONGOOSE—a comprehensive covert action against Castro, aimed at killing him if possible. The newly established Directorate for Science and Technology did not have all the CIA science and technology under its control. There was also a Technical Services Division under the Deputy Director for Plans—the "gadget shop," as it was quaintly known, conjuring up an image of the type of hardware supplied to fictional spy JAMES BOND. But hidden in all these layers of bureaucracy were more than gadgets. There were laboratories to concoct poisons and lethal viruses and bacteria for CIA assassins.

None of the assassination plots against Castro worked. The CIA also had plans to kill Patrice Lumumba, Prime Minister of the Republic of the Congo (now Zaire), but indications are that political enemies killed Lumumba before the CIA got a chance to do it.

The CIA appeared to perform well during the Oct. 1962 CUBAN MISSILE CRISIS, which was precipitated by Air Force–piloted U-2 spyplanes (provided by the CIA) discovering that Soviet ballistic missiles that could reach the United States were being installed in Cuba. But the U.S. INTELLIGENCE COMMUNITY was later found to have badly estimated the Soviet effort—an estimated 8,000 Soviet troops were believed to be in Cuba but the real number was more than 40,000; no Soviet nuclear warheads were detected in Cuba, but 134 had been actually landed.

But soon after the Cuban crisis, as President Johnson replaced the assassinated Kennedy and ratcheted up the U.S. commitment to the conflict in Vietnam, the CIA used VIETNAM as its new stage for secret operations. Once again the CIA's reputation suffered because of its covert actions and assassinations of the PHOENIX program and its clandestine operations in Laos. "The CIA ran the war there," recalled a former CIA officer who led a band of Hmong tribesmen and Thai mercenaries in Laos. (See SPECIAL OPERATIONS GROUP.)

CIA intelligence efforts in Vietnam had mixed results. When acting objectively, the CIA was often right. In July 1965, for example, the CIA analyzed the U.S. bombing of North Vietnam and concluded that it had only a marginal effect and would not change North Vietnamese policy. But CIA analysts sometimes tried to follow the current U.S. line on the war. By March 1966 the CIA was arguing for the bombing of Hanoi and Haiphong Harbor despite their analysis of the previous year. Those contradictory evaluations weakened the CIA's position in government councils and at the same time strengthened the feeling inside and outside the agency that the war was draining the CIA's independence and integrity.

THE REVELATIONS

The 1972 WATERGATE scandal, which ultimately drove President Nixon from office, badly tarnished the CIA. E. Howard Hunt, one of the White House PLUMBERS, was supplied with a disguise from the CIA's Technical Service Division for the BLACK BAG JOB at the Watergate hotel and apartment complex in Washington, D.C. Hunt also hired ex-CIA employees for the Watergate break-in and the CIA lent the plumbers a POLYGRAPH expert to help track down leaks. Although DCI RICHARD HELMS did not carry out all the White House requests regarding Watergate, he did not erect a wall between the CIA and Nixon because of his belief that he must serve the President: "I work for the President of the United States," he declared. That loyalty cost him and the CIA another loss of public faith.

If Watergate hurt the CIA, what happened in the next few years nearly destroyed the agency altogether. On Dec. 22, 1974, Seymour Hersh, a reporter for *The New York Times*, revealed a litany of abuses of power by the CIA, including 20 years of mail interception that formed part of a DOMESTIC INTELLIGENCE operation, which was prohibited by law. (See CHAOS.) DCI WILLIAM E. COLBY confirmed the story but insisted that the practice had ended.

In the wake of the *Times* story came new disclosures, the most sensational being the CIA's plans for assassinating Castro, Lumumba, and Dominican Republic dictator Rafael Trujillo, who had been killed in an ambush on May 30, 1961. (The killers were not from the CIA, but the weapons probably were.)

Later came still more revelations. There was a long series of mind-control experiments—at least one of them fatal. (See MKULTRA.) The National Student Association and magazines—including *Der Monat* in Germany and *Encounter* in Britain—had been used as covers for CIA activities. American journalists, professors, and clergymen had been recruited as spies.

President Ford reacted by establishing the Rockefeller Commission to investigate CIA activities within the

United States. The House of Representatives set up a Select Committee on Intelligence to investigate allegations of "illegal or improper" activities of federal intelligence agencies; it became known as the PIKE COMMITTEE after its second chairman, Otis G. Pike, a New York Democrat. The Senate formed the Select Committee to Study Government Operations with Respect to Intelligence Activities, popularly known as the CHURCH COMMITTEE. Out of those committee hearings came a report that inspired an executive order from President Carter explicitly prohibiting the CIA from engaging, directly or indirectly, in assassinations.

Charles McCarry, who left the CIA to write novels and to become a senior editor for *National Geographic Magazine*, once observed that there were two kinds of people he never met at the CIA: an assassin and a Republican. (See LITERARY SPIES.) The Church Committee did not find any assassins either.

President Carter, when he entered the White House in January 1977, appointed a Naval Academy classmate—whom he did not really know—to be DCI, Adm. Stansfield Turner. In response to the unfavorable press that the CIA was suffering, Turner let go some 600 men and women engaged in covert operations. This resulted in major demoralization at the agency. Peter Scott, co-author with Jonathan Marshall and Jane Hunter of *The Iran-Contra Connection* (1987), declared:

> When all these covert operators were fired in the 1970s, they didn't just start opening restaurants or working in bookstores. They were people who were very skilled in covert manipulation of political processes, and they essentially ganged up to find and elect a candidate who would put them back in the covert operations business, and Reagan and Bush were only too eager to be that kind of candidate.

KEEPING CLOSER WATCH

The investigations into the CIA led to the establishment in May 1976 of the permanent Senate Select Committee on Intelligence to oversee the nation's intelligence organizations. Then in July 1977 the House's permanent Select Committee on Intelligence was formed.

Since the Church Committee disclosures, a series of executive orders has explicitly restricted CIA activities. The agency cannot put people under SURVEILLANCE within the United States, place BUGS, tamper with their mail, or monitor them in any way. But if the CIA believes there is a connection between someone in the United States and a foreign government, it can secretly request the FBI to perform surveillance. The FBI can then go to the FOREIGN INTELLIGENCE SURVEILLANCE COURT and request legal authorization.

Before committing the agency to a covert operation, the CIA must get authorization from the President. The congressional oversight committees must be told of such actions in a "timely fashion." Congressional scrutiny is now routine. In a typical year, CIA officials and analysts give more than 1,000 substantive briefings to specific members of Congress and congressional committees.

As part of his crusade against the Soviet "evil empire," President Reagan appointed as DCI an OSS veteran, WILLIAM J. CASEY, a vigorous champion of covert action. Reagan made Casey a member of the cabinet and reconstituted the PRESIDENT'S FOREIGN INTELLIGENCE ADVISORY BOARD to give Casey even more backing. To protect sensitive information, a special law exempts the CIA from many requirements of the FREEDOM OF INFORMATION ACT.

The CIA faced another round of investigations over the Reagan administration's decision to make an end run around Congress by providing funds to the anti-Sandinista Contra rebels in Nicaragua. The money came from indirectly selling arms to Iran via Israel to win the release of American hostages held in Lebanon by Iranian-controlled guerrillas. (See IRAN-CONTRA AFFAIR.) After long, acrimonious Senate hearings, the majority report said that "certain NSC and CIA personnel" had deceived Congress. Again the issue of state-approved murder arose. *Psychological Operations in Guerrilla Warfare*, a manual prepared with CIA help for use by the *Contras*, advocated the use of bribery and blackmail and hinted at the efficacy of assassination.

Another test—in the public spotlight—was to come. In Feb. 1994 FBI agents arrested ALDRICH H. AMES, a CIA counterintelligence officer who had been spying for the Soviets and then the Russians for at least eight years. For most of that period Ames, who lived lavishly, had not been suspected, although CIA security officials knew that a MOLE was in their midst and that they were being fed questionable information from Moscow agents who had almost certainly been TURNED. Intelligence reports given to Presidents Reagan and Clinton were thus tainted, but CIA officials did not admit it. The Ames affair, charges of sexual harassment within the agency, the holding back of promotions for women, and other agency problems led to the early resignation of R. JAMES WOOLSEY, President Clinton's first DCI.

Clinton's next choice for DCI was retired Adm. BOBBY RAY INMAN. This decision soon turned into a public relations disaster as Inman, a longtime Washington "insider," took himself out of consideration because of his concern over press harassment. His withdrawal led to the appointment of JOHN M. DEUTCH, a highly respected former Deputy Secretary of Defense.

But Deutch, who feuded with the clandestine service and became a target of ridicule and scorn, lasted only 20 months. By the time he stepped down in Dec. 1996, the CIA was an embattled agency, seemingly unable to cope with its role in the post–Cold War world.

Deutch put the CIA on a faltering course toward a new mission, to counter the spread of weapons of mass destruction, drug trafficking, and international organized crime, as well as of INDUSTRIAL ESPIONAGE. He also ordered the clandestine service to end its relationship with about 100 foreign agents who had been involved in such crimes as assassination, torture, and terrorism. About one-half of the fired agents worked in Latin America.

To replace Deutch, President Clinton chose national security adviser Anthony Lake. But Lake withdrew his name when it became clear that his confirmation was in doubt because several Senators questioned his fitness to run the CIA. When Lake withdrew his name, Deputy DCI GEORGE J. TENET took over as acting DCI; he was finally given the post in July 1997 because the Senate, where he had previously been a staff worker, would confirm him.

As Tenet took over, the CIA was enduring its worst public relations disaster since the Bay of Pigs debacle. As *The New York Times* put it in July 1997, "The CIA's public record over the last four years has been a nearly unbroken litany of bad news." This litany included the discovery of two traitors—Ames and HAROLD J. NICHOLSON—and the exposure of clumsy covert operations in France, India, Japan, Italy, and Iraq. In the most serious disaster, Iraqi security services penetrated a CIA operation to topple the Iraqi government and executed more than 100 Kurds who had been aiding the CIA.

In April 1997 the Inspector General of the Department of Justice issued a report that said the CIA "must bear the primary responsibility" for failing to ferret out Ames. The report noted that "potentially incriminating information" about Ames had been available to the CIA in late 1989 but "was not properly referred to the FBI for investigation." Early involvement of the FBI, the Inspector General said, "would have had the potential to accelerate significantly his eventual identification as the source" of blown operations and the loss of agents in the Soviet Union.

The agency also mishandled revelations about the presence of chemical weapons in an Iraqi munitions dump blown up by U.S. troops shortly after the Persian Gulf War. (Two senior analysts publicly resigned over what they said was a coverup of documents showing that tens of thousands of U.S. troops may have been exposed to the Iraqi weapons.)

Other disclosures included information about the teaching of assassination and mental torture techniques to security forces in Latin America; the revoking of the security clearance of a senior State Department official because he had informed members of Congress about the CIA's involvement in the murder of an American citizen in Guatemala; and the acknowledgment that the CIA remained silent for 30 years about lies it told in relation to unidentified flying objects, confusing the public so as to conceal work on spy planes.

Because of the CIA's record of distortion and deception regarding out-of-date secrets, the agency had little credibility to draw upon when it denied a sensational story, first published by *The San Jose* (Calif.) *Mercury News* in Aug. 1996. The newspaper claimed that in the 1980s large quantities of crack cocaine were smuggled into the United States and sold, primarily to black citizens of the Watts district of Los Angeles, in order to finance the U.S.-backed Nicaraguan Contras.

In Sept. 1996, as a political firestorm raged over the story, Deutch appeared before the Congressional Black Caucus and dignified the claim by promising an investigation. His performance was widely criticized within the administration, and many observers believe that it contributed to the decision to end his DCI tenure.

Subsequent investigations by the Los Angeles County Sheriff's Department—and by the *Mercury News* itself—raised serious questions about the story. The sheriff's department said there was no evidence of CIA involvement in drug trafficking. In May 1997 the executive editor of the newspaper repudiated the story, saying that it "fell short of [his] standards."

The terrorist air attacks on the World Trade Center and Pentagon on Sept. 11, 2001, was rigorously investigated in 2004 by an independent presidential commission, which said that the CIA claimed to have been "at war" against terrorism since 1998 but "There was no comprehensive estimate of the enemy."

While little was then publicly known of the CIA's warnings or lack of warnings about such terrorist acts, it soon became evident that the CIA operatives were active in several Arab countries. Subsequently, as the Bush administration initiated a war on terrorism with the invasion of Afghanistan in 2002 and Iraq in 2003, the CIA had people on the ground and (unmanned) aircraft aloft. The first American combat casualty in Afghanistan was MICHAEL (JOHNNY) SPANN, a CIA covert operations officer. He was killed in a prison revolt near Mazari-Sharif in northern Afghanistan in Nov. 2001. He had been interrogating prisoners when the uprising started.

Other CIA officers, some working directly with U.S. SPECIAL OPERATIONS FORCES, operated throughout Afghanistan and subsequently in Iraq as conventional U.S. forces engaged in open conflict.

The CIA "air force" in this period included the unmanned PREDATOR, an Air Force UNMANNED AERIAL VEHICLE developed for the TACTICAL INTELLIGENCE role. Beyond using them for reconnaissance, the CIA armed Predators with Stinger air-to-air missiles and employed them against suspected terrorists traveling by automobile in both Yemen and Afghanistan.

From the beginning of the Iraqi War in March 2003, the CIA came under intense scrutiny because of its conclusion that Iraq had an active program to develop chemical, biological, and nuclear weapons. In Aug. 2003 DCI Tenet, in an unusual move, released a NATIONAL INTELLIGENCE ESTIMATE, created in Oct. 2002, on "Iraq's Continuing Programs for Weapons of Mass Destruction" (WMD). He said, "We stand by the judgments in the NIE." However, by mid-2004, no such weapons had been found. Tenet's release of the estimate did not mean he was opening the CIA files. Asked about the size of its budget, he told a federal court that such a revelation "could cause serious damage to the national security." The agency had released the figure for fiscal 1997 ($26.6 billion) and fiscal 1998 ($26.7 billion).

Criticism of CIA post–Sept. 11 analyses, especially WMD reports, produced a significant change: In Feb. 2004 officials said Tenet had ordered that details about clandestine sources be given to analysts. By long practice, analysts had not been given such sensitive information, especially facts about agents who provide the data that the analysts must evaluate. CIA analysts who had produced WMD reports had believed that the data had been confirmed by many sources rather than from a single source.

Counter-terrorist efforts became the agency's principal role at the start of the 21st century.

DIRECTORS OF CENTRAL INTELLIGENCE

Three DCIs served as heads of the CIG before the CIA was founded: Rear Adm. Sidney W. Souers, Lt. Gen. HOYT S. VANDENBERG, and Rear Adm. Roscoe H. Hillenkoetter. Hillenkoetter became DCI in May 1947 and was in that post when the CIA was created in Sept. 1947. He served as DCI until Oct. 1950.

Oct. 1950–Feb. 1953	Lt. Gen. WALTER BEDELL SMITH, USA
Feb. 1953–Nov. 1961	ALLEN W. DULLES
Nov. 1961–April 1965	JOHN A. McCONE
April 1965–June 1966	Vice Adm. WILLIAM F. RABORN, JR., USN
June 1966–Feb. 1973	RICHARD McG. HELMS
Feb. 1973–July 1973	JAMES R. SCHLESINGER
July 1973–Sept. 1973	Lt. Gen. Vernon A. Walters, USA (acting DCI)
Sept. 1973–Jan. 1976	WILLIAM E. COLBY
Jan. 1976–Jan. 1977	GEORGE H.W. BUSH
Jan. 1977–March 1977	E. Henry Knoche (acting DCI)
March 1977–Jan. 1981	Adm. STANSFIELD TURNER, USN
Jan. 1981–Jan. 1987	WILLIAM J. CASEY(ROBERT M. GATES served as acting director during Casey's illness from Dec. 18, 1986, until May 26, 1987.)
May 1987–Aug. 1991	WILLIAM H. WEBSTER
Sept. 1991–Nov. 1991	Richard J. Kerr (acting DCI)
Nov. 1991–Jan. 1993	Robert M. Gates
Feb. 1993–May 1994	R. JAMES WOOLSEY
May 1994–Dec. 1996	JOHN M. DEUTCH
Jan. 1997–July 1997	GEORGE J. TENET (acting DCI)
July 1997–	George J. Tenet

Cicero

(b. 1905 d. 1970)

German CODE NAME for Elyeza Bazna, who spied on the British ambassador in Turkey during World War II.

An Albanian, Bazna worked as chauffeur for the first secretary at the British Embassy in Ankara and was then promoted to private valet to the British ambassador, Sir Hughe Knatchbull-Hugessen. As the ambassador's valet from Oct. 1943 to April 1944, he had access to highly classified documents at the ambassador's residence, where security was negligent. He photographed documents to sell to the Germans, being paid £300,000—most, however, in forged £5 bank notes.

Among the secrets this espionage garnered for Germany were information about the Casablanca Conference, at which President Roosevelt conferred with Prime Minister Churchill; details of Allied bomber operations; and the code word Overlord for the Normandy invasion.

His spying was compromised when a secretary at the German Embassy in Ankara who had knowledge of the Cicero operation defected to the British. Cicero escaped.

The story was recounted in the book *Operation Cicero* (1950) and the film *Five Fingers* (1952), in which James Mason played Cicero. Confronted with the story, British Foreign Secretary Ernest Bevin admitted in the House of Commons that "the Ambassador's valet succeeded in photographing a number of highly secret documents in the Embassy and selling the films to the Germans." The autobiographical *I Was Cicero* was published in 1962.

Cicero, having served a prison sentence for using counterfeit money, was a night watchman in Munich at the time of his death.

CIDG

SEE CIVILIAN IRREGULAR DEFENSE GROUP

CIG

SEE CENTRAL INTELLIGENCE GROUP

Cinnamon and Shrimp

Local pacification project sponsored by the CIA in South Vietnam in the early 1960s. The 500-man paramilitary group was sponsored by wealthy businessmen in Saigon to keep the Saigon–Vung Tao road, an area in which communist guerrillas operated, open to commercial traffic.

The group was generally successful while also providing useful intelligence about the area to the South Vietnamese Army.

The CIA sponsored numerous paramilitary groups in South Vietnam in this period; see CIVILIAN IRREGULAR DEFENSE GROUP.

CIPA

SEE CLASSIFIED INFORMATION PROCEDURES ACT

Cipher

A method of CRYPTOGRAPHY that involves the replacement of each letter in a message with another letter or a number. There are two basic kinds of cipher—transposition and substitution. The main difference between a cipher and CODE is that a cipher works on the principle of replacing a single letter, whereas a code works on the principle of substitution of complete words or phrases.

In transposition the actual letters of the message are rearranged. Thus, the PLAIN TEXT word BATTLESHIP could become ATLEBSPITH in a transposition cipher. Obviously, such ciphers can be easily "broken" because of the frequency of certain letters in different languages.

In English, for example, the letter E is the most frequently used, while more words begin with the letter S than any other. Also, certain words, such as *to* and *from* at the beginning of a message, would be easily understood.

In substitution, the plain-text letters are replaced by another letter or number. Although a cipher can be produced by hand, machine-generated ciphers permit a more complex cipher system to be installed, with a different number replacing the same letter every time it is used up to some astronomical number of uses. Thus, a word such as BOMBER could be LKJHGF the first time it is used and QWERTY the second time, even in the same message.

The most significant cipher machines used in World War II were the German ENIGMA, the Japanese Alphabetical Typewriter (see PURPLE), the British TYPEX, and the U.S. SIGABA.

Cipher Bureau

SEE HERBERT O. YARDLEY

Cipher Disk

Concentric disks, one of which has a standard alphabet and the other a scrambled or inverted alphabet (or arbitrary symbols). Thus a PLAIN TEXT message could be enciphered by rotating the scrambled or inverted alphabet disk to match actual letters of the message.

The device was apparently conceived in the 15th century by LEON BATTISTA ALBERTI. The cipher disk came into large-scale use in the United States for the first time during the Civil War. The Union Army's chief signal officer patented a version of the cipher disk—very similar to the original Italian disk—for use in flag signaling from point to point.

At the end of the 19th century, the U.S. Army adopted a similar version of the cipher disk in which one alphabet was standard and the other inverted (reverse standard). Although technically this was a step backward from the scrambled alphabet on one disk, there were compensating advantages, since the regularity of the alphabets tended to reduce errors.

The Army continued using cipher disks at the tactical level through World War I and into the 1920s to provide a cipher system that could be easily carried and used. Although easily deciphered if the message was intercepted, the method could give a few hours of protection to tactical messages.

The cipher disk formed the basis for the cipher cylinder concept that had been invented by Thomas Jefferson while he was Secretary of State (1790–1793). The French cryptologist Etienne Bazeries essentially re-invented Jefferson's device in 1891.

Also see M-94 CIPHER MACHINE.

Cipher Key

The specifications for setting a CIPHER machine so that it can convert an enciphered message into PLAIN TEXT.

The key for ENIGMA and other cipher machines of the type developed by BORIS HAGELIN was the settings of the ROTORS. In more modern cipher machines, the key is the arrangement of letters. The longer the cipher key, the more difficult it is to break it. JAMES BAMFORD in *The Puzzle Palace* (1982) notes that a 56-bit key would have about 70 quadrillion possible combinations before a letter would be repeated in place of the same letter in a message. The longest publicly known key was the 126-bit one developed by IBM for its Lucifer cipher. Most keys are significantly shorter.

Keys are changed periodically in an effort to defeat CRYPTANALYSIS. During World War II the Germans changed their high-priority Enigma ciphers every day. During the Cold War keys were changed even more frequently. A key used only once is invulnerable to cryptanalysis.

Cipher keys are vulnerable to cryptanalysis because of misuse and theft. Cipher machine operators misuse them, repeating the same key more than once.

The keys can also be stolen. For example, U.S. Navy communications specialists JOHN A. WALKER and JERRY WHITWORTH provided cipher keys to the Soviet intelligence services. In the U.S. Navy, every month sealed packets with a month's worth of daily keys or key lists for the cipher machines were given to various naval communications centers and ships. The key lists they stole resembled perforated IBM punch cards.

Walker would take the key lists, usually at the beginning of the key list month, and photocopy them in the communications spaces. Or, if necessary, he would take them into his office and photograph them. Photography

A Confederate cipher disk from the American Civil War. Cipher disks date at least to the 15th century, and continued in widespread use through World War II. Cipher disks have also been popular as a children's toy. (COURTESY OF INTERNATIONAL SPY MUSEUM)

was quicker than copying, and avoided the risk of someone coming over to use the machine and seeing him handling the sacrosanct key lists. It would take 20 to 30 minutes to photograph a month's key material for one CRYPTOSYSTEM.

Because the key lists were supposed to be destroyed as they were used (although in practice a batch would be destroyed every few days), it was easier for Walker, and subsequently Whitworth, to copy the lists in one session, near the beginning of the month.

Also, if an enemy can obtain copies (electronic or printed) of messages that have been deciphered, and the transmissions in cipher were recorded, he can go back through message files and compare the clear text with the enciphered text and possibly use that information to break into other ciphers in use at that time. From 1970 to 1973, while he was on board the replenishment ship *Niagara Falls*, Walker was able to copy and pass along to the Soviets nearly "one hundred percent" of the keys handled by the KW-7, KWR-37, KG-14, KY-8, and KL-47 cipher machines. (See KW SERIES.) He would periodically rendezvous with KGB officials, usually at six-month intervals, to deliver his packets of film.

At the espionage trial of Jerry Whitworth, Walker told how easy it was to steal them: "There was no difficulty in [stealing key lists] . . . anyone in the radio room could have gotten the material." If the packets that he wanted were sealed, he would simply break the seal. Reaffixing the seal? "Sometimes as simple as masking . . . or Scotch tape."

Cipher Pad

SEE ONE-TIME PAD

Ciphony

The technology of concealing or uncovering secret messages transmitted in telephone conversations. Derived from *ci*pher and tele*phony*.

Circus

Fictional name for the headquarters of the British Secret Intelligence Service (MI6), which was actually located at BROADWAY from 1924 to 1966. Reputedly named for Cambridge Circus circle—at the intersection of Shaftesbury Avenue and Charing Cross Road and several other streets—the "Circus" was popularized by master spy novelist JOHN LE CARRÉ. Although the headquarters of MI6 was not found at Cambridge Circus, British intelligence services may well have had subsidiary offices in the area, which is inundated with theaters and bookstores.

In *The Honourable Schoolboy* (1977), le Carré explains that the name "was derived from the address of that organization's secret headquarters, which overlooked a famous intersection of London streets." When his super spy-sleuth GEORGE SMILEY takes charge of the

Circus, le Carré tells of his "scruffy throne-room on the fifth floor of the Edwardian mausoleum in Cambridge Circus. . . ."

The American edition of NIGEL WEST's history of the Security Service (MI5) from 1945 to 1972 is named *The Circus* (1982); in Britain the book had the title of *A Matter of Trust*.

Civil Air Transport

(CAT)

Airline operated by the CIA to provide clandestine support to U.S. intelligence operations in the Far East. Civil Air Transport (CAT) was founded in 1946 by American flier Claire L. Chennault, head of the "Flying Tigers" fighter unit in China and subsequently a major general in the U.S. Army Air Forces. The airline was established with support from the Nationalist Chinese government of Chiang Kai-Shek and the UNITED NATIONS Relief and Rehabilitation Administration. (It was formally named Civil Air Transport on Oct. 26, 1946.)

After the communist takeover of China, CAT flew from bases in Japan and South Korea as well as from Taiwan to carry out commercial cargo operations and clandestine missions supporting U.S. intelligence activities in the Far East. CAT subsequently became an AIR PROPRIETARY of the CIA in the early 1950s.

During the communist siege of the French garrison at Dien Bien Phu in Vietnam in 1954, CAT aircraft—C-119 Flying Boxcar heavy cargo planes—joined French planes in dropping supplies to the beleaguered troops. Of 29 C-119s that flew in support of Dien Bien Phu, 24 were flown by CAT pilots. One C-119 was shot down, crashing in a violent explosion as its cargo of six tons of ammunition blew up; the two pilots, James B. McGovern and Wally Buford, were the only known American combat fatalities of the French war in Indochina.

CAT pilots also flew B-26 Invader bombers in Indochina, carried a raiding party into Tibet that captured Chinese government documents, and flew in support of secret U.S. operations in Vietnam and Laos. In 1959 AIR AMERICA became the new corporate name for CAT, Inc.

The CIA liquidated the holdings of CAT in 1973, with the U.S. Treasury Department receiving about $30 million from the transaction.

Civilian Irregular Defense Group

(CIDG)

Force of tribal fighters in South Vietnam organized by the CIA from late 1961 to fight communist guerrillas. The isolated tribal minorities populated most of South Vietnam's rugged interior mountain and jungle areas.

By 1963 the CIDG force included some 12,000 indigenous troops in more than 200 villages, assisted and trained by CIA advisers and U.S. Army SPECIAL OPERATIONS FORCES (Green Beret) counterinsurgency teams. The force, armed mostly with rifles and submachine guns, was highly effective in halting communist inroads in these areas. The effort was critical as U.S. and South Vietnamese regular military forces concentrated their efforts in the cities, located mostly along the coast of South Vietnam.

As a result of these early successes, ethnic Cambodians within South Vietnam's borders and paramilitary Catholic youth groups joined the CIDG, bringing the total force to about 75,000 in 1964.

But the effectiveness of this force was soon undermined by the shift of CIA paramilitary operations to the U.S. Army in Oct. 1963, the turnover being called Operation Switchback. With the changeover the CIDG absorbed several other CIA border patrol and SURVEILLANCE activities involving more than 6,000 Vietnamese.

Under Army control the CIDG's role began to change from a defensive force to one that carried out offensive operations, with strikes being carried out into communist-controlled areas. The CIDG continued as an effective force into the late 1960s, when the U.S. role in the Vietnam War began to decline. In 1970 U.S. special forces withdrew from the CIDG. Some of the units became Ranger (commando) units in the South Vietnamese Army.

Also see CINNAMON AND SHRIMP and VIETNAM.

CL-282

Aircraft designed by CLARENCE L. (KELLY) JOHNSON in early 1954 as a private venture by the Lockheed Aircraft Corp, developed in the firm's SKUNK WORKS. It was to be a high-altitude RECONNAISSANCE version of the firm's F-104 Starfighter to meet the requirements of the U.S. Air Force and the CIA.

The CL-282 was designed as a wide-wing variant of the turbojet-powered F-104, which first flew in 1954 and became operational in 1958. The reconnaissance variant—designated CL-282—was to have a wingspan of 70⅔ feet. For ground handling and takeoff the aircraft would rest on a dolly, which would be jettisoned as the aircraft became airborne (as with the German Messerschmitt Me 163 rocket aircraft).

The CL-282's maximum altitude would be just over 70,000 feet, with a 2,000-mile range. In many respects Johnson had designed a jet-propelled glider.

The Air Force, however, rejected the CL-282 design. reportedly, when it was briefed to Gen. Curtis LeMay, the outspoken commander of the U.S. Strategic Air Command (SAC), halfway through the briefing LeMay stood up, took his cigar out of his mouth, and told the briefers that if he wanted high-altitude photographs he would put cameras in his B-36 PEACEMAKER bombers and that he was not interested in a plane that had no wheels or guns. The general then left the room, remarking that the whole business was a waste of his time.

After being rejected by the Air Force, the CL-282 design became the basis for the U-2 spyplane, which was developed under the aegis of the CIA). It was subsequently adopted by the Air Force.

CL-400

Envisioned as a successor to the U-2 spyplane, the CL-400 was a product of Lockheed Aircraft Corp.'s SKUNK WORKS. In early 1956 Lockheed designer CLARENCE L. (KELLY) JOHNSON submitted a proposal to the U.S. Air Force for a hydrogen-fueled, high-altitude, supersonic RECONNAISSANCE aircraft.

A contract was issued in April 1956 for two CL-400 prototypes, followed by an order for six additional aircraft. However, neither Lockheed nor the Air Force was satisfied with the predicted aircraft range. The project was therefore terminated in Oct. 1957, and the almost complete prototypes were scrapped.

The aircraft was to have had two hydrogen-fueled engines fitted on the tips of thin trapezoidal wings. It would have been a two-seat aircraft with a cruising speed of Mach 2.5 at altitudes of 95,000 to 100,000 feet.

The A-12 OXCART was developed in place of the CL-400.

Clancy, Tom

(b. 1947)

Best-selling American author and master of the "techno-thriller," whose first book, *The Hunt for Red October*, introduced Jack Ryan, a CIA intelligence analyst whose ever-rising career is covered in 10 Clancy novels (to date).

Clancy, born and educated in Baltimore, Md., was an insurance agent when he wrote *The Hunt for Red October* (1984). With no intelligence or military background, his sources of information were the reference books *Guide to the Soviet Navy* and *Combat Fleets of the World*, and the board game "Harpoon." The inspiration for the "hunt" was the abortive mutiny on the Soviet frigate *Storozhevoy* in Nov. 1975.

In *The Hunt for Red October*, Ryan determines that the captain of a Soviet ballistic missile submarine is defecting to the West—with his submarine. Clancy's fast-moving narrative and graphic technical descriptions captured the imagination of President Reagan, who publicly praised the book. Sean Connery and Harrison Ford starred in the film version (1990).

Jack Ryan appears in nine more Clancy novels: *Patriot Games* (1987), *The Cardinal of the Kremlin* (1988), *Clear and Present Danger* (1989), *The Sum of All Fears* (1991), *Debt of Honor* (1994), *Executive Order* (1996), *Rainbow Six* (1998), *The Bear and the Dragon* (2000), and *Red Rabbit* (2002). In those books Ryan proceeds from analyst to troubleshooter to DIRECTOR OF CENTRAL INTELLIGENCE to President of the United States.

Clancy has written one other work of fiction—*Red Storm Rising* (1986), about a conflict between the United States and Soviet Union, as well as several nonfiction works. The latter include a series of books in collaboration with senior U.S. military commanders. With John D. Gresham he has written a series of "military tour" books describing U.S. miliary forces and operations.

Classification

The protection of material against unauthorized disclosure in the interest of national security is classified by government agencies.

In the United States there are three levels of military classification; in ascending order of secrecy, they are CONFIDENTIAL, SECRET, and TOP SECRET. In addition, certain CODE WORDS, or terms, are used to indicate special or COMPARTMENTED classifications, which means that an individual must be given specific ACCESS to that intelligence.

The U.S. Department of Energy (formerly Atomic Energy Commission) uses a different set of classifications: RESTRICTED DATA, L CLEARANCE, and Q CLEARANCE. (This "restricted" classification differs from the former military "restricted," which is no longer in use; the latter ranked below "confidential.")

There are other "restrictions" on the release of information to the public, such as FOR OFFICIAL USE ONLY. These are not security classifications, but U.S. government officials have periodically employed them to keep information from the public.

A landmark Defense Department study in 1985, directed by retired Army Gen. Richard Stilwell, stated in its report *Keeping The Nation's Secrets* (1985), "it is clear that the volume of classified documents is enormous. Obviously, the Department [of Defense] needs to protect much of what it is doing with classification controls. Nevertheless, too much information appears to be classified and at much higher levels than is warranted. . . ."

Examples of overclassification abound. The Defense Department refused to make public any photos of the Soviet air-cushion assault craft of the Pomornik class in 1986 because they were being "saved" for a report by Secretary of Defense Caspar Weinberger, scheduled for publication in 1987. However, Allies in the NORTH ATLANTIC TREATY ORGANIZATION made the photographs available to interested U.S. journalists.

Similarly, the Pentagon withheld SATELLITE photos of new Soviet fighter aircraft after Air Force Lt. Gen. Lawrence A. Skantze had them published as an accompaniment to his congressional testimony to impress Congress that the Soviets were pursuing advanced aircraft developments.

Senator Sam Nunn told of attending a classified briefing at which all of the charts used by the briefers were classified secret, including one that simply said, "We must not fail." When Nunn asked why the four words were secret, nobody could give him an answer. So he provided his own: "When you are classifying a whole lot of things, you tend to classify everything. . . . By trying to protect everything, you protect nothing."

"For official use only" and "restricted distribution" are also used—illegally—to withhold information from the public. After congressional staffer William S. Lind wrote a hard-hitting critique of the Army's unclassified manual *FM 100-5 Operations*, the Army slapped the following unclassified "classification" on the document:

DISTRIBUTION RESTRICTION. This publication contains technical or operational information that is for official government use only. Distribution is limited to US government agencies. Requests from outside the US government for release of this publication under the Freedom of Information Act or the Foreign Military Sales Program must be made to Commander, TRADOC [Training and Doctrine Command], Fort Monroe, VA 23651-5000.

The Army still handed out the document to members of Congress, staffers, and anyone perceived as a potential ally who would help sell Army thinking. To others, it was simply "unavailable."

The Navy did the same thing with the *Monthly Ships Progress Report*. This periodical lists the yards in which Navy ships are being built, along with the dates of their past and future keel laying, launching, and commissioning. After severe congressional criticism in the 1970s over delays in ship programs, the issuing Naval Sea Systems Command "restricted" circulation of the document by marking it "For Official Use Only." The information in the document was readily available through a telephone call to the Pentagon's information offices, a mile from the Naval Sea Systems Command offices. The Pentagon would give the dates and shipyard information, as did press releases issued at the Pentagon for every ship contract award, launching, and commissioning. When journalists appealed the "For Official Use Only" designation, the document's restriction was quickly changed to read as follows:

DISTRIBUTION STATEMENT B
Distribution limited to U.S. Government Agencies only; ADMINISTRATIVE/OPERATIONAL USE; [DATE]. Other requests for this document shall be referred to COMNAVSEA [Commander Naval Sea Systems Command] (SEA 907).

Finally, after several appeals to higher-level government officials, in 1994 the Naval Sea Systems Command again made the document available to the public.

The epitome of classification game playing occurred when the Navy refused to release a list of the cryptographic machines that were in the spy ship *PUEBLO*, which was captured by North Korean forces in Jan. 1968. Copies of such lists existed not only at the NAVAL SECURITY GROUP headquarters on Nebraska Avenue in Northwest Washington, D.C., but also in Pyongyang and in Moscow—probably with the machines themselves. Playing such games with security classifications accomplishes little and makes a mockery of the entire system designed to keep the nation's real secrets from getting to places like Pyongyang and Moscow.

Perhaps the ultimate U.S. military security absurdity happened in 1987, when the U.S. Air Force asked its civilian employees with SECURITY CLEARANCES to sign an agreement calling on them not to discuss or publish classified information and information that could be classi-fied *in the future*. Thus, to the concept of classified infor-mation was added the bizarre idea of "classifiable" information—ordinary data that *someday* might undergo a transformation into secret data. The Air Force branded those reluctant to sign the agreement as lacking in "personal commitment to protect classified informa-tion." Procedures were being initiated to punish those who did not sign or to dismiss them from government service when, under threat of legal action, the Air Force withdrew the requirement for the nondisclosure agree-ment. However, the "future secret" idea developed a life of its own. By the fall of 1987, some 1.7 million Air Force civilian and military employees had signed the form.

But such absurdities have occurred: In the late 1980s the Navy's submarine community attempted to reclassify the design speed (35 knots) of the nuclear submarine *Sea-wolf* although it had been previously published in the congressional testimony of the Chief of Naval Opera-tions (the submarine is faster). In the 1990s the same community reclassified all discussion of polymers as a means of making submarines faster despite scores of ear-lier articles in U.S. and Soviet publications on the subject.

The desire to withhold virtually all information per-taining to defense and national security tends to reduce the effectiveness of meaningful U.S. classification policies and hence damages American security in general.

Classified Information Procedures Act

(CIPA)

U.S. statute enacted in 1980 to establish procedures for the relevance and admissibility of classified information for use in espionage trials. The CIPA protects security in-formation by allowing a judge to decide on ways to keep secret material out of trials. Under the act, a judge, in a closed hearing, can decide how to balance protection of secrets with the standards for a fair trial.

Enactment of CIPA was inspired by fears of what legal observers call GRAYMAIL, a veiled threat by the de-fense that the cost of prosecution would be the exposure of secrets in the courtroom and hence to the public. Graymail can thwart justice by forcing the Department of Justice either to drop the case or to arrange a plea bar-gain beneficial to an admitted spy.

Through the CIPA, secrets may be examined, under tight security arrangements, by defense attorneys, clerks, and others involved in the trial. Such examinations take place in closed hearings, and those handling the classified documents are sworn to secrecy.

In the SAMUEL L. MORISON case the Department of Justice invoked CIPA, but the government went far be-yond the ordinary provisions of the act, in which attor-neys who will be seeing classified material simply agree to a "protective order" issued by the presiding judge and sign a pledge never to divulge the secrets in the docu-ments they have seen. In the Morison case the govern-ment demanded that his lawyers be fingerprinted, obtain full-scale SECURITY CLEARANCES, and allow the FBI to in-spect confidential records "including, but not limited to, academic, achievement, attendance, athletic, personal history and disciplinary records; medical records, and credit records."

Those extraordinary demands, which the lawyers considered demeaning and unwarranted, were also su-perfluous. No secrets were revealed during the trial, which lasted seven days and ended with the jury finding Morison guilty.

Clean

An AGENT or intelligence material or facilities—including an ACCOMMODATION ADDRESS or SAFE HOUSE—that has never been used operationally and is thus probably un-known to enemy intelligence services.

Clear

A message sent in PLAIN TEXT rather than CIPHER or CODE.

Clickbeetle

CODE NAME for the initial phase of U.S. Navy spy ship op-erations in the Far East that were conducted beginning in the late 1960s by the USS *Banner* and PUEBLO. Operation Clickbeetle called for a series of four- to six-week cruises to "conduct tactical SURVEILLANCE and intelligence collec-tion against Soviet naval units and other targets of op-portunity."

The Clickbeetle orders also directed the ships to re-main at least one mile outside claimed territorial waters, i.e., 13 miles. (The *Banner* made a total of 16 patrols in 1967–1970; the *Pueblo* was captured on her first patrol.)

Cline, Dr. Ray S.

(b. 1918 d. 1996)

A deputy director of the CIA and one of the nation's most experienced and respected INTELLIGENCE OFFICERS.

Cline earned his undergraduate and graduate de-grees at Harvard, and also studied at Oxford. He became a U.S. Navy cryptanalyst in 1942 and served in the OF-FICE OF STRATEGIC SERVICES in 1943–1945. He then served as an Army historian from 1945 to 1949, writing the of-ficial history of Army decision making during World War II, *Washington Command Post* (1951).

Subsequently joining the newly established CIA in 1949, Cline served in London from 1951 to 1953 in var-ious CIA headquarters positions and supervised opera-tions against mainland China from Taiwan from 1958 to 1962. As Deputy Director for Intelligence at the CIA from 1962 to 1966, he played a major role in the CUBAN MISSILE CRISIS.

After policy disagreements with the DIRECTOR OF

CENTRAL INTELLIGENCE, Vice Adm. WILLIAM F. RABORN, Cline was assigned as CIA station chief in Frankfurt, Germany, in 1966, and acted as adviser to the U.S. Embassy in Bonn from 1966 to 1969. Afterwards he directed the BUREAU OF INTELLIGENCE AND RESEARCH in the State

Department from 1969 to Nov. 1973, when he retired from government service. He was awarded the nation's highest intelligence decoration, the CIA's Distinguished Intelligence Medal.

In 1973 he became executive director of studies at Georgetown University's Center for Strategic and International Studies in Washington, D.C., and after that chairman of the U.S. Global Strategy Council.

A prolific author of articles and monographs on intelligence, Dr. Cline wrote *Secrets, Spies, and Scholars* (1976) and *The CIA Under Reagan, Bush & Casey* (1981).

Clipper Bow

Planned U.S. Navy SATELLITE for ocean RECONNAISSANCE employing synthetic aperture radar. The program was canceled before development completed. (The Soviet Union did deploy a similar RADAR OCEAN RECONNAISSANCE SATELLITE.)

Also see LACROSSE.

Cloak and Dagger

Traditional symbols of the intelligence profession—the cloak to hide and the dagger to kill. The term is used as slang for a spy operation or activity.

Also see Rear Adm. SIDNEY W. SOUERS.

Club, The

SEE THE ROOM

Cluster

U.S. NAVAL INTELLIGENCE prefix for CODE WORDS for projects and activities related to the Soviet Union during the Cold War. For example, the names Cluster Bay and Cluster Gulf were assigned to Soviet mines, and Cluster Lance to a seafloor acoustic system.

Cluster Carve and Cluster Island were the names of U.S. Navy systems with dual gamma and neutron detection capabilities for detecting nuclear weapons on Soviet ships. Those could be carried in small boats operated by the Navy's TASK FORCE 157.

Cluster Spade was an operation to measure the gravitational effects along missile trajectories in the Mediterranean Sea, conducted jointly by TF 157 and the Defense Mapping Agency in the 1970s. This project was also carried out by a disguised ship, this one a small freighter.

Cluster Neptune was a classified study produced in 1973 by the OFFICE OF NAVAL INTELLIGENCE to analyze the probable Soviet perceptions of the Vietnam War and their impact on Soviet naval planning and strategy.

Coastwatchers

Australians and New Zealanders who hid out in the Solomon Islands and Bismarck Islands to report on Japanese movements during World War II. Sheltered by anti-Japanese natives, the coastwatchers also radioed reports of Japanese air raids, alerting Allied fighter control centers.

The Royal Australian Navy established the Coastwatcher Service before World War II, and by 1941 there were more than 100 watching stations. Typically, a coastwatcher was a solitary scout—a planter, missionary, colonial bureaucrat, or policeman—who volunteered to serve when the Japanese arrived in the area. Adventurous, independent, and undisciplined, these scouts lived under primitive conditions, continually hunted by the Japanese, who sometimes used HIGH-FREQUENCY DIRECTION FINDING techniques to track down their radio transmissions. When captured, they were killed or brutally tortured, as were natives found helping them. (Their radios and supplies required porters whenever they moved.)

After the 1942–1943 Guadalcanal campaign, Adm. William F. Halsey said, "The coastwatchers saved Guadalcanal and Guadalcanal saved the Pacific." Their exploits included the rescue of Lt. (jg) John F. Kennedy in the Solomons after his *PT 109* was run down and sunk by a Japanese destroyer and Kennedy led his surviving crewmen to an uninhabited island. An Australian watcher on Kolombangara Island arranged for their rescue.

In April 1944 a coastwatcher recovered papers from the body of Vice Adm. Mineichi Koga, commander-in-chief of the Japanese Combined Fleet, after a plane carrying the admiral crashed off the Philippine island of Cebu, killing all on board. Some of the papers had to do with the Japanese plan for defense of the Philippines. The papers were rushed to American commanders for use in planning their operations in the western Pacific.

Civilians also served as coastwatchers on isolated islands in the Philippines. These coastwatchers, however, did not operate as independently as the Australian-trained variety. The Philippine coastwatchers were armed, and many worked with Filipino guerrilla forces—which is not what a coastwatcher was to do. "If your watcher gets involved in something like guerrilla warfare," a U.S. Navy intelligence officer wrote after the war, "he quickly spoils his usefulness as an observer and as a reporter."

According to Army historian Edward Drea in *MacArthur's ULTRA* (1992), "Beyond their tactical reports, perhaps the coastwatchers' finest service was to shield, albeit unknowingly, the ULTRA secret in the Southwest Pacific Area." The Allies were able to use ULTRA intelligence in areas where there were coastwatchers, for the Japanese would believe that their ships and aircraft had been spotted, not that such movements were derived from Allied codebreaking efforts.

The coastwatching network was directed by the Australian-U.S. ALLIED INTELLIGENCE BUREAU.

Cobbler

Russian term for a forger; see SHOE and SHOEMAKER.

Coberly, Alan D.

A deserter from the U.S. Marine Corps, Coberly was observed entering the Soviet Embassy in Manila in June 1983. He was judged an apparent WALK-IN with secrets to sell, although he held no SECURITY CLEARANCE and not much chance to gain access to secrets. He was apprehended by U.S. authorities, court-martialed, sentenced to 18 months at hard labor, and given a bad conduct discharge.

Code

Method of CRYPTOGRAPHY that involves the replacement of all words and phrases with code words or code numbers. A code book or dictionary of code words or code numbers is required for the sender and intended recipient to employ a code.

The principal difference between a code and a CIPHER is that a code works on the principle of substitution of complete words or phrases, whereas a cipher works on the principle of replacing a single letter.

Thus, to send the message TWO BATTLESHIPS SUNK IN HARBOR, ONE CARRIER DAMAGED, one would require a code book that has most or all of these words with either letter or number substitutes:

Word	Letters	or	Numbers
Battleship	ATMN		9827
Carrier	BSIM		5389
Damaged	SKTL		9012
Harbor	BWTS		7624
In	TDAU		8914
One	RCBU		4780
Sunk	PTMB		3589
Two	PCST		9367

Note that there is no order to the arrangement of letters or numbers. Also, the word "in" may not appear in the code book, but may—like other such words—be understood.

Accordingly, the message could be transmitted as follows:

PCST ATMN PTMB TDAU BWTS RCBU BSIM SKTL or 9367 9827 3589 8914 7624 4780 5389 9012

Such codes could have hundreds or even thousands of such substitutions. The code words employed in coded communications are different from CODE WORDS that are used to indicate a classified program or level of CLASSIFICATION.

Code Name

(1) An alias or a symbolic designation used by a spy for security in transmitting messages that might be intercepted; always used by the operator of a clandestine radio transmitter.

(2) Word or term assigned to a project, program, or operations, which may or may not be classified; if classified, it is intended to help safeguard the meaning or intention. Also known as a code word.

Code Talkers

American Indians whose native languages were used as CODES for voice communications in World War I and World War II.

The idea of using Indian language "code talkers" began in World War I when the U.S. Army, with no secure system for battlefield voice communications, used Choctaws for radio communications and for transmitting and receiving field telephone messages in France. (The Allies had belatedly learned that the Germans were tapping phone lines.)

During World War II, the Army made code talkers of Comanches, Choctaws, Kiowas, Winnebagos, Seminoles, Navajos, Hopis, Cherokees, and warriors from other tribes, who were used in the European Theater. The Marine Corps used Navajos in every Marine division and raider battalion in the Pacific theater.

Because some military terms did not exist in the Navajo language, the Navajos coined words from their language, such as *besh-lo* ("iron fish," meaning submarine) and *dah-he-tih-hi* ("hummingbird," for fighter plane.) To see a code talker dictionary, see *www.history.navy.mil/faqs/faq61-4.htm.*

Code Word

SEE CODE NAME

Codford

Planned operation by the British Special Operations Executive (SOE) against post–World War II activities by Nazis in neutral countries. It was expected that Nazi leaders would attempt to hide funds, art treasures, and other assets in occupied countries to be used after hostilities were over. It was envisioned that the SOE would locate those assets by penetrating the smuggling routes and building up contacts with art dealers and financial institutions.

Cohen, Eliahu ben Shaul

(b. 1924 d. 1965)

Born in Alexandria, Egypt, Cohen was an Arab linguist who became a highly successful spy for the Israeli MOSSAD. He was the first Israeli spy caught and executed

Two U.S. Marine Corps code talkers of the Navaho tribe on Bougainville in the Solomon Islands in 1943. In both world wars the United States used American Indians to prevent the enemy from intercepting tactical radio and telephone communications. (NATIONAL ARCHIVES)

as an Israeli (as opposed to another nationality).

He immigrated to Israel in 1957, as politically active Jews were expelled from Egypt following the Suez campaign (1956). He had secretly visited Israel in 1955 for a short course in radio and sabotage.

In Israel, Cohen served briefly in the Army and was recruited by the Mossad in May 1960 to infiltrate the ruling Baath Party in Syria. Leaving his wife and children behind in Israel, Cohen arrived in Damascus in early 1962 using the name Kamal Amin Taabet, carrying an Argentinian passport (claiming to have lived there since 1947), and declaring himself to be a Lebanese of Syrian descent. He set up a business in Damascus as a furniture and tapestries exporter and made a wide circle of friends as he hosted lavish parties. His new friends included important members of the business community, the military, the Baath Party, and, eventually, Amin al-Hafez, who at the beginning of 1965 was about to be named Deputy Minister of Defense. He later became President.

Cohen was very successful in providing the Mossad with details of Syrian military activities, including fortifications on the critical Golan Heights. He delivered his information to the Mossad by clandestine shortwave radio transmissions.

Cohen's popularity with the Syrian leadership led to his being considered for the post of Deputy Defense Minister. Reportedly, Cohen was caught when Syrian officials ordered a halt to all diplomatic broadcasts from Damascus to test new Soviet electronic equipment. Naturally, Cohen was not notified, and when he continued to broadcast during the blackout period, his transmissions were detected.

He was arrested on Jan. 18, 1965, tortured, tried for espionage by a military tribunal, and sentenced to death. He was hanged on May 18, 1965, in Damascus's Marjeh Square before a cheering crowd of more than 10,000, with television cameras showing the event. There are reports that 17 Syrian Army officers were executed because of their relationship with Cohen.

There are also stories that the Israeli government attempted to "buy" Cohen's life from Syria through a French contact. Allegedly, $1 million was offered.

Former Mossad chief ISSER HAREL told Craig S. Karpel, writing for *Penthouse* magazine: "What if I were to tell you that there are many Eli Cohens? And that if they are successful, you will never hear of them?"

Cohen's Israeli CODE NAMES were Operative 88 and "Menashe."

Cohen, Morris

(b. 1910 d. 1995)

With his wife, Lona, Morris Cohen was a major Soviet AGENT, first in the United States, where he worked with RUDOLF ABEL, and subsequently in Great Britain, where he worked with GORDON LONSDALE. The Cohens operated mostly under the COVER names of Peter John and Helen Kroger.

Morris Cohen was born in New York City of Russian immigrant parents. He joined the Communist Party in 1935 and two years later joined the Abraham Lincoln Brigade to fight for the Republicans in the Spanish Civil War. While recovering from wounds, he was recruited by Soviet intelligence to spy after he returned to the United States.

In 1941 Cohen married Leontina Petra (b. 1913), also a communist. Both of them spied for the Soviet Union during World War II while he was in the U.S. Army and she worked in a defense plant. He also worked for AMTORG, the Soviet military procurement organization in the United States.

They were associated with JULIUS ROSENBERG and his wife, Ethel, as well as with Soviet spymaster Abel. After Morris Cohen's death, the Soviet newspaper *Komsomolskaya Pravda* declared, "Thanks to Cohen, designers of the Soviet atomic bomb got piles of technical documentation straight from the secret laboratories in Los Alamos."

On the day that Julius Rosenberg was arrested for espionage (July 17, 1950) the Cohens fled the United States. They traveled extensively. In New Zealand they took on the names of a deceased couple, Peter John and Helen Kroger. They arrived in England in 1954, posing under those names as a Canadian couple. In London,

Peter ran a small secondhand bookstore at 190 The Strand; he specialized in books on sadomasochism and torture. The bookstore was a good cover for a spy ring because of the pedestrian traffic, the need to travel to the continent to buy books, and the regular international mailings.

The Cohens lived in a large bungalow in Ruislip, a suburb west of London. Among their visitors was a man they introduced to neighbors as a young friend from Canada, Gordon Lonsdale. In 1960 he briefly stayed at the Ruislip cottage.

As the net closed in on Lonsdale, in Nov. 1960 the Cohens were put under SURVEILLANCE by MI5, the British security service. Their bungalow was watched until Jan. 7, 1961, when Lonsdale was arrested and British officials entered the house and took the Cohens into custody. When MI5 officers searched their house—a nine-day process—they found photographic equipment, a hidden shortwave radio, code books, ONE-TIME PADS, microfilm inside a hollowed-out Bible, several thousand U.S. dollars, and seven forged passports. The Cohens' home had been Lonsdale's communications center.

The suspects' fingerprints revealed that they really were the Cohens, wanted in the United States in connection with the ATOMIC SPY RING.

Tried for espionage in Britain, both were convicted and sentenced to 20 years in prison. They served only eight years; on Oct. 24, 1969, they were exchanged in a complex SPY SWAP for several British citizens held by the Soviets. They were flown to Poland and later went on to the Soviet Union. (Lona died in Moscow in 1992.)

COI

SEE COORDINATOR OF INFORMATION

COINTELPRO

COUNTERINTELLIGENCE PROGRAM; SEE FBI

Colby, William E.

(b. 1920 d. 1996)

U.S. DIRECTOR OF CENTRAL INTELLIGENCE (DCI) from Sept. 1973 to Jan. 1976.

Colby graduated from Princeton University in 1941 and joined the Army, being assigned to airborne units. He volunteered for the OFFICE OF STRATEGIC SERVICES (OSS) in 1943 and was parachuted into German-occupied France in the summer of 1944, and into German-occupied Norway in 1945. A major at the time of the Norwegian jump, he was decorated for action in that operation.

After the war Colby attended Columbia Law School and then entered private law practice with WILLIAM DONOVAN, the wartime head of the OSS. Colby joined the National Labor Relations Board and, shortly after the Korean War began in June 1950, entered the CIA. He served at the U.S. Embassy in Stockholm from 1951 to

1953 and then in Rome from 1953 to 1958; and he was CIA station chief at the U.S. Embassy in Saigon from 1959 to 1962. He returned to CIA headquarters in 1962.

Colby returned to Vietnam in 1968 under the COVER of the U.S. Agency for International Development, serving with the rank of ambassador. There he helped to run the CIA's PHOENIX program. In 1971 he was reassigned to the State Department but in reality rejoined the CIA, where in 1973 he took the important post of Deputy Director for Operations. Later that year he was named DCI.

Soon after he became DCI, Seymour Hersh, a reporter for *The New York Times*, obtained information on Operation CHAOS and asked Colby about it. Colby admitted the mail intercept, which was the gist of Hersh's story. But he claimed that it was a COUNTERINTELLIGENCE operation, thus blaming it on JAMES JESUS ANGLETON, whom Hersh had not previously heard of. Colby was planning on firing Angleton.

Getting rid of Angleton, head of CIA's counterintelligence activities, was a high priority for Colby because of Angleton's obsession that there was a high-ranking MOLE within the CIA. (Reportedly, Colby was one of his suspects.)

Colby retired from government service in 1976 to write and lecture. His book *Honorable Men: My Life in the CIA* was published in 1977 amidst controversy. Colby had signed secrecy agreements at the CIA stating that as a former employee he had to obtain agency approval of his writings to ensure that they contained no CLASSIFIED information. Although Colby's American publisher knew and understood this proviso, copies of the manuscript had been sent to a French publisher before the CIA could excise certain sensitive passages.

This was, in the words of a Justice Department official, a "breach of Colby's obligation." Colby settled the dispute by paying the government $10,000 and assuring that he would adhere to his agreement in the future.

Colby died in a canoeing accident near his Chesapeake Bay vacation home in May 1996.

Cold

The psychological terrain of a spy in enemy territory—beyond the easy reach of his "side." JOHN LE CARRÉ brought the term to life in his novel *The Spy Who Came In from the Cold* (1963), an intriguing story of a double bluff, in which the hero-spy, Leamas, cannot come in from the cold without bringing along his girlfriend, Liz Gold. (The book was made into a powerful film of the same name in 1965 starring Richard Burton.)

Cold Approach

Attempt to recruit a foreign national as an AGENT or informer without any prior indication that the person might be receptive to such an offer. A cold approach may be undertaken because of cursory evidence that the individual needs money or is unhappy with his job, lifestyle, or family.

A cold approach is highly risky, as an individual who rejects such an approach may inform police or government officials, possibly in the hope of gaining a reward.

Coldfeet

CODE NAME for a U.S. Navy project to parachute two INTELLIGENCE OFFICERS onto an abandoned Soviet ice station in the Arctic to assess Soviet research in several scientific areas and possibly in anti-submarine warfare.

The officers, Air Force Maj. James F. Smith and Navy Lt. (jg) Leonard A. LeSchack, parachuted onto the deteriorating drift station on May 28, 1962. (The location was too far to reach by helicopter.) The two men carefully examined the debris and equipment that remained on the ice. After three days they were "snatched" from the ice during flyovers by a CIA-owned B-17 bomber that had been modified with the Fulton skyhook recovery system.

(For the recovery the officers put on special harnesses that were attached to a recovery line that was carried aloft by balloons. The aircraft, fitted with a hook-on device in the nose, flew over, captured the line suspended beneath the balloon, and crewmen reeled them into the plane. The procedure was carried out perfectly for the recovery of both officers and their find.)

According to LeSchack's account, *Project Coldfeet* (1996), coauthored with William M. Leary, the classified operation provided "first hand observation of the nature, extent, and sophistication of the Soviet Arctic research program." The two officers brought back 83 Soviet documents and 21 pieces of equipment, plus extensive notes that they had made and photographs taken while on the ice.

Colepaugh, William C.

(b. 1918)

American sent from Germany to spy in the United States during World War II.

Colepaugh, born in Niantic, Conn., attended Admiral Farragut Academy in New Jersey and the Massachusetts Institute of Technology, where he studied naval architecture and engineering. In Oct. 1942 he joined the U.S. Naval Reserve but he was discharged in less than a year "for the good of the service."

The FBI became interested in Colepaugh because he was reported to have German sympathies. The FBI did not know at the time that in the spring of 1941 Colepaugh had sailed on a British ship from the United States to Scotland and back to gather information about convoy formations for the German Consulate in New York City.

FBI agents tried to stop him when they learned that he had sailed on Jan. 10, 1944, apparently as a merchant seaman, on board the *Gripsholm*, a liner of neutral Sweden that was repatriating Germans to Germany via Portugal.

Under the name of Carl Curt Gretchner, Colepaugh went to Germany where the SS sent him to a SPY SCHOOL at The Hague in the Netherlands. He was told that he would be sent back to the United States as a spy. Among the TRADECRAFT lessons he learned was a German technique for safe correspondence between the United States and Germany: He was given the names and addresses of American prisoners of war. He was to write innocuous letters to the prisoners, concealing the real messages in SECRET WRITING. The letters would be intercepted by German INTELLIGENCE OFFICERS who would forward the messages to proper authorities. He was to get information on U.S. rocket, aircraft, and shipbuilding activities.

Colepaugh did not speak German, hence it was necessary to team him with someone who did. At the school Colepaugh met ERICH GIMPEL, a German AGENT who had just returned from Spain. Gimpel would accompany Colepaugh to the United States, with $60,000 in cash, a pocketful of diamonds to supplement the cash, and MICRODOT instructions on how to build a radio and communicate with BERLIN. On Oct. 6, 1944, the pair left for the United States on board the SUBMARINE *U-1230*.

On the night of Nov. 10 the submarine surfaced off the coast of Maine. A rubber boat was put over the side, and crewmen rowed the two spies ashore to an isolated beach in Frenchman Bay near Bar Harbor. They hiked and then took a taxi to Bangor. From Bangor they went by train to Boston and then to New York City, where they spent several days looking for an apartment suitable for a spy nest and to begin radio communications with Germany.

While the FBI was still searching for two suspicious strangers seen along a lonely road in Maine, Colepaugh looked up a friend, told him what was happening, and gave himself up to the FBI. Gimpel was picked up in New York a few days later.

Tried before a military tribunal on Feb. 6, 1945, both men were found guilty of espionage and sentenced to be hanged. President Truman later commuted their sentences to life imprisonment.

Colepaugh was paroled after 15 years in prison. He remained in the United States and settled in Pennsylvania.

Collins, Martin

SEE RUDOLF ABEL

Colonel Boone

Term used at the beginning of an enciphered message sent by U.S. military or naval intelligence activities to President Roosevelt when he was traveling overseas during World War II to indicate that the intelligence in a message, although paraphrased and abbreviated, was derived from MAGIC intercepts.

Colonel Passy

SEE ANDRÉ DEWAVRIN

Colossus

British high-speed calculating machine installed at BLETCHLEY PARK during World War II. More advanced than the BOMBE, the Colossus was described as a "pioneer programmable electronic digital computer," capable of reading approximately 25,000 bits per second—the speed achieved by "real" computers in the early 1950s.

The Colossus had 1,500 vacuum tubes. It was originally developed for breaking the German FISH (*Geheimschreiber*) CIPHER machine.

The Mark I model of the Colossus was first used at Bletchley Park in Feb. 1944, followed by the improved Mark II in June 1944. The latter was a faster and more versatile machine with 2,400 vacuum tubes. The Mark II was rushed into service to make it available to decipher German communications related to D-DAY—"just in time to make an invaluable intelligence contribution to the success of Operation Overlord," according to F. HARRY HINSLEY and his coauthors of *British Intelligence in the Second World War* (1984). By the end of the war there were 10 Colossus machines in service.

Colossus undoubtedly served as the basis for post–World War II codebreaking equipment developed by the United States and Great Britain.

Combat Electronic Warfare and Intelligence (CEWI)

U.S. Army process that began in the mid-1970s to integrate diverse electronic disciplines in field organizations. Beginning at that time the Army allocated each division an organic intelligence company; however, almost simultaneously the first CEWI battalion, derived from the 522nd MILITARY INTELLIGENCE Battalion, became part of the 2nd Armored Division.

(Previously the Army was reluctant to make military intelligence units organic to divisions because linguistic and other requirements could vary greatly under different theater conditions.)

The CEWI battalion—now assigned to each U.S.

Army division and some higher commands—provides intelligence collection management, COUNTERINTELLIGENCE, prisoner interrogation, and ELECTRONIC INTELLIGENCE (ELINT) capabilities. The last includes a platoon of helicopters configured for ELINT collection.

In addition to CEWI battalions at the division level, independent brigades and armored cavalry regiments were assigned CEWI companies.

Combat Intelligence

The knowledge of the enemy, weather, and geographic features required by a commander for the planning and conduct of tactical operations.

The term TACTICAL INTELLIGENCE has essentially the same meaning, and the two terms are often used interchangeably.

Comics

Many comic strips have featured spies. American cartoonist Milt Caniff, who began "Terry and the Pirates" in 1934, often had his hero fight spies, mostly "Japs" (rarely did the word *Japanese* appear in the strip). Caniff introduced a new hero to newspaper readers in 1947: Steve Canyon, a sophisticated U.S. Air Force officer, also fought spies—now called "Commies." Canyon, who won his pilot's wings in 1942, according to his "official" U.S. Air Force file, worked against Soviet and Chinese INTELLIGENCE OFFICERS until he was retired in 1989.

Surviving in the spy field is *MAD* magazine's regularly featured comic strip "Spy Vs. Spy," drawn by "El Mundo." Formerly a political cartoonist in Cuba, El Mundo fled the Castro regime in 1960 and a year later began the simplistic *MAD* strip, which features a White Spy and a Black Spy engaged in laughable and unending combat. There is sometimes a female "gray" spy—the strip being renamed "Spy Vs. Spy Vs. Spy"—to add a bit of sex to the strip. She always beats the Black and White Spies.

CROCK RECHIN & WILDER

Panel 1: HERE ARE YOUR SPY ORDERS. I WROTE THEM IN INVISIBLE INK

Panel 2: HOW DO I READ THEM? 4.27

Panel 3: WITH THESE GLASSES

©1996 by North America Syndicate, Inc. World rights reserved.

Spying can be a humorous matter, as in the comic strip "Crock" by Rechin and Wilder. Shown here are nomads from the strip, invariably plotting to attack Crock and his legionnaires. (© 1996, NORTH AMERICAN SYNDICATE)

COMINT

SEE COMMUNICATIONS INTELLIGENCE

Commercial Espionage

SEE ECONOMIC INTELLIGENCE and INDUSTRIAL ESPIONAGE

Committee of Secret Correspondence

The first American agency for collecting foreign intelligence. The Continental Congress established the committee on Nov. 29, 1775, "for the sole purpose of Corresponding with our friends in Great Britain, Ireland and other parts of the world."

The unstated purpose was the gathering of intelligence. BENJAMIN FRANKLIN ran the committee, drawing on his experience in foreign affairs. Before the Revolution he acted as a colonial agent in London for Massachusetts, Georgia, and Pennsylvania. When the Revolution began, he assumed control of foreign affairs. Other members of the committee included James Lovell, whose interest in CRYPTOANALYSIS aided the American cause, and John Jay, a future Chief Justice of the United States.

One of the first people with whom the committee had dealings was JULIEN ACHARD DE BONVOULOIR, a French AGENT whose mission was to help the United States. Franklin obtained from Bonvouloir the assurance that France no longer had an interest in Canada, which France had lost to Britain in the Seven Years' War (1756–1763). The committee then sent its own agent, Silas Deane of the Continental Congress, to France in April 1776. Deane had a second mission, as a member of the committee, to buy arms for the Continental Army. The British learned of the covert work of the committee and penetrated American intelligence with EDWARD BANCROFT, a DOUBLE AGENT. But the French-American alliance had been forged, assuring powerful support for the revolutionaries.

In 1777 the committee was dissolved and its duties transferred to a Committee of Commerce in the American Mission to France.

Committee on Foreign Intelligence

(CFI)

Established by President Ford on Feb. 19, 1976, with control over budget preparation and resource allocation for the U.S. NATIONAL FOREIGN INTELLIGENCE PROGRAM. The committee was part of a series of measures related to INTELLIGENCE COMMUNITY reforms and restructuring put into effect by Ford, several of which elevated the status of the DIRECTOR OF CENTRAL INTELLIGENCE (DCI).

The committee is chaired by the DCI, the other members being the Under Secretary of Defense (Intelligence) and the Deputy Assistant to the President for National Security Affairs.

Communications Intelligence

(COMINT)

Intelligence derived from the intercept of communications; in modern times, a subset of SIGNALS INTELLIGENCE. Communications intercepts can be of value to an enemy even if they cannot be deciphered through radio TRAFFIC ANALYSIS in determining the location, movement, and even strength of forces.

COMINT is always sent from one command to another via special, highly secure communication links, referred to as COMINT channels. (See COPEK.)

Also see CRYPTANALYSIS.

Communications Security

(COMSEC)

Procedures and methods employed to deny one's communications to an enemy. The failure to practice effective communications security has caused many military disasters.

One of the earliest COMSEC failures in the era of radio communications occurred in World War I. At the beginning of the conflict in East Prussia the Russian armies scored massive victories over their Austrian enemies in heavy fighting in the Tannenberg campaign (Aug. 1914). However, Russian victory turned to defeat when smaller German forces completely routed the Russian armies because the German commanders were able to intercept Russian radio messages that were being transmitted "in the clear." The Russian officers had a total disregard for communications security, whereas the Germans were keenly aware of the value of radio security and intercept.

With this advantage, at Tannenberg the smaller German force destroyed almost four Russian corps, killed thousands of Russian troops (including the army commander), took almost 90,000 prisoners, and captured hundreds of artillery pieces and massive quantities of supplies. Tannenberg made the reputation of Gen. Paul von Hindenburg, who almost brought victory to the German armies in the later stages of World War I.

(The U.S. Army continues to use the Tannenberg campaign in East Prussia as a fundamental example of excellent defensive tactics—made possible through German radio intercept of Russian communications.)

Also in World War I, poor German COMSEC enabled the British to read a considerable number of German communications. (See ROOM 40 and ZIMMERMANN TELEGRAM.)

Between the world wars the failure of Japanese COMSEC enabled the United States to read communications between Tokyo and the Japanese negotiators at the Washington Naval Conference in 1921–1922. (See BLACK CHAMBER.)

In World War II the Allied military successes were often due to Allied radio TRAFFIC ANALYSIS and CRYPTANALYSIS efforts. These were the ENIGMA, MAGIC, and ULTRA programs, which read German and Japanese communications (military and diplomatic, respectively). The

Allied successes against German U-boats in the Battle of the Atlantic were due in large part to poor German COMSEC. Significantly, the German Navy's commanders refused to believe that their communications were being read by the Allies despite several indications. Similarly, on the eve of World War II the Japanese had indications that their diplomatic code was being read by the Americans, but made no efforts to protect their communications (see PURPLE).

The major German—or Japanese—success in penetrating Allied COMSEC was the German B-DIENST effort against Anglo-American convoy communications.

During the Cold War era (1945–1991), the communications of the United States and other NORTH ATLANTIC TREATY ORGANIZATION countries were compromised mainly by Soviet and East German spies who had access to CIPHER KEYS and other communications material. U.S. cryptologists long believed that even if their encryption machines were compromised, their transmissions would still be secure because of the continual changing of keys; however, Soviet efforts, ably abetted by JOHN WALKER and JERRY WHITWORTH, provided extensive access to America's most secure communications.

The advent of the electronic typewriter began a new era of challenge for COMSEC, since each key of an electronic typewriter was in effect a switch that, when depressed, produced an electronic signature that could be read by an appropriate eavesdropping device. In a famous spy case, electronic typewriters en route to the U.S. Embassy in Moscow were bugged by KGB electronic experts prior to being delivered to the embassy. For a time the KGB was able to reproduce every character being typed at the embassy with those machines.

The COMSEC situation was exacerbated as personal computers replaced electronic typewriters in preparing classified documents; electronic emissions from the computers could also be detected and intercepted. The U.S. countermeasure to these potential COMSEC violations by electronic typewriters and computers is a program known as TEMPEST.

Communist Party of the United States of America (CPUSA)

Company, The

Term used within the CIA for that organization. People employed by the CIA resent its use by outsiders.

Comparator

First in a series of high-speed computational machines planned in the 1930s by the U.S. NAVY COMMUNICATIONS INTELLIGENCE organization, OP-20-G. The machines were intended to revolutionize CRYPTANALYSIS. The Navy had a contract with Dr. Vannevar Bush at the Massachusetts Institute of Technology (MIT) to design and develop the calculating machines, which would have been the most capable in the world. The project was canceled around 1939 because of lack of funds.

Bush later served as Director of the Office of Scientific Research and Development, which initiated the U.S. efforts to build the atomic bomb. A distinguished scientist and engineer, Bush was president of the Carnegie Institute and vice president of MIT.

Compartmented

Having a separate procedure for handling sensitive intelligence material. Compartmented material is limited to individuals with special SECURITY CLEARANCES. For example, certain clearances are necessary for access to TALENT KEYHOLE or SATELLITE and other OVERHEAD photography.

Compromise

The known or suspected exposure of classified personnel, information, or other material to unauthorized persons.

Computer Espionage

The tapping of computers to gain access to classified information or to alter the data stored in the computer. Ordinarily, computer-tapping AGENTS seek information. But computers can also be illegally entered for other purposes: "Viruses" can be inserted to degrade or destroy a computer's data, or a "software mole" can create false orders. Like an invisible time bomb, the subverted software lies hidden in the computer system, ready to explode in the form of catastrophic commands at a preset time.

The vulnerability of computer systems in U.S. Navy warships has been known since at least 1975. About that time the Department of Defense formed "tiger teams" whose mission was to try to penetrate sensitive defense computers. The tiger teams broke into—and took over—every computer system that they attempted to enter. The lack of adequate computer protection was conceded in the Department of Defense computer security manual that was in effect when Navy radioman JERRY WHITWORTH was serving in the nuclear-propelled aircraft carrier *Enterprise* in 1982–1983 and selling secrets to the Soviets. "Operating in a true multilevel security mode," the manual said, "remains a desired operational goal. . . . However this goal cannot generally be obtained with confidence due to the limitations in the currently available hardware/software state-of-the-art."

In 1989 West German police uncovered a Soviet-run computer spy ring that stole U.S. military software and data. Five persons were charged with passing to Soviet HANDLERS information gained from tapping more than 30 computers used by U.S. military units and military contractors. The German computer tapping was first discovered by Dr. Clifford Stoll, an astronomer and expert on computer security, who worked at the Lawrence

Berkeley Laboratory in Berkeley, Calif. The laboratory did highly classified work on nuclear weapon design.

A 75¢ accounting error in the Berkeley Laboratory computer system first alerted Stoll to the presence of an unauthorized hacker in the system. Stoll made up a fake Strategic Defense Initiative file—named SDINET—and used it as bait for the hacker. In his account of the chase, *The Cuckoo's Egg* (1989), Stoll told of working with the little-known National Computer Security Center, which helps to protect data in both government and commercial data banks.

The center's own network was entered by a graduate student in 1986. Since then the NSA has developed a "Blacker" project using an "end-to-end" encryption system: Everything in the network is encoded. Blacker is used to transmit classified information over secure government computer networks.

Intrusions of U.S. computers were also detected at the nuclear research centers at LOS ALAMOS, N.M., and at the Argonne National Laboratory in Argonne, Ill. West German officials said that the hacker-spies had been paid in money and drugs by KGB recruiters beginning in 1985. Also tapped were government computers in West Germany, Britain, France, Italy, Japan, and Switzerland.

In 1989 the FBI set up a "sting" operation in Washington, D.C., to trap a Soviet diplomat attempting to obtain information showing how U.S. government computers were protected. The diplomat, Lt. Col. Yuri Pakhtusov, an assistant military ATTACHÉ, approached a U.S. military officer and asked for such documents. The officer reported the approach to the FBI, which told him to agree to supply Pakhtusov with the information. The Soviet was arrested as the transfer took place. The U.S. State Department ordered his expulsion.

Federal investigations of PETER H. LEE and WEN HO LEE showed that sensitive data stored in computers could easily be removed. Unlike the documents, MICRODOTS, and Minox camera negatives of traditional espionage, computer files can be be made to disappear instantly. Investigators claim, however, that only the absolute destruction of a hard drive can guarantee the untraceable loss of its contents.

The use of computers in COUNTERINTELLIGENCE was revealed in the investigation of ALDRICH H. AMES. Although the FBI did not disclose details, electronic SURVEILLANCE of Ames's personal computer probably involved the planting of a computer BUG in his home. The bug might have picked up his keystrokes (each produces a distinctly different electronic signal) or turned on his computer in his absence, allowing the FBI to scan and download his files.

Computers became battlefields for Israeli security when in 1997 they reportedly tried to "crash" a Hezbollah Web site by overloading it with e-mail messages. The Hezbollah retaliated by sending the messages back—with computer viruses embedded in them. Such "computer warfare" has led the U.S. DEFENSE INTELLIGENCE AGENCY to monitor numerous INTERNET sites believed to be related to terrorist organizations.

In a 1997 report on computer security, a Pentagon task force stated that at least 65 percent of the Department of Defense's unclassified systems were vulnerable. In 1995 outsiders broke into Defense computers at least 200,000 times. Only about two percent of the intrusions were detected at the time. In one of the intrusions, hackers broke into the Air Force's Web page and replaced it with anti-government slogans and a pornographic image.

COMSEC

SEE COMMUNICATIONS SECURITY

Confidential

(C)

U.S. security classification for national security information, the unauthorized disclosure of which could be expected to cause damage to national security. This is the lowest U.S. security classification.

Also see SECRET, TOP SECRET.

Confirmed Intelligence

U.S. term for information or intelligence reported by three independent sources. According to the U.S. Army manual FM 34-130 *Intelligence Preparation of the Battlefield* (1994), "Analytical judgment counts as one source. Ensure that no more than one source is based solely on analytical judgment."

Confusion Agent

An individual dispatched to confuse the intelligence or COUNTERINTELLIGENCE apparatus of another country rather than to collect information.

Conrad, Sgt. 1st Class Clyde Lee

(b. 1947 d. 1998)

U.S. Army noncommissioned officer who was introduced to communist intelligence AGENTS from Czechoslovakia and Hungary in 1975 while serving as a classified document custodian with the 8th Infantry Division in West Germany. Over the next 10 years Conrad passed numerous classified documents to these intelligence services.

In addition, Conrad recruited his assistant, Sgt. RODERICK J. RAMSAY, who served with him from 1983 to 1985, to help in his espionage.

Conrad received a large amount of money during his 10-year spying escapade—some estimates say up to $5 million, although such a large amount seems highly unlikely for Eastern Bloc intelligence services. Ramsay received about $20,000.

Conrad and several civilians involved in the spy ring were arrested in Aug. 1988 and brought to trial in West Germany. Conrad was found guilty of having "endangered the entire defense capability of the West" and sentenced to life in prison.

Conrad, Joseph

(b. 1857 d. 1924)

Author of *The Secret Agent* (1907), a powerful early spy novel. Born Josef Teodor Konrad Korzeniowski in Russian-ruled Poland, Conrad became one of the greatest novelists in the English language.

Conrad went to sea at the age of 17 and in 1886 shipped to England. He learned English and earned his master mariner's certificate, but gave up the sea for writing in 1893. *The Secret Agent*, set in a world of anarchists, takes place in London. In it, Conrad explores the COUNTERINTELLIGENCE efforts of British operatives as they try to unravel an anarchist bomb plot. The story was based on an attempt to bomb London's Greenwich Observatory in 1894.

Although better known for his masterpieces *Lord Jim* (1900) and *Heart of Darkness* (1902), Conrad brought to fictional espionage a sense of despair and betrayal, elements that reappeared in the novels of JOHN LE CARRÉ. Another Conrad novel, *Under Western Eyes* (1911), tells of a Russian student named Razumov who finds himself being drawn into the betrayal of another student involved in an assassination plot.

Writing to a friend about his pessimistic view of life, Conrad said, "There is . . . a machine. It evolved itself . . . and behold!—it knits. . . . It knits us in and it knits us out. It has knitted time, space, pain, death, corruption, despair and all the illusions—and nothing matters. I'll admit however that to look at the remorseless process is sometimes amusing."

Consortium for the Study of Intelligence

Group established by American social scientists, historians, and specialists in foreign policy and international and constitutional law to encourage teaching in the intelligence field at both the undergraduate and graduate levels, and to encourage research in the intelligence field.

Formed in April 1979, the consortium has sponsored conferences on intelligence and a series of monographs and other publications. The monographs, published by the National Strategy Information Center, a nonprofit educational organization, began with the series *Intelligence Requirements for the 1980's*.

Consumer

Person or agency that uses information or intelligence.

Continental Air Services

(CAS)

AIR PROPRIETARY established by the CIA in the 1960s with the takeover of Bird & Son, a small, privately owned airline. Continental Air Services (CAS) provided cargo services, rescue, and forward air control for air strikes in Laos during the 1960s and early 1970s while the United States was engaged in the Vietnam War.

(The air strikes were flown by U.S., Thai, and Laotian pilots.) CAS pilots flew a variety of transport and utility aircraft, including H-34 helicopters. Their largest aircraft were twin-engine C-123 Provider and four-engine C-130 Hercules transports.

Also see AIR AMERICA and CIVIL AIR TRANSPORT.

Control

(1) Physical or psychological pressure exerted on an AGENT to ensure that he or she responds to directions from an intelligence agency or service.

(2) Organization or individual that directs an intelligence operation.

(3) Fictional head of British intelligence in JOHN LE CARRÉ novels—a takeoff on the traditional "C" used to designate the head of the British Secret Intelligence Service (MI6). Le Carré has had several Controls during the course of his novels—even his hero, spycatcher GEORGE SMILEY [F] served in that role. The descriptions of Control are like those of many le Carré characters, quite graphic, as in this excerpt from *Tinker, Tailor, Soldier, Spy* (1974):

> It was Control's time for looking exceptionally youthful. Smiley remembered how Control had lost weight, how his cheeks were pink, and how those who knew him little tended to congratulate him on his good appearance. Only Smiley, perhaps, ever noticed the tiny beads of sweat that in those days habitually followed his hairline.
> Control detested failure as he detested illness, and his own failures most. He knew that to recognise failure was to live with it; that a service that did not struggle did not survive. He detested the silkshirt agents, who hogged large chunks of the budget to the detriment of the bread-and-butter networks in which he put his faith. He loved success, but he detested miracles if they put the rest of his endeavour out of focus. He detested weakness as he detested sentiment and religion. . . .

Controlled Foreign Agent

Term used by U.S. military services to describe a DOUBLE AGENT. Sometimes referred to as a controlled foreign ASSET.

Cook, 2nd Lt. Christopher M.

(b. 1955)

U.S. Air Force officer assigned to a Titan strategic missile launch center who walked into the Soviet Embassy in Washington, D.C., and offered to sell information on U.S. strategic missiles. His earlier telephone calls to the embassy were rebuffed, the Soviet officials probably believing that he was an AGENT PROVOCATEUR. On Dec. 23, 1980, he visited the Soviet Embassy in Washington,

D.C., and was paid $50 for handwritten notes that he had copied from classified documents.

After the Christmas holidays he returned to Mc-Connell Air Force Base in Kansas where he was assigned. He gathered classified material and tried to again enter the embassy on May 2, 1981, but it was closed.

Cooke was tracked down because he had placed a call from the Soviet Embassy to his home in Richmond, Va., during his Dec. 1980 visit. Taps on the embassy telephones by the FBI led to his capture. Although he admitted committing espionage, because of a bungled interrogation, a military court ruled that he could not be court-martialed. He was released from the Air Force, in which he had served for one year.

Cooke held a master's degree, probably making him the most highly educated American to be a WALK-IN to a foreign embassy. When dealing with the Soviets he used the alias Mark Johnson and gave himself the CODE NAME "Scorpion."

Cooking the Books

Politicizing or slanting of intelligence analysis to support political views or objectives. The term came into use in espionage circles during the early 1990s.

Cookie Lady

Initially believed to part of a major espionage ring in Saigon during the Vietnam War, the "Cookie Lady" turned out to be a cookie lady. In early 1970 an informant told a U.S. Navy INTELLIGENCE OFFICER that a Vietnamese national working at the U.S. Navy offices in Saigon was selling discarded Navy documents from "burn bags" to the lady who sold cookies on a nearby street corner.

Expecting that it had discovered the first elements of a major spy ring, the NAVAL INVESTIGATIVE SERVICE sent an officer to look over the cookie lady. He bought three cookies from her, which she obligingly wrapped up for him—in a U.S. Navy CONFIDENTIAL message!

She had been buying scrap paper from the Navy employee to wrap her cookies—and neither she nor the Navy employee could read English. "What we had was a case of competitive free enterprise rather than espionage. But what we also had was a lousy physical security situation. . . ." wrote Rear Adm. Thomas A. Brooks and Capt. William H. Manthorpe in the *Naval Intelligence Professionals Quarterly*.

Cooper, James Fenimore

(b. 1789 d. 1851)

First major U.S. novelist, whose second novel, *The Spy* (1821), was his first great success. *The Spy* was a historical novel based on the activities of HARVEY BIRCH [F], an unpaid spy for Gen. GEORGE WASHINGTON in the American Revolution. Jurist John Jay had told Cooper about the exploits of Enoch Crosby, who served as Cooper's model for Birch.

The book's full title is *The Spy: A Tale of the Neutral Ground*. Cooper wrote many more novels, his most famous probably being *The Last of the Mohicans* (1826).

Cooper, raised on the American frontier, served in the U.S. Navy from 1806 to 1811. He subsequently settled in upstate New York, planning to became a gentleman farmer. But on the occasion of reading aloud to his wife, he told her that he could write a better novel than he had in his hands. She challenged him to do so, and his first, *Precaution*, was published in 1820. It had little success, but the immediate success of *The Spy* led to his devoting himself to writing.

Cooper was also a social critic, and his novels stressed individual freedoms and the rights of property owners.

Coopted Agent

National of a country who assists a foreign intelligence service. Also called a coopted worker.

Coordinator of Information

(COI)

Title given to WILLIAM DONOVAN when he began his career as an INTELLIGENCE OFFICER. President Franklin D. Roosevelt appointed Donovan COI on July 11, 1941, directing him to

> collect and analyze all information and data which may bear upon national security, to correlate such information and data and make the same available to the President and so such departments and officials of the Government as the President may determine, and to carry out when requested by the President such supplementary activities as may facilitate the securing of information important for national security not now available to the Government.

When Donovan became COI the agency was budgeted to have a payroll of 92 people. By Dec. 15, 1941, it employed 596 people and was on its way to becoming Donovan's own creation, the OFFICE OF STRATEGIC SERVICES (OSS).

Col. Edwin L. Sibert, who later became an intelligence officer under Gen. Dwight D. Eisenhower, told Donovan biographer Anthony Cave Brown that when he visited COI headquarters in Washington, D.C., it "closely resembled a cat house in Laredo on a Saturday night, with rivalries, jealousies, mad schemes, and everyone trying to get the ear of the director. But I felt that a professional organization was in the making, and I am glad to say that I was right."

Many of Donovan's early moves would greatly influence U.S. intelligence policy for decades to come. He created a Research and Analysis Division. And he turned to the Ivy League for talent: As the head of R&A, as it became known, he selected James Phinney Baxter, president of Williams College. Baxter was soon replaced by William L. Langer, a professor of history at Harvard (and a combat veteran of World War I). Under Langer, R&A developed into a huge organization staffed by psychologists, economists, geographers, and anthropologists. Archibald MacLeish, the Librarian of Congress, was the chief recruiter for R&A. Others lured by the intrigue promised by the COI included Estelle Frankfurter, daughter of Supreme Court justice Felix Frankfurter; John Ford, who had just directed the filming of *The Grapes of Wrath*; and Merian C. Cooper, the director of the film *King Kong*.

The most secret branches of COI were known as SA/B and SA/G. They were designated as training branches that would become active in the event of American entry into the war in Europe. In the structuring of COI (and later the OSS), "SA" meant Special Activities, and the letter after the slash indicated the initial of the man in charge. SA/B was an intelligence branch under David K. E. Bruce and SA/G was a sabotage branch under M. P. Goodfellow.

Donovan put the overseas propaganda program—officially, the Foreign Information Service (FIS)—under the direction of Robert E. Sherwood, a distinguished playwright and occasional presidential speech writer. Sherwood set up shortwave monitoring stations to listen to German propaganda broadcasts. The FIS promptly issued responses to anti-American propaganda. Among Sherwood's FIS aides were prominent authors, including Thornton Wilder and Stephen Vincent Benét. Marine Capt. James Roosevelt, the President's eldest son, was made Donovan's military adviser.

The COI vanished with the creation of the OSS, which became official on June 13, 1942.

Copek

CIPHER system used by the U.S. Navy during World War II for technical exchanges between cryptologists at different locations.

Coplon, Judith

(b. 1922)

U.S. Department of Justice employee who spied for the Soviet Union.

Coplon, born in Brooklyn, N.Y., studied Russian at Barnard College. After graduation she began her career as a Justice Department employee in 1943 in New York City, transferring in 1945 to the department's Washington headquarters. There she worked in the foreign agents registration section. In that seemingly innocuous job she gleaned a great deal of information, because FBI reports were often included in files of registered foreign agents—including those the FBI suspected of being Soviet operatives.

In 1948, when the FBI first suspected that she was a COURIER for a Soviet spy ring, J. EDGAR HOOVER, director of the FBI, wanted her simply fired as a security risk. But COUNTERINTELLIGENCE officials recommended that she be kept on and closely watched. Hoover, who was not comfortable with espionage work, finally agreed. Coplon was placed under SURVEILLANCE and her phone was tapped. On her frequent journeys between Washington and New York she was observed handing over documents to her Soviet contact, Valentin Gubitchev, a Soviet INTELLIGENCE OFFICER whose COVER was an employee of the UNITED NATIONS (UN).

The FBI prepared a fake secret memo signed by Hoover and passed it under Coplon's unsuspecting eyes. She had it in her handbag, along with other FBI documents, in New York City in March 1949 when agents arrested her and Gubitchev. The Soviet government's claim of diplomatic immunity for Gubitchev was unsuccessful because although he had entered the United States as a member of the Soviet delegation to the UN, he had subsequently become an employee of the UN Secretariat. The job shift lost him his immunity.

Coplon, tried for theft of government documents and attempted theft of national defense documents, was convicted, as was Gubitchev. He was deported, in a deal engineered by the State Department. Coplon's conviction was set aside by an appeals judge on two legal issues: Records of the wiretap should have been shown to her defense attorney, and her arrest should have been made with a warrant. (Congress soon thereafter passed a law authorizing warrantless arrest in espionage cases.)

She remained under bond, awaiting new trial, until 1967, when the Justice Department closed the case.

VENONA intercepts showed that Coplon's CODE NAME was "Sima."

Copperhead

British DECEPTION operation in 1944 to lead German intelligence into believing that the Allies played operations in the Mediterranean rather than the D-DAY invasion of western France. British Security Service (MI5) induced actor M. E. Clifton-James to impersonate Gen. Bernard L. Montgomery, a senior British commander, and be seen at Gibraltar and Algiers, where he was certain to be seen by Axis AGENTS. The ruse—also known as Operation Hambone—was considered a success.

Born in Australia in 1888, Clifton-James served in the British Army during World War I, seeing combat in France, where he suffered serious injuries in a gas attack. After the war he took to the stage but rejoined the Army in World War II. He was a lieutenant in the Pay Corps when he received a call from Lt. Col. David Niven, the actor phoning on behalf of MI5. Clifton-James accepted the role.

After the war he wrote of his adventures in *I Was Monty's Double* (1954), published in the United States as *The Counterfeit General*, and made into the 1958 film *I Was Monty's Double*. Clifton-James played both Montgomery and himself in the film.

He died in 1963.

Cordrey, Pvt. Robert E.

A U.S. Marine, Cordrey was an instructor at the Nuclear, Biological, and Chemical Defense School at Camp Lejeune, N.C., in 1984 when he attempted to contact INTELLIGENCE OFFICERS of the Soviet Union and Czechoslovakia to sell classified information. According to federal officials, the case was not disclosed until Jan. 1985 "due to the extremely sensitive nature of the investigation." Cordrey, who did not contest the charges of attempting contact, was sentenced to 12 years at hard labor.

Cornwall, David

SEE JOHN LE CARRÉ

Corona

U.S. photographic SATELLITE employed for RECONNAISSANCE of the Soviet Union, China, the Middle East, and other areas of the world from 1960 to 1972. Corona was the world's first spy satellite.

The CIA and Air Force began development of Corona in 1956 as a successor to the U-2 aircraft, initially known as Air Force Weapon System (WS) 117L. The spy satellite concept had its origins in a 1946 study by the RAND Corp. exploring the feasibility of orbiting artificial satellites. Developments in ballistic missiles (to boost a satellite into orbit), long-range cameras, and techniques for aircraft to snatch film canisters being parachuted down from satellites led to the Corona program. The U.S. government decision to develop and deploy Corona was made eight weeks after the Soviets had orbited *Sputnik I*, the world's first artificial satellite, on Oct. 4, 1957.

Corona had a stabilized camera that would turn on and off automatically as it passed over preselected target areas. Once the film was exposed, the film packet was ejected over the Pacific Ocean, where an Air Force aircraft snatched it in flight as it descended by parachute.

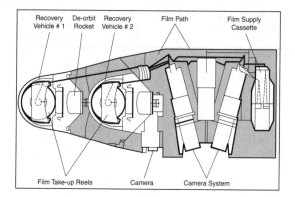

Corona KH-4B reconnaissance satellite.

The first version of Corona was the KEYHOLE or KH-1 system. Beginning in February 1959 and extending through June 1960, an even dozen launches were attempted, eight with satellites carrying cameras. All were failures, and no film canisters were retrieved from orbit. Learning from these failures, the Air Force–CIA–industry team intensified its efforts. Finally, on Aug. 18, 1960, the 13th Corona satellite was launched into orbit and successfully photographed portions of the Soviet Union. The film canister was ejected from the satellite the following day and snatched with its parachute by an Air Force plane. That one mission provided more photographic coverage of the Soviet Union than had all previous 23 U-2 spyplane missions. The 3,000 feet of recovered film showed 1.6 million square miles of Soviet territory.

Over the next decade the satellites and their cameras were continually upgraded. Under the CODE NAME TALENT KEYHOLE, the 1960 target list for photographs of the Soviet Union included (1) strategic/ballistic missiles, (2) heavy bombers, and (3) nuclear energy activities, with the principal emphasis on Soviet ICBM deployments. Subsequently, the overhead target list was expanded, as more satellites and improved cameras and film became available, enabling satellites to carry out multiday missions. For example, on July 24, 1968, Vice Admiral H. G. Rickover, head of the U.S. Navy's nuclear propulsion program, told the Joint Committee on Atomic Energy that "the Soviets have for some time had the largest nuclear submarine building and repair facilities in the world. . . . Yet, despite this, they continue to expand their facilities." His description of the massive shipyard No. 402 at Severodvinsk in the Soviet Arctic was based on Corona photography.

The satellite photos became invaluable in U.S. strategic assessments and planning, as well as technical evaluations of Soviet ships, aircraft, and other combat systems; production and transportation capabilities; and the myriad other aspects of military activity.

The final Corona mission was flown in May 1972. A total of 95 successful or partially successful KH missions were flown; 26 missions failed. (A mission might be partially successful if one of two cameras in a later satellite

A U.S. Air Force C-119 *Flying Boxcar* snags a Corona film canister (beneath parachute) during a recovery above the Pacific Ocean. Each Corona satellite ejected two such canisters during a mission. Later satellites could down-link images to ground stations or ships at sea. (CENTRAL INTELLIGENCE AGENCY)

failed, or if only one of two film canisters was recovered.) The final Corona series—the KH-4B—had a mission life of 19 days and carried 32,000 feet of film, parachuted to earth in two packets.

While the principal Corona targets were in the Soviet Union, China was also extensively covered, as were portions of Southwest Asia and the Middle East. A few flights photographed areas of the United States for calibration purposes.

Into the 1990s the Corona program was highly classified. At the time Corona was active the satellite launches were given the cover name of DISCOVERER and publicly referred to as research satellites. In one of his first public statements after being appointed DIRECTOR OF CENTRAL INTELLIGENCE, on May 23, 1995, Dr. JOHN M. DEUTCH hailed the Corona system as a classic example of an effective decision-making process by government, of industry-government cooperation, and of the significance of intelligence collection. Corona, he noted, "profoundly altered the course of the Cold War."

A Corona satellite is on exhibit in the National Air and Space Museum in Washington, D.C.

Corporation

Soviet KGB term for communist parties in other countries.

Cosmic

Highest classification for defense material of the NORTH ATLANTIC TREATY ORGANIZATION, applied exclusively to TOP SECRET documents. The CODE WORD was adopted in the early 1950s in place of METRIC.

Costello, John

(b. 1943 d. 1995)

Controversial British intelligence historian. After reading economics and law at Cambridge, he worked in television before becoming a freelance writer.

As a historian he had a reputation for great energy and perseverance. His major intelligence-related works were *And I Was There* (1985), the autobiography of Rear Adm. EDWIN T. LAYTON, on which he collaborated

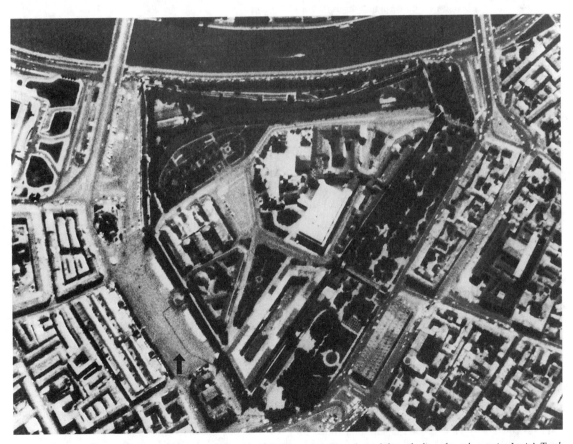

A Corona satellite photo of the Kremlin, Moscow, on May 28, 1970. The arrow points (lower left) to the line of people entering Lenin's Tomb in Red Square. Corona was developed and orbited to succeed the U-2 spyplane in detecting Soviet nuclear weapons and delivery systems. (CENTRAL INTELLIGENCE AGENCY)

with the former U.S. Pacific Fleet INTELLIGENCE OFFICER; *Mask of Treachery* (1989), about ANTHONY BLUNT; and *Deadly Illusions* (1994), the story of NKVD official ALEKSANDR ORLOV, on which he collaborated with former KGB officer Oleg Tsarev.

The Times of London wrote of Costello in his obituary:

> The truth about Costello's merits as a historian lay, not surprisingly, somewhere between the two extreme views of his achievements. Even his severest detractors acknowledged his ability to unearth new and fascinating material. Where he fell down—to the . . . academic eye at any rate—was in what was regarded as a prose style that sometimes seemed to coarsen conclusions that might have been more interestingly argued. He also sometimes ignored evidence that did not fit in with the thesis he wanted to make. Conversely he accepted—was gullible about, some might have said—information from sources such as a KGB operative with an axe of his own to grind.

He was found dead on a commercial flight from London to Miami, apparently a victim of food poisoning.

Cotton, F. Sidney

(b. 1894 d. 1969)

Pioneer in aerial intelligence. An Australian who served in Britain's Royal Naval Air Service in World War I, from 1932 onward Cotton was involved in the commercial film business as well as flying. At the time of Munich conference in Sept. 1938 he was approached by French intelligence to make RECONNAISSANCE flights over Germany using a business COVER.

Beginning on March 25, 1939, under the cover of a firm called the Aeronautical Research and Sales Corp., Cotton made several high-altitude photographic flights over western Germany, Italy, and Italian-held areas of North Africa, including two flights into BERLIN. Cotton's flights were sponsored by the French government through April, and afterward by the British (with his first modified Electra turned over to the French in late April and another one later in the year). His copilot-engineer was Flying Officer R. H. Niven, a Canadian with the Royal Air Force (RAF), who in late Aug. 1939 piloted a commercial Beechcraft aircraft on reconnaissance flights over German ports.

Cotton flew specially modified twin-engine Lockheed 12-A Electras fitted with hidden cameras. His second aircraft had three main cameras under the cockpit—one pointing down vertically and the others set at angles of 40°, to photograph an overlapping strip 11½ miles wide from an altitude of 21,000 feet. Additional cameras could be fitted in the wings. On the ground the camera ports were covered, giving the plane the guise of a business aircraft. This second Electra had additional fuel tanks fitted to provide an increase in range from the normal 700 to 1,600 miles.

After World War II began in Sept. 1939, Cotton flew additional photo-reconnaissance missions over Germany to spy out ports and warship locations. He continued to use a Lockheed 12-A Electra because available British military photo planes were ineffective for such missions.

Cotton was commissioned as a squadron leader in the RAF and appointed to command the first specialized RAF photo-reconnaissance unit.

When the war was over Cotton continued his private and commercial flying, often becoming embroiled in revolts and disaster relief. *The Times* of London wrote that he had established "a record of ruggedly individualistic, superbly unconventional behaviour, second only to his reputation for courage and resourcefulness."

Counterespionage

Activities to protect classified material from foreign collection efforts.

Counterintelligence

(CI)

Activities to protect against foreign assassination, espionage, sabotage, and intelligence collection efforts.

Countermeasures

Means of countering a specific or generic enemy threat, especially ELECTRONIC COUNTERMEASURE.

Courier

Messenger responsible for delivery and security of classified documents or other classified material. A person may be an unknowing courier, asked by a "friend" to deliver a package or envelope to another friend.

Cousins

British slang for the U.S. INTELLIGENCE COMMUNITY, especially the CIA.

Cover

Protective guise used by a person, organization, or installation to prevent identification with clandestine activities or to conceal true affiliation or sponsorship.

Covert Action

Activities carried out in a concealed or clandestine manner, primarily to make if difficult, if not impossible, to trace the activities back to the sponsoring intelligence service or agency.

Covert Action Information Bulletin

Anti-CIA periodical founded in the 1970s, listing alleged CIA AGENTS working under diplomatic COVER in various countries. Former CIA officer PHILIP AGEE was on the publication's board of advisers.

The publication's "Naming Names" column was dropped in 1982 after the Intelligence Identities Protection Act became law. This made it a crime for anyone with access to classified information to disclose information that identifies a covert agent. In 1992 the publication became the *Covert Action Quarterly*.

CPUSA

COMMUNIST PARTY OF THE UNITED STATES OF AMERICA

Legal U.S. political party transformed by Soviet intelligence agencies into a source for AGENTS carrying out missions dictated by THE CENTER in Moscow.

American Communist Party members recruited by the GRU (Soviet MILITARY INTELLIGENCE), NKVD, and, later, KGB included EARL BROWDER, head of the American Communist Party from 1930 until he was deposed in 1945; JULIUS ROSENBERG and others in the ATOMIC SPY RING; ALGER HISS of the State Department; HARRY DEXTER WHITE of the Treasury Department; JUDITH COPLON of the Justice Department, and White House aide LAUCHLIN CURRIE. Agents in the federal government not only conducted routine espionage, such as photographing and delivering secret government documents, but also attempted to influence others who, while not members of the party, were sympathetic to some of its causes.

The CPUSA (as U.S. COUNTERINTELLIGENCE officers usually called it) was so tied to Moscow that a CODE WORD for CPUSA members was "Fellow Countrymen." That code word, along with many more, appeared in Soviet espionage messages exposed by the VENONA decrypts (see Appendix A). Not until their release, beginning in 1995, was there overwhelming evidence of the Soviet espionage offensive channeled through the CPUSA. Augmenting the Venona messages are documents discovered by historians when Soviet espionage archives opened after the collapse of the Soviet Union.

British historian CHRISTOPHER ANDREW, carrying the Soviet-CPUSA PENETRATION to its possible extreme, wrote, in the wake of the Venona revelations, that if President Roosevelt had not replaced Vice President Henry Wallace, a Soviet sympathizer, with Harry S. Truman in 1944, when Roosevelt died in 1945 the country would be governed by "a pre-planned KGB-controlled administration with Henry Wallace as president, agent Lauchlin Currie as secretary of state, and agent Harry Dexter White as secretary of treasury."

The idea of using national communist parties for espionage came in 1919 when Russian party leaders created the Communist International (later known as Comintern) to use "all available means (for the overthrow of the international bourgeoisie and for the creation of an international Soviet republic as a transition stage to the complete abolition of the State."

CPUSA members who agreed to spy on behalf of the USSR were usually inspired by a belief that they were contributing to the better world forecast by Leninist rhetoric. In the 1930s the rhetoric appealed to the jobless and the hopeless. Even when the party line veered drastically, many still clung to a faith in communism that eclipsed patriotism. The faithful never faltered when a call for U.S. neutrality at the beginning of World War II suddenly became a call for U.S. assistance to the Soviet Union after Germany invaded the USSR in June 1941. By the end of the war, membership was estimated at between 50,000 and 75,000.

In 1948, reacting to spy accusations from former CPUSA members ELIZABETH BENTLEY and WHITTAKER CHAMBERS, the Department of Justice moved against the U.S. Communist Party under the Smith Act, which prohibited advocating the violent overthrow of the government. "There are today many communists in America," said Attorney General J. Howard McGrath in April 1949. "They are everywhere—in factories, offices, butcher stores, on street corners, in private businesses. And each carries in himself the germ of death for society."

The FBI arrested 145 Communist Party leaders. Many of the 109 convictions came from trials at which FBI informants, planted in the party, appeared as star government witnesses. The most successful FBI penetration of the party involved informers who met consistently with Soviet leaders in Moscow. (See SOLO.)

The release of Venona and MASK decrypted messages in the 1990s, along with documents from long-secret Soviet archives, showed conclusively that the CPUSA had been deeply engaged in espionage. One document is a Comintern accounting sheet listing payments to Americans in 1919 and 1920 amounting to the equivalent of almost $3 million, a fortune at the time. Other documents show that ARMAND HAMMER, later head of Occidental Petroleum, laundered Soviet money so that Comintern funds could not be traced to Moscow.

In *The Secret World of American Communism* (1996) Harvey Klehr of Emory University and John Earl Haynes of the Library of Congress, working with Russian archivist Fridrikh Igorevich Firsov, document the CPUSA espionage directed from Moscow and conclude:

> It is no longer possible to maintain that the Soviet Union did not fund the American party, that the CPUSA did not maintain a covert apparatus, and that the key leaders and cadres were innocent of connection with Soviet espionage operations. . . . Both the Soviet Union and the American Communist leadership regarded these activities as normal and proper. Their only concern was that they not become public.

Crabb, Lt. Comdr. Lionel

(b. 1910 d. 1956)

Merchant sailor, gas station attendant in the United States, English businessman, photographer, and Royal Navy diver. He was killed while on an intelligence collection mission against a Soviet cruiser. Known as "Buster" Crabb, he was one of the Royal Navy's best-known underwater sabotage experts and divers.

When World War II began Crabb was a merchant seaman. In 1940 he joined the Royal Navy Patrol Service and was given a commission in 1941, although a weakness in his left eye prevented him from going to sea. He volunteered for mine and bomb disposal and was assigned to that work at Gibraltar in 1942. There Crabb and other Navy divers defended British warships against attacks by Italian frogmen and "human torpedoes." When the Allied offensive began, he worked on clearing Italian harbors.

Crabb left the Navy in 1948 but returned to active duty in diving work from 1952 to 1955. On the morning of April 19, 1956, Crabb dived into Portsmouth Harbor, reportedly on a secret mission for MI6, to examine the underwater hull of the new Soviet cruiser *Ordzhonikidze*, which had brought Soviet leaders Nikita Khrushchev and N. A. Bulganin to England the previous day. A headless body was later found floating in the harbor, presumably the remains of Crabb. He was officially listed as "presumed dead" by the British government.

Crib

Incorrect practices used with CODE or CIPHER machines or devices that enable enemy cryptologists to break into the code or cipher. Most codebreaking successes are due primarily to cribs.

For example, if a message is sent by a command to several units in different codes or ciphers, one of which is partially or fully read by the enemy, this is a crib for gaining access to the second code or cipher. Similarly, communication practices such as always issuing a weather report at a certain time or beginning a message with the same salutation facilitate cribs.

Another example of a crib that the Allies used during World War II was the transmission by the German high command of birthday greetings to Adolf Hitler on April 20, sometimes in PLAIN TEXT as well as in code or cipher!

Cribs could also be forced or created. For example, during World War II the British would send bombers to lay sea mines in a specific area, knowing that the Germans would issue a report of the minelaying effort. The knowledge of the addressees and general contents of such reports helped to break into certain ENIGMA keys.

Crippie

U.S. military slang for a cryptologist; not a derogatory term. Also "crypie."

Critical Infrastructure Information Act

U.S. law aimed at aiding in the gathering of TERRORIST INTELLIGENCE by having private companies, such as power plants, voluntarily share information about vulnerabilities with the Department of HOMELAND SECURITY (DHS).

Although the law calls for federal officials to keep such information secret, some companies expressed concern that knowledge about potential problems could aid competitors—or terrorists—if there were LEAKS. The law, however, allows the DHS to certify such data is "protected" from disclosure under state and federal laws, including environmental laws and the FREEDOM OF INFORMATION ACT.

"Our aim," said a DHS official, "is to provide a platform for the private sector that will enable them to give us the information we need to advise and assist them to make the country safer. We are not trying to provide a mechanism that people can use to hide damaging information from regulators or the public."

Critical Intelligence

Information or intelligence of such urgent importance that it is transmitted to the chief of state and other national decision-making officials.

Crosby, Enoch

SEE JAMES FENIMORE COOPER and HARVEY BIRCH [F]

Cryptanalysis

The process of converting encrypted or encoded messages into PLAIN TEXT without initial knowledge of the appropriate key. (See CIPHER KEY.)

The late JAMES JESUS ANGLETON, chief of COUNTERINTELLIGENCE for the CIA from 1954 until he left the agency in 1974, wrote: "The ultimate is to break down the other man's signals security. . . . to protect your signals and penetrate the other guy's signals security."

Breaking into an enemy's communications—"reading his mail"—has been the goal of spies and intelligence services since the beginning of recorded history. Many battles have been won or lost because one side or the other could read its opponents' intercepted messages (see COMMUNICATIONS SECURITY).

The term *cryptanalysis* was coined in 1921 by American codebreaker WILLIAM F. FRIEDMAN to mean the breaking of CIPHERS and CODES. Previously the term CRYPTOGRAPHY was used for both making and breaking codes.

The need to understand coded messages dates to the most ancient times. The Book of Daniel, relating events of the 6th century B.C., tells of mysterious writing appearing on the wall of the banquet hall of the king of Babylon: MENE, MENE, TEKEL, UPHARSIN.

Then came in all the King's wise men: but they could not read the writing, nor make known to the king the interpretation. Then was king Belshazzar greatly affrighted, and his countenance was changed in him, and his lords were perplexed. (Daniel 5:8–9)

Only the Hebrew prophet Daniel could decipher the message. He told Belshazzar: "Thou art weighed in the balances, and art found wanting. . . . Thy kingdom is divided and given to the Medes and Persians." (Daniel 5:26–28) The diplomatic and military history of the world since that time is overflowing with secret messages and communications that required the services of a codebreaker like Daniel.

For example, the English had a considerable interest in codebreaking to help in the defense of the realm. The extensive intelligence activities of Sir FRANCIS WALSINGHAM to protect Queen Elizabeth I in the late 1500s, mainly from Catholic threats to her crown, included an elaborate cipher organization whose main purpose was to intercept and read coded correspondence from abroad to Catholics in England. This English interest in codebreaking continued through the centuries (see JOHN THURLOE, JOHN WALLIS, EDWARD WILLES).

At the beginning of the 20th century the use of radio communications—coupled with the other modern technologies of war—made cryptanalysis at once more difficult and, because of its immediacy, more important.

WORLD WAR I

Radio became an important tool of military commanders in World War I, leading to a related interest in radio or COMMUNICATIONS INTELLIGENCE. Codes and ciphers at that time, even those employed to transmit the most sensitive information, were simple by current standards. They were implemented by hand, usually overlying double-entry code books. Attacking those codes and ciphers took time and patience, but they could invariably be broken.

By World War I the British Army and Royal Navy both had established codebreaking agencies. It was the latter's ROOM 40 that was undoubtedly the most important cryptanalysis organization of the war. It not only broke into the German Navy's codes but also read coded cable communications from the German Foreign Office to German embassies abroad, including the so-called ZIMMERMANN TELEGRAM, which was a key factor in precipitating the entry of the United States into the war as an ally of Britain and France in April 1917.

When the French Cipher Bureau, under the brilliant cryptologist Capt. GEORGES PAINVIN, was able to break into the German ADFGX CIPHER, this success enabled the Allies to defeat the Germans' spring 1918 offensive in France. There were other wartime codebreaking successes, some of which were achieved by the Germans, mostly against the Russians.

Modern U.S. cryptanalysis had begun in 1916, when 27-year-old HERBERT YARDLEY became chief of the Army Signal Corps cryptology section. His efforts during World War I were highly successful, establishing standards for future U.S. military cryptologic operations. (The U.S. Navy's fledgling cryptologic activity was quickly closed after a review of Yardley's program.)

BETWEEN THE WARS

In 1919 Yardley established the BLACK CHAMBER, which was able to decipher Japanese diplomatic codes on the eve of the international naval conference in Washington, D.C., in 1921. The American negotiators, armed with Yardley's success, were able to push the Japanese delegation as hard as possible to derive the best possible terms for the United States.

With the postwar reductions in the size of the Army, Yardley's Black Chamber was funded mostly by the State Department. Yardley's efforts continued until 1929, when newly appointed Secretary of State Henry Stimson closed down the codebreaking operation, reportedly declaring, "Gentlemen do not read each other's mail."

A year later the Army established the SIGNAL INTELLIGENCE SERVICE (SIS), headed by one of the most successful cryptologists of all time, William F. Friedman. There were few foreign military communications for the U.S. Army to intercept, and the SIS soon centered its codebreaking attempts on the Japanese PURPLE diplomatic code.

Yardley's dismissal and the Army's failure to make him head of the new SIS left him bitter. He revealed his World War I successes in *The American Black Chamber* (1931). Beyond the embarrassment to the United States, the book's revelations led the Germans and Japanese to employ machine-generated ciphers, which were considerably more difficult to break than hand- or book-derived codes and ciphers. Indeed, with proper security a machine cipher was—in theory at least—impossible to break.

The U.S. Navy established a major NAVY COMMUNICATIONS INTELLIGENCE effort between the wars. Navy ships monitored Japanese communications during exercises, later supplemented by intercept stations ashore in China and the Philippines. The Navy was particularly successful in both conducting radio TRAFFIC ANALYSIS of Japanese naval operations and breaking into some of their secondary codes. The Navy codebreakers were also aided by BLACK BAG JOBS, surreptitious break-ins of Japanese offices in the United States to copy code books.

Japan's aggressive actions in China and Indochina inspired the U.S. Army and Navy to collaborate on breaking the Purple code. The codebreakers succeeded against the Japanese in Aug. 1940. Friedman called his codebreakers "magicians," giving the Purple decriptions the CODE NAME of MAGIC. The Japanese naval ciphers proved more elusive, although there were some breakthroughs in early Dec. 1941.

Meanwhile, in Britain the codebreakers of Room 40 had mostly dispersed after World War I. Many were soon employed by the GOVERNMENT CODE AND CYPHER SCHOOL, established in 1919 as Britain's codebreaking agency. This organization had some successes against the Italian ciphers employed in the crisis and conflicts of the

1930s, especially the Italian invasion of Abyssinia (Ethiopia) and the Spanish Civil War.

In the late 1930s, despite the German military buildup, many in the British government believed that rapprochement with Adolf Hitler was possible. The government of Poland, adjacent to Germany, knew better, and beginning in 1932 the BIURO SZFROW made remarkable strides in breaking into ciphers generated by German ENIGMA machines—ably assisted by a Pole who worked in the factory that produced the machines.

As war shadows fell over Europe in 1939, the Polish codebreakers revealed their successes against Enigma to their French and British counterparts. Thus, the Allies began the war with some success in breaking into German military ciphers. At the same time, in an unprecedented sharing of CRYPTOMATERIAL, the United States provided the British with one of its few Purple analog machines, and an exchange between U.S. and British codebreakers began that still continues almost six decades later. (See BRUSA AGREEMENT.)

WORLD WAR II

The war in Europe began in Sept. 1939 with the onslaught of German bombers and Panzer columns against the outnumbered and outgunned Polish Army. The rapid German victory in Poland was followed by the so-called phony war, in which the British and French had declared war on Germany but there was no fighting on land. At sea there was violent conflict, with German surface warships and submarines wreaking havoc on British merchant shipping, vital for the island nation.

The land war began in April 1940, when German legions and air forces overran Denmark and Norway; a month later they defeated France, Belgium, and the Netherlands, and pushed the surviving British Army off the continent of Europe. With Winston Churchill, a firm believer and user of the ULTRA intelligence derived from breaking Enigma ciphers, as its new leader, Britain fought on alone.

The breakthroughs in Ultra did lead to some British successes at sea, but they were few and far between. The British were able to capture some cryptomaterial from German weather trawlers and, on rare occasions, from a captured or sunken submarine.

The U-boats, joined early in the war by surface warships, merchant raiders, and land-based bombers, were winning the Battle of the Atlantic. If its merchant ships were driven from the sea, Britain would fall. The British had so far been unable to break the principal keys used in Enigma communications with U-boats. In Nov. 1942 alone, the Allies lost 109 merchant ships—721,700 gross tons. Thirteen U-boats were lost that month.

When the British at last broke into the U-boat operational key on Dec. 13, 1942, the effect was immediate: That month merchant ship losses fell to 44 and in Jan. 1943 to only 33. At the same time, U-boat sinkings increased. A record 19 U-boats were sunk in Feb. 1943, 15 were sunk in both March and April, and 41 in May. The U-boats were withdrawn from the major Atlantic convoy routes.

The distinguished German naval historian Jürgen Rohwer, in *The Critical Convoy Battles of March 1943* (1977), wrote of this period: "It is clear therefore, that the cracking of the German code systems was a crucial factor in the convoy battles of April and May [1943] which were seen later to have been the turning point of the U-Boat war." Several factors led to this Allied victory over the U-boats: increased numbers of long-range patrol aircraft, improved radar, more escort ships, better antisubmarine tactics, and—in some ways most significant—success in breaking the U-boat Enigma ciphers.

As early as 1941, Vice Adm. Karl Dönitz, head of the U-boat arm (and later commander of the German Navy), noted how periodically the convoys evaded his U-boat groups; the diary of the U-boat command stated: "Coincidence alone it cannot be—coincidence cannot always work on one side and experiences extend over almost nine months. A likely explanation would be that the British from some source or other gain knowledge of our concentrated dispositions and avoid them, thereby running across only [U-]boats proceeding singly."

Dönitz biographer Peter Padfield explained the German logic in examining this problem in *Dönitz: The Last Führer* (1984):

> The three ways they could get this information were by spies—everything had been done to exclude this possibility—or by deciphering radio messages—the experts in crypt-analysis at High Command considered this *out of the question*—or by "a combination of U-boat radio traffic and reports of sightings." [Emphasis added]

Both the German Navy commanders and the rest of the German military establishment refused to believe that the Allies could have broken into their cherished Enigma system.

The most successful cryptanalysis by the Axis powers during World War II was undoubtedly carried out by the German Navy's B-DIENST organization. In particular, the Germans were able to read the Allied convoy codes, which enabled U-boats to be vectored toward the merchant ships. With the British and Americans reading the U-boat ciphers, the convoys would be rerouted, and this codebreaking cat-and-mouse game would continue for days on end.

On land the German Army was able to break into Soviet tactical communications; on the Eastern Front the Germans gained an estimated 70 percent of their most reliable COMBAT INTELLIGENCE from the intercept of Soviet tactical radio communications. Ironically, the best intelligence available to the British on Soviet forces and operations was through Ultra intercepts of German Air Force communications from the Eastern Front. Relatively little of this German intelligence was officially provided by the British to the Soviets (see below).

Allied successes with Japanese ciphers also helped

win the war in Europe. The Japanese ambassador to BERLIN, Gen. HIROSHI OSHIMA, had special and close relations with the Nazi leadership, including Adolf Hitler. Oshima regularly sent to Tokyo reports of his discussions with Hitler and other Reich officials, as well as technical papers on German military plans, weapons, and defenses.

WAR IN THE PACIFIC

In the Pacific, Navy codebreakers were partially cracking the Japanese Navy's principal JN-SERIES CIPHERS from Dec. 1941—the month of the Japanese PEARL HARBOR ATTACK. This intelligence was soon put to use: On Jan. 27, 1942, the U.S. submarine *Gudgeon* was sent to a spot in the ocean by Navy codebreakers. The *Gudgeon* detected and sank the Japanese submarine *I-73* running on the surface. She was the first Japanese warship to fall victim to an American submarine.

The Navy's codebreakers at Pearl Harbor (station HYPO) were able to advise Adm. Chester W. Nimitz, the American commander in the Pacific, that the Japanese would attack Port Moresby, New Guinea, in their drive toward Australia. U.S. carriers stopped the Japanese force in early May 1942 in the Battle of the Coral Sea, the first setback for the Japanese.

Next the codebreakers told Nimitz that the Japanese would mount a major assault against MIDWAY atoll to draw out the American fleet for a decisive battle. Forewarned, Nimitz was able to deploy his few, outnumbered warships in a position from which they could surprise the Japanese. In the Battle of Midway in early June 1942, the Japanese lost four large aircraft carriers, along with all of their aircraft and many of their pilots; the United States lost one carrier. Midway was the turning point of the Pacific War.

After Midway the U.S. forces went on the offensive in the Pacific. On the morning of April 17, 1943, a U.S. Navy radio intercept station at Dutch Harbor in the Aleutian Islands intercepted a message from the battleship *Yamato*, flagship of the Japanese fleet. Recognizing the name of the flagship even with the message in code, the Aleutians station flashed the message to Washington. There, codebreakers were able to decipher the message, which revealed that the commander in chief of the Japanese Fleet, Adm. ISOROKU YAMAMOTO, was making an inspection of bases in the Southwest Pacific. Details of his schedule were provided.

Nimitz and his subordinate commander, Vice Adm. William F. Halsey, ordered an aerial interception of Yamamoto during his inspection. Yamamoto was shot down and killed on April 18, 1943.

Ultra-Magic helped the U.S. Navy in operations through the remainder of the war. Decripts enabled the U.S. destroyer escort *England* to sink six Japanese submarines in 12 days, making her the most successful antisubmarine ship of any navy in either world war.

The Navy provided decripts of Japanese naval communications to Gen. Douglas MacArthur, commander of the U.S. Southwest Pacific Area. Japanese transports and naval aircraft were directly involved in Army operations, hence their value to MacArthur. Not until 1944 were major Japanese Army codes deciphered.

The Japanese had little success against Allied ciphers, mainly because of their limited interest and emphasis on intelligence activities, and the lack of cooperation between the (small) codebreaking activities of the Army and Navy. Indeed, the U.S. SIGABA appears to have been the only enciphering machine not "broken" by an enemy. (The Japanese were able to break into Chinese codes with relative ease.)

THE COLD WAR

By the start of World War II the United States and British were regularly intercepting Soviet communications to their diplomats and AGENTS abroad. Virtually no progress, however, was made in decoding these communications because the Soviets used ONE-TIME PADS to encode their messages. This method was probably the most secure scheme possible.

The Soviets, however, had successes against their enemies as well as their allies during the war. In part because of Josef Stalin's massive purges of military officers in the late 1930s, Soviet codebreaking efforts were relatively primitive when Germany launched operation BARBAROSSA against the Soviet Union in June 1941. By the end of the year some Enigma machines had been captured from the Germans, apparently with appropriate keys. Further, the Soviets had access to British codebreaking successes: JOHN CAIRNCROSS, a Soviet MOLE, was assigned to BLETCHLEY PARK, the wartime home of the British Government Code and Cypher School, during 1942–1943.

Other moles in the British government, especially the members of the CAMBRIDGE SPY RING, provided the Soviets with highly classified government papers, including messages. These CRIBS helped the Soviets break into British-American communications at least into the 1950s. The Soviet codebreakers were also helped by the continual communication between President Roosevelt and Stalin; these were sent by U.S. Navy communication circuits—in cipher—but they were lengthy messages, and the U.S. Navy officers who handled the President's messages in Moscow were ordered not to change a single word. Thus, the Soviets were given an excellent crib into U.S. military communications.

The principal British spy who gave the Soviets access to ciphers was GEOFFREY PRIME of the Government Code and Cypher School. In the United States there was a parade of traitors: WILLIAM H. MARTIN and BERNON F. MITCHELL, cryptanalysts from the NSA, who defected to the USSR; Army Sgt. JACK DUNLAP, driver for the head of NSA with access to his classified papers, which he sold to the Soviets; Warrant Officer JOSEPH HELMICH and Sgt. ROBERT S. LIPKA, soldiers assigned to the NSA, who also provided cipher material; one or more U.S. Marines at the American Embassy in Moscow, who may have given Soviets access to TOP SECRET communication spaces; JOHN A. WALKER and JERRY WHITWORTH, Navy communications specialists who sold the keys for cipher machines to the Soviets.

The last two men inflicted the most damage on American communications security. In Jan. 1968 the North Koreans captured the U.S. spy ship *PUEBLO*, obtaining numerous cipher machines, albeit damaged, as well as maintenance manuals and copies of classified messages. The North Vietnamese had captured numerous U.S. cipher machines—some sources say 32—during the Vietnam War, most from South Vietnamese troops when the war ended in 1975. Those machines undoubtedly were made available to the Soviet Union.

U.S. officials felt that their ciphers were still secure because the all-important keys, changed every day with very carefully controlled distribution, were still safe. But Walker and Whitworth gave the Soviets the keys. When the Walker-Whitworth spy ring was revealed in May 1985, opinion varied as to the damage the radio operators had inflicted on the defense establishment. To many U.S. naval officers, the implications were beyond their ability to comprehend. Assessing the impact of the Walker-Whitworth betrayal a month after their arrest, Adm. James D. Watkins, the Chief of Naval Operations, declared that the Navy had the problem "bounded and can leave it in the dust behind us. . . . We believe we are on the downside of the problem. . . . We believe we have surrounded it."

Asked specifically about the possible vulnerability of U.S. submarines because of the espionage efforts, Watkins, at a Pentagon press conference, was even more sanguine. He declared that there was no indication that the Soviets had broken the codes that would permit them to detect the U.S. undersea craft "and therefore, we remain convinced that our SSBN [strategic missile submarine] force is still one hundred percent survivable."

But other officials were much more concerned than Watkins appeared to be. Rear Adm. John Butts, director of NAVAL INTELLIGENCE at the time, in a staff meeting estimated the damage done by Walker-Whitworth: "On a scale of one-to-ten . . . a twelve!" More than a year after the spy ring was broken, a new Chief of Naval Operations, Adm. Carlisle A. H. Trost, stated that code material could have given the Soviets the advantage over the United States in a war at sea. Trost's director of Naval Intelligence, Rear Adm. WILLIAM O. STUDEMAN, said, "We will likely never know the true extent to which our capabilities have been impaired by the traitorous and infamous acts of Jerry Whitworth."

"Had conflict erupted between the two superpowers," Trost said, "the Soviets would have been exploiting information with the potential to have powerful war-winning implications for the Soviet side."

Summing up Soviet codebreaking capabilities, historian DAVID KAHN has implied that they have had great success: "We know that there are three things which are often associated with success in codebreaking: ability in chess, ability in music, and ability in mathematics." Historically, the Russians have excelled in all three areas.

It is more difficult to ascertain the U.S. success in breaking into Soviet communications. During World War II the United States intercepted and recorded Soviet communications with diplomats and agents in the United States. After the war, in 1947, an American cryptologist, MEREDITH GARDNER, was able to begin reading some of the messages because of a Soviet error in distributing onetime pads during the war. (See VENONA.) This breakthrough—shared with the British—enabled parts of some messages to be read, revealing the extent of Soviet spy activities in the United States. (See MASK.)

The British also placed BUGS in the Soviet Embassy in London that revealed some intelligence related to ciphers, but these were soon detected and rendered impotent. And undoubtedly, some of the many Soviet INTELLIGENCE OFFICERS and military officers who spied for the West or defected brought some cryptomaterial with them. This material, coupled with the tremendous batteries of computers and the efforts of cryptologists at the NSA and the Government Code and Cypher School, undoubtedly made inroads into Soviet communications.

In the latter part of the 20th century the major intelligence services continued their efforts to break into the codes and ciphers of potential enemies. With the enormous increase in computer-processing capabilities, some governments began to express increased concern over the development of commercially available data-scrambling software. This software permits private citizens and commercial firms to transmit data over telephone lines with little or no possibility of its being read by anyone other than the intended receiver.

In an effort to curtail the use of this technology by individuals as well as by multinational firms, in 1996 the Clinton administration placed restrictions on the export of some forms of data-scrambling software. Clinton officials classified such software as a "munition," imposing many of the same export restrictions as those imposed on missiles and other weapons.

The administration's rationale was that such "unbreakable" computer programs could help criminals and terrorists. FBI director LOUIS FREEH told a congressional panel that such software sold in the United States should be required to contain a feature that would enable law enforcement agencies to read scrambled communications.

Computer software firms and others immediately attacked the Clinton administration proposals as a violation of free speech. On Dec. 18, 1996, in San Francisco, U.S. District Judge Marilyn Hall Patel ruled that the government's attempts to stop a professor of mathematics from exporting an encryption program that he had created was an unconstitutional restriction of his right to freedom of expression. The decision did not directly declare all encryption export controls illegal, but it stands as a substantial court victory for opponents of such controls.

The exporting of encryption techniques is still under federal watch. Highly technical controls are maintained by the Department of Commerce's Bureau of Industry and Security, whose missions include regulating the export of sensitive goods and technologies.

Cryptogram

A message in CIPHER or CODE.

Cryptography

The science of secret writing, the term being derived from the Greek *kryptos* (secret) and *graphos* (writing). Cryptography is employed in intelligence and espionage activities to send messages in such a way as to conceal the real meaning from everyone but the sender and the intended recipient.

There are two principal kinds of cryptography: CODE and CIPHER. (See SECRET WRITING.)

The term *cryptography* also meant the "breaking" of codes until 1921, when American codebreaker WILLIAM F. FRIEDMAN coined the term CRYPTANALYSIS.

Crypie

SEE CRIPPIE

Cryptologic Service Groups

NSA units that work directly with senior U.S. military commanders and civilian officials to provide cryptologic support on a real-time basis. The groups have been described as "miniature NSAs."

Cryptomaterial

Documents, devices, equipment, apparatus, and other material for the encryption, decryption, or authentication of communications.

Cryptonym

A false or COVER name assigned to an AGENT or classified operation or project; a CODE NAME.

The CIA in the past assigned cryptonyms with two-letter prefixes or digraphs that indicated a particular subject or area; thus, in MKULTRA the MK indicated a project of the CIA's Technical Services Staff, and MHCHAOS indicated the CIA aspect of the domestic Operation CHAOS, the MH indicating U.S. international security.

Cryptosecurity

Methods and procedures for protecting CIPHERS and CODES, both the CRYPTOSYSTEMS and operating procedures.

Cryptosystems

Material and equipment for encryption and decryption.

Crystal

SEE KENNAN

CSP
(CODE & SIGNAL PUBLICATIONS)

U.S. Navy designation for CRYPTOMATERIAL, including equipment, documents, and instructions.

Cub (An-12)

Soviet cargo/transport aircraft, one of the most important aircraft of that category in Soviet military and civilian operation. A number were configured for the ELECTRONIC INTELLIGENCE (ELINT) role for carrying out SURVEILLANCE of Western warships.

Beyond operating from Soviet bases, from 1967 to 1972 ELINT-configured Cubs were among the Soviet planes based in Egypt to support Soviet naval activities in the eastern Mediterranean. Some of these planes had Egyptian markings but appear to have been flown only by Soviet crews. The aircraft have also flown from bases in other Third World countries aligned with the Soviet Union.

The Antonov-designed Cub has a high-wing configuration to provide clear cargo space and is propelled by four turboprop engines; the main landing gear is housed in pods on the fuselage to avoid cutting into floor space. The sharply upswept rear fuselage incorporates an underside rear-loading ramp. A tail-gun position for a twin 23-mm turret is provided in most aircraft (some with civil markings); although there is no fire-control radar for the guns, armed An-12s usually have a tail-warning radar. As cargo aircraft they can lift up to 44,000 pounds, or almost 100 troops.

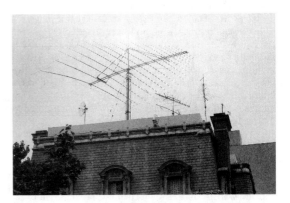

The first step in cryptanalysis is the interception of communications. These aerials on the roof of the Soviet military attaché offices on Belmont Road in Washington, D.C., provided communications to Moscow for the GRU and "raw material" for U.S. cryptanalysis efforts. (N. POLMAR)

A variety of military electronic configurations of the Cub have been observed since 1970. The U.S. designation Cub-B covers ELECTRONIC COUNTERMEASURES aircraft, with antenna domes faired into the fuselage and tail; Cub-C is used for ELINT aircraft, with ventral antenna housings and other features indicating their FERRET role; Cub-D is a special maritime surveillance/ELINT version. (The Soviet designation for the basic cargo/transport aircraft is An-12BP.)

The An-12 first flew in 1955 and entered military service in 1959; a civil version was flying with Aeroflot about 18 months later. Some 850 aircraft were produced, most for military use. Beyond the Soviet/Russian Air Forces, An-12 variants were flown by Warsaw Pact and several Third World air forces.

Cuba

"A menace 90 miles from U.S. shores." For decades that was how American policymakers described Cuba as they tried to topple the island's communist leader, Fidel Castro. Cuba is the only place in the world where the United States and the Soviet Union faced off in a nuclear confrontation, the only place in the Western Hemisphere where communism came and stayed, and the only place ruled by a leader whom U.S. INTELLIGENCE OFFICERS planned to assassinate—with the aid of the Mafia crime syndicate. Castro, far more than Cuba, has been a TARGET, not as a source of intelligence but as a source of irritation.

The United States hailed Castro as a liberator for a short time when he overthrew dictator Fulgencio Batista in Dec. 1959 after a lengthy guerrilla campaign. Soon, however, Castro seized U.S. property in Cuba, collectivized farms, and openly espoused communism. He also began accepting what would be 30 years of massive economic and military support from the Soviet Union. The United States clamped an economic embargo on Cuba and began making plans to get rid of Castro.

The first of two U.S. crises with Cuba came in March 1960 when President Eisenhower approved a CIA plan to overthrow Castro by training anti-Castro Cuban exiles in Florida and infiltrating them into Cuba to stir up a rebellion. Leaders of the exiles would then land and proclaim themselves the provisional government of "Free Cuba." The CIA had succeeded in supporting pro-U.S. coups in Iran and Guatemala, and Cuba was expected to be the agency's third such success.

Veterans of the previous coups were among the men assembled in the Cuban Task Force under RICHARD M. BISSELL, the chief of the CIA's clandestine service. The director of the task force was Jacob D. Esterline, who, while serving in the OFFICE OF STRATEGIC SERVICES during World War II, had fought behind Japanese lines in Burma. Also on Esterline's task force was E. HOWARD HUNT, who had worked on the Guatemala operation and was now charged with organizing Cuban exile groups. The CIA set up a front—Frente Revolucionario Democrático—for recruiting the Florida émigrés.

They were flown in unmarked aircraft from Florida to a military training base, Camp Trax, that Bissell had set up in the mountains of Guatemala. On Swan Island, off the coast of Honduras, the CIA set up Radio Swan, supposedly a commercial station. It broadcast news, music, and anti-Castro programs, ostensibly produced by Cuban exiles in Florida.

The CIA established contact with guerrilla units in isolated mountain areas of Cuba and began dropping supplies to them. Anti-Castro AGENTS were also sent in by boat. What the CIA did not know at the time was how much Castro knew of these operations. His secret police and his intelligence agency, Direccion General de la Inteligencia (DGI), understood completely what was happening.

In July 1960 Castro sent his brother Raul to the Soviet Union to ask for a Soviet commitment of more protection from an expected U.S. invasion. Soviet Premier Nikita Khrushchev increased military aid to Cuba, sending more weapons and more advisers. When the CIA detected the arms buildup, Bissell enlarged his plan, calling for amphibious landings of hundreds of men, along with air cover. The U.S. Air Force lent the CIA a colonel who bought several B-26 Invader light bombers, surplus from the Korean War era.

Many countries, including Cuba, had B-26s. Directing what had bloomed into a major paramilitary operation, Bissell decided that the B-26s could provide a COVER for the invasion. One of the B-26s would be painted to look like a Cuban Air Force plane and pocked with bullet holes. An émigré pilot would then fly it from a secret airfield in Nicaragua to Miami, where he would ask for political asylum. He would claim to be a Cuban Air Force pilot who had been shot at by some of his comrades who were not joining the revolt. But, he would contend, most of the Cuban armed forces were joining in a general revolt against Castro.

As the time neared for the invasion, so did the 1960 presidential election in the United States. President Eisenhower postponed the operation. Vice President Richard Nixon, who knew some details of the original Cuban plan, was running against John F. Kennedy. During the election campaign ALLEN W. DULLES, the DIRECTOR OF CENTRAL INTELLIGENCE, told Kennedy vaguely that an operation was planned against Cuba. But not until after Kennedy's election did Dulles brief him on the scope of the plan. And not until Jan. 28, 1961, eight days after he was inaugurated, did Kennedy ask the Joint Chiefs of Staff (JCS) to examine the military aspects of the operation.

The JCS judged that the plan had a "fair" chance of success—if the landings triggered an uprising. However, there was no chance that the invaders alone could defeat Castro's armed forces, estimated to number 200,000.

Guatemala was pressuring the United States to get the Cuban trainees—BRIGADE 2056, as the group was known—out of the country. There was also pressure from the exiles themselves, more than 1,400 men, armed and desperate to return to their homeland.

On March 11 Kennedy convened a meeting of his

top advisers. "Don't forget that we have a disposal problem," Dulles told the meeting. "If we have to take these men out of Guatemala, we will have to transfer them to the United States, and we can't have them wandering around the country telling everyone what they have been doing." Kennedy ratified Dulles's pragmatic view: "If we have to get rid of these 800 men [he did not then know the real number], it is much better to dump them in Cuba than in the United States, especially if that is where they want to go."

The planned site for the amphibious landing had been the city of Trinidad, near the Escambray Mountains, where anti-Castro guerrillas were hiding. Men landed there could quickly vanish into the mountains. Because a small airstrip there could not accommodate the B-26s, they would have to fly to and from the base in Nicaragua. Kennedy, however, wanted the planes to be flown to Cuba and then operated from Cuban soil, bolstering the cover story that they belonged to the Cuban Air Force. He also wanted a less populated location for the landings.

That meant that the invasion site had to be shifted from Trinidad to the Bay of Pigs, where there was an airstrip long enough for a B-26. The invaders were to seize three beaches along a 40-mile stretch of shore, then cross a swamp and slog 50 miles to reach the mountains. Some paratroops would be dropped to capture roads that crossed the swamp. The Bay of Pigs also put the troops closer to Havana and the strongest concentrations of Cuban armed forces. The invaders were told that if they held the beaches for three days, 500 guerrillas would join them, the rebellion would begin, and the whole country would rise against Castro.

At that point the concept of PLAUSIBLE DENIAL had long since been overtaken by reality. Newspapers in Latin America had reported the recruiting of exiles in Miami, where the streets were buzzing with rumors of an imminent invasion. Among the exiles were DGI agents reporting back to Havana. On April 12 Kennedy, attempting to quell the rumors, told a news conference, "There will not be, under any conditions, an intervention in Cuba by the United States Armed Forces. . . ." Still, Free Cuba leaders believed that U.S. forces would support the invasion.

The landings—the CIA referred to them as a "lodgment"—had been scheduled for April 5. Kennedy postponed them until April 12, then until April 17.

THE INVASION BEGINS

On the morning of April 15, nine B-26s took off from Nicaragua. Eight bombed airfields in Cuba. The ninth flew to Miami, where the pilot landed, showed the fake bullet holes on his aircraft, and told the Cuban Air Force defection cover story. At the UNITED NATIONS, U.S. Ambassador Adlai Stevenson, who did not know the pilot was lying, used the Cuban's story to explain charges that the United States had mounted an attack on Cuba.

A second air strike had been scheduled for April 16, as the invasion force neared the shore. But Kennedy, concerned about credibility, canceled it.

The first invaders landed shortly after 1 A.M. on April 17 and came under heavy attack from Castro's tanks, artillery, and infantry. Cuban aircraft attacked the ships offshore, sinking the one carrying most of the reserve ammunition early in the battle. Castro himself appeared on the scene. He knew the location well; it was a favorite fishing spot of his. Hemmed in, few of the invaders escaped—some to the mountains, where the guerrillas were supposed to be, others to U.S. warships waiting offshore to pick up survivors.

In one last attempt to aid the men on the beach, Kennedy reluctantly permitted a mission impossible: On the 18th, U.S. aircraft carriers were directed to send unmarked aircraft within 15 miles of the beach to ascertain the situation. Soon the planes were allowed to fly over the beaches, but only to carry out RECONNAISSANCE and not to engage Cuban air or ground forces—although they were subsequently ordered to provide some support for anti-Castro B-26s from Nicaragua.

The elaborate rules of engagement mattered little. Due to a mixup over time zones, the B-26s arrived over the beach an hour before the Navy aircraft. Two B-26s were shot down and four Americans—CIA contract fliers—were killed. One of them, Maj. Thomas Ray from the Alabama Air National Guard, survived when his plane crashed, but was killed by Castro soldiers.

The would-be members of the provisional government beseeched the Kennedy administration to send in U.S. Marines, launch massive air raids, save the men on the beach, and evacuate the brigade. U.S. destroyers, with air cover, did search the waters off of the Bay of Pigs for survivors. Nothing else was done. Adm. Arleigh Burke, the Chief of Naval Operations, joined other officials in a midnight meeting at the White House on the night of April 18–19. The issue of whether or not to permit carrier planes to gain control of the air over the beach was discussed. Reportedly, Burke pleaded, "Let me take two jets and shoot down the enemy aircraft," according to Peter Wyden in *Bay of Pigs* (1979).

President Kennedy responded, "No." He said he had repeated "over and over again" that he would not commit U.S. forces to the invasion. Burke asked that unmarked carrier aircraft be permitted to fly low over the beaches as a show of force, with order not to fire. Again Kennedy refused. Burke suggested sending in a destroyer to provide fire support, especially to knock out Castro's tanks.

The President got angry. "Burke, I don't want the United States involved in this," he said sharply.

Burke, feeling he had "never been so distressed," raised his voice. He wanted to be "as forceful as I could be in talking to the President." He said, "Hell, Mr. President, but we *are* involved!"

Reportedly, the fighting on the beach killed about 1,650 of Castro's troops and 114 of the invaders. Castro's forces took 1,189 prisoners. There was no uprising. Anyone who might have joined in a rebellion was already in jail. Castro's secret police, well aware of the impending invasion, had rounded up at least 100,000 potential rebels, perhaps as many as 200,000.

Castro held the prisoners for 18 months before releasing them for a ransom of $62 million in medicine and food raised by private corporations that were gently prodded by the Kennedy administration.

Kennedy's refusal to provide air cover became the popular explanation for the invasion's failure. Inside the CIA, however, the blame was squarely placed on Bissell for his failure to consult the agency's own experts on Cuba as well as more qualified military experts. The elite OFFICE OF NATIONAL ESTIMATES was not asked for an assessment of the possibility of an insurrection. The "lodgment" plan was so obviously flawed that some CIA critics of Bissell believed that the plan held a hidden design: Trapped on the beach, Brigade 2056 would have to be saved by a massive U.S. intervention, a true invasion of Cuba.

After a decent interval, Dulles and Bissell resigned. The debacle only intensified the Kennedy administration's desire to get rid of Castro. In Nov. 1961 Kennedy approved a COVERT ACTION sabotage and subversion plan with the CODE NAME MONGOOSE under Maj. Gen. EDWARD LANSDALE, an expert on insurgency. Mongoose was controlled by the cabinet-level SPECIAL GROUP (AUGMENTED). In Miami the Mongoose activities were code-named Task Force W and directed by WILLIAM K. HARVEY, a CIA veteran.

Task Force W, operating on an annual budget of $50 million, had 400 Americans and 2,000 Cuban exiles on the payroll and a fleet of fast boats. Task force operatives contaminated sugar being exported by Cuba, sabotaged a shipment of ball bearings being sent to Cuba from Europe, and made raids along the Cuban coast.

Another group, known as Alpha 66, also raided Cuba, but it was not under CIA control. In Aug. 1961 Alpha operatives sped along the shore of a resort area and strafed a hotel, killing about 20 Cubans and Soviet advisers. A month later Alpha 66 shelled British and Cuban merchant ships in the area. Although the raids were launched from the United States, U.S. officials said that the émigrés would not be prosecuted and warned foreign shippers that they took risks if they traded with Cuba.

Meanwhile, under presidential direction, the commander-in-chief of the unified U.S. Atlantic Command was directed to prepare plans for the military invasion of Cuba. Known as Operational Plans (OPLANs) 314 and 316, they initially were developed to be executed with warning time of only four and two days, respectively, for the participating U.S. units; those times were later extended to provide more time for bombing Cuban defensive weapons and positions. Either OPLAN would have been one of the largest American military ventures since World War II: Each projected two of Marine amphibious and two Army airborne divisions assaulting Cuba, followed by additional heavy Army formations. The invading forces would be transported by an array of amphibious shipping, along with every transport aircraft

that the services could muster. Massive air strikes were to precede the landings, with a sustained air campaign based from airfields throughout the southeastern United States. The plans and material were to be ready by about Oct. 1962. Neither plan seems to have considered the possibility of Soviet intervention of any kind.

THE SECOND CRISIS

Khrushchev continued to provide Cuba with defensive arms and advisers from the USSR and Eastern Bloc countries. Then, to help ensure that the United States would not invade Cuba and to compensate for shortcomings in the Soviet long-range missile program, in April 1962 Khrushchev decided to send ballistic missiles to Cuba that could strike the United States. This move triggered a confrontation with the United States in Oct. 1962 that could have exploded into nuclear war. (See CUBAN MISSILE CRISIS.)

After the Oct. 1962 crisis subsided, U.S. and Soviet representatives met in New York City for the delicate task of negotiating details of the missile withdrawal. Even as they met, Mongoose went on. On Nov. 8 a Task Force W sabotage team blew up a Cuban factory. At least two other teams were also in Cuba during the negotiations, but their efforts had no effect on the talks.

Mongoose by then was the largest clandestine operation being run by the CIA. The Miami station was the largest in the world; it comprised 600 case officers and some 3,000 agents, most of whom were émigrés—and an unknown number of whom were DGI DOUBLE AGENTS.

Lansdale, ever seeking action, suggested that rumors be spread that Jesus Christ was about to make his second coming and had chosen Cuba as the site—but not until that godless communist Castro was gone. To confirm the rumors, a U.S. Navy SUBMARINE was to surface one night off Havana and produce a pyrotechnic display that would look celestial in origin.

Nothing developed from that idea, or from many other equally unrealistic plans: spraying hallucinogenic chemicals in a radio studio just before Castro arrived to speak, so that he would sound disoriented over the air; putting chemicals in his shoes so that his body would absorb and make his beard fall off; spraying hallucinogenic chemicals on his cigars. (The CIA was deeply involved in hallucinogens at this time; see MKULTRA.)

Economic sabotage continued. A team of CIA-trained Cubans went to Paris and contaminated a shipment of Cuba-bound oil so that it would lose its lubricating properties and destroy machinery. Agents inside Cuba sabotaged sugar refineries.

ENTER THE MAFIA

In the summer of 1960 plans to discredit and topple Castro turned into plans to kill him. On July 21 Bissell asked a CASE OFFICER whether a newly recruited agent would be able take care of "possible removal [of] top three leaders"—Castro, his brother Raul, and their revolutionary comrade, Che Guevara, who had become renowned as a communist missionary in Latin America. Meanwhile, Harvey met in Miami with John Rosselli, a Mafia kingpin, and discussed how to kill Castro. Rosselli had recruited two other Mafia chiefs, Sam Giancana and Santos Traffi-cante. They began finding Cubans to form a hit squad.

The Mafia motive was simple. Castro had shut down Havana's notorious gambling casinos and driven the Mafia out of Cuba. The end of Castro and the emergence of Free Cuba would almost certainly mean the return of gambling and related vices—and the Mafia's profits would soar.

In April 1962 Harvey again met Rosselli in Miami and gave him four poison pills prepared by the CIA's Technical Services Staff. Rosselli later reported that the pills were in Cuba, along with a three-man hit team.

Nothing happened. Almost certainly that hit team and a subsequent one were detected by Castro's highly efficient secret police agency, the Committee for the De-fense of the Revolution, which, as a defector once said, has operatives "in every block and factory." In June, Harvey, who had been removed as director of Task Force W, met with Rosselli in Miami and ended the CIA-Mafia arrangement. The FBI, which had been keeping Rosselli under SURVEILLANCE, monitored the meeting, without knowing what it was about.

The plotting against Castro continued. On Nov. 22, 1963, a CIA officer in Paris met with a Cuban who was supposed to assassinate Castro. The officer gave the Cuban a poison-filled fountain pen that was to be jabbed into Castro. As the meeting ended, the CIA officer learned that President Kennedy had been assassinated in Dallas. The timing was to haunt investigations into the Kennedy assassination and led to unsubstantiated suspi-cion that a vengeful Castro had been involved in Kennedy's murder.

THE AGENTS WHO TURNED

For years some CIA officers worried that the extensive networks of agents in Cuba had been penetrated by the DGI. Publicly, at least, there were no indications of pen-etration. There was also concern that Cuba had become a haven for international terrorists. The notorious terror-ist "Carlos (the Jackal)" (Ilyich Ramirez Sanchez) was trained at Camp Manjanzas in Havana by instructors who included a KGB general, according to reports from Cuba.

But how reliable was that intelligence? In March 1983, Jesus Raul Perez Mendez, an operations chief of the DGI, defected in Miami and revealed details about the DGI's success in implanting agents into the large Cuban communities in Miami and Key West, Fla. The DGI, he said, also used its contacts for importing nar-cotics into the United States.

Another DEFECTOR, Maj. Florentino Azpillage, chief of intelligence in the Cuban Embassy in Prague, provided CIA debriefers with a list of 38 U.S. agents in Cuba who had been TURNED by the DGI and were being run as DOU-BLE AGENTS despite their having been regularly cleared in BACKGROUND INVESTIGATIONS, including POLYGRAPHS. He

believed that probably all U.S. agents in Cuba were under DGI control. That meant that for an unknown time many of the CIA's NATIONAL INTELLIGENCE ESTIMATES on Cuba had been tainted. CIA specialists on Cuba had been telling their CONSUMERS that they were getting extraordinary in-telligence out of Cuba. Now the CIA discovered that much of the intelligence had been extraordinarily faked and was DISINFORMATION. (Double agents continued to plague U.S. intelligence on Cuba, as evidenced by the return to Cuba of a false defector as late as Feb. 1996.)

Meanwhile, U.S. intelligence officials reported that Soviet technicians were continuing to upgrade the huge communications intercept installation at LOURDES, Cuba. The facility intercepted telephone, fax, and other com-munications relayed overseas from the U.S. mainland by SATELLITE. The Lourdes facility was staffed at its peak by about 6,000 men and women.

THE END OF A PARTNERSHIP

The end of the Cold War and the breakup of the Soviet Union in Dec. 1991 shut off Soviet financial support for Castro. But the Lourdes listening station remained in op-eration for a few years as Soviet technicians and advisers quickly departed Cuba.

The Bay of Pigs reverberated for years. Stories had to be concocted about the casualties. There was, for exam-ple, Maj. Ray, the Alabama pilot killed after his plane crashed. Immediately after his death, his widow was told that her husband had been "working as a mercenary for a rich Cuban exile corporation and had been killed in the crash of his cargo plane." She did not believe this and began a campaign to uncover the truth, which was not revealed until 1978. The Cubans kept Ray's body until Dec. 1979, when it was sent to his family. (See BOOK OF HONOR.)

Invasion veterans were involved in WATERGATE and in the 1976 bomb assassination, in Washington, D.C., of for-mer Chilean Ambassador Orlando Letelier, a critic of U.S.-supported Gen. Augusto Pinochet. Brigade 2056 remained as a symbol and became a powerful Miami lobbying group against lifting U.S. economic restrictions on Cuba.

Some U.S. success had come in 1998 when the FBI said it had cracked the largest Cuban spy ring ever dis-covered. Documents showed that the ring's members were trying to get jobs on U.S. military bases. One of the accused spies had acquired a false identity by using the 1965 birth certificate of a Texas infant who had died at seven months. The FBI eventually rounded up 14 mem-bers of the ring, known as the Wasp Network.

In June 2001 five members of the ring were con-victed of espionage against the United States and were sentenced to prison terms ranging from 15 years to life. The leader of the ring, known as Gerardo Hernandez, was found guilty of contributing to the death of four fliers from the Brothers to the Rescue exile group. The fliers were killed when Cuban fighters shot down their two planes in Feb. 1996.

Meanwhile, the DGI, which the FBI now calls the Cuban Intelligence Service (CIS), continued to enjoy successes against the United States. In 2003, for example, Castro jailed 75 dissidents after about a dozen informers among them provided intelligence officers with names and information about the dissidents' connections with U.S. diplomats in Cuba. Some of the Cuban agents were so trusted that they were allowed to use U.S. diplomats' computers. Other informers were known to be at large in Florida, mingling with members of anti-Castro exile groups.

U.S. designation of Cuba as a "terrorist state" was reexamined by Congress in 1998, but the designation was retained.

Also see ANA BELEN MONTES.

Cuban Missile Crisis

The Cuban missile crisis of Oct. 1962 was both a triumph and a failure for U.S. intelligence. The crisis erupted after Soviet leader Nikita Khrushchev attempted to place ballistic missiles with nuclear warheads in Cuba to (1) prevent a U.S. invasion of Cuba and (2) help redress the increasing imbalance of strategic weapons between the United States and the Soviet Union.

The movement of strategic missiles to Cuba—along with protective Soviet air, naval, and ground forces—was given the Soviet CODE NAME ANADYR. The original plan called for the shipment of 36 medium-range ballistic missiles (Soviet designation R-12, U.S. SS-4 Sandal) and 24 intermediate-range missiles (Soviet R-14, U.S. SS-5 Skean). All would have nuclear warheads and all 60 missiles could reach targets in the United States. There would also be nuclear warheads for coastal defense missiles and artillery rockets, and six nuclear bombs, along with Il-28 Beagle light bombers, all intended to stop U.S. invasion forces. In all, more than 50,000 Soviet troops, sailors, fliers, military technicians and mechanics, and other support personnel were to be brought to Cuba.

The issues were quite clear to the Soviets. One retired Soviet naval officer, Dr. Georgi Sviatov, recalled that in the fall of 1962, as a young engineer-lieutenant engaged in submarine construction, "Cuba came as a simple decision." To put strategic missiles into Cuba reflected

> First, the simplicity of strategic weapon deployments—to put missiles into Cuba was the same as our crash programs to put ballistic missiles in our submarines.
> Second, we were supporting Cuba . . . "the romantic revolution."
> And, our missiles in Cuba were simply the equivalent of the American Jupiter missiles placed in Turkey.

Soviet and Eastern Bloc merchant ships carrying the men and matériel—mostly well concealed—began arriving in Cuba on July 26, 1962. It was a remakable achievement for the Soviet armed forces, which had never before deployed a large military force overseas, especially under a high degree of secrecy. That summer U.S.

political and military leaders were preoccupied with problems in BERLIN and crises in Vietnam. There was already some speculation among senior U.S. officials that the Soviets might be bringing bombers or long-range missiles into Cuba, although there appears to have been no hard evidence.

The CIA had flown U-2 spyplane flights over Cuba since Oct. 1960. Under JOHN MCCONE, the DIRECTOR OF CENTRAL INTELLIGENCE appointed by President Kennedy in Nov. 1961, the number of high-altitude flights over Cuba had increased. By late summer 1962 many intelligence sources were providing the Kennedy administration with information on the Soviet arms buildup in Cuba. But there were no indications that long-range nuclear weapons were being sent to Cuba. Four NATIONAL INTELLIGENCE ESTIMATES developed by the U.S. INTELLIGENCE COMMUNITY in 1962—the last dated Sept. 19—declared that the Soviets would not send nuclear weapons to the island.

There were four CIA U-2 missions over Cuba in June 1962. Their photographs showed the first indications that Cubans were installing Surface-to-Air Missiles (SAMs), although the missiles themselves were not evident at the time. When the next U-2 flight was flown on Aug. 5 it revealed more indications of SAM sites being prepared.

McCone and others considered the possibility that the Soviets might try to move long-range missiles as well as the SAMs into Cuba, and McCone ordered an increase in the RECONNAISSANCE flights to four a month. Also, U.S. officials began to discuss possible actions against the SAM sites, although they were unquestionably defensive weapons. A blockade was discussed on Aug. 10, but there was concern that any action taken against Cuba would lead the Soviets to retaliate in Berlin.

PHOTOGRAPHIC INTERPRETATION of the U-2 film was being done by the Air Force Strategic Air Command (SAC) at Offutt Air Force Base, Neb. McCone, wanting a broader interpretation of the photos, directed the Naval Photographic Interpretation Center in Washington, D.C., to also analyze the photos. This was not interservice rivalry; McCone simply wanted the best and most objective explication.

In additon to high-altitude U-2 photos, U.S. national leaders and military commanders were being provded with COMMUNICATIONS INTELLIGENCE and SIGNALS INTELLIGENCE garnered by electric reconnaissance aircraft flying in international air space, and by the INTELLIGENCE COLLECTON SHIP Oxford, operating off the coast of Cuba.

Photos from the U-2 mission of Aug. 29 clearly showed the SAM sites, with missile transporters, radar, and launchers in place. Those photos also showed coastal defense missiles being installed. The U-2 flight of Sept. 5 revealed more SAM sites being readied and Soviet MiG-21 high-performance fighters. On Aug. 28 a U-2 had photographed the crated Il-28 bombers being brought into Cuba. The U-2 flights continued.

Late that month Col. JOHN R. WRIGHT, JR., of the DEFENSE INTELLIGENCE AGENCY, while looking at U-2 photos, was the first American to realize that the pattern of SAM deployments near San Cristobal resembled those in the Soviet Union used to protect strategic missiles. Mc-Cone ordered more intensive photo coverage of Cuba.

But who would fly the missions? Given the risks posed by the newly installed SAMs, Secretary of Defense Robert S. McNamara felt that the pilots should be uniformed military officers. McCone objected, on the basis that Cuba was still an intelligence operation and, as such, within its jurisdiction, and the CIA had later, more capable variants of the U-2.

President Kennedy decided to have the Air Force fly the missions, but with the better-equipped U-2C aircraft of the CIA. Two Air Force pilots, Maj. Richard S. Heyser and Maj. RUDOLPH ANDERSON, JR., were hurriedly qualified in the U-2C. Early on Oct. 14 Heyser overflew Cuba in a U-2C, followed by Anderson in a second U-2C. Moments after Heyser's aircraft touched down at McCoy Air Force Base in Florida, the film rolls were flown to Offutt and to Washington, D.C. That day the photo evidence became clear: The Soviets were putting offensive nuclear missiles into Cuba.

Airman 1st Class Michael Davis, a photo interpreter at Offutt, was the first American to actually see the SS-4 ballistic missiles in Cuba. On the morning of Oct. 16, Dr. RAY CLINE, the Deputy Director for Intelligence at the CIA, went to the White House to brief the President's special assistant for national security affairs, McGeorge Bundy. He in turn informed President Kennedy that there was hard evidence of offensive missiles in Cuba.

As officials discussed the building crisis, it was decided to fly six U-2 sorties over Cuba on Oct. 17 to obtain full high-altitude coverage of the island. Those flights revealed the installation of two types of ballistic missiles were underway, the SS-4 and SS-5, as well as a massive buildup of conventional weapons. (None of the latter missiles actually reached Cuba.) President Kennedy immediately convened a committee of his top advisers to consider possible American responses. Robert Kennedy later recalled in his book *Thirteen Days* (1969), "the dominant feeling was one of shocked incredulity. We had been deceived by Khrushchev, but we had also fooled ourselves. No official within the government had ever suggested to President Kennedy that the Russian buildup would include [offensive] missiles."

The buildup led President Kennedy to order a national military alert on Oct. 19. Three days later the Joint Chiefs of Staff issued a directive to prepare for a blockade of the island, the Strategic Air Command kept some 65 B-52 strategic bombers—with four nuclear weapons and target folders—on airborne alert and all other bombers were placed on a high state of alert, with some dispersal to satellite airfields to reduce losses from a surprise Soviet bomber or missile attack. In great secrecy, President Kennedy had U-2 photos flown to the capitals of Britain, Canada, France, and West Germany to garner other Western governments' support for U.S. responses.

On the night of Oct. 22, President Kennedy addressed the American people:

Within the past week, unmistakable evidence has established the fact that a series of offensive mis-

siles sites is now in preparation on that imprisoned island. The purpose of those bases can be none other than to provide a nuclear strike capability against the Western Hemisphere. . . .

He ordered a naval blockade to halt the flow of offensive missiles into Cuba. Navy warships encircled the island, while Navy carrier-based planes and land-based patrol planes scoured the Atlantic and Caribbean for Soviet ships and submarines. The SAC sent 16 KC-97 piston-engine tankers and five photo-reconnaissance variants of the B-47 STRATOJET aircraft on low-level, overwater searches around Cuba.

Simultaneously, preparations began for massive aerial strikes against the Soviet missile sites. Air, ground, and naval forces began moving into position for a possible invasion of the island in accord with Operational Plans (OPLANs) 314 and 316, which had been drawn up following the Bay of Pigs landings.

As the U.S. blockade of Cuba began, the high-flying U-2 reconnaissance flights were supplemented by low-level passes by Navy F8U CRUSADER photo planes and, subsequently, photo versions of the Air Force F-101 VOODOO. Low-level photography was needed to reveal the state of readiness of the missiles and other details.

Late on Oct. 25, aerial photography revealed that work on the missile sites was proceeding at a very rapid rate. The following evening, photos showed that the Il-28 Beagle light bombers were being speedily uncrated and assembled.

Two days later, on Oct. 27, after Fidel Castro had ordered his own anti-aircraft artillery to fire at the low-flying U.S. aircraft, a Soviet local air defense commander—without authorization—ordered an SA-2 surface-to-air missile battery to fire on a high-altitude U-2. Maj. Anderson had taken off from the McCoy base on the morning of Oct. 27 for another flight over Cuba. While over the eastern end of the island, his U-2 aircraft was hit by an SA-2 missile. Anderson died when his plane crashed on an island in the Banes-Antilla area.

Robert Kennedy wrote in *Thirteen Days* of the reaction when news of Anderson's loss reached the White House:

"How can we send any more U-2 pilots into this area tomorrow unless we take out all of the SAM sites?" the President asked. "We are now in an entirely new ball game."

At first, there was almost unanimous agreement that we had to attack early the next morning with bombers and fighters and destroy the SAM sites. But again the President pulled everyone back. "It isn't the first step that concerns me," he said, "but both sides escalating to the fourth and fifth step—and we don't go to the sixth because there is no one around to do so. We must remind ourselves we are embarking on a very hazardous course."

No action was taken in response to the Anderson shootdown; both the U-2 flights and low-level reconnaissance continued. Anderson was to be the only U.S. combat casualty of the Cuban missile crisis. (At least one other U-2 was fired on by an SA-2 missile.)

Tensions reached an even higher level. Castro readied his forces to repel an invasion. He advised Khrushchev by a cable (sent early on Oct. 27) that in the event of a U.S. assault on the island, they should strike the United States with nuclear weapons rather than concede the initiative to Kennedy.

For Castro, "an invasion to wipe out communism in Cuba would be the start of a global war between Socialism and Imperialism." For Khrushchev, "it would be no such thing, and the Soviet Union must be kept from being drawn into a war in Cuba," wrote political historian Raymond Garthoff in a 1992 paper on the Cuban crisis.

The Cuban crisis was resolved diplomatically. There were secret, direct communications between President Kennedy and Premier Khrushchev, and there were equally important "back channel" exchanges between the two leaders, most using Robert Kennedy, American journalists, and two KGB officials in Washington, GEORGI BOLSHAKOV and ALEKSANDR FEKLISOV. The latter exchanges could be more candid, as Khrushchev did not have to discuss those messages with the Politburo.

A low-level reconnaissance photo of Soviets ships in the Cuban port of Mariel, taken in early November 1962 by a U.S. Navy RF-8 Crusader. The photo shows a variety of ballistic missile support equipment and three Soviet merchant ships. (U.S. NAVY)

On Oct. 28 the Soviet government agreed to remove the ballistic missiles from Cuba. The blockade continued as the strategic missiles were dismantled and removed from the island. On Nov. 20, President Kennedy announced the lifting of the quarantine against Cuba as dismantling of the Il-28 bombers began. The quarantine had succeeded, demonstrating American resolve while not bringing attacks upon Soviet forces in Cuba. Khrushchev withdrew the offensive missiles from Cuba (as well as three of the four ground combat regiments); President Kennedy agreed not to invade Cuba and to withdraw the Jupiter ballistic missiles from Turkey.

INTELLIGENCE FAILURES

While U.S. reconnaissance aircraft had provided the detailed photos needed to show the world Soviet actions and duplicity, the intelligence community had failed to detect the early signs of the Soviet buildup of Cuba and the nature and size of that buildup. U.S. sources believed that only some 8,000 Soviet military personnel had reached the island by the time of the quarantine. The actual number was 41,900!

Perhaps most important, the U.S. intelligence community concluded that no nuclear weapons had been landed in Cuba. In fact, the first warheads had arrived in the freighter *Indigiirka* on Oct. 4. This shipment included 36 warheads for SS-4 missiles, 80 for the coastal defense missiles, 12 for the short-range Luna artillery rockets, and six bombs for the Il-28 bombers—a total of 134 nuclear weapons. (Another merchant ship had also arrived with 24 nuclear warheads for SS-5 missiles, but they were not unloaded.)

The White House also had a secret source of intelligence: Col. OLEG PENKOVSKY, an officer in Soviet MILITARY INTELLIGENCE (GRU). During 1961–1962 he had passed highly secret data on Soviet weapons and readiness to the British and Americans. This intelligence, together with earlier U-2 flights over the Soviet Union, showed Kennedy the low level of Soviet readiness for a nuclear war.

Intelligence—good and bad—and U.S. superiority in nuclear weapons were the critical factors needed for President Kennedy to achieve a negotiated success in the Cuban missile crisis. An official Air Force history of the crisis notes,

> The processing and exploitation of the raw intelligence data was as vital to national security as the flying of the collection missions. The Cuban crisis was a fast-developing situation in which intelligence had to be quickly processed and analyzed, with the results delivered to national decisionmakers in time for them to act upon it.

Culper Ring

Highly successful spy operation that directly supplied intelligence to Gen. GEORGE WASHINGTON during the American Revolution.

In June 1778, as Gen. Sir Henry Clinton, the new commander of British forces in America, occupied New York City, Washington's troops were scattered around New York, New Jersey, and Connecticut. In need of intelligence on Clinton's forces and intentions, Washington ordered Maj. BENJAMIN TALLMADGE to set up an espionage net.

Tallmadge, a native of Long Island, recruited ABRAHAM WOODHULL of Setauket, Long Island, across Long Island Sound from Connecticut. Long Island, like New York City, was occupied by the British. Woodhull took the COVER name Samuel Culper. He then recruited ROBERT TOWNSEND, a New York City businessman. Because he was a Quaker, Townsend had not spoken out about the revolution and could easily assume the role of a Tory. Later he joined a Tory militia. Woodhull became "Culper Senior" and Townsend "Culper Junior."

Tallmadge developed a code, making four handwritten copies. He kept one and gave the others to Woodhull, Townsend, and Washington. Townsend was 723, Woodhull 722, and Washington 711. Many historians believed that "355" was a mysterious woman AGENT romantically involved with Townsend. But 355 merely meant the word "lady" in the code. Townsend wrote his reports in coded SECRET WRITING at the specific instructions of Washington, who gave him instructions: "He should occasionally write his information on the blank leaves of a pamphlet, on the first, second, and other pages of a common pocket book, or on the blank leaves at each end of registers, almanacks, or any new publication or book of small value." He also suggested interlining the secret writing in letters to friends.

Washington, who did not know the identities of the spies, told Tallmadge that "Culper Junior" should "mix as much as possible among the officers and Refugees, visit the Coffee Houses, and all public places. He is to pay particular attention to the movements by land and water in and about the city especially." Washington preferred spies who, like Townsend and Woodhull, "live with the other side; whose local circumstances, without subjecting them to suspicions, give them an opportunity of making observations."

A Townsend sub-agent, James Rivington, wrote a gossip column for a Tory newspaper whose other contributors included Maj. JOHN ANDRÉ, who wrote poetry when he could spare time from spying and conspiring with Maj. Gen. BENEDICT ARNOLD. Townsend's reports were taken to Woodhull by Austin Roe, a Setauket tavern keeper, who traveled regularly to and from New York City to get supplies. He deposited them in a DEAD DROP on Woodhull's farm.

The dead drop was serviced by CALEB BREWSTER, a sailor who took the messages across the Sound to Tallmadge or one of his COURIERS and then delivered them directly to Washington. The messages gave Washington day-by-day knowledge of the deployment of Clinton's troops—information that was to prove invaluable for Washington's strategy.

When French troops arrived in Newport, R.I., in 1780 to aid the Americans, Clinton decided to embark most of his troops by ship to Newport and attack the

French before they marched to join the Americans. Townsend saw the troops preparing to embark and sent a report that reached Washington in time for him to make it appear that he was marching on Manhattan. This DISINFORMATION fooled Clinton, who called off the embarkation and waited for the American attack that never came.

Cumming, Capt. Sir Mansfield

(b. 1859 d. 1923)

First head of the British Secret Intelligence Service (MI6), appointed director of the service—initially designated MI1c—in 1909 at the age of 50. His name was not officially made public, and he was generally known by the name "C," a tradition carried on by his successors (none of whose names began with that initial).

A naval officer, he suffered from severe bouts of seasickness and he lost a leg in 1914. A legend claimed that after being injured in an automobile accident in France in 1914 he amputated his own leg with a penknife. Actually, both legs were broken in the accident and one had to be surgically amputated the following day. He was fitted with a wooden leg. (His son was killed in the accident.)

Under his direction MI6 enjoyed several successes. Among his AGENTS was the indefatigable SIDNEY REILLY, who carried out missions for Cumming in several areas of the world. (Cumming was not always certain of where Reilly's true loyalties lay, but he certainly admired Reilly's skills.)

He built up a major intelligence organization, and after World War I he successfully protected MI6 when control was passed from the War Office to the Foreign Office. He was also successful in gaining control of the GOVERNMENT CODE AND CYPHER SCHOOL, Britain's codebreaking establishment.

Cumming served as director of MI6 until early 1923, when he retired because of ill health and was knighted. He died a few months later. After marrying, he took his wife's family name, changing his to Mansfield George Smith-Cumming.

Current Intelligence

Intelligence summaries and analyses of recent events.

Currie, Lauchlinn

Aide to President Franklin D. Roosevelt who spied for the Soviet Union.

Currie was first named as a Soviet AGENT by ELIZABETH BENTLEY, a COURIER who defected from the American Communist Party (CPUSA) and testified about espionage before the House Un-American Activities Committee. Bentley also told a federal grand jury that an aide to President Roosevelt had learned that American codebreakers had nearly cracked "the Russian secret code." The news stunned the codebreakers, working on the VENONA operation that decrypted Soviet espionage messages.

Because Currie had access to White House SIGNALS INTELLIGENCE, he probably heard rumors about the Russian code work.

During World War II Currie, then a special assistant to the president, had twice gone on confidential trips to China, which was embroiled in civil war of great interest to the Soviet Union, because nationalist Chiang Kai-shek was pitted against communist leader Mao Tse-tung.

In the Venona decrypts his CODE NAME was "Page."

Cut-Out

A third person used to conceal the contact between two people—usually between an AGENT and a HANDLER who do not want to meet because one or both may be under SURVEILLANCE.

Cynthia

(1) See AMY ELIZABETH THORPE.

(2) British intelligence operation in World War II to break into CIPHERS used by the Vichy French government.

D-21

Air-launched unmanned RECONNAISSANCE aircraft developed by the United States. It was to be launched by high-altitude A-12 OXCART and SR-71 BLACKBIRD spyplanes. The unusual D-21 was somewhat similar to the A-12/SR-71 in appearance.

The D-21 flew only four operational missions, all launched from B-52H strategic bombers for photo-reconnaissance flights over China. One drone, however, veered northward and flew over Soviet Siberia. It came down in Soviet territory, and some parts were later recovered. Apparently the program was canceled because of cost of the nonrecoverable drones, problems in recovering their exposed film, and the availability of reconnaissance SATELLITES.

The D-21 was developed as a high-speed (Mach 3.5) reconnaissance aircraft to overfly TARGETS where manned aircraft could not be used for political reasons or because of enemy air defenses. The drone was to be carried by the A-12/SR-71 aircraft and launched from high altitudes. Several trial launches were conducted. However, after an A-12 crashed while launching a D-21, the large, eight-engine B-52H was substituted as the launch platform. Two of the bombers were modified to operate with the D-21 drones, each being able to carry two D-21s on underwing pylons. They flew only from Beale Air Force Base in northern California and the Groom Lake test facility in Nevada. The CODE NAME for the B-52/D-21 operation was SENIOR BOWL.

For four operational missions, the carrying B-52 took off from a U.S. base and flew to a launch position over the western Pacific. After it launched the D-21, the B-52 could land at any available airfield. The drone flew its mission and then streaked out over the sea where the film canister, camera, and certain instruments were jettisoned. They would be "captured" in descent by a recovery plane snagging the parachute, as was done with satellite packages (see CORONA). The D-21 itself would then self-destruct into small, hopefully unidentifiable pieces.

The four B-52/D-21 missions over China were flown from 1969 to 1971. None of the film/equipment packages was ever recovered.

The D-21 was developed by the Lockheed SKUNK WORKS, which built 38 drones between 1964 and 1969. The vehicle had an elongated delta wing without horizontal tail surfaces; the principal material used in construction was titanium. A single ramjet engine was fitted, with a camera bay in the fuselage. Weighing about 11,000 pounds fully loaded with fuel, it was 42¾ feet long and had a wingspan of 19 feet. Maximum range was approximately 3,500 miles, and it could fly at altitudes of about 95,000 feet (slightly higher than the SR-71).

Two A-12 aircraft were modified for trials and operations with the D-21 and referred to as M-12. When "mated" they were referred to as MD-21—Mother and Daughter. The code name for this scheme was "Tagboard." The MD-21 program ended on July 30, 1966, with the remaining D-21s modified for B-52 launch.

The surviving drones were then placed in storage from 1968 to 1976 and subsequently discarded, with at least 17 being placed in open storage at Monthan Air Force Base, Ariz. (In 1994 the National Aeronautics and Space Administration acquired four of the D-21s for possible research projects.)

D-21 was a generic designation, with the D-21B being modified for B-52 launch; combat drones were labeled GTD-21. The number "21" is said to have been chosen because it was the reverse of the "12" in A-12.

Also see UNMANNED AERIAL VEHICLES.

Dames Blanches

World War II Allied intelligence organization composed of Belgian women who counted the cars of troop trains. The COVER for their SURVEILLANCE work: They sat knitting at the windows—where they could watch for troop trains—because they needed the light.

Daniloff, S. Nicholas

American journalist in Moscow whose trumped-up arrest for spying by the KGB nearly wiped out a planned summit meeting between President Reagan and Soviet leader Mikhail Gorbachev.

Daniloff, Moscow correspondent for *U.S. News & World Report*, was arrested in Moscow on Aug. 30, 1986, exactly one week after the FBI arrested a Soviet KGB officer who worked for the UNITED NATIONS. (For details of the FBI case against the Soviet, see GENNADI ZAKHAROV.)

Daniloff met a Russian acquaintance in the Lenin Hills, a park near his Moscow apartment. The Russian handed Daniloff a packet, saying that it contained newspaper clippings. Instead, it contained part of a map of Afghanistan marked SECRET, a diagram of where Soviet military installations were on the map, and 26 photos of Soviet soldiers. Eight KGB officers promptly appeared from a van parked nearby and arrested Daniloff.

Gorbachev condemned Daniloff as a "spy who was caught in the act." Daniloff angrily denied the charge. A White House spokesman called the arrest of Daniloff "nothing other than seizure of a hostage." Talk of a SPY SWAP immediately began, but American officials declared that no deal could be made, because Daniloff was not a spy. The Soviets claimed Daniloff was linked to Paul M. Stombaugh, a political officer at the U.S. Embassy in Moscow, who had been expelled as a spy in 1985, and Murat Natirboff, an embassy officer the Soviets had identified as the CIA station chief in Moscow. Natirboff had left the Soviet Union shortly before Daniloff's arrest.

Daniloff, who had been ending a five-and-a-half year assignment in Moscow when he was arrested, was held in Lefortovo, a czarist-era prison in Moscow, for 13 days and then released, as was Zakharov; both men were placed in the custody of their respective ambassadors.

In the midst of the negotiations to release Daniloff, the Reagan administration charged that 25 Soviets in the United Nations were KGB officers. (A numbers game had been going on about how many Soviets should be in the Soviet mission to the United Nations.)

The end of the Zakharov-Daniloff affair came on Sept. 30, 1986, when the United States and the Soviet Union announced that President Reagan and Gorbachev would meet for a summit conference in Iceland on Oct. 11–12. The announcement about the summit was made by Tass, the Soviet press agency, at 9:50 A.M. Four minutes later, Zakharov entered a plea of no contest to the espionage charges in Federal Court in Brooklyn, N.Y. He then left for Washington, D.C., where he boarded a Soviet Aeroflot flight that departed from Dulles International Airport at 3:15 P.M. Daniloff arrived in Washington at 4:40 P.M. on the last leg of a journey from Moscow that had begun the day before. A Soviet dissident and his wife were also released as part of the exquisitely timed swap—which the Reagan administration officially described as not a swap. Also released was a former leader of a dissent movement in the Soviet Union and his wife.

Western COUNTERINTELLIGENCE officials later said they believed that the KGB had begun setting up Daniloff in Dec. 1984, when a Russian claiming to be a priest arrived at Daniloff's office and told him he had been imprisoned for his faith. Although Daniloff later said that he was not convinced the man was priest, the correspondent nevertheless agreed to deliver a letter from him to the U.S. Embassy. In Jan. 1985 the priest left an envelope in Daniloff's mailbox. In it was another envelope, addressed to the U.S. ambassador. And in that envelope was a third, addressed to the DIRECTOR OF CENTRAL INTELLIGENCE, who was then WILLIAM J. CASEY. That innermost envelope contained data on Soviet military weapons.

In Feb. 1985, Daniloff was asked to come to the embassy, where he was taken to a secure room and questioned by an embassy official he assumed was a CIA officer under diplomatic COVER. He gave the officer the name and phone number of the presumably bogus priest. A few months later Daniloff was again called to the embassy, and in the secure room a CIA officer told him the priest was apparently connected with the KGB. Shortly afterward, Stombaugh was expelled as a spy, presumably for attempting to contact the so-called priest.

According to the Soviets, the evidence connecting Daniloff to Stombaugh of the CIA included a letter written by Stombaugh. As published by the Soviets, the letter said, "Dear and respected friend, We would like to assure you that the letter passed by you to the journalist on Jan. 24 got to the designated address. We highly appreciate your work."

Daniloff, after his release, pieced together what had happened. "If I knew then what I know now," he said, "I would have burned the letter instead of taking it to the embassy."

(For other examples of how Americans were set up as spies in the Soviet Union, see RUSSIA-SOVIET UNION.)

Dar, Maj. Avraham

Israeli INTELLIGENCE OFFICER who set up an intelligence NETWORK in Egypt that proved to be a total disaster.

Born in Palestine, Dar worked in Europe after World War II helping Jews to immigrate to the future state of Israel. During the Israeli War of Independence (1948–1949) he was an officer in the Palmach (commandos) and worked in Arab countries. He briefly left the Army, but rejoined in 1951, being assigned to AMAN, Israeli MILITARY INTELLIGENCE.

In May 1951 he entered Egypt on a British passport in the name of John Darling. He set up an underground network although, as noted by Ian Black and Benny Morris in *Israel's Secret War* (1991), "The objective of this network—Jewish self-defence, assistance to illegal immigration, espionage or anti-Egyptian sabotage—was not clear at first to . . . Dar or the young Jews [in his network]." Most of his AGENTS, men and women, were rank amateurs.

Dar left Egypt, and the members of his network traveled to Israel, usually through France, for brief schooling in clandestine communications, espionage, and sabotage. However, since the network was not broken up into CELLS, the members all knew the others involved.

By the end of 1953 the agents had been trained and were back in Egypt obtaining explosives and identifying potential targets for sabotage. In 1954 Avri El-Ad was sent into Egypt to take command of the network. In June the CODE WORD to activate the network—Operation Susannah—was broadcast from Tel Aviv in response to the military takeover of Egypt. It was hoped that acts of sabotage would discredit the military-nationalist government. Beginning in July the network started detonating bombs in Cairo and Alexandria. Their targets were libraries, the U.S. Information Center, post offices, and cinemas—not military targets, as some Aman officials believed they would be. When one member of the network was captured attempting to plant a bomb in a movie theater, he was forced to reveal the others. All were arrested.

Their trial began on Dec. 11, 1954. One was beaten to death during interrogation, and one committed suicide during the trial. Two others were sentenced to death and executed, four were given prison sentences ranging from seven years to life, and two men were acquitted.

Dar continued in Aman, and during the Israeli-British-French assault on Egypt in Oct. 1956, Dar, a major, and two other Aman operatives were assigned to the MOSSAD and flown into Port Said on a French aircraft to liaise with French intelligence and carry out special missions as required. In Operation Tushia (Hebrew for "wisdom"), on Nov. 11, Dar and two others, wearing French uniforms and posing as Jewish soldiers in the French Foreign Legion, made contact with the Jewish community in Port Said. With the help of the French, they arranged the movement of one-third of the community, 65 persons, to Israel by ship on Nov. 17–18.

In 1957 Dar resigned from the Army in protest that the Israeli government had not forced Egypt to release the imprisoned members of his Cairo network in exchange for the 6,000 Egyptian soldiers captured in the Suez campaign of Oct.–Nov. 1956. (Unknown to the Israelis, among the Egyptian prisoners was Gen. Mohammed Digwi, the governor of Gaza, who had served in 1955 as president of the court that had sentenced the two Cairo operatives to death. (The four imprisoned members of Dar's network were released in 1967 when MEIR AMIT, head of the Mossad, personally appealed to President Gamal Abdel Nasser.)

Darragh, Lydia

(b. 1729 d. 1789)

Quaker whose family spied for the colonies in the American Revolution.

Lydia Darragh lived on Second Street in Philadelphia in a house almost opposite the headquarters of Gen. Sir William Howe, commander of British forces in America until June 1778. As a Quaker, she was believed to be anti-war and thus above suspicion as a spy. She collected MILITARY INTELLIGENCE from what she heard and saw. She may also have known a captain on Howe's staff and gained information from him without his realizing it.

Her husband, William, wrote her reports in a shorthand CODE and hid them in cloth-covered buttons, which were popular at the time. The Darraghs' teenage son John slipped off to the American camp at Whitemarsh, outside Philadelphia, cut off the buttons, and gave them to his elder brother, Lt. Charles Darragh, who transcribed the shorthand for Gen. GEORGE WASHINGTON.

In Nov. 1777, the Darragh family members were ordered out of their house on Second Street so that Howe could use it. Lydia protested and Howe agreed to take only one room as a council chamber. On Dec. 2 an officer ordered Lydia to send her family to bed early because the staff "wished to use the room that night free from interruption." Sensing an important meeting was in the offing, Lydia eavesdropped, probably while hiding in a closet adjoining the council chamber. She heard that a massive assault aimed at destroying the Continental Army would come on Dec. 4.

Like many women, Lydia had a pass for going through British lines to a mill located between Philadelphia and Whitemarsh. On Dec. 3 she passed through the lines and hurried on to the camp, where she told American officers what she had heard.

Howe did march out of Philadelphia on Dec. 4, but Washington's forces were so well prepared that he did not fight. Word of the Whitemarsh standoff reached London by the end of December, and British officials used it as an example of how impossible was the conquest of America. AGENTS of spymaster BENJAMIN FRANKLIN passed this word to him in France, and he spread it among his French supporters.

The Philadelphia Quakers later requested Charles Darragh to leave the Friends Meeting because he had fought in the war. Some sources also say that Lydia was expelled when the Quakers heard of her spying.

Data Mining

The scanning of billions of bits of data in search of information about a specific intelligence TARGET. In the wake of the Sept. 11, 2001, attacks on the United States, data mining was often cited as a means for obtaining TERRORIST INTELLIGENCE. The technique is in use by the FBI and the Department of HOMELAND SECURITY, along with the Transportation Security Administration in its efforts to develop a new airline passenger profiling system.

By one description of the process, it uses "a combination of machine learning, statistical analysis, modeling techniques, and database technology" to find "patterns and subtle relationships in data" with the aim of finding "rules" that could lead to "the prediction of future results."

Data mining has been watched carefully by non-government organizations concerned with possible invasions of privacy, because the mining sites include personal and commercial databases.

Davies, Staff Sgt. Allen J.

Former U.S. Air Force enlisted man who offered the Soviets classified information on RECONNAISSANCE programs, including electronic and infrared technologies. Davies, who had been in the Air Force for 10 years, had a SECRET-level SECURITY CLEARANCE.

Davies had been "involuntarily separated" from the U.S. Air Force in 1984 for poor job performance. He sought revenge by offering to spy for the Soviets. Although the government did not reveal how his offer was first discovered, telephone taps of Soviet diplomatic offices apparently played a role. At the time he made the call he was working as a laboratory technician at Ford Aerospace Communications Corp. in Palo Alto, Calif.

When Davies contacted the Soviet Consulate in San Francisco, his call was intercepted by FBI telephone monitoring. In Oct. 1986 an FBI agent, posing as a Soviet contact, called Davies and set up a meeting. The FBI said that Davies provided the agent with "detailed verbal information" and a "hand drawing" of classified reconnaissance technology. He told the agent that he had obtained the information in 1983–1984 while he was stationed at Rhein Main Air Base in West Germany.

Davies was arrested while attempting to pass the classified documents to the agent. He was convicted of espionage charges and sentenced to five years in prison.

Davilia, Maj. Rafael

U.S. National Guard intelligence officer arrested in 2003 for stealing TOP SECRET military documents. The FBI said that he had taken some 300 documents, many of which pertained to chemical and biological warfare. At the time of his arrest he was assigned to the National Guard's 96th Troop Command, based at Tacoma, Wash. Federal officials said he had pilfered documents throughout his 30-year Army career. None of the documents were found when he was charged. His ex-wife was also arrested, but her lawyer said she was cooperating with prosecutors.

Davis, Spcl. 4th Class James T.

(b. 1936 d. 1961)

Army intelligence specialist who was the first U.S. soldier killed in combat in Vietnam. On Dec. 22, 1961, Davis was in a jeep operating a AN/PRD-1 direction finder, searching for clandestine Viet Cong radios, when he and 10 South Vietnamese soldiers were ambushed by the Viet Cong. Only one of the Vietnamese soldiers survived the firefight.

Davis, assigned to the 3rd Radio Research Unit at the Tan Son Nhut Air Base near Saigon, was one of about 60 soldiers from the ARMY SECURITY AGENCY serving in Vietnam. They had been sent there in May 1961 as part of the military advisory group that preceded U.S. commitment of combat troops three years later.

Davis, Pvt. Sam

(b. 1842 d. 1883)

A private with the 1st Tennessee Regiment in the American Civil War who was executed as a spy. Davis was serving as a COURIER for a Confederate unit known as Colman's Scouts when he was captured by Union troops near Pulaski, Tenn., in Nov. 1863.

He was interrogated for several days but refused to reveal any information about Confederate units. When offered freedom in return for information, he is reported to have declared: "I would sooner die a thousand deaths than betray a friend or be false to duty." He was hanged on Nov. 27, 1863. The Confederate press praised him as a latter-day NATHAN HALE.

Dayton, Brig. Gen. Elias

(b. 1737 d. 1807)

Continental Army officer who ran a highly effective spy ring for Gen. GEORGE WASHINGTON during the American Revolution.

Washington's instructions to Dayton, issued on July 26, 1777, were a precise description of Washington's own views on MILITARY INTELLIGENCE:

> The necessity of procuring good Intelligence is apparent & need not be further urged—All that remains for me to add is, that you keep the whole matter as Secret as possible. For upon Secrecy, Success depends in Most Enterprizes of the Kind, and for want of it, they are generally defeated, however well planned and promising a favorable issue.

Dayton, commanding officer of the 1st (Essex County) New Jersey Militia, ran a ring that centered on Staten Island, N.Y., which was occupied by British forces. John LaGrange Mersereau, unable to fight in the Continental Army because of a disabled right arm, was Dayton's principal AGENT. Mersereau worked from behind British lines on the island, sending information to Dayton via a COURIER named John Parker. Dayton was in New Jersey, across the Hudson River from Staten Island.

When Parker died in British custody, Mersereau took the risk of delivering the intelligence himself. He crossed at night to Shooter's Island, off the Jersey shore, by raft, towing a bottle full of reports. If he were caught, he would cut the bottle's tether and sink it. Through light signals between the island and shore, DEAD DROPS were set up, where Mersereau left the bottle and picked up instructions.

The constant flow of intelligence from Dayton's ring was reported by Washington to the Continental Congress on July 5, 1777: "I keep people constantly on Staten Island, who give me daily information of the operations of the enemy."

At times Dayton had 20 agents working for him, including two American officers who posed as sellers of provisions to the British on Staten Island. The ring operated from 1777 to 1780, and some aspects of it are still unknown. In reports that survive there are COVER names but no identification of agents. There is also a hint, but no details, suggesting that Dayton's ring penetrated the British Army.

Dayton was promoted to brigadier general in 1783.

DCI

SEE DIRECTOR OF CENTRAL INTELLIGENCE

D-Day

Name given to the date of the invasion that initiated the climactic battles of World War II in Western Europe. Allied intelligence agencies developed many COVER and DECEPTION schemes intended to protect the location of the Normandy landings and the date, June 5 and then June 6, 1944. See BIGOT LIST, FIRST U.S. ARMY GROUP, FORTITUDE, and TWENTY COMMITTEE.

The dates of most Allied amphibious operations were given the designation D-Day, although *the* D-Day invariably refers to the day of the Normandy landings.

Deacon, Richard [p]

Pseudonym for Donald McCormick, the British author of several authoritative books on espionage.

Born in 1911, McCormick served in the Royal Navy in World War II. He did "some field work" for IAN FLEMING, an INTELLIGENCE OFFICER who later became the creator of JAMES BOND [F].

After the war McCormick resumed his career as a journalist. He was the foreign manager of the *Sunday Times* from 1963 to 1973. Under both his pseudonym and his real name he is the author of more than 50 books. His espionage volumes include *A History of the British Secret Service* (1969), *A History of the Russian Secret Service* (1972), *The Chinese Secret Service* (1974), *Kenipei Tai: The Japanese Secret Service Then and Now* (1982), and *Spyclopaedia* (1989).

Dead Drop

Prearranged hidden location for depositing and picking up messages and money in a clandestine manner, without the parties involved—usually an AGENT and his HANDLER—being present at the same time. See JOHN WALKER for a description of a classic dead drop operation.

Also see DROP, DUBOK.

de Batz, Jean

(b. 1754 d. 1822)

SECRET AGENT for King Louis XVI during the French Revolution.

De Batz, although loyal to the crown, started out as a reformer in the states-general legislature. As the revolution began brewing in 1789, he secretly worked for the king, conspiring to restore the monarchy. Like the fictional SCARLET PIMPERNEL, de Batz rescued aristocrats and aided them in their flight from France.

When the palace was stormed in Aug. 1792 and King Louis and Queen Marie Antoinette were imprisoned, de Batz and his NETWORK tried to free them. In a daring plan that faltered, de Batz even tried to save the king on his way to the guillotine in Jan. 1793. He similarly failed in an attempt to save the queen, who was beheaded on Oct. 16, 1793.

De Batz continued to conspire against the revolutionaries and fight at the barricades in the Paris insurrection of 1795, which was put down by Gen. Napoléon Bonaparte. After a brief imprisonment, de Batz remained a loyal monarchist under Louis XVIII, who rewarded de Batz for a lifetime of service to the throne.

de Bettignies, Louise

(b. 1880 d. 1918)

Spy for the British and French during World War I.

Born in Lille, she spoke French, German, English, and Italian. When the Germans overran northern France in 1914, she fled to England. British intelligence officials asked her to return, both to spy and to help Allied prisoners of war escape.

Under the COVER name Alice Dubois, she and another woman, Marie van Houtte, ran the "Alice Service," as their ring of spies and prisoner helpers was known. Both de Bettignies and van Houtte were captured by the Germans and court-martialed as spies. Van Houtte was sentenced to prison, de Bettignies condemned to death, a sentence that was commuted. She died in prison and was awarded a posthumous Croix de Guerre.

de Bonvouloir, Julien Archard

(b. 1749 d. 1783)

Frenchman who spied on Americans in 1775 to determine whether France should support the colonists against Great Britain. De Bonvouloir, claiming to be a European merchant, talked to American revolutionary leaders, including BENJAMIN FRANKLIN, to sound out sentiments.

Franklin and others realized that de Bonvouloir was an AGENT and began asking him about France's attitude toward them. The result was a favorable report to Paris on the Americans from de Bonvouloir, and a subsequent French decision to aid the Americans, which was a decisive factor in the American Revolution.

de Broglie, Count Charles François

(b. 1719 d. 1781)

Spy for King Louis XV. A nobleman who entered the diplomatic service, Count de Broglie directed the King's Secret, the private royal intelligence service.

The king placed de Broglie in a position familiar to spymasters of any age: He was to appear to carry out one public policy while clandestinely carrying out another. De Broglie, as ambassador to Poland, publicly supported the French policy of working toward putting a Pole on the throne of the kingdom of Poland. Secretly, however, he worked to get a Frenchman crowned. As director of the King's Secret, de Broglie became the center of European intrigue and plots perpetrated by King Louis and his agents. At the same time, the French Foreign Ministry was advancing a foreign policy that the king, through de Broglie's intelligence network, was able to undermine at will. The result was turbulence and a decline in French power both in Europe and abroad.

de Bussy, François

(b. 1699 d. 1780)

French diplomat who spied for Britain.

De Bussy was secretary to the French ambassador in VIENNA from 1725 to 1728 and chargé d'affaires there from 1728 to 1733. He and a British diplomat, Lord Waldgrave, became close friends. De Bussy, the bastard son of a French noble, was debt-ridden and unlikely to obtain funds from legitimate sources. Waldgrave bided his time.

In 1733, when de Bussy was working for the Foreign Ministry in Paris, Waldgrave, then the British ambassador, recruited de Bussy as a spy. De Bussy passed documents and made verbal reports to Waldgrave. When he went to London on official business, de Bussy passed secrets directly to INTELLIGENCE OFFICERS in the British government. He continued to spy until 1749, when his colleagues, suspicious about his wealth, forced him to end his espionage career.

Decade of the Spy

Phrase coined by the authors of this book to reflect the large number of Americans—particularly military personnel—arrested for espionage during the 1980s. Nearly 60 servicemen and civilian employees in the Department of Defense alone were accused of spying or serious violations of security regulations. Since the 1970s the driving force for espionage has been greed, not the ideology that inspired virtually all members of the ATOMIC SPY RING and CAMBRIDGE SPY RING of the pre-Cold War era. In a previous book, *Merchants of Treason* (1988), the present authors wrote, "The spy-for-pay era is driven as much by the client's need for data as by the mercenary spy's need for cash."

Deception

Measures to mislead an enemy by manipulating, distorting, or falsifying evidence to induce a mistaken perception.
    Also see COVER.

DeChamplain, Master Sgt. Raymond

DeChamplain, a U.S. Army enlisted man, was recruited by the Soviet KGB in Bangkok, Thailand, sometime in the early 1970s. The way in which his recruitment was detected was not made public by U.S. officials. When DeChamplain was arrested he was assigned to the joint U.S. Military Advisory Group in Bangkok. In Nov. 1971, DeChamplain was court-martialed and sentenced to seven years at hard labor.

Dedeyan, Sahag K.

A mathematician at the Johns Hopkins University Applied Physics Laboratory in Maryland. In March 1973 Dedeyan, a Lebanese-born naturalized U.S. citizen who held a SECURITY CLEARANCE, took from the laboratory an analysis of U.S. policies toward the NORTH ATLANTIC TREATY ORGANIZATION and showed it to a relative, Sarkis Paskalian, who was an AGENT of the KGB. Dedeyan did not know that Paskalian had been recruited and trained by the KGB some years earlier. Paskalian photographed the document and passed it to the Soviets.

Paskalian's action became known in an undisclosed way to the FBI. When FBI agents arrested him, Paskalian admitted his guilt. He was sentenced to 22 years in prison for espionage. Dedeyan, charged with violating security regulations, was sentenced to three years in prison.

Defector

A person who repudiates his or her country and may be in possession of information of value to another country.

Defector in Place

DEFECTOR who denounces his or her country but does not leave. Usually such a defector chooses to become a MOLE, remaining in a place where valuable intelligence can be given to another country. Among the significant Soviet defectors in place during the Cold War were Col. OLEG PENKOVSKY and OLEG GORDIEVSKI. Their opposite numbers from the West included GUY BURGESS, JOHN CAIRNCROSS, HAROLD (KIM) PHILBY, DONALD MACLEAN, and EDWARD LEE HOWARD.

Defence Intelligence Staff

The Defence Intelligence Staff (DIS) is part of Britian's Ministry of Defence (MOD) and, although funded with

Defence votes, is also an essential element of the national intelligence machinery.

Created in 1964, by the amalgamation of the three service intelligence staffs and the civilian Joint Intelligence Bureau, it forms an integrated body able to support the Ministry of Defence, the armed forces, and other government departments. The DIS's principal task is to analyze information, from both overt and covert sources, and to provide intelligence assessments, advice, and strategic warning to the Joint Intelligence Committee, the MOD, Military Commands, and deployed forces. The DIS also controls two defense agencies—the Defence Geographic and Imagery Intelligence Agency (DGIA) and the Defence Intelligence and Security Centre (DISC), which are responsible for providing imagery, geographic products, and intelligence training.

Air Marshal JOE FRENCH, who took office in Nov. 2000, found himself in newspaper headlines in 2003 when the Foreign Affairs Select Committee investigated Prime Minister Tony Blair's statements about Iraq's nuclear weapons program. (See IRAQ.) French was also the Chief of Defence Intelligence (CDI). In addition to his role as head of the DIS, the CDI is responsible for the overall coordination of intelligence throughout the armed forces and single service commands. A report on DIS in 2003 said it had about 4,600 military and civilian workers.

Also see JOINT INTELLIGENCE COMMITTEE.

Defense HUMINT Service

(DHS)

Organization within the U.S. DEFENSE INTELLIGENCE AGENCY (DIA) that uses AGENTS for the collection of HUMAN INTELLIGENCE (HUMINT).

The DHS was created by JOHN M. DEUTCH when he was Deputy Secretary of Defense. It was formally established on Nov. 2, 1993. The little-known DHS took on added significance in May 1995 when Deutch became DIRECTOR OF CENTRAL INTELLIGENCE (DCI). As DCI, his responsibilities included directing the U.S. INTELLIGENCE COMMUNITY, including the DIA. Deutch said he was encouraging the DIA's recruitment and use of overseas agents—a major mission of the DHS.

The CIA has been the paramount organization for recruiting and running agents. The first hint of change came when, as DCI, Deutch created the position of associate DCI for military support and placed a uniformed officer, Vice Adm. Dennis Blair, in that post. Thus Blair—and "military support"—were placed above the CIA chain of command. This change also enhanced the status of the DHS, a newcomer in the spy community. (Blair subsequently was promoted to full admiral and served as commander of the U.S. Pacific Command from 1999 to 2003.)

During the Cold War, when the Soviet Union was the major TARGET for U.S. intelligence, the recruiting and running agents was the mission of the CIA's Directorate of Operations (also known as the clandestine service).

The CASE OFFICERS for agents were traditionally CIA INTELLIGENCE OFFICERS operating under diplomatic COVER in U.S. embassies and consulates. There were also NCOs, officers in NON-OFFICIAL COVER, who worked outside of the agency under cover as business executives or the like.

As the Cold War was ending and the CIA was beginning to focus on new missions, such as ferreting out terrorists and drug dealers, the old system became less effective. Agents had to look beyond embassy cocktail parties for likely recruits. So, as the CIA sought to enter a darker world of espionage, the DHS emerged as a new source of back-alley intelligence.

Under the 1996 law that covered the secret funding of U.S. intelligence agencies, Congress authorized the DHS to run PROPRIETARY COMPANIES and other front establishments for clandestine agents overseas. Congress gave the DHS a three-year trial period to carry on commercial activities "to provide cover security to intelligence collection activities undertaken abroad." At that time the DHS had about 1,000 employees and had its headquarters in Clarendon, Va.

The DIA had asked for permanent authorization for DHS, but Congress had decided on the three-year trial, a House of Representatives report said, to allow for the "development and oversight of a track record on the use of this authority without encouraging overuse of it, and particularly its more elaborate and sophisticated applications."

This was a cautious warning to the DHS to avoid another scandal over clandestine activities. In the mid-1980s, U.S. ARMY INTELLIGENCE became enmeshed in legal problems stemming from COVERT ACTIONS. (See YELLOW FRUIT.)

In July 1995, Chinese intelligence officials apprehended two DIA HUMINT operatives who were under diplomatic cover as ATTACHÉS stationed in Hong Kong. They were accused of spying in restricted military zones along China's southeastern coast. In Jan. 1996, Lt. Col. Bradley Gerdes, the U.S. assistant military attaché in Beijing, and a Japanese military attaché were accused of spying at a military airport, near the headquarters of the South China Fleet.

Defense Intelligence Agency

(DIA)

U.S. Department of Defense agency established on Oct. 1, 1961, for coordinating the intelligence activities of the military services. The DIA serves as the intelligence agency for the joint Chiefs of Staff (JCS) as well as for the Secretary of Defense and the U.S. unified or theater military commanders.

Under the Defense Reorganization Act of 1958, several unified military commands were created, but as long as each individual service had its own intelligence organization, the unified commands would not be receiving unified intelligence. The services had set up barriers that prevented the free exchange of intelligence data.

Complaints about vastly different estimates and bureaucratic infighting inspired the creation of the DIA under the Kennedy administration, although the specific efforts by the Department of Defense "to put its house in order" with respect to intelligence dates to 1959. In his first State of the Union message, President Kennedy said, "The capacity to act decisively at the exact time action is needed has too often been muffled," creating "a growing gap between decision and execution, between planning and reality."

Thus Secretary of Defense Robert S. McNamara created the DIA, giving it as a prime mission the coordinating of intelligence estimates, which previously had been individually produced by the services. The DIA is a member of the INTELLIGENCE COMMUNITY and as such in theory comes under the nominal responsibilities of the DIRECTOR OF CENTRAL INTELLIGENCE (DCI) as well as the Secretary of Defense. Further, as originally set up, the Director DIA assumed the functions of the J-2 (intelligence) within the JCS; the DIA still provides support for the J-2.

The classified *Plan for the Activation of the Defense Intelligence Agency* (1961) called for a maximum of 250 personnel—military and civilian—at DIA headquarters.

The military services retained their intelligence agencies (see AIR FORCE INTELLIGENCE, ARMY INTELLIGENCE, NAVAL INTELLIGENCE) and responsibilities for intelligence training, developing doctrine for COMBAT INTELLIGENCE, internal security, and COUNTERINTELLIGENCE within their respective services. Other duties retained by the services, but available to the DIA for its mission, included the collection of TECHNICAL INTELLIGENCE and intelligence support for JCS studies.

The DIA has frequently struggled, through reorganizations and Pentagon lobbying, to increase its importance within the intelligence community. But in fulfilling its charter to collect military and military-related intelligence, the DIA must rely upon the NATIONAL RECONNAISSANCE OFFICE for military information obtained by SATELLITES and STRATEGIC RECONNAISSANCE AIRCRAFT; the NSA for the making and breaking of codes; and the CIA for military intelligence gained from foreign intelligence agencies. If, for example, the CIA TURNS a Russian GRU officer, the DIA must depend upon the CIA to obtain the GRU officer's information.

By 1975 the DIA had more than 4,600 employees and an annual budget estimated at more than $200 million. Its growth had become the subject of inquiries by Congress. Testifying before the PIKE COMMITTEE in June 1974, Lt. Gen. DANIEL GRAHAM, then DIA director, listed the prediction of Turkey's invasion of Cyprus as one of the major achievements of the DIA that year. "That was not terribly difficult," Chairman Otis Pike responded. "It was being threatened on Turkish radio."

A report from the Pike Committee, leaked in Feb. 1976, recommended the abolition of the DIA because it duplicated work being done by other intelligence agencies. Graham, who had retired by then, called the report "a rotten piece of work" written by "youngsters turned loose and determined to find some scandal."

The DIA survived the Pike-Graham imbroglio, but criticism persisted. "Because the DIA is self-conscious about living within the shadow of the more capable CIA," former DCI STANSFIELD TURNER wrote in 1986, "it often takes contrary positions just to assert its independence. . . . More often than not, when the DIA does produce a differing view, it cannot—or will not—support it." Turner, like many other CIA officials down the years, also criticized the DIA for being unable to dominate the competing military services.

During the Persian Gulf War of 1991, some 2,000 DIA personnel were directly assigned to supporting U.S.-led coalition forces in Kuwait and Iraq. But military commanders complained that they did not get timely battlefield intelligence.

There were changes in intelligence network and routing systems to speed up intelligence to battlefield and at-sea commanders. In Feb. 1991 the DIA began producing a closed-circuit telecast to about 1,000 defense intelligence and operations officers in the Pentagon and at 19 military commands in the United States. The Defense Intelligence Network show is encrypted so that it can be watched only by authorized monitors. Ingredients for the telecasts include aerial and satellite reconnaissance images and audio reports from the NSA. "We've got to do to intelligence what CNN has done to news," a Pentagon official told *The Washington Post*.

The DIA has also provided intelligence to UNITED NATIONS peacekeeping forces and to U.S. responses to terrorist actions. The DIA also aids law enforcement agencies involved in anti-drug operations. There has been an improvement in performance as the military establishment changed its attitude toward intelligence, which had been seen as a dead end for non-specialist officer career paths. Although the DIA was conceived as a military agency, by the mid-1980s about 60 percent of the DIA staff were civilians.

A possible renaissance for the DIA came in 1995 with the appointment of JOHN M. DEUTCH, former Deputy Secretary of Defense, as DCI. During his time in the Pentagon, Deutch had taken a close interest in the DIA and had created within it the DEFENSE HUMINT SERVICE (DHS), which is authorized to run AGENTS and PROPRIETARY COMPANIES overseas.

After the capture of Saddam Hussein in Dec. 2003, the CIA was chosen to lead his interrogation. But specialists in the DIA, which had operated extensively in Iraq, were also part of the interrogation team. DIA analysts were also involved in the hunt for weapons of mass destruction.

The DIA is organized into five directorates and the JOINT MILITARY INTELLIGENCE COLLEGE (formerly Defense Intelligence College). The directorates are:

Administration
Analysis
Human Intelligence (HUMINT)
Information Management and Chief Information Officer
Intelligence Joint Staff
MASINT and Technical Collection

DIA headquarters is in the Pentagon. The Defense Intelligence Analysis Center is at Bolling Air Force Base in southwest Washington, as is the Joint Military Intelligence College.

DIA is usually headed by a vice admiral or a lieutenant general appointed by the Secretary of Defense. The directors have been:

Oct. 1961–Sept. 1969	Lt. Gen. Joseph F. Carroll, USAF
Sept. 1969–Aug. 1972	Lt. Gen. Donald V. Bennett, USA
Aug. 1972–Sept. 1974	Vice Adm. Vincent P. de Poix, USN
Sept. 1974–Dec. 1975	Lt. Gen. Daniel O. Graham, USA
Jan. 1976–May 1976	Lt. Gen. Eugene F. Tighe, Jr., USAF
May 1976–Aug. 1977	Lt. Gen. Samuel V. Wilson, USA
Sept. 1977–Aug. 1981	Lt. Gen. Eugene F. Tighe, Jr., USAF
Sept. 1981–Sept. 1985	Lt. Gen. James A. Williams, USA
Oct. 1985–Dec. 1988	Lt. Gen. Leonard H. Perroots, USAF
Dec. 1988–Sept. 1991	Lt. Gen. Harry E. Soyster, USA
Sept. 1991–Nov. 1991	Dennis M. Nagy (civilian, acting)
Nov. 1991–Sept. 1995	Lt. Gen. James R. Clapper, Jr., USAF
Sept. 1995–Feb. 1996	Lt. Gen. Kenneth A. Minihan, USAF
Feb. 1996–July 1999	Lt. Gen. Patrick M. Hughes, USA
July 1999–Oct. 2002	Vice Adm. Thomas R. Wilson, USN
Oct. 2002–	Vice Adm. Lowell E. Jacoby, USN

Defense Intelligence College

SEE JOINT MILITARY INTELLIGENCE COLLEGE

Defense Intelligence Officer

U.S. intelligence specialist, a title created in 1974 by Army Lt. Gen. DANIEL O. GRAHAM, then the director of the DEFENSE INTELLIGENCE AGENCY (DIA). Graham, stormy and outspoken, was in charge during one of the times the DIA was finding a role for itself within the INTELLIGENCE COMMUNITY. As part of his buildup of the DIA, he designated as defense INTELLIGENCE OFFICERS his personal staff representatives for specific intelligence matters, such as military coups in Ethiopia and militarily-led independence movements in Africa.

Defense Investigative Service

(DIS)

SEE DEFENSE SECURITY SERVICE (DSS)

Defense Security Service
(DSS)

U.S. Department of Defense agency that conducts security investigations of military personnel, Department of Defense civilian employees, and applicants for employment with firms having contracts for work involving classified information.

The agency had been known as the Defense Investigative Service (DIS), which had been established on Jan. 1, 1972, as a separate defense agency reporting to the Secretary of Defense.

The DSS investigates persons seeking SECURITY CLEARANCES in factories and other facilities operated by defense contractors. DSS says that its 1,300 interviewers are responsible for 500,000 BACKGROUND INVESTIGATIONS each year. There is no official mention of backlogs, but they are considerable. About 230 other DSS employees oversee more than 11,000 facilities where Department of Defense contract work is performed. The DSS COUNTERINTELLIGENCE office helps contractors spot suspected foreign intelligence-collection operations.

The DSS also administers the complex regulations that govern CLASSIFICATION of documents and other secret material used by the defense industry. The major mission of the DSS, the processing of clearance applications, was handled by the Defense Industrial Security Clearance Office (DISCO). In the wake of several espionage cases involving defense industry employees, the U.S. Senate investigated DISCO practices between the fiscal years 1980 and 1984. In those years DISCO supervised security investigations of 138,252 people. Only 118 were turned down, an incredible acceptance rate of 99.91 percent.

Reacting to the report, Senator Sam Nunn, the leading Senate authority on defense matters, said, "That suggests to me either virtually all of the applicants are of a sterling character, and this is just a remarkable character profile among the people who apply, or that we have a system which is basically ineffective and incapable of weeding out people who should not have security clearance."

DIS BACKGROUND INVESTIGATIONS were conducted either by DIS investigators or by private investigators hired by the DIS. There had been frequent criticism about such DIS investigations, particularly after a DIS-cleared employee was arrested for espionage. For example, JONATHAN JAY POLLARD lied about his previous employment and educational record, and the drug use of CHRISTOPHER BOYCE was not discovered.

WILLIAM H. BELL, a Hughes Aircraft Corp. employee who became a spy, said after his arrest that he had displayed "all the signals, all the classical reasons" for being a spy: financial problems that were quickly followed by unexplained wealth; dissatisfaction with his job; and an open relationship with a national of a communist nation. But no one at Hughes or in the DIS reacted to his spying. His TOP SECRET clearance had not been reviewed for 28 years. He was unmasked only when a DEFECTOR named him.

Subsequently, the responsibility for background investigations was transferred to other agencies and DIS was reorganized into the DSS. In 2003 its principal missions were listed as investigations related to terrorism, "product substitution," cyber crimes, including computer intrusion, technology transfers, and such categories of fraud as bribery, corruption, and major thefts.

Defense Special Missile and Astronautics Center (DEFSMAC)

NSA organization, established by Secretary of Defense Robert S. McNamara in 1964 to augment the North

American Air Defense Command (NORAD). Its director is an NSA civilian with a military officer from the DEFENSE INTELLIGENCE AGENCY as his deputy.

"Today the organization operates as the nation's chief warning bell for the launch of foreign rockets," author JAMES BAMFORD wrote in *Body of Secrets* (2001). Bamford quoted a former NSA official as stating that the organization also has the "capability to relatively immediately determine what kind of vehicle has been launched" and whether it represents a threat to the United States or its allies. In an NSA statement of 1998 the DEFSMAC was described as providing the "initial analysis and reporting on all foreign space and missile events."

Defense Support Program

SEE MIDAS

Defoe, Daniel

(b. 1660 d. 1731)

British writer and spy, whose *Robinson Crusoe* is one of the world's most famous books. Born as Daniel Foe, he combined D. Foe into a single surname and became quite adept at assuming names. He was educated at Newington Green because, while his family could have afforded to send him to Cambridge or Oxford, his father was a Nonconformist.

Defoe, who has been called the "father of the British SECRET SERVICE," became a merchant but was plagued with financial difficulties. Interested in politics, he wrote political pamphlets and volunteered to spy for the speaker of the House of Commons in 1703. Sometimes using the COVER of a tradesman named "Alexander Goldsmith," he traveled extensively in Britain, reporting not only about political foes but also watching for plots against the throne by Jacobites, the supporters of the son of the deposed James II.

He set up a spy ring devoted to obtaining DOMESTIC INTELLIGENCE. Later, during negotiations for the union of the parliaments of England and Scotland in 1706, he passed himself off to Scots as a nongovernmental supporter of union. He also so ingratiated himself with the Jacobites that he was able to edit their newspapers and subtly expose their true sympathies.

Soon after publication of *Robinson Crusoe* in 1719 his spy career came to an end. He subsequently wrote *Moll Flanders* (1722) and other works.

Deighton, Len

(b. 1929)

Writer of spy thrillers. Deighton, unlike such other British spy writers as IAN FLEMING, GRAHAM GREENE, and JOHN LE CARRÉ, has no experience in the intelligence field.

Deighton was a railway clerk before performing his national service in the Royal Air Force as a photographer

attached to the Special Investigations Branch. After his discharge in 1949 he attended art school. But while working part time as a waiter he developed an interest in cookery, which led to his producing a comic strip in the Sunday *Observer* newspaper and writing two cookery books. He subsequently worked as an illustrator in New York and as art director for a London advertising agency.

Deighton decided to devote himself to writing after the publication of his first spy thriller, *The Ipcress File* (1962), a novel about a low-grade INTELLIGENCE OFFICER who discovers that one of his superiors is a spy. It was an instant success and was made into a film, starring Michael Caine, in 1965.

Funeral in Berlin (1964) established Deighton as a writer of spy thrillers in the tradition of le Carré rather than Fleming, for Deighton's agent-heroes are disillusioned men who depend on their own survival instincts rather than gadgets and derring-do. His heroes are targets of treachery on guard against their compatriots as well as Soviet agents.

In Deighton's trilogy *Berlin Game* (1983), *Mexico Set* (1985), and *London Match* (1985), the hero, Bernard Sampson, goes from his desk job in Whitehall to East BERLIN. Nearly everyone Sampson meets, so-called friend or so-called foe, betrays him or someone else. The trilogy was launched in England and became a television miniseries in the United States. Sampson also appears in Deighton's *Spy Hook* (1988) and *Spy Line* (1989).

Other Deighton espionage books include *Spy Story* (1974), *Yesterday's Spy* (1975), *Twinkle, Twinkle, Little Spy* (1976) (published in America as *Catch a Falling Spy*), *SS-GB* (1978), *XPD* (1981), *Goodbye, Mickey Mouse* (1982), and *Winter* (1987). The especially fascinating *SS-GB* describes a Britain under German rule following the country's conquest by Nazi Germany in 1940.

To date, Deighton has published some 50 books, including several nonfiction aviation books.

Also see LITERARY SPIES.

Denied Area

Region that cannot be easily penetrated to gain intelligence. A denied area can be part of a country prohibited to diplomats (and thus LEGALS under diplomatic COVER). Or an entire country, such as China prior to U.S. recognition, could be denied. In such an area intelligence agencies must rely upon ILLEGALS, indirect observations (such as interrogation of refugees and visitors), and AIRCRAFT, SATELLITE, and ELECTRONIC INTELLIGENCE.

Denning, Vice-Adm. Sir Norman

(b. 1904 d. 1979)

Founder of the Royal Navy's OPERATIONAL INTELLIGENCE CENTRE (OIC) in World War II, which used ULTRA and other intelligence to plot the destruction of the German surface fleet and U-boat force.

In June 1937, Denning, then a paymaster lieutenant commander, was tasked to establish an intelligence center that could combine intelligence derived from various sources and advise the Navy's leadership on courses of action. It was a refinement of ROOM 40 in World War I, which had begun as a codebreaking office but had evolved into such a center.

Denning started with one clerk, no office, and no background in intelligence. But he was the right man for the job. First he spent four weeks at the GOVERNMENT CODE AND CYPHER SCHOOL (GC&CS), where Comdr. ALASTAIR DENNISTON gave him a good grounding in British codebreaking efforts, which at that time were successful only against Italian communications, not German. Denning then studied the Room 40 files.

Before he could go much further he was being called upon to provide intelligence related to the Spanish Civil War, which had already been raging for a year. The GC&CS was able to provide him with some intelligence, while HIGH-FREQUENCY DIRECTION FINDING efforts enabled him to plot Italian submarines that were supporting the Nationalist (fascist) forces. Starting a card index of intelligence and setting up plots of ship locations, he began a process that has continued to this day, albeit now computerized and employing ALL-SOURCE INTELLIGENCE.

Under Denning's direction the OIC grew until it had soon become the de facto operations center for the war at sea against Germany. As demonstrated in naval histories—and the film *Sink the Bismarck* (1960)—the OIC directed successful operations that found and sank the German battleship *Bismarck* in May 1941, and eventually won the Battle of the Atlantic against the U-boats. (That battle was "won" in May 1943 but continued until Germany capitulated in May 1945.)

OIC veteran PATRICK BEESLY wrote in *Very Special Intelligence* (1977): "Denning, throughout the whole war, spent six days and six nights a week in the Admiralty. He was almost continuously on call." He created an OIC that was efficient, helpful, reflective, and invaluable.

Denning served as the penultimate DIRECTOR OF NAVAL INTELLIGENCE, from 1959 to 1964 (with that position being abolished with establishment of a unified Defense Staff). Subsequently, Denning served as the first Deputy Chief of Defense Staff (Intelligence), when that staff was established in 1964 by Lord Louis Mountbatten. That was the No. 2 intelligence post in the British armed forces, and Mountbatten himself selected Denning.

Denning retired from the Navy in 1965.

Denniston, Comdr. Alastair G.

(b. 1881 d. 1961)

Head of Britain's GOVERNMENT CODE AND CYPHER SCHOOL (GC&CS), located at BLETCHLEY PARK during World War II. Under his leadership from 1921 to 1944, the GC&CS broke into Italian CODES and much of the German ENIGMA enciphered communications.

Although christened Alexander, Denniston used the name Alastair. He was educated at Bowden College in England, Bonn University, and the Sorbonne. Denniston

played hockey for Britain in the Olympics, and taught French and Latin at a boys' school. In 1912 he went to the naval college at Osborne to teach foreign languages. When World War I began he was assigned to the Admiralty's codebreaking effort known as ROOM 40.

After the war he joined the GC&CS, which succeeded Room 40 in 1919. Two years later he was named head of the agency, which was responsible for compiling and printing all codes and CIPHERS used by the British government as well as attempting to penetrate foreign communications. The GC&CS attempts to penetrate German communications met with very limited success; however, inroads were made into Italian codes during the European political crises of the 1930s.

Denniston visited Warsaw in July 1939 to meet with the codebreakers of the Polish BIURO SZFROW, where the Poles revealed that—with French help—they had broken into the German Enigma ciphers. The subsequent delivery of an Enigma machine to Denniston by the Poles, as well as assistance from the French, was to open the way for the GC&CS to break into virtually all German communications.

In Aug. 1939, as World War II was about to erupt in Europe, Denniston moved the GC&CS from the Secret Service (MI6) headquarters at No. 54 BROADWAY in London to Bletchley Park to escape the expected air raids on the British capital.

In Aug. 1941 Denniston made the first of three trips to the United States to discuss codebreaking issues with the U.S. Army and Navy. Those meetings evolved into the unprecedented BRUSA AGREEMENT of May 1943.

The GC&CS grew rapidly under Denniston's guidance, but the strain was tremendous. Further, he became involved in infighting over the handling of decrypts. In Jan. 1942 Denniston, while technically remaining head of the GC&CS, moved to London to run the diplomatic and commercial codebreaking efforts, while Comdr. Edward W. Travis took over the military efforts at Bletchley Park. Denniston became ill with a stone in his bladder and was forced into retirement in 1944 (with Travis becoming head of the entire GC&CS operation).

Ill, depressed, and upset at his "firing," Denniston died before the British successes in breaking into the Enigma ciphers were revealed.

d'Éon, Chevalier Charles Genevieve Louis

(b. 1728 d. 1810)

SECRET AGENT who sometimes posed as a woman to carry out his undercover missions for King Louis XV. He was an excellent swordsman and held degrees as a doctor of civil and canonical law.

In 1755 he became the French ambassador to Russia, where he often dressed as a woman. Legends swirled around him—that he was the czarina's maid of honor, that painters wanted to make portraits of this beautiful woman.

After the French court intrigued to destroy him, d'Éon fled to England, where he became associated with

the British SECRET SERVICE (although he was also supposedly conducting TACTICAL INTELLIGENCE about British
roads for potential French invaders). Ordered home,
d'Éon refused to obey and threatened to become a DE-
FECTOR. The king sent another agent, PIERRE BEAUMAR-
CHAIS, to pay off d'Éon and negotiate a settlement
requiring him to dress as a woman for the rest of his life,
as a way to guarantee that he would not conspire against
the throne. Beaumarchais believed that d'Éon was dangerous only as a male.

Secret agent d'Éon remained in England. There were
several investigations to determine his gender. He was
buried as a male.

Department of Internal Security

SEE SHIN BET

Deputy Chief of Staff (Intelligence)

General officer in U.S. Army headquarters with responsi-
bility for intelligence activities; also the de facto head of
G-2. The Army's staff abbreviation code is DCS (INT).
The position is analogous to the U.S. Navy's DIRECTOR OF
NAVAL INTELLIGENCE.

Formerly the Assistant Chief of Staff (Intelligence).

Deriabin, Maj. Peter Sergeyevich

(b. 1921 d. 1992)

KGB officer who defected in VIENNA in 1954 and later
worked for the CIA.

Deriabin, a native of Siberia, served in the Red Army
during World War II. After being wounded four times he
was assigned to the Higher Military Counterintelligence
School from June 1944 to April 1945 and emerged as a
military COUNTERINTELLIGENCE officer. After a brief time
as a state security officer in Siberia, he was transferred to
the Ministry of State Security, then known as the NKGB
(see NKVD) in Moscow. As an officer in the Guard Directorate, he was responsible for keeping watch on the uniformed and plainclothes security personnel in the
Kremlin.

In May 1952, Deriabin was assigned to the Austro-
German section of the Second Directorate, which dealt
with foreign intelligence. From there, in Sept. 1953 he
was posted to the Soviet mission in Vienna, which was
still under Allied occupation. After a relatively uneventful five months in Vienna, in Feb. 1954 he walked into
the U.S. military headquarters and asked for political
asylum. At the time he was a major, the highest-ranking
Soviet INTELLIGENCE OFFICER to become a DEFECTOR.

Deriabin left a wife and child behind in what seemed
to be an impulsive decision. The CIA got Deriabin out of
Vienna by shipping him as freight on a train that had to
pass through the Soviet occupation zone around Vienna.
For five years the CIA kept Deriabin hidden while he was
debriefed and brought into the agency. One of his most

intriguing revelations was a remark he had heard while
serving in Moscow: a senior intelligence official called
SDECE, the French intelligence agency, "that prostitute I
put in my pocket." This bit of information became extremely valuable seven years later when the CIA heard
reports from other Soviet defectors that the SDECE had
been penetrated by the KGB. Deriabin also reliably
named ANATOLY GOLITSYN as a possible defector.
(Golitsin confirmed the SDECE penetration.)

Deriabin became an agency authority on the history
and techniques of Soviet intelligence. He taught CIA
classes, lectured at the Defense Intelligence College, and
translated the material for *The Penkovsky Papers*
(1965), a book secretly produced by the CIA from its
files on Col. OLEG PENKOVSKY, the highest-ranking Soviet
military official known to have aided the West.

With Frank Gibney, Deriabin wrote an autobiography, *The Secret World* (1959). Deriabin's other books
were *Watchdogs of Terror* (1972) on Soviet intelligence;
The KGB: Masters of the Soviet Union (1982); and, with
Jerrold L. Schecter, *The Spy Who Saved the World*
(1992), a book about Penkovsky.

Derivative Classification

U.S. government term for a determination that information derived from a document or file is in substance the
same as the original information and that the application
of the same level of security CLASSIFICATION is justified.

Desheng, Hou

Chinese military ATTACHÉ detained by the FBI in 1987 for
attempting to obtain material from NSA from a federal
employee working under FBI direction. Desheng was
taken into custody at a restaurant in Washington's Chinatown after accepting what he believed to be classified
NSA documents.

Arrested at the same time was Zang Weichu, a Chinese consular official in Chicago. Both diplomats were
asked to leave the country as a result of "activities incompatible with their diplomatic status." They were the
first Chinese diplomats expelled since formal relations
were established between the United States and China in
1979.

Designated Countries

U.S. government term for countries whose interests are
considered inimical to those of the United States. Persons
holding SECURITY CLEARANCES must report contacts by
anyone from designated countries and cannot travel to
such countries without advising their security officer.

In 1991, on the eve of the collapse of the Soviet
regime, the designated countries listed by the U.S. government were Afghanistan, Albania, Angola, Bulgaria,
Cuba, Czechoslovakia, Ethiopia, Hungary, Iran, Iraq,
Kampuchea (formerly Cambodia), Laos, Libya, Mongo-
lian People's Republic (Outer Mongolia), Nicaragua,

North Korea, People's Republic of China (including Tibet), Poland, Rumania [sic], South Yemen, Syria, Union of Soviet Socialist Republics (including Estonia, Latvia, Lithuania, and all other constituent republics, Kurile Islands, and South Sakhalin), Vietnam, and Yugoslavia.

Since the end of the Cold War the list has been in a continual state of flux.

In 2003, there were 49 Designated Countries, divided into four groups. Those with which the United States has no diplomatic relations; countries under U.S. sanction or embargo; countries of "missile technology concern"; and countries accused of supporting terrorism. The focus has been on terrorism. In that category were Cuba, Iran, North Korea, Libya, Sudan, and Syria.

DESOTO

CODE NAME for U.S. Navy destroyer patrols in the Gulf of Tonkin off North Vietnam in the early 1960s. The purpose was the collection of ELECTRONIC INTELLIGENCE. A controversial attack on a DESOTO warship precipitated a crisis that led to the Vietnam War.

In Jan. 1964, about the time the DESOTO patrols began, the NATIONAL SECURITY COUNCIL approved the highly classified Plan 34A, which authorized support by the CIA of covert South Vietnamese operations against North Vietnam. The plan had two parts: the infiltration of South Vietnamese AGENTS into North Vietnam by aircraft and boat, and hit-and-run attacks against North Vietnamese shore installations by high-speed craft manned by South Vietnamese or mercenaries hired by the CIA.

"Although some individuals knew of both 34A operations and DESOTO patrols, the approval process for each was compartmentalized, and few, if any, senior officials either planned or followed in detail the operational schedules of both," former Secretary of Defense Robert S. McNamara wrote in his memoir, In Retrospect (1995), adding, "We should have."

On the night of July 20, 1964, South Vietnamese patrol boats, as part of Plan 34A, attacked two North Vietnamese islands in the Gulf of Tonkin. The next morning the U.S. destroyer Maddox, on DESOTO patrol, steamed into the gulf. On Aug. 2 the Maddox, in international waters about 25 miles off the coast, reported being under attack by high-speed torpedo boats. Another destroyer, the Turner Joy, was sent to aid the Maddox.

On Aug. 4 another Plan 34A attack took place along the North Vietnamese coast, and a few hours later the Maddox and the Turner Joy both reported night attacks by small boats, two of which were reportedly sunk by the destroyers' guns. A U.S. aircraft carrier, the Ticonderoga, launched fighter aircraft to aid the two destroyers.

Ever since that night, controversy has swirled around the Aug. 4 attack. Some naval officers who were on the scene said no attack had occurred. North Vietnamese radio transmissions, intercepted by the NSA, were disputed. But President Johnson, seizing on the attack as a provocation by North Vietnam, ordered a retaliatory strike on Aug. 4. Aircraft from the Ticonderoga and a second carrier, the Constellation, flew 64 sorties against North Vietnamese patrol boat bases and an oil storage complex.

At the time, Plan 34A was known to few administration or congressional leaders. In the congressional debate that followed, there was no public mention of CIA support of the South Vietnamese raids. There was the possibility that the North Vietnamese were reacting to those raids by attacking U.S. warships. But in the furor over the attacks, the raids were forgotten. Johnson pushed through Congress what became known as the Tonkin Gulf Resolution, giving him the power "to take all necessary steps, including the use of armed force," to aid South Vietnam.

McNamara went to Hanoi in Nov. 1995 on what he said was an attempt to learn more about the origins of the Vietnam War. While there he met with Gen. Vo Nguyen Giap, commander of North Vietnam forces in the war. In his postscript to the Tonkin Gulf Resolution and the disputed Aug. 4 attack, McNamara said that after meeting with Giap, "I am prepared to say, without a doubt, there was no second attack."

Subsequent interviews with Vietnamese torpedo boat commanders confirmed that the first attack did take place, but not the second.

Deutch, Dr. John M.

(b. 1938)

DIRECTOR OF CENTRAL INTELLIGENCE (DCI) appointed in May 1995 to, in his words, take the CIA "beyond the horror" of the discovery that ALDRICH H. AMES, who had been a Soviet MOLE in the agency. Deutch was the first DCI since WILLIAM J. CASEY to be made a member of the President's cabinet.

The honor was short-lived. Deutch resigned in Dec. 1996 after he realized that President Clinton, newly elected to his second term, was not going to reappoint him.

During his 20 months as DCI, Deutch was in a continuous feud with the CIA's Directorate of Operations, the clandestine service. He fired two senior officers in the wake of CIA abuses committed in overt operations in Guatemala. Deutch also had publicly criticized unnamed officers of the clandestine service as arrogant and ineffective. In an interview with The Washington Post following his resignation, Deutch said that officers in the clandestine service had ritually condemned him with an attitude he translated as, "You don't know what you're doing, you're not experienced, you're not one of us."

Deutch also lost the confidence of high-level Clinton administration officials because of the way in which he handled several incidents that plagued the CIA during his short tenure. He was especially criticized for personally appearing before a group of Los Angeles citizens to deny an unfounded link between the CIA and the introduction of crack cocaine into the city.

Deutch replaced R. JAMES WOOLSEY, who was DCI when Ames was arrested by the FBI in Feb. 1994. Woolsey was forced to resign after he failed to crack down on CIA officials who had mishandled the internal investigation of Ames. Deutch left no doubt about his attitude: "The extent of the damage was due mostly to inexcusable laxity on the part of the professionals of the Directorate of Operations and others at the CIA. It is an intelligence calamity of massive proportions."

Deutch was the first foreign-born DCI. Born in Belgium, he was four years old when he, his sister, and his parents arrived in the United States, a Jewish family fleeing the Nazis. The family settled in a suburb of Washington, D.C., where Deutch's father, an engineer, worked for the War Production Board developing synthetic rubber. Deutch, following in his father's footsteps, earned a degree in chemical engineering at the Massachusetts Institute of Technology (MIT) while simultaneously getting a history degree from Amherst. While working for the Department of Defense as a policy planner from 1961 to 1965, Deutch received a doctorate in physical chemistry from MIT.

After teaching chemistry at Princeton, he returned to MIT and became the chair of the chemistry department in 1976. He retained his Pentagon ties, working for the RAND Corp., a defense think tank. On Deutch's office door at MIT was a sign that said, "On defense matters, I'm a hawk. On social issues, I'm a liberal. On departmental issues, I'm a raving maniac."

During the Carter administration (1977–1981) he worked for the new Department of Energy, becoming the undersecretary responsible for nuclear weapons programs. When President Reagan succeeded Carter, Deutch returned to MIT and became provost. During the Bush administration (1989–1993) Deutch served on the PRESIDENT'S FOREIGN INTELLIGENCE ADVISORY BOARD.

On his 50th birthday colleagues gave him a T-shirt inscribed with the words FIRE, AIM, READY—a vivid description of his charge-ahead leadership and rapid-fire decision making. Deutch brought those qualities to the Pentagon when President Clinton's Secretary of Defense, Les Aspin, appointed him undersecretary for acquisitions and technology. He enjoyed the Pentagon job so much that he turned down President Clinton's offer of the post of DCI after Woolsey resigned in Dec. 1944. Clinton's next choice, retired Air Force Gen. Michael P. C. Carns, dropped out after a BACKGROUND INVESTIGATION showed that he might have violated immigration and labor laws in aiding a young Filipino to enter the United States. Clinton turned to Deutch again, and he reluctantly accepted.

He was not reluctant in describing his role, however. Soon after becoming DCI he said he saw himself charged with reestablishing the reputation of the CIA after the Ames affair. Deutch also believed that he had a pivotal role in defining post–Cold War missions for the CIA and the INTELLIGENCE COMMUNITY. Espionage, he said in Sept. 1995, is still "the core mission" of the CIA, and the ability to perform COVERT ACTIONS must continue. "If we do not take such risks because we are afraid to fail or we are afraid of controversy, then we will fail as an intelligence service," he said.

"I am personally outraged by this," Deutch said before the House Intelligence Committee during a hearing on the Ames case. "I was personally misled," he declared, emphasizing the fact that CIA officers, aware that AGENTS in Russia had almost certainly been TURNED, had supplied the White House and Pentagon with tainted intelligence. Deutch did not elaborate in public sessions, but sources said that he had based recommendations about the F-22 fighter aircraft on tainted information about Soviet anti-aircraft capabilities.

In rebuilding and reorganizing the CIA he listed the four major post–Cold War challenges as the spread of chemical, biological, and nuclear weapons of mass destruction; actions of hostile nations, such as North Korea, Iran, and Iraq; the threat of international crime, terrorism, and drugs; and the need to preserve U.S. economic security. Responding to suggestions that the last challenge sounded like INDUSTRIAL ESPIONAGE, Deutch said, "We should know if foreign governments are penetrating our corporations."

Deutch also set in motion a plan to consolidate IMAGERY INTELLIGENCE and tighten the DCI's grip on the big-spending NATIONAL RECONNAISSANCE OFFICE (NRO). After learning of careless handling of NRO funds, Deutch fired the two top officials of the agency, NRO director Jeffrey K. Harris and deputy director Jimmie D. Hill. The DEFENSE HUMINT SERVICE, a Pentagon organization that he had created within the DEFENSE INTELLIGENCE AGENCY, seemed destined to play a bigger role in COVERT ACTIONS.

As Deutch put his mark on the CIA, agency officials exposed to his blistering, demanding style began calling CIA headquarters "Deutchland." He and his executive director, former Assistant Secretary of the Navy Nora Slatkin, disciplined 17 officers for infractions in the Ames case and for mishandling information about a CIA agent allegedly involved in the 1990 murder of an American in Guatemala. (Woolsey had only given letters of reprimand to 11 officers accused of laxity in the Ames case.)

Deutch, ranking Slatkin on the same level as the director of the DIA and the NSA, has made himself the chief executive of U.S. intelligence, as the term DCI implies. He initiated the development of a Joint Space Management Board to buy SATELLITES and the establishment of the NATIONAL IMAGERY AND MAPPING AGENCY.

Deutch had his security clearance suspended in Aug. 1999 as a result of a CIA security investigation that revealed he had kept TOP SECRET documents on his home laptop computer, which could easily have been entered through its connection to the INTERNET. The classified documents included memos to President Clinton and Cabinet officials. There was also classified material from the time Deutch served as deputy defense secretary. (A Pentagon investigation concluded in Jan. 2001 that there was "no evidence" that Deutch's actions had compromised national security.) Under a Justice Department plea agreement, Deutch admitted to unauthorized retention of classified material, a misdemeanor. Clinton, on his last day as president, pardoned Deutch.

Deuxième Bureau

(DB)

French Army General Staff's intelligence section, formed after the French defeat in the Franco-Prussian War of 1870–1871.

The bureau got its name from the French Army General Staff system, which had four principal bureaus: Premièr (first) Bureau—personnel; Deuxième (second)—intelligence; Troisième (third)—operations; and Quatrième (fourth)—supply. (The U.S. Army General Staff system copied this arrangement, i.e., G-2 for intelligence.)

Intelligence had fallen to its lowest ebb in the French Army by the time the Franco-Prussian War began in 1870. The army of Napoléon III lacked even useful maps of Prussia. Defeated in 1871, the French Army General Staff was reorganized, using the Prussian Army as a model. Out of this reorganization came the Deuxième Bureau. One of the officers in its key unit, the Section de Statistiques et de Reconnaissances Militaires, was Capt. ALFRED DREYFUS. His conviction in 1894 on trumped-up espionage charges—and the scandal that followed—undermined French trust in the DB and its subordinate section, the Service de Renseignements (Information Bureau) or SR.

The DB provided the French general staff with excellent intelligence about German planning prior to World War I and during the opening battles of Aug. 1914. However, the intelligence was largely discarded by the military leadership. As the war progressed, the DB's effectiveness declined until, as the Germans were about to begin their great offensive of March 1918, the head of the DB said, "I am the best-informed man in France, and at this moment I no longer know where the Germans are." The DB, as a MILITARY INTELLIGENCE organization, did, however, usher in modern intelligence techniques with aerial RECONNAISSANCE, radio intercepts, and fast-reaction codebreaking.

The DB became enormous during and immediately after World War I, running French military espionage and COUNTERESPIONAGE both inside and outside France. Members of the DB took a special oath that bound them to keep bureau secrets forever.

After the war the DB was caught up in the "Red Scare" that swept Britain, France, and the United States. Working sometimes with the SÛRETÉ GÉNÉRALE and sometimes competing against it, the DB in the 1920s and 1930s sought communist spies in the armed forces and defense industry. DB officers focused especially on aviation units and aircraft factories.

One of the DB's stars of the period between the world wars was GUSTAVE BERTRAND, head of French CRYPTANALYSIS. He was instrumental in helping the Poles break into the ENIGMA CIPHERS on the eve of World War II and in obtaining Enigma machines for France and Britain.

During France's short-lived combat role in the war, the DB provided adequate intelligence, but its military leaders were locked into preordained strategy. They ignored warnings of the May 1940 German attack that swept across France, gaining a swift victory. In wartime France—half German-occupied, the other governed by the pro-Nazi Vichy regime—the DB disappeared along with the defeated French Army. But Capt. Paul Paillole and other INTELLIGENCE OFFICERS set up an anti-German intelligence agency in the Vichy region under the COVER of Enterprise des Travaux Ruraux, ostensibly a company for aiding rural travelers. Paillole ran the group until Nov. 1942, when the Anglo-American invasion of French North Africa led to German occupation of all of France. Paillole fled to Britain, where he joined the BCRA, a new intelligence service established by Gen. Charles de Gaulle, head of the Free French with his headquarters in London.

When the European War ended in the spring of 1945, the French Army was reborn, and with it the Deuxième Bureau. Once again the DB was not only a military intelligence organization but also a quasi-military secret service, especially in France's colonial empire, which erupted in anti-French rebellions after the war.

In Indochina, the DB and a new postwar rival, the SDECE, both tried to work with guerrilla groups or infiltrate the Vietminh communist insurgents. The DB must share in the responsibility for France's defeat in the French-Indochina War (1946–1954), but the lack of good military intelligence was overshadowed by a political refusal to acknowledge the strength of the Vietminh forces.

The Geneva peace conference of 1954 divided Vietnam, setting up two nations, with the Vietminh getting North Vietnam and the south becoming the Republic of South Vietnam. French troops, together with the DB and SDECE, were relocated to South Vietnam. Some DB and SDECE officers continued to work closely with a notorious criminal organization, Binh Xuyen opium-runners of Saigon, providing ways to get opium and gold to France. As the French role in Indochina was ending and the U.S. chapter in Vietnam was beginning, DB operatives often skirmished with their opposite numbers from the CIA. (See Col. EDWARD G. LANSDALE, UNITED STATES, VIETNAM.)

Today the DB coordinates the military intelligence coming from the French Army, Navy, and Air Force, including information provided by the ATTACHÉS of each service. It also operates a Center for the Exploitation of SCIENTIFIC AND TECHNICAL INTELLIGENCE and a Center for Intelligence Exploitation. Since 1992 the DB has been under the Military Intelligence Directorate, as has the DPSD.

Dewavrin, André

(b. 1911 d. 1998)

Director of intelligence for the Free French forces during World War II. As "Colonel Passy"—a name borrowed from a Paris Métro stop—he ran BCRA, Gen. Charles de

Gaulle's intelligence agency in London. An engineering officer who earlier taught fortifications at the French military academy of Saint-Cyr, Dewavrin was assigned to a French unit being formed in Britain when France fell. He joined de Gaulle's Free French in London and was immediately given the task of forming an intelligence service that was ultimately named BCRA, for Bureau Central de Renseignements et d'Action (Central Bureau for Information and Action).

Dewavrin, an artillery officer who knew nothing about intelligence, was put under the wing of Sir Claude Dansey, assistant chief of British MI6. A courageous man but a reckless intelligence chief, Dewavrin entered German-occupied France in Jan. 1943.

He continued to serve as de Gaulle's intelligence chief until Feb. 1946, after de Gaulle's resignation as France's interim president. Dewavrin was arrested in May 1946 on what appear to have been trumped-up charges that he had embezzled BCRA funds during the war. He was later cleared, but resigned from the Army.

French journalist and naval officer Robert Mengin, who said that Dewavrin's ideas were "the exact opposite of mine," nonetheless wrote in *No Laurels for de Gaulle* (1966), "Colonel Passy was a courageous, highly intelligent, dedicated man. . . ."

DGER

Direction Générale des Études et Recherches (General Directorate of Studies and Research), the French foreign intelligence agency that succeeded the DGSS in 1944.

Historically, French intelligence agencies were controlled by the military. Like its predecessor, the DGSS, the DGER broke with tradition, reporting to the War Ministry and later to the Prime Minister. The new arrangement was the work of Gen. Charles de Gaulle, who created the DGER when he established his provisional government after the liberation of France in 1944.

The director of DGER was ANDRÉ DEWAVRIN, who, under the nom de guerre "Colonel Passy," ran de Gaulle's wartime BCRA (Central Bureau for Information and Action). Dewavrin ordered the DGER's AGENTS to collect intelligence on political parties and resistance movements; they were also to watch for acts of subversion, particularly by communists. The Directorate of Technical Control tapped telephones and intercepted mail (an old French tradition; see BLACK CHAMBER). Agents kept thousands of citizens in German-occupied France under SURVEILLANCE.

The DGER's 10,000 agents swarmed around France in the wake of liberating Allied armies in 1944, seeking out collaborators—and finding caches of ill-gotten gains hidden by collaborators. Agents counterfeited documents (a skill learned during the occupation) for people who suddenly needed new identities, blackmailed politicians, and conducted illegal currency transactions. Disgusted French said the agency should have been called Direction Générale des Escroqueries et Rapines (General Directorate of Fraud and Plunder). Communists also had

a name for the DGER: Direction Générale des Ennemis de la République.

The DGER operated from Nov. 1944 to Jan. 1946, when de Gaulle resigned as interim President of France. The agency was quickly abolished and replaced by the SDECE, Service de Documentation Extérieure et de Contreespionnage (the Service of External Documentation and Counterespionage).

DGSE

Direction Générale de la Sécurité Extérieure (General Directorate for External Security), the French intelligence agency that succeeded the notorious SDECE in 1981.

When Socialist François Mitterrand was elected president in 1981, he abolished the SDECE, at least in name, and established the DGSE, with Pierre Marion, former head of Air France and an aerospace company, as its chief. Eighteen months later Marion resigned and was replaced by Adm. PIERRE LACOSTE, the first naval officer to run a major French intelligence agency.

Lacoste reorganized the agency, which had about 2,800 full-time employees (1,300 of them military). Under Lacoste's plan, Division 1 collected and analyzed intelligence; Division 2 handled COUNTERINTELLIGENCE and security to prevent penetration by hostile intelligence agencies; Division 3, the "action" component of DGSE, was a new version of the SDECE's Action Service.

The hope that the DGSE would be more responsible than the SDECE was dashed in 1985 when DGSE "action" officers blew up and sank the *RAINBOW WARRIOR*, a ship owned by the environmental organization Greenpeace and sent into the Pacific to protest French nuclear weapons tests. A photographer was killed on the ship, which was blown up at a dock in New Zealand. Lacoste was forced to resign in the international uproar that followed the disclosure of DGSE's involvement in the sinking of the *Rainbow Warrior*.

Claude Silberzahn, who became head of the DGSE in 1989, had to reallocate the agency's resources for the post–Cold War world. He chose INDUSTRIAL ESPIONAGE. DGSE spying on the U.S. aerospace industry became so flagrant that in 1993 the CIA warned U.S. aircraft companies to beware of French spying at the annual Paris Air Show. Some companies boycotted the show. The warning was based on evidence showing that the DGSE had plotted to steal technological information from the more than 40 U.S. companies that had signed up for the show.

Silberzahn, in a tacit admission that the CIA warning was warranted, was removed as director of the agency. But in defense of French tactics, he insisted that modern espionage "is essentially economic, scientific, technological and financial."

Officials of the FBI have said that French intelligence AGENTS remain among the most active in carrying out industrial espionage against U.S. corporations. In France, the DGSE planted agents inside IBM, Texas Instruments, and Corning branches and obtained valuable trade secrets.

DGSE agents are alleged to have bugged Air France flights between Paris and New York to listen in on traveling U.S. businessmen. U.S. officials also claim that the DGSE has tried to place industrial MOLES in European branches of U.S. corporations, has wiretapped state-owned communications lines used by U.S. companies in France, and has tried to steal bids of U.S. firms competing against French companies for an Indian fighter aircraft contract. It is also alleged that French consular officials in Texas have searched the trash at the homes of U.S. executives in the hope of finding technological information and electronically monitored flight tests of the Boeing 747–400 aircraft for the benefit of Airbus, the European aircraft consortium.

DGSS

Direction Générale des Services Spéciaux (General Directorate of Special Services). This French intelligence agency emerged from a political struggle during World War II between Gen. Charles de Gaulle, leader of the Free French, and his rival, Gen. Henri-Honoré Giraud.

After the Anglo-American invasion of North Africa in Nov. 1942, de Gaulle wanted his intelligence agency, the London-based BCRA, to merge with Giraud's SR, and Military Security Service, which had operated in Vichy-controlled France. The merger finally took place with the SR becoming the technical division of a new agency, the DGSS. As its director, de Gaulle selected Jacques Soustelle, a civilian with no intelligence experience. The fact that the DGSS reported to de Gaulle, not the military leadership, marked a historic change for the future of French intelligence agencies.

Following the D-DAY landings on June 6, 1944, the DGSS began operations not only in France but also in the Middle East and Eastern Europe. The DGSS also used French citizens in the United States to get intelligence on U.S. activities that affected France. After de Gaulle set up his provisional government in a liberated Paris, the DGSS became the DGER, *Direction Générale des Études et Recherches* (General Directorate of Studies and Research), an internal intelligence agency.

DIA

SEE DEFENSE INTELLIGENCE AGENCY

Dickinson, Velvalee

(b. 1893 d. ?)

One of the very few Americans who spied for Japan during World War II.

Velvalee Dickinson and her husband, Lee, learned to appreciate Japanese culture while living in California, where Lee was a stockbroker with many Japanese-American clients.

The couple moved to New York City in 1935, and made the acquaintance of Japanese diplomats attached to the consulate there. When a Japanese official asked if they would spy for Japan, they agreed. After America's entry into World War II in Dec. 1941, the Dickinsons toured the West Coast, observing the location and condition of U.S. Navy warships, particularly those that had sailed to California ports for repairs following Japan's PEARL HARBOR ATTACK.

Velvalee had set up a doll shop in New York City, and she used this as a COVER, sending information in a "doll code" to a Japanese ACCOMMODATION ADDRESS in Buenos Aires. She used the names of customers for the return address on her letters, which spoke of "a doll in a hula skirt" about a ship newly arrived from Hawaii or "three new dolls" for the transfer of three warships from the Atlantic to the Pacific.

When the Japanese agent at the accommodation address moved away, the Buenos Aires post office sent her undelivered letters to the return addresses. Mystified by the strange letters they were receiving, several women reported the letters to U.S. postal authorities. The letters were turned over to the FBI, whose laboratory established that the signatures were forgeries and that the contents contained information hidden by a doll code.

Suspecting a spy plot, the FBI tracked the letters down to Velvalee. (Lee Dickinson had died in 1943.) She had a safe-deposit box containing $15,940, most of it in $100 bills that the FBI traced to prewar currency in Japanese banks.

Labeled the "Doll Woman" by the tabloid press, Dickinson was charged with espionage and violations of wartime censorship laws. In 1944, after pleading guilty to the lesser charge, she was sentenced to 10 years in prison and fined $10,000. She was paroled in 1951.

Dickstein, Samuel

(b. 1885 d. 1954)

Only known member of the U.S. Congress to have spied for the Soviet Union. Dickstein, a member of the House of Representatives from 1923 to 1944, was the founder of what became the House Un-American Activities Committee (HUAC).

Dickstein's spying came to light in VENONA intercepts of Soviet AGENT messages between the United States and Moscow. Dickstein spied for money and so often importuned his HANDLERS for funds—in an era of ideological spying (see MICHAEL STRAIGHT and CPUSA)—that he was given the Soviet CODE NAME "Crook."

Born in Lithuania, he was six years old when his parents immigrated to the United States and moved into New York's Lower East Side, which Dickstein would later represent. In 1906 he received a law degree from New York Law School and entered politics, first as a deputy state attorney general, then as a member of the New York City Board of Aldermen, and then the New York state legislature. In 1923 he won election as a Democrat to the U.S. House of Representatives. This was the first of his 11 consecutive congressional terms.

Because there were so many immigrants in his district, he focused on immigration issues and gradually turned his interest to what he called "un-American" activities. Ironically, he is credited by some for introducing that term to Congress.

His investigative committee at first was known as the McCormack-Dickstein or Dickstein Committee. In 1936, Martin Dies, a conservative Democrat from Texas, beat Dickstein and took over the chairmanship. The Dies Committee next became known as the House Un-American Activities Committee. While it was hunting down communists in government, Dickstein was on the payroll of the NKVD.

As Allen Weinstein and Alexander Vassiliev recount Dickstein's espionage in *The Haunted Wood* (1999), the first NKVD contact was made in July 1937 by an ILLEGAL who said that he wanted to become an American citizen. Dickstein asked for funds that sounded like a bribe to the illegal, code-named "Buby." Maj. Gen. GAIK OVAKIM, the NKVD RESIDENT in New York, later indignantly told Moscow that Dickstein was "heading a criminal gang that was involved in shady businesses, selling passports, illegal smuggling of people, getting the citizenship."

In Dec. 1937 Dickstein called on the Soviet ambassador to the United States, inspiring a message to Moscow that said Dickstein had "professed a friendly attitude toward the Soviet Union," offered to pass information his committee uncovered about Russian fascists, for which "he would need 5–6 thousand dollars." Despite the ambassador's skepticism, NIKOLAI VEZHOV, head of the NKVD, approved making Dickstein a paid agent.

Dickstein and his handlers constantly bickered over money. In May 1938, soon after the founding of the HUAC, Dickstein and the NKVD came to an agreement: $1,250 per month for "documentary materials" and "to guide" the committee toward subjects the NKVD would like investigated. But soon his handler was complaining to THE CENTER that Dickstein was "unscrupulous," "greedy for money," and "a very cunning swindler."

When Dickstein was dropped from the committee later in May he became far less valuable to the Soviets, who wanted to renegotiate the agreement. Dickstein, infuriated, said, according to still another message, that he had been far better treated when he "worked for" Polish and British intelligence agencies.

Again, Dickstein won. His handler even suggested to THE CENTER that money be given to the congressman as part of a general program to aide friendly lawmakers. The Venona intercepts do not include any response to this intriguing message. But it is clear from another intercept that in Sept. 1938, when Dickstein began publicly attacking the HUAC for hunting down communists, he was doing the bidding of the NKVD. When asked to penetrate U.S. intelligence agencies, Dickstein balked—because Moscow did not offer him enough money.

Early in 1940, Moscow broke with Dickstein, after paying him more than $12,000, which, as Weinstein and Vassiliev point out, is equivalent to about $133,000 in current dollars. Dickstein's work for the NKVD was not revealed during his lifetime. In 1945 he capped his congressional career by running successfully for the New

York State Supreme Court. In a sensational 1948 incident, Judge Dickstein once more dealt with the Soviets—this time ordering Soviet diplomats to produce in court a woman who had "leaped to freedom" from the Soviet Consulate in New York. Mrs. Oksana Kasenkina, whose leap was widely publicized, was a teacher of diplomats' children who had refused to obey an order to return to the Soviet Union. Dickstein shared in the publicity and the patriotism displayed by the teacher. He continued serving as a judge until he died in 1954.

Diello, Ulysses

SEE CICERO

Dinar

SEE UMBRA

Direction Finding

SEE HIGH-FREQUENCY DIRECTION FINDING

Direction de la Surveillance du Territoire

SEE DST

Director of Central Intelligence

(DCI)

Head of the CIA and the leader of the INTELLIGENCE COMMUNITY, the grouping of U.S. government organizations that carry out intelligence activities.

The term was first used in 1946, when President Truman created the NATIONAL INTELLIGENCE AUTHORITY (NIA), which was to coordinate U.S. foreign intelligence activities through a CENTRAL INTELLIGENCE GROUP (CIG) headed by a Director of Central Intelligence. The NIA and the CIG were dissolved when the CIA was founded on Sept. 20, 1947. The head of the CIA was simultaneously designated as the Director of Central Intelligence.

Under the National Security Act of 1947 the DCI was to direct the CIA, the nation's principal intelligence agency, and coordinate overall U.S. intelligence programs and activities, the work of other components of what became known as the "intelligence community." However, because of a combination of weak or uninterested DCIs and the bureaucratic strengths of the other members of the community, the DCI's non-CIA functions historically have been limited.

Under a reorganization of the Intelligence Community in 1971, the DCI was made responsible for "planning, reviewing, coordinating and evaluating all intelligence programs and activities and in the production of national intelligence." Members of the Intelligence Community advise the DCI through their membership on committees dealing with intelligence matters of common concern. Chief among those groups are the NATIONAL INTELLIGENCE BOARD and the NATIONAL INTELLIGENCE COUNCIL, both of which the DCI chairs.

The DCI also chairs the NATIONAL SECURITY COUNCIL's Senior Interagency Group, which deals with interagency intelligence matters and monitors the execution of intelligence policies and decisions.

The Deputy Director of Central Intelligence (DDCI) assists the DCI and acts for and exercises the powers of the DCI in his absence or disability or between the tenure of one DCI and the appointment of a new one.

See DIRECTOR OF NATIONAL INTELLIGENCE; see CIA for a listing of DCIs.

Director of Military Intelligence

(DMI)

The position of Director of Military Intelligence was established in the British War Office in 1887 to strengthen the office's intelligence branch. Prior to the institution of the General Staff, the DMI was responsible for home defense and mobilization, as well as for foreign intelligence.

The DMI post was abolished in 1904, with intelligence functions being incorporated into the Intelligence and Mobilisation Department of the War Office. But the DMI was reintroduced in 1916 because the need for a separate intelligence staff was demonstrated early in World War I.

The DMI position was again abolished in 1922 when a combined Directorate of Operations and Intelligence was set up. The separate DMI was once more established within the War Office in Sept. 1939 following the outbreak of World War II in Europe, and it continued through the conflict.

Director of National Intelligence

(DNI)

Position proposed by several studies to provide a senior official to manage the U.S. INTELLIGENCE COMMUNITY. The idea came up again in 2004 during hearings before the independent presidential commission investigating the Sept. 11, 2001 terrorist attacks.

In 1971 the report of a panel chaired by JAMES R. SCHLESINGER discussed creation of the position of DNI, but did not formally propose the position. (Schlesinger subsequently served as DCI from Feb. 1973 to July 1973, when he became Secretary of Defense.) There were other studies that did recommend such a senior intelligence authority.

In 1992 proposed legislation introduced by Senator David L. Boren and Representative David McCurdy called for a DNI with programming authority over the entire intelligence community, and the ability to temporarily transfer personnel among intelligence agencies. Their proposal was not passed into law.

In a paper published in CIA journal *Studies in Intelligence* (No. 1, 2003), Larry C. Kindsvater, the CIA's ex-

ecutive director for intelligence community affairs, proposed such a supra position, although he retained the title DCI for the position.

Director of Naval Intelligence

(DNI)

The position of Director of NAVAL INTELLIGENCE was established in the British Admiralty in 1886, the Naval Intelligence Division (NID) (originally known as the Foreign Intelligence Committee) having been established in 1882. The DNI staff were originally responsible for fleet mobilization and war plans as well as foreign intelligence collection and were organized into two divisions: (1) intelligence and (2) mobilization. In 1900 a third division was added to deal with issues of strategy and defense, and in 1902 a fourth division took on questions related to the protection of merchant shipping.

The importance of the NID was rapidly recognized. By 1902, wrote historian Arthur J. Marder in *The Anatomy of British Sea Power* (1940), "no question of any greater importance than the, say, change of an article of uniform, is decided without the N.I.D. having its say."

During World War I the NID was responsible for the Royal Navy's highly successful cryptographic efforts. (See ROOM 40.)

The first British head of naval intelligence, appointed in 1882, was Capt. William Henry Hall.

The U.S. Navy established the position of DNI (initially called Chief Intelligence Office) in 1882; Lt. THEODORUS B.M. MASON was its first director.

Also see OFFICE OF NAVAL INTELLIGENCE, NAVAL INTELLIGENCE, U.S.

DIS

(1) DEFENCE INTELLIGENCE STAFF; (2) Defense Investigative Service; see DEFENSE SECURITY SERVICE

Discard

Intelligence slang for an AGENT betrayed by his own intelligence service or agency to protect a more valuable source of information.

Discoverer

COVER name for the world's first SATELLITE employed for photographic RECONNAISSANCE. As the CORONA spy satellite was being developed, on Dec. 3, 1958, the U.S. government issued a press release identifying the Discoverer as a test vehicle; later launches were to carry aloft satellites to explore the environmental conditions of space. Biomedical specimens, including live animals, were to be carried into space, and their recovery would be attempted after orbit.

The Discoverer I was launched on Feb. 28, 1959, to test the Thor-Agena booster rockets that would be used in the Corona program. Additional test satellites were lifted aloft, preparing the way for Corona. The first attempt to launch an actual spy satellite carrying a camera occurred on June 25, 1959; that failed launch had the cover name Discoverer IV.

The Discoverer III was launched on June 3, 1959, after several abortive attempts. It was the only Discoverer to carry animals—four black mice. (The Soviets had orbited a live dog in their Sputnik 2 satellite, which had been placed in orbit on Nov. 3, 1957. Neither the satellite nor the dog, Laiika, survived.)

The Discoverer cover was used through the Corona launch of Feb. 27, 1962, that mission having the designation Discoverer XXXVIII. The Corona program continued until 1972, when it was succeeded by more effective spy satellites.

The Soviet government was able to discern the true nature of the Discoverer satellite soon after the first camera-fitted versions were launched. By the end of 1960 several Soviet magazines revealed that the Discoverer satellites were spy platforms, although it is not clear if those early stories were accusations or based on real knowledge of their true mission. However, given Soviet knowledge of satellite technology, the several Americans passing secrets to the Soviets at that time, and open speculation in American newspapers, it was inevitable that the Soviets would soon discover the real purpose of Discoverer.

Disinformation

The creation and dissemination of misleading or false information to injure the image of the targeted enemy. The term is attributed to the Soviet KGB, which made frequent use of the practice. Typical KGB disinformation operations involved forged documents designed to discredit the United States.

In June 1957, for example, KGB disinformation specialists fed Egyptian newspapers copies of letters allegedly written by Abba Eban, Israel's ambassador to the United States, to Charles Malik, Foreign Minister of Lebanon. Eban supposedly wrote that "bitter hostility between our countries . . . cause me as much distress as they cause you." Both Israel and Lebanon denounced the forgeries. But they had been so widely broadcast and published in Egyptian media that many Egyptians did not believe the denials. That is one of the purposes of disinformation: By the time the truth is known, the damage has been done.

In another forgery incident, the Soviets in 1986 distributed to U.S. news media copies of a fake letter purportedly from an official of the U.S. Information Agency to Senator Dave Durenberger, chairman of the SENATE SELECT COMMITTEE ON INTELLIGENCE, laying out a propaganda plan to exploit the Chernobyl nuclear power plant catastrophe. The committee later published the forgery and an analysis of how the disinformation deed was done. In 1981 the KGB forged a letter from President Reagan to the king of Spain; the forgery was discovered, and no incident resulted.

The Soviets used the term "active measures" to describe such operations. Usually, they were short-term. But some lasted a long time, such as a persistent campaign to discredit U.S. policy in India by claiming that the CIA was aiding separatist movements to split the country.

U.S. Army Sgt. ROBERT LEE JOHNSON, who spied for the Soviets in Europe, handed them a copy of a war plan that included a list of European targets for tactical U.S. nuclear weapons. In the early 1980s, versions of these documents surfaced in Europe. The KGB, having used them militarily to analyze U.S. strategy, then recycled them for propaganda purposes during antinuclear campaigns in Europe. The documents were authentic only up to a point. KGB disinformation specialists could not resist adding more Western European "targets" to the actual list.

The KGB coined the Russian word *dezinformatsia*. It came into the English language as *disinformation*.

DMI

SEE DIRECTOR OF MILITARY INTELLIGENCE

DNI

SEE (1) DIRECTOR OF NATIONAL INTELLIGENCE; (2) DIRECTOR OF NAVAL INTELLIGENCE

D Notice

Formal British censorship request issued by the Defence Press and Broadcasting Advisory Committee, which includes government and news media representatives. The D notice is confidentially circulated to editors asking restraint in publishing certain material. It is a letter of advice or request, warning that an item may be protected under the OFFICIAL SECRETS ACT and that although its publication may not be illegal, it would be contrary to the national interest.

Doctor

Russian intelligence term for police. If an AGENT is arrested, he or she suffers an ILLNESS; agents who are taken to jail are in HOSPITAL.

Document X

SEE ENGLAND-GREAT BRITAIN-UNITED KINGDOM

Dodd, Martha

American socialite who spied for the Soviet Union.

Dodd accompanied her father, William Dodd, when he went to Germany in 1933 as American ambassador. In BERLIN she fell in love with a Soviet diplomat and became an AGENT, passing diplomatic information to the Soviets. She became a devout communist, even sleeping with Nazi officials to obtain information.

She fell in love with another Soviet diplomat, who gave her the CRYPTONYM "Juliet #2." A friend of MILDRED FISH HARNACK, heroine of the anti-Nazi RED ORCHESTRA espionage and resistance NETWORK, Dodd never knew that her two Soviet lovers were conducting their romances under official direction.

When the Dodd family returned to the United States in Dec. 1937, she was passed to ISSKHAK AKHMEROV, the brilliant NKVD ILLEGAL in New York. He advised her to seek out useful information from her Washington contacts, who included President and Mrs. Roosevelt. He gave her the cryptonym "Liza."

In June 1938 she married financier Alfred Stern. Moralistic NKVD officials distrusted her, calling her in one report "a typical representative of American bohemia, a sexually decayed woman ready to sleep with a handsome man." She and Stern contributed little in the way of intelligence, mostly because Stern, dubbed the "Red Millionaire" by the press, was openly a communist. But he did subsidize a publishing firm to be used as a PROPRIETARY COMPANY where Soviet ILLEGALS could find COVER jobs.

During the communist-hunting era of the 1950s the couple fled to Mexico, then to Czechoslovakia, with a sojourn to Cuba. After vainly asking for a jail-free return to the United States, they settled in Czechoslovakia and faded away.

Doder, Dusko

American journalist accused of accepting money from the KGB. The accusation, without supporting evidence, was made in Dec. 1992 in *Time* magazine. The source was VITALY YURCHENKO, a KGB officer who defected in Aug. 1985. Doder was working as a freelance journalist in Yugoslavia when *Time* published the story. In Aug. 1996 *Time* apologized to Doder in a London court and paid him $262,000 in damages.

Yurchenko alleged that Doder, while Moscow bureau chief for *The Washington Post*, had been paid $1,000 by the KGB. Doder filed a libel suit against *Time*. (Yurchenko voluntarily returned to the Soviet Union in Dec. 1985, throwing doubt on his defection.)

The *Post* asked for a "review of the Doder file" by YEVGENY PRIMAKOV, director of the FSK, the Russian successor to the Soviet KGB. Through a spokeswoman, Primakov replied, "We have no evidence to show that Doder accepted $1,000 from KGB officials."

Other former KGB officers said that Doder was a TARGET for KGB recruitment, but there is no evidence that he had ever cooperated with the KGB.

Richard Cohen, a *Post* columnist writing about Dusko's career, said that when Doder reported a scoop—the death in 1984 of Soviet leader YURI ANDROPOV—the CIA asked the *Post* not to publish the story. *Post* editors shifted Doder's dispatch from the front page to the back

of the paper. "Doder was right, the CIA wrong," Cohen wrote. "Possibly the CIA is now getting even."

After his assignment in Moscow, Doder worked for the *Post* in Washington, D.C. The FBI told the *Post* that Doder was "under suspicion," according to Cohen. An investigation by the *Post* "came up with nothing."

A letter published by the *Post* in July 1995 quoted Arthur Hartman, former U.S. ambassador to the Soviet Union, as saying, "The U.S. Embassy in Moscow closely monitored the articles written by Mr. Doder that were published in *The Washington Post*. As a result of reports I received I concluded that articles by Mr. Doder often contained the same or similar information that the Embassy knew from independent sources was being put out by the KGB." Hartman's implication that Doder was being fed DISINFORMATION essentially reflected the position of the FBI and CIA.

Dog Drag

Device developed by the U.S. OFFICE OF STRATEGIC SERVICES during World War II that released a "persistent aromatic scent" when dragged behind an AGENT to throw dogs off the scent of the agent during a chase. The British employed a hot-pepper device, but it burned the dogs' nostrils and thus revealed that an agent was in fact being followed.

Dog Skin Report

Intelligence report written by a French AGENT in Indochina while it was under Japanese control during World War II. The agent shaved his dog, wrote his report on the dog's skin in indelible ink, waited for the dog's hair to grow back, and then escaped with the dog—and the report.

French INTELLIGENCE OFFICER Philippe L. Thyraud de Vosjoli, who worked under the CODE NAME of LAMIA, read the report in 1944 when he was assigned to the Indochinese section of the French intelligence service BCRA. "The information contained in it might have been of value at the time," he recalled, "but it was now over a year old and obsolete."

Doihara, Maj. Gen. Kenji

(b. 1883 d. 1948)

Japan's most important INTELLIGENCE OFFICER in Manchuria in the 1930s, dubbed "Lawrence of Manchuria" by the Western press. "His task," wrote American journalist John Gunther, "was to create trouble and then smooth it over to the advantage of the Japanese."

As an AGENT PROVOCATEUR, Doihara created "incidents" that purportedly demonstrated Chinese aggression toward Japan. The most significant of these incidents came on Sept. 18, 1931, when Japanese troops, claiming that Chinese saboteurs were tampering with the roadbed of the Japanese-owned South Manchuria Railway, seized the Chinese city of Mukden (now Shenyang). Its mayor happened to be Doihara.

Doihara established the Tokumu Kikan (Special Service Organization), which spread its tentacles throughout Manchukuo (Manchuria), carrying out Doihara's mandate to "eliminate every organization or society which is not sincerely friendly to the Japanese." Chinese leader Chiang Kai-shek executed several generals on charges that they were AGENTS of Doihara.

One of Doihara's legendary agents was Yoshiko Kawashima, a Chinese-born woman who often disguised herself as a man. She was said to have persuaded the deposed ex-Emperor of China, Pu Yi, to become Doihara's puppet emperor of Manchukuo. She was also reputedly the daring agent who delivered the consort of Pu Yi from exile in Tientsin (Tianjin) to Manchukuo. She was arrested by Chinese COUNTERINTELLIGENCE officers in Peking (Beijing) in Nov. 1945 and executed as a traitor.

Doihara became the commander-in-chief of the 7th Army Area with headquarters at Singapore from March 1944 to April 1945, and the CinC of the 1st Army Area in Japan until the end of the war. His arrest was ordered on Sept. 21, 1945, and he was tried as a war criminal by the Allied war crimes tribunal; judged guilty, he was hanged on Dec. 23, 1948.

Dolce, Thomas J.

Civilian research analyst at the U.S. Army's Aberdeen Proving Ground in Maryland who supplied classified documents to the Republic of South Africa between 1979 and 1983. The documents concerned U.S. evaluations of Soviet military equipment.

He pleaded guilty in 1988 to a single count of espionage. He admitted passing documents 40 or more times to military ATTACHÉS at the South African Embassy in Washington and at South African missions in London and Los Angeles.

Dolce, who was ideologically motivated, had moved to South Africa in 1971, but later returned to the United States in search of a job. Before 1971, Dolce had been a U.S. Army specialist on clandestine warfare.

In April 1989 he was sentenced to 10 years in prison and fined $5,000.

Dolnytsin, Maj. Gen. Anatoli [p]

False name released by British intelligence officials in 1963 when the *Daily Telegraph* sought the identity of a Soviet DEFECTOR being debriefed in London.

The defector was actually ANATOLI GOLITSYN. But, in preparing a D NOTICE requesting the press not to publish anything on the defector, the Security Service (MI5) officer drafting the notice misspelled Golitsin's name. (The British used the spelling Golytsin; the typist made it Dolnytsin.)

The *Daily Telegraph* decided to defy the D Notice and published a story headlined "Soviet Spy Gets British

Asylum." An infuriated Golytsin, knowing that the misspelling would not throw off the KGB, fled Britain, returning to his debriefers at the CIA in the United States.

Compounding the error was the fact that in Sept. 1961 there had been a diplomat named Anatoly Alexander Dolnytsin in Britain. Journalists speculated that he was the defector. The MI5 man who had made the mistake expected to be reprimanded; instead, he was congratulated. "The Security Service," wrote NIGEL WEST in *A Matter of Trust* (1982), "had gained a small advantage and in future journalists would be misled into relying on the official, erroneous version of Dolnytsin. This indeed is exactly what happened."

Domestic Intelligence

Intelligence relating to activities or conditions within a country that, according to the government, threaten internal security. In authoritarian countries, the search for domestic intelligence is an extension of the COUNTERINTELLIGENCE activities of state security organs. In democracies, the gathering of domestic intelligence produces charges that the government is threatening civil rights.

Also see FBI, J. EDGAR HOOVER, HUSTON PLAN, PLUMBERS, WATERGATE.

Donald E.

SEE TOP HAT

Donovan, Maj. Gen. William

(b. 1883 d. 1959)

Director of the U.S. OFFICE OF STRATEGIC SERVICES (OSS) during World War II. Donovan directed the U.S. clandestine intelligence and special operations organization from its establishment in 1941. The OSS was the precursor of the CIA.

When World War I began in 1914, Donovan, a prominent and prosperous New York lawyer, went to Europe to help Herbert Hoover in famine relief efforts. He was recalled to the United States in 1916 for active Army duty and saw action fighting Pancho Villa's raiders on the Mexican-U.S. border. Returning to New York in March 1917, Donovan was given command of a battalion in the legendary 69th "Fighting Irish" Infantry regiment (New York National Guard). Shipped to Europe in Nov. 1917, the regiment saw extensive combat as part of the U.S. Rainbow Division. Donovan was wounded three times in 19 months in France. His valor on the battlefield made him one of the most decorated soldiers of the war: He received the Medal of Honor, Distinguished Service Cross, Légion d'Honneur, Order of the British Empire, and Croix de Guerre with palm and silver star.

Donovan's faith in the BLACK arts of intelligence began in the years following World War I when State Department officials sent him on a mission to revolution-torn Russia, where he served briefly as U.S. liaison officer to the White Russian (anti-communist) forces under Adm. A. V. Kolchak. He returned to the United States in late 1920 and resumed his law career. He became, successively, a U.S. attorney, an assistant U.S. attorney general, and a private attorney with an international practice; his clients included Winston Churchill.

Insatiably curious and often footloose, he traveled in the 1930s as a private citizen to see for himself the Italian-Ethiopian war and the Spanish Civil War. In the late 1930s he was a special ambassador for President Franklin D. Roosevelt, traveling throughout Europe and the Middle East. Donovan's most important mission came in July 1940, when he went to Britain, ostensibly to make a "survey of the British defense situation." Joseph P. Kennedy, U.S. ambassador in London, who believed Britain would soon be defeated by Germany, vigorously opposed the trip.

Donovan met with Rear Adm. John Godfrey, Britain's DIRECTOR OF NAVAL INTELLIGENCE, Maj. Gen. Sir STEWART MENZIES, head of MI6, and other intelligence officials. He was not officially informed about a new British agency for engaging in subversive warfare, the SOE (Special Operations Executive). Donovan impressed those he met and, as a British historian later wrote, "stored up a fund of personal goodwill" and "helped set in motion the wheels leading to the development of initial intelligence cooperation between the two countries." The trip, enthusiastically supported by British officials, convinced Donovan that, with American aid, Britain could hold out against the German onslaught. He later credited himself with recommending the controversial deal in which Roosevelt, evading U.S. neutrality laws, swapped 50 aging U.S. destroyers for long-term leases on several British bases in the western Atlantic and Caribbean.

Late in 1940, accompanied by WILLIAM STEPHENSON, director of British intelligence operations in the United States, Donovan left on a dangerous, 25,000-mile trip through the war fronts and spy centers of the European War—Britain, Gibraltar, Malta, Egypt, Greece, Yugoslavia, Turkey, Portugal, and Spain—in what his biographer Anthony Cave Brown described in *The Last Hero* (1982) as "an unending procession of generals, admirals, air marshals, spies, politicians, sheikhs, priests, mullahs, princes, colonels, and kings."

Prime Minister Churchill, bent on bringing the United States into the war, was so impressed that he telegraphed Roosevelt, saying that Donovan "has carried with him throughout an animating, heart-warming flame." The Director of Naval Intelligence cabled the commander-in-chief of the Mediterranean Fleet, "There is no doubt that we can achieve infinitely more through Donovan than through any other individual."

When Donovan returned to Washington in March 1941 word of his interest in intelligence matters had preceded him, presumably through U.S. military and naval attachés in London. On April 8, Maj. Gen. Sherman Miles, chief of U.S. ARMY INTELLIGENCE, wrote to Gen. George C. Marshall, the Army chief of staff, saying "there is considerable reason to believe that there is a movement on foot, fostered by Col. Donovan, to establish a super agency controlling all intelligence. . . . such a move would appear to be very disadvantageous, if not calamitous." At the same time, J. EDGAR HOOVER, director of the FBI, was pushing to have his Special Intelligence Service spread from Latin America to Europe and Asia.

The distaste that Miles and Hoover had for Donovan was intensified by the fact that they already had to contend with another amateur: socialite VINCENT ASTOR, Roosevelt's yachtsman friend. The President had named Astor, an officer in the Naval Reserve, the New York area controller for Army intelligence, the OFFICE OF NAVAL INTELLIGENCE, and the FBI. There were rumors in Washington that Roosevelt was going to create the feared "super agency" and put Astor in charge.

Urged on by Secretary of the Navy Frank Knox, Donovan wrote a memo on June 10, 1941, urging the creation of a clandestine U.S. intelligence service. Such an agency, Donovan said, should be headed by a "Coordinator of Strategic Information," appointed by the President and "directly responsible to him and to no one else." The agency would be financed through a secret fund controlled "solely at the discretion of the President."

Donovan diplomatically agreed that the proposed agency should not take over "the home duties now performed by the F.B.I." and that it should not interfere with "the intelligence activities of the Army and the Navy."

Maj. Gen. William Donovan. (NATIONAL ARCHIVES)

But it would coordinate, classify, and interpret "all information from whatever source obtained. . . ."

While Knox lobbied for the idea and senior Army and Navy officers fought it, Roosevelt stalled. The British saw Donovan as an advocate for active support of their war effort. In what was later described as an attempt to "hurry on the process," British officials called on Godfrey, head of British Naval Intelligence, and his personal aide, Lt. Comdr. IAN FLEMING (future creator of JAMES BOND [F]). At a White House dinner, Godfrey told Roosevelt that America needed an intelligence agency headed by Donovan.

On July 11, 1941, Roosevelt appointed Donovan director of a new foreign intelligence collection agency, giving him the title of COORDINATOR OF INFORMATION (COI). When Roosevelt announced Donovan's appointment, Stephenson cabled to Menzies: "You can imagine how relieved I am . . . that our man is in a position of such importance to our efforts."

Roosevelt initially intended Donovan to return to active duty and serve as COI director in uniform. But Army and congressional opposition forced the President to put that idea aside temporarily. Donovan thus began his intelligence career as a civilian. He took over so quietly that newspaper reporters dubbed him "Hush Hush Bill." (After Dec. 7, 1941, he went back in uniform. Although he was often referred to as "General Donovan," he did not become a brigadier general until March 1943; he was made a major general in Nov. 1944.)

Opposition to Donovan began to disappear when Brig. Gen. WALTER BEDELL SMITH convinced his superiors in the Army that, since Donovan had easy access to the White House and important Roosevelt administration officials, it would be a good idea to tuck his new organization under the Joint Chiefs of Staff (JCS), which had been created early in 1942 to coordinate U.S. war strategy with the British chiefs of staff. Donovan's organization became the OSS under JCS jurisdiction on June 13, 1942. (Smith served as DIRECTOR OF CENTRAL INTELLIGENCE from 1950 to 1953.)

A month later Donovan almost lost his OSS by authorizing a series of burglaries of the Spanish Embassy in Washington, D.C., to gather diplomatic messages needed as intelligence for the North African invasion. As Hoover fumed, the JCS intervened, saving Donovan and the OSS.

Donovan spent much of his time fighting off a variety of opponents—ranging from British intelligence officials, who saw him as a rival in Europe, to Gen. Douglas MacArthur, who barred the OSS from his Southwest Pacific theater. And Hoover was always waiting for a chance to stab him in the back. "The ABWEHR [German MILITARY INTELLIGENCE] gets better treatment from the FBI than we do," Donovan once said.

But Donovan was a master at bureaucratic infighting. One of his European operatives, WILLIAM CASEY (another future DCI) described him as "a roly-poly man, soft of voice and manner belying the sobriquet 'Wild Bill' he had never been able to shake." The press also liked to call him "Wild Bill," a name reputedly earned in his heroic Army days. Friends said that no one ever called him that to his face.

On June 7, 1944, the day after the D-DAY invasion of German-occupied France, Donovan and his aide David Bruce broke U.S. and British regulations prohibiting ULTRA-cleared officers from risking capture. They landed on Utah beach and almost immediately were pinned down by German machine-gun fire. Donovan turned to Bruce and said, "We know too much." He drew a pistol and added, "If we are going to get captured, I'll shoot you first. Then myself. After all, I'm the commanding officer." They were safely back aboard a command ship before nightfall.

During the Italian campaign, Donovan visited Capri, where he instructed an OSS officer to keep an eye on La Fortino, the villa of a New York society friend and political supporter. The request triggered a diatribe from the officer, and, as Robin W. Winks tells it in *Cloak & Gown* (1987):

> Donovan at that moment had an epiphany about the complexity of his work. The situation had reached the point, he later said, where he had to have two shovels, one to dig a hole for himself and the other to shovel the shit that flowed into it.

Winks also says that someone who knew Donovan well once remarked that when e e cummings asked, "And how do you like your blue-eyed boy, Mister Death," he could have been thinking of Donovan, a charismatic man with piercing blue eyes.

By late 1944 Donovan was lobbying for the creation of a permanent, post-war version of the OSS. During this prelude to the Cold War, the FBI and military intelligence agencies worked behind the scenes to kill the proposed agency before it was born. But the OSS was a colossus by then, with agents and offices throughout much of the world; as the European War was ending, Donovan was laying plans to spy against the Soviets in Europe.

Donovan had his own inner vision about how to handle the Soviets, giving them some help here and fighting them there. His vision often got him in trouble with policymakers. After Germany's surrender, Wilhelm Höttl, a former chief of German intelligence in the Vatican and the Balkans, gave himself up to the Americans. He said he operated his network against the Soviets and would turn it over to the OSS if it were used against Soviet interests. Washington officials were already anticipating the need to use former Nazis against the Soviets. (See REINHARD GEHLEN and GEHLEN ORGANIZATION.)

Learning of Höttl's offer through ALLEN DULLES, Donovan suggested that the OSS team up with Soviet intelligence to wipe out the network; to him, a Nazi was a Nazi. Although the JCS initially protested the act, records indicate that the affair had gone so far that it could not be stopped. There is no known record that shows exactly what happened next, but Höttl was released from prison in one of many U.S. accommodations toward former Nazis.

The death of President Roosevelt on April 12, 1945,

foreshadowed the end of Donovan's influence in Washington. Donovan never managed to develop a rapport with President Truman, whose immediate focus was on the Pacific theater of war. When the European war ended, there was little for Donovan's OSS to do. On Sept. 20, 1945, a little more than a month after the fighting stopped in the Pacific, Truman abolished the OSS.

Although the CIA evolved out of the OSS, Donovan had no role in the creation of the new agency. Many of Donovan's influential friends lobbied for Donovan to be named the first Director of Central Intelligence, but Truman never considered him.

Donovan served as associate prosecutor at the postwar Nuremberg trials of German war leaders. He was appointed American ambassador to Thailand in August 1953 but had to resign 18 months later because of ill health. When he died, President Eisenhower exclaimed, "What a man! We have lost the last hero."

Dooley, Dr. Thomas A.

(b. 1927 d. 1961)

U.S. Navy physician who became renowned for his humanitarian work in Vietnam. It was not known at the time that he was working for the CIA.

After France's defeat in the Indochina War, the 1954 Geneva Conference divided Vietnam into North and South Vietnam. Dooley was a U.S. Navy medical officer; he left the Navy in 1956 to do medical work in North Vietnam and Laos. He had a double mission: Openly he aided Catholic refugees; covertly, as a CIA operative, he urged them to head south and join the Catholics of South Vietnam. This was part of a U.S. policy to support Prime Minister Ngo Dinh Diem of South Vietnam.

Dooley's humanitarian labors were real. He was known as the "jungle doctor of Laos." His work for the CIA included turning U.S. public opinion against the communists, and propaganda often eclipsed reality. In his best-selling book *Deliver Us from Evil* (1956) he told of atrocities committed by communists upon Vietnamese Christians.

After Dooley's death (from cancer at age 34) a movement began to make him a saint. The sainthood process ended when his ties to the CIA were discovered during the canonization investigation. Posthumous inquiries also established that he was a HOMOSEXUAL who was forced out of the Navy after an OFFICE OF NAVAL INTELLIGENCE investigation.

Dora

SEE LUCY SPY RING

Dorian

U.S. Air Force proposal in 1964 to employ the MANNED ORBITAL LABORATORY (MOL) for military RECONNAISSANCE. It was to have been fitted with the KH-10 camera.

The proposal was abandoned with the cancellation of the MOL project in 1969.

Double Agent

AGENT engaged in clandestine activity for two or more intelligence services who provides information to one service about the others, or about each service to the others. A double agent may be unwittingly manipulated into such a position.

Double-Cross Committee

SEE DOUBLE-CROSS SYSTEM and TWENTY COMMITTEE

Double-Cross System

The extraordinarily successful British scheme to TURN German AGENTS during World War II. The heart of the system was the mixture of true and false secrets that the DOUBLE AGENTS transmitted by radio to a completely deceived ABWEHR, the German military intelligence agency. The Germans not only accepted the false intelligence but also sometimes acted on it—fulfilling the committee's hope to "influence and perhaps change" German plans.

The scheme was rooted in the prewar espionage activities of Arthur Owens, a Welsh electrical engineer who made business trips to Europe and passed information to the British Admiralty. Dissatisfied with what the British paid him, Owens offered his services to the Germans. Abwehr officer NIKOLAUS RITTER gave Owens the CODE NAME "Johnny" and in the summer of 1939 sent him for training to Hamburg, where he learned to send Morse code and to build a radio transmitter.

Owens returned to Britain just as the war began in the fall of 1939 and told the British Security Service (MI5) about his contact with the Abwehr. While Owens was briefly interned, from his jail cell he transmitted to the Abwehr data on the Royal Air Force, ship movements, and other bits of intelligence that his MI5 HANDLERS expected the Germans to appreciate.

Owens—"Johnny" to the Abwehr—got the code name "Snow" from the British. Other agents in Britain followed: G.W., Biscuit, and Celery, all recruited by MI5 and accepted as agents by the Abwehr. When Germany began infiltrating agents into Great Britain by SUBMARINE and parachute, they were told to use Snow, Germany's "master spy in England," as their contact. The double-cross system emerged successfully from this first round of deception.

The system was run by the TWENTY COMMITTEE, a mixture of professional INTELLIGENCE OFFICERS and amateurs. (The committee's name came from the pun produced by the Roman numeral XX and the agents' double-cross work.) As Sir JOHN MASTERMAN, chairman of the Twenty Committee, put it, "By means of the double-cross system we actively ran and controlled the German espionage system in this country."

The system, he said, had seven objectives: (1) to control the enemy's own spy system; (2) to catch spies; (3) to learn about the methods and personalities of the Abwehr and other German intelligence agencies; (4) to break into German CODES and CIPHERS; (5) to learn German intentions by studying the requests sent to the doubled agents; (6) to influence German plans through the information sent back by the doubled agents; and (7) to deceive the Germans about Allied plans.

The British Security Service established a special section called B1(a) to find and handle German agents. Beginning in Oct. 1941, the Twenty Committee provided B1(a) with the deceptive information to be passed on to Germany.

The outstanding achievement of the double-cross system was buttressing, through the agents' false reports, BODYGUARD, the DECEPTION plan for the Allied invasion of Europe. The plan was developed to help hide the real date, time, and details of D-DAY, the June 1944 Normandy landings. (A nonexistent military force, the FIRST U.S. ARMY GROUP, was part of the deception.)

Ultimately, the system's efforts convinced the German high command that the main invasion force would land at the Pas de Calais, not Normandy. Incredibly, the double-crossers continued the deception for weeks after D-Day. On the continent, the 212 Committee ran double-cross agents while the Twenty Committee continued to operate in Britain. Special COUNTERINTELLIGENCE units turned German stay-behind networks and operated them under the double-cross system.

The system also discovered German intentions. When the Abwehr asked its British agents about coastal defenses in southeast England, for example, the question indicated plans for an invasion in that area. Or, asked about British preparations for gas warfare, a controlled agent sent back, in Masterman's words, "a glowing account of the excellence of British preparations, and implied that gas warfare would be of greater advantage to the British than to the Germans."

According to British records, MI5 captured every German agent sent to Britain by the Abwehr. Those who refused to cooperate were executed. Double-cross ran about 120 double agents, of whom 39, such as "Mutt and Jeff," were long-term. Sent to Britain as saboteurs, they were turned, committed fake acts of sabotage, and, as trusted agents, were believed when they repeatedly warned of an imminent British landing in Norway. One turned agent, "Tate," was awarded German citizenship by radio so that he could be given, also by radio, the Iron Cross both First and Second Class for his work. GARBO was awarded the Iron Cross and made a Member of the British Empire for his deception activities.

The Twenty Committee could frequently confirm its successes because of ULTRA, the secret operation that broke German codes and read German radio traffic. Ultra was a deep secret within the secret of the Twenty Committee. Even when the double-cross system was finally revealed by Masterman in *The Double-Cross System in the War of 1939–45* (1972), he did not disclose the Ultra secret. (For details about efforts to get the book published, see Sir JOHN MASTERMAN.)

When the Germans began launching V-1 and V-2 missiles against Britain in the summer of 1944, the committee's agents gave false reports on where they were striking, diverting many to unpopulated areas. Special counterintelligence units were set up to continue the committee's work on the continent after the D-Day landings, continuing the deception far beyond the time expected. The committee had orchestrated its work to climax with the invasion, believing that the Abwehr would not be tricked into believing that agents had managed to move from Britain to the continent. But the double-cross system continued until the end of the war in Europe.

There was suspicion toward the end of the war that one of the double agents, code-named "Treasure," was actually a TRIPLE AGENT, also working for the Soviet Union. Masterman was vague about Treasure, whom he described as "a French citizen of Russian origin." She was allowed to operate a transmitter for only a short time because, Masterman wrote, "she proved exceptionally temperamental and troublesome." Some sources identify her as Lily Sergueiev and claim that she had given Allied military plans to the Soviets.

Also see DUSKO POPOV.

Downey, John

(b. 1930)

CIA officer who was captured in China on Nov. 29, 1952.

The CIA recruited Downey at Yale University shortly before he graduated in 1951, when many Yale men were in the CIA. Downey was a fine prospect: captain of the wrestling team and a guard on the football team. After training in the United States, he was sent to Japan as part of a covert CIA operation to send AGENTS into China. Chiang Kai-shek, defeated by the Chinese communists under Mao Zedong, had fled to Taiwan (then called Formosa). U.S. policy called for "unleashing" Chiang's army to retake the mainland. As part of that policy, Downey and other CIA operatives were training Formosans at a secret base in Japan and infiltrating them into China.

Downey did not have to fly with the men being dropped into China, but he did. Friends say he had flown at least one mission before his unmarked C-47 Dakota took off on Nov. 29, 1952. With Downey on the plane were CIA officer RICHARD FECTEAU, two Formosan pilots, and seven Formosan agents who were to be dropped in the mountains of Manchuria to set up a communications base. Before dropping off the agents, the plane was to swoop over a spot where an agent was to be scooped up in a sling.

As the plane swooped down, Chinese anti-aircraft guns began firing, forcing the plane to land. The Chinese, who learned about the pickup of the agent through radio intercepts, captured Downey and Fecteau. The Formosans were taken away separately, almost certainly to execution.

The U.S. State Department, using a prearranged cover story, announced that an aircraft was missing on a routine flight between Seoul and Tokyo and that the passengers included two Department of Defense employees, Downey and Fecteau. They were given up for dead.

Downey spent the first ten months of his sentence in leg irons under continual questioning, during which he admitted that he was a CIA officer. In Dec. 1954 China announced the capture and trial for espionage of two CIA operatives. Downey was sentenced to life imprisonment. Fecteau, because he was subordinate to Downey, was given a 20-year prison term. The two men were transferred from a rural prison to one in Beijing. There they met the crew of a B-29 SUPERFORTRESS RECONNAISSANCE plane that had been shot down.

By then the Korean War was over and the United States was arranging a prisoner-of-war exchange with China. On the U.S. list were 129 Chinese, mostly scientists and economists who had been working in the United States. On the Chinese list were 40 Americans, including the B-29 crewmen in prison with Downey and Fecteau. But Downey and Fecteau themselves were not on the list because the United States would not admit that they were CIA officers. The B-29 fliers were released in Aug. 1955, and one of them reported to the CIA that a Chinese official told him, "The only way they will ever get out will be for your government to admit they are CIA agents."

China and the United States did not have diplomatic relations, but in 1957 China again offered in an indirect way to release the two CIA officers. The offer, however, was rejected by Secretary of State John Foster Dulles (whose brother, ALLEN W. DULLES, was then DIRECTOR OF CENTRAL INTELLIGENCE).

After President Nixon acknowledged, without fanfare at a press conference, that Downey and Fecteau were indeed CIA officers, they were finally released—Fecteau in 1971, Downey in 1973.

In 2002 China authorized a search for the bodies of the aircraft in which Downey had been flying. He accompanied a U.S. search team that went to northern China. The team found pieces of wreckage but no crew remains or signs of graves.

DPSD

Direction de la Protection de la Sécurité de la Défense (Directorate for the Protection of Defense Security), a French intelligence organization responsible for internal security at military bases and defense facilities.

An agency known as the Sécurité Militaire was originally responsible for these activities. But it sometimes strayed into DOMESTIC INTELLIGENCE, and it kept files on the political beliefs of members of the armed forces. In the French tradition of responding to an intelligence agency's misdeeds by changing its name, in 1981 the Sécurité Militaire became the DPSD.

Since 1992 the DPSD has been under the Military Intelligence Directorate, as has the DEUXIÈME BUREAU.

Dreyfus, Capt. Alfred

(b. 1859 d. 1935)

French Army officer falsely accused of spying in a case that rocked France and inspired a public distrust of French intelligence agencies that persists to this day.

A Jew born in Alsace, Dreyfus and his family left the province after it was annexed by Germany in 1871 following the Franco-Prussian War. The family moved to Paris, where Dreyfus attended the École Polytechnique and entered the Army. He had an outstanding record in the Army staff college and seemed destined for a brilliant military career.

Then, in Oct. 1894, he was accused of passing French Army secrets to the German military ATTACHÉ. The accusation was based on an unsigned note discovered by an AGENT of the Section de Statistiques et de Reconnaissances Militaires, the unit of the deuxième bureau concerned with foreign intelligence and COUNTERINTELLIGENCE. The agent was a cleaning woman who worked in the German Embassy in Paris and passed to her French HANDLER the contents of embassy wastepaper baskets. One of her finds included a letter in which the embassy's principal INTELLIGENCE OFFICER referred to French war plans obtained from "that scoundrel D."

Dreyfus was selected as the "D" on the basis of flimsy and concocted evidence. Convicted in a secret court-martial in 1895, he was marched before an assembly of troops, was ceremonially stripped of his rank and insignia, had his sword broken, and was dismissed from the Army in disgrace. He was then sent to the notorious French penal colony of Devil's Island in French Guiana.

In 1896 the Statistics Section obtained an incriminating note—this one from a German intelligence officer to Maj. Ferdinand Esterhazy of the French General Staff. Investigation clearly showed that Esterhazy, not Dreyfus, was the spy. But the new evidence was suppressed. Subsequently, Esterhazy was acquitted in a rigged court-martial, the officer who had found the new evidence was dismissed from the Army, and official knowledge of Dreyfus's innocence led to a cover-up that reached to the highest levels of the Army.

In 1898 novelist Émile Zola wrote "J'Accuse," an open letter to the French president charging the Army with having framed Dreyfus. The Dreyfus affair polarized France, with the left supporting him and the right denouncing him. The pressure grew for a reexamination of the case. An appeals court in 1899 overturned the earlier conviction. Although the court did not entirely clear Dreyfus, the new finding led the President of the Republic to pardon him.

Dreyfus fought for reinstatement, which he finally won in 1906. Restored to the rank of captain, he retired in 1907, but returned to the Army to serve in World War I.

Driscoll, Agnes Meyer

(b. 1889 d. 1971)

Senior cryptanalyst of the U.S. Navy's cryptologic organization, OP-20-G, in the period from between the two World Wars until shortly after World War II. She was a key participant in the exploitation of several Japanese CODE and CIPHER systems, mostly naval, but also diplomatic.

A graduate of Ohio State University in 1911, she had a short teaching career, after which she joined the U.S. Navy in 1918. She was assigned to the Code and Signal Section of the Director of Naval Communications. In 1919, she was discharged and remained in the office as a civilian.

The following year she was asked to join the Department of Ciphers at George Fabyan's Riverbank Laboratory where she trained in cryptology, working under WILLIAM F. FRIEDMAN. In the latter part of 1920, she worked for about three months at HERBERT O. YARDLEY'S BLACK CHAMBER in New York City.

Returning to Washington, D.C., she spent two years developing and testing cryptographic systems for the Navy. One, a device named the "CM," was jointly developed with Lt. Cdr. William Gresham. (It earned her and Gresham's widow a cash award from the U.S. Congress in 1937.)

In 1923 she was hired away from the Navy by EDWARD H. HEBERN, who wanted to sell the Navy Department his patented cipher wheel device and hoped that she could provide the necessary technical expertise. However, in 1924, the machine was rejected and Hebern's company failed. She rejoined the Navy Department (the branch known as OP-20-G) that same year.

With her return, the Navy's cryptographic work centered around the newly formed research and training unit, which she shared with Lt. LAURANCE SAFFORD. The first major success for the desk was the exploitation of the Japanese Navy's 1918 operational code known as the RED BOOK. Although the codebook had been stolen by the OFFICE OF NAVAL INTELLIGENCE in 1922, the overlaying cipher was broken by Driscoll in 1926.

In 1930 the Japanese Navy replaced it with a new code called the BLUE BOOK by OP-20-G. Driscoll's recovery of this code was considered by Safford a feat equal to that of the Army's breaking of PURPLE because she had no CRIBS, or translations, as did Friedman's team. This effort also heralded the first serious use of machine technology in code breaking.

Her efforts were not limited to naval codes. Around 1935, she worked on the Japanese M-1 cipher machine, CODE NAMED Orange, used by Japan's naval ATTACHÉS. This machine was similar to one used by Japanese diplomats, known as Purple, and broken by Army cryptologists.

In 1937, Driscoll was injured in a traffic accident that kept her away from her work for about a year. In 1939 Safford set her to work on the Japanese Navy's new general purpose cipher, familiarly known as JN-25 (see JN-SERIES CIPHERS). After some success, she was put to work on the German ENIGMA cipher machine. Despite about 2½ years of work, her team made little headway against the Enigma. Partly, it was because she was working against a variant far more advanced than the Poles had broken in 1932; also, she resisted advice from visiting British cryptanalysts. The Allied exchange on Ultra, finished in mid-1943, ended OP-20-G work on the Enigma, and Driscoll was transferred to work against the Japanese naval attaché cipher machine, known as Coral. Whether she had any effect on its exploitation is unknown.

Although she was named OP-20-G's principal cryptanalyst by the end of the war, her career began a slow fade from the center of cryptologic activity. In the postwar years, she did spend some time in a vain effort against the Soviet VENONA system. She was part of the cryptologic consolidations, first transferred to the ARMED FORCES SECURITY AGENCY, and later to the NSA.

She retired in 1958.

Drones

SEE UNMANNED AERIAL VEHICLES

Drop

The action of placing material in a clandestine location or DEAD DROP to be picked up by a specific individual.

Drug

Interim British CODE NAME for the VENONA codebreaking project. It was initially known as "Bride."

Drummond, Yeoman 1st Class Nelson C.

The first black American convicted of espionage. Drummond, a clerk at the U.S. Naval Headquarters in London, had SECURITY CLEARANCES at the TOP SECRET and COSMIC levels.

A Soviet-hired TALENT SPOTTER, noting that Drummond, a chronic gambler, was constantly in dire straits financially, passed his name to a Soviet contact, probably working out of the Soviet Embassy in London. One night in 1957 a stranger in a bar gave Drummond a small amount of money and asked for a favor: a Navy identification card so that his friends could use the Navy exchange. From there the demands went higher until Drummond was supplying classified documents.

When Drummond was transferred to a job where he had no access to classified documents, his Soviet HANDLER broke off contact, warning Drummond that he was under investigation. The OFFICE OF NAVAL INTELLIGENCE was in fact conducting a secret inquiry about missing documents; several sailors, including Drummond, were under suspicion. Some of the missing documents were not ones that Drummond had given his handler. That meant that the Soviets not only had inside information about the probe but had also probably recruited, in addition to Drummond, at least one sailor or civilian employee in the London office.

In 1958 Drummond was assigned to duty in the United States, where for the next four years he continued his espionage work by passing secrets he picked up during duty tours in Boston, Mass., Norfolk, Va., and Newport, R.I. His contacts were diplomats assigned to the Soviet mission to the UNITED NATIONS. He passed information on naval weapons systems, anti-submarine systems, and submarine maintenance data.

Because the Soviets at the United Nations were under SURVEILLANCE by the FBI, it may have been the FBI efforts that led to Drummond's arrest. But it is also possible that a tip on Drummond may have come from Maj. Gen. DIMITRI POLYAKOV, a Soviet GRU officer who spied for the United States for nearly 20 years. (Polyakov was one of the U.S. AGENTS betrayed by ALDRICH H. AMES, a Soviet MOLE in the CIA.)

After being discovered, in 1963 Drummond was tried and convicted of espionage and sentenced to life imprisonment for selling secrets to the Soviet Union. His six years of spying had earned him about $28,000.

Dry Cleaning

Actions taken to determine if one is under SURVEILLANCE. For example, a driver might make a sudden U-turn to observe if a following car does the same. In sophisticated surveillance practices, such dry cleaning is expected. A subject may, for example, be followed by several cars on parallel routes. The U-turn would be picked up by a second car.

DST

Direction de la Surveillance du Territoire (Directorate for Surveillance of the Territory), the French intelligence agency founded in 1944. Charged with COUNTERINTELLIGENCE and anti-terrorism, the DST replaced the counterintelligence branch of the SÛRETÉ GÉNÉRALE known as ST (for Surveillance du Territoire).

The DST falls under the Ministry of the Interior and is traditionally headed by a police officer who has previously served as a police commissioner. According to its official mission statement, the DST "is responsible for detecting and preventing, on the territory of the French Republic, the activities inspired, engaged in or sustained by foreign influences of nature that menaces the security of the country. . . ."

DST is reputed to have better files and resources than its Ministry of Defense rival, the DGSE (previously the SDECE). During the French-Algerian conflict in the 1950s a DST AGENT inadvertently revealed an SDECE operation. The DST did succeed in infiltrating the Algerian insurgency, but its accomplishments were overshadowed by the more spectacular—and controversial—actions of the SDECE and the DEUXIÈME BUREAU.

During the Cold War DST's primary mission was guarding against Soviet subversion within France and Soviet penetration of the French government, particularly the intelligence agencies. The KGB maintained one of its largest stations in France—at one time controlling an estimated 700 operatives there, most of them operating in Paris under the direction of the Soviet Embassy.

The DST taps embassy telephones, monitors clandestine radio communications, and attempts to gain intelligence from LEGALS residing in France. In one of its most spectacularly successful cases, a KGB DEFECTOR, given the CODE NAME "Farewell," provided DST with information that resulted in the expulsion in 1983 of 47 Soviets accused of spying: 40 diplomats, five trade representatives, and two who were using the COVER of the Soviet news agency Tass.

Three more Soviet diplomats were expelled in 1987 after the DST broke a space technology spy ring that involved five Frenchmen. The Soviets were attempting to get information about the French rocket Ariane, which lifts SATELLITES into space.

DST has been the source of many controversies. In 1973, for example, it planted BUGS in the offices of Le Canard Enchaîné, a muckraking, satirical, anti-Gaullist weekly. The bugs were discovered and DST's involvement revealed. In 1980, when Le Canard Enchaîné moved to new offices, its staff found new bugs reportedly installed by the indefatigable DST. When the DGSE was accused of involvement in the sinking of the RAINBOW WARRIOR, the DST, showing its police bias, cooperated with New Zealand police by providing information on DGSE operatives. (Ironically, one of the French newspapers that revealed the DGSE involvement was Le Canard Enchaîné.)

About one-fourth of the DST's resources are said to be devoted to combating terrorism in France. One of the DST's most famous anti-terrorist triumphs was the apprehension of Abu Daoud, Palestinian leader of Black September, when he appeared in France in 1976. However, when DST officials tried to hand him over to the West German authorities, who had linked him to the massacre of Israeli athletes at the Munich Olympic Games in 1972, they were outraged to learn that Daoud had entered France on a "safe conduct" from the SDECE (the previous name for the DGSE) and had to be released.

Dubberstein, Waldo H.

(b. 1907 d. 1983)

Retired employee of the CIA who was found dead the day he was indicted on charges of selling U.S. military secrets to Libya.

A career INTELLIGENCE OFFICER, Dubberstein was an authority on the Middle East. After studying to be a Lutheran minister, he shifted to studies in ancient civilizations, earning a doctorate at the Oriental Institute of Chicago University. He was among the first analysts to work for the CIA when it was created in 1947. He was an area expert and analyst during his long, uneventful tenure at the agency.

After retiring from the CIA in 1970, he worked for the DEFENSE INTELLIGENCE AGENCY (DIA) and taught at the National War College in Washington, D.C. In the 1970s Dubberstein was an associate of EDWIN P. WILSON, a former CIA officer who was convicted of plotting to kill people accusing him of smuggling weapons and explosives to Libya.

"I am not guilty," Dubberstein said in a note found by his body on April 29, 1983. Authorities said he shot himself in the head with a shotgun. His body was found in a basement storage room of the apartment house in Arlington, Va., where he lived. The note was dated April 24. He had purchased the shotgun on April 26. Dubberstein and Wilson met while they both worked for the CIA. Sometime in 1977 Wilson asked Dubberstein for help on a "special mission" involving Libya. (Wilson had been working for a secret U.S. Navy project. See TASK FORCE.) Dubberstein went to Libya in 1978, apparently without the knowledge of the DIA. The U.S. government accused Dubberstein of selling Libya information on U.S. military strength in the Middle East for $32,000. At the time Libya had close connections with the Soviet Union, raising the possibility that the Soviets also received the information.

Dubok

Russian term for DEAD DROP.

Duggan, Laurence

State Department official accused of spying for the Soviets. A social friend of NOEL FIELD, another State Department official, Duggan worked for the State Department's Latin American Division and the UNITED NATIONS Relief and Rehabilitation Administration. Investigations stemming from VENONA discoveries produced a copy of a 1943 cable Duggan allegedly sent to Moscow, reporting on plans for the Allied invasion of Italy.

On Dec. 11, 1948, the FBI questioned Duggan about information on communist espionage supplied by WHITTAKER CHAMBER. Nine days later, Duggan plunged to his death from the sixteenth floor of his office building.

Dukes, Sir Paul

(b. 1889 d. 1967)

British intelligence operative in Russia at the time of the Bolshevik Revolution.

Dukes, the son of a clergyman, studied music in St. Petersburg and was living there in 1915, hoping to become a conductor, when he started working for the Anglo-Russian Commission, which coordinated the two nations' efforts in World War I.

Back in London after the Bolsheviks seized power in 1917, he was asked by British intelligence to return to Russia. He entered via Helsinki and, as AGENT ST 25, infiltrated the Bolsheviks. Fluent in Russian and a master of disguise, he once masqueraded as a member of the CHEKA, the Bolshevik secret police. As "Comrade Piotrovsky" he was a member of the Communist Party.

He made contact with the anti-Bolshevik White Russians and obtained information on resistance to the revolution. To get his reports into British hands, he rowed a dinghy to a rendezvous in the Baltic Sea with patrol ships of the Royal Navy.

At great risk, Dukes stayed in Russia until Sept. 1919, when his NETWORK was smashed by the Cheka and he fled to Finland. He was knighted for his work.

In 1939 he was asked again to become an agent, this time to investigate the disappearance of a Czech businessman who had vanished after Nazi Germany took over Czechoslovakia. Dukes suspected that the body of a tailor, found mutilated on railroad tracks, was actually the body of the missing businessman. He forced the Germans to exhume the body and proved its real identity.

Dulles, Allen W.

(b. 1893 d. 1969)

DIRECTOR OF CENTRAL INTELLIGENCE (DCI) from Feb. 1953 to Nov. 1961 and a spymaster since he began his espionage career in the OFFICE OF STRATEGIC SERVICES (OSS) during World War II.

Grandson of one Secretary of State and nephew of another, Dulles joined the U.S. Diplomatic Service in 1916 hoping someday to become the third Secretary of State in the family. (His brother, John Foster Dulles, who had similar aspirations, did achieve the goal.) As a young man, he read Rudyard Kipling's *Kim* and for the rest of his life was fascinated by the GREAT GAME as seen by the spy hero of the book, KIM.

His first posting was to the U.S. Embassy to the Austro-Hungarian Empire in VIENNA. In April 1917, after the United States declared war on Germany, Dulles was posted to the U.S. Legation in Bern, Switzerland. He was on duty one day when a man claiming to be Vladimir Ilyich Lenin called the legation and asked for a meeting. Dulles brushed him off as a mentally ill émigré. Next day, Lenin, his talk with a U.S. diplomat not to be, was on his way from Germany to Russia in the now famous sealed train. Years later, as DCI, Dulles would tell the story to new recruits, urging them not to make snap judgments about people.

Dulles also served in Constantinople (now Istanbul) and at the Versailles Peace Conference following World War I. He resigned from the State Department in 1926 and joined the Wall Street law firm of Sullivan and Cromwell, which had an international client list of powerful men and corporations. John Foster Dulles was already there as a law clerk when Allen joined the firm.

Sullivan and Cromwell had extraordinary access to high-ranking U.S. government officials and firm ties with European banking, investment, and industrial interests. Allen Dulles, like many in the law firm, often took on temporary government assignments, serving as an adviser to U.S. delegations at international conferences, mingling with the men he would see again during his spymaster career. He also met historic figures, including Italian dictator Benito Mussolini in Nov. 1932 and German chancellor Adolf Hitler in April 1933. (Coincidentally, future DCI RICHARD HELMS also met Hitler in the 1930s; as a United Press correspondent he interviewed Hitler in 1936. Oddly, Dulles never mentioned his Hitler meeting to Helms.)

After the United States entered World War II Dulles was recruited into the OSS by its director, Maj. Gen. WILLIAM DONOVAN. Dulles worked for a time in the OSS headquarters in New York, next to the BRITISH SECURITY COORDINATION, the MI6 station set up by WILLIAM STEPHENSON. Without telling most of them what he was doing, Dulles recruited some of his business acquaintances for the OSS. His work was supposedly secret, but on Sept. 17, 1942 *The New York Times* published a short story quoting the Republican Committee of New York County as saying that Dulles was being replaced as committee treasurer because of his "war work with the government Office of Strategic Services."

In Nov. 1942, when he arrived in Bern to open the OSS station there, his real career in espionage began. The debut of the amateur spymaster was brilliant. Although attached to the U.S. Embassy for diplomatic COVER, he worked out of his home at Herrengasse 23 and was vaguely known as a special emissary with White House connections. The OSS designated him Agent 110 or "Mr. Bull." Diplomats in Bern, again a spy nest, knew that he was the U.S. intelligence chief in Europe. He recruited workers among the Americans trapped in Switzerland by the war. Among them were U.S. Army Air Forces fliers who had crash-landed in Switzerland and were interned with nothing to do.

Another recruit was MARY BANCROFT, a 38-year-old American whose husband was an accountant frequently absent from Bern. She became Dulles's assistant and mistress. Bancroft was a friend of the famed psychoanalyst Carl Jung, who was fascinated by the way Dulles trusted the advice of a woman. Men like Dulles, Jung told Bancroft, "needed to listen to what women were saying in order to exercise their best judgment and not go off the deep end."

Dulles's most valuable AGENT was Fritz Kolbe, a German Foreign Office official who handled cable traffic. Kolbe went to Bern to volunteer as a spy for the Allies. Rebuffed by Dulles's British counterpart in Bern, Kolbe turned to Dulles, who accepted him as bona fide. Dulles gave him the code name "George Wood." By the spring of 1944 Kolbe had delivered 1,200 documents, none of which was more than two weeks old. Among the secrets was a report that the British ambassador in Ankara, Turkey, had a valet who was a spy (see CICERO). From Dulles also came information on German work on an atomic bomb and missiles.

Dulles could only send digests of Kolbe's material to Allied spymasters in Washington and London, who at first were skeptical. But after having the cables analyzed, Donovan cabled Dulles: "I now firmly believe in the good faith of Wood, and I am ready to stake my reputation on the fact that these documents are genuine."

Maj. Gen. KENNETH STRONG, head of Gen. Dwight D. Eisenhower's intelligence staff, called Dulles "undoubtedly the greatest United States professional intelligence officer of his time, although he was perhaps stronger and more interested in matters concerned with collection and short-term evaluation than in the business of long-range estimating."

When the war ended Dulles returned for a time to the practice of law. But, watching the old OSS evolve into the CIA, he marked time, expecting that he would soon resume his government service. At the request of Secretary of Defense James Forrestal, Dulles wrote a study of the CIA, which criticized the new agency as not living up to its promise. He worked with the campaign of Thomas E. Dewey, who opposed President Truman in 1948. When Truman won, Dulles expected that he would be ignored as a candidate for an intelligence post. But the new DCI, Gen. WALTER BEDELL SMITH, asked him to become Deputy Director for Operations. He accepted, suggesting that "plans" be substituted for "operations" to keep his work—supervising spies and COVERT ACTION—less revealing. He went to work for the CIA in Jan. 1951 and in August became the deputy director.

President Eisenhower appointed him DCI in Feb. 1953 and he served until 1961. During his long and historic tenure, the CIA became a global force, engaging in covert actions from South America to the Middle East, digging the BERLIN TUNNEL, and developing the U-2 spyplane.

Leftist writer Ilya Ehrenburg labeled Dulles "the most dangerous man in the world," writing, "If Dulles got into heaven by mistake, he would start organizing coups and shooting at angels." This was published in a Soviet newspaper, and, as Peter Grose wrote in *Gentleman Spy* (1994), Dulles enjoyed quoting it.

Under Dulles, the CIA planned and carried out the

Allen W. Dulles. (NATIONAL ARCHIVES)

Bay of Pigs invasion of Cuba in April 1961. That debacle ended his career. Subsequently, he spent much of his time managing the construction of the new CIA headquarters at LANGLEY, Va., and in Nov. 1961 he resigned.

He returned to private life, wrote *The Craft of Intelligence* (1963), and served his nation one last time as a member of the President's Commission on the Assassination of President Kennedy.

Duncan, Helen

(b. 1897 d. 1956)

Spiritualist accused of disclosing military secrets in séances that supposedly allowed British servicemen, killed in action, to speak to their next of kin. She was tried in Old Bailey in March 1944 under a 1735 witchcraft act because of fears that she would reveal secret information.

After two Royal Navy officers accused her of fraud for gulling the bereaved kin of servicemen, an official investigation revealed an incident that stunned INTELLIGENCE OFFICERS then concerned about the keeping of D-DAY secrets: During a séance that Duncan had conducted in Portsmouth, site of a major Royal Navy base, she purported to show a bereaved mother her dead son *before* the mother knew that he had been killed in action. The sailor had been one of 862 men killed when the battleship *Barham* was torpedoed in the Mediterranean on Nov. 25, 1941. The séance occurred before official announcement of the sinking.

Investigators believed that Duncan had picked up news about the sinking from loose-lipped sailors in Portsmouth. Similarly, in March 1944, with Portsmouth selected as the principal port for the D-Day invasion fleet, intelligence officials feared that Duncan might learn D-Day secrets and spread them through her séances. That was the alleged reason for her trial.

Duncan and her three sitters were accused of pretending "to exercise or use human conjuration that through the agency of Helen Duncan spirits of deceased dead persons should appear to be present." She was sentenced to nine months in prison, keeping her "voices from the dead" silenced until after D-Day, June 6, 1944; she was released from prison on Sept. 22, 1944.

Duncan was born in Callender, Scotland. From an early age she displayed the gift of medium with the spirit world. She made a living by conducting séances throughout Britain, during which the spirits of the dead were alleged to appear, talking and touching their relatives. She eventually became minister to a network of Spiritualist churches and private parties.

Some British papers referred to her as "the last witch."

Dunlap, Sgt. Jack F.

U.S. Army sergeant assigned to the NSA who spied for the Soviets. A wounded, decorated combat veteran of the Korean War, Dunlap was a driver for Maj. Gen. Garrison Cloverdale, assistant director and chief of staff at NSA.

After TOP SECRET meetings with officials in Washington, D.C., Cloverdale often left his briefcase with the sergeant and told him to return to his office. Dunlap photographed the contents of the briefcase and passed the film to his Soviet HANDLER, whom Dunlap knew only as "the bookkeeper." Besides what he found in the briefcase, Dunlap also stole and copied a number of other classified documents that he managed to find at the NSA.

Dunlap, who was married and had five children, lived high on his spy money. He bought a cabin cruiser, a Jaguar, and drove a late-model Cadillac to and from the tightly guarded NSA compound at FORT MEADE, midway between Washington and Baltimore, Md. He never came under suspicion as a spy.

Because he was a soldier, he had not been required to take a POLYGRAPH test when the Army assigned him to the NSA. But when he applied to leave the Army while remaining at the agency, he was given a polygraph examination. The tests, which showed that he had engaged in some "petty thievery" and "immoral conduct," triggered a deeper investigation. He was assigned to a job where he had no access to classified documents.

Shortly after the investigation began, Dunlap tried to kill himself with sleeping pills. Subsequently, he drove to an isolated spot, put a hose from the exhaust pipe into the partially open window of his car, and died of carbon monoxide poisoning. His body was found the next day.

Dunlap was buried with full military honors at Arlington National Cemetery on July 25, 1963. The following month his widow turned over to the FBI a stack of classified papers she had found while going through his belongings.

The extent of his espionage was never revealed and the "bookkeeper" was never found. But it seems likely that Dunlap had been unmasked not by the polygraph but by Maj. Gen. DIMITRI POLYAKOV, a Soviet GRU officer who spied for the United States for nearly 20 years. Polyakov was one of the U.S. ASSETS betrayed by ALDRICH H. AMES, a CIA officer arrested in 1994 as a Soviet MOLE.

Duquesne Spy Ring

German spy ring in the United States during World War II, named after Frederick J. Duquesne, a South African veteran of the Boer War who emigrated to the United States from Bermuda in 1902 and was known to British intelligence as an anti-British adventurer with an interest in explosives.

From the age of 17 on, Duquesne spied for Germany, first against Britain in the Boer War, then in World War I and World War II. Duquesne took credit for signaling the German U-boat that sank the cruiser *Hampshire* in June 1916; among the victims was a distinguished passenger, Lord Kitchener, chief of staff of the British Army. Duquesne's autobiographical *The Man Who Killed Kitchener* (1932), published under the pseudonym Clement Wood, told how he allegedly got on board the cruiser, used a flashlight to signal a U-boat to torpedo the ship, and slipped off the ship before she was hit. Actually, the cruiser was sunk by a mine. In his fraudulent book Duquesne claimed the use of the aliases Fritz Joubert Duquesne, Frederick Fredericks, Capt. Stoughton of the West Australia Horse, and Piet Niacoud. He alleged that he was arrested in the United States during World War I but escaped.

The actual spy case began in 1939 when 40-year-old WILLIAM G. SEBOLD, who worked at the Consolidated Aircraft Corp. in San Diego, Calif., returned to his native Germany to visit his family. During his visit he was recruited by Maj. NIKOLAUS A. RITTER, the ABWEHR officer in charge of espionage against the United States and Britain. Sebold went to the U.S. Consulate in Cologne and reported what had happened. He agreed to become a DOUBLE AGENT. (His story became the basis for *The House on 92nd Street*; see MOVIES.)

Back in the United States, under control of the FBI, Sebold followed German instructions to contact Duquesne and HERMAN LANG, who worked for the L. C. Norden Co., which manufactured the TOP SECRET Norden bombsight. Secretly aided by the FBI, Sebold set up a shortwave radio on Long Island and, beginning in May 1940, transmitted to Germany almost every day. At the time the United States was not at war with Germany.

The FBI surreptitiously photographed Duquesne-Sebold meetings and developed a large amount of evidence against Duquesne, who had been instructed by the Abwehr to engage in both espionage and sabotage. Information that he mailed to Germany—via ACCOMMODATION ADDRESSES in Portugal, Brazil, and elsewhere—was often carried to Europe by merchant ship crewmen who were in the ring.

In Jan. 1942, less than a month after the Japanese PEARL HARBOR ATTACK, the FBI tracked down the Duquesne spy ring: another 32 German AGENTS. All were tried, convicted, sentenced to a total of more than 300 years in prison, and fined a total of $18,000. Their capture ended the work of the largest single spy ring in U.S. history. Of the 32, two were native-born Americans, five were German aliens, and 25 were naturalized U.S. citizens.

Duquesne received an 18-year sentence and a $2,000 fine. Evelyn Clayton Lewis, a sculptor and toymaker, and his live-in girlfriend, were sentenced to a year and a day. Lang, whose spying was considered particularly serious, received an 18-year sentence.

These are the names of the other convicted spies and their sentences: Paul Bante, a member of the pro-Nazi German-American Bund, 18 months and $1,000 fine; Max Blank, a book clerk, 18 months and $1,000 fine; Alfred E. Brokhoff, mechanic for the U.S. Lines, five years; Heinrich Clausing, ship's cook, eight years; Conradin O. Dold, chief steward on American Export Lines ships, two years and $1,000; Rudolf Ebeling, shipping foreman for Harper and Brothers publishers, five years and $1,000; Richard Eichenlaub, waiter, 18 months and $1,000 fine; Heinrich C. Eilers, U.S. Lines steward, two years and $1,000 fine; Paul Fehse, ship's cook and head of the marine division of the German espionage system in the United States, 15 years; Edmund C. Heine, former Ford Motor Co. sales executive in Germany, two years and $5,000; Felix Jahnke, radio operator temporarily employed as a soda jerk, 20 months and $1,000; Gustav W. Kaercher, engineer who designed power plants and naval bases, 22 months and $2,000 fine; Josef Klein, a photographer and lithographer, five years; Hartwig R. Kleiss, ship's cook, eight years; Rene E. Mezenen, waiter and ship's steward, eight years; Carl Reuper, factory worker, two years; Everett M. Roeder, firearms inventor, 16 years; Paul A. W. Scholz, clerk in German bookstores, two years; George G. Schuh, 18 months and $1,000 fine; Erwin W. Siegler, ship's butcher, two years; Oscar R. Stabler, ship's barber, two years; Heinrich Stade, musician and waiter, 15 months and $1,000 fine; Lilly Barbara Carola Stein, manager of a women's apparel store, 10 years; Franz J. Stigler, sailor, two years; Erich Strunck, seaman, two years; Leo Waalen, ship's painter, 12 years; Adolf H. A. Walischewski, seaman, five years; Else Weustenfeld, secretary at the German Consulate in New York City (who lived with the brother of spy director Ritter), five years; Axel Wheeler-Hill, truck driver and German-American Bund official, 15 years; Bertram W. Zenzinger, dental student, nine years, six months, $1,000 fine.

Dust

SEE SPY DUST

Dzerzhinsky, Feliks Edmundovich

(b. 1877 d. 1926)

Founding director of the CHEKA, the forerunner of Soviet intelligence ORGANS. Dzerzhinsky established the Cheka in 1917 and remained head of the Soviet secret police through its name changes (GPU and OGPU) until 1926. He was also given responsibility for the welfare and education of children made homeless in the Russian Revolution (1917) and ensuing Civil War (1917–1920).

Born in Poland, Dzerzhinsky wanted to be a Catholic priest until he plunged into political movements in Russia. An anti-government agitator in the 1905–1906 revolution in Russia, he was imprisoned by the czarist regime. Hailed as the "Knight of the Proletariat" during the Bolshevik Revolution in 1917, he became commandant of Smolny Institute in St. Petersburg, the former school for wealthy girls that became Bolshevik headquarters. As one of Lenin's closest friends, he was responsible for the security of senior party leaders. After an assassination attempt on Lenin in Aug. 1918, Dzerzhinsky launched a massive terror campaign, jailing, torturing, and killing scores of suspects. The Cheka, which initially employed 23 people when Dzerzhinsky founded it, had 37,000 employees by Jan. 1919.

British diplomat-spy ROBERT BRUCE LOCKHART, in *Memoirs of a British Agent* (1932), his eyewitness account of the revolution, described Dzerzhinsky as "a man of correct manners and quiet speech but without a ray of burnout in his character. The most remarkable thing about him was his eyes. Deeply sunk, they blazed with a steady fire of fanaticism. They never twitched."

Dzerzhinsky set up a secret police structure that endured through to the KGB: First Directorate, to work against prospective subversives outside Soviet borders; Second Directorate, to seek out subversives within the Soviet Union; and Third Directorate, to watch for subversion and possible coups within the armed forces. His secret police also helped the Communist Party control the economy and the transportation system.

During the Allied interventions against the Bolsheviks in 1917–1919, Dzerzhinsky broke up a small spy NETWORK operating out of the U.S. Consulate. He also had operatives raid a suspected French intelligence office in Moscow, arresting six AGENTS and explosives. Reaching beyond Russia, he set up the AMTORG, a Soviet purchasing mission that served as a COVER for Dzerzhinsky's agents in the United States.

When Lenin ordered the first concentration camps, Dzerzhinsky established them on Solovetsky Island in 1922. He deported thousands of men who later perished in the Arctic climate or from the harsh conditions of the camps. In 1922 he supported Stalin's efforts to conquer Georgia. Dzerzhinsky's passion for protecting the Revolution—and for searching out and destroying counterrevolutionaries—led to the first significant overseas intelligence efforts of the Soviets. (See THE TRUST.) Czarist officials and White Russian officers were sought out in Europe and even in the United States. They were watched, reported on, and sometimes murdered.

This first Soviet spymaster is reported to have died of a stroke during an argument with Stalin on July 20, 1926. Conclusive evidence is lacking, but rumors persist that the stroke suffered by the 48-year-old Dzerzhinsky was induced by something more violent than Stalin's arguments.

Dzerzhinsky Square

Historic site of the LUBYANKA, longtime headquarters for Soviet security organs (e.g., NKVD, KGB), at No. 2 Dzerzhinsky Street, a short distance from the Kremlin, in Moscow. Seven streets come out of the square, which also contains a subway station, *Detsky Mir* (Children's World) department store (the largest in Russia), and the Polytechnical Museum.

A 40-foot, 14-ton bronze statue of FELIKS DZERZHINSKY by sculptor Ye. Vuchetich and architect G. Zakharov was erected in the square in 1958 at the direction of Soviet leader Nikita Khrushchev. The statue was taken from its pedestal on the night of Aug. 22, 1991, by democratic supporters after the abortive coup against Mikhail Gorbachev. The statue was not destroyed but was dumped on its back in a Moscow sculpture park. At

A Muscovite and canine friend rest on the statue of Feliks Dzherzhinsky, founder of the Soviet state security apparatus. The statue, which once stood in the square bearing his name, was torn down during he tumultuous days of August 1991. It now lies in a Moscow sculpture park, along with other Stalin-era statues. (WIDE WORLD)

that time the square was renamed Lubyanka Square and the former Dzerzhinsky Metro became the Lubyanka Metro.

The square was the scene of many historic events dating back to the early 1600s. In this century, meetings were held there in Oct. 1905 during the first Russian Revolution; on Oct. 20 a 200,000-strong political demonstration filed through the square, following the coffin of a prominent revolutionary killed by the czarist police. The square was the scene of fighting in the Oct. 1917 revolution and the starting point from which revolutionaries launched an attack on the Kremlin through Nikolskaya Street (later October 25 Street) and Teatralny Avenue (later part of Marx Prospekt).

Dzhurtchenko, Vitaly

High-ranking member of the KGB who defected to the United States in Aug. 1985. Dzhurtchenko was operating under diplomatic COVER in Rome when he defected. Some sources identified him as the fifth-ranking officer in the KGB. After Dzhurtchenko defected, there were a number of East-West defections, including chief of the KGB's London operations, OLEG GORDIEVSKY.

837th Signal Service Detachment

SEE CENTRAL BUREAU

Earhart, Amelia

(b. 1897 d. 1937?)

Popular American aviatrix suspected of flying spy flights over Japanese-held islands before World War II. Earhart achieved many firsts—she was the first woman to fly across the Atlantic, to fly across the Atlantic alone, and the first female passenger on a flight across the Atlantic. She wrote a book about the last experience, the first of several books she wrote about her adventures.

After nursing wounded soldiers in Canada during World War I, she attended Columbia University in New York. However, she dropped out of school to work to earn money for flying lessons.

In 1928 Earhart took a passenger flight across the Atlantic and in 1932 she made a solo flight across the Atlantic; she was the first woman to fly across the United States in both directions. A 1935 solo flight by Earhart from Hawaii to California covered a greater distance than the transatlantic flight.

With flight engineer Fred Noonan, Earhart attempted an around-the-world flight in 1937. After she had flown more than two-thirds of the journey, her plane vanished near Howland Island in the Pacific. Although there are theories and some indications that she landed on an uninhabited island, there is no definitive evidence. Another theory is that the Japanese captured and imprisoned or executed her for attempting to spy on islands that they controlled. She most likely came down at sea, the most probable cause being her lack of knowledge of radio navigation.

The theory that she was spying on Japanese naval bases in the area was first popularized in a 1943 MOVIE *Flight for Freedom*, in which Rosalind Russell plays the spying aviatrix. Her boyfriend in the film, played by Fred MacMurray, uses the intelligence she collects to lead a Navy dive-bombing mission against the Japanese islands. Interestingly, on her 1937 flight, Earhart flew the same basic type of aircraft, a twin-engine Lockheed Electra, that was flown by SIDNEY COTTON on his clandestine RECONNAISSANCE flights over Germany.

Ears Only

Material that is so highly classified that it cannot be committed to writing but must only be discussed orally and even then only in special facilities.

Eastland Document

The only known documentary assessment by either the U.S. or British governments of what information was available to DONALD MACLEAN, longtime Soviet MOLE in the British government. The document was a letter written by the U.S. State Department to Sen. James Eastland, chairman of the Senate Internal Security Subcommittee, which suggested investigating damage done to the U.S. by Maclean and GUY BURGESS. The letter, dated Feb. 21, 1956, attempted to assess the damage to U.S. nuclear activities caused by Maclean's former access to both Anglo-American nuclear exchanges and a considerable amount of highly classified information on U.S. nuclear weapon programs.

Also see ATOMIC SPY RING.

ECCM

SEE ELECTRONIC COUNTER-COUNTERMEASURES

Echelon

CODE NAME for a worldwide surveillance network operated by the NSA in cooperation with similar intelligence intercept agenices in Britain, Australia, Canada, and New Zealand.

Echelon's computers search through intercepted messages for keywords or for fax and e-mail addresses. The highly secret program was described in a report issued in 2001 by the European Parliament. The U.S. Congress, concerned about the DOMESTIC INTELLIGENCE aspects to such a program, added a requirement for NSA to the fiscal 2000 intelligence budget: report on its legal standards for intercepting communications. "Echelon," said Representative Robert L. Barr Jr. (R-Ga.), "gives every appearance of a program that is far broader than it ought to be and poses serious questions about constitutionality."

U.S. officials said that NSA followed the provisions of the FOREIGN INTELLIGENCE SURVEILLANCE ACT (FISA), which prohibits NSA from eavesdropping on Americans either in the United States or overseas, unless the agency can show that there is reason to believe that they are AGENTS of a foreign government committing espionage or some other crime. If any information is accidentally intercepted, the law forbids its dissemination and it must be destroyed within 24 hours unless it contains "a threat of death or serious bodily harm."

ECM

(1) Electrical Cipher Machine (see SIGABA); (2) ELECTRONIC COUNTERMEASURES

Economic Intelligence

Information collected to supplement political and MILITARY INTELLIGENCE. Most economic intelligence is easily obtained from OPEN SOURCES. But sometimes the intelligence must be obtained through clandestine means.

Since the passsage of the Economic Espionage Act in 1996, theft of trade secrets has been a federal crime.

Sherman Kent, chief of the OFFICE OF NATIONAL ESTIMATES in the CIA, defined the span of economic intelligence in *Strategic Intelligence for American World Policy* (1949); an intelligence agency, he wrote

> must watch for new crops and the development of new methods of agriculture, changes in farm machinery, land use, fertilizers, reclamation projects, and so on. It must follow the discovery of new industrial processes, the emergences of new industries, and the sinking of new mines. . . .

Economic intelligence is the grist for an intelligence analyst. Most of it is relatively easy to obtain from OPEN

SOURCES, especially commercial SATELLITE photography and infrared imagery.

Since its founding the CIA has routinely monitored world oil production, key crops, foreign economic policies, and world trade developments. Some countries that are TARGETS of intelligence may not produce open economic reports, or produce ones filled with DISINFORMATION. Analysts must search for and weigh what information they can obtain.

China, for example, keeps such a tight hold on economic statistics that in 1996 it announced that it would also restrict the flow of financial news *into* the country. China has long considered that the unauthorized disclosure of any financial information is as serious a breach of security as the disclosure of military information.

ROBERT M. GATES, speaking in 1991 when he was DIRECTOR OF CENTRAL INTELLIGENCE, said that requests for economic information from the CIA outnumber all others. Nearly one-half of the intelligence requirements in 20 policymaking agencies and departments, he said, "are economic in nature."

The difference between economic intelligence and INDUSTRIAL ESPIONAGE is sometimes difficult to define. Even while he was discussing economic intelligence, Gates noted that "special focus" was needed on countries that "try to steal our technology or seek unfairly or illegally to disadvantage American business."

One country's economic intelligence is another country's espionage: In Nov. 1971 the chief of France's economic intelligence service told Count ALEXANDRE DE MARENCHES, head of the French intelligence agency DGSS, that the United States would devalue the dollar the next month. Marenches passed on the information to French President Georges Pompidou. He in turn informed the Bank of France, which made millions selling dollars and buying francs on world markets.

In Sept. 1993, President Clinton—with the chief executive officers of the General Motors, Ford, and Chrysler corporations at his side—announced that the U.S. government would cooperate with the three automobile firms in an attempt to build a car with a fuel-efficiency three times that of current models. In this "new partnership between government and industry," a White House statement said that

> superstrong, lightweight materials developed for advanced weapons systems, ultracapacitors from "Star Wars" projects, superefficient motors and fuel cells from the [Defense] Advanced Research Projects Agency, virtual design and prototyping from the Army Tank Command, and many other technologies will be available for the project.

Some observers saw the possibility of industrial espionage because the Pentagon, through the INTELLIGENCE COMMUNITY, would have information on other nations' manufacturing techniques. Passing this on to U.S. car manufacturers would be either economic intelligence or industrial espionage—depending upon one's viewpoint.

According to a 2001 report by the Office of Counterintelligence Executive, economic espionage cost the U.S. business community at least $100 billion in lost sales in 2000. Most of the espionage, the report said, involved manufacturing processes and research development.

Eden, William

(b. 1744 d. 1814)

British statesman and head of the British SECRET SERVICE at time of the American Revolution. Eden was Undersecretary of State to the colonies in 1772 when he reorganized the British Secret Service in an effort to acquire detailed information on the colonies' relations with foreign governments. He became one of five commissioners to the American colonies in 1778, dispatched in a fruitless attempt to obtain a peace agreement.

He was appointed Chief Secretary for Ireland in 1780 and Vice Treasurer for Ireland in 1783; and subsequently ambassador to Spain and then Holland among other government posts. His last office was president of the Board of Trade (1806–1807).

Eden was created Baron Auckland in the Irish peerage in 1789 and in the British peerage in 1793.

Edmonds, Emma S.

(b. 1839 d. 1898)

Canadian-born woman who successfully operated behind Confederate lines as a Union spy during the American Civil War. She was probably the only spy in history who was both transvestite and "transracial."

Edmonds came to the United States from New Brunswick, Canada, in 1856. When the Civil War began in 1861 she adopted the name Frank Thompson and volunteered to serve as a male nurse for the Union Army. She was present at the first Battle of Bull Run, the first major combat between Union and Confederate troops. After serving as a male nurse for two years, Edmonds volunteered to serve as a spy behind Confederate lines. Disguising herself as a young black man by dyeing her skin, getting her hair cropped short, and wearing a wig, she managed to cross the front lines near Yorktown, Va.

Although claiming to be a free black when confronted by an overseer, Edmonds was put to work on Confederate fortifications. After a day of backbreaking work, she was able to make a sketch of the fortifications and an accounting of the guns being installed. The next day she carried water for the workers and then food to the troops. Impressed as a sentry at one point, she was able to defect back to Union lines during a rainy night, carrying her Confederate rifle as a trophy.

After three days behind Confederate lines, Edmonds brought back useful military information. During the coming months she successfully accomplished 11 more missions behind Confederate lines without being detected. On one occasion she went as an Irish peddler woman, other times she posed as a dry goods clerk, and once she claimed to be the grieving friend of a dead soldier.

Eventually contracting malaria while on a spy mission, she deserted after returning to Union lines, fearing that medical treatment would reveal her sex.

EEI

SEE ESSENTIAL ELEMENTS OF INFORMATION

Eitan, Rafael

(b. 1929)

Israeli intelligence AGENT and spymaster, who directed the espionage activities of American spy JONATHAN JAY POLLARD.

Born in Palestine of Russian parents who had emigrated there in 1922, as a young boy Eitan saw a spy movie with his mother, after which he told her, "I want to be a spy like MATA HARI." Eitan joined the Haganah (Jewish defense force) at age 12 and went on to enter the Palmach, its elite commando component. During and after World War II, before the state of Israel was established in 1948, he carried out clandestine operations to help refugees enter Palestine illegally after the British mandate authorities imposed an almost total ban on Jewish immigration to appease the Arab community. This work included blowing up a British radar station on Mount Carmel. He earned his nickname "Rafi the Smelly" because he had to wade through sewers to reach the radar site.

He was wounded on May 15, 1948, Israel's first full day of statehood. He then served with Army intelligence during the War of Independence (1948–1949). When the war was over Eitan went into cattle farming, but after six months he entered the intelligence service (later named MOSSAD) and subsequently the domestic security service (SHIN BET), becoming chief of operations for the latter in the late 1950s. Among his successes, Eitan discovered in 1958 that Lt. Col. ISRAEL BEER, aide to Prime Minister David Ben-Gurion, was a Soviet spy.

In May 1960, Eitan performed his most daring exploit, as a member of the Mossad-Shin Bet team that captured Nazi war criminal Adolf Eichmann in Argentina and brought him to Israel to stand trial. This feat made Eitan a national hero. (Eichmann was tried, found guilty, and hanged.)

Eitan transferred to the Mossad in 1963, such shifts being normal in the Israeli intelligence services. While with the Mossad he participated in the hunt for German rocket scientists and engineers who were working on Egyptian weapon projects. At the same time, Eitan claims that he established the first Israeli connections with Egyptian President Gamal Abdel Nasser. Eitan was also said to be the head of the Israeli vengeance squad that tracked down and killed the Palestine Liberation Organization's Black September terrorists who murdered 11 Israeli athletes at the 1972 Munich Olympics.

In 1972 Eitan left the Mossad because he was passed over for the position of director. He undertook several business ventures, including raising tropical fish, but was unsuccessful and reentered the government in 1978 when Prime Minister Menahem Begin appointed him his adviser on terrorism. In that position he organized and directed several anti-terrorist operations. In addition, in 1981 he was named head of the Defense Ministry's LAKAM—Lishka LeKishrei Mada (Liaison Bureau for Scientific Affairs). Lakam was the COVER for a clandestine, TECHNICAL INTELLIGENCE agency that was independent of the Army's AMAN and other Israeli intelligence agencies. Thus, Eitan simultaneously held two intelligence positions, reporting independently to the Prime Minister on terrorist issues and to the Minister of Defense for Lakam's expanding activities.

In 1984, when Jonathan Pollard, working at the Anti-Terrorism Alert Center of the U.S. NAVAL INVESTIGATIVE SERVICE, offered to sell secrets to the Israeli government, he was put in contact with Lakam. Eitan met with Jonathan Pollard and his fiance, Anne Henderson, in Paris in Nov. 1984. The Israelis wined and dined their new agent (and bought a $10,000 ring for Anne). In 1985 the American spies again met with Eitan in Israel. Part of Eitan's interest in Pollard may have been the opportunity to demonstrate the superiority of his Lakam over the Mossad.

After the Pollard espionage story broke when the American spy and his wife were arrested on Nov. 21, 1985, the U.S. Department of Justice claimed that Eitan had masterminded the Pollard affair. As a result of the Pollard debacle, Lakam was disbanded in 1986 and Eitan was appointed head of Israel's state-owned chemical company.

Despite the Pollard affair, Eitan is widely regarded as an intelligence hero in Israel, even by many of his critics.

Ekipa Z

CODE NAME for the 15 Polish cryptologists from the BIURO SZFROW working at the French CRYPTANALYSIS center BRUNO from Oct. 1939 to May 1940.

Electric Cipher Machine (ECM)

SEE SIGABA

Electro-Optical Intelligence

(ELECTRO-OPINT)

Intelligence other than SIGNALS INTELLIGENCE derived from optical monitoring of the electromagnetic spectrum from the ultraviolet (0.01 micrometers) through the far infrared (1,000 micrometers).

Electronic Counter-Countermeasures

(ECCM)

Actions taken to retain the effectiveness of one's own use of the electromagnetic spectrum—radar, radio, and the like—against hostile ELECTRONIC WARFARE (EW) efforts.

Methods of ECCM include multiple-frequency radars, wherein the radar frequency changes while it sweeps to reduce possible enemy interference, and "burst" radio transmissions, which are highly condensed messages transmitted at very high speeds that reduce their vulnerability to enemy detection and interception.

ECCM devices are fitted in surface warships, submarines, and combat aircraft. Extensive TECHNICAL INTELLIGENCE about foreign EW systems is needed in the design of ECCM equipment.

Electronic Countermeasures

(ECM)

Methods used to detect hostile threats to friendly forces and to inhibit or degrade the effectiveness of enemy weapons and sensors. For example, against enemy radars the ECM devices attempt to interfere with the radar through jamming and deception; changing the electrical properties of the air between the radar and (friendly) target, mainly through chaff (airborne foil strips); and changing the reflective properties of the (friendly) target through radar-absorbing (anechoic) materials or paint, and through electronic and mechanical echo (blip) enhancers or decoys.

Most surface warships, SUBMARINES, and combat aircraft have ECM systems to help protect them against hostile detection and attack. In addition, there are specialized ECM aircraft that assist other aircraft in penetrating heavily defended areas. U.S. ECM aircraft have included the EF-111A Raven and EA-6B Prowler.

Extensive TECHNICAL INTELLIGENCE about foreign EW systems is needed for the design of ECM equipment.

Electronic Intelligence

(ELINT)

Intelligence derived from electromagnetic radiation other than radio communications; the principal source of ELINT is radar transmissions.

Surface warships, INTELLIGENCE COLLECTION SHIPS, SUBMARINES, and specialized AIRCRAFT are employed in ELINT collection. The last have included specialized variants of the A3D SKYWARRIOR, C-121 CONSTELLATION, C-135 STRATOTANKER, P2V NEPTUNE, P3V ORION, and the P4M-1Q MERCATOR.

Electronic Security

The detection, identification, evaluation, and location of foreign electromagnetic radiations. In COUNTERINTELLIGENCE operations, for example, this means being able to detect communications from foreign AGENTS to embassies or foreign countries.

See ELIAHU COHEN—an Israeli spy detected through electronic security—and RAFTER.

Electronic Surveillance

The detection, intercept, location, recording, and analysis of electromagnetic radiations, such as radar and radio communications. Electronic surveillance is generally passive, seeking to detect the presence of an enemy or military forces (including ships and aircraft) through "listening" for radio and radar emissions.

Electronic Surveillance Measures

(ESM)

Military equipment and activities for the detection, interception, location, recording, and analysis of electromagnetic radiations, such as radar and radio. ESM provides the TECHNICAL INTELLIGENCE for ELECTRONIC COUNTERMEASURES (ECM) and ELECTRONIC COUNTER-COUNTERMEASURES (ECCM). ESM systems are passive.

ESM systems are installed in ground stations and specialized vehicles, surface warships, INTELLIGENCE COLLECTION SHIPS, SUBMARINES, and specialized AIRCRAFT (see ELECTRONIC INTELLIGENCE).

Electronic Warfare

(EW)

Overall term for efforts to detect, locate, exploit, reduce, or prevent an enemy's use of the electromagnetic spectrum, and actions that retain one's own use of the electromagnetic spectrum. There are several components of electronic warfare:

> ELECTRONIC COUNTER-COUNTERMEASURES (ECCM)
> ELECTRONIC COUNTERMEASURES (ECM)
> ELECTRONIC SURVEILLANCE MEASURES (ESM)
> SIGNALS INTELLIGENCE (SIGINT)

Also see MEASUREMENT and SIGNATURE INTELLIGENCE (MASINT).

Elicitation

The acquisition of intelligence from a person or group when the collector does not disclose the intent of the interview or conversation.

ELINT

SEE ELECTRONIC INTELLIGENCE

Elliot, Rita

Soviet spy in Australia who set up a spy NETWORK in 1955 using the COVER of a circus tightrope walker. She was very successful until Australian COUNTERINTELLIGENCE officials noticed that she entertained many men who were connected with nuclear research and other secret work. After being warned by Moscow to stop her spying activities, she left Australia in 1961 to perform in India and Pakistan.

No more was heard of her after that. Her real name was Esfir Yurina.

Ellis, Col. Charles Howard (Dick)

(b. 1895 d. 1975)

British Secret Intelligence Service (MI6) officer who sold information to both German and Soviet intelligence agencies.

Born in Australia, Ellis served in the Middlesex Regiment of the British Army during World War I. Between the wars he studied at Oxford and the Sorbonne, and in 1924 joined MI6. Under COVER of the Foreign Office, he served in BERLIN and Paris, collecting intelligence and as a TALENT SPOTTER and recruiter.

In Aug. 1940 he went to New York where, with the rank of colonel, he became deputy head of BRITISH SECURITY COORDINATION (BSC) under WILLIAM STEPHENSON. Again, Ellis had diplomatic cover, being listed as the British consul in New York. While with BSC he assisted WILLIAM DONOVAN in establishing the U.S. OFFICE OF STRATEGIC SERVICES.

He returned to MI6 headquarters in London in 1944. Two years later he was appointed field officer in charge of Southeast Asia and the Far East, being based in Singapore. He was sent to Australia in 1950 to advise the new AUSTRALIAN SECURITY AND INTELLIGENCE ORGANIZATION (ASIO).

In 1951 information came to light about a British "Captain Ellis" who had given the German ABWEHR intelligence about MI6 during World War II, including the revelation that the British had tapped into the secret telephone links between Joachim von Ribbentrop, the German ambassador in London, and Adolf Hitler in Berlin. Earlier indications that there was a spy named Ellis had been ignored by British intelligence after the head of the MI6 Soviet desk at the time—HAROLD (KIM) PHILBY—had seen the report. He wrote, "Who is this man Ellis?" and noted that no further action was needed. (At the time Ellis worked in an office a few doors away from Philby.)

Although the possibility that Ellis was a MOLE—for the Germans if not the Soviets—was investigated, it was dropped when Ellis announced in 1953 that he would retire from MI6. It was two years before normal retirement at age 60, but Ellis cited health problems.

He sailed for Australia, where he immediately signed a two-year agreement to work for ASIO. But two months later Ellis broke his contract and sailed back to Britain, shortly after learning that VLADIMIR PETROV, a Soviet INTELLIGENCE OFFICER in Canberra, was about to defect. On his arrival in London, in 1954, Ellis immediately contacted Philby, apparently telling him of Petrov's impending defection.

Meanwhile, the Security Service (MI5) began searching files for indications that Ellis had been a foreign agent (see FLUENCY). (In Washington, D.C., the FBI was also conducting inquiries into Ellis's activities.)

Ellis was now taken on part time by MI6 to supplement his pension. His job was to review the MI6 archives—destroying files that were felt to be no longer of value!

Finally, MI5 investigators concluded that Ellis had been a paid agent of the Abwehr from before the war until May 1940, when Germany invaded France and Holland, and that subsequently the Soviets may have blackmailed him into spying for them. Indeed, Ellis may have worked for the Soviets from the late 1920s.

The decision was made in 1966 to interrogate him, and he was placed under SURVEILLANCE by the SPECIAL BRANCH of Scotland Yard, which tapped his phone to thwart any attempt to defect. During the interrogations Ellis alleged that upon going to work for MI6 in the 1920s without adequate training, he had begun giving his agents trivial information about British intelligence so that they could feed it to the Soviets, who paid them for it. Then, to supplement his own pay, he had provided his agents with information they could sell to the Germans as well as to the Soviets. Thereafter, he was threatened with exposure unless he provided better intelligence.

He denied, however, that he worked directly for Soviet intelligence. As he was questioned over several weeks, the Australians—but not the FBI—were told of his duplicity. He was neither exposed nor tried before his death, and lived out his life on his government pension.

Ellis, Lt. Col. Earl H.

(b. 1880 d. 1923)

U.S. Marine Corps officer who spied out Japanese islands in the western Pacific and was a leading proponent for American development of an amphibious capability to assault those islands. Ellis's impact on the development of U.S. Marine amphibious doctrine in the 1920s and 1930s was considerable.

Ellis enlisted in the Marine Corps in 1900 and was commissioned the following year; he served in the Far East and distinguished himself in France during World War I. Immediately after World War I, "Pete" Ellis began lecturing on the role of the Marine Corps in seizing bases in the Pacific in time of war so that the U.S. fleet could deny them to the Japanese. His 50,000-word plan, submitted to the commandant of the Marine Corps in July 1921, was a blueprint for a Marine advance across the Pacific. It began: "In order to impose our will upon Japan, it will be necessary for us to project our fleet and land forces across the Pacific and wage war in Japanese waters." His assault targets in the 1921 plan included the Marshall, Caroline, Peleliu, and Ryuku Islands (including Okinawa)—most of them sites of future World War II amphibious assaults. He listed specific atolls to be captured and the troop requirements, as well as the weapons, reef-crossing vehicles, and tactics to be used.

In Aug. 1921, Ellis began an extensive tour of the Pacific to gather intelligence on prospective amphibious targets. In 1922 in Yokohama, Japan, he was admitted to the U.S. naval hospital and diagnosed as suffering from alcoholism. After being hospitalized a second time at Yokohama, he sailed for Saipan and then the Marshall Islands. He was again hospitalized but continued his tour of Japanese islands—a thoroughly inept intelligence undertaking. A biographer, Dirk Anthony Ballendorf, observed in the *Marine Corps Gazette,*

> As a spy, he does not receive high marks. From a military standpoint, only the most dismal appraisal could be made of his mission's execution: a seriously ill, neurotic, sometimes drunken Marine officer, absent without leave, with a code book, openly discussing his mission with American nationals, and, in full view of the Japanese, traipsing through the islands making notes and maps. American naval authorities would have been embarrassed had they known of Ellis' whereabouts. At several stops in the Japanese islands he became ill.

Everywhere he went he charted the islands and reefs, and listed other items of potential interest for amphibious operations. His presence did not go unnoticed. Throughout his travels Ellis was carefully watched by the Japanese, but he managed to slip a packet of information to at least one businessman, asking that it be mailed for him in the United States. Ellis was hospitalized again for two weeks on Jaluit in the Marshalls. Then, back in the Carolines, on Koror in the Palau group, he moved in

Lt. Col. Earl H. Ellis. (U.S. MARINE CORPS)

with the native royalty, who had befriended him, and was provided with a wife, Metauie, a beautiful woman 25 years his junior. His behavior grew ever more erratic. He continued to drink heavily, mainly beer and sake. He would sometimes rant and rave, and once pranced around "like a soldier and punched his arm through the wall," according to an eyewitness.

Finally, in May 1923, he became violently ill and confided to his wife and their houseboys that he was "an American spy sent by higher authority from New York." He still drank when he could manage it, and refused to take medicine that was prescribed for him. He died on May 12 and was buried on Koror. His belongings, including maps and notes and—reportedly—a CODE book, were confiscated by the Japanese.

When the U.S. government was informed of Ellis's death, an attempt was made to have a U.S. Navy ship call at the island for his remains, but the Japanese refused permission. However, a U.S. Navy chief pharmacist was allowed to travel on a Japanese ship to Koror, where Ellis's remains were exhumed, photographed, and cremated. They were then returned to Japan with Chief Pharmacist Lawrence Zembsch.

Obviously, the Japanese had a keen interest in Ellis's mission. But he could have collected no information about defenses and fortifications in the Caroline and Marshall Islands. The Japanese did not fortify those islands until the 1930s.

Ellis, Robert W.

A U.S. Navy enlisted man stationed at the Moffett Field Naval Air Station in California, Ellis contacted the Soviet Consulate in San Francisco in 1983 and offered to provide classified documents for $2,000.

He was arrested as he attempted to sell the documents to an FBI agent posing as a Soviet INTELLIGENCE OFFICER. Although the government did not reveal how his offer was first discovered, telephone taps of Soviet offices apparently played a role. Ellis was given a dishonorable discharge and sentenced to five years at hard labor. His sentence was later reduced to three years.

EMCON

SEE EMISSION CONTROL

Emission

Electronic impulses emanating from radars, radios, and other electronic equipment. They can be detected, intercepted, recorded, and analyzed to reveal a variety of intelligence.

Emission Control

(EMCON)

Practice of avoiding or reducing the use of radio and radar to prevent hostile forces from detecting or intercepting the emissions.

Emission Security

Measures taken to deny intelligence to enemy activities from the interception and analysis of electronic emissions. These measures include EMISSION CONTROL.

Employee

American slang for a person employed by, assigned to, or detailed to a U.S. intelligence agency.

England–Great Britain–United Kingdom

The deep roots of intelligence in England are intertwined with the detection of treason, which created the need for DOMESTIC INTELLIGENCE. For centuries the intelligence services of the Crown were concerned primarily with keeping the reigning monarch alive and on the throne. In the 14th and 15th centuries this meant seeking out treasonous Scots and other foreigners. But there was no agency for ridding England of spies. Beginning in 1351 the legal basis for finding and executing enemies of the monarch was the Treason Act, which defined high treason as crimes against the king and the realm, including the crime of counterfeiting. People could lose their heads even for "imagining the death of the king."

Treason encompassed spying against the Crown, but espionage was eclipsed by treason, the ultimate crime. Mary, Queen of Scots, and Sir Walter Raleigh were among the many people tried and executed under this act, which was also invoked in modern times to try British traitors during both World Wars. (For example, see WILLIAM JOYCE.)

The monarchy's need for foreign intelligence became acute in 1570, when Pope Pius V excommunicated Queen Elizabeth I. Fearing papist plots by Englishmen, Elizabeth built up an extensive domestic intelligence organization under Sir FRANCIS WALSINGHAM, who began serving as her Secretary of State in 1573. (One of Walsingham's spies was poet-dramatist CHRISTOPHER MARLOWE.) Walsingham extended his intelligence NETWORK to the continent, with Catholics as his intelligence TARGET. He bribed "Priests, Jesuits and Traitors" to "bewraye the practises against this Realm." A spy in Rome reported hearing plots to have the queen's "flesh torn from her by dogs."

Walsingham's network seems to have ended at his death in 1590. Not until the 17th century and the rise of Lord Protector Oliver Cromwell was there another substantial intelligence system in the realm. One of Cromwell's "Intelligencers," JOHN THURLOE, reported that his spymaster employed "a great number of subtil and sly fellowes" and secretly intercepted mail going through the General Letter Office. (See JOHN WALLIS.) Under Cromwell mail of interest was examined by a "Secret Man" in a room set aside for this use.

THE SECRET OFFICE

Espionage became a permanent government fixture after the Glorious Revolution, which saw the rise and fall of James II and the ascendancy of Parliament entrenched in the 1689 Bill of Rights. Writer DANIEL DEFOE, who has been called the father of the British SECRET SERVICE, volunteered to spy for the Speaker of the House of Commons in 1703, watching for plots against the throne by Jacobites, as the supporters of the son of the deposed James II were known. In the 18th century came the creation of an official "Decypherer" for breaking CODES (see Bishop EDWARD WILLES) and a SECRET OFFICE under the Secretary of State.

The Secret Office was later attached to the Post Office, where mail continued to be routinely intercepted. (See BODE FAMILY.) In 1782 the duties of the Secretary of State were redefined: A Foreign Office handled affairs outside Britain, and a Home Office dealt with British matters. The division was reflected in the collection of intelligence, with one agency for internal security and another for foreign intelligence collection.

The American Revolution of 1775–1781 tested British intelligence efforts, as AGENTS were needed in the American Colonies, both for COUNTERINTELLIGENCE and MILITARY INTELLIGENCE, as well as in France, which supported the revolutionaries. (See BENEDICT ARNOLD, JOHN ANDRÉ, and EDWARD BANCROFT.)

Meddling with the mail continued, despite an inquiry in Parliament in 1844. A letter writer had placed tiny seeds in an envelope with the letter and, noticing their disappearance, brought it to the attention of Parliament. Despite protestations, British intelligence services have continued to open mail. A major focus for British intelligence during most of the 19th century was the GREAT GAME—the struggle between Russia and Britain for control of Central Asia. The Russians wished to expand into the region, while the British sought to secure the northern approaches to India. British officials chose Meshed in the Khorassan province of Persia (now Iran) as the spy center for the Great Game. They bribed journalists, pilgrims, postal workers, and refugees to get information. A contemporary report tells of a sailor spying on a Russian steamship in the Caspian Sea, adding, "But it is just possible that he may be in Russian pay." The Meshed operation continued until World War I.

SECRET MONEY

From 1782 British intelligence efforts had been secretly funded. Parliament, in a secret vote, provided the Secretary of State with the money, which was not publicly audited. Diplomats returning to London from foreign tours took oaths that they had spent the secret money honestly. Records show that money was spent on agents (who were considered long-term) and informants (who provided information occasionally) in Germany, Russia, Italy, the Ottoman Empire, and Spain.

Large sums of money were passed out in Prussia and Russia to get those countries to join in an alliance against France in 1807. The fund also supported Secret Service

pensioners, including relatives of diplomats whose connection with intelligence was dubious.

Diplomats, military ATTACHÉS, and journalists were among the spies who roamed the British Empire in the twilight of the 19th century. From 1894 to 1898 secret funds were also paid to Reuters news agency, which supplied confidential reports from its correspondents and agreed to let the Foreign Office use the service to publish propaganda in foreign newspapers.

Both the War Office and the Admiralty had established formal intelligence branches by 1883. But there was an undercurrent of amateurism to British spying until the Boer War (1899–1902) revealed the need for a permanent, professional approach to intelligence and counterintelligence. Maj. Gen. Sir ROBERT BADEN-POWELL, the hero of the siege of Mafeking in 1900, introduced innovative intelligence techniques during this war. Those innovations helped to kindle new interest in reorganizing the Secret Service to provide intelligence in the event of a European war. The plan, developed around 1905, called for "observers" in enemy territory to pass intelligence to "carriers"—salesmen, Gypsies, and women were suggested for the role. They would journey to neutral countries, where "collectors" would analyze the intelligence and take it to the nearest British Embassy for encoding and transmission to London. The collectors were to be supplied by the War Office's Directorate of Military Intelligence.

The plan was never carried out, but in 1909 a subcommittee of the Committee of Imperial Defence recommended the establishment of a Secret Service Bureau that was to take responsibility for counterintelligence in Britain, funded by the Secret Service fund of the War Office. The Bureau had a Home Section and a Foreign Section. The Home Section became the Security Service, designated MI5 (for the fifth branch of Military Intelligence) and the Foreign Section became the Secret Intelligence Service, designated MI6.

WORLD WAR I

In the trenches of World War I British TACTICAL INTELLIGENCE was ineffective. At the Somme, for example, the British sustained heavy casualties when the Germans learned of British operational plans by eavesdropping on field telephones. A brigade major, despite warnings, had read his orders over the phone! (The transcript was later found in a German trench.) "Hundreds of brave men perished," a British historian wrote, "as the result of this one act of incredible foolishness." Some useful intelligence was supplied, however, by AIRCRAFT carrying out RECONNAISSANCE missions over German lines, and by observation BALLOONS.

But British codebreakers distinguished themselves by cracking virtually all German codes and CIPHERS. The deciphering of the ZIMMERMANN TELEGRAM by the Royal Navy codebreakers of ROOM 40 had a profound impact on the war. The message, from the German Foreign Minister to the German ambassador in Mexico, offered the Mexicans reconquest of U.S. territory in return for helping Germany. When the telegram was revealed, American wrath over its contents helped to push the United States into the war. To preserve British codebreaking prowess the GOVERNMENT CODE AND CYPHER SCHOOL (GC&CS) succeeded Room 40 after the war.

The war educated a generation of individuals who would become pillars of future British intelligence and counterintelligence, among them Sir STEWART MENZIES, who worked in Army intelligence and would someday head MI6. During the war Menzies developed a card index filing system that classified people according to their potential as friend or foe. Under his system, people were either BS (British subjects), AS (Allied subjects), NS (neutral subjects), or ES (enemy subjects). They were then given an intelligence rating, ranging from AA for "Absolutely Anglicised" to BB for "Bad Boche." This was a crude model for the compartmentalization scheme employed at Menzie's later MI6.

To hide the actual size of the American Expeditionary Force sent to France in 1917, U.S. and British INTELLIGENCE OFFICERS worked together to create an elaborate DECEPTION plan, known as Document X. Neutral Mexican and Spanish diplomats were fed bits of a fake report on America's industrial and military buildup. As expected, they spread the inflated figures to German contacts. The British and French contributed to the plan by making similar moves. British codebreakers confirmed the success of the deception.

German intelligence thus heard reports of U.S. regiments that were actually battalions, and of divisions that were actually regiments. Divisions became armies, and armies became army groups. Document X worked so well, a British intelligence officer later wrote, "that some of our own high Staff Officers never knew the exact position, and strangely over-estimated the strength of the American Force on the Western Front."

After the war Britain preserved the intelligence apparatus and aimed it at a new target—Bolsheviks. Fearing a Bolshevik-inspired civil uprising similar to those sweeping Russia and Germany, British intelligence created a new secret agency, M04, whose mission was to gather information about threats of civil uprisings or mutiny in the armed forces.

Wartime cooperation between British and U.S. intelligence continued into the postwar years. Winston Churchill, who had served as First Lord of the Admiralty early in the war, encouraged the cooperation, showing a keen personal interest in intelligence matters. At his suggestion, Prime Minister Lloyd George centralized British intelligence, placing MI6 under the Foreign Office and authorizing the agency to run agents and conduct operations outside British territory. Its most famous agent was SIDNEY REILLY, who operated in Bolshevik Russia—and many other places where the British had interests.

Intelligence officers attached to the War Office, such as Menzies, remained there as COVER, but they actually worked for MI6.

In 1927 Britain broke off diplomatic relations with the Soviet Union over the ARCOS AFFAIR. A Soviet firm doing business in England, Arcos was primarily an espionage effort. After the breakup of the Arcos ring, the Soviets shifted from LEGAL agents—diplomats and attachés—to ILLEGALS, Russians and British subjects under cover. The Soviet Union enlisted Communist Party members in Britain as spies, setting up a spy ring specifically to steal secret plans from the British ordnance factory at Woolwich Arsenal.

The British counter-intelligence agency, MI5, assigned 25-year-old Olga Gray to penetrate the ring. She became a member of Friends of the Soviet Union, joined the Communist Party, and was such a trusted comrade that she ran a SAFE HOUSE for the NKVD, giving MI5 a great deal of intelligence on the party and its espionage activities. When the ring was smashed by MI5, she feared for her life. Assuming a new identity, she immigrated to Canada.

As Adolf Hitler rose to power in the early 1930s, British intelligence shifted from concerns over domestic enemies to the preparation for another war with Germany.

WORLD WAR II

In 1938, after Prime Minister Neville Chamberlain promised "peace in our time" when he made his pact with Hitler at Munich, an offer came to Menzies from Col. F.N. MASON-MACFARLANE, British military attaché in BERLIN, and WILLIAM S. STEPHENSON, a British intelligence officer who later directed British intelligence efforts in the United States. They offered to assassinate Hitler with their sporting rifles. Lord Halifax, the Foreign Secretary, rejected the offer, saying, "We have not reached that stage in our diplomacy when we have to use assassination as a substitute for diplomacy."

With such eccentric and desperate ideas as their banners, British intelligence went to war. In Aug. 1939, when war against Germany was imminent, Parliament passed the Emergency Powers Act, a law that gave the government the authority to impose sweeping restrictions on civilians. Regulation 18B, produced by fiat rather than Parliament, gave the Home Secretary the right to arrest and jail suspects indefinitely without trial if it was suspected that they were involved in "acts prejudicial to the public safety or the Defence of the Realm." Under the regulation, intelligence officers moved against such organizations as the British Union of Fascists, the Anglo-German Fellowship, and the Right Club, which was involved in the espionage of ANNA WOLKOV and U.S. code clerk TYLER KENT.

Germany invaded Poland on Sept. 1, 1939, and two days later Britain and France declared war on Germany. But the war was fought initially at sea. During this period, incorrectly called the "phony war," Menzies authorized two of his officers to attempt to make contact with German dissidents who wanted to overthrow Hitler. The result was disaster. (See Capt. S. PAYNE BEST.)

Meanwhile, German intelligence services, principally the ABWEHR, sought to infiltrate agents and to recruit agents in Britain. The British TWENTY COMMITTEE quickly

TURNED most German spies into DOUBLE AGENTS and ran the amazingly successful DOUBLE-CROSS SYSTEM, which tricked German intelligence into believing that it was running a spy network that actually was being run by the British. Secrecy surrounded dealings with captured spies, who were told: Turn or die. Eighteen Axis spies—16 in Britain and two Spaniards in Gibraltar—were executed; 15 were hanged. Josef Jakobs (alias George Rymer), age 43, broke his leg parachuting into Britain and could not stand on the gallows; he was tied to a chair on the grounds of the Tower of London and shot by a firing squad. One spy was reportedly acquitted, rearrested in court, and jailed for the rest of the war on charges of violating the OFFICIAL SECRETS ACT. Only one German spy is known to have reached the United Kingdom during the war and evaded capture (see J. W. TER BRAAK).

One of the most important British victories of the war took place not on a battlefield but at BLETCHLEY PARK, secret site of the superb codebreaking efforts of the GC&CS. From there came ULTRA, the deciphered German radio intercepts that enabled U.S. and British political and military leaders to get inside German planning and decision making.

To aid resistance groups and commit sabotage in Nazi-occupied Europe, British intelligence created the Special Operations Executive (SOE). It was, as historian M. R. D. Foot has noted, "true to the tradition of English eccentricity . . . an essentially unorthodox formation, created to wage war by unorthodox means in unorthodox places."

Hovering over these intelligence triumphs was Prime Minister Winston Churchill, who took office in May 1940. He provided all of the resources and support required for the British to exploit codebreaking and other intelligence sources. His passion for intelligence was seen in his note to the Chief of the Imperial General Staff on Nov. 24, 1940: "The great thing is to get the true picture, whatever it is."

He reviewed many of the Ultra communications personally and forced his commanders to employ them in their strategy. Even when he was not in London, he received decrypts through a SPECIAL LIAISON UNIT that accompanied him. Throughout the war Churchill took special efforts to disguise his sources of intelligence so that the German military leadership would not realize that most of their secret military communications had been penetrated by British codebreakers. (See BONIFACE, BODYGUARD.)

In the intelligence war, Britain clearly outmatched GERMANY. Throughout the war, as David Kahn noted in *Hitler's Spies* (1978), "the Allies usually knew to within a division the strength of the German forces in France." Knowledge gleaned from Ultra was the key to winning the Battle of the Atlantic, the lengthy and critical campaign against German U-boats. The shrewdly handled double-cross system orchestrated an elaborate deception operation for D-DAY so perplexing the German General Staff that it could not decide whether the invasion was a feint even as Allied troops were landing at Normandy.

COLD WAR

As soon as the war against Hitler ended in May 1945, Britain's war against its former Soviet allies and their intelligence agencies began. As Hugh Trevor-Roper, historian and wartime intelligence officer, observed, MI5 did not realize that "the same philosophy of penetration which had yielded such good results against Germany" was being used against Britain. The Soviets, recruiting spies from within British society, were doing to MI5 and MI6 what the double-cross system had done to the Abwehr.

The list of British traitors during the Cold War was very long: GUY BURGESS, DONALD MACLEAN, HAROLD (KIM) PHILBY, Sir ANTHONY BLUNT, JOHN CAIRNCROSS, all of the CAMBRIDGE SPY RING—named after that favorite recruiting ground of Soviet TALENT SPOTTERS. Those men delivered to Soviet intelligence agencies some of the most closely held secrets concerning Anglo-American intelligence, national policy, codebreaking, and even the atomic bomb. Also compromising British secrets were GEORGE BLAKE, JOHN VASSALL, GORDON LONSDALE, LEO LONG, and GEOFFREY PRIME. The sex-and-secrets PROFUMO AFFAIR caused great political embarrassment but appears to have divulged no secrets.

Former MI5 intelligence officer PETER WRIGHT, in *Spycatcher* (1987), a book that Prime Minister Margaret Thatcher attempted to suppress, claimed that Sir ROGER HOLLIS, the head of MI5, was himself a Soviet MOLE. Wright also claimed that a group of MI5 operatives plotted against Prime Minister Harold Wilson in the 1960s.

Inside MI5 and MI6 security was notoriously lax. HOMOSEXUAL liaisons exposed officers to Soviet blackmail. Burgess and Maclean were notorious drunks, Philby an occasional one. Dame Rebecca West, responding to the recurrent scandals, wrote that "[we] would have been spared a great deal of trouble if we had simply kept our cupboards locked and had removed from our public service officials who were habitually blind drunk."

The Cold War kept the World War II intelligence structure functioning. GC&CS turned its eavesdropping to Soviet installations and to any embassies, companies, and individuals deemed worthy of SURVEILLANCE—collaborating closely with the United States in codebreaking efforts under the BRUSA AGREEMENT. MI6, in concert with the COUSINS—the U.S. CIA—successfully ran Col. OLEG PENKOVSKY of the GRU, probably the most important source of Soviet military intelligence that the West had in the 1960s.

In addition, British pilots flew U.S. spyplanes that performed OVERHEAD reconnaissance of the Soviet Union. Indeed, the first intentional overflight of the Soviet heartland came in 1952 when—at the request of the CIA—a British CANBERRA photo plane overflew a Soviet missile test facility. At least one more Canberra overflight followed, with Royal Air Force pilots also flying over Soviet territory in reconnaissance variants of the B-45 TORNADO and the U-2 spyplane.

POST-COLD WAR

After Wright succeeded in getting *Spycatcher* published in 1987, Parliament tightened the Official Secrets Act to permit former intelligence officers to be prosecuted for revealing past operations. Yet secrecy was giving way as the Cold War ended. For the first time, the directors of intelligence agencies were publicly named, and MI5 was openly described in a brochure. The existence of the joint Intelligence Committee was acknowledged and an official booklet, *Central Intelligence Machinery*, was published, describing for the first time how intelligence services work.

STELLA RIMINGTON, named head of MI5 in Dec. 1991, became the first woman to head a British intelligence agency and the first to be publicly named. She was appointed as an increasing number of women were being recruited into MI5. By 1991 an estimated 40 percent of MI5's operatives were women and the percentage was growing. Women now working in the field, especially in Northern Ireland, include officers from both MI5 and the SPECIAL BRANCH of Scotland Yard, which works closely with MI5. Rimington was succeeded in 2002 by another woman with extensive operational experience, ELIZA MANNINGHAM-BULLER.

Like other Western intelligence communities, Britain's intelligence services have taken up counterterrorism and halting narcotics as key missions. In 1992 MI5 was assigned to lead the fight against members of the Irish Republican Army (IRA) and the Irish Nationalist Liberation Army (INLA). MI5 estimated, in an unusual display of openness, that by the mid-1990s anti-terrorism efforts were consuming about 70 percent of its resources.

The openness startled longtime observers. "Secrecy is as essential to intelligence as vestments to a Mass, or darkness to a spiritualist seance, and must at all costs be maintained, quite irrespective of whether or not it serves any purpose," according to author MALCOLM MUGGERIDGE, a former intelligence officer who has talked and written extensively about his old craft.

Engulf

Series of British operations in the 1950s and 1960s to break into Egyptian and French CIPHER communications by detecting the noises made by the setting of cipher machines (especially derivations of those developed by BORIS HAGELIN).

The British were able to BUG the cipher room of the Egyptian Embassy in London in 1956, as tensions rose between Britain and Egypt, culminating in the 1956 Suez campaign. Officers of the British Security Service (MI5) were able to enter the cipher room after the Post Office induced problems with the embassy's telephones and the officers entered under the COVER of telephone repair workers to plant the bugs.

According to former MI5 officer PETER WRIGHT, in his book *Spycatcher* (1987),

The single most important intelligence which we derived from the cipher break was a continuous account of Egyptian/Soviet discussions in Moscow, details of which were relayed into the Egyptian Embassy in London direct from the Egyptian Ambassador in Moscow. The information from this channel convinced the Joint Intelligence Committee (JIC) that the Soviet Union were indeed serious in their threat to become involved in the Suez Crisis on the Egyptian side.

Another cable, Wright contends, prompted Prime Minister Anthony Eden to agree to an early cease-fire at Suez, while the sharing of this intelligence with the United States under the BRUSA AGREEMENT probably made an important contribution to shaping U.S. policies toward Britain, France, and Israel over the Suez War.

Significantly, according to Wright, the Soviets sent a team of SWEEPERS to the Egyptian Embassy as a goodwill gesture to search for bugs and microphones. The Soviets discovered the telephone bug planted by MI5 but neither removed it nor warned the Egyptians, apparently because the Soviet government wanted the British to know precisely their position on Middle East issues.

The British also bugged the French Embassy as part of Engulf; that operation was given the CODE NAME of STOCKADE.

In still another variation of Engulf, when the Soviet cruiser *Ordzhonikidze* visited Stockholm, Sweden, in 1959, the British attempted to detect cipher noises from the warship. While the warship was moored at a pier, the British hid microphones in a warehouse opposite the ship's communications spaces. Although the microphones were able to detect what were believed to be cipher machine noises, they did not lead to any deciphering success.

Enigma

Electrical CIPHER machine used by the German armed forces and government ministries during World War II. The Allies were able to break into many of the Enigma ciphers during the war through an effort generally known as ULTRA. The ability to read German, Japanese, and Italian military and diplomatic CIPHERS helped to achieve many Allied successes, especially in the Battle of the Atlantic, the lengthy battle by Anglo-American forces against German U-boats (1939–1945).

Enigma was an electrical-mechanical enciphering machine about the size of a portable typewriter with a standard typewriter-style keyboard and a series of separate letters that could be internally illuminated. Enigma machines were simple to operate and suitable for field, truck, and shipboard use, being battery-powered and portable. After setting the machine (see below), the operator simply typed out the message in PLAIN TEXT. This action would illuminate the enciphered letters, allowing another operator to write down the enciphered message for radio transmission; the process was reversed for incoming messages.

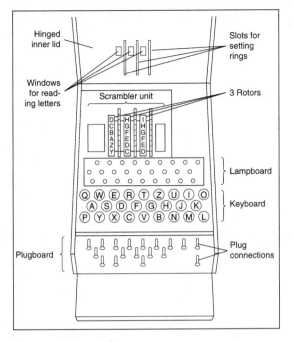

Hinged inner lid

Windows for reading letters

Scrambler unit

Plugboard

Slots for setting rings

3 Rotors

Lampboard

Keyboard

Plug connections

Three-rotor Enigma machine.

Enigma could provide electromechanical enciphering through nonrepeating ciphers by using three to five interchangeable wheels, or ROTORS, and several plugboard connectors. With three rotors it would take 17,000 permutations before a plain-text letter would have the same enciphered letter; with a five-rotor Enigma six sextillion (6,000,000,000,000,000,000,000) permutations were possible for each letter of the alphabet. The rotor settings could be rapidly changed—up to several times per day—to complicate codebreaking efforts even further. Enigma's principal disadvantage was that it did not print out messages and hence required two or more persons to operate efficiently. Also, it was not "on line," meaning that it was not directly connected to a radio or teletype.

The Enigma machine was invented by the German engineer ARTHUR SCHERBUIS for use by commercial firms to keep business secrets in their communications. Its formal name was the "Glow-lamp Ciphering and Deciphering Machine Enigma." The machine was first exhibited in 1923. Enigma, the manufacturer's name for the machine, was reportedly based on the intricate "Enigma Variations" by British composer Sir Edward Elgar.

The U.S. Army purchased an Enigma machine for evaluation in 1928—paying $144 plus $12.30 for packing and shipping—and the British Foreign Office acquired one at about the same time. But neither country put the machine into service.

The first military use of Enigma machines was by the Swedish Army and the German Navy, both of which initially acquired the Enigma machine in 1926, followed by

the German Army in 1928 and the German Air Force in 1935. By 1939 there were more than 20,000 Enigma machines of different models in use by German military, diplomatic, and police services. The Japanese Navy and diplomatic service began using an Enigma in 1934, although the Japanese would primarily use the Alphabetical Typewriter 97 and its variants through World War II (see PURPLE). By the early 1930s the commercial Enigma machines were withdrawn from the open market.

BREAKING ENIGMA

German officials believed that the Enigma machines were immune to enemy CRYPTANALYSIS efforts, even if one were captured. The settings for the rotors—the Enigma keys—were changed regularly (once a day after World War II began), preventing the use of captured machines and rotors. But during World War II Allied codebreakers were able to penetrate most of the Enigma-generated ciphers, which had major influences on many of the battles and campaigns.

As early as the end of 1932 the Polish BIURO SZFROW was able to break into German Enigma ciphers. This was done with the help of French codebreakers. The French provided documents obtained by HANS-THILO SCHMIDT, a French AGENT with the CODE NAME Asché, who had access to German Enigma secrets. The Poles completed the first deciphering of an entire German radio message in the last week of Dec. 1932. They made steady progress in reading secret German communications, and by 1938 were reading German Army and Air Force radio traffic enciphered with Enigma almost daily.

This success ended in Sept. 1938, when the Germans changed the operating procedures for their Enigma machines. Although the keys had always been changed periodically, previously message after message had been sent with the rotors in the same position. Now the rotor settings were changed each day. (By the end of World War II the rotor settings would be changed three times per day; however, the plugboard settings would not be changed, reflecting German confidence in the security of Enigma.)

The Poles asked the French and British for assistance, sharing reconstructed Enigma machines with them. When German forces invaded Poland in Sept. 1939, several Polish codebreakers fled to France (and, eventually, some to Britain). Subsequently, the British took the lead in breaking into Enigma ciphers.

Initially the Enigma machines used only three rotors. Then, on Feb. 1, 1942, the German Navy introduced the M4 variant with four rotors into the U-boat force. This was one of the most significant events in German cryptology in World War II, making the codebreakers' efforts considerably more difficult; this machine, code-named SHARK by the British, was not broken on a regular basis until Dec. 1942. Eventually the German Navy employed Enigmas with up to five rotors, whereas the other services used a maximum of four rotors.

The British codebreaking effort was aided by the capture of CRYPTOMATERIAL from German weather ships

sages, plus some hundreds of GESTAPO and diplomatic service communications.

The British provided Soviet dictator Josef Stalin with information derived from Enigma cryptanalysis, but without revealing its source. However, JOHN CAIRNCROSS and other Soviet MOLES revealed the British successes against Enigma by the spring of 1941, while the Soviets were able to capture Enigma machines from the Germans by late 1941.

Soviet records reveal that it was during their offensive at Klin, some 50 miles northwest of Moscow, in early Dec. 1941, that they captured their first German Enigma machine. The device was taken to Moscow—and temporarily stolen off the back of a truck when the two soldiers assigned to deliver it stopped, briefly, to visit one of their parents. Children carried it off, believing it to be a typewriter, and sold it to a local dealer for scrap! When it was recovered, the device was turned over to the Soviet security service (NKVD).

According to intelligence historian DAVID KAHN in *The Codebreakers* (1967), the Soviets were able to read Enigma messages by 1942. By mid-1943 the Soviets are known to have also captured a naval Enigma machine, and they were reading some German Air Force ciphers. Upon learning this, the British provided the Soviets with another captured Enigma machine and an instruction book but did not provide help in solving the ever-changing Enigma settings. Subsequently, the Soviets captured numerous Enigma machines and code documents as the German forces fell back, losing hundreds of thousands of troops and their equipment.

Because of the rapid cipher changes possible with the Enigma, simply having the machines was not enough to break the code. However, the availability of the machines, previous settings, *and* German communications personnel as prisoners of war undoubtedly enabled Soviet cryptologists to break into Enigma during the later part of the war.

The Germans used the Enigma throughout the war, although the Army employed the FISH at higher command levels and a new Navy cipher machine, the TUNNY, was being introduced. The Enigma's longevity in German service—almost two decades—was based on its simplicity, portability, wide use, and presumed security, as well as on the problems of introducing a new machine and training user personnel in wartime. Further, the Germans had no direct evidence at any time that the Allies had broken into Enigma; although there were some suspicions, as David Kahn notes, "There was no smoking gun."

From 1926 through the end of World War II in the spring of 1945, as many as 100,000 Enigma machines were delivered to German services and agencies, according to some reports. A lesser but still impressive number was more probable.

German soldiers appear to be having problems with their Enigma machine in a command vehicle during the 1940 campaign in France. Gen. Heinz Guderian, standing in the vehicle, had a key role in the development of German mechanized forces. (IMPERIAL WAR MUSEUM)

and submarines. Like the Poles, who shared their Enigma knowledge with the French and British, the British codebreakers at BLETCHLEY PARK shared theirs with the Americans prior to U.S. entry into the war on Dec. 7, 1941. This led to the unprecedented collaboration between U.S. and British codebreakers during the war (see BRUSA AGREEMENT).

The wide use of Enigma gave the British codebreakers vast volumes of enciphered intercepts to break into. Their success was extraordinary: In early 1942 the codebreakers at Bletchley Park deciphered an average of 25,000 German Army and Air Force and 14,000 Navy messages per month. From the fall of 1943 until the end of the war in Europe, the monthly average was 48,000 Army and Air Force messages and 36,000 Navy mes-

ENIGMA KEYS

Different Enigma keys (rotor settings) were used not only by all of the German military services (including the SS) but also by the Gestapo, the ABWEHR, the diplomatic ser-

Enigma advertisement.

vice, and even the Todt construction organization, as well as by major commands within those services and agencies.

For security reasons there would be periodic changes in keys (beyond the daily rotor settings), and as the war progressed, widely used keys were broken into smaller groups to reduce the number of enciphered messages in each key, thus reducing the potential CRIBS for Allied codebreakers.

Scores of Enigma keys were broken by British codebreakers at Bletchley Park. Some keys were broken for specific periods and then "lost" when the Germans made changes in rotor settings; however, most were broken again through cribs or simply "brute force" cryptanalysis—putting more BOMBES and people to work on the key.

A few keys were broken by being captured by Allied armies, such as Armadillo (Air Force key broken in April 1944) and Swan (German First Army in Aug. 1944). Several keys were broken as soon as they appeared, such as Gadfly (Air Force Fliegerkorps X in Jan. 1942) and Hornet (Air Force Fliegerkorps IV, also in Jan. 1942). A few keys were never broken, such as Puce (Air Force Luftflotte 4 in the Soviet Union) and TGD (Gestapo key named after its BERLIN call sign).

REVEALING ENIGMA

Remarkably, secrecy about breaking Enigma was largely maintained from the early 1930s until the early 1970s. Many thousands of persons had access to the Enigma/

Ultra secrets during the war, and some of them were captured by the Germans (see Brig. Gen. ARTHUR W. VANAMAN). Indeed, most members of the Polish codebreaking staff were captured by the Germans in Sept. 1939, as were French codebreakers in May 1940. Yet none of them betrayed the secrets of their success, even though doing so could have brought direct benefits—possibly including survival—to themselves and their families.

According to Kahn, 30,000 men and women knew of the British and U.S. successes in breaking Enigma. They included codebreakers and communications specialists at Bletchley Park, ARLINGTON HALL, and the U.S. Navy's facility at Massachusetts and Nebraska avenues in Washington, D.C.; several hundred high-ranking recipients in London and Washington as well as in the field; and several thousand officers and enlisted men in the SPECIAL LIAISON UNITS (SLUs) that handled transmission of the information for field commanders.

Not one of these men or women is known to have broken faith with Enigma/Ultra until the first public revelation in a garbled story told by Michel Garder in *La Guerre Secrèe des Services Spéciaux Français, 1935–45* (1967). The book did not use the term Enigma. But it led French Brig. Gen. GUSTAVE BERTRAND, one-time head of French cryptanalysis activities, to write an account of the Enigma effort, *Enigma ou la plus Grande Énigme de la Guerre 1939–1945* (1973). This book created considerable controversy and led to counterclaims within intelligence circles, although it gained little public attention.

The next book on the subject—and one that made

worldwide headlines—was *The Ultra Secret* (1974) by RAF Group Capt. F. W. WINTERBOTHAM, a British intelligence officer who had set up the Allied distribution system for Ultra (i.e., SLUs). More details—as well as counterclaims to Winterbotham's story—appeared two years later when Col. Paul Paillole, former chief of French COUNTERESPIONAGE, took issue with the British contention that the secrets of the Enigma were first revealed by a Pole who had worked at the Enigma factory. Paillole's claims were published as "Now the French claim their Spy found the Code" in the *Sunday Times* on June 27, 1976.

A flood of articles and books followed Winterbotham's revelations. Among the more important works subsequently published in this field are *The Enigma War* (1979) by Józef Garliński, a Kiev-born Pole; the official, four-volume *British Intelligence in the Second World War* (1979–1990), edited by F. H. HINSLEY, et al.; and, especially, Ronald Lewin's *Ultra Goes to War* (1978). David Kahn's *Seizing Enigma* (1991) provides a valuable look at the race to break the German U-boat Enigma ciphers—mostly by seizing Enigma machines and material from German weather ships and submarines. Edward Drea's *MacArthur's ULTRA* (1992) and Ronald H. Spector's *Eagle Against the Sun* (1985) provide excellent accounts of the value of Ultra to U.S. military operations in the Pacific.

Thousands of Americans had knowledge of Ultra and MAGIC during the war. The latter originally referred to the reading of Japanese diplomatic codes, but the efforts were largely merged during the war. (There was a major U.S. security leak during the war when journalist STANLEY JOHNSTON revealed in an article in the *Chicago Tribune* that the United States was reading Japanese communications on the eve of the Battle of Coral Sea in May 1942; several other revelations were made after the war, in part because of the extensive investigations and congressional hearings into the PEARL HARBOR ATTACK.)

Also see NAVY COMMUNICATIONS INTELLIGENCE, SIGNAL INTELLIGENCE SERVICE.

Enterprise, The

SEE IRAN-CONTRA AFFAIR

Epsilon

British operation to eavesdrop on German scientists interned in Britain during World War II.

ESM

SEE ELECTRONIC SURVEILLANCE MEASURES

Espionage Act

U.S. law passed in June 1917 because of fears of German spies and saboteurs. It resulted in thousands of arrests and convictions, but not one was for active spying; most were for dissent.

The first person to be charged for espionage under the law was Daniel Ellsberg, who leaked the PENTAGON PAPERS to the press and Congress in 1971. However, efforts by President Nixon's staff to build a case against Ellsberg—including breaking into his psychiatrist's office—led to the charges being dismissed before he was brought to trial.

The second American to be charged under the espionage act was SAMUEL L. MORISON.

Accused spies are usually tried under Title 18, Part I, Chapter 37 of the U.S. Code. That chapter's section 794 calls for punishment up to, and including, the death penalty for "gathering or delivering defense information to aid foreign government" with "intent or reason to believe that it is to be used to the injury of the United States or to the advantage of a foreign nation." Other related statutes cover "protected communications," codes, and diplomatic correspondence. There are also prohibitions against gathering, transmitting, or losing defense information, photographing or sketching defense installations, and disclosing classified information.

Depending upon the decision of the Department of Justice and the severity of the alleged offense, members of the armed services may be tried under the espionage article of the Uniform Code of Military Justice.

Essential Elements of Information

(EEI)

Critical items of information regarding the enemy and the environment needed by a military commander at a particular time to integrate with other available information and intelligence to assist him in reaching decisions.

The nature and number of EEIs will vary with the type and phase of an operation. For example, in the preparation of plans for a parachute assault, EEIs could include (1) the geography of the drop zone, including obstructions; (2) enemy air defenses in the area; and (3) ground forces that could counter the parachutists. After the plans are developed, when the commander is deciding whether or not to execute the assault, only the last item—ground forces that could counter the parachutists—may be an EEI, the other factors having already been determined and provided for.

Also see INTELLIGENCE PREPARATION OF THE BATTLE-FIELD.

Established Source

A standard or accepted source of intelligence, the validity of whose material does not have to be checked.

EW

SEE ELECTRONIC WARFARE

Ewing, Sir Alfred (James)

(b. 1855 d. 1935)

British scientist who established modern British code-breaking activities. When World War I began in Aug. 1914 the DIRECTOR OF NAVAL INTELLIGENCE, Rear Adm. Henry F. Oliver, asked Ewing, the Director of Naval Education, to see if he could exploit German radio signals that were being intercepted.

In *The Codebreakers* (1968), DAVID KAHN writes that when Ewing began to develop the Royal Navy's codebreaking effort, he

> was then 59, a short, thickset Scot with blue eyes beneath shaggy eyebrows, a quiet voice, and the manner of a benign physician. He had been knighted three years before for his contributions to science, which included pioneering studies of Japanese earthquakes, of magnetism, and of mechanical lagging effects in stressed materials (now known by a word he coined, "hysteresis"), and for his public services, notably his naval education directorship.

Ewing, who had been head of naval education since 1903, grabbed at the opportunity to establish a codebreaking office and immediately began researching CODES at the library of the British Museum, Lloyd's of London, and the General Post Office (where commercial code books were on file). He simultaneously assembled a staff to attack the German codes. His first recruits were faculty members, particularly German instructors, at the Royal Naval Colleges of Darmouth and Osborne, who were on their summer leave at the time. Among them was ALASTAIR DENNISTON, a German teacher at Osborne. (Later, Ewing recruited professors from Cambridge, seeking mostly classicists and linguists.)

Soon the group became known as ROOM 40 and enjoyed great success against German codes. (After World War I the codebreaking effort became known as the GOVERNMENT CODE AND CYPHER SCHOOL.) Ewing headed Room 40 from its founding in 1914 until 1917, when he left the Navy to serve as principal and vice chancellor of the University of Edinburgh.

Executive Action

Euphemism for assassination, usually sanctioned or, if not approved, at least not prevented or censured by an intelligence agency. The term appeared in documents of the CIA obtained by the CHURCH COMMITTEE, which investigated the CIA in 1975.

Also called an executive operation.

Exfiltrate

To get an AGENT or other individual out of a country or area by clandestine means.

Exploitation

Process of obtaining information from any source.

Eyes Only

Security restriction for documents indicating that they may only be read and should not be discussed orally except under certain, highly restrictive conditions.

Ezhov, Commissar-Gen. of State Security Nikolai Ivanovich

(b. 1895 d. 1940)

Head of Soviet State Security (NKVD) in 1935–1938 and briefly also the chief of Soviet MILITARY INTELLIGENCE (GRU) in 1938. The major purges of the Stalin regime began under his direction.

He was "a petty official who only joined the Bolsheviks when it became clear that they had won," in the words of VIKTOR SUVOROV in *Inside Soviet Military Intelligence* (1984). Ezhov—called the "blood-thirsty dwarf" by his enemies and some colleagues—was about five feet tall. He held minor, provincial party posts until 1927, when he was brought to Moscow and assigned to Josef Stalin's personal secretariat. He rose rapidly through the government ranks and in 1935 became the Communist Party secretary for secret police NKVD work. The following year, on Sept. 26, 1936, he was appointed Commissar for Internal Affairs (NKVD) and Commissar-General for State Security.

Under Ezhov's leadership Stalin's "great purge" began in 1937. It started as a purge of NKVD personnel and was then extended to the Army and other institutions, including the Communist Party itself. Tens of thousands of government and Party officials and workers were arrested and executed or imprisoned. Ezhov is said to have personally shot several victims. With the purge of Soviet General Staff and GRU officials in 1938, he took control of the GRU, probably in July of that year. Because he retained his state security posts, Ezhov established a monopoly of secret activities and intelligence work in the Soviet Union.

That was too much power in the hands of one man for Stalin to tolerate. In Dec. 1938 Ezhov was removed from all posts except that of Commissar of Water Transport. He was arrested, apparently in Jan. 1939, and later executed, although details of his fate are lacking. According to some reports, he was shot in April 1940; others say that he was castrated and buried alive at the NKVD sanatorium at Sukhanovo near Moscow, possibly on June 4, 1940. IVAN SEROV—a future chairman of the KGB as well as chief of the GRU—is said to have had a direct role in Ezhov's execution.

Ezhov's name was also commonly transliterated as Yezhov.

1st Weather Reconnaissance Squadron

(PROVISIONAL)

The first U.S. unit established to operate U-2 spyplanes. The U.S. Air Force squadron was formed at Groom Lake, Nev., in April 1956. The U-2 pilots were flying under contract to the CIA, on leave from the U.S. Air Force. The squadron had an Air Force commanding officer and CIA executive officer.

The squadron was moved to the Royal Air Force base at Lakenheath, northeast of London, in July 1956, and in September 1956 to the U.S. air base at Wiesbaden, West Germany. The first U-2 overflights of the Soviet Union took place from Wiesbaden, but because of probable Soviet knowledge of the Wiesbaden operations, the squadron moved to a more remote West German base at Giebelstadt.

The squadron was disbanded in Nov. 1957, and U-2 operations were then undertaken by the newly established 2nd and 3rd Weather Reconnaissance Squadrons (Provisional), flying from Adana, Turkey, and Atsugi, Japan, respectively. U-2 operations continued out of West German bases as well as from Lahore and Peshawar, Pakistan; Bahrain; Britain; Bodö, Norway; Okinawa; Taiwan; the Philippines; and the Charbatia air base near Cuttack, India.

The 1st and subsequently 2nd squadrons were also known as Detachment 10/10.

14 Intelligence Company

Elite British Army SURVEILLANCE unit set up in Northern Ireland in about 1973 to provide better intelligence in the Army's search for terrorists. It was originally named the RF, for Reconnaissance Force, and operated under a series of COVER names.

Both the Secret Intelligence Service (MI6) and the Security Service (MI5) were operating in Northern Ireland when British troops were sent in to deal with rising violence between Protestants and Catholics there in 1969. But the Army found an increasing need for its own intelligence. It tried several approaches, from standard methods of gathering TACTICAL INTELLIGENCE to the creation of 14 Intelligence Company for the highly specialized mission of providing intensive, "on-the-ground" surveillance.

According to Mark Urban in *Big Boys' Rules* (1992),

> Most missions carried out by 14 Intelligence Company involved either setting up static observation posts (Ops) or watching people from unmarked cars (Q cars). A OP in an urban area might be a derelict house or, in the countryside, a roadside ditch. Q cars were fitted with 'covert radios', invisible to the casual observer.

In 1987 the intelligence unit was placed under the same Army administrative control as Britain's anti-terrorist organizations, the Special Air Service (SAS), the Special Boat Service (SBS), and the Royal Marine Special Forces. At times, 14 Intelligence Company used the SAS as a cover to prevent the IRA from knowing that there was a highly trained Army unit dedicated to surveillance.

The work was highly dangerous. Soldiers of 14 Intelligence Company were often in close contact with the SAS, which was especially targeted by the IRA. The SAS and 14 Intelligence Company killed 20 IRA men between 1983 and 1987. IRA gunmen killed four members of the unit between 1974 and 1984, the height of the IRA war against British troops.

The unit was also referred to as 14 Intelligence and Security Company.

5412 Committee

Panel of advisers established in 1955 by the U.S. NATIONAL SECURITY COUNCIL to provide White House–level approval of important or sensitive covert operations. On the committee were ALLEN W. DULLES, the DIRECTOR OF CENTRAL INTELLIGENCE, and representatives of President Eisenhower, the Department of State, and the Department of Defense.

Eisenhower's 5412 Committee, later named the Special Group, was particularly charged with examining any covert operations that could cause political damage to the Eisenhower administration. (The Dulles doctrine of PLAUSIBLE DENIAL was designed to ease such damage.)

After the exposure of the BERLIN TUNNEL in 1956, Eisenhower also wanted direct knowledge of any COVERT ACTION that infringed on another nation's sovereignty.

Dulles decided that the U-2 spyplane was too sensitive and secret to be brought before the 5412 Committee. Thus, as Michael R. Beschloss observed in *Mayday: Eisenhower, Khrushchev and the U-2 Affair* (1986), Eisenhower "took a role essentially as U-2 project manager, making critical choices on when and sometimes where the planes should fly." When a U-2, piloted by FRANCIS GARY POWERS, was shot down over the Soviet Union on May 1, 1960, the weight of the damage fell on Dulles and the CIA, not the 5412 Committee.

F-101 Voodoo

U.S. Air Force fighter aircraft, modified in the RF-101 configuration for low-level photo-RECONNAISSANCE. The RF-101 and the Navy's F8U CRUSADER were the source of low-level photography during the CUBAN MISSILE CRISIS of 1962, providing detailed intelligence of the Soviet military buildup on the island. The RF-101 also was the principal Air Force tactical reconnaissance aircraft in the Vietnam War from 1961 to 1965.

The F-101 was designed by McDonnell Aircraft to serve as a long-range "penetration" fighter to escort B-36 PEACEMAKER strategic bombers attacking the Soviet Union. But before the first F-101 took off, the Air Force canceled the bomber escort requirement. The fighter was then produced for tactical fighter, air defense, and strike roles. The RF-101 photo-reconnaissance variant was produced in large numbers (with 10 RF-101C photo aircraft being transferred to Taiwan).

The F-101 was developed from two XF-88 prototypes. A relatively large, single-seat aircraft with swept-back wings, it was powered by two turbojet engines, giving the aircraft a speed of just over 1,000 mph at about 35,000 feet. Most fighter variants had four 20-mm cannon and could carry air-to-air missiles under the wings and in an internal weapons bay. The F-101C could carry a nuclear bomb on a centerline pylon, whereas some aircraft could carry air-to-air rockets with nuclear warheads

The RF-101 photo aircraft had four cameras installed in an elongated nose and two more cameras fitted in the weapons bay. No guns were fitted. The planes could carry out night photo missions using flares. At the time of the Cuban missile crisis the F-101 was fitted with KA-1 and KA-2 cameras, which were found unsuitable for high-speed, low-level photography. Only after KA-45 cameras produced for the Navy by Chicago Aero Industries were installed could the F-101s undertake the Cuban photo missions, beginning on Oct. 26 (three days after the first Navy photo missions).

The first F-101 flew in 1954, and squadron deliveries began in 1957; the first reconnaissance variant, a YRF-101A, flew in 1956. A total of 604 F-101 aircraft and 203 RF-101 aircraft were produced. Subsequently, 84 F-101 fighters were converted to RF-101s for Air National Guard use.

The last F-101s were retired from active Air Force service in 1971; the Air National Guard flew the planes until 1983.

F4H Phantom (F-4)

The principal all-weather, multi-purpose fighter flown by the U.S. Air Force, Navy, and Marine Corps in the 1960s and 1970s, as well as by 11 other air forces and the Royal Navy. The specialized RF-4 photo-RECONNAISSANCE variant was flown in greater numbers than any other Western reconnaissance aircraft of the Cold War.

Developed from the outset as a carrier-based aircraft, the Phantom has served in the fighter-interceptor, fighter-escort, and attack roles as well as in the anti-radar (Wild Weasel) and reconnaissance roles. U.S. Air Force variants could carry nuclear weapons. From 1958 to 1979, McDonnell Douglas produced 5,045 aircraft for U.S. and foreign service, and Japan built 127 F-4EJ variants. Of those, 701 were photo-reconnaissance variants, being flown by the U.S. Air Force and Marine Corps, and the air forces of West Germany, Greece, Iran, Israel, Japan, and Turkey.

The Phantom is a large, twin-engine, swept-wing fighter with a large nose radar housing. There is tandem seating for the two crew-members under a single canopy. Up to 16,000 pounds of missiles, rockets, bombs, and fuel tanks could be carried on six wing pylons and three fuselage attachment points by the "straight" fighter-attack aircraft. (By contrast, the B-17 "heavy bomber" of World War II could carry only 8,000 pounds of bombs, albeit with greater range.) Top speed for the RF-4C model in a "clean" condition was 1,485 mph at altitude (Mach 2.25).

The elongated photo-reconnaissance variants have three cameras fitted plus electronic, radar, and infrared sensors. The Air Force RF-4 models could also carry nuclear weapons.

The Phantom was flown extensively in combat by the U.S. services in the Vietnam War and by the Israeli Air Force in several Middle East wars. All five U.S. fighter aces of the Vietnam War—one Navy pilot and one Air Force pilot, and one Navy and two Air Force "backseaters"—scored their kills of MiG-type aircraft in Phantoms; of the 57 aerial kills by U.S. aircraft in that conflict, 36, plus several probables, were made by Phantoms.

Most of the 665 U.S. Air Force RF-4C and RF-4E aircraft were used for tactical reconnaissance in the Vietnam War, as were the 46 Marine RF-4B aircraft. U.S. Air Force F-4G Wild Weasel aircraft were used in the 1991 war in the Persian Gulf.

The first flight of the XF4H-1 Phantom occurred in May 1958; the aircraft entered Navy service in July 1961, and the Air Force began using it in July 1963. In 1996, the last U.S. Phantoms were retired, those being F-4G Wild Weasel aircraft flown by the Air Force and RF-4C and F-4G aircraft flown by the Air National Guard. However, several other air forces continue to fly the aircraft.

Originally designated F4H by the U.S. Navy and F-110 by the U.S. Air Force, all American variants were changed to F-4 in 1962.

F8U Crusader (F-8)

U.S. Navy carrier-based fighter that, in the F8U-1P photo-RECONNAISSANCE variant, provided vital low-level photography of targets in Vietnam and Cuba. (See CUBAN MISSILE CRISIS.) F8Us were flown by both Navy and Marine units in the fighter and reconnaissance roles.

Six Navy F8U-1P aircraft, flying from Key West, Fla., undertook the first U.S. low-level overflights of Cuba on Oct. 23, 1962. Those flights were made at speeds of 400 mph at altitudes of about 400 feet. After landing at Cecil Field near Jacksonville, Fla., the planes' exposed film was quickly removed and rushed into the adjacent Navy photo laboratory. The flight leader, Comdr. William B. Ecker, commander of photo squadron VFP-62, was told to take off immediately and fly to Andrews Air Force Base near Washington, D.C. Upon reaching Andrews he was whisked by helicopter to the Pentagon, still wearing his flight suit but relieved of his revolver. There he was ushered into the Joint Chiefs of Staff to give the military leaders firsthand impressions of the flight.

When Ecker apologized for being "sweaty and smelly," the outspoken Gen. Curtis E. LeMay, the Air Force chief of staff, interrupted, "God damn it, you've been flying an airplane, now, haven't you? You ought to sweat and smell. Sit down!"

Fighter variants of the F8U saw extensive combat in the Vietnam War, Navy aircraft flying from carriers and Marine aircraft flying from land bases. Both services flew the F8U-1P photo variant, fitted with five cameras under the forward fuselage. No guns were installed in the photo aircraft.

In 1964 F8Us were among the first U.S. combat aircraft to fly in the Vietnam conflict. Photo Crusaders were used to get photographic coverage of the area, especially Laos. In May 1964 a photo plane from the carrier *Kitty Hawk* piloted by Lt. Charles F. Klusmann was hit by antiaircraft fire over Laos. Although his plane burned for 20 minutes, he made it back to the carrier. But two weeks later, on June 6, while flying another photo mission Klusmann's plane was again hit. This time the damage was severe and he had to parachute near communist positions. He was captured—apparently the first American flier to be taken in the Vietnam conflict. After three months in captivity he escaped, along with several Laotian prisoners. Hiding for two days in the jungle, he was then able to reach a government camp and was eventually rescued by U.S. forces.

Built by Chance Vought, the F8U had a swept wing that angled upward to reduce the aircraft's landing speed. The single-seat aircraft had a single turbojet engine. The fighter variants had four 20-mm cannon and could carry air-to-air missiles or 5,000 pounds of bombs under the wings. The Crusader was the first U.S. aircraft to achieve a speed of more than 1,000 mph in level flight to enter series production. Marine Maj. John Glenn, later an astronaut and U.S. senator, flew an F8U-1P in a record-breaking flight across the United States on July 16, 1957: 3 hours, 23 minutes at an average speed of 723.5 mph.

In total, 1,075 F8U fighters plus 144 F8U-lP photo planes were produced. Another 42 F8U fighters were built for French carrier service.

The prototype, XF8U-1 took off for the first time in 1952; the first specialized F8U-lP flew in 1957. Squadrons began receiving F8U fighters in 1957 and the planes were in active naval service until 1982; the last U.S. Navy unit flying the Crusader was Naval Air Reserve squadron VFP-206, which stood down its Photo Crusaders in 1986. (The French Navy still operated the Crusader from its aircraft carriers until 1999.)

In the 1962 redesignation of U.S. military aircraft the Crusader became the F-8 and the photo variants RF-8.

Fabian, Capt. Rudolph J.

(b. 1908 d. 1984)

U.S. Navy cryptologist who commanded the BELL codebreaking station in Australia during World War II.

A 1931 graduate of the Naval Academy, Fabian was a lieutenant in charge of CAST station on the island of Corregidor in the Philippines when the Japanese struck U.S. bases on Dec. 7, 1941 (see PEARL HARBOR ATTACK). When it became obvious that the Japanese would overrun the Philippines, the Commander-in-Chief U.S. Fleet, Adm. E. J. King, personally ordered Fabian and his codebreakers out of the Philippines to avoid capture by the Japanese.

On the night of Feb. 4–5 the SUBMARINE *Seadragon* surfaced in Manila Bay and took aboard 23 torpedoes, two tons of submarine spare parts, and 3,000 pounds of radio equipment, including the Cast station's CIPHER machine for PURPLE. During the day the submarine remained on the bottom of the bay to evade Japanese aircraft and artillery fire. On the night of Feb. 5 the *Seadragon* again surfaced to take on board Fabian, 16 of his sailors, and 8 Army and Navy officers.

The *Seadragon* then put to sea and safely delivered them to Australia. (The *Seadragon* made a second trip to Manila Bay, as did the submarine *Permit*, taking off all 75 members of the Navy codebreaking unit.)

In Melbourne, Fabian established a codebreaking station known as Fleet Radio Unit Melbourne (FRUMEL) or, more commonly, station Bell. The cryptographers were soon joining with their colleagues at Pearl Harbor and in Washington, D.C., in deciphering Japanese naval and diplomatic communications. (See NAVY COMMUNICATIONS INTELLIGENCE.)

Fabian commanded the Bell unit until Jan. 1944, when he left to join the British Eastern Fleet in the Indian Ocean to coordinate U.S. codebreaking activities with the British force. After the war he served in other cryptologic assignments. He retired in 1961 with the rank of captain.

False Flag

Approach by a hostile INTELLIGENCE OFFICER who misrepresents himself or herself as a citizen of a friendly country or organization. The person who is approached may give up sensitive information believing that it is going to an ally, not a hostile power.

When U.S. Navy Chief Warrant Officer JOHN A. WALKER first recruited Senior Chief Radioman JERRY A. WHITWORTH, for example, he told Whitworth that the material was for the reference book *Jane's Fighting Ships*, rather than the Soviet Union.

In another case, an American of Armenian ancestry was approached by an Armenian who claimed to be a distant relative. He claimed to need help in trying to reclaim lost Armenian lands from Turkey. He was actually an AGENT for the KGB who succeeded in getting classified information he would never have gotten if he had not flown a false flag.

Farm, The

SEE CAMP PEARY

Family Jewels

List of illegal activities carried out by the CIA.

The list was compiled at the direction of JAMES R. SCHLESINGER during his short tenure (Feb.–July 1973) as DIRECTOR OF CENTRAL INTELLIGENCE (DCI). Schlesinger, appointed in the wake of the WATERGATE scandal and the resignation of DCI RICHARD HELMS, asked the CIA inspector general for a report on past CIA activities that were probably illegal.

According to Thomas Powers in his authoritative biography of Helms, *The Man Who Kept the Secrets* (1979), the files went first to WILLIAM E. COLBY, Deputy Director for Operations, who was to succeed Schlesinger. The preliminary summary was called "Potential Flap Activities." The CIA's director of security, passing his files to the inspector general for inclusion in the report, jokingly called them "the Family Jewels." That name, according to Scott D. Breckinridge, the former deputy inspector general, "caught on and came to be applied familiarly to the entire collection."

Included were details on Operation CHAOS, the CIA side of the FBI's secret and illicit COINTELPRO DOMESTIC INTELLIGENCE program. Also cited were the CIA's actions in the HUSTON PLAN, a domestic intelligence project concocted by the Nixon White House; contacts with the White House PLUMBERS, including former CIA officer E. HOWARD HUNT; illegal wiretaps and BLACK BAG JOBS; unauthorized mail opening; and CIA plans for assassinations. (See CIA, CUBA.) According to the Powers book, Helms had already destroyed files on the experimental use of hallucinogenic drugs in "brainwashing" experiments (see MKULTRA) and 4,000 to 5,000 pages of his own private files. But some information on the brainwashing was included in the Family Jewels files.

In *The CIA and the U.S. Intelligence System* (1986) Breckinridge gave this description of the Family Jewels assembly of files:

> They were assembled into a set of files, which were divided into activities involving the separate directorates, including a section for specialty sensitive material. . . . Later, when the files were reviewed by the Department of Justice to determine if there were prosecutable offenses, each piece of paper was numbered in sequence. Including routing slips, blank pages, and dividers between sections, the total came to slightly more than 690. The media, upon learning of that number, reported some 690 instances of wrong-doing. As it happened, no prosecutions resulted from these cases.

In June 1973 Colby decided to tell congressional oversight committees about the files, insisting that the revealed "excesses" could never happen again. But the secrets of the Family Jewels began to circulate. In Dec. 1974, *New York Times* reporter Seymour Hersh, having heard about Chaos, asked DCI Colby about it. According to Powers, Colby told Hersh about Chaos and then went on to talk about other activities, including a mail-opening program run by JAMES JESUS ANGLETON, head of CIA COUNTERINTELLIGENCE.

After the *Times* published the Hersh report on domestic intelligence abuses, President Ford got a shorter version of the Family Jewels from Colby. Shocked at the report on assassinations, Ford mentioned it "off the record" at a luncheon with Arthur Ochs Sulzberger, publisher of the *Times*. The newspaper did not publish it, but CBS correspondent Daniel Schorr heard a rumor about assassinations. When he asked Colby, Colby retorted, "Not in this country." Schorr broke the story, saying that the CIA had assassinated several foreign officials. That was not true. As Schorr later reported, "It turned out as Helms said, that no foreign leader was directly killed by the CIA. But it wasn't for want of trying."

Out of these reports came hearings and reports in which virtually all of the Family Jewels were disclosed: *Report to the President by the Commission on CIA Activities Within the United States*, issued in June 1975 (also known as the Rockefeller Commission Report; it was conducted by Vice President Nelson A. Rockefeller) and the *Final Report of the Select Committee to Study Governmental Operations with Respect to Intelligence Activities* (also known as the CHURCH COMMITTEE), issued in 1976.

Farewell

SEE COL. VLADIMIR I. VETROV

Farnsworth, Lt. Comdr. John S.

(b. 1893)

Former U.S. Navy officer who spied for Japan. Farnsworth graduated from the U.S. Naval Academy in 1915 and served in destroyers during World War I. He had an uneventful naval career, attaining the rank of lieutenant commander.

After marrying a society woman, he got heavily in debt, and borrowed money from an enlisted man, which he refused to repay. Farnsworth was subsequently court-martialed and resigned from the Navy in 1927.

Disgruntled and in need of money, he began spying for Japan, which attempted to recruit Americans for espionage in the 1920s and 1930s. He got most of his information from former Navy comrades who were unaware of his spying. He told them he needed the information for "magazine articles." At that time Navy security was relatively lax.

During an investigation into the disappearance of a Navy manual, officers from the OFFICE OF NAVAL INTELLIGENCE (ONI) heard that Farnsworth had been flashing large sums of money. Further investigation revealed that he had borrowed CODE books and signal books and had been asking questions about tactics, new ship designs, and weapons. He was placed under SURVEILLANCE by the ONI and the FBI.

Farnsworth, apparently believing that investigators had built a case against him, told a journalist that he appeared to be a spy but was actually a DOUBLE AGENT. The journalist turned him in and he was arrested. He was convicted in Feb. 1939 of unlawfully disclosing information affecting the national defense to a representative of a foreign nation. He was sentenced to a prison term of four to 12 years.

Faust

OFFICE OF STRATEGIC SERVICES (OSS) operation for the PENETRATION of Nazi Germany during World War II.

The operation, pointedly named after Goethe's knowledge-seeking Dr. Faust, began following the Allied D-DAY landing in Normandy in June 1944. Under the direction of WILLIAM J. CASEY (a future DIRECTOR OF CENTRAL INTELLIGENCE) the OSS dispatched over 200 AGENTS into Nazi Germany.

According to information made public by the CIA in 2002, during the recruitment of agents, an OSS officer made contact with JÜRGEN KUCZYNSKI, a communist, who passed information about the operation to his sister, known as Ruth Weber, a Soviet agent with the CODE NAME Sonia. Her HANDLERS instructed her to get communists into the operation. One of them, Erich Henschke, alias Karl Kastro, hired as an OSS consultant, passed to the Soviets, via Sonia, the cover stories and CODES used by the OSS.

FBI

(FEDERAL BUREAU OF INVESTIGATION)

Principal U.S. COUNTERESPIONAGE agency, which investigates possible violations of U.S. espionage laws by American or AGENTS of foreign intelligence organizations. The FBI also serves as a national police force for crimes that cross state lines. The FBI is part of the U.S. INTELLIGENCE COMMUNITY but not primarily as an intelligence gatherer. Rather, the FBI is mandated by federal authority as the "lead" or foremost agency in the investigation of espionage.

The FBI describes its intelligence activities as counterespionage—the protection of classified material from foreign collection efforts, as opposed to COUNTERINTELLIGENCE, which involves attempts to stop hostile intelligence collection.

There are two major differences between the FBI and the CIA: (1) FBI agents are law enforcement officers who can make arrests; CIA INTELLIGENCE OFFICERS cannot make arrests, and (2) the FBI can conduct operations only within the United States, while the CIA cannot operate within the United States. The geographical ban is strictly enforced for the CIA. But for the FBI the restriction has been stretched to allow FBI agents to work in U.S. embassies as "legal ATTACHÉS," who handle overseas cases stemming from U.S. transnational law enforcement agreements. (U.S. courts have ruled that the FBI can arrest suspects overseas and bring them to the United States for trial.)

Despite the label of "lead agency" for espionage investigation, the FBI does not possess total knowledge of other Intelligence Community counterespionage activities. Further, few of the FBI's 10,000 agents specialize in counterespionage activity due to the FBI policy of rotating agents through various duties and field offices to make them eligible for promotion as fully rounded agents. As the principal investigative arm of the U.S. Department of Justice, the FBI conducts investigations into a wide spectrum of federal crimes. The FBI also provides support for national security, such as conducting BACK-

GROUND INVESTIGATIONS of nominees to sensitive government positions.

The FBI is represented in the Intelligence Community by an assistant director of the FBI National Security Division (formerly the Intelligence Division), which handles espionage, sabotage, and subversive activities—including terrorism—for which the FBI is the lead agency. This assistant director is also the FBI representative on the NATIONAL FOREIGN INTELLIGENCE BOARD and the NATIONAL INTELLIGENCE COUNCIL.

The FBI evolved from a Department of Justice force of "special agents," created in July 1908 by President Theodore Roosevelt's Attorney General, Charles J. Bonaparte. The new investigative service was called the Bureau of Investigation. It later became the U.S. Bureau of Investigation and then the Division of Investigation. The special agents also investigated the relatively few federal white-collar crimes, such as bankruptcy frauds and antitrust violations.

The Bureau of Investigation's first venture into espionage came in World War I when its agents aided military counterespionage efforts (see ARMY INTELLIGENCE, U.S.). Like the military, the bureau used the voluntary services of the American Protective League, whose members reported suspected subversives, and sometimes even conducted their own vigilante investigations.

German sabotage in the United States was effective during the war. Some 50 suspicious explosions damaged or leveled munitions and chemical plants. The most spectacular was the Black Tom explosion on July 30, 1916, when hundreds of tons of munitions exploded on Black Tom Island, raking New York Harbor with shrapnel. The bureau concluded that the explosion was an accident, but postwar investigations established that it had been sabotage.

THE G-MAN ERA

In 1920, with the advent of Prohibition, liquor production and consumption became a federal crime. With Prohibition came gangsters who kidnapped people and robbed banks, and then drove across state lines to make a safe escape. But in 1932 Congress passed a federal kidnapping law, the first of several extending the powers of the Bureau of Investigation.

Also in the early 1920s came the Red Menace, a reaction to the fear of a worldwide Bolshevik conspiracy in the wake of the Russian Revolution. A young Bureau of Investigations (BOI) bureaucrat, J. EDGAR HOOVER, began making a reputation for himself as a zealous pursuer of anarchists, radicals, and Reds for the General Intelligence Division of the BOI. In 1924 he became director of the BOI, and, as the nation's concerns shifted from subversives to crime, he responded by looking for crooks instead of revolutionaries. His agents were called "G-Men," reputedly because when gangster George (Machine Gun) Kelly was being captured in Sept. 1933 he shouted, "Don't shoot, G-men!"

In March 1933 the German ambassador asked the U.S. Secretary of State to investigate an American who had written a letter to the German Embassy threatening to kill Adolf Hitler. This gave the BOI an excuse to begin an investigation into pro-Nazi organizations in the United States.

Under President Franklin D. Roosevelt the bureau was upgraded to the Division of Investigation. Roosevelt supported legislation that gave Hoover more independence, creating what in July 1935 became the Federal Bureau of Investigation. That same year James Cagney starred in *G-Men,* the first of a long line of MOVIES extolling the gang-busting exploits of the FBI.

Although the spotlight usually shone on the FBI's crime fighting, Hoover never ceased his crusade against subversives. Roosevelt recognized this, secretly ordering Hoover to engage in DOMESTIC INTELLIGENCE by gathering information on isolationists, such as aviation hero Charles Lindbergh and the America First Committee. In June 1939 Roosevelt also secretly ordered all federal agencies to report to the FBI any data considered to be "bearing directly or indirectly on espionage, counterespionage, or sabotage."

WORLD WAR II

The FBI thus became the key agency for looking for spies. Unlike the Bureau of Investigation of World War I, the FBI of World War II organized an extremely competent counterintelligence effort. In 1940 the FBI had 898 agents; by 1945 there were 4,886. The phenomenal growth of the FBI during the war was due to a steady increase in federal laws, a wartime surge into intelligence, and Hoover's lobbying of a Congress that had great faith in Hoover and his FBI. Before America's entry into World War II, Hoover warned of a FIFTH COLUMN of traitors, an "enemy within"—people who "hold that the Government of the United States can be overthrown." There never was a fifth column. Nevertheless, Congress saw the FBI as a bulwark against all enemies, and the agency grew in size—and in power.

Congress had prohibited wiretapping in the 1934 Communications Act. But the FBI nevertheless conducted wiretaps under a Justice Department interpretation that the act banned not wiretapping in and of itself but rather the disclosure of information obtained by wiretaps. And in May 1940 Roosevelt issued a secret directive allowing wiretaps of people suspected of subversive activities. As soon as World War II began in Europe in Sept. 1939, Hoover ordered all FBI field offices to prepare reports on people of "German, Italian, and Communist sympathies." Their names were to be put in a Custodial Detention Index so that they could be rounded up if the United States entered the war. Hoover also authorized surreptitious break-ins (dubbed BLACK BAG JOBS by agents). He had no legal authority for either the planned detention or the break-ins.

President Roosevelt, readying the nation for war, asked local police departments to turn over to the FBI any information about espionage or subversive activities.

He ordered the FBI to "act as the coordinating head of all civilian organizations furnishing information relating to subversive movements." Army Intelligence and the OFFICE OF NAVAL INTELLIGENCE were to handle cases involving members of the armed services and civilian employees in the Panama Canal Zone and other locations outside of the United States.

In June 1940 a new FBI unit, the Special Intelligence Service, was established to fight Nazi infiltration and espionage in Latin American nations. This gave the FBI its first mission as an intelligence agency operating outside the United States. Hoover declined to cooperate with WILLIAM STEPHENSON, who had been sent to New York City by the British Secret Intelligence Service (MI6) to set up an intelligence operation under the COVER name of BRITISH SECURITY COORDINATION. Hoover's distaste for foreign intelligence agencies and personal dislike for DUSKO POPOV, a brilliant DOUBLE AGENT working for MI6, spoiled a British plan to have Popov run a bogus U.S. spy ring for the Germans.

The FBI went to war on Dec. 8, 1941, the day after the PEARL HARBOR ATTACK, when FBI agents began rounding up pre-designated enemy aliens. By Dec. 10 the FBI had detained 2,342 Japanese, German, and Italian aliens. (The subsequent mass detention of Japanese-Americans from the U.S. West Coast was handled by the Army.)

Hoover, in his vigil for subversives, chose particularly to watch newspapers published for African-American (then called Negro) readers. Hoover suspected these newspapers of antiwar, communist sympathies because of editorial complaints about segregation in the armed services and discrimination in war industries. Hoover tried to get black newspapers indicted under the ESPIONAGE ACT but Attorney General Francis Biddle blocked the move.

Despite Hoover's dislike of espionage, the FBI adapted its crime-fighting techniques to spy fighting and developed a good record as a wartime hunter of spies and saboteurs. Its first major case began in 1940 when WILLIAM G. SEBOLD, a German-American, told the FBI that the Nazis had threatened to harm his family in Germany if he did not agree to spy on the United States. The FBI instructed him to accept and, by running him as a double agent, cracked the DUQUESNE SPY RING, arresting 33 persons, many of whom had been under SURVEILLANCE for nearly two years. All were found guilty of espionage charges.

The FBI TURNED Grace Buchanan-Dineen, a Canadian who had been recruited by Nazi intelligence officers to be the main contact for spies operating in the Detroit, Mich., area. After wiring her apartment and setting up a hidden movie camera, FBI agents arrested seven people, including a Detroit physician and a professor of German at a university in Detroit. The FBI's well-honed investigative skills also led to the arrest and conviction of VELVALEE DICKINSON, an American doll seller who spied for Japan.

In June 1942 four saboteurs were put ashore by a German U-boat on the Atlantic shore of Long Island, N.Y., and four others near Jacksonville, Fla. They carried high explosives and more than $174,000 in U.S. currency. (Some bills were U.S. gold notes no longer in circulation; there were also bills with Japanese writing on them.) Spotted by a U.S. Coast Guard officer on beach patrol, the Long Island saboteurs were quickly rounded up; the Florida group scattered, but they were tracked down by the FBI in New York and Chicago within 10 days of their landing. They were tried and convicted before a military commission appointed by President Roosevelt. In Aug. 1942 six of them were hanged; two, who aided in the arrest of the others, were imprisoned.

Another U-boat landed American-born WILLIAM C. COLEPAUGH and ERICH GIMPEL at Frenchman Bay, Maine, in 1944. Both had been trained at a German SPY SCHOOL and had been prepared for their mission by NIKOLAUS RITTER, chief of espionage against the United States and Britain for the ABWEHR, the German MILITARY INTELLIGENCE service. Before the two would-be spies went to work, Colepaugh confessed to the FBI, which quickly found Gimpel.

The FBI missed some spies, such as HERMAN LANG, who passed information to the Germans about the secret Norden bombsight, and SIMON E. KOEDEL, a SLEEPER who had been activated in Sept. 1939 and was not caught until Oct. 1944. But neither the Germans nor the Japanese successfully established espionage NETWORKS in the United States during the war.

In Latin America the FBI's Special Intelligence Service was effective primarily because agents teamed up with the secret police agencies of totalitarian governments. At its peak the special unit had 360 agents in Latin America, many of them with diplomatic status as legal attachés. Information they produced led to the arrest of 389 spies, 30 saboteurs, and 281 German propagandists. Since most of the countries preferred to ally themselves with the United States, the local police cooperated with the FBI in curbing Nazi attempts to infiltrate the region.

The FBI's wartime accomplishments in espionage were overshadowed by the success of WILLIAM DONOVAN, who outmaneuvered Hoover by creating an overseas intelligence operation—an intelligence niche that Hoover wanted for the postwar FBI. In July 1941, over the objection of Hoover and the military intelligence agencies, President Roosevelt appointed Donovan COORDINATOR OF INFORMATION, a quasi-intelligence agency. A year later Donovan became the head of the OFFICE OF STRATEGIC SERVICES (OSS), precursor of the CIA.

Ironically, Hoover played an indirect role in launching the intelligence career of JAMES JESUS ANGLETON, future counterintelligence chief of the CIA. Hoover had fired Melvin Purvis, the G-man hero renowned for setting up the ambush of gangster John Dillinger. When the war began, Purvis became an Army INTELLIGENCE OFFICER. Among the recruits Purvis brought into intelligence work was Angleton, who joined the OSS.

HUNTING COMMUNISTS

Hoover fought President Truman's decision to establish a national foreign intelligence agency. But when Truman created the CIA in 1947, Hoover saw that the FBI's future lay in fighting the Cold War through DOMESTIC INTELLIGENCE.

The FBI concentrated its resources on what Hoover viewed as the protection of national security. This view was ratified in 1947 when Truman gave the FBI the responsibility for investigating the loyalty of federal employees and applicants for federal employment. In 1948, the Department of Justice moved against the U.S. Communist Party under the Smith Act, which prohibited the violent overthrow of the government (See CPUSA).

The FBI was given the mission of arresting and developing cases against 145 Communist Party leaders. Many of the 109 convictions came from trials at which FBI informants, planted in the Communist Party, appeared as star government witnesses.

The postwar years ushered in many of the dilemmas that would perplex U.S. counterespionage actions for decades. FBI officials and agents began to learn that conducting CLOAK AND DAGGER operations was more complicated and more frustrating than playing cops and robbers. FBI counterespionage agents discovered that they could not make arrests even after they had built what, for other crimes, would have been a good case.

As the Cold War started, the FBI had two public images: There was the anonymous FBI agent, a coolly efficient supercop, as portrayed by the press, movies, and radio. And there was Hoover himself, the relentless foe of communism, appearing before congressional committees, issuing stern warnings about communism, and working, usually backstage, to further the anti-Red crusade—and the growth of his own agency.

Hoover leaked to congressional committees reports about communists making American movies and writing American books. The FBI had files on writers John Dos Passos, Dashiell Hammett, and Lillian Hellman, among others. FBI files on Hollywood figures included actors Errol Flynn and Clark Gable. Hoover had several Hollywood sources, including Screen Actors Guild president Ronald Reagan, who was a "confidential informant" of the FBI's Los Angeles field office. Thurgood Marshall, a civil rights lawyer who would become a Supreme Court justice, also served as an informant during the 1950s.

While he made headlines, Hoover did not win cases. He secretly authorized the black bag jobs that produced the AMERASIA CASE, but the trials that grew out of the case were spoiled by evidence illegally obtained.

The FBI concentrated on building better cases. Hardworking agents, guided by deciphered Soviet communications, smashed the ATOMIC SPY RING, digging up the evidence that convicted JULIUS ROSENBERG, his wife, Ethel, and others. Hoover authorized illegal phone taps on JUDITH COPLON, a Justice Department worker who was a COURIER for a Soviet INTELLIGENCE OFFICER. (An appellate court overturned her conviction because of the wiretap and lack of a warrant.) FBI agents, following such clues as a hollow nickel, caught Soviet master spy RUDOLPH ABEL, who was convicted and imprisoned. Although Soviet courier ELIZABETH BENTLEY went first to the FBI,

Hoover's leaks to favored members of Congress made her an anti-communist celebrity, not a convicted spy. Similarly, Hoover secretly helped Congressman Richard Nixon in his crusade against ALGER HISS, who was jailed for perjury, not espionage.

FBI counterintelligence operatives serving in the Soviet Espionage Squad staked out the UNITED NATIONS in New York City as a prime hunting ground for spies and potential double agents. Two of the squad's most celebrated DEFECTORS IN PLACE were TOPHAT and FEDORA, whose disclosures so fascinated Hoover that he made sure the information went directly to the White House.

Hoover's interest in espionage, however, was eclipsed by his preoccupation with subversion. The black bag jobs continued—the Washington Office of the Jewish Culture Society, the Hellenic American Brotherhood, and the Chinese Hand Laundry Alliance were just three victims—until July 1966, when Hoover officially ended the practice. But in fact the FBI continued its illegal break-ins. In 1968 Hoover's agents entered the Chicago headquarters of the Students for a Democratic Society, a leading anti-Vietnam War group.

THE REACH OF COINTELPRO

From 1955 to 1975 the FBI conducted 740,000 investigations into "subversive matters." By 1975 the Bureau had 6½ million domestic intelligence files. Much of it was produced by a secret operation called COINTELPRO for Counterintelligence Program, which was launched in 1956 after Hoover advised the NATIONAL SECURITY COUNCIL that he had a plan to "infiltrate, penetrate, disorganize, and disrupt" the U.S. Communist Party, or CPUSA. The concept was not to find spies but to destroy the party to prevent its members from spying.

COINTELPRO soon went beyond the infiltration of the Communist Party. Hoover authorized FBI monitoring of any organization that might, in his view, thwart the aims of the U.S. government. The counterintelligence operation targeted the Socialist Workers Party, the Ku Klux Klan, and black nationalist groups. As protests grew against the Vietnam War in the 1960s, COINTELPRO turned to the antiwar movement. From 1967 to 1972 COINTELPRO expanded to include an FBI directed CIA operation, given the CODE NAME CHAOS.

Behind the Chaos-COINTELPRO effort was the theory—advanced by both the Johnson and Nixon administrations—that protests against the Vietnam War were being directed by the Soviet Union. The CIA's Chaos investigation used employees who joined antiwar groups before going overseas to seek out possible Soviet connections. The CIA, which developed files on 7,200 Americans during Chaos, found no evidence of Soviet influence.

The FBI's COINTELPRO, however, plunged on, seeking subversion in black extremist groups, the Puerto Rican independence movement, Clergy and Laity Concerned about Vietnam, and the American Christian Action Council. Driven by Hoover's obsessive belief that black leader Martin Luther King, Jr., was a communist—

and a sexual degenerate—FBI agents turned in 39,237 pages of reports on King. Several TARGETS of COINTEL-PRO later successfully sued the Justice Department for illegal spying and attempts to disrupt antiwar groups by seeking to instigate violence. In one incident, the FBI sent black activists a leaflet supposedly written by white activists. "We consider you and your kind as black bandits," the leaflet said.

Hoover also believed that the University of California at Berkeley was "infiltrated with a lot of communists." JOHN MCCONE, the DIRECTOR OF CENTRAL INTELLIGENCE from Nov. 1961 to April 1965, was an alumnus of the university and a generous supporter. He asked Hoover to supply a regent with evidence of communists on campus. Hoover had an agent provide the regent with "public source information" on people who were "causing trouble," but apparently no names of communists were given to McCone.

According to Athan G. Theoharis and John Stuart Cox in *The Boss* (1988)

> A tacit agreement had been reached. Hoover was accorded broad latitude to conduct sensitive operations—operations that no attorney general could approve because of the necessary resort to illegal methods—on the assumption that these investigations were limited to suspected foreign agents and their American operatives. . . . Hoover saw no need to brief them, having been encouraged to believe that they wished the FBI to monitor and destabilize "subversive" activists without creating any written record.

Hoover's death in 1972 while in office was the end of the Hoover FBI and the beginning of a new FBI. Three decades later columnist Robert D. Novak, commenting on the conduct of FBI Director ROBERT MUELLER, described the difference in *The Washington Post* on May 12, 2003:

> The change is typified by the way [Robert] Mueller reacts to criticism. When I wrote a column about the director's failure to respond to internal whistle-blowers and senatorial critics, he asked me in for a chat at the J. Edgar Hoover Building. When I criticized Director Hoover more than 30 years ago, Hoover ordered the Washington field office to tap my home telephone (as reported to me by an assistant FBI director, who said he overrode the illegal order).
>
> Mueller also has deviated from the bureau's customary practice, which persisted longer after Hoover, of insisting that it could do no wrong.

Relations between the CIA and the FBI—the two principal U.S. civilian intelligence agencies—had been cool at best under Hoover. It warmed under his successors. The FBI became more of a working member of the Intelligence Community. But cooperation meant learning a new way to operate.

LIVING BY NEW RULES

On the day after Hoover died, President Nixon appointed L. PATRICK GRAY acting director of the FBI. Less than a month later the WATERGATE scandal began and Gray was drawn into it. He resigned under a cloud that was finally lifted only when CLARENCE KELLEY, Kansas City, Miss., chief of police, became director.

In the aftermath of Watergate, Congress exposed a long record of illegal activities in both the CIA (see MKUL-TRA and FAMILY JEWELS) and the Hoover FBI. President Carter's Attorney General, Edward Levi, set new guidelines for FBI counterintelligence investigations. This led to a new law, the FOREIGN INTELLIGENCE SURVEILLANCE ACT, which tightened control over wiretaps and BUGS, and created the FOREIGN INTELLIGENCE SURVEILLANCE COURT to rule on petitions for electronic surveillance.

Counterintelligence now was more complicated. The number of Soviet and Eastern European spies in the United States at least doubled between 1966 and 1978. No longer could an FBI field office independently move against a suspected spy; the spy might be wittingly or unwittingly under the control of U.S. HANDLERS in a counterintelligence operation unknown to the field office. A man who looks like a suspect from the vantage point of a San Francisco FBI surveillance team may in fact be an American working as a double agent, or a KGB officer in the process of being turned or being fed DISINFORMATION.

The intelligence community and knowledgeable officials in the Department of Justice made the decisions about who was to be arrested and who was to be left alone. In 1978 Attorney General Griffin B. Bell had to weigh the conflicting claims of the FBI and CIA in the case of RONALD L. HUMPHREY, a U.S. State Department officer who passed information to David Truong, a South Vietnamese believed to be a spy. Truong's courier was being run by the CIA, which wanted to protect her identity. The FBI wanted her as a witness in court. Bell ruled for the FBI.

Major spy cases of the 1980s—the DECADE OF THE SPY—were typically exposed by defectors rather than by FBI detective work. What the FBI was extremely good at was bringing in the evidence that enabled U.S. prosecutors to present a solid case in court. Only one espionage trial, that of RICHARD C. SMITH, has been lost, and the loss was the result of bungling by the CIA and Army intelligence, not because of the FBI.

It was Kelley's successor, Judge WILLIAM H. WEBSTER, who presided over the Decade of the Spy. The FBI successfully developed their cases and all but one of which ended in convictions.

As the Decade of the Spy was ending, so was the Cold War, and as Webster left the FBI to become Director of Central Intelligence, counterintelligence became a less important mission of the FBI. In 1991 the FBI drew up a "national security threat" list. On the list was INDUSTRIAL ESPIONAGE, as manifested in foreign intelligence agency attempts to obtain information about U.S. technology. Until the war on terrorism began after the Sept. 11, 2001, attacks, industrial espionage was a major FBI mission.

Soon after the list was created, the FBI reassigned

425 counterintelligence agents to the investigation of violent crimes. In 1994 the name of the FBI's Intelligence Division was changed to the National Security Division. Also in 1993 the FBI set up an office in Moscow to help Russian police fight organized crime. Subsequently Legal ATTACHÉS were established in capitals around the world.

POST-COLD WAR

For some FBI agents, counterintelligence meant calling on libraries and asking whether people with "East European or Russian-sounding names" had been checking out any books on technology. Librarians complained, and the practice died down. Like the image of FBI agents working in Moscow, the library visits seemed to symbolize the end of traditional spy hunting. Then, on Feb. 21, 1994, the FBI arrested ALDRICH H. AMES, a CIA counterintelligence officer who had been spying for the Soviets and then the Russians for at least nine years. Lack of cooperation between the CIA and the FBI—a recurrent theme over the years—was blamed for the failure to detect Ames's treachery earlier. President Clinton issued a directive transferring responsibility for counterintelligence to the FBI and placed an FBI official in charge of a national center for policymaking on counterintelligence issues. Every four years the directorship of the center is rotated through the CIA, FBI, and military intelligence agencies.

The new directive seemed to help in the investigation of HAROLD J. NICHOLSON, another CIA officer who spied for Russia, and EARL EDWIN PITTS, an FBI agent who was arrested in Dec. 1996 after a 16-month "sting" operation. Pitts was later convicted.

The cases showed that the FBI still hunts spies. But the emphasis in the bureau had shifted to anti-terrorism and anti-drug investigations. Overseas investigations, which sometimes clash with CIA activities, require the approval of the host country. In 2003 there were FBI legal attachés in 46 countries. There are also agents working with Russian police to monitor "Russian Mafia" activities in the United States.

Rapid advances in communications technology are also affecting FBI electronic surveillance techniques. FBI director LOUIS J. FREEH said in 1995 that the FBI and the telephone industry "are working together to find reasonable and affordable solutions that will keep pace with technology." He stressed that the FBI has "no intention to expand the number of wiretaps or the extent of wiretapping." To work against COMPUTER ESPIONAGE the FBI set up a National Computer Crime Squad.

Meanwhile, during Freeh's tenure the FBI was racked by several blunders, among them: the probe of the Atlanta (Ga.) Olympic Park bombing in 1996, in which the FBI wrongly identified a security guard as the main suspect and was then unable to locate the man eventually charged; the handling of the WEN HO LEE case, in which a Taiwan-born nuclear scientist at the LOS ALAMOS nuclear laboratory was accused of mishandling classified information; the arrest of FBI agent ROBERT HANSSEN, who pleaded guilty to 15 counts of espionage; and the mishandling of hundreds of documents in the Oklahoma City bombing investigation.

President George Bush replaced Freeh less than a year after he entered the White House. Replacing him as head of the FBI was ROBERT MUELLER, who became director on Sept. 4, 2001.

FBI priorities changed radically one week later, on Sept. 11, 2001, when terrorists destroyed the World Trade Center and attacked the Pentagon. Immediately the FBI began rounding up suspects, many of whom had been under surveillance since the first terrorist bomb attack on the World Trade Center in 1993. Ironically, the FBI had had a MOLE within the terrorist group that made that attempt. But the agency claimed he had not been an active informant for some seven months.

Following the 2001 attacks, there were major recriminations as agents in FBI field offices revealed that they had provided warnings of such an attack to headquarters that went unheeded. Much criticism focused on the handling of Zacarias Moussaoui, a French citizen of Moroccan descent, dubbed "the twentieth hijacker" by some investigators.

Moussaoui, like the other 19 hijackers in the Al Qaeda plot, had been under cover in the United States for some time. He enrolled in a flight school in Minnesota, paying in cash and telling instructors he was particularly interested in learning to fly big jets. The flight school called the FBI in Aug. 2001 and reported suspicions about Moussaoui. FBI agents questioned him, and because he had overstayed his visa, they turned him over to immigration officers who jailed him.

Agents investigating Moussaoui wanted a FOREIGN INTELLIGENCE SURVEILLANCE COURT (FISC) warrant, but higher officials in Washington held up the application, saying there was no evidence connecting him to a known terrorist group. According to French sources, French intelligence officials told the FBI that they had linked Moussaoui to Osama bin Laden and Al Qaeda, tracing him to a suspected terrorist training camp in Afghanistan. French intelligence then put him on a watch list of probable terrorists. But this information apparently did not get to the officials holding up the application for the FISC warrant.

Moussaoui was charged in 2002 with planning to destroy an aircraft, along with other counts that can be punished with the death penalty. Prosecutors believe he was to have been the fifth hijacker of the United Flight 93 aircraft, the only flight with four, rather than five, hijackers aboard. That aircraft, en route from Newark to San Francisco, crashed into a field in Somerset County, Penn., after passengers struggled with the hijackers.

Whatever the results of the investigations, the 25,000 employees of the FBI began concentrating on the agency's highest priority mission: stopping terrorism.

CHIEFS AND DIRECTORS

The predecessor of the Federal Bureau of Investigation was the Bureau of Investigation (BOI), whose chiefs were

Stanley W. Finch (July 1908–April 1912); A. Bruce Bielaski (April 1912–Feb. 1919); William E. Allen (acting, Feb. 1919–July 1919); William J. Flynn (July 1919–Aug. 1921); William J. Burns (Aug. 1921–May 1924). J. Edgar Hoover became chief of the BOI in May 1924 and continued in that role through the name changes that followed. In July 1932 the BOI became the U.S. Bureau of Investigation and in Aug. 1933 the Division of Investigation (which included the Bureau of Prohibition). In July 1935 the organization was renamed the Federal Bureau of Investigation (FBI), and Hoover became its first director. FBI directors were:

July 1935–May 1972	J. Edgar Hoover
May 1972–April 1973	L. Patrick Gray (acting)
April 1973–July 1973	William D. Ruckelshaus (acting)
July 1973–Feb. 1978	CLARENCE M. KELEY
Feb. 1978–May 1987	William H. Webster
May 1987–Nov. 1987	John Otto (acting)
Nov. 1987–July 1993	WILLIAM S. SESSIONS
July 1993–Sept. 1993	Floyd L. Clarke (acting)
Sept. 1993–Sept. 2001	LOUIS J. FREEH
June 2001–Sept. 2001	THOMAS J. PICKARD (acting)
Sept. 2001–	ROBERT MUELLER

FBIS

FOREIGN BROADCAST INFORMATION SERVICE

FBQ Corporation

PROPRIETARY COMPANY or COVER established by the U.S. OFFICE OF STRATEGIC SERVICES (OSS) in 1942 to erect radio intercept stations at Bellmore (Long Island), N.Y., and Reseda, Calif. The radio stations were an attempt by the OSS to enter the field of CRYPTANALYSIS because of the limited amounts of MAGIC and ULTRA decrypts made available to the OSS by the Joint Chiefs of Staff. FBQ's installations were used to intercept and analyze commercial radio traffic.

The stations were soon taken over by the U.S. Army's SIGNAL INTELLIGENCE SERVICE.

Fecteau, Richard

CIA INTELLIGENCE OFFICER who was captured in China when his spyplane was shot down on Nov. 29, 1952. Charged with espionage by the Chinese, Fecteau was imprisoned until 1971.

Fecteau, fellow CIA officer JOHN DOWNEY, and seven AGENTS were on board an unmarked C-47 Dakota that took off from a secret CIA base in Japan. The pilots, like the agents, were recruited on Formosa (Taiwan), where Chiang Kai-shek, defeated by the Chinese communists under Mao Zedong, had fled. To support U.S. policy to enable Chiang to retake the mainland, the CIA was infiltrating Formosans into mainland China.

In Dec. 1954 China announced the capture and trial for espionage of two CIA operatives. Downey was sentenced to life imprisonment. Fecteau, because he was subordinate to Downey, was given a 20-year prison term.

By then the Korean War was over and the United States was arranging a prisoner-of-war exchange with China. But neither Fecteau nor Downey was on the U.S. list for exchange because the United States would not admit that they were CIA officers.

Although China and the United States did not have diplomatic relations, in 1957—in an indirect way—China again offered to release the two CIA officers. The offer was, however, rejected by Secretary of State John Foster Dulles (whose brother, ALLEN W. DULLES, was then DIRECTOR OF CENTRAL INTELLIGENCE).

Subsequently, after President Nixon acknowledged at a press conference that Fecteau and Downey were CIA officers, they were finally released, Fecteau in 1971, Downey in 1973.

Fedora

U.S. CODE NAME for a Soviet INTELLIGENCE OFFICER who provided information to the FBI, the CIA, and British intelligence agencies. Information that he gave to the FBI reverberated for years, echoing in the PENTAGON PAPERS incident and the WATERGATE scandal. He may also have been a DISINFORMATION source whose mission was to confuse U.S. intelligence agencies.

Fedora has never been officially identified. The most authoritative identification was Aleksei Kulak, who was a KGB officer under COVER as a scientific ATTACHÉ in the Soviet Mission to the UNITED NATIONS. He has also been identified as Victor Lessiovski, a KGB officer with similar cover. The conflicting identities for Fedora symbolize the confusion caused by his disclosures.

Fedora began his career as a DEFECTOR IN PLACE sometime in 1962, soon after DMITRI POLYAKOV, an officer in Soviet MILITARY INTELLIGENCE (GRU), had done the same. Polyakov had been given the code name TOP HAT, and the FBI decided to continue the hat motif with Fedora. (Later there was Homburg.)

FBI CASE OFFICERS were running Soviet defectors from the United Nations, and J. EDGAR HOOVER, director of the FBI, often took Fedora's information directly to the White House. When President Nixon attempted to get a court to stop publication of the Pentagon Papers, for example, Fedora told the FBI that a set of the papers—secret documents on the Vietnam War—had been delivered to the Soviet Embassy in Washington, D.C. This made Nixon believe that Daniel Ellsberg, who had exposed the papers in an antiwar move, was a possible Soviet AGENT. Nixon's aides then sent the PLUMBERS on a search for incriminating information about Ellsberg.

But much of what Fedora said was doubted by JAMES JESUS ANGLETON, chief of COUNTERINTELLIGENCE in the CIA. Angleton believed that Fedora and Top Hat were both DOUBLE AGENTS whose mission was the discrediting of a real Soviet defector, ANATOLI GOLITSIN. Angleton's unproven theory was that the Soviets desperately wanted to discredit Golitsin because he had revealed that a MOLE had penetrated the CIA.

The mystery story of the defectors began when YURI NOSENKO approached a CIA officer in Geneva in Jan. 1964 and defected. Following President Kennedy's assassination in Nov. 1963, an investigation into the background of the assassin, Lee Harvey Oswald, showed that he had lived in the Soviet Union after renouncing his American citizenship. According to Nosenko, who claimed to be the KGB officer who had handled Oswald's case during his three years in the USSR, the KGB had had no dealings with Oswald.

Golitsin insisted that Nosenko had been sent to discredit him. Fedora backed up Nosenko, which made Angleton believe that Fedora, too, was a disinformation agent. The dispute over what the CIA called the "bona fides" of Fedora sharpened the long-running feud between Hoover's FBI and the CIA.

Fedora did lead British intelligence officers to a possible spy in a British atomic weapons facility, but there was not sufficient evidence to arrest the suspect. The British tended to distrust Fedora, believing that his accusations about British spies were designed to disrupt the U.S.-British intelligence alliance.

Doubts about Fedora began to surface in 1971, but not until Hoover's death in 1972 did rigorous investigation begin. Edward Jay Epstein's book on Oswald, *Legend* (1978), asserted that Fedora and Nosenko were disinformation agents. One of Epstein's sources, William C. Sullivan, former deputy director of the FBI, doubted Fedora. Angleton was also believed to have been one of Epstein's sources.

The matter seemed to be settled in Oct. 1981, when an article in *The Reader's Digest* named Fedora as a Soviet agent under KGB control during the years he was supplying information to the FBI. *The Reader's Digest* had a close tie to the FBI for many years through an editor, JOHN D. BARRON, and a denunciation of Fedora in the magazine probably reflected FBI policy.

Fedora returned to the Soviet Union sometime after 1977 and, according to CIA sources, died there of natural causes in about 1983. The CIA differed with the FBI, according to author David Wise, who was given extraordinary access to CIA personnel for his book *Nightmover* (1995), about the ALDRICH H. AMES case. Wise said that the CIA "acknowledged" Fedora "as a true source in 1975, a year after the departure of Angleton. . . ."

Fedorchuk, Army Gen. Vitaly Vasilievich

(b. 1918)

Career Soviet intelligence apparatchik, who served as chief of the KGB from May to Dec. 1982, and subsequently Minister of Internal Affairs (MVD).

Fedorchuk joined the NKVD security police in 1939. During World War II he served in the military COUNTERINTELLIGENCE organization SMERSH. After the war he continued in military counterintelligence with the NKVD-KGB (Smersh was abolished in 1946), and in the late 1960s he became head of the Third Directorate of the KGB, responsible for counterintelligence/internal security within the armed forces. In 1970 Fedorchuk left MILITARY INTELLIGENCE activities to become chief of the KGB apparatus in the Ukraine.

In May 1982, Fedorchuk replaced YURI ANDROPOV when the latter stepped down as head of the KGB to join the Communist Party secretariat. Scientist-historian Zhores A. Medvedev, in his biography *Gorbachev* (1986), wrote, "Fedorchuk was not even a member of the Central Committee and in retrospect his appointment seems to have been an attempt [by Andropov] to neutralize the KGB in the power struggle which was taking place over [Leonid] Brezhnev's successor."

Andropov succeeded Brezhnev as General Secretary of the Communist Party and head of the Soviet Union in Nov. 1982. A month later he made Fedorchuk Minister of Internal Affairs with the rank of army general and charged him with cleaning up corruption and waste in the MVD. Fedorchuk's ineptness and unpopularity led Mikhail Gorbachev to transfer him in 1986 to the position of military inspector, ending his long career in intelligence-police work.

He was considered by most of his peers to be an arrogant bumbler.

ALSO TRANSLITERATED AS FYDORCHUK.

Feedback

CODE NAME for a series of studies by the RAND Corporation in 1951–1954 for the U.S. Air Force to justify the development of a SATELLITE RECONNAISSANCE system. Feedback was a major factor in the startup of the U.S. CORONA program.

Federal Bureau of Investigation

SEE FBI

Feklisov, Aleksandr

(b. 1914)

Senior NKVD and KGB officer who was HANDLER for JULIUS ROSENBERG and other American members of the ATOMIC SPY RING. Subsequently, Feklisov worked with ABC News State Department correspondent John Scali to establish a back channel for communications between President Kennedy and Prime Minister Nikita Khrushchev during the CUBAN MISSILE CRISIS.

Feklisov was born into a poor family in a rough section of Moscow; his father was a railroad switchman. He showed an early interest in engineering and was able to matriculate in the Moscow School of Communications. In school he was a good student, capable athlete, and active member of the *Komsomol*, the communist youth league.

Completing his training as a radio technician in 1939, he was selected for NKVD service. After a year of English language training as well as studying espionage skills, he was dispatched to the United States, arriving in

New York in late February 1941 via the Siberian-Pacific route. Working for the Soviet consulate in the mornings, his main assignment was to operate a clandestine radio for the NKVD.

Julius Rosenberg had already been recruited by the NKVD to steal classified documents from his job with the Army Signal Corps. A short time later Feklisov became Rosenberg's handler and, beyond garnering secrets from Rosenberg and his colleagues, he used the American engineer as a conduit for secrets of the U.S. atomic bomb project.

Feklisov met with Rosenberg about 50 times. He never met Rosenberg's wife, Ethel, who also participated in her husband's espionage activities. After 5½ highly successful years in the United States, Feklisov returned to the USSR in Oct. 1946. After a brief stay in Moscow he was assigned to the Soviet Embassy in London, arriving in Sept. 1947. There he was in charge of technical intelligence collection, and again engaged in nuclear espionage, serving as handler for KLAUS FUCHS.

After another successful tenure, Feklisov went back to Moscow in Dec. 1955 and was given responsibility for supervising political espionage against the United States and Canada. He participated in Khrushchev's visit to the United States in 1959 as part of the KGB security contingent.

In Aug. 1960 Feklisov returned to the United States as the RESIDENT, head of KGB operations. "To manage the Rezidentura in the main enemy's country was a real challenge," Feklisov wrote in his autobiographical *The Man Behind the Rosenbergs* (2001). Also, "I knew that before sending me off to America, the [KGB] had obtained my file at MI5 and the FBI. I was listed as a diplomat, nothing more"—an indication of the success of the Soviets in penetrating Western intelligence.

With offices in Washington, his COVER was embassy press ATTACHÉ. Among the many friends and acquaintances he made in Washington was John Scali, ABC news reporter and moderator of the weekly Sunday talk show *Issues and Answers*. Scali was close to a number of senior Kennedy administration officials, including his next-door neighbor, presidential adviser Ken O'Donnell. Feklisov had met with Scali on a number of occasions, most recently the Monday afternoon of President's televised speech on the evening of Oct. 22, 1962, revealing that the United States knew that the Soviets were installing ballistic missiles in Cuba. On Oct. 26, Feklisov telephoned Scali—who had been assigned the KGB CODE NAME "MIN"—and suggested that they meet for lunch.

Choosing the Occidental Grille on Pennsylvania Avenue, two blocks from the White House, the two men began to discuss the missile crisis. Sensing that Scali was listening and ready, Feklisov made the offer he had been ordered to deliver—that there was room for negotiations on the crisis. Scali, realizing that Feklisov might be making an important back-channel invitation to the Kennedy administration, left quickly and contacted Secretary of State Dean Rusk. The Feklisov offer was presented to President Kennedy and his brother Robert Kennedy that afternoon. Deciding that this might be a real initiative to achieve a breakthrough, Scali was sent back for a second meeting with Feklisov. During those days, in Oct. 1962 the world stood closer to nuclear conflict than at any time during the 45-year Cold War. Scali and Feklisov had established the back-channel communications link that led to the peaceful resolution of the crisis.

Feklisov served in Washington until March 1964. While in the United States he used the name Alexander Fomin. He related in his 2001 autobiography that he then

> participated in other secret operations that are still too recent to be told. I trained intelligence officers at the Andropov Institute . . . I have done research on intelligence matters and defended a doctoral dissertation in history.

He permanently retired from the KGB in 1986.

Felfe, Heinz

(b. 1918 d. ?)

A DOUBLE AGENT who spied for the Soviet Union while head of COUNTERINTELLIGENCE against Soviet penetration for West Germany's BND (Bundesnachrichtendienst, or Federal Intelligence Agency).

The son of a Nazi officer, Felfe served during World War II in the SS and the SD. After the war, as a prisoner of war he was recruited by Soviet intelligence and, under Soviet control, worked briefly for British INTELLIGENCE OFFICERS in Germany. He then joined BND, becoming chief of the Soviet counterintelligence department during the 1950s.

When Felfe was arrested in West Germany in Nov. 1962, he possessed 14 rolls of microfilm and a miniature recording tape. He was accused of giving the names of more than 100 BND agents to the Soviets. Tried and convicted in 1963, he was sentenced to 14 years in prison. After serving six years, he was exchanged for six prisoners held by the Soviets.

Leaving his wife and children in West Germany, he settled in East Berlin and became a professor of criminology at Humboldt University. "It was absolutely clear to me that the hope of the future lay with the Soviet Union and not in the United States," he said when he published his Soviet-approved autobiography, *In Service of the Adversary* (1986).

Fellers, Brig. Gen. Bonner F.

(b. 1896 d. 1973)

U.S. military ATTACHÉ in Cairo, Egypt, from Oct. 1940 to July 1942, whose extensive reports to the U.S. War Department on British military operations were intercepted and deciphered by the Germans.

A 1918 graduate of the U.S. Military Academy at West Point, N.Y., Fellers subsequently served in coast artillery units and as an aide to senior officers. In Feb. 1936 he became assistant to Gen. Douglas MacArthur, the military adviser to the president of the Philippines Commonwealth. He returned to Washington, D.C., in 1938–1939 to attend the Army War College, then went to Spain as assistant military attaché, and in Oct. 1940 became the military attaché in Cairo.

After the Servizio Informazione Militare (Italian MILITARY INTELLIGENCE) burgled several foreign embassies in Rome in 1941, the Italians obtained a copy of the U.S. Black CODE used by attachés, which they then shared with the German ABWEHR. At the same time, cryptologists with Gen. Erwin Rommel's Afrika Korps also broke into the U.S. CIPHER. The Germans were able to intercept and decipher Fellers' messages within a few hours of their dispatch. (Those codebreaking efforts helped Rommel several times in battles with British forces.)

Fellers asked questions and kept his eyes open, according to historian DAVID KAHN in *The Codebreakers* (1968). "The British let him in on some of their secrets, hoping that this would improve American equipment lend-leased to Britain's desert forces. . . . Fellers soaked up this great quantity of information and poured it out to Washington in voluminous and detailed reports."

The Germans were able to read virtually all of Fellers' reports being sent to Washington, D.C. Finally, in the summer of 1942 a German prisoner of war told the British that Fellers' communications were being decrypted. (The British had themselves intercepted and broken the code.) Fellers was ordered back to the United States but was not told about his inadvertent assistance to the enemy. In 1942 the U.S. Army awarded Fellers the Distinguished Service Medal for his service as military attaché, the citation noting, "His reports to the War Department were models of clarity and accuracy."

In Sept. 1943 he was assigned to the staff of Gen. MacArthur, the Commander-in-Chief, Southwest Pacific Area, and was promoted to brigadier general. He remained on MacArthur's staff until he retired from active duty in 1946. After leaving the Army, he was an adviser to Sen. Robert A. Taft and wrote *Wings for Peace: A Primer for a New Defense* (1952), which advocated a strong defense based on air power.

Fence

Russian slang for the border with another country; the term is used in relation to both military and intelligence activities.

Ferret

Originally a vehicle, usually an aircraft, used to investigate foreign radar systems by approaching them so as to cause them to be turned on (see AIRCRAFT and *GRAF ZEPPELIN*). It has subsequently become a term for ELECTRONIC INTELLIGENCE collection by SATELLITES, which generally do not elicit radar activity.

Field, Noel

(b. 1904 d. 1970)

Former U.S. diplomat who disappeared in 1949 shortly before his name emerged at the trial of ALGER HISS, a former U.S. State Department official accused of stealing U.S. government documents in the 1930s. Field had been recruited by German communists to aid world communism.

British-born Field joined the State Department in 1926 after graduating from Harvard. He resigned in 1936 to work for the League of Nations in Geneva and later for the Unitarian Services Committee in Switzerland. There he was drawn into the NETWORK run by Gen. WALTER KRIVITSKY, chief of Soviet MILITARY INTELLIGENCE in Europe, who defected to the West in 1939.

In Switzerland, Field met an old family friend, ALLEN W. DULLES, Bern station chief of the OFFICE OF STRATEGIC SERVICES (OSS). Field joined the OSS, while ostensibly working for the Unitarian Services Committee aiding refugees. The OSS had him make contact with the German Communist Party (KPD). The KPD's leader in exile, JÜRGEN KUCZYNSKI, while working for the OSS, organized networks to operate against the Nazis.

After the war Field returned to the United States and tried, through Hiss, to return to the State Department. But when Hiss testified at his perjury trial that Field was a communist, Field fled with his wife to Czechoslovakia and later to Hungary, seeking political asylum in the Soviet bloc. There he was thought to be an agent of the CIA and was jailed by the AVH, the Hungarian secret police. He testified in show trials designed to purge Hungarian leaders unacceptable to the Soviets.

After being held for five years in Hungary, he was released from custody. He elected to remain in Hungary and continued to seek asylum rather than return to the West. Following the abortive 1956 Hungarian uprising he issued a statement defending the Soviet suppression of the revolt. The State Department stripped him of his citizenship.

He died in Budapest in 1970.

Fifth Column

Term coined in 1936 by Nationalist Gen. Emilio Mola in the Spanish Civil War to describe Nationalist supporters in Madrid who would support his four army columns assaulting the city.

The British later applied the term to people who spied for or sympathized with Nazis in occupied countries, particularly France. Ernest Hemingway established the term in the United States through his play about the Spanish Civil War, *Fifth Column*. A shadowy fifth column was blamed for the swift fall of France in 1940, and British officials worried about the existence of a fifth column amid the refugees who fled to England from the Continent.

Prime Minister Winston Churchill borrowed the fifth column idea when he ordered the creation of the SOE

(Special Operations Executive), which was "to set Europe ablaze." Minister of Economic Warfare Hugh Dalton, the director of the SOE, said it would be similar "to the organizations which the Nazis themselves have developed so remarkably in almost every country in the world." President Roosevelt also believed in the existence of such a Nazi organization, speaking in a fireside chat on May 26, 1940, about the "fifth column that betrays a nation unprepared for treachery." In fact, there was no such Nazi organization.

WILLIAM DONOVAN, sent to England by Roosevelt on a fact-gathering mission in July 1940, coauthored a series of syndicated newspaper articles and a pamphlet "Fifth Column Lessons for America," which played a major role in creating hysteria over possible infiltration of Nazi agents into the United States. The pamphlet warned that the Nazis could count on a "German colony of several million strong" in the United States, including thousands of domestic workers and "German waiters." Many of the German-Americans in this mythical fifth column, the pamphlet said, would act "to destroy their own country, to sabotage its defenses, weaken its war effort, sink its ships, kill its soldiers and sailors for the benefit of a foreign dictator and his alien political philosophy."

After the war the term died out, probably because no real fifth column had ever emerged in the Allied countries in World War II.

Fifth Man

Label applied to a fifth member of the CAMBRIDGE SPY RING, that is, a Soviet spy who infiltrated British intelligence, either MI5 or MI6.

Former Security Service (MI5) official PETER WRIGHT believed that the fifth man was ROGER HOLLIS (who became head of MI5), as did historian JOHN COSTELLO. KGB defector OLEG GORDIEVSKY believed that the fifth man was JOHN CAIRNCROSS—who subsequently claimed that he was in fact the fifth man.

Also see FLUENCY COMMITTEE, FOURTH MAN, and THIRD MAN.

Firm, The

Popular term for the CIA among employees who work there—and those who do not. Other terms are THE COMPANY and, for its headquarters, LANGLEY, in the Washington, D.C., suburb of McLean, Va.

First U.S. Army Group

(FUSAG)

Phantom army created by the Allies in 1944 to make German commanders believe that an assault force was in England ready to cross the channel to Pas de Calais. The FUSAG DECEPTION, given the CODE NAME of FORTITUDE, was part of BODYGUARD, a complex overall deception plan.

Lt. Gen. George S. Patton was designated as commanding general of FUSAG, whose order of battle was transmitted to Germany by DOUBLE AGENTS in Britain under the control of the TWENTY COMMITTEE.

To create what appeared to be a massive military buildup along the Kent coast, Allied deception specialists built tent encampments with fake tanks and other vehicles, put dummy landing crafts in the Thames estuary and allowed Luftwaffe RECONNAISSANCE aircraft to fly over the area.

Realistic radio traffic flowed from Patton's bogus headquarters and Allied aerial bombing concentrated on the Pas de Calais area right up to D-DAY on June 6, 1944. The deception continued for a time after D-Day in an attempt to convince the Germans that the Normandy invasion would soon be followed by even larger forces landing on the Calais beaches. At least 19 German divisions remained in Calais for weeks after D-Day.

Fish

Advanced German, on-line CIPHER machine. Fish—called both Geheimschreiber and Sägefisch by the Germans—differed from the more widely used ENIGMA in that it was a non-Morse-code system that could simultaneously encrypt and transmit or simultaneously receive and decrypt messages.

When an operator typed a message into the machine it automatically produced teleprinter impulses in the Baudot telegraph code for radio transmission. The receiving machine produced teleprinter PLAIN TEXT tapes that were cut apart and pasted directly onto military message sheets. Thus, Fish was easier to use and faster than the Enigma. But, unlike Enigma, Fish was not portable.

Fish was more secure than Enigma because of its speed; it was fitted with 10 ROTORS (compared to a maximum of five in Enigma), as well as other advanced features. It was nonetheless broken by British codebreakers.

Intercepts of this type of machine were first made by British Y-SERVICE intercept stations as early as 1932. Those were early, unenciphered, experimental transmissions. The first enciphered, operational messages were intercepted in 1940. The machine appears to have entered service the following year.

Fish—the name given to the machine by the British GOVERNMENT CODE AND CYPHER SCHOOL (GC&CS)—was employed above the field army level of German military forces, transmitting orders and position statements to and from the highest authorities of the armed forces and the government. By the end of 1941 the GC&CS decided to concentrate its available codebreaking resources on German Army communications (Tunny). There were considerable Fish communications by the Air Force, while few Navy communications in Fish were intercepted.

Those communication links, identified with Lorenz-produced, Schlüsselzusatz Series 40 machines, were named Tunny by the British, and the subsequent Siemens

T52 variants were called Sturgeon. This set the British pattern of using fish names for various links and CIPHER KEYS in the system.

The GC&CS codebreakers at BLETCHLEY PARK were initially stumped by Fish. But when the Eighth Army in North Africa captured two Fish machines, the British succeeded in breaking the cipher. BOMBE calculating machines were modified to work the Fish ciphers with the COLOSSUS, an early programmable electronic, digital calculator, developed especially for attacking this cipher. By the end of the war 10 of the massive Colossus machines were at work on Fish ciphers.

According to F. H. HENSLEY and his coauthors of *British Intelligence in the Second World War* (1984), "Success against Fish resulted from a combination of events, including mistakes [in German transmissions], but the delay in producing Fish decrypts was offset by the high quality of the intelligence they yielded."

The average delay in producing Fish decrypts, according to Hinsley, was three days in 1943 and 1945, and during 1944 it was as much as seven days. But the high level of Fish communications made such delays less significant than delays in German ciphers at the tactical and operational levels. Some Fish ciphers, however, such as the German Army's Wehrkreis link—which the British named Thrasher—were never broken.

Flashlight

SEE MANDRAKE

Flavius Vegetius Renatus

Fourth century A.D. Roman military expert who wrote what is often considered the most influential military treatise in the Western world, *Rei militaris institute*, also called *Epitoma rei militaris* (The Military Institutions). A strong believer in the value of intelligence to military operations, Flavius wrote: "Our spies should be constantly abroad. We should spare no pains in tampering with their men, and giving encouragement to deserters. By these means we may get intelligence of their present or future designs."

His work stressed constant drill, severe discipline, the employment of reserves, and battlefield tactics as well as intelligence collection.

While his writings had little impact on the armies of the rapidly declining Roman empire, his work had great influence on Medieval and subsequent western military doctrine.

A patrician and a reformer, Flavius had little personal military experience.

Fleet Intelligence Center

(FIC)

U.S. Navy intelligence command, located ashore, that provided comprehensive intelligence support to operating fleets. The first such center was established in July 1942 as the Intelligence Center Pacific Ocean Area (ICPOA) to support Adm. Chester W. Nimitz, who was both Commander-in-Chief U.S. Pacific Fleet and Commander-in-Chief Pacific Ocean Areas. In the latter post he commanded all U.S. air, naval, and ground forces in the Pacific to the 160th degree of east longitude.

ICPOA was a Navy command, but with liaison officers assigned from the other services. When established, it had 17 officers and 29 enlisted men. ICPOA's first officer-in-charge was Comdr. JOSEPH ROCHEFORT, who also continued as head of Navy codebreaking at Pearl Harbor. (See HYPO.) In Sept. 1942 he was relieved as head of ICPOA by Capt. ROSCOE HILLENKOETTER.

As ICPOA grew it became too large for its quarters in the Pearl Harbor Navy Yard and was moved to a new facility on the rim of Makalapa Crater, near Adm. Nimitz's massive headquarters complex. The center was reorganized on Sept. 7, 1943, to cope with the expanding size of Nimitz's forces and the massive operations those forces were undertaking. Renamed the Joint Intelligence Center Pacific Ocean Area (JICPOA), it was placed under Army Brig. Gen. Joseph J. Twitty, an experienced cartographer who had been the Army's liaison to the Navy ICPOA.

The center continued to expand. In Jan. 1945 it had 500 officers from all of the services and 800 enlisted men and women. That month, as Nimitz had established an advanced command post on Guam, JICPOA established an office there. Eight months later, when the war ended, the center had more than 1,800 personnel in Hawaii plus hundreds of personnel on numerous islands and fleet flagships.

JICPOA was involved in every phase of intelligence, from PHOTOGRAPHIC INTERPRETATION to map production, preparation of intelligence analyses and reports, radio intelligence, the handling of MAGIC and ULTRA material, prisoner interrogations, and so on. Every month JICPOA produced an average of 2 million sheets of printed intelligence and more than 150,000 photo prints for use by all of the armed forces in the Pacific.

After World War II the Navy's operating fleets had small intelligence staffs that relied on the OFFICE OF NAVAL INTELLIGENCE in Washington, D.C., to provide support and additional specialists when needed.

The first postwar FIC was established at the U.S. naval air station at Port Lyautey (now Kenitra), Morocco. Named the Fleet Intelligence Center Eastern Atlantic and Mediterranean, the command provided support to the Navy area headquarters in London and to U.S. naval forces afloat. This support included providing intelligence specialists for forward operations, such as the 1958 U.S. landing of Marines into Lebanon. In 1960 the FIC was renamed Fleet Intelligence Center Europe (FICEUR).

When Morocco ended U.S. base rights in 1964, the center was moved to Jacksonville, Fla. By 1970 FICEUR had 52 Navy and Marine officers, 115 enlisted men and women, and nine civilians.

Late in 1955, the Atlantic Fleet's intelligence office at Norfolk, Va., began operating as a FIC, although it was not designated as Atlantic Intelligence Center (LANTINTCEN) until 1961 and not changed to FICLANT until 1968. Regardless of name, the center's responsibilities grew rapidly to include all of the Atlantic, the Caribbean, and the Indian Ocean. It provided critical intelligence support to U.S. naval forces being readied to intercede in the abortive Bay of Pigs invasion of 1961 (see CUBA) and the CUBAN MISSILE CRISIS of 1962. By 1970 FICLANT had 53 Navy and Marine officers, 128 enlisted men and women, and 27 civilians.

The two Navy intelligence centers on the East Coast, FICEUR and FICLANT, were merged in 1974 to create the Fleet Intelligence Center Europe-Atlantic (FICEURLANT).

The Pacific Fleet's intelligence center (FICPAC) was established in 1955 on Ford Island in the center of Pearl Harbor, Hawaii. In the early 1960s, responding to the crises in Southeast Asia, FICPAC produced specialized photo intelligence reports for the area as well as "evasion and escape" folders for aviators in case they were shot down. A forward FICPAC facility was set up at Cubi Point in the Philippines in Aug. 1964 to provide more immediate photographic interpretation support to U.S. aircraft carriers that were flying strikes against North Vietnam.

FICPAC was a principal source of intelligence for U.S. Navy and Marine forces fighting in Vietnam and operating offshore. By 1970—at its peak strength during the war—FICPAC had 75 Navy and Marine officers, 214 enlisted men and women, and 24 civilians. (The largest FIC was FICEURLANT, which by 1991 had 500 active duty personnel plus reservists on temporary active duty.)

During the 1980s the role of unified or area commanders-in-chief, who direct all U.S. military operations in a geographic area, increased in importance and authority. Accordingly, in 1991 FICEURLANT and FICPAC were disestablished, and their functions taken over by JOINT INTELLIGENCE CENTERS at the unified command headquarters.

Fleet Radio Unit Melbourne

(FRUMEL)

SEE BELL

Fleet Radio Unit Pacific

(FRUPAC)

The U.S. NAVY COMMUNICATIONS INTELLIGENCE unit for the Pacific Fleet. Established before World War II, FRUPAC was located at Pearl Harbor Navy Yard, on Oahu, Hawaii. During the war it had the COVER name Combat Intelligence Unit.

In 1941 FRUPAC had 10 officers and 20 enlisted men at Pearl Harbor, and almost 60 more at outlying stations in the Pacific area. Short-handed when the war

began, the unit was then assigned the musicians from battleship *California*, which had been sunk in the PEARL HARBOR ATTACK. They proved so able at CRYPTANALYSIS that the Navy began to pay special attention to recruiting men with musical backgrounds for CIPHER work.

In July 1942, FRUPAC became subordinate to the newly established Intelligence Center Pacific Ocean Area (ICPOA) at Pearl Harbor. In the Sept. 1943 reorganization of intelligence activities in the Pacific, FRUPAC was placed under the Pacific Fleet commander. (Although Adm. Chester W. Nimitz was both Commander-in-Chief Pacific Ocean Area and Commander-in-Chief Pacific Fleet, there were separate staffs for the two commands.)

When Nimitz moved his forward headquarters to Guam in Jan. 1945, part of FRUPAC went with him.

FRUPAC provided invaluable COMMUNICATIONS INTELLIGENCE to U.S. forces in the Pacific during the war, and supervised the Radio Intelligence Units assigned to fleet and task force commanders. By the end of the war several hundred men and women were assigned to FRUPAC.

Fleming, Chief Petty Officer David

U.S. Navy submariner convicted in 1988 of stealing classified photographs and training manuals. When he was arrested in Oct. 1987, Fleming was photographer aboard the nuclear-proplled submarine *La Jolla*, based at San Diego, Calif.

A military court convicted Fleming under statutes that apply to espionage. But there was no evidence that he planned to provide classified materials to representatives of another country. He was sentenced to four years in prison and was given a bad conduct discharge. He was released on parole in 1990.

Fleming, Ian

(b. 1908 d. 1964)

British NAVAL INTELLIGENCE officer and the creator of JAMES BOND [F], one of the most famous spies in modern fiction. After short careers as a journalist and stockbroker, in 1939 Fleming was recruited into naval intelligence as personal assistant to the director and was commissioned a lieutenant commander in the naval reserve. Fleming's boss, Rear Adm. John Godfrey, the DIRECTOR OF NAVAL INTELLIGENCE (DNI), and Maxwell Knight, head of MI5's countersubversion department, were models for Bond's boss, "M." Fleming was also inspired by the tales of his brother Peter, who worked for the British SOE (Special Operations Executive). Godfrey greatly admired Fleming for his initiative and dependability, once commenting that "Ian should have been DNI and I his naval adviser."

Most of Fleming's espionage work was cerebral and deskbound, although he usually carried a commando knife and a fountain pen that he said contained tear gas. Legends of his derring-do during the war abound, but the stories appear to have been concocted after the James Bond novels became popular. Fleming is, however, credited with the creation of 30TH ASSAULT UNIT, an intelligence-gathering commando unit.

A wartime trip to the United States included a stopover in Lisbon, where Fleming gambled in a casino at nearby Estoril. This experience later gave him the setting for *Casino Royale* (1953), the first Bond book. When Fleming arrived in New York he met with WILLIAM STEVENSON, head of British intelligence in the United States and, like Bond, a devotee of the perfect martini. Fleming also met JAMES DONOVAN, who later became the head of the OFFICE OF SPECIAL SERVICES (OSS).

Later President Kennedy gave James Bond a boost in America by saying that *From Russia with Love* (1957) was one of his 10 favorite books. By the 1960s Fleming was writing a Bond book a year, and the books were as popular in the United States as in England. Many were made into films (see MOVIES). Fleming's other Bond books are *Diamonds Are Forever, Doctor No, For Your Eyes Only, From Russia with Love, Goldfinger, Live and Let Die, The Man with the Golden Gun, Moonraker, Octopussy, On Her Majesty's Secret Service, The Spy Who Loved Me, Thunderball,* and *You Only Live Twice.*

Floater

Person used for a one-time or occasional intelligence operation. Generally a floater is a low-level person, sometimes used without his or her knowledge. A floater might be a waiter sent to a hotel room with a bottle of champagne—allegedly from the management—to ascertain who is in the hotel room.

Fluency Committee

British group established in Oct. 1964 to investigate a possible Soviet MOLE in a senior position in the British intelligence community. The Fluency Committee was a joint effort of the D Branch (investigations) of the Security Service (MI5) and the COUNTERINTELLIGENCE Division of the Secret Intelligence Service (MI6). Chairman of the group was PETER WRIGHT of MI5.

The investigation was based on the confessions earlier that year of Soviet spies ANTHONY BLUNT, JOHN CAIRNCROSS, and LEO LONG along with material from several Soviet DEFECTORS. In particular, the committee reviewed indications of a mole that had previously pointed to HAROLD (KIM) PHILBY. Upon reexamination, the information pointed to the existence of a Soviet spy in MI5 run by Soviet MILITARY INTELLIGENCE (GRU). Philby had served in MI6 working for the NKVD/NKGB.

Wright felt that all indications pointed to two career MI5 officers—Graham Mitchell and ROGER HOLLIS—the latter the Director-General of MI5 at the time the Fluency Committee was convened. (Hollis retired in Dec. 1965.)

In 1965 the committee submitted its report to MARTIN FURNIVAL JONES, the new head of MI5, and DICK

WHITE, head of MI6. It showed indications of almost continuous Soviet penetration of MI5 from 1942 to at least 1962. The committee's candidates for an undiscovered Soviet mole in MI5 were Hollis and Michael Hanley, at the time a branch director in MI5 and a probable successor to Furnival Jones. Wright recorded Furnival Jones' reaction:

> Where's this going to end, Peter—you've sent me a paper which says that my predecessor and most likely my successor are both spies. Have you thought this through? Have you stopped to think about the damage that will be done if we act on these recommendations? It will take a decade to recover from this, even if there's nothing at the end of it.

Wright responded, "I stand by what we have written, F.J. [Furnival Jones], and what's more, so does every other member of the Fluency Working Party, and I can assure you if there were other candidates, you would have had them."

Furnival Jones approved a limited investigation and then interrogation of Hanley, given the MI5 CODE NAME Harriet. He was cleared and continued his career in MI5.

Finally, in 1969 the Fluency files were turned over to a branch of MI5 and an interrogation of Hollis was approved. For two days he was politely "grilled," with MI5 analysts (including Wright) listening to and recording the sessions. Hollis neither revealed nor admitted anything, and the Hollis file was closed. (In 1981, Prime Minister Margaret Thatcher told the House of Commons that, after further review, it had been concluded that Hollis was *not* a spy.)

The Fluency Committee had aided general MI5 investigations and helped to break into additional VENONA messages. But the apparent senior mole was never found, although Wright, CHAPMAN PINCHER, and others continued to believe that Hollis was a Soviet AGENT.

Flutter

American slang for a lie detector test; to "flutter" someone is to administer a lie-detector (POLYGRAPH) test.

Foote, Alexander

(b. 1905 d. 1958)

Member of the Soviet LUCY SPY RING during World War II.

A British subject, Foote served in the International Brigade on the Republican side in the Spanish Civil War, returning to England in 1939 when the war ended. After a time as a COURIER for Soviet intelligence in England, he was recruited to work in Switzerland for a Soviet espionage network operated by RUDOLF ROESSLER, whose CODE NAME was Lucy. The network was being run against Nazi Germany.

Foote, whose code name was Jim, became the key radio operator for transmitting information from Germany and Switzerland to Moscow. Unbeknownst to him, some of the intelligence he passed to Moscow was diluted ULTRA material, which the British at BLETCHLEY PARK decided to pass on to their Soviet allies without revealing the source as Ultra.

Responding to German pressure, in Nov. 1943 the Swiss Security Service arrested Foote, who destroyed his transmitter and burned incriminating papers while the Swiss broke down the door of his apartment. Released from a Swiss prison in Sept. 1944, he went to Paris, reported to the Soviet Embassy, and was ordered to Moscow for training as an AGENT in the United States. Sent to the Soviet intelligence station in BERLIN, he defected to the British there. In his debriefing he gave his interrogators from the Security Service (MI5) information that linked a woman code-named Sonia to the British branch of the Lucy ring. (She was also a courier for KLAUS FUCHS; see URSULA KUCZYNSKI.)

Foote ostensibly wrote an espionage biography entitled *Handbook for Spies* (1949). But according to NIGEL WEST, the book was actually written by Courtney Young of MI5, which took "the opportunity to score a few propaganda points," including a suggestion that Soviet spy networks were probably operating "both in England and the United States."

MI5 arranged for Foote to get a job with the Ministry of Agriculture and Fisheries, and he resumed his life as an ordinary citizen.

For Official Use Only

(FOUO)

U.S. designation applied to information that has not been given a security CLASSIFICATION. The designation allows officials to withhold information from the public even though disclosure of the information would not affect national security. FOUO is often invoked to protect information containing trade secrets or commercial or financial information from firms doing business with the government, as well as information about individuals.

But FOUO is also stamped on government information whose release could embarrass a bureaucrat or thwart a questionable government project being developed in secrecy. (See CLASSIFICATION.)

Foreign Armies East

Fremde Heere Ost (Foreign Armies East), the German Army General Staff's 12th branch, concerned with MILITARY INTELLIGENCE on the Eastern (Russian) Front in World War II. It was established on Nov. 10, 1938, as Adolf Hitler began planning for an assault on the Soviet Union.

Like FOREIGN ARMIES WEST, this branch collected intelligence from a variety of sources—spies, codebreaking,

prisoner interrogation, aerial RECONNAISSANCE, front-line observers, and so on. However, the ABWEHR—the intelligence branch of the military high command—had its own intelligence collection activities, including spies and frontline observers.

When war began in Sept. 1939, Foreign Armies East was located at Zossen, 20 miles south of BERLIN, site of the General Staff's field headquarters. When the Germans invaded the Soviet Union in June 1941, Foreign Armies East moved with other parts of the Army's General Staff to the Führer's headquarters in East Prussia, near Lake Mauersee (now Lake Marnry in Poland).

Foreign Armies East, especially under Col. REINHARD GEHLEN, who became head of the branch in April 1942, had a high degree of success in identifying and evaluating the Soviet forces fighting against Germany. Intelligence historian DAVID KAHN wrote in *Hitler's Spies* (1978):

> Gehlen's accuracy was one of the major factors both in fortifying his personal position and in changing the German army's negative attitude toward intelligence. Another was his discreet propaganda. He issued a booklet of his predictions contending that he had "succeeded in correctly recognizing the enemy's intentions—sometimes months in advance." A third factor was circumstance. The Germans were on the defensive [after the winter of 1942–1943], which requires knowledge of the enemy more than the offensive. Moreover, their strength was declining, and since intelligence enables a commander to magnify his available strength, the German generals gratefully accepted Gehlen's assistance.

But Foreign Armies East also made major errors in its evaluations and predictions of the Soviet plans and intentions. For example, on June 22, 1944—the third anniversary of the German invasion—the equivalent of four Soviet army groups smashed into the center of the German front, precisely where Gehlen predicted there would be no action. The German front collapsed, and before the Germans could make a stand they had lost several hundred miles of territory.

A further complicating factor for Foreign Armies East and West was that Hitler disliked intelligence officers and often disregarded their appraisals as defeatist. Also, as Germany went on the defensive in 1942–1943, staff officers, especially at the Führer's headquarters, tended to downgrade intelligence estimates, in turn forcing the intelligence staffs to inflate their estimates.

Indeed, as Hitler was raging at his generals on March 28, 1945, Heinz Guderian, one of the war's leading tank commanders, shouted, "Has Gen. Gehlen in his intelligence estimate 'misinformed' about the strength of the Russians? No!" Hitler screamed back, "Gehlen is a fool!"

Guderian was fired on the spot. Gehlen was relieved of Foreign Armies East on April 9, 1945—a month before the end of the Third Reich.

Foreign Armies West

Fremde Heere West (Foreign Armies West), the German Army's General Staff's third branch, concerned with MILITARY INTELLIGENCE on the Western Front in World War II. Previously designated the Foreign Armies branch, in 1938, as Adolf Hitler began planning an assault on the Soviet Union, the section concerned with Eastern Front intelligence became the FOREIGN ARMIES EAST branch of the General Staff.

According to intelligence historian DAVID KAHN in *Hitler's Spies* (1978), the two intelligence branches divided the world on the principle that "People who wear their shirts inside their pants belong to the west, those who wear theirs outside, to the east."

Foreign Armies West, initially with headquarters in BERLIN, was more dependent upon the ABWEHR for its intelligence sources than was Foreign Armies East. After the war began, in Sept. 1939, Foreign Armies West relocated to Zossen. Subsequently, the intelligence staff moved forward with the chief of the General Staff as preparations were made for war in the West. By May 1940, when the Germans attacked France, the intelligence branch had located 122 of the 123 French and British divisions in France.

But as Kahn observed, "It was not perfect: it once lost sight of an entire Belgian army of half a million men." Although Foreign Armies West did provide the Army with valuable intelligence and assessments, it failed to predict the American-British invasion of French North Africa in Nov. 1942, was misled by a British DECEPTION operation known as MINCEMEAT into believing that the Allies would invade the Balkans rather than Sicily, was unable to give warning of Allied landings at Anzio and Nettuno, and was misled again by Allied deception on D-DAY at Normandy.

Foreign Armies East proved more successful than its counterpart in the West, in part because of the diverse nationalities, geography, and tactics involved on the Western Front compared to the nature of the war against the Soviet Union.

Also see WALTHER NICOLAI.

Foreign Broadcast Information Service

(FBIS)

CIA unit that monitors foreign media, especially radio and television broadcasts. A component of the CIA's Directorate of Science and Technology, the FBIS translates, summarizes, and analyzes broadcasts of both open and classified radio stations. The FBIS also procures other forms of foreign OPEN SOURCE information, including newspapers, journals, books, newsletters, commercials annual reports, telephone directories, CD-ROMs, and databases.

The FBIS dates to 1941, when the U.S. Federal Communications Commission established a Foreign Broadcast Monitoring Service at the request of the State Department. During World War II the monitoring service, overseen by the U.S. Army, concentrated on listening to German, Italian, and Japanese propaganda broadcasts.

After the war the CENTRAL INTELLIGENCE GROUP took over the service. When the CIA was created broadcast monitoring became one of its responsibilities. The FBIS made an agreement with the monitoring service of the British Broadcasting Corp. (BBC), dividing the responsibility for monitoring most of the world's pertinent news broadcasts and others of interest to intelligence analysts. (The BBC also occasionally provided COVER for CIA INTELLIGENCE OFFICERS.)

FBIS transcripts are made available to scholars and researchers. Daily reports are widely distributed within the U.S. government and subscribers in the media and the academic community. The transcripts are also electronically transmitted to U.S. and British offices throughout the world.

LARRY WU-TAI CHIN, arrested in 1986 as a spy for China, worked for the FBIS. His arrest revealed that the FBIS also handled classified material, but the nature of it was not revealed.

Foreign Intelligence Surveillance Act

U.S. legislation enacted in 1976 (to become law two years later), which provides for legal handling of clandestine SURVEILLANCE of espionage suspects.

When the executive branch decides to seek electronic surveillance of an individual in an espionage case, the Chief Justice of the United States selects a district court judge to hold a closed session to decide if the government should have the authority to conduct such surveillance. The FOREIGN INTELLIGENCE SURVEILLANCE COURT usually performs this task.

The act amended the U.S. Code by adding a new chapter, "Electronic Surveillance Within the United States for Foreign Intelligence Purposes." The law recognized the need to establish legislative controls over telephone taps and electronic BUGS.

Foreign Intelligence Surveillance Court

Clandestine court unique in American justice, which some legal observers have described as a modern version of England's notorious royal star chamber. The inspiration for the secret court emerged from congressional investigations of wiretapping abuses. The leading architect of the secret court was Sen. Edward Kennedy, who in 1976 introduced the court's legislative underpinning, the FOREIGN INTELLIGENCE SURVEILLANCE ACT, which became law in 1978.

No defense attorney can enter this court, for it serves only the federal government and admits before it only officers of the government. All briefs presented to the court are secret, as are all of its actions and decisions. Records of the proceedings of the court are sealed under security measures established by the Chief Justice of the United States and the Attorney General.

The court originally had seven judges, each appointed by the Chief Justice of the United States for seven-year, nonrenewable terms. Each had to be from a different circuit, with the terms staggered so that a new judge came to the court each year.

In 2001, the USA PATRIOT ACT increased the number of FISC judges to 11, "of whom no fewer than 3 shall reside within 20 miles of the District of Columbia." The act also extended the life of FISC-authorized surveillance from 90 days to 120 days, with a possible extension to one year. Investigators were given "roving authority," enabling them to obtain a generic court order that would cover shifting situations, such as a change in the TARGET's telephone company or internet service provider. (Previously, such a change would necessitate a return to the court for new authorization.) In an "emergency situation," electronic surveillance that would otherwise require court authorization may now be conducted for up to 72 hours. During that time the investigators must either obtain court authorization or end the surveillance.

The Justice Department's Office of Intelligence Policy and Review represents the United States before the FISC, preparing applications authorization of electronic surveillance and physical searches by U. S. intelligence agencies in investigations involving espionage and international terrorism. If such surveillance produces prospective evidence to be used in a trial, the office handles all the motions and briefs.

The court convenes in an electronically secure room on the restricted sixth floor of the Department of Justice building on Constitution Avenue in Washington, D.C. The court's constitutionality stands virtually unchallenged by either liberal or conservative guardians of the Bill of Rights. Democrats and Republicans across the political spectrum support the court.

Since the war on terrorism began in 2001, the issuance of approvals for surveillance has soared. In 1994, for example, there were 576 requests for wiretaps and BUGS, all of which, as usual, were approved. In the year 2002, there were 1,228 applications; 1,226 were approved and two had to be "modified" before subsequent approval. The modifications came as a result of the first Department of Justice appeal to the equally secret Court of Review since the passage of the law that created the court and its clandestine procedures.

The only judge of this court to speak publicly about it, Judge Royce C. Lamberth, told an American Bar Association group in 1997 that when an application comes before him, "I get into the nitty gritty. I know exactly what is going to be done and why. And my questions are answered. . . ." Commenting on "rubber stamp" charges because applications are routinely granted, he said, "Some have been revised, some have been withdrawn and resubmitted with additional information. . . ."

He revealed that the clandestine search of the home of CIA spy ALDRICH AMES—a search legally different from a clandestine entry to plant BUGS—had been authorized by Attorney General Janet Reno and not by the court. Had Ames gone to trial, Lamberth said, "that would have been a hotly litigated issue." The statute has now been amended so that searches must be authorized by the court itself. (See USA PATRIOT ACT.)

Fort Holabird

Former site of the U.S. Army's MILITARY INTELLIGENCE training. Located in Baltimore, Md., "The Bird," as it was affectionately known, was founded as a quartermaster depot in 1918 to serve the needs of the Army in World War I. Between the wars the Quartermaster Corps manufactured trucks at Holabird and the specifications for the famed World War II jeep were drawn up there.

After World War II Holabird became the site for Army COUNTERINTELLIGENCE training. The U.S. Army Intelligence School opened there in May 1955, and the curriculum was expanded to teach combat intelligence and regional studies.

During the Vietnam War the Intelligence School became so crowded that a second site was needed. With the growing need for ELECTRONIC INTELLIGENCE, Army intelligence officials selected Fort Huachuca, in the remote high desert of southeastern Arizona, an area relatively free of electronic signal traffic. The move was made in 1971; Fort Huachuca was named the "Home for Military Intelligence," and the school was renamed the Intelligence Center and School. "The Bird" was closed down as a military intelligence facility in 1973.

Fort Meade

Site of the NSA and related MILITARY INTELLIGENCE activities since 1957. The Army base, near Laurel, Md., encompasses the NSA, providing a vast secure area surrounded by fences. Fort George G. Meade—its official name—is about midway between Baltimore, Md., and Washington, D.C. It was selected in 1952 as the site of what was then the ARMED FORCES SECURITY AGENCY (AFSA).

U.S. codebreaking efforts centered on the Washington area during World War II. After the war, concerned that a single attack on Washington could wipe out all U.S. codebreaking capabilities, the Joint Chiefs of Staff decided to consolidate AFSA facilities and move them out of the Washington area. In 1950 Fort Knox, Ky., was chosen as the site. But many of AFSA's 5,000 employees would not move, and the loss of even a small percentage of the highly skilled work force would cripple the agency. Thus, in 1952 the search began for a new site within 25 miles of Washington. One choice was the Bureau of Public Roads Laboratory in LANGLEY, Va. Another was Fort George G. Meade. (Langley became the home of the CIA.)

The base, founded in 1917, was named after Maj. Gen. George Gordon Meade, a Union hero of the battle of Gettysburg. More than 100,000 World War I "Doughboys" were trained at Fort Meade. In 1928 the post was renamed Fort Leonard Wood, but Pennsylvanians, stung by the loss of a Gettysburg remembrance, vigorously protested. The Pennsylvania delegation in the House of Representatives added a mandatory name change to the Regular Army Appropriation Act, and it once more became Fort George G. Meade.

The base again served as a training center during World War II and was the headquarters of the U.S. Second Army when it was selected as AFSA's new home. To keep the relocation of AFSA secret, the move to Fort Meade and the widespread construction there were given the CODE NAME Project K. Soon after the relocation decision was made, the clandestine National Security Agency was created by secret presidential order.

Fort Meade is also location of the National Cryptologic MUSEUM.

Fortitude

CODE NAME for the part of the DECEPTION plan for D-DAY specifically related to Allied landings in Normandy in June 1944. (BODYGUARD was the overall code name for the entire set of deception operations to provide the German high command with DISINFORMATION.)

There were two basic code names: Fortitude North for the nonexistent Allied army in Scotland, reported by British-controlled German agents to be planning to invade Norway, and Fortitude South for the nonexistent FIRST U.S. ARMY GROUP (FUSAG) under Lt. Gen. George Patton, which was reported to be preparing to land at Pas de Calais. At least 19 German divisions remained in Calais for weeks after D-Day.

Forty Committee

The NATIONAL SECURITY COUNCIL (NSC) group that was assigned the task of approving COVERT ACTIONS conducted by the CIA.

"Forty" was a 1970s name for an ongoing function with frequently changing names. Since the 1950s there had been some NSC mechanism for deciding on covert actions.

James R. Gardner, a retired State Department official who was a liaison officer to the committee in Oct. 1975, told the House Intelligence Committee (PIKE COMMITTEE) that nearly 40 actions had been approved between 1972 and 1974 without a meeting of the Forty Committee. Gardner said that the committee chair, Henry Kissinger, national security adviser and later simultaneously Secretary of State, preferred to make the decisions by "telephone votes," rather than through meetings. He likened the Forty Committee to President Lincoln's cabinet, in which only Lincoln's vote counted; on the Forty Committee it was Kissinger's.

Other members of the Forty Committee were WILLIAM E. COLBY, the DIRECTOR OF CENTRAL INTELLIGENCE; William P. Clements, Jr., Deputy Secretary of Defense; Gen. George S. Brown, Chairman of the Joint Chiefs of Staff; and Joseph J. Sisco, Under Secretary of State for political affairs.

Gardner, an officer of the State Department's BUREAU OF INTELLIGENCE AND RESEARCH, said that Kissinger was usually the only member of the committee who had detailed knowledge of the proposed covert actions.

FOUO

SEE FOR OFFICIAL USE ONLY

Fourth Man

The label for the British spy believed to have aided the THIRD MAN, (HAROLD [KIM] PHILBY), who in turn had been in league with two other MOLES in the British government, GUY BURGESS and DONALD MACLEAN. In 1963, when Philby was unmasked as a Soviet spy, British intelligence officials sought a fourth man, long suspected to be Sir ANTHONY BLUNT, a former INTELLIGENCE OFFICER and a highly respected art historian who was the curator of the queen's paintings. Blunt was, in fact, the fourth man and speculation arose about a "fifth man" (see JOHN CAIRNCROSS and ROGER HOLLIS).

Also see CAMBRIDGE SPY RING.

Fox, Edward L.

American writer who was the ghost writer of *The Secrets of the German War Office* (1914), supposedly written by a German spy known as Dr. Armgaard K. Graves. The book was a best-seller in Britain. In reality, Graves was a fraud and impostor.

Fozie

SEE KURT FREDERICK LUDWIG

France

France has long been a country of intrigue and espionage, much of it directed at its traditional enemy, England. As far back as the prelude to the Battle of Agincourt in 1415, King Henry V of England discovered three traitors, or MOLES, within his entourage—men who were selling intelligence to the French about the English plans: Richard, Earl of Cambridge; Henry, Lord Scroop of Masham; and Sir Thomas Grey, knight of Northumberland.

William Shakespeare's *Henry V* (1599) describes the young king confronting the traitors: "What shall I say to thee, Lord Scroop—thou cruel, Ingrateful, savage, and inhuman creature? Thou that didst bear the key of all my counsels [secrets], That knew'st the very bottom of my soul, That almost mightst have coin'd me into gold."

All three, then arrested for high treason for spying for France, were forthwith sent to their death. (In Sir

Laurence Olivier's film version of *Henry V*, made during World War II and sponsored by the British government, the scenes about the traitors were cut from Shakespeare's script in keeping with wartime sentiments.)

In 1590, when French King Henry IV established the *Poste aux Lettres*, he began the long French tradition of the *cabinet noir*, the "BLACK CHAMBER," where letters were opened, read, and resealed. The work inspired the recruitment of experts in the art of restoring broken seals, made France Europe's leader in the field of espionage, and spawned the development of CRYPTOSYSTEMS for encrypting and decrypting letters.

Mail tampering was one of the grievances proclaimed by the revolutionaries of 1789, but the practice continued through the Napoleonic era (and on into the 20th century). Similarly, the machinations of CARDINAL DE ARMAND JEAN RICHELIEU during the reign of Louis XIII in the 17th century set a pattern for court plots and counterplots throughout the age of kings that required extensive spying within the court.

During the American Revolutionary War, BENJAMIN FRANKLIN, diplomat and spy stationed for a time in Paris, called France "the intriguing nation." Spies had flair. CHEVALIER CHARLES GENEVIEVE LOUIS D'ÉON sometimes posed as a woman to carry out his undercover missions for King Louis XV. Another AGENT, PIERRE BEAUMARCHAIS, was known for his wise adage on the value of secrecy in statecraft: "A project once disclosed is a project doomed to failure."

Under Napoléon Bonaparte, France established a central espionage system, with internal security the domain of the prefect of police, Joseph Fouché, who worked assiduously to follow Napoléon's maxim that "a leader has the right to be beaten, but never the right to be surprised." Fouché's Ministry of General Police ran a secret police agency, the SÛRETÉ GÉNÉRALE (later known as the Sûreté Nationale and usually simply called the Sûreté), which oversaw the black chamber of the Napoleonic era. Its staff read not only the letters of government officials and diplomats but also the letters of the Bonaparte family. Eventually, the black chamber expanded to include branch offices in Amsterdam, Hamburg, VIENNA, and other major cities in Europe.

Napoléon demanded high-quality TACTICAL INTELLIGENCE during his campaigns, and sometimes his generals got it themselves, by donning disguises and mingling with the sutlers and other camp followers. Other agents developed superb maps or kidnapped civilians to get information about what lay on the road ahead. Napoléon's principal intelligence agent was KARL SCHULMEISTER, renowned as "the emperor of spies" during the Napoleonic Wars.

DISINFORMATION specialists for Napoléon produced an enduring piece of forgery, the "Testament of Peter the Great," in which the czar supposedly disclosed Russian plans to conquer much of the world and gain a warmwater port. Although discredited as a counterfeit, the testament endured through the 19th and 20th centuries as a rationale for politicians to warn of Russian—and, later, Soviet—plans for expansion.

Intelligence had fallen to its lowest ebb in the French Army by the time the Franco-Prussian War began in 1870. The army of Napoléon III lacked even useful maps of Prussia. Defeated in 1871, the French Army General Staff reorganized, using the Prussians as models. Out of this reorganization came the DEUXIÈME BUREAU. Officers in its key unit, the Section de Statistiques et de Reconnaissances Militaires, included Capt. ALFRED DREYFUS. His conviction and subsequent presidential pardon rocked France and created a public distrust of French intelligence agencies that persists to this day.

The G-series of staff designations later adopted by many Western armies originated with the French Army in the late 1800s, when several staff bureaus were designated for various functions—hence today G-2 indicates intelligence.

French espionage extended throughout the French empire in the 19th century. To hold on to colonies in North Africa, French INTELLIGENCE OFFICERS often had to pit Arab chieftains against each other. Once, to convince some chieftains of the weakness of a group of anti-French chiefs, French agents had the opposition chiefs bring in warriors and have them lift what looked like ordinary wooden chests. The French had rigged the chests with electromagnets, making them impossible for the bewildered warriors to lift.

WORLD WAR I

In the years leading to World War I, French intelligence agencies focused on Germany (when they were not looking for French subversives) and did anticipate German strategy. But French politicians canceled out intelligence gains. In May 1913 CODEBREAKERS of the Sûreté decoded messages showing that the French foreign minister and the Vatican were holding secret meetings. An enraged minister of the interior revealed the messages at a cabinet meeting. (France had broken diplomatic ties with the Vatican following revelations of Catholic Church involvement in the Dreyfus affair.) The Cabinet ordered the *Sûreté* to stop reading diplomatic messages.

Shortly thereafter, the French prime minister asked the German ambassador for copies of German diplomatic messages. In the conversation the German ambassador became of aware of the French codebreaking; the Germans therefore changed their codes. Thus, when France went to war in 1914, French codebreakers, who had become highly skilled, operated under the dual handicaps of a hiatus in diplomatic interceptions and changes in the diplomatic codes of Germany and other nations.

The French played a leading role in aerial RECONNAISSANCE, which augmented traditional intelligence methods during World War I. By the end of the war, planes carried cameras with film so sensitive that small details—sometimes even footprints—could be perceived in photos taken from 15,000 feet. (See AIRCRAFT.) The French also pioneered the first primitive ELECTRONIC INTELLIGENCE system by intercepting German radio communications, many of which were made in the clear. Carrier pigeons were often used to carry encoded tactical intelligence messages. (See PIGEON POST.) An attempt to use BALLOONS in the same way failed.

On the battlefield, German intelligence won over French intelligence, particularly in the masking of maneuvers. By simply moving at night and using effective camouflage, Germany could move scores of divisions without French detection. Clever disinformation and DECEPTION also aided the Germans. As the Germans began the great offensive of March 1918, the head of the Deuxième Bureau said, "I am the best-informed man in France, and at this moment I no longer know where the Germans are." But if World War I showed the French to be weak in tactical intelligence, their use of aircraft, radio intercepts, and fast-reaction codebreaking ushered in the modern age of MILITARY INTELLIGENCE.

HUNTING THE BOLSHEVIKS

After the war, French intelligence interest focused on Russia; as the Bolsheviks rose to power, refugees, including many White Russians from the czarist court, fled to Paris—often with Red agents in pursuit. The French intelligence agencies were kept busy tracking both the White Russians and the Reds who followed them, mostly to Paris, where their titles and lavish spending—for many thought their exile from St. Petersburg was temporary—made French surveillance and counterespionage activities complex. There were also rivalries among the White Russian groups, at times exacerbated by British agent SIDNEY REILLY. (See BOLSHEVIK LIQUIDATION CLUB and THE TRUST.)

Augmenting the welter of French intelligence agencies was the new Service de Contrôle et d'Assistance des Indigènes en France des Colonies (CAI), which operated out of the Colonial Ministry. CAI agents trailed people from French colonies, especially Indochinese suspected of being communists. Continuing the French tradition, COUNTERINTELLIGENCE operatives sifted through mail from Indochina. Among the suspects were Ho Chi Minh, the future leader of anti-French (and later anti-American) communist forces in Vietnam.

In the 1920s and 1930s Soviet spies were deeply entrenched in France. The Air Ministry, a favorite recruiting target for the Soviets, produced so many spies that a French writer compared it to Cambridge University, source of Britain's CAMBRIDGE SPY RING. The French Communist Party was directly connected to the Soviet Embassy in Paris, and communists were found at all levels of society.

French intelligence faltered in the interwar years. Internecine warfare between agencies threatened the delivery of dependable information to military and political leaders. As war with Germany threatened, however, the *Deuxième Bureau* intensified its work and supplied the General Staff with warnings of German blitzkrieg tactics. And from military ATTACHÉS came reports of German advances in aircraft and tank design. The attachés also alerted the Army to German plans to occupy Czechoslovakia in March 1939 and astutely interpreted German war games as a simulated invasion of Poland.

But most French generals and politicians ignored this intelligence and, following Britain's lead, chose appeasement over preparation for war. On Sept. 1, 1939, however, when Germany invaded Poland, war could no longer be avoided. France mobilized, and, with Britain, on Sept. 3 declared war on Germany.

WORLD WAR II

When France went to war the French Army's command structure consisted of four widely scattered army headquarters and the War Ministry in Paris; intelligence was likewise uncentralized and unfocused. Air reconnaissance, which France had pioneered in World War I, failed in this war, primarily because the French Air Force quickly lost command of the air to the German Luftwaffe. The Deuxième Bureau overestimated German forces along the Dutch border and underestimated those on the Luxembourg frontier.

From Sept. 1939 to May 1940—the so-called phony war—French troops, joined by the British Expeditionary Force, manned defensive lines and awaited an attack that was not predicted, due to poor French intelligence and the failure of French generals to accept the possibility of a German strike through the Ardennes. On May 10, 1940, Germany simultaneously invaded the Netherlands, Belgium, and Luxembourg, which all fell quickly. On May 13 the Germans established a bridgehead at Sedan, the gateway into France, easily outflanked the much vaunted Maginot Line, and sped through the Ardennes.

On June 10, the government evacuated Paris. Prime Minister Paul Reynaud resigned. His successor, Marshal Henri Philippe Pétain, surrendered his retreating army. The Germans reannexed the Alsace and Lorraine areas as parts of Germany and occupied northern and western France. The rest of France was left unoccupied and was administered, along with French colonies, by a collaborationist government at Vichy, 200 miles southeast of Paris.

On June 28, Brig. Gen. Charles de Gaulle, who had escaped to England, was recognized by the British government as the "leader of all Free Frenchmen." De Gaulle set up the anti-Vichy Free French movement in London. The Vichy regime tried de Gaulle in absentia for desertion and sentenced him to death. "Whatever happens," de Gaulle declared, "the flame of the French resistance must not go out and will not go out."

Resistance became the rallying cry in occupied France, where thousands of men and women formed guerrilla units, many known simply as the maquis. De Gaulle set up a French intelligence service, ultimately named the BCRA, Bureau Central de Renseignernents et d'Action (Central Bureau of Information and Action), to link the Free French in London with the Resistance and work with the British SOE (Special Operations Executive) to send agents into France.

French officers, including military intelligence officers, in Vichy France were considered "officers of the armistice." Many of them would be condemned after the war as collaborators. The Surveillance du Territoire, the intelligence branch of the Sûreté, continued to function for Vichy, which also set up a paramilitary organization, the Milice, which hunted down members of the Resistance. Joseph Darnand, a celebrated hero of the French Army, ran the Milice, transforming it into a Vichy version of the German GESTAPO. (When France was liberated, Darnand fled to Germany but was caught and executed by France for treason in 1945.)

To the French, all German secret service terror was attributed to the GESTAPO, although that branch of the secret political police acted independently of the principal German intelligence agency of the occupation, the SD. One of the most brutal of the SD officers in France was KLAUS BARBIE, "the Butcher of Lyon," who escaped justice until long after the war.

Few Resistance members spoke German, but most learned enough to get by, and all knew the significance of two words, *streng geheim* (TOP SECRET). Because a Resistance legend, René Duchez, recognized these words, he was able to steal a map, about 10 feet long and two feet wide, showing the "Atlantic Wall," the German defense complex along the French coast. He snatched it while posing as a wallpaper hanger for a firm engaged in building some of the defenses. The map showed underwater obstacles, which were blown up before the Anglo-American troops landed on D-DAY, June 6, 1944. On the eve of D-Day the Resistance created wholesale sabotage, knocking out telephone and electric lines and disrupting railroads.

De Gaulle, who had declared himself the head of the de facto government of France, entered Paris in triumph on Aug. 26, 1944, behind French and American troops. French politics became increasingly complex, and so did the intelligence picture, with pro–de Gaulle and anti–de Gaulle agencies openly warring. The BCRA was disbanded and replaced by the DCSS (Direction Générale des Services Spéciaux).

After liberation, de Gaulle ordered the DGSS to report directly to him, not to the military high command—a historic change for French intelligence. The service was soon renamed the DGER (Direction Générale des Études et Recherches). But after scandals involving rampaging DGER agents, it was replaced by the SDECE (Service de Documentation Extérieure et de Contreespionage).

France by now had a swarm of intelligence services. The Interior Ministry had the DST (Direction de la Surveillance du Territoire) and the Renseignements Généraux, both under the Sûreté Nationale, and the Paris Prefecture of Police's own Renseignements Généraux, a Napoleonic relic. The DST took over some Army counterintelligence work, but there still existed the Army's Sécurité Militaire, which watched for subversive soldiers. The Colonial Ministry's Bureau had its own spy agency, the Bureau Technique de Liaison et de Coordination.

"Rather than serving the interests of the French state," wrote Douglas Porch in *The French Secret Services* (1995), "the secret services became the Fourth Republic's Achilles' heel. . . . Rivalries born of fragmentation and politicization joined with an atmosphere boiling with intrigue, rumors of Gaullist coups and communist insurrection, to tempt the services into the political arena."

POSTWAR INTELLIGENCE

The Gaullists set up the machinery for a postwar election that produced a new constitution and a new legislative body, which elected de Gaulle interim president. However, denied the mandate he desired, he resigned on Jan. 20, 1946, setting in motion postwar political turmoil.

After the hunt for wartime collaborationists died down, the competing intelligence agencies concentrated on looking for communist infiltrators in government. Not until the breaking of NKVD codes in the late 1940s did French intelligence officials learn how high the infiltration had been. (See VENONA.)

Soviet spies included Pierre Cot, a Minister for Air and a scientist at the French Air Ministry. Charles Hernu, Defense Minister from 1981 to 1985, reportedly passed intelligence reports to Bulgarian, Romanian, and Soviet spymasters in the 1950s and 1960s, when he was a rising Socialist politician. More disturbing news came in 1996, when a French counterintelligence official said that Hernu had been given $60,000 for his unsuccessful bid for the French National Assembly in 1958. Hernu died in 1990. French intelligence learned of Hernu's spying in 1992 from a Romanian intelligence official.

Because of the power of the French Communist Party, which had members in the French parliament, British and American intelligence agencies were reluctant to work closely with their French opposite numbers. In 1949, for example, when the Minister of Air was a communist, his chief of security was caught handing secret documents to the Yugoslav military attaché. Soviet defectors reported that the NKVD had infiltrated French security services and had even recruited a French ambassador through a HONEY TRAP baited by a prostitute in NKVD employ.

COLONIAL CONFLICTS

Intelligence services played a controversial role in France's attempt to resume control of Laos, Vietnam, and Cambodia after World War II. The communist Viet Minh, led by Ho Chi Minh, had seized power in Vietnam when Japanese occupation came to an end in Aug. 1945. France responded by landing troops at Haiphong and occupying Hanoi. The French hunted down communists, with the help of Nationalist Chinese officers who had worked for China's CENTRAL BUREAU OF INVESTIGATION AND STATISTICS.

The need to keep track of thousands of Indochinese in France led to the creation of still another intelligence agency, the Service de Liaison avec les Originaires des Territoires Français d'Outremer, which coordinated intelligence collected by the Deuxième Bureau, the SDECE, and military intelligence.

During the brutal Indochina war, Deuxième officers

attached to combat units routinely tortured and murdered suspected communists. The SDECE played a major role in Indochina, although more restrained. But how much a lack of SDECE intelligence led to France's humiliating defeat at Dien Bien Phu in 1953–1954 is still debated by historians. The Army must be blamed for the choice of site—an outpost in an isolated valley that could be resupplied only by air. The Deuxième Bureau provided Army commanders with enough intelligence about Viet Minh strength to alert the Army to extreme danger. But the Army chose to stand and fight, suffering a disastrous defeat in May 1954 that effectively ended the war in victory for the Viet Minh.

When bombs exploded throughout Algeria in Nov. 1954, French intelligence agencies, which had few ASSETS in the colony, were as surprised as their political masters. The explosions signaled the start of a war that would end with intelligence agencies, particularly the SDECE, disgraced by criminal conduct. Using gangsters and murderous mercenaries as "honorable correspondents," the SDECE tortured suspected insurgents, assassinated and kidnapped leaders of the FLN (Front de Libération Nationale), and aided renegade French officers who mutinied, formed the OAS (Organisation Armée Secrète), and launched an insurrection in May 1958.

In the midst of the crisis, the French parliament gave de Gaulle dictatorial power, and he cracked down on both the Army and intelligence services. But de Gaulle's return did not restore U.S. and British confidence in the French intelligence apparatus. Their suspicions were dramatically confirmed in Dec. 1961, when ANATOLI GOLITSIN, a KGB agent who had defected to the U.S. CIA, said that a Soviet spy ring, code-named SAPPHIRE, had deeply penetrated de Gaulle's government.

Establishment of effective, legitimate intelligence services was expected to be a hallmark of de Gaulle's Fifth Republic. But in Oct. 1965 the SDECE kidnapped and presumably murdered Moroccan nationalist Mehdi Ben Barka, and again the agency was discredited and reorganized.

Paris had one of the largest KGB foreign stations in the world. The Soviets were attracted by what U.S. and British intelligence officials saw as slack French security. But in the 1970s, when the intelligence agencies were under stricter oversight, French counterintelligence moved skillfully against the Soviets. Between 1974 and 1980, French officials ordered the expulsion of some 40 Soviet and East European diplomats. There were additional mass expulsions in 1983 and 1987.

France's intelligence apparatus got notorious publicity in 1985 when the DGSE, the French external security service, blew up the RAINBOW WARRIOR, a ship owned by the Greenpeace environmental organization, in the harbor at Auckland, New Zealand. That botched operation "can safely be said to be a prototype case through which relations between the state and intelligence services in France can be analyzed," wrote Porch in The French Secret Services. One man drowned when the ship was sunk. New Zealand authorities quickly unraveled the DGSE

plot behind the sinking. The French government, Porch added, fell into "what British spy novelist John le Carré called 'the oldest trap in the trade,' the belief that the real world's imperfections can be redressed by the secret world."

In the uproar that followed, as in the Barka case, the French parliament attempted to find ways to gain oversight over the French secret world. But again the intelligence agencies, aided by strong military allies, managed to have the oversight proposals shelved.

As the Cold War ended, French counterintelligence officials became concerned about terrorists. Because of France's liberal attitude toward granting political asylum, terrorists and potential terrorists could easily enter the country. They concentrated on Paris, which holds "the gold medal for terrorism in all categories," according to the magazine L'Express. Without Soviets to pursue, the DGSE turned to INDUSTRIAL ESPIONAGE, which became so blatant that in 1993 the CIA warned U.S. aircraft companies to beware of French spying at the annual Paris Air Show.

France continued the industrial espionage war in 1995 by asking five Americans, including CIA officers with diplomatic COVER, to leave the country because they had been caught attempting to bribe French officials in an attempt to obtain political and economic intelligence. One American was immediately sent home in a tacit admission of guilt.

French intelligence officials reportedly shared with the FBI information about Zacarias Moussaoui, a French citizen dubbed by U.S. investigators "the twentieth hijacker" in the Sept. 11, 2001 Al Qaeda attacks on the World Trade Center and the Pentagon. The French had linked Moussaoui to Osama bin Laden and Al Qaeda, tracing him to a suspected terrorist training camp in Afghanistan. French intelligence then put him on a watch list of probable terrorists. The FBI could have obtained this information, but there was a breakdown in communications between the French and the FBI. (Mishandling of the Moussaoui case would become a major issue when congressional critics looked into FBI anti-terrorist operations.)

Franklin, Benjamin

(b. 1706 d. 1790)

American statesman, diplomat, inventor, and publisher who established intelligence NETWORKS during the American Revolution. Franklin was the key member of the first U.S. agency for collecting foreign intelligence: the Committee of Secret Correspondence, set up by the Continental Congress on Nov. 29, 1775, "for the sole purpose of Corresponding with our friends in Great Britain, Ireland and other parts of the world."

Franklin's experience in foreign affairs began before the Revolution, when he acted as a colonial agent lobbyist in London for Massachusetts, Georgia, and Pennsylvania. The Continental Congress appointed him minister plenipotentiary, essentially ambassador to France, in Sept. 1778. He was also in control of diplomacy and foreign intelligence collection.

Franklin's main goal was to convince France that the best way to hurt Britain was to form an alliance with America. Franklin also worked covertly, dealing with JULIEN ACHARD DE BONVOULOIR, a French AGENT sent to America.

Franklin's own agent, Silas Deane, a Connecticut delegate to the Continental Congress, was, like Franklin, a member of the Secret Committee set up by the Congress to buy arms and other matériel. The French dealt with Deane through PIERRE BEAUMARCHAIS, ostensibly a merchant but actually an agent of the French Foreign Ministry.

Beaumarchais, drawing on his own funds and money from King Louis XVI and others in France and Spain, set up what is known in modern espionage as a PROPRIETARY COMPANY, a firm designed to hide intelligence or COUNTERINTELLIGENCE activities. The British SECRET SERVICE learned of the real purpose of the purported import-export firm, *Hortalez et Compagnie*, but Beaumarchais was able to get substantial amounts of arms to America.

Through agents in London, Franklin also kept track of British political and military activities. In Jan. 1778 Gen. Lord Cornwallis, reporting in London on the progress of the war in the colonies, said that the conquest of America was impossible. His words were quickly passed to one of Franklin's agents in London, who managed to get the report speedily to Franklin in France. Franklin used the intelligence to bolster his successful arguments for an American-French alliance.

Also see UNITED STATES.

Franks, Sir Arthur

(b. 1920 d. ?)

Head of the British Secret Intelligence Service (MI6) from 1978 to 1981. A veteran of the World War II SOE (Special Operations Executive), Franks served MI6 in Iran and BERLIN.

Fraser-Smith, Charles

(b. 1904 d. 1992)

Inventor of spy devices for the British government during World War II. His devices were the inspiration for "Q"— the wizard of spy equipment in IAN FLEMING's JAMES BOND [F] novels and the movie adaptations.

Fraser-Smith attended Brighton College, which he left at 17 to briefly become a preparatory schoolmaster. Undistinguished academically, he was an ardent rugby player. After studying agriculture in 1926 he farmed in Morocco.

He returned to Britain in 1940 to join the fight against Germany. There he was recruited by the Ministry of Supply to develop special devices for the Secret Intelli-

gence Service (MI6). Fraser hid spy cameras in cigarette lighters, maps in smoking pipes, SECRET WRITING gear in shoe heels, and a myriad of other devices in unlikely spots. He worked out hiding places for compasses so that British fliers taken prisoner could secrete them during searches. Besides MI6 operatives, he developed devices for the SOE (Special Operations Executive) and SAS (Special Air Service).

In 1947 he retired from government service to farm again, this time in England. He wrote of some of his activities in *The Secret War of Charles Fraser-Smith* (1981). His coauthored *Men of Faith in the Second World War* (1986) discusses the religious views of 10 heroic figures in the war. The *Four-Thousand Year War* (1988), which he coauthored with David Porter, his biographer, describes the role of God in humankind's struggle to be free.

Frauenknecht, Alfred

(b. 1927 d. 1991)

Swiss engineer who sold Israeli intelligence the plans for the French Mirage fighter in the late 1960s. Frauenknecht was a senior engineer at the Sulzer Brothers firm in Switzerland with responsibility for producing Mirages for the Swiss Air Force.

Israeli intelligence learned that Frauenknecht was having financial problems (in part because he was supporting a mistress) and was unhappy with his firm. Although not Jewish, he felt great sympathy for the Jewish state and was angry that France had withheld the delivery of 50 Mirage fighters already paid for by Israel. In a joint effort by the secret Israeli intelligence agency LAKAM, the Israeli MILITARY INTELLIGENCE agency AMAN, and the Israeli Air Force technical staff, Frauenknecht was approached by an Israeli military officer who befriended him and persuaded him to steal blueprints of the highly classified Mirage aircraft.

In 1968–1969, Frauenknecht, with the help of a nephew, photocopied both the Mirage plans and blueprints for the special machinery needed to produce the aircraft and handed them over to the Israelis. The total haul amounted to hundreds of thousands of documents. Frauenknecht was paid $200,000 by the Israelis—the specific amount he requested—a trifle considering the real value of the plans.

He was arrested by Swiss police after a carton of secret blueprints had been misplaced. When arrested he declared: "I did it to help Israel on moral grounds for conscience. For them it was a question of survival. For myself, a devout Christian, I am still haunted by the memory of Dachau and Auschwitz." Charged with espionage, Frauenknecht confessed, was tried in 1971 and convicted. He was sentenced to 4½ years at hard labor.

Israel used the Mirage plans as the basis for its next generation fighter aircraft. Although ignored by the Israeli government after his release from prison, Frauenknecht maintained his affection for the country.

Freedom of Information Act

(FOIA)

Federal law that directs government agencies to disclose classified information upon request.

The law, in effect since 1967, opened up long-classified government records. Frequent amendments expanded people's rights to documents. The FBI, for example, had been essentially exempt, but in 1975 new amendments opened up FBI files. By 2003, however, historians, researchers, and ordinary citizens had access to more than 6 million pages of FBI documents released under FOIA requests. After the Sept. 11, 2001, attacks on America, the Justice Department told federal agencies that if they resisted FOIA requests, they would be given support in most cases.

The FOIA has several exemptions that add protection to such documents as intelligence sources and methods or virtually any PRODUCT of the NSA.

The FOIA applies only to federal agencies and does not create a right of access to records held by Congress, the courts, or by state or local government agencies. Each state has its own version of the FOIA.

Requests for agency records about oneself can also be made under the Privacy Act of 1974, which allows anyone the right to see personal records and to correct them if necessary. Both laws give people the right to sue the federal agency official who refused the request.

For detailed information about FOIA procedures, see www.usdoj.gov/04foia.

Freeh, Louis J.

(b. 1950)

Director of the FBI. Freeh became director in Sept. 1993, replacing WILLIAM S. SESSIONS, who was dismissed when he refused to resign after an inquiry into his abuse of the perquisites of his office. Freeh has served longer than any director of the FBI except for J. EDGAR HOOVER.

Freeh joined the FBI in 1975, after earning a law degree from Rutgers University. He spent several years investigating the infiltration of organized crime into the longshoremen's union.

In 1981 he became a U.S. attorney. His prime interest as a federal prosecutor was bringing cases against leaders of organized crime. In 1987 Freeh led the prosecution team that convicted defendants in the "pizza connection," an international Mafia drug ring. The trial ended in the conviction of 17 defendants who had used pizzerias as fronts for money.laundering. Freeh was appointed a federal judge by President Bush in 1991.

Freeh inherited a task that Sessions had not carried out: changing the FBI's Cold War mission. He gave priority to anti-terrorism, the drug war, and international organized crime. He opened an FBI office in Moscow to cooperate with Russian police authorities in the fight against international crime. But his efforts in increasing FBI activities overseas raised concern at the State Department and opened a new turf war with the CIA, a rival with the FBI for COUNTERINTELLIGENCE resources. But he and JOHN M. DEUTCH, the DIRECTOR OF CENTRAL INTELLIGENCE from 1994 to 1996, began working on ways to explore the roles of both agencies in the post–Cold War world.

Freeh also opened a new debate on wiretapping when he said that new technical ways must be found to balance personal privacy against what he saw as a need to create a U.S. communications system that would allow new electronic SURVEILLANCE procedures in an age of rapidly advancing technology. "Court-ordered wiretapping," he said, "is the single most effective investigative technique used by law enforcement to combat illegal drugs."

Freeh, who was replaced by ROBERT MUELLER on Sept. 4, 2001, survived the post–Sept. 11, 2001, recriminations against the FBI for failing to detect the terrorist plots to destroy the World Trade Center in New York City and targets in Washington, D.C.

Fremde Heere Ost

SEE FOREIGN ARMIES EAST

Fremde Heere West

SEE FOREIGN ARMIES WEST

French, Capt. George J.

U.S. Air Force officer arrested in 1957 after offering to sell nuclear bomb secrets to the Soviets. He made his offer by tossing a letter onto the grounds of the Soviet Embassy in Washington, D.C. His toss apparently was seen by FBI agents, who kept the embassy under SURVEILLANCE. In a secret court-martial he was sentenced to life imprisonment. Additional details of the case were not revealed.

Friedman, Lt. Col. William F.

(b. 1891 d. 1969)

American cryptologist who broke the Japanese PURPLE CODE in 1940.

The son of Russian Jews who emigrated to United States in 1892, Friedman was cited as "unquestionably one of the greatest cryptanalysts of all time," by World War II codebreaking historian DAVID KAHN.

Friedman graduated from Cornell University in 1914 with a degree in genetics. George Fabyan, a wealthy eccentric interested in both genetics and CIPHERS, hired Friedman to work at Fabyan's Riverbank Laboratories, an early "think tank" in Geneva, Ill. Friedman worked with his patron on ciphers that were supposed to prove whether Francis Bacon wrote the plays and sonnets attributed to William Shakespeare.

The U.S. Army and Navy sent CIPHER problems to Riverbank because there was no government-conducted CRYPTANALYSIS facility at that time. Friedman directed the Riverbank cryptanalytic operations and training from 1916 to 1920, except for a year as an Army 1st lieutenant working on German codes for the American Expeditionary Force in France.

In 1920 he went to Washington, D.C., where he worked for the Army Signal Corps, becoming chief cryptographer in 1922. Seven years later he became the chief of the new SIGNAL INTELLIGENCE SERVICE, which replaced the Cipher Bureau run by HERBERT O. YARDLEY. Friedman had six assistants to help him. (In 1935 an Army officer was assigned as military head of the group.)

Friedman, a leader in the evolution from pencil-and-paper to machine codebreaking, began attacking the top-level Japanese diplomatic codes—called Purple by U.S. codebreakers—in 1938. In Aug. 1940, after 20 months of intensive work, he and his colleagues solved their first Purple message. While breaking the Purple code did help U.S. military activities in the Pacific, its primary value was in deciphering communications from Japanese diplomatic and military missions in Nazi Germany to Japan.

In 1943 Friedman visited BLETCHLEY PARK in England to further the exchange of Anglo-American codebreaking knowledge. He continued his codebreaking work during the war and in 1952 became the first cryptologist to join the new NSA. In 1958 Friedman, Navy Capt. LAURANCE SAFFORD, and Frank B. Rowlett each received $100,000 from Congress for their contributions to the development and improvement of electrical enciphering machines. (See SIGABA.)

In an assessment of Friedman's contributions, the NSA's Center for Cryptologic History noted that his writings—beginning with his Riverbank publications and including *The Index of Coincidence* and *The Elements of Cryptanalysis*—"enabled cryptanalysts to make the transition into the modern age. Friedman's writings, which included his own techniques plus the ideas of others, formed a body of knowledge which served as a foundation upon which the new science was created."

Friedman and his wife, Elizabeth Smith Friedman, coauthored *The Shakespearean Ciphers Examined* (1957), in which they debunked the Bacon theory. Elizabeth Friedman, a cryptanalyst who first learned the art at Riverbank, testified as an expert witness in the trial that convicted VELVALEE DICKINSON, an American, of spying for Japan during World War II. (Dickinson had used a "doll code" for passing information to the Japanese.) Elizabeth Friedman died in 1980.

Friendly, Maj. Alfred

(b. 1911 d. 1983)

U.S. Army officer who worked at the BLETCHLEY PARK codebreaking facility during World War II.

Friendly, a captain in MILITARY INTELLIGENCE, arrived at Bletchley Park in 1944 as part of the American detachment there.

A reporter for *The Washington Post* before entering the Army, Friendly returned to the *Post* after the war, served briefly as the press officer for the Marshall Plan, the postwar European recovery effort, and returned once more to the *Post*, becoming the assistant managing editor and then managing editor. He stifled his journalist's instinct to write about Bletchley Park until Group Capt. FREDERICK W. WINTERBOTHAM revealed the role of the facility in his book *The Ultra Secret* (1974). Friendly then broke his silence and gave an account of his work in the *Post*.

Friends

General slang for members of an intelligence service; specifically British slang for members of the Secret Intelligence Service (MI6).

FSB

The Russian Federal Security Service, established in April 1995, reorganized from the FSK.

A government spokesman, Maj. Gen. Alexander Mikhailov, said of the change, "We have been gradually given other tasks such as fighting organized crime and gangs, contraband and corruption-fascist elements." Under the new legislation the agency can operate its own prison system, infiltrate foreign organizations and organized crime, create commercial enterprises as fronts for investigative work, and demand information from private firms.

Lt. Gen. SERGEI STEPASHIN, the third and last head of the FSK, briefly directed the new agency. The volatile politics of Moscow led to his replacement in July 1995 by Col. Gen. Mikhail Barsukov. He, in turn, was replaced on June 20, 1996, by his deputy, Col. Gen. Nikolai Kovalev. Russian President Boris Yeltsin fired the hawkish Barsukov on the eve of the presidential runoff vote. (At the time Yeltsin sacked several military and security service generals as well as his first deputy premier.) According to Kovalev, economic COUNTERINTELLIGENCE would be the agency's highest priority.

The FSB also has responsibility for safeguarding classified government material, and it provides security for the armed forces and other government organizations.

As evidence of its modern approach to state security, in July 1996 the FSB released to the public a six-hour CD-ROM providing a history of Soviet intelligence and security activities. The history is revealed through 60 interviews with former intelligence officers and historians.

FSB spokesman Yuri Kobaladze explained, "We released this on CD-ROM because that is a modern way to communicate with people. We want to be modern. Even in this sphere we still want to be better than everyone else. Now let the British make a CD-ROM about their intelligence service, and then let the Americans do it. But we will always be first."

The organization of the FSB set out on May 22, 1997, provided for the following structure:

Counterintelligence Department
Anti-terrorism Department
Analysis, Forecasting, and Strategic Planning Department
Organizational and Personnel Work Department
Support Services Department
Investigation and Curtailment of Criminal Organization
Activity Directorate
Investigations Directorate
Operational Search Directorate
Operational Technical Measures Directorate
Personal Security Directorate
Directorate of Affairs
Detention Center
Scientific Research Center

The FSB had four directors in its first four years. VLADIMIR PUTIN served as head of the FSB in 1998–1999, and from March 1999 additionally was chairman of the Russian Security Council. Yeltsin appointed him Prime Minister in August 1999, and on Dec. 31, 1999, he succeeded Yeltsin as President of the Russian Federation.

Directors of the FSB have been:

Mar. 1994–July 1995	SERGEY VADIMOVICH STEPASHIN
July 1995–June 1996	Mikhail Ivanovich Barsukov
July 1996–July 1998	Nikolay Dmitriyevich Kovalev
July 1998–Aug. 1999	VLADIMIR VLADIMIROVICH PUTIN
Aug. 1999–	Nikolay Platonovich Patrushev

FSK

The Russian Federal Counterintelligence Service, responsible for internal Russian law and order—and COUNTERINTELLIGENCE activities—from Dec. 1991 to Apr. 1995. It was succeeded by the FSB.

The FSK was established by Russian President Boris Yeltsin as one of the successor agencies to the KGB. The FSK was subordinate to the short-lived MB (Ministry of Security).

The FSK's first general director was VIKTOR BARANNIKOV, appointed in Jan. 1992. He was replaced in July 1993 by Col. Gen. NIKOLAY M. GOLUSHKO, whom President Yeltsin in turn removed from office in Feb. 1994; Golushko's principal deputy, Lt. Gen. SERGEI STEPASHIN, was then promoted to head the FSK—its third and last director.

Golushko declared that "According to Statute, the task of the FSK is to work to expose, avert, and suppress intelligence-gathering and subversive activity by foreign special services and organizations and illegal encroachments on Russia's constitutional system, sovereignty, territorial integrity, and defense capability."

The FSK unified and incorporated the various regional and territorial COUNTERINTELLIGENCE activities as well as those of the armed forces, Border Guard Troops, and Internal Troops. In 1994 the Russian trade newspaper *Trud* estimated that the FSK had a strength of 75,000 military and civilian employees.

The agency's name was changed from the Federal Counterintelligence Service to the Federal Security Service (FSB) on April 12, 1995. The change was part of legislation signed by Yeltsin that gave the agency far broader authority to help counter the increasing crime and corruption in the Russian Federation.

Fuchs, Emil Julius Klaus

(b. 1911 d. 1988)

British nuclear physicist who spied for the Soviets. As a key member of the ATOMIC SPY RING, he gave the Soviets technical information that accelerated the building of their atomic bomb and early knowledge that the United States was pursuing a hydrogen bomb.

Fuchs, born in Germany into a minister's family, attended the University of Leipzig, where he was an organizer for the SPD, the German Socialist Party. He later attended the University of Kiel and joined the German Communist Party, which Hitler outlawed soon after coming to power in 1933. With the aid of the party underground, Fuchs slipped out of Germany and arrived in England in Sept. 1933 as a refugee from Nazi Germany.

He began studying physics at the University of Bristol, where he completed his doctorate in 1936. He was an active member of the Society for Cultural Relations with the Soviet Union and considered himself a member in exile of the German Communist Party. In 1939 he applied for naturalization as a British citizen, but Britain went to war against Germany in Sept. 1939, before the application was processed, and Fuchs was classified an enemy alien.

During a FIFTH COLUMN scare in 1940, he and thousands of other refugees were interned. He was put first in a camp on the Isle of Man and then sent to Canada. After a few months in Canada, Fuchs was allowed to return to England, and in 1941, even though he was an alien, he became one of the many German physicists who were working on the secret U.S.-British effort to build an atomic bomb. He signed a standard form placing him under the OFFICIAL SECRETS ACT and thereby received a high-level SECURITY CLEARANCE. In June 1942 he became a naturalized British citizen.

Besides working on the design of an atomic bomb Fuchs also aided Britain's Secret Intelligence Service (MI6) in attempts to learn how far Germany had progressed in its own atomic work. At the same time he was working for the GRU, the Soviet MILITARY INTELLIGENCE agency. He regularly delivered reports on Tube Alloy, the CODE NAME for the British project, to a COURIER whose name he did not know. (She was URSULA KUCZYNSKI, sister of JÜRGEN KUCZYNSKI, leader of the German Communist Party, who was then living in Britain.)

In Dec. 1943, Fuchs was sent to the United States as a member of a British mission to work on the Manhattan Project, the code name for the U.S. atomic bomb effort. There he met with U.S. officials planning the gaseous diffusion plant in Oak Ridge, Tenn., and thus learned of the U.S. approach to developing the weapon, although he knew of Oak Ridge only as "Site X."

Fuchs returned to the United States in 1944 under instructions to make contact with a courier he knew only as Raymond. The courier was HARRY GOLD, whose original HANDLER was Semon Semonov, a Soviet INTELLIGENCE OFFICER who directed INDUSTRIAL ESPIONAGE operations in the United States. In early 1944 Semonov was replaced by Anatoli Yakovlev and at Yakovlev's instruction Gold met Fuchs in New York City several times to receive packages of documents.

Fuchs was next sent to the bomb design and assembly laboratory in Los Alamos, N.M. There, according to Hans Bethe, a fellow scientist, "He worked days and nights. He was a bachelor and had nothing better to do, and he contributed very greatly to the success of the Los Alamos project."

In Feb. 1945, when Fuchs went to visit his sister in Cambridge, Mass., Gold met him and he was given a "quite considerable packet" of information. Unable to travel after that due to security restrictions, Fuchs next met Gold in June when Gold made a dangerous, two-stop courier run. He went first to Santa Fe, N.M., where Fuchs gave him sketches and notes about the plutonium (Fat Man) bomb, which was about to be tested. Then Gold went to Albuquerque, N.M., where he gave $500 to an American solder assigned as a technician at Los Alamos. The soldier was Tech. Cpl. DAVID GREENGLASS, another member of the atomic spy ring.

In Sept. 1945, with the war ended by the atomic bombing of Hiroshima and Nagasaki, Fuchs met again with Gold and gave him highly classified information. Gold also gave Fuchs instructions on how to make contact with his Soviet handler when he returned to London.

Britain was attempting to build its own atomic bomb after collaboration with the United States ended after the war. Fuchs went to work on it. By 1950 he was head of the theoretical physics division of Britain's atomic energy establishment at Harwell. In England he continued his espionage activities. On Sept. 28, 1947, he had his first meeting with his new handler—ALEKSANDR FEKLISOV, who had earlier directed the atomic spy ring in the United States. He was now in charge of collecting technical and scientific intelligence in England.

While Fuchs and other members of the atomic spy ring took no money for their services, Feklisov reported

that at the end of one meeting he gave Fuchs an envelope with £200 to pay for treatment of his brother, who was seriously ill in Switzerland. Fuchs, upon being told the amount, immediately opened the envelope and handed back £100 to Feklisov.

In Nov. 1949 the FBI took suspicions about Fuchs's possible espionage to the Atomic Energy Commission, which had replaced the Manhattan Project in control of U.S. atomic programs. The FBI did not reveal then (or for decades later) that the information came from VENONA, a highly secret U.S. program for the decryption of Soviet intelligence messages transmitted to Moscow in the 1940s. The Venona messages showed that a source with the code name "Charles" had provided information "of great value" about "the electromagnetic method of separation of ENORMOZ" (the code name for the atomic bomb). The FBI deduced that Charles was Fuchs.

The FBI opened a case file on Fuchs in Sept. 1949 and notified the British intelligence liaison in Washington, HAROLD (KIM) PHILBY, who was himself a Soviet spy. Philby knew that if he tried to stop the investigation his own role as a MOLE could be BLOWN. "I en-

Klaus Fuchs. [NO CREDIT]

joyed an enormous advantage over people like Fuchs, who had little or no knowledge of intelligence work," he later wrote. His last meeting with Feklisov was on May 25, 1949, when Fuchs passed over a packet of documents.

On Dec. 21, 1949, William J. Skardon, an officer with the British Security Service (MI5), began questioning Fuchs at Harwell. On Jan. 27, 1950, Fuchs confessed and was formally arrested. Evidence provided by Fuchs led the FBI to Harry Gold, David Greenglass, and JULIUS ROSENBERG, helping to crack the atomic spy ring. After arresting Fuchs, MI5 identified his communist background, complete with German Communist Party card number, in Gestapo records that MI5 had seized at the end of the war.

Fuchs, trying to explain his ability to spy for the Soviet Union, said:

I used my Marxist philosophy to establish in my mind two separate compartments. One compartment in which I allowed myself to make friendships, to have personal relations, to help people and to be in all personal ways the kind of man I wanted to be. . . . I could be free and easy and happy with other people without fear of disclosing myself because I knew that the other compartment would step in if I approached the danger point. . . . Looking back at it now the best way of expressing it seems to be to call it a controlled schizophrenia.

The secrets that Fuchs passed included details about the complex gaseous-diffusion method U.S. scientists had developed for separating uranium-235, the fissionable material for the bomb, from uranium-238. Knowledge of this process saved the Soviet Union long and costly experiments.

Charged with violating the Official Secrets Act, Fuchs was tried at the Old Bailey. Because the secrets involved a weapon of mass destruction, the judge who sentenced Fuchs described his crime as "only thinly differentiated from high treason." He could not be tried for high treason, which called for the death sentence, because that crime is defined as spying for an enemy whereas the Soviet Union had been an ally at the time. Fuchs pleaded guilty and was sentenced to 14 years in prison, the maximum sentence.

"The mind of Fuchs," said a British prosecutor, "may probably be unique and create a new precedent in the world of psychology." Half of Fuchs's mind, according to the prosecutor, "was beyond the reach of reason and the impact of fact." The other half "lived in a world of normal relationships and friendships with his colleagues and human loyalty." Fuchs had "produced in himself a classic example of the immortal duality in English literature, Jekyll and Hyde."

Fuchs, a model prisoner, was released in June 1959 and went to East Germany, where he worked in atomic research, becoming director of the Central Institute for Nuclear Physics. He retired in 1979 and continued living in East Germany until his death.

Fukushima, Maj. Gen. Baron Yasumasa

(b. 1858 d. 1919)

Japanese MILITARY INTELLIGENCE officer at the time of the Russo-Japanese War (1904–1905).

Son of a samurai family, Fukushima joined the Imperial Japanese Army at an early age and almost immediately was posted to the General Staff. He served as a military ATTACHÉ in China and Germany. On what appeared to be a whim, he told German officers he could ride his horse from BERLIN to Vladivostok. Urged on by his colleagues, he made the 9,000-mile horseback journey—and collected intelligence along the way. In other travels through Mongolia, Manchuria, and Korea, he obtained valuable information.

During the Russo-Japanese War he was director of intelligence for the Japanese First Army. Gen. Sir Ian Hamilton, attached to the First Army as a British military observer, described Fukushima as a "very able" INTELLIGENCE OFFICER who smoothly carried out his mission, which, Hamilton wrote, was to "baffle and thwart in every possible way all the foreigners who have dealings with him, whilst, to enable him the more effectively to execute this disagreeable duty, he is officially described as their mentor and assistant."

Looking back on Japan's intelligence accomplishments in the war, Fukushima felt that SUN-TZU, the Chinese sage of intelligence, would be proud. "He would have said that we had followed his textbook to the very last sentence," Fukushima was quoted as saying. "But we know that we did better than that. We started a new book where he left off."

After the war Fukushima was given rank equivalent to a governor-general in the Kwantung province of China, a post he held from 1912 to 1917.

Furnival Jones, Sir (Edward) Martin

(b. 1912 d. 1997)

Director-General of the British Security Service (MI5) from 1965 to 1972, a most difficult period for British COUNTERINTELLIGENCE.

Following his studies at Cambridge, Furnival Jones became a solicitor. In 1940 he entered the Security Service. After the Allied invasion of Normandy in June 1944, he served on the security staff of Gen. Dwight D. Eisenhower's headquarters in Europe. For that service he was mentioned in dispatches and awarded the U.S. Bronze Star.

After the war Furnival Jones remained with MI5, serving successively as head of the military liaison, protective security, and COUNTERESPIONAGE branches. In 1963 he became the Deputy Director General of MI5. At the time MI5 was in a depression because of the revelations of several MOLES in British intelligence and allegations that ROGER HOLLIS, the Director General of MI5, was a mole (see FLUENCY COMMITTEE).

After Hollis retired in 1965, Furnival Jones became head of MI5. He had a troubled tenure, having to approve interrogations of Hollis as well as Michael Hanley, who was to be his successor as head of MI5. Neither of those two men was ever charged with espionage. In a positive vein, Furnival Jones played a key role in the mass expulsion of 105 Soviets from the Soviet Embassy in London, wrecking KGB and GRU espionage activities in Britain.

He retired in 1972.

FUSAG

SEE FIRST U.S. ARMY GROUP

Fusion

The process of examining and integrating all available sources of intelligence and information to derive a complete assessment of foreign activities, capabilities, and intentions.

G-2

Intelligence staff of a U.S. Army organization at the division level and above.

In Aug. 1903 the War Department implemented the recently authorized General Staff Corps for the Army and organized the General Staff into three divisions; "Military Information," designated as the Second Division, evolved into the intelligence staff. Subsequently, the basic staff for the headquarters of a battalion and larger units had four sections: G-1 Personnel, G-2 Intelligence, G-3 Operations, and G-4 Supply. (During World War II two additional staff functions, G-5 Civil Affairs or Military Government and G-6 Public Relations and Psychological Warfare, were provided at theater and higher headquarters.)

The G-series of staff designations originated with the French Army in the late 1800s, with several staff bureaus being designated for various functions (see FRANCE). Initially three staff bureaus were established, the second bureau being responsible for handling matters concerning information on the enemy.

S-2 is used for the intelligence staff at the brigade, regiment, and battalion levels.

(The U.S. Army Air Forces—established in 1941—used A-1, A-2, A-3, and A-4 to denote staff sections during World War II.)

G2A6

Radio intelligence section of the G-2 staff of the American Expeditionary Force in France during World War I. At its peak the Army unit had 72 men, including two lawyers, a reporter, a music critic, a language professor, an architect, a chess expert, and an archaeologist—all of whom, it was hoped, could help decrypt intercepted German communications.

Gambit

U.S. photographic RECONNAISSANCE SATELLITE of the KEY-HOLE series. First launched on July 12, 1963, the Gambit series differed from the earlier CORONA in being a "close-look" satellite, using the KH-7 camera for clear, detailed photographs of small areas. The Gambit series satellites were developed primarily to provide details of Soviet intercontinental missile installations.

The initial Gambit missions were not fully successful because of problems with the orbital control mechanism, but those problems were soon solved. There were 38 Gambit launch attempts through June 4, 1967—almost 10 per year. Two launches failed; the others were successful, with their two film canisters being parachuted down for aircraft in-flight snagging.

Gamekeeper

Slang used by British INTELLIGENCE OFFICERS for a controller, that is, an officer who controls AGENTS. See HANDLER.

Gamma

U.S. special intelligence operation during the 1960s against American citizens who visited North Vietnam during the Vietnam War. The program, jointly run by the DEFENSE INTELLIGENCE AGENCY and the NSA, used four-letter suffixes (Gilt, Goat, and the like) to indicate specific activities such as mail opening.

Garbo

CODE NAME of Juan Pujol Garcia, a Spaniard who was taken on by Germans in World War II to spy on the British. He became one of the most effective DOUBLE AGENTS in history.

Garbo worked against the Germans because of his dislike of Spanish dictator Francisco Franco. He believed that only an Allied victory in the war could depose Franco. After offering his services to British intelligence and being rejected, Garbo was accepted by the German ABWEHR. He departed Madrid in July 1941, ostensibly en route to England, carrying SECRET WRITING materials, lists of questions for German AGENTS in Britain, money, and ACCOMMODATION ADDRESSES.

Garbo actually went to Lisbon, where he tried unsuccessfully to contact British intelligence. He told the Germans that he had reached Britain, and in July 1941 he began writing reports about British naval and shipping matters, which he sent to the Abwehr. He also told them of the NETWORK that he was establishing in Britain.

In Jan. 1942 Garbo, still in Lisbon, finally met with British intelligence officials and once more offered himself as a double agent. After infighting between the British Secret Intelligence Service (MI6) and Security Service (MI5) over who would control him, Garbo arrived in Britain in April 1942 and remained there for the rest of the war, operating as a double agent under the control of the TWENTY COMMITTEE. (His wife and young son went with him.)

In London he established a paper network of NOTIONAL AGENTS to improve his credibility with the Germans. He told the Abwehr that he had 14 agents and 11 well-placed contacts. He also gave himself a deputy, a substitute radio operator, and several assistants scattered throughout Britain.

One of Garbo's imaginary agents was a "Wren," as members of the WRNS (Women's Royal Naval Service) were called. Garbo said the Wren was sent to the headquarters for the Southeast Asia theater in Ceylon, where she passed information to him for the Abwehr. The Germans in turn passed the phony information to the Japanese military ATTACHÉ in BERLIN to be passed on to Tokyo.

The Germans were extremely impressed with Garbo's reports, most of which were sent by post to Abwehr addresses. One report, ostensibly written before the Anglo-American landing in North Africa in Nov. 1942, reached the Germans after the landings. The Abwehr responded that "your last reports are all magnificent but we are sorry they arrived late, especially those relating to the Anglo-Yankee disembarkation in Africa." The postal delays led the Germans to establish radio links with Garbo.

Garbo's activities forced the Germans to reveal several of their real agents to British intelligence. (See DOUBLE-CROSS SYSTEM.) And the Germans paid for the deceptive operation, clandestinely sending about $340,000 to Garbo to pay for his network. The Germans awarded Garbo the Iron Cross (in absentia) for his information on the D-DAY Allied invasion of France (June 6, 1944). The British government made him a Member of the British Empire for the same phony information, which he sent to the Germans by British-controlled radio.

"Garbo" was his British code name; his German code name was "Rufus." He later wrote an account of his career as a double agent entitled simply *Garbo* (1986).

Garcia, Juan Pujol

SEE GARBO

Garcia, Master-at-Arms 1st Class Wilfredo

U.S. Navy petty officer found guilty in 1988 of attempting to sell classified Navy documents to representatives of a foreign government.

Garcia was arrested after an investigation by the NAVAL INVESTIGATIVE SERVICE (NIS) and the FBI. The investigation began late in 1985 when a civilian in Vallejo, Calif., reported to NIS and FBI officials that a sailor, later identified as Garcia, had sold him confidential documents for $800,000. The businessman promised more money to Garcia after they were resold to a foreign government. The documents were taken to the Philippines for that sale. NIS in Manila entered a home with a search warrant and recovered the documents.

Garcia, who had served in the Navy for 15 years, was found guilty of espionage and several other charges. He was sentenced to 12 years in prison.

Gardening

British term for undertaking an activity that will force an enemy to send a message in CIPHER or CODE, thus giving codebreakers a CRIB to help in their cryptographic efforts.

Intelligence historian NIGEL WEST described in *The SIGINT Secrets* (1986) a classic World War II gardening operation by British cryptologists at BLETCHLEY PARK:

> This involved the Royal Navy undertaking provocative operations with the intention of generating predictable wireless traffic. A particular favorite was the laying of mines in an area thought by the Germans to have been cleared. Once a new mine was discovered, it would be reported and minesweepers would be deployed until the short signal "route cleared" was transmitted.
> Interception of this single message was often enough for Bletchley [BLETCHLEY PARK] analysts to isolate the text and discover the daily change in the cipher.

Gardner, Meredith Knox

(b. 1912 d. 2000)

U.S. cryptologist credited with breaking the CIPHERS

employed by Soviet INTELLIGENCE OFFICERS in the United States during and immediately after World War II.

A former university language teacher, Gardner was recruited by the Army's SIGNAL INTELLIGENCE SERVICE (SIS) shortly after the U.S. entry into World War II on Dec. 7, 1941. Gardner was fluent in several languages, including Russian.

Radio messages sent from the Soviet intelligence activities in the United States to Moscow during the war were intercepted by the SIS but could not be decoded until the summer of 1946. At that time Gardner, like others at the Army's ARLINGTON HALL facility, noted similarities in the patterns of several messages. Those messages had been encoded with ONE-TIME PADS, which were considered unbreakable. However, because of wartime problems, the Soviet NKVD had allowed the use of duplicated pads.

Gardner was successful in his efforts, and in Dec. 1946 he decoded a message that contained the names of several scientists working on the atomic bomb project. More coded messages were partially or completely read during the coming months, leading to close cooperation between the Army and the FBI to break into the Soviet-run ATOMIC SPY RING. This massive decoding effort—soon joined by the British—was given the CODE NAME VENONA.

When the magnitude of the espionage was discovered, Gardner also wrote special reports recording what he was finding in the messages, so that U.S. intelligence officials could be alerted more rapidly. The subjects of the special reports, released in 1997, included atomic spying, the code names of British spy DONALD MACLEAN, the network of JULIUS ROSENBERG, and the NKVD hunt for a DEFECTOR from the Soviet trade mission in Washington, D.C.

Venona was a major factor in the arrest and conviction of several Soviet spies in the United States and Britain.

Gardner retired from government service in 1972.

Gates, Robert M.

(b. 1943)

DIRECTOR OF CENTRAL INTELLIGENCE (DCI) from Nov. 1991 to Jan. 1993 and previously long-time Deputy DCI.

Gates joined the CIA in 1966 as an assistant NATIONAL INTELLIGENCE officer for strategic programs. He had a master's degree in Eastern European history and a doctorate in Russian history and language. A skilled analyst with a penchant for crisp sentences, Gates rapidly gained a reputation for knowing how to write concise reports. This skill won him an assignment in 1974 to the staff of the NATIONAL SECURITY COUNCIL (NSC), where he remained until 1979.

On his return to CIA headquarters in LANGLEY, Va., in 1979, Gates served as national intelligence officer for the Soviet Union, a key post on his way to appointment as Deputy Director for Intelligence (DDI) in Jan. 1982. As DDI he was responsible for all CIA analysis. In Sept.

1983 he assumed the additional post of chairman of the NATIONAL INTELLIGENCE COUNCIL, with oversight of all NATIONAL INTELLIGENCE ESTIMATES prepared by the INTELLIGENCE COMMUNITY.

Gates was acting DCI in Feb. 1987 when a dying WILLIAM J. CASEY resigned as DCI. President Reagan nominated Gates to replace Casey. At 43, Gates would have been the youngest person ever to become DCI. But Gates withdrew his name during confirmation hearings after members of the Senate Intelligence Committee criticized him for not knowing about the IRAN-CONTRA AFFAIR. Casey had helped Marine Lt. Col. Oliver North of the NSC staff mastermind the illegal transaction. As Senators William S. Cohen and George J. Mitchell wrote in *Men of Zeal* (1988), members of the committee believed that Gates had "not been vigorous enough in searching out the facts" for Casey in the testimony he was giving to Congress.

Gates continued as deputy DCI under Casey's successor, WILLIAM H. WEBSTER. In Dec. 1988 President-elect George H. W. Bush named Gates deputy national security adviser, a post that did not require Senate confirmation. In May 1991 Bush nominated Gates to be DCI. Senator David Boren, chairman of the Senate Intelligence Committee, said of the nomination, "Bob Gates was an exceptional deputy to Webster, an honest liaison to the congressional committees, and an invaluable aide to the President in the White House."

At his subsequent Senate confirmation hearings, high-ranking CIA officials testified that Gates had received warnings about Iran-Contra, contradicting Gates's previous assertions that he had not been told. Gates was nevertheless confirmed and became DCI in Nov. 1991.

Early in his tenure he promised to speed up the declassification of CIA files and created an "Openness Task Force" for that purpose. He continued the agency's move away from the Cold War, focusing on the issues of nuclear proliferation, terrorism, drugs, and the future of the former Soviet Union.

In Oct. 1992 Gates became the first DCI to enter the Kremlin when he met with Russian President Boris Yeltsin and YEVGENY PRIMAKOV, director of the Russian Foreign Intelligence Service (SVR). In a conciliatory gesture, Gates gave Yeltsin information on the 1974 CIA Operation JENNIFER to raise a sunken Soviet submarine. (See HUGHES GLOMAR EXPLORER.)

After the inauguration of President Clinton, Gates resigned as DCI and retired from the CIA. His first book, *Out of the Shadows* (1996), was described as "an insider's story of five presidents and how they won the Cold War."

GC&CS

SEE GOVERNMENT CODE AND CYPHER SCHOOL

GCHQ

SEE GOVERNMENT COMMUNICATIONS HEADQUARTERS

Geheimschreiber

SEE FISH

Gehlen, Lt. Gen. Reinhard

(b. 1902 d. 1979)

Head of German MILITARY INTELLIGENCE for the Eastern (Russian) Front during World War II and postwar head of the BND, West Germany's foreign intelligence agency.

Gehlen served in various assignments in his early Army career, mostly in artillery. He was a liaison officer for senior commanders during the May 1940 campaign in France and was assigned to the General Staff as an adjutant in July 1940. Subsequently he was sent to the Eastern Front, and in April 1942, with the rank of lieutenant colonel, he became the senior intelligence officer on the General Staff dealing with the Russian front—head of the General Staff's FOREIGN ARMIES EAST Branch. On Dec. 1, 1944, he was promoted to generalmajor (brigadier general), one of the few German officers to gain promotion to this rank without senior command experience. His staff produced generally realistic assessments of Soviet forces and their intentions, which often fell on deaf ears within the Nazi leadership because of a basic distrust of intelligence estimates, especially by Adolf Hitler. (When German Gen. Hans Guderian presented Gehlen-supplied intelligence on Soviet forces at a conference with Hitler, the Führer raved that Gehlen ought to be committed to an insane asylum.) It was another Gehlen report on Soviet strength and intentions that led Hitler to dismiss Gehlen on April 9, 1945.

Gehlen had already begun making plans for his own future. His comprehensive files on the Soviet armed forces, aerial photographs of Russia, and other material were already being sealed in 50 steel drums, to be buried in several locations for future use. As Hitler's Germany underwent its final days, he and his key staff members went into hiding, in part because of fears of assassination by HEINRICH HIMMLER.

After the war ended in early May 1945, Gehlen surrendered—accompanied by his principal assistants, and with his files—to U.S. forces on May 22. After interrogation by U.S. officers, in Aug. 1945 he was flown to Washington, D.C., with six of his officers for discussions with senior U.S. ARMY INTELLIGENCE officers. He remained in the United States for almost a year, sailing back to Germany in July 1946 to establish the GEHLEN ORGANIZATION. The goal of the organization was to help the United States make use of Gehlen's intelligence NETWORK in Soviet-controlled areas.

In April 1956 his organization became the BND, West Germany's Federal Intelligence Service, with Gehlen as director. (He also held the rank of lieutenant general in the Army reserve.) Having served both the Nazis and Americans as a spymaster, Gehlen now served West Germany, albeit not as well as he had served former sponsors. He failed to predict the building of the Berlin Wall and other East German-Soviet activities. Furthermore, he

began collecting intelligence on the West, helped Egypt establish its intelligence service, and even worked with the Israelis (in his anti-Soviet efforts).

When HEINZ FELFE, chief of his COUNTERESPIONAGE department, was uncovered in 1961 as a communist DOUBLE AGENT, Gehlen's credibility came into question. Although Felfe's exposure hastened the fall of the government of Konrad Adenauer in 1963, Gehlen remained in charge of the BND for another five years, although with less influence and power.

His memoirs were published under the title *The Service* (1972).

Gehlen Organization

Intelligence agency established by the United States in West Germany after World War II, ostensibly to collect intelligence on the Soviet Union's military forces.

In July 1946, after a year of discussions with U.S. ARMY INTELLIGENCE officials in the United States, REINHARD GEHLEN returned to West Germany to unearth intelligence files that he had buried there at the end of the war and to reassemble his staff, who had served in FOREIGN ARMIES EAST on the German General Staff.

The Gehlen Organization worked under the direction of the U.S. Army, which funded its staff and operations, provided equipment, and offered other assistance as needed. Its headquarters were established, from late 1947, on an estate in the village of Pullach, five miles south of Munich.

The group was able to "awaken" some of its SLEEPERS in East Germany and the western Soviet Union, AGENTS who had stayed behind when the Soviet armies rolled westward in 1944–1945. But mostly it collected intelligence from interrogations of East German refugees who had fled to the West and from spies who had been sent into the East.

The organization was not appreciated by all Allied officials: U.S. Army Gen. Arthur Trudeau called Gehlen's organization "that spooky Nazi outfit." But the U.S. Army was pleased with his efforts. Following the establishment of the U.S. CIA in 1947, three-way discussions began with the U.S. Army and Gehlen about the future sponsorship of the organization. Accordingly, on July 1, 1949, U.S. control of the organization passed to the CIA.

While most of Gehlen's intelligence operations were against East German and Soviet military TARGETS, on one occasion his agency TURNED an NKVD officer.

The West German government was established on Sept. 12, 1949, but after preliminary discussions with the new government, Gehlen was forbidden from having anything further to do with it. However, a year later Gehlen met West German chancellor Konrad Adenauer, and a cordial relationship followed.

On May 5, 1955, West Germany became a member of the NORTH ATLANTIC TREATY ORGANIZATION and regained its sovereignty. Adenauer decided that the Gehlen Organization would become West Germany's Federal Intelligence Service (Bundesnachrichtendienst, or BND). The transmutation began on April 1, 1956, with the BND attached—not subordinated—to the chancellor's Office.

Also see INDISPENSABLES.

Genetrix

CODE NAME for the 1950s U.S. Air Force RECONNAISSANCE program that used BALLOONS to photograph TARGETS in the Soviet Union. Of a reported 287 camera-carrying balloons launched from Europe, only 44 were recovered in the Pacific; the others were never recovered although several were found in the Soviet Union.

Earlier code names for this project were Gopher, Grandson, and Grayback.

Also see MOBY DICK.

Genyosha

SEE BLACK OCEAN SOCIETY

George, Claire E.

(b. 1930)

U.S. Deputy DIRECTOR OF CENTRAL INTELLIGENCE (DCI) for Operations during the 1980s and a principal figure in the IRAN-CONTRA AFFAIR. George was the first senior official of the CIA to be convicted in a trial for felony offenses while carrying out official duties. (The only other senior CIA official to be convicted was former DCI RICHARD M. HELMS, who pleaded no contest to a misdemeanor charge.)

George joined the CIA in 1955 after two years in the Army. He first served in South Korea and was then sent to Hong Kong in 1957. He subsequently served in Africa, India, and Greece, as well as at CIA headquarters. After becoming the Deputy DCI for Operations he became involved in the attempts to trade arms to Iran in return for the release of Americans held hostage in Lebanon.

George was tried for obstruction, perjury, and making false statements to the intelligence committee of the House of Representatives on Oct. 14, 1986, which at the time was attempting to determine if the U.S. government had been involved with a cargo aircraft that was shot down over Nicaragua on Oct. 5, 1986. The aircraft was carrying arms to Contra rebels.

His first trial, in Aug. 1992, ended in a mistrial. George was then retried and found guilty on Dec. 9, 1992, of two counts of lying to Congress. Sentencing was planned for early 1993, but on Dec. 24, 1992, President GEORGE H. W. BUSH pardoned George, along with five others involved in the Iran-Contra affair.

George Smiley [f]

Principal hero of JOHN LE CARRÉ's detective and spy books. In le Carré's first two novels, *Call for the Dead* (1962) and *A Murder of Quality* (1963), Smiley did detective work. Then, in the roles of spy and spymaster,

Smiley appeared in the le Carré successes *The Spy Who Came In from the Cold; Tinker, Tailor, Soldier, Spy; The Honourable Schoolboy;* and *Smiley's People.* He was described precisely as the ideal intelligence AGENT in *A Murder of Quality:*

> Obscurity was his nature, as well as his profession. The byways of espionage are not populated by the brash and colorful adventurers of fiction. A man who, like Smiley, has lived and worked for years among his country's enemies learns only one prayer: that he may never, never be noticed. Assimilation is his highest aim, he learns to love the crowds who pass him in the street without a glance; he clings to them for his anonymity and his safety. His fear makes him servile—he could embrace the shoppers who jostle him in their impatience, and force him from the pavement. He could adore the officials, the police, the bus conductors, for the terse indifference of their attitudes.
>
> But this fear, this servility, this dependence, had developed in Smiley a perception for the colour of human beings: a swift, feminine sensitivity to their characters and motives. He knew mankind as a huntsman knows his cover, as a fox the wood. For a spy must hunt while he is hunted, and the crowd is his estate. He could collect their gestures and their words, record the interplay of glance and movement, as a huntsman can record the twisted bracken and the broken twig, or as a fox detects the signs of danger.

While a master of intrigue (and the organization of intelligence), Smiley is certainly not the popular image of a spy: His marriage to the "delicious" Ann is a disaster, he is neither young nor handsome, he wears thick glasses, and at times he lacks overt boldness.

Sir MAURICE OLDFIELD, lunching with John le Carré and Sir Alec Guinness, who played Smiley in the television version of *Tinker, Tailor, Soldier, Spy,* said, "We are definitely not as our host here describes us." Guinness had wanted to meet a real spymaster, and le Carré arranged the lunch. After the television series was broadcast, Oldfield wrote to Guinness, "I still don't recognize myself."

When Oldfield died in 1986, *The Times* reported that he had been the model for Smiley. But le Carré told *The Times:* "I never heard of Sir Maurice either by name or in any other way until long after the name and character of George Smiley were in print."

Gerhardsen, Verna

(b. 1912 d. 1970)

Wife of Norwegian Prime Minister who was targeted as a source of high-level intelligence for the Soviet Union by an attempt to involve her in a sexual relationship with a KGB officer.

Verna Gerhardsen's husband, Einar Gerhardsen, was, except for a short break, Prime Minister of Norway from 1945 to 1965. He was 15 years her senior. He was mayor of Oslo when Germany invaded Norway in 1940, spent the rest of World War II in a concentration camp, and emerged to become his nation's leader. He died in 1987.

In the early 1950s Verna Gerhardsen was a member of a left-wing youth group that made connections with the Soviet Union's Young Pioneers. In 1954, while on a trip to the Soviet Union with a youth delegation, she stayed at the Intourist hotel in Yerevan, the capital of Soviet Armenia. Yevgeni Belyakov, a young KGB officer assigned to exploit the delegation, was staying in a "plus-room"—a regular hotel room that also contained equipment for recording and filming. There he is said to have seduced Verna.

The story emerged in 1993 from Bogdan Dubensky, a retired KGB general officer, in an interview with *The Times* of London. He said that the young KGB officer was then posted to the Soviet Embassy in Oslo to continue the relationship. "She was never blackmailed," Dubensky said, speaking delicately about the use of SEX by the KGB. Belyakov told her they had been filmed together at the hotel, claiming not to have known that his superiors had arranged it.

According to Dubensky, Verna passed information to the KGB about Norway's positions on UNITED NATIONS and NORTH ATLANTIC TREATY ORGANIZATION matters. She also gave Belyakov information about members of the Norwegian *Storting* (parliament). "We worked out from that who would therefore be our next targets for KGB recruitment," recalled Dubensky, who was then the KGB resident at the Oslo embassy. The affair ended after three years, he said, after Belyakov got drunk, beat up his wife, and had to be recalled to the Soviet Union because of "danger of a public scandal."

Gerhardt, Commo. Dieter Felix

(b. 1935)

South African naval officer who spied for Soviet MILITARY INTELLIGENCE (GRU).

Born in BERLIN, Gerhardt and his family went to South Africa before World War II. An introverted, ungainly young man of great height, he was nicknamed "Jumbo." In the Navy he seemed dedicated and a stern disciplinarian.

Gerhardt was recruited by the GRU in 1960 while he was in Britain as a young officer assigned to the Royal Navy. He was an apparent WALK-IN to the Soviet Embassy in London. His motivation may have been the imprisonment of his German father in South Africa by the British during World War II.

Gerhardt divorced his first wife and married a Swiss woman, Ruth Johr, who was already a Soviet AGENT. The marriage may have been suggested by the GRU. She acted as his COURIER, making frequent trips to Geneva, ostensibly to visit her mother.

He was alleged to have been paid $250,000 for information on South Africa's Navy, which used British,

French, and Israeli ships and equipment. Also, he moved in the highest defense circles, where he could easily pick up political as well as military information, and was personally acquainted with Premier P. W. Botha. Also of interest to the Soviets, Gerhardt had access to intelligence from Silvermines, the extensive South African SURVEILLANCE system of offshore waters. In addition, he did TALENT SPOTTING for the Soviet intelligence services.

By the time his activities were found out, Gerhardt was commander of the Simonstown naval shipyard. His lavishly furnished home at the Simonstown naval base near Cape Town and his high living standard were explained away as being made possible by a small inheritance from his mother in Germany and by his success in playing racehorses, winning the lottery, and investing in the stock market.

In 1982 he attended Syracuse University, in New York State, taking an advanced course in mathematics. Gerhardt was detained in the United States in Jan. 1983 by the U.S. FBI and South African agents. After 11 days of interrogation, he was flown back to South Africa under guard.

The South African government had believed that there was a Soviet MOLE in the country since 1967 when Yuri Loganov, a Soviet agent, was captured in Johannesburg. But they did not identify Gerhardt as the spy until MOSSAD (Israeli intelligence) agents in Moscow had observed Gerhardt sitting with his wife at the Bolshoi Ballet on two of at least five visits he made to Moscow. The trips to the Soviet Union were not authorized, and he had failed to submit the proper reporting documents after his visits.

Tried for high treason and espionage during a three-month trial held in camera, in Dec. 1983 Gerhardt was found guilty and sentenced to life imprisonment; his wife was sentenced to 10 years.

Germany

By the middle of the 19th century, the European continent was a cauldron of unrest. Karl Marx had published his *Communist Manifesto*. In France revolutionaries had driven Louis Philippe, the "citizen king," from his throne. The Russian czar feared he would be next. The German states argued over unification. Prussia prepared for a war against Austria that could unite that cluster of German states into Europe's major military power. To accomplish that, Prussia had a powerful army—and good spies.

Prussia had begun engaging in modern espionage earlier than its continental rivals. And with the creation of its first permanent General Staff, Prussia had a structure that could accommodate a permanent intelligence service. The endless planning of the General Staff had revealed the need for a modern type of MILITARY INTELLIGENCE: information not merely about a battlefield but about an entire country—its railroad lines and armories, its war plans, and weapons production.

Knowledge of a potential enemy's railroads, for example, would provide data about the signs and probable speed of mobilization. Knowledge of its arms manufacturing could be translated into the numbers and quality of arms in battle. As the Prussian General Staff declared in 1816, Prussia must have "the most exact knowledge of this country and of other European states in military matters."

Beyond the General Staff, Prussia was also developing a permanent, civilian-controlled espionage service. Its founder was WILHELM STIEBER, who began as an AGENT PROVOCATEUR seeking out radicals and socialists and later became a spymaster overseeing the largest NETWORK in Europe. (On one of his missions he went to London to spy on Marx.) While Stieber was setting up his Central Intelligence Bureau and spying on Austria, Helmuth Count von Moltke, chief of the Prussian General Staff, prepared for war against Austria in 1866 by establishing a temporary intelligence bureau to gather information about Austrian war plans. Stieber also set up the Prussian Army's COUNTERINTELLIGENCE unit, the Field Security Police.

Moltke's major AGENT was Baron AUGUST SCHLUGA, a young, Hungarian-born Austrian who brought Moltke the Austrian ORDER OF BATTLE. Schluga, a former Austrian Army officer, had posed as a journalist in VIENNA to obtain the information. Using military intelligence and the POLITICAL INTELLIGENCE supplied by Stieber's spies, Moltke beat the Austrians in seven weeks and became a firm believer in a permanent intelligence bureau.

Stieber's next espionage TARGET was France, where he hired thousands of spies, including prostitutes. The use of SEX for blackmail and gathering secrets was a frequent Stieber script.

Prussian Premier Otto von Bismarck goaded France into war in 1870 by using DISINFORMATION to convince the Germans that France was threatening Prussian sovereignty and to convince the French that King William of Prussia had insulted the French ambassador to Prussia. Bismarck rightly believed that the other Germanic states would join Prussia against France, leading to the creation of a united Germany with the most powerful army in Europe. In the Franco-Prussian War (1870–1871), Moltke again showed his genius as a strategist, but his brilliance was greatly aided by the intelligence that Stieber provided. Because generals typically believe that it is they who win wars, however, chronicles of Moltke's triumphs fail to acknowledge Stieber and his spies.

WORLD WAR I

Moltke's intelligence bureau became Section b of the IIIrd Oberquartiermeister (Chief Quartermaster) and was known by its location on the General Staff's densely full table of organization: III b. Schluga, the agent who had provided Moltke with the Austrian order of battle, became "Agent 17" in Paris, one of the many cities in Europe where III b had spies. One of them was the exotic dancer MATA HARI, trained as a spy in Germany and sent to France. She found no secrets but was executed by the French government, her continuing fame based more on legend than on fact.

Schluga, the dean of German spies, kept his sources and methods secret even from his superiors. In his greatest triumph, he obtained a copy of a document revealing France's mobilization plans on the eve of World War I. When war came in 1914, it brought with it a new era in espionage: instantaneous COMMUNICATIONS INTELLIGENCE.

Anticipating U.S. entry into the war, Germany moved boldly: By 1917, III b had over 330 agents in Allied countries, including the United States, where their main mission was sabotage rather than espionage.

During the early days of the war, a German radio station at Königsberg, East Prussia, picked up Russian transmissions. The Russians were transmitting in the CLEAR because radio was so new that the idea of interception had not occurred to them. The Germans were able to piece together Russian plans and virtually wiped out an entire Russian army at Tannenberg as a result. The battle, says intelligence historian DAVID KAHN in *Hitler's Spies* (1978), "gave Russia its first great push toward defeat. And it opened German eyes to a form of intelligence they had never really considered."

On the Western Front, British, American, and French forces eventually discovered the advantages and perils of radio and trench telephone communications. On the Eastern Front the Germans' interception net had an important role in the defeat of Russia. German skills at encoding communications did not match French efforts at codebreaking. But France's efforts in pioneering aerial RECONNAISSANCE were offset by German efficiency in producing and interpreting aerial photographs.

The Imperial German Navy had an Intelligence Branch that also produced communications intelligence. Some 24 intercept and HIGH-FREQUENCY DIRECTION FINDING stations were set up along the coast. The Military-Political Branch and Foreign Navies Branch analyzed the intelligence. The Army's Intelligence Branch had a Foreign Armies Branch that analyzed Allied strategy, accurately predicting the Allied Somme offensive in the summer of 1916.

Ultimately, intelligence was of little significance in this war of attrition, muddy trenches, machine guns, and poison gas. The German Army was defeated, but III b had proved its worth and it would be retained as a permanent army unit.

In April 1919 the Weimar Republic, a shaky, unpopular democracy born of Germany's postwar chaos, sent a delegation to the postwar conference at Versailles, France, under the assumption that Germans would negotiate a treaty with the Allies. But there were no negotiations. The Germans were simply handed the Versailles Treaty, which stripped Germany of more than 27,000 square miles of territory. The treaty also abolished the General Staff and allowed only a small army without an Intelligence Branch. A secret intelligence substitute, known as the Troops Department, was founded as part of the general clandestine resurrection of German military services.

A sullen, desperate society was ready for politicians who would promise a better tomorrow—with or without a democracy. Adolf Hitler, dynamic leader of the National Socialist German Workers' Party, better known as the Nazi Party, presented himself as a savior against the communists, Jews, and exploiters.

NAZI POWER AND ESPIONAGE

Elections in March 1933 would decide whether the Nazis had grown strong enough to gain a clear parliamentary majority in the Reichstag. The German Communist Party was the largest in Europe outside the Soviet Union. On Feb. 27, the Reichstag building went up in flames. Hermann Göring, head of the Nazi political police, blamed the communists and announced that the fire signaled the start of a revolution. Hitler, given emergency powers, outlawed every political party except the Nazis, ended the Weimar Republic, and proclaimed the Third Reich.

Even before he came to power, Hitler had relied on crude intelligence services to seek out and destroy his enemies. His earliest organization, the SA (*Sturmabteilung*, "storm detachment"), composed of gangs of Nazi street fighters, began in 1920 as a legion of thugs—storm troopers who guarded party meetings, brawled with communists, and had a primitive counterintelligence unit. Hitler's elite personal guard, the SS (Schützstaffel, "protection detachment"), wiped out the SA leadership in the bloody "Night of the Long Knives," on June 30, 1934. The SS grew into a political police force with its own intelligence service, the SD (*Sicherheitsdienst*, Security Service). The SS, run by HEINRICH HIMMLER, was both a secret police and a terror organization that ran concentration camps. Later, it would run death camps and murder squads. The SD's task was to "discover the enemies of the National Socialist concept."

WORLD WAR II

By the time Hitler's blitzkrieg forces invaded Poland in Sept. 1939, Germany had a complex intelligence apparatus, part of it controlling the civilian society and part of it functioning as traditional military intelligence services. The SD, under REINHARD HEYDRICH, created the RSHA, or Reichssicherheitshauptamt (Reich Security Organization). Through a vast network of informers and agents throughout Germany and conquered Europe, the SD worked closely with the most dreaded members of Himmler's secret police, the GESTAPO, an acronym for Geheime Staatspolizei (Secret State Police). Hitler had made Himmler both head of the SS and chief of the national police. The Gestapo was the political arm of the plain-clothes police. Later, as a part of the RSHA, the Gestapo became a law unto itself. The Gestapo had absolute power over the lives of people believed to be acting against the state. Its victims were sent to concentration camps or were tortured and slain. Sometimes, in a sham of legality, the accused were brought before the Gestapo-controlled People's Courts, whose judges were notorious for their unremitting stream of death verdicts.

All of these actions took place directly under Hitler's command. In 1938 he had abolished the Ministry of War and made himself the director of the armed services and established the OKW, or Oberkommando der Wehrmacht (Armed Forces High Command)—a "military staff directly under my command," as he put it. Military intelligence was the responsibility of the ABWEHR, which recruited and controlled agents and also operated a Cipher Branch for intercepting foreign military and non-military communications.

Two Army intelligence organizations reported to the OKW: FOREIGN ARMIES WEST and FOREIGN ARMIES EAST. During the war against the Soviet Union, Foreign Armies East was directed by Brig. Gen. REINHARD GEHLEN, who developed a large, productive network of agents reporting on the Soviet Union as well as analysts who poduced quality reports. Foreign ECONOMIC INTELLIGENCE was gathered and analyzed by a branch of the War Economy and Armaments Department, which became, under Albert Speer, the Ministry for Armaments and Munitions.

The German's second blitzkrieg—the May 1940 offensive against Belgium, France, Holland, and Luxembourg—was preceded by a brilliant display of TACTICAL INTELLIGENCE. Acting on information on France gained through aerial reconnaissance, CRYPTANALYSIS, and agents, the German Army conquered western Europe in little more than a month. According to a study of signals intelligence in the campaign, French communications security was so careless that "no movement and no dislocation remained concealed from the Germans. The French Air Force was most incautious in its use of radio and the ground stations gave countless clues." German intelligence was so efficient that some historians contend that it had a decisive role in the swift conquest of France.

Germany occupied part of France and set up the pro-Nazi Vichy regime in the rest of the conquered nation. In occupied France the Abwehr, the SD, and the Gestapo all dealt with the French Resistance movement, which was somewhat controlled from London by the BCRA, France's intelligence agency in exile. Using informers and terror, the SD and the Gestapo waged merciless war on the Resistance. In Feb. 1944, when Vice Adm. WILHELM CANARIS was removed as head of the Abwehr, many of the Abwehr's people in France were transferred to the SD.

The Germans killed 100 French hostages for every German killed by the French underground, mostly by guerrilla units known as the maquis. The Germans are known to have executed 29,660 French hostages; another 40,000 French men and women perished in German custody. Others were taken away and never heard from again—killed and *vernebelt* ("turned into mist") under the Nacht und Nebel Erlass ("Night and Fog Decree"), carried out by the SD. Hitler had issued the decree in Dec. 1941 as a way of preventing the creation of "martyrs" by public execution.

Under the NN, as the SD called the decree, citizens of occupied countries were taken to Germany secretly to "vanish without leaving a trace," with "no information . . . given as to their whereabouts or their fate."

BREAKING CODES

In the overall area of communications intelligence, foreign diplomatic codes were routinely broken by German cryptanalysts in what was known as Pers Z (ostensibly a section of the Personnel and administrative branch of the Foreign Office). Pers Z codebreakers solved some of the codes of the United States, Britain, France, Japan, Italy, and Spain—but not of the Soviet Union.

Germany's most sensational display of communications espionage was the interception and unscrambling of the transatlantic telephone calls between President Roosevelt and Prime Minister Winston Churchill. KURT VETTERLEIN identified the Roosevelt-Churchill link and developed the means of breaking into it.

After the German invasion of the Soviet Union in June 1941, German cryptanalysts broke the Turkish diplomatic code, enabling German strategists to learn indirectly about Soviet plans, for the neutral Turkish ambassador in Moscow made accurate and detailed reports on activities of interest to Germany. It was through broken Turkish codes that Germany learned about such matters as the amounts and types of U.S. war matériel arriving in the Soviet Union.

The German codebreaking effort, however, was eclipsed by the Allied triumphs of ENIGMA, the U.S.-British operation at BLETCHLEY PARK, which succeeded in breaking German CIPHERS throughout much of the war. Enigma intercepts also contributed to the humiliating defeat that the Abwehr suffered in its attempt to spy on Britain. The British DOUBLE-CROSS SYSTEM made DOUBLE AGENTS of the Abwehr agents supposedly spying in Britain.

Assessing Germany's defeat, Kahn wrote in *Hitler's Spies*, "Germany lost the intelligence war. At every one of the strategic turning points of World War II, her intelligence failed. It underestimated Russia, blacked out before the North African invasion, awaited the Sicily landing in the Balkans, and fell for thinking the Normandy landing a feint."

Allied success against German Navy communications to and from U-boats was a key factor in winning the Battle of the Atlantic, the longest and one of the most important campaigns of the war (Sept. 1939–May 1945). Further, when Adm. Karl Dönitz, head of the German submarine force, ordered investigations of possible Allied penetration of the naval Enigma, the response was always that the naval Enigma was impenetrable. Rather, the cause must be French spies at submarine bases, or Allied radar, or some other security compromise, but not that German ciphers were vulnerable.

SPYING IN TWO GERMANYS

After Germany surrendered in May 1945, the Allies divided the country into four zones of occupation—American, British, French, and Soviet—each with its own intelligence and counterintelligence operations. The Americans and British continued their wartime cooperation; the French, behaving much as they did during the war, did little sharing. All three worked against the Soviets. Out of the three Western zones emerged West Germany. The Soviets installed a communist government in their zone, which became East Germany. BERLIN was divided into two cities, and West Berlin, surrounded by East Germany, became the spy center of Europe.

In fact and fiction, West Berlin's Checkpoint Charlie became the key Cold War passage through the Berlin Wall, which East Germany erected in Aug. 1961 to stop the flight of its citizens to the West. The Berlin Wall also marked the boundary between competing intelligence operations—in the East, MFS, the Ministerium für Staatssicherheit, or Stasi (Ministry for State Security), headed by ERICH MIELKE, and on the West, a combination of West German, U.S., and British intelligence services. In East Germany, with a population of 18 million, the Stasi had 500,000 informers, 85,000 agents, and files on 6 million people.

Nothing like that level of DOMESTIC INTELLIGENCE existed in West Germany, but Berlin, the spy nucleus for both Germanys, had more spies in the 1960s and 1970s than any other city on earth. So strong was the presence of British and U.S. intelligence in West Germany that the workings of West German agencies were relatively unimportant to the West. One of the most celebrated U.S.–British spy projects was the BERLIN TUNNEL, an underground penetration of Soviet–East German communications links. Not for years did the West realize that the Soviet KGB had known about the tunnel even before it was dug.

As West Germany rapidly evolved from conquered enemy to Cold War ally, the Americans and British realized that West Germany needed to develop a national intelligence system that would directly counter the Stasi. Reinhard Gehlen, the former head of Foreign Armies East, was an important player in this undertaking. When Germany surrendered in 1945, Gehlen was one of scores of Nazis who were accepted by the West as good prospective ASSETS to use against the Soviets.

Gehlen and his organization were theoretically an "autonomous apparatus" outside of the U.S. intelligence activities, but in fact he was directly connected with U.S. CIA operations in West Germany. After the founding of the Bundesrepublik, the Federal Republic of Germany (West Germany) in 1949, the Gehlen intelligence organization became the BND or Bundesnachrichtendienst (Federal Intelligence Agency). Gehlen remained its head until he retired in 1968. U.S. and British intelligence agencies also helped to set up the BFV or Bundesamt für Verfassungsschutz (Agency for Constitutional Protection), West Germany's counterintelligence agency.

Gehlen had made a deep penetration of the East German government; his agents at one time included a member of the cabinet. But in the spy wars of the Cold War, the Stasi was the winner. HEINZ FELFE, chief of counterintelligence against the Soviets under Gehlen, for example, was arrested in 1961 on charges of having spied on the Soviets for a decade. The information came from an East German DEFECTOR in what became a depressingly standard event: the penetration of the BND or the BfV by Stasi agents. OTTO JOHN, the head of West Germany's counterintelligence operations, was revealed as a Soviet agent. So was HANS JOACHIM TIEDGE, who had been in the West German counterintelligence service for 19 years and had headed the department that searched for East German spies.

The Stasi's greatest achievement was the placing of a spy at the side of West German Chancellor Willy Brandt. In the 1950s GÜNTER GUILLAUME, a Stasi agent, slipped into West Germany and joined the Social Democratic Party, working his way up the party ranks to become Brandt's personal aide. Brandt was forced to resign when Guillaume was exposed in 1974. Between the arrest of Guillaume and 1979, West Germany announced the capture of more than 100 people believed to be Eastern Bloc spies.

Stasi operatives often used SEX as an intelligence weapon, making videotapes of Westerners in compromising situations for blackmail purposes. Another way of learning about sexual habits was by installing Stasi BUGS in confessionals in Roman Catholic churches.

The Stasi sent handsome male agents—dubbed "Romeos" by Western intelligence officials—to West German and NORTH ATLANTIC TREATY ORGANIZATION offices specifically to charm secretaries whose offices were targeted for espionage. Among them were a secretary in the Defense Ministry and a German woman employed at NATO headquarters in Brussels. Several other secretaries were arrested between 1960 and the end of the Cold War. The last of the secretary-spies were released and pardoned as part of a spy exchange in 1990.

GERMAN REUNIFICATION

In March 1990 East Germany announced that it was closing its foreign espionage service and recalling its agents. The Stasi espionage section was cut from 4,000 employees to 250, who were to supervise the withdrawal of agents. The shutting down of the espionage section was the last step in the dissolution of the Stasi. In Oct. 1990, formal reunification occurred—and immediately the quest for information from the archives of the Stasi began.

The revelations provided by the archives destroyed many lives: wives betrayed by husbands, students betrayed by teachers. An East German who was supposedly a courageous human rights lawyer was an informer. A minister learned that his depression had been caused by drugs his physician had prescribed under Stasi orders. A group of former Stasi officers and agents formed the Insiders' Committee for Reexamination and asked for compassion and acceptance of their treachery.

In 1999 the CIA agreed to give Germany copies of 320,000 Stasi files that the United States had obtained in a secret operation whose CODE NAME was Rosewood. Officials said that the data included the real and code names of Germans. The names of foreigners who worked for the Stasi in the United States and other countries were not turned over. The CIA had previously given Germany information that aided in the identification of about 2,000 former Stasi agents, including RAINER RUPP, who was convicted of giving NATO secrets to East Germany.

MARKUS WOLF surrendered to authorities, was tried for treason, and was convicted and sentenced to six years in prison. Others who served in the Stasi were arrested and faced similar trials. Then, in May 1995, Germany's highest court of appeals ruled that East Germans who had worked solely in their country could not be tried for treason because they had not betrayed their country. Although a new trial was ordered for Wolf, observers believed that the court ruling had the effect of a general amnesty and that he would never go to prison.

As Germany celebrated its reunion, the BND, like other spy agencies that had served in the Cold War, found new missions: ECONOMIC INTELLIGENCE and COMPUTER ESPIONAGE. Critics of the BND in Germany say that the agency has now targeted U.S. corporations in search of secrets that will help German industries.

Also see ERICH MIELKE.

Gessner, Pvt. George John

U.S. Army private and nuclear weapons technician who, after deserting from Fort Bliss, Texas, in 1960, delivered classified data to Soviet INTELLIGENCE OFFICERS in Mexico City in 1960–1961.

Apprehended by U.S. authorities, he served a brief sentence for desertion at the Leavenworth federal penitentiary in Kansas. Upon release from Leavenworth in 1962, he was arrested and charged with espionage. In June 1964 he was convicted and sentenced to life in prison.

Gessner was the first person to be tried under the 1946 Atomic Energy Act's provision against transferring nuclear information to unauthorized persons. Upon appeal, in March 1966 a court dismissed the espionage charges against Gessner.

Gestapo

The Gestapo—an acronym for Geheime Staatspolizei (Secret State Police)—ruthlessly dealt with all opposition to Nazi Germany both inside Germany and in Nazi-occupied territory, conducted intelligence and subversive activities in other countries, and administered the concentration and death camps of the Nazi regime. The official designation of the agency was the Division for Investigation and Liquidation of Opposition.

It was originally formed by Hermann Göring in 1933 to replace the Prussian political police, a regional agency. With Rudolf Diels as its chief, the Gestapo was initially employed by Göring to arrest and murder opponents of the Nazi Party. But with the appointment of HEINRICH HIMMLER to head the Gestapo in April 1934, the agency began to expand as the police arm of the SS, the paramilitary force of the Nazi Party, also headed by Himmler. (Also see SD.)

When Himmler was promoted to Reich Commissioner for the strengthening of the Third Reich and given control of newly annexed Poland in Oct. 1939, he was succeeded as head of the Gestapo by HEINRICH MÜLLER. Müller directed the Gestapo in its notorious wartime activities, and played a key role in the "final solution of the Jewish question." He was last seen in the BERLIN Führerbunker on April 28, 1945. His disappearance left the Gestapo without direction as the Allies overran the last Nazi-held areas of Germany.

The basic law covering the Gestapo, enacted on Feb. 10, 1936, gave it absolute power over the lives of persons believed to be acting against the state. The Gestapo operated throughout Germany and the Nazi-occupied countries. Victims were sent to concentration camps or were simply tortured and slain. Some accused were brought before the Gestapo-controlled People's Courts, and almost inevitable death sentences. Gestapo actions and orders, however, were not subject to judicial review. As Dr. Werner Best, a Himmler henchman, said, "As long as the police carries out the will of the leadership, it is acting legally."

The Gestapo was Section IV of the RSHA (Reich Security Headquarters).

Gideon

Canadian CODE NAME for a Soviet ILLEGAL who entered Canada in 1952 for the purpose of developing a LEGEND prior to crossing the border into the United States. However, Gideon met and fell in love with a Canadian woman, which was strictly against Soviet regulations.

Not wanting to leave Canada—and by this time possibly not wanting to be a spy—Gideon advised the Soviet CENTER that it was too difficult to emigrate to the United States. Accordingly, he was directed to serve as an illegal RESIDENT in Canada, responsible for running other illegals throughout the country.

Because of the workload and his own sluggishness, he quickly fell behind in carrying out his complex assignments. Finally, Gideon told his lover about his real work and decided to reveal his true identity to the authorities.

The ROYAL CANADIAN MOUNTED POLICE (RCMP), in charge of counterespionage activities at the time, decided to turn Gideon into a DOUBLE AGENT. For a year he performed his duties as resident under the close supervision of the RCMP, which observed his activities, monitored his radio communications, and debriefed him on Soviet TRADECRAFT.

In 1955 the KGB recalled Gideon to Moscow for debriefing. Although initially reluctant to do so, Gideon returned to the Soviet Union. He was never heard from again. Some RCMP officials believed that after his initial defection, Gideon was subverted by Soviet intelligence and continued to deal with the RCMP in a deception operation by the Soviets. Either way, the RCMP and British intelligence services learned much from Gideon.

Gilbert, Otto Attila

Hungarian-born American who spied for Hungary in the United States. In the only operation revealed by U.S. authorities, he unwittingly dealt with a U.S. Army officer acting as a DOUBLE AGENT.

Gilbert arrived in the United States in 1957 in the wave of Hungarians fleeing the Soviet occupation of their homeland following the unsuccessful revolution of 1956. He became a naturalized citizen in 1964. Sometime in the late 1970s he was drawn into a U.S. Army penetration attempt being run by the Hungarian intelligence service.

The plot began in Dec. 1977, when U.S. Army Warrant Officer Janos Szmolka, also a Hungarian-born naturalized U.S. citizen, made a trip to Budapest to visit his mother. Szmolka was assigned to the Army's Criminal Investigation Detachment at Mainz, West Germany. Szmolka was in his mother's home when a family friend took him aside and told him that a "representative of the government" wanted to talk to him privately. The man introduced himself as Lajos Perlaki and identified himself as a Hungarian INTELLIGENCE OFFICER. Perlaki said that Hungary wanted Szmolka to spy in exchange for "favorable treatment" of Szmolka's mother and married sister, his closest blood kin. Szmolka knew from Army briefings that what was happening to him had happened numerous times to soldiers with relatives in Eastern Bloc countries. How many of them had reported such blackmail threats no one knew.

Szmolka subsequently reported the meeting and, under U.S. Army COUNTERINTELLIGENCE instructions, played along, continuing with the deception after he was assigned in 1980 to Fort Gordon, near Augusta, Ga. Szmolka met with Perlaki in VIENNA and mailed innocuous material to ACCOMMODATION ADDRESSES in Hungary and Paris. In an early 1981 meeting in Vienna, Perlaki paid Szmolka $3,000 for 16 rolls of film of unclassified documents. Reemphasizing that he wanted secret documents, Perlaki offered $100,000 for classified material on weapons and CRYPTOSYSTEMS.

Szmolka asked for a face-to-face meeting with a Soviet AGENT in the United States. On April 17, 1982, Gilbert, who lived in Forest Hills, N.Y., appeared in Augusta. Szmolka handed classified documents to Gilbert, who paid him $4,000. FBI agents, observing the exchange, arrested Gilbert. Faced with the possibility of life imprisonment, Gilbert entered into a plea bargain by pleading guilty to conspiring to receive and transmit classified military documents. Three other counts of espionage were dropped. He was sentenced to 15 years.

Gilmore, John

(b. 1908 d. ?)

Writer, illustrator—and spy. Born in Germany as Willie Hirsch, he was sent to the United States at age 14 to live with relatives. As an author and illustrator he earned bylines in *Collier's* and *The Saturday Evening Post*, sold drawings to *Life* magazine, and produced the books *New York, New York* and *City of Magic*.

Gilmore went to the Soviet Union in 1936 while working for the magazine *Soviet Russia Today*. Upon returning to the United States he began collecting aerial photographs for the GRU, Soviet MILITARY INTELLIGENCE. He also enlisted other individuals to help him collect material for the Soviets; two were DOUBLE AGENTS who reported Gilmore's efforts to the FBI.

Following a series of meetings with IGOR MELEKH, a Soviet employee at the UNITED NATIONS, he was arrested on Oct. 23, 1960. Although indicted for espionage by a federal grand jury in Chicago, he was not brought to trial, because Melekh was released on condition that he leave the country. Accordingly, Gilmore was released, and on July 21, 1961, he and his family sailed for Germany, en route to Czechoslovakia, where he took up residence.

His release was part of the SPY SWAP for two U.S. Air Force fliers who had survived their AIRCRAFT being shot down by Soviet fighters on July 1, 1960. (See AIRCRAFT SHOT DOWN.)

Gimpel, Erich

(b. 1910 d. 1996)

German spy landed in the United States by SUBMARINE during World War II. Gimpel, a native-born German, accompanied WILLIAM COLEPAUGH, an American-born spy, when they came ashore from a U-boat on the coast of Maine in 1944.

The two men had met at a SPY SCHOOL operated by the SS in The Hague in the Netherlands. Gimpel had just returned from Spain, where he had been a German AGENT. On Oct. 6, 1944, they left for the United States on board the *U-1230*. They were put ashore on the night of Nov. 28 in a rubber boat at an isolated beach in Frenchman Bay, near Bar Harbor, Maine. (For details of events following their landing, see WILLIAM COLEPAUGH.)

Gimpel was recruited as a spy in 1935 while working for a German radio company in Peru. An ATTACHÉ at the German Embassy in Lima told him to keep watch on ships and cargoes entering and leaving port. In Jan. 1942, shortly after the U.S. entry into World War II, Peru sided with the United States and severed relations with Germany. Gimpel was deported to the United States and held in an alien detention camp in Texas until he was repatriated to Germany in Aug. 1942 on a neutral Swedish ship.

Under the repatriation agreement, he could not become a member of the German armed forces. Thus, because of his proficiency in Spanish, he went to work for the German Foreign Office as a COURIER between BERLIN and the German Embassy in Madrid. The Spanish city was a spy nest for both Allied and Axis agents.

In the summer of 1944 Gimpel got his first formal espionage training at the school, where he was given the alias Wilhelm Coller. The Gimpel-Colepaugh spy operation, expected to last for two years, had the CODE NAME Magpie. The pair was told to send information about the 1944 presidential campaign (which had already ended with President Roosevelt's reelection in November 1944 to a fourth term). They were also ordered to collect technical data from OPEN SOURCES, such as engineering journals, and transmit their material by radio or by MICRODOTS or in SECRET WRITING, send letters to ACCOMMODATION ADDRESSES in neutral countries. (The microdot-producing equipment was so heavy that Gimpel left it on the U-boat.) They were not to set up a NETWORK.

Five days after the spies had landed, the FBI, noting that a British freighter had been torpedoed eight miles off Maine, suspected that a U-boat that close to shore in late 1944 might have dropped off AGENTS. But an FBI search along the Maine coast turned up nothing. The spies, meanwhile, were spending an average of $100 a day enjoying New York City. On Dec. 21 Colepaugh slipped away from Gimpel, and on Dec. 26 he gave himself up to the FBI and provided a description of Gimpel, including a suit and overcoat he had just bought. After an intensive manhunt in New York City, FBI agents arrested Gimpel on Dec. 30 at a newspaper stand in Times Square.

Tried before a military tribunal on Feb. 6, 1945, Gimpel and Colepaugh were found guilty of espionage and sentenced to be hanged. President Truman later commuted their sentences to life imprisonment.

Gimpel was paroled and repatriated to West Germany in 1956, where he died in 1996.

Ginsberg, Samuel

SEE WALTER KRIVITSKY

Gisevius, Hans Bernd

(b. 1904 d. 1974)

German diplomat in Switzerland during World War II who served as liaison between the U.S. OFFICE OF STRATEGIC SERVICES (OSS) and the anti-Hitler forces in the German Army.

A political conservative, Gisevius joined the GESTAPO in the early 1930s, shortly after the Nazis came to power, but he soon became disillusioned with Adolf Hitler. After the "Night of the Long Knives," June 30, 1934, he left the government for private business.

Gisevius compiled dossiers on Nazi officials that he took to WILHELM CANARIS, head of the ABWEHR, German military intelligence. In 1939 Canaris employed Gisevius as chief of special projects, and the following year Gisevius was sent by the ABWEHR to the German consulate in Zurich, where he made contact with ALLEN DULLES of the U.S. OFFICE OF STRATEGIC SERVICES (OSS).

He agreed to serve as a liaison for Dulles with German military officers and civil officials who opposed the Nazi regime. He also assisted FRITZ KOLBE, who was providing Dulles with classified Foreign Office documents.

Gisevius returned to Germany, but after the failed July 1944 plot to assassinate Hitler, he fled back to Switzerland. After the war he returned to Germany and served as a key witness for the prosecution at the Nuremberg Trials in the case against Hermann Göring, his former chief in the Prussian Ministry of the Interior.

Subsequently, with the help of the OSS, he went to the United States, but after failed business ventures, he retired to Germany.

His autobiography, *Bis zum Bitteren Ende* ("To the Bitter End"), published in 1946, was a strong indictment of the Nazi regime, many of whose leading members Gisevius knew personally, as well as of the German people, who, Gisevius claimed, pretended not to know about the atrocities being committed in their name.

Glavnoye Razvedyvatelnoye Upravlenie

SEE GRU

Global Hawk

U.S. UNMANNED AERIAL VEHICLE (UAV) developed for very long-range RECONNAISSANCE missions. The Global Hawk was used on a limited basis during counter-terrorist operations in Afghanistan in 2002 and in the Gulf War of 2003. It is considered a potential replacement for the U-2 spyplane.

Built by Northrop Grumman's Ryan Aeronautical Center in Rancho Bernardo, Calif., for the U.S. Air Force, the Global Hawk has the designation RQ-4, indicating reconnaissance (R) and unmanned vehicle (Q). The Global Hawk is a very large drone, 44 feet long with a wingspan of 116¼ feet, and weighs some 23,000 pounds when fully loaded with fuel and sensors—electro optical/infrared sensors and synthetic aperture radar. It has a turbofan engine with a cruise speed of some 300 mph. The Global Hawk can fly 6,000 miles and have a 24-hour loiter time or, without loiter, fly 13,500 miles. It can reach 65,000 feet and is provided with a variety of sensors that can provide real-time intelligence to ground commanders or to operation centers via relay links to SATELLITES or other UAVs.

The Global Hawk first flew in Feb. 1998 and subsequently entered service with the U.S. Air Force. During flight tests a Global Hawk flew from Edwards Air Force Base in California to Alaska, and returned, on Oct. 19–20, 1999, a 24-hour, unrefueled, nonstop flight.

In an operational demonstration of its capabilities, in April 2001 a Global Hawk UAV took off from Edwards Air Force Base in California and flew 8,600 miles in 22 hours, landing at an airfield near Adelaide, Australia. That flight represented only 60 percent of the Global Hawk's range. The drone then participated in U.S.-Australian exercises. A minor problem on its fourth local flight was quickly fixed. On local flight No. 6—which lasted 25 hours—the Global Hawk reached 63,000 feet and took 200 reconnaissance photos, which it downloaded via datalink to Australian ground stations and the U.S. aircraft carrier *Kitty Hawk*.

Subsequently, Global Hawks were used operationally to collect intelligence over Iraq and Afghanistan (mission details are classified). However, during the Gulf War of 2003, images from a Global Hawk were downlinked to a ground station and immediately uplinked to a U.S. Navy F/A-18 Hornet attack aircraft that was able to strike a target within a few minutes of its detection. Similarly, the attack on a restaurant where Saddam Hussein and one or more of his sons were meeting on April 7, 2003, may have been similarly targeted by a Global Hawk, with the target being passed rapidly to a B-1 bomber in flight, which attacked with guided bombs. According to *Aviation Week & Space Technology* (April 14, 2003), the four GBU-31 weapons were dropped within 12 minutes of the order for the Oman-based bomber to attack.

Because of its great endurance and large payload, there have been proposals to employ the Global Hawk in support of counter-terrorist operations in the United States and, in a separate effort, as part of a national ballistic missile defense system. Also, the U.S. Navy in 2003 was planning to evaluate the Global Hawk as part of a Broad-Area Maritime Surveillance (BAMS) program.

Glomar Explorer

SEE *HUGHES GLOMAR EXPLORER*

Gold

SEE BERLIN TUNNEL

Gold, Harry

(b. 1910 d. 1972)

American chemist who conspired with Soviet atomic spy KLAUS FUCHS. Born in Russia as Heinrich Goldodnitsky, Gold came to the United States with his family in 1914 and became a U.S. citizen in 1922. He studied chemical engineering at the University of Pennsylvania and also attended Drexel Institute of Technology and Xavier University.

Gold apparently worked for Soviet intelligence from 1934 until 1945. He passed to the Soviets secret data on the U.S. atomic bomb program that he received from Fuchs, a British scientist, and from DAVID GREENGLASS, a machinist at the LOS ALAMOS atomic laboratory in New Mexico. Gold had seven or eight meetings with Fuchs in New York City at which atomic secrets were handed over. In Feb. 1945, he met Fuchs again in Cambridge, Mass., and received a "quite considerable packet" of information.

Gold next met Fuchs in June 1945, making a dangerous, two-stop COURIER run. He went first to Santa Fe, N.M., where Fuchs gave him sketches and notes about the plutonium (Fat Man) atomic bomb, which was about to be tested. Gold then went to Albuquerque, N.M., where he gave $500 to Tech. Cpl. David Greenglass, a solder assigned to Los Alamos.

In Sept. 1945, after the atomic bombing of Hiroshima and Nagasaki ended the war, Fuchs met with Gold again and gave him data that included the production rate of uranium-235. Gold gave Fuchs instructions on how to make contact with his Soviet HANDLER in London.

Gold was dropped by the Soviets in 1946 for a breach in security. When Fuchs was detected in 1949, his trail led to Gold, who was arrested on espionage charges by the FBI on May 22, 1950. Gold confessed and named Greenglass, MORTON SOBELL, and JULIUS ROSENBERG and his wife, Ethel, who were all arrested. Tried and found guilty on Dec. 9, 1950, Gold received a 30-year prison sentence. He was released on parole in 1965 and settled in Philadelphia.

He was awarded the Order of the Red Star by the Soviet Union. Gold's Soviet CODE NAMES were "Goose" and "Raymond."

Also see ATOMIC SPY RING.

Goldfinger

U.S. Navy intelligence operation employing a modified P3V ORION maritime RECONNAISSANCE aircraft to monitor nuclear weapons being transported by ship by the Soviet Union. The aircraft was employed in the late 1960s and early 1970s to complement the monitoring efforts of Navy surface ships and craft (see TASK FORCE).

Although ostensibly named for the JAMES BOND [F] novel of the same name, the CODE NAME Goldfinger was derived from the name of the U.S. DIRECTOR OF NAVAL INTELLIGENCE from 1968 to 1971, Rear Adm. F. J. (Fritz) Harlfinger.

Goldfus, Emil R.

SEE RUDOLF ABEL

Goldstein, Wolff

(b. 1921)

The first Soviet spy known to operate against Israel. Born to Jewish parents in Eastern Europe, Goldstein embraced communism at a young age and was recruited by the NKVD, reportedly from the outset to spy against the state of Israel.

He arrived in Israel during the War of Independence (1948) and went to work for the economics department of the Foreign Ministry. As was common among new arrivals, he Hebraicized his name, becoming Ze'ev Avni. During the 1950s the Foreign Ministry posted Goldstein to Brussels and, subsequently, to Belgrade. He had access to Israeli government communications as well as secret negotiations, all of which he passed to the KGB (which succeeded the NKVD in 1954 as the Soviet foreign intelligence agency). The KGB thus gained access to all Israeli diplomatic communications, including those intended for Israeli intelligence operatives operating under diplomatic COVER.

The Israeli SHIN BET internal security force began to suspect Goldstein while he was assigned to the Israeli Embassy in Belgrade because of his willingness to work

extra shifts in the embassy's classified communications area. Recalled to Israel under a pretext, he was interrogated, and soon confessed to his activities on behalf of the KGB. He was tried in secrecy, sentenced to prison, and served 10 years, after which he returned to Switzerland, where he had lived as a young man.

A few years later, with the agreement of Israeli intelligence officials, Goldstein returned to Israel, was given a new identity, and went to work for the Israeli Army as a psychologist.

Golienewski, Col. Michal

Polish INTELLIGENCE OFFICER who defected to the West and provided information leading to the arrest of GEORGE BLAKE, a Soviet spy in the British Secret Intelligence Service (MI6), and HARRY HOUGHTON, a civilian employee of the Royal Navy base at Portland.

Golienewski was working as a MOLE for the KGB within Polish intelligence at the time of his defection in 1960. He thus had extensive knowledge of Soviet espionage activities as well as Polish. The previous year he had written 14 letters to U.S. CIA station chiefs throughout Europe, signing himself "Sniper." His letters contained useful information, including clues to Houghton's espionage activities. Finally, in Dec. 1960 he defected to the CIA in West Berlin, accompanied by his mistress.

When he came to the West he revealed a cache of hundreds of rolls of film of classified documents that he had hidden in Europe. He gave his American and British debriefers useful information on the KGB's activities and spies. But Golienewski also claimed that he was the Grand Duke Aleksei Nikolaevich Romanov, who had escaped from the Bolsheviks to Poland in 1917.

In 1963 he told of a KGB spy operation involving an AGENT with the CODE NAME Bor, who was really Henry Kissinger, a Harvard professor (and future secretary of the NATIONAL SECURITY COUNCIL and Secretary of State). He also indicated that the British Security Service (MI5) officer Michael Hanley, a future head of MI5, was also a Soviet agent.

According to British intelligence officer PETER WRIGHT, by 1963 "the CIA suspected he was going clinically insane." Also, CIA official JAMES JESUS ANGLETON and future director RICHARD HELMS became convinced that Golienewski had fallen back under KGB control before he defected and that Blake and Houghton had been given away to Western intelligence to protect more important spies.

Golikov, Marshal of the Soviet Union Filipp Ivanovich

(b. 1900 d. 1980)

Senior Soviet Army commander and chief of the GRU, Soviet MILITARY INTELLIGENCE, during the critical period 1940–1941. A favorite of Soviet dictator Josef Stalin, he had a surprisingly long career despite failures both as a commander and as an intelligence chief.

Golikov, of peasant origins, volunteered to serve in the Red Army in 1918 and took an active part in the suppression of anti-Bolshevik peasant riots while on the staff of the 3rd Army Special Punitive Brigades. After the Russian Civil War he commanded a regiment, a brigade, a division, and then a corps. In the brief Soviet campaign in Poland in Sept. 1939 he commanded the 6th Army.

In June 1940, with the introduction of general ranks in the Red Army, he became a lieutenant general and that year was appointed chief of the GRU. Golikov was largely responsible for the rehabilitation of the GRU into an effective intelligence service following the murderous purges of the late 1930s. Although the GRU gave Stalin warning of the pending German assault (which Stalin ignored), Golikov was not dismissed—or worse—by Stalin after the Soviet-German conflict began on June 22, 1941. Rather, while remaining chief of the GRU he led the first Soviet missions seeking military assistance (and secrets) in London and Washington, D.C.

In Oct. 1941 Golikov returned to the Soviet Union to command the 10th Army in the defense of Moscow during the winter of 1941–1942. He then commanded the 4th Assault Army and later the Voronezh Front, one of the largest field commands in the Soviet Army. In 1942–1943 he was deputy commander of the Stalingrad Front. Nikita Khrushchev, in his autobiographical *Khrushchev Remembers* (1970), wrote of receiving

> a message from an officer in Stalingrad informing us that Golikov had gone completely off his head and was behaving like a madman. His presence in the [Stalingrad] army wasn't doing us any good, and he was even becoming a liability to us. . . . We relieved Golikov of his duties and had him recalled.

Stalin later reproached Khrushchev for recalling Golikov and in April 1943 he appointed Golikov both chief of the Main Personnel Directorate of the Red Army and a deputy minister, posts he held until 1950. He was also put in charge of the forced repatriation of Soviet prisoners of war and others to the Soviet Union after World War II. Former SMERSH officer A. I. Romanov wrote of the repatriation administration:

> Everybody who knew what was what realised that Golikov was no more than a 'front', a man who signed official documents, reports and appeals. The repatriation administration was also a 'front' to delude outsiders, our foreign allies in particular. All the real work was done by . . . Smersh and the Main Secret Political Administration of the NKGB.

Some reports contend that Golikov was also imprisoned for two years—probably 1949–1950. Regardless, he held major Army positions from 1950 to 1957, when he was simultaneously given the important posts of head of the Political Directorate of the Soviet Army and director of a Party Central Committee Department. Surviving the death of Stalin, in 1961 he was promoted to the highest military rank, Marshal of the Soviet Union.

Golikov retired from active duty in May 1962. His awards included the vaunted Hero of the Soviet Union.

Golitsyn, Maj. Anatoli Mikhailovich

Soviet KGB officer who defected to the United States from his post in Helsinki, Finland, in Dec. 1961. Golitsyn—who was known as Anatoli Kilmov when he defected—advised U.S. officials that there was a Soviet MOLE in the CIA.

He was born in the Ukraine of a Ukrainian mother and Russian father. He served in the Red Army during World War II and attended COUNTERINTELLIGENCE school. Subsequently, Golitsyn was assigned to the NKVD and its successor, the KGB. He had assignments in NKVD/KGB headquarters, and from 1953 to 1955 served in VIENNA, spying on Soviet émigrés. In 1960 he was assigned to the KGB station in Helsinki. He cited disillusionment with communism and infighting in the KGB as the reasons for his defection.

Golitsyn provided information on scores of Soviet spies and intelligence operations. He helped the British Secret Intelligence Service (MI6) conclude the case against HAROLD (KIM) PHILBY, a mole in British intelligence, and exposed JOHN VASSAL, a Soviet spy in the British Admiralty. This and other information led to the establishment of the British FLUENCY COMMITTEE to examine his leads, including a report of Soviet penetration of the Security Service (MI5).

His information about Soviet activities in France caused the resignation of two French intelligence chiefs, the departure of President de Gaulle's intelligence adviser, and, in 1983, the sentencing of Professor Hugh Hambleton, a Canadian, to 10 years in a British prison for giving classified NORTH ATLANTIC TREATY ORGANIZATION documents to the KGB. Golitsyn met with intelligence chiefs in several Western countries to discuss Soviet activities.

CIA officials found Golitsyn temperamental and difficult to deal with. He demanded access to all files held by the CIA and British intelligence and reportedly wanted to establish his own institute to study Soviet disinformation and a worldwide COUNTERINTELLIGENCE agency to work against the KGB—paid for by the CIA. However, his claim that there was a Soviet mole in the CIA endeared him to JAMES JESUS ANGLETON, head of CIA counterintelligence. Angleton gave him access to considerable sensitive CIA material, and his leads led to the ruination of several CIA officers against whom there was no other evidence or indication of disloyalty.

Two other Soviet defectors, FEDORA and YURI NOSENKO, both attempted to cast doubt on the validity of the information that Golitsyn gave to the West.

MI5 gave him the CODE NAME "Kago."

Golushko, Col. Gen. Nikolay Mikhaylovich

(b. 1937)

Second and last minister of the MB (Ministry of Security) for the post-Soviet Russian Federation.

Golushko graduated from the law department of the Tomsk State University in 1959 and worked for four years as a procuracy investigator. In 1963 he went to work for the KGB as deputy inspector for the KGB directorate of the Kemerovo region. From 1974 on he held major positions in KGB headquarters in Moscow.

In 1982 he became head of the KGB Secretariat, where he remained until 1985. He was chairman of the Ukrainian KGB from 1987 through 1991, when he was relieved of those duties because of his support for advocates of a change in the Soviet government.

In Jan. 1992 President Boris Yeltsin appointed him a deputy and then First Deputy Minister of the MB. Yeltsin made him minister on July 28, 1993, although the ministry was abolished later that year. (Golushko replaced VIKTOR BARANNIKOV as minister.)

Gordievsky, Oleg

(b. 1938)

British MOLE in the KGB. After spying for the British for 11 years, Gordievsky was betrayed in 1985 by a ALDRICH AMES, a Soviet mole in the U.S. CIA. He was able to escape from the Soviet Union and defect to Britain.

Gordievsky attended the Moscow Institute of International Relations, after which, in 1962, he joined the KGB. Following a year of training, in 1963 his first assignment at KGB headquarters was to analyze ILLEGALS working in the West. In Jan. 1966 he was assigned to Copenhagen to direct the KGB network in Denmark. He served in Copenhagen until 1970 and again from 1973 to 1978. (While in Moscow on leave in 1977, he attended the first KGB lecture given by HAROLD [KIM] PHILBY.)

Reportedly, when the Soviets invaded Czechoslovakia in 1968 he decided to help the West. He began to spy for the British Secret Intelligence Service (MI6) in 1974, while still in Copenhagen. He returned to Moscow from 1978 to 1982, when he was assigned to the Soviet Embassy in London. In early 1985 he was appointed the KGB RESIDENT in London.

In May 1985 Gordievsky was summoned back for consultations to Moscow, where he was interrogated and accused of betraying the Soviet Union. He denied all accusations. Although shadowed by the KGB, he was able to contact British intelligence. He jogged regularly and on the afternoon of July 19, dressed in jogging clothes, he went out for a run. He never returned to his apartment. Aided by the British, he was able to escape from the Soviet Union, but he left behind his wife, Leila, and two daughters.

After he "surfaced" in London in Sept. 1985, the British government expelled 25 Soviet diplomats, journalists, and others who had been identified by Gordievsky as having engaged in intelligence activities.

In 1990 the head of the KGB, VLADIMIR KRYUCHKOV, claimed that Gordievsky could have been reunited with his wife the year before had the communists not lost power in Czechoslovakia. At a Moscow press conference Kryuchkov said that the family reunion was a legitimate offer, but Gordievsky called it "just another trick. The KGB obviously hoped that when I had seen my wife and my two daughters, I would be persuaded to return to Moscow." Soon after Gordievsky defected, his wife divorced him; if she had not done so, it is unlikely that she could have retained a job or kept their children in preferred schools.

His wife and daughters were allowed to leave the Soviet Union in 1991, but Gordievsky and his wife did not get back together.

With CHRISTOPHER ANDREW he wrote the comprehensive *KGB: The Inside Story* (1990).

Gottlieb, Sidney

(b.1918 d. 1999)

CIA official who led the agency's controversial and unsuccessful experiments in mind control.

Gottlieb was head of the CIA's Technical Services Division for more than 20 years. His most notorious work involved the CIA MKULTRA program, in which drugs, including LSD, were given to unwitting subjects. He also developed poisons that were to be used in attempts to assassinate Cuban leader Fidel Castro. (See CUBA.)

Often described as "a kind of genius" and "a real Dr. Strangelove," Gottlieb supervised or personally carried out experiments that twisted a person's mind while searching for spiritual meaning in his own life. During the 1950s and early 1960s, his mind-altering drugs were given to hundreds of victims, including prisoners and mental patients. One patient was given LSD every day for 174 days.

Gottlieb, who took LSD frequently, went to India after his retirement and managed a leper hospital. After about a year and a half, he retired in Virginia, where he spent time folk dancing and raising goats.

Gouzenko, Igor Sergeievitch

(b. 1919 d. 1982)

CIPHER clerk in the Soviet Embassy in Ottawa, Canada, whose defection provided the West with information on Soviet spy activities. The primary purpose of those activities was to steal atomic bomb secrets. (See ATOMIC SPY RING.)

Gouzenko attended the Moscow Engineering Academy and the Moscow Architectural Institute. He was sent to MILITARY INTELLIGENCE school in Moscow in 1941 and was then posted to the GRU, the Red Army's intelligence service. He served in combat in World War II, earning a commission. In the summer of 1943 he was sent to Ottawa to serve as a cipher clerk in the Soviet Embassy. He flew; his wife, Svetlana, pregnant with their first child, was allowed to go to Canada, traveling by sea.

In Canada he successfully carried out his duties and while he and his wife came to enjoy life in the West. In Sept. 1944 he received unexpected orders to return to the Soviet Union. His return was subsequently delayed, and he and his wife decided that they would never go back to their homeland.

He attempted to defect with Svetlana, again pregnant, and their young son to the Canadian government on Sept. 6, 1945. Canadian officials initially declined to give him asylum. A neighbor, a sergeant in the Royal Canadian Air Force, gave him shelter. Finally the government, realizing his importance and the fact that he was in danger, gave him sanctuary.

Gouzenko's revelations and the documents that he brought with him revealed a major Soviet espionage ring in Canada. These led to the exposure of Col. NIKOLAI ZABOTIN, the GRU RESIDENT in Ottawa, and atomic scientist ALAN NUNN MAY, as well as other atomic spies. May and nine others involved in atomic espionage in Canada were sent to prison. Gouzenko also implicated ALGER HISS, a U.S. State Department official, as a Soviet spy but the evidence he provided was inconclusive.

Canadian officials provided Gouzenko and his family with a home in a secret location and another name. Periodically he would appear on Canadian television to discuss Soviet espionage, but always with a black hood over his head. Gouzenko subsequently wrote a book about his defection, *This Was My Choice* (1948), the basis for the later film *The Iron Curtain*. He then wrote novels while continuing to live in Canada.

Government Code and Cypher School

(GC&CS)

British cryptologic agency from 1919 until 1940, when it was renamed the GOVERNMENT COMMUNICATIONS HEADQUARTERS.

The GC&CS was established on Nov. 1, 1919, both to study foreign CIPHER and CODE systems and to advise the government on the security of classified British communications. The new agency was formed by 25 veterans of the Royal Navy's ROOM 40 and the War Office's MI (b) cryptologic section. It was initially placed under the Admiralty for administration purposes, but in 1922, along with the Secret Intelligence Service (MI6), the GC&CS was placed under the Foreign Office, which also funded its operation. The head of MI6—invariably known by the initial "C"—was also placed in charge of the codebreaking operations. However, the actual direction of the GC&CS was left largely to a committee representing MI6 and the military services. In 1922 Comdr. ALASTAIR DENNISTON, from Room 40, became head of the GC&CS.

The codebreakers were at first located in the former Marconi wireless offices at Watergate House, near the Savoy Hotel in London; subsequently, they moved to MI6's building, No. 54 BROADWAY, opposite St. James's Park and adjacent to QUEEN ANNE'S GATE in London.

A specific Navy section of the GC&CS was organized in 1924, an Army section in 1930, and an Air section in 1936. Those sections were expected to specialize only in cryptologic matters of interest to their respective services. The Admiralty and War Office reserved the right to withdraw their respective sections from the new agency. The withdrawal of those sections would have crippled British cryptologic efforts because of the complexity and synergistic aspects of codebreaking.

Soviet communications had been read by the GC&CS since shortly after the Revolution of 1917, although the adoption of ONE-TIME PADS brought those efforts to a virtual halt (until the post–World War II VENONA effort). In the early 1930s the main TARGETS of the GC&CS were the military communications of the Soviet Union and Germany, both of which were rebuilding their armed forces. The agency achieved significant successes against both countries, although because of the relatively low amounts of encrypted radio traffic, not all ciphers could be broken. By the late 1930s the German communications became more difficult to intercept because the Germans were now using ENIGMA encryption machines for their military and police radio communications.

In 1936 the British contacted Capt. GUSTAVE BERTRAND, the head of French Army codebreaking efforts, and began a promising exchange of information between the two agencies to break into Enigma ciphers. There was already extensive French-Polish coordination, and on Jan. 9–10, 1939, Bertrand hosted a conference in Paris of the top cryptologists from France, Poland, and Britain. The meeting afforded Britain, the only country to survive the coming German onslaught, the basis for breaking into German ciphers during the war. (See BIURO SZFROW.)

By the late 1930s the cryptologists at the GC&CS were fully integrated in their efforts against their principal target: the German ciphers generated by ENIGMA machines. (The attempts to break into Japanese Navy ciphers were left largely to the British codebreaking station in Hong Kong.)

The political triumphs of Adolf Hitler at Munich and his takeover of the Rhineland, Austria, and Czechoslovakia left little doubt in the minds of British military leaders that war in Europe was coming. In Aug. 1939, a month before the war erupted, Comdr. Denniston moved the GC&CS from its Broadway offices to BLETCHLEY PARK, an estate north of London, to escape expected German air attacks. (At the time of the Munich crisis in Sept. 1938, there was a trial move to Bletchley Park.)

A few months later—the precise date is unknown—the GC&CS was renamed Government Communications Headquarters (GCHQ) in an effort to disguise its true activities.

During the war the GC&CS at Bletchley Park enjoyed considerable successes against Enigma communications (see ENIGMA and BLETCHLEY PARK). After Germany invaded the Soviet Union on June 22, 1941, Prime Minister Winston Churchill decided that the Soviet regime should be treated as an ally. On that date it was decided that all deciphering of Soviet signals should stop for the duration of the war. This was a boon for Soviet AGENTS operating in Britain, whose secret communications were now made without fear of British interception.

The strain of the codebreaking efforts affected Denniston, and in Jan. 1942, after 20 years as head of the GC&CS, he moved to London, where he ran the diplomatic and commercial codebreaking efforts. Although technically still head of the GC&CS, in practice Denniston was replaced by Comdr. Edward W. Travis, who took over the military efforts at Bletchley Park. Denniston was forced into full retirement in 1944.

Unlike Room 40 after World War I, there was no question that the GCHQ—still referred to as the GC&CS by most codebreakers—would be retained in the Cold War era. The successes against Enigma and the very existence of the codebreaking effort were kept secret into the 1970s. The codebreaking activities were moved from Bletchley Park to Cheltenham, in Cotswold, some 40 miles south of Birmingham. The move provided for the construction of specialized facilities, with more space than currently available at Bletchley Park. (The older facility was retained for training activities; it is now a Post Office training facility.)

Virtually all aspects of GCHQ/Cheltenham are kept secret from the public, although the Soviets have had considerable knowledge of British codebreaking activities. In World War II the secrets of Bletchley Park were given to the Soviets by JOHN CAIRNCROSS and possibly others; in the Cold War era GEOFFREY PRIME passed them the secrets of Cheltenham.

Government Communications Headquarters (GCHQ)

The GOVERNMENT CODE AND CYPHER SCHOOL (GC&CS), Britain's codebreaking agency from 1919, was renamed Government Communications Headquarters in 1942 in an effort to hide its activities. Most codebreakers continued to refer to it as GC&CS—and some still do today.

While little has been publicly revealed about GCHQ, the organization appears to have four major operating divisions:

Division H: CRYPTOANALYSIS
Division J: Special SIGNALS INTELLIGENCE (SIGINT)
Division K: General SIGINT
Division X: Computers

Since the passage of the Anti-Terrorism Crime and Security Act of 2001, GCHQ has provided not only SIGNALS INTELLIGENCE (SIGINT) but has stepped up its "information assurance" mission, helping to keep government communication and information systems safe from hackers and other threats. The agency also provides similar help to the "UK's critical national infrastructure," including power, water, and civilian communications. Even the names of the directors of GCHQ have remained closely guarded. The following are the directors since World War II:

1944–1952	Comdr. Edward W. Travis, RN
1952–1960	Group Capt. Eric Jones, RAF
1960–1964	Clive Loehnis
1965–1973	Leonard Hooper
1973–1978	Arthur Bonsall
1978–1983	Brian Tovey
1983–1989	Peter Marychurch
1989–1996	John Anthony Adye
1996–1997	David Omand
1998–2003	Francis Richards
2003–	David Pepper

Also see BRUSA AGREEMENT, UKUSA AGREEMENT.

GPU

SEE CHEKA

GRAB

(GALACTIC RADIATION AND BACKGROUND EXPERIMENT)

The world's first spy SATELLITE to be orbited, it was designed for the collection of ELECTRONIC INTELLIGENCE (ELINT). Developed in great secrecy at the Naval Research Laboratory (NRL) in Washington, D.C., the first GRAB satellite was launched on June 22, 1960—two months before the successful CORONA mission was launched. GRAB had an unclassified mission as it carried a publicly announced experiment to measure solar radiation (hence its name). But GRAB's primary purpose, not revealed until June 1998, was to record emissions from radars within the USSR.

For more than two years, GRAB satellites collected electronic emissions from Soviet air defense radars. The data were recorded on magnetic tape and later processed and analyzed by the NSA and the U.S. Strategic Air Command.

The project was begun at NRL in 1958. Keith Hall, director of the NATIONAL RECONNAISSANCE OFFICE, speaking at the NRL on June 17, 1998, said:

> You can say that GRAB got its start on the Pennsylvania Turnpike. Research engineer Reid Mayo of NRL originated the concept of an ELINT satellite early in 1958 on his way back from a family trip to Michigan. He was stranded by a snowstorm at a Howard Johnson's restaurant on the turnpike. While his wife and children slept, he made initial calculations on a paper place mat. Those notes evolved into a satellite that was a remarkable piece of technology in its time.

President Eisenhower approved the first launch of a GRAB satellite on May 5, 1960, four days after the U-2 spyplane flown by FRANCIS GARY POWERS was shot down over the Soviet Union. The first GRAB satellite got a "free ride" into space on June 22, 1960, aboard the Navy's third Transit navigation satellite. GRAB carried two electronic payloads—the classified ELINT package and instrumentation to measure solar radiation. The second successful GRAB launch occurred on June 29, 1961.

The two successful GRAB satellites were operational from July 1960 and until Aug. 1962.

Graduated

Russian slang for a MOLE who succeeds in moving from a low position to a more important or sensitive one in a foreign government office or agency, or military service.

Graf, Ronald Dean

SEE DONALD KING

Graf Zeppelin

German passenger airship, employed in 1939 for electronic SURVEILLANCE of British RADAR installations. The *Graf Zeppelin*—the second German airship of that name—was completed in 1938. It was the most advanced commercial airship ever built.

The *Graf Zeppelin* carried out flying trials but did not enter passenger service. Based at Frankfurt, the airship was placed in service as a FERRET for the German Air Force in the spring of 1939 to measure the wavelength of British radars and to pinpoint the location of the radar sites. The airship was used because existing airplanes lacked endurance and the space for the electronic equipment necessary for such work. The *Graf Zeppelin* made its first surveillance flight in late May 1939.

No useful data were acquired because of problems with the electronic equipment. The second flight, in early Aug. 1939, also failed to acquire useful information. While the *Graf Zeppelin* was tracked by British radar on its first flight, it escaped unnoticed on the second. But the airship was sighted visually, and after the *London Daily Telegraph* newspaper revealed the flight, the German government denied that the aircraft had left Germany or approached the coast of England. After the outbreak of war in Europe, the *Graf Zeppelin* was grounded.

This second *Graf Zeppelin*, given the designation *LZ.130*, was the final rigid airship constructed by Germany, the 130th to be built.

(The previous *Graf Zeppelin* was completed in 1928 and employed in commercial passenger service for 10 years, making 590 flights before being decommissioned in June 1937. That *Graf Zeppelin* made its first long-range trip across the Atlantic to the United States in 112 hours. The airship subsequently flew around the world in 1929, a journey with numerous stops and extensive flights over Siberia that took just over 21 days, with seven days spent at ports. That same year the craft surveyed the Arctic, and in 1930 it pioneered regular German airship service to South America.)

Both of the *Graf Zeppelin* airships were broken up in 1940. Hermann Göring, head of the Luftwaffe, wanted their aluminum for combat aircraft.

Granville, Christine

(b. 1915 d. 1952)

Highly successful British AGENT in World War II. Born Countess Krystina Skarbek of Polish nobility, she was tall, attractive, and graceful, winning a Miss Poland contest when in her teens.

She was in Addas Abba (Ethiopia) when war began in Sept. 1939. She abandoned her husband and traveled to Britain, where she offered her services to the Secret Intelligence Service (MI6). The British sent her to Budapest where, working as a journalist, she repeatedly went into Poland to smuggle out Poles. Reportedly, she was arrested by the Germans during one of her sojourns into Poland but managed to escape. She was also said to have been arrested on the Yugoslav border while helping to smuggle downed Allied fliers to freedom; she talked her captors into releasing her.

She next served in the Middle East. Subsequently, under the auspices of the British Special Operations Executive (SOE), she parachuted into southern France to serve as a COURIER with the French Resistance.

At the end of the war she was awarded the George Medal and the Order of the British Empire.

Without other means of support, after the war she served as a stewardess on an ocean liner, where she was stabbed to death in a lovers' quarrel.

Gray, J. Patrick

(b. 1916)

Acting director of the FBI who was forced to resign because of his involvement in the WATERGATE scandal.

President Nixon appointed Gray acting director on May 3, 1972, the day after the death of J. EDGAR HOOVER, who had been director for 48 years. On June 17 five men were arrested for breaking into the Democratic National Committee headquarters at the Watergate hotel-office-apartment complex in Washington, D.C. The resulting scandal, triggering an attempt at a cover-up by the White House, soon touched Gray.

Because the burglars had connections with the CIA, Nixon pressured RICHARD M. HELMS, the DIRECTOR OF CENTRAL INTELLIGENCE, to use his influence to stop the FBI investigation into the affair. Helms had his deputy, Lt. Gen. Vernon A. Walters, go to Gray. Walters later quoted Helms as saying, "You must remind Mr. Gray of the agreement between the FBI and the CIA, that if they run into or appear to expose one another's assets, they will notify one another."

Gray reined in the FBI, but FBI officials, sensing a cover-up, complained. Gray then called Walters to request a written CIA statement asking the FBI to hold up its probe. No statement came, and the FBI investigation resumed. But Gray was tainted. While still awaiting what would undoubtedly be a brutal Senate confirmation hearing, Gray resigned on April 27, 1973. Charges of authorizing warrantless break-ins (BLACK BAG JOBS) were later made against Gray, but they were dropped in Dec. 1980.

Graymail

Threat by a defendant in a trial to expose intelligence activities or other classified information if prosecuted.

Great Britain

SEE ENGLAND-GREAT BRITAIN-UNITED KINGDOM

Great Game

The massive British intelligence activities in India during the 1800s. The term is usually credited to Rudyard Kipling in his novel KIM (1901). Historians later appropriated it to describe the open and covert operations of China and Russia in their attempts to gain control of Central Asia. Some sources credit the term to a British officer, Capt. Arthur Connolly, who in 1840 wrote in a letter to a friend:

> We are on the eve of stirring times; but if we play the great game that is before us, the results will be incalculably beneficial to us [the British] and to the tribes whose destinies may change from turmoil, violence, ignorance and poverty to peace, enlightenment and varied happiness.

The British government used large numbers of civilians and military men in intelligence, security, and COUNTERESPIONAGE work in the empire prior to World War I. The largest task was in India, where only a few thousand troops were available to control a large, rebellious territory.

Greene, Graham

(b. 1904 d. 1991)

English novelist and AGENT for the Secret Intelligence Service MI6).

Greene summed up his own attitude toward writing and espionage in *A Sort of Life* (1971): "I suppose . . . that every novelist has something in common with a spy; he watches, he overhears, he seeks motives and analyses character. . . ."

His fascination with espionage began in 1924, when he was still a student at Oxford. Using funds supplied by the German Embassy in London, he toured a still-occupied Germany, looking for signs of French-organized revolts in the Vichy area. He worked on the editorial staff of *The Times* from 1926 to 1930 and became a movie critic for *The Spectator* until 1939. By the time World War II began, Greene was also an established novelist, well

known for the 1932 thriller *Stamboul Train* (published as *Orient Express* in the United States) and other works of fiction. His *Confidential Agent* (1939) foreshadowed his wartime work.

Greene's sister, Elisabeth, who worked in an office of MI6, lured him into the service. His SECURITY CLEARANCE was snagged by the revelation that he had a court record: a libel action had been brought against him by studio executives who were outraged by his claim that the movies of Shirley Temple, the child actress, were sexually suggestive. As a result, Greene's acceptance into MI6 had to be personally approved by the head of the agency.

Greene's case officer was HAROLD (KIM) PHILBY. "No one could have been a better chief," Greene later wrote. "He had all the small loyalties to his colleagues, and of course his big loyalty was unknown to us."

Greene's first intelligence assignment was to Freetown, Sierra Leone, where he handled agents and kept watch over a waterfront renowned for smugglers and spies. While in Freetown he wrote *The Ministry of Fear* (1943). Philby next sent him to neutral Portugal, a hotbed of espionage. In 1945 Greene moved from MI6 to the Foreign Office's political intelligence department, although he soon departed.

After the war he wrote *The Heart of the Matter* (1948), drawing upon his experiences in West Africa. When he went to occupied VIENNA to work on the screenplay for *The Third Man* (based on his 1935 short story, "The Basement Room"), Soviet INTELLIGENCE OFFICERS there suspected that he was still in MI6. An intelligence officer's remark about criminals' use of Vienna's sewers inspired Greene to use them for chase scenes. Many believed that Harry Lime, the central character in the movie, was based on Kim Philby. Greene himself wrote in a newspaper article that he was using the phrase "the THIRD MAN" long before it became the label for Philby the spy.

After Philby was exposed as a spy, Greene said, "I liked him. I've often asked myself what I would have done if I'd discovered he was a secret agent at that time. . . . I think, perhaps, if in a drunken moment he had slipped a hint, I would have given him twenty-four hours to get clear and then reported him."

Greene's knowledge of intelligence practices is served up as humor in *Our Man in Havana* (1958), but in *The Human Factor* (1978) espionage is presented as a bleak, amoral art. Maurice Castle, the DOUBLE AGENT in *The Human Factor*, was not modeled on Philby, Greene later said. "I know very well from experience," he wrote, "that it is only possible for me to base a very minor and transient character on a real person." According to a biographer, Greene sent a copy of the manuscript to Philby in Moscow and asked for his opinion. In the novel, a British intelligence officer who is a Soviet MOLE tells the Soviets about a secret British–South African treaty drawn up to keep South African gold from the Soviets. After the novel was published, a similar treaty became public. Biographers point to such phenomena to bolster speculation that Greene never really lost contact with British intelligence.

The Quiet American (1955)—and the 2002 movie of the same name—were inspired by Greene's experiences as a journalist in French Indochina, where he met U.S. guerrilla war specialist EDWARD G. LANSDALE, the model for Pyle, his protagonist. There he also witnessed the manipulations of agents of the CIA. In the novel, after a bomb goes off in a crowded square, Pyle looks at the wet on his shoes and asks, "What's that?" The Englishman narrator (Greene) replies, "Blood. Haven't you ever seen it before?" At that moment, when the American is "seeing a real war for the first time," the U.S. involvement in Vietnam is fatefully ordained. Once again Greene had found in his travels through the underbrush of espionage the small events of history and preserved them in a novel.

Graham's eldest brother, Herbert, spied briefly for the Japanese in the 1930s, handing over to a contact in London phony secrets culled from published sources. He was also a spy for the rebels during the Spanish Civil War, which is the background for *Confidential Agent* (1939). A bungling con man, Herbert was probably the basis for the vacuum-cleaner salesman who becomes a British spy in *Our Man in Havana* (made into a film in 1960—see MOVIES).

Greenglass, Tech. Cpl. David

(b. 1922)

The LOS ALAMOS contact for Soviet atomic spy HARRY GOLD, brother-in-law of JULIUS ROSENBERG. Greenglass entered the U.S. Army in 1943 and, after technical training, was assigned to the Los Alamos nuclear laboratory in a minor position related to building the atomic bomb. He provided the Soviets with plans of the Los Alamos laboratory complex as well as a rough sketch of the plutonium (Fat Man) atomic bomb that would be dropped on Nagasaki on Aug. 9, 1945.

He was arrested on June 16, 1950, on espionage charges, having been linked to a Soviet spy ring by Gold, who was in turn also collecting secret material from KLAUS FUCHS. In addition, a Soviet intelligence message intercepted by U.S. MILITARY INTELLIGENCE in 1944 that was decrypted in 1950 narrowed the search to Greenglass. (See VERONA.)

He was tried and sentenced to a 15-year prison term. He gave evidence against the Rosenbergs, apparently to have his own sentence reduced. Greenglass was released from prison in 1960.

His Soviet CODE NAME was "Caliber."

Also see ATOMIC SPY RING.

Greenpeace

SEE *RAINBOW WARRIOR*

Gregory, Staff Sgt. Jeffrey E.

Member of the CLYDE LEE CONRAD spy ring, whose members sold NORTH AMERICAN TREATY ORGANIZATION (NATO) secrets to Hungarian and Czechoslovakian AGENTS. Gregory was arrested in April 1993 at Fort Richardson, Alaska, in a joint FBI-U.S. Army Intelligence investigation that had lasted for more than a decade.

Like the other members of the ring, Gregory was assigned to the 8th Infantry Division in Bad Kreuznach, Germany, in the mid-1980s. As a staff driver, he helped to maintain the commanding general's mobile command center. His duties included the updating of maps showing military maneuvers and he had access to classified messages and correspondence. An FBI official reported that Gregory once stole a military flight bag stuffed with 20 pounds of classified documents. The documents included NATO "war plans."

Greif

German CODE NAME for a commando operation during the World War II Battle of the Bulge. *Greif* literally means "griffin," the mythical eagle-lion, but was translated as "snatch" for the beast's kidnapping habits.

The Greif unit was created for the Battle of the Bulge in Dec. 1944. Some 3,500 German troops, under the command of OTTO SKORZENY, were to dress in U.S. uniforms and, using captured American vehicles, weapons, and equipment, sow confusion behind American lines while also capturing bridges over the Meuse River. About 150 English-speaking German soldiers were included in the commando force.

Skorzeny's ersatz GIs cut communications wires, changed road signs, and gave confusing, GI-to-GI information to U.S. troops stunned by the sudden German attack. At the headquarters of the Allied Expeditionary Forces at Versailles, just outside Paris, extra security was thrown around Gen. Dwight D. Eisenhower because of planted rumors that a Skorzeny-led assassination squad had targeted Eisenhower.

Four of the fake Americans were captured in U.S. uniforms and executed as spies.

Grillflame

SEE PSYCHIC INTELLIGENCE

Group 300

CODE NAME for the 15 Polish cryptologists from the BIURO SZFROW working at the French cryptanalysis center CADIX from mid-1940 until Oct. 1942. Subsequently, the Poles went to Great Britain.

GRU

Glavnoye Razvedyvatelnoye Upravlenie (Chief Intelligence Directorate of the General Staff), the Soviet-Russian MILITARY INTELLIGENCE directorate.

In the post-Soviet era, with the reduction in the size and capabilities of the KGB's successor agencies, the im-

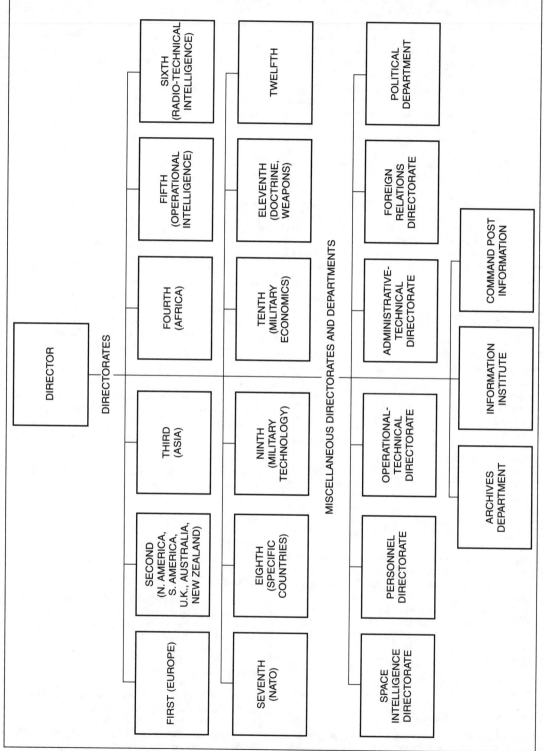

DIRECTOR

DIRECTORATES

| FIRST (EUROPE) | SECOND (N. AMERICA, S. AMERICA, U.K., AUSTRALIA, NEW ZEALAND) | THIRD (ASIA) | FOURTH (AFRICA) | FIFTH (OPERATIONAL INTELLIGENCE) | SIXTH (RADIO-TECHNICAL INTELLIGENCE) |

| SEVENTH (NATO) | EIGHTH (SPECIFIC COUNTRIES) | NINTH (MILITARY TECHNOLOGY) | TENTH (MILITARY ECONOMICS) | ELEVENTH (DOCTRINE, WEAPONS) | TWELFTH |

MISCELLANEOUS DIRECTORATES AND DEPARTMENTS

| SPACE INTELLIGENCE DIRECTORATE | PERSONNEL DIRECTORATE | OPERATIONAL-TECHNICAL DIRECTORATE | ADMINISTRATIVE-TECHNICAL DIRECTORATE | FOREIGN RELATIONS DIRECTORATE | POLITICAL DEPARTMENT |

| ARCHIVES DEPARTMENT | INFORMATION INSTITUTE | COMMAND POST INFORMATION |

GRU Organization.

portance of the GRU's foreign intelligence activities has increased.

The GRU was created on Nov. 5, 1918, as the Registered Directorate of the Field Staff of the Workers and Peasants Red Army by V. I. Lenin at the urging of his war commissar, Leon Trotsky. (The designation GRU was not formally assigned until June 1942 although it was in use during most of the earlier Soviet period.) The new intelligence ORGAN was not intended to detract from the importance of intelligence services of the Red Army's existing front and army commands, but to coordinate their activities and appraise the central staff of the military situation.

In addition to the collection of STRATEGIC INTELLIGENCE and OPERATIONAL INTELLIGENCE, the GRU has emphasized the gathering of military scientific data since the earliest days of Soviet military intelligence. Indeed, a favorite anecdote of GRU officers tells of a scientist ordered to penetrate into a foreign country illegally, become a naturalized citizen, and spy out scientific-technical information for the GRU. The scientist agreed to the assignment but pointed out that he did not know the language of the country to which he was going.

"Don't worry about it," he was told. "Act like a mute."

"And what if I suddenly talk in my sleep?" the scientist asked.

"It won't happen," a GRU official assured him. "We'll cut your tongue out."

From its beginning, the GRU had a charter for foreign intelligence collection. And unlike the CHEKA and its successor agencies, which were all involved in internal police and criminal investigation functions as well as intelligence activities, the GRU has never been concerned with internal police work. The only exceptions occurred in the late 1930s, when the GRU was used in the purge of NKVD officials, and again in 1953, when it operated against members of the MVD, which was responsible for internal security.

Obviously there has been considerable duplication and overlap between activities of the GRU and the state security organs (e.g., NKVD, KGB), but this was not necessarily regarded as a shortcoming. Efficiency and cost-effectiveness were never a Soviet consideration with regard to intelligence. More information was always considered to be better, and duplicative intelligence activities served to check one another.

But as John Erickson, the West's leading analyst of Soviet military-political history, wrote in The Soviet High Command (1962), "The army and the secret police were fatally entangled and fearfully taken up in a protracted struggle the one against the other. It was to become a struggle to the death."

Early in its existence the GRU underwent a purge, or "blood-letting," predating the horrifying purges of the military establishment during the Stalinist era. The first purge of the GRU occurred in Nov. 1920, when Lenin ordered hundreds of INTELLIGENCE OFFICERS shot for having given incorrect evaluations of the situation in Poland. Time in position was very brief for the early chiefs of the GRU; some were removed for incompetence (usually from a political viewpoint), and some probably because they were too good and their services were needed elsewhere in the tumultuous Civil War, which lasted until 1922.

The GRU was quickly rehabilitated, and the Red Army reorganization of 1926 established military intelligence as the Fourth Department of the Red Army (General) Staff. (The other departments were Operations, Organization-Mobilization, and Military Communications, respectively.) Bolstered by this formal status, the GRU enjoyed many successes in the 1920s and 1930s, garnering secret military information from Germany, Britain, and the United States.

STALINIST PURGES

In 1929–1930 Josef Stalin ordered a purge against certain "rightists" in the Soviet Union. Several senior military officers were purged, but only some five percent of the military leadership were arrested, less than one-half the number for other government groups, without impact on the GRU. When the far-reaching Stalinist purge was begun secretly in 1935, the initial arrests and executions were of NKVD officials, especially those overseas; the executions were carried out by GRU officials. YA. K. BERZIN, head of the GRU, traveled from Moscow to the Far East with several trusted assistants to eliminate specific NKVD officials. (During his absence in the Far East and subsequently in Spain, Berzin technically remained head of the GRU; however, S. T. URITSKI was named as acting chief of military intelligence.)

The second purge of the Soviet military establishment was initiated by Stalin in 1937. Hundreds of Army officers were executed and thousands more imprisoned; the acting head of the GRU, Uritski, was arrested and shot. Operatives of the NKVD traveled to other countries, where they murdered both GRU ILLEGALS and intelligence officers of the GRU and NKVD who had refused to return to the Soviet Union—a reversal of the Berzin effort against the NKVD in 1935! One of the NKVD executioners was I. A. SEROV, a young officer recently transferred from the Army to the security agency; he later served as head of the KGB and, subsequently, the GRU. At that point the GRU was devastated: According to VIKTOR SUVOROV in his Inside Soviet Military Intelligence (1984), "In the course of the 1937 purge the GRU was completely destroyed—even down to the lavatory attendants and cooks on its payroll."

Although the GRU recovered its strength within a year, it lost all of its power during another wave of terror in the summer of 1938. The previous year the brilliant Marshal of the Soviet Union M. N. Tukhachevsky was arrested, tried, and shot, initiating a wave of terror against the Red Army. Tens of thousands of officers were executed or imprisoned. The General Staff was liquidated, including all senior GRU officers. Former GRU chief Berzin, who had gone to Spain and virtually commanded the Republican forces during the Spanish Civil War, was executed on July 29, 1938, after returning to

Moscow. The brief but unexpectedly difficult Soviet campaign against Finland in 1939–1940 apparently convinced Stalin of the need to rebuild the General Staff, which he had so recently destroyed. In this context the GRU was quickly revived under the command of FILIPP GOLIKOV. One of the numerous failures of the conflict with Finland was an operation designated *Spetsnaz*, which was carried out by about 50 special troops of the GRU under Gen. Khadzhi-Umar Mamsurov. He had successfully led special units to attack Nationalist transport and other activities behind the front lines in the Spanish Civil War. Mamsurov's men had tried to capture Finnish soldiers for intelligence interrogation but were unable to do so. Still, the effort defined a new area of special operations for the GRU.

On the eve of the German invasion of the Soviet Union on June 22, 1941, the GRU was able to give the Soviet leadership warning of the pending assault; however, all such information was rejected by Stalin. In the fall of 1941 the GRU was divided into two branches; the operation of the overseas AGENTS of the GRU was placed under a newly established Chief of Intelligence Directorate of the Supreme High Command, which reported directly to Stalin. The strategic and operational intelligence activities remained under the GRU, directly supporting the Soviet General Staff and the GRU.

WORLD WAR II

During World War II Soviet military intelligence was relatively effective. However, the massive German assault of June 22, 1941, largely destroyed Soviet tactical and theater intelligence capabilities, and the GRU was ineffective during the first year of the Great Patriotic War (the Soviet term for their participation in the European conflict). By the Battle of Stalingrad in the winter of 1942–1943, the GRU had again made a comeback. Col. David Glantz, a leading U.S. Army analyst of Red Army intelligence, has observed:

> While Soviet numerical superiority remained the biggest factor in their achievement of victory, effective intelligence work contributed to the Soviet ability to generate that superiority without German knowledge. [Intelligence] contributed to the rapid development of the [tactical] penetration operation by forming an accurate picture of German tactical dispositions. Once the operation had begun, sound intelligence insured the initiative would remain in Soviet hands until time and distance had taken its toll on advancing Soviet forces. This, in part explained the extraordinary depth of the Soviet advance.
>
> * * *
>
> The Soviets characteristically have left much unsaid [about military intelligence in the war]. Without German archival materials, one would have to rate Soviet intelligence as good. When available German materials are taken into account, that evaluation rises even higher. It is likely full Soviet disclosure of

their own archival materials will indicate an even greater Soviet capability.

During the war GRU agents were able to penetrate the German General Staff (Operation Dora—see LUCY SPY RING) through Switzerland and steal atomic secrets by way of Canada (Zaria); the GRU also controlled RICHARD SORGE, the legendary Soviet agent in Japan. More overtly, Soviet military ATTACHÉS in the United States and Great Britain collected tons of documents on war plans and weapons (in addition to the planes, ships, aircraft, and tanks actually transferred during the war). The premier award of Hero of the Soviet Union was issued to 121 men and women associated with the GRU for their wartime service.

The GRU was not responsible for COUNTERINTELLIGENCE within the armed forces, that role being assigned to the state security organ. From Dec. 1918 there were Special Departments (Osobye Otdely) within the state security organs that were responsible for counterintelligence within the military establishment. There was a very brief period, from Feb. to July 1941, when Stalin did allow the military to take charge of its own counterintelligence activities. During those months a Special Department was retained in the NKGB and NKVD to carry out security functions within their respective military units, after which the Army and Navy Special Departments were again subordinated to the NKVD.

In 1941 the Soviets established the SMERSH organization within the NKVD specifically to combat espionage within the armed forces and also to track down traitors and deserters behind the front lines, shoot retreating soldiers, and arrest Soviet troops who escaped from German captivity. In 1943 Smersh became a separate agency under the State Defense Committee. Its activities were incorporated into the newly created MGB (Ministry of State Security) on March 16, 1946.

In 1947 Stalin chose to remove intelligence functions from both the Army and the MGB. A new intelligence organization for foreign intelligence was created—KI, or Komitet Informatsii (Committee of Information)—under the direction of V. M. Molotov, the Commissar of Foreign Affairs. That organization lasted until 1951, although the GRU was able to withdraw from the KI arrangement in mid-1948.

Significantly, Gen. of the Army SERGEI SHTEMYENKO, head of the GRU from 1946 to 1948, was promoted to chief of the General Staff in late 1948 but was subsequently broken. He then returned to head the GRU in 1956–1957, was again demoted, and was ultimately promoted a third time to senior rank.

The head of the GRU has often been a senior officer from the state security organ (NKVD or KGB). For example, from 1958 to 1962 the GRU was headed by Col. Gen. Serov, a former Smersh officer and chairman of the KGB. Under Serov the GRU became thoroughly corrupt.

Gen. of the Army PETR IVASHUTIN, a former NKVD/KGB officer, served as head of the GRU for 24 years (1963 to 1987), bringing the agency's graft, corruption, and failures to an unprecedented level; several senior GRU officers defected to the West during his tenure. (Under Serov, GRU officers voluntarily made contact with Western services and gave them much more valuable information than they took from them.)

Gen. of the Army VLADLEN MIKHAYLOV, head of the GRU from 1987 to 1991, had no military intelligence background and little competence; day-to-day operations were taken in hand by three of his deputies, who rotated as acting chairmen. Finally, on the eve of the demise of the Soviet Union, Mikhaylov was replaced for a short time by Col. Gen. YEVGENIY TIMOKHIN, an air defense officer without intelligence experience. In 1992 he in turn was replaced by Lt. Gen. FEDOR LADYGIN.

Ladygin, subsequently promoted to colonel general, in Nov. 1996 told Komsomolskaya Pravda that his main priorities included military-related ECONOMIC INTELLIGENCE and TECHNICAL INTELLIGENCE to prevent Russia from sinking "to the status of a third world country."

By the late 1980s, before the breakup of the Soviet Union, the Soviet Army's GRU components—which collected operational intelligence—included about 180 reconnaissance battalions (340 men each) and some 700 reconnaissance companies (55 men) plus the intelligence staffs of higher formations of the Ground Forces and the 15 Military Districts within the Soviet Union (more than 100,000 personnel). Similarly, intelligence staffs at naval fleet headquarters and operational formations, as well as major staffs of the Strategic Rocket Forces, Air Forces, and Air Defense Forces, were under the aegis of the GRU. The GRU's Space Intelligence Directorate coordinated intelligence collection SATELLITES, while the Sixth Directorate coordinated the GRU's SIGNALS INTELLIGENCE complex of electronic listening posts around the world at sea in INTELLIGENCE COLLECTION SHIPS.

GRU espionage efforts against the United States were by this time reported to be greater than those of the KGB. Reportedly, the GRU had the lead responsibility in obtaining classified U.S. military technology.

The GRU now also controls the country's special warfare forces, known by the Russian acronym SPETSNAZ (for Chasti Spetsial'nogo Naznacheniya). The Spetsnaz forces are somewhat similar to the U.S. SPECIAL OPERATIONS FORCES, like the Army's Green Berets and Delta Force, and the Navy's SEAL teams. The Spetsnaz troops are controlled by the GRU for training and administration, and for wartime operations. However, in the Soviet period they were assigned to KGB control for special operations, such as the initial military operations in Czechoslovakia during the 1968 Soviet occupation of that country and the assassination of Afghanistan's president in Dec. 1979.

There were reported to be Spetsnaz brigades of some 900 to 1,300 officers and enlisted men assigned to each of the four groups of forces in Europe as well as to several of the major military districts. There were also naval Spetsnaz brigades assigned to each of the four Soviet fleets. According to former Soviet intelligence officer Suvorov, writing in 1984, there were 20 Spetsnaz brigades

plus 41 separate companies. Thus, the total strength of Spetsnaz forces could be in the order of 30,000 troops within the Soviet armed forces.

Several educational institutions trained GRU officers in a three- to five-year course of study. The principal school for GRU officers was the Military-Diplomatic Academy in Moscow, but GRU officers were also trained by intelligence faculties at the Training Center of Illegals, Frunze Military Academy, Naval Academy, Military Signals Academy, Military Institute of Foreign Languages, Cherepovetski Higher Military Engineering School for Communications, Higher Naval School of Radio Electronics, and Spetsnaz Faculty of the Ryazan Higher Airborne School. In addition, GRU agents were trained in various aspects of the spy TRADECRAFT at special SPY SCHOOLS.

The GRU reportedly has 18 directorates, the principal ones being numbered from one through 12 (see diagram). GRU headquarters are located on Khoroshevskiy Highway in Moscow, near the old Khodynka airfield. The complex's main building is a nine-story structure with walls entirely of glass, giving rise to the Western nickname "Aquarium," although GRU officers usually refer to it as Steklyashka (piece of glass). The building was originally designed as a military hospital.

CHIEFS OF THE GRU

Note the great disparities in length of service. M. A. Shalin, Ya. K. Berzin, and S. M. Shtemyenko twice served as head of military intelligence.

Oct. 1918–July 1919	S. I. Aralov
July 1919–Dec. 1919	S. I. Gusev
Dec. 1919	D. I. Kurskiy
Jan. 1920–Feb. 1920	G. L. Pyatakov
Feb. 1920–Aug. 1920	V. X. Aussem
Aug. 1920–Apr. 1921	Ya. D. Lentzman
Sept. 1921–Mar. 1924	A. Ya. Zaybot
Mar. 1924–Apr. 1935	Ya. K. Berzin
Apr. 1935–June 1937	S. P. Uritski
June 1937–Aug. 1937	Ya. K. Berzin
Sept. 1937–Oct. 1938	S. G. Genden
Oct. 1938–Apr. 1939	A. G. Orlov
Apr. 1939–July 1940	I. I. Proskyov
July 1940–Oct. 1941	F. I. Golikov
Oct. 1941–July 1942	A. P. Panfilov
July 1942–1943	I. I. Ilichev
1943–1946	F. F. Kuznetsov
1946–1948	S. M. Shtemyenko
1949	V. V. Kurasov
1949–1952	M. V. Zakharov
1951–1956	M. A. Shalin
1956–1957	S. M. Shtemyenko
1957–1958	M. A. Shalin
1958–1962	Ivan A. Serov
1963–1987	Petr I. Ivashutin
1987–1991	Vladlen M. Mikhaylov
1991–1992	Yevgeniy L. Timokhin
1992–1997	Fedor I. Ladygin
1998–	Valentin V. Korabelnikov

Grunden, Airman 1st Class Oliver E.

U.S. Air Force enlisted man arrested for attempting to sell classified information on the U-2 spyplane. Grunden was assigned to the 100th Organizational Maintenance Squadron at the Davis Monthan Air Force Base, Ariz.

Only 19 years old, he was caught by a team of agents from the Air Force OFFICE OF SPECIAL INVESTIGATIONS and the FBI. He was court-martialed and received a five-year prison sentence and a dishonorable discharge. The U.S. court of military appeals overturned his conviction because of procedural errors; he was retried, again found guilty, and had his sentence reduced to time already served.

Guardians

Super security group proposed by PETER WRIGHT, a British intelligence officer, whose function would be to watch for Soviet penetration of the Security Service (MI5) and Secret Intelligence Service (MI6).

Guardrail

U.S. Army name for an airborne SIGNALS INTELLIGENCE program. In 1971 the National Security Agency (NSA) desired to demonstrate the value of a remote airborne COMMUNICATIONS INTELLIGENCE system for use in Europe. This system became known as GUARDRAIL I. Three aircraft were converted from U-21G airframes. No mission equipment operators were carried in the aircraft; the operators were in ground trailers that received the intercepts over a datalink.

The Guardrail program expanded, becoming Army-wide. The program is now based on several AIRCRAFT—the RC-7, derived from the commercial DASH-7, and RC-12 Super King Air as well as the EH-60 Blackhawk helicopter. Those aircraft are fitted with several electronic intercept systems to provide direct support to ground commanders by identifying enemy radar and radio transmissions.

(Earlier, RC-21 and UH-1 Huey aircraft were used in the Guardrail program.)

Guillaume, Günter

(b. 1927 d. 1995)

Personal assistant to West German Chancellor Willy Brandt—and an East German spy. He was unquestionably the best of several MFS (Stasi) agents who penetrated the West German government between 1949, when the East German regime was established, to 1990, when the two Germanys merged.

During World War II Guillaume's father, a physician, had given shelter and medical treatment to Brandt when he was being hunted by the GESTAPO. In 1955 the senior Guillaume contacted Brandt, then mayor of West BERLIN, to help his son escape from the East. Through Brandt's help, Günter came to the West in 1956 as a political refugee. At the time the younger Guillaume, trained by the KGB, was in the East German Army and working for the Stasi. He later said that he had been sent to the West as a SLEEPER with instructions to "become a West German citizen, settle down, look for an apartment, and look for work."

Brandt got him a position with his Social Democratic Party (SDP), and he rose through party ranks to become Brandt's personal assistant in 1970. There Guillaume had access to the most secret plans and documents of Brandt's administration as well as the NORTH ATLANTIC TREATY ORGANIZATION. He also accompanied the Brandt family on vacations. In *Who's Who in Espionage* (1984), Ronald Payne and Christopher Dobson observed, "Guillaume seemed harmless enough. Double-chinned, podgy-faced, and owlish behind his steel-rimmed glasses, he looked and acted like the ideal functionary."

In April 1974 Guillaume and his wife were arrested for espionage. During interrogations Guillaume admitted working for the Stasi. Tried and convicted, Guillaume was sentenced to 13 years in prison. Guillaume's wife, Christel, was also convicted of treason. The scandal over Guillaume led to Brandt's resignation as chancellor in May 1974.

Both returned to East Germany in 1981 as part of an exchange for West German citizens being detained in the East. Guillaume was subsequently decorated by the Soviet government.

Testifying in the 1993 treason trial of former East German spymaster MARKUS WOLF, Guillaume portrayed himself a "partisan for peace" whose information helped to preserve a military balance between the West and East. One of the sensitive documents he passed to the East Germans was a personal message to Brandt from President Nixon.

Wolf later called the Guillaume affair a major failure, for Brandt's fall was a severe blow for East-West relations.

Gun, Katharine

Employee of Britain's GOVERNMENT COMMUNICATIONS HEADQUARTERS (GCHQ) who was the source of a LEAK of a TOP SECRET Jan. 2003 NSA memo that asked GCHQ for cooperation in an eavesdropping operation on UNITED NATIONS members. She was charged under the OFFICIAL SECRETS ACT with disclosing secret government information. The targeted UN diplomats were discussing resolutions pertaining to U.S.–British plans to invade Iraq.

As published in the British *Observer,* the NSA memo said the agency was "mounting a surge particularly directed at the UN Security Council (UNSC) members (minus US and GBR of course) for insights as to how membership is reacting to the ongoing debate RE: Iraq, plans to vote on any related resolutions, what related policies/negotiating positions they may be considering, alliances/dependencies, etc—the whole gamut of information that could give US policymakers an edge in obtaining results favorable to US goals or to head off surprises." The "surge" included SURVEILLANCE of the UN diplomats' office and home phones. NSA neither confirmed nor denied the authenticity of the memo.

Gun, 29 years old, was a Chinese-language translator and analyst at GCHQ, which cooperates with NSA under the UKUSA AGREEMENT.

The government, without comment, later dropped charges against Gun.

Gustavus

SEE BENEDICT ARNOLD

H

H-21

SEE MATA HARI

Haeger, John Joseph

SEE CHARLES SCHOOF

Hagelin, Boris C. W.

(b. 1892 d. 1983)

CIPHER machine inventor. Hagelin was born in the Russian Caucasus, where his father worked in the oilfields. He studied for three or four years in St. Petersburg and then went to Sweden, where he graduated from the Royal Institute of Technology in 1921. He began to develop his interest in cipher machines in the A.B. Cryptograph firm, acquired that year by Dr. Emmanuel Nobel, with his father, Karl W. Hagelin, owning a share of the firm. (The firm had been established in 1915.)

They had concluded that cipher machines could have a decisive role in sensitive business communications. Hagelin first exhibited the "Glow-lamp Ciphering and Deciphering Machine Enigma" in 1923. Although machines were purchased by the U.S. Army and the British Foreign Office, it was the Swedish Army and then German military and police forces that adopted the Enigma machine for their classified communications.

Hagelin's next success was his "tactical" cipher machine or C-series machine. It was initiated in 1934 at the request of the French DEUXIÈME BUREAU to develop a "pocket" cipher machine that printed out its encipherment. He adopted an unfinished concept for a calculating change-making machine to develop his C-series

machine. When the French saw the machine they ordered 5,000.

Hagelin tried for several years to sell the C machine to the U.S. military services. He finally achieved success in 1940 when it was accepted for Army use. An initial batch of 50 was shipped by air from Sweden to Washington, D.C. It was designated the M-209 CIPHER MACHINE or "converter" by the U.S. Army, and production was undertaken in the United States by L. C. Smith & Corona Typewriters, Inc., which achieved a daily output of up to 500 machines. By the end of World War II more than 140,000 units had been produced in the United States.

After four years in America, Hagelin returned to Sweden in 1944. While he was gone, the firm's workshop in Stockholm was selling C machines to several countries, among them Germany and Italy; one even went to Japan, smuggled out of the country by the Japanese military ATTACHÉ and taken to Japan by a German U-boat. According to Hagelin's accounts, toward the end of the war Germany produced about 700 of the machines for its own use.

After World War II improved models of the C machine were also produced in France as well as Germany.

In 1959 Hagelin moved his firm, Crypto, from Sweden, where the government can take over inventions for reasons of national security, to Switzerland. He met several times with his friend WILLIAM F. FRIEDMAN, the U.S. cryptographer, in circumstances that suggested Friedman was working on behalf of NSA. In *Puzzle Palace* (1982), JAMES BAMFORD wrote that it appeared likely that Hagelin "was asked to supply to the NSA details about various improvements and modifications made to the cipher machines his company had supplied to other governments. . . ." Speculation about NSA relationships with Crypto continued into the 1990s, when the company formally denied that it had ever allowed any intelligence agency access to the production of its machines.

Haguewood, Petty Officer 3rd Class Robert D.

U.S. Navy enlisted man convicted in 1986 of selling unclassified documents, which he thought were government secrets, to an undercover police officer. In a plea bargain, he was sentenced to two years and given a dishonorable discharge.

Haguewood was stationed at the Pacific Missile Test Center at Point Mugu, Calif. He was arrested in March 1986 when he sold an aircraft ordnance loading manual to an undercover police officer for $400. Watching the transaction were agents of the FBI and the NAVAL INVESTIGATIVE SERVICE.

Haifisch (Shark)

Major German DECEPTION operation planned in 1941 to disguise Germany's intention of mounting a surprise invasion of the Soviet Union (see BARBAROSSA). Shark (*Haifisch*), which was approved in late April 1941, along with HARPOON, consisted of assembling ships and landing craft on the western European coast, onloading and offloading exercises, and RECONNAISSANCE flights over England. Also, rumors were spread in German-occupied areas that the long-delayed invasion of England was to be carried out. (The original invasion plan—Operation Seelöwe ([Sealion])—had been prepared for the fall of 1940 but canceled because of the failure of the German Air Force to defeat the Royal Air Force.)

The *Haifisch* deception was to make the British and Soviets believe that there would be airborne landings to help capture beachheads and airfields, followed by landings of eight infantry divisions at four locations along England's southeastern coast. The landings would be quickly followed by four Panzer and two motorized divisions, with a third wave of six infantry divisions coming ashore to extend German control over the entire area and envelop London.

When the Germans assaulted the Soviet Union on June 22, 1941, the deception activities did not immediately cease. Rather, the German High Command sought to continue the ruse, wanting the British to believe that after a rapid German victory in the East, the triumphant German forces would again turn West.

Although the ULTRA codebreaking effort gave the British leadership an excellent appraisal of German plans to attack the Soviet Union, fear of an invasion of Britain continued even after that assault began. Finally, on Aug. 1, 1941, in reaction to the situation on the Soviet front, the Prime Minister and chiefs of staff decided to relax the high state of readiness to resist a German invasion that was then in effect in Britain.

Hale, Capt. Nathan

(b. 1755 d. 1776)

American spy in the Revolutionary War, executed by the British. A 1773 graduate of Yale, Hale taught school in New London and East Haddam, Conn., before enlisting in the Continental Army. He was a captain in Sept. 1776, when he volunteered to spy on the British for Gen. GEORGE WASHINGTON, an ardent believer in the importance of MILITARY INTELLIGENCE.

Hale apparently sailed in a small boat from Connecticut to Long Island and, slipping behind British lines in Manhattan, identified himself as a schoolteacher, a natural COVER. But he did not easily pass unnoticed, for he was tall and had scars on his face from a gunpowder explosion. He spent several days spying on the British before being captured while trying to return to American lines.

Little was known about his capture until 2003, when James H. Hutson, chief of the Manuscript Division of the Library of Congress, revealed that a long-suppressed account had Hale tricked and seized by Maj. Robert Rogers, a bold British officer known for his cunning. The account is contained in a manuscript, written by a Connecticut Tory, or British sympathizer, and donated to the Library of Congress by his descendants in 2000. The account "fits the facts as we know them" and "one is tempted to accept it as being substantially true," Hutson said. According to the manuscript, Rogers was searching in Long Island ports for Tory recruits when he spotted Hale as a probable American spy. Rogers, switching to civilian clothes, claimed to be head of a ring spying on the British and got Hale to admit he also was a spy—with members of Rogers' "spy ring" as witnesses. As Hale relaxed with his newfound friends, he was arrested. He tried to change his story. But it was too late.

Rogers, once a New Hampshire farmer, had created "Rogers' Rangers" during the French and Indian War (1754–1763). After the war Rogers went to England. When he returned to America and offered his services to the Revolution, Washington, fearing that Rogers was a British INTELLIGENCE OFFICER, had him arrested. Rogers escaped, joined the British, and again organized a rangers unit.

Gen. Sir William Howe, commander in chief of British forces in North America, ordered Hale's execution, without benefit of a trial, on Sept. 22, 1776. Denied the comfort of a clergyman or even a Bible, Hale stood on the scaffold and said brave words that have come down through the years in two versions: "I only regret that I have but one life to lose for my country" or "I only regret that I have one life to give for my country." (Some historians believe the last words were inspired by lines from Joseph Addison's 1713 play *Cato*: "What pity is it / That we can die but once to serve our country!")

Hale's last words, revealed years later by a British officer, were reportedly suppressed, and his last letters destroyed, because the British did not want to make a martyr of him. But he did become an enduring hero.

In 1914 a statue of Nathan Hale was placed on the Yale campus. The likeness was imaginary, for no portrait of Hale existed. The statue portrays a handsome young rebel, noose around his neck, hands tied behind him. A copy of the statue, erected in 1973, stands near the entrance of the headquarters of the CIA in LANGLEY, Va. In 1985 Connecticut's General Assembly made Hale the state's official hero.

Hall, Warrant Officer James W., III

U.S. Army officer who spied for East Germany.

Hall pleaded guilty to espionage in March 1989 after being court-martialed for giving his HANDLER documents and photographs about U.S. SATELLITES, NORTH ATLANTIC TREATY ORGANIZATION war plans, and electronic eavesdropping practices and equipment. U.S. officials called the loss of secrets through Hall "a massive hemorrhage."

While stationed in BERLIN from 1981 to 1985 and in Frankfurt from 1986 to 1987, Hall was an ELECTRONIC WARFARE and SIGNALS INTELLIGENCE specialist. Much of his work involved the interception of electronic and communications signals emanating from Warsaw Pact countries.

Hall was caught in Georgia when he boasted of his spying to an FBI undercover operative posing as a Soviet AGENT. Hall had begun spying in 1982 and continued until his arrest in Dec. 1988. His handler, known as "Meister," was Huseyin Yildrim, a Turkish-born mechanic who taught car repairing at a U.S. Army base in Berlin.

The East German government kept Hall on a $30,000 annual retainer and also gave him cash bonuses. The Army estimated that he was paid between $100,000 and $200,000 and given an East German medal. In 1987 he made a $30,000 cash down payment on a $92,000 ranch house in Richmond Hill, Ga. (His Army salary was $21,221.20 a year.)

After pleading guilty and weeping over his "feeling of betrayal," he was sentenced in March 1989 to 40 years in prison, fined $50,000, and given a dishonorable discharge.

Hall, Theodore Alvin

(b. 1926 d. 1999)

American physicist who was a member of the Soviet ATOMIC SPY RING during World War II.

In NSA documents declassified and released in 1996, Hall was linked with KLAUS FUCHS, a British physicist whose espionage for the Soviet Union was revealed in 1950. Like Fuchs, Hall had worked at the nuclear laboratory in LOS ALAMOS, N.M., where the United States designed and built the atomic bombs that were dropped on Hiroshima and Nagasaki.

The NSA documents were the transcripts of intercepted and decrypted messages sent to and from Soviet INTELLIGENCE OFFICERS communicating with Moscow during World War II (see VENONA). NSA analysts decided that the AGENT with the CODE NAME "Mlad" was Hall.

In an interview with Joseph Albright and Marcia Kunsel for their book *Bombshell: The Secret Story of America's Unknown Atomic Spy Conspiracy* (1997), Hall said that as an 18-year-old physicist at Los Alamos he was "worried about the dangers of an American monopoly of atomic weapons" and decided that the information should be shared with the Soviet Union. He made contact with a Soviet HANDLER through AMTORG, the Soviet purchasing company that also served as an intelligence front.

The Soviets arranged for Hall's Harvard roommate, Saville S. Sax, to be the CUT-OUT for passing secrets from Hall to Soviet intelligence. (In the Verona cable intercepts Sax has the code name "Star.") Hall's next cut-out was a far more experienced spy, Lona Cohen, who appears in the intercepts under the code name Leslie. She and her husband, MORRIS COHEN, also worked with another atomic spy, JULIUS ROSENBERG, and with the Soviet operatives RUDOLF ABEL and GORDON LONSDALE.

Hall passed an extraordinarily important secret: Los Alamos scientists were working on an "implosion" principle using plutonium. He also provided the Soviets with a diagram of an atomic bomb.

Hall emigrated to Britain in 1962. He was a biophysicist at Cambridge University, where he became a renowned scientist specializing in biological X-ray microanalysis. When the NSA documents were released in 1996, Hall was in ill health, suffering from cancer and Parkinson's disease, and Sax was dead.

Hall's older brother, Edward N. Hall, graduated from City College of New York in 1936; one of his classmates was JULIUS ROSENBERG. The older Hall later joined the Army Air Forces, where he had a distinguished career as an engineer, later receiving the coveted Robert A. Goddard award for his contribution to liquid-rocket technology. In 1955, as an Air Force colonel, he was placed in charge of development of the Titan intercontinental ballistic missile. And, in 1958, he was assigned by the U.S. government to help France with its missile program. He retired the following year after 20 years of military service and entered the corporate world.

As in several other cases of alleged spies identified through Venona, no action was taken when the Soviet communications were broken for fear of revealing the U.S. codebreaking success to the Soviets.

Hall, Virginia

(b. 1906 d. 1982)

American journalist who was an AGENT for the British SOE and the U.S. OFFICE OF STRATEGIC SERVICES (OSS) during World War II. She later served in the CIA.

Hall was a European correspondent for the *New York Post* when World War II began in Europe in Sept. 1939. She volunteered to work for the SOE before America's entry into the war. Early in 1942, she ran an SOE SAFE HOUSE in Lyons. Although she had a wooden leg, she became a courier, disguising herself as a peasant and carrying messages between members of SOE networks. She was known by two CODE NAMES: "Diane" and "René."

In March 1944, as SOE and French Resistance forces began preparations for the Allied invasion of Normandy, she helped to form the first OSS network in France. What neither the SOE or OSS knew was that, through treachery by DOUBLE AGENTS, the German ABWEHR knew her identity and her previous work for the SOE. But she was not betrayed, and her preinvasion mission succeeded.

After the war, when the OSS was disbanded, she remained in intelligence, joining the OSS's successor, the CIA. She served as a senior intelligence officer in Latin America.

Hall, Adm. Sir William Reginald

(b. 1870 d. 1943)

Britain's DIRECTOR OF NAVAL INTELLIGENCE (DNI) during World War II. He established the Royal Navy's code-breaking organization, ROOM 40, which decoded the ZIMMERMANN TELEGRAM, the contents of which had a major impact on the U.S. decision to enter World War I. Room 40 also achieved numerous other significant intelligence successes. (Hall had the nickname "Blinker," which referred to one of his eyes that would "flash like a Navy signal lamp.")

In their official history *British Intelligence in the Second World War* (1979), F. H. HINSLEY, et al., observe that Hall wielded his control vigorously, "building up his own espionage system, deciding for himself when and how to release intelligence to other departments, and acting on intelligence independently of other departments in matters of policy that lay beyond the concerns of Admiralty." In response to Hall's independence, "in 1918 there was a considerable body of naval opinion, supported by the Foreign Office, in favour of abolishing the posts of DNI and [Deputy] DNI."

The son of Capt. William Henry Hall, the first director of the Intelligence Division at the British Admiralty (1882–1889), "Blinker" Hall entered the Navy in 1884. He rose to command the cadet training ship *Cornwall*, the armored cruiser *Natal*, and, in 1913–1914, the new battle cruiser *Queen Mary*. He introduced many reforms, including the now standard three-watch system, in which one-third of the crew was normally on duty. (Historically, warships of all navies had two watches—port and starboard.)

Hall became DNI in Nov. 1914 and served in that post until Jan. 1919. He built up the naval intelligence organization during the war, encouraged radio-intercept and codebreaking efforts, and provided the fleet with good intelligence. He was promoted to rear-admiral in 1917, rose to the rank of vice-admiral, and became a full admiral in 1926.

The American ambassador to London in World War I, Dr. Walter Page, wrote to President Wilson in March 1918:

Hall is one genius that the war has developed. Neither in fiction nor in fact can you find any such man to match him. Of the wonderful things I know he has done, there are several that it would take an ex-

citing volume to tell. The man is a genius—a clear case of genius. All other secret service men are amateurs—a clear case of genius.

He also served as a conservative member of the House of Commons. With Amus J. Peaslee, Hall wrote *Three Wars with Germany* (1943). Hall began an autobiography, but he stopped work after a few chapters. His biographer, Adm. Sir William James, concluded in *The Eyes of the Navy* (1955) that Hall's "loyalty and skill enabled him to exercise a dominating influence on world affairs at a critical period of history."

Halperin, Maurice

OFFICE OF STRATEGIC SERVICES (OSS) officer who spied for the Soviets. He was chief of the OSS Latin American research division. His CODE NAME (Hare) became known in VERONA decrypts. FBI investigations into the decrypts tied the "Hare" to Halperin through the revelations of ELIZABETH BENTLEY, an American who served as a COURIER and then as a DEFECTOR who revealed her spy work to the FBI and congressional committees.

Hambleton, Hugh George

(b. 1922)

Economist for the NORTH ATLANTIC TREATY ORGANIZATION (NATO) who spied for the Soviet Union.

Born in Ottawa, Hambleton spent several years in Europe, where his father was a journalist. In 1937 he returned to Canada and subsequently attended school in California. After graduating in 1940 he joined a Free French unit being formed in Canada. He was sent to Algiers and, after the liberation of France in 1944, to Paris, where he worked in French MILITARY INTELLIGENCE and was later assigned as a liaison officer to the U.S. Army. He was later transferred to a Canadian Army intelligence unit.

Back home in Ottawa after the war, he met a Soviet diplomat who asked him to obtain some routine, unclassified information. Hambleton ignored the request. The two met again when Hambleton went to France to study for an economic degree at the University of Paris. No further attempt to recruit Hambleton was made until 1956, after he became an economic analyst at NATO, handling highly classified documents. Hambleton's Soviet HANDLER arranged for a truck to be parked near their rendezvous; in the truck KGB technicians photographed the documents he brought so that he could quickly get them back to his office.

From the documents, wrote JOHN BARRON in *KGB Today* (1983), "the Russians could read what the West, correctly or incorrectly, thought was true, and sometimes what it intended to do. They could see what the West did and did not know about them and their intentions." The KGB handler said the material was "pure gold." Hambleton never took money for his work. His motive was the furtherance of world peace.

Hambleton, cracking under his reluctant espionage, quit NATO in 1961 to study at the London School of Economics, although he spent most of his time in Spain. Later, while on the faculty of Laval University in Quebec, he traveled as a scholar to Israel, Peru, Austria, and the Soviet Union, always providing the KGB with reports from his travels, including his assumption that Israel had built atomic weapons. On a KGB-arranged visit to Moscow he had a singular honor—dinner with YURI ANDROPOV, then chief of the KGB. Andropov, echoing one of Hambleton's handlers, asked him to try to find a position with the Hudson Institute, an American think tank whose work included nuclear war studies.

In Nov. 1978, during a rendezvous in VIENNA, Hambleton's KGB handler warned him that he was under investigation by a Western security service and should break off all contact. He spent a sabbatical year in Europe and returned to Laval University in Sept. 1979. Soon officers of the ROYAL CANADIAN MOUNTED POLICE appeared with an arrest warrant. They found spy paraphernalia but, because he had not spied on Canada, Canadian authorities did not prosecute him.

In June 1982 Hambleton flew to London on a holiday. He was arrested and charged with violating the OFFICIAL SECRETS ACT by passing classified information to the Soviet Union. Hambleton claimed that he had been a DOUBLE AGENT working for French intelligence. When that plea failed, he admitted passing "thousands" of NATO documents to the Soviets but insisted that two-thirds were unclassified. Those that were classified included many classified as COSMIC, NATO's highest CLASSIFICATION. He admitted his guilt under cross-examination during his trial at the Old Bailey and was sentenced to 10 years in prison.

Sources vary in explaining how Hambleton was exposed as a spy so long after his NATO employment. British sources point to ANATOLI GOLITSYN, a KGB DEFECTOR, who defected in Dec. 1961 and had earlier spent time at THE CENTER, KGB headquarters in Moscow, summarizing reports on NATO for his superiors. Although Golitsyn did not know the names of the AGENTS feeding NATO intelligence to the Soviets, he could provide identifying information. The FBI has unofficially linked Hambleton's unmasking to another defector, RUDOLF A. HERRMANN [P], a KGB officer who was TURNED by the FBI between 1977 and 1979.

Hambone

SEE COPPERHEAD

Hamilton, Victor N.

(b. 1917 d. 1998)

NSA research analyst who defected to the Soviet Union in 1963.

An Arabic-speaking specialist on the Near East, Hamilton was working as a bellhop in a hotel in Georgia when a U.S. Army officer recruited him for the NSA in 1957. Hamilton, whose original name was Hindah, was living in Libya in the 1950s when he met an American woman. They married and moved to Georgia, where he legally changed his name and became a naturalized American citizen.

About one and a half years after he went to work at the NSA he was judged to have mental problems, but the agency kept him on because of his language skills. He was working in the Near East Sector of NSA's ALLO (All Other countries) unit, which he said consisted of handling intercepts from what was then the United Arab Republic of Egypt and Syria, a short-lived union that lasted from 1958 to 1961, along with other Middle East and North African countries. In June 1959, when, the agency said, he was "approaching a paranoid-schizophrenic break," he was discharged.

In July 1963 Hamilton surfaced in Moscow and revealed NSA secrets, which the Soviet newspaper *Izvestia* published. Hamilton claimed that the NSA had fired him because he wanted to make contact with relatives in Syria.

Little was heard publicly from Hamilton until 1992, when he was discovered by the Ark Project, an organization that searches for members of the U.S. armed forces declared prisoners of war or missing in action. He was found in Special Hospital No. 5 in Troitskoye, about 30 miles southwest of Moscow. He was described as suffering from paranoia and other mental problems. Hospital officials said he had refused treatment and was unaware of the breakup of the Soviet Union.

Hammer, Armand

(b. 1898 d. 1990)

American capitalist who was a secret AGENT OF INFLUENCE for the Soviet Union during most of his life. Hammer was usually portrayed as a successful businessman who acted as a kind of unofficial ambassador between the United States and the Soviet Union. In reality, he laundered money for the Soviet Union and, according to FBI informants, he was involved in Soviet espionage in the United States.

In Nov. 1980, when ALEXANDRE DE MARENCHES, then Director-General of the SDECE, was briefing President-elect Ronald Reagan on French knowledge of Soviet espionage, he used the term *agent of influence* to warn Reagan of Hammer. SDECE had compiled a dossier on Hammer after learning of his extensive contacts with Soviet officials, including high-ranking KGB officers.

Hammer's relationship with the Soviet Union began in 1921 when he traveled to Moscow with a letter of introduction to V. I. Lenin from Hammer's father (see AMTORG). A friend of presidents from Franklin Roosevelt to GEORGE H. W. BUSH, he used his influence to build up his oil empire. But as Edward Jay Epstein revealed in *Dossier* (1996), much of Hammer's life was a fraud. While portraying himself as a "bridge builder" to the Soviet Union, he was more interested in maintaining secret connections with Soviet political and intelligence officials.

In the West, Hammer gained prestige and influence by reaching out to powerful figures, including Sen. Al Gore Sr., and Prince Charles, lavishing gifts on him and Princess Diana, and contributing generously to the royal couple's favorite charities.

Handler

INTELLIGENCE OFFICER, coopted person, or CASE OFFICER who is directly responsible for the operations of AGENTS.

Hankey, 1st Baron Maurice

(b. 1877 d. 1963)

One of the more intriguing and influential figures of 20th century Britain, who wielded considerable influence over intelligence activities.

Lord Hankey began his public career as a Royal Marine officer on the battleship *Ramillies*. While in the fleet he so impressed Admiral Sir John Fisher that when Fisher became Second Sea Lord at the Admiralty in 1902, he brought Capt. Hankey with him to London as a member of his staff.

Hankey returned to sea in 1907 as the INTELLIGENCE OFFICER for the Mediterranean Fleet, but in less than a year he was appointed assistant secretary to the important Committee on Imperial Defence, a promising post. His superior was Sir Charles Ottley, who had just retired from the Navy as DIRECTOR OF NAVAL INTELLIGENCE. The committee created the forerunners of the Security Service (MI5) and Secret Intelligence Service (MI6) in 1909.

Hankey succeeded to the post of secretary of the Committee in 1912. Upon becoming secretary of the War Cabinet in 1916, which was meeting almost daily, he had a considerable degree of influence for a young officer. At the end of the war he was named British secretary to the peace conference in Paris. For his efforts he was formally thanked by both Houses of Parliament with a grant of £25,000, then a very considerable sum.

Between the wars he served as secretary of both the cabinet and the Committee on Imperial Defence, as well as secretary for several major conferences. In the early 1930s he was deeply involved in intelligence matters and produced some of the first detailed reports on Germany's massive rearmament programs. Retiring in 1938, he was raised to the peerage the following year. With the outbreak of World War II in Sept. 1939, Hankey was made a member of the War Cabinet as Minister without Portfolio.

In Dec. 1939 Prime Minister Neville Chamberlain commissioned Hankey to undertake a study of MI5 and MI6 as well as the GOVERNMENT CODE AND CYPHER SCHOOL in the wake of complaints from the military services that they were receiving poor intelligence from MI6. JOHN CAIRNCROSS became Hankey's private secretary. (Cairncross was later revealed to be a Soviet spy, a member of the CAMBRIDGE SPY RING.)

Hankey was dismissed from the cabinet after Winston Churchill became Prime Minister in May 1940, but Hankey's reports influenced Churchill's handling of the intelligence services and the establishment of the Special Operations Executive (SOE). (After Hankey left the government, Cairncross was assigned to the Government Code and Cypher School, where he passed intercepted and decrypted ULTRA material to the Soviets.)

Hankey's writings included the books *Government Control in War* (1945) and *Politics—Trials and Errors* (1949), the latter condemning the policy of unconditional surrender and the trials of war criminals. His memoir, *The Supreme Command, 1914–18*, was published in 1961.

Hanssen, Robert P.

(b. 1943)

FBI agent convicted of spying for the KGB and its successor, the SVR, for more than two decades. Investigators called him "the most damaging spy in FBI history."

Hanssen, a COUNTERINTELLIGENCE specialist, used his expertise to avoid detection for more than 20 years. His Russian HANDLERS did not know his name nor the fact that he was a highly trained and experienced FBI agent. His colleagues learned of his betrayal not through their own investigation but only when receiving an intelligence file from a Russian ASSET. Information in the file did not identify him by name but provided enough information to point to Hanssen. The Russians paid him in diamonds and cash for a total of more than $600,000. His superiors never questioned a life style that was far beyond his means.

In 1990, Hanssen's brother-in-law, FBI Special Agent Mark Wauck, learned that that Hanssen's wife had found $5,000 in cash in Hanssen's dresser drawer. Wauck reported this, along with other suspicions, to a supervisor. Neither he nor anyone else in the FBI bothered to check the tip.

During his 25-year FBI career, Hanssen was assigned to counterintelligence in New York City and Washington, D.C. He also worked at FBI headquarters and the State Department in positions that gave him access to a wide spectrum of highly secret counterintelligence and military information, including, according to reliable sources, the existence of an eavesdropping TUNNEL under the Russian Embassy in Washington.

He was arrested on Feb. 18, 2001 as he was placing his latest collection of classified information in a DEAD DROP in a Virginia park, in a suburb near Washington. Hanssen had been under SURVEILLANCE for some time.

He pleaded guilty to espionage on July 6, 2001, and, under a plea agreement in which he promised to cooperate with investigators, he was sentenced to life imprisonment.

The damage that Hanssen did is incalculable. He gave his handlers the identities of dozens of agents, at least three of whom were executed. The highly classified documents and computer disks that he handed over in dead drops included information about U.S. nuclear-war strategy and developments in military weapons. He also kept the Russians apprised of several espionage cases by revealing secrets of the U.S. INTELLIGENCE COMMUNITY's Soviet counterintelligence program.

Because there was no trial, there seemed to be little likelihood that the public would be made aware of the extent of his betrayal. But the Senate intelligence oversight committees demanded an investigation, and some results of that investigation were revealed in Aug. 2003.

The investigation was conducted by a team directed by the Justice Department's office of Inspector General. The team analyzed 368,000 pages of material from the FBI, the CIA, the Justice Department, the NSA, and the State Department. The entire 674-page report was given a CLASSIFICATION beyond TOP SECRET because it contained "extremely sensitive classified information." A 383-page report, classified SECRET, was made available to certain executive and congressional officials. All that was made public was a 31-page unclassified executive summary.

That summary shows that Hanssen's spying began in Nov. 1979, three years after he joined the FBI, and "continued intermittently" until his arrest in Feb. 2001, two months before his mandatory retirement date. According to the report, Hanssen's espionage spanned three separate time periods: 1979–1981, 1985–1991, and 1999–2001.

Hanssen's first spying period did not give the KGB much significant information. According to the report:

Hanssen's first period of espionage ended in the spring of 1981, when his wife Bonnie inadvertently discovered him reviewing a GRU communication in the basement of their home. Although Hanssen minimized his espionage in discussions with his wife, he says that he confessed his espionage to an Opus Dei priest within days of Bonnie's discovery. According to Hanssen, the priest granted him absolution and told him that he did not have to turn himself in, but suggested that he donate the money he had received from the GRU to charity. Hanssen said that he broke off contact with the GRU and made multiple $1,000 donations to Mother Teresa's "Little Sisters of the Poor."

But during the next period he had access to high-level secrets that he passed to the Russians. They acted on the information, shutting down FBI and CIA operations and producing that the report calls "catastrophic and unprecedented losses of Soviet intelligence assets."

The wipeout of assets triggered a desperate search for a MOLE in the U.S. INTELLIGENCE COMMUNITY. In Jan. 1992, Hanssen became chief of the National Security Threat List Unit at FBI Headquarters. It dealt with such issues as ECONOMIC INTELLIGENCE and nuclear proliferation. At this time he was able to hack into the FBI's computer system and get highly secret counterintelligence information. He boldly reported his own hacking, claiming that he did it to prove the vulnerability of the system. Meanwhile, the FBI was stepping up its PENETRATION investigations. This turned up the CIA's ALDRICH AMES, who was arrested in 1994. But the hemorrhaging did not stop. Further penetration investigations led the FBI counterintelligence sleuths to focus on a CIA INTELLIGENCE OFFICER

who was put under surveillance. The FBI even asked the Justice Department to prosecute the CIA suspect, who was ultimately cleared and never prosecuted. But the investigation ruined his career.

Hanssen, meanwhile, was watching such investigations from afar. He was no longer at FBI headquarters because he had been transferred out in a move to apparently improve office morale. A moody loner who did not get along well with his colleagues, he was reprimanded once for a physical assault on a female employee. As a devout Catholic and ultra-conservative, he bored fellow workers with his preaching. Privately, he had sides to himself no one in the FBI suspected. Using a closed-circuit video system he had installed in his bedroom, he videotaped his wife and himself making love—and showed the tape to a friend. In a bizarre platonic affair, he befriended a stripper, giving her money, jewels, a Mercedes Benz, and a credit card but he said he never slept with her.

His superiors at FBI headquarters decided to get him out of their sight, and in Feb. 1995 he was assigned as an FBI liaison agent to the State Department. Unsupervised, he did little work—except for spying. During his six years at the State Department, the FBI never gave him a performance evaluation. According to the report, he spent "hours each day out of the office, surfing the Internet and watching movies on his personal laptop computer, and visiting friends and acquaintances." He also continued to have access to the FBI's Automated Case Support (ACS) files, a computer system containing thousands of internal FBI classified documents. He frequently checked the ACS system for his own name to see if he was the subject of one of the FBI's counterintelligence espionage investigations.

One file he came across involved FELIX BLOCH, a senior State Department official suspected of providing information to the KGB. Hanssen's tip-off to the KGB was relayed to Bloch and the case against him collapsed.

Around this time Hanssen seemed to be unraveling. He suggested to his handlers that they try to recruit his best friend, a man with no intention of spying and who was then serving as a military attaché at the U.S. Embassy in Bonn. In late 2000, in ways not officially disclosed, the FBI decided that Hanssen was a spy. He was transferred back to FBI headquarters and placed under total surveillance. On Feb. 12, 2001, FBI agents found, at one of Hanssen's dead drops, a package containing $50,000. Six days later, as Hanssen was serving another dead drop with a package of documents and computer disks, fellow agents arrested him.

Hanssen had maintained his anonymity throughout his spy career, using the alias "Ramon" or "Ramon Garcia."

Harari, Mike

(b. 1927)

Israeli MOSSAD and SHIN BET officer. Born in Tel Aviv, he became an intelligence operative at the same time that Is-

rael became a nation in May 1948. Subsequently, as an officer in Shin Bet, Israel's internal intelligence agency, he was involved in two controversial events.

Harari led the secret Israeli vengeance squad assigned to assassinate the Black September terrorists responsible, directly or indirectly, for the kidnapping and massacre of 11 Israeli athletes at the Olympic Games in Munich in 1972. In less than a year Harari's Paris-based squad killed 12 Palestinians whom the Mossad linked to Black September. (Three other Palestinians were killed by Harari's team in revenge for the slaying of an Israeli INTELLIGENCE OFFICER in Madrid.)

But those operations were sullied by the assassins' killing of a wrong man, a Moroccan waiter living in Norway and married to a Norwegian. Harari escaped when Norwegian police closed in on the Mossad group, but his teammates were caught. Many details of the vengeance operation became public during the investigation, and the six Mossad operatives who were arrested received short prison terms.

After the Norwegian fiasco, Harari was ordered to Mexico City, a key Israeli intelligence station for Latin America. Among his contacts in the area was Col. Manuel Noriega, then chief of MILITARY INTELLIGENCE for the dictator of Panama, Gen. Omar Torrijo. When Torrijo died in a plane crash in 1981, Noriega, who supplied information to the CIA, succeeded him. Harari, who had retired from Israeli intelligence, became an aide to Noriega (and honorary Panamanian consul in Tel Aviv). Harari set up Noreiga's security and grew wealthy brokering sales of Israeli weapons to Panama.

In 1988, when the United States indicted Noriega for drug running, rumors spread about Harari's close association with the dictator. When U.S. forces invaded Panama in Dec. 1989, another spate of rumors suggested that Harari had been arrested as an accomplice. But he managed to slip out of Panama. He surfaced in Israel, where, in an uncharacteristic move for a shadowy operative, he appeared on television. The interview, however, disclosed little about his career or his years working for Noreiga.

Harbrink

SEE DAVID BARNETT

Harel, Isser

(b. 1912 d. 2003)

Director of SHIN BET, Israel's domestic security agency, from 1948 to 1952; director of the MOSSAD, Israel's foreign operations agency, from 1952 to 1963; and commander of AMAN, the Israeli MILITARY INTELLIGENCE service, from 1962 to 1963.

Born Isser Halperin in Russia, he immigrated to Palestine in 1931 and changed his name to Harel. After being dismissed from the British constabulary, he joined the Haganah, the Jewish underground defense organization, and began his intelligence career.

In the tumult following Israel's birth in May 1948, widespread and expensive intelligence organizations were created. Harel, a close friend of Prime Minister David Ben-Gurion, became the guiding hand that stabilized intelligence activity and gave it not only respectability but a power unknown in most democracies.

After the disgrace and fall of ISSER BE'ERI, Israel's first military intelligence chief, in 1949, Harel became the director of Shin Bet. On Ben-Gurion's orders, he was also designated the MEMUNEH—the one in charge of Israeli intelligence activities. He reported directly to Ben-Gurion on both international and domestic security matters. Harel formally became director of the Mossad in 1952 after the first director, REUVEN SHILOAH, had served but 18 months.

Some of Harel's most controversial actions occurred early in his tenure. He placed a BUG in the offices of the lefist Mapam Party in 1953. He later placed a journalist under "administrative detention" and funded a magazine to attack publications critical of Israeli intelligence activities.

Among his positive accomplishments, Harel set up a Nazi-hunting unit in the Mossad and developed a list of "most wanted" Nazis who had escaped Allied war crimes trials. High on the list was the name of Adolf Eichmann, the Nazi functionary who had officiated over the killing of millions of Jews during the Holocaust. Harel also developed evidence indicating that Eichmann had been aided in his escape from Germany by the ODESSA, a secret organization of former SS officers. The Mossad believed that the South American end of the Odessa escape route was Buenos Aires, Argentina.

(An Israeli intelligence team went to Argentina in May 1960 and kidnapped Eichmann. He was placed on trial in April 1961 for crimes against humanity, crimes against the Jewish people, and crimes in violation of international laws on the conduct of war. He was convicted and was hanged on May 31, 1962.)

Under Harel's direction, Israeli agents infiltrated Egyptian and West German intelligence agencies, using terrorist tactics to stop German scientists from working for Egypt. In 1963 two Mossad agents were arrested in Switzerland for intimidating the daughter of a German scientist working on an Egyptian missile program, and two other Mossad agents were arrested in West Germany on suspicion of similar activities.

Ben-Gurion, then engaged in negotiations to strengthen Israeli-West German relations, turned against Harel. He reprimanded him for his campaign against the scientists, having lost confidence in the man he had dubbed the Memuneh. Harel resigned from government in March 1963.

Harper, James D.

(b. 1934)

Self-employed electronics engineer who sold information on U.S. missiles to the SB (Sluzba Bezpieczenstwa), the Polish intelligence service, whose American work was directly supervised by the KGB.

Harper had been trained in electronics in the U.S. Marine Corps. After being honorably discharged in 1955 he worked in several electronics firms. By 1975 he had his own firm for manufacturing digital stopwatches. That same year, a business associate, William Bell Hugle, introduced Harper to two Poles who gave him a "shopping list" of high-tech information and devices, including a tank-launched rocket.

Harper did not have a SECURITY CLEARANCE and was not working on any defense contracts. But he provided enough technological information to earn a trip to Geneva in Nov. 1975, when he turned over the information for at least $5,000. He later described the information as unclassified. In July 1979 he and Hugle met in Warsaw with Zdzislaw Przychodzien, ostensibly an executive of the Polish Ministry of Machine Industry and actually a lieutenant colonel in the SB. Harper then began a long-term system to provide the Poles and KGB with American defense secrets.

Harper's girlfriend was Ruby Louise Schuler, who held a SECRET clearance as an executive secretary at Systems Control, Inc. (SCI), in Palo Alto, Calif. SCI was doing research for the U.S. Army on ballistic missile defense. The SCI research focused on efforts to make Minuteman missiles and other U.S. strategic missile systems less vulnerable to Soviet missiles. Schuler opened an SCI safe after hours and systematically removed secret documents. She got them out of the plant by putting them in her pocketbook or strapping them to her body.

In June 1980, Harper met in Warsaw with Przychodzien and sold 100 pounds of documents, waterlogged from their hiding place near a river. Przychodzien and other SB agents worked through the night separating the pages and restoring the documents so that they were decipherable. The next day, says the U.S. COUNTERINTELLIGENCE report on the case, "the documents were brought to the Soviet Embassy where a team of 20 KGB experts, flown in specially from Moscow, declared them to be genuine and extremely valuable." Harper was paid $100,000, and Przychodzien and his unit received a commendation from KGB Chairman YURI ANDROPOV.

At his next meeting in Warsaw in Sept. 1980, Harper brought the register of the classified documents in the safe that Schuler was regularly rifling. Przychodzien and his aides selected exactly what documents they wanted. On delivering them later that year, Harper received another $20,000.

In Dec. 1980, under instructions from Przychodzien, Harper met in Mexico City with a Polish agent with the CODE NAME "Jacques"; Harper's was "Jimmo." Jacques paid Harper $10,000 on account. Subsequently, Harper passed copies of 17 secret documents and was paid another $100,000.

In Sept. 1981 Harper, fearing betrayal by Schuler, anonymously called an attorney, hoping to begin a process of gaining immunity from prosecution in exchange for cooperation, including possible use as a DOUBLE AGENT. But the CIA and FBI were already on Harper's trail. A CIA ASSET—almost certainly Col. WLADYSLAW KUKLINSKI—had reported the extraordinary Andropov

commendation, saying that he had overheard the words "California" and "missile research." Eventually, this tip led the FBI to Harper, who was arrested in Oct. 1983.

Shown what the government knew about his espionage, Harper opted for a plea bargain instead of a trial. He received a life sentence.

Schuler died in June 1983. Hugle, who once ran as a Democratic candidate for Congress, slipped out of the United States and was not prosecuted.

Harpoon

Major German DECEPTION operation proposed to hide the plans for a surprise invasion of the Soviet Union in June 1941 (see BARBAROSSA).

HAIFISCH (Shark), the main deception effort, sought to make the British believe that an assault was planned on the English coast. Harpoon was a deception within a deception, designed to make the British believe that the landings would be along the coast of Scotland and the southern coast of England, at Lyme Bay, with the latter German forces then thrusting northward toward Bristol.

Harriet

SEE FLUENCY COMMITTEE

Hart, Edith Tudor

(b. 1908 d. 1973)

Soviet COURIER and TALENT SPOTTER whose discoveries included HAROLD R. (KIM) PHILBY.

Born in VIENNA, she traveled to England in 1925. Trained in the Montessori method, she worked as a kindergarten teacher. She married Dr. Alex Tudor Hart, a left-wing British physician. He later served with the Republican forces during the Spanish Civil War.

Edith divorced him and became a well-known British photographer. (She took one of Philby's favorite photographs, in which he poses smoking a pipe.) She was a friend of Philby's first wife, Litzi Friedman, in Vienna, and through her later became involved in the espionage activities of the Communist Party of Great Britain. Scotland Yard's SPECIAL BRANCH at times kept her under SURVEILLANCE but never was able to build a case against her.

She is believed to have first met Philby in Vienna and is credited in Soviet intelligence archives as having introduced him to the NKVD officer who recruited Philby as a spy. She is also known to have discovered at least one other potential spy, known only by the CODE NAME "Scott." GUY BURGESS in 1938–1939 used her to contact Soviet intelligence in Paris.

She was the owner of a small antiques shop in Brighton when she died, her spy career publicly unknown. In *The Crown Jewels* (1999), intelligence historian NIGEL WEST said, "While the Soviet spies recruited at Cambridge have now acquired international notoriety, very little is known about the other network known to have been drawn at roughly the same time from Oxford

University." The recruitment at Oxford, West added, was the work of Hart, "a key figure in Soviet espionage operations in Britain."

Harvey, William King

(b. 1915 d. 1976)

Former FBI special agent who became a senior official of the CIA.

Harvey joined the FBI in 1940, three years after graduating from Indiana University with a law degree. He was assigned to COUNTERINTELLIGENCE work and grew to like it. In 1947 Harvey resigned from the FBI and, much to the displeasure of FBI Director J. EDGAR HOOVER, joined the CIA as an INTELLIGENCE OFFICER working in counterintelligence.

When HAROLD (KIM) PHILBY was assigned to the British Embassy in Washington as MI6 liaison officer with the FBI and CIA, Harvey was one of Philby's contacts. Harvey got to know both Philby and his fellow spy, GUY BURGESS. When the latter insulted Harvey's wife, Libby, during a party at Philby's home, Harvey began checking into the backgrounds of both Burgess, whom he loathed, and Philby, whom he suspected as a MOLE. But he was not able to gather enough evidence to prove his growing suspicions.

In 1952, Harvey, known as Big Bill, led the CIA effort to build the BERLIN TUNNEL (affectionately called Harvey's Hole), for tapping Soviet communications in East Berlin.

Harvey, who drank heavily and carried a .45-caliber pistol, was part of the MONGOOSE operation against Fidel Castro (see CUBA), which President Kennedy ordered in 1961. He was also aware of plans to assassinate Castro and organized an EXECUTIVE ACTION group for the killing. Attorney General Robert Kennedy, President Kennedy's brother and the prime force behind Mongoose, accused Harvey of moving too slowly. Once, while Robert Kennedy was touring the CIA station in Miami, Fla., he and Harvey argued; at another meeting, Harvey criticized the President and the Attorney General in their presence. He was dropped from Mongoose.

RICHARD HELMS, head of the Directorate of Plans (clandestine service) in CIA, got Harvey out of Washington in 1963, assigning him as chief of station in Rome. His drinking and erratic behavior intensified, but he stayed on until 1969, when he resigned.

Harvey Birch [f]

Fictional hero of JAMES FENIMORE COOPER's *The Spy* (1821), a novel about espionage in the American Revolution. Harvey Birch is a peddler who lets people suspect he is in the pay of the British while he spies for "Harper," a fictionalized Gen. GEORGE WASHINGTON.

Birch's exploits are based on the real adventures of Enoch Crosby, a New York shoemaker. Crosby served in the Army at the beginning of the Revolution. He dropped out because of ill health, but he reenlisted in 1776. While hiking to an American camp in New York, was mistaken by a Tory for a British sympathizer. Crosby played along and learned about a Tory military plot to join up a Tory militia with regular British forces.

Crosby took his information to John Jay, a revolutionary leader, who enlisted him as a DOUBLE AGENT. After staging an "escape" from American hands, Crosby rejoined the Tories. When American troops captured them, they pretended that Crosby was one of the enemy.

He slipped away again and continued as Jay's SECRET AGENT, following a pattern of infiltrating Tory military units and then exposing them until he became notorious and a target for vengeance. After the war Crosby settled in New York as a farmer and deputy sheriff. He eventually received $250 for his spy services.

After hearing tales about Crosby from Jay, Cooper wrote *The Spy*. A true account of Crosby's espionage activities by H. L. Barnum, *The Spy Unmasked*, was published in 1829.

Hawkins, Col. Gains B.

(b. 1920 d. 1987)

U.S. Army INTELLIGENCE OFFICER who touched off a controversy about the manipulation of estimates of *Vietcong* strength during the Vietnam War.

Hawkins served in the Army in World War II, afterwards joined the reserves, and was called to active service for the Korean War. He learned Japanese and pursued Far Eastern studies at Stanford University. In 1966 he volunteered for Vietnam, believing that it was "the ultimate test for intelligence officers." In 1966 and 1967 he was the Army's authority on Vietcong strength.

Hawkins estimated in 1967 that the Vietcong had mustered 500,000 men—not the 300,000 previously estimated. "During the weeks that followed," he wrote in *The Washington Post* in 1982, "my superiors put the emphasis on reducing our estimates of the enemy's personnel strength. By a process of rationalization I chose what seemed to be the only practical course. Without any good analytical reason, I sliced and cut away the strength figures in those categories where our intelligence was the least solid."

The manipulating of the figures became an issue when Gen. William C. Westmoreland sued the CBS network, which in 1982 had broadcast a television documentary, "The Uncounted Enemy: A Vietnam Deception." At the libel trial Hawkins testified that Westmoreland had told him that the 500,000 figure was "politically unacceptable" because it would indicate that no progress had been made in the war. After Hawkins testified, Westmoreland withdrew the suit.

Hebern, Edward H.

(b. 1869 d. 1952)

Inventor of the first CIPHER machine to make use of RO-TORS to provide random encipherment. Raised in a Soldiers' Orphan Home in Illinois, he was able to get only a high school education. He held a variety of jobs as a young man, and into his adult life worked as a carpenter.

For unknown reasons, at age 40 he became interested in CRYPTOGRAPHY. Beginning in 1912 he filed patents for a number of cryptologic devices. In 1914 he devised an arrangement with two electric typewriters connected by 26 wires arranged in random order; when a key on one typewriter was depressed it printed a letter in cipher on the other. Although every letter on the first typewriter reproduced the same substitute letter on the second, a shift could produce a different substitute. Thus was born electromechanical encipherment and the concept of changing the substitution.

In 1921, while in Oakland, Calif., Hebern reduced his electromechanical encipherment concept to a rotor system, which he produced the following year. He advertised his "unbreakable" cipher in a magazine, which caught the attention of Agnes Meyer, a cryptanalyst in the Navy Department. When contacted by the Navy, Hebern came to Washington, D.C., demonstrated his machine, and filed his first rotor patent. The Navy was interested in procuring his cipher machines.

Also in 1921, Hebern had incorporated the Hebern Electric Code, the first cipher machine company in the United States. Although he had little trouble selling $1 million in stock, the Navy's orders were slow and he went bankrupt. Undeterred, Hebern founded another company and in 1928 sold four five-rotor machines to the Navy at $750 per machine and $20 per rotor, a considerable amount for the time.

The four machines were tested ashore and in the fleet. Their success was reflected when the Navy purchased 31 more machines in 1931. But when an improved cipher machine Hebern submitted to the Navy in 1934 turned out to be a failure, the Navy turned against him. No more Hebern machines were purchased and, as they wore out, they were replaced by other cipher devices.

A few were still in use in World War II, however, and the Japanese captured two of them in the Pacific. The U.S. military services purchased no more of Hebern's machines, although he claimed that his ideas were being used in other machines. He was unable to collect on his claims—which certainly had some validity. He died in 1952 following a heart attack.

Hediger, Seaman Yeoman David A.

In Dec. 1982 Hediger, a crewman on a U.S. Navy submarine tender, called the Soviet military ATTACHÉ office in Washington, D.C. (then a Soviet facility separate from the embassy). Apparently his call was monitored by the FBI and reported to the Navy. Hediger was listed as an "espionage case" by the Navy, but there is no public record of any action being taken against him.

Helmich, Warrant Officer Joseph G., Jr.

Retired U.S. Army officer who was arrested in July 1981 for selling CRYPTOMATERIAL to the Soviet Union.

A former Army CODE custodian stationed in Paris from 1962 to 1964, Helmich was a lavish spender who lived beyond his means and was continually in debt. So many of Helmich's checks bounced at military clubs that in early 1962 his commanding officer warned him that if he did not clear up at least $500 worth of them he would be court-martialed. The officer gave Helmich a deadline for making good on the checks.

Helmich unsuccessfully tried to get a bank loan. Then, a day before the court-martial deadline, he became a WALK-IN—a volunteer spy who walked into the Soviet Embassy in Paris and offered up, for cash, secrets about U.S. and NORTH ATLANTIC TREATY ORGANIZATION (NATO) communications. As a warrant officer in the communications center of the Supreme Allied Commander, Europe, Helmich had access to U.S.-NATO diplomatic and military communications. He sold the Soviets a maintenance manual, technical information, rotors, and key lists for the KL-7 CRYPTOSYSTEM, the TOP SECRET Army code machine in wide use by U.S. and allied military services and embassies. He also had knowledge of the operation of the KW-26, another code machine.

His espionage continued in the United States when he was posted to Fort Bragg, N.C. To exchange his secrets for cash, he met Soviet HANDLERS in Mexico and in France. He was paid more than $131,000 for the information. Although U.S. INTELLIGENCE OFFICERS suspected the source of Helmich's sudden wealth, they could not prove he was spying. He retired from the Army in 1961 and eventually opened a tile company in Florida.

The FBI, which apparently did not discover evidence of Helmich's espionage until 1980, began questioning him in August of that year. Helmich said at first that he had got some money from the Soviets but that he had not given them any valuable information.

Early in 1981, in need of money for his company, Helmich went to Ottawa and contacted the Soviet Embassy there. He was spotted by Canadian intelligence officers, who passed the information on to the FBI. Helmich was arrested, tried for espionage, convicted, and sentenced to life imprisonment.

Helms, Richard McG.

(b. 1913 d. 2002)

First career INTELLIGENCE OFFICER to become the U.S. DIRECTOR OF CENTRAL INTELLIGENCE (DCI). Helms served as DCI from June 1966 to Feb. 1973, having been deputy DCI from April 1965 to June 1966.

Soon after graduating from Williams College, Helms became a foreign correspondent in Europe for the United Press. While working in Germany, he interviewed Adolf Hitler. He later became a newspaper advertising manager. Commissioned as a lieutenant (j.g.) in the Naval Reserve in July 1942, he was called to active duty and, after training and staff assignments, joined the OFFICE OF STRATEGIC SERVICES (OSS) in Aug. 1943. He served in Britain, Luxembourg, and Germany, where he first confronted the reality of postwar intelligence: The Cold War had started and the United States had to enlist German intelligence, in the form of the GEHLEN ORGANIZATION, to work against the Soviets.

After his discharge from the Naval Reserve in 1946, Helms became a civilian employee of the War Department, which had taken over part of the disbanded OSS and named it the Office of Special Operations (OSO). Helms became chief of OSO intelligence and COUNTERINTELLIGENCE for Austria, Germany, and Switzerland. With few resources, he relied mostly on British intelligence operatives.

When the CIA was created in July 1947, COVERT ACTION was handled by the Office of Policy Coordination (OPC) under the State Department, and run by FRANK WISNER, an OSS veteran. When the OPC was absorbed into a new Directorate for Plans at CIA, Wisner became Deputy Director for Plans. (He was called the DDP, and the initials came to be used for the directorate itself; the DDP was also called, more accurately, the Clandestine Service.) Helms became acting chief of operations in the DDP in July 1952 and frequently took over the DDP during the long period of Wisner's physical and mental breakdown. An administrator with experience in the field and at headquarters, Helms seemed destined to succeed Wisner as DDP. Covering this period in *The Man Who Kept the Secrets* (1979), Thomas Powers wrote of Helms:

> As chief of operations, he was a kind of middle man between the field and Washington policymakers, approving and even choosing the wording of cables to the field describing "requirements"; and passing on concrete proposals for operations from the local CIA stations before handing them up to the policy-making apparatus for final approval. . . .

If Helms did not exactly decide what the DDP ought to do, he nevertheless had a solid margin of control over how its operations were carried out, and he certainly had an unprecedented breadth of knowledge of what was in fact going on. He was one of the very few men in the CIA, in fact, who had a legitimate "need to know" virtually everything.

When Wisner left the DDP in 1958 to become chief of station in London, Helms was expected to succeed him. But ALLEN W. DULLES, the DCI, gave the post to RICHARD M. BISSELL. After Bissell directed the Bay of Pigs fiasco in April 1961 (see CUBA), both Bissell and Dulles resigned. In 1962 the new DCI, JOHN A. MCCONE, appointed Helms DDP.

During Helms's tenure as DDP, the CIA's involvement in the Vietnam War grew, and so did dissension within the agency about the war. Many officers in the Directorate of Intelligence (DDI) believed that the war would be a disaster; in the DDP, under Helms, the covert actions in VIETNAM continued. (See PHOENIX.)

When President Johnson appointed Helms DCI in June 1966, dissent within the agency over the Vietnam War escalated. In Sept. 1967 Helms asked the most experienced intelligence analyst in the OFFICE OF NATIONAL ESTIMATES to "set forth what the United States stake is in the struggle." He sent the analysis to Johnson alone, in a sealed envelope. Its contents were classified until former Secretary of Defense Robert S. McNamara revealed them in his memoir *In Retrospect* (1995). The analysis concluded that the risks of defeat in Vietnam were "probably more limited and controllable than most previous argument has indicated."

Straight, honest assessments were what Helms sought. But it would be what happened to the CIA under Helms, not what the CIA did, that would be his legacy. When the WATERGATE scandal broke Helms learned that E. HOWARD HUNT, a former CIA officer, was involved. Then President Nixon, through aides, tried to get the CIA to claim national security concerns as a justification for keeping the FBI from tracing Watergate money to the White House. (See L. PATRICK GRAY.) Helms would not let the CIA be dragged deeper into the scandal. He believed that intelligence work was not dirty work. "The nation must to a degree take it on faith that we too are honorable men, devoted to her service," he once said.

Helms also declined to give Nixon CIA files on the Bay of Pigs invasion of Cuba, the coup that overthrew President Ngo Dinh Diem of South Vietnam in 1963, and the assassination of Dominican Republic dictator Rafael Trujillo in 1961. The events occurred during the Kennedy presidency, and speculation was that Nixon would somehow use information in those files to defend himself from possible impeachment.

In Feb. 1973 Nixon, interpreting Helms's loyalty to the agency as a betrayal, fired Helms, easing the act by appointing Helms ambassador to Iran, then a key U.S. ally in southwest Asia. In the aftermath of Watergate, congressional investigative committees pounced on the CIA. Dark CIA secrets, which became known as the FAMILY JEWELS, were made public. (See MKULTRA.)

One of these secrets was CIA participation in an attempt to prevent Salvador Allende, the elected President of Chile, from assuming office in 1970. During the Senate hearing on his confirmation as ambassador to Iran, Helms was asked whether the CIA had tried to overthrow Allende. He answered, "No, sir." Those two words were the basis of a perjury indictment in 1977, after he had resigned as ambassador. In a plea bargain with the Department of Justice, Helms was fined $2,000 and given a two-year suspended sentence.

"You stand before this court in disgrace and shame," the judge said in 1977. Six years later President Reagan awarded Helms the National Security Medal, the highest decoration for intelligence work. After leaving public life, Helms formed a consulting firm, the Safeer Company; *safeer* is Farsi for ambassador.

In his posthumously published autobiography, *A Look Over My Shoulder: A Life in the Central Intelligence Agency* (with William Hood, 2003), he attempted to counter criticism of agency faults by pointing out the president, not the CIA, orders covert operations. Writing about his perjury conviction, he wrote that he believed he acted correctly in his testimony before the committee because of Nixon's orders and because he wanted to protect agents in the field.

Hentsch, Oberstleutnant Richard

(b. 1869 d. 1918)

German INTELLIGENCE OFFICER responsible for Germany's decision to halt its armies in northern France in 1914.

The chief of the Foreign Armies section (chief of foreign intelligence) of the German General Staff at the start of World War I, Hentsch also served in the important role of liaison officer between the General Staff and the commanders of the five German armies invading northern France.

On Sept. 8, 1914, he met with Col. Gen. von Moltke, Chief of the General Staff and de facto commander-in-chief of the German forces invading France. Hentsch then set out by car to visit each of the army headquarters and thus evaluate the battle situation. He convinced the five army staffs that a withdrawal from battle was required. His recommendations—he had no written orders from Moltke—led to the German defeat in the Battle of the Marne, which was more a psychological than a physical victory for the British and French forces. Had the Germans not halted their advance, it is highly possible that they could have surrounded, if not captured, Paris in this early campaign of World War I.

Reportedly, as the German armies fell back, Moltke told the Kaiser: "Your Majesty, we have lost the war!" A German inquiry in 1917 into the pullback of the armies exonerated Hentsch of any improper action.

German intelligence under Hentsch was "incompetent and misleading," wrote historian Correlli Barnett in his biographical history *The Swordbearers* (1964).

Herman [p]

Romanian-born U.S. Air Force master sergeant recruited by the KGB while assigned to U.S. Air Force intelligence in Europe in 1959. Fluent in six languages, Herman served in several intelligence positions until 1968, when he became a suspect in an investigation by the Air Force Office of Special Investigations (OSI). Because he made no admissions following his arrest in 1970, he was not punished. He was honorably retired after 30 years of military services.

The OSI report on him identifies him only by the pseudonym "MSgt. Herman."

Herrmann, Rudolph A. [p]

Soviet INTELLIGENCE OFFICER who operated in the United States as an ILLEGAL in the 1960s.

Herrmann, a Czech who was recruited by the KGB, was given a new identity—that of Rudolph Herrmann, a German soldier who was killed in the Soviet Union during World War II. After KGB training in East Germany and Moscow, in 1961 he was sent to Canada under the COVER of being an immigrant from West Germany. After several years as a member of the large Soviet intelligence apparatus in Canada, he was ordered to enter the United States legally. He obtained a U.S. visa and in 1968 moved to Hartsdale, N.Y., a suburb of New York City. Accompanying him were his German-born wife, who had also been trained by the KGB, and their two Canadian-born sons.

They bought a house selected according to KGB specifications: no nearby high-tension wires (which could interfere with radio reception), out of view of other houses, on a height, and clear of any obstructions to the east, the direction of the Moscow CENTER's radio transmissions.

In the United States Herrmann did not seek out classified information. As a RESIDENT, he would take over control of AGENTS run by the LEGALS operating under diplomatic cover, in the event that the Soviet diplomatic relations with the United States were broken or in time of war. Herrmann, who, unlike the legals, could travel freely, also found sites in various places in the United States for DROPS through which to exchange messages, money, and pilfered material with agents.

"He was given an assignment to assume an identity and just be available for specific assignments," according to an agent of the FBI familiar with the Herrmann case. "He was told to do such things as take a picture of that house or get to casually know this man. He never knew what he was doing in terms of the full picture." (According to JOHN BARRON, known for his close ties to the FBI, Herrmann—whose birth name was Ludek Zernenek—was frequently asked to find drops near U.S. military bases, where Americans were presumably spying for the Soviets.)

Herrmann freelanced, with great success, as a photographer and filmmaker. He instructed his older son, Peter, in espionage TRADECRAFT and enlisted him in the KGB, which put Peter on a path that would lead from Georgetown University to law school and perhaps ultimately to a sensitive government post or high elective office, all under KGB direction.

Peter was a junior at Georgetown in 1977 when the FBI turned him and his parents into DOUBLE AGENTS. The FBI apparently had had Herrmann and his family under SURVEILLANCE for some time. During his debriefing, according to Barron, Herrmann exposed a Canadian, HUGH HAMBLETON, as a longtime KGB agent.

After two years of running Herrmann, the FBI feared that the KGB was becoming suspicious. The FBI gave the defector family another identity—a new LEGEND appliquéd over the old KGB one—and moved it to a new location.

Herzog, Maj. Gen. Chaim

(b. 1918 d. 1997)

Twice head of Israeli MILITARY INTELLIGENCE (1949–1950, 1959–1962) and from 1983 to 1993 the President of Israel, Herzog is the only known head of military intelli-

Upon retiring from active military service in 1962, Herzog headed an industrial group in Israel and then entered law practice, simultaneously becoming a leading military and political commentator.

He became the first military governor of the West Bank of Jordan in 1967 and, subsequently, the Israeli ambassador to the United Nations from 1975 to 1978. He was elected to the *Knesset* (parliament) in 1981 and in 1983 he became President of Israel, serving in that largely honorary position until May 1993.

He has written several books in the military field, among them the classics *The War of Atonement: October 1973* (1975) and *The Arab-Israeli Wars* (1982). He is also coauthor of *Battles of the Bible* (1978).

Hexagon

SEE BIG BIRD

Heydrich, Reinhard

(b. 1904 d. 1942)

Chief of the Nazi RSHA, Reichssicherheitshauptant (Reich Security Organization) and one of the principal planners for the "final solution"—the massacre of Europe's Jewish population.

The son of an actress and an opera singer-composer who was also the director of the Conservatory of Music at Halle, Heydrich was named after a character in Wagner's *Tristan und Isolde*. A naval officer from 1922 to 1931, he was forced to resign his commission for "conduct unbecoming to an officer and gentleman" after seducing a young girl. That same year he became affiliated with the Nazi Party and subsequently the Schützstaffel (protection detachment), soon to be known by its dreaded initials, SS. He later became the first chief of the SD, the Sicherheitsdienst, the intelligence-collection and espionage section of the SS.

After swiftly and mercilessly carrying out the "blood purge" of SA leader Ernst Röhm in 1934, Heydrich became a brigadeführer (lieutenant general) and a close associate of SS chief HEINRICH HIMMLER, who in 1936 gave Heydrich command of the GESTAPO, the Nazi secret police. Heydrich issued the secret orders for the "spontaneous demonstrations" for *Kristallnacht* (Crystal Night), the nationwide, orchestrated assault on German Jews in Nov. 1938.

Using blackmail and intelligence gathered by a huge network of informers, he manufactured the evidence that purged Gen. Werner von Blomberg and Gen. Werner Freiherr von Fritsch, chief of the High Command of the German Army, alleviating opposition to Adolf Hitler's plans.

Heydrich also engineered the fake incident (CODE NAME Canned Goods) that gave Hitler a trumped-up reason to invade Poland: On Aug. 31, 1939, the eve of the scheduled invasion, Heydrich crafted a Polish "raid" on a German border radio station. The raiders were SS

Chaim Herzog, 1951. (COURTESY CHAIM HERZOG)

gence of any nation to become chief of state. (Soviet YURI ANDROPOV and American GEORGE H. W. BUSH were heads of national intelligence organizations prior to becoming chiefs of state.)

Born in Ireland, Herzog emigrated to Palestine as a boy when his father was appointed Chief Rabbi of Palestine. The younger Herzog was educated at the Universities of Cambridge and London. He served as an INTELLIGENCE OFFICER in the British Army during World War II, attaining the rank of lieutenant colonel.

After the war, as a British Army officer, he helped to interrogate Nazi war criminals. On his release from the British Army he joined the Haganah, the Jewish defense force in Palestine. He was named deputy chief of military intelligence shortly after the state of Israel was established in May 1948; and when the chief, ISSER BE'ERI, was removed in Jan. 1949, Herzog became head of the agency, serving in that position until 1950. In addition to twice directing Israeli military intelligence, he was the Israeli defense ATTACHÉ in Washington, D.C., from 1950 to 1954 and commander of the Jerusalem Brigade from 1954 to 1957.

men dressed in Polish uniforms. For proof, he supplied bodies in Polish uniforms. The victims were German concentration camp prisoners, killed by fatal injection, and then shot at the scene. Similar deceptions, using other murdered prisoners, were staged elsewhere under his direction. (SS men who took part were later "put out of the way," a Nazi testified at the Nuremberg war crimes trials.)

When the war began, Heydrich launched Operation Reinhard, the plan for the systematic extermination of the Jews of Poland. The Blond Beast, as Heydrich was called, became Deputy Reich Protector of Bohemia and Moravia (as Germany designated western Czechoslovakia) in Sept. 1941 and continued mass executions there. In Jan. 1942 he called the Warmsee Conference, whose agenda was "the final solution of the European Jewish Question."

To protect AGENTS in occupied Europe—especially in France, where Heydrich was expected to move aggressively against the Resistance—the British Secret Intelligence Service (MI6) decided to assassinate him. MI6 also believed that Heydrich was the most formidable Nazi INTELLIGENCE OFFICER. He was probably about to purge WILHELM CANARIS, the head of the ABWEHR, a man whom MI6 knew to have anti-Hitler sentiments.

In Dec. 1941 the British Special Operations Executive (SOE) parachuted into Czechoslovakia two Czech assassins, a radio operator, and three CIPHER experts. On May 23, 1942, a clockmaker fixing a clock in Heydrich's office noticed a paper listing Heydrich's itinerary for May 27. He threw the paper into the wastepaper basket, and the cleaning woman—like the clockmaker, a member of the Czech underground—passed it to the assassination team. On May 27, at a sharp bend in the Prague–Dresden road, the two assassins ambushed Heydrich's Mercedes, firing at him and his bodyguard and rolling a bomb under the car. There is some evidence that the British experts who constructed the bomb added a vial of deadly germs. Wounded but quickly treated, Heydrich nevertheless died, apparently of infection, on June 4.

In an orgy of bloody reprisals, SS men razed the Czech village of Lidice and killed all of its male inhabitants; more than 1,000 Czechs elsewhere were sentenced to death; and 3,000 inmates of the Theresienstadt camp for Jews were sent to their deaths.

WALTER SCHELLENBERG, chief of the SD, called Heydrich "the secret pivot on which the Nazi regime turned." Canaris called Heydrich a "fanatical barbarian and by far the most intelligent of all those brutes."

High-Frequency/Direction Finding

(HF/DF)

A means of determining the direction and, through the use of multiple receivers, the location of the source of radio transmissions. It is employed to locate enemy military forces on land and at sea as well as individual, clandestine radio transmitters.

HF/DF—also called "Huff-Duff"—was first used on an extensive basis in wartime to locate German submarines (U-boats) during World War II. German submarine tactics, especially when multiple-submarine "wolf packs" were used, required that the submarine detecting a convoy come to the surface and broadcast the position to draw in other U-boats.

The Royal Navy was the first navy to adopt HF/DF, employing both land-based and shipboard intercept systems. The British had begun the establishment of listening stations—primarily to intercept radio transmissions for codebreaking activities—in the late 1920s. The efforts were accelerated in the late 1930s because of the threat of British naval involvement in the Abyssinian (Ethiopian) crisis and the Spanish Civil War. In particular, during the Spanish conflict it became important to identify the "pirate" (Italian) submarines attacking merchant ships carrying supplies to the Republican forces.

The Royal Navy began providing HF/DF systems to warships in the late 1930s. Subsequently, the Canadians developed a device that automatically recorded the bearings of the radio transmissions. As a further improvement, employing the services of French research scientists who had fled the Nazis, the U.S. Navy developed a device that automatically plotted the bearings to the transmitting U-boat as visual images on a screen. That device helped direct an attack on the U-boat by continuing to indicate the bearings of even a brief radio signal after transmission had ceased. The prototype version of this HF/DF system was tested at sea in a destroyer in March 1940, and installation in U.S. Coast Guard and Navy ships began in late 1942.

While shore-based stations were valuable for both the detection and recording of U-boat transmissions (for subsequent deciphering and decoding under the ULTRA effort) and the rerouting of convoys, the availability of HF/DF on convoy escort ships revealed the location of "shadowing" submarines and helped to set up attacks by escorts or accompanying aircraft. When a convoy escort intercepted a U-boat transmission, generally the submarine was not more than 15 to 20 miles away. (This was the "ground bounce" phenomenon of high-frequency transmissions.) As the intercept provided a bearing, it was possible to dispatch an escort ship or aircraft to hunt for the U-boat. Even if the escort failed to sink the submarine, by forcing the submarine to submerge and cease broadcasting, the convoy could radically alter course and probably escape.

During the war the German submarine high command consistently underestimated the vulnerability of U-boat operations to HF/DF detection.

Hill, Capt. George

British INTELLIGENCE OFFICER who served with master spy SIDNEY REILLY in Russia during the Bolshevik Revolution.

Hill, as an enlisted man in the British Army, was wounded at Ypres in World War I. Fluent in Russian and German, he was then assigned to the British Security Service (MI5) and given a commission. Posing as a Bulgarian, he slipped into an internment camp in the Balkans and gathered intelligence. Later, he learned to fly with the Royal Flying Corps and flew British AGENTS behind enemy lines. In Aug. 1914 he was sent to Russia as a liaison to the Russian Army and to collect intelligence about German troop movements. His CODE NAME was IK8.

In the fall of 1917 he was transferred to the Secret Intelligence Service (MI6) and sent to Petrograd (formerly St. Petersburg) to gather intelligence on the Bolshevik revolution. He established contact with the Bolsheviks and for a time became air adviser to revolutionary leader Leon Trotsky. But he went on a mission of his own, deciding to get the Rumanian crown jewels and currency reserves out of Moscow and into Bucharest. He succeeded on that mission but lost contact with the Bolsheviks.

In April 1918 MI6 again tried to get intelligence, sending in a volunteer, Capt. Sidney Reilly of the Royal Flying Corps. Under Reilly's leadership, the two did elaborately plan an anti-Bolshevik campaign. But before they could get it started, the Bolsheviks began killing suspected enemies and hunting down Hill and Reilly. In Aug. 1918 they both went underground. By one account they escaped by making their way across the Baltic and into Sweden, where they found a Scotland-bound ship. Sir ROBERT BRUCE LOCKHART, a British diplomat-agent who knew both Reilly and Hill, wrote of Hill, "He was as brave and as bold as Reilly."

Hill was later sent to southern Russia to try, in vain, to coordinate White Russian intelligence organizations during the Russian Civil War. In World War II Hill taught sabotage to MI6 recruits. He was later stationed in Moscow as the representative of the Special Operations Executive (SOE) and liaison officer to the NKVD.

Hillenkoetter, Vice Adm. Roscoe H.

(b. 1897 d. 1982)

The first DIRECTOR OF CENTRAL INTELLIGENCE (DCI), serving from May 1, 1947 to Oct. 7, 1950.

A graduate of the Naval Academy, he served as assistant naval ATTACHÉ at the U.S. Embassy in Paris from 1933 to 1935 and again from 1938 to 1940. When France fell in the spring of 1940, the United States recognized the Vichy regime and President Roosevelt named a former naval officer, William D. Leahy, as ambassador. Hillenkoetter remained as naval attaché, making an impression on Leahy, who would serve both President Roosevelt and President Truman as a trusted military adviser.

Hillenkoetter, as a commander, was executive officer of the battleship *West Virginia* during the PEARL HARBOR ATTACK on Dec. 7, 1941. In Sept. 1942, as a captain, Hillenkoetter became the officer in charge of the Intelligence Center Pacific Ocean Area (ICPOA) at Pearl Harbor. He relieved Capt. JOSEPH J. ROCHEFORT, the Navy's top codebreaker, who was still running the NAVY COMMUNICATIONS INTELLIGENCE operation in the Pacific. Hillenkoetter managed the growth of the new

organization, which included Rochefort's FLEET RADIO UNIT PACIFIC. Hillenkoetter was detached from ICPOA early in 1943.

He commanded a destroyer tender in 1943–1944 and in Nov. 1945 he became commanding officer of the battleship *Missouri*, one of the most prestigious commands in the fleet. Hillenkoetter, who had been promoted to rear admiral in Nov. 1946, was again the naval attaché at the U.S. Embassy in Paris when President Truman summoned him home to become the director of the CENTRAL INTELLIGENCE GROUP, the predecessor to the CIA.

He became DCI on May 1, 1947. Under the National Security Act that established the CIA, he was reappointed on Nov. 24, 1947, on the basis of the new law and was confirmed by the Senate on Dec. 8 as the first director of the CIA.

The new agency, full of veterans of the wartime OFFICE OF STRATEGIC SERVICES, was searching for a role when Hillenkoetter took over. That role soon became clear when he was asked what the CIA could do to assure a communist defeat in the crucial Italian elections, scheduled for April 1948. Told by the agency's counsel that the new National Security Council had vested broad but vague power in the CIA, Hillenkoetter acted. By authorizing a secret operation to finance pro-Western candidates in Italy, he launched the CIA's first COVERT ACTION.

He also presided over the CIA's first crisis. President Truman and the rest of the U.S. government were stunned when North Korean troops struck South Korea on June 25, 1950. But in a *New York Times* interview published on June 26, Hillenkoetter insisted that the CIA had known that "conditions existed in Korea which could have meant an invasion this week or next." The implication was that Truman had been warned but had ignored the warning. In reality, the CIA had known of a buildup on the border but had no intelligence about North Korea's intentions.

Hillenkoetter let it be known that he would like to go to sea, and Truman gladly obliged. In October the admiral was given command of a force of cruisers and destroyers deployed to guard Formosa (Taiwan). Promoted to vice admiral in April 1956, he became inspector general of the Navy and retired in 1957 to enter private business.

Himmler, Heinrich

(b. 1900 d. 1945)

Director of state security in Nazi Germany.

Reichsführer-SS (leader of the SS, the Nazi secret police) and overseer of death camps, Himmler also managed a Bavarian chicken farm on the side. His pince-nez and diffident manner cloaked the ruthless personality of a Nazi who was an architect, though never a practitioner, of horror and terror.

An Army veteran of World War I, Himmler was an early follower of Adolf Hitler, working his way up from commander of political police in Bavaria to a place of power that ultimately was second only to Hitler's.

Among his first acts as SS chief was the establishment in 1933 of Dachau as a "model" concentration camp for dissidents. In 1934 he engineered the Night of the Long Knives, the blood purge against Ernst Röhm, thus destroying Röhm's SA police apparatus and assuring the rise of his own SS, the Schützstaffel (protection detachment). Himmler put SS men in charge at Dachau, establishing the precedent that the SS would run concentration camps and carry out Hitler's orders to murder perceived enemies of the state.

When Germany went to war in Sept. 1939, Hitler made Himmler the Commissar for Consolidation of German Nationhood, which translated into the mass murder of Jews and others whose genealogy or beliefs were contrary to Nazi ideology. Himmler set up Nazi stud farms where unwed "German women and girls of good blood" could bear the children "of soldiers setting off to battle." He supervised the forced eviction of Poles to the East to make room for ethnic Germans. He ordered the systematic killing of concentration camp inmates at Auschwitz and oversaw the massacre of the Warsaw Ghetto.

Under his guidance, the Nazi "euthanasia action" killed more than 50,000 Germans judged mentally or chronically ill or otherwise unfit for work. "There is no more living proof of hereditary and racial laws than in a concentration camp," he once said. "You find there hydrocephalics, squinters, deformed individuals, semi-Jews: a considerable number of inferior people."

The war also gave Himmler the opportunity to transform his SS into a military force, the Waffen SS, which carried out on the battlefield and in civilian enclaves behind the line the instructions that he gave a group of SS officers in Oct. 1943:

> Whether or not 10,000 Russian women collapse from exhaustion while digging a tank ditch interests me only in so far as the tank ditch is completed for Germany.... We Germans, who are the only people in the world who have a decent attitude to animals, will also adopt a decent attitude to these human animals. But it is a crime against our own blood to worry about them....

Appointed Minister of the Interior in Aug. 1943, he became the administrator of concentration camps, organized conquered peoples for slave labor in war plants, and approved barbaric "medical experiments" in the camps. He also established the Einsatzgruppen sent into occupied countries to exterminate Europe's Jews. (See RSHA.)

Himmler's SS swiftly rounded up and doomed the conspirators of the July 20, 1944, plot against Hitler, who rewarded Himmler with command of the reserve army that was to make Germany's last-ditch stand in BERLIN. Himmler was at the peak of his power.

But as Germany crumbled in the spring of 1945, Himmler desperately attempted to negotiate a peace settlement through the Swedish Red Cross. Hitler learned of the talks and, in the political testament that contains his last words, expelled Himmler from the Nazi Party. When the war ended, Himmler, in disguise, was captured near Bremen by British troops. On May 23, 1945, he killed himself by swallowing a vial of poison.

Hinsley, Francis Harry

(b. 1918 d. 1998)

Official historian of British intelligence activities during World War II. Hinsley was assigned to work at BLETCHLEY PARK in Oct. 1939, when he was a third-year student at Cambridge. He initially specialized in the signals organization of the German Navy. He subsequently became the liaison between Bletchley Park and the Admiralty's OPERATIONAL INTELLIGENCE CENTER and, from the summer of 1944, engaged in negotiations with U.S. intelligence agencies on the exchange of SIGNALS INTELLIGENCE, between the two countries.

After the war he returned to academia and became vice chancellor and professor of the history of international relations at the University of Cambridge.

Hinsley is the principal author, with E. E. Thomas, C. F. G. Ransom, R. C. Knight, and C. A. G. Simkins, of the official four-volume history *British Intelligence in the Second World War* (1979–1990). (A fifth volume in the series, on strategic DECEPTION, was authored by Michael Howard and published in 1990.) Subsequently, with Alan Stripp, Hinsley edited a collection of remembrances by workers at Bletchley Park entitled *Code Breakers* (1993).

Hirsch, Capt. John V.

U.S. Air Force INTELLIGENCE OFFICER who was investigated in an espionage case but not prosecuted.

Hirsch had access to U.S. ELECTRONIC INTELLIGENCE programs while assigned to the 690th Electronic Security Wing at Tempelhof Airport in West BERLIN in the late 1980s. He was chief of the engineering and installation branch at the unit, which monitored the radar and communications transmissions of Warsaw Pact countries. He had a TOP SECRET clearance.

During a routine SECURITY CHECK in the summer of 1989 he was given a POLYGRAPH examination that indicated deceptive answers. Air Force investigators then found classified documents in his car and discovered bank accounts totaling $120,000. Further investigation showed records of recent travel to Austria, France, and Italy.

Hirsch was transferred to the headquarters of the Electronic Security Command at Kelly Air Force Base in San Antonio, Tex., while the Air Force Office of Special Investigations and the FBI continued to probe his background. Defense officials said that Hirsch declined to take a second polygraph test.

Air Force Secretary Donald P. Rice said that investigators had used "reasonable judgment" in investigating Hirsch, but no espionage charge was brought against him. He requested and received an honorable discharge.

Hirsch, Willie

SEE JOHN GILMORE

Hiss, Alger

(b. 1904 d. 1996)

U.S. State Department official accused of spying for the Soviet Union. Convicted and imprisoned for perjury, he was never convicted of espionage. But in 1996 decrypted Soviet intelligence messages of the 1940s released by the NSA linked him to espionage. (See VENONA.)

Hiss, born in Baltimore, attended Johns Hopkins University and Harvard Law School. After graduating from Harvard he served as a law clerk to Supreme Court justice Oliver Wendell Holmes, practiced law in Boston and New York, and then went to Washington, D.C., as a member of President Roosevelt's New Deal administration. He served in the Agricultural Adjustment Administration and the Justice Department before entering the State Department in 1936.

Hiss was a key State Department official in the formative era of the UNITED NATIONS, serving as secretary general at the 1945 San Francisco meeting where the United Nations was founded. His duties often put him in contact with DONALD MACLEAN, a British Foreign Office diplomat who was later revealed to be a spy for the Soviet Union. Hiss also advised President Roosevelt at the wartime Yalta Conference where Roosevelt, British Prime Minister Winston Churchill, and Soviet dictator Josef Stalin met.

British diplomat Robert Cecil in *A Divided Life* (1988), a "personal portrait" of fellow diplomat Maclean, says the Soviet spy "had a good relationship" with Hiss. After Hiss was convicted of perjury, Cecil wrote, "Maclean heatedly championed him on occasions when it would have been in his own best interest to have kept silent." About 20 years after Maclean's defection to Moscow, Cecil met Hiss at a social function and asked him how well he had known Maclean. "I know why you ask that question," Hiss replied, saying no more.

In 1939 WHITTAKER CHAMBERS, a former member of the U.S. Communist Party (see CPUSA), had told Assistant Secretary of State Adolf Berle that Hiss, who then worked under Berle, was a communist. Berle scoffed at the charge. Similar information came from French intelligence sources. IGOR GOUZENKO, a Soviet DEFECTOR, said that an Assistant Secretary of State was a Soviet spy, and the FBI secretly targeted Hiss as the suspect but could not prove the charge.

Hiss quietly left the State Department to become, in 1947, the president of the eminent Carnegie Endowment for International Peace. In July 1948 Chambers, a senior editor for *Time* magazine, told the House Un-American Activities Committee that Hiss had been a fellow communist in the 1930s and had given Chambers State Department documents that he passed to a Soviet HANDLER.

(Earlier, ELIZABETH BENTLEY, an admitted Soviet AGENT, told the committee that she had passed docu-

Alger Hiss, convicted of perjury in 1950, always pled innocent to charges of spying for the Soviet Union. However, the Venona decrypts of Soviet communications indicate the Hiss was in fact the American code-name Ales, who provided important government information to the Soviets.

ments from high-ranking U.S. government officials to her Soviet handlers.)

Hiss, denying the charges, sued Chambers for libel. To back up his accusation, Chambers produced handwritten memos and typewritten summaries of State Department documents. Introduced as evidence was a Woodstock typewriter that experts identified as the one that had typed both copies of documents given to Chambers and Hiss family letters. Hiss and experts on his side claimed that the typewriter had been tampered with in order to produce the similarities.

Chambers had held back strips of 35-mm film and three undeveloped rolls. The existence of this additional evidence reached the Un-American Activities Committee, and one of its members, Representative Richard M. Nixon, issued a subpoena for Chambers' holdings. Chambers led congressional investigators to a pumpkin patch on his Maryland farm. Hidden in a hollowed-out pumpkin were what became known as the "pumpkin papers."

Nixon was catapulted to instant fame when newspapers showed photographs of him with a magnifying glass peering at prints of the film—State Department documents of the 1930s. The prints, but not the three rolls of undeveloped film, were introduced at the perjury trial. (In 1975, using the Freedom of Information Act, Hiss got the rolls of film. One was blank; the others showed dim images apparently from pages of Army and Navy manuals of the 1930s.)

A federal grand jury, which could not indict him for espionage because the statue of limitations had run out, charged him with two counts of perjury. His first trial ended in a hung jury. In 1950, he was convicted at a second trial and was sentenced to five years in prison. After serving 44 months, he was released in Nov. 1954. Hiss continued to insist that he was innocent of espionage. In 1992 a Russian historian who had gained access to Soviet intelligence files of the 1950s said that espionage accusations against Hiss had been "completely groundless." But this did not convince those who believed that the evidence against Hiss had been strong.

In 1996 came the release of the Venona messages. One, dated March 30, 1945, refers to an American code-named "Ales"; the message notes that a Soviet agent working in the State Department accompanied President Roosevelt to the 1945 Yalta Conference and then flew on to Moscow. There, the message indicates, Ales met Soviet Andrei Vyshinsky, the Commissar for Foreign Affairs, and was cited for his aid to the Soviets. NSA analysts said that Ales could only have been Hiss.

Höke, Margarete

(b. 1935)

Secretary in the office of West German President Richard von Weizsacker arrested on charges of espionage.

Officials of the BFV (Federal Office for the Protection of the Constitution) said that she had worked for West German presidents from 1959 until her arrest in Aug. 1985. She was one of many secretaries targeted by KGB and Stasi INTELLIGENCE OFFICERS, who used SEX as an accompaniment to spying. She was arrested after being named by OLEG GORDIEVSKY, a DEFECTOR from the KGB.

Höke's HANDLER was her lover, Franz Becker, a Soviet intelligence officer. She was accused of passing him copies of more than 1,700 classified documents, along with reports she had seen from Western embassies. Becker managed to flee when Höke was arrested. In 1987 she was sentenced to eight years in prison.

Also see HANS JOACHIM TIEDGE.

Hollis, Sir Roger

(b. 1905 d. 1973)

Director-General of the British Security Service (MI5) from 1956 to 1965 and the suspected FIFTH MAN in the CAMBRIDGE SPY RING. Suspicions about Hollis split British intelligence in the 1970s and 1980s, with some defending Hollis as a victim of insider gossip and others trying to lay out a case convicting him—after his death.

Leading those who suspected Hollis to be a MOLE in the COUNTERINTELLIGENCE agency was PETER WRIGHT, an MI5 officer from 1949 to 1976, who accused Hollis in his book *Spycatcher* (1987). It was during Hollis's tenure that the members of the Cambridge ring—HAROLD (KIM) PHILBY, GUY BURGESS, DONALD MACLEAN, AND ANTHONY BLUNT—had all penetrated British intelligence.

Hollis, the son of a Church of England bishop, went to Oxford, not Cambridge, but left before he earned a degree. Instead, in 1927 he sailed to Shanghai, where he became employed by the British American Tobacco Co. In 1934, suffering from tuberculosis, he returned to England. Four years later he joined MI5, where he was assigned to the section dealing with the Communist Party of Great Britain and, during World War II, the Soviet Union. For a time he was acting head of Section F, which dealt with the Soviet Union and the Soviet Bloc.

After the war, Hollis was sent to Australia, where he helped to form the AUSTRALIAN SECURITY AND INTELLIGENCE ORGANIZATION. By then he was head of the C Division, which dealt with MI5 internal security. In 1953, Sir DICK WHITE, Director-General of MI5, appointed Hollis his deputy.

ANATOLI GOLITSYN, a senior KGB officer who became a DEFECTOR in Dec. 1961, told Western intelligence officers that Burgess and Maclean, who defected to the Soviet Union in 1951, were two of the "Ring of Five," as the KGB sometimes referred to the British spy ring. Philby was the THIRD MAN and Blunt, an MI5 officer during World War II, was the FOURTH MAN. Wright, who spent six years debriefing Blunt and trying to unravel the Ring of Five claim, zeroed in on Hollis as the FIFTH MAN. In 1961 Hollis was four years away from ending his tenure as Director-General.

The case that Wright and others built against Hollis began with his years in China. They believed that he might have been recruited there by someone in the Shanghai NETWORK, then being run by master Soviet spy RICHARD SORGE. But exhaustive checks of records about Sorge failed to establish any contact with young Hollis. Similarly, examination of leaks and bungled cases under Hollis did not produce any evidence of treachery on his part. During his tenure MI5 tracked down GEORGE BLAKE and broke the GORDON LONSDALE ring. (See HARRY HOUGHTON, PORTLAND CASE.)

But Wright was not convinced. Besides Hollis, he also wondered about Graham Mitchell, head of COUNTERESPIONAGE in MI5 and later Deputy Director-General under Hollis. "By the beginning of 1964," Wright wrote in *Spycatcher*, "both Arthur [Martin, a senior MI5 COUNTERINTELLIGENCE officer] and I were convinced that Hollis, rather than Mitchell, was the most likely suspect for the spy we were certain had been active inside MI5 at a high level."

The investigation continued after Hollis retired. In 1969 he was interrogated for two days by an MI5 officer in one room in a SAFE HOUSE, while in another room MI5

officers (including Wright) listened and recorded the sessions. Hollis neither revealed nor admitted anything, and the Hollis file was closed.

British authorities tried to suppress Wright's book prior to its publication in 1987. No such action had been taken against CHAPMAN PINCHER, whose book *Their Trade Is Treachery* (1981) had made similar charges against Hollis. But because Pincher was a journalist, his accusations carried less weight than Wright's accusation, which came from a man who had actually worked in MI5.

Responding to Pincher's book, Prime Minister Margaret Thatcher stated in March 1981 that two investigations had cleared Hollis. "It is very often impossible to prove innocence," she said in a statement in Parliament. "But no evidence was found that incriminated him, and the conclusion reached at the end of the investigation was that he had not been an agent of the Soviet intelligence service." She said that the book "contains no information of security significance which is new to the security authorities. And some of the material is inaccurate or distorted."

After Hollis retired, his wife of 31 years divorced him, and he married his secretary, with whom he had had a long affair. British INTELLIGENCE OFFICERS doubted whether the affair could have been used by the Soviets as the basis for blackmail, given the British establishment's tolerance for sexual straying of various kinds.

Holmes, Capt. Wilfred Jay

(b. 1900 d. 1986)

U.S. Navy CRYPTANALYST on the staff of the U.S. Pacific Fleet and Pacific Ocean Areas command at Pearl Harbor during World War II.

"Jasper" Holmes, a 1922 graduate of the Naval Academy, served on surface ships and submarines. A physical disability forced him to leave active service in 1936 while he was in command of the submarine *S-30*. He joined the engineering facility of the University of Hawaii and, under the pen name Alec Hudson, became a well-known short story writer for *The Saturday Evening Post*.

Recalled to active naval service in June 1941, Holmes was assigned to the codebreaking staff at Pearl Harbor. In late May 1942, U.S. Navy codebreakers knew that the Japanese Fleet was preparing for an attack, but could identify their objective only by the letters "AF." Holmes is usually credited with conceiving an ingenious method of making the Japanese reveal the meaning of AF, leading to the American victory (see MIDWAY).

Holmes remained in codebreaking work until after the end of the war, retiring in Nov. 1946. He returned to the University of Hawaii as chair of the Engineering Department. He wrote a comprehensive account of U.S. and Japanese submarine operations in the war in *Undersea Victory* (1966) and revealed much of the U.S. Navy's intelligence operations in World War II in his *Double-Edged Secrets* (1979).

Holystone

SEE SUBMARINES

Homeland Security

Following the terrorist attacks on the World Trade Center in New York City and the Pentagon in Washington, D.C., on Sept. 11, 2001, the U.S. INTELLIGENCE COMMUNITY concentrated its effort to a major extent on TERRORIST INTELLIGENCE.

The largest organization change in the government was establishment of the Department of Homeland Security (DHS), the third largest of the Cabinet-level departments. Congress, critical of the failure of the FBI and CIA to foresee and warn of the terrorists' plans, responded by endorsing the Bush administration plan for the merger of 22 domestic agencies into one department designed to protect the nation against terrorist threats.

The new department, which began operations on Jan. 24, 2003, was envisioned as the principal customer of terrorist intelligence, although its own ability to gather and process intelligence was to be confined to a small component, not to duplicate the efforts of other U.S. intelligence agencies. Initially, the department's principal function was to issue warnings, based on a color code, about the threat level to the nation: red for severe, orange for high, yellow for elevated, blue for guarded, and green for low.

The major organizations drawn into the DHS were the U.S. Coast Guard, the Federal Emergency Management Agency (FEMA), the U.S. SECRET SERVICE, and a new version of the immigration service, now called the Bureau of Citizenship and Immigration Services.

DHS started out with an organization of five directorates:

Border and Transportation Security: encompasses the Transportation Security Administration, U.S. Customs Service, the border security functions of the Immigration and Naturalization Service, Animal & Plant Health Inspection Service, and the Federal Law Enforcement Training Center.
Emergency Preparedness and Response: takes over FEMA's traditional role as responder to natural disasters and adds terrorist attacks.
Science and Technology: described as "preparing for and responding to the full range of terrorist threats involving weapons of mass destruction."
Information Analysis and Infrastructure Protection: apparently where the intelligence component of DHS will be placed. Officially, this directorate "merges the capability to identify and assess a broad range of intelligence information concerning threats to the homeland under one roof, issue timely warnings, and take appropriate preventive and protective action."
Management: handles budget, management, and personnel issues.

Many members of the Intelligence Community saw the DHS as blurring the traditional lines between DOMESTIC

INTELLIGENCE, primarily the responsibility of the FBI, and the international intelligence-gathering done by the CIA and the NSA, which are prohibited from operating in the United States. Four agencies absorbed into the DHS—the Coast Guard, Customs Service, Secret Service, and Border Patrol—had meager intelligence-collection functions.

Homosexuals

Just as heterosexual relations are frequently involved in espionage, so are homosexual relations. Several British INTELLIGENCE OFFICERS were homosexuals, for example, and their sexuality played a role both in their activities and in their fears of blackmail. Not until the more tolerant 1980s and 1990s did homosexuality become less likely to inspire an attempt at blackmail. Even so, in 1980 MAURICE OLDFIELD, the retired Director-General of MI6, resigned as coordinator of British security and intelligence in Northern Ireland after having admitted to being a homosexual.

Homosexual AGENTS have been TURNED through threats of exposure. Col. ALFRED REDL, a senior Austrian intelligence officer, was one such victim in the early 1900s. Russian TALENT SPOTTERS, knowing that Redl was a homosexual, supplied him with young men as well as money and blackmailed him into spying for Russia. In 1937 an American clerk in the office of the military ATTACHÉ of the U.S. Embassy in Moscow reported that NKVD agents had photographed him while he was engaged in a homosexual act and had given him 72 hours to provide them with U.S. military CODES. The clerk was immediately sent home.

An FBI report on other activities in the same embassy discovered two more homosexuals. According to the report, the FBI agent who made the investigation "points out that Moscow is a most undesirable post of assignment for these persons since . . . their sex conduct . . . could readily be used as a lever to pry confidential information from them." The report recommended that only married couples be sent to Moscow.

When ALLEN W. DULLES became the European spymaster for the OFFICE OF STRATEGIC SERVICES (OSS) in World War II, the OSS heard of reports of a homosexual group of upper-class men who might be valuable to Dulles. "Such were the social inhibitions of the era," wrote Peter Greece in Gentleman Spy (1994), that Dulles was not given leads to the group. The OSS officer who learned of the group decided that Dulles "could not cope with this rather special affinity group." According to Greece, Dulles did not understand the physical aspects of homosexuality and had to have homosexuality explained to him when he found a reference to it as a criminal offense under Nazi law. Homosexual behavior was also against the law in England. The brilliant British codebreaker ALAN TURNING killed himself in 1954 after being convicted of being a practicing homosexual.

Links between secret sexual behavior and espionage abound: GUY BURGESS and ANTHONY BLUNT of the CAMBRIDGE SPY RING were homosexuals; and another member, DONALD MACLEAN, who was bisexual, often had homosexual affairs. All three were members of a secret society, the Apostles. Andrew Sinclair wrote in The Red and the Blue (1986)

> The strong homosexual element among the Apostles did buttress their oath of secrecy and separate them more from conventional society. To be an open homosexual was to ruin one's career and risk legal prosecution and prison. . . . Those Marxists who were homosexual were even more tightly bound together in worlds of subterfuge and deceit. . . . With a blindness that defies belief, they chose not to know the fact that Stalinist Russia persecuted homosexuals even more than England did.

U.S. Army Sgt. JAMES A. MINTKENBAUGH was recruited to spy for the KGB in Germany in the 1950s by another soldier-spy. Mintkenbaugh was a homosexual—"and this fact," says a government report on the case, "interested the KGB handlers since the homosexual frequently is shunned by society and made to feel like a social outcast. Such a personality may seek to retaliate against a society that has placed him in this unenviable position." Blackmail was the tool used by Soviet intelligence to recruit JOHN VASSALL, a clerk in the British Admiralty, as a spy. A Soviet defector's recollection that a spy in the Admiralty was "a homosexual" led to Vassall's arrest in 1962.

After KGB SURVEILLANCE operatives noted that a French diplomat looked interested in a Soviet police captain guarding the French Embassy in Moscow, the captain was ordered to set up an affair. Compromising photos were taken and shown to the diplomat in an effort to blackmail him into espionage. The diplomat, whose homosexuality was known to his superiors, smiled and thanked the KGB for the photos.

In 1960 WILLIAM MARTIN and BERNON MITCHELL, two CRYPTOGRAPHY specialists at the U.S. National Security Agency (NSA), defected to the Soviet Union, saying that they had left the NSA because they did not approve of U.S. intelligence-gathering methods. There was no indication that they had been blackmailed into defecting. But their betrayal of the NSA triggered a hunt for other homosexuals in the agency; dozens of employees were fired or forced to resign because they were suspected of homosexual behavior.

Twenty years later, as recounted by JAMES BAMFORD in The Puzzle Palace (1982), the NSA attempted to pressure a homosexual employee to resign. When he went to a lawyer, the NSA agreed to retain him provided that he tell his family that he was a homosexual and agree to report to the NSA "any attempt to blackmail [him] or subject [him] to coercion or duress because of [his] sexual preference. . . ." In a similar case in 1982, an employee admitted to having engaged in homosexual acts while on vacation abroad. This led to his discharge—not for his sexual activities, the NSA claimed, but because of an "indiscriminate pattern of activity which invites the risk of security exploitation."

J. EDGAR HOOVER, director of the FBI for 48 years, was obsessed by reports about homosexuality—whether directed at him or at prominent Americans. For their biography of Hoover, *The Boss* (1988), Athan G. Theoharis and John Stuart Cox obtained, through the Freedom of Information Act, the index to Hoover's Official and Confidential File, which was full of references to homosexuality associated with "prominent persons."

One report alleged that [name and title deleted] "was a homosexual and Communists were using this to blackmail [name deleted] to place other Communists on the [name of office deleted] staff. During interviews information received which linked [name deleted] with [name deleted] as a homosexual." Another file contained "personal background data relative to . . . alleged homosexual tendencies."

Another 647-page file, compiled by the FBI and U.S. ARMY INTELLIGENCE on members of Congress and other prominent persons, was withheld. But its index mentioned that "[name deleted], a self-admitted homosexual, alleged to an informant of the military that former [name of congressman deleted] and other prominent persons had engaged in homosexual activities."

In Aug. 1995, in an overhaul of SECURITY CLEARANCE practices, President Clinton signed an executive order prohibiting the denial of clearances to homosexuals simply because of their sexual orientation. The order said that the test for clearances would be whether a person's character was "consistent with the national security interest of the United States."

Honeyman, John

(b. 1730 d. 1823)

New Jersey man who spied for Gen. GEORGE WASHINGTON during the American Revolution, providing valuable intelligence for Washington's brilliant foray against the Hessian troops at Trenton, N.J., on Dec. 26, 1776.

An Irish-born veteran of the French and Indian War, Honeyman had served with the British in Canada and had helped to carry the body of Gen. James Wolfe from the Plains of Abraham when Wolfe was killed defeating the French at Quebec in 1759. He may have met Washington in Philadelphia when the general was attending meetings of the Continental Congress in 1775.

When Washington's Continental Army was retreating across New Jersey in 1776, Washington wanted to "get some person in to Trenton" as an AGENT. He recruited Honeyman, telling him to use the COVER of being a Tory. Honeyman's association with the heroic Wolfe guaranteed his acceptance by the enemy garrison at Trenton, Washington realized.

Posing as a Tory, Honeyman, a butcher and weaver from Griggstown, N.J., thus fled to Trenton, where he convinced other pro-British colonials that he was being sought as a traitor by Washington himself. The DECEPTION plan was so believable that a mob of American patriots raided Honeyman's house in Griggstown. Washington

saved Honeyman's wife and children from harm by giving the family a signed document that, while calling Honeyman a "notorious Tory," ordered that his family not be molested.

After reconnoitering Trenton and assessing the low quality of the Hessian mercenaries there, Honeyman, as part of the deception plan, wandered toward American lines, got himself captured, and was taken directly to Washington. Honeyman gave his report and was allowed to "escape" to make his way back to Trenton. There he told the Hessian commander of his capture and reported that the Continental Army was in such a low state of morale that they would not attack Trenton.

His tale was believed. The Hessians relaxed security, and on Christmas Day Washington crossed the Delaware River to New Jersey with 2,400 troops. The next day Washington's forces surprised the Hessians in a rout that gave the Americans a desperately needed victory.

Honeyman left Trenton after the battle. After the war his mission became known and his neighbors learned that he had always been a loyal patriot.

Honey Trap

Slang for use of men or women in sexual situations to intimidate or snare others. This use of SEX to trap or blackmail an individual is standard practice in intelligence operations.

Also see HOMOSEXUALS.

Honorary Agents

Secret informants used by the German SD. WALTER SCHELLENBERG wrote in *The Schellenberg Memoirs* (1956) that the honorary agents were

> trusted informants placed strategically in all walks of life, in every profession and industry. They were usually men of wide experience in their own fields and were thus in a position to furnish very valuable information, giving special attention to reports on public opinion and reactions to legislation, decrees and other measures taken by the government.

Hoover, J. (John) Edgar

(b. 1895 d. 1972)

Director of the investigative arm of the U.S. Department of Justice—and America's leading foe of subversives—from 1924 until his death in 1972. He was the director of the FBI from its founding in 1935.

Hoover went to work as a file clerk for the Department of Justice in 1917 and in 1919 was appointed a special assistant to the Attorney General. In 1921 he became the assistant director of the Department of Justice's Bureau of Investigation and in 1924 he was named director. The bureau later became the U.S. Bureau of Investigation, the Division of Investigation, and finally, in 1935, the FBI. By then, Hoover's agents were popularly known as "G-men" (short for "government men").

During his long reign Hoover *was* the FBI. Representative Emanuel Celler, chairman of the House Judiciary Committee, once said that Hoover was powerful because "he was the head of an agency that in turn had tremendous power, power of surveillance, power of control over the lives and destinies of every man in the nation. He had a dossier on every member of Congress and member of the Senate." At times he seemed more powerful than the presidents he served.

Born in Washington, D.C., he became a third-generation civil servant. He went to work as a file clerk at the Library of Congress while studying at George Washington University, where he earned a bachelor of law degree in 1916 and a master of law degree a year later. A bachelor, he resided with his widowed mother in Washington until her death in 1938 and then lived in the family home for the rest of his life.

After completing his education, Hoover went to work as a clerk in the Department of Justice. When the United States entered World War I in 1917, his career as a hunter of subversives began. Anxiety about enemy aliens rapidly expanded the work of the Justice Department's Bureau of Investigation (BOI). Hoover was assigned to the alien enemy registration section, which became a focal point in the U.S. reaction to fears that the Bolshevik revolution in Russia would spread to other countries.

Attorney General A. Mitchell Palmer, leading a crusade against the "Red menace," set up a General Intelligence Division within the BOI and made Hoover his special assistant for developing cases against radicals. Hoover soon had files on more than 200,000 people and organizations. He rounded up more than 200 members of the Union of Russian Workers and found "anarchistic propaganda" that was "atheistic in tendency and immoral and vicious in purpose." The Russians were deported in Dec. 1919. Hoover orchestrated another raid on radicals in Jan. 1920, this time arresting 10,000 people in more than 30 cities. Most of them were quickly released; of the 3,500 held for deportation, only 556 were eventually deported.

In May 1924 Hoover was appointed acting director of the BOI, and in Dec. 1924 he became director, overseeing what was evolving into a national police force with 441 "special agents" and field offices in major cities. The work of the BOI vastly increased in 1933 when the Prohibition Bureau—the Justice Department office set up to enforce the constitutional amendment barring the production, sale, and transport of liquor—was placed under the BOI. (Prohibition was repealed in Dec. 1933.) As the nation's concerns shifted from subversives to crime, Hoover responded by looking for crooks instead of revolutionaries.

Under President Franklin D. Roosevelt the bureau was upgraded to the Division of Investigation. Roosevelt supported legislation that gave Hoover more independence, creating what in July 1935 became the Federal Bureau of Investigation (FBI).

When war broke out in Europe in 1939, Hoover, with Roosevelt's blessing, shifted the FBI's mission to the hunting down of subversives, spies, and saboteurs. But Hoover's crime-fighting instincts did not prepare him for the subtleties of espionage.

With Roosevelt's knowledge, the British Secret Intelligence Service (MI6) set up an intelligence operation, BRITISH SECURITY COORDINATION (BSC), in New York City in 1940. WILLIAM STEPHENSON, the director of the BSC, met Hoover through their mutual friend, former world heavyweight boxing champion Gene Tunney. Hoover had insisted that no British INTELLIGENCE OFFICERS were to operate in the United States. But Stephenson convinced the FBI chief that both nations could benefit from mutual cooperation. Playing to Hoover's vanity, Stephenson allowed the FBI to get credit for detecting any German saboteurs and spies discovered by the British.

Stephenson, in search of deeper cooperation between U.S. and British intelligence agencies, found it not in Hoover but in WILLIAM DONOVAN, whom Roosevelt had appointed COORDINATOR OF INFORMATION to head a quasi-intelligence agency directly responsible to President Roosevelt. Hoover fought Donovan and his emergence as chief of what eventually became the OFFICE OF STRATEGIC SERVICES (OSS), which was placed under the Joint Chiefs of Staff. The two men had met at the Justice Department when Hoover was director of the BOI and Donovan was the assistant attorney general who supervised the bureau. Donovan had left Justice in 1929, but Hoover remembered him as a man he disliked—flashy, sophisticated, coolly unbureaucratic.

Donovan, maneuvering to create the OSS, assured an FBI official (Hoover would not meet with him) that he would not interfere with the FBI. To still the turmoil, Roosevelt appointed his son James as a liaison between Donovan and the FBI. Hoover did collect information about the well-traveled Donovan's associations with "German activities" and communists, but given Roosevelt's backing of Donovan, Hoover prudently did not try to exploit this information.

Meanwhile Hoover, who had built up the reputation of the FBI through shrewd use of publicity in the gangster era, used similar techniques to make his G-men heroes of the U.S. war effort. He put his byline over magazine articles portraying the FBI as a relentless hunter of Nazi and Japanese spies.

In Aug. 1941, the British introduced the FBI to DUSKO POPOV, a DOUBLE AGENT who was under MI5 control while being run by the ABWEHR, the German MILITARY INTELLIGENCE organization. The Abwehr had sent Popov to the United States to set up a spy ring. At the request of the Germans' Japanese allies, the MICRODOT instructions he carried included questions about Pearl Harbor, the U.S. Navy base in Hawaii. But Hoover, believing that Popov was a German spy who had duped the British, dismissed him as a "Balkan playboy" and refused to allow him to go to Hawaii. (In the April 1946 issue of *The Reader's Digest* Hoover claimed credit for discovering the microdot scheme when the FBI "captured" a German spy. The "spy" was Popov, and the credit should, of course, go to the British.)

Although by Aug. 1941 the United States and Japan were on a collision course and many U.S. officials considered war likely, Hoover ignored the microdot questions about Pearl Harbor, failing to see the possible significance of the German interest in the base. (Revelations about the Pearl Harbor questions were first revealed by Sir JOHN MASTERMAN; see DOUBLE-CROSS SYSTEM.)

Not until Sept. 30 was some of Popov's message passed on to the Army and Navy intelligence staffs. And even then the significance of the Pearl Harbor inquiries continued to be disregarded.

On Jan. 13, 1942, more than a month after the PEARL HARBOR ATTACK, Hoover wrote a memo to Maj. Gen. Edwin M. Watson, President Roosevelt's appointments secretary. In it Hoover mentioned neither Popov nor the Pearl Harbor queries, noting merely that he thought the President might want to see "one of the methods used by the German espionage system in transmitting messages to its agents." Hoover enclosed a 400x enlargement of a portion of the microdot message and an FBI translation. The portion that Hoover chose to show the President did not refer to Pearl Harbor. The translation referred to the part of the message that sought information about American aircraft production.

While the FBI tracked down spies, Hoover preached, warning of a FIFTH COLUMN of traitors, an "enemy within"—composed of people who believed "that the Government of the United States [could] be overthrown." Perhaps because of the AMERASIA case, which involved Soviet espionage, he clung to his belief that communist subversives perpetually threatened the United States. (See DUQUESNE SPY RING, WILLIAM C. COLEPAUGH, VELVALEE DICKINSON.)

As the war was ending, Donovan, at Roosevelt's request, submitted a plan for a peacetime intelligence service. Hoover managed to get a copy of the plan and leaked it to *The Chicago Tribune*, which labeled it a "super spy system for the postwar New Deal." (The *Tribune* remained in favor with Hoover even though the newspaper—and STANLEY JOHNSTON, one of its reporters—had been accused of revealing U.S. codebreaking efforts during the war.)

Hoover gave FBI cooperation to the makers of the 1945 film *The House on 92nd Street* (see MOVIES). The film, using a documentary technique that suggested the story was true, was based on a successful FBI double-agent operation (see WILLIAM G. SEBOLD). But the film went on to give the impression that the FBI had prior knowledge of a real German sabotage plot; in fact, the arrival of German saboteurs by SUBMARINE stunned the FBI.

Hoover was obsessed with obtaining secrets about politicians and celebrities. In June 1940 FBI agents broke into the New York office of the American Youth Congress and photographed correspondence that included letters from First Lady Eleanor Roosevelt. A report was sent to Hoover. The BLACK BAG JOB had been inspired by Hoover's

concern over "agitation among Negroes." Hoover was told about "Negro maids allegedly demanding their own terms for working and at the same time stating they were members of an Eleanor Roosevelt Club. . . ."

After President Roosevelt's death in April 1945, Hoover tried to get the Truman administration to kill the Donovan proposal. But Truman, who disliked Hoover, paid him little heed and authorized the creation of the CIA. During Hoover's reign there would be little cooperation between the FBI and the CIA.

Hoover-authorized break-ins continued through the 1940s and into the 1950s, especially against organizations that he considered subversive, including civil rights organizations and labor unions. Hoover also ordered wiretaps of the phones of Jehovah's Witnesses because they opposed the draft and refused to salute the American flag. Hoover personally approved "misur" (microphone surveillance) in many cases, and in the 1960s was still tracing his authority to a ruling made by the Attorney General in 1938.

He cooperated with the congressional committees searching for communists in government, testifying about the threat. But he more frequently worked backstage, leaking documents to the House Un-American Activities Committee and the Senate Internal Security Committee. In the ALGER HISS case Hoover was especially helpful to a young congressman, Richard M. Nixon.

Hoover for the most part stayed clear of President Eisenhower, allying himself with Senator Joseph R. McCarthy, the communist-hunting senator who was Eisenhower's political foe. Hoover dug up information on Eisenhower's wartime mistress, Kay Summersby, but never used it against him.

In 1956 Hoover launched a secret operation, COINTELPRO (for COUNTERINTELLIGENCE programs), which involved gathering DOMESTIC INTELLIGENCE about people and organizations that Hoover judged to be disloyal to the government. During the Vietnam War he concentrated COINTELPRO on anti-war activists and drew in the CIA (see CHAOS). COINTELPRO became the longest-lived and most penetrating domestic intelligence operation in American history. In the face of unprecedented criticism by civil rights groups and by elected officials, Hoover ended COINTELPRO in 1971.

"If it hadn't been for Edgar Hoover," President Johnson told his successor, President-elect Nixon, in Dec. 1969, "I couldn't have carried out my responsibilities as Commander in Chief. Period. Dick, you will come to depend on Edgar. He is a pillar of strength in a city of weak men. You will rely on him time and time again to maintain security. He's the only one you can put your complete trust in."

President Nixon started out trusting Hoover, but the White House began its own domestic intelligence program (see HUSTON PLAN) and no longer had great faith in Hoover. After being reelected in 1972, Nixon almost certainly planned to ask for Hoover's resignation. But Hoover died before that happened. Nixon missed him when the WATERGATE scandal broke. Talking to White House counsel John W. Dean III in Feb. 1973, Nixon

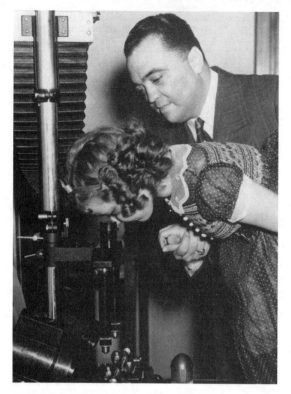

J. Edgar Hoover with child actress Shirley Temple. (FEDERAL BUREAU OF INVESTIGATION)

said, "Well, Hoover performed. He would have fought. That was the point. He would have defied a few people. He would have scared them to death. He had a file on everybody."

After Hoover's death, long-suppressed rumors surfaced about his private life. Claims that he was a closet HOMOSEXUAL, while intriguing, were not proved. In assessments of his long career, his record as a political infighter seemed to transcend his record as a crime or spy fighter. In Feb. 1975 Attorney General Edward Levi, in congressional testimony, said that Hoover's "Official and Confidential" office file included derogatory information on many people, including members of Congress and presidents. In 1976 the House and Senate intelligence committees revealed the abuses of COINTELPRO.

All of Hoover's locked office files marked "personal" had been destroyed, and many of the files to which Levi referred remained classified. In *The Boss*, biographers Theoharis and Cox obtained some files through the Freedom of Information Act. They found "derogatory personal information on two presidents, a First Lady, a cabinet member, and countless other prominent personalities." But the man who had started as a file clerk knew that there were many ways to keep files. He had arranged the most sensitive ones in such a way— "neither indexed nor recorded in the Bureau's central

records system," according to the biographers—that his office file "technically did not exist."

Hori, Maj. Eizo

(b. 1913 d. 1995)

Japanese Army INTELLIGENCE OFFICER who earned the label "MacArthur's staff officer" from his colleagues.

A 1934 graduate of the Military Academy, Hori was commissioned as a cavalry officer. He was immediately assigned to the staff at Imperial Headquarters, after which he served extensively overseas—in Britain, Germany, the Soviet Union, and the United States. For most of World War II he was assigned to the Second Division (intelligence) of the Army General Staff and then to the intelligence staff of the 14th Army in the Philippines.

Throughout the war Hori showed a remarkable talent for anticipating U.S. operations. He made his predictions by trying to think like his principal enemy, Gen. Douglas MacArthur. It was Hori's amazingly accurate forecasts that prompted fellow officers to give him his nickname. For instance, when his superiors believed that MacArthur would thrust toward Japan after U.S. forces assaulted Saipan in June 1944, Hori insisted, correctly, that he would invade the Philippines.

Hori also analyzed U.S. bomber flights over Japan, determined which ones were probably for RECONNAISSANCE, and deduced that Kyushu was getting a great deal of attention. Then, after walking Kyushu beaches, he picked Ariake Bay (now Shibushi Bay) on the southwestern coast of the island as a likely invasion site. He knew that weather would play a role. Landings early in the fall risked typhoons, which were unlikely after October. Freezing or near-freezing weather came in December and January, when U.S. troops would be fighting on southern Kyushu. But at least they would be dry, for rain was rare and the rice fields would be drained. Taking all this into consideration, Hori decided on late October as the probable date. As it turned out, U.S. strategists had selected Nov. 1 for the Kyushu landings.

Demobilized after the war, Hori entered the Ground Self-Defense Force (that is, the Army) in 1954. He again received intelligence assignments, serving as military ATTACHÉ in West Germany and chief of the intelligence section of the Joint Chiefs of Staff before retiring in 1967. He subsequently became a professor of German at Osakagakuin University from 1974 until the late 1980s.

Hot Lines

During the DECADE OF THE SPY the U.S. military services and other government agencies established telephone hot lines for reporting possible espionage activities or foreign attempts to recruit American military personnel.

The U.S. Army's toll-free, hot line was 800-CALL SPY (225-5779). It was still in use in 2004. Soldiers throughout the United States received the hot-line number on a slip of paper with their paychecks, along with a page of "tips" for spotting spies. Among the tips passed on to the soldiers were:

- Look for people whose first task of a morning is to replace a classified document in a safe.
- At best, it could be someone who has taken work home—a security breach in itself. And at worst, it could be someone who's feeding the documents to foreign AGENTS.
- Pay attention to those who say they are taking many short trips to the beach or mountains but who return bearing souvenirs from abroad.
- Beware the comrade-in-arms who brags about doing classified work or of "being in JAMES BOND [f]" kinds of activities.

The telephones are answered 24 hours a day by experienced COUNTERINTELLIGENCE agents at FORT MEADE, Md. Callers are allowed to provide anonymous tips.

Horton, Seaman 2nd Class Brian P.

U.S. Navy sailor who attempted to sell classified information to the Soviet Union. Between April and Oct. 1982 Horton attempted five times to contact the Soviet Embassy in Washington, D.C., offering to sell information on U.S. strategic war plans for $1,000 to $3,000. Although federal authorities did not disclose how they had learned of Horton's phone calls, it seems highly likely that they heard his four telephone calls through taps on the embassy.

Horton also sent a letter that U.S. investigators were also aware of. No secrets were sold. Horton was court-martialed for making an unreported contact with a foreign embassy. His lawyer claimed that the sailor was merely working on a novel. He was sentenced to six years in prison.

Hospital

Russian slang for prison. See ILLNESS.

Houghton, Harry Frederick

(b. 1906 d. ?)

Royal Navy employee whose espionage for the Soviet Union was revealed by MICAL GOLIENEWSKI, a Polish INTELLIGENCE OFFICER who became a DEFECTOR.

Houghton joined the Royal Navy in 1937, served during World War II, and was discharged after the war as a chief master-at-arms. He then joined the civil service and in 1951 was posted to Warsaw as a clerk to the naval ATTACHÉ in the British Embassy. He dabbled in the black market and made enough untaxed extra income to live far beyond his clerk's pay.

After returning to Britain in Oct. 1952 he went to work in the highly sensitive Admiralty Underwater Weapons Establishment at Portland, Dorset. There Polish intelligence officers recruited him as a spy, and once

more he earned extra money, this time for giving the Poles information, which they passed on to their Soviet colleagues. When Houghton was transferred to a repair shop, where he had access to fewer secrets, his girlfriend, Ethel (Bunny) Gee, who also worked at the Navy station, obligingly got classified documents for him. Twice in 1956 he was reported as a security risk, and his ex-wife had told the security officers at Portland that Houghton regularly met a foreigner in London and had amassed a large amount of cash—the KGB gave Houghton a bonus of £400 in Dec. 1955 and again in Nov. 1956, and £500 in July 1957. Her suspicions were ignored.

Then, in the form of letters signed "Sniper," came Golienewski's revelations to the CIA. (Golienewski had not yet been identified.) Sniper claimed that the KGB had a spy in the British Admiralty. The CIA passed the information to the British Security Service (MI5), which found no one in the Admiralty but noted Houghton's service in Warsaw. In 1960 MI5 put him under SURVEILLANCE and noted that he met regularly with a man later identified by his espionage pseudonym—GORDON LONSDALE.

Lonsdale was trailed to a house occupied by Peter Kroger and his wife, Helen (also espionage pseudonyms; see MORRIS COHEN). In Jan. 1961 detectives of the SPECIAL BRANCH of Scotland Yard arrested Houghton, Gee, and Lonsdale as they met for a transfer of documents; the Krogers were also arrested.

The PORTLAND CASE, as it was called in the press, ended in March 1961 with the conviction of all five on espionage charges. MI5 turned down Houghton's offer to cooperate in exchange for leniency. Houghton and Gee received sentences of 15 years in prison; Lonsdale, 25 years; and the Krogers, 20 years each. Only Houghton and Gee completed their sentences; Lonsdale was exchanged in a SPY SWAP for GRENVILLE WYNNE in 1964, and the Krogers were exchanged for university lecturer Gerald Brooke in 1969.

Houghton and Gee were released in 1970 and were married in 1971. Houghton wrote an account of his espionage in *Operation Portland: The Autobiography of a Spy* (1972).

Lonsdale's CODE NAME for Houghton was "Shah."

House

Russian slang for THE CENTER, headquarters of Soviet espionage establishment. Also referred to as "Big House."

Howard, Edward Lee

(b. 1951 d. 2002)

Former CIA officer who defected to the Soviet Union in 1985 after being identified as a Soviet AGENT—possibly to deflect U.S. MOLE hunters away from ALDRICH H. AMES.

Howard was born in Alamogordo, N.M., near the site of the world's first atomic bomb test. His father was a U.S. Air Force missile specialist stationed at the nearby

Holloman Air Force Base. His mother was a descendant of a Hispanic-American family from New Mexico. He moved frequently, as his father was transferred from base to base in the United States and overseas. After graduating from the University of Texas in 1972, he worked for a time for Exxon Corp. in Ireland and then joined the Peace Corps, working in Colombia, where he met his future wife, also a Peace Corps volunteer.

After leaving the Peace Corps in 1975 he earned a master's degree in business administration and became a loan officer in Peru for the U.S. Agency for International Development. Back in the United States in 1979, he worked for an environmental firm in Chicago when the CIA contacted him in 1980, responding to an application that he had sent about a year before.

Howard spent a year as a "career trainee," including an 18-week course in TRADECRAFT at CAMP PEARY, a CIA training site in Virginia. He was then assigned to the Directorate of Operations, which runs the CIA's routine clandestine services. Howard accepted an offer to become an INTELLIGENCE OFFICER operating under diplomatic COVER out of the U.S. Embassy in Moscow. He would work as a CASE OFFICER, running Soviet nationals who were spying for the United States. His wife, Mary, hired to work in the same directorate, did secretarial assignments for the Deputy Director for Operations.

As part of a new personnel policy, Mary Howard was given training as a support worker who would aid her husband and other case officers in the embassy-based CIA operation in Moscow. She might, for example, act as a lookout or counter-SURVEILLANCE operative while her husband or another case officer serviced the Moscow DEAD DROPS. One of the Howards' trainers was MARTHA PETERSON, a CIA officer who had outwitted KGB watchers until they picked her up in 1977.

But Howard failed POLYGRAPH tests and was dropped by the CIA in May 1983.

According to the CIA, Howard used drugs, had an alcohol problem, and was a petty thief—he had once slipped money out of a woman's purse on an airliner in flight. The drug use showed up on his first routine polygraph test; the other aberrations appeared in later tests.

Howard got a job as an economic analyst with the New Mexico state legislature. He, Mary, and their newborn son moved to El Dorado, a subdivision south of Santa Fe. Howard continued to drink heavily and was arrested on Feb. 6, 1984, after a drunken brawl in which he fired a .44-caliber magnum revolver. He was put on probation for five years.

In Sept. 1984 Howard admitted that he had made a trip to Europe. According to the FBI, he had met with KGB officers in VIENNA and received money for information he provided. Presumably, that information had to do with what he had learned during his training and short tour in the CIA. Another possibility was that he hoped to provide information on the nearby LOS ALAMOS National Laboratory, a research center for nuclear weapons and "Star Wars" technology. He may also have intended to be a KGB support agent or COURIER for a spy

in the area. Howard's fluency in Spanish and his CIA background made him a good candidate for reporting on the CIA's Latin American operations centered on Santa Fe.

In March 1985 Howard and his wife made another trip to Europe, telling friends in Santa Fe that they were visiting Germany. In June 1985 Paul M. Stambaugh, a CIA officer under COVER as a second secretary in the U.S. Embassy in Moscow, was arrested, along with the Soviet agent he was to meet, A. G. TOLKACHEV, a Soviet missile and avionics expert. The arrests were not revealed at the time. Tolkachev was executed on Sept. 24, 1986, but his death was not announced until Oct. 22.

(Later, Tolkachev's betrayal would be blamed on Howard. But in Feb. 1994, after the arrest of Ames, a CIA COUNTERINTELLIGENCE officer, Tolkachev was made Ames's victim. Howard, in an interview with writer David Wise in 1991, insisted, "I didn't bust him." Ames said he had given his first information to the KGB in June 1985. Intelligence officials are now inclined to believe that both were responsible; Howard by giving broad information about Moscow ASSETS and Ames by specifically pointing out Tolkachev.)

Howard met with a former CIA employee in July 1985 and said that he had been giving information to the Soviets; word of that meeting reached the CIA, but no action seems to have resulted. A month later, VITALY YURCHENKO, a senior KGB officer who had defected in Rome, told CIA debriefers that a former CIA employee who had been assigned to Moscow had met with KGB officers in the fall of 1984 and had given up agency secrets about CIA spies in the Soviet Union. The CIA and FBI began looking for the mole, whose name Yurchenko claimed not to know.

The FBI, contacted by the CIA, put Howard under surveillance in Sept. 1985 and got authorization for wiretaps from the FOREIGN INTELLIGENCE SURVEILLANCE COURT. On Sept. 20 FBI agents confronted Howard, who feigned an interest in cooperating. The next day, Howard and his wife drove to Santa Fe, followed by an FBI surveillance team. At some point on the trip to and from the city, Howard jumped out of the car, his wife activating a crude version of a JACK IN THE BOX, a dummy. (See TRADECRAFT.)

On Sept. 23, the FBI obtained a warrant for Howard's arrest. By then he was on his way to Moscow via New York, Copenhagen, and Helsinki, where his EXFILTRATION was handled by KGB officers in the Soviet Embassy who put him in the trunk of an embassy car and crossed into the Soviet Union at Viborg.

The subsequent arrest of Michael Sellers, a second secretary at the U.S. Embassy in Moscow, and Eric Sites, military ATTACHÉ at the embassy, was attributed to Howard, as were the arrests of Stambaugh and Tolkachev. (The discovery in 1994 of Ames's treachery readjusted the who-betrayed-whom list, with some betrayals previously blamed on Howard now being attributed to Ames.)

Howard surfaced in Moscow in Aug. 1986, when the Soviet Union announced that it had given him political asylum for "humane considerations." He was granted Soviet citizenship. He later appeared on television, saying, "I love my country. I have never done anything that might harm my country."

Howard, in a self-serving book, *Safe House* (1995), claimed that he made a furtive return to the United States with a KGB-supplied fake passport, learned through a KGB source that the FBI had probably compromised his wife, and decided to return to Moscow, where he founded a consulting company for U.S. firms wishing to set up offices in Russia.

Howard died in Moscow on July 12, 2002, from a fall in his residence.

Hudson, Col. Duane T.

(b. 1910 d. 1995)

British INTELLIGENCE OFFICER who served in Yugoslavia during World War II. Hudson, a handsome, swashbuckling man, was one of the real models for JAMES BOND [F].

A graduate of the Royal School of Mines and a champion amateur boxer, Hudson in 1935 became manager of an antimony mine in Yugoslavia, where he became fluent in Serbo-Croatian. In 1936 he married a White Russian ballerina who had fled the Soviet Union. They later divorced.

Hudson was one of the first members of Section D of the Secret Intelligence Service (MI6). Section D, formed in 1938 as the Statistical Research Department of the War Office, was devoted to "ungentlemanly war." He joined soon after Britain went to war in Sept. 1939 and was assigned to Zagreb. Although Yugoslavia was neutral, pro-German Croats were working to prepare the way for a Nazi takeover. Hudson recruited saboteurs against ships of the Axis powers operating in Dalmatian ports.

When the Special Operations Executive (SOE) was formed to carry sabotage-and-espionage operations into Nazi-occupied Europe, Hudson was transferred to the SOE. He was landed by SUBMARINE off the coast of Montenegro in Sept. 1941 with orders to "discover who is fighting the enemy" and to "coordinate all elements of resistance."

Hudson tried to negotiate a settlement between the rival communist and anti-communist resistance groups. But he found himself caught in between, and for months he was on his own, living off the land and twice escaping from pro-German captors. Embroiled in the Yugoslavian civil war, Hudson tried in vain to persuade both sides to join in a common attack on the Germans.

In his final mission for the SOE, he commanded a British mission to aid the Home Army in Poland in the final months of World War II in Europe. The Soviet government, striving to crush the Home Army, had Hudson arrested by the NKVD and imprisoned him for a short time in Moscow's notorious LUBYANKA.

Huff-Duff

SEE HIGH-FREQUENCY/DIRECTION FINDING

Hugel, Max

(b. 1925)

Stockbroker and entrepreneur who, in a controversial appointment, briefly headed the Directorate of Operations at the CIA.

Hugel, a confidant of WILLIAM J. CASEY during their work on the 1980 Reagan presidential campaign, became Casey's special assistant when Casey took over as DIRECTOR OF CENTRAL INTELLIGENCE (DCI) in Jan. 1981. Chafing at that job, however, Hugel asked for more responsibilities. Casey made him Director of the Directorate of Operations (DDO), the most sensitive post in the CIA. As DDO, Hugel was in charge of the CIA's clandestine activities, including AGENTS and COVERT ACTION.

Three previous DCIs—ALLEN W. DULLES, RICHARD HELMS, and WILLIAM E. COLBY—had been DDO before attaining the top intelligence position. That was the caliber of DDOs, Hugel was reminded by critics in the media. "It's like putting a guy who is not an M.D. in charge of the cardiovascular unit of a major hospital," a former CIA officer told *The Washington Post*.

The Hugel appointment touched off a silent storm of protest within the CIA, especially in the ranks of the DDO. After Hugel was appointed, Richard F. Stolz, Jr., a veteran CIA officer who had run the Soviet Division, resigned. He had been in line for DDO. (Stolz was later made DDO by Casey's successor, WILLIAM H. WEBSTER.)

Brooklyn-born and rough-hewn, Hugel was given to lavender leisure suits and heavy gold chains. He was described as having had some experience in U.S. MILITARY INTELLIGENCE in the years following World War II, but details of his work were not made known in May 1981, when he was suddenly catapulted into the DDO post.

In July two brothers, Thomas R. and Samuel F. McNell, Jr., formerly business associates of Hugel, accused him of improper stock trading by providing them with insider information. Sixteen audiotapes of conversations between Hugel and the brothers were sent to the *Post*. On the tapes Hugel also threatened the brothers: "I'll cut your balls off. . . . I'll get my Korean gang after you . . ."

Hugel, while denying the accusations, resigned immediately after the *Post* published a story on the tapes, having let him and Casey listen to the tapes before publication. He remained active in Republican politics.

Hugger-Mugger

Term of unknown origin meaning secret or stealthy. It also means confused or disorderly, a description suitable for some intelligence operations.

Hughes, Capt. William H., Jr.

U.S. Air Force officer who had knowledge of highly classified communications programs. He mysteriously disappeared after being sent to the Netherlands. His fate is not publicly known, but he was classified as a deserter in 1983.

Hughes Glomar Explorer

Salvage ship built by the CIA specifically to lift the remains of the Soviet submarine *K-129*, a Golf-class ballistic missile submarine that sank in the mid-Pacific in 1968 after an internal explosion. This was the most ambitious deep-ocean location and salvage operation ever undertaken.

The ship was built under the cover name *Hughes Glomar Explorer*, ostensibly by eccentric millionaire Howard Hughes for seafloor mineral mining. The ship was launched in 1972 and completed the following year. She was manned by a crew specially selected by the CIA. The ship had a heavy lift system that included a grappling claw that could be attached clandestinely to the ship by a submersible barge (designated *HMB-1*). Reportedly, the barge would also have been used to hide the Soviet submarine had the entire 330-foot undersea craft been salvaged.

After the U.S. SUBMARINE *Halibut*, towing a seafloor camera for lengthy periods, located the sunken *K-129*, the *Glomar Explorer* arrived at the submarine lift site on July 4, 1974. During the month-long operation, it lifted the forward portion of the submarine from a depth of three miles in a clandestine operation given the code name JENNIFER. The submarine broke during the lift operation; the after portion of the submarine, containing two ballistic missiles with nuclear warheads, fell back to the seafloor.

The forward section was recovered. It contained torpedoes, including two with nuclear warheads, and other important equipment. The remains of the submarine were studied within the salvage ship, then cut apart and packaged for further analyses or jettisoned. The bodies of six sailors recovered from the salvaged section were buried at sea with military honors. (Ninety-eight men were lost in the sinking.)

A follow-on effort to recover the remainder of the submarine was planned but canceled following U.S. press revelations of the original salvage effort.

Following the operation, the ship was turned over to the Navy, renamed simply *Glomar Explorer*, and laid up in reserve at Suisun Bay, Calif. After several abortive efforts to lease the ship for use in commercial deep-sea drilling operations, in 1996 the ship was leased to a joint venture of Chevron, EEX, and Enterprise Corporations for deep-depth oil drilling. The ship was extensively converted during a 135-day yard period in the first half of 1997. In fall 1998 the ship achieved a world undersea drilling record of 7,718 feet.

The U.S. Navy retains ownership of the *Glomar Explorer*.

Human Intelligence

Intelligence derived from information collected by people, usually in a foreign territory; synonymous with spying.

Humphrey, Ronald L.

Official of the U.S. Information Agency (USIA) who provided classified material to a South Vietnamese working for the Vietnamese communists.

Humphrey was a career foreign service officer for the U.S. State Department, of which the USIA is a part. The FBI, while keeping a young Vietnamese under SURVEILLANCE in 1977, had linked him to Humphrey. The FBI had been watching David Truong, son of Truong Dinh Dzu, who had run as a peace candidate in South Vietnam against then President Nguyen Van Thieu in 1967 and had been jailed.

Deep-ocean salvage ship Hughes Glomar Explorer.

Spies can be anywhere: A World War II poster. (IMPERIAL WAR MUSEUM)

Truong had moved to the United States to attend Stanford University and in 1975 had founded the Vietnamese-American Reconciliation Center in Washington, D.C. He became an anti-war activist, a source of information on Vietnam for many members of Congress, and a friend of many influential officials, including WILLIAM E. COLBY, who was DIRECTOR OF CENTRAL INTELLIGENCE from Sept. 1973 to Jan. 1976.

An FBI tap on Truong's phone produced the Truong-Humphrey link. David Truong was passing intelligence to representatives of the Vietnamese communist government in Paris. But his COURIER, Dung Krall, the young Vietnamese-American wife of a U.S. naval officer, was actually a DOUBLE AGENT working for the CIA. The documents included U.S. reports on political, military, and intelligence matters in China, Ethiopia, Laos, Singapore, Thailand, and Vietnam.

Believing Humphrey to be the source of the documents, the FBI asked Attorney General Griffin B. Bell to authorize the secret installation of a closed-circuit television monitor in the USIA communications room, where Humphrey was a watch officer. Truong and Humphrey were arrested on Jan. 31, 1978.

Humphrey told the FBI that he had been supplying documents to Truong in the hope that Vietnamese authorities would release his common-law Vietnamese wife, with whom he had lived when he had been stationed in Vietnam. Truong said he had been working to try to improve relations between the United States and the new Socialist Republic of Vietnam.

Although evidence in the espionage cases against both men had been collected through warrantless surveillance, the Department of Justice decided to go to trial. Both men were convicted of espionage and sentenced to 15 years. On appeal, lawyers for the two men challenged the warrantless taps and searches that had produced the damning evidence. The appeals were unsuccessful, and in 1982 both men began serving their prison terms. However, the court challenges exposed the shaky legal grounds for electronic surveillance and highlighted the need for a new judicial process. Out of the case came the FOREIGN INTELLIGENCE SURVEILLANCE ACT and the FOREIGN INTELLIGENCE SURVEILLANCE COURT.

Hunt, E. Howard

(b. 1918)

INTELLIGENCE OFFICER and author.

Hunt was medically discharged from injuries after a fall while serving in the U.S. Navy aboard a destroyer during World War II. He then worked for a time as a war correspondent for *Life* magazine. After that, he enlisted in the U.S. Army and volunteered for the OFFICE OF STRATEGIC SERVICES (OSS), serving in China.

Hunt translated his Navy experiences into fiction in first novel, *East of Farewell* (1942). It was a fictionalized account of his service in the U.S. Navy on convoy duty in the North Atlantic. After the war, Hunt resumed writing novels and also tried his hand at screenwriting. Restless and intrigued by his life in the OSS, Hunt joined the agency's successor, the CIA, and served in the Balkans, the Far East, Guatemala, Mexico, and Uruguay.

In 1964, when RICHARD HELMS was DIRECTOR OF CENTRAL INTELLIGENCE (DCI), Hunt was asked to write a series of spy novels that his U.S. publisher hoped would be the American response to JAMES BOND [F]. Helms, like DCI ALLEN DULLES, believed that spy novels of the James Bond type helped to popularize an agency that could do little to publicize itself. Helms approved Hunt's moonlighting as a spy novelist, provided that each manuscript was submitted in advance for review. Hunt's intrepid AGENT was named Peter Ward.

Hunt wrote under the pseudonym David St. John, but the Library of Congress copyright card, available in any public library, also showed his real name. When the first book was published, Hunt later recounted, he was sent abroad and resigned from the CIA because his novels were "in a sense agency-inspired" and his work as a spy novelist might embarrass the agency. The CIA later took him on as what was described as a "contract agent."

Hunt injects tantalizing parallels to real-life espionage in his books. One, *The Berlin Ending* (1973), suggests that West German Chancellor Willy Brandt was a Soviet-controlled agent. (See GERMANY.) Another novel, *The Hargrave Deception* (1980), is based on the duel of wits between CIA COUNTERINTELLIGENCE chief JAMES JESUS ANGLETON and HAROLD (KIM) PHILBY. The fictional Soviet MOLE, Peyton James, like Angleton, is a fly-fisherman; the character based on Philby is an American, Roger Hargrave, educated at Oxford (Philby went to Cambridge). Hargrave defects to the Soviet Union but is really an American DOUBLE AGENT whose true identity is known only to James. The plot follows the bizarre line of reasoning of some CIA officers, diehard followers of Angleton, who believed that Angleton was actually running Philby.

When Anthony Masters, author of *Literary Agents* (1987), asked Hunt whether the exploits of the Peter Ward character in Hunt's spy novels were based on his own CIA experiences, Hunt "replied that he did not think that the agency would like him to be specific as to which books utilized actual experiences: 'I dealt more with the methodology of espionage than I did with actual cases.'" He also said that he did not care for the James Bond books because they looked as if they had been written by

> a poseur, by a well intentioned amateur and . . . my impression was that he was a sort of gofer or bag carrier for the then wartime director of Naval Intelligence. . . . Bond's adventures were, of course, preposterous. . . . They were tongue-in-cheek, they were pure entertainment, and by contrast in the Ward series I tried to stay very strictly with reality.

In his nonliterary life, Hunt ran the psychological and political aspects of the CIA effort to engineer a coup in Guatemala in the 1950s. Because Hunt was stationed in Mexico in 1963 and Lee Harvey Oswald was watched there by the CIA, Hunt is often a shady character in imagined conspiracies surrounding Oswald's assassination of President Kennedy.

Hunt was hired by the Nixon administration in 1971 as a member of a Special Investigation Unit known as the PLUMBERS. He was a key figure in the Plumbers' WATERGATE burglary and the break-in at the office of Daniel Ellsberg's former psychiatrist after publication of the PENTAGON PAPERS, which Ellsberg had stolen. For the latter BLACK BAG JOB the CIA outfitted Hunt with what could have been props for a character in a spy novel: a wig, a camera, false identification papers, and a speech-altering device.

For his illegal activities he was tried, convicted, and sentenced to eight years in prison and a fine of $10,000. He served 33 months.

Hush Most Secret

British World War II–era classification for highly sensitive material; a higher classification than MOST SECRET. Such material was transmitted only by hand and carried by an officer.

Huston Plan

Nixon administration blueprint for monitoring anti-war dissidents in the 1970s. Officially it was the "Domestic Intelligence Gathering Plan: Analysis and Strategy," but it became known as the Huston Plan after its principal architect.

Tom Charles Huston was a White House staffer whose duties included matters of DOMESTIC INTELLIGENCE. A lawyer who had served in U.S. ARMY INTELLIGENCE, Huston became convinced that the government had to monitor "foreign Communist support of revolutionary youth activities in this country." He was referring primarily to the anti-Vietnam demonstrations that began to plague the administration soon after President Nixon took office in 1969.

The Huston Plan was created in July 1970 after Nixon, at a meeting of leading officials of the INTELLIGENCE COMMUNITY, established the INTERAGENCY COMMITTEE ON INTELLIGENCE (AD HOC). Its chairman was J. EDGAR HOOVER, director of the FBI.

Huston got the plan approved by Nixon, outmaneuvering Hoover, who particularly did not want to use the FBI to resume surreptitious entry (BLACK BAG JOBS), which he had been prohibiting since 1966. Hoover told Attorney General John Mitchell that the FBI would not carry out such break-ins without specific written instructions from the President.

Mitchell convinced Nixon to withdraw the Huston Plan file days after it was approved. John Dean, who would later play a major role in the WATERGATE scandal, soon replaced Huston as the White House specialist in domestic intelligence.

Dean set up the INTELLIGENCE EVALUATION COMMITTEE to explore the possible use of some aspects of the discredited Huston Plan.

Hyde, H. Montgomery

(b. 1907 d. 1989)

British historian who served during World War II as an INTELLIGENCE OFFICER working for WILLIAM STEPHENSON and, subsequently, on the staff of Gen. Dwight D. Eisenhower.

Educated at Queen's University, Belfast, and Magdalen College, Oxford, Hyde entered the British Army's Intelligence Corps in 1940. He was the security officer attached to the British Secret Intelligence Service (MI6) in Bermuda when he and Stephenson began tracking down KURT LUDWIG, a major German AGENT.

Early in 1944 Hyde was posted to New York City to work with Stephenson, who ran BRITISH SECURITY COORDINATION (BSC), the British intelligence COVER organization that operated out of Room 3603 in Rockefeller Center. Later Hyde was assigned to Gen. Eisenhower's staff in Europe.

Hyde left the Army after the war with the rank of lieutenant colonel. He wrote more than 50 books, including a biography of Stephenson, *Room 3603* (1963),

first published in Britain as *The Quiet Canadian* (1962), and his own account of British intelligence, *Secret Intelligence Agent* (1982).

Hypo

Code name for U.S. Navy CRYPTANALYSIS station located at Pearl Harbor, Hawaii, from the late 1930s through World War II. When the Japanese attacked Pearl Harbor on Dec. 7, 1941, the Hypo station was commanded by Comdr. JOSEPH ROCHEFORT; he served in that position from June 1941 until Oct. 1942, when he was relieved by Capt. William B. Groggins, who commanded Hypo through the end of the war.

Hypo—for Hawaii—was the phonetic word for the letter *H* in military communications at the time. Hypo was generally known as FLEET RADIO UNIT PACIFIC (FRUPAC) during the war.

Ic

Designation of an INTELLIGENCE OFFICER on a staff at various levels of the German Army during World War II.

IC

SEE INTELLIGENCE COMMUNITY

Ichthyic

U.S. CODE NAME for planned intelligence collection activities by the U.S. Navy spy ships *Banner* and PUEBLO off the coasts of North Korea and Soviet Siberia during 1968. The program was canceled after the capture of the *Pueblo* by North Koreans on Jan. 23, 1968.

Idealist

The BYEMAN CODE NAME for the American U-2 spyplane.

Ignatiev, Semyon Denisovich

(b. 1904 d. 1983)

Head of the MGB, Soviet Ministry of State Security, from 1951 to 1953.

A party apparatchik working for the Central Committee, Ignatiev took control of the MGB in Dec. 1951. He replaced Col. Gen. VIKTOR ABAKUMOV, a protégé of LAVRENTY BERIA. Abakumov was purged from the post by Josef Stalin, apparently as a means of limiting Beria's power. Subsequently, Ignatiev had a leading role in the alleged "Doctor's Plot" against Stalin in 1952–1953, which was used to rationalize a new wave of purges, par-

ticularly against the Jewish intelligentsia. This was the most anti-Semitic endeavor in the history of the Soviet intelligence ORGANS.

Within 24 hours of Stalin's death, on March 5, 1953, Beria merged the MGB into an enlarged Ministry of Internal Affairs (MVD), which took on the functions of state security and foreign intelligence. On March 7, Ignatiev was dismissed by Beria from the now defunct MGB, but he was neither arrested nor executed, an early indication of the massive changes being made in the Soviet leadership. Some historians, including Robert Conquest, chronicler of the Stalinist purges, believe that Nikita Khrushchev protected Ignatiev.

Ignatiev was transferred to the Communist Party secretariat, but he was subsequently fired and exiled to a provincial post. He died of natural causes, a most unusual ending for the chief of a Soviet intelligence service.

Ilichev, Lt. Gen. Ivan Ivanovich

Chief of the GRU, Soviet MILITARY INTELLIGENCE, in 1942–1943. Although some reports contend that he was executed during the war, he served after World War II, from June 1953 to July 1955, as the high commissioner of the Soviet zone of Austria.

Little more is known about his career.

Illegal

Soviet INTELLIGENCE OFFICER performing intelligence work in a foreign country while passing himself off as a foreigner and not as a Soviet citizen. The illegal's main job is to recruit AGENTS who will penetrate secret TARGETS. A transiting illegal is called "an artist on tour."

Illegal Agent

An AGENT who is operated either by an ILLEGAL RESIDENT or directly by the headquarters of a foreign intelligence service.

Illegal Net

An intelligence-collection operation or a unit with multiple AGENTS operating under the control of an ILLEGAL RESIDENT.

Illegal Operation

Activities conducted by INTELLIGENCE OFFICERS or AGENTS under the direction of a RESIDENT or an intelligence agency's headquarters.

Illness

Russian slang for someone under arrest. See HOSPITAL.

Imagery Intelligence

(IMINT)

Intelligence derived from visual photography, infrared sensors, lasers, electro-optics, and radar sensors. The latter includes synthetic aperture radar wherein images of objects are reproduced optically or electronically on film, electronic display devices, or other media.

Indispensables

Former Nazi intelligence and COUNTERINTELLIGENCE experts taken into the GEHLEN ORGANIZATION after its establishment in West Germany in 1947. Those ex-Nazis also worked for Dr. OTTO JOHN, head of the BFV, the West German counterintelligence agency.

The Gehlen organization and BfV were ostensibly established to operate against Soviet and East German (communist) activities. In reality the Indispensables operated mainly against right-wing political groups.

Industrial Espionage

Commercial spying, primarily to gain advantages not obtainable easily or legitimately. On the private level, commercial firms have long spied on competitors. But since the 1980s the term has come to mean state-sponsored spying by one nation against the industrial and commercial interests of another.

Unlike ECONOMIC INTELLIGENCE, which relies heavily on OPEN SOURCE efforts, industrial espionage involves illegal activities, just as traditional intelligence collection does. In recent years there appears to have been a significant increase in this form of espionage. (See CHINA, FRANCE.)

Since 1994 a little-known organization, the NATIONAL COUNTERINTELLIGENCE CENTER (NACIC), has coordinated what the United States knows about industrial espionage against U.S. firms or technologies. The NACIC distributes reports on that intelligence to selected U.S. corporations.

Within the United States the CIA monitors foreign intelligence activities targeted against U.S. economic and industrial interests. Potentially criminal information gathered by the CIA outside the United States—such as state-supported unfair trading practices or bribery of contractors—is turned over to the FBI. Informally and unofficially, the CIA alerts targeted U.S. companies.

The State Department's Overseas Security Advisory Council (OSAC), which in the 1990s was running an electronic bulletin board for exchanging information between the U.S. government and the U.S. private sector, changed its emphasis after Sept. 11, 2001. The OSAC began to provide its 2,300 registered "constituents" with such issues as "business and legal challenges in Russia," the "increasing threat to maritime interests in Sub-Saharan Africa," and the vulnerability of "soft targets" to terrorist attacks. The OSAC gives its constituents annual briefings, often delivered by the Secretary of State. In 2002, for example, Secretary Colin L. Powell talked about "carjackings in South Africa, unrest in Argentina, and tensions between India and Pakistan," as examples of what the OSAC "helped guide the way through."

The NSA, whose global eavesdropping activities are highly classified, sometimes discovers evidence of industrial espionage. This sometimes results in SANITIZED "FBI threat notifications" that the FBI may pass on to potentially targeted firms.

The NSA's ECHELON project, a worldwide surveillance network, has inspired allegations by European companies that eavesdropping, aimed at gathering TERRORIST INTELLIGENCE, is also being used to commit industrial espionage. And, inside the U.S. business community, there are frequent charges of spying. In 2003, for example, Lockheed sued Boeing, charging that Boeing had used industrial espionage to secure a lucrative rocket contract. Boeing apologized for the unethical conduct of some employees but insisted that the company maintained high ethical standards.

Although the FBI may suspect, or even confirm, the involvement of a foreign power, it focuses only on those incidents that can produce a criminal case. Such cases are rare and usually involve traditional espionage methods. In the 1980s the FBI said that the KGB and Eastern Bloc countries were not only using traditional methods of recruitment to develop industrial spies but were also setting up dummy firms and using false licenses to acquire manufacturing equipment they were legally unable to import. A case did emerge from this espionage (see WILLIAM H. BELL), but in later years the United States has depended far more on spreading information than in trying to make court cases.

In 1994, for example, the CIA learned that a French company was offering bribes to Brazilian officials controlling a $1.4 billion telecommunication project. The U.S. government informed Brazil, and a U.S. company, matching the legitimate French bid, won the contract.

The seriousness of the problem was underscored in 1995 with the passage of a U.S. law that required the President to report to the Congress on foreign industrial espionage that makes U.S. industry intelligence TARGETS. The law defined foreign industrial espionage as "industrial espionage conducted by a foreign government or by a foreign company with direct assistance of a foreign government against a private United States company and aimed at obtaining commercial secrets."

SILICON VALLEY, Calif., the highest concentration of computer-technology industry in the United States, has been a major target of industrial spies. In Jan. 2003 Chinese businessman Qing Chang Jiang, president and sole U.S. employee of EHI Group USA Inc./Araj Electronics, was arrested for allegedly shipping three microwave amplifiers to China. They could be used to improve the quality of long-distance telephone calls—or to make intercontinental ballistic missiles more accurate.

Jiang was at least the fourth Chinese native indicted since Oct. 2002 on charges involving the shipment of equipment or trade secrets to China from Silicon Valley. U.S. prosecutors said that Jiang, a Chinese citizen, shipped the amplifiers without a license to a company in Shijianzhuang, China, that shares its address with the 54th Research Institute, a Chinese military agency. Prosecutors alleged that Jiang shipped the amplifiers for use by the Chinese military. Most exports to the military agency are outlawed. (Jiang had lived in the United States legally since 1995; he had a wife and son in China.)

SPYING ON FRIENDS

Traditional allies in the Cold War are not allies in the technological wars. France, Israel, and Japan have been named as operating major intelligence-collection efforts against U.S. industries. The CIA estimated in 1987 that 80 percent of Japan's intelligence resources are directed toward U.S. industry. The FBI reported in 1992 that French intelligence was "operating against" IBM and Texas Instruments. In 1992 Recon/Optical, a suburban Chicago military contractor, accused Israel of trying to steal plans for an airborne spy camera. The Israelis settled the case out of court, reportedly for $3 million in damages.

In 1993 the CIA warned U.S. aircraft companies to beware of spying at the annual Paris Air Show, which has since become less attractive to U.S. firms. Hughes Aircraft pulled out of the 1993 show after being warned that it would be a target of French intelligence. Also targeted were Boeing, General Dynamics, Lockheed Martin, Northrop Grumman, and other leading U.S. aerospace contractors. According to the CIA, U.S. financial institutions and the LOS ALAMOS National Laboratory were additional targets.

Defending French industrial spying, a French intelligence official was quoted in news accounts as saying that modern espionage "is essentially economic, scientific, technological and financial." By some estimates, 80 percent of French intelligence gathering involves open sources, such as trade journals and computer databases. The other 20 percent, critics say, comes from bribery, infiltration of industrial spies, and BLACK BAG JOBS into company offices and COMPUTER ESPIONAGE.

The U.S. campaign against French spying apparently inspired a French counterattack. Early in 1995 France accused a CIA INTELLIGENCE OFFICER of trying to obtain unpublished government information from a French official. The official did provide her with the information, believing that she represented an American foundation interested in the world economy. When someone else became suspicious, French intelligence put her under SURVEILLANCE and later reported that she was seen giving money for unauthorized financial information. When France complained to the U.S. Embassy, Ambassador Pamela Harriman could honestly say that she knew nothing about the incident. The CIA officer was under NON-OFFICIAL COVER, meaning that she was not connected with the embassy.

France made the most of the incident, demanding that the United States recall her and four others accused of espionage. She did return to the United States, but there was no U.S. admission of guilt.

Adm. STANSFIELD TURNER, who was DIRECTOR OF CENTRAL INTELLIGENCE (DCI) from March 1977 to Jan. 1981, spoke more bluntly about industrial espionage than any DCI before or since: "We steal secrets for our military preparedness. I don't see why we shouldn't stay economically competitive." He did not say "steal for economic reasons," but the implication was clearly there.

While Turner was DCI, the CIA routinely sponsored briefings at the Commerce Department for executives of U.S. corporations. They heard about foreign developments in such areas as semiconductors and aircraft technology. At one briefing, executives with interests in major electric power projects were briefed on what the CIA knew about China's plans to build hydroelectric plants.

When Turner was succeeded as DCI by WILLIAM J. CASEY, a Reagan appointee, speculation grew as to whether specific foreign firms engaging in trade practices considered unfair by U.S. corporations would be targeted. No such specific targeting is ever known to have taken place. Casey, however, encouraged what a former aide called an "informal" relationship between the CIA and U.S. industry. Such a relationship went on throughout the Cold War, when the Pentagon routinely passed to defense contractors SCIENTIFIC AND TECHNICAL INTELLIGENCE, including highly secret information from the Argonne, Lawrence Livermore, Oak Ridge, and Los Alamos national laboratories.

Casey's successor, ROBERT M. GATES, vigorously fought off attempts to add industrial espionage to the CIA's missions. He summed up his reaction by recounting what he said an agent told him: "Mr. Gates, I'm prepared to give my life for my country but not for a company."

R. JAMES WOOLSEY, the first DCI under President Clinton, insisted that the CIA would not engage in industrial espionage. But in Dec. 1993, Woolsey said that the CIA was working to find out "who in foreign countries is bribing who else in order to get contracts that American companies are losing." The French exposure of the CIA officer happened shortly before Woolsey was succeeded by JOHN M. DEUTCH, who became DCI in May 1995. Deutch shied away from any open discussion of industrial espionage or economic intelligence. DCI GEORGE TENET reiterated the policy in 2000. While admitting that SIGNALS INTELLIGENCE did provide economic information to the U.S. government, he said that the NSA is "just not in the business of conducting industrial espionage."

SECRETARIES AND STUDENTS

A 1995 White House report on industrial espionage said that recruiters from unnamed countries were looking for material from secretaries, computer operators, technicians, and maintenance workers. Such workers "frequently have good, if not the best, access to competitive information," the report said. "In addition, their lower pay and rank may provide fertile ground for manipulation by an intelligence agency." Sometimes industrial spies break into an office and, tipped off by an insider, steal a certain laptop or set of disks, knowing that they contain targeted information.

Some countries export students trained as spies. China has a technical college that Western intelligence agencies describe as a school for industrial espionage. Students get scientific and technical training to prepare for trips, supposedly as students, to the United States, Britain, France, Germany, and Japan. During a tour of a French photographic firm, Chinese students were seen dipping their ties into chemicals to acquire a sample of the chemicals.

In at least one country (unnamed in the White House report), students can evade military service by traveling to more advanced countries as spies. As graduate students they offer to serve as assistants at no cost to professors doing research in a field targeted for spying by the student's country.

Experts and consultants with ties to Western manufacturers are recruited, sometimes not subtly. "Do you have advanced/privileged information of any type of project/contract that is going to be carried out in your country?" asked an advertisement published in the *Asian Wall Street Journal* in 1991. "We hold commission/agency agreements with many large European companies and could introduce them to your project/contract. Any commission received would be shared with yourselves." The ad included a phone number in Western Europe. U.S. intelligence officials pointed to the ad as a bold invitation to industrial espionage.

Industrial Security Manual

(ISM)

SEE NATIONAL INDUSTRIAL SECURITY PROGRAM

Infiltration

The placement of an AGENT in a TARGET area, group, or organization. Such an infiltration into a foreign country may be overt, as when an agent under COVER legally visits or immigrates to a country, or clandestine, as when an agent sneaks across a border or is brought into a country by SUBMARINE or small boat.

Information Bureau

SEE BUREAU OF INFORMATION

Informer

Person who provides information or intelligence; he or she may do so wittingly or unwittingly.

Infrared Intelligence

(IRINT)

Intelligence derived from infrared sensors. In modern times a subset of IMAGERY INTELLIGENCE.

Inman, Adm. Bobby Ray

(b. 1931)

Successively the U.S. DIRECTOR OF NAVAL INTELLIGENCE (DNI), Director of the NSA, and the Deputy DIRECTOR OF CENTRAL INTELLIGENCE (DCI).

A graduate of the University of Texas, Inman entered the Navy in 1951 and served in surface warships before becoming an intelligence specialist. He became DNI in Oct. 1974 with the rank of captain, being promoted to rear admiral in July 1975. A year later Inman became a vice director of the NSA, and in July 1977 he was appointed director of the NSA with the rank of vice admiral. He served in that position until Feb. 1981, when he became the Deputy DCI.

In Feb. 1981, Inman became the first U.S. Navy INTELLIGENCE OFFICER to be promoted to the rank of full admiral. (The only other naval intelligence officer to attain four-star rank is WILLIAM O. STUDEMAN, who became Deputy DCI in 1992, having also previously served as Director of the NSA.) Inman held the deputy director position for 14 months, until his retirement from the Navy in July 1982. Reportedly, he left the intelligence position because of personality conflicts with DCI WILLIAM CASEY. He then briefly served as an unpaid adviser to the House Committee on Intelligence but quickly quit, claiming that the Democratic-controlled committee was politically partisan.

Inman subsequently served in senior positions in the business world. On Dec. 16, 1993, President Clinton announced his intention to nominate Inman to be his Secretary of Defense, but Inman publicly withdrew his nomination on Jan. 18, 1994, declaring that he would not take the position because of continued attacks on him by newspaper columnists (Senate confirmation was assured). He would have been only the second career military officer to hold the top Defense post, the first having been Gen. of the Army George C. Marshall in 1950–1951.

INR

SEE BUREAU OF INTELLIGENCE AND RESEARCH

INSCOM

SEE ARMY INTELLIGENCE AND SECURITY COMMAND

Integrated Operational Intelligence Center

(IOIC)

U.S. Navy facility installed in large aircraft carriers from 1962 to 1979 to provide rapid processing and analysis of multi-sensor RECONNAISSANCE data and other TACTICAL INTELLIGENCE collected by the RA-5C aircraft (see A3J VIGILANTE).

The IOIC could produce photographic prints of TARGET areas within 10 minutes of an aircraft's return to a carrier. The IOIC could also handle ELECTRONIC INTELLIGENCE and INFRARED INTELLIGENCE. The RA-5C tested the use of motion picture photography of target areas, but it was not adopted for that aircraft.

When the RA-5C systems worked they produced the best photographic and other tactical intelligence available. However, the RA-5C was a sophisticated aircraft that was difficult to maintain, and several were shot down in flights over North Vietnam during the Vietnam War.

Intel Puke

Derogatory term used within the U.S. military services for an INTELLIGENCE OFFICER or any intelligence specialist. The word "puke" is used for any specialty—such as "supply puke" or "communications puke."

Intelligence and Warning

(I&W)

Intelligence activities intended to detect and report time-sensitive intelligence information that could relate to a direct threat to a country or its allies. I&W includes forewarning of enemy actions or intentions; the imminence of hostilities or insurgency or terrorist action; or hostile action against RECONNAISSANCE operations.

Also see STRATEGIC INTELLIGENCE.

Intelligence Appreciation

British term for an INTELLIGENCE ESTIMATE—an assessment relating to a specific subject or area, intended to describe the subject or area and to identify potential courses of action open to an enemy and the probability of their being used.

Intelligence Collection Ships

Surface ships—and in the 20th and 21st centuries SUBMARINES—have been used extensively for intelligence collection. In World War II the warships of major navies began carrying HIGH-FREQUENCY DIRECTION FINDING (HF/DF) equipment and, subsequently, ELECTRONIC INTELLIGENCE (ELINT) collection equipment. Every naval ship and submarine is a de facto intelligence collection ship as it observes and reports information on foreign navies, merchant shipping, ports, and other subjects.

SOVIET UNION

Specialized "spy" ships were initiated in the 1950s when the Soviet Union employed modified trawler-type ships to collect intelligence in overseas areas and to observe Western naval operations. The former requirement was due to the lack of Soviet overseas electronic listening posts (except for embassies and consulates), in contrast to the ring of U.S. intelligence installations that were being installed in Allied and some neutral countries around the Soviet Union.

Although often depicted in the Western press as "disguised" fishing trawlers, the Soviet intelligence collection ships were readily identifiable. All were Navy manned and were fitted with extensive electronic antennas, and some were armed. However, Soviet fishing craft, as well as merchant ships, undoubtedly collected intelligence as opportunities permitted. But most Soviet intelligence ships—designated AGI by Western intelligence—were built on trawler hulls because the latter's large, insulated cargo holds were readily adaptable to electronic equipment bays and crew berthing spaces. Trawler hulls also provided long endurance, had good seakeeping qualities, and were in series production.

The later and larger Soviet (now Russian) AGIs were designed specifically for intelligence collection. The large ships of the *Primor'ye* class (3,700 tons, 278 feet) and *Bal'zam* class (5,400 tons, 346 feet) were capable of on-board intelligence processing as well as collection, thus accelerating the delivery of intelligence data to fleet and regional commanders. The larger Soviet AGIs have light anti-aircraft guns and many have been observed with shoulder-fired anti-aircraft missile launchers.

By the late 1980s—just before the demise of the Soviet regime—some 60 of these ships were being operated by the Soviet Navy. Those AGIs normally kept watch off the U.S. strategic submarine base at Holy Loch, Scotland, and off the southeastern coast of the United States—a position enabling surveillance of submarine bases at Charleston, S.C., and Kings Bay, Ga., and the missile activity off Cape Canaveral, Fla. The AGIs also operated in important international waterways, such as the Strait of Gibraltar, the Sicilian Straits, and the Strait of Hormuz, and AGIs regularly kept watch on exercises by warships of the U.S. Navy and other NORTH ATLANTIC TREATY ORGANIZATION fleets. During the Vietnam War a Soviet AGI off the island of Guam and another operating near U.S. carriers in the Gulf of Tonkin are believed to have provided some warning of U.S. air strikes to the North Vietnamese.

Soviet surface warships also conducted surveillance of Western naval forces at sea. Those Soviet ships and AGIs that engaged in close trailing operations were generally referred to as "tattletales." The USSR also made wide use of submarines for intelligence collection.

UNITED STATES

In the post–World War II period the U.S. Navy relied on aircraft, both carrier- and land-based as well as surface warships and submarines, for intelligence collection. Two U.S. destroyers engaged in electronic collection off the coast of North Vietnam in 1964 led to the so-called Gulf of Tonkin incident, which escalated U.S. participation in Vietnam. (See DESOTO.)

The first specialized U.S. intelligence collection ships were acquired to compensate for the lack of electronic listening posts in South America and Africa. Those were World War II–era cargo ships converted after 1960, when the NSA was authorized to acquire ELINT ships to TARGET Third World countries.

The Soviet intelligence collection ship Gidrofon *watching a U.S. aircraft carrier in the Gulf of Tonkin in 1969, during the Vietnam War. Soviet AGIs were not disguised fishing ships and were easily identified by their mass of antennas, naval pennant numbers, and navy crews.* (U.S. NAVY)

The first NSA conversion was the *Pvt. Jose F. Valdez* (T-AG 169), which deployed in Nov. 1961, operating for the next 10 years off the coasts of Africa carrying out ELINT missions with the COVER of "extended hydrographic survey cruise." The *Valdez* was followed by two other NSA-sponsored conversions, the *James E. Robinson* (T-AG 170) and *Sgt. Joseph E. Muller* (T-AG 171). These ships were operated by civilian merchant crews and NSA technicians, the T-AG designation indicating civilian-manned (T), miscellaneous auxiliary (AG) ships.

Simultaneously, the U.S. Navy entered into intelligence collection in collaboration with the NSA. A series of ELINT ships was converted from wartime cargo ships and manned by Navy and Marine personnel from the NAVAL SECURITY GROUP that would collect against both NSA and Navy targets. The first Navy-operated ship was the *Oxford* (AG 159), built as a cargo ship in 1945. According to the U.S. Naval Historical Center's *Dictionary of American Naval Fighting Ships* (1970), she was placed in Navy commission on July 8, 1961 to conduct research "not only in electromagnetic reception, but also in oceanography and related areas."

During the fall of 1962 the *Oxford* operated in the Caribbean, intercepting radio communications from Cuba as the Soviet Union moved troops and weapons onto the island. The *Oxford* was redesignated AGTR, indicating miscellaneous auxiliary (AG) technical research (TR). Four similar conversions of large cargo ships followed: the *Georgetown* (AGTR 2), *Jamestown* (AGTR 3), *Belmont* (AGTR 4), and *LIBERTY* (AGTR 5). These ships were manned by Navy personnel but operated under the aegis of the NSA with some civilian specialists on board. They were easily recognized as intelligence ships because of their operations, antenna arrays, and comments in naval reference books about them. The ships carried a minimal armament of machine guns and small arms.

The *Georgetown* operated primarily off South America; the *Jamestown* operated off Africa, in the Caribbean, and in the South China Sea; the *Belmont* remained in the Caribbean (supporting the American troop landing in the Dominican Republic); and the *Liberty* was dispatched to the eastern Mediterranean, to meet her fate off the coast of Sinai in June 1967.

The Navy, the Department of Defense, and the NSA subsequently considered a fleet of smaller cargo or even trawler-type ships for the ELINT role. These ships were intended to operate closer to "target" areas than were the larger AGTR conversions. The initial AGERs were three small (176-foot) cargo ships that were converted for the ELINT role in the mid-1960s, the first being the *Banner*, designated AGER 1. Those letters indicated miscellaneous auxiliary (AG) environmental research (ER).

The *Banner*, operating out of Yokosuka, Japan, began ELINT collection against Soviet Siberia, North Korea, and China in 1967 under the CODE NAME CLICK-BEETLE. On occasion the ship was harassed by Soviet naval ships.

The *Banner* was followed to the Far East in late 1967 by her sister ship *PUEBLO* (AGER 2), with a third ship, the *Palm Beach* (AGER 3), also being placed in commission for ELINT operations in another area. Like the AGTRs, these ships carried a minimal armament of machine guns and small arms.

Additional AGER conversions were planned, but the U.S. passive ELINT ship program was abandoned after the Israeli air and torpedo boat attacks on the *Liberty* in 1967 and the capture of the *Pueblo* by North Korea in Jan. 1968.

Also see SUBMARINES.

Intelligence Commando

SEE 30TH ASSAULT UNIT

Intelligence Community

(IC)

The term *Intelligence Community* refers to the aggregate of those parties of the U.S. executive branch that conduct the various intelligence activities that make up the total national intelligence effort. The DIRECTOR OF CENTRAL INTELLIGENCE (DCI) is head of the U.S. Intelligence Community as well as de facto head of the CIA; under the DCI's direction, the Deputy DCI for Community Management oversees the cordination of community activities.

In addition to the CIA, the Intelligence Community comprises:

> AIR FORCE INTELLIGENCE
> ARMY INTELLIGENCE
> DEFENSE INTELLIGENCE AGENCY
> Department of Energy
> Department of HOMELAND SECURITY
> Department of State
> Department of Treasury
> Federal Bureau of Investigation (FBI)
> Marine Corps Intelligence
> National Geospatial Intelligence Agency
> NATIONAL RECONNAISSANCE OFFICE
> National Security Agency (NSA)
> NAVAL INTELLIGENCE

as well as the intelligence elements of the Department of the Treasury, the Department of Energy, the Drug Enforcement Administration, and staff elements of the Office of the Director of Central Intelligence. The DIA, NRO, NSA, and four military intelligence services are components of the Department of Defense. The FBI, restricted by law to police activities only within the United States, is mandated by federal authority as the "lead" or principal agency for COUNTERESPIONAGE operations.

Intelligence Community Staff

(ICS)

Special staff of the U.S. DIRECTOR OF CENTRAL INTELLIGENCE (DCI), providing support for his role as head of

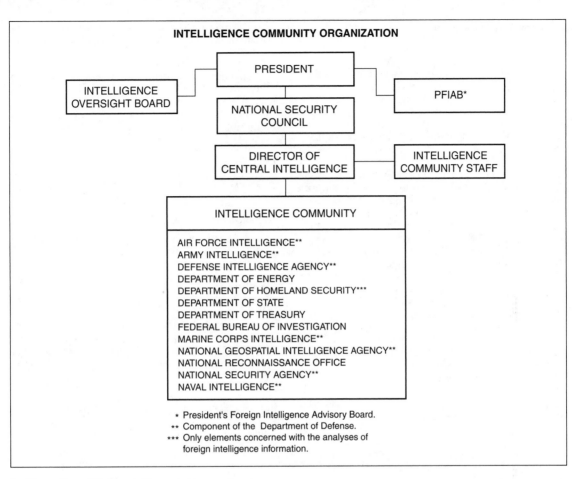

INTELLIGENCE COMMUNITY ORGANIZATION

PRESIDENT

INTELLIGENCE OVERSIGHT BOARD

PFIAB*

NATIONAL SECURITY COUNCIL

DIRECTOR OF CENTRAL INTELLIGENCE

INTELLIGENCE COMMUNITY STAFF

INTELLIGENCE COMMUNITY

AIR FORCE INTELLIGENCE**
ARMY INTELLIGENCE**
DEFENSE INTELLIGENCE AGENCY**
DEPARTMENT OF ENERGY
DEPARTMENT OF HOMELAND SECURITY***
DEPARTMENT OF STATE
DEPARTMENT OF TREASURY
FEDERAL BUREAU OF INVESTIGATION
MARINE CORPS INTELLIGENCE**
NATIONAL GEOSPATIAL INTELLIGENCE AGENCY**
NATIONAL RECONNAISSANCE OFFICE
NATIONAL SECURITY AGENCY**
NAVAL INTELLIGENCE**

* President's Foreign Intelligence Advisory Board.
** Component of the Department of Defense.
*** Only elements concerned with the analyses of foreign intelligence information.

Intelligence Community Organization

the INTELLIGENCE COMMUNITY, and therefore separate from the internal staff of the CIA.

The head of the ICS has long been a three-star military officer (vice admiral or lieutenant general). However, in 1996 the Congress established the position of Deputy DCI for Community Management, who oversees the ICS.

Intelligence Cycle

The processes by which information is acquired and converted into intelligence and made available to customers. There are usually five steps in the cycle:

Planning and direction: determining intelligence requirements, preparing a collection plan, issuing orders and requests for information collection, and checking on the productivity of collection entities.

Collection: acquiring information and providing this for processing and/or production activities.

Processing: converting collected information into a form more suitable for the production of intelligence;

this could include translations or reformatting computer data.

Production: converting information into finished intelligence through the integration, analysis, evaluation, and interpretation of all available data and the preparation of intelligence products in support of customer requirements.

Dissemination: distributing intelligence to customers.

Intelligence Estimate

The appraisal of available intelligence relating to a specific situation or condition for the purpose of determining the courses of action available to an enemy or potential enemy.

Intelligence Officer

Professional member of an intelligence organization; he or she may be in the military or a civilian with specialized intelligence training.

Intelligence Oversight

A major factor in U.S. intelligence organization and activities since World War II. The National Security Act of July 26, 1947, as amended, provides for intelligence oversight of the CIA, whose duties are defined "under the direction of the National Security Council. . . ." Thus, the CIA is accountable to the President of the United States through the NATIONAL SECURITY COUNCIL.

Subsequently, additional oversight agencies have been established, the most influential probably being the PRESIDENT'S FOREIGN INTELLIGENCE ADVISORY BOARD (PFIAB), set up by President Eisenhower in 1956 as the President's Board of Consultants on Foreign Intelligence activities. The members are distinguished citizens with experience in business, international relations, and intelligence. Beyond the PFIAB, there is an Intelligence Oversight Board, established by President Carter in 1978, composed of three members appointed by the President. This group reviews questions of legality and propriety concerning the U.S. INTELLIGENCE COMMUNITY. The board is chaired by a member of the PFIAB, ensuring close ties between the two groups.

In addition, the Office of Management and Budget (OMB) provides fiscal and management oversight of issues related to the Intelligence Community. (The OMB was established within the executive branch in 1970.)

Congress also oversees U.S. intelligence activities through special committees. Two examples are the CHURCH COMMITTEE and PIKE COMMITTEE, which investigated allegations of wrongdoing by the CIA and NSA. Subsequently, the Senate established the Senate Select Committee on Intelligence on May 19, 1976, and the House set up the House Permanent Select Committee on Intelligence on July 14, 1977. Certain CIA-sponsored programs, as well as intelligence activities of the military services, Department of State, and the FBI are regularly reviewed by specific standing committees, as well as by appropriate committees in both houses of Congress.

Intelligence Preparation of the Battlefield
(IPB)

Term that gained currency with the U.S. Army in the 1980s to indicate a systematic integration of information on the enemy, weather, and terrain to provide the basis for situation development, target value analysis, intelligence collection, RECONNAISSANCE and SURVEILLANCE planning, and battlefield decision-making.

Army Field Manual FM 34-130, *Intelligence Preparation of the Battlefield* (1994), begins

> IPB is the best process we have for understanding the battlefield and the options it presents to friendly and threat forces. . . . IPB is a systematic, continuous process of analyzing the threat and environment in a specific geographic area. It is designed to support staff estimates and military decision making. Applying the IPB process helps the commander

selectively apply and maximize his combat power at critical points in time and space on the battlefield. . . .

According to an Army lesson plan on the subject, "IPB provides a mode that ensures uniformity in how intelligence personnel within each echelon of command are to analyze environment and evaluate the effects of each on threat and friendly courses of action."

Intelligence Process

SEE INTELLIGENCE CYCLE

Intelligence Producer

Intelligence agency or staff that participates in the production stage of the INTELLIGENCE CYCLE.

Intelligence Requirement
(IR)

A subject—general or specific—on which intelligence is required. In U.S. usage, also the intelligence report developed on a specific subject. A list of IRs is often issued by senior planners for implementation by intelligence agencies.

Interception of Oral Communication

Euphemism for employing a BUG to overhear conversations.

Interdepartmental Intelligence

U.S. term for the synthesis of intelligence collected by various agencies and departments that is required by agencies and departments for the performance of their missions. Such intelligence transcends the exclusive needs or intelligence production capabilities of a single department or agency.

International Spy Museum

A MUSEUM and study center dedicated to the history of espionage. Located in downtown Washington, D.C., it is the largest publicly accessible facility of its kind.

The museum was opened on July 17, 2002.

Internet

Worldwide computer network (sometimes called the World Wide Web) that has numerous sites providing information on U.S. intelligence agencies and intelligence in general.

Begun as a means of transmitting U.S. military information, the Internet has become a system for transmitting nearly every kind of information imaginable. U.S. intelligence agencies, like other government entities, have joined the Internet, giving millions of computer users the chance to get intelligence information—all, of course, unclassified.

The Internet evolved in the 1970s out of an effort to connect a U.S. Department of Defense Advanced Research Projects Agency (ARPA) computer network (the ARPAnet) with other government and academic networks involved with ARPA. The ARPAnet itself was an experimental network, originally designed to support government research.

ARPAnet enabled all computer subscribers in the system to be equally capable of sending and receiving messages (electronic mail)—a departure from hierarchical computer network systems. As a byproduct of this design, the Net could route message traffic around any damaged or destroyed nodes in the event of a disaster. The Internet evolved from that concept.

Today the public can access Internet intelligence sites on the World Wide Web by using the Web site addresses given here. (Addresses may change without notice, but new addresses can usually be found by searching with key words, such as "espionage" or "CIA." Note also that many (though not all) addresses are case sensitive, that is, "CIA" and "cia" are not necessarily equivalent.)

The CIA and other U.S. intelligence organizations have decided to use the Internet as a public communications tool. It is a testament to the openness of U.S. society that virtually all intelligence agencies maintain a presence on the Internet. At the CIA Internet site, visited some 120,000 times a week, there is a "CIAWEB" offering a virtual tour of CIA headquarters, biographies of DIRECTORS OF CENTRAL INTELLIGENCE and their deputies, historical information about the agency, the latest edition of the CIA's *World Factbook*, maps, and a bibliography of books on intelligence, including Norman Polmar and Thomas B. Allen's *Merchants of Treason* (1988) and *Spy Book*.

Swedish hackers broke into the CIA home page in Sept. 1996, changing the greeting to "Welcome to the Central Stupidity Agency." After that, CIA home page put up this message:

You are entering an Official United States Government System, which may be used only for authorized purposes. Unauthorized modification of any information stored on this system may result in criminal prosecution. The Government may monitor and audit the usage of this system, and all persons are hereby notified that use of this system constitutes consent to such monitoring and auditing.

China and Cuba have drastically curbed Internet use as a means of restricting public access to certain Web sites.

Most intelligence agencies have their own secret computer networks, sealed off from the outside world by security programs, that include a parallel and classified version of the World Wide Web, intended for uses as various as the delivery of intelligence photos and the distribution of information to diplomats (see COMPUTER ESPIONAGE).

Canada's Royal Commission on Espionage
www.rcespionage.com
CIA
www.cia.gov
COUNTERINTELLIGENCE
www.cicentre.com
DEFENSE INTELLIGENCE AGENCY
www.dia.mil
Defense and International Security Literature (UK)
www.mpr.co.uk/scripts/sweb.dll/li_home
Espionage Cases 1975–1999
www.dss.mil/training/espionage/index.htm
Espionage cases and information from Federation of American Scientists
www.fas.org
FBI FREEDOM OF INFORMATION ACT Electronic Reading Room: Declassified FBI files on famous spy cases, including ANTHONY BLUNT, GUY BURGESS, DONALD MACLEAN, HAROLD (KIM) PHILBY, and JULIUS ROSENBERG
www.foia.fbi.gov/spies.htm
GRU (Soviet Military Intelligence)
www.fas.org/irp/world/russia/gru
Homeland Security
www.whitehouse.gov/homeland
Israeli Defense Forces
www.idf.il
MI5
www.mi5.gov.uk
NATIONAL COUNTERINTELLIGENCE CENTER
www.nacic.gov
NATIONAL IMAGERY AND MAPPING AGENCY (NIMA). Provides access to products that can be released to the public.
www.geoengine.nima.mil.
NATIONAL RECONNAISANCE OFFICE
www.nro.gov
NSA (National Security Agency)
www.nsa.gov
NKVD "crimes and victims"
www.nkvd.org
Russian Federation's defense-related agencies
199.221.15.210/rusmil
Russian Foreign Policy and Security Watch
www.rferl.org/securitywatch
Russian security and intelligence organizations, from the OPRICHNINA of Ivan the Terrible to present.
www.industrialsecurityservices.com/soviet_intel.pdf
Terrorism (UK)
www.homeoffice.gov.uk/terrorism
UK documents declassified by Public Record Office
www.pro.gov.uk
VENONA
www.nsa.gov/docs/venona
Intrepid
SEE WILLIAM STEPHENSON

Invisible Ink

SEE SECRET WRITING

IOIC

SEE INTEGRATED OPERATIONAL INTELLIGENCE CENTER

IPB

SEE INTELLIGENCE PREPARATION OF THE BATTLEFIELD

IR

SEE INTELLIGENCE REQUIREMENT

Iran-Contra Affair

A complex, illegal scheme to free American hostages held in Lebanon by selling arms to Iran and then diverting the money from the sale to support the Nicaraguan anti-Sandinista Contras.

The scheme was conceived by Marine Lt. Col. Oliver North, assistant deputy director for political-military affairs on the NATIONAL SECURITY COUNCIL (NSC), with the help of Vice Adm. John Poindexter, President Reagan's national security adviser, and WILLIAM J. CASEY, who, as DIRECTOR OF CENTRAL INTELLIGENCE (DCI), was a member of Reagan's cabinet. Several active and former CIA officers, including a future DCI, ROBERT GATES, were drawn into the swirl of investigations that followed the disclosure of these highly secret operations.

The roots of the Iran-Contra Affair go back first to Nov. 1979, when the United States imposed an embargo on arms shipments to Iran, and then to Sept. 1983, when President Reagan signed a secret directive authorizing COVERT ACTION in Nicaragua to overthrow the Sandinistas, members of a left-wing Nicaraguan political group, the Sandinista National Liberation Front (FSLN). The group took its name from Augusto Cesar Sandino, a former revolutionary leader. In 1979, launching attacks from Costa Rica and Honduras, the FSLN brought down the regime of Anastasio Somoza Debayle and set up a left-wing junta that nationalized industries. Right-wing opposition forces, known as the Contras, were covertly financed by the United States.

In 1981 the CIA began advising the House and Senate intelligence oversight committees that it was funding the Contras. This led to the passage, on Sept. 27, 1982, of a classified section of the intelligence authorization bill that specifically prohibited the CIA from using its funds for "the purpose of overthrowing the government of Nicaragua." On Dec. 21, Congress passed the Boland Amendment, named after Rep. Edward P. Boland, chairman of the House Intelligence Committee; it substantially stated publicly what had been classified. When it became apparent that the administration was still supporting the Contras, a second amendment, known as Boland II, even more explicitly prohibited the funding of a government overthrow in Nicaragua.

That was the legal situation when President Reagan met with his senior advisers on June 25, 1984, to discuss ways to fund the Contras while still abiding by the congressional restraints. Casey suggested funding the Contras through other countries. (Robert C. McFarlane, Reagan's national security adviser, had already begun soliciting contributions from other countries.) Later, funds were solicited from American private citizens.

About that time North recruited former U.S. Air Force Maj. Gen. Richard V. Secord, who had shadowy CIA connections (see EDWIN P. WILSON). Secord formed a partnership, called "The Enterprise," with Albert Hakim, an Iranian expatriate, setting up a web of offshore bank accounts, shell corporations for arms procurement, and other entities to provide North with a framework for the scheme.

In the spring of 1985 the first arms purchased through The Enterprise reached the Contras. In May, Michael Ledeen, a consultant to the NSC, drew Israel into the scheme when he learned from Israelis that the Iranians wanted American TOW (Tube-launched, Optically tracked, wire-guided) missiles. Arrangements were made for Israel to handle the sales. The Reagan administration believed that all American hostages would be released after the shipment of arms from Israel reached Iran in Aug.–Sept. 1985. Then McFarlane was told that only one hostage could be returned and he had to choose. Asked, in his words, "to play God," he chose WILLIAM BUCKLEY, the kidnapped CIA station chief in Beirut. When the Iranians refused McFarlane—without telling him that Buckley was already dead—he chose the Reverend Benjamin Weir.

The middleman for the hostage-arms swap was Manucher Ghorbanifar, who flunked a CIA-administered POLYGRAPH test, resulting in an agency "BURN notice." CIA official CLAIR GEORGE, Deputy Director of Operations at that time, later admitted that it was the third time the CIA had "sent a notice around the world that the individual that we are speaking about should not be dealt with because he's dishonest and untruthful." As for Secord, George said, he "was an individual with whom I would not do business." Soon George realized he was "not playing with the whole deck," because Casey had shifted the scheme out of the CIA and into the hands of North; essentially Casey became North's CASE OFFICER.

Ghorbanifar's name appeared in news reports again in 2003. Newspapers, in stories apparently stemming from Pentagon LEAKS, reported that Defense officials met with him during talks in Paris over the future of Iran. The meetings, set up by a Defense Department intelligence entity known as the Near East, South Asia and Special Plans Office, reportedly focused on regime change in Iran.

While hundreds of TOW missiles and spare parts for Hawk missiles flowed to Iran, Reagan denounced Iran publicly. On July 8, 1985 he called Iran part of a "confederation of terrorist states . . . a new international version of Murder Inc. America will never make concessions to terrorists." In Dec. 1985, when Poindexter succeeded McFarlane as national security adviser, he gave Reagan a covert action "finding" that retroactively approved the sending of missiles to Iran in exchange for hostages.

North now had the operation running smoothly. In Jan. 1986 he obtained KL-43 encryption devices from the NSA to distribute among his group so that they would have secure communication (see KW SERIES). On April 4, in a report to Poindexter, North indicated that profits from the Iranian arms sales would be diverted to the Contras. On Oct. 5, a plane piloted by Eugene Hasenfus was shot down in Nicaragua. Hasenfus, captured by the Contras, said that he was working for the CIA.

Four days later, as a congressional storm broke over the apparent violations of the Boland Amendments at the White House, W. Robert Pearson, NSC deputy executive secretary and deputy general counsel at the NSC, sent an e-mail message to Poindexter, recommending that two issues be emphasized: "Administration support for democratic resistance remains unchanged, and NSC has done nothing beyond the law with respect to any activities in Central America, and in particular has had no connection whatever with the downed plane or Hasenfus."

Next, a Lebanese newspaper revealed the arms sales. The scheme was beginning to unravel. Casey and North talked about a "fall-guy plan," with Poindexter possibly having to be "a fall guy." On Nov. 13, in an address to the nation, President Reagan said, "We did not—repeat—did not trade weapons or anything else for hostages nor will we." Over the next few days Poindexter and North began shredding documents and erasing e-mail files, not realizing that backup files existed.

DISCLOSURE AND AFTERMATH

Ordered by President Reagan to investigate the arms sales, Attorney General Edwin Meese disclosed on Nov. 25, 1986, that money derived from selling weapons to Iran had been diverted to the Contras. Reagan stated that he had no previous knowledge of the diversion.

In reaction, the House and Senate created a select committee to determine whether any laws had been broken and whether new laws were needed. Reagan appointed a special board, chaired by former Senator John Tower, whose report provided a foundation for the select committee. But it was the committee's public hearings, with their parade of witnesses, that laid bare the Iran-Contra Affair. And lengthy as those hearings were, they did not reveal all that could have been disclosed.

"Many questions were not asked or could not be answered," wrote Republican Senator William S. Cohen and Democratic Senator George J. Mitchell, both of whom served on the committee. In their jointly authored book, *Men of Zeal* (1988), they continued,

Although the Committee scrutinized more than three hundred thousand documents, others, some crucial, were reduced to confetti in shredding machines or to ashes in burn bags. Many of the more than five hundred witnesses . . . appeared to offer candid testimony, but others suffered from curious cases of accommodating amnesia. . . . Top officials were in flat contradiction on key facts. Some were lying, others merely mistaken.

The select committee filed two reports on Nov. 19, 1987, one by a bipartisan majority of 15 Democrats and three Republican senators, the other by six House Republicans and two Republican senators. The majority report summed up the affair:

The Iran initiative succeeded only in replacing three American hostages with another three, arming Iran with 2,004 TOWs and more than two hundred vital spare parts for HAWK missile batteries, improperly generating funds for the Contras and other covert activities (although far less than North believed), producing profits for the Hakim-Secord Enterprise that in fact belonged to U.S. taxpayers, leading certain NSC and CIA personnel to deceive representatives of their own government, undermining U.S. credibility in the eyes of the world, damaging relations between the Executive and the Congress, and engaging the President in one of the worst credibility crises of any administration in U.S. history.

A special counsel, acting independently of and in conflict with Congress, investigated possible crimes. In March 1988 North, Poindexter, Secord, and Hakim were indicted on multiple counts that included conspiracy to defraud the United States, theft of government property, obstruction of justice, wire fraud, false statements, and the destruction and removal of documents.

North, who retired from active duty after being indicted, was convicted of obstructing Congress, unlawfully mutilating government documents, and taking an illegal gratuity (a home security fence). During North's trial federal judge Gerard A. Gesell criticized "an absurd situation in which the press is accurately reporting information in the public domain while the court is confronted with representations that the same facts must never be officially acknowledged." He had discovered that a SANITIZED memorandum that the prosecution introduced in his court had been offered as evidence in a civil court action without having been sanitized.

North was sentenced to two years' probation and fined $150,000. A federal appeals court set aside two convictions and dismissed the third on procedural points. Poindexter was convicted of lying to Congress, obstructing congressional investigators, and conspiring to cover up the arms sale and diversion of funds. His convictions were also set aside.

McFarlane, who had attempted to kill himself in Feb. 1987, pleaded guilty to five misdemeanor counts of withholding information from Congress. Secord pleaded guilty to lying to congressional investigators and was sentenced to two years' probation. Hakim pleaded guilty to the misdemeanor of providing an illegal gratuity (North's security fence). Sentenced to two years' probation and fined $5,000, he also agreed to give up any claim to the $7.3 million earned in the arms sales.

Carl R. Channell, who raised funds from conservative donors, pleaded guilty to tax fraud and was sentenced to two years' probation. Richard R. Miller, a public relations executive, was sentenced to two years' probation and 120 hours of community service for conspiring to supply the Contras with military equipment paid for by tax-deductible contributions. Clair George was found guilty of lying to Congress. He was pardoned by President GEORGE H. W. BUSH, whose own involvement in the Iran-Contra Affair remained elusive. Cohen and Mitchell concluded that Bush certainly knew about the weapons sale. "I went along with it," he said in an interview with CBS News anchor Dan Rather. Bush did so, the two senators concluded, "either out of loyalty to the President or because he, too, was consumed by the passion to obtain the freedom of the hostages."

Iraq

A country carved out of the fallen Ottoman Empire after World War I. Iraq in 1920 became a League of Nations mandate territory (under Britain) and it was declared an independent kingdom in 1932.

Iraq became a TARGET of the U.S. INTELLIGENCE COMMUNITY soon after Saddam Hussein came to power in 1968 when he led a revolt that made the Ba'ath Party (formally the Ba'ath Arab Socialist Party) Iraq's only political organization. In 1979 Saddam deposed the president and took over Iraq, establishing his rule with a complex network of secret police organizations.

He also established nuclear, chemical, and biological weapons programs, and used poison gas against dissident groups in his own country. On June 7, 1981, Israeli aircraft bombed Iraq's Osirak nuclear facility, near Baghdad, to prevent Saddam from creating nuclear weapons. Israeli planners may have used U.S. SATELLITE photographs provided by JONATHAN POLLARD.

Saddam led Iraq into an inconclusive eight-year war (1980–88) against Iran following the revolt in that country against American-backed Shah Mohammed Reza Pahlavi. The United States provided technical and possibly intelligence assistance to Saddam during that conflict.

After Iraq invaded Kuwait in 1990, a U.S.-led UNITED NATIONS coalition attacked Iraq in the Gulf War of Jan.–Feb. 1991 (Operation Desert Storm). Following the coalition's liberation of Kuwait and invasion of Iraq, the UN Security Council required Iraq to dispose of all weapons of mass destruction and long-range missiles, and to permit UN verification inspections. For a brief period those inspections were supported by U-2 spyplanes, which provided UN inspectors with aerial photography of suspected arms facilities.

To prevent the Iraqi use of air support to suppress internal dissidents, the U.S.-led allies established "no fly zones" in northern and southern Iraq. Those zones provided a means for U.S. AIRCRAFT to maintain almost continued RECONNAISSANCE of the country to supplement satellites in that role.

Continued Iraqi noncompliance with UN arms resolutions led to President George W. Bush's decision to wage a preemptive war to prevent Iraq from using weapons of mass destruction. Bush ordered an invasion of Iraq in March 2003 (Operation Iraqi Freedom). Some 250,000 American soldiers and Marines were augmented by troops from a coalition of nations, including 45,000 from Britain and small contingents from several other nations. The massive coalition attack was overwhelming, rapid, and decisive.

A unit headed by a CIA INTELLIGENCE OFFICER, the 1,400-member Iraq Survey Group, searched for weapons of mass destruction, but had not found any by mid-2004, and many of the group's analysts and other specialists were detailed to intelligence activities tracking down information about insurgents attacking occupation troops.

Ba'athists and others began a guerrilla war against the coalition troops, using car bombs, rockets attacks, and ambushes. Red Cross and UN activities were also attacked in the indiscriminate killing. Military and civilian intelligence operatives took on a new mission: seeking insurgent cells and developing information to forestall attacks. Elements of Iraq's former intelligence services were recruited to aid the occupation forces.

U.S. ARMY INTELLIGENCE had the principal role in the capture of Saddam on Dec. 13, 2003. He was found in a "spider hole" on a farm in Adwar, near Tikrit. Army Lt. Angela Santana and Cpl. Harold Engstrom developed a complex chart—nicknamed "Mongo Link"—that showed links between some 300 tribal and family sources and Saddam. Their work in the 104th Military Intelligence Battalion, assigned to support the 4th Infantry Division, was a stellar example of real-time information delivered directly to troops in the field: the 600 soldiers and SPECIAL OPERATIONS FORCES raided the farm complex where Saddam was hiding within 11 hours of the relevant information being acquired.

Secretary of Defense Donald Rumsfeld gave to the CIA the primary responsibility for the interrogation of Saddam and control of information produced by the interrogation. But DEFENSE INTELLIGENCE AGENCY officers also participated in the interrogation.

Ironbark

U.S. classification for secret Soviet documents obtained by GRU Col. OLEG PENKOVSKY for U.S. and British intelligence.

ISM

INDUSTRIAL SECURITY MANUAL

SEE NATIONAL INDUSTRIAL SECURITY PROGRAM

Israel

A U.S. INTELLIGENCE OFFICER, rating intelligence agencies, once said that the United States, Britain, and the Soviet Union—in that order—did the best intelligence collection. "But if I were in a dark alley and scared," he added, "I would call on Israel's MOSSAD. . . . They are really tough cookies."

That has been the essence of Israel's intelligence agencies since the beginning: tough, dedicated to the survival of their nation, and possessing a power unknown in most democracies. In Israel's War of Independence (1948), the new nation repulsed assaults by Arab states not only by force of arms but also by an intelligence system that predated the founding of the state.

Before the birth of Israel, Palestine, as a mandate of the League of Nations under British administration, became a magnet for Jews fleeing Nazi persecution. The flood of Jewish immigrants drastically changed the social fabric of Palestine. In 1919 there were 65,300 Jews in the territory; by 1936 the number had risen to 400,000, representing 28.5 percent of Palestine's population. The British straddled the issue of Jewish immigration, trying to cut it back while simultaneously using Jewish units to maintain order.

In 1940 the British Special Operations Executive (SOE) formed an all-Jewish commando unit made up of volunteers drawn from the Haganah, the underground Jewish defense force. Many of the commandos had been in a special Haganah unit called the Palmach ("strike company"), organized to fight as guerrillas if the Germans invaded Palestine. The Haganah evolved into an underground Jewish army with an intelligence branch called SHAI, for Sherut Yediot (information service).

With AGENTS scattered throughout the British establishment in Palestine, Shai thus became the first Israeli intelligence agency, for it already existed when Israel became an independent nation on May 14, 1948. Shai was abolished in July 1948 with the establishment of a MILITARY INTELLIGENCE service, the AMAN, and a domestic security service, the SHIN BET.

There was also the Aliyah Bet, which had been established in 1937 by the Haganah to help Jews immigrate illegally from "hostile areas" after the British imposed drastic immigration restrictions. This was in many respects an intelligence agency. After statehood, drawing on intelligence provided by other agencies as well as its own sources in those countries, Aliyah Bet was highly successful in bringing hundreds of thousands of Jews to Israel from the Soviet Union and Arab countries by overt as well as clandestine means.

For the intelligence services, scandal came quickly. ISSER BEERI, the first chief of Aman, was court-martialed for incidents involving the torture and execution of men suspected of traitorous acts. ISSER HAREL took over as Israel's spy chief, although he was titularly in charge only of Shin Bet. Later, MEIR AMIT, as head of Aman, steered away from the adventures of the early days toward a professionalism that soon put Israel's security agencies in the same league with those of the United States, Britain, and France.

In 1951, however, when Israel's intelligence organizations were in disarray, the coordinator of secret intelligence within the Foreign Ministry came back from a trip to the United States with news about the new American CIA. He suggested to Prime Minister David Ben-Gurion that a similar agency, answerable only to the Prime Minister, be established in Israel. Out of that recommendation came the Mossad Letafkidim Meyuchadim, the Central Institute for Intelligence and Special Duties—the MOSSAD. Israel's vaunted Mossad became the agency that could do anything: kidnapping, assassination, rescue of hostages, and collection of secret information. Mossad agents are backed up by the Sayeret Matkal, the General Reconnaissance Unit, a secret Army unit. Ad hoc intelligence groups were set up for special operations.

Next to be formed was the Defense Ministry's Science Liaison Bureau, secretly referred to as LAKAM (an acronym of its Hebrew letters). It was set up in 1957 so secretly that even the top Israeli intelligence officer, Isser Harel, did not know it had been established. Its prime original purpose was the security of Israel's development of nuclear weapons.

Israel's intelligence agencies were highly effective in many other countries. Sometimes it was their own agents that garnered wanted intelligence, at other times foreign military officers whom they had trained, or foreign government agencies that wanted Israeli assistance, often covert, in the military, economic, or even agricultural sector. This plethora of agents and "friends" provided Israel with invaluable intelligence; one Israeli source in the Soviet Union was said to have provided the Israelis with a copy of Nikita Khrushchev's highly secret report to the 20th Communist Party Congress in Moscow in 1956 at which he denounced Josef Stalin. The report was promptly passed to the CIA. (There was later speculation that the source was the KGB, acting under Khrushchev's orders.)

WARS FOR SURVIVAL

In 1956, as Israel joined with Britain and France in planning the abortive British-French strike to seize the Suez Canal from Egypt, Israeli intelligence could take some highly qualified credit. It had been an Aman NETWORK set up in Egypt in 1954 that had been the harbinger of the 1956 action. The Aman scheme was to have its agents attack British and U.S. property in Egypt, discrediting President Gamal Abdel Nasser, who had made nationalization of the Suez Canal one of his priorities.

But the Aman project had been a disaster. After U.S. Information Service libraries were bombed in July 1954, Egyptian COUNTERINTELLIGENCE discovered and widely publicized the Israeli plot. In Israel and the United States it was Aman that had been discredited (see AVRAHAM DAR).

When Nasser nationalized the canal in 1956, however, Britain and France were eager to work with Israel, respecting its ability to penetrate Egypt. The war rapidly ended through a cease-fire arranged by the UNITED NATIONS, strongly endorsed by the United States and the Soviet Union. During the Suez operation, amid official U.S. condemnation of the invasion, the CIA gave the Mossad some support, thanks primarily to JAMES JESUS ANGLETON, chief of CIA counterintelligence and ex officio head of Israeli affairs within the CIA.

Israel also established long-term ties with British intelligence. Britain's Secret Intelligence Service (MI6) sent a veteran officer, Nicholas Elliott, to Tel Aviv as a liaison. He overcame Mossad suspicions of the British by mingling with Israeli officers. One day he went swimming in the nude with senior Mossad officers. One of the Israelis, seeing he was circumcised, said, "My God, your Service thinks of everything!"

A great Israeli intelligence triumph came early in the morning of June 6, 1967, when intelligence monitors intercepted a radio-telephone conversation between Nasser in Cairo and King Hussein of Jordan in Amman planning a plot to accuse the United States and Britain of planning to send aircraft to assist Israel in what became known as the Six Day War. The incident showed the audacity of Israeli intelligence, which revealed major secrets—the Arab leaders' carelessness and the successful eavesdropping.

Israel's stunning victory in the Six Day War of 1967 was marked by the mistaken Israeli attack on the LIBERTY, a U.S. INTELLIGENCE COLLECTION SHIP steaming off the Sinai coast. Angry U.S. defense officials blamed trigger-happy Israelis for the attack, in which 34 Americans were killed and 171 wounded. Despite the *Liberty* tragedy, CIA officials saw the war as another example of the proficiency of Israeli intelligence. That was not so, however, in the Yom Kippur War in 1973, when Egypt and Syria launched a successful surprise attack against Israel.

In Sept. 1973 Israeli intelligence reported that Syria was placing anti-aircraft missiles near the Israeli border and that Egypt was moving troops toward the Suez Canal. Soviet-provided anti-aircraft missiles were also appearing in Egyptian armored units. Radio monitors picked up Egyptian appeals for blood donors, a civil defense mobilization, and orders to black out cities. On Oct. 4, Soviet advisers left Egypt and Syria. A Mossad agent in Egypt reportedly arrived back in Israel with actual plans for the attack. Aman officers, who had the responsibility for warning of war, were later said to have dismissed the attack plans as DISINFORMATION.

The signs of approaching war simply did not fit into Aman preconceptions, signs that were in part an excellent Egyptian DECEPTION effort. There was also fear that if Israel started a mobilization and there was no war, Israeli society would be disrupted. There had been false alarms and "cry wolf" warnings in the recent past.

At 3 A.M. on Oct. 6, Yom Kippur—the holiest day of the Jewish calendar—the head of Aman finally decided that an attack was imminent. It came at 2:05 P.M. and it was devastating. In the first hours of the war the Egyptians successfully crossed the Suez Canal and smashed through the thin Israeli defenses on the eastern bank, and thrust into the Sinai.

In the search for culpability that followed Israel's hard-won victory in 1973, the AGRANAT COMMISSION, established in the wake of the war, focused the blame on Aman. The Mossad thus lost little of its stellar reputation from the Yom Kippur War. In the aftermath of the war, Prime Minister Golda Meir and chief of staff Moshe Dayan resigned.

"Israel's intelligence and security services are among the best in the world," according to a secret evaluation by the CIA in the 1970s. "Their expert personnel and sophisticated techniques have made them highly effective, and they have demonstrated outstanding ability to organize, screen and evaluate information obtained from recruited agents, Jewish communities, and other sources throughout the world." (The report was among the shredded documents pieced together and made public by Iranians who took over the U.S. Embassy in Tehran in 1979.)

The Mossad's exploits include the 1960 capture of Nazi war criminal Adolf Eichmann in Argentina with Shin Bet help, the tracking down and killing of the Black September terrorists who murdered 11 Israeli athletes at the 1972 Munich Olympics, and the rescue of kidnapped passengers at Entebbe Airport in Uganda in 1976, a joint operation with the Israeli Army and Air Force. (See MIKE HARARI.)

AN ERA OF UNENDING TROUBLES

In 1985 Lakam was in operational control of the recruitment and running of an American spy, JONATHAN POLLARD. The Pollard case incensed American officials, many of whom had been well aware of earlier Israeli espionage against the United States. The cases rarely made headlines, and few became publicly known until that of Pollard, who did tremendous harm to U.S.-Israeli relations and split the Jewish community in the United States. There were some strange links to the Pollard case. In 1965, the Nuclear Materials and Equipment Corp. (NUMEC) of Apollo, Pa., admitted to federal authorities that the company could not account for 200 pounds of highly enriched uranium. Experts estimated that at least six nuclear weapons could be made from the lost uranium. An investigation turned up incriminating evidence tying NUMEC to Israeli ownership. One of the Israelis linked to NUMEC was RAFAEL EITAN. A legendary intelligence officer, Eitan had run Pollard through Lakam, which ostensibly was disbanded after the arrest of Pollard.

In March 1978, Stephen D. Bryen, a member of the Senate Foreign Relations Committee staff, met with a group of Israeli officials in the coffee shop of a Washington, D.C. hotel. Michael Saba, a representative of the National Association of Arab Americans, said that he sat by chance at an adjacent table. Saba later swore in an affidavit that he had overheard Bryen say, "I have the Pentagon document on the bases, which you are welcome to see." The remark, investigators said, referred to a report on bases in Saudi Arabia. Bryen, who denied providing Israelis with classified materials, was, at the time of the Pollard arrest, a Deputy Undersecretary of Defense, overseeing the export of defense-related U.S. technology.

The same 1979 CIA report that praised Israeli intelligence said that Shin Bet "tried to penetrate the U.S. Consulate General in Jerusalem through a clerical employee who was having an affair with a Jerusalem girl. They rigged a fake abortion case against the employee in an unsuccessful attempt to recruit him. Before this attempt at blackmail, they had tried to get the Israeli girl to elicit information from her boyfriend." The report told of several wiretaps and hidden microphones in U.S. offices and residences in Israel, as well as "two or three crude attempts to recruit Marine guards for monetary reward."

Israel has enjoyed a long-standing special understanding with the U.S. INTELLIGENCE COMMUNITY. The understanding is that Israel gets whatever is needed to help in its defense. Essentially, this has meant routine access to photographs and other intelligence data obtained by U.S. SATELLITES.

But the relationship has been seriously damaged at least twice: in 1981, when Israel successfully bombed an Iraqi nuclear reactor being readied to produce nuclear weapons, and in 1985, when Pollard was unmasked as an Israeli spy. According to Adm. BOBBY RAY INMAN, the Deputy DIRECTOR OF CENTRAL INTELLIGENCE at the time of the Iraqi raid, Israel was able to bomb the reactor because it had obtained intelligence that was not provided under the understanding between the two countries. Inman made the revelation in 1994 (as he was withdrawing his nomination for Secretary of Defense): "I looked at the distance on the map from Israel to Baghdad, and thought, I wonder how and where they got the targeting material?" He said he learned that in the previous six months Israel had drawn not only on information about Baghdad but also about Pakistan and Libya. Inman ordered that Israel's access be limited to areas within 250 miles of its borders; beyond that, special permission would have to be obtained. WILLIAM J. CASEY, the Director of Central Intelligence, later upheld the decision, Inman said. (Ironically, U.S. Army Gen. Norman Schwarzkopf, after the Gulf War of 1991, sent a note of thanks to the Israeli prime minister, saying that if the Iraqi reactor had not been bombed 10 years earlier the U.S. troops fighting in Iraq might have faced nuclear weapons.)

While many have criticized U.S. assistance to Israel as a one-way deal, in reality the U.S. Intelligence Community has benefited greatly from the Israelis. Some benefits have been political, like the Khrushchev speech denouncing Stalin, but most have been military: Every Israeli victory over its Arab neighbors brought a bounty of Soviet weapons and other equipment, often the latest. After these were minutely examined by the Israelis, their reports—and sometimes the hardware—were passed on to the United States.

Among the more spectacular noncombat intelligence successes were the planting of a spy, ELIAHU COHEN, in the highest levels of Syrian society; having an advanced MiG-21 fighter flown to Israel in 1966 by a Mossad-induced Syrian DEFECTOR while providing safe passage out of Syria for his family; collecting some 200,000 technical documents on the Mirage aircraft from Swiss engineer ALFRED FRAUENKNECHT; and stealing an entire Soviet P-12 radar installation from Egyptian territory in 1969, lifting it out by helicopter in a daring night operation. Those were intelligence coups of the first order, and the results of most were shared with Israel's American colleagues.

But Israeli intelligence has also been marked by monumental failures, including penetration by Soviet spies (see WOLFF GOLDSTEIN and SHIMON LEVINSON) and even by an agent in the pay of the United States (see YOSSI AMIT). Even the super-sleuth agency *Lakam* failed to prevent MORDECHAI VANUNU from revealing details of the Israeli atomic bomb program.

In the 1980s, wrote Dan Raviv and Yossi Melman in *Every Spy a Prince* (1991), "Israeli citizens lost much of their confidence in their secret services. Instead of assuming that they could sleep safely at night because the Mossad, Shin Bet, and Aman were protecting them, Israelis tossed and turned because of profound doubts about the intelligence community." The historians of Israeli's intelligence agencies quoted Gen. Shlomo Gazit, former chief of military intelligence, as saying that professionalism has been slipping "in both the advisory and operational levels of the security services."

AGAINST THEIR NEIGHBORS

In the 1980s popular and political support for the Mossad and Shin Bet declined in the wake of accusations that intelligence operatives had tortured and killed alleged Palestinian terrorists. To combat the *intifada*—the Palestinian revolt against Israeli occupation of the West Bank and Gaza—clandestine Israeli military units, with the CODE NAMES Cherry and Samson, donned kaffiyehs and, speaking Arabic, stalked Palestinians.

The image of Israeli intelligence suffered another blow on Sept. 25, 1997, when Mossad agents failed in an attempt to poison Khaled Meshal, the chief of the political bureau of the militant Islamic group *Hamas*. The assassination attempt came shortly after suicide bombers had exploded bombs in crowded Jerusalem streets.

Two men carrying Canadian passports attacked Meshal outside his office in Amman, Jordan, and injected a toxic substance into his left ear. The would-be assassins were arrested, and King Hussein of Jordan reportedly asked President Bill Clinton to obtain information on the poison. Meshal was near death. Shortly thereafter, Israeli Prime Minister Binyamin Netanyahu agreed to provide the antidote for the poison in return for the release of the Mossad agents.

The sophisticated methods and successful agents used by Israel to collect information about the armies, weapons, and plans of surrounding Arab states were of little use in ensuring internal security against Arab terrorists who intended to penetrate Israeli borders. The Shin Bet developed other tactics and methods for dealing with this internal threat. The territories acquired in Israel's wars—the Sinai, the Gaza Strip, Golan Heights, and the West Bank—produced new geography and new problems for the security services. Unlike Israeli citizens—Jews, Christians, and Arabs—the Arab residents of the territories had no affection for Israel. Some Arab states supported the Palestinians in those territories, while some also supported terrorist operations against Israel and some against the United States.

Similarly, intelligence agencies had difficulty in reacting to their home-grown terrorists, religious and nonreligious. As a former Shin Bet official said, "groups of

Jewish extremists who are religiously motivated are difficult to penetrate. They are more committed and coherent than secular extremists."

After Israel signed the peace agreement with the Palestine Liberation Organization (PLO) in Sept. 1993, Israeli intelligence agencies began to discover that right-wing extremists were venting their hate more at Israeli leaders than at the PLO. Shin Bet did move against some right-wingers, but the traditional fear prevailed: subversion from the left. Most resources were devoted to secular left-wing groups, not religious extremists.

The culmination of years of public criticism of Israeli intelligence came in Nov. 1995, following the assassination of Israeli Prime Minister Yitzhak Rabin by a Jewish religious extremist. The Shin Bet was the target of most of the criticism, both for failing to keep track of rabid anti-government zealots and for failing to give the Prime Minister adequate protection.

Following Rabin's assassination on Nov. 4, 1995, there were calls for a reorganization and reorientation of the Shin Bet. Rear Adm. AMI AYALON, former head of the Israeli Navy, became head of the Shin Bet in Jan. 1996, replacing Karmi Gilon, who took full responsibility for the Shin Bet's failure to prevent Rabin's assassination. (Rabin had earlier asked Ayalon to take the post.)

The challenges facing the Shin Bet when Ayalon took charge were enormous: still the threat of foreign infiltration (especially from Syrian-controlled Lebanon), from Palestinians in Gaza and the West Bank, and from right-wing Israelis opposed to the Arab-Israeli peace accords. The situation escalated in the late 1990s when it appeared that the PLO would reach an accommodation with Israel; Palestinian extremists began a deadly series of suicide bombings that racked the society as shopping malls, restaurants, and bus stations were targeted. Israeli intelligence activities turned to both prevention of such attacks and retribution, most of the latter by assassination of extremist political leaders, and using the Army to cordon off portions of Palestinian territory, destroying suspected terrorist centers and arms factories, and even the homes of the suicide bombers. But the vicious bombings continued into 2004.

And the Pollard case lived on: In 1996 Israel made him an Israeli citizen and some officials petitioned President Clinton to release him. A vigorous, unrelenting lobbying campaign to free him continued. But he remained incarcerated.

Israeli espionage in the United States did not end. The U.S. DEFENSE INVESTIGATIVE SERVICE in Oct. 1995 warned military contractors that Israel was "aggressively" spying in the United States. The warning was withdrawn two months later because it referred to the Israelis using "strong ethnic ties" to recruit spies. The Pentagon felt that the notice had indelicately singled out Jewish citizens. The Anti-Defamation League of B'nai B'rith charged that the warning "borders on anti-Semitism."

The notice covered both military and nonmilitary spying, especially INDUSTRIAL ESPIONAGE aimed at aiding Israel's state-owned and independent defense, aerospace, and electronics industries by providing them with U.S.

technology. Those intelligence operations had been run by Lakam, which theoretically had been abolished after Pollard's arrest. U.S. intelligence sources believe, that, while Lakam may no longer exist, its work continues in the hands of a variety of uncoordinated government agencies—often without knowledge of the Mossad or Aman.

Significantly, while Israel's internal security problems have increased over the past few years, the external threats and, consequently, foreign intelligence requirements have actually been decreasing. Syria is currently (in 2004) the only Arab state that could directly threaten Israel with military action. Thus, conventional intelligence requirements about foreign military capabilities and political intentions have been replaced to a large degree by concern about nonconventional weapons development: chemical, biological, and nuclear weapons. Those threats far outweigh traditional concerns for the numbers of tanks, fighter aircraft, or missile boats in the arsenals of Arab states.

Those concerns have led to a shift in Mossad and Aman tactics and policies, and in equipment. In Sept. 1988 Israel launched the first OFEK SATELLITE, prototype for photographic SURVEILLANCE satellites to watch its Arab neighbors. Thus, the people who first used the term *spy* (see BIBLICAL SPIES) are today employing the most sophisticated spy systems in existence.

Also see CENTER FOR SPECIAL STUDIES.

Ivanov, Igor Alexandrovich

(b. 1931)

Undoubtedly the only person to be convicted of espionage and let free on bond. A chauffeur for the Soviet trade agency AMTORG, Ivanov arrived in the United States in March 1962. Within a year the FBI identified four Soviet citizens and an American engineer, JOHN BUTENKO, trying to obtain classified plans related to the U.S. Strategic Air Command.

In Oct. 1963 the FBI caught them attempting to obtain the documents. Three of the Soviets, who were working for the UNITED NATIONS and had diplomatic immunity, were declared persona non grata and told to leave the United States, but Ivanov and the American were arrested and charged with espionage.

In Dec. 1964 both men were tried and sentenced to 30 years in prison. Ivanov, however, was immediately freed on $100,000 bond, posted by the Soviet Embassy, while his conviction was appealed through the American court system.

The following year the Soviets attempted to exchange Ivanov for Newcomb Mott, an American textbook salesman who as a tourist had strayed across the poorly marked border between Norway and the Soviet Union. After three months in solitary confinement, Mott was brought to trial, found guilty of illegal border crossing, and sentenced to 18 months in a labor camp.

The U.S. government refused the proposed exchange. (Mott died under mysterious circumstances in

Jan. 1966.) Ivanov was, however, permitted to return to the Soviet Union in 1971 on condition that he return to the United States for his next court appearance. He never returned to the United States.

Ivanov, Capt. 1st Rank Yevgeny Mikhailovich

(b. 1926 d. 1994)

Assistant Soviet naval ATTACHÉ in London from 1960 to 1963 who played a key role in the PROFUMO AFFAIR. Ivanov was the son of a Red Army officer. His father's family was of peasant stock, and his mother's family came from the nobility. The younger Ivanov had an early interest in the military and entered the Pacific Higher Naval School of Vladivostok in 1943. He served briefly in the Pacific War against the Japanese, returning to school in Baku to graduate in 1947.

After serving two years on the battleship *Sevastopol*, in 1949 he entered the Military-Diplomatic Academy in Moscow, which trained officers for the GRU, Soviet MILITARY INTELLIGENCE, in a four-year course. Ivanov was posted as assistant naval attaché to Oslo, Norway, in 1953, where he was successful in garnering military secrets. Subsequently, he was assigned to the Soviet Embassy in London.

Soon after his arrival in March 1960 he was befriended by artist-osteopath Stephen Ward. He met Ward's protégés Christine Keeler and Mandi Rice-Davis, and had sex with Keeler and possibly Rice-Davis. Through Ward, Ivanov met the cream of British society, including Prince Philip, Sir Winston Churchill, Lord Astor, and Secretary of State for War John Profumo. Ivanov was able to steal documents—some secret—and socially interrogate many of the people he met. Gregarious and a sportsman, he fit in easily at parties and dinners.

He returned to Moscow from Britain in Jan. 1963 and attended the prestigious Academy of the General Staff. He graduated and was promoted to Captain 1st Rank in 1968. He served as a head of the GRU's analysis department until retiring in 1981.

His wife since 1953, Maya Ivanov, served with her husband in London, as a CODE clerk, but the couple were rarely seen in public together.

Ivanov's autobiography, *The Naked Spy*, written with Gennady Sokolov, was published in 1992.

Ivashutin, Gen. of the Army Petr Ivanovitch

(b. 1909 d. ?)

Chief of the GRU, Soviet MILITARY INTELLIGENCE, from 1963 to 1987. Appointed chief of the GRU in March 1963 after the forced retirement of Col. Gen. I. A. SEROV, Ivashutin had a career that coincided closely with the tenure of Leonid Brezhnev as head of the Communist Party and Soviet government.

Ivashutin volunteered for Red Army service and entered Army COUNTERINTELLIGENCE in 1931. During World War II he was assigned to SMERSH, and in 1944–1945 he was chief of the Smersh units of the 3rd Ukrainian Front. In the latter role he fought against Ukrainian insurgents and helped to establish communist regimes in Bulgaria, Hungary, and Yugoslavia. It was during this period that he met Brezhnev and that the careers of the two men became linked.

At the end of the war Ivashutin also participated in the forced repatriation of Soviet citizens to the USSR and helped to execute Soviets who had served in the German-sponsored Russian Liberation Army.

After the disbanding of Smersh in 1946 he served in the NKVD under LAVRENTY BERIA, becoming head of the Third Chief Directorate (Armed Forces). He remained with the NKVD and its successor, the KGB, after Beria's demise. Following the dismissal of Serov, on Brezhnev's orders he was appointed to head the GRU. While Ivashutin staunchly defended the interests of the defense establishment, even against the KGB, a high level of corruption continued in the GRU. An article in the Moscow newspaper *Nezavisimaya Gazeta* in 1991 described the misconduct of Ivashutin's tenure:

> The period of rule of General of the Army P.I. Ivashutin, who headed the GRU for 24 years, ended with this major (Polyakov) and several minor . . . traitors. An entire era! This era was also famous because expensive gifts were presented to each new chief of the General Staff (especially on the anniversary), which had been purchased with GRU field funds and, of course, with hard currency.

Ivashutin survived the deaths of Soviet leaders Brezhnev, YURI ANDROPOV, and Konstantin Chernenko to serve as head of the GRU until the eve of the dissolution of the Soviet Union. His longevity was due to powerful support from the military leadership, who saw his value as a counterweight to KGB influence.

He was awarded the honor of Hero of the Soviet Union in 1985.

Ivy Bells

U.S. Navy operation to plant an intercept device on a Soviet underwater communications cable at a depth of some 400 feet in the Sea of Okhotsk. SUBMARINES periodically serviced the device and recovered tapes from it. The cable, between Soviet bases on the Kamchatka Peninsula and the Soviet Far Eastern coast, carried highly classified military as well as civilian communications.

The BUG was placed on the cable by the U.S. nuclear-propelled submarine *Halibut*, which also replaced the tapes from the start of the operation until 1976, when the nuclear-propelled submarine *Parche* took on the job. Both submarines had been extensively modified for seafloor work and recovery operations.

Although the communications on the tapes were weeks or months old, they were still valuable to intelligence analysts. Some of the communications pertained to future events that could be monitored when they took place. The data also provided TECHNICAL INTELLIGENCE.

Ivy Bells continued until 1981 when U.S. SATELLITE photos showed Soviet salvage ships working over the exact spot where the intercept device had been attached to the seafloor cable. Subsequently, when the *Parche* went in to replace the tapes, the device was missing. The Navy and other intelligence agencies were unable at the time to determine how or exactly when Ivy Bells was compromised.

With the arrest of NSA analyst RONALD PELTON in 1985 the government learned that he had revealed the clandestine Navy operation to the Soviets in about Jan. 1980. (One of the seized seafloor recording devices is now on display in the MUSEUM at the former KGB headquarters in Moscow.)

The first comprehensive account of Ivy Bells appeared in the best-selling *Blind Man's Bluff* (1998) by journalists Sherry Sontag and Christopher Drew. Many naval officers believed that *Blind Man's Bluff* should not have been allowed to be published because of their unwavering view that all submarine operations should remain secret—in keeping with the traditional name of the underwater Navy, the Silent Service.

I&W

SEE INDICATIONS AND WARNING

Izmaylov, Col. Vladimir

Soviet GRU MILITARY INTELLIGENCE officer serving as an assistant military ATTACHÉ in Washington, D.C., who was expelled from the United States in June 1986. He attempted to recruit a high-level U.S. Air Force officer with access to highly classified data on strategic defense programs and radar-evading (stealth) technology.

J

J-2

Intelligence element of a U.S. joint (multiservice) staff. The J-2 of the U.S. Joint Chiefs of Staff has the title Director for Intelligence and is a rear admiral or lieutenant general.

Also see G-2 and S-2.

Jack in the Box

A dummy—sometimes inflatable—placed in a car to deceive enemy SURVEILLANCE about the number of persons in the vehicle.

Also see TRADECRAFT.

Jahnke, Kurt

German spy and saboteur in the United States during World War I and a mysterious Nazi intelligence official in World War II.

German-born, Jahnke became a naturalized American citizen and claimed to have been in the U.S. Marine Corps and to have been a U.S. border guard along the Mexico-U.S. border prior to World War I. He also said he made a thriving business out of making coffins for deceased Chinese whose relatives wanted the bodies shipped home.

Before the United States entered the war, Jahnke was recruited as a saboteur by Franz von Bopp, German consul general in San Francisco, where Jahnke got a job in a shipyard, presumably to commit acts of sabotage there. Von Bopp directed sabotage operations on the U.S. West Coast, but he may have dispatched Jahnke to the East Coast for a special project, the sabotage of the huge munitions depot on Black Tom Island on the New Jersey side of New York Harbor on July 30, 1916. Jahnke and another von Bopp recruit, LOTHAR WITZKE, were prime suspects in the Black Tom disaster. Jahnke was also suspected of being part of a German effort to foment strikes on the docks in East Coast ports.

Sometime in 1917 Jahnke went to Mexico and was the subject of a Nov. 1917 cable, apparently from von Bopp to BERLIN: "Kurt asks for further instructions. . . . He proposes that a naval expert should be sent to Mexico. . . ." The cable was intercepted and decrypted by British intelligence.

The reply came in a cable from Madrid to the German legation in Mexico City, telling Jahnke to try to send an AGENT into the United States. Jahnke sent three: Witzke; William Altendorf, a former Mexican Army officer; and William Gleaves, a black Canadian who was given two assignments—to infiltrate an American union and to create dissension among blacks in the U.S. Army stationed around El Paso, Texas. Both Altendorf and Gleaves, unknown to each other, were MOLES. Altendorf had been recruited by U.S. ARMY INTELLIGENCE and Gleaves by a British INTELLIGENCE OFFICER in Mexico City. Witzke was caught soon after crossing the border.

Back in Mexico, Jahnke, who was supposedly in charge of sabotage operations in the United States, was challenged by a new arrival, Capt. Frederick Hinsch, a German merchant ship captain. Berlin was told in a cable that Hinsch should take over because he "is a German" and "Jahnke is not self-reliant." Jahnke fought back and, after a flurry of cables (all intercepted by the British), was made "sole Naval Confidential Agent in Mexico."

Jahnke apparently remained in Mexico until the war ended and then made his way to Germany. He next appears in intelligence chronicles at the end of Aug. 1939, shortly before Germany invaded Poland, starting World War II. David Boyle, posing as a king's messenger (diplomatic COURIER), was sent to Berlin by the British Secret

Intelligence Service (MI6) to see if a high-ranking Nazi could be drawn into talks that would stave off war. In Berlin Boyle met Jahnke, who by then had become chief of the Jahnkebüro, the private intelligence service set up by Foreign Minister Joachim von Ribbentrop.

There was suspicion, never entirely dispelled, that Jahnke was a DOUBLE AGENT, working for Germany and acting at least as a contact for British intelligence. When Deputy Führer Rudolf Hess flew to Scotland in May 1941, an enraged Adolf Hitler suspected that Jahnke was somehow involved. Jahnke, under von Ribbentrop's protection, survived Hitler's distrust. He next became a political adviser to Brigadeführer WALTER SCHELLENBERG, the chief.

Schellenberg once heard that Jahnke had gone to Switzerland to meet a British intelligence officer. An investigation turned up no evidence, and Jahnke was cleared. Then, in Nov. 1944, a German officer using the name Karl Marcus appeared in recently liberated France. Although apparently a deserter, Marcus told French interrogators that he had been sent "to get in touch with the British."

Marcus managed to make contact with the British by going to the Chinese Embassy and asking someone there to reach a British intelligence officer attached to the headquarters of Gen. Dwight D. Eisenhower. When a British officer appeared, Marcus told him that he was Jahnke's secretary, sent to speak to the British about working with Germany to thwart Soviet postwar plans. Believing that his real mission was to drive a wedge between the Allies, British and U.S. officials dismissed him.

Intelligence officers with long memories, however, remembered that Jahnke had once had a Chinese coffin business and probably still had a connection that could get him into a Chinese Embassy.

James, Lew [p]

Alias of the last CIA officer to leave Vietnam.

James was captured by the North Vietnamese on April 16, 1975, as they closed in on Saigon. When the last Americans fled Vietnam on April 30, James was not among them. His fate unknown, the CIA listed him as a missing "consular officer."

He had been captured with South Vietnamese Army officers, beaten during a lengthy interrogation, and then taken to Hanoi and imprisoned. James had been under "light" COVER, with an identification card that listed him as an "employee of the U.S. Embassy" and a "Foreign Service Reserve Officer." But he had no real embassy job and so could not fool his captors for long. After questioning him repeatedly, the North Vietnamese interrogators showed him captured documents revealing his true identity.

James was freed more than six months later under what FRANK SNEPP, in his book *Decent Interval* (1977), called a 'professional arrangement' worked out by the CIA through another western intelligence organization. He was indeed the last CIA operative in Vietnam."

Snepp, the CIA's chief strategy analyst in Vietnam, also wrote that when Tucker Gougelmann, a retired CIA officer who had worked in Saigon, returned to look for Vietnamese friends, he was captured and died in captivity a year later after being questioned by the KGB and other intelligence organizations. "What he disclosed under questioning has not been determined," Snepp wrote. "His knowledge of CIA operations and personnel both in Vietnam and elsewhere in Asia was considerable."

The CIA publicly acknowledged Gougelmann in 2001, reporting that he had died in Vietnam in 1976 after being interrogated and tortured for nearly a year. He had retired from the CIA in 1972, but was captured in 1975 when he returned to Saigon to try to aid a group of orphans he had befriended. (See BOOK OF HONOR.)

James Bond [f]

Hero of the phenomenally successful spy novels written by IAN FLEMING and the many MOVIES based on those books. Bond was Agent 007, an intrepid British secret AGENT whose 00-prefix CODE NAME indicated that he had the authority to kill.

In tales full of fantasy, there are touches of reality. Bond's frequent adversary SMERSH was an actual Soviet intelligence organization. A Bulgarian writer, A. Gulyashi (reportedly on commission from the KGB), wrote an anti-Bond book to counter the disrespectful image of Smersh and the Soviets. The book, *Zakbov Mission*, published as *Avakum Versus 007* in serial form in *Komsomolskaya Pravda*, pits a communist hero against Bond. Bond's boss was known as "M." Max Knight, head of MI5's section B5(b), which operated against subversives, called himself M, in imitation of "C," as the head of the MI6 was known.

Fleming's death in 1964 did not mean the death of Bond. Agent 007's publishers enlisted John Gardner to keep Bond alive. Gardner had spoofed Bond with a bumbling character named Boysie Oakes in *The Liquidator* (1964) and several other Boysie Oakes books. His first Bond imitation, *License Renewed*, was published in Britain and the United States in 1981. Others followed annually.

For titles and dates of James Bond books and films see IAN FLEMING and MOVIES.

Jamestown Foundation

Washington-based organization that helps Soviet and Eastern Bloc DEFECTORS adjust to life in the United States. At the end of the Cold War, when numerous East European INTELLIGENCE OFFICERS were offering secrets to the CIA, many tried to defect to the foundation rather than to the United States. The foundation has close ties to the INTELLIGENCE COMMUNITY.

Jamestown Foundation was set up in 1984 to help ARKADY SHEVCHENKO write his book, *Breaking With*

Moscow. Later, similar help was given to Ion Pacepa, a former top Romanian intelligence officer. Through such connections, the foundation has developed a post–Cold War mission to develop information for U.S. policymakers through a network of "former high-ranking government officials and military officers, political scientists, journalists, scholars and economists."

Japan

After centuries of feudalism and warring clans, Japan began a rapid evolution in 1868, when a new generation of young, tradition-shattering leaders proclaimed a restoration of the emperor and the creation of a modern nation. Japan, which had long isolated itself from foreign influence, would develop military and industrial skills to compete with the West. A charter issued by the emperor declared, "Knowledge shall be sought throughout the world so as to strengthen the foundations of imperial rule."

The quest for knowledge at first would not include espionage. Not until 1878 would the Japanese government have a formal intelligence organization, an Army Intelligence Service, established in conjunction with the creation of a Japanese Army General Staff. The buildup of the Imperial Japanese Army had been rapid, beginning with an Imperial Force of 10,000 men in 1871 and growing with the issuing of a conscription law in 1873.

In 1881 came the KEMPEI TAI, born as military police but destined to enter Japanese society as a dreaded secret police. The same year that saw the creation of the Kempei Tai also witnessed the founding of Japan's first modern intelligence-collecting agency, the BLACK OCEAN SOCIETY, founded in 1881 to expand Japanese influence in Asia and to obtain intelligence from China, Korea, Manchuria, and Russia.

Spying had an ancient and revered history in Japan. Ninja spies were among the elite of the samurai. The Ninja samurai was, as defined by a Japanese-English dictionary, a man who had "mastered the art of making himself invisible through some artifice and is chiefly engaged in espionage." As Japan modernized, however, reliance on Ninjas lessened and the need for MILITARY INTELLIGENCE increased.

China was also modernizing its military, and in 1894, in a clash over Korea, the two nations went to war. It was a clash of military doctrine as well, for Japan had built up both its army and navy while China, the great land power, had ignored sea power. Japan, which had made China a TARGET for intelligence, knew the military strengths and weaknesses of China. Japan's navy defeated China's and won the eight-month war.

The peace treaty ceded Taiwan (Formosa) to Japan, along with the Kwantung Peninsula in southern Manchuria, and recognized the independence of Korea. Russia, with France and Germany, pressured Japan into abandoning its claim on Manchuria, which in 1898 Russia took over with a 25-year lease.

20TH-CENTURY ESPIONAGE

At the dawn of the 20th century Japanese military and political strategies were based on the theory that it had two enemies—China and Russia. China was no longer an immediate threat. Russia, with its takeover of Manchuria, needed to be dislodged.

Government and commercial interests were tightly layered in Japan, and at times one of the two interests acted with seeming independence of the other. The decision to make Russia a target of intelligence collection came from what today would be called the "private sector." The decision was made by Ryohei Uchida, a leading member of the Black Ocean Society, who in 1901 founded the BLACK DRAGON SOCIETY. The new society was powerful enough to dictate the naming of Japanese military ATTACHÉS sent abroad. Their best operative was Col. MOTOJIRO AKASHI, a baron who had been on the Imperial Headquarters Staff during the Sino-Japanese War. A painter, poet, and persuasive man, Akashi performed brilliantly, even getting master spy SIDNEY REILLY, who already worked for Britain and Russia, to do some work for the Japanese cause.

The Japanese Navy relied on its own officers to obtain NAVAL INTELLIGENCE. Two officers learned not only the Russian language but also the rites of the Russian Orthodox Church to work under COVER in a shipping company in St. Petersburg. The Japanese were well aware that Russians, like most other Europeans, tended to look at all Asian people as vaguely the same, so the officers were seen as Asians, not Japanese. One became engaged to a Russian woman to keep his cover. They provided the Japanese naval attaché with information on Russian naval movements and a steady stream of other intelligence.

In Sept. 1904 the Russian secret police arrested them. The Russian fiancée was a Russian AGENT.

THE RUSSO-JAPANESE WAR

The Russians built a branch of the Trans-Siberian Railway into Manchuria and down to Port Arthur (now Lushun), a prize port also enviously eyed by China and Japan. Russia, with a legal right only to southern Manchuria, proceeded to take possession of all of Manchuria. Japan believed that Korea would be next on the Russian road of conquest.

In Feb. 1904 Japan launched a surprise torpedo attack on the Russian fleet at Port Arthur on shore. The Japanese knew the location of every ship and even every searchlight. On land, Japan had detailed knowledge of Russian military strength and was able to use DECEPTION and DISINFORMATION as a dazzling part of its overall strategy.

Gen. Sir Ian Hamilton, attached to the Japanese First Army as a British military observer, was amazed at the detailed Japanese intelligence figures on the Russian troops in Manchuria. He was shown an assessment that indicated the exact locations of about 200,000 men in Oct. 1903. The Japanese let Hamilton (and presumably

Russian AGENTS) believe these figures. But the Japanese knew that the Russians had been reducing their troops and by May 1904 would have a force of only about 80,000 men. The director of intelligence for the First Army was Maj. Gen. Baron YASUMASA FUKUSHIMA, who was also in charge of disseminating disinformation, particularly for foreigners like Hamilton.

Black Dragon operatives, aided by Japanese officers in civilian clothes, gathered much of the military intelligence. By one later Western estimate, one in 10 of the thousands of Chinese coolies working for the Russians in Manchuria was a Japanese agent. The Chinese were paid by Japanese HANDLERS to provide bits and pieces of information that Japanese analysts built into accurate estimates.

In Manchuria, the Black Dragon Society organized Chinese guerrilla units and hired Manchurian thugs to harass the Russians. At the same time, Akashi was meeting with Russian dissidents in Sweden, urging them to return to their homeland and rise in revolt against the warmongers. While Japanese armies, well supplied with TACTICAL INTELLIGENCE, invaded the peninsula and defeated the Russians in a series of battles, subversion back in Russia was also helping to end the war in Japan's favor.

Japan's resident agent in Port Arthur was a soldier of fortune who called himself Gen. Rafael de Nogales and said that he had fought as a teenager in the Spanish-American War of 1898. Posing as a salesman of Swiss watches, he sometimes worked closely with a Chinese agent who smuggled messages on bits of rice paper hidden in his hollow gold teeth. The use of non-Japanese operatives became a frequent Japanese intelligence tactic, but Japan, like other countries using nonnationals, did not trust them.

The Japanese Navy, controlling the waters off Port Arthur, sank some Russian ships and bottled up the rest. Whatever hope Russia had lay in the arrival of the Baltic Fleet from halfway around the world. After some of its ships had steamed 18,000 miles, in May 1905 the Baltic Fleet entered the Strait of Tsushima, which separates Japan from Korea, to do battle. Of the 38 ships in the Russian fleet, 34 were sunk, captured, or interned in a neutral port. The Japanese lost three small ships. The battle essentially ended the war, but it was already lost in Russia itself, where revolutionaries were threatening revolt. Akashi financed some of the unrest in a highly successful COVERT ACTION.

In Sept. 1905 a treaty, brokered by President Theodore Roosevelt, gave Japan rights to Port Arthur and the peninsula, along with the southern half of the island of Sakhalin. Russia also evacuated Manchuria and recognized Japan's interests in Korea.

TOWARD MILITARISM

Convinced that Russia had been subdued for some time, Japan—and Japanese intelligence—turned to the United States as a target. In Jan. 1932 Japan sent the tanker *Erimo* from the naval base at Yokosuka, near Tokyo, to Hawaii. Electronic monitors on the tanker collected SIGNALS INTELLIGENCE from U.S. Navy ships taking part in an exercise that involved taking a notional expeditionary force from the U.S. West Coast to Hawaii. From analysis of the traffic, Japanese codebreakers were able to break a two-digit Navy CODE. Later, Japan set up intercept stations in Pacific islands and Mexico. In a Japanese BLACK BAG JOB that paralleled similar U.S. efforts, operatives broke into the U.S. Consulate at Kobe and photographed the diplomatic "gray" code book to confirm that Japanese codebreaking of the gray code was accurate.

While operatives in Hawaii were accumulating what would become thousands of reports on the U.S. Navy, the U.S. OFFICE OF NAVAL INTELLIGENCE was hampered in reciprocating because of a lack of funds and a lack of high-level government interest. America, wrote RICHARD DEACON in his book Kempei Tai (1990 ed.), "was then paying the penalty for the orthodox view in her military and naval hierarchies that intelligence work was something underhand and criminal."

Japanese intelligence also used Black Dragon contacts to establish connections with progressive elements in China, including Sun Yat-sen, whose Nationalist Party would usher China into the modern age. Japanese agents trained Chinese police, gaining influence in China and inserting agents into the Chinese police-intelligence structure.

Because it had a military pact with Britain, Japan entered World War I on the Allied side. Although playing only a limited role in the war, the Japanese shared in the spoils, under the Versailles Treaty obtaining the Pacific islands that had belonged to Germany. These included the Marshall Islands, the Caroline Islands, and all of the Mariana Islands except Guam, which the United States had acquired after the Spanish-American War. The islands were not to be fortified. But Japan would secretly convert many of the islands into air and naval bases that threatened the shipping lanes between Hawaii, Australia, and the American-administered Philippines.

Japan and China, in a military agreement made in 1918, agreed to cooperate to develop military intelligence in Siberia and "the North-East territory" (northern Manchuria), where "intelligence agencies may be established and the two countries shall exchange intelligence information." Japan's most important INTELLIGENCE OFFICER in Manchuria was Maj. Gen. KENJI DOIHARA. "His task," wrote American journalist John Gunther, "was to create trouble and then smooth it over to the advantage of the Japanese."

Japanese agents working under Doihara created "incidents" that purportedly demonstrated Chinese aggression toward Japan. The most significant of these incidents came on Sept. 18, 1931, when Japanese troops, claiming that Chinese saboteurs were tampering with the roadbed of the Japanese-owned South Manchuria Railway, seized the Chinese city of Mukden (now Shenyang), whose mayor was Doihara. The bogus "Mukden incident" launched a swift Japanese conquest of northeastern China, where the Japanese set up the state of Manchukuo ("the state of Manchu") and put the deposed Emperor of China, Pu Yi, on the throne as Doihara's puppet emperor.

Japan's march toward a military state continued with the signing, on Nov. 25, 1936, of the Anti-Comintern Pact with Germany. The pact, aimed at combating the international communism sponsored by the Soviet Union, pledged the safeguarding of "common interests" against threats by the Soviet Union. Japan continued to maintain an intelligence network in the Soviet Union.

Internal security became the responsibility of the Kempei Tai, which became known as the secret police. Another intelligence organization also watched over the populace. This was the "thought police," whose officers spied for the Thought Section of the Criminal Affairs Bureau, created by the Ministry of Justice in 1927 to root out members of the outlawed Communist Party and other subversives. There were also Special Higher Police, who operated out of the Home Ministry.

Then came the Peace Preservation Law, which prohibited any plans to change the government. Enforcement of this law was given to the thought police, which also censored books and sent spies into colleges. Sometimes thought police and the Kempei Tai had spies, unknown to each other, in the same classrooms. The thought police announced in 1930 that it would "welcome secret communications from citizens," setting up a national spy-on-your-neighbor system through the police-operated Neighborhood Association. From 1928 to 1943 a total of 68,508 persons were arrested for violating the Peace Preservation Law.

WORLD WAR II

Japan again moved against China in 1937, when another staged event was used as a pretext for attacking Chinese troops near Peking (Beijing). The undeclared war, which Japan always called the "China Incident," was envisioned by the Japanese militarists as a way to create another puppet state similar to Manchukuo. In one of the early actions of the war, Japanese warplanes bombed the U.S. Navy gunboat *PANAY*, prompting the first of an escalating set of protests from the United States.

Although China was torn by internal strife, armies under Chiang Kai-shek and Mao Zedong managed to cooperate enough at the beginning to slow down Japan's conquest. The war put a strain on Japan's resources but at the same time spurred creation of the Greater East Asia Co-Prosperity Sphere, a "new order" that would change the balance of power in the Far East—unquestionably in Japan's favor.

After the Germans defeated France in May 1940, Japan received German approval to occupy French Indochina, from which supplies had been flowing to anti-Japanese forces in China. On Sept. 27, 1940, Japan, Germany, and Italy signed the Tripartite Pact, which called for each nation to provide military assistance in case of attack by any nation not yet in the war. The pact was aimed at giving the United States pause about intervention against what was now a three-nation Axis.

Anticipating war with the United States, Japan set up several intelligence operations. Japanese naval intelligence officers were dispatched to the U.S. West Coast in fishing ships with special radio equipment, and intelligence officers disguised as seamen sailed in merchant ships. An agent in Panama City organized Japanese barbers into a network. In Mexico, Japanese operatives scouted for places where Japanese submarines could cache fuel. In California intelligence officers, under cover as students studying English, trolled for U.S. sailors who would sell secrets. The U.S. OFFICE OF NAVAL INTELLIGENCE discovered two spies, Lt. Comdr. JOHN S. FARNSWORTH and former Navy yeoman HARRY T. THOMPSON, who, while unemployed at San Pedro, Calif., spied for the Japanese against the U.S. Navy in 1934–1935. (See VELAVEE DICKINSON.)

In Hawaii the Japanese established a resident family near the Pearl Harbor naval base: Dr. BERNARD KUEHN, who claimed to be an anthropologist; his wife, who acted as a COURIER to Tokyo; and a young woman posing as their daughter. All were German agents on loan to the Japanese. Also watching the naval base was Ens. TAKEO YOSHIKAWA, a Japanese Navy intelligence officer under cover as vice consul in Honolulu.

Elsewhere in Asia, the Japanese had extensive intelligence networks. Their resources included male brothels for entertaining and blackmailing HOMOSEXUAL Javanese who were administering Dutch holdings in the Dutch East Indies (now Indonesia). They also had caches of bicycles for Japanese Army couriers. In some areas, Japanese loggers cleared forests in such a way as to create landing strips. A Japanese intelligence officer who had studied in the United States worked under cover as a steward in an officers' club at a British naval base in Singapore.

Prior to the PEARL HARBOR ATTACK Japan had a worldwide intelligence-gathering network, staffed primarily by diplomatic, commercial, and military personnel. Japanese Naval Intelligence operated out of what was called the Third Department of the Japanese Naval General Staff. (The other departments handled war plans, supply, and communications.) When war began with the United States, the Third Department had 29 officers plus one officer with the Combined Fleet. By the end of the war, the number of officers had increased to 97, with 42 in the Fifth Section (intelligence on North and South America, U.S. territories, and front-line intelligence).

The Third Department received its information from communications (analyzing traffic, since U.S. codes were not broken), captured documents, extensive monitoring of foreign news broadcasts, analysis of newspapers and magazines obtained through neutral countries, and naval attachés in Sweden, Switzerland, Portugal, and Spain. Postwar records, analyzed by U.S. intelligence officials, showed that the Japanese also obtained significant intelligence from the interrogation of prisoners of war. A U.S. study of Japanese intelligence said that "certain data about U.S. forces, known to the Japanese, can be traced to no other source."

The Japanese manual on interrogation of prisoners

stated that torture "is the most clumsy method and only to be used when all else fails." Nevertheless, survivors of Japanese interrogation told of American prisoners being beaten during interrogation and of being executed, often by decapitation. Some tortured prisoners gave the Japanese tactical information on ships and aircraft. But little of the information was of real value.

A postwar U.S. report on Japanese military and naval intelligence said that "the most lucrative sources of information available to the Japanese became (1) analysis of Allied communications transmissions and (2) Allied short and medium wave radio broadcasts coupled with information from Allied newspapers and magazines purchased by Japanese representatives in neutral countries." And, because the Japanese launched what was expected to be a short war, "neither the Army nor the Navy developed an intelligence organization containing within itself the means of collecting, processing and disseminating intelligence throughout all levels of command." (See NAKANO.)

As for spying against Japan, by far the most successful spy was RICHARD SORGE, a Soviet intelligence officer who became RESIDENT director of military intelligence for the Far East. Spying against both Japan and Germany, Sorge was able to warn Moscow that Germany would invade the Soviet Union, that Japan would not help Germany by invading Siberia, and that Japan planned to attack the United States.

On the battlefields of the Pacific, Japan fought what an intelligence officer later called "an abacus war," relying more upon intuition than hard intelligence. One officer, Maj. HORI EIZO, was nicknamed "MacArthur's staff officer" because of his uncanny ability to predict U.S. moves. A major intelligence advantage of the United States was in CRYPTOLOGY; the breaking of Japanese codes enabled the United States to read Japanese military and diplomatic messages. Such information was the key to the crucial Battle of Coral Sea (May 1942) and the decisive Battle of MIDWAY (June 1942), and to the killing of Adm. ISOROKU YAMAMOTO (April 1943), the commander-in-chief of the Combined Fleet. Despite press leaks (see STANLEY JOHNSTON) and other indications, the Japanese military leadership refused to believe that the Americans could have broken into their secret communications.

Japanese codebreakers never achieved any substantial penetration of American codes. But when B-29 bombing raids began in 1944, the monitoring of the B-29s' radio traffic enabled Japanese intelligence analysts to predict the targets of air raids more than 70 percent of the time. Later, with the coming of more planes and more raids, the prediction rate dropped sharply. In the last significant intelligence analysis of the war, Japanese experts were able to determine at once that Hiroshima had been destroyed on Aug. 6, 1945, by an atomic bomb.

The Japanese Army's Tokumu Bu (Special Service Organization) was a strange and sinister agency, loosely administered and operated in deep secrecy. Its activities ranged from intelligence gathering and sabotage to assassination and FIFTH COLUMN operations. Its units followed Japanese military conquerors, setting up "liaison organi-

zations" in China, India, Burma, and elsewhere in Southeast Asia.

Anyone who even spoke of the Tokumu Bu was threatened with arrest. Sometimes units of it went under the innocuous name Renkraku Bu (Liaison Department). A newspaperman who claimed to know about the organization told interrogators, "No records were kept; it was the rule to pass on the names of these secret agents to one's successor, but, of course, this was sometimes unintentionally or intentionally forgotten." Military officers in Tokumu Bu rarely appeared in uniform.

Japanese intelligence had little effect on the war effort. Again and again, for example, Japanese intelligence officers accepted exaggerated reports of planes shot down or battles won against Allied forces. Intelligence assembled for the Pearl Harbor attack was solid and extensive. But as the war progressed, sources of intelligence diminished and the Japanese were forced to rely on speculation to predict Allied moves.

In the weeks between surrender and the arrival of occupation troops, the Japanese burned or hid information about CRYPTANALYSIS, struck the names of codebreakers from unit rosters, and even declared some of them dead.

PEACETIME ESPIONAGE

Allied occupation authorities abolished the thought police, the Kempei Tai, and all other intelligence organizations. Japan, under a new, American-dictated constitution, denounced war and shaped its military establishment into a self-defense force. The collection of intelligence officially resumed in July 1952 with the creation of the Public Security Investigation Agency (Koan Chosa Cho) under the Ministry of Justice and the Security Agency, Hoancho. Like the Kempei Tai, Hoancho primarily worked with the military but had domestic missions as well. In 1954 Japan authorized the Police Agency (Keisatsu Cho) to have a unit, named Keibu Bu (Guard Division), for investigating subversives.

Both the Soviet Union and China restored intelligence networks in Japan, the Soviets using the old Russian stronghold in Harbin as their headquarters and the Chinese using the International Red Cross as a cover. North Korea also gathered intelligence, using repatriated Koreans as carriers, primarily of TECHNICAL INTELLIGENCE.

The U.S. CIA, in a sustained COVERT ACTION, poured millions of dollars into the coffers of Japan's Liberal Democratic Party in the 1950s and 1960s to preserve the conservative party, gain intelligence, and weaken the political left. Cash payments went to individual party members, including one who became Prime Minister. The Liberal Democrats dominated the Japanese parliament for 38 years, ending their rule in 1994 after scandals over cash contributions by Japanese favor seekers.

Soviet money went to liberal and left-wing candidates. Both the United States and the Soviet Union saw the need to establish ways to influence Japan and to collect intelligence there. STANISLAV LEVCHENKO, a Soviet DEFECTOR who ran a KGB spy network in Japan in the

1970s, said in 1983 that prominent officials and journalists were among his agents. In 1980 a retired major general and two active-duty officers in Japanese military intelligence were arrested for selling secrets to Soviet military attachés. They were the first known espionage arrests in Japanese history. Under the law, the maximum prison sentence for espionage was one year. The retired general got the maximum, the others received eight-month sentences.

As Japan developed into an economic superpower, the nation became both a source and a consumer of IN-DUSTRIAL ESPIONAGE. In 1990 three major Japanese companies—the aerospace arm of Nissan Motor, Mitsubishi Heavy Industries, and Ishi-kawajima-Harima Heavy Industries (rockets and jet engines)—bought software from an American executive who was arrested for selling military technology without a license. The software, banned from export, was developed for the Strategic Defense Initiative ("Star Wars") program. Since then, both the United States and Japan have claimed that the other is conducting industrial espionage. Both countries deny official sanction of industrial espionage, but there is little doubt that this kind of spying represents the intelligence gathering of the future.

In 1996 Japan's Public Security Investigation Agency, which then had about 2,000 employees, was reorganized. One new mission was a specific concern about religious cults suspected of subversive activities. This development came in the wake of criticism about the agency's failure to have substantial intelligence on the Aum-Shinrikyo cult, which carried out fatal attacks on Tokyo subways with sarin gas.

Jedburghs

Members of American-British teams who secretly arrived in France to aid the French Resistance during World War II. A Jedburgh team normally consisted of an American working for the OFFICE OF STRATEGIC SERVICES (OSS), a Briton from a British intelligence service, usually the Special Operations Executive (SOE), and a Free French officer or enlisted man. All wore uniforms when they were parachuted into France, in the hope that if they were captured the Germans would not execute them as spies.

One of the team members was a radio operator. The teams provided communications, leadership, and advice to local guerrilla organizations. The teams also assured Allied officials that arms and other equipment being dropped to guerrillas were being used properly and in keeping with Allied strategy.

U.S. and British aircraft dropped 93 Jedburgh teams into France following the Normandy invasion of June 6, 1944. Other teams also parachuted into Belgium, Holland, and Norway. The teams were recruited and trained in a joint effort of the OSS and the SOE.

Although there is a town called Jedburgh in southeast Scotland, it had no apparent connection with the team name, which supposedly was a randomly selected CODE WORD. But some hidden British wit may have inspired it, for "Jedburgh justice"—punishing malefactors first and trying them afterward—was a phrase known at least to Scots.

Jeffries, Randy Miles

A messenger for a Washington, D.C., company that transcribed congressional hearings who in 1985 gave some classified documents to a Soviet official. Later he attempted to sell others to an undercover agent of the FBI posing as a Soviet INTELLIGENCE OFFICER named "Vlad." One of the documents was a TOP SECRET transcript on military communications programs.

Officials said that he had given the Soviets transcripts on closed hearings about U.S. plans for nuclear war, information about Trident submarine operating areas in the Pacific, security techniques for preventing Soviet eavesdropping on U.S. computers and telephone systems, and U.S. radar capabilities.

Jeffries' meeting with the Soviet contact had been detected by FBI electronic interception when he called the Soviet Military Office in Washington, D.C. The building, separate from the Soviet Embassy until the new embassy was opened on Wisconsin Ave. in 1991, was kept under FBI electronic and often manned SURVEILLANCE. Jeffries pleaded guilty to one count of espionage and received a 10-year prison sentence.

Jennifer

CODE NAME for the deep-ocean salvage operation by the U.S. CIA to retrieve the sunken Soviet ballistic missile submarine *K-129* from the ocean floor in 1968. The submarine's destruction was detected by the U.S. Navy's SOUND SURVEILLANCE SYSTEM (SOSUS), and the location of the wreckage was pinpointed by the SUBMARINE *Halibut* towing cameras along the ocean floor.

The CIA constructed and manned a special salvage ship, the *HUGHES GLOMAR EXPLORER*, which successfully lifted the forward portion of the *K-129* from a record depth.

JIC

SEE (1) JOINT INTELLIGENCE CENTER; (2) JOINT INTELLIGENCE COMMITTEE

JN-Series Ciphers

U.S. designation for Japanese Navy CIPHERS. U.S. Navy CRYPTANALYSIS efforts first penetrated the Japanese Navy's JN-25 cipher in Sept. 1940. That was the Japanese Navy's operational cipher. (This brief penetration occurred almost three years before the U.S. Army was able to break into Japanese Army ciphers.)

JN-25, which had come into use on June 1, 1939, was the most widely used Japanese Navy cipher. It was a five-digit, two-part code: there were 33,333 groups in a "dictionary" book, to which were added by "false" arithmetic (no borrowing or carrying from column to column) a five-digit number selected in sequence according to a second book of random additives. The resulting encipherment consisted of series of five-digit numbers, all divisible by three to provide a convenient check against garbling. The second edition of the cipher—referred to as JN-25b—came into force on Dec. 1, 1940.

By Nov. 1941 some messages could be partially read by U.S. Navy codebreakers. Most authoritative estimates place U.S. success against JN-25 at that time at 10 to 15 percent. There are indications that British and Dutch cryptologists were having more success with JN-25 at the time. (See CRYPTANALYSIS.)

Prior to the PEARL HARBOR ATTACK on Dec. 7, 1941, the head of U.S. NAVY COMMUNICATIONS INTELLIGENCE had assigned the breaking of the JN-25 cipher then in use to Station CAST in the Philippines and to the OP-20-G (NEGAT) organization in Washington, D.C. A small British codebreaking unit at Singapore was also working on JN-25. The U.S. Navy's third codebreaking unit, Station HYPO at Pearl Harbor, was assigned to break into the Japanese flag officers' cipher. Cast and OP-20-G (as well as the U.S. Army) were already reading the Japanese PURPLE diplomatic cipher.

On Dec. 4, 1941, new additive books came into effect, halting the limited American readings in the cipher. Four days later, however, Station Cast, on Corregidor, under Lt. RUDOLPH J. FABIAN, broke into this new encipherment. (In early 1942, with the fall of the Philippines, Fabian's codebreakers were taken to Australia by submarine, where they established Station BELL.)

On Dec. 10, 1941, the Hypo unit was ordered to join in the assault on JN-25. By the end of the month portions of JN-25b were being read by the Navy codebreakers. Enough decrypts were made rapidly enough to lead to the U.S. Navy's Coral Sea victory in May 1942.

The Japanese introduced JN-25c on May 28, 1942, but progress by U.S. codebreakers was rapid. Both the Battle of MIDWAY victory in June 1942 and the assassination of the Japanese Combined Fleet's commander-in-chief, Adm. ISOROKU YAMAMOTO, in April 1943, were due to the codebreakers. Through CRIBS virtually every change made by the Japanese was rapidly overcome by the codebreakers, leading to further U.S. Navy successes in the Pacific. After a reporter, STANLEY JOHNSTON, wrote in the *Chicago Tribune* on June 7, 1942, of American knowledge of Japanese forces before the battle, there was fear among U.S. naval leaders that the article might reveal Allied codebreaking successes to the Japanese. However, that article never reached Japan. The Japanese High Command remained ignorant of American successes in breaking into JN-25 until after the war.

The Navy's ability to decipher Japanese naval communications directly benefited Gen. Douglas MacArthur's Southwest Pacific Area and Adm. Chester W. Nimitz's Pacific Ocean Areas in their operations against the Japanese.

Joan Eleanor

Nickname for a very small (6½ x 2¼ x 1½ inches) radio transmitter-receiver used by the U.S. OFFICE OF STRATEGIC SERVICES during World War II. The four-pound radio was invented by Navy Lt. Comdr. Steve Simpson, an RCA engineer in civilian life, and DeWitt R. Goddard, another RCA engineer who was given a Navy commission to work with Simpson.

The radio was battery-powered and transmitted to a larger unit, connected to a recorder, in a plane circling overhead. Because of its design and the wavelength on which it broadcast, the transmitter was difficult for German direction finders to detect. Joan Eleanor was the CODE NAME for the system, Eleanor being the unit on the ground and Joan (named for Maj. Joan Marshall of the Women's Army Corps) being the unit in the plane.

Joe K

SEE KURT LUDWIG

John and Jane Doe [p]

Pseudonyms used in court papers in 2004 for a husband and wife who claimed to have spied in a Soviet republic for the CIA. Mr. Doe told the court that the CIA had persuaded him to remain in his position and spy for the United States, after which the CIA would arrange the Does' defection and resettlement, and ensure their personal and financial security for the rest of their lives.

The couple was brought to the United States and all was fine for the couple for some time, with their false identities and backgrounds. But then the American bank that Mr. Doe worked for in Seattle, Wash., merged with another, and he was laid off. The CIA left him without assistance, despite an earlier promise to resume financial aid if he became unemployed. The Does sued for an order directing the CIA to provide them with due process and to pay them the money that they were promised.

The courts refused under the long-established precedent that lawsuits could not be brought to enforce U.S. intelligence agencies' promises, because that would require exposure of matters that must be kept secret in the interest of effective foreign policy. (See WILLIAM A. LLOYD.)

In the Jan. 2004 opinion by the U.S. Court of Appeals for the Ninth District (Seattle), judges expressed the opinion that little could be worse for the country's ability to engage spies than insecurity about whether they will get what was promised to them. "If what the Does allege is true," said the court's majority opinion, "a serious injustice has been done to them, and the injustice to them is seriously harmful to the long-term security interests of the United States.

"Nevertheless, the judicial branch cannot right such a wrong without disclosure of the engagement's existence, which, as said, must remain forever secret. It will not do to have word circulating in whatever former Iron Curtain country the Does come from that the collapse of its totalitarian regime was brought about partly by CIA spies and not wholly by its own people's thirst for freedom." And, the opinion added, "Joshua needed spies, Lincoln needed spies, we needed spies to deal with the Soviet empire, and spies will be needed as long as there are men on earth."

John, Dr. Otto

(b. 1909 d. 1997)

West German intelligence official who worked for MFS (Stasi), the East German intelligence agency, and was convicted of treason by West Germany.

In 1933 John joined Lufthansa, the German civil airline, working in the legal offices of the firm until 1944. During World War II he worked with Generalmajor HANS OSTER, chief of staff of the ABWEHR, German MILITARY INTELLIGENCE. Both men strongly opposed Hitler and were involved in the July 20, 1944, plot to kill him. John's brother was executed for participating in the plot.

Four days after the plot failed, John flew to Madrid, defected to British INTELLIGENCE OFFICERS there, and was taken to Britain. He spent the rest of the war working for a radio station broadcasting BLACK PROPAGANDA. After the war he helped the British in the political screening of German prisoners and assisted in the prosecution of senior German military officers.

In Dec. 1950, John was made acting director of the BFV, West Germany's COUNTERINTELLIGENCE organization. Despite opposition by former German Army officers, he was permanently appointed in Dec. 1951.

On July 20, 1954, while in East BERLIN for a commemoration of the 1944 assassination plot, he defected to East Germany. He spent the next six months in the Soviet Union, returning to East Berlin in Dec. 1954, when he joined the staff of the Stasi.

John returned to West Berlin on Dec. 13, 1955, with the help of a Danish journalist. Although he claimed that he had been kidnapped, he was tried, convicted of treason in a West German court, and sentenced to four years at hard labor. He was released from prison on July 28, 1958, and moved to Austria.

Johnson

SEE RICHARD SORGE

Johnson, Clarence L. (Kelly)

(b. 1910 d. 1990)

Legendary aircraft designer who directed the design and production of the U-2 and SR-71 BLACKBIRD spyplanes during his long reign at Lockheed's SKUNK WORKS.

Johnson studied aeronautical engineering at the University of Michigan, graduating in 1933. He went to work for Lockheed as a tool designer, and after a series of assignments—stress analyst, wind tunnel engineer, weight

Clarence L. (Kelly) Johnson stands with a U-2 spyplane, one of the highly innovative aircraft produced by Johnson and the Lockheed Corporation's Skunk Works. Johnson's team also designed the U-2's successors, the supersonic A-12 Oxcart and SR-71 Blackbird. (LOCKHEED)

engineer—in 1938 he became chief research engineer. Besides being an outstanding engineer he was also a convincing salesman, getting the Royal Air Force (RAF) to buy Lockheed's Hudson bomber in 1938. Johnson was proud to see that a Hudson was the first RAF airplane to destroy an enemy aircraft in World War II (a Dorier Do 18 flying boat on Oct. 8, 1939). He also worked on the twin-boom P-38 Lightning, one of the most famous U.S. aircraft of World War II.

"I have known what I wanted to do ever since I was 12," he once said. "There has never been any change since that time in my desire to design airplanes."

In 1952 he was named chief engineer at the Lockheed plant in Burbank, Calif. He designed 40 aircraft, including the first U.S. combat jet, the F-80 Shooting Star—designed and built in 143 days—and the F-104 Starfighter. But he was best known for his spyplanes and the founding of the Skunk Works, a TOP SECRET design shop (formally known as the Advanced Development Projects facility), where spy SATELLITES and electronic jamming devices were also developed.

Johnson had a reputation for never spending a dime more than he had to spend. He gave back to the U.S. government about $2 million when the first U-2 was built at less than had been allocated. He designed the hydrogen-fueled CL-400 as a proposed successor to the U-2. When he saw that it would not perform adequately, he stopped working on it.

When Johnson retired as a Lockheed senior vice president in 1975, *Time* magazine called him "perhaps the most successful aviation innovator since Orville and Wilbur Wright." He remained on the Lockheed board of directors until 1980 and later served as a senior management adviser. He received the Air Force's highest civilian medal and three presidential citations, including the Medal of Freedom.

Johnston, Sgt. Robert Lee

(b. 1920 d. 1972)

U.S. Army sergeant recruited as a spy by the Soviets in BERLIN during the 1950s and early 1960s. Johnson was living with an Austrian-born mistress, by whom he had a son. Disgruntled over his failure to advance in rank, he decided to get even with the Army. "I did not want to have anything further to do with the Army or the American way of life. . . . I decided to seek asylum with the Soviets," he later said.

Through his mistress, he contacted Soviet INTELLIGENCE OFFICERS in East Berlin. At a meeting in Feb. 1953, Soviet officers persuaded Johnson to stay in the Army and work for Soviet intelligence. Meanwhile, Johnson married his mistress and was transferred out of his infantry unit to the Berlin Command's intelligence staff as a file clerk.

With a camera supplied by the Soviets, Johnson, in charge of classified files, systematically photographed every paper that looked important. His wife carried the film to Johnson's Soviet HANDLER. She, like Johnson, had been given a short course in TRADECRAFT.

When an Army friend, Sgt. JAMES A. MINTKENBAUGH, joined Johnson in his Berlin assignment, Johnson recruited him as a spy. In 1956 Johnson was discharged from the Army, but Mintkenbaugh—plus $500 from the KGB—convinced him to reenlist. Transferred to the Armed Forces Courier Transfer Station at Orly Airfield, near Paris, he began supplying the KGB with richer intelligence.

To and from the COURIER center were dispatched extremely valuable secret documents, including CIPHER KEYS for cipher machines. War plans and contingency plans, bulky documents too long and sensitive to transmit by cipher machine, also move through courier centers. The Orly center handled CRYPTOMATERIAL and highly classified documents destined for the NORTH ATLANTIC TREATY ORGANIZATION (NATO), the U.S. European Command, and the U.S. Sixth Fleet in the Mediterranean. Johnson had access to the vault where the secrets were kept between the time that they arrived from Washington, D.C., and the time couriers took them to their destination.

Told by his handler to penetrate the courier station vault for access to classified pouch envelopes, Johnson volunteered for permanent weekend duty. By making use of wax impressions of the key used to open the padlock and by using a Soviet-supplied radioactive device to X-ray the combination lock and read the combination, Johnson gained access to the vault from Nov. 1962 to the spring of 1963 and methodically passed the pouches to his handler, who opened them, photographed the contents, and then resealed them.

Two of the documents Johnson passed along were *CINCEUR* [Commander-in-Chief Europe] *Operation Plan NR 100-6*, which detailed U.S. plans for war in Europe, and *Nuclear Weapons Requirements Handbook*, which listed European targets for U.S. tactical nuclear weapons. These were later used for Soviet DISINFORMATION operations against NATO.

When Johnson was transferred to the United States, he did not continue spying. Fearing betrayal by his wife, he deserted the Army and became a drifter. In 1965, haunted by fear and conscience, Johnson gave himself up and implicated Mintkenbaugh, who was quickly arrested. Johnson's wife independently confirmed that both she and her husband had committed espionage.

In 1965 Johnson and Mintkenbaugh were each sentenced to 25 years in prison. On May 19, 1972, Johnson's 22-year-old son, Robert Lee Johnson, Jr., went to the federal prison in Lewisburg, Pa., to visit his father, whom young Robert had not seen for many years. Born just before Johnson had begun spying for the Soviets, Robert had seen both his father and mother dishonored by espionage. He had tried to retrieve his name and honor by serving in the Army and was in Vietnam. Robert ended his visit by plunging a knife into his father, killing him instantly.

Johnston, Stanley

American journalist who in 1942 revealed the U.S. Navy's codebreaking success against the Japanese Navy.

Johnston, a reporter for the *Chicago Tribune*, was on board the U.S. aircraft carrier *Lexington* during the Battle of the Coral Sea on May 7–8, 1942. In history's first carrier-versus-carrier battle, a Japanese force heading for Port Moresby on New Guinea was turned back, but the carrier *Lexington* was sunk. When the "*Lex*" was abandoned, Johnston was taken aboard the U.S. cruiser *Chester* and then transferred to the transport *Barnett* for return to the United States.

On board the cruiser a naval officer showed Johnston a deciphered Japanese radio message containing the Japanese operations order for the subsequent Battle of MIDWAY on June 4–5. Shortly after the battle, on June 7, the *Chicago Tribune* published a front-page story with the headline "NAVY HAD WORD OF JAP PLAN TO STRIKE AT SEA." Several affiliated papers also ran the story. The owner of the *Tribune* was Col. Robert McCormick, a rabid isolationist and opponent of the Roosevelt administration; on the eve of the PEARL HARBOR ATTACK he had published the purported U.S. war plans.

The June 7 story in the *Tribune* had no byline, but it was written by Johnston. It claimed that the U.S. Navy had advance knowledge of the strength and disposition of the Japanese force, even citing the names of major warships in the Japanese task forces.

The story was in fact based on a highly classified May 31 intelligence bulletin sent out by the NAVY COMMUNICATIONS INTELLIGENCE unit at Pearl Harbor (see HYPO and FLEET RADIO UNIT PACIFIC). The bulletin gave precise details on the Japanese force and gave the lie to Johnston's subsequent claim that the story was based on reference books, knowledge of Japanese losses at Coral Sea, and other OPEN SOURCE material.

Some Navy officers insisted on prosecuting Johnston for espionage, and the Department of Justice reluctantly began proceedings against Johnston and the *Tribune* under the 1917 ESPIONAGE ACT. The testimony of several witnesses before a grand jury in Chicago soon made it evident that Johnston had been shown the May 31 message by the *Lexington*'s executive officer while on board the *Chester*. "This violated every security rule in the book, but the grand jury refused to return an indictment. *The Chicago Tribune* beat the rap because the intelligence estimate had been volunteered to Johnston without any injunction about its being secret," wrote Rear Adm. EDWIN T. LAYTON, then the Pacific Fleet's INTELLIGENCE OFFICER, in *And I Was There* (1985). Significantly, at that time U.S. censorship rules did not prohibit newspapers from publishing information about enemy naval forces.

There is no evidence that the Japanese saw the *Tribune* story. Although they changed their ciphers in August 1942, no evidence has ever been uncovered that the change was related to Johnston's indiscretions.

Johnston almost immediately wrote a book about the Coral Sea battle entitled *Lexington: Queen of the Flat-Tops* (1942). The first page noted, "The information herein has been inspected by the Office of Censorship, which found no objection."

(Internationally known newscaster Walter Winchell also said that the Navy had advance notice of the Japanese movements at the Battle of Midway. On July 5 he made reference to the Coral Sea and Midway, asserting in his gossip column in the *New York Daily News*, "When the history of these times is written it will be revealed that twice the fate of the civilized world was changed by intercepted messages." On July 7 he referred to the *Tribune* story, reinforcing the codebreaking thesis. But Winchell's statements were not pursued by U.S. officials.)

Joint Intelligence

U.S. term for intelligence produced by more than one military service.

Joint Intelligence Center

(JIC)

U.S. intelligence center for a unified, or joint, command (a command containing forces from two or more military services). The JIC is responsible for providing intelligence support to the joint commander and to the component commands.

Joint Intelligence Committee

(JIC)

Senior British intelligence coordinating body, in some respects similar to the U.S. NATIONAL SECURITY COUNCIL.

The Joint Intelligence Committee was established as the Joint Intelligence *Sub*-Committee (JIC) of the British Joint Chiefs of Staff in 1936. Its membership consisted of a chairman, the Deputy DIRECTOR OF NAVAL INTELLIGENCE, Deputy Director of Intelligence (Air), and Head of the MI1 branch of the General Staff.

The War Cabinet and Chiefs of Staff Committee on May 17, 1940, spelled out the responsibilities of the JIC:

> taking the initiative in preparing, at any hour of the day or night, as a matter of urgency, papers on any particular development in the international situation whenever this appears desirable to any member. . . . The object of these papers, *which should be as brief as possible*, will be:
>
> (i) To draw attention to any information received in the Foreign Office or the Service Departments which appears to be of special importance, to assess its value, and to supplement it with any other information available so as to present the board deductions which are to be drawn concerning the particular situation in question.
>
> (ii) To summarise broadly the available evidence regarding the intentions of the enemy or developments in any of the "danger spots" in the international situation, and to set out the conclusions which may be drawn therefrom.

The JIC met regularly to evaluate and coordinate available military intelligence and to make recommendations; at times the Security Service (MI5) and Foreign Office turned to the JIC with questions. The military service intelligence departments initially considered the JIC to be superfluous and a time-consuming exercise. Still, the role and influence of the JIC increased, as more military and government agencies looked to the JIC for appraisals. Of particular interest was the JIC's daily intelligence summary. In the summer of 1941 a JIC office was established within the British Joint Staff Mission in Washington, D.C.

The JIC survived World War II and, with changing memberships and an expanding role, continues today. Its current charter, according to the official publication *National Intelligence Machinery* (2002) begins:

> under the broad supervisory responsibility of the Permanent Secretaries' Committee on the Intelligence Services, to give direction to, and to keep under review, the organisation and working of British intelligence activity as a whole at home and overseas in order to ensure efficiency, economy and prompt adaptation to changing requirements.

The current membership of the JIC, which meets weekly, consists of: the Intelligence Coordinator (chairman), the heads of the three military service chiefs of intelligence, two members from the Foreign and Commonwealth Office, one member from the Department of Trade and Industry, one member from Treasury, and the heads of the security agencies—MI5 and MI6. The position of chairman is appointed, and is not necessarily the Intelligence Coordinator, who would then be a member of the JIC.

Also see DEFENCE INTELLIGENCE STAFF.

Joint Military Intelligence College

U.S. Defense Department educational institution operated by the DEFENSE INTELLIGENCE AGENCY (DIA). The college was established as the Defense Intelligence School in 1962, in part through the merger of the Army's STRATEGIC INTELLIGENCE School and the Navy's postgraduate intelligence curriculum. Renamed the Defense Intelligence College in 1981, it became the Joint Military Intelligence College in 1993. The college is located at Bolling Air Force Base, in southwest Washington, D.C.

Students include military and civilian intelligence specialists seeking career development. Military officers selected for duty as defense ATTACHÉS in U.S. embassies also train at the college, which offers senior-level instruction aimed at broadening the careers of intelligence professionals. In 1980 Congress authorized the school to award the degree of master of science in strategic intelligence, and, in 1997, a bachelor of science in intelligence.

Students come from the military services, including the Coast Guard: the CIA, DIA, FBI, and NSA; as well as other government agencies. Military personnel may be officers or senior noncommissioned officers. The college has an off-campus program at the National Security Agency (NSA) and has encouraged a steady increase in enrollment from civilian agencies. On campus it has added two part-time graduate programs, one designed specifically for military reservists.

The college also sponsors research opportunities for the students and faculty.

Joint Ocean Surveillance Information Centre

British agency established in January 1990 at Northwood, north of London, to support various military commands and operating forces. It is operated by the Maritime Air Force (18th Group of the Royal Air Force) and Commander-in-Chief Fleet, which are also located at Northwood.

Joint Reconnaissance Center

SEE NATIONAL RECONNAISSANCE OFFICE

Jones, Geneva

U.S. State Department secretary arrested in 1993 for helping to pass classified information to rebels who were trying to overthrow the Liberian government. Jones, who had worked for five years in the State Department's Bureau of Politico-Military Affairs, was accused of copying more than 130 cables, smuggling them out of the State Department, and turning them over to two journalists. One of them was Dominic Ntube, editor of a U.S.-based newspaper about Africa and a resident alien. He was also charged with stealing the documents and faxing them to the rebels.

Some of the documents related to U.S. military operations in Somalia and Iraq; portions of them appeared in West African magazines. Other classified U.S. documents were found in the command post of rebel leader Charles Taylor, who later overthrew the Liberian government and, in a reign of terror, killed thousands before stepping down under international pressure in 2003. Accompanying the cables were fax cover sheets bearing Ntube's Washington, D.C., telephone number. Federal investigators who searched his home found thousands of U.S. government documents, including many from the CIA.

Jones pleaded guilty to 21 counts of theft and two counts relating to unlawful communication of national defense information. She was sentenced to 37 months in prison.

Jones, Sir John

(b. 1923 d. 1998)

Director-General of the British Security Service (MI5) from 1981 to 1985. He was the first head of MI5 since Sir ROGER H. HOLLIS (1956 to 1965) who did not have personal experience in COUNTERESPIONAGE operations.

Jones, like Hollis, had worked in F Branch, which dealt with DOMESTIC INTELLIGENCE, primarily gathering information on the Communist Party of Great Britain, left-wing groups, and people suspected of subversion.

Under Jones, MI5 developed more technical and electronic forms of SURVEILLANCE using wiretaps, computer taps, and BUGS, relying on devices more than AGENTS. Jones was "a forceful advocate" for technical surveillance, wrote PETER WRIGHT in *Spycatcher* (1987) because he believed "he could not infiltrate his officers into these left-wing groups since many of them lived promiscuous lives, and there were some sacrifices even an MI5 officer would not make for his country."

Jones, Staff Sgt. John P.

U.S. Air Force technician arrested in Korea in 1952 with Staff Sgt. GIUSEPPE CASCIO for conspiring to "give intelligence to the enemy." Jones suffered a nervous breakdown and was not charged after a medical board declared him to be insane and unfit to stand trial.

Josephine

SEE KARL-HEINZ KRÄMER

JOSIC

SEE JOINT OCEAN SURVEILLANCE INFORMATION CENTRE

Joyce, William

(b. 1906 d. 1946)

"Lord Haw Haw," who broadcast propaganda to England from Germany during World War II. Although he was not a spy, he was deeply involved in espionage through his association with pro-German operatives in England. ANNA WOLKOFF, who received U.S. Embassy documents from code clerk TYLER KENT, secretly sent potential topics for anti-British propaganda to Joyce.

Joyce got his nickname from British listeners because he used an assumed aristocratic accent to deliver his pro-Nazi broadsides. A member of Sir Oswald Mosley's British Union of Fascists, he went to Germany in 1939 and became one of Propaganda Minister Josef Goebbels's radio stars.

Born in Brooklyn, N.Y., to an English mother and Irish-American father, Joyce moved to Great Britain with his family in 1921. He claimed to be an American citizen when he was put on trial for treason in London's Old Bailey after the war. The court held that as the holder of a British passport he was a subject of the Crown. He was found guilty and hanged on Jan. 3, 1946.

J-STARS (E-8 aircraft)

U.S. SURVEILLANCE aircraft used extensively in the Gulf War of 1991 against Iraq, although the plane was still in the development stage. Given the military designation E-8, the J-STARS—for Joint Surveillance and Target Acquisition Radar Systems—is a joint Army–Air Force project to provide high-quality radar detection and tracking of moving vehicles on the ground.

Interest in such a surveillance capability was initiated in the 1970s by the Air Force with a radar project called Pave Mover. The project was given impetus by experience in the Arab-Israeli conflicts of the period. In 1985 the Air Force and the Army, which had been seeding a helicopter-carried surveillance radar, combined their requirements to develop J-STARS.

The J-STARS aircraft is based on a Boeing 707-320 airframe with a 24-foot, canoe-shaped pod under the forward fuselage housing an AN/APY-3 phased-array, multimode radar. Truck-size targets can be detected at distances of up to some 125 miles, with both moving and fixed targets presented with a high degree of resolution, invaluable for both intelligence collection and targeting. J-STARS can simultaneously track hundreds of ground stations in real time.

The aircraft has a normal mission time of 11 hours; with one in-flight refueling, that can be extended to 21 hours. The J-STARS system can operate at night and in virtually all weather conditions. The E-8 is manned by a crew of 21; for longer missions additional crewmen are carried.

The first of two prototype E-8A aircraft, converted from commercial 707s, flew on April 1, 1988. Both aircraft were employed to track Iraqi ground forces during the Gulf War in Jan. 1991, enabling the targeting of Iraqi vehicles, including Scud-type missile launchers. The two planes flew 49 missions, each averaging 11 hours, with at least one aircraft aloft for most of the period of the air war.

At the time of the Gulf War of 2003—in which J-STARS aircraft participated—the Air Force had 14 of the aircraft. All are assigned to the USAF 116th Air Control Wing at Robins Air Force Base, Ga.

Ju 88

Highly versatile and effective German Junker medium bomber that flew throughout World War II on every battle front where the Germans fought. The widely flown RECONNAISSANCE variants took high-altitude photos of the Soviet Union before the German invasion.

In many respects similar to the British MOSQUITO aircraft, the twin-engine Ju 88 was produced in greater numbers than any other German bomber. It was flown in the bomber, torpedo, anti-tank, day-and-night-fighter, photo-reconnaissance, and training roles. The Ju 88 was also used to carry Me 109 and Fw 190 fighters on *Huckepack* (piggyback) bombing missions, on which the explosive-laden, unmanned bomber would be dispatched against targets after the piloted fighter broke away. As Allied fighters improved and brought down large numbers of Ju 88 bombers, their crews dubbed them "flying coffins."

The Junker's bomber was developed in response to a 1935 Air Ministry requirement, and the prototype Ju 88V1 flew on Dec. 21, 1936, just 11 months after design work had commenced. Additional prototypes and pre-production models followed, with changes being made in engines and wingspan as well as other features. The first Ju 88s entered Luftwaffe service early in 1939 as high-speed bombers. They were used extensively in the Battle of Britain but suffered heavy losses in the daylight raids. Improved Ju 88s were used in bombing attacks against Britain in the spring of 1944 as well as in March 1945, including an audacious night fighter sweep to shoot down Allied bombers over Britain.

Most Ju 88s had a large glazed cockpit and nose, which afforded the pilot excellent visibility. Reconnaissance variants had fuel and cameras in the bomb bay and additional fuel in underwing drop tanks. The early Ju 88A4 bombers had a maximum speed of 273 mph and a range of 1,550 miles. They could carry up to 3,960 pounds of bombs in their internal bay and another 2,205 pounds of bombs under the wings for short, overload fights. The bombers' defensive armament consisted of several 20mm cannon and machine guns; the bomber variants normally had a crew of four. The C-6 fighter variant had a top speed of 311 mph; its armament consisted of three 20-mm cannon in the nose and several machine guns. The fighters flew with a crew of three, with a fourth man added to night fighters that entered service in 1944.

Several specialized camera-carrying variants were built. The Ju 88H was an ultra-long-range reconnaissance aircraft with increased fuel and a range of 3,200 miles; some H models had three built-in cameras as well as radar.

Total Ju 88 production was about 9,000 bomber variants and about 6,000 nonbombers—a total of 14,676 production aircraft, plus several prototypes being built in seven plants.

"K"

SEE MAJ. GEN. SIR VERNON KELL

KAEOT

British COUNTERINTELLIGENCE slang for "keep an eye on them," referring to people suspected of espionage.

Kahn, David

(b. 1930)

Journalist who has become the leading U.S. historian of codebreaking. Kahn, who earned his doctorate in modern history at Oxford University, was a writer for the New York newspaper *Newsday* and associate professor of journalism at New York University. He has also been distinguished visiting historian at the NSA.

He has produced several outstanding books in the field of communications intelligence: *The Codebreakers* (1968), *Hitler's Spies: German Military Intelligence in World War II* (1978), *Seizing Enigma: The Race to Break the German U-boat Codes, 1939–1943* (1991), *The Codebreakers: The Comprehensive History of Secret Communications from Ancient Times to the Internet* (1996).

His *Kahn on Codes* (1983) is a compilation of his articles and essays.

Kaltenbrunner, Gruppenführer Ernst

(b. 1903 d. 1946)

An ardent Nazi, Kaltenbrunner was an SS official and, after the assassination of REINHARD HEYDRICH in June 1942, the director of the RSHA (Reich Central Security Office). An early functionary of the Nazi Party in his na-

tive Austria, Kaltenbrunner, a lawyer, became the leader of the Austrian SS, and following the German takeover of Austria in 1938 became the chief of internal security in Austria, with the SS rank equivalent to lieutenant general.

After he took over Heydrich's post, he concentrated on rounding up Jews and, through his aide Adolf Eichmann, had a major role in directing the Holocaust. He took a personal interest in the methods of execution in camps under his control, especially the gas chambers.

Late in 1944, as he realized Germany had lost the war, Kaltenbrunner tried in vain to negotiate peace talks with ALLEN DULLES, the head of the U.S. OFFICE OF STRATEGIC SERVICES in Switzerland. When the war ended in early May 1945, he was picked up by U.S. soldiers and tried at Nuremberg by the Allies. The evidence against him included his signature on numerous documents ordering mass killings of Jews as well as prisoners of war. He was sentenced to death and hanged.

Kalamatiano, Xenophon

(b. 1882 d. 1923)

An American who spied against the Bolshevik regime in Russia.

Kalamatiano was born in Austria of a Greek father and a Russian mother. After his father's death in 1894, his mother remarried and the family moved to the United States, where Kalamatiano attended the Culver Military Academy in Bloomington, Ill., and then the University of Chicago. After graduation, he remained at the latter to teach Russian.

In 1907 he was hired by a farm tools firm as its representative in Russia. He established his own farm implement company in Moscow in 1912, rapidly prospered, and in 1913 married a member of the czarina's court.

While on a trip back to the United States in 1914, he was asked by a representative of Secretary of State Robert Lansing to report to the U.S. government on the situation in Russia. A few months after this request, in Aug. 1914, Russia was plunged into World War I and Kalamatiano's information became vital to the development of foreign policy by the Wilson administration.

When the United States entered the war in April 1917, Kalamatiano's relationship with the government was formalized, and he became a paid confidential employee. According to F. C. Brown in the *Naval Intelligence Professionals Quarterly* (fall 1996),

> Kalamatiano was given funds with which to hire informants, rent a safe house, and cover incidental expenses. He was provided with a US passport in the name of Sergei Nikolaevich Serpukhovsky, and was assigned a Moscow-based controller.... In addition, Kalamatiano began a news service, which enabled him to justify travel.

As conditions in Russia deteriorated, he sent his wife and son to the United States. Kalamatiano now devoted his full energies to espionage, activities that were quickly reported to FELIKS DZHERZHINSKY, head of the CHEKA, the Bolshevik secret police. From about Oct. 1917, the Cheka had an informant in the U.S. consulate who was able to obtain copies of Kalamatiano's reports.

Kalamatiano was allowed to remain at liberty until fall 1918, when the Cheka began arresting foreign intelligence AGENTS in Russia. Kalamatiano, away from Moscow at the time, initially eluded the Bolshevik guards posted at the consulate and his home. Still, he was found and arrested.

Placed on trial with others accused of plotting to overthrow the Bolshevik regime, he was found guilty and sentenced to death. Although twice brought out of his cell for execution, he languished in prison. In Aug. 1921, he was released through the efforts of future President Herbert Hoover, who was coordinating the feeding of starving millions in Europe.

Upon his arrival in Washington he received no debriefing; he was simply paid off and given a train ticket to California, where his wife and son were living. He became a language professor at his alma mater, Culver Military Academy. After suffering a frozen foot while hunting during the winter of 1922–1923, he died in Nov. 1923 from blood poisoning.

Brown's appraisal of Kalamatiano's perceptive views on the new communist state and espionage activities was that "his legacy, studied in depth by the KGB, was never so much as examined here in his adopted homeland."

Kalugin, Maj. Gen. Oleg Danilovich

(b. 1934)

Longtime head of Soviet KGB operations in the United States and later critic of the KGB.

Kalugin attended Leningrad State University and,

subsequently, a SPY SCHOOL before coming to the United States in 1958 as an exchange student, studying journalism at Columbia University in New York. After a year at Columbia he became a Radio Moscow correspondent at the UNITED NATIONS. In 1965—after five years in New York—he returned to Moscow to serve under the COVER of press officer in the Soviet Foreign Ministry.

He was then assigned to Washington, D.C., with the cover of deputy press officer for the Soviet Embassy. In reality he was the KGB RESIDENT for POLITICAL INTELLIGENCE, a key position during the Cold War. He held that post for 12 years. He was for a time HANDLER of an American WALK-IN, JOHN WALKER.

His success in the United States led to his being promoted to general in 1974, the youngest in the KGB. He returned to KGB headquarters to become head of the foreign COUNTERINTELLIGENCE or K branch of the First Directorate of the KGB.

His promising career was derailed in 1980 when differences between Kalugin and the KGB leadership led to his being "exiled" from KGB headquarters to become the deputy head of the Leningrad KGB. Kalugin's continuing criticism of the KGB's policies, methods, and "demonization" of the U.S. CIA caused VIKTOR CHEBRIKOV to dismiss Kalugin from the KGB in 1987.

As the Soviet Union underwent changes under Mikhail Gorbachev, Kalugin became more vocal and public in his criticism of the KGB, denouncing Soviet security forces as "Stalinist." Finally, in 1990, on Gorbachev's orders he was stripped of rank, decorations, and pension. Still—despite opposition supported by the KGB—in Sept. 1990 he was elected to Parliament, a people's deputy for the Krasnodar region.

Kalugin became a firm supporter of Boris Yeltsin, head of the Russian Republic. During the Aug. 1991 abortive coup against Gorbachev he led crowds to the Parliament building ("White House"), center of anticoup efforts, and induced Yeltsin to address the crowds. He then became an adviser to the new KGB chief, VADIM BAKATIN. (Bakatin, however, was fired from that post in Nov. 1991.) Ever vocal, Kalugin told the press that in the future the KGB would have "no political functions, no secret laboratories where they manufacture poisons and secret weapons." He continued to speak out, both in Russia and in the United States, in favor of oversight of Russian intelligence activities.

After several speaking engagements in the United States and visits with his former opponents in the U.S INTELLIGENCE COMMUNITY, in 1997 Kalugin sought to become a permanent resident of the United States. His application was revealed and thus opposed by several retired U.S. INTELLIGENCE OFFICERS.

In a speech in Arlington, Va., after receiving an award from the magazine *Sources,* Kalugin sought to explain his character:

> "I never defected. I never betrayed my country. I never cooperated with any agency of the United States or any other country. I am a Russian citizen trying to make my life decent and live in dignity."

In 2002 he was convicted of treason in absentia, and sentenced to 15 years in prison. In 2003 he became an American citizen. Kalugin has published two books about his former intelligence activities, *Burning Bridges* (1992) and *The First Directorate* (1994). He also serves as a member of the board of the INTERNATIONAL SPY MUSEUM in Washington, D.C.

Kampiles, William P.

(b. 1955)

Former CIA watch officer who sold a TOP SECRET manual on the BIG BIRD SATELLITE to the Soviet Union.

A graduate of Indiana University, Kampiles worked at CIA headquarters in LANGLEY, Va., from March to Nov. 1977. Chided for poor performance, his dream of becoming an INTELLIGENCE OFFICER shattered, he resigned from the CIA, walking out with a copy of the 64-page Big Bird manual under his jacket. On Feb. 19, 1978, Kampiles flew to Athens, where he sold the manual for $3,000 to a military ATTACHÉ at the Soviet Embassy. The GRU officer gave him guidance about other subjects of interest and instructions for subsequent meetings.

Upon returning to the United States, Kampiles told a friend at CIA that he had "conned" the Soviets out of $3,000, omitting to say that he had actually sold them the manual. His ploy was to get the CIA to rehire him as an intelligence officer. His friend suggested that he put his proposal in writing, which he did.

Until Kampiles sold the manual, Soviet intelligence officials were apparently unaware that the Big Bird was both a SIGNALS INTELLIGENCE and photo SURVEILLANCE satellite. Analysts at the NATIONAL PHOTOGRAPHIC INTERPRETATION CENTER knew that something had gone wrong when they noticed that the Soviets were changing their camouflage methods for military installations and strategic missile silos.

Then came the letter from Kampiles to his superiors in the CIA, describing his dealings with the Soviet—again omitting the fact that he had actually delivered the manual. The letter "remained unopened for two months at the CIA," according to Griffin B. Bell, U.S. Attorney General at the time. Bell later wrote that the INTELLIGENCE COMMUNITY "had come to believe that every time you prosecuted a spy, you would lose the secret, and that it was better public policy—the lesser of two evils—to let the spy go and keep the secret. But I had the idea that you could prosecute these cases without losing the secret." An informal CIA–Justice Department agreement essentially gave the CIA veto power over espionage prosecutions.

Bell had successfully fought the intelligence community to prosecute RONALD L. HUMPHREY, a U.S. Information Agency officer, and David Truong, the Vietnamese AGENT Humphrey had been providing with government documents. Bell, learning of Kampiles' espionage, told the CIA that he wanted to put Kampiles on trial. The CIA wanted his betrayal kept secret. Bell went to President Carter to get approval. Kampiles was arrested in Chicago by the FBI on Aug. 17, 1978.

The Kampiles case was a turning point for espionage prosecution. Kampiles was convicted of espionage and sentenced to 40 years in prison. His theft revealed that the CIA's internal security procedures were "surprisingly lax," according to Adm. STANSFIELD TURNER, who was DIRECTOR OF CENTRAL INTELLIGENCE at the time. "When we learned that one [Big Bird manual] was missing," he wrote in *Secrecy and Democracy* (1985), "we also found we could not account for thirteen others!"

K'ang Sheng

(b. 1899 d. 1975)

Director of Chinese intelligence activities under Mao Zedong.

Born Chao Yuri, the son of a wealthy landlord, he changed his name as an act of opposition to his father. While attending Shanghai University he joined the Communist Party in 1925 and became a labor organizer.

K'ang apparently began intelligence work in the 1920s, supplying local Communist leaders with intelligence. He was in Moscow in 1928 and again in the 1930s to study Soviet intelligence and security techniques. According to most reports, however, he never fully trusted the Soviets. He wrote a book in the 1930s, intended for Soviet audiences, entitled *Revolutionary China Today*.

He become head of the She-hui pu (Social Affairs Department), or main security organ, from about 1939 until 1946. During World War II he infiltrated some of his AGENTS into the rival Nationalist intelligence service of Chiang Kai-shek. After the war K'ang's intelligence activities supported the Chinese revolution and, subsequently, the quest for intelligence from the West on atomic weapons.

K'ang became a member of the Central People's Government Council and the Chinese *Politburo* in 1949, marking him as a national leader. He was in Moscow again in 1959, accompanying Prime Minister Chou En-lai, and in 1960 for meetings with Warsaw Pact representatives.

However, he fell from favor after the Cultural Revolution of the mid-1960s.

Kao, Yen Men

Chinese national arrested for attempting to illegally procure and export classified and embargoed high-technology military items from the United States.

Kao, who lived in Charlotte, N.C., was arrested in Dec. 1993, after a six-year investigation into a spy ring seeking information about advanced naval weapons and technology. COUNTERINTELLIGENCE officials said Kao "and several other Chinese nationals" conspired to illegally export the Navy's Mk 48 Advanced Capability (ADCAP) Torpedo, two F 404-400 General Electric jet engines used to power the Navy's F/A-18 Hornet fighter, and fire-control radar for the F-16 Falcon fighter. None of those systems were delivered to China. In an FBI sting operation, he paid an FBI informant $24,000 for a SATELLITE component. An immigration judge ordered his deportation to Hong Kong for overstaying his visa and for "committing acts of espionage against the United States."

Prosecutors decided against a trial to avoid offending the Chinese government and to protect counterintelligence sources and methods.

Kao, who reportedly owned two Chinese restaurants in Charlotte, had been under FBI SURVEILLANCE for several years, while he was in communication with Chinese INTELLIGENCE OFFICERS.

An obsessive gambler, Kao reportedly squandered money sent to him by his Chinese HANDLERS. Fearing reprisal, he requested deportation to Hong Kong rather than mainland China. He left behind his wife, a naturalized U.S. citizen, and two children.

Kappa

SEE FRITZ KOLBE.

Karla [f]

Soviet espionage chief and main villain of several JOHN LE CARRÉ [P] novels. East German master spy MARKUS WOLF has been cited as the model for Karla, but in reality there appear to have been few similarities between the men other than their profession and relative success.

Karlow, Serge Peter

(b. 1921)

U.S. CIA employee branded a MOLE—in error. Karlow was a veteran of the OFFICE OF STRATEGIC SERVICES (OSS) and, subsequently, the CIA.

Born in the United States, Karlow spent part of his childhood in Germany, from where his parents had emigrated. He was attending Swarthmore College (on a full scholarship) when, in July 1942, he was commissioned as an ensign in the U.S. Navy and assigned to the OSS. He served in the Mediterranean with high-speed PT boats that supported OSS operations. He lost a leg when a captured Italian PT boat he was riding struck a mine and blew up. (He received the Bronze Star for that mission.) Karlow returned to Washington, D.C., and in 1946 was assigned with KERMIT ROOSEVELT to write a history of the OSS (published in 1976 as *War Report of the OSS*).

Upon joining the CIA he worked both in the United States and in West Germany on high-tech gadgets and materials needed for espionage TRADECRAFT. Karlow described his work to David Wise for his book *Molehunt* (1992): "We dealt with guns, locks, paper. We made the tools you need to send people into denied areas.... Clothing with correct labels, identity papers, union membership cards, employment documents, ration cards."

Karlow had a successful career in the CIA, mostly in the Technical Services Division, until COUNTERINTELLI-GENCE agents of the CIA and FBI came to believe that they had found a Soviet mole given the CODE NAME Sasha. The tenuous identification was based on leads provided by two DEFECTORS from the KGB—ANATOLI GOLITSYN and YURI NOSENKO.

In 1962 Karlow was assigned as the CIA's representative at the State Department's operations center in order to deny him access to more politically SENSITIVE information than available at the CIA. Late in 1962 he was confronted by the FBI in what appeared to be a routine investigation. On Feb. 11, 1963, Karlow was told that he was under investigation. After extensive investigation and interrogation, he was fired from the CIA.

Karlow went to work for a commercial firm and concentrated on clearing his name. He was still a "prime suspect" for Sasha, but there was no proof and hence no formal charges were brought against him. In a strange twist of fate, the head of CIA counterintelligence who had helped to build the case against Karlow was JAMES JESUS ANGLETON, who was himself fired from the agency in Dec. 1974. The two knew each other well, and now Karlow pumped his former adversary for information that would help him clear his name.

With additional laws having been passed that allowed greater access to CIA files, Karlow intensified his efforts to clear his name. He and WILLIAM J. CASEY, then DIRECTOR OF CENTRAL INTELLIGENCE (DCI), both spoke at an OSS reunion in Oct. 1986. Casey promised to have the case reopened, but Casey died a few months later. The new DCI, WILLIAM H. WEBSTER, reviewed the case and decided that Karlow had been unjustly discharged from the CIA.

In 1988 Congress passed a special provision to permit payment to Karlow. The following year he was paid almost $500,000. He was also given a medal and a citation in recognition of 22 years of service to the CIA.

(Additional payments totaling some $200,000 were also made to former CIA employees Paul Garbler and Richard Kovich, also suspected of being Soviet spies. Both had been given relatively unimportant assignments and allowed to retire from the CIA. They were given the additional compensation in 1981.)

Katyn Massacre

The mass slaughter of Polish officers in 1940 by the Soviet NKVD. On April 12, 1943, German radio announced that the bodies of 4,143 Polish officers, all bound and shot in the back of the head, had been found in eight communal graves in the Katyn Forest near Smolensk. The Germans said the officers had been killed by the Soviets.

The Soviets had taken about 200,000 Polish prisoners of war in late 1939 as the Soviet Union joined Nazi Germany in assaulting Poland. About 15,000 of the prisoners—including 8,700 officers—were never seen again. The Soviets claimed that Germans had killed the Poles during the German invasion of the Soviet Union.

Not until 1989 did the Soviet government officially

begin to admit that the Poles had been murdered by NKVD units. The mass killings took place in the spring of 1940 when Soviet troops held the area, before the German invasion of July 1941. The murders were said to have been ordered by Josef Stalin because of his deep hatred of Poles. Another reason, put forth by a Soviet researcher in 1990, held that the NKVD was evacuating prison camps to make room for deportees from Estonia, Latvia, and Lithuania. The other vanished Polish prisoners were never accounted for. Similar executions were reported elsewhere, with some mass graves still unlocated; other prisoners were reportedly loaded on barges that were scuttled in the White Sea. (The CHEKA had used a similar drowning method for mass executions in the Russian Civil War.)

Historian and Soviet expert Robert Conquest wrote in *Stalin: Breaker of Nations* (1991):

> The repercussions of Katyn were severe and long lasting. . . . Stalin's attitude to human life, and to truth, let alone to international law, emerges very clearly. His precise state of mind when he decided on the executions in March 1940 is beyond our knowledge. In a broad sense he presumably thought, "They might give trouble in the future, so let us shoot them."

The NKVD was the obvious agency to undertake that assignment.

Kauder, Fritz

(b. 1903 d. ?)

Principal player in a highly successful Soviet DECEPTION operation against the Germans in World War II. Assigned the CODE NAME Max by the ABWEHR, Kauder forwarded bogus intelligence to the German armed forces for three and a half years.

Kauder was born in VIENNA to a Jewish mother and a father who had converted to Judaism but was later baptized as a Christian. Working mainly as a journalist and businessman in the early 1930s, Kauder lived in Budapest, where he became friendly with influential Hungarians and helped in some illegal matters, such as the obtaining of fraudulent visas. He also befriended German intelligence officials and American diplomats in Budapest.

When the war began in Europe, despite being Jewish he began selling documents and information to the Abwehr and the SD. Operation Max began about the time of the German invasion of the Soviet Union in July 1941, with former White Russian officers offering to send the Abwehr intelligence about the Soviets. The Germans provided two radio transmitters, which were set up in Moscow and in central Russia with the code names Max and Moritz, respectively. The latter soon disappeared, but Max continued to send information until early 1945.

Intelligence from Max included strategic and tactical material, all ostensibly of the highest CLASSIFICATIONS, indicating that Max was a spy within the Kremlin. Some in Germany thought he was a physician who attended Stalin; others believed Max was a tap on Kremlin telephone lines.

Probably the most astounding Max message was that of Nov. 4, 1942, which revealed the timeliness and high level of the source:

> On 4 November war council in Moscow presided over by Stalin. Present: 12 marshals and generals. In this war council the following principles were set down: a) Careful advance in all operations, to avoid heavy losses. b) Losses of ground are unimportant. *** f) Carrying out all planned offensive undertakings, if possible, before 15 November, insofar as the weather situation permits. Mainly: from Grozny [out of the Caucasus] . . .; in the Don area at Voronezh; at Rzhev; south of Lake Ilmen and Leningrad. The troops for the front will be taken out of the reserves. . .

Initially, Vienna was the reception point for radio messages from Max in Moscow. However, near the end of 1941 the reception point was moved to Sofia, Bulgaria, and Kauder took over that post. He received messages from Moscow and retransmitted them to Vienna, which forwarded them to Abwehr headquarters in BERLIN for further distribution to the military services.

The possibly unprecedented duration of the deception operation testifies to its success. According to some sources, NKVD commissar LAVRENTY BERIA personally directed the operation from Moscow. The British interception of many of the Max messages through ULTRA led ANTHONY BLUNT, a Soviet MOLE in MI5, to advise the Soviets of the "leak." But German intelligence apparently never questioned the validity of Max's information. While periodic questions were raised about the validity of the whole operation, too many German officials found the information correct (to the extent that it could be checked) and declared it was vital for the war. Reportedly, Adolf Hitler, who knew of the operation, heard that Max was a Jew and refused to accept further information from that source. The German High Command argued for Max's importance regardless of his religious heritage.

Late in the war the Abwehr decided that the operation was a Soviet deception effort, but by that time the Abwehr was being ignored by the German leadership. The German armed forces believed Kauder's information until the messages from Max ceased in Feb. 1945, when the Soviet Army was marching eastward.

As in Operation SCHERHORN, Max demonstrated the Soviet expertise in such deception activities.

Kauder also used the name Richard Klatt.

Kauffman, Capt. Joseph P.

U.S. Air Force officer court-martialed in West Germany in 1962 for having passed unspecified "military secrets" to East German intelligence. Kauffman was exposed by a DEFECTOR who had been an East German INTELLIGENCE

OFFICER. He was convicted and sentenced to 20 years at hard labor. On appeal the sentence was reduced to two years.

Kearn, Operations Specialist 1st Class Bruce L.

While serving on the U.S. tank landing ship *Tuscaloosa*, Kearn left the ship on an unauthorized leave in 1984, taking with him classified documents, including CRYPTO-MATERIAL. Sentenced to four years at hard labor and given a dishonorable discharge, he plea-bargained and was sentenced to one and a half years.

Kedrov, Mikhail Sergeyevich

(b. 1878 d. 1941)

Soviet INTELLIGENCE OFFICER who, along with his son, was executed for reporting on illegal actions of LAVRENTY BERIA. Kedrov's famed "last letter" was cited by Nikita Khrushchev when he exposed the excesses of Soviet dictator Josef Stalin at the 20th Communist Party Congress in 1956.

An early Bolshevik, Kedrov was head of the secret police—the CHEKA—in the Archangel area during the Russian civil war (1917–1920). Subsequently, in 1921, while head of the special division of the OGPU (the renamed Cheka), he investigated the secret police situation in Azerbaijan, where Beria was vice chairman of the OGPU. He found that Beria had released enemies of the Soviet regime and had condemned innocent people. He wrote to Moscow recommending that Beria be removed. Nothing happened.

Kedrov was himself a brutal interrogator and ran the forced labor division of the state intelligence apparatus. He extracted false confessions from his victims when they were required.

He retired in 1939, by which time his son Igor was an investigator for the Soviet intelligence service, renamed the NKVD. When Beria was appointed Commissar of Internal Affairs and head of the NKVD in 1939, both Kedrov and his son, and several of their friends, wrote a number of letters of protest to Stalin during Feb.–March 1939.

Igor Kedrov was immediately arrested and shot. The senior Kedrov was arrested in April 1939 and imprisoned. There he penned a letter to Communist Party Secretary A. A. Andreyev:

> From a gloomy cell in Lefortovskaia Prison, I appeal to you for help, Hear my cry of horror, don't pass on by, intercede, help to destroy a nightmare of interrogations, to discover the mistake. . . . I am an innocent victim. Believe me. Time will show. I am not an agent-provocateur of the tsarist secret police, not a spy, not a member of an anti-Soviet organization, as I am accused on the basis of slanderous declarations. And I have committed no other crimes against the Party or the homeland. I am a stainless old Bolshevik; for almost forty years I have fought honorably in the Party ranks for the good and happiness of the people. . . . Now the investigators are threatening me, an old man of sixty-two, with measures of physical coercion even more severe, cruel, and humiliating.

The letter continued, expressing his faith in the party and the Soviet government.

Kedrov's innocence was obvious. The Military Collegium of the Supreme Court completely exonerated him, an almost unique occurrence during the Stalinist purges. But Beria would not release him, and in Oct. 1941 he received the customary single bullet in the back of the head. A new, backdated verdict was drawn up after his murder.

At the 20th Communist Party conference in Moscow in 1956, Nikita Khrushchev quoted Kedrov's letter to Andreyev. In his memoir, *Khrushchev Remembers* (1970), Khrushchev, one of Stalin's most trusted lieutenants, wrote that after Stalin died and Beria had been deposed, "I remember I was particularly shocked at the revelation that Kedrov had been executed as an enemy of the people."

Keeler, Christine

SEE PROFUMO AFFAIR

Kell, Maj. Gen. Sir Vernon

(b. 1873 d. 1942)

Founder and first head of MI5. A graduate of the Royal Military Academy at Sandhurst, Kell fought in the BOXER Rebellion in China in 1900. Displaying an early facility for languages—he was fluent in French, German, Italian, and Polish from home schooling—he served and studied in China and Russia. He was an INTELLIGENCE OFFICER on Gen. Lorne Campbell's staff in Tientsin while also the foreign correspondent for the *Daily Telegraph*, an interesting mix of occupations.

From 1902 to 1906 Kell was head of the German section in the War Office. During this period he suffered from severe asthma and was unable to continue on active military service. In 1906, accordingly, he was given the task of organizing the Security Service (initially M05 and, from 1916, known as MI5). He began using the initial "K" on official documents, as a result of which that letter became a synonym for the position of head of MI5.

When Kell organized the Security Service in 1906 he was given one room in the War Office. By 1914 he had a staff of 14, and by 1918 the number had grown to 700. He continued to head MI5 after the war and through the 1930s, although he had officially retired from the Army in 1923.

Kell was sacked by Prime Minister Winston Churchill on May 25, 1940. Several events led to his dismissal, the principal cause being the fact that a German U-boat sank the British battleship *Royal Oak* inside the naval base at

Scapa Flow in the Orkneys on Oct. 14, 1939. Newspapers ran front-page stories speculating that German espionage had caused or at least contributed to the sinking. After an explosion at the Royal Gunpowder factory at Waltham Abbey in Jan. 1940, there was again speculation of sabotage. More reports of sabotage followed, and finally, Churchill confronted Kell privately in the Prime Minister's office. His dismissal stunned Kell and surprised the staff of MI5. (Churchill did not mention Kell's name in his six-volume memoir of World War II.)

Kempei Tai

Japanese intelligence organization founded in 1881 as a military police agency. It became a dreaded secret police organization, reaching the peak of its power in World War II.

Kempei Tai exerted immense control over civilians and searched for signs of subversion with a ruthlessness comparable to that of Germany's GESTAPO. During World War II, when it dealt continually with civilians, the Kempei Tai remained under the War Ministry. Because the Imperial Navy existed as a separate source of power, however, the Kempei Tai was frequently impeded by the Navy.

Many Kempei Tai agents came from distinguished Japanese families. Entry was restricted to candidates who passed rigorous mental and physical examinations. Units of 1,000 or so men were attached to each army, which used the Kempei Tai for COUNTERINTELLIGENCE, including the interrogation and handling of prisoners of war. Many Allied prisoners suffered torture and death at the hands of Kempei Tai interrogators.

Sometimes working in uniform, sometimes in civilian clothes, Kempei Tai agents could arrest soldiers and determine punishment without resort to courts. Their power extended to civilians and to foreigners. A few women were also employed as Kempei Tai agents.

The Kempei Tai is sometimes referred to as the "thought police," but that was a separate organization. The Thought Section of the Criminal Affairs Bureau was created by the Ministry of Justice in 1927 to root out members of the outlawed Communist Party and subversives. Later, the Peace Preservation Law, which prohibited any plans to change the government, was put under Thought Section jurisdiction.

After World War II, U.S. occupation authorities in Japan abolished the Kempei Tai along with the secret societies that had engaged in espionage. (See JAPAN.)

Kennan

U.S. spy SATELLITE carrying the KH-11 camera system (see KEYHOLE). This system provided first real-time viewing, with photo images of long, narrow strips of the earth being transmitted in digital form to relay satellites that send the signals to a ground receiving station at Fort Belvoir, Va., south of Washington, D.C. (Later, other ground stations were able to pull down KH-11 imagery.)

The first KH-11 launch occurred on Dec. 19, 1976, and the first pictures were transmitted on Jan. 20, 1977. Not being limited by the amount of film carried, as were previous photo satellites, the Kennan had a useful orbital life of more than two years (the first was in orbit for 770 days; later KH-11s were in orbit in excess of 1,000 days). Some KH-11s exceeded four and a half years in orbit.

KH-11 satellites initially flew in company with KH-8 and KH-9 photo satellites but subsequently succeeded them. Two KH-11s were usually in orbit during the next several years, providing detailed photography of the Soviet Union, China, and other areas of interest to U.S. political and military leaders. A KH-11 was used to locate the American hostages inside the U.S. Embassy compound in Teheran after its takeover by Iranian militants in 1980; this provided the intelligence needed to plan the abortive raid on the embassy.

A KH-11 photo was probably the first U.S. spy satellite view to be publicly shown, when a shot of the Soviet Tu-160 Blackjack bomber appeared in the Dec. 14, 1981, issue of the magazine *Aviation Week and Space Technology*. According to its caption, the photo showed the bomber at the Ramenskoye research facility near Moscow and had been taken little more than two weeks earlier. It was, of course, classified.

KH-11 satellites continued to be orbited into the 1990s, the name having been changed from Kennan to Crystal in 1982. There were continued improvements to the KH-11 camera system, with the satellite's weight increasing to some 16 tons.

The KH-11 flew in an orbit approximately 165 to 287 miles above the Earth. The signal from the KH-11s was transmitted to one of two Satellite Data Systems (SDS) orbiting over the Earth, the first SDS being launched in 1976. It was the SDS—which performed several functions—that relayed the KH-11 signal to the ground.

The Kennan/KH-11 vehicle has been reported as cylindrical in shape, some 64 feet long, 10 feet in diameter, and initially weighing some weighing 15 tons.

Also see BIG BIRD.

Kent, Tyler G.

(b. 1911 d. 1988)

CODE clerk in the U.S. Embassy in London who smuggled highly secret cables and other documents to a pro-German organization during World War II.

Kent was born in Manchuria, where his father was the U.S. consul. After graduating from Princeton, he studied Russian at the Sorbonne. He became a State Department employee, working as a clerk in the U.S. Embassy in Moscow for William C. Bullitt, first American ambassador to the Soviet Union. There Kent was promoted to code clerk.

He was transferred to the U.S. Embassy in London, beginning work there on Oct. 5, 1939. Winston Churchill had just been appointed First Lord of the Admiralty. He was communicating regularly with President Franklin D.

Roosevelt, and both men expected that he would eventually become Britain's wartime Prime Minister.

As soon as Kent arrived in London, he was seen in the company of a suspected German AGENT who was being tailed by detectives of Scotland Yard's SPECIAL BRANCH. He also frequented the Russian Tea Room, a rendezvous for White Russians run by Adm. Nikolai Wolkoff, the former Imperial Russian naval ATTACHÉ in London, and his wife, a former maid of honor to the czarina. Through their daughter Anna, Kent met Irene Danischewsky, wife of a naturalized British merchant who frequently visited the Soviet Union. She became Kent's mistress. Both she and her husband were under SURVEILLANCE by the Security Service MI5 as possible spies for the Soviet Union.

The cables that Kent stole included some sent to Roosevelt by Churchill before and after the latter became British Prime Minister. Disclosure of them at the time would probably have ruined U.S.-British relations, for the documents showed that Roosevelt was looking at ways to evade U.S. neutrality laws to help Britain survive the German onslaught.

When MI5 officers arrested Kent on May 20, 1940, they found 1,929 official documents in his apartment. Besides copies of Churchill's cables, there was a book containing the names of people under surveillance by the Special Branch and by MI5. Searchers also found keys to the U.S. Embassy's CODE room.

After Kent had been held for 11 days under secret arrest, the U.S. State Department announced that he had been fired and "detained by order of the Home Secretary." The statement did not say that he had been arrested for violating the OFFICIAL SECRETS ACT. ANNA WOLKOFF was arrested on the same day and similarly charged.

A State Department official made a confidential assessment: "[the documents] are a complete history of our diplomatic correspondence since 1938. . . . It means not only that our codes are cracked . . . but that our every diplomatic maneuver was exposed to Germany and Russia. . . ." Later investigation established, however, that Kent had not seriously compromised State Department codes.

On Oct. 23 the secret trial of Kent began at the Old Bailey. Brown paper was pasted on the windows and glass door panels. The only spectators were official observers, including MALCOLM MUGGERIDGE, representing MI6. Two of the witnesses against Kent were Maxwell Knight, head of countersubversion for MI5, and Capt. Archibald Maule Ramsay, who was interned by Knight on the Isle of Man because he had seen the documents. British officials knowledgeable about the papers believed that if their contents were revealed Roosevelt's bid for re-election would fail. (Ramsay had founded the Right Club, whose members believed in a conspiracy of Jews, Bolsheviks, and Masons.)

Kent was specifically charged with obtaining documents that "might be directly or indirectly useful to an enemy" and letting Wolkoff have them in her possession. He was also accused of stealing documents that were the property of the American ambassador to London, Joseph P. Kennedy. (Kennedy, the father of John F. Kennedy, was skeptical about Britain winning against Germany.)

Kent admitted that he had also taken documents from the U.S. Embassy in Moscow and had hidden them away, vaguely thinking that someday he might show them to U.S. senators who shared his isolationist and anti-Semitic views. He said he had burned the Moscow documents before being assigned to London. (In Moscow he had fallen in love with an interpreter who also worked for the NKVD, and this led to suspicions that he may have had Soviet contacts. His predecessor as a code clerk in Moscow, Henry W. Antheil Jr., had passed information to the Soviets. He was killed in a commercial plane crash in 1940, before formal charges were made against him.)

When news of Kent's arrest broke, the U.S. and British governments tried to play down the affair. Anti-Roosevelt rumors spread that Kent had been imprisoned to keep him quiet, allegedly because he had found evidence that Churchill and Roosevelt were conspiring to involve the United States in the war. The documents, finally released in 1972, did not support the conspiracy rumor. The papers that Kent conveyed did indicate Anglo-American naval cooperation. But they also showed that Roosevelt was reluctant to go further without congressional or public approval.

Kent was released in Sept. 1945 and deported to the United States. He never changed his opinions. After marrying a wealthy woman, he became the publisher of a weekly newspaper that attacked blacks, Jews, and the late President Roosevelt. He condemned President John F. Kennedy as a communist and charged that he was killed by communists because he was abandoning his communist leanings.

Despite his anti-communist writings, officials in the FBI still suspected him to be a secret Soviet sympathizer. Between 1952 and 1963, Ray Bearse and Anthony Read wrote in *Conspirator* that there were six FBI investigations of Kent, "all ending inconclusively."

Key List

SEE CIPHER KEY

Keyhole

(KH)

U.S. designation for IMAGERY INTELLIGENCE collected by spy AIRCRAFT and SATELLITES. The Keyhole (KH) designations were assigned to the camera systems. For example, the CORONA satellite cameras were designated KH-1 through KH-4; ARGON cameras were KH-5; and LANYARD cameras were KH-6.

Later satellites have been designated KH-7, KH-8, KH-9 (BIG BIRD), and KH-11 (KENNAN and, subsequently, Crystal). There was a planned KH-10, but before it could be produced the more advanced KH-11 design became available. While KH-12 and KH-13 satellites have been mentioned in books and articles, the NATIONAL RECONNAISSANCE OFFICE reportedly ceased using the designation scheme in the late 1980s with KH-11 the last used.

The CIA lists the following early KH missions:

KH Ground

Program	Camera	Operational	Successes	Failures	Resolution
Corona	KH-1	1960	1	9	40 ft
Corona	KH-2	1960–61	4	6	25 ft
Corona	KH-3	1961	4	2	12–25 ft
Corona	KH-4/A/B	1962–72	86	9	6–25 It
Argon	KH-5	1962–64	6	6	460 ft
Lanyard	KH-6	1963	1	1	6 ft

In 1962, when Corona satellites were orbiting with the KH-4 camera, all previous Corona missions were retroactively given the KH-4 designator, leading to some confusion in satellite histories.

Also see LACROSSE, TALENT KEYHOLE.

KG 200

Kampfgeschwader (Bomber Wing) No. 200, or KG 200, was a "special duties" group of the German Air Force in World War II that was used extensively for clandestine operations. The *Luftwaffe* established KG 200 on Feb. 20, 1944, primarily to drop AGENTS behind enemy lines in support of operations by the ABWEHR and the SS. KG 200 had a key role in Operation ZEPPELIN, the alleged German attempt to assassinate Soviet dictator Josef Stalin.

The wing flew a variety of aircraft, German as well as captured American, British, French, and Italian planes. The more unusual planes on the KG 200 roster included captured U.S. four-engine B-17 Flying Fortress and B-24 Liberator bombers as well as the six-engine Ju 390 very long-range transports and multiengine flying boats. In addition to dropping agents by parachute and landing them behind enemy lines, the wing also used the PAG drop device to deliver people.

KGB

Komitet Gosudarstvennoy Bezopasnosti (Committee for State Security) was the Soviet agency responsible for state security from Mar. 1954 until Oct. 1991—the eve of the demise of the Soviet Union in Dec. 1991. Subsequently, the principal foreign intelligence functions of the KGB were assigned to the newly established Central Intelligence Service. In addition, from 1960 to 1966 the KGB was also responsible for the internal security of the Soviet Union (see NKVD).

The KGB's functions included COUNTERESPIONAGE, foreign intelligence collection and analysis, COUNTERINTELLIGENCE for the armed forces, protection of land and maritime borders, and certain special security functions, among them the control of nuclear weapons, communications for the national leadership, and provision of the Kremlin guards. The KGB was the world's largest intelligence and police agency, probably larger than all Western intelligence agencies combined. For most of its existence

it was responsible for the functions that in the United States are carried out by the CIA, NSA, FBI, DEFENSE INVESTIGATIVE SERVICE, Marine Corps embassy guards, military service counterintelligence agencies, Border Patrol, Coast Guard, and SECRET SERVICE.

KGB agents have generally been depicted in the Western media as being large, bull-necked, strong, and stupid. Many were. In *Breaking with Moscow* (1985), Soviet defector ARKADY SHEVCHENKO, former Under Secretary-General of the UNITED NATIONS, described one KGB operative in New York as "muscular, and blonde, he looked like the incarnation of a Gestapo stereotype," who liked to talk about the skyscrapers in Manhattan. "All those shining towers," he said, "they look so strong, so tall, but they're just a house of cards. A few explosions in the right places and *do svidaniya* [goodbye]."

MODUS OPERANDI

Murder, kidnapping, and intimidation have been the tools of the trade for Soviet security-intelligence organs, from the CHEKA to the KGB. But there were many recent examples of KGB (as well as GRU) operatives acting in a sophisticated and innovative way. On one occasion a U.S. government employee was contacted by a Soviet intelligence operative. After some discussions, the contact was allowed to drop. But two or three years later, after the American had moved, divorced, and changed his car, the same Russian met him in a drugstore to renew the contact.

More devious and concealed operations have also occurred. DONALD ULTAN, a 30-year-old Brooklyn-born employee of the American Embassy in VIENNA, was a target for Soviet intelligence because he was a CODE clerk—the highest priority for KGB and GRU efforts. The complex and somewhat bizarre plan had a Soviet agent who was a naturalized citizen of a Western country invite a close friend of Ultan for a drink. Thus was arranged a "chance" meeting in a café with a semi-retired Belgian businessman who was, of course, a KGB officer. This, in turn, was maneuvered into a meeting with Ultan. The KGB officer never appeared to be particularly interested in Ultan but instead scheduled more encounters with Ultan's friend. There followed many hours of friendly meetings in cafés and coffee houses, chess playing, and an occasional outing. Ultan—Jewish and fluent in French—began a pleasant association with the Belgian, who claimed to be Jewish (with relatives in Israel) and who also spoke French.

Only after five months did the KGB agent ask Ultan to provide code information for money. After a brief delay, Ultan went to the embassy security officer and revealed the KGB contact. The Soviet effort against Ultan was sophisticated and, in the words of a U.S. intelligence report on the incident, "well-planned."

Ultan and other Americans involved with codes—such as Navy communications specialists JOHN WALKER and JERRY WHITWORTH—have been the top TARGETS of Soviet espionage. According to the U.S. government's classified manual *Soviet Intelligence Operations Against*

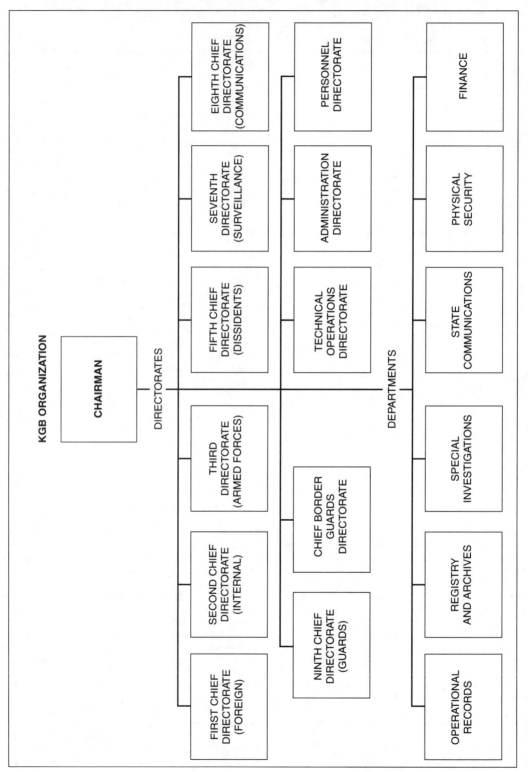

KGB ORGANIZATION

CHAIRMAN

DIRECTORATES

FIRST CHIEF DIRECTORATE (FOREIGN)

SECOND CHIEF DIRECTORATE (INTERNAL)

THIRD DIRECTORATE (ARMED FORCES)

FIFTH CHIEF DIRECTORATE (DISSIDENTS)

SEVENTH DIRECTORATE (SURVEILLANCE)

EIGHTH CHIEF DIRECTORATE (COMMUNICATIONS)

NINTH CHIEF DIRECTORATE (GUARDS)

CHIEF BORDER GUARDS DIRECTORATE

TECHNICAL OPERATIONS DIRECTORATE

ADMINISTRATION DIRECTORATE

PERSONNEL DIRECTORATE

DEPARTMENTS

OPERATIONAL RECORDS

REGISTRY AND ARCHIVES

SPECIAL INVESTIGATIONS

STATE COMMUNICATIONS

PHYSICAL SECURITY

FINANCE

KGB Organization.

Americans and U.S. Installations, "It is this broad category of code clerks, secretaries, Marine guards, etc., which the Soviets regard as particularly vulnerable since (in the words of one KGB directive) 'they do not belong to the privileged class and are worse off financially.'" The last point is critical: Most of the Americans who have betrayed America to the Soviets have done so for money.

A notable exception may have been the Marine guards at the American Embassy in Moscow in the mid-1980s, several of whom were accused of betraying classified access to offices and materials in return for sexual favors. At least in the initial stages of the investigation of the Marines stationed in Moscow and Leningrad (now St. Petersburg), money was not seen as a motive.

The KGB continued to try to introduce "class wars" into spy recruiting; blacks and a full-blooded American Indian were major targets among the Marine guards at the U.S. embassy in Moscow. However, one Marine officer who served at the Embassy in this period was quick to point out that the Soviet efforts to turn embassy staff and guards into spies constituted "a blanket operation."

"These [American] people are in Moscow for a short time, two years," he told the authors of this book. "The Soviets go after them all; certainly some appear more vulnerable to their attempts than others, but almost everyone at the embassy—especially the junior people and enlisted Marine guards—are the subject of KGB attention."

Thus, the KGB employed virtually all aspects of intelligence TRADECRAFT to garner information. Women were a particularly effective weapon, and the HONEY TRAP was often employed against Americans and other foreigners in the Soviet Union and, on at least one occasion, in the United States (see RICHARD MILLER).

PERSPECTIVE

The KGB was established as a state committee under the Council of Ministers in 1954 in an effort by the Soviet leaders who followed Josef Stalin and LAVRENTY BERIA to ensure control over the state security agency. With Beria's demise the internal security function was assigned to the MVD and state security (including foreign intelligence) to the KGB. In July 1978 the KGB was changed to a state committee of the Soviet Union, elevating the agency to ministerial status 24 years after its establishment.

The significance of the KGB to the Soviet system has been described by John J. Dziak, a lecturer on Soviet intelligence at George Washington University, in an interview with the *Washington Times*: "The KGB is the cutting edge of the [Soviet] system. The Soviet system can't survive without it." Raymond G. Rocca, deputy chief of counterintelligence for the U.S. CIA until 1974 and a lecturer at the JOINT MILITARY INTELLIGENCE COLLEGE, who was also interviewed by the *Washington Times*, regarded the KGB as a major player in the theory and practice of communist ideology. "It's the linchpin of the communist system," he said.

The first head of the KGB was IVAN SEROV (1954–1958), who had previously been deputy chief of the GRU; in Dec. 1958 he returned to head that intelligence agency as its chief. (Most chiefs of the GRU had previously served in the KGB and its predecessor agencies.) ALEKSANDR SHELEPIN, head of the KGB from 1958 to 1961, attempted to rebuild the agency into an effective intelligence and counterintelligence service.

Under the chairmanship of YURI ANDROPOV (1967–1982) the KGB assumed a relatively high level of respectability and power. Upon the death of Leonid Brezhnev, Andropov left the KGB to become head of the Communist Party and de facto ruler of the Soviet Union. He was second only to Beria in longevity as head of the principal Soviet intelligence service.

VITALY FEDORCHUK briefly succeeded Andropov in 1982 but was transferred to the post of Minister of Internal Affairs when Andropov replaced Brezhnev, reflecting the Soviet leader's confidence in him.

VLADIMIR KRYUCHOV, who had become head of the KGB in 1988, was one of the plotters in the abortive Aug. 1991 coup to overthrow Mikhail Gorbachev. He was dismissed and promptly arrested. Also among the 13 men charged in the plot were KGB Lt. Gen. Yuri Plehanov, head of the Kremlin's presidential guard, who had helped keep Gorbachev under house arrest in the Crimea; Vladimir Grushko, deputy head of the KGB; and Vyacheslav Generalov, deputy head of the Kremlin guard. None of those men would be brought to trial.

Leonid Shebarshin was briefly named head of the KGB following the attempted coup. He had served in Afghanistan, Iran, and India before becoming KGB deputy chief in 1987. But Shebarshin was unacceptable to some of the Soviet leadership and that same month he was succeeded as head of the KGB by VADIM BAKATIN.

Bakatin had been fired as Minister of Interior in Dec. 1990 by Kremlin hard-liners. Under his direction the KGB changed its composition and mission; its border troops became a separate agency, its combat forces were transferred to the Soviet Army (Ground Forces), and the Kremlin guard and communications troops were made directly responsible to the Soviet government (see below). Former KGB Maj. Gen. OLEG KALUGIN, an adviser to Bakatin, in Aug. 1991 said that in the future the KGB would have "no political functions, no secret laboratories where they manufacture poisons and secret weapons."

Bakatin's tenure lasted only until the beginning of Oct. 1991, when he was replaced by YEVGENY PRIMAKOV, to whom it fell to preside over the dismantling of the KGB, which was formally abolished on Oct. 22, 1991 (although Primakov appears to have retained the position of head of the KGB into Dec. 1991). The KGB's components were reorganized into three separate services: the MB (Russian Ministry of Security), in existence from 1991 to 1993, when it changed to the FSK and then FSB; the Inter-Republic Council for Security; and the State Border Guards Service.

KGB ORGANIZATION

The basic organization of the KGB in its later years provided for nine chief directorates:

First Chief Directorate: Foreign intelligence, active measures, counterintelligence, analysis.

Second Chief Directorate: Domestic counterintelligence, countersubversion, industrial security.

Third Chief Directorate: Counterintelligence and countersubversion within the Soviet armed forces, including the Special Departments (Osobye Otdely, or OO).

Fourth Chief Directorate: Embassy security and internal security.

Fifth Chief Directorate: Dissidents.

Sixth Chief Directorate: Economic, secret political, and transport.

Seventh Chief Directorate: Surveillance equipment.

Eighth Chief Directorate: SIGNALS INTELLIGENCE, COMMUNICATIONS SECURITY.

Ninth Chief Directorate: Protection of national leadership and sensitive installations, including the Kremlin guards.

In the late 1960s the Fourth through Sixth Chief Directorates were absorbed by the Second Chief Directorate; however, in 1969 the Fifth Chief Directorate was established to deal with political, social, and cultural dissidents.

Officers of the Third Chief Directorate of the KGB—responsible for counterintelligence within the armed forces—were assigned to all branches of the armed forces; they generally wore standard military uniforms but were readily recognized as KGB officers, reported through a special the KGB chain of command, and operated a network of "informers." In the Navy, uniformed KGB officers were assigned to large surface ships as well as to shore bases.

In his book *Inside the KGB* (1990), Soviet defector Aleksei Myagkov, a former KGB officer, described being told that "when recruiting informers, you must not only convince them but also compel them to work for us. The KGB has enough power for that." He added:

The KGB had the rights and the power needed. If it was an officer [wanted as an informer], then his career could be threatened (without KGB approval no officer can be sent to a military academy or get promotion). With regular [enlisted] servicemen it was even simpler; they could just be dismissed from the army. Any Soviet citizen's life, too, could be threatened; he could be barred from an institute or from work in any undertaking, or be forbidden to travel abroad.

During the 1980s the KGB was estimated to number more than 400,000 personnel, including 230,000 to 250,000 border troops and approximately 50,000 signal and security troops supporting the national and Communist Party leadership. There were also several hundred thousand KGB informers within Soviet society, including the government and armed forces.

It had been estimated that between 40 and 60 percent of Soviet Embassy officials in Washington, D.C., were attached to the KGB. Officers of the KGB also served in combat areas, supporting Soviet military and state interests. From 1954 to 1989 a total of 572 KGB personnel were killed "rendering military-technical assistance to other countries"—including Arab countries, North Vietnam, and Afghanistan—and in border conflicts.

KGB headquarters were located at No. 2 DZERZHINSKY SQUARE in Moscow, the location of its predecessor and successor agencies. During the 1970s the KGB's First Chief Directorate (foreign operations) moved to a modern, Finnish-designed office building at Yaseenevo on the Moscow Ring Road.

The KGB and its predecessors operated a large education and training network, with several SPY SCHOOLS to train Soviet and Eastern European intelligence and security personnel. The training facility at Pushkina, near Moscow, was used extensively to train Arab terrorists.

KGB CHAIRMEN

The following were chairmen of the KGB:

Mar. 1954–Dec. 1958	I. A. Serov
Dec. 1958–Nov. 1961	A. N. Shelepin
Nov. 1961–Apr. 1967	V. Y. Sernichasmy
May 1967–May 1982	Yu. V. Andropov
May 1982–Dec. 1982	V. Fedorchuk
Dec. 1982–Aug. 1988	V. M. Chebrikov
Aug. 1988–Aug. 1991	V. A. Kryuchov
Aug. 1991	Leonid Shebarshin
Aug. 1991–Oct. 1991	Vadim Bakatin
Oct. 1991–Dec. 1991	Yevgeny Primakov

KH-Series Satellites

SEE KEYHOLE

Khaki

CIPHER system used by the U.S. Navy during World War II for secure communications between major intelligence activities, especially for the transmission of MAGIC and ULTRA material.

Also see NAVY COMMUNICATIONS INTELLIGENCE.

Khokhlov, Capt. Nikolay Y.

A trained Soviet assassin and one of the first significant Soviet DEFECTORS of the Cold War.

Khokhlov was recruited into Soviet intelligence (NKVD) in 1941. About 12 years later, he was assigned to assassination or WET AFFAIRS operations. He was to kill Georgi Sergeevich Okolovich, an influential Russian émigré and official of the Popular Labor Alliance of Russian Solidarists, an anti-Soviet party based in West Germany. Three years earlier a Soviet attempt to kidnap Okolovich had failed.

Khokhlov's weapon was an electrically operated gun, fitted with a silencer and concealed in a gold cigarette case. It fired cyanide-tipped bullets that would probably lead a pathologist, after seeing a non-fatal bullet wound, to diagnose the cause of death as heart failure.

On Feb. 18, 1954, Khokhlov called at Okolovich's apartment and told him that he had been sent to assassinate him. Then, with his wife, he defected to the U.S. CIA. He also revealed the identities of two other Soviet AGENTS, sent to assist him, who corroborated his revelations. After extensive debriefings by the CIA, on April 20, 1954, he gave a press conference, revealing the unusual assassination gun and the plan to kill dissidents living overseas.

Khokhlov subsequently wrote *In the Name of Conscience* (1959), publicly revealing many of the excesses of the NKVD. On Sept. 15, 1957, while attending a conference in Frankfurt, he fell ill. He was found to have a severe blood disorder that would soon lead to his death. Transferred to a U.S. military hospital, he was kept alive by intravenous feeding and massive blood transfusions while a variety of "miracle" drugs were tried on him. He survived, and it was subsequently determined that he had been poisoned with thallium that had been subjected to intensive radiation in a complex Soviet assassination attempt.

KI

Komitet Informatsii, or KI, was the Soviet agency charged with all foreign intelligence and clandestine operations that previously were carried out by the MGB and the GRU (MILITARY INTELLIGENCE). Soviet dictator Josef Stalin established the Committee of Information in Oct. 1947 under the control of the Council of Ministers. As such, the KI was chaired by a succession of officials from the Foreign Ministry: V. M. Molotov, Yakov Malik, Andrei Vyshinskiy, and Valeriy Zorin.

The KI responsibilities were

(1) Military and political espionage abroad
(2) Operations against all anti-Soviet organizations abroad
(3) COUNTERINTELLIGENCE for Soviet embassies, missions, consulates, trade delegations, and citizens abroad
(4) Intelligence operations in other Communist countries

Certain, limited clandestine activities—such as assassinations—were still directed by the MGB.

The KI concept was a complete failure, in part because there were now four state security ORGANs—the MGB, GRU, and MVD, as well as the KI—resulting in overlap, shortfalls, and confusion. In mid-1948, Marshal of the Soviet Union N. A. Bulganin, himself a former CHEKIST, prevailed upon Stalin to permit the GRU to withdraw its foreign intelligence operations from the KI. Later that year counterintelligence and some other elements previously conducted by the MGB were returned to that agency.

A year after its establishment the KI was left with only the tasks of collecting foreign political and economic intelligence. Those, too, were returned to the MGB in 1951, ending an awkward and (from a Soviet viewpoint) perilous arrangement.

The true rationale for the establishment of the KI is not clear. It may have been either a power play by Molotov or Stalin's attempt to reduce the power of the state security organs.

Killian, Dr. James R., Jr.

(b. 1904 d. 1998)

American scientist who had a profound effect on U.S. intelligence, SATELLITE, and strategic weapon programs. In describing his role as President Eisenhower's science adviser, Killian wrote, "Only when Jefferson was his own science adviser and Vannevar Bush was advising Franklin Roosevelt during World War II was science so influential in top government councils as it became in Eisenhower's second term."

Killian, a Massachusetts Institute of Technology (MIT) graduate, was editor of the school's *Technology Review* from 1930 to 1939. He became a vice president of the college in 1943 and president in 1948. President Truman appointed Killian a member of the Scientific Advisory Committee of the Office of Defense Mobilization in 1951.

In the spring of 1954 Killian was the president of the MIT when President Eisenhower, a year after entering the White House, asked Killian to establish a Technological Capabilities Panel to look into the potential of long-range, strategic missile developments. Long-range missiles were under development in the Soviet Union, and the threat of a surprise attack by such weapons was a major concern of U.S. political and military leaders.

Inevitably called the Killian Committee for its chairman, the panel consisted of some 50 distinguished scientists and engineers from academia, laboratories, and the government who served in several subpanels that looked into various aspects of strategic offensive weapons, strategic defense, and STRATEGIC INTELLIGENCE technologies. The panel issued its report—"Meeting the Threat of Surprise Attack"—on Feb. 14, 1955. It recommended acceleration of U.S. strategic missile development, with the emphasis on 1,500-nautical-mile missiles launched from overseas land bases and from ships (or submarines). Significantly, the report also laid the foundation for the U-2 spyplane and satellite programs to provide RECONNAISSANCE of strategic TARGETS in the Soviet Union.

The intelligence subpanel, led by Edwin H. Land of Polaroid fame, stated in the report:

> We must find ways to increase the number of hard facts upon which our intelligence estimates are based, to provide better strategic warning, to minimize surprise in the kind of attack, and to reduce the danger of gross overestimation or gross underestimation of the threat. To this end, we recommend the adoption of a vigorous program for the extensive use, in many intelligence procedures, of the most advanced knowledge in science and technology.

The intelligence portion of the report was considered so sensitive that President Eisenhower forbade even the

NATIONAL SECURITY COUNCIL to be briefed on it for fear of leaks. In their several private meetings with Eisenhower, Killian and Land discussed a variety of OVERHEAD reconnaissance systems that could provide factual intelligence on Soviet strategic weapons developments, both manned bombers and missiles.

President Eisenhower embraced the Killian Committee's recommendations, accelerating the nation's strategic missile program (including the Polaris sea-based missile) and pursuing the proposed strategic reconnaissance efforts. Killian was also influential in convincing Eisenhower that the strategic reconnaissance programs (the U-2 aircraft and satellites) should be under the control of the CIA and not the military services. According to Killian, when discussing the U-2 program, Eisenhower "stipulated that it should be handled in an unconventional way so that it would not become entangled in the bureaucracy of the Defense Department or troubled by rivalries among the services." In particular, Gen. Curtis LeMay, head of the Strategic Air Command, which needed data on Soviet targets, demanded control of overhead reconnaissance systems.

When Eisenhower established the PRESIDENT'S FOREIGN INTELLIGENCE ADVISORY BOARD in 1956 (originally known as the President's Board of Consultants on Foreign Intelligence Activities), he named Killian as the first chairman. Killian served in that role until 1963.

After the Soviets orbited the world's first artificial satellite on Oct. 4, 1957, Killian was named President Eisenhower's science adviser and asked to organize and chair the President's Scientific Advisory Committee.

Killian's memoir, *Sputnik, Scientists, and Eisenhower,* was published in 1977.

Kim [f]

Hero of Rudyard Kipling's popular 1901 novel of the same name. An Irish orphan raised as a Hindu in India, Kim was an exemplar to many who, in real or imagined life, played what Kipling called the GREAT GAME. Kim could slip from one identity to another—now a Hindu, now a Muslim, now a European, now an Indian. He was the ideal AGENT: He could spy and accurately report what he had seen.

Words in *Kim* became an anthem for players and spectators of the Great Game:

> From time to time, God causes men to be born—and thou art one of them—who have a lust to go ahead at the risk of their lives and discover news. Today it may be of far-off things, tomorrow of some hidden mountain, and the next day of some nearby man who has done a foolishness against the State. . . . When he comes to the Great Game, he must go alone—alone and at the peril of his head. Then, if he spits, or sits down, or sneezes other than as the people do whom he watches, he may be slain.

HAROLD (KIM) PHILBY got his nickname from the hero-spy. And, as Peter Grose notes in *Gentleman Spy*

(1994), a biography of ALLEN W. DULLES, a DIRECTOR OF CENTRAL INTELLIGENCE, Dulles had a lifelong attachment to the book. It was at his bedside when he died.

Kim, Robert C.

(b. 1940)

OFFICE OF NAVAL INTELLIGENCE computer specialist who gave classified documents to South Koreans. Kim, a naturalized U.S. citizen born in South Korea, pleaded guilty to conspiring to gather national defense information. In July 1997 he was sentenced to nine years in prison.

He denied that he was a spy, insisting that he had passed the documents so that South Korea would buy a computer system being sold by his brother's company.

FBI wiretaps, authorized by the FOREIGN INTELLIGENCE SURVEILLANCE COURT, recorded conversations in which he and his brother discussed plans for a multi-million-dollar deal involving the system, which tracks ship movements.

King, Donald Wayne

Navy Airman assigned to the Naval Air Station in Belle Chasse, La., who pleaded guilty in 1989 to conspiracy to commit espionage and larceny of government property following his arrest by agents of the NAVAL INVESTIGATIVE SERVICE (NIS). Arrested at the same time was another airman, Ronald Dean Graf.

The pair had delivered $150,000 worth of sensitive and classified aircraft parts and technical manuals to an undercover NIS agent they believed was a foreign government representative. The stolen material pertained to the Navy's P3V ORION, an anti-submarine RECONNAISSANCE aircraft.

King was sentenced to five years, Graf to five years.

King, Capt. John H.

CIPHER clerk in the British Foreign Office who gave information to the Soviet Union. He was specifically recruited by the NKVD because of his sensitive position.

King served in the British Army during World War I and was commissioned as a captain. Becoming a cipher specialist, he served in Damascus, Paris, and—after the armistice of 1918—in Germany. He joined the communications department of the Foreign Office in 1934.

Estranged from his wife, in 1953 he met an American woman in Geneva who became his mistress. King increasingly found it difficult to live within his income. His recruitment to work for the Soviets was slow and deliberate, being undertaken by Henri Christiaan Pieck, a successful Dutch artist. Pieck and his wife entertained King and his mistress and took them on expensive European holidays.

Finally, visiting London, Pieck undertook a FALSE FLAG operation, telling King that he was anxious to obtain inside information on international relations for a

Dutch banker. King could both help Pieck's friend and make much-needed money. He agreed to the proposal.

He began supplying Pieck with classified documents, which were photographed in a London apartment and returned to him. Some of the documents—secret cables between British officials—were considered important enough to be passed directly to Soviet dictator Josef Stalin.

NKVD officer WALTER KRIVITSKY, who had defected in 1937, led the British to conclude that a well-placed spy was providing the Soviets with high-level political secrets. By 1939, the suspicions of the security department of the Foreign Office pointed to King. Two security officials met King one evening and, in a pub on Curzon Street, bought him whiskey after whiskey. Intoxicated, King admitted that he was working for the Soviets.

Arrested, he was brought to a secret trial at the Old Bailey on Oct. 18, 1939, and admitted his guilt. He was sentenced to 10 years but was released after the war with full remission for good conduct.

Kingfisher

High-performance strategic RECONNAISSANCE aircraft proposed by the Convair Corp. to succeed the U-2 spyplane. The new plane was intended to be carried aloft beneath a B-58 Hustler turbojet bomber and then to be released after the "mother" plane exceeded the speed of sound. The project was not pursued.

Kites

Periodically, efforts have been made to employ tethered kites for military RECONNAISSANCE. In the late 1800s the U.S. Army experimented with kites carrying observers and unmanned kites fitted with cameras. Although successful, these experiments showed how kites were totally dependent upon winds. Serious interest in kites soon ended.

The reconnaissance kite concept was resurrected in Germany in World War II when the Focke-Achgelis firm developed the Fa 330 "automotive kite," an unpowered kite towed by surfaced SUBMARINES to increase their reconnaissance range. It had a three-blade rotor that enhanced lift as it was towed. The Fa 330 had a steel tubular construction with a conventional tail assembly that could be folded and disassembled and stowed within the submarine. Some 200 to 500 feet of steel cable were usually winched out for the operation; a telephone line imbedded in the cable permitted communication with the submarine. The kite flew at an altitude of about 300 feet.

Several of the approximately 200 Fa 330s that were built were operated from U-boats. Their pilots, usually enlisted, trained in a wind tunnel at Chalais-Meudon, France. Some kites were fitted with wheels and a tail skid so that they could be towed behind light observation planes for in-flight training.

Knightley, Phillip

(b. 1927)

British investigative reporter who has written extensively in the field of espionage.

Born in Australia, he came to London in the early 1950s and became a prominent journalist. He was a special correspondent for the *Sunday Times* for 21 years and a leader of its celebrated Insight team of investigative reporters. He is the author of the exemplar work *The First Casualty*, the latest edition of which has the subtitle *The War Correspondent As a Hero and Myth-Maker from the Crimea to Kosovo* (2002). He helped to uncover the HAROLD (KIM) PHILBY spy scandal, and played a central role in exposing the 1963 PROFUMO scandal. He is one of only two journalists to have been twice named journalist of the year in the British Press Awards.

He left the *Sunday Times* in 1985 to concentrate on writing books. These include several in the field of espionage: *The Philby Conspiracy* with Bruce Page and David Leitch (1981), *The Second Oldest Profession: Spies and Spying in the Twentieth century* (1987), *Philby: The Life and Views of the K.G.B. Masterspy* (1988), and *An Affair of State: The Profumo Case and the Framing of Stephen Ward* with Caroline Kennedy (1987).

He has also written and lectured extensively on the changing role of journalism in wartime and the role of the investigative reporter.

Koch, Hugo Alexander

Dutch engineer who registered a patent for an enciphering machine in 1919. His "secret writing machine" concept was the precursor of the ENIGMA CIPHER machine. Koch's patent for a secret writing machine declared that "steel wires on pulleys, levers, rays of light, or air, water, or oil flowing through tubes could transmit the enciphering impulse as well as electricity did."

Koch established a company to produce secret writing machines and sold patents to ARTHUR SCHERBIUS, a German engineer.

Kocher, Karl F.

(b. 1934)

Former employee of the CIA who provided classified U.S. information to the Czechoslovak Intelligence Service (CIS). He was the first known Eastern Bloc spy to have penetrated the CIA.

Born in Czechoslovakia, Koecher had undergone training as an INTELLIGENCE OFFICER by the CIS from 1962 to 1965. He and his wife, Hana, "defected" to Austria in 1965 and entered the United States as immigrants on Dec. 4, 1965. He claimed that he was a DEFECTOR from the CIS. After studying at Indiana University, he moved to New York and attended Columbia University.

The Koechers became American citizens in 1971. They led an adventurous social life, reportedly attending wife-swapping parties and frequenting SEX clubs as well as a nudist colony, possibly seeking to recruit additional AGENTS for Eastern Bloc intelligence agencies.

An ILLEGAL AGENT, Koecher was ordered to seek employment with a U.S. intelligence agency. The FBI undertook a SECURITY CHECK on Koecher, and he passed a CIA POLYGRAPH test in Oct. 1972. (Later investigations revealed that CIA technicians had misread the polygraph test results.)

From 1973 to 1975 Koecher worked as a translator at the CIA and held a SECURITY CLEARANCE at the TOP SECRET level. Subsequently, he worked as a CIA contract employee in New York from 1975 to 1977. Information about Koecher's activities before he worked for the CIA has not been revealed by the U.S. government. He came under suspicion when he was observed meeting with CIS officers during a routine FBI SURVEILLANCE operation.

One of the documents that Koecher passed to the CIS compromised ALEKSANDR D. OGORODNIK, a Soviet diplomat in Moscow who was a CIA MOLE. (When confronted by Soviet officials in 1977, Ogorodnik committed suicide.)

Koecher was arrested in his apartment in New York City on Nov. 27, 1984, while preparing to fly to Switzerland. He was charged with conspiracy to commit espionage. His wife was described in court papers as having served as a COURIER between Koecher and the CIS from 1974 to 1983. Although she was held as a material witness in the case, she was not charged, because the FBI had violated legal guidelines by continuing to interview her after she had requested a lawyer.

Held without bail, Koecher had not yet stood trial when he was exchanged for Soviet dissident Anatoly Scharansky. (The government-to-government exchange was called a SPY SWAP, but Scharansky was not a spy.) The Koechers crossed the Glienicker Bridge from West to East Germany in BERLIN on Feb. 11, 1986, half an hour after Scharansky had crossed the bridge to the West.

Author Ronald Kessler, writing in the *Washington Post*, gave this description of the couple at the time of their exchange for Scharansky: "With his mustache and fur-lined coat, [he] looked like nothing so much as a fox. His wife, Hana, wore a mink coat and high white mink hat. Blonde and sexy, with incredibly large blue eyes, she looked like a movie star."

Kessler interviewed the Koechers in Prague in 1987. Karl still worked for the CIS. His field of expertise: the United States.

Koedel, Simon E.

(b. 1881 d. ?)

American who spied for Germany during World War II.

Koedel, born in Bavaria, came to the United States when he was 22, served in the U.S. Army for three years, and became an American citizen. From afar he followed the rise of Adolf Hitler and ardently supported him. Sometime in the early 1930s he traveled to Germany and offered his services as a spy. The ABWEHR trained him,

began paying him a stipend, and told him to return to the United States as a SLEEPER and await instructions.

In Sept. 1939, as Germany was invading Poland, the "awakening" order came: a cable from Germany containing the CODE WORD "alloy" and signed "Hartmann."

Although Koedel was a movie projectionist with no knowledge of the U.S. defense industry, he joined the American Ordnance Association and used this connection to gain entry to the U.S. Army arsenal at Edgewood, Md. After his tour, he wrote a long report on weapons development at Edgewood.

Through the ordnance association he became acquainted with Senator Robert R. Reynolds of North Carolina, who provided him with, among other information, a list of U.S. ports "capable of handling ships loading oil and coal as well as general cargo." The Abwehr had asked for precisely that in March 1940 to gauge what supplies could come from the United States in response to the planned German offensive.

Koedel was an industrious and ingenious spy. To gather shipping information he would ride the Staten Island ferry, crossing New York Harbor, checking the names of ships in port. Sometimes he posed as a longshoreman. Koedel's information went to Germany via the German Embassy in Washington, D.C., and through ACCOMMODATION ADDRESSES in neutral countries.

Koedel's daughter, Marie, went to New York waterfront bars to pick up intelligence for her father. She also recruited a British sailor, Duncan Scott-Ford, who provided information about convoys. (Scott-Ford was hanged as a spy by the British in Nov. 1942.) Koedel was finally caught in Oct. 1944 after Marie's former fiancé went to the FBI with his suspicions. Koedel was imprisoned and deported after the war.

Kolbe, Fritz

A WALK-IN to the U.S. OFFICE OF STRATEGIC SERVICES (OSS) in Switzerland during World War II who provided the Allies with invaluable copies of hundreds of official German communications.

Kolbe was the special assistant to Ambassador Karl Ritter, a Foreign Office official who handled many of the most important German diplomatic missions as the confidant of Foreign Minister Joachim von Ribbentrop. In that role Kolbe had access to virtually all important German diplomatic communications as well as documents related to the armed forces.

Kolbe was a 20-year veteran of the German diplomatic service whose wife and son were in South Africa (controlled by the British).

In Aug. 1943 Kolbe had approached the British military ATTACHÉ in Bern, Col. HENRY CARTWRIGHT, who had ejected Kolbe from his office because Cartwright feared a German "provocation." The next day a friend of Kolbe's was able to take sample documents to the U.S. Embassy in Bern where ALLEN DULLES, the OSS representative, was startled to see the documents. As his biographer, James Srodes, wrote in *Allen Dulles: Master of Spies* (1999),

"Even the normally enthusiastic Dulles drew back from bait like this; it smelled just too good to be true."

But it was true. Kolbe met with Dulles later that week and provided the OSS officer with copies of German messages and more than 100 other items. Srodes described them:

> The reports covered troop morale on the Eastern Front, an assessment of *maquis* sabotage in France, the Berlin visit of a Japanese ambassador, and various conferences between Foreign Secretary von Ribbentrop and other Nazi officials. Among other treasures Kolbe brought were a hand-drawn map of Hitler's secret Eastern Front headquarters at Rastenburg, the location of the railway siding nearby for the special trains that the top Nazis use to get there, and one of the German one-time cipher pads.

Beyond the intrinsic value of the documents, the copies of German communications were CRIBs that would help the cryptologists at BLETCHLEY PARK and ARLINGTON HALL STATION break further into the ENIGMA machines used by the Foreign Office and armed forces. Kolbe wanted no payment for his invaluable documents. He asked only that he be considered for a high government position after the war—when the Allies won.

Also serving as a COURIER between Berlin and Bern for the German Foreign office, he returned with an even larger cache of material the following month. As the flow continued and the documents were authenticated, on Jan. 10, 1944, WILLIAM DONOVAN, the head of the OSS, personally showed a collection of the Kolbe documents to President Roosevelt with "cautious endorsement."

Subsequently, beginning in May 1944—under the CODE NAME "Boston Series"—collections of the Kolbe documents were distributed to 11 of the most senior U.S. civilian and military officials in Washington, D.C., including Roosevelt.

Meanwhile, Kolbe had teamed up with an Alsatian doctor working in Berlin. They set up a secret photography laboratory at the doctor's clinic where Kolbe could copy key documents. The flow of material to the Bern OSS office continued until the end of the war.

After the war Dulles was instrumental in getting Kolbe into the United States, with the OSS paying him $10,000. There were difficulties with the State Department in obtaining his entry because he had been in the German government. But Kolbe's business efforts failed and he and HANS GISEVIUS, who had assisted him in Berlin as an OSS AGENT IN PLACE, returned to Germany—"to live out rather dismal lives, reviled as traitors to the nation they had tried to save," wrote Srodes.

Kolbe was given the code name "George Wood" by the OSS; his documents were given the name "Kappa."

Kometa

Fourth-generation Soviet SURVEILLANCE SATELLITE. This further refinement of the earlier ZENIT satellites was fitted with solar panels for recharging its batteries, thus extending its operational life. Some reports credit later versions of this satellite—employed for topographic mapping—with a life of up to 45 days.

Komitet Gosudarstvennoy Bezopasnosti

SEE KGB

Kondor (Condor)

CODE NAME for German effort to plant AGENTS of the ABWEHR in Cairo, the capital of British-held Egypt, in 1942. The operation was planned in anticipation of German troops entering the city.

Krämer, Dr. Karl-Heinz

(b. 1914 d. ?)

German air ATTACHÉ in Stockholm, Sweden, during World War II who struck the fear into British intelligence services that there was a major spy NETWORK operating in Britain.

Krämer was attending the University of Hamburg in 1939 when he was drafted into the German Air Force with the rank of specialist lieutenant and assigned to the ABWEHR's intelligence station in Hamburg. He handled AGENT operations in the Low Countries, Hungary, and Turkey, supervising several successful operations. He was also able to get valuable information from Sweden on British aircraft production and plants. He was sent to Stockholm in Oct. 1942.

After his arrival in Stockholm, Krämer engaged a maid who was anti-Nazi and especially disliked Krämer's wife, Eva. Peter Falk, an officer of the British Secret Intelligence Service (MI6) in Stockholm, made contact with the maid through a mutual friend. She began to report Krämer family gossip to Falk and also provided scraps from Krämer's wastebasket. Then she made a mold of the key to his desk and, after Falk had a key made, she was able to provide the British with copies of numerous intelligence documents. Since most of the communications between the German Embassy in Stockholm and BERLIN went by land line and cables, the British ULTRA intercepts of German radio communications were useless.

The maid's work was vital to the British. The documents she purloined helped MI6 to identify several German intelligence sources. Then there was a shock: German sources with the CODE NAMES Hektor and Josefine were supplying important material from Britain, including details of the secret telegrams passing between President Roosevelt and Prime Minister Winston Churchill. Early in World War II the British Security Service (MI6) had captured and incarcerated or TURNED all German agents. (See DOUBLE-CROSS SYSTEM.)

Wrote NIGEL WEST in MI6: British Secret Intelligence Service Operations 1909–1945 (1983):

The prospect of a major Abwehr network operating in London filled MI5 [British Security Service] with dread. Many of its double-agent operations relied on there being no independent agents at liberty, and several important strategic deception plans were likely to be endangered if the Germans had the capability to double-check their information, Krämer's information appeared authentic and, on occasion, enough to jeopardize major operations.

MI5 put one of its best people on the case: ANTHONY BLUNT, who, unknown to the British, was a major Soviet spy. Still, Blunt performed well. He was able to identify Hektor as Col. Count Johan Oxenstierna, the Swedish naval attaché in London, and William Strang, a junior official at the Foreign Office.

Strang underwent "a painful interview," wrote West. Oxenstierna was fed what MI5 called BARIUM—carefully provided information, which began showing up in Krämer's Hektor-Josefine reports. Oxenstierna was declared persona non grata by the British government and left Britain, whereupon the Hektor-Josefine network ceased to operate.

A follow-up Swedish investigation found that Oxenstierna was sending his reports to the Swedish Defense Staff, not to Krämer, who had recruited a secretary on the staff. She had taken material that Oxenstierna had reported, some based on discussions with Strang, and passed it to Krämer. MI5 apologized to Strang.

After the war Krämer, interrogated by MI5, confirmed the true source of his reports to Berlin.

Krasney Kapel

SEE RED ORCHESTRA

Kreml

(KREMLIN)

Successful German DECEPTION operation against Soviet forces in May–June 1942. After winning the battle for Kharkov, 400 miles south of Moscow in late 1941, the German High Command planned an offensive to destroy the Soviet forces toward the southern end of the Eastern Front. To divert Soviet attention from that thrust (which would lead to the decisive Battle of Stalingrad), on May 29, 1942, the German High Command ordered "the earliest possible resumption of the attack on Moscow" by Army Group Center. Kreml was the CODE NAME for the deception operation.

U.S. Army historians Earl F. Ziemke and Magna E. Bauer, in *Moscow to Stalingrad: Decision in the East* (1985), observed:

KREML was a paper operation, an out-and-out deception, but it had the substance to make it a masterpiece of this somewhat speculative form of military art. In the first place, it coincided with So-

viet thinking—which, of course, the Germans did not know. In the second, its premise—to simulate a repeat of the late 1941 drive on Moscow—was solid; in fact, it made better strategic sense than did that of BLAU [the southern operation].... The army group directive, which assigned two panzer armies the identical missions they had received in the previous fall, could have been taken for the real thing even by German officers who were not told otherwise, and most were not.

As part of Operation Kreml, the German Air Force increased RECONNAISSANCE flights over and around Moscow, prisoner-of-war interrogators were given lists of questions to ask about Moscow's defenses, the German intelligence staff sent "swarms" of AGENTS toward Moscow, and sealed packets of Moscow maps were distributed down to the regimental level. A readiness date of Aug. 1 was announced.

Postwar Soviet accounts contend that Kreml failed, but the Soviet High Command (*Stavka*) had in fact believed that Moscow was again the target of the German offensive. On June 28, 1942, Operation Blau—the main German attack eastward—began. It was a highly successful thrust.

Kremlin, The

Slang for the offices of the OFFICE OF STRATEGIC SERVICES (OSS) at 2430 E Street N.W., in Washington, D.C., during World War II. It subsequently was used by the successor agencies to the OSS, the CENTRAL INTELLIGENCE GROUP and the CIA, until the latter organization moved to the Washington suburb of LANGLEY, Va.

The U.S. Navy had built the complex in the 1930s for medical facilities. It is on a slight rise and overlooks the Lincoln Memorial and the Potomac River.

Krivitsky, Maj. Gen. Walter

(b. 1899 d. 1941)

The first senior Soviet INTELLIGENCE OFFICER to defect to the West.

Born in Russian-controlled Poland with the name Samuel Ginsberg, Krivitsky joined the Bolshevik Party in 1917 and subsequently began his career with the GRU, Soviet MILITARY INTELLIGENCE. In Germany in 1923 he attempted to foment a communist revolt, after which he worked for the Red Army staff and in GRU headquarters in Moscow. He was transferred to the NKVD in 1934. Both his GRU and NKVD service involved foreign intelligence activities.

As the NKVD RESIDENT in the Netherlands, he was responsible for Soviet military intelligence throughout Western Europe. He returned to Moscow in May 1937 during the Stalinist purges, which included decimating the ranks of the intelligence ORGANS and military services. After making his reports, Krivitsky was allowed to return to The Hague. But in Sept. 1937 he was ordered to return to Moscow. Fearing that he was to become a victim of the purges, Krivitsky decided to defect. He went to Paris and sought asylum at the French Ministry of the Interior. Along with his wife and four-year-old son he was able to reach the United States safely despite two reported attempts by Soviet AGENTS to assassinate him while he was still in France.

Krivitsky's revelations were of great interest to U.S., British, and French security services. He traveled to Britain in 1939, where his revelations gave early evidence of the penetration of the British government by Soviet MOLES and led directly to the arrest of JOHN H. KING. He also called attention to another Soviet spy in Britain, "a young English journalist" for a London newspaper who covered the Spanish Civil War. Although not identified at the time, this was HAROLD (KIM) PHILBY.

As NIGEL WEST wrote in *MI5: British Security Service Operations 1909–1945* (1981), "The real value of Krivitsky's information lay in his ability and willingness to identify NKVD men working under diplomatic cover in Britain and even a few of their sources." Krivitsky revealed that 61 Soviet agents worked in Britain and the Commonwealth, although he could not specifically identify them all. Three, he said, were in the Foreign Office and three in British intelligence services. John King was identified by Krivitsky but was said to be in the Cabinet secretariat.

He also wrote articles (including one for *The Saturday Evening Post* in 1939) exposing Soviet espionage, and he testified before the U.S. House Un-American Activities Committee in 1939. His autobiography *In Stalin's Secret Service* was published that same year (the British title was *I Was Stalin's Agent*).

Krivitsky checked into Room 524 of the Hotel Bellevue on Capitol Hill, in Washington, D.C., on Sunday afternoon, Feb. 9, 1941. He paid $2.50 for the night. The next morning a maid found him dead from a gunshot to the temple; the room had been locked and there were three suicide notes. The Metropolitan Police ruled his death a suicide, but he was undoubtedly murdered by a Soviet assassin.

His Soviet CODE NAME was Groll.

Kroger, Peter

SEE MORRIS COHEN

Kruglov, Col. Gen. Sergei Nikiforovich

(b. 1903 d. ?)

Senior Soviet INTELLIGENCE OFFICER who served as head of internal security (MVD) from Dec. 1945 to March 1953, and of the "super" MVD responsible for both internal and state security from June 1953 to Feb. 1956.

A career intelligence-security officer, from 1941 to 1945 he was deputy head of the NKVD, the state security-intelligence ORGAN. Specifically, from 1943 until the end of 1945, Kruglov was deputy to VIKTOR ABAKUMOV, head

of SMERSH, the military COUNTERESPIONAGE organization. In that position Kruglov ran the security detail at the Tehran conference in Nov.–Dec. 1943, attended by Soviet dictator Josef Stalin, President Roosevelt, and Prime Minister Churchill, and again at Yalta in Feb. 1945. At Yalta, which had been a Black Sea resort of the czars, the NKVD provided lavish hospitality to the American and British leaders, personally supervised by Kruglov. Joan Bright of the British secretarial staff described Kruglov as "the most powerful-looking man I had ever seen, with huge shoulders, face, hands and feet."

But more important, Kruglov's minions provided the Allied leaders with a careful and rapid response to their every whim and desire, while providing security. And of course, his specialists unquestionably conducted SURVEILLANCE of the American and British leaders and their staffs.

(For his services at Tehran and Yalta, Kruglov was later awarded an honorary British knighthood, becoming the only Soviet intelligence officer to be so honored.)

In Dec. 1945 Stalin removed his chief of intelligence and repression, LAVENTRY BERIA, from the head of the internal security apparatus, the MVD, and gave that post to Kruglov. In March 1946, the MVD was raised from a commissariat to a ministry, with Kruglov being promoted to minister. Although Kruglov had been appointed to the important Smersh position by Beria, he was not considered a Beria loyalist, and Stalin wished some balance to the increasing powers and honors being accorded to Beria in the postwar period.

Kruglov held the MVD position for more than seven years. On March 7, 1953, two days after Stalin's death, the Soviet government merged the MVD and the MGB, the state security agency, into a single "super" MVD under Beria. "Kruglov of the MVD and [Semyon] Ignatiev of the MGB were dropped with equally speeded dispatch, but neither man was arrested or shot, a clear departure from the norm for fallen leaders of organs," wrote U.S. intelligence analyst John J. Dziak in his *Chekisty: A History of the KGB* (1988). "Indeed," Dziak noted, "Kruglov was retained as Beria's deputy. That was a mistake for Beria."

On June 26, 1953—almost four months after Stalin's death—Beria was arrested. Kruglov sided with the anti-Beria faction and was rewarded by succeeding him as Minister of Interior. Kruglov appears to have had a key role in the fall of Beria, including the arrest of his other deputies. Indeed, some reports cite that Kruglov's wiretapping of Beria's telephones had revealed that Beria was planning his own coup on June 27 to take over the government.

Kruglov continued as head of the MVD, which in March 1954 was downgraded with the establishment of the KGB, which became the agency responsible for state security, the MVD reverting to internal security activities. He was fired by Nikita Khrushchev on the eve of the 20th Party Congress in Feb. 1956, at which Khrushchev revealed the excesses and terror of Stalin and his police-intelligence organs—activities in which Kruglov had been a major participant.

Reportedly, Kruglov subsequently committed suicide, fearing that the retribution against the state terrorists would reach out to him.

Kryuchov, Col. Gen. Vladimir Aleksandrovich

(b. 1924)

Head of the KGB from 1988 to 1991. After brief service in the Soviet Army, Kryuchov studied at the Law Institute. Following graduation he served in the Public Prosecutors Office in the early 1950s. He was subsequently posted to the Soviet Embassy in Budapest, Hungary. From 1957 to 1967 he served in the Central Committee department responsible for foreign communist parties, at the time headed by YURI ANDROPOV.

When Andropov was promoted to chairman of the KGB in 1967, Kryuchov was made head of a department within that ORGAN. By 1978 he was serving as head of a chief directorate of the KGB with the rank of lieutenant general. He was promoted to deputy chairman of the KGB prior to becoming head of the organization in 1988.

As head of the KGB he launched a campaign to improve the agency's image and to "win the minds" of Western politicians. He took part in the attempted coup against President Mikhail Gorbachev on Aug. 18, 1991, was arrested as a "betrayer of the Motherland" and imprisoned, although not prosecuted. The government of Boris Yeltsin released him in 1993, and he retired to write his memoirs.

Kuczynski, Dr. Jürgen

(b. 1904 d. 1997)

Soviet AGENT in Britain; he was the brother of the Soviet spy known as Sonia (see URSULA KUCZYNSKI).

Kuczynski joined the German Communist Party (KPD) in 1930. Subsequently, he was recruited by the GRU and posted to BERLIN in 1936 to help the communists in their brief effort to overthrow the Nazi regime.

He went to England before World War II as a refugee and became a leader of the underground section of the KPD there while continuing to serve the GRU. In England he promoted relations with the British Communist Party and organized communist groups in several cities.

Kuczynski was interned in Jan. 1940, being considered a security risk, but was released after three months. He remained an active GRU agent during the war. It was Kuczynski who introduced British nuclear physicist KLAUS FUCHS to a Soviet intelligence contact in 1941.

The U.S. Embassy in London asked Kuczynski in Sept. 1944 to participate in the American Strategic Bombing Survey to help evaluate the impact of the Allied bombings on the German war effort. That required that he be appointed a lieutenant colonel in the U.S. Army. The information he received in that role was passed on via Sonia's radio to Moscow. Other, more valuable U.S.

intelligence was also passed to Kuczynski, who was now on various U.S. military distribution lists.

He disappeared into East Germany in Nov. 1945.

His Soviet CODE NAME was "Karo."

Kuczynski, Robert René

(b. 1876 d. 1947)

Father of Soviet spies JÜRGEN KUCZYNSKI and URSULA KUCZYNSKI. Polish-born, Kuczynski was an economist and ideological communist. He was deeply involved with German left-wing politics until 1933, when he went to Britain.

The senior Kuczynski knew about his daughter's espionage activities on behalf of the Soviet Union and helped her when she arrived in Britain in 1941.

Kuczynski, Ursula

(b. 1907 d. 2000)

Soviet AGENT who was a member of the RED ORCHESTRA and the LUCY SPY RING during World War II and served as a COURIER for KLAUS FUCHS in the ATOMIC SPY RING. CHAPMAN PINCHER, author of *Too Secret Too Long* (1984), called her "the most successful female spy in history." She was also known as Ruth Weber and Ruth Hamburger Beurton.

Born in BERLIN to a communist father, Kuczyninski joined the Communist Youth Union when she was 17. The family moved to Britain and, as early as 1928, according to Fuchs' biographer, Robert Chadwell Williams, in *Klaus Fuchs: Atom Spy* (1987), the British Security Service MI5 opened a file on her, her father, and her brother, Jürgen.

In 1929 she married Rolf Hamburger in Germany, and the following year she was ordered by Soviet intelligence to go to Shanghai. There she met AGNES SMEDLEY, RICHARD SORGE, and probably ROGER HOLLIS. Sorge persuaded Ruth to work as an ILLEGAL for the GRU, Soviet MILITARY INTELLIGENCE. She allowed her apartment to be used as a meeting place for Sorge and also served as courier for the group. Sorge gave her the CODE NAME "Sonia," which she is believed to have used for the rest of her career.

In Dec. 1932 Sorge reported to Moscow that Sonia was a capable agent. She was sent to Mukden, the capital of Japanese-controlled Manchuria, in April 1934 to maintain contact between Moscow and the Chinese partisans fighting the Japanese. She was subsequently sent to Peking (Beijing) in May 1935, but she soon left China when Sorge's successor in Shanghai was arrested.

Back in Europe, she visited her parents in London and then accompanied the Hamburgers to Poland, where Rolf also worked for the GRU. Sonia went to Moscow June 1937 for advanced training and to be decorated with Order of the Red Banner, the highest honor then available to a non-Soviet citizen; she was made a major in the GRU.

In 1938 she was sent her to Switzerland, hub of the Red Orchestra and the Lucy network, one of whose members was ALEXANDER FOOTE, a British subject who had served in the International Brigade in the Spanish Civil War. He introduced her to Len Beurton, also a brigade veteran. The GRU ordered her to divorce Rolf and to marry Beurton to enable her to become a British citizen and be eligible for a British passport. She married Beurton on Feb. 23, 1940, and received a British passport in May. She made her way to England, with Len following soon after.

"Ollo," who had been Kuczyninski's nanny in Germany, wanted to go to England with the family. Told she could not go, she revealed Kuczyninski's and Beurton's espionage activities to the British consular representative in Montreux, Switzerland, but she was ignored. When Sonia and her two children arrived in Britain in Feb. 1941, she moved into a home near Oxford and began radio transmissions to the USSR in the spring of 1941.

Sometime in 1942, Fuchs made contact with her brother Jürgen Kuczynski. They knew each other from their past communist ties. Jürgen put Fuchs in touch with Ursula, who sent Fuchs' information about atomic bomb work to her Soviet HANDLERS in London or by radio to Moscow.

In June 1947 two MI5 officials and a local detective attempted to question Ursula and her husband about alleged spy activities (possibly because she had been named by Foote, who had defected to the West). "They left us calmly and politely, but empty-handed," she later wrote. There was apparently no further interest in the family by COUNTERESPIONAGE officials.

Sonia and two of the children went to East Germany for a vacation in 1950—the day before Fuchs went on trial for violation of the OFFICIAL SECRETS ACT. Beurton joined her in East Germany later in 1950. "Either it was complete stupidity on the part of MI5 never to have connected me with Klaus, or they may have let me get away with it, since every further discovery would have increased their disgrace," she wrote under her pen name Ruth Weber in her autobiography, *Sonya's Report* (published in 1977 in East Germany, in 1991 in Britain). In an afterword to the British edition she wrote: "I had not worked those 20 years with Stalin in mind. We wanted to help the people of the Soviet Union in their efforts to prevent war, and when war broke out against German fascism, to win it."

She never returned to Britain. In 1969 she received her second Order of the Red Banner. She was awarded the Order of Karl Marx in 1984.

Kuehn, Dr. Bernard

German spy in Hawaii on the eve of World War II, along with his wife and Ruth Kaethe Suse, who posed as their daughter. All three worked for the German ABWEHR and also collected intelligence for Japanese NAVAL INTELLIGENCE.

Kuehn joined the Nazi Party in 1930. He visited Japan, and in 1935, following meetings with the Japanese naval ATTACHÉ in BERLIN, he agreed to spy for Japan. He was to receive $2,000 per month plus a $6,000 bonus at the end of each year.

To carry out his espionage, Kuehn, his wife, and Suse traveled to Hawaii in 1936. He was ostensibly to study Japanese at the University of Hawaii. In March 1939 he was given a portable radio transmitter fitted in a suitcase. The transmitter had a range of only 100 miles. Thus, it is assumed that he was to contact Japanese SUBMARINES operating off Hawaii. (There is no record of any such communications nor of Japanese submarine operations in the Hawaiian area prior to Dec. 1941.) The Kuehns worked closely with TAKEO YOSHIKAWA, the Japanese Navy's most important AGENT in Hawaii.

Sometime around early 1939 Kuehn came under suspicion as a spy by U.S. authorities, but no action was taken against him.

It is unlikely that Kuehn contributed any intelligence to the Japanese Navy for the PEARL HARBOR ATTACK. A Japanese INTELLIGENCE OFFICER made the following estimate of Kuehn in 1950: "so poor and primitive that it was feared he would not be able to get sufficient information for our intention of launching an air strike upon Pearl Harbor. . . . it was decided to use him only when other means were of no avail. . . ." He also developed a useless scheme for signaling submarines offshore with a combination of lights, radio advertisements, and markings on sailboats.

During the PEARL HARBOR ATTACK on Dec. 7, 1941, Kuehn was reported by an American intelligence officer to be sending light signals from his attic window to the Japanese consul. But such an action seems unlikely—what could Kuehn have been telling the Japanese at that point?

After the attack, Kuehn and Suse were arrested by the FBI, which later arrested Mrs. Kuehn as well. Kuehn was at first sentenced to death for his attempted espionage, but he gave U.S. authorities information on foreign intelligence, and his sentence was commuted to 50 years' imprisonment. In 1946 he was freed.

Mrs. Kuehn and their "daughter" were deported at the end of the war.

Kuklinski, Col. Ryszard

(b. 1930 d. 2004)

Polish Army officer who provided the U.S. CIA with intelligence on Soviet military planning from 1970 until he defected in 1981.

In early Nov. 1981, Kuklinski, his wife, and at least one son were helped to leave Poland for the West by the CIA. Kuklinski had been involved in planning the martial law crackdown on the Solidarity trade union, which occurred Dec. 13, 1981.

Polish authorities first realized his espionage activities when he failed to report for work on Nov. 6, 1981. He was tried and convicted in absentia and sentenced to death. He had passed an estimated 35,000 pages of classified documents to the CIA.

He was described in *The Washington Post* in 1986 as "a very brave man who became an agent [for the CIA] not for money but because he detested what the Soviets and [Polish] military government had done to his country." In 1997 the Polish government dropped the charges against him. He returned to Poland for a visit in April 1998, receiving a mixed reception.

Kunkle, Chief Petty Officer Craig D.

(b. 1949)

Former U.S. Navy chief aviation antisubmarine operator who pleaded guilty to espionage charges after trying to sell secrets to two undercover FBI agents posing as Soviet INTELLIGENCE OFFICERS.

Kunkle, a veteran of 11½ years in the Navy, had been discharged in 1985 for multiple acts of indecent exposure. At the time of his attempted espionage in 1988 he was working as a hospital security guard. He said that he wanted to spy for the Soviets to make money and have revenge on the Navy for his discharge.

Beginning in Dec. 1988, Kunkle made contact six times with a man he believed to be from the Soviet Embassy in Washington, D.C. The man was an FBI agent, and after offering secret information—based on what he remembered from being an instructor in anti-submarine warfare—Kunkle was paid $5,000. Hidden FBI cameras recorded the meetings, and Kunkle was arrested on Jan. 11, 1989.

After pleading guilty to charges of espionage, Kunkle was sentenced to 12 years in prison.

How the FBI was able to intercept Kunkle's attempts to contact the Soviets has not been revealed, but it was probably through wiretaps on Soviet Embassy telephones.

Kurasov, Gen. of the Army Vladimir Vasilievich

(b. 1897 d. 1973)

Soviet Army commander and chief of the GRU in 1949.

A czarist officer who went over to the Bolshevik side after the October Revolution of 1917, Kurasov served mainly on staffs through 1940, when he was made deputy chief of the Operations Directorate of the Soviet General Staff. He held this position until World War II began, when he became commander of the 4th Shock Army.

After the war he served as commander in chief of the Group of Soviet Forces in Austria. Promoted to general of the Army, he became chief of the GRU in Feb. 1949. Later that year he was transferred to become head of the General Staff Academy (the senior war college). From 1956 to 1961 he was deputy chief of the General Staff.

Kuznetsov, Col. Gen. Fedor Fedorotovich

(b. 1904 d. 1979)

Chief of the GRU from 1943 to 1946; he also had a major role in the murderous purges of the military, both before and after World War II.

Kuznetsov was a factory worker in Moscow and an active member of the Communist Party when he was called up into the Army in 1938 as deputy head of the Chief Political Directorate. In that position he was active in the Stalinist purges of the Red Army, including the GRU.

In 1943 he was named head of the GRU, after the sudden removal of his predecessors. He helped to organize the Churchill-Roosevelt-Stalin conference at Tehran (Iran) from Nov. 28 to Dec. 1, 1943, after which he was promoted to the rank of colonel-general. Subsequently, he had key roles in the Allied conferences at Yalta (Crimea) and Potsdam (Germany) in 1945.

Under Kuznetsov's direction the GRU emphasized espionage efforts to steal U.S. atomic technology in this period (see ATOMIC SPY RING).

In 1948 he was made head of the Chief Political Directorate of the armed forces. Kuznetsov held that position until Stalin's death in March 1953, after which he was demoted to head the Chief Personnel Directorate of the armed forces. He was later head of a military academy and ended his career as chief of the Political Directorate of the Northern Group of Forces. He retired in 1969.

KW-Series Cipher Machines

U.S. post–World War II CIPHER machines. KG, KL, and KY series are also designations used for U.S. cipher machines and associated equipment.

These machines encipher and decipher messages at high speeds. The KW designations were sometimes assigned the suffix letters R and T, indicating that they were allocated to Receiving and Transmitting functions, respectively. Because of the difficulty in keeping track of the designations, various KW- and KY-series cipher machines were also assigned mythological names, such as Creon, Jason, Nestor, and Pontis.

During the 1960s and 1970s the KW-7 Orestes was the most widely used cipher machine in the U.S. military services; those machines were also used by other government agencies as well as several allied nations. U.S. naval ships, for example, had from one KW-7 in small ships to some 25 in the nuclear-propelled aircraft carrier *Enterprise*.

The KW-7 was housed in a plain gray box about the size of a teletype printer. The vital parts of the machine were encased in shielding material to prevent the emission of electronic signals that could be intercepted by a nearby intercept device.

A message was typed into the KW-7 in PLAIN TEXT English. The signals went through cryptographic circuits within the box and were encrypted according to a cipher preset for that day by the numbers on the CIPHER KEY. The message was then transmitted via radio as a stream of grouped numbers. At the receiving end, the message entered another KW-7, where the message could be decrypted only if the machine had been set with the same key. Messages were entered on a teletype keyboard; incoming messages were printed out electronically through the teletype component of the machine.

The cipher keys, or "key lists," evolved in form through the years. The key—the daily set of numbers that activates the machine—was once simply printed on what was called a key list. The radioman operating the cipher machine would punch keys corresponding to those numbers, and the machine would then align its logic to decipher the messages being received that day or to encipher and transmit the day's outgoing messages.

Later, the key list became the "key card," which resembled an early IBM computer punch card (still referred to as the key list). Using the card version, the radioman opened a compartment on the side of the cipher machine, pressed the card against an electronic sensor, and closed the compartment. The sensor translated the card's holes into signals that gave the machine the day's key numbers. The cards were still being used in post–Cold War years. But some machines accepted keys in the form of cassette tapes. The key numbers were electronically imprinted on an ingeniously designed spool of tape that could not be rerolled back into its container and hence could only be used once.

Like the key lists and cards, the tape was merely a medium for what Navy radiomen called "filling" the machine with the day's key numbers. Some machines also demanded the simultaneous use of a key card and a CRIB (Card Reader Insert Board), which has a function similar to the key card. But whether the radioman used lists, cards, or tapes, the system was the same: a machine, a key, and—what is sometimes overlooked in descriptions of the system—a radioman. (This is the U.S. Navy designation for both male and female radio operators.)

Although the method of "filling" the cipher machines kept changing through the years, there were relatively few changes in the machines, especially the long-serving KW-7. The cost to replace machines is considerable, especially when one considers that at the turn of the 20th century many thousands were in use by the U.S. military services and other government agencies (as well as allies).

(Even the White House used these machines, as do the President and White House officials when traveling, although they usually made use of military communications systems. Marine Lt. Col. Oliver North used a portable KL-43 when overseas while running the IRAN-CONTRA AFFAIR.)

CIPHER SECURITY

Security for cipher machines is maintained through physical security of the machines and, especially, the key lists. The rules to protect the key lists are the heart of the Clas-sified Materials System (CMS), which was developed by the NSA and administered by a string of handlers, beginning with the COURIERS who carry keying materials, in tamper-proof packages, from the NSA's tightly guarded printing plant at FORT MEADE, Md., to secure NSA depots around the world. From there they are carried by members of the Armed Forces Courier Service to the machines' operators—embassies, military bases, intelligence-agency offices, and Navy ships.

In the U.S. Navy, the final destination for this complex delivery system is a Navy radioman designated as the CMS custodian. Ashore or aboard ship, the key lists are signed for, carefully kept track of, stored in safes, and destroyed after use. Only personnel with TOP SECRET and special "crypto" COMPARTMENTED clearances are allowed to handle the key lists.

At least that was the way the system was designed to work.

Many Americans and some foreigners with detailed knowledge of cipher machines and access to key lists provided information about U.S. cipher machines—and key lists—to the Soviet Union during the Cold War and, probably, to its successor, Russia. And the Soviets have obtained numerous U.S. cipher machines.

The Soviets received firsthand information on U.S. cryptologic efforts and cipher systems in 1960, when NSA cryptologists WILLIAM H. MARTIN and BERNON F. MITCHELL defected to the Soviet Union. Then in 1963–1964, Warrant Officer JOSEPH G. HELMICH, an Army communications specialist, sold details of cipher machines to the Soviets. He provided key lists for the KL-7 and possibly for the KW-26 as well as other equipment. (At his 1981 trial the government stated "the residual impact of the compromise continues to the present time because the KL-7 was continuously in use and still is.")

Five years after Helmich sold out, in January 1968, with the capture of the USS PUEBLO, a U.S. Navy–NSA spy ship, the Soviets obtained several U.S. cipher machines, including the KW-7, KWR-37, and KG-14. At the time the KW-7 used a worldwide key list, meaning that anyone with a machine and key list could read military communications (for the period of the list) anywhere in the world.

More machines were lost in 1975 as North Vietnamese troops overran the South, and the U.S.-supplied Saigon forces hastily retreated, leaving their weapons and cipher machines in their wake. The North Vietnamese and their Soviet allies probably captured some 30 U.S. cipher machines; the exact number 32 has been mentioned by some sources.

From at least 1968, U.S. Navy Chief Warrant Officer JOHN A. WALKER and his comrade in betrayal, Senior Chief Radioman JERRY WHITWORTH, supplied the Soviets with key lists and innumerable other documents and manuals, permitting them to recover past classified U.S. and Allied communications, and probably enabling them to develop competence for reading real-time transmissions on the cipher machines in their possession. Further, the materials and information provided by Walker and

Whitworth and other American and non-Americans enabled the Soviets to break into ciphers used by machines not in their possession.

Walker and Whitworth supplied so much cryptologic information that the Soviets began discriminating about what they wanted. In particular they wanted the KW-7 key lists; they did not want messages carried on the KW-8 system, encoded voice circuits, or other intelligence information, which they obviously preferred to obtain from other sources.

Also, in the late 1970s the Soviets obtained information on the KW-7 as used by the CIA from CHRISTOPHER BOYCE and ANDREW D. LEE. Boyce had access to sealed plastic envelopes that contained the key lists. He removed the lists from the envelopes, photographed them, and then replaced them and resealed the envelope with an iron or a carelessly applied touch of glue. Once, when he had messed up a resealing, a government inspector checked the botched packet but ignored the broken seal.

Beyond key lists and cipher documentation, the American spies provided the Soviets with technical manuals for the machines, which, according to NSA engineers, could enable them to construct such devices—in addition to the machines, even damaged, recovered in Vietnam and from the USS *Pueblo*. Because the KW-7 and certain other U.S. cipher systems were in use by numerous other nations, one could speculate that CRYPTOMATERIAL was also compromised by foreign sources.

"We knew the KW-7 was vulnerable," a retired U.S. Navy admiral with expertise in communications told the authors of this book in 1987. "We never heard that NSA said there was a [security] problem with the key list, except for some being lost once. We heard that they had been lost in [aircraft] crashes. And 30 machines had been lost in Vietnam. But having the machines was not enough. The Soviets did not have computers that could calculate fast enough to understand the algorithm." (The algorithm is the mathematical logic that translates a message's number groups into electronic signals that can be read by the machine's teletype system.)

But the Soviets had previously made inroads into reading Western codes and ciphers.

Also see CRIB, CRYPTANALYSIS.

Lacoste, Adm. Pierre

(b. 1924)

Director of France's DGSE Direction Générale de la Sécurité Extérieure (General Directorate for External Security), who was dismissed in Sept. 1985 after it became publicly known that GSE operatives had sunk the Greenpeace ship *RAINBOW WARRIOR* in the harbor of Auckland, New Zealand, on July 10, 1985.

After attending the French Naval Academy during World War II, Lacoste served with the Free French Navy in the Mediterranean. After the war, he served in naval assignments both ashore and at sea, and he saw action in Indochina. After studying at the French Center for Higher Military Studies and the National War College, he became deputy military executive to the Minister of Defense (1972–1976) and then Commander of the Naval War College (1976–1982).

Lacoste took over the DGSE in 1982 after the resignation of its first director, former aerospace executive Pierre Marion, who served only 18 months. Lacoste was the first naval officer to run a major French intelligence agency.

After the sinking of the *Rainbow Warrior,* Lacoste denied that he had ordered the operation, but French intelligence sources later said that Lacoste was aware that some "action" was planned against the ship. She was to have sailed into an area where France was about to test nuclear weapons. The ship, owned by the Greenpeace environmental organization, was blown up by a bomb. One man drowned as the ship sank. Eleven crew members and visitors survived.

Defense Minister Charles Hernu was forced to resign, although he, too, took the PLAUSIBLE DENIAL route out of the debacle.

After departing DGSE, on July 1, 1986, Lacoste was named President of the Foundation for the Studies of National Defense. A frequent speaker on defense and intelligence issues, he has written numerous magazine articles and several books in those fields.

Lacrosse

U.S. SATELLITE program developed to overcome the problem of cloud cover over the Soviet Union, which was hindering RECONNAISSANCE by spy satellites. Cloud cover was a serious impediment to monitoring the Soviet Union, limiting the effectiveness of early photographic satellites. For example, a CORONA satellite first detected the possible Soviet deployment of an antiballistic missile system near Tallinn in Estonia in 1961. However, it was eight years before additional, detailed satellite photography could be obtained, mainly because of clouds.

The solution was to employ radar—the reflection of focused radio waves—that could penetrate cloud cover as well as darkness. The U.S. SEASAT-A experimental ocean surveillance satellite, orbited on June 27, 1978, carried a Synthetic Aperture Radar (SAR) with a resolution of 82 feet (that is, capable of detecting objects of that size from an altitude of some 780 miles above the earth). The relatively small antenna of the SAR makes use of the movement of the satellite to enhance radar.

The space shuttle *Columbia* went into orbit on Nov. 12, 1981, carrying imaging radar that, unexpectedly, was able to penetrate down 16 feet into the dry sands of the eastern Sahara desert. On Oct. 5, 1984, the shuttle *Challenger* went aloft on another imaging radar mission, "photographing" several North American cities. JEFFREY T. RICHELSON wrote in *America's Secret Eyes in Space* (1990):

Given the cloud cover that blanketed many of the targets, the mission was a dramatic demonstration of the additional capability provided by radar imaging. The mission produced excellent photographs that have a clear indication of what radar imaging could do over Eastern Europe and the USSR in autumn and winter during cloud cover or night.

The Lacrosse satellite began life at the CIA under the CODE NAME Indigo, to carry a SAR system that would electronically downlink images to receiving stations on earth. While Lacrosse was intended to provide reconnaissance of ground targets, an ocean reconnaissance satellite employing SAR was initiated for the Navy. (That program, called Clipper Bow, was later canceled; the Soviet Union already had an operational RADAR OCEAN RECONNAISSANCE SATELLITE.)

The CIA initially planned to have the SAR fitted "piggyback" to the KH-11 camera satellite (see KEYHOLE). The proposal was vetoed by Secretary of Defense Harold Brown, who believed that the plan placed too many surveillance assets on too few satellites.

Meanwhile, costs of development increased rapidly in the Lacrosse program, and questions were raised in Congress about the accuracy of cost estimates produced by the CIA and the NATIONAL RECONNAISSANCE OFFICE. But there was considerable pressure in Congress for Lacrosse because it could help to verify Soviet compliance with arms limitation treaties.

Launching of the first Lacrosse satellite was delayed because of the *Challenger* explosion on Jan. 28, 1986, which essentially grounded U.S. space launches. The use of the shuttle as virtually the only U.S. satellite launch vehicle had helped to justify the high cost of the shuttle system. Not until Dec. 2, 1988, was a Lacrosse satellite carried into orbit as the payload aboard the shuttle *Atlantis*. Even then there were problems; the launch facility at Vandenberg Air Force Base in California was having technical problems, and launching the shuttle from Cape Canaveral, Fla., provided a flight path that prevented coverage of the Soviet submarine bases and building yards on the Kola Peninsula, many strategic missile bases, and the space launch facility at Plesetsk.

Once deployed from the shuttle, the Lacrosse satellite's twin, 150-foot solar panels and a data-link antenna were extended; the solar panels provided power for the radar. Several weeks after it was orbited at an altitude of almost 300 miles, the Lacrosse used on-board rockets to attain a permanent orbit of between 415 and 437 miles.

The Lacrosse launched in late 1988 joined two KH-11 (KENNAN/Crystal) camera satellites already in orbit. Additional Lacrosse satellites have been placed in orbit into the 1990s, although details are still classified.

Ladygin, Lt. Gen. Fedor Ivanovich

Chief of the GRU, Russian MILITARY INTELLIGENCE, from 1992 to 1997. A career GRU officer, Ladygin served from 1990 to 1992 as chief of the legal-treaty directorate of the Russian General Staff with additional duty in the Ministry of Foreign Affairs.

He has a reputation within the Russian Army as a capable administrator and a disciplinarian. He once described the major objective of the GRU was to keep Russia from sinking "to the status of a third world country."

Lahousen, Generalmajor Erwin von

(b. 1897 d. 1955)

Chief of German sabotage during World War II and plotter who played a key role in an attempt to assassinate Adolf Hitler.

An Austrian from an aristocratic family, Lahousen served in the Austrian Army during World War I. After the war he became chief of Austrian COUNTERINTELLIGENCE. When Nazi Germany took over Austria in 1938, the Austrian intelligence services were absorbed into Germany's and Lahousen was posted to the ABWEHR, headed by WILHELM CANARIS, a German naval officer.

Canaris quickly forged a bond with Lahousen, who shared his anti-Nazi feelings. "He hated Hitler, his philosophy, his system and to an even greater degree his methods," Lahousen later said of Canaris. Lahousen's diary reflected his dilemma: loyalty to Germany, disloyalty to Hitler and the Nazis. Lahousen, speaking for Canaris, tried in vain, for example, to prevent the killing of Russian prisoners as dangerous Bolsheviks. *Spies and Saboteurs* (1958), by Charles Wighton and Günter Peis, is based on Lahousen's diary.

Canaris appointed Lahousen head of Abwehr Section 11, which was concerned primarily with sabotage. He handled the successful sabotage aspects of the German invasion of Poland in Sept. 1939. But because Canaris believed that sabotage was not as important as espionage, Lahousen ordered that AGENTS being sent to Britain be trained primarily in spying, not sabotage. His agents failed miserably (see DOUBLE-CROSS SYSTEM), and saboteurs landed in the United States were quickly rounded up. (See FBI.)

In 1943 Lahousen was ordered to the Eastern Front and escaped the final days of the Abwehr, which, along with Canaris, had fallen into disfavor. Lahousen later said that he had supplied the bomb used on July 20, 1944, in the attempt to kill Hitler during a conference at his field headquarters in Rastenburg in East Prussia. The officer who placed the bomb and about 200 accused plotters, including Canaris, were later executed; thousands were imprisoned. Lahousen escaped punishment even though the bomb was British-made and it was known that such sabotage bombs were confiscated and stored by the Abwehr. He later testified against Nazi leaders at the Nuremberg trials.

Lakam

A highly secret Israeli intelligence agency founded to guard Israeli efforts to build nuclear weapons. In the fall of 1956, as Israeli, British, and French officials met secretly to plan the abortive British-French strike to seize the Suez Canal from Egypt, the Israeli government initiated efforts to obtain from France a nuclear reactor capable of producing material for nuclear weapons.

Two Israeli intelligence agencies, the MOSSAD and AMAN, had worked on the TOP SECRET plan to make Israel a nuclear power. But both Prime Minister David Ben-Gurion and his chief defense aide, Shimon Peres, director-general of the Defense Ministry, believed that a new agency was needed so that nuclear information could be tightly held. Accordingly, the agency was set up in 1957 under BINYAMIN BLUMBERG, a veteran officer of SHIN BET, Israel's domestic security agency.

At first Blumberg's agency was called the Office of Special Assignments, operating secretly out of the Defense Ministry. Later it became the Lishka LeKishrei Mada (Science Liaison Bureau), secretly known as Lakam, an acronym of its Hebrew letters. Even ISSER HAREL, the top Israel intelligence officer (the MEMUNEH, "the one in charge") did not know of the existence of Lakam when Peres founded it. Scientific ATTACHÉS sent to Israeli embassies in the United States and Europe reported to Lakam. The agency also gently pressured Israeli scientists, asking them to be patriotic about knowledge they picked up abroad.

Lakam oversaw security for the building of the reactor in the Negev Desert, claiming that the project was a textile factory. French intelligence officials, well aware of the nature of the project, infiltrated the area to learn what the Israelis were doing. U.S. intelligence was alerted by PHOTOGRAPHIC INTELLIGENCE.

While Israel publicly insisted it was not building an atomic bomb, U.S. and French intelligence agencies were skeptical. As French support weakened, Lakam developed a new source of supply, the Nuclear Materials and Equipment Corp. (NUMEC), of Apollo, Pa. In 1965 the U.S. Atomic Energy Commission discovered that NUMEC, which supplied uranium for U.S. nuclear reactors, had somehow "mislaid" 200 pounds of enriched uranium. U.S. intelligence officials established that NUMEC had been in touch with the Israeli scientific attaché in Washington, D.C.—a Lakam operative. The NUMEC incident convinced the United States that Israel was developing nuclear weapons.

In 1981 Blumberg was succeeded by RAFAEL EITAN, a legendary Mossad officer who had been a major figure in Israeli intelligence since the birth of the nation in 1948. Eitan, already an adviser on counterterrorism to Prime Minister Menachem Begin, retained that post while heading *Lakam*. In his latter job he reported to Ariel Sharon, longtime military figure and Minister of Defense. Sharon, who had fought in the several Arab-Israeli wars, took a keen interest in *Lakam*.

Sharon, distrustful and contemptuous of the Mossad, built up Lakam as his private worldwide intelligence agency. Lakam's targets included the United States, despite the fact that Israel and the States had an agreement not to spy on each other. Through Lakam, for instance, krytrons—devices that can be used as nuclear bomb detonators—were smuggled out of the United States. When the FBI uncovered the smuggling plot, Is-

rael officially apologized and returned all detonators, except those ostensibly for medical research.

Another Lakam operation—CODE NAME Plumbat—carried out with the aid of the Mossad, got uranium to Israel through a complicated plot: About 200 tons of uranium oxide, bought by a German firm from a Belgian firm, was loaded onto the German-flag freighter *Scheersberg* in Antwerp in late 1968. The ship never reached its supposed destination, Genoa. When the ship did reappear, she was at a Turkish port, empty. The uranium cargo had been transferred at sea to an Israeli ship.

Lakam probably would have remained an anonymous intelligence agency if an American spy, JONATHAN J. POLLARD, had not blurted out Eitan's name on a tapped telephone as the FBI closed in on Pollard in Nov. 1985. Pollard, an American working as a civilian intelligence analyst for the U.S. Navy, had approached an Israeli official in New York City and offered to spy for Israel. The Mossad was not interested, but Lakam was.

Eitan instructed his operatives—"scientific attachés" in Washington and New York—to work as Pollard's HANDLERS. Eitan met Pollard and personally ordered specific documents for Pollard to filch, copy, and return to intelligence files. To handle the thousands of papers Pollard stole, Lakam set up a high-speed copying system at an apartment in Washington.

When Pollard was arrested, Israel officially denied knowledge of the operation, although American officials assumed that Pollard had been directed by the Mossad. In Israel, Mossad officers brooded over the incident, which made that reputable organization look so amateurish.

Peres, the founder of Lakam, was Prime Minister when Pollard was arrested. He claimed that he was unaware that intelligence information he was receiving came from an American spy working for Lakam. Eitan, however, was quoted in the Israeli newspaper *Hadashot* as saying that all his actions, including the running of Pollard, "were done with the knowledge of those in charge."

Lakam was quietly dissolved in 1986.

Lalas, Steven J.

Employee of the U.S. Embassy in Athens who spied for Greece from at least 1977 to April 1993, when he was arrested. U.S. COUNTERINTELLIGENCE officers first suspected a leak in the embassy when, in conversations between U.S. and Greek officials, the Greeks disclosed information that was classified.

Lalas was placed under SURVEILLANCE and was videotaped copying documents. Information he stole included the names of AGENTS of the CIA, cables about terrorist organizations sent to Athens from the Washington, D.C., headquarters of the FBI, assessments by the DEFENSE INTELLIGENCE AGENCY of troop strength and deployments in Europe, cables between Athens and the White House, and information about U.S. intelligence activities in Bosnia.

Lalas began his espionage career in 1977 when he was in the U.S. Army. From 1983 to 1993 he worked for the State Department. His motive, officials said, was greed. His espionage earned him $24,000 in two years, but his other spy income figures were not revealed.

U.S. authorities arrested him and took him to Alexandria, Va., where the FBI prefers to hold trials because there is a higher rate of convictions in the U.S. District Court there than in its counterpart in Washington, D.C. (Federal prosecutors attribute the reason to the differing racial compositions of juries.) Lalas pleaded guilty to conspiracy to commit espionage and received 14 years, instead of the maximum life term, in return for cooperating with CIA counterintelligence officials.

The CIA was concerned about what Lalas turned over to his Greek HANDLERS. Although Greece, a member of the NORTH ATLANTIC TREATY ORGANIZATION, is officially a U.S. ally, CIA officials believed that Greece, acting in its own self-interest, could have traded the intelligence from Lalas for information the Greeks wanted from the Soviet Union and later Russia.

Lamia

CODE NAME for Philippe L. Thyraud de Vosjoli, a French INTELLIGENCE OFFICER whose assignment in the United States was marked by crisis and misadventure.

De Vosjoli also used *Lamia* as the title of his book, published in 1970 as the memoir of a man named Lamia; he worked so long as Lamia that the name de Vosjoli seems hardly to have existed.

A member of the French Resistance when he was 19 years old in 1940, de Vosjoli managed to make his way to Free French Algeria via Spain. He joined the Algerian branch of the BCRA, the intelligence service begun by Gen. Charles de Gaulle in exile in London. He later served in India as part of the French Military Mission.

After the war he served successively in the series of postwar French intelligence agencies—the DGSS, the DGER, and the SDECE. After serving as a confidential aide to Henri Ribiére, head of SDECE, in April 1951 he was sent to Washington as SDECE station chief.

One of his first duties, he wrote in *Lamia,* was at the request of Gen. WALTER BEDELL SMITH, the DIRECTOR OF CENTRAL INTELLIGENCE (DCI). Smith said that Joseph Kennedy, former U.S. ambassador to Britain, was serving as a member of the U.S. Intelligence Advisory Committee. Kennedy's son, John F. Kennedy, was running for the U.S. Senate from Massachusetts. Smith told de Vosjoli that, since there were many people of French origin in Massachusetts, "it would be helpful to his campaign" if France awarded a posthumous Legion of Honor to John's brother Joseph, who had been killed in a bomber accident in World War II. France did so—after Kennedy won the election.

De Vosjoli was in CUBA on Jan. 1, 1959, when Fidel Castro's forces took over Havana and proclaimed victory in the revolution. He had set up a NETWORK in Cuba, where anti-French Algerians of the Front de Libération

Nationale (FLN) were training for guerrilla warfare in Cuban training camps.

Back in Cuba in March 1961 he found Havana "transformed into a military camp." De Vosjoli heard rumors there and in Washington that a U.S. invasion of Cuba was imminent. The abortive Bay of Pigs fiasco did come the following month. Before and after the invasion Castro rounded up thousands of suspected subversives and U.S. AGENTS. But, de Vosjoli later claimed, his net survived.

In July 1962 he began getting reports of the presence of Soviet ships. Shortly before the CUBAN MISSILE CRISIS in Oct. 1962, he said he had advised JOHN A. MCCONE, the DCI, about the presence of offensive missiles on the island.

De Vosjoli's tenure as SDECE's man in Washington came to an abrupt end as a result of the accusations made by ANATOLI GOLITSYN, a KGB officer who defected in Dec. 1961. Golitsyn, code-named Martel by the French, claimed that the SDECE was riddled with Soviet MOLES. The KGB defector sketched a Soviet network code-named SAPPHIRE and indicated that it reached into the inner circle of President Charles de Gaulle.

Outraged, de Gaulle suspected a plot against him concocted by the CIA. In turn the CIA, concerned about the lack of French response to Golitsyn's revelations, suspected he was right. JAMES JESUS ANGLETON, head of CIA COUNTERINTELLIGENCE and a friend of de Vosjoli, engineered a BLACK BAG JOB to break into the French Embassy in Washington.

De Vosjoli's superiors in Paris accused him of collaborating with Angleton. He was concerned that Soviet agents within the SDECE wanted to derail his career because of his efforts to prove that Sapphire did exist. He even feared for his life. He resigned in Oct. 1963 and fled to Mexico.

In 1967 *Topaz,* a novel by American author Leon Uris, was published amid publicity asserting that it was a thinly veiled account of the Sapphire ring. De Vosjoli successfully sued Uris for basing a character too closely on him.

Lamphere, Robert J.

(b. 1918 d. 2002)

COUNTERINTELLIGENCE supervisor for the FBI.

Lamphere supervised FBI investigations into such major spies as HAROLD (KIM) PHILBY, JULIUS ROSENBERG, and KLAUS FUCHS. He also participated in one of the most secret operations of the Cold War—the interception and deciphering of Soviet intelligence messages that contained the names of Americans working for the Soviet Union. The operation was code-named VENONA.

"We had no idea that such a thing as the Rosenberg case would develop when, in the spring of 1948, we began these investigations based on the 1944–45 K.G.B. messages," Lamphere said in his memoir, *The F.B.I.-K.G.B. War: A Special Agent's Story* (1986), written with Tom Shachtman. Lamphere, working clue by clue, name by name, was a key operative in the cracking of the ATOMIC SPY RING.

Lamplighters

British term for support personnel in intelligence operations. The term was made popular in JOHN LE CARRÉ novels.

Land, Edwin H.

(b. 1909 d. 1991)

Distinguished American inventor, scientist, and business executive who played a key role in U.S. development of spyplanes and photographic SATELLITES. Land is best known as inventor of the Polaroid Land camera, the world's first practical instant camera.

His efforts to develop air and space spy systems began in the early 1950s, when President Truman appointed him to the Scientific Advisory Committee of the Office of Defense Mobilization. In the spring of 1954, when JAMES R. KILLIAN, then president of the Massachusetts Institute of Technology, was asked by President Eisenhower to establish a Technological Capabilities Panel to look into the potential of long-range, strategic missile developments, Killian selected Land to head the intelligence subpanel.

Land's report was an important factor in President Eisenhower's approving the U-2 spyplane program. His involvement in the U-2 program and its successor, the A-12 OXCART, continued, and he was instrumental in the start-up of the CORONA satellite program. Often he served as the go-between for RICHARD M. BISSELL and both Killian and President Eisenhower. He was involved in the technological developments to improve these systems—in the words of one CIA participant in these efforts, Don Welzenbach, "Land was always pushing the envelope,"—that is, he continually strove for better systems.

After the Soviets brought down the U-2 spyplane piloted by FRANCIS GARY POWERS, President Eisenhower wanted to halt further OVERFLIGHTS. Land and Killian argued against this so effectively that Eisenhower changed his mind and approved satellite RECONNAISSANCE of the Soviet Union.

Land also served on Eisenhower's Board of Consultants on Foreign Intelligence Activities (see PRESIDENT'S FOREIGN INTELLIGENCE ADVISORY BOARD).

In the business world, Land demonstrated his first instant cameras in 1947 and introduced color film in 1963. Many other photographic developments came from his imaginative mind. He retired as president of Polaroid in 1975 and as chairman of the board in 1982.

Lang, Hermann

(b. 1902 d. ?)

German-born worker who gave Germany the U.S. plans for the TOP SECRET Norden bombsight.

Lang immigrated to the United States in 1927 and eventually found a job at the Norden Co., a small factory in New York City that was working on the Norden bombsight, an aiming device for high-altitude bombers. It was named after Carl L. Norden, a Dutch-American inventor who started developing it in 1928 with Theodore Barth, an engineer.

In 1937 NIKOLAUS RITTER, an officer of the ABWEHR, the German intelligence service, traveled to New York City and met Lang through an informant. Ritter was head of espionage against the United States and Britain. Lang told Ritter that he had blueprints of the bombsight. Lang, an inspector, slipped blueprints out of the factory, brought them home, and, while his wife was asleep, traced the blueprints. He returned them the next day.

The tracings were large and needed to be rolled, not folded. Ritter had a COURIER conceal the rolls in an umbrella and take them aboard a German liner docked in New York. Lang later traced other bombsight plans, which he sent to Germany through intermediaries by cutting them up and concealing them in newspapers bound for Germany. Acquisition of the bombsight plans was Ritter's most important intelligence coup in the United States.

Lang made a trip to Germany in 1938, was thanked by the Luftwaffe, and was recruited as an AGENT by the Abwehr. But when Lang returned to the United States and his Norden inspection job, he could not top his previous achievement. He did, however, join the DUQUESNE SPY RING.

The bombsight had a high degree of accuracy, although not as good as claimed by its boosters, who said it could "drop a bomb into a pickle barrel from 25,000 feet." The bombsight first got widespread use in U.S. heavy bomber raids over German-occupied Europe in 1942. The device was so secret that Norden bombsights were not used in the B-25 bombers of the Doolittle raid on Japan in April 1942 lest the bombsight fall into Japanese hands. Well before then, the German Luftwaffe had incorporated Norden principles into German bombsights. Details of the bombsight were kept classified until 1947.

Lang was identified by WILLIAM G. SEBOLD, a DOUBLE AGENT working for the FBI and was sentenced to 18 years in prison following his trial in 1942.

Langley

Term sometimes used by employees of the CIA to designate their workplace. CIA headquarters is in Langley, Va., part of the Washington, D.C., suburb of McLean. See FIRM, COMPANY.

Lansdale, Maj. Gen. Edward

(b. 1908 d. 1987)

U.S. Army officer who became a clandestine operative in the Philippines and Vietnam, and an important figure in the backstage U.S. campaign to topple Fidel Castro's regime in Cuba.

Lansdale was attracted to the military life as a high school student in Los Angeles, where he enrolled in the Junior Reserve Officer Training Corps (JROTC) in 1923, obtaining a commission via ROTC, which he later resigned when he entered the University of California at Los Angeles. He left college before graduating and drifted into the glamorous new world of advertising. After the PEARL HARBOR ATTACK on Dec. 7, 1941, Lansdale, married and the father of a baby boy, requested recommissioning as an Army second lieutenant but did not pass the physical examination. He appealed, and in Feb. 1943 he was commissioned as a first lieutenant and assigned to the San Francisco field office of the Army's Military Intelligence Service (MIS) "for limited service only."

Soon afterward he was recruited by the OFFICE OF STRATEGIC SERVICES (OSS). He simultaneously worked for the OSS and the MIS, developing a frequent use of MILITARY INTELLIGENCE as a COVER for deeper COVERT ACTION.

During World War II most of Lansdale's duties involved writing OSS training manuals and gathering basic intelligence information, often finding specialists on remote Pacific areas where U.S. forces planned actions.

When the war ended, he was sent to the Philippines, where he launched his career as a clandestine operator. Left-wing Filipino insurgents, who evolved from guerrilla groups fighting the Japanese, were threatening the stability of the government. One group had become the de facto government in much of Luzon; the Hukbo ng Bayan Laban Sa Habon in Tagalog—the Huks to Americans. Lansdale targeted the Huks as he sought to find ways to aid the Philippine government. But he had to leave the Philippines in 1948 after he was transferred to the recently created U.S. Air Force and sent to an intelligence school in Colorado.

In 1949 he was assigned to the Office of Policy Coordination, the highly secret covert action organization run by FRANK WISNER independent of the new CIA. In Washington, D.C., Lansdale met Ramón Magsaysay, a member of the Philippine Congress, and mapped out a way to make him an anti-Huk President of the Philippines.

Once again Lansdale used intelligence as a cover. He supposedly was a military intelligence adviser to the President of the Philippines, Elpido Quirino, while simultaneously running the covert U.S. effort to create a political power base for Magsaysay, who, under U.S. pressure, had been appointed Secretary of Defense by Quirino. Lansdale used bizarre tactics, such as spreading rumors that a local vampire was pursuing Huks and then having Filipino anti-Huk units kill Huks by puncturing their throats and draining their blood. Or he had Huk leaders thanked for their help in order to make their comrades believe they had been betrayed.

In June 1953, as Magsaysay's American backers directed his campaign, Lansdale traveled in Indochina for six weeks to observe French anti-guerrilla warfare against insurgents of the Associated States of Vietnam,

Laos, and Cambodia. Magsaysay won a landslide victory over Quirino, launching Lansdale's reputation as America's leading expert in beating communist guerrillas.

In July 1954, following their disastrous defeat at Dien Bien Phu, the French agreed to partition Vietnam along the 17th parallel, with a communist North Vietnam under Ho Chi Minh in the capital of Hanoi, and a Republic of South Vietnam, with Saigon as its capital. This was to be a temporary measure, pending Vietnam-wide elections in 1956.

ALLEN W. DULLES, the DIRECTOR OF CENTRAL INTELLIGENCE, ordered Lansdale to Saigon, upsetting both the CIA and the French, who distrusted Lansdale. The CIA and the SDECE, the French intelligence service, were regularly exchanging intelligence information. Both sides feared that Lansdale would jeopardize the cooperation because he already had a reputation as a lone wolf. To soothe the French, Dulles made a deal: a large supply of CIA radios in exchange for a tolerance of Lansdale. His cover was assistant U.S. air ATTACHÉ while he directed the CIA-run Saigon Military Mission. Lansdale was to help set up a stable, anticommunist South Vietnam government and work out ways to oppose Ho Chi Minh. Lansdale, by then an Air Force lieutenant colonel, ran into immediate opposition from the CIA's Saigon station chief, who was running his own covert programs. Dulles had set it up so that Lansdale would operate outside the control of the station chief. Thus was born, in confusion and animosity, the U.S. involvement in Vietnam.

Lansdale backed Ngo Dinh Diem, a former French colonial functionary, to be president of the Republic of South Vietnam. To Lansdale, Diem was potentially another Magsaysay. Lansdale also conceived of the idea of a propaganda campaign ("psywar," he called it) to get nearly 1 million Catholics in the north to migrate south. The refugees massed in the North Vietnamese port of Haiphong, badly in need of aid. Lansdale got the U.S. Navy to bring in medical supplies and food and the CIVIL AIR TRANSPORT, a CIA PROPRIETARY COMPANY, to airlift refugees to South Vietnam. One of the propaganda stars was Dr. THOMAS DOOLEY, whose work for the refugees was highly publicized in the United States by reporters who did not know Dooley was part of a CIA operation.

Having set up Diem as the American-approved President of South Vietnam, Lansdale returned to Washington, where he became a major adviser on special operations to the Secretary of Defense; his job essentially gave him control of military support for CIA covert operations.

Around that time Lansdale earned some fame when literary critics wrote that he was the model for Alden Pyle, a character in *The Quiet American* (1955), by GRAHAM GREENE. Pyle was a zealous CIA agent under cover in Vietnam during the Eisenhower administration. (Greene, who often denied any specific person was a model for a fictional character, said that he would never use Lansdale "to represent the danger of innocence.") Lansdale fared better as the model for the title character in *The Ugly American* (1958), by William J. Lederer, a former U.S. Navy officer who knew Lansdale in the

Philippines, and Eugene Burdick, a political scientist sympathetic to the U.S. policies Lansdale carried out. The so-called quiet American was Col. Edwin Barnum Hillandale, who connected with the people and won more respect than the stuffy diplomats. *The Ugly American* became a best-seller, endorsed by Sen. John F. Kennedy and other U.S. senators and was cited as an inspiration for the Peace Corps. (The ironic title referred to an unhandsome engineer, Homer Atkins, who was actually a good American working hard for the natives of Sarkhan, a fictional Southeast Asian country.) In Jean Lartéguy's novel, *Le Mal Jaune,* published in the United States as *Yellow Fever* (1965), Lansdale is thinly veiled as the anti-French Col. Lionel Teryman, a new COL. THOMAS L. LAWRENCE.

In 1960, as the Eisenhower administration began looking to CUBA as a new trouble spot, Lansdale, by then a brigadier general, learned of the plan to invade Cuba and vigorously opposed it. After the abortive Bay of Pigs invasion the Kennedy administration began Operation MONGOOSE, an intensive covert action campaign against Cuba, and had the CIA develop plans to assassinate Castro. Lansdale got into that side of the project by suggesting that "gangster elements" might be recruited for a "special target" operation and "liquidation of leaders." He also suggested nonlethal poisoning of sugar field workers to stop the Cuban sugar harvest and the creation, with fireworks, of an apparition that would convince Catholic Cubans that Castro was the anti-Christ.

The CUBAN MISSILE CRISIS ended Mongoose, and Lansdale was soon on his way to Venezuela and Bolivia to inspect anti-guerrilla activity. In Sept. 1963 his Pentagon post was abolished, and he was forced into retirement. In his biography *Edward Lansdale* (1988), Cecil B. Currey writes:

> The Joint Chiefs viewed him as a bizarre variation from normal officers of flag rank . . . [Secretary of State] Dean Rusk . . . could not countenance his diplomacy of concern and friendship. . . . His approach to foreign policy at once appealed to Kennedy and horrified the bureaucracy. His very effectiveness in what he did became a double-edged sword that others now used against him.

Even in retirement Lansdale continued to serve. He returned to Vietnam in Aug. 1965 as a special assistant to U.S. Ambassador Henry Cabot Lodge and to Lodge's successor, Ellsworth Bunker, until June 1968. His autobiographical book, *In the Midst of Wars,* appeared in 1972.

Lanyard

An unsuccessful U.S. spy SATELLITE developed to provide high-resolution photographs of suspected antiballistic missile sites in the Leningrad (St. Petersburg) area of the Soviet Union.

Lanyard was expected to provide high-resolution imagery—a resolution of about two feet (i.e., identifying objects that size on the ground). But its best performance was only six feet, using a KH-6 camera (SEE KEYHOLE). Employing modified CORONA technology, the single Lanyard mission was launched into orbit on July 31, 1963. The camera failed after 32 hours.

(There had been two previous attempts to fly the KH-6 camera: On March 18, 1963, the Agena booster failed and orbit was not achieved; on May 18, 1963, a KH-6 orbit was achieved, but the system failed.)

The single successful Lanyard orbit was at an altitude of 98 to 255 miles.

Laos

SEE VIETNAM

Laser Intelligence
(LASINT)

Intelligence derived from laser systems. LASINT is a subset of IMAGERY INTELLIGENCE.

Latz, T. D. [p]

COVER NAME of a CIA official, a former U-2 pilot, who was the senior AIR AMERICA officer at U.S. Embassy in Saigon in April 1975. He was responsible for the helicopter evacuation of a large number of Americans and South Vietnamese nationals, many involved in intelligence operations, when communist forces assaulted the city.

Lawrence, Col. Thomas E.
(b. 1888 d. 1935)

British INTELLIGENCE OFFICER who operated extensively behind Turkish lines in Arabia during World War I, collecting intelligence and leading an Arab revolt. In many respects he was the West's leading Arabist of the period—invariably known as Lawrence of Arabia.

Born the second of five illegitimate sons of Sarah Maden and Sir Thomas Chapman, Lawrence attended Oxford University. While a student he developed an intense interest in the Arab world, traveling to Syria in 1909 to research his thesis. While there he was engaged to work on the archaeological dig at Carchemish in Syria.

He returned to Oxford in 1913. The following year he came back to the Middle East to join a British expedition, led by a British intelligence officer, ostensibly to search for the route used by Moses, although in reality the group was mapping the northern Sinai. (From this trek Lawrence and C. Leonard Woolley wrote *The Wilderness of Zin* [1915], the first of his 10 books.)

Lawrence was commissioned as a 2nd lieutenant in Oct. 1914, after the outbreak of World War I, and assigned to a British intelligence unit in Cairo. There he produced maps of Arabia, interrogated prisoners, handled communications, and performed other tasks as the British fought the Turks (Germany's ally) in the Middle East.

He was one of several junior officers sent to work with Arab forces to harass the Turks. Lawrence particularly impressed the Emir Feisal, and the British command directed him to serve as the Emir's military adviser. Lawrence subsequently led Arab raids against Turkish rail lines and collected intelligence for the British. Against specific orders, Lawrence led a force that captured the key city of Aqaba (ancient Elath), a port on the Gulf of Aqaba, on July 6, 1917. This move turned the Turkish flank and allowed British troops under Gen. Edmund H. H. Allenby to take Jerusalem in Dec. 1917.

During this period Lawrence was captured by the Turks, who tortured and sodomized him. (Some reports indicate that he was betrayed by a guide.) He escaped his captors and in Oct. 1918 led Arab forces in the capture of the Syrian capital of Damascus. But when the Anglo-French command refused to recognize Feisal as head of an independent Arabia, Lawrence—believing that he had been betrayed and had in turn betrayed the Arabs—returned to England. At the time he held the rank of colonel in MILITARY INTELLIGENCE.

Back in England, and at the Paris peace conference of 1919, he advocated independence for Arabia. When King George V was to invest Lawrence with the Order of Bath, he refused the honor, greatly embarrassing the monarch. He did return to the Middle East with Winston Churchill for the 1921 Cairo conference that established the borders of Iraq and Transjordan. His book *The Seven Pillars of Wisdom* (1926) sought to demonstrate that the Arabs were entitled to their own land and had been betrayed by the Allies.

Obsessed with the need to do penance for his failures, Lawrence enlisted under an alias in the Royal Air Force (RAF) and later in the Royal Tank Corps. Friends of Lawrence, concerned for his sanity, were able to have him transferred to the RAF and assigned to India. He then served in England from 1929 until his discharge in Feb. 1935, leading a relatively happy and quiet life.

While riding a motorcycle on May 13, 1935, he was in a road accident. He lay in a coma for six days before dying of his injuries. The heavy security at the military hospital where he was taken after the accident raised questions about the possible involvement of British intelligence organizations in his death.

Layton, Rear Adm. Edwin T.

(b. 1903 d. 1984)

Head of intelligence for the U.S. Pacific Fleet during World War II. Layton was largely responsible for intelligence derived from breaking Japanese codes being used by the fleet commander at the battles of Coral Sea and MIDWAY, as well as later Pacific campaigns.

A 1924 graduate of the U.S. Naval Academy, during the 1920s and 1930s Layton served in surface ships, interspersed with tours ashore—in Japan for language

training, in Peking and later Tokyo as assistant naval ATTACHÉ, and in Washington, D.C. After a little more than a year as commanding officer of a destroyer-minesweeper, in Dec. 1940 then-Lt. Comdr. Layton became intelligence officer for the fleet commander at Pearl Harbor, Adm. James O. Richardson. He continued to serve in that role for Richardson's successors, Adm. Husband E. Kimmel (1941) and Fleet Adm. Chester W. Nimitz (1942–1945).

Layton's codebreakers at Pearl Harbor made major inroads in reading the Japanese naval codes and analyzing radio transmissions for ship movements. However, just before the outbreak of war there was a constant struggle between Layton and the intelligence staff in Washington. Layton later charged that the refusal of those in Washington to share information with his staff contributed to the failure to know the location of Japanese warship movements at the outbreak of the Pacific War. His autobiographic study of naval intelligence in the Pacific War—"*And I Was There*"—was published in 1985, the year after his death. The book cited incompetence, bureaucratic feuding, and empire building in Washington, particularly by Capt. Richmond Kelly Turner, then director of Navy war plans.

Layton was a champion user of codebreaking information to plan operations, and he had a strong supporter in Adm. Nimitz. At the end of the war Layton, then a captain, was ordered by Nimitz to join him at the surrender ceremony on the USS *Missouri* in Tokyo Bay on Sept. 2, 1945, as a mark of the admiral's regard for his staff's intelligence work.

From Feb. 1946, Layton held several shore assignments, including the task of setting up the U.S. Navy's intelligence school and serving as naval attaché in Rio de Janeiro, Brazil. As a rear admiral he was assistant director of intelligence for the Joint Chiefs of Staff and assistant chief of staff to the Commander in Chief Pacific Fleet. He retired in Nov. 1959.

L Clearance

U.S. SECURITY CLEARANCE given by the Department of Energy (formerly Atomic Energy Commission) to DOE employees, personnel of other government agencies, and contractors. An L clearance is valid for access to RESTRICTED DATA at the CONFIDENTIAL level and to national security information at the SECRET level.

An L clearance is necessary for access to nuclear weapon materials.

See Q CLEARANCE.

LCS

SEE LONDON CONTROLLING STATION

Leak

The deliberate disclosure of classified information. This is often done for political reasons, that is, to garner support for a controversial program or to release a "trial balloon." The term is sometimes loosely applied to the inadvertent release of information to unauthorized persons. See PLUMBERS.

Some leaks are criminal. Under the Intelligence Identities Protection Act of 1982, for example, it is a crime to knowingly reveal the identity of a covert operative. Britain can also prosecute a leak under the OFFICIAL SECRETS ACT. (See VALERIE PLANE and KATHARINE GUN.)

Le Carré, John [p]

(b. 1931)

Pseudonym of David Cornwell, an INTELLIGENCE OFFICER in British Security Service (MI5) who became an internationally acclaimed master of the espionage novel. Although his novels seemed to well up from the underworld of spy and counterspy, the authenticity stemmed from his characters rather than their activities.

He wrote of espionage as a profession that psychologically crippled its practitioners. Serving a nation that no longer served them, his characters either cynically went through the motions, answering their own code of honor, or they deceived and even betrayed each other.

The traitor Bill Haydon in *Tinker, Tailor, Soldier, Spy* (1974; adapted for television in 1980) reflects le Carré's belief that as British values eroded, so did the nation's secret services. Le Carré said HAROLD (KIM) PHILBY, the real-life traitor in MI5, was "a creature of the postwar depression, of the swift snuffing out of the Socialist flame, of the thousand-year sleep of [British political leaders] Eden and Macmillan." Underscoring the Haydon-Philby connection, le Carré has a character refer to Haydon as "our latter-day Lawrence of Arabia" (see COL. THOMAS E. LAWRENCE)—a clear reference to Philby's father, an Arabist who had been likened to Lawrence. Also, Haydon, like Philby, was educated at Cambridge.

Le Carré's first two novels—*Call for the Dead* (1961) and *A Murder of Quality* (1962)—starred a shadowy, middle-aged intelligence officer named GEORGE SMILEY [f]. Not until his third novel, *The Spy Who Came In from the Cold* (1963), was le Carré established as a major spy writer. The book was acclaimed both in Britain and the United States and became a movie in 1966, with Richard Burton playing the title role. (See MOVIES.)

Le Carré was the son of a debt-ridden, womanizing father who lived a life of lies. "So we found ourselves, my brother and I, often living in the style of millionaire paupers," le Carré wrote about the lifestyle his father imposed. His father, described by le Carré as "a fantasist, perhaps a schizophrenic" who "liked using several names," appears as a thinly veiled fictional character in *A Perfect Spy* (1986; adapted for television, 1988).

After a boyhood and youth in what he called "occupied territory," le Carré spent a year in Switzerland as a student. He learned German there, and when he was drafted into the British Army he was assigned to intelligence in Germany, where he interrogated displaced persons in refugee camps.

When he completed his Army service, he went to Lincoln College, Oxford, where he graduated with first-class honors. After a stint of teaching at Eton, he became a freelance illustrator. One of his commissions was the drawings in *Talking Birds,* by Maxwell Knight, for many years the head of MI5's countersubversive department. Knight recruited le Carré into MI5, whose Director-General was Sir ROGER HOLLIS, one of the many real people who are believed to have been models or partial models for le Carré characters.

In 1960 le Carré was transferred to MI6 and sent to the British Embassy in Bonn under diplomatic COVER as a second secretary. He was later given the cover of consul in Hamburg.

Of Smiley le Carré said in 1980: "I think he stands where I stand; he feels that to pit yourself against any 'ism' is to strike a posture which is itself ideological, and therefore offensive in terms of practical decency. In practice almost any political ideology invites you to set aside your humanitarian instincts."

Alec Leamas, the spent, cynical, but honorable hero of *The Spy Who Came In from the Cold,* sees himself engaged in a war—"fought on a tiny scale, at close range." He sees "people cheated and misled, whole lives thrown away, people shot and in prison, whole groups and classes of men written off for nothing."

George Smiley is introduced in *Call for the Dead* as a scholar who had served in intelligence during World War II. He is called back into intelligence because "the revelations of a young cipher-clerk in Ottawa had created a new demand for men of Smiley's experience." (In real life, IGOR GOUZENKO was such a clerk.) Smiley's estranged wife, Ann, describes him as "breathtakingly ordinary," an advantage for a field man. "Short, fat, and of a quiet disposition, he appeared to spend a lot of money on really bad clothes, which hung about his squat frame like a skin on a shrunken toad," according to Ann.

Smiley was often presented as being modeled on SIR MAURICE OLDFIELD, Director-General of MI6. But, when Oldfield died in 1986 and *The Times* made that assertion, le Carré denied it, telling *The Times*: "I never heard of Sir Maurice either by name or in any other way until long after the name and character of George Smiley were in print."

Most intelligence officials in Britain hated the spy world that le Carré portrayed. In *Literary Agents* (1987), Anthony Masters quotes from an unpublished manuscript by John Bingham, who was both an intelligence officer and a writer. Clearly targeting le Carré, Bingham wrote, "The belief encouraged by many spy writers that Intelligence officers consist of moles, morons, shits and homosexuals makes the Intelligence job no easier."

RICHARD HELMS, who was DIRECTOR OF CENTRAL INTELLIGENCE when le Carré emerged, detested his novels because of their cynicism and themes of betrayal.

When the Cold War ended, le Carré announced that he, too, had entered a new era. In the post–Cold War world, he said in 1993, "what espionage looks like now is what it always was: a sideshow got up as major theater."

He writes all of his novels in longhand on yellow pads. After his wife subsequently types the manuscripts, they are sent directly to the publisher, without a review by the author.

Le Carré's other novels include *The Looking Glass War* (1965), *A Small Town in Germany* (1968), *The Honourable Schoolboy* (1977), *Smiley's People* (1977), *The Little Drummer Girl* (1983), *The Russia House* (1989), *The Secret Pilgrim* (1991), *The Night Manager* (1993), *Our Game* (1995), *The Tailor of Panama* (1996), *Single & Single* (1999), *The Constant Gardener* (2003), and *Absolute Friends* (2003).

Lee, Andrew D.

(b. 1952)

American who sold SATELLITE secrets to the Soviets. Conspiring with CHRISTOPHER BOYCE, for nearly two years Lee carried to Soviet HANDLERS film containing photographs of TOP SECRET documents that Boyce had photographed. Lee was caught after he threw something onto the grounds of the Soviet Embassy in Mexico City, trying to get the attention of his HANDLER. When Mexican police, thinking he was a terrorist, started questioning him, Lee asked for help from a U.S. diplomat. At police headquarters, police opened an envelope Lee had been carrying. It was full of film strips. The police developed the film and gave the prints to U.S. officials, who knew about Lee because of the incident at the embassy. The photos were of U.S. documents marked top secret.

Lee, who was arrested on Jan. 6, 1977, implicated Boyce, who was arrested on Jan. 18 (See CHRISTOPHER BOYCE for details of the case.) Tried and convicted of espionage, Lee was sentenced to life imprisonment, Boyce to 40 years.

Lee, Maj. Duncan

(b. 1914 d. 1988)

U.S. OFFICE OF STRATEGIC SERVICES (OSS) officer who spied for the Soviet Union. Lee was a close friend and key aide to WILLIAM DONOVAN, head of the OSS. He is the most senior OSS officer known to have been a Soviet AGENT.

A descendant of Confederate Gen. Robert E. Lee, he was born of missionary parents in China. He studied at Cambridge in England and in 1939 graduated from Yale Law School, where he and his wife joined the American Communist Party. (See CPUSA.) He joined Donovan's law firm, where Donovan took him under his wing.

He gave his reports in the form of briefings to his HANDLERS, declining to take and copy documents. He delivered information from U.S. ambassadors, along with such high-level information as reports of German peace feelers and the way Chiang Kai-shek decided to deal with his communist rivals. On March 3, 1944, Lee disclosed the highly classified information that the allied invasion

of Normandy (D-DAY) would be between mid-May and the beginning of June. (D-Day was June 6.)

Lee's espionage career ended after he and a COURIER, Mary Price, became lovers. She quit and was replaced by ELIZABETH BENTLEY, who reported that Lee had decided to stop spying. Bentley, who had become involved with her handler, later defected.

Also see MAURICE HALPERIN.

Lee, Peter H.

(b. 1939)

China-born physicist at LOS ALAMOS nuclear weapons laboratory who pleaded guilty to passing classified national defense information to Chinese scientists on a visit to Beijing in 1985; he also admitted to lying when he described, on a form for obtaining a SECURITY CLEARANCE that a 1997 visit to China was for pleasure. During that trip he had several meetings with Chinese scientists.

Lee had also worked in the United Kingdom as a member of the British-U.S. Radar Ocean Imaging Programme, which examined ways of tracking nuclear SUBMARINES.

In March 1998 Lee pleaded guilty to "willfully passing national defense information to Chinese scientists" and lying on the security clearance form, which enabled him to work for TRW, a major California defense contractor that in 2002 was acquired by Northrop Grumman. (TRW figured in a spy case in the 1970s; see CHRISTOPHER BOYCE.)

He received a suspended five-year prison term, one year of incarceration, three years of supervised probation, a $20,000 fine, and 3,000 hours of community service.

The FBI investigation of Lee had the CODE NAME "Royal Tourist."

Lee, Wen Ho

(b. 1939)

Taiwanese-American nuclear weapons engineer suspected of spying for China.

Subject of a long and inconclusive FBI investigation, Lee frustrated suspicious COUNTERINTELLIGENCE officials for five years. Finally, in Dec. 1999 he was indicted on 59 counts of illegally removing classified data from LOS ALAMOS nuclear laboratory. Authorities said that he had in his possession computer files full of information about U.S. nuclear weapons. He was not accused of espionage but he was held in jail pending trial

FBI interest in Lee's activities at Los Alamos was tied to CIA analysis of nuclear weapons test explosions in China between 1992 and 1994. The CIA believed that China, in a technological breakthrough had developed small thermonuclear warheads. Then, in 1995, a Chinese official seeking to defect provided the CIA with documents showing that the Chinese warhead resembled the

U.S. warhead known as W-88 and developed at Los Alamos. Suspicion focused on Lee.

In Sept. 2000, Lee was freed after pleading guilty to one of the counts: illegally downloading nuclear weapons design secrets to a non-secure computer when he was working at Los Alamos. He said he could not remember how many cassette tapes he made from the downloaded data and that he that he had thrown them away. Officials said he had downloaded 1.4 gigabytes of data, the equivalent of about 400,000 pages. FBI agents sifted through tons of debris in a landfill in a vain search for the tapes. Officials at Los Alamos discovered the downloading after Lee had been discharged in March 1999 for security violations.

The judge who freed Lee had apologized on behalf of the nation, reflecting the emotion that swirled around the case. Then came a Congressional inquiry, inspired by claims that he had been singled out because he was of Chinese descent. At the hearing, Attorney General Janet Reno and LOUIS FREEH, director of the FBI, both denounced Lee. "He is not an absent-minded professor," Reno said. "He is a felon. He committed a very serious calculated crime and he pled guilty to it. He abused the trust of the American people by putting at risk some of our core national security secrets."

Lee had traveled twice to China and at least 10 times to Taiwan, where he was a visiting scholar at the Chung Shan Institute of Science and Technology, center of Taiwan's nuclear research.

Another chapter to the Lee mystery story case was added in 2003, after the arrest of KATRINA LEUNG. Run by the FBI as an AGENT for spying on China, Leung actually was a DOUBLE AGENT. Investigators wondered whether DISINFORMATION provided by Leung might have affected the FBI's handling of the Lee case.

Legal

Intelligence AGENT who comes into a country using an official position as his COVER, such as commercial ATTACHÉ or clerk.

Legal Attaché

SEE ATTACHÉ

Legend

False identity that an AGENT builds up through forged documents and other means, such as living under the name of the person whose identity he assumes.

Le Queux, William Tufnell

(b. 1864 d. 1927)

English novelist and amateur spy who said he based his spy books on his experiences in the SECRET SERVICE. His claim was never officially confirmed; if it was true, Le

Queux was the first in a long line of British INTELLIGENCE OFFICERS turned writer. (See LITERARY SPIES.)

His 1896 thriller, *A Secret Service,* was taken seriously by some British officials, who used the book as a call for preparedness. The book told of an impending German invasion of Britain (a theme echoed by ERSKINE CHILDERS in 1903). In 1905 Le Queux claimed that a friend in BERLIN had revealed to him the existence of a huge German spy NETWORK in Britain. He also claimed to know about British traitors who belonged to a secret organization called the "Hidden Hand."

Le Queux continued writing thrillers and spy novels until his death. His other works included *Guilty Bonds* (1890*), Secrets of Monte Carlo* (1899)*, An Observer in the Near East* (1907), and *Where the Desert Ends* (1923).

Lessenthien, Machinist's Mate 1st Class Kurt G.

(b. 1966)

U.S. sailor convicted of attempting to sell military secrets to Russia. An instructor at the Navy Nuclear Power School in Orlando, Fla., Lessenthien admitted that he had offered information about U.S. nuclear submarine technology to a Russian government representative. He had served on three U.S. submarines.

The FBI learned of the sailor's alleged contact apparently through electronic SURVEILLANCE of the Russian Embassy in Washington, D.C. An FBI agent posing as a Russian then contacted Lessenthien. In March 1996, a Navy official said, Lessenthien offered a Russian TOP SECRET data for "tens of thousands of dollars."

He was charged with 22 counts of attempted espionage and failure to safeguard classified material. He was accused of photographing classified equipment on a Trident missile submarine and removing classified documents from it. He was taken into custody after he mailed classified material to the "Russian" AGENT as a "show of good faith." At a meeting he handed over more material and was arrested.

In a plea bargain he was sentenced to 27 years in prison. He said he needed the money to pay off debts. The jury that convicted him had recommended the maximum life term.

Leung, Katrina M.

AGENT for the United States, accused of being a DOUBLE AGENT for China while being run by the FBI. When she was arrested in 2003, her HANDLER, an FBI COUNTER-INTELLIGENCE specialist, was also arrested and identified as her lover. Officials also said that she had been the lover of another FBI agent.

Federal officials said that over a 20-year period the FBI had paid Leung $1.7 million for the information she gathered. But, at the same time, according to the federal charges, she was taking classified data from her handler,

FBI agent James J. (JJ) Smith, and passing it on to China. Smith, 59 years old when he was arrested, was charged with gross negligence. Leung, 49 years old, was married, as was Smith, who had retired. They were accused of being lovers throughout their espionage relationship. Leung and Smith pleaded not guilty to the charges.

If the allegations are true, two decades of U.S. information about China are tainted by DISINFORMATION that Leung's Chinese handlers in MSS (Ministry of State Security) would have manufactured for her to pass on.

She was considered an especially important U.S. agent because of her family connections in China. U.S. officials said that the Chinese-American businesswoman had access to former President Jiang Zemin, former Premier Zhu Rongji, and the late President Yang Shangkun. Some of her reports went directly to the White House, officials said.

Information provided by Leung may have had effects on at least two other major FBI cases with Chinese connections. One was the failed prosecution of WEN HO LEE, a Chinese-American nuclear weapons engineer who worked at LOS ALAMOS National Laboratory. The other involved election campaign donations that had been illegally channeled from China to American candidates; that investigation centered on Ted Sioeng, a multimillionaire businessman who later fled the country. Smith had been the lead FBI agent in at least one aspect of that investigation.

Former Senator Fred D. Thompson, a Tennessee Republican who had led the congressional investigation into the Chinese donations, asked bluntly, "Did she dampen the FBI's ardor on campaign finance?"

A search of Leung's home produced an FBI document that mentioned an operation with the CODE NAME Royal Tourist. This was the espionage investigation of PETER LEE, who worked for the California firm TRW (which figured in a spy case in the 1970s; see CHRISTOPHER BOYCE.)

Both Leung and her husband, Kam, who lived in San Marino, Calif., were socially prominent and active in Southern California Republican politics. She was a director of the Los Angeles World Affairs Council. In 1996 U.S. intelligence officials warned that China was planning to pour $3 million into U.S. election campaigns. Congress did discover that hundreds of thousands of illegal funds had been passed from Chinese sources to the Democratic National Committee. Smith worked for the FBI from Oct. 1970 until his retirement in Nov. 2000.

The other former FBI agent, also said to have been Leung's lover, was William Cleveland, Jr. Government sources said he had warned that Leung might have been a double agent. When she was arrested, Cleveland resigned as chief of security at Lawrence Livermore National Laboratory, another U.S. nuclear weapons research site. During the late 1970s and early 1980s, Cleveland was in charge of espionage investigations at Lawrence Livermore.

Leung was born Man Ying Chan in Guangzhou, China. Officials said her MSS code name was Lou; her MSS handler was known as Mao. One of her FBI code names was Parlor Maid.

Levchenko, Maj. Stanislav Aleksandrovich

(b. 1941)

Former KGB officer who defected to the United States. Levchenko grew up as the privileged son of a military school faculty member. He attended Moscow University's Institute of Oriental Studies and studied Japanese in the hope of becoming a diplomat stationed in the Far East. After graduating in 1964, the following year he became an interpreter for the Central Committee of the Communist Party and made several trips to Japan.

In 1966 he was drafted into the Army and was ordered into the GRU (MILITARY INTELLIGENCE). In 1971 he was assigned to the First Directorate (foreign operations) of the KGB and, after another year of training, to the Japanese desk at THE CENTER. He was given the COVER of a journalist and in Feb. 1975 was sent to Tokyo as a correspondent for the magazine New Times. There he cultivated contacts with Japanese political, military, and economic leaders.

He became bitter over his treatment by the KGB, and in Oct. 1979, after seeking out U.S. INTELLIGENCE OFFICERS in Tokyo, he defected and named many of his KGB colleagues as well as Japanese contacts. He alleged that the KGB was paying at least 200 Japanese, although not all were active spies. He named some, but not all, fearing some would commit suicide if their identities were revealed. He subsequently testified before the House of Representatives Permanent Select Committee on Intelligence in July 1982, describing KGB programs directed against the United States.

Levchenko was sentenced to death in absentia by a Soviet court in 1981 while he was living in the United States. His book, On the Wrong Side (1988), recounted his life in the GRU and KGB.

Levinson, Col. Shimon

(b. 1933)

Israeli INTELLIGENCE OFFICER and security chief for the Prime Minister's office who was convicted of spying against Israel for the KGB.

He entered the Israeli Army as an enlisted man. Subsequently commissioned, Levinson was the Israeli military representative on the Israeli-Jordanian cease-fire committee from 1954 to 1961. He joined AMAN, Israeli MILITARY INTELLIGENCE, in 1963, undertaking various assignments until he rejoined the cease-fire committee in 1967. After the Six Day War (1967) he became a liaison officer to UNITED NATIONS forces. He later became the chief military liaison officer to the United Nations, a position he held until 1978.

The following year he took leave of the Army to work in counter-drug activities in Southeast Asia. About 1983, while in Bangkok, Levinson volunteered to work for the KGB, apparently for financial reasons. Levinson testified that over the next six years he met with his KGB controllers in European cities on 11 occasions.

He returned to Israel in 1983 and two years later was appointed security chief for the Prime Minister's office.

Levinson was arrested on May 12, 1991, as he was returning from abroad after his contacts with the KGB apparently broke down.

Israeli officials declared that Levinson had passed the highest secrets related to nuclear and military matters to the KGB. However, former Israeli intelligence official RAFAEL EITAN said that the only important information passed by Levinson that could help the Soviets was about senior Israeli officials.

A trial in camera, held in 1992–1993, is believed to have been the longest spy trial in history. In July 1993 Levinson was convicted of giving information to the enemy, espionage, and having contact with a foreign AGENT. He was sentenced to 12 years in prison. He received only about $30,000 from the KGB for his services.

Liberty

U.S. Navy INTELLIGENCE COLLECTION SHIP attacked by Israeli air and naval forces on June 8, 1967, when she was in the Mediterranean off the Sinai coast during the Arab-Israeli Six Day War.

The Liberty was collecting ELECTRONIC INTELLIGENCE (ELINT) from both Israeli and Egyptian forces fighting in that area when Israeli aircraft and torpedo boats, misidentifying the ship, attacked her. In the attack 34 crewmen were killed, 171 were wounded, and the ship was severely damaged.

The ship was launched in May 1945 as Simmons Victory, a Victory-class cargo ship for carrying supplies to Allied forces in the Pacific during World War II. She performed the same role during the Korean War, being decommissioned in 1958. The U.S. Navy purchased the ship in Feb. 1963, refitted it as an intelligence collection ship, and assigned it the classification AGTR, indicating miscellaneous auxiliary (AG)—technical research (TR). As the fifth AGTR ship, she was designated AGTR5. She was renamed Liberty and, after commissioning in Dec. 1964, was sent along the African coast, under control of the NSA.

In May 1967, under the command of Comdr. William McGonagle, she was ordered to Rota, Spain, where she took on supplies and six Arabic linguists— three from the NSA and three U.S. Marines—and proceeded to an operations area off Port Said, at the northern end of the Suez Canal. A crisis was brewing between Israel and Egypt, with Syria and Jordan allying with Egypt. Egyptian President Gamal Abdel Nasser announced a blockade of the Strait of Tiran at the tip of the Sinai Peninsula.

As the Liberty headed toward Israel, the Six Day War started, and the ship was ordered to keep 25 miles from the coast. A second order would have put her 100 miles off the coast. She did not get that order. Besides, for her mission the electronic eavesdroppers on board needed to be close to the coast to intercept tactical communications.

Early on June 8 an Israeli Air Force patrol plane spotted the Liberty about 70 miles west of Gaza and correctly identified her as a U.S. ship. In the maelstrom of

battle between Israeli and Egyptian, an Israeli pilot reported to the Israeli Air Force command center (Tel Aviv) that an unidentified ship had fired on him. There were also reports, which later proved to be false, that Israeli troops in the Egyptian coastal town of El Arish were being shelled by a ship. Israeli torpedo boats were dispatched to investigate. They detected the Liberty by radar at extreme range and manually calculated that her speed was 28 to 30 knots. The speed estimates were wrong. The torpedo boats were working with the Navy command center (Haifa) and called for air attacks because they could not intercept a ship at the estimated speed at the distance the Liberty was from them.

At about 2 P.M., two Israeli Mirage jet aircraft sighted the Liberty, identified her as an enemy ship (the Egyptian troop transport El Quseir), and strafed her. They did not see her American flag. Two Israeli Super-Mystère aircraft, diverted from another mission, arrived and dropped napalm on the ship. One napalm bomb may have struck her.

The aircraft broke off their attack when one of the pilots identified the letters CTR-5 [sic] on her hull. Three Israeli torpedo boats now approached and asked the smoke-engulfed ship to identify herself. Getting what was later described as an evasive answer, the boats launched five torpedoes. One hit the ship below the waterline, destroying an intelligence compartment and opening it to the sea; 25 technicians, attached to the NAVAL SECURITY GROUP intercept unit, were killed in the explosion or drowned. As the torpedo boats maneuvered for another attack the Israelis learned that it was a U.S. ship that they were attacking. (The three boats had launched five of the six torpedoes that they carried.)

On board the listing Liberty, Comdr. McGonagle, his right leg torn by shrapnel, his executive officer and operations officer dead or dying, commanded a floating inferno. He rejected Israeli offers of assistance and conned his crippled ship out of the area. She sailed through the night by the north star and at dawn rendezvoused with U.S. Navy ships and helicopters, which took off her dead and wounded. McGonagle stayed on board and sailed his ship to Malta.

Israel rapidly tried to end a diplomatic uproar by setting up a court of inquiry. It reported that the attack "was perpetrated as a result of a chain of three errors"— the false report that El Arish was being shelled, the wrong estimate of the Liberty's speed, and the misidentification of the ship as the El Quseir. Critics of Israel's findings wondered how the 10,680-ton, 455-foot Liberty could be mistaken for the 2,640-ton, 275-foot El Quseir. Controversy was heightened by discrepancies between the Israeli and U.S. battle reports.

The Israeli government paid $3,323,000 directly to the families of the 34 men who were killed; $3,566,547 was paid in compensation to those wounded. After years of claims and counterclaims, in 1980 Israel paid the U.S. Navy $6 million for damage to the Liberty (with no admission of liability). For many, particularly those in the NSA and Navy with close attachments to the ship and its operations, Israel remained unforgiven. But on a government-to-

A U.S. SH-3 *Sea King* helicopter hovers over the U.S. intelligence ship Liberty *after she was attacked by Israeli aircraft and torpedo boats in a tragic mistake during the Arab-Israeli conflict of June 1967. The damage from a torpedo is visible on the starboard side, forward.* (U.S. NAVY)

government level, the attack on the *Liberty* was sadly accepted as a tragic incident in the fog of war.

There have been three official Israeli and 10 U.S. investigations—five by Congressional panels—into the attack on the *Liberty*. All found either that the attack was definitely a tragic mistake or that there was no evidence that it was intentional. These views were confirmed in the 1990s with revelation that an U.S. Navy EC-121 ELINT aircraft was in the area at the time, recording Israeli radio transmissions, with at least two Hebrew linguists on board. (See C-121 CONSTELLATION.)

The intercept supervisor in the EC-121, Chief Petty Officer Marvin E. Nowicki, a Hebrew linguist, later wrote in the *Wall Street Journal*, "My position . . . is that the attack, though terrible and tragic especially to the crew members and their families on that ill-fated day in June 1967, was a gross error." Following the attack the *Liberty* was decommissioned and the U.S. Navy ended its program of passive intelligence collection ships. Comdr. McGonagle was awarded the Medal of Honor for his actions during the attack and several other crewmen were also decorated.

In a 2002 book, *The Liberty Incident,* A. Jay Cristol, a sitting Federal judge and former naval aviator, wrote that the attack was an accident in the fog of war, not a deliberate Israeli operation to destroy the ship. The controversy over what happened, he wrote, stemmed from the fact that both the United States and Israel had decided to keep much of the information about the *Liberty* incident classified for more than a decade.

Libi

Abbreviation of the NKVD CODE NAME for JULIUS ROSENBERG, which was used by his Soviet HANDLER, ALEXANDR FEKLISOV.

Lie Detector

SEE POLYGRAPH

Lindberg, Lt. Comdr. Arthur E.

U.S. Navy officer who helped the FBI in a scam to trap Soviet INTELLIGENCE OFFICERS. Following an elaborate FBI scenario, Lindberg boarded the Soviet cruise ship *Kazakhstan* for a weeklong New York-to-Bermuda voyage in the summer of 1977. As Lindberg was leaving the ship, he handed an officer a note saying that he was "interested in making additional money prior to [his] retirement." Soviets did contact him, and he provided them with information about underwater acoustics and detection techniques used in the hunting of Soviet submarines. Navy anti-submarine warfare experts doled out the information, which Lindberg photographed. He placed the film at DEAD DROPS near New Jersey highways. In May 1978 FBI agents staked out a drop in Woodbridge, N.J., and arrested three Soviets who serviced the drop. Two of them were UNITED NATIONS employees; the third was an ATTACHÉ in the Soviet United Nations mission and had diplomatic immunity. He was expelled.

The other two Soviets did not have immunity and were to be put on trial—over the objections of the Navy, which feared that submarine-hunting secrets would be revealed in testimony; of the CIA, which feared reprisals against its own agents in the Soviet Union; and of the State Department, which worried about the possible effect of the arrests on a forthcoming summit meeting planned between President Carter and Soviet leader Leonid Brezhnev.

In Moscow the KGB retaliated by arresting an American businessman for smuggling and by revealing the previously undisclosed arrest and expulsion of MARTHA

PETERSON, a CIA CASE OFFICER in Moscow. Meanwhile, the two Soviets were tried and convicted of espionage; each was given a 50-year sentence. They were then traded to the Soviet Union for five Soviet dissidents and "other considerations," which some sources said included a Soviet promise not to execute an imprisoned CIA agent. The American businessman was convicted on a lesser charge, given a five-year prison sentence, and expelled.

Link Encryption

The application of on-line CRYPTOSECURITY to a communications system, or "link," so that all information passing over the link is totally encrypted.

Lipka, Robert S.

(b. 1946)

U.S. Army intelligence analyst accused of spying for the Soviets while working at the NSA. In Sept. 1997, after pleading guilty to conspiracy to commit espionage, he was sentenced to 18 years in prison.

Lipka, who worked at the NSA from 1964 to 1967, was not arrested until Feb. 1996. The FBI was alerted to Lipka when his former wife called the FBI in 1993 and said that he had been spying for the Soviets.

Lipka was assigned to the NSA as an intelligence analyst when a young soldier. He worked in the central communications room, where he removed highly classified documents from teleprinters and distributed them around the agency. He was told he was replacing Army Sgt. JACK F. DUNLAP, who had spied for the Soviets and killed himself when he came under suspicion.

Lipka's age and actions coincide with a "young soldier" who was a WALK-IN volunteer spy, as described by former KGB Maj. Gen. OLEG KALUGIN in his book *The First Directorate: My 32 Years in Intelligence and Espionage Against the West* (1994). "The young soldier," Kalugin wrote, "was involved in shredding and destroying NSA documents and could supply us with a wealth of material," giving his HANDLER "whatever he got his hands on, often having little idea what he was turning over." These included the NSA's "daily and weekly top secret reports to the White House, copies of communications on U.S. troop movements around the world and communications among the NATO allies." Kalugin said that the soldier used the money he received—$500 to $1,000 for each package he delivered—to finance his college education. Authorities said he was paid about $27,000 for the documents, which he photographed with cameras supplied by his handler.

After leaving the Army, Lipka attended Millersville University in Millersville, Pa., and received a bachelor's degree in education in 1972. He became a schoolteacher and worked on the side as a coin dealer. He and his wife, Patricia, divorced in 1974.

After his former wife made her accusations to the FBI, an agent posing as "Sergey Nitikin" called on Lipka and said he was a Russian MILITARY INTELLIGENCE officer who wanted to resume contact. They met four times and in the conversations, the FBI said, he admitted having been a spy while at the NSA.

The FBI said Lipka used classic TRADECRAFT in making his deliveries in one place (such as the men's room in a restaurant) and picking up his payment at a DEAD DROP. The FBI also said that the KGB gave him a "roll-over" camera, which snapped photos as it was rolled over a document.

According to FBI sources, a man and wife, identified as Peter and Ingeborg Fischer, acted as CUTOUTS between the KGB and Lipka. They were under SURVEILLANCE during the 1960s, but as far as is publicly known, they were not apprehended.

Literary Spies

Writing about espionage is as old as writing itself (see BIBLICAL SPIES). The earliest source for spy stories is Ti Jenchieh, a seventh-century Chinese spymaster, whose exploits were fictionalized in 18th-century stories known as the *Dee Goong An*. They were translated and adapted in recent times by a Dutch diplomat, R. H. Van Gulik, who published them as the "Judge Dee Stories." Thus, even these tales, although rooted in ancient sources, are, like other spy fiction, relatively young.

In Western literature JAMES FENIMORE COOPER is generally credited with writing the first spy novel, *The Spy* (1821), which was based on the real espionage of a Patriot in the American Revolutionary War (see HARVEY BIRCH [f]). Then follows a long period without spy fiction in America, other than the highly embellished memoirs that poured out of the pens of spies who served on both sides of the American Civil War.

In England, DANIEL DEFOE worked as a spy against the Jacobites before writing *Robinson Crusoe* (1719), but he did not merge his two careers. Charles Dickens wove espionage into the plot of *A Tale of Two Cities* (1859). Then, as in America, there was a dry spell for fictional spies. At the end of the 19th century, two prolific British authors turned to espionage for plots and launched the genre in Britain. E. Phillips Oppenheim sometimes gets the credit for the first British spy novel, *Mysterious Mr. Sabin* (1898), but his contemporary, WILLIAM TUFNELL LE QUEUX, preceded him with *The Secret Service* (1896). Oppenheim's *The Great Impersonation* (1920) is the best known of his spy novels.

In *Kim* (1901), Rudyard Kipling uses the GREAT GAME as the background for the tale of an Indian lad recruited by a British INTELLIGENCE OFFICER. DOUBLE AGENT HAROLD (KIM) PHILBY got his nickname from Kipling's eponymous hero. BARONESS EMMUSKA ORCZY invented *The Scarlet Pimpernel* (1905), a British aristocrat who aids hapless French aristocrats during the French Revolution.

In 1903 came *The Riddle of the Sands* by ERSKINE CHILDERS, who had become convinced that Germany planned to invade Britain. His novel, about two British yachtsmen stumbling onto German invasion plans, inspired the British Admiralty to create a North Sea Fleet. Childers launched a wave of British spy novels, including two by JOSEPH CONRAD: *The Secret Agent* (1907) and *Under Western Eyes* (1911). In *The Secret Agent*'s somber world of anarchists Conrad anticipates the haunted AGENTS of GRAHAM GREENE and JOHN LE CARRÉ. G. K. Chesterton, in *The Man Who Was Thursday* (1908), uses a conspiracy to take over the world—a plot device that foreshadows the would-be world conquerors confronted by IAN FLEMING'S JAMES BOND [f].

SOMERSET MAUGHAM, himself a British agent in World War I, drew upon his experiences to write *Ashenden* (1928). "Of all fictitious spy stories," Anthony Masters wrote in *Literary Agents* (1987), "*Ashenden*'s adventures come nearest to the real-life experiences of his creator." *Ashenden,* le Carré told a Maugham biographer, influenced him in his espionage writing. Maugham, said le Carré, "was the first person to write anything about espionage in a mood of disenchantment and almost prosaic reality."

In the 1930s spy thrillers began appearing as serials in pulp magazines (so called because they were published on cheap newsprint). The most popular were the fantastic adventures of Secret Service Operator 5, "America's Undercover Ace," also known as Operator 5 (and sometimes Operator Z7).

Cyril Henry Coles, a British intelligence officer in World War I and World War II, collaborated with Adelaide Frances Manning to write a series of some 25 books under the pseudonym Manning Coles. The hero of the series is Tommy Hambledon, an agent working for the "British Intelligence Service." The Manning Coles books include *Drink to Yesterday, Pray Silence* (both 1940), and *They Tell No Tales* (1941). F. van Wyck Mason, more famous as an author of murder mysteries, used "Hugh North of Army intelligence" as a hero in *Seeds of Murder* (1930).

ERIC AMBLER wrote of a Europe moving toward war in his series of prewar novels. Graham Greene also anticipated the war with his *The Confidential Agent* (1939). Later would come *Our Man in Havana* (1958) and *The Human Factor* (1978), realistic novels of the Cold War. In *The Quiet American* (1955) Greene used at least some elements in the work of a real U.S. COVERT ACTION operative, U.S. Maj. Gen. EDWARD LANSDALE, as the model for Alden Pyle, a zealous CIA agent under COVER in Vietnam during the Eisenhower administration. Lansdale had the paradoxical distinction of being such a good SECRET AGENT that he became the model for aspects of characters in three works of fiction: *The Ugly American* (1958) by William J. Lederer and Eugene Burdick, who portrayed Lansdale as Col. Edwin Barnum Hillandale, who reached the hearts and minds of the people; and Jean Lartéguy's novel *Le Mal Jaune,* published in the United States as *Yellow Fever* (1965), in which Lansdale is thinly veiled as the anti-French Col. Lionel Teryman.

During World War II many writers worked in intelligence, some gaining experience they would later use as novelists. Greene was an AGENT for MI6; IAN FLEMING, creator of JAMES BOND[f], was a British NAVAL INTELLI-

GENCE officer. British author Angus Wilson started his writing career as a result of his wartime work as a cryptographer at BLETCHLEY PARK, where he had a nervous breakdown and was advised by a psychotherapist to take up writing.

Novelist John P. Marquand worked for the OFFICE OF STRATEGIC SERVICES (OSS). Among his projects was the testing of German prisoners of war for antitoxins in an attempt to learn whether they were being protected against biological warfare agents that Germany might use against the Allies.

The two world wars produced a time and a setting for relatively few spy novels compared to the rich offerings of the Cold War, which became the arena for countless novels pitting agents of the West against agents of the East. Heroes and villains spied for the CIA, MI6, and the KGB. Intelligence agencies emerged from the shadows and appeared on pages of fiction when little about their real work was appearing on pages of nonfiction books.

Most spy novels were thrillers featuring as heroes spies who in no way resembled real INTELLIGENCE OFFICERS, HANDLERS, or agents. Writer MALCOLM MUGGERIDGE, who was an intelligence officer during World War II, commented that thriller writers took to espionage "as easily as the mentally unstable become psychiatrists or the impotent pornographers."

James Bond—Agent 007—burst into spy fiction in *Casino Royale* (1953), the first of 11 Bond novels portraying the spy as a superhero. President Kennedy, who said that Bond's creator, IAN FLEMING, was one of his favorite authors, helped put James Bond novels on U.S. best-seller lists. So did Bond films. (For titles and dates of James Bond films, see MOVIES.)

JOHN LE CARRÉ introduced a realistic spy, a brooding, tormented man who saw himself as playing a role he did not fully understand. Le Carré's weary GEORGE SMILEY [f] appears in *Call for the Dead* (1961), but it was his *The Spy Who Came In from the Cold* (1963) that established him as a master of the espionage tale.

Charles McCarry's adept writing about espionage is based on his career in the CIA. He considers himself simply a novelist, not a spy novelist. But his authentic hero, Paul Christopher, works for a CIA-like agency and uses the COVER of a magazine writer. His first novel, *The Miernik Dossier* (1973), was hailed by ERIC AMBLER as "wholly convincing." The book consisted of 89 documents concerning Taddeus Miernik, who may be a master spy. McCarry's other novels include *The Tears of Autumn* (1975), *The Secret Lover* (1977), *The Last Supper* (1983), and *Shelley's Heart* (1995). (After leaving the CIA, McCarry served for several years as a senior editor on *National Geographic* magazine.) Other authors followed le Carré's realistic style, using TRADECRAFT and authentic situations to portray the life of the spy. Ken Follett, who sometimes built plots around INDUSTRIAL ESPIONAGE, offered realism in *The Shakeout* (1975), *The Key to Rebecca* (1980), *The Man* from *St. Petersburg* (1982), and *Five Tigers* (1985).

William F. Buckley, a conservative writer and former CIA officer, straddled the spy style, putting his character,

Blackford Oakes, somewhere between an American James Bond and a realistic hero. Oakes, who resembles Buckley at least politically, is a former CIA agent recalled for special projects. His cycle of 10 Oakes novels ended in 1994 with *A Very Pretty Plot*.

Novelist Norman Mailer entered the world of espionage with *Harlot's Ghost* (1996), a 1,253-page saga that encompasses much of the Cold War. Philip Roth, whose career has clearly been that of a literary novelist, mystified readers (and spy novel fans) with his *Operation Shylock* (1993), which at least some U.S. bookstores put on the "spy thriller" shelves. Roth has a character named Philip Roth work in Athens as an Israeli spy. Readers and critics assumed that the book was a novel, but Roth later insisted that what he had written was indeed true. At the end of the book a MOSSAD operative tells "Roth" that it is in his interest to say that the book is fictional. "And I became quite convinced that it was in my interest to do that," Roth added, explaining, "I'm just a good Mossadnik."

LEN DEIGHTON established himself with his first book, *The Ipcress File* (1962). Other books included *Funeral in Berlin* (1964), *Twinkle, Twinkle, Little Spy* (1976), and a trilogy: *Berlin Game* (1983), *Mexico Set* (1984), and *London Match* (1985). In *The Day of the Jackal* (1971) Frederick Forsyth stepped up the pace of the spy story by adding an assassin and counterintelligence officers racing against the clock. His other novels include *The Odessa File (1972), The Dogs of War* (1974), and *The Fourth Protocol* (1984). Leighton's *Hope* (1995) takes his Bernard Samson, the weary British intelligence officer, through the ebbing Cold War. *The Fist of God* (1994) took Deighton into the Persian Gulf War.

Trevanian (the pen name of Rod Whitaker) added brutality to the realism of *The Eiger Sanction* (1972), *The Loo Sanction* (1973), and *Shibumi* (1979). Robert Ludlum, a prolific writer, placed himself somewhere between Fleming's outlandish tales and le Carrés realism. Complex global conspiracies abound in Ludlum's novels, which include *The Scarlatti Inheritance* (1971), *The Matarese Circle* (1979), *The Bourne Supremacy* (1986), and *The Icarus Agenda* (1988). Ludlum died in 2001.

With the arrival of TOM CLANCY'S *The Hunt for Red October* (1984) high-tech talk about military weapons systems and SATELLITES was added to espionage, but Clancy's intrepid CIA hero, Jack Ryan, was much more a young executive who ran intelligence operations than a spy in the mold of George Smiley. Clancy's Ryan, like le Carré's Smiley, is found in successive novels.

THE REAL AND UNREAL

The lines between fiction and nonfiction often become hazy. Fictional accounts of espionage are often so authoritative that the CIA began a library of spy novels published throughout the world. This secret library is the setting for a fictional thriller in *Six Days of the Condor* (1974) by James Grady, one of the innumerable spy novels that became the basis for movies about spies. The hero of Grady's book and movie is a low-level CIA employee caught up in a swirl of intrigue and murder.

Former intelligence officers become authors of novels, and novelists with no experience in espionage write about it, sometimes basing their work on solid research and sometimes letting their imagination do the research.

Intelligence agencies frown on officers who put away the cloak and dagger and pick up the pen. SIR COMPTON MACKENZIE was tried and convicted of violating the OFFICIAL SECRETS ACT in 1932 for publishing his World War I memoirs. The British intelligence establishment sharply criticized le Carré and Greene for their portrayals of that establishment. Prosecution under the Official Secrets Act was contemplated when Greene's *Our Man in Havana* was published. (For other examples, see PHILIP AGEE, SIR JOHN MASTERMAN, FRANK SNEPP, and PETER WRIGHT.)

RICHARD HELMS, DIRECTOR OF CENTRAL INTELLIGENCE (DCI) did not like le Carré's spy novels—especially *The Spy Who Came In from the* Cold—because of their cynicism and themes of betrayal. Helms authorized HOWARD HUNT to write spy novels while he was on the CIA payroll. There was hope that Hunt would produce the American answer to James Bond, but Hunt's novels never achieved anything like the popularity of Fleming's. Helms, like DCI ALLEN W. DULLES, believed that spy novels of the James Bond variety helped popularize an agency that could do little to publicize itself.

Le Carré noted that intelligence agencies had frequently recruited writers and did not realize the price that had to be paid. "Writers are a subversive crowd, nothing if not traitors," le Carré told the *Sunday Times* in 1986. "The better the writer, the greater the betrayal tends to appear, a thing the secret community has learned the hard way, for I hear it is no longer quite so keen to have us aboard."

Often, the discriminating reader does not know where reality begins or ends. The popularity of Tom Clancy's novels stemmed from the reliability of his research into weapons; for his readers, high-tech was reality enough. But when an ex-agent decides to write a nonfiction book, the reality has to come from within the author. The prime example of this true-or-false nonfiction is *My Silent War* (1968), in which Philby writes of his double agent career working for both MI6 and the KGB. Philby's book is self-serving and has its share of settling old debts, but it did not ooze propaganda. Graham Greene called the book "far more gripping than any novel of espionage I can remember."

HISTORY AND ESPIONAGE

Unlike other facets of history, the role of intelligence in world events does not get the coverage it deserves. Most historians, facing the chasms of misinformation inherent in intelligence, abandon attempts to write about it. When information about ULTRA and other World War II codebreaking was finally released, for example, most historians failed to credit the importance of CRYPTANALYSIS in winning and losing battles.

Robin W. Winks of Yale University is one of the few historians who carefully examined intelligence. Looking primarily at the culture that produced the first recruits of the Office of Strategic Services, Winks wrote an informative, witty, and well-documented book, *Cloak & Gown* (1987), which he called "a history of a peculiar kind."

Historians, he noted, "traditionally rely upon documentation," but intelligence relies "on the denial, the falsifying, and the destruction of documentation." And even when documentation is provided to the archives, it is often jumbled and deliberately riddled with inaccuracies.

Espionage literature, Winks wrote:

> tends either to partake of the special pleading generally associated with the memoir, which is natural to a person who has come to the field through participation in it; or to be defensive—one not very hidden agenda being a plea for understanding that spying is essential to the protection of an open and democratic society from its closed enemies—or wildly, arrogantly angry, as with the work of Philip Agee and the "disclosers."

(For a list of nonfiction espionage books that the authors of this book found reliable, see the Recommended Reading list at the back of this book.)

The search for truth in spy fiction can be as frustrating as the search for truth in supposedly well-documented nonfiction treatments of espionage. Rupert Allason, the leading writer on the subject of British intelligence in the 1970s and 1980s (writing under the pseudonym NIGEL WEST), said in *MI6* (1983), "The dangers of placing faith in documentary records was pointed out by one particular retired Head of Station who told me that much of the information in his Station's Registry was pure fiction."

Lloyd, William A.

(b. ? d. 1868)

Employed personally as a spy for the Union by President Abraham Lincoln.

Lloyd was a well-known transportation agent and was thus able to roam, more or less freely, to Richmond, Savannah, Chattanooga, and New Orleans. His unpaid compensation became a landmark court case.

Lincoln had personally hired Lloyd in 1861 to spy behind Confederate lines for the duration of the war, agreeing to pay him $200 per month—a princely wage in those days.

When Lloyd died, his administrator sued the government. The Supreme Court held, in the broadest terms, that contracts for clandestine service to the government can never be sued upon. It said that such agreements necessarily contain the proviso that the parties' lips were to be forever sealed—a condition implied in all secret employments of the government in time of war, or upon matters affecting our foreign relations. The courts ruled that the service stipulated by the contract was a secret service; the information sought was to be obtained clandestinely, and was to be communicated privately; the employment and the service were to be equally concealed.

Apparently, because of Lincoln's death, Lloyd's estate was never paid. Lloyd's case endured as a precedent, which was cited in a spy-suit case in 2004. (See JOHN AND JANE DOE.)

Lockhart, Sir Robert Bruce

(b. 1887 d. 1970)

British diplomat who played a complex role during the Bolshevik Revolution in 1917–1918.

Born in Scotland, Lockhart later proclaimed, "There is no drop of English blood in my veins." He was educated in Germany and France and, after completing his studies, went to Malaya to work on a rubber plantation, where, at great personal risk, he made a sultan's ward his mistress.

After a time in Japan and Canada, he returned to Scotland, but soon accepted an appointment as British vice consul in Moscow, the center of radicalism in Russia, then heavily engaged in disastrous World War I battles. He became consul in 1915, as German victories on the Russian front were demoralizing the home front. A year later, with the war going even worse for the Russians, the British mounted a propaganda effort, with Lockhart getting pro-British, pro-war articles into Russian newspapers.

In the summer of 1917 the British ambassador sent him back to Britain, ostensibly due to fears about his health; in reality Lockhart, who was married, had become involved with a married Russian woman, and the ambassador felt that his removal would end the affair. He arrived back in England six weeks before the Bolshevik Revolution began.

Sent back to Russia after the Nov. 1917 revolution to make contact with the revolutionaries, he arrived in the capital of Petrograd (St. Petersburg) while Bolshevik negotiator Leon Trotsky was at Brest-Litovsk arranging a separate peace with Germany. After the Bolshevik press hailed Lockhart's arrival, a U.S. INTELLIGENCE OFFICER in Petrograd reported that Lockhart was a dangerous revolutionary. Lockhart found himself caught between those who supported the Bolsheviks and those who believed that a democratic state was possible.

After his first meeting with Trotsky, Lockhart wrote in his diary, "He strikes me as a man who would willingly die for Russia provided there was a big enough audience to see him do it."

As Allied diplomats began leaving Russia, Lockhart arranged to get them Bolshevik-stamped passports. He got most approved, but a functionary made a pile of rejects, including one belonging to a Col. Keyes, a British intelligence officer under diplomatic COVER. The woman stamping the passports was pretty, Lockhart recalled. "I talked to her gently, and she smiled. I continued to talk, and, as we talked, I began to fiddle with the passports. As I was whispering to her, I slipped Keyes's passport into the large pile. And, God bless her blue eyes, she stamped it!"

The last Allied diplomats left Petrograd on Feb. 28,

1917. Lockhart volunteered to stay and, as the sole British diplomatic representative in Russia, moved to Moscow when the Bolsheviks relocated the government there. Remaining with Lockhart was a NAVAL INTELLIGENCE officer. To prevent Germany from getting the Russian Baltic Fleet, he recruited AGENTS who would try to scuttle the ships if necessary.

In May 1918 Lockhart was told that a British officer had appeared in Moscow and demanded to see Lenin, claiming to have been sent by Prime Minister Lloyd George. The man was master spy SIDNEY REILLY, sent by British intelligence (MI6) to undermine the Bolsheviks. In August, as Lockhart was preparing to leave Russia, agents of the CHEKA, the Bolshevik secret police, arrested him at gunpoint, took him to the LUBYANKA, the Cheka prison, and demanded to know the whereabouts of Reilly.

Lenin had been shot and grievously wounded, and a British-backed plot was suspected. The Bolshevik press proclaimed a "Lockhart Plot"—a plan to murder Lenin and Trotsky and set up a military dictatorship. Reilly, who had vanished, was also cited as a plotter (which he was). Lockhart was picked up again and held in solitary confinement for more than a month before being exchanged for Maxim Litvinov, a Soviet agent being held in Britain.

Celebrated by British newspapers as the "Boy Ambassador," Lockhart arrived in Britain a hero. He later wrote that he had been tempted to remain in Russia and had been offered employment in the Cheka. After leaving the foreign service in 1928, he became a journalist and author.

In his book *Memoirs of a British Agent* (1932) he provided a penetrating, close-in view of the Russian Revolution, introducing readers to Lenin, Leon Trotsky, and FELIKS DZERZHINSKY, head of the Cheka. He also met and "paid little attention" to a "strongly-built man with a sallow face, black moustache, heavy eyebrows, and black hair"—Josef Stalin. The book was a sensation in Britain and the United States. Subsequent editions were published in French, German, Italian, Swedish, Danish, Polish, and Finnish.

Lockhart's memoirs were republished in 1974 and 1984, with an introduction by his son, Robin Bruce Lockhart, who served in World War II. The younger Lockhart later wrote *Reilly: Ace of Spies* (1967), which subsequently became a TELEVISION miniseries.

In 1966 the Soviet newspaper *Izvestia*, resurrecting the old charges that Lockhart and Reilly had tried to subvert the revolution, claimed that Cheka agents had penetrated the plot and that Lockhart had known more about Reilly's plans than he had later admitted.

Lody, Lt. Carl Hans

German naval reserve officer who spied for Germany in Britain during World War I.

As a tourist guide for the Hamburg-Amerika Line, Lody learned to speak English with an American accent. Recruited as an AGENT by German MILITARY INTELLIGENCE, he arrived in Edinburgh, Scotland, on a U.S. passport, posing as an American tourist. German intelligence had stolen the passport from an American in BERLIN.

Lody's CASE OFFICER was Adolf Burchard in Stockholm, Sweden. Lody sent a cable that announced his arrival in Scotland—and also delighted in recent German military losses. The cable had been routinely intercepted by the British Security Service (MI5), which thought the language and tone of the cable peculiar. Lody was placed under SURVEILLANCE.

He continued to send messages to Burchard, but MI5 let only one reach him: a false rumor that Russian troops were passing through Scotland on their way to the Western Front.

Lody was arrested and court-martialed in London in Oct. 1914. He was found guilty and sentenced to death by firing squad. On the grounds of the Tower of London on Nov. 6, supposedly, he turned to the officer in charge of the firing quad and said, "I suppose you will not shake hands with a spy?" The officer replied, "No, I will not; but I will shake hands with a brave man."

Lody was one of 30 spies arrested in Britain during World War I. He and 11 others were executed; one killed himself, and the others were imprisoned. After Lody's "well-publicized execution," Phillip Knightley wrote in *The Second Oldest Profession* (1986), there was "a distinct lack of volunteers" in Germany. Like most German spies of that time, Knightley wrote, Lody was "scandalously ill-prepared" and was one of a "pathetic group of inadequates" drawn to espionage in search of easy money or the fulfillment of fantasies.

Lomenech, Daniel

(b. 1922 d. 1996)

Royal Naval Sub-Lieutenant officer who during World War II set up an intelligence-collecting network in French ports.

Lomenech, born in France, escaped to England when France fell in 1940. He was one of four British AGENTS landed in France in March 1941 for Operation Allah, aimed at learning about German Navy activities in Brest and other French ports. Twice nearly captured by the GESTAPO, he escaped in July 1941 by boarding a fishing boat that delivered him to the British submarine *Sealion*.

Later he became captain of a patrol boat disguised as a French fishing vessel, with Lomenech and his crew in the smocks and peaked caps of Breton fishermen. On one of his missions, he picked up a French agent—and his wife and four children—and delivered all safely in England.

His father, a member of the British network, was captured and hanged. His mother died in a concentration camp and his sister died soon after her release at the end of the war.

London Cage

Mansion in Kensington Palace Gardens, London, where British INTELLIGENCE OFFICERS conducted interrogations of German prisoners of war during World War II. Often their rooms had BUGS, and British officers listened to their private conversations.

London Controlling Station

(LCS)

Secret Allied unit that organized DECEPTION plans to mislead German strategists during World War II. Prime Minister Winston Churchill established the unit, which was usually referred to as the LCS. The chief of the LCS was called "the Controller of Deception."

LCS invented and developed deception plans—such as A FORCE, a phantom army of inflatable tanks and dummy parachute troops—but did not carry out operations. Those were conducted by such agencies as the TWENTY COMMITTEE, MI6, SOE, and the OFFICE OF STRATEGIC SERVICES. For the D-DAY deceptions, LCS worked with the Anglo-American Deception Unit of the Supreme Headquarters Allied Expeditionary Force and the U.S. Joint Security Control.

Lonetree, Cpl. Clayton J.

(b. 1961)

Marine Corps guard at the U.S. Embassy in Moscow in 1984–1986 who divulged classified information to the KGB. He was the first U.S. Marine ever convicted of espionage. The KGB, which sought to subvert U.S. minorities, made him a TARGET.

Lonetree, grandson of the chief of the Winnebago Indians of Wisconsin and nephew of a Marine who won the Medal of Honor in the Korean War, enlisted in the Marine Corps in 1980. In 1984 he volunteered for embassy guard duty and took a six-week embassy service course. After being given a SECURITY CLEARANCE at the TOP SECRET level, along with all of the other graduates, he awaited assignment.

In 1984 he was ordered to the U.S. Embassy in Moscow. There, like all other Marines assigned to Moscow, Lonetree signed a nonfraternization agreement and promised to report all contacts with Soviet citizens. In letters home Lonetree said he had become a minor celebrity, "surrounded" by Muscovites who gawked at him because they had never seen an American Indian. But for all the attention, he was often lonely and morose. He drank more than he should have; according to a Marine officer familiar with Lonetree's record, he was "a loner and a loser."

One day he met a pretty 25-year-old Russian employee of the embassy, Violetta A. Seina, at a Moscow metro stop. "Violetta said she was going home but continued to talk with me after missing her train stop," Lonetree later recalled. "We got off together at a later stop and began a long walk together, talking about various subjects, including American movies, books, food, likes and dislikes." They walked and talked for about two hours. Their friendship soon developed into a sexual relationship.

Their dating was interrupted when Lonetree, despite his poor disciplinary record, was sent to Geneva as part of the security force for the Nov. 1985 summit meeting of President Reagan and Soviet leader Mikhail Gorbachev.

When Lonetree returned to Moscow, his romance with Violetta deepened. "We both agreed that it was not safe for us to be seen together in public or near her house," Lonetree later recounted. "I would utilize counter-surveillance techniques in leaving the embassy and going to Violetta's house."

In Jan. 1986 Violetta introduced Lonetree to her "Uncle Sasha," who was really Aleksiy Yefimov, a KGB INTELLIGENCE OFFICER. Uncle Sasha asked the Marine if he would like to be a friend of the Soviet Union. "At that time," according to Lonetree, "he began asking me a series of questions which were written on a list he held on his lap. He said the list had been prepared by a friend of his who is a general in the KGB and also a member of the Central Committee."

Yefimov showed Lonetree photos of Marines and other people who worked at the U.S. Embassy. There were also some snapshots of men and women. Lonetree rearranged the photos to show Uncle Sasha who was married to whom. Lonetree also described in detail the layout of the ambassador's office. What else Lonetree told Uncle Sasha—and what he did for him and Violetta—may never be known. But he had obviously become the victim of a KGB HONEY TRAP operation.

On March 9, 1986, the day before Lonetree's departure for the Marine guard force at the U.S. Embassy in VIENNA, Yefimov gave Lonetree a piece of paper to sign that said, "I am a friend of the Soviet Union. I will always be a friend of the Soviet Union, and will continue to be their friend." At this or another meeting with Uncle Sasha, Lonetree was asked to place a BUG in the ambassador's office. He later said that he had refused, but that he did provide "plans" not otherwise described.

Lonetree agreed to meet Yefimov in Vienna, where the Marine provided information on Americans in that embassy and handed over a floor plan of the embassy, a phone directory, and the names of the Austrian cleaning women, along with the rooms each woman was responsible for. He was paid a total of $2,500 in U.S. currency and the equivalent of $1,000 in Austrian currency.

Yefimov wanted to know whether any Marines were HOMOSEXUALS or had alcohol problems, and asked Lonetree what he knew about the ambassador's secretary. Later, alone one night on guard duty, Lonetree slipped top-secret documents out of the embassy and hid them in a drainpipe on the roof of the building where the Marines lived. He also stole the contents of a burn bag—about 120 documents that included information on America's position on negotiations for a Mutual Balanced Forces Reduction agreement with the Soviet Union.

On Dec. 12, 1986, Yefimov turned Lonetree over to "George," a KGB officer named Yuri Lysov, who asked questions similar to the ones Yefimov had asked. There was also talk about getting Lonetree back to Moscow and his beloved Violetta, perhaps with the aid of a Soviet diplomatic passport. But on Dec. 14, 1986, Lonetree told the CIA station chief what had been happening. Some sources say that the CIA instinctively moved to make Lonetree a DOUBLE AGENT. But the Department of Defense refused to let Lonetree be TURNED. His case was handed to the NAVAL (CRIMINAL) INVESTIGATIVE SERVICE (NIS).

Lonetree was charged with espionage, but the investigation did not end there. The NIS began questioning other Marines. Cpl. Arnold Bracy and Lonetree were accused of allowing KGB operatives into the embassy at night and giving them access to secret documents and cryptographic equipment.

In the panic that followed, embassy officials, fearing that the KGB had bugged communications rooms, cut back messages to and from Washington. All 28 Marines in Moscow were replaced. Secretary of Defense Caspar Weinberger said that the United States had suffered "a very great loss." Congressional critics clamored for the razing of the unfinished building that was to be the new U.S. Embassy, which was said to be riddled with bugs.

A third Marine, Staff Sgt. Robert S. Stufflebeam, deputy leader of the Moscow guard unit, was charged with failing to report fraternizing with Soviet women. The cases against Bracy and Stufflebeam were dropped, and the NIS was severely criticized for its handling of the situation.

Lonetree was court-martialed in 1987 for supplying classified information, conspiring to commit espionage, disclosing the identities of covert agents, and other offenses. He was sentenced to 30 years, but his sentence was shortened because he cooperated with COUNTERINTELLIGENCE officers after his arrest. He was released in Feb. 1996 after having served nearly nine years.

Long, Leo

Member of Britain's CAMBRIDGE SPY RING recruited by ANTHONY BLUNT.

Long entered Cambridge University, where he concentrated on French studies, in 1935. The son of an unemployed carpenter and a bitter critic of British society, Long became a member of the Communist Party cell at the university. He also joined The Apostles, a secret Cambridge society whose members included Blunt and GUY BURGESS, another member of the Cambridge ring.

During World War II Long worked in British MILITARY INTELLIGENCE as a uniformed officer and gained access to highly secret codebreaking work at BLETCHLEY PARK, passing this information to Blunt, also a Soviet AGENT. Later, at Blunt's urging, Long was assigned to the military intelligence section that assessed German SIGNALS INTELLIGENCE. His information on German intercepts supplemented that being sent to the Soviets via another Blunt recruit, JOHN CAIRNCROSS.

After the war, Long worked for the British Control Commission in Allied-occupied Germany as deputy head of military intelligence. When Blunt retired from the Security Service MI5, he tried unsuccessfully to have Long appointed in his place. Long left intelligence work and, presumably, espionage in 1951.

PETER WRIGHT, the MI5 officer who interrogated Blunt, got Long's name from him and then questioned Long, who, like Blunt, was promised immunity from prosecution in exchange for giving information. "Far from being helpful in his debriefing," Wright wrote in *Spycatcher* (1987), "his attitude, when challenged on a point, was invariably to say that we would just have to take his word for it."

Lonsdale, Gordon Arnold

(b. 1922 d. 1970)

The assumed name of a Soviet ILLEGAL sent to the United States as a potential spy at the age of 11. The man known as Lonsdale carried the name of a child who had been born in Canada and taken by his mother to Finland, where he died, possibly during the Finno-Soviet War in 1939–1940. Soviet espionage operatives obtained Lonsdale's Canadian birth record and passport and used the documents to manufacture an identity for Conon Trohmovich Molody, the Moscow-born son of a Soviet science writer.

When Conon was 11, his mother sent him to live in California with her sister, who posed as his mother. After five years in California, he returned to the Soviet Union, where he received a commission in the Red Navy and was trained in espionage. A Soviet grain ship carried him to Vancouver, where, with the Lonsdale documents, he established a Canadian identity. He attributed his odd accent—American English tinged with Russian—to his days as a lumberjack far from civilization.

Sometime after World War II, Lonsdale wrote in his book *Spy* (1965) that he went to the United States and met a Soviet AGENT who appears to have been RUDOLF ABEL. "I do not propose to describe in any detail my experiences in the United States," he wrote coyly. "Any reader will understand my reason for this." He claimed that the FBI had been unable to learn what he did in the United States. The manuscript was prepared with the aid of the KGB.

In 1955 Lonsdale journeyed to England, where he spied out British defense secrets under COVER of a businessman whose enterprises included renting jukeboxes and manufacturing bubblegum machines. One of his TARGETS was a Royal Navy underwater weapons facility.

In 1960 revelations of Lt. Col. MICHAL GOLIENEWSKI, a DEFECTOR from the Polish Intelligence Service, inspired a security investigation at the facility. This led to Lonsdale's arrest and the roundup of four members of his ring. Two of them, Helen and Peter Kroger (see MORRIS COHEN), also had identities created by the KGB and its predecessors.

Tried and convicted at London's Old Bailey for conspiring to pass information "which might be directly or indirectly to an enemy," Molody-Lonsdale was sentenced to 25 years in prison. In 1964 he was exchanged for British AGENT GREVILLE WYNNE. The SPY SWAP had been originated by Lonsdale's wife and Mrs. Wynne.

Lonsdale, hailed as a hero when he returned to Moscow, became part of the ex-spy community there. He was particularly friendly with GEORGE BLAKE, a British spy Lonsdale had met in prison when both were serving their espionage sentences.

The MI5 CODE NAME for Lonsdale was "Last Act."

Also see PORTLAND CASE, HARRY HOUGHTON.

Lord Haw Haw

SEE WILLIAM JOYCE

Los Alamos

U.S. nuclear weapons laboratory that was a key TARGET of Soviet intelligence during World War II and the early part of the Cold War. Subsequently, it became a major target of Chinese espionage efforts.

In early Oct. 1942, Maj. Gen. Leslie Groves, the head of the U.S. atomic bomb program, began a seeking a suitable location for a laboratory where the atomic bombs would be designed and constructed. Initially consideration was given to establishing the laboratory at Oak Ridge, Tenn., because most of the plants to produce uranium-235 would be located there, or in Chicago, where a major laboratory complex already existed.

But Groves believed that the project required a more remote site, a climate that permitted year-round construction, safety from enemy attack (i.e., not near the coast), and access to power, water, and fuel. It would also have to be near to an adequate test location for bomb components and possibly the atomic bombs. And, Groves wanted a natural bowl ringed by hills that could help secure the site and contain any accidental explosions.

After considering several sites, Los Alamos, New Mex., was selected. It met most of the criteria set out by Groves. The site, some 60 miles from Albuquerque, contained a large boys' school, whose building would be suitable for housing the senior scientists and for other purposes. The site was decided upon in Nov. 1942, although the school was allowed to operate until Feb. 1943 so that the approximately 40 students could complete the term.

Construction was already underway as the students were packing. The Army took over 54,000 acres of semi-arid forest and grazing land that was already controlled by the federal government; another 8,900 acres was purchased in from private owners.

A flood of men and women arrived at Los Alamos: top scientists and engineers, laboratory technicians, a medical staff, Army cooks and bakers, Navy officers (who were ordnance experts), and hundreds of military policemen to insure security of the installation. By Jan. 1944 there were 3,500 "permanent residents" at Los Alamos; a year later there were almost 6,000. Hundreds of workmen labored continuously to build the work spaces and accommodations for them—fortunately, Groves had demanded a site where year-round construction was possible.

Groves set up a nursery school for working mothers, some of whom were scientists; others were starting new careers as secretaries and teachers. There was a grammar school and a high school and there was small-scale democracy in the form of a community advisory council. So many babies were born in the small hospital that Groves seriously ordered J. Robert Oppenheimer, the scientific director of Los Alamos to do something about it. Oppenheimer refused. His wife had their second baby there on Dec. 7, 1944.

"From the standpoint of security," Groves wrote in *Now It Can Be Told* (1962), "Los Alamos was quite satisfactory. It was far removed from any large center of population, and was reasonably inaccessible from the outside. . . . Also, the geographically enforced isolation of the people working there lessened the ever-present danger of their inadvertently diffusing secret information among social or professional friends outside."

People assigned to Site Y, as the facility was officially known, were allowed only to use a Santa Fe post office address, Box 1663. All outgoing mail had to be submitted, in unsealed envelopes, to military censors. If a censor deemed the letter could be sent, he would send it, but without the usual censors' mark. All incoming mail also went to the censors. Friends and relatives on the outside, for the most part, did not know exactly where Box 1663 was or what the people who were there did for the war effort. One of the rumors was that Los Alamos was a home for pregnant women soldiers (WACs).

But despite all precautions, Los Alamos was readily penetrated by the Soviet ATOMIC SPY RING. Soviet attempts to penetrate Los Alamos unquestionably continued during the Cold War, while the WEN HO LEE case made it clear that Chinese intelligence had also marked the laboratory on its maps.

Lotz, Wolfgang

(b. 1921 d. 1995)

German-born Israeli INTELLIGENCE OFFICER who operated in Cairo from 1959 to 1964.

Lotz's father was a Gentile, his mother a Jew. His father died when he was quite young. In 1937, fleeing Nazi persecution of Jews, Lotz and his mother emigrated to Palestine, then under British control. The boy joined the Haganah, the Jewish defense force, and after the European War began in Sept. 1939, he volunteered for the British Army. Lotz became a commando and fought in North Africa.

After the war, Lotz returned to Palestine and took part in the Israeli War of Independence in 1948, running arms and then fighting in the Israeli Army. He ended his war service as a major.

Sometime after that he was recruited by the MOSSAD, the Israeli intelligence service. Tall, blond, and fluent in German, Lotz was an ideal operative to infiltrate the Nazi colony that had sprung up in Cairo. Lotz's LEGEND was that he was a former German officer who had fought in Rommel's Afrika Korps in the desert war in Egypt and had moved to Australia, where he had made a fortune as a racehorse owner and breeder. He spent a year in Germany to harden his COVER story.

Lotz opened a riding school and stud farm near Cairo and strutted around like a dedicated Nazi expatriate. Rumors spread that he had been an SS officer. He became friends with the head of the Egyptian police and with scientists among the ex-Nazis. (The Israelis were concerned about possible Egyptian use of former rocket developers and weapons specialists.)

To complete his cover, the Mossad arranged for Lotz, whose wife and child were in Israel, to take a blond, Nordic-looking German wife named Waldraut Neumann. A fake wedding ceremony took place in Munich. (He later claimed that he had met her on the Orient Express and married her without telling her that he was a Mossad operative.)

Lotz, who periodically made secret trips to Israel to see his family, continued living his double life until 1964. By then Egypt had developed an efficient Secret Service, with officers trained by British, U.S., and Soviet intelligence services. Aided by Soviet experts in radio-detection techniques, the Egyptian Secret Service traced his transmissions and found his clandestine radio hidden in a bathroom scale.

The Secret Service arrested, interrogated, and tortured Lotz, who insisted that he was a German working for Israeli money; the fact that he was not circumcised helped him sustain his cover. If the Egyptians had known he was an Israeli, he probably would have been executed. Put on trial as a formality, he was sentenced to life imprisonment at hard labor. Waldraut, who had also been arrested and tried, was sentenced to three years.

Lotz was freed in 1968 in exchange for nine Egyptian generals captured the year before in the Six Day War.

Lotz, who divorced his wife in Israel and truly married Waldraut, wrote about his adventures in *The Champagne Spy* (1972). The title came from the Mossad nickname for the high-living Lotz. Waldraut, who converted to Judaism, died in 1973. Lotz moved to Germany, where he married twice more before his death.

Lourdes

Site of massive Soviet-Russian SIGNALS INTELLIGENCE facility near Havana, CUBA. Called the most sophisticated Soviet spy base outside the Eastern Bloc when it was publicly revealed by the U.S. government in March 1985, it was credited with being able to monitor telephone conversations in the southeastern United States, space activities at Cape Canaveral, Fla., and transmissions by U.S. commercial and military SATELLITES.

At that time the facility was operated by 2,100 technicians, military and civilian.

The facility was established in the mid-1960s, following the CUBAN MISSILE CRISIS of 1962. The importance of Lourdes to Russia in the post–Cold War era was demonstrated in Nov. 1996 when Col.-Gen. FEDOR LADYGIN, head of the Main Intelligence Directorate (GRU), arrived in Cuba to discuss the continued operation of the intelligence facility. At the time Russia was reported to be paying an annual rent of about $200 million for Lourdes.

However, on Oct. 17, 2001, Russian President VLADIMIR PUTIN announced the closure of the facility at Lourdes (and at the same time Russian withdrawal from the Cam Ranh Bay naval base in Vietnam). The implementation of the withdrawal orders were to begin on Jan. 1, 2002. Reportedly, most of the facility was shut down by the end of the 2002.

Subsequently, Cuban leader Fidel Castro decided that the massive Lourdes facility would become a center for computer learning, research, and production. "We will make Cuba the computer center of the Caribbean," said a Cuban Foreign Ministry official.

Lowe, Thaddeus S. C.

(b. 1832 d. 1913)

BALLOON enthusiast who served as an aerial spy for the Union Army during American Civil War. Interested in balloons from the age of about 25, in 1860 he came to the Smithsonian Institution in Washington, D.C., to propose making a balloon flight across the Atlantic Ocean.

When the war began in 1861 he offered his services to the Union Army. President Lincoln invited him to dine at the White House and listened to his proposals for military use of observation balloons. On June 18, 1861, he went aloft in a balloon over Washington with a telegraph key and sent what is believed to be the first message ever transmitted electrically from the air. It was addressed to Lincoln.

Paid $5 per day while constructing balloons for the Army and $10 per day while an "aeronaut", Lowe began producing and flying balloons for the Army. The Balloon Corps of the Army of the Potomac was formally established with four balloons in Nov. 1861. Lowe was the first man known to observe artillery fire from the air and to telegraph corrections back to the cannoneers. He may also have been the first man to use a camera effectively from a balloon for gathering intelligence about enemy forces, and he was the first to collect intelligence from a balloon tethered to a barge (in the Potomac River).

Lowe and the other Union balloonists were never really supported by the Army, although their missions were often successful. He left Army service in May 1863.

He continued his interest in science and is credited with being the first person to manufacture artificial ice.

L-Pill

Lethal or poison pill, traditionally carried by spies to be used if a spy is captured to prevent his being tortured and revealing secrets. During World War II some lethal pills consisted of cyanide encased in glass. They could be concealed in a false tooth and worked loose by the AGENT'S tongue if necessary. He would then bite into the capsule, breaking the glass, and would die almost instantly. If the pill broke loose while the agent was sleeping, however, it would pass harmlessly through his digestive track.

Of course, an agent caught with an L-pill who was not able to use it would immediately be identified as a spy.

Records of the U.S. OFFICE OF STRATEGIC SERVICES (OSS) indicate that an L-pill was used only twice by OSS agents. When OSS chief WILLIAM DONOVAN and his aide David Bruce visited the Normandy beaches on June 7, 1944, the day after the Allied landings, they had no L-pills. Donovan, fearful of capture, told Bruce he would kill them both with his pistol if they were in danger of capture.

ALEKSANDR OGORODNIK, a Soviet diplomat working for the United States, was caught at a DEAD DROP by the Soviets in 1977 (See MARTHA PETERSON.) He agreed to sign a confession and asked to use his pen. He bit off the top where cyanide L-pill was hidden and died instantly.

During the Cold War American spies could employ more sophisticated methods of suicide if caught. Initially, pilots of U-2 spyplanes were issued cyanide pills. GARY FRANCIS POWERS, whose U-2 was shot down over the Soviet Union in 1960, was issued what looked like ordinary silver dollars fitted with a metal loop that could be fastened onto a key chain or a chain worn around the neck. But this charm was lethal: When unscrewed, it revealed a thin needle carrying curare, a deadly poison. (When Powers was shot down his captors immediately took the silver dollar and discovered the poison needle; it is now on display at the KGB MUSEUM in Moscow.)

Lubyanka

Longtime headquarters of Russian-Soviet state security ORGANS. Located at No. 2 Dzerzhinsky Street, just off DZERZHINSKY SQUARE, the building became synonymous with the terror of Soviet intelligence-security agencies. The building served as organ headquarters, prison (with rooftop exercise yard), and execution center.

Before the Bolshevik Revolution of 1917 the large, gray stone building had housed the insurance companies called "Anchor" and "Russia." The single Soviet insurance company, which had taken over the functions of these two as well as other czarist companies, was called *Gosstrakh*. This was an acronym from the words *gosudarstvennoye* and *strakhovaniye*, Russian for "state insurance company." NKVD officer A. I. Romanov, in his autobiographical *Nights Are the Longest There* (1972) told how "In Russian the word Strakh, the second part of the acronym, means terror, and people used to say jokingly, 'It used to be Gosstrakh, now its Gosuzhas', which we must translate as, 'It used to be state terror, now it's state horror.'"

Countless numbers of men and women were incarcerated in Lubyanka. The term THE CELLAR was often used as the threat of imprisonment in Lubyanka. In fact, the cellar was used for executions; there are no cells there. Robert Conquest wrote in *The Great Terror: Stalin's Purges of the Thirties* (1968):

> The cellars of the Lubyanka were really a sort of basement divided into a number of rooms off corridors. Later on, in ordinary routine, the condemned handed in their clothes in one of these rooms and changed into white underclothes only. They were taken to the death cell and shot in the back of the neck with a TT eight-shot automatic. A doctor then

signed the death certificate, the last document to be put in their files, and the tarpaulin on the floor was taken away to be cleaned by a woman specially employed for that purpose.

The Lubyanka's principal internal prison is located on the sixth floor of the building. (Much larger was Moscow's Lefortovo prison—where during the height of the Stalinist purges of the late 1930s, up to 70 men per day were executed with a shot to the back of the neck.)

The cells in Lubyanka could be kept cold, very cold, hot, or very hot; if a prisoner's attitude so warranted, lights would be kept on for 24 hours. When a prisoner being taken for an examination passed another, one would be faced to the wall so there could be no recognition. Sometimes guards escorting prisoners would continually snap their fingers to announce their presence, the noise preventing an accidental meeting of escorted prisoners. Interrogations (often torture sessions) were conducted by trained interrogators aided by assistants known as "bone crushers."

The chairman of state security (at times combined with internal security—(see RUSSIA-USSR)—had his office on the third floor, as did most other officers of the executive branch of the agency. Hidden in the labyrinth is a MUSEUM, which in recent years has grown to considerable size, and a wall honoring state intelligence and security officers who have been awarded the honor of Hero of the Soviet Union.

After World War II the Lubyanka complex was expanded. The workmen were German prisoners of war, who had retained for several years (or until they died).

The headquarters and certain directorates of the KGB were later moved from Lubyanka into modern office buildings in another Moscow location, all linked by computer and telex networks. Major KGB offices were relocated to the 31-story SEV building at the Tchaikovsky Street end of Kalinia Prospect, one of Moscow's major boulevards.

Following the collapse of the Soviet Union in 1992, selected foreigners and Russians were being given guided tours of parts of Lubyanka for $30 per person.

Lucy Spy Ring

World War II Soviet espionage operation named after Lucy, CODE NAME for Karl Sedlacek, a Czech military INTELLIGENCE OFFICER who worked in Switzerland under COVER as a journalist named Thomas Selzinger.

One of the Soviets running the ring was Sando Rudolfi. Hungarian-born, he became a communist in 1919 and began working for Soviet intelligence. As an undercover agent for the Comintern, he spied in Paris in the early 1930s and in 1936. After changing his name to Alexander Rado, with the anagram code name Dora, he became the resident director of the Soviet intelligence network in Switzerland.

The other key members of the ring were RUDOLPH ROESSLER, an anti-Nazi German with connections in the

German Army, and ALEXANDER FOOTE, a British leftist who became the radioman for the ring. He transmitted to Moscow almost daily. The Soviet AGENT URSULA KUCZYNSKI, who also served the ring, as did Rachel Duebendorfer, a Pole code-named "Sissy," who sometimes got direct orders from Moscow, and Christian Schneider, code-named "Taylor," who was Duebendorfer's CUT-OUT with Roessler. In 1943 Soviet intelligence officials asked Duebendorfer to find out the Lucy's identity. She refused.

Through tight compartmentalization and a series of CUT-OUTS, members of the ring did not meet one another. Rado, using Duebendorfer and Schneider as cut-outs, never met Roessler. Foote later said he only once met Roessler face to face.

The ring produced amazing intelligence. From it came a warning of the German invasion of the Soviet Union, giving the exact date, June 22, 1941, and the ORDER OF BATTLE. The Lucy ring also gave the Soviets the exact time of a planned German offensive at Kursk, giving the defenders in that battle a great advantage. ALLEN W. DULLES, European spymaster stationed in Switzerland for the OFFICE OF STRATEGIC SERVICES, said that the ring got intelligence from the German High Command "on a continuous basis, often less than twenty-four hours after its daily decisions concerning the Eastern front were made." Incredibly, intelligence officers in Moscow, reflecting the paranoia of Soviet dictator Josef Stalin, often rejected the material coming from the ring. The most glaring rebuff was the refusal to act on the forecast of the German invasion. (See BARBAROSSA.)

Some British sources claimed that British intelligence, aware of the Lucy ring, saw to it that Rado and Foote got sanitized ULTRA intelligence from the BLETCHLEY PARK codebreakers. But British intelligence historian F. H. HINSLEY wrote, "There is no truth in the much publicised claim that the British authorities made use of the Lucy ring . . . to forward intelligence to Moscow."

Swiss authorities had been tolerant of the ring because Roessler also provided them with intelligence on Germany. In Nov. 1943, perhaps over concern about Swiss neutrality, Swiss security officers arrested Foote. Roessler was prevented from communicating with Moscow and was finally arrested in May 1944, as were Duebendorfer, her daughter Tamara, and Boetcher. The Swiss, who may have been protecting them from German SD officers, released Foote, Roessler, and the others in Sept. 1944. Rado, meanwhile, had slipped off to liberated Paris.

Duebendorfer and Boetcher, who went to the Soviet Union in 1945, were imprisoned for long terms, probably because Josef Stalin did not want to acknowledge that anti-Nazi Germans had aided the Soviets. Foote and Rado flew to Moscow from liberated Paris in Jan. 1945. When the Soviet plane made a routine landing in Cairo, Rado left it and disappeared. He was later found by Soviet intelligence officers, who took him to the Soviet Union, where he was imprisoned until Stalin's death in 1953. He returned to Hungary, where he died in 1981. Foote defected from Soviet intelligence and managed to get back to his native England.

Roessler ended his days in Switzerland after another sojourn into spying in the 1950s, resulting in his conviction on espionage charges in West Germany and a one-year prison sentence.

Ludwig, Kurt Frederick

(b. 1903 d. ?)

Head of the "Joe K" German spy ring in the United States in 1940–1941.

The ring was known as the Joe K because that was the signature used on letters sent to BERLIN addresses giving information on Allied shipping in New York Harbor. Ludwig also used the CODE NAME Fouzie—and at least 50 other male and female aliases.

Born in Ohio, Ludwig was taken as a child to Germany, where he grew up and married. He visited the United States several times in the 1920s and 1930s. He was arrested for espionage in Austria in Feb. 1938 after police noticed that he had been photographing bridges near the Austro-German border; but the case was delayed, and Ludwig was not tried because the Nazis entered into Austria in March. Ludwig remained in Germany until March 1940, when he returned to the United States to establish a spy ring. (It was separate from, but had connections to, the DUQUESNE SPY RING, also broken by the FBI.)

American and British authorities knew that a spy ring was operating out of New York City, sending information on Allied shipping to Germany by letters mailed to Berlin and to ACCOMMODATION ADDRESSES in neutral Spain and Portugal. The first break came at the secret mail-intercept operation in Bermuda, run by BRITISH SECURITY CO-ORDINATION (BSC), a COVER for the Secret Intelligence Service (MI6). In 1940 the British operatives intercepted a letter from New York, signed "Joe K," to "Lothar Frederick," known to be an alias used by REINHARD HEYDRICH, chief of the RSHA, the main Nazi secret police organization. BSC experts in Bermuda opened letters, read their contents, and resealed the envelopes so well that their recipients did not detect tampering.

Joe K had shown up as the signature on many letters sent to accommodation addresses. In March 1941 BSC chemists detected SECRET WRITING in a Joe K letter; the secret message referred to a duplicate letter sent to "Smith" in China. The BSC mail-intercept operation was run in cooperation with the FBI—even though J. EDGAR HOOVER, head of the FBI, and WILLIAM STEPHENSON, head of the BSC, did not get along. The FBI traced the Smith letter and found that it contained a plan of U.S. defenses at Pearl Harbor. (There is another German connection to the PEARL HARBOR ATTACK—see DUSKO POPOV.)

Another Joe K letter, also followed up by the FBI, contained a panicky secret message about a car in New York's Times Square deliberately running down and killing "Phil." The BSC told the FBI that Phil had been Ulrich von der Osten, a German MILITARY INTELLIGENCE officer who had been "removed from circulation" a month after his arrival in the United States via Japan.

Piecing together a reference in dead Phil's notebook, an intercepted cable from Portugal to "Fouzie," and information from the Joe K letters, the FBI found Fred Ludwig, who had fled the scene when von der Osten had been struck down on March 18.

Ludwig was being paid through the German Consulate in New York City and was recruiting AGENTS and COURIERS through the German-American Bund. With the death of von der Osten, Ludwig was the ranking German spy in the United States. Under FBI SURVEILLANCE, Ludwig was seen visiting the docks in New York Harbor and U.S. Army posts around New York. In May, accompanied by an 18-year-old secretary, he traveled to Florida, stopping along the away at Army camps, airfields, and factories. Ludwig met with an agent in Miami and sent back reports through a mail drop arranged by a U.S. Army enlisted man stationed on Governor's Island in New York Harbor.

In Aug. 1941, apparently sensing he was under surveillance, Ludwig drove to Montana, stored his car, leaving behind his shortwave radio—and took a bus to the West Coast. Believing that he was planning to go to Japan and make his way from there to Germany, the FBI arrested him near Seattle, Wash. The FBI then rounded up eight others, including the secretary and the soldier. Put on trial for espionage in March 1942, Ludwig was convicted and sentenced to 20 years in prison, as was the soldier. The young secretary, who testified for the government, was sentenced to five years. The five others received sentences of 10 to 15 years.

A ninth member of the ring, known only as "Robert," was tracked down by the FBI through papers obtained from a janitor in the building housing the German Consulate; the janitor regularly put papers into the furnace as Germans watched, then pulled them out, doused the flames, and passed the singed sheets to the FBI. Robert turned out to be Paul Borchardt, a German Army veteran and scientist who, though fired from his university post for being a Jew, agreed to come to the United States as a refugee and spy. He said he did it as a German patriot. He was sentenced to 20 years. (He and the others escaped the death penalty because their spying was undertaken before the outbreak of war.)

Luminaire

Soviet CIPHER machine of the 1960s that was plugged into a radio receiver. The machine translated sound signals into numbers that appeared on 10 small dials in the top of the machine. The numbers were an enciphered message that was solved by a ONE-TIME PAD. The Luminaire was designed for agents who did not know Morse code or who needed to have a silent method of receiving messages.

M-94 Cipher Machine

Hand-held cylinder, used by the U.S. Army from 1934 through World War II, that permitted simple enciphering of messages. Based on the concept of the CIPHER DISK, the aluminum cylinder was constructed of 25 individual disks with the 26 letters of the alphabet set in the edge of each disk in random sequences.

The M-94 was six inches long and had a diameter of two inches. No two disks had the same sequence of letters. The disks could be fixed in any arrangement, with an external bar running the length of the cylinder to aid in aligning the disks and reading the resulting cipher.

The user arranged the disks to spell the first 25 letters of his message, then read the enciphered message off another row. The recipient set up the enciphered message on his device and then read the PLAIN TEXT message. The M-94 provided a fast and efficient method of enciphering and deciphering messages, although security was limited.

M-134

SEE SIGABA

M-209 Cipher Machine

A small, compact mechanical cipher machine used by U.S. military forces in World War II. The device, intended for field use, was encased in a metal box and had the benefits of simple operation and having a built-in tape printer. Encryption was done by six rotors or wheels, set by hand.

The M-209 could encipher a PLAIN TEXT message by substituting a letter for a letter, automatically printing the enciphered text on a paper tape; it could reverse the process, deciphering a message that had been previously enciphered by another M-209. The device—officially called a "converter"—offered a high degree of security when used properly. However, in the field it was difficult and slow to use.

The M-209 weighed 7¼ pounds, including carrying case and tools.

Macartney, Lt. Wilfred F. R.

(b. 1899 d. ?)

Former British Army INTELLIGENCE OFFICER who led a Soviet spy ring. His espionage activities followed a truly remarkable, albeit brief, Army career.

In 1915, at the age of 16, Macartney failed an Army medical examination because of poor eyesight. He was able to join the Royal Army Medical Corps as an ambulance driver. He was sent to France, where he gained a commission in the Royal Scots. But after several months his eyes deteriorated and he was forced to resign his commission. After treatment he was again commissioned, this time in the Essex Regiment, and sent first to Malta and then to Egypt.

He was then assigned to work for Capt. COMPTON MACKENZIE, the Royal Marine officer in charge of British intelligence activities in the Eastern Mediterranean. Sent back to France in Sept. 1917, he was taken prisoner by the Germans at the Battle of Cambrai. He escaped by jumping from a train near Aix-la-Chapelle. He was cited for his audacity.

At the end of the war in Nov. 1918, 19-year-old Macartney was assigned to the Berlin-Baghdad Railway Mission at Constantinople. He left the Army in Aug. 1919 as a lieutenant.

In 1926, Macartney smashed the window of a jeweler's shop, was arrested, and was sentenced to nine months in prison. When he got out, he contacted a Lloyd's underwriter and inquired about arms shipments to Finland. The Lloyd's employee who willingly provided the information was surprised when Macartney gave him £25. Macartney explained that he was working for the Soviets and asked for some information about the Royal Air Force.

Thoroughly alarmed, the Lloyd's employee sought advice and was introduced to Sir REGINALD HALL, who promptly passed him on to VERNON KELL, head of the Security Service (MI5). Kell decided to set a trap, by having a secret RAF manual passed to Macartney, who was then observed passing the document to a member of the Soviet Trade Delegation in London.

Using this secret document as an excuse, Kell and the SPECIAL BRANCH of Scotland Yard planned an elaborate raid on the Soviet trade delegation, which was located in the same building as ARCOS Ltd., a company registered in Britain. Although it had long been suspected of carrying out espionage activities, the trade delegation had diplomatic immunity. The raid, the British government would explain, was only to seek the secret document in the Arcos offices. The May 12–13 raid gave British officials an excuse to sift through thousands of documents.

The RAF manual was never found, but other documents of political interest were. On May 26, 1926, the British government published a White Paper and announced that relations with the Soviet Union, established in 1921, would be ended.

Macartney was allowed to continue at liberty in the hope that he would lead MI5 to other Soviet contacts. When this did not happen, he was arrested on Nov. 16, 1927, tried at the Old Bailey, and convicted under the OFFICIAL SECRETS ACT of "attempting to obtain information on the RAF." He was sentenced to 10 years in prison and two years at hard labor.

He was released early and quickly produced two books, *Walls Have Mouths* (1936) and *Zigzag* (1937). He joined the International Brigade in the Spanish Civil War, fighting on the Republican side, and became the first commander of the brigade's British battalion. He was wounded in an accident in 1937 and returned to Britain.

Later he was again prosecuted under the Official Secrets Act, this time for having revealed in a magazine article the World War II exploits of a German DOUBLE AGENT, Edward Chapman (CODE NAME Zigzag). He was given a nominal fine.

Mackenzie, Sir Compton

(b. 1883 d. 1973)

British secret AGENT and author who was prosecuted for violating the OFFICIAL SECRETS ACT. Mackenzie, an accomplished writer and naval officer, attained the rank of captain in the Royal Marines and subsequently served with the Navy in the ill-fated Dardanelles landings of 1915. Invalided out of the service that same year, he became a secret agent in Greece in 1916. Mackenzie directed British intelligence activities in Syria in 1917.

Mackenzie had the misfortune to have an early spy novel, *Extremes Meet,* published in 1928, the same year that SOMERSET MAUGHAM's *Ashenden* was published. He complained that Maugham was getting more attention even though he had so few real adventures as a secret agent.

He subsequently described his own secret activities in his autobiography, *Greek Memories* (1932). This book led to his being tried under the Official Secrets Act; the book was seized by the British government and withdrawn from publication. Mackenzie's offenses included revealing the pseudonym "C" used by Capt. MANSFIELD CUMMING, first head of MI6. Despite the fact that Cumming was dead and the other revelations dated, Mackenzie was found guilty and fined £100 plus court costs. The government's ban on the book was lifted, and it was published again in 1940 as *Aegean Memories.*

These events were described in his subsequent book *Greece in My Life* (1960). Mackenzie also wrote several plays and novels and in 1933 published a spoof on the British intelligence services, *Water on the Brain.* "It has indeed become impossible for me to devise any ludicrous situation the absurdity of which will not soon be surpassed by officialdom," he wrote in a preface to the 1954 edition.

In World War II he served as a captain in the Home Guard. He was knighted in 1952.

Also see LITERARY SPIES.

Maclean, Donald Duart

(b. 1913 d. 1983)

Member of the CAMBRIDGE SPY RING, he was among history's most successful spies, penetrating both British and American secrets at the highest levels.

Maclean was the son of a lawyer who became a distinguished member of Parliament, being knighted in 1917. As the son of a privileged and good family, Maclean naturally went to Cambridge, where many men of his class were being introduced to communism. At Cambridge, like GUY BURGESS, HAROLD (KIM) PHILBY, and ANTHONY BLUNT, he was recruited to spy for the Soviet Union. Following the orders of his recruiters, Maclean stopped being an active communist at Cambridge in preparation for entering the Foreign Office. When he applied for the diplomatic service, he told interrogators that he had had communist leanings while a student and had never completely abandoned them. His clever candor helped ease his way into a Foreign Office where pedigree was considered sufficient grounds for patriotism and a fling at communism was considered a mere youthful indiscretion.

After being accepted into the diplomatic service in 1935, he was assigned to the Central Department of the Foreign Office, which was responsible for Belgium, Germany, and France. In 1938 he was posted to Paris, where he undoubtedly worked as an AGENT for NKVD officers connected to the Soviet Embassy. The Soviets may not have gotten much from the junior diplomat, but they were biding their time. In Paris, Maclean met an American, Melinda Marling. They were married in June 1940 just after France had been overrun by German troops. Soon after they arrived back in London, Melinda left for the United States, where she gave birth to their first child, who lived only for a few days. She returned to London in the fall of 1941.

Maclean's work as a Soviet agent began in earnest in 1944 when he was sent to the British Embassy in Washington as first secretary. He also substituted for the head of chancery. The two positions gave him the opportunity to see and photograph every message and paper of importance received by the ambassador. Melinda delayed joining her husband in America until she had another baby. When she did come, she lived with her mother in New York City, giving Maclean an excuse for frequent visits, during which he met with a Soviet HANDLER in New York. After Melinda moved to Washington, Maclean continued his trips to New York, leading his embassy colleagues to conclude he kept a woman there. Soviet message traffic about the visits to New York would in later years make Maclean a suspected spy.

Since Maclean was also Britain's secretary on the Combined Policy Committee on Atomic Development, he was able to pass along—from the very minutes of the committee meetings—information on such subjects as British-U.S. postwar policy on atomic energy and the planning and stockpiling of nuclear weapons. He also had access to the new U.S. Atomic Energy Commission. He was a busy man, a busy atomic spy. "No task was too hard for him; no hours were too long," wrote fellow diplomat Robert Cecil in *A Divided Life* (1989). "He gained the reputation of one who would always take over a tangled skein from a colleague who was sick, or going on leave, or simply less zealous. In this way he was able to manoeuvre himself into the hidden places that were of the most interest to the NKVD."

Maclean worked with ALGER HISS, a U.S. State Department official, on the creation of the UNITED NATIONS. One issue taken up at Maclean-Hiss meetings involved discussions about U.S. military units overseas, including how many were in South Korea. Assessors of Maclean's treachery believe that he was thus able to pass to the Soviet Union intelligence of great value to North Korea and communist China prior to the Korean War.

Maclean's New York work enabled him to make contact with Soviet intelligence agents in the United Nations and at the Soviet Consulate in New York City. One of the pieces of information that helped to unmask Maclean was the cracking of a 1946 NKVD message from New York noting the visit of an agent named Homer to New York on the occasion of the birth of his child. (See VENONA.) The message, decrypted in 1951, showed that Homer's visit coincided with Maclean's trip to New York in July 1946 when Melinda gave birth to their son Donald. Maclean delivered to his Soviet contact in New York two cables sent by Prime Minister Winston Churchill to President Truman on June 5, 1945. The cables had to do with talks in Moscow between Soviet dictator Josef Stalin and Harry Hopkins, the longtime adviser to President Roosevelt who had assumed the same role for Truman. The CIPHER clerk at the Soviet Consulate in New York, transmitting a coded cable to Moscow, included the serial numbers of the Churchill-Truman cables. Thus, when this 1945 cable traffic was decrypted, U.S. intelligence analysts could easily determine who handled those specific cables, narrowing the search for a MOLE to a few people, including Maclean.

But it was another event that touched off an immediate investigation: On June 15, 1945, muckraking columnist Drew Pearson published a magazine article disclosing the Stalin-Hopkins talks and a Churchill cable to Truman. The FBI began probing the LEAK, suspecting that Pearson's source was a Soviet agent, particularly since the article portrayed Stalin sympathetically. The FBI suspected a leak in the British Embassy but could not prove it.

Around this time the FBI had Maclean under SURVEILLANCE because of his drunken escapades in Washington, often with known HOMOSEXUALS The possibility of blackmail based on homosexuality probably inspired the FBI surveillance.

In Aug. 1948 Maclean left Washington and after a brief time in London went on to his next post: counselor and head of chancery of the British Embassy in Cairo. The youngest in the diplomatic service to hold that position, he seemed destined for a successful career and perhaps a knighthood. But after several binges and drunken brawls, he was recalled to London in May 1950. A forgiving Foreign Office attributed Maclean's bizarre behavior to stress and suggested medical help. He began seeing a psychiatrist but did not change his ways. He kept on drinking and, when his wife temporarily left him, picking up male lovers.

Early in 1951 he was given charge of the American Department in the Foreign Office. At social occasions he spoke out openly against the immoral policies of the West as contrasted with the enlightened policy of the Soviets. Later that same year he was appointed head of a Foreign Office delegation to the United States. Among the papers he saw, and presumably passed to the Soviets, was a report on Prime Minister Clement Attlee's visit to President Truman in Dec. 1950 to get assurance that Gen. of the Army Douglas MacArthur would not be permitted to use the atomic bomb in Korea. Maclean also gave the Soviets every cable sent from Foreign Minister Anthony Eden to Lord Halifax, Britain's ambassador to Washington.

In 1949 Philby had been assigned to the British Embassy in Washington, as liaison between MI5 and both the CIA and the FBI. In Jan. 1951 Philby learned about the codebreaking that exposed Homer and realized that Maclean was in peril. Philby wanted to warn Maclean, then in London, but could not risk cabling or telephoning him. Accordingly, Burgess, who was also then assigned to the British Embassy, managed to get himself expelled from the embassy and sent back to London, where he could personally warn Maclean.

In London, Burgess immediately contacted Blunt, who passed the warning on to his Soviet handler, YURI MODIN. Alerted by Modin, Moscow authorized Maclean's flight to the Soviet Union. By then TOP SECRET documents were being withheld from Maclean and he was under surveillance by Scotland Yard's SPECIAL BRANCH. Maclean did not want to leave; Melinda was about to have another child.

But Modin and Burgess set up an escape plan and forced it on Maclean. On Friday, May 25—Maclean's 38th birthday—Burgess invited himself to dinner, the signal for flight. Maclean was to be interrogated on Monday, and, given his precarious mental state, probably would have broken down. (No authority, British or Soviet, has ever satisfactorily explained the coincidence of Maclean's flight just before interrogation.)

Burgess rented a car and elaborately acted as if he were going off on a holiday with a male lover. Instead, he picked up Maclean at his suburban home in Tatsfield, Kent. The two men sped to Southhampton, where they abandoned the car and boarded a ferry that was just about to leave for a weekend cruise along the French coast. The ferry made stops at French ports, but customs officials did not ask for papers, out of discretion for unmarried couples on board. On the morning of May 26 they disembarked at St. Malo and took a cab to Rennes, where they boarded a train to Paris. From there they took another train to Bern, where they picked up false British passports at the Soviet Embassy. They then traveled on to Zurich and boarded a plane to Stockholm, but left it at Prague. From there Soviet INTELLIGENCE OFFICERS flew them to Moscow.

On Monday, May 28, Melinda Maclean called the Foreign Office, ostensibly looking for her husband. British security officers kept the escape secret, but on June 7 a British paper broke a story about "two Britons" being sought. By then Melinda had her baby, a girl. In July, Melinda, the children, and Melinda's mother traveled to Switzerland. Meanwhile, the KGB had deposited £2,000 in a Swiss bank account in Melinda's name.

Eighteen months after Donald Maclean defected, Modin approached Melinda in London to arrange her migration to Moscow. In My *Five Cambridge Friends* (1994), Modin tells of signaling Melinda by showing her half of a postcard. "The other half had been handed to Melinda by her husband a year and a half before, with orders that she should trust nobody who did not produce its match." (Modin claimed that Melinda had known about Maclean's espionage for many years. Other writers dispute this.)

Melinda first moved to Switzerland. Then in Sept. 1953 she and the children boarded a train on a KGB-arranged trip that ended in Moscow.

In 1956 the Soviets officially revealed that Burgess and Maclean were in Moscow. They said in a joint statement that they had not been Soviet agents and that they had gone to the Soviet Union "to further understanding between East and West." Although Burgess learned only enough Russian to get by, Maclean seriously studied the language and went to work for the Institute of World Economics. He also wrote *British Foreign Policy Since Suez,* which was published in the Soviet Union and in Britain in 1970.

Donald Maclean. (ARCHIVES PHOTO)

In 1964 Philby began an affair with Melinda Maclean. In 1966 she left Maclean, who was drinking heavily, and moved in with Philby. She returned to the United States in 1979. Maclean's three children married in the Soviet Union but eventually left, two to Britain, one to the United States. Maclean died in 1983, and his ashes were taken to Britain, as had been the ashes of Burgess, who had died in 1963.

Assessments of Maclean's value to the Soviets range widely. But many intelligence officials who have studied his case conclude that his information from Foreign Office and embassy sources far outweighed what Philby and Burgess were obtaining from intelligence files. He was in a position to tell his Soviet handlers the most intimate details of U.S.-British thinking on such subjects as the future of nuclear weapons and the founding of the NORTH ATLANTIC TREATY ORGANIZATION. An official U.S. appraisal of Maclean's work said: "In the fields of US/UK/Canada planning on atomic energy, US/UK postwar planning and policy in Europe, all information up to the date of [Maclean's] defection undoubtedly reached Soviet hands."

Madsen, Yeoman 3rd Class Eugene L.

U.S. Navy yeoman who worked on the strategic warning staff in the Pentagon. He was arrested in 1979 for attempting to sell classified information to the Soviet Union. He was sentenced to eight years.

Magdeburg

German "small" cruiser sunk in the eastern Baltic early in World War I. The recovery of one of the ship's CODE books provided British codebreakers in ROOM 40 with the means of breaking into secret German military communications. In *Seizing the Enigma* (1991), codebreaking historian DAVID KAHN called the incident "the most fateful accident in the history of cryptology."

The fast, small (4,570-ton) ship set out from Memel, at the eastern extreme of Prussia, to join other German warships attacking Russian ships at the entrance of the Gulf of Finland. At 12:37 A.M. on Aug. 26, 1914, the ship ran aground off the island of Osdensholm. While efforts were made to free the ship, most of the code books and CIPHER KEYS were destroyed; some were retained, however, for communicating with rescuers. Unable to free the cruiser, her captain decided to destroy the ship because of approaching Russian warships. The scuttling charges were lit, and the crew hastily abandoned the ship. Some of the code books were lost in the commotion as the charges exploded. Fifteen men died.

The Russians quickly took possession of the wreck of the *Magdeburg* and the surviving crewmen, who had not been taken off by a German torpedo boat. Russian officers searching the hulk found a code book forgotten at the bottom of a locker. Later, Russian divers found another code book that had been thrown overboard and a third lost during the abandoning of the ship.

Realizing the value of the code books and cipher keys, the Russians immediately offered the undamaged one to their British allies. The prize was carried to Britain by a British warship via Archangel, arriving at the British Admiralty on Oct. 13. The code book was handed to Winston Churchill, First Lord of the Admiralty.

The *Magdeburg* code book became the basis for British code-breaking successes in Room 40.

(The myth has often been repeated that the Russians found the *Magdeburg* code book clutched in the arms of a drowned German sailor who was washed ashore.)

Magen, David

Israeli INTELLIGENCE OFFICER in Egypt who became a DOUBLE AGENT, spying for Egypt against Israel.

Born in the early 1920s in Hungary as Theodore Gross, he emigrated with his family to South Africa. He subsequently went to Italy to study music, becoming an accomplished singer with an international reputation. When World War II erupted he joined the British Army and served as an intelligence officer, apparently going behind German and Italian lines on special operations.

When conflict broke out in Palestine in 1948 on the eve of Israeli independence, Gross went to Israel to join the newly formed Israeli Army. With his intelligence background and knowledge of languages, he was recruited for the Political Department, the precursor to the MOSSAD. In Israel—as was the custom—he Hebraicized his name, using *Magen*, Hebrew for "shield."

Under the name Ted Cross he was dispatched to Italy to run a NETWORK of Arab AGENTS who were collecting intelligence for Israel. In 1950 he was sent into Egypt to operate a network of local informers.

The Israeli COUNTERESPIONAGE service, the SHIN BET, discovered that Magen was in contact with Egyptian intelligence officers. He was ordered back to Israel in 1952, arrested upon arrival, and charged with espionage—the first Israeli to be arrested on that charge. He was tried secretly, convicted, and sentenced to 15 years.

Without authorization—or reporting to the Mossad—Magen had made contact with Egyptian intelligence officers. His defense was that he was trying to become a TRIPLE AGENT loyal to Israel, a standard excuse for those convicted of becoming double agents. Magen had many supporters and their efforts led to his release in 1959. Upon release he changed his name and continued to live in Israel, believing until his death in 1973 that he had been unjustly treated.

Magic

Intelligence derived by the U.S. Army and Navy (and later British) from the codebreaking effort against the Japanese diplomatic CODE, given the U.S. designation PURPLE.

In March 1939 the Japanese began to employ the new Purple code machine and CIPHER. This code was first broken in the fall of 1940 by a U.S. military cryptologist team directed by WILLIAM F. FRIEDMAN, the chief cryptanalyst of the Army's SIGNAL INTELLIGENCE SERVICE. Friedman referred to his staff as "magicians." This apparently is the origin of the term *Magic* that was used for Purple-derived intelligence. Subsequently the term *Magic* was applied to a much broader category of Allied codebreaking operations in the war against Japan.

Magnum

The third major U.S. SATELLITE for the collection of COMMUNICATIONS INTELLIGENCE (COMINT) and TELEMETRY INTELLIGENCE (TELINT). The successor to the CHALET system, the first Magnum satellite was orbited on Jan. 24, 1985, to monitor Soviet and Chinese microwave communications as well as telemetry data transmitted during the two nations' intercontinental ballistic missile tests.

That first launch was to be highly classified. After an Air Force spokesman declared that such launches from Cape Canaveral, Fla., would come under new rules to deny America's adversaries as much information as possible, on Dec. 19, 1984, the *Washington Post* ran a front-page story reporting that the shuttle *Discovery* would be carrying a "new military intelligence satellite that is to collect electronic signals and retransmit them to a U.S. receiving station on earth." Secretary of Defense Caspar Weinberger promptly denounced the *Post* and the Air Force spokesman was reassigned.

The Magnum satellite, unlike its predecessors Chalet and RHYOLITE, was initially placed in a highly elliptical orbit with an apogee of 21,543 miles and a perigee of only 212 miles. According to William E. Burrows in his revealing *Deep Black* (1986), Magnum's initial orbit was:

a temporary so-called parking orbit where it was stabilized before being rerouted to geosynchronous [i.e., a 22,300-mile orbit] . . . . thereby attempting to undo what [the Air Force] saw as the damage that had been done by the earlier disclosures. This was a neat bit of what was later to be officially called a deliberate policy of disinformation by the Defense Department.

Also see GRAB.

Magpie

CODE NAME for German operation during World War II for spying on U.S. defense sites. Magpie was never carried out because the would-be director, American-born WILLIAM COLEPAUGH, gave himself up to the FBI soon after he had been landed by a U-boat in Maine. See ERICH GIMPEL.

Mail Cover

Request made by an intelligence service to a postal agency to examine the exterior of mail addressed to or from a particular individual or organization believed to be possibly involved with espionage. The mail is not opened and the person or organization involved is not made aware of the examination.

Mail Drop

SEE ACCOMMODATION ADDRESS

Major Martin [f]

Maj. William Martin, Royal Marines, was the fictional persona given to a human body used by the British to deceive the Germans in Operation MINCEMEAT in 1943.

Malinovsky, Roman

(b. ? d. 1918)

Czarist MOLE in the Bolshevik leadership prior to the Russian Revolution of 1917.

Malinovsky was a Moscow worker whose criminal record for burglary gave him connections to the police, leading to his spying on the Bolsheviks for the Okhrana, the czarist secret police. He was apparently recruited in 1910. The Okhrana intended to have Mahnovsky help the Bolshevik Party to continue the split with the Menshevik Party, thereby preventing unification of the Russian revolutionary movement.

His success in infiltrating the Bolshevik movement

was demonstrated by his being elected in 1912 as one of the six Bolshevik deputies to the Duma, the czarist parliament. He became head of the Bolshevik faction among the 13 Social Democratic Party deputies in the Duma and became treasurer of the newly founded Bolshevik newspaper *Pravda* ("Truth"). The latter position enabled him to provide the Okhrana with details of the party's finances and membership (the paper's editor, Miron Chernomazov, was also an Okhrana spy).

Early on Malinovsky was suspected as a police spy. But V. I. Lenin, head of the Bolshevik Party, steadfastly defended him, calling him an "outstanding leader." American intelligence analyst John J. Dziak, in *Chekisty: A History of the KGB* (1988), wrote: "Lenin protected Malinovsky almost to the end, hurling venomous charges of 'malicious slanderers' at . . . [those] who in 1914 demanded a nonfactional Social Democratic Party investigation of Malmovsky."

The director of the state police, S. P. Beletsky, described Malinovsky as "the pride of the Okhrana." During his spy career Beletsky increased Malinovsky's pay from 50 to 700 rubles per month as he submitted detailed reports on the Bolshevik leadership. But Malinovksy's double life was taking its toll. He was induced to resign from the Duma and fled from St. Petersburg with 6,000 rubles from the Okhrana, which told him to go abroad and begin a new life.

Malmovsky was captured by the Germans and placed in a prisoner-of-war camp, where he promptly began spreading Bolshevik propaganda to the captured Russians. When released, he began a correspondence with Lenin. In 1917 Lenin was called upon to testify about Malinovsky before the CHEKA as that Bolshevik ORGAN investigated earlier Okhrana operations and provocations. Dziak wrote of Lenin, "He emphatically exonerated Malinovsky on the grounds that everything he did benefited the Bolshevik faction, which gained far more than did the Okhrana."

Malinovsky returned to Russia in Oct. 1918, a year after the Russian Revolution, insisting that he could not "live outside the revolution." He demanded to be arrested and brought to see Lenin. Lenin agreed to the arrest but refused to see Malinovsky, who was brought before a tribunal on Nov. 6, 1918, and charged with spying for both the Okhrana and the Germans. Found guilty, he was shot within hours after the verdict was delivered.

Dziak speculates, "Was Malinovsky's bravado [in returning to Russia] driven by a stricken conscience or did he expect a deserved exoneration and welcome from a Bolshevik leadership whose double agent he really was?"

Malpas

SURVEILLANCE efforts by the British Special Operations Executive (SOE) during World War II to monitor and prosecute diamond smuggling from the neutral West African states to enemy countries. The effort was carried out in cooperation with the Secret Intelligence Service (MI6) and British consular offices.

Maly, Theodor

(b. ? d. 1937)

Soviet INTELLIGENCE OFFICER who reportedly recruited HAROLD (KIM) PHILBY to spy for the Soviet Union.

Generally described as large and handsome, Maly was Hungarian by birth and had been ordained as a Catholic priest prior to World War I. During the war he served as a chaplain in the Austro-Hungarian Army and was taken prisoner by the Russians in the Carpathian campaign. After suffering in several prisoner-of-war camps, Maly gave up his religious beliefs and joined the Bolsheviks.

Despite twinges of conscience over the atrocities of the Bolsheviks during the Revolution and Civil War, Maly remained a staunch supporter of their cause, serving in the OGPU, the state intelligence service. Late in 1932 he was sent as an ILLEGAL to Germany and then assigned to VIENNA.

Philby was working in Vienna at this time as a COURIER between the outlawed Communist Party and contacts in Paris and Prague. Maly recruited Philby for Soviet intelligence in May 1934, sending him back to Britain.

Maly was sent to Britain in April 1936 as chief of the ILLEGAL station in London; he and his wife used false Austrian passports. One of his most important responsibilities was management of the growing CAMBRIDGE SPY RING, and in early 1937—on orders from Moscow—he sent Philby to Spain with the COVER of a journalist.

Maly was recalled to Moscow in July 1937. By that time both veteran Bolsheviks and officers of Soviet intelligence (at the time NKVD) serving abroad were being purged by Stalin. Maly certainly knew what was happening to returning NKVD officials. He nevertheless went back to Moscow, perhaps because a commendation from Stalin the previous year led Maly to believe that he would be immune to the fate of his colleagues. He may also have understood the fate awaiting him, as he told a friend that he "decided to go there [Moscow] because nobody can say, 'That priest may have been a real spy after all.'" Upon returning to Moscow he was arrested; late in the year he was shot.

While he was an illegal in Europe, Maly's principal reporting name was Mann, but he was known to the Cambridge recruits as Theo.

Mamba

Operation by British Special Operations Executive (SOE), beginning in 1944, to suborn ex-Soviet soldiers in German service in Germany and occupied nations of Europe. The British dropped fake documents and subversive equipment (such as clandestine radios) to known Soviet-manned German units to encourage the Germans to believe that there was a resistance movement within the units.

SOE officials believed that these operations forced the Germans to replace the Soviet units in northern France with troops. Operations Cafeka and Restinga were components of Mamba.

Mandrake (Yak-25RD)

Soviet high-altitude RECONNAISSANCE aircraft whose effectiveness was somewhat curtailed by the shooting down of the U.S. U-2 spyplane in 1960. The Mandrake—the CODE NAME assigned by the NORTH ATLANTIC TREATY ORGANIZATION—was derived from the Yak-25 Flashlight, a twin-jet, swept-wing fighter developed specifically for night and all-weather operations. That plane—armed with 23mm cannon, carrying a long-range radar, and having a maximum speed of 677 mph—first flew in 1953 and entered service two years later. But it was already outdated by the advanced U.S. B-47 STRATOJET bomber, which was almost as fast as the Yak-25.

The Mandrake had straight wings with a span of 75 feet, more than twice that of the swept-wing fighter. The wings were also set higher on the fuselage than in the Flashlight, with twin turbojet engines in wing-mounted nacelles. Cruise altitude was about 60,000 feet, although the aircraft may have been able to reach 70,000 feet. The Yak-25s had a crew of two.

Sometimes called the "Soviet U-2," the straight-wing Mandrake flew reconnaissance flights over Western Europe in the late 1950s, as well as over areas adjacent to the Soviet Union. The flights over the West are believed to have halted abruptly following the shooting down of a U-2 on May 1, 1960, as the Soviets probably wished to avoid having aerial spying charges leveled at them.

Apparently some fighters were rebuilt as reconnaissance variants (as well as modified to electronic warfare configurations). Total Yak-25 production through about 1958 was some 1,000 aircraft of all types—fighter, bomber, and reconnaissance. The basic arrangement of the Yak-25 was further refined in the much-improved Yak-28 Brewer bomber and Firebar fighter aircraft.

Manned Orbiting Laboratory

(MOL)

U.S. Air Force program to maintain a manned spacecraft in orbit, primarily for RECONNAISSANCE purposes. This most ambitious proposal did not come to fruition because of costs and the "black hole" of the Vietnam War that soaked up all available funds.

As initially proposed, the orbit of the craft was not to overfly the Soviet Union, and there were no plans to carry out intelligence collection. When the proposal was put forward in Jan. 1964, Secretary of Defense Robert S. McNamara rejected it, failing to see a need for the Air Force to put men in space.

Two major changes were proposed for the MOL: a large radar antenna and a camera system to take photos of intelligence quality, the latter making the "laboratory" part of the KEYHOLE program. The revised MOL concept was given the CODE NAME DORIAN.

The MOL was to consist of a two-man Gemini space capsule attached to a 41-foot cylindrical laboratory and living chamber; it would weigh about 25,000 pounds, including 6,000 pounds for the Gemini B capsule and 5,000 pounds for the reconnaissance payload. They would be launched into orbit together, carried into space by a Titan 3C rocket. The MOL would be placed in orbit at an altitude of about 150 miles. Orbiting the earth once every 90 minutes, the MOL would remain aloft for several years, with the crew and supplies being replaced by replenishment capsules. A 30-day mission was envisioned for the two-man crews.

The proposed MOL camera system would have a four-inch resolution, meaning it would be able to sight an object that size on earth. However, atmospheric distortions would reduce the effective resolution to about nine inches, still a valuable capability.

JEFFREY T. RICHELSON, in *America's Secret Eyes in Space* (1990), wrote:

> It was hoped that putting a man in the loop and in space would heighten the value of the photos that would be produced. Detection and high-resolution photography of a new target might take weeks or months using unmanned satellites, but men could spot and photograph a new target without delay. In addition, rather than wasting film where there was clearly no activity of interest, certain areas could be bypassed. Thus, the astronauts would serve as part time photo-interpreters as well as determining some of the targets for the MOL camera.

A major selling point for the MOL project was its predicted ability to continuously monitor Soviet missile and bomber deployments, helping to verify arms control agreements. At the same time, it would provide more flexibility than unmanned reconnaissance SATELLITES (see CORONA), and would be used simultaneously for man-in-space research. Also, the Navy hoped that MOL could be employed in ocean SURVEILLANCE activities.

But some Pentagon officials considered the MOL project little more than an Air Force "toy," while the CIA, partially responsible for developing reconnaissance satellites, felt that the incursion was duplicative and unnecessary. The lack of CIA support was a significant factor in all OVERHEAD reconnaissance decisions.

Furthermore, several members of Congress from Florida, upon hearing that the MOL would be sent aloft from Vandenberg Air Force Base in California rather than Cape Canaveral, began to oppose the project. They feared it would cost jobs in Florida. The plan was to launch the MOL from Vandenberg because to reach a polar orbit from Canaveral would require cutting the payload by 2,500 to 5,000 pounds, severely reducing MOL's effectiveness. (The difference was caused by the reluctance to fly the spacecraft over populated areas during launch, necessary for a polar orbit from Canaveral.)

Development of MOL proceeded with the first, unmanned launch scheduled for April 15, 1969, and the first manned launch for Dec. 1969. Meanwhile, the MOL's weight increased to more than 15 tons, greater than a Titan 3C missile could lift. A new version of the Titan, designated 3M, would have to be developed.

MOL components were being tested, some in space flight, but the entire project was not to be. Increasing costs and diminishing political support caused its demise. McNamara was gone from the Pentagon, and the increasing U.S. efforts in the Vietnam War were forcing cancellation or delay of many projects not related to the war. Also, the Air Force was initiating a new bomber (the B-1) and the Navy a new strategic missile submarine (the Trident). The MOL was the largest "nonwar" item in the Air Force's research and development budget, which, wrote Richelson, "made an inviting target." Meanwhile, the first unmanned MOL flight was pushed to late 1970, the first manned flight to mid-1971.

There were continued cost increases and flight delays until the project was canceled. The public announcement was made on June 10, 1969. The project had "soaked up" about $1½ *billion*.

Marchetti, Victor L.

Coauthor with JOHN D. MARKS of the controversial *The CIA and the Cult of Intelligence* (1974), which the CIA tried to stop from publication.

Marchetti served in the U.S. Army in the early 1950s. After earning a degree in Soviet studies at Pennsylvania State University, he joined the CIA in 1955. Working as an analyst in the Soviet field, from 1966 to 1969 he served on the immediate staff of the DIRECTOR OF CENTRAL INTELLIGENCE (DCI). However, during the late 1960s he became disenchanted with the CIA, and resigned in 1969. At the time he was executive assistant to the Deputy DCI.

Upon leaving the CIA he wrote a novel, *The Rope Dancer* (1971), and then, with John Marks, began writing a book about the CIA's policies and operations. According to Alfred A. Knopf, their publisher, the book was "the first in American history to be subjected to prior government censorship."

The CIA claimed right of prior censorship through Marchetti's employment agreement with the agency. Marchetti's claim of First Amendment infringement was upheld in the first trial about the book. That verdict was overturned at the appellate level; the Supreme Court did not hear the case.

Referring to the book, President Nixon later recalled in his memoirs "the visible concern" on the face of DCI RICHARD HELMS, "over the possible publication of a book by two [sic] disaffected CIA agents. Helms had asked if I would back up legal action by the CIA, despite the fact that there would be cries of 'suppression.' I had told him that I would."

A first review of the Marchetti-Marks manuscript resulted in about 350 passages being censored by the CIA—from single words to entire pages. Following demands by the authors, lawyers, and publisher, the CIA yielded on almost 200 deletions. After several delays, the book was published in 1974, with the cuts on which the CIA had yielded indicated in boldface type. The word DELETED—also in boldface—was printed, with appropriate "white space," wherever material was excised from the book.

Examples of material originally cut by CIA censors and then restored:

> The National Security Agency tuned its huge antennae in on Soviet shipping and Cuban communications. ITT had operated much of the Cuban communications system before Castro's nationalizations, and the company worked closely with the CIA and NSA [National Security Agency] to intercept messages.

The CIA learned that Soviet military personnel were being secretly used in combat roles as submarine crews in Indonesia and as bomber crews in Yemen, a drastic departure from previous Soviet practice.

Some of the original deletions were strictly political:

> Vice President Spiro Agnew gave an impassioned speech on how the South Africans, now that they had recently declared their independence, were not about to be pushed around, and he went on to compare South Africa to the United States in its infant days. Finally, the President [Nixon] leaned over to Agnew and said gently, "You mean Rhodesia, don't you, Ted?"

Even after the final cut list was agreed to, the CIA still opposed publication of the book. Reportedly, one proposal made at LANGLEY was simply to purchase every copy of the book to prevent its being made available to the public. That course of action was not pursued.

More former deletions were inserted into an edition of the book published in 1983. By then, Marchetti said, about 110 deletions still had not been restored. The entire book, in measured tone and apparently factual, was highly critical of the CIA. The final chapter began:

> ["]It is a multi-purpose, clandestine arm of power . . . more than an intelligence or counterintelligence organization. It is an instrument for subversion, manipulation, and violence, for the secret intervention in the affairs of other countries." Allen Dulles wrote those words about the KGB in 1963 so that Americans would better understand the nature of the Soviet security service. His description was a correct one, but he could just as accurately have used the same terms to describe his own CIA.

Marenches, Count Alexandre de

(b. 1924)

Director-General of the SDECE, the major French foreign intelligence service, from 1970 to 1981, under Presidents Pompidou and d'Estaing.

Marenches joined the French Resistance in German-occupied France when he was 18. Still in his teens, he made his way across France to neutral Spain, and thence to the Free French forces in North Africa. After training there he was commissioned a lieutenant, and in 1944 he was posted to a Moroccan unit fighting with Allied forces in Italy. He was wounded in combat. Marenches later served as an officer in the French liaison mission attached to the Supreme Headquarters Allied Expeditionary Force. There he met and translated for Gen. Charles de Gaulle, the Free French leader.

After the war Marenches founded a machinery business and spent 15 years earning enough money to devote time to what he called duties "of a confidential and delicate nature" for the French government, both as a civilian and as a lieutenant colonel in the French Army Reserve. On one mission—a broad intelligence-gathering trip to Hawaii, Guam, and Japan—his COVER (with U.S. intelligence approval) was "Col. David Alexander" of the U.S. Army.

President Georges Pompidou had contemplated abolishing the SDECE when he took office in 1969. Instead, at the urging of Marenches, Pompidou kept the agency and appointed Marenches the Director-General.

The SDECE, when Marenches took over, was more like a criminal gang than an intelligence agency. "Some agents were running drugs and guns; others were engaged in kidnapping, murder, and the settling of the most bloody scores," he later said. His staff, wrote JEFFREY T. RICHELSON in *Foreign Intelligence Organizations* (1988), "ranged from gangsters and fascist Gaullists to incompetent military men and Soviet agents." The scandal-rocked SDECE had engendered a distrust that extended from ordinary citizens to political leaders. Soviet penetration of the agency added to the distrust. Marenches, known for his dry wit, said that the Soviets' extreme efforts to get SDECE secrets showed the value of those secrets. (See LAMIA, SAPPHIRE.)

On his first day as Director-General he fired a number of senior officers, beginning a cleanup and reorganization that transformed the SDECE into a professional organization. Because of his own pro-American sentiments, he also led the agency toward more cooperation with the U.S. CIA—while still engaging in INDUSTRIAL ESPIONAGE against the United States. He also set up a cooperative intelligence arrangement with China.

The SDECE predicted that the Soviet Union would attack Afghanistan well in advance of the Dec. 1979 invasion. To develop intelligence ASSETS in the Middle East, Marenches had AGENTS in Iran and, after the U.S. Embassy staff was held hostage in Tehran in 1979, he developed a plan to kidnap the Ayatollah Khomeini and hold him for exchange of the hostages. The United States vetoed the plan.

Marenches developed close personal ties with President Reagan and his DIRECTOR OF CENTRAL INTELLIGENCE, WILLIAM J. CASEY. The French intelligence chief came close, as he told it, to setting up Operation MOSQUITO, in which the French would set up a drug network in Afghanistan to demoralize Soviet troops with drugs seized by U.S. Drug Enforcement Agency and smuggled into Afghanistan by the SDECE.

Following Pompidou's death in March 1974, Marenches continued to serve under President Valéry Giscard d'Estaing and served briefly under his successor, François Mitterrand.

After leaving the SDECE Marenches became a private consultant. With David A. Andelman, he wrote *The Fourth World War: Diplomacy and Espionage in an Age of Terrorism* (1992). He maintained that radical religious fanatics, terrorists, and drug traffickers of the Southern world—including Iran, Libya, and Syria—were waging undeclared war against the nations of the North. He urged Northern nations to use joint military and intelligence resources against these threats to international security.

Markov, George

The first known fatality of the infamous "umbrella gun" developed by the KGB for specialized assassinations. Markov, a Bulgarian émigré writer living in Britain, was a former protégé of Todor Zhivkov, general secretary of the Bulgarian Communist party. He had fled to Britain, where he broadcast for the BBC World Service and publicized the abuses of the Zhivkov regime.

The KGB technical directorate developed an umbrella gun that fired a metal pellet, the size of a pinhead, containing the highly toxic poison ricin, made from castor-oil seeds. The KGB RESIDENT in Washington, D.C., purchased the umbrellas and sent them on to Moscow for modification. The umbrellas were probably fitted with a compressed gas cylinder as well as a firing mechanism. The umbrella guns were then taken to Sofia, where officers of the Bulgarian secret police, the Durzhavna Sigurnost, were instructed in their use.

An assassination team armed with the umbrellas was then sent to London; the target was Markov. In Sept. 1978 he was "accidentally" prodded by an umbrella when he was bumped by a stranger on London's Waterloo Bridge. The man apologized and disappeared.

Markov fell ill and was taken to a hospital. Before he died on Sept. 11 he was able to recall the accidental prodding. A tiny stab wound and the pellet were found in his right thigh; the ricin had decomposed by the time of the autopsy.

Markov was not the first victim of an umbrella gun attack. Another Bulgarian émigré, Vladimir Kostov, had been similarly "bumped" in Paris on Aug. 26, 1978. Word of the Markov assassination led to an operation on Kostov on Sept. 25. A steel pellet similar to the one that killed Markov was removed intact from his back.

An earlier version of the umbrella gun may have also been used against Nobel Prize winner Aleksandr Solzhenitsyn in Aug. 1971, while he was still in the Soviet Union. According to Solzhenitsyn, he was stricken by a mysterious ailment while standing in a food line. His body subsequently became covered with terrible blisters, and he was bedridden for almost three months before recovering.

Marks, John D.

Coauthor with VICTOR L. MARCHETTI of the controversial *The CIA and the Cult of Intelligence* (1974), which the CIA tried to stop from being published.

Marks is often identified with Marchetti as one of two CIA employees who wrote the book; however, he was never in the agency. Marks was employed by the State Department from 1966 to 1970 as an analyst and then as staff assistant to the intelligence director at the State Department. He left to become executive assistant to Sen. Clifford Chase. (See MARCHETTI entry for details about the book.)

Marks also wrote *The Search for the "Manchurian Candidate": The CIA and Mind Control* (1979), which reported on MKULTRA, the CIA project involving hallucinogenic drugs.

Marlowe, Christopher

(b. 1564 d. 1593)

English poet and dramatist who served as a spy for Sir FRANCIS WALSINGHAM, the 16th-century diplomat and spymaster for Queen Elizabeth I.

The son of a shoemaker, Marlowe was recruited while a student at Cambridge, long a fruitful campus for spy TALENT SPOTTERS (see CAMBRIDGE SPY RING). Marlowe's most significant period in espionage appears to have begun when he suddenly left Cambridge in Feb. 1587 and, pretending to be a Catholic sympathizer, traveled to Rheims to infiltrate Catholic conspirators plotting against Elizabeth's regime. When he returned to Cambridge in July, he was arraigned for leaving without permission and for visiting a Jesuit seminary in Rheims, where he protested against the Protestant establishment in England. A letter from the Queen's Privy Council, which declared Marlowe to have been engaged "on matters touching the benefit of his country" and denying he had any intention of entering the college at Rheims, enabled him to gain his master's degree.

Little is known of his other endeavors on behalf of Walsingham, the focus of his life unquestionably being his brilliant literary efforts. Still, there is evidence that his secret life continued; indeed, even his death had innuendoes of the secret world: He was allegedly stabbed to death during a drunken brawl in Deptford on May 30, 1593. (The site is often described as a tavern; it was a hired room in a house owned by a widow with connections in the royal court—and may have been a SAFE HOUSE.) Marlowe's murderer, Ingram Frizer, claimed that Marlowe had drawn a dagger and that he had seized it as the two argued about the bill. Frizer was fully pardoned a month later.

Never explained was the presence of Robert Poley in an upstairs room of the tavern. Poley, a known spy for

Walsingham, had been a steward to Lady Sidney, Walsingham's daughter and a participant in his espionage activities. Informers had already come forth with alleged evidence that Marlowe was guilty of treason. Was Marlowe assassinated—conceivably on Walsingham's orders—because of his tendency to be outspoken and unguarded in conversation? Or was he involved in an espionage operation that went wrong?

Marquand, John P.

(b. 1893 d. 1960)

Pulitzer Prize–winning novelist who worked for the OFFICE OF STRATEGIC SERVICES (OSS) during World War II. Marquand won the Pulitzer Prize in 1938 for *The Late George Apley.*

While in the OSS, among his projects was the testing of German prisoners of war for antitoxins in an attempt to learn whether they were being protected against biological warfare agents that Germany might use against the Allies. Marquand was also director of intelligence and information for biological warfare research, although little information about this was ever released.

Also see LITERARY SPIES.

Martin, William H.

(b. 1931)

Cryptologist for the NSA who, with BERNON F. MITCHELL, defected to the Soviet Union in 1960. Their defection, wrote JAMES BAMFORD in *The Puzzle Palace* (1982), was the "worst scandal in the history of NSA."

A math genius, "Ham" Martin had finished high school in two years instead of three, having spent his summers studying college subjects. After a year of college he enlisted in the Navy. Following cryptographic training, he was assigned to the NAVAL SECURITY GROUP radio intercept station in Kamiseya, Japan. There he met Mitchell. After his Navy enlistment was over in 1954, Martin remained in Japan for a year as a civilian with the ARMY SECURITY AGENCY. Subsequently, he returned to the United States to study mathematics at the University of Washington.

He and Mitchell maintained their friendship and both began working at the NSA on July 8, 1957. They soon became disillusioned with the NSA's activities, however, and after an abortive attempt to tell a U.S. congressman about their views, they began planning to defect to the Soviet Union.

In 1959 Martin was awarded an NSA scholarship for a master's degree in mathematics at the University of Illinois, the first two-year scholarship ever awarded by the NSA. At Illinois he excelled, earning a straight A average, while also taking a Russian course and associating with members of the Communist Party. In Dec. 1959 he and Mitchell flew to CUBA and probably met with Soviet diplomats—against NSA rules.

Martin and Mitchell took leave together in late June 1960, going first to Mexico City, and then on to Cuba the next morning to board a Soviet cargo ship. The NSA initiated a search when the two failed to return from vacation in July. In a safe-deposit box in Mitchell's name, NSA officials found a letter explaining "why we have sought citizenship in the Soviet Union."

On Aug. 1 a Pentagon news release stated that two NSA employees had failed to return from vacation and that they were missing and unaccounted for. Five days later Pentagon officials revised the statement, adding, "It must be assumed that there is a likelihood that they have gone behind the Iron Curtain."

Nothing was heard from them until Sept. 6, 1960, when they appeared on a televised Moscow news conference to reveal the "unscrupulous" NSA spying on other nations, including U.S. allies. They said that the NSA was breaking the CODES of at least 40 nations. Obviously the two men were able to provide Soviet intelligence officials with a considerable amount of information on U.S. electronic spying activities. President Eisenhower labeled Martin and Mitchell "self-confessed traitors," and former President Truman declared that "they ought to be shot."

After their defection it was revealed that Martin and Mitchell were HOMOSEXUAL lovers. In a subsequent purge, the NSA fired 26 employees for "indications of sexual deviation."

In the Soviet Union the defectors were given Soviet citizenship. Martin changed his name to Sokolovsky, enrolled in an advanced education course, and got married.

Mask

British CODE NAME for intercepted and decrypted secret Soviet espionage messages between Moscow and AGENTS who were Communist Party members in several countries, including the United States. So many messages passed between Moscow and the Communist Party of the U.S.A. (CPUSA) that an officer from the Comintern's International Liaison Department was stationed in the United States to operate the party's shortwave radio station.

The messages, sent between 1934 and 1937, principally concerned NKVD espionage operations involving Communist Party members recruited for spying. The recruitment was done through the International Liaison Department (also known as the Liaison Service) of the Comintern, the Soviet organ responsible for coordinating communist policy through national parties.

Several messages appealed for candidates to be trained in Moscow as operators of clandestine radios. The trainees—female stenographers or music students were preferred—had to have been party members for at least two years. "Perfect health essential," one message said. "Most important that their eyes, ears and hands should be in perfect order, and they should not be suffering from any contagious disease." One trainee was Marguerite Browder, sister of U.S. Communist Party leader EARL R. BROWDER. The National Cryptologic Museum library has a complete set of Mask intercepts.

Mason, Lt. Comdr. Theodorus B. M.

(b. 1848 d. 1899)

First U.S. Navy Chief Intelligence Officer (predecessor of the DIRECTOR OF NAVAL INTELLIGENCE. Mason, an 1868 graduate of the Naval Academy, held the chief intelligence position from June 1882 to April 1885. He was a lieutenant at the time of his appointment.

He retired from the Navy in 1894.

Mason-MacFarlane, Lt. Gen. Sir Noel

(b. 1889 d. 1953)

INTELLIGENCE OFFICER for the British military forces in France in 1940 when they were routed by the German Army.

Educated at the Royal Military Academy at Woolwich, Mason-MacFarlane entered active service in 1909 as an artillery officer. He served in France, Belgium, and Mesopotamia during World War I and was heavily decorated. He was British military ATTACHÉ in VIENNA from 1931 to 1934, and, after attending the Imperial Defence College and commanding an artillery brigade, he served on the Army staff and as attaché in Copenhagen and BERLIN.

In 1939, as a major general, he was appointed the director of MILITARY INTELLIGENCE for the British Expeditionary Force in France under Gen. Sir John Gort. Deprived of his staff by Gort's order to maintain a small headquarters in France, Mason-MacFarlane was unable to provide proper intelligence to his superior during the ill-fated campaign in France, which led to the German victory and the British evacuation from Dunkirk. As the British forces retreated, Mason-MacFarlane hastily assembled stragglers and support troops to form an effective force that fought its way to the beaches against heavy German opposition.

In the summer of 1941 he was named head of the British military mission to the Soviet Union. Leaving Moscow in early 1942, he later served as governor of Gibraltar. In 1944 he underwent extensive medical treatment and retired from the Army the following year.

Massingham

CODE WORD for British Special Operations Executive (SOE) activities in German-occupied Europe carried out from bases in North Africa.

Masterman, Sir John Cecil

(b. 1891 d. 1977)

Chairman of the TWENTY COMMITTEE, which during World War II ran the DOUBLE-CROSS SYSTEM, the ingenious scheme that transformed captured German AGENTS in Britain into DOUBLE AGENTS. To German INTELLIGENCE OFFICERS, the TURNED agents appeared to be operating successfully because they were transmitting back to Ger-

many information that seemed to be valid. Masterman credited DICK WHITE of the Security Service (MI5) with inventing the idea, but Masterman ran the system.

An Oxford don who had been trapped in Germany during World War I, Masterman polished his German during four years in a prisoner-of-war camp in Rühleben. After the war he returned to Oxford, becoming vice chancellor and provost of Worcester College. He was regarded as a fine player of cricket, tennis, and field hockey.

Information about the Double-Cross System remained secret after the war. In 1961 Masterman began pressing the British intelligence establishment for permission to publish a book on the system. ROGER HOLLIS, Director General of MI5, refused to authorize publication, as did Prime Minister Alexander Douglas-Home.

Revelations about the CAMBRIDGE SPY RING devastated British intelligence in the 1960s. Masterman, "depressed by the low state of the reputation of the Security Service," believed that publication would help restore public confidence. He drolly listed the book before it was published in his *Who's Who* entry, then vaguely sketched the system in a mystery novel, *The Case of the Four Friends* (1957).

In April 1970, when the British government again declined permission, Masterman decided to publish the book in America, beyond the reach, he believed, of the OFFICIAL SECRETS ACT. He called this secret effort "Plan Diablo."

Aiding in the effort was Norman Holmes Pearson, a member of the Yale University faculty, who suggested Yale University Press as the publisher. Pearson, head of X-2, the COUNTERINTELLIGENCE branch of the OFFICE OF STRATEGIC SERVICES (OSS) during the war, had served on the Twenty Committee. Yale had contributed many scholars and students to the OSS, and Chester B. Kerr, director of the press, saw the book as both important and a potential commercial success.

For a time British authorities threatened legal action against Masterman, but they then reluctantly decided to grant permission as long as about 60 passages in the manuscript were deleted. Kerr would delete only a dozen. The *book, The Double-Cross System in the War of 1939–45*, was published in Feb. 1972, with a foreword by Pearson, who did not refer to his work on the Twenty Committee. Nor did Masterman reveal that ULTRA codebreaking, still highly secret, had greatly aided the Double-Cross System.

Mata Hari [p]

(b. 1876 d. 1917)

The most renowned woman spy in history—although she probably wasn't one. She was naïve, easily duped, and trapped by her "friends" as well as her enemies during World War I. The *Oxford English Dictionary* describes her as "Prototype for seductive spy."

Born in Holland as Margaretha Gertrud Zelle to a well-to-do Dutch shopkeeper and his Javanese wife, she attended a school for teachers but was expelled for having sex with the headmaster. At age 18 she married a Dutch army officer who was 20 years her senior. They

Mata Hari, clothed, in 1915.

gated. British officials warned her not to go to Germany and sent her back to Spain. There she met and had an affair with the German military ATTACHÉ, Maj. Kalle. He sent a message to Berlin in a CODE that he knew the Allies could read, saying that spy "H-21" had proved valuable.

Mata Hari returned to Paris on Jan. 4, 1917, and was arrested on Feb. 13. Although the French and British intelligence services suspected her of spying for Germany, neither could produce definite evidence against her. Secret ink was found in her room—incriminating evidence in that period. She contended that it was part of her makeup. She admitted to taking money from Germans but claimed that it was for love, not spying.

Still, she was tried by a closed court-martial, found guilty, and executed by a French firing squad on Oct. 15, 1917. Refusing a blindfold or to be bound to the stake, she blew a kiss to the 12-man firing squad before their rifles shattered the morning stillness. Neither former lovers nor family claimed her body, and her remains were taken to a Paris hospital for dissection by medical students.

Three films attempted to capture the drama of her life: *Mata Hari,* a 1931 classic melodrama, starred Greta Garbo, Ramon Novarro, and Lionel Barrymore. The French version, *Mata Hari, Agent H21* (1964) starred Jeanne Moreau, while the third, *Mata Hari* (1985), was an absurd attempt to trade on the name of an exotic nonspy.

Mata Hari's memory is kept alive in a permanent exhibit at the Fries Museum in Leeuwarden, the Netherlands. Included in the exhibit are her two personal scrapbooks and an Oriental rug embroidered with the footsteps of her fan dance.

Maugham, W. Somerset

(b. 1874 d. 1965)

Author and spy. Maugham, clubfooted and too old and short to serve in the British armed services, became an ambulance driver in World War I. Then, because he was fluent in German and French, he was recruited in 1915 as an AGENT for the British SECRET SERVICE BUREAU. His first major literary success, *Of Human Bondage,* had just been published. So his COVER—an author writing a book—was a natural one. He went to Switzerland, where for about a year he kept watch on suspected German spies, contacted other Allied agents, and made regular reports to the Secret Service Bureau. He worked without pay as a patriotic gesture.

In 1917 he believed that his Secret Service career was over. But Sir WILLIAM WISEMAN, chief of British intelligence in America, persuaded Maugham to go to Russia on a mission to support the Mensheviks and counter the Bolshevik plans to pull Russia out of the war. Under the CODE NAME Somerville, Maugham went to Russia, posing as a writer for U.S. publications. Maugham met with Aleksandr Kerenski, the socialist leader, who sent Maugham to London with a desperate request to the Allies to raise an anti-Bolshevik army.

Maugham wrote a number of stories based on his experiences. Warned prior to publication that some sto-

soon moved to the Dutch East Indies and had two children, but divorced in 1906.

She went to Paris in 1905, assuming the name Mata Hari (Eye of the Dawn) and the persona of a Javanese princess. She made her debut as an erotic dancer at the Oriental Studies Museum, followed by performances to ecstatic audiences throughout Europe and in Egypt. She also began having wealthy and influential lovers.

During World War I Mata Hari had an affair with a 25-year-old Russian pilot flying with the French, Capt. Vadim Maslov, son of a Russian admiral. When Maslov was wounded in the summer of 1916, she asked permission to visit him in a forward hospital. French officials at the DEUXIÈME BUREAU gave her permission—in return for her agreeing to spy on Germans, including possibly the crown prince, whom she knew. She was to receive 1 million francs for her efforts.

To carry out her assignment, Mara Hari traveled to Spain en route to neutral Holland, from which she could cross over into Germany to rendezvous with the crown prince. En route to Holland, her ship stopped over in Falmouth, England, where she was detained and interro-

ries violated the OFFICIAL SECRETS ACT, Maugham burned them. The rest, including an account of a mission to Russia, were published in *Ashenden* (1928), the name of Maugham's alter ego in *Of Human Bondage* and hero of the book. (He also uses Somerville as a name in the book.) "The work of an agent in the Intelligence Department is on the whole monotonous," he wrote in the foreword to *Ashenden.* "A lot of it is uncommonly useless." He is believed to be the first author of spy books to write from the perspective of being a former spy. Assessing Maugham's contribution to espionage literature, *The Times Literary Supplement* said *of Ashenden,* "Never before or since has it been so categorically demonstrated that counterintelligence work consists often of morally indefensible jobs not to be undertaken by the squeamish or the conscience-stricken."

"*Ashenden* had a lasting influence on post-war espionage writing," Anthony Masters wrote in *Literary Agents* (1987), his book on authors who spied. "Eric Ambler, Graham Greene, John le Carré and Len Deighton all created middle-aged and often cynical heroes who were locked into a particular series of Intelligence rituals. But of all fictitious spy stories, Ashenden's adventures come nearest to the real-life experiences of his creator."

During World War II, Maugham did some intelligence work for Sir WILLIAM STEPHENSON, head of MI6 in the United States. But Stephenson indicated to Maugham's biographer, Ted Morgan, that Maugham had not performed any important missions. Maugham, Stephenson said, was typical of volunteers who did not have "much taste for the business and became involved because they saw no alternatives."

Max

SEE FRITZ KAUDER

Maxwell Smart [f]

Central character of an American TELEVISION series, *Get Smart,* produced in the 1960s. Smart, also known as Agent 86, was a bumbling intelligence AGENT who was helped in his duels against KAOS by Agent 99, a woman who was supportive and much brighter. They work for a secret intelligence agency known only as Control.

Don Adams played Max and Barbara Feldon was Agent 99.

May, Allan Nunn

(b. 1912 d. 2003)

British nuclear physicist who spied for the Soviet Union while working in Canada on the atomic bomb.

May had been a communist since his student days at Cambridge University, from which he graduated in 1933. Other members of the communist cell at Cambridge included HAROLD (KIM) PHILBY and DONALD MACLEAN, two members of the CAMBRIDGE SPY RING. May had also been

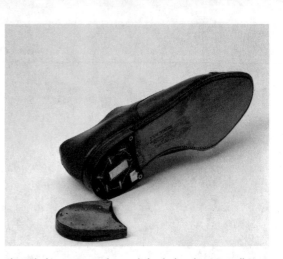

Shoe telephones were used not only by the bungling Maxwell Smart in the TV series Get Smart, *but by real secret agents. Shoes, including this artifact of the Cold War, were also useful for hiding a variety of spy tools—lock picks, alternative identity papers, recording devices, and cameras.* (COURTESY OF INTERNATIONAL SPY MUSEUM)

a radical in the Cambridge branch of the Union of Scientific Workers.

In 1942 May joined the secret British atomic bomb project, CODE NAME Tube Alloys, working first at a laboratory in Cambridge. Sometime late in 1944 or early in 1945 he was sent to Canada. He visited a project site at Chalk River, about 200 miles northwest of Ottawa, and talked to American scientists working on the atomic bomb, under the code name Manhattan Project, at the University of Chicago. While in Ottawa he was recruited for espionage by Col. NIKOLAI ZABOTIN, the military ATTACHÉ at the Soviet Embassy and an INTELLIGENCE OFFICER. May then worked at Chalk River, where one of his physicist colleagues was BRUNO PONTECORVO, a suspected spy who later defected to the Soviet Union.

May reported to Soviet intelligence on the successful U.S. test of the atomic bomb at Alamogordo, N. Mex., on July 16, 1945, although the report did not reach Moscow until Aug. 9, three days after the atomic bombing of Hiroshima. May also gave Zabotin samples of uranium 235, the critical material in the Hiroshima bomb.

The embassy played a crucial role in the Soviet-run U.S.-Canadian-British ATOMIC SPY RING. On Aug. 2, 1945, Zabotin's superiors in Moscow had asked him to "take measures to organize acquisition of documentary materials on the atomic bomb! The technical processes, drawings, calculations."

This was one of the many messages supplied to Western intelligence by IGOR GOUZENKO, a CIPHER clerk in the Soviet Embassy. Gouzenko defected in Sept. 1945, the same month that May returned to Britain and a position at King's College in London.

He was placed under SURVEILLANCE by the British Security Service (MI5) and interrogated in Feb. 1946. MI5 knew he had three times failed to show up for meetings at the British Museum with his Soviet HANDLER. Stunned at MI5's knowledge of his spying, May confessed, saying that he had passed secrets from Feb. to Aug. 1945. "The whole affair was extremely painful to me and I only embarked on it because I felt this was a contribution I could make to the safety of mankind," he said. "I certainly did not do it for gain." (He had, in fact, accepted $700 and two bottles of whiskey from his Soviet handler. He later said that he burned the money because it was insulting.)

He was arrested on March 4, 1946, by the SPECIAL BRANCH of Scotland Yard. After a one-day trial at the Old Bailey, he was found guilty and sentenced to 10 years in prison. Released in 1952 after time off for good behavior, he later became a professor of physics at the University of Ghana. When he died he was living in Cambridge.

He was code-named Alek by the Soviet intelligence and Primrose by MI5.

MB

The Russian Ministry of Security, the initial successor to the KGB. The MB, which existed from 1991 to 1993, was established by a decree of Russian President Boris Yeltsin, issued on Dec. 19, 1991. The first minister was Marshal VIKTOR BARANNIKOV, through July 1993, when he was replaced by Col. Gen. NIKOLAY GOLUSHKO.

The ministry was abolished in 1993. Its principal intelligence components were the Foreign Intelligence Service (SVR) and the Federal COUNTERINTELLIGENCE Service (FSK).

Also see RUSSIA-USSR

McCone, John A.

(b. 1902 d. 1991)

DIRECTOR OF CENTRAL INTELLIGENCE (DCI) during the CUBAN MISSILE CRISIS. McCone was appointed DCI by President Kennedy after the abortive Bay of Pigs invasion in April 1961 (see CUBA). Following the long-serving ALLEN W. DULLES, McCone held the DCI position from Nov. 1961 to April 1965.

A 1922 graduate of the University of California at Berkeley with a degree in engineering, McCone held various engineering and then corporate executive positions. On several occasions he left industry for government appointments.

He was a member of the president's Air Policy Committee in 1947–1948, Deputy Secretary of Defense in 1948, Under Secretary of the Air Force in 1950–1951, and Chairman of the Atomic Energy Commission in 1958–1960 before becoming DCI.

During the missile crisis of 1962 he was a member of President Kennedy's EXCOMM, which met almost daily for six weeks to advise the president. McCone was one of those who advised Kennedy against an invasion of Cuba. Robert F. Kennedy wrote in *Thirteen Days* (1969):

John McCone said everyone should understand that an invasion was going to be a much more serious

undertaking than most people had previously realized. "They have a hell of a lot of equipment," he said, "And it will be damn tough to shoot them out of those hills, as we learned so clearly in Korea."

Subsequently, McCone had a key role in the development of U.S. intelligence activities and sources in Vietnam.

He was considered an outsider by most at the CIA when he was appointed DCI, having had no previous intelligence or military experience (other than as a civilian executive in the Pentagon). However, he was relatively close to both John F. and Robert Kennedy and helped to rebuild the CIA's image after the Bay of Pigs disaster.

DCI was McCone's last position in Washington, D.C. After retiring from government service, McCone served as the U.S. government representative to the Vatican.

McCormick, Donald

SEE RICHARD DEACON

Measurements and Signatures Intelligence

(MASINT)

An intelligence discipline first recognized by the INTELLIGENCE COMMUNITY in 1986. It joined HUMAN INTELLIGENCE (HUMINT), SIGNALS INTELLIGENCE (SIGINT), and IMAGERY INTELLIGENCE (IMINT). In 1992, the Central MASINT Office was established in the DEFENSE INTELLIGENCE AGENCY (DIA).

The DIA defines MASINT as "technically derived intelligence that detects, locates, tracks, identifies, and describes the specific signature of fixed and dynamic target sources," including "radar, laser, optical, infrared, acoustic, nuclear radiation, and radio frequency, spectroradiometric, and seismic sensing systems as well as gas, liquid, and solid materials sampling and analysis."

Medical Intelligence

(MEDINT)

Intelligence derived from foreign medical, bioscientific, and environmental information that is of interest to military planners, especially medical personnel. For example, details of diseases in a potential combat area, or medical problems being encountered by enemy forces, are invaluable to military planners.

Melekh, Lt. Col. Igor Yakovlevich

Career Soviet INTELLIGENCE OFFICER caught spying while assigned to the UNITED NATIONS in New York City.

A graduate of the Military Institute of Foreign Languages and later an instructor at the Military Diplomatic Academy, which trains officers for the GRU, Melekh was sent to the United States in 1958. He was assigned to the United Nations secretariat.

Melekh was observed meeting in New York City with Willie Hirsch, who was already under FBI SURVEILLANCE at the time (see JOHN GILMORE). The FBI put Melekh under surveillance as well. On Oct. 23, 1958, at another meeting, this time in Chicago, Melekh, accompanied by Hirsch, handed $200 to a man who was to provide aerial photographs and maps of the Chicago area.

The man was a DOUBLE AGENT, called Agent X by the FBI. Agent X had helped to entrap Hirsch and was now operating against Melekh as well. Some time later Melekh telephoned Agent X and told him to come to New York, where Melekh gave him another $200 and demanded action in getting the Chicago photos and maps.

Another Melekh-Agent X rendezvous was arranged in Jan. 1959, at a subway station in Brooklyn, N.Y. On the evening of Jan. 17 Melekh and Agent X, closely watched by FBI agents, met at the underground station. A package was exchanged for an envelope from Melekh containing $500.

The FBI waited for Melekh to arrange further dealings with Hirsch or Agent X. Finally, on Oct. 27, 1960, the FBI took both Melekh and Hirsch into custody in New York City. That day a federal grand jury in Chicago had charged them both with espionage—"conspiracy to obtain information pertaining to our national defense for transmittal to Soviet Russia."

Melekh, who did not have diplomatic immunity, was released on bail after a brief stay in jail and was forbidden to leave Manhattan. Hirsch remained in jail. Melekh was not brought to trial. He was released on condition that he leave the United States, which he did on April 8, 1961.

There was considerable criticism in the American press of the Kennedy administration's dismissal of the charges against Melekh. Although President Kennedy denied any link between Melekh and the release of two U.S. fliers who had survived when their aircraft was shot down by Soviet fighters on July 1, 1960, the actions were related. (See AIRCRAFT SHOT DOWN.)

(Hirsch was also released on condition that he leave the country; the case against him fell apart when it was decided to free Melekh. Hirsch, too, was involved in the tenuous SPY SWAP for the two B-47 aviators.)

Memuneh

Israeli term for "the one in charge," the honorific given by Prime Minister David Ben-Gurion to ISSER HAREL in 1957. At the time Harel was director of the MOSSAD, the Israeli foreign intelligence service. He had previously been director of the SHIN BET, the domestic security service, over which he continued to have controlling influence; he simultaneously chaired the intelligence coordinating committee known as Varash, making him de facto head of all Israeli intelligence activities until he stepped down as director of the Mossad in 1963 (when Ben-Gurion also ended his tenure as Prime Minister).

Harel was the only person to hold the title of Memuneh.

Mendez, Antonio J.

CIA disguise expert who helped get U.S. hostages out of Iran in a daring escape caper.

In 1979 he EXFILTRATED six U. S. Embassy employees from Iran during the hostage crisis. Mendez created elaborate LEGENDS for the employees, designating each one as a member of a film production company seeking locations in Iran. He spread knowledge of the production in Hollywood and even advertised it in *Variety*. All escaped safely.

Mendez, while working on a mission in Bangkok, met Jonna Heistand, his future wife, who later succeeded him as the CIA's chief of disguise. He retired in 1990, they married in 1991, and she retired the following year.

"We were Q," says Jonna Mendez, referring to the gadgetry creator in JAMES BOND films. (The fictional Q was based on the real CHARLES FRASER-SMITH.)

The two disguise experts worked in the CIA Office of Technical Affairs (OTA), also called "the Magic Kingdom." Besides providing disguises, the office also created fake documents. The CIA authorized a rare look at the OTA by clearing Antonio Mendez's book, *Master of Disguise* (1999). But at least one of his disguises, a paper-thin mask that can be put on quickly, is still classified.

To demonstrate the CIA's disguise prowess, Jonna Mendez once visited President GEORGE H. W. BUSH in disguise, then whipped off her realistic mask in the Oval Office, startling the president.

Menzhinsky, Vyacheslav Rudolfovich

(b. 1874 d. 1934)

Head of the Soviet OGPU, the secret police-security ORGAN, from 1926 to 1934 (see CHEKA). Successor to FELIKS DZHERZHINSKY, Menzhinsky was also of Polish noble origins. He was the first deputy chief of the GPU from 1923 to 1926, before succeeding as head of the organization.

U.S. intelligence analyst John Dziak described Menzhinsky in his *Chekisty: A History of the KGB* (1988): "A gifted linguist and intellectual dabbler, Menzhinsky was either sickly or a hypochondriac, all of which made, in his case, for a weak leader. This suited Stalin's technique, because Menzhinsky's deputy [Genrikh] Yagoda already was one of Stalin's henchmen."

Menzhinsky fell victim to a heart attack on May 10, 1934. He was known to have had a heart condition and was under the care of Kremlin physicians. In July 1934 the OGPU was abolished and absorbed into the Main Administration of State security (GUGB) within the NYKVD (Commissariat of Internal Affairs). Menzhinsky's principal deputy chairman was GENRIKH YAGODA, who succeeded him as head of Soviet intelligence.

Menzies, Maj. Gen. Sir Stewart G.

(b. 1890 d. 1968)

Director of MI6, the British Secret Intelligence Service, from 1939 to 1953. Menzies (pronounced MEN-SING) was responsible for much of Britain's intelligence activities during World War II, including operations at BLETCH-LEY PARK, and the early period of the Cold War.

Educated at Eton, Menzies subsequently served briefly as an officer in the Grenadier Guards and then in the Army's Life Guards from 1910 to 1939. He saw action in France during World War I and was decorated by the king for bravery. As a colonel he was deputy to Adm. Sir HUGH SINCLAIR (head of MI6 from 1923 until his death in 1939), and then succeeded to the directorship of MI6. His position was particularly difficult during the war in that he worked for Prime Minister Winston Churchill, who had an insatiable appetite for intelligence and secret projects.

A strong proponent of codebreaking, Menzies enthusiastically sponsored efforts at Bletchley Park to develop the BOMBE machines that began deciphering the German ENIGMA machine CIPHER in 1940. Promoted to major general in 1945, he remained the head of MI6 until 1953, when he retired in the aftermath of the defection of DONALD MACLEAN and GUY BURGESS to the Soviet Union.

Menzies left the day-to-day operation of MI6 to his subordinates: "Don't expect me to read everything that's put on my desk," he told them. Maintaining MI6's relationship with the ministries was his primary occupation. "In personal relationships he was always polite, but never warm—'hard as granite under a smooth exterior' is the description of one SIS officer's wife. He was a clubman, loved horses and racing, and drank heavily," wrote Phillip Knightley in *The Second Oldest Profession* (1986).

Many in the intelligence services believed that Menzies was the illegitimate son of Edward VII. This was certainly not true, but the myth was possibly fostered by Menzies himself.

Merkulov, Vsevolod, Nikolayevich

(b. ? d. 1953)

Head of the NKGB (People's Commissariat of State Security) from Feb. to July 1941, and again from April 1943 until March 1946. Merkulov was a member of the so-called Georgian mafia of LAVRENTY BERIA, head of the NKVD.

"Arrests, deportations, executions, and prison camps increased, mandating reorganized and expanded security forces," following the separation of Soviet intelligence agenies after the Soviet takeover of Latvia, Lithuania, and Estonia," wrote John J. Dziak in *Chekisty: A History of the KGB* (1988). The "1943 changes came after the Battle of Stalingrad, when Soviet advances offered the prospect of reconquered lands and populations."

Merkulov worked successively for the CHEKA, GPU, and OGPU from 1921 to 1931, after which he did party work in Georgia for the next seven years. He became Beria's first deputy at the NKVD in Dec. 1938 (first deputies of intelligence/security ORGANS generally succeeded to the chief position).

Hungarian diplomat Nicholas Nyaradi, in My *Ringside Seat in Moscow* (1953), wrote of Merkulov:

> A paradox: a man of great kindness and bestial cruelty, one who is deadly earnest while being quite witty. He has the patience of Job and yet he chainsmokes 40 to 50 cigarettes during a business day. A man of such prominence that Russian ambassadors stand to attention in his presence, Merkulov is always diffident, a shy smile playing about his lips as he speaks. Merkulov was the man who personally supervised the liquidation of nearly two million Estonians, Lithuanians and Latvians with heartless efficiency; but, like a gangster who bursts into tears at the strains of Brahms' "Lullaby", he has the typical Russian sentimentality about children, and, after I knew him better, he once showed me with welling eyes a photo of his soldier son.

When not directing the NKGB, Merkulov worked directly for Beria within the NKVD. After the death of Josef Stalin in 1953, Beria was arrested; so were many of his henchmen, including Merkulov. He was one of six Beria aides tried by the Soviet Supreme Court on multiple charges from Dec. 18 to 23, 1953, and executed on Dec. 23. (Beria had already been shot.)

Metric

The highest security CLASSIFICATION used by the Atlantic Union from 1948 and then by the NORTH ATLANTIC TREATY ORGANIZATION. It was changed to COSMIC in the early 1950s.

MfS

Ministerium for Staatssicherheit, the East German Ministry for State Security. Established in April 1950, the MfS was modeled on the Soviet security apparatus—the MGB and its predecessors, the NKGB and NKVD. (The Soviet Union established the German Democratic Republic—East Germany—on Oct. 7, 1949.)

MfS was developed from several smaller intelligence activities that supported Soviet internal security in the one-third of Germany that was the Soviet zone of occupation from May 1945 until Oct. 1949. Even after the establishment of East Germany in the former Soviet zone, the Red Army's intelligence agency (GRU) and other Soviet intelligence ORGANS continued to be highly active.

Invariably known as the STASI, the MfS had headquarters in East BERLIN, from where it carried out repression at home and espionage abroad. The latter operations were most often a surrogate for the agency's Soviet "senior." The foreign intelligence arm of the Stasi was the Chief Administration, Intelligence (HVA). Its principal TARGET was West Germany, although other Western European countries and U.S. military forces in Europe were also targeted.

At home, the Stasi carried out repression of the East German population through a massive NETWORK of informers, often with members of the same family reporting on others (and being paid). The pre-Stasi organizations had made use of several former German police and intelligence officials, many ex-GESTAPO and officers. Even after the establishment of the MfS, their employment continued; one of them was Lt. Gen. Rudolf Bamler, former head of COUNTERESPIONAGE for the ABWEHR. (The same, of course, was being done in the West; see GEHLEN ORGANIZATION.)

East Germany was stark and cold; the Stasi fit in perfectly, as depicted in JOHN LE CARRÉ's classic book *The Spy Who Came In from the Cold* (1963). But the Stasi was effective in penetrating the West German government, and subverting officials, at virtually every level. (See GERMANY.)

When East Germany merged with West Germany on Oct. 3, 1990, the Stasi was reported to have 173,000 registered informers out of a population of less than 17 million, or about one per 100 citizens. This number was in addition to a full-time MfS staff of more than 90,000 uniformed and civilian personnel.

After the union of the two Germanys, several former East German intelligence officials were tried for their previous activities and indiscretions as well as border police and some informers. After several trials of former Stasi officials, including the East German spymaster MARKUS WOLF, the unified Germany's Constitutional Court ruled on May 23, 1995, that former Stasi officials could not be prosecuted for conducting Cold War espionage against the West. The 5-to-3 ruling effectively gave amnesty to Wolf and other former East German intelligence officials.

MI

(1) MILITARY INTELLIGENCE; (2) Designation for British intelligence/security activities. The term was derived from the pre–World War I establishment of branches within the War Office, with their original designation having the prefix MO for Military Operations. They were changed to MI for *Military Intelligence* in 1916.

The principal MI organizations were

MI1	Directorate of Military Intelligence
MI1(b)	CYPTOANALYSIS Section (incorporated into the GOVERNMENT CODE AND CYPHER SCHOOL in 1919)
MI1(c)	Foreign Section
MI3	European Country Section
MI3(b)	German sub-section (changed to MI14 in 1940
MI5	Security Service (originally Security Intelligence Service)
MI6	SECRET INTELLIGENCE SERVICE
MI8	Radio Security Service 1
MI9	Escape and Evasion Service
MI11	Field Security Police
MI14	German Section
MI19	Combined Services Detailed Interrogational Center
MI(L)	War Office Liaison with Allied Intelligence Services

Not all of the above organizations were in existence at the same time.

MI5

British Security Service responsible for COUNTERESPIONAGE activities in the United Kingdom.

In March 1909, according to historian F. H. HINSLEY in *British Intelligence in the Second World War* (1990), "to the accompaniment of mounting public concern about alarming spy stories and lurid invasion novels . . .," a subcommittee of the Committee on Imperial Defence was set up to consider the nature and extent of the foreign espionage in Britain—and who should attempt to counter such activity. The report, issued in July 1909, found no doubt that "an extensive system of German espionage exists in this country. . . ." And that there was "no organization for . . . accurately identifying its extent and objectives."

In response to the report, the SECRET SERVICE BUREAU—formally the Imperial Security Intelligence Service—was created on Oct. 1, 1909, to serve as an intermediary between the War Office, the Admiralty, and Britain's spies and AGENTS abroad, as well as to undertake counterespionage functions for the British government. The bureau was divided into a Home Section and a Foreign Section.

Although the Secret Service Bureau was to be separate from any government department, it was placed administratively under the War Office's MO5, the special branch of the Military Operations Directorate responsible for questions relating to foreign aliens. Initially the bureau was organized into a naval branch, under Capt. MANSFIELD CUMMING, and a military branch, under Capt. VERNON KELL. Subsequent reorganizations gave Cumming, soon known by the designation "C," the responsibility for foreign intelligence collection while Kell, using "K," was assigned the spy-catching responsibilities of the bureau.

The bureau was busy as the British sought intelligence on Germany's military and naval buildups, while 12 spies were arrested in Britain before the outbreak of World War I. Further, there was evidence of a spy NETWORK in Britain that would be activated when war began.

At the outbreak of World War I, in Aug. 1914, the Home Section was placed directly under the War Office (MO5), being changed to MI5 when a new directorate of MILITARY INTELLIGENCE was established. The Foreign Section became MI1(c) and was made responsible for COUNTERESPIONAGE outside the British Empire as well as intelligence collection abroad.

Again, there were extensive espionage activities abroad and counterespionage work at home. At the start of the war the bureau arrested 21 suspected spies (one other escaped). Another 35 were apprehended during the war, and by 1916 there were probably no spies loose in Britain.

By the end of World War I the Foreign Section was moved to the Foreign Office and became known as the Secret Intelligence Service (SIS) with the designation of MI6. Cumming remained its chief until 1923. The Home Section evolved into the Security Service with the designation MI5. Kell held the position of Director-General of

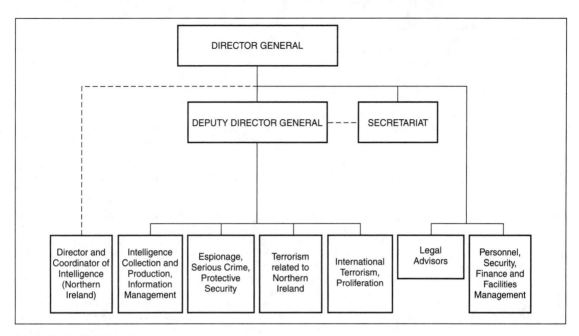

```
                    ┌─────────────────────┐
                    │  DIRECTOR GENERAL   │
                    └─────────────────────┘
                              │
      ┌───────────────────────┼───────────────────────────┐
      ┊            ┌──────────────────────┐   ┌──────────────────┐
      ┊            │ DEPUTY DIRECTOR      │- - -│   SECRETARIAT    │
      ┊            │ GENERAL              │   └──────────────────┘
      ┊            └──────────────────────┘
```

Security Service (MI5) Organization.

| Director and Coordinator of Intelligence (Northern Ireland) | Intelligence Collection and Production, Information Management | Espionage, Serious Crime, Protective Security | Terrorism related to Northern Ireland | International Terrorism, Proliferation | Legal Advisors | Personnel, Security, Finance and Facilities Management |

MI5 until 1940. (Although he used the initial "K," his successors never adopted it to the extent that the heads of MI6 employed the pseudonym "C".)

THE BOLSHIE THREAT

Between the world wars there were periodic efforts to restructure the British intelligence services, especially to combine MI5 and MI6. But in the period when Germany was not yet a threat, there was the threat of bolshevism as Soviet Russia sought to export world revolution. A high point in the MI5 efforts to uncover "bolshie" plots came in May 1927, when a massive MI5 and police raid was conducted against Soviet front activities in Britain (see ARCOS AFFAIR; MACARTNEY WILFRED). Indeed, despite the growth of fascist movements in Britain, especially the one led by crowd-drawing Blackshirt leader Sir Oswald Mosley, the Security Service and police believed that communists were a much graver threat to British society.

However, by the late 1930s it was obvious that Germany was again a threat to Britain, and there was renewed concern over potential German espionage. This concern was exacerbated as tens of thousands of refugees from Hitler's terror began to arrive in Britain.

The head of MI5 for most of World War II was Sir DAVID PETRIE, who served in that post from Nov. 1940 until 1946. Upon his appointment Petrie was given three simultaneous ranks in the Army Intelligence Corps: 2nd lieutenant, acting colonel, and local brigadier.

The MI5 organization appears to have been highly successful. Sixteen German spies were captured and executed in Britain during the war, and two Spaniards were

executed as spies at Gibraltar. Many other German agents were TURNED and forced to participate in a massive British DECEPTION scheme that made the German intelligence services—and Adolf Hitler himself—believe that they had an extensive and effective spy NETWORK in Britain. (See DOUBLE-CROSS SYSTEM.)

Only one man is known to have spied in Britain during the war and evaded capture or being "turned," JAN WILHELM TER BRAAK. At least two other men claimed to have parachuted into Britain during the war and successfully returned to Germany without being detected, but their stories can not be substantiated.

The basic wartime organization of MI5 had five major divisions:

A Administration
B Counterespionage
C Security
D Military Liaison
E Aliens
F Overseas Control

COLD WAR TRIBULATIONS

The successes that MI5 enjoyed in World War II were not to carry over into the lengthy Cold War period. There were several highly successful MI5 operations against the Soviet, French, and Egyptian embassies in London (see ENGULF). In addition, a number of Soviet agents operating in Britain were captured, mostly by MI5 sleuthing.

But during and after the war the British government was infiltrated by several Soviet MOLES, mostly young men recruited at Cambridge University (see CAMBRIDGE

SPY RING). Over time these men rose to senior positions in the Foreign Office, MI6, and other agencies.

The flight of DONALD MACLEAN from Britain in 1949 and of HAROLD (KIM) PHILBY from Beirut in 1963, both to the Soviet Union while under active MI5 investigation, led to public as well as official dismay about the agency. Indeed, there was concern—and even evidence—that MI5 itself was infiltrated by Soviet moles.

In 1963 it was discovered that ANTHONY BLUNT, who had served in MI5 during the war, was a Soviet mole. There were more suspects. A major 1960s investigation by a joint MI5-MI6 panel—given the CODE NAME of the "FLUENCY COMMITTEE"—investigated the charges and concluded that there were indications of almost continuous Soviet penetration of MI5 from 1942 to at least 1962. The committee's candidates for undiscovered Soviet moles in MI5 were Michael Hanley, at the time a branch director in MI5, and ROGER HOLLIS; at the time Hollis was the Director-General of MI5 and Henley later became Director-General.

Hanley and Hollis were interrogated, in a friendly manner, and although the results were inconclusive, their files were closed. (In 1981 Prime Minister Margaret Thatcher told the House of Commons that, after further review, it had been concluded that Hollis was not a spy. MI5 also announced that the accusation against Hollis was unfounded—a finding confirmed by former KGB INTELLIGENCE OFFICER OLEG GORDIEVSKY.

Hollis's successors, especially MARTIN FURNIVAL JONES, faced a considerable challenge to restore confidence in the agency, including helping sagging internal morale. Of particular concern to Furnival Jones and his successors was the reestablishment of close, open relations with the United States through the FBI and CIA, whose leaders regarded the penetration of British intelligence and the Foreign Office, as well as the U.S. atomic bomb project, as a major British security failure. Despite earlier suspicions that he was a Soviet mole, Michael Hanley succeeded Furnival Jones in 1972, causing much consternation in the U.S. INTELLIGENCE COMMUNITY, which felt that it had been "burned" continuously by the British failure to discover either the British members of the ATOMIC SPY RING or the Cambridge spy ring.

Two decades later, in Dec. 1991, the British public were surprised—and some old-timers were shocked—to open their morning newspapers and read that a 56-year-old mother of two had been named to head MI5. STELLA RIMINGTON was the first woman named to head an intelligence agency in any major country. She was also the first head of MI5 to be named officially in the press. However, the official statement announcing her appointment noted: "no photographic or interview facilities are being provided in connection with this appointment." (In 1993, for the first time, the head of MI6, Sir Colin McColl, was officially identified.)

The official revelations continued when, on July 16, 1993, MI5 published the glossy 36-page booklet *The Security Service.* Inside were details of MI5's activities, the exact wording of its charter, and even an organization chart. It was revealed that MI5 had a staff of 2,000 employees. Also released at the time were photos of Rimington, the head who brought the Security Service out of the shadows of the Cold War.

The Security Service listed six functions of MI5: (1) counter-terrorism ("Irish organisations currently pose the principal terrorist threats to the security of the United Kingdom"); (2) counterespionage ("It is a fact that the old threat [Soviet Union and Warsaw Pact] no longer exists, but it is equally true that spying continues"); (3) countersubversion ("Since the collapse of Soviet Communism . . . [these efforts] now represent less than five percent of the investigative work of the Service"); (4) protective security; (5) security intelligence; and (6) record keeping.

Counterterrorism efforts take up some 70 percent of the Security Service's resources, with about 26 percent being allocated to international security threats and 44 percent to Irish and domestic concerns. In October 1992 responsibility for leading the intelligence effort against Irish terrorism in the United Kingdom was transferred to the Metropolitan Police. But MI5 continued to supply intelligence to the police and, between 1992 and 1999, this work led to 21 convictions for terrorist-related offenses. The intelligence also prevented several terrorist attacks, including potentially disastrous bomb explosions in London. In 1996, Parliament gave MI5 the power to support law enforcement agencies in solving "serious crime," a category that seems to be left purposely vague.

MI5 works closely with MI6 and the military intelligence activities—including the Special Air Service and Special Boat Service—in carrying out counterterrorism and TERRORIST INTELLIGENCE activities.

Upon taking over as Director-General of MI5 from Rimington on April 1, 1996, Stephen Lander emphasized further the counterterrorism role in the wake of a renewed bombing campaign by the Irish Republican Army (IRA). Lander, former director of Irish counterterrorism in MI5, was known to have strong feelings on this issue.

The second woman to head MI5 is Eliza Manningham-Buller, who took office in Oct. 2002. A career MI5 officer, she was born Elizabeth Lydia Manningham-Buller, a daughter of Sir Reginald (later Lord Dilhorne), who served as Attorney General and Lord Chancellor in the Conservative administrations of Harold Macmillan and Alec Douglas-Home. She read English at Lady Margaret Hall, Oxford, where it is believed MI5 first attempted to recruit her, much to her father's distress. She joined MI5 three years later, in 1974. Manningham-Buller is considered to be an expert on counter-terrorism.

DIRECTORS-GENERAL

The Directors-General of MI5 were:

1909–1940	Maj. Gen. Sir Vernon Kell
1940–1946	Sir David Petrie
1946–1953	Sir PERCY SILLITOE
1953–1956	Sir DICK WHITE
1956–1965	Sir ROGER HOLLIS
1965–1972	Sir Martin Furnival Jones
1972–1978	Sir Michael Hanley

MI6

British Secret Intelligence Service (SIS), responsible for foreign intelligence. The SIS also had its origins in the SE-CRET SERVICE BUREAU created in 1909 (see MI5, above).

Upon the outbreak of World War I in Aug. 1914, the bureau's Foreign Section became MI1(c) and was made responsible for COUNTERESPIONAGE activities outside of the British Empire as well as intelligence collection abroad. The Foreign Section was shifted back to the War Office from 1916 to 1918, when it was placed under the aegis of the Foreign Office. In 1921 the Secret Intelligence Service (SIS) was established as Britain's foreign intelligence agency under the control of the Foreign Office. Capt. MANSFIELD CUMMING (known as "C") was head of the Foreign Section/SIS/MI6 from 1909 until 1923, stepping down a few months before his death.

The principal TARGET of Cumming's AGENTS at this time was Germany. The intelligence staff of the British Expeditionary Force in France, which was responsible for TACTICAL INTELLIGENCE, was performing poorly. Cumming's efforts, involving higher levels of intelligence collection, yielded greater success. He placed local directors of intelligence, who reported to his headquarters, in all of the theaters.

Cumming became involved in POLITICAL INTELLIGENCE as well. When Czar Nicholas II abdicated on March 16, 1917, it became expedient for Britain to support the efforts of Aleksandr Kerensky to form a new government that would keep Russia in the war against Germany. To this end, the British government sent him funds via an office that Cumming had set up in New York City. The courier used to carry the funds was Cumming's agent W. SOMERSET MAUGHAM. Maugham then became a go-between for Prime Minister Lloyd George and Kerensky. Meanwhile, other British intelligence agents were at work in revolution-torn Russia, most notably Maj. STEPHEN ALLEY and the irrepressible SIDNEY REILLY.

It is not clear what Reilly's mandate was, nor from whom he got it. He had earlier been in Russia representing Cumming—whom he referred to, sometimes even affectionately, as "that one-legged bastard"—as well as German shipyards, and himself. Reilly, a staunch royalist, met with Bolshevik leaders and then tried to foment a counterrevolution. He was unquestionably involved in the attempted assassination of Bolshevik leader V. I. Lenin, which left Lenin badly wounded.

Reilly's complex and grandiose plans to retake Russia (and set himself up as prime minister) ended in disaster. Cumming never again employed him—at least not officially. But he continued to send his other agents abroad. The March 1921 trade agreement between Britain and Russia, which constituted de facto recognition of the Bolshevik regime, prohibited each country from undertaking espionage activities against the other. This, however, did little to deter Cumming or his Russian counterpart, FELIKS DZERZHINSKY, from their profession. The British were particularly concerned that the Russians might interfere in the ongoing conflict in Ireland. And there was soon evidence that the Russians were both spying in Britain and supporting a communist movement, which was particularly troublesome as the economic situation in Britain deteriorated.

(Significantly, in 1919 the highly successful Admiralty CRYPTANALYSIS program, known as ROOM 40, and the small War Office cryptanalysis effort were merged to establish the GOVERNMENT CODE AND CYPHER SCHOOL, which was also placed under Cumming's overall direction. It was soon able to break the diplomatic cipher used by the Russians to communicate with their embassy in London.)

Reilly became a major problem for MI6 in 1924. Although by that time living in the United States, he was financially supporting anti-Bolshevik movements in Europe. In 1924 he was lured back to the Soviet Union (established in 1922) by a DECEPTION operation known as THE TRUST. When he disappeared across the Finnish border, his wife began demanding help from MI6 officers in determining his fate. (The Trust was in fact a front for the Russian intelligence service, then known as OGPU.)

In 1923 the Secret Intelligence Service gained a new Director-General, another Navy officer, Rear Adm. HUGH SINCLAIR, who had served as DIRECTOR OF NAVAL INTELLIGENCE immediately after the war. There was overlap in his intelligence efforts against the Soviets and the German situation. Under the terms of the Versailles Treaty, the Germans were forbidden from developing military aviation as well as certain other weapons. German leaders—including Hermann Göring—went to Russia to establish secret training facilities and programs and to work with the Soviets in weapons development. And, as the Soviet Union began its own industrial and military rebuilding after revolution and civil war, it considered Great Britain its principal enemy.

Germany began rebuilding its military strength in the 1930s, causing MI6 agents to work harder to determine the size and scope of the rearmament efforts. But MI6 resources were too little for the foreign intelligence effort needed to support Britain's worldwide interests. There was little warning of Italy's African adventure into Abyssinia (Ethiopia) in 1935, or of Germany's occupation of the Rhineland that same year. MI6 also provided insufficient notice of Hitler's intentions—and capabilities—when Germany took over the Sudetenland and invaded Czechoslovakia (1938) and Poland (1939).

British intelligence historian NIGEL WEST[p] describes the state of MI6 at the beginning of World War II in *MI6: British Secret Intelligence Service Operations 1909–45* (1983):

Admiral Hugh Sinclair's first sixteen years as Chief of SIS were made extremely difficult for him because he was starved of funds. This made him close much needed [foreign] Stations and keep on too many rundown old pros from the Great War. Nor did he use what monies he had to great advantage: he spent too much on Russian intelligence from gullible emigre sources and too little elsewhere. As a result, he was caught napping by the rise of Nazism.

During the inter-war period, SIS lacked clout in Whitehall. Cumming's Russian reports had lost the Service credibility, so that when officers . . . did field useful data, they were not believed. This lack of enthusiasm for SIS deepened in Whitehall when the Abyssinian and Rhineland *coups d'état* arrived unforeseen and unheralded by SIS. Sinclair's belated recognition of Germany as its principal target had meant that when Whitehall's demands for German intelligence began to increase, Sinclair was in no position to deliver. Good sources take years to develop and the hostile security climate in Nazi Germany made SIS's task an arduous one.

In 1938, MI6 formed the innocuous sounding Statistical Department of the War Office, which was to be devoted to "ungentlemanly war." Two months after the war began, on Nov. 4, 1939, Adm. Sinclair died in office. His successor, Col. STEWART MENZIES, also held the post for well over a decade. Menzies, later promoted to major general, was responsible for much of Britain's successful intelligence activities during the war, including the ULTRA cryptanalysis efforts. There were some successes in the months before Britain went to war. For example, Group Capt. F. W. WINTERBOTHAM was able to carry out extensive collection missions to Germany—even meeting Adolf Hitler. Another success was obtaining high-altitude aerial photography of Germany. The Royal Air Force had no photographic RECONNAISSANCE unit; beginning in March 1939, MI6 and the French sponsored an Australian, SIDNEY COTTON, who made spy flights over Germany in a commercial aircraft with hidden cameras.

But there were also monumental failures. In the VENLO INCIDENT on the Dutch-German frontier, two MI6 officers were kidnapped by the Germans in Nov. 1939. The two officers, Capt. PAYNE S. BEST and Maj. H. RICHARD STEVENS, subsequently revealed many of MI6's secrets, including the names of British agents, to the Germans.

Despite this inauspicious beginning, MI6 achieved considerable success in World War II. Together with the ULTRA successes against German communications (see ENGIMA, CRYPTANALYSIS), MI6 was able to provide Allied leaders with extensive and useful knowledge of German and Italian capabilities and, to a large degree, intentions.

Menzies was able to work well with U.S. and the other British intelligence agencies. There were many problems, especially in dealing with the U.S. OFFICE OF STRATEGIC SERVICES (OSS) and British Special Operations Executive (SOE), but in the course of the overall war effort they were minor. (This is demonstrated by the actual cooperation among the services, and the awarding of decorations; Menzies was awarded the U.S. Legion of Merit.)

During World War II, MI6 comprised two major branches, designated Y for headquarters activities and YP for overseas stations. Y had the following sections:

I   Political
II   Military
III Naval
IV   Air
V   COUNTERESPIONAGE
VI   Industrial
VII Financial
VIII Communications
IX   CIPHER
X   Press

In the summer of 1944 a new section was established, given the (existing) designation IX: Soviet espionage and subversion. The head of the new section was a veteran of Section V (counterespionage). He was HAROLD (KIM) PHILBY, one of the Soviet Union's most successful spies.

The Cold War brought new challenges to British intelligence, as former ally Josef Stalin was rapidly transformed into the new enemy. Soviet intelligence had gained a major foothold in the British intelligence services during the war, mainly through the efforts of the CAMBRIDGE SPY RING. Besides Philby, who had been considered a rapidly rising star in MI6—possibly even a future director-general—there was JOHN CAIRNCROSS, who served at the GOVERNMENT CODE AND CYPHER SCHOOL as well as in MI6, and GEORGE BLAKE who began spying for the Soviets after the Korean War. Further, the close relationship between MI5 and MI6 meant that ANTHONY BLUNT and other Soviet MOLES in the Security Service often had access to MI6 material.

(One of the strangest cases was that of CHARLES H. ELLIS, an MI6 officer in World War II who sold intelligence to both the Germans and Soviets; his spying for the Soviets may have continued after the war.)

These Soviet penetrations revealed much of British and American intelligence operations to the Soviet intelligence services. The Allied failures during the Cold War that can definitely be attributed to these penetrations include the loss of agents sent into Albania and elsewhere, and the Soviet knowledge of the BERLIN TUNNEL project. Scores of other British-U.S. intelligence operations were also compromised.

MI6 itself was responsible for several intelligence failures (and embarrassments). In 1956, for example, MI6 sent overage and overweight ex-Navy diver LIONEL CRABB on a secret mission in Portsmouth Harbor to examine the underwater hull of the new Soviet cruiser *Ordzbonikidze,* which had brought Soviet leaders Nikita Khrushchev and N. A. Bulganin to Britain. He never returned, and a headless body was later found floating in the harbor, presumably the remains of Crabb.

Still, MI6 recorded several major successes. Soviet intelligence officer OLEG PENKOVSKY had first approached the U.S. CIA seeking to reveal military secrets of the Soviet armed forces. Ignored by the Americans, he approached a British businessman, GREVILLE WYNNE, who passed on the contact to MI6. Although the British had to "share" Penkovsky with the CIA, for a brief period in the early 1960s Soviet military policies and weapons were laid bare to the British and American political and military leaders.

There have been other MI6 successes, although few as dramatic and productive as the short-lived Penkovsky triumph. The Secret Intelligence Service, unlike the Security Service beginning with STELLA RIMINGTON, has not yet "gone public." It is unlikely to do so as, despite the end of the Cold War, MI6 agents are still being sent into foreign lands on dangerous missions. Even so, in the spirit of going public, MI5 has revealed its address: 85 Albert Embankment, Vauxhall Cross, London (known to MI5 workers there as "Legoland").

Like MI5 and the intelligence agencies of many other nations, MI6 has given its its highest priority to TERRORIST INTELLIGENCE. Soon after the Sept. 11, 2001, terrorist attacks in the United States, MI6 began rapidly expanding its counter-terrorism unit. MI6's budgets had been drastically cut back following the end of the Cold War. "Priorities and the working environment have both changed," an official said. "This will not be like VIENNA or Geneva."

During the 2004 debate in the United States and Britain over the accuracy of reports that Iraqi leader Saddam Hussein was developing "weapons of mass destruction," MI6 chief Sir Richard Dearlove had a key role in the controversy. However, when the Foreign Office announced in Aug. 2003 that Dearlove would step down the following August, the official spokesman strongly rebutted rumors that he was leaving early because of differences with other ministers over Iraqi weapon issues.

A report in *The Observer* newspaper had suggested that Dearlove had decided to retire early because he was dismayed by "the visible rift between his organization and Downing Street" [i.e., the Prime Minister] on intelligence on Iraq. But a Foreign Office spokesman told CNN it was a scheduled retirement and media reports linking the decision to intelligence on Iraq were "entirely fabricated." The official said that when Dearlove goes he would have been in the post for five years—the normal term of duty for "C."

DIRECTORS-GENERAL

The Directors-General of MI6 were:

1909–1923	Capt. Sir Mansfield Cumming
1923–1939	Adm. Sir Hugh Sinclair
1939–1952	Maj. Gen. Sir Stewart Menzies
1953–1956	Sir John Sinclair
1956–1968	Sir DICK WHITE
1968–1973	Sir John Rennie
1973–1978	Sir MAURICE OLDFIELD
1979–1982	Sir Arthur Franks
1982–1985	Sir Colin Figures
1985–1989	Sir Christopher Curwen
1989–1994	Sir Colin McColl
1994–1999	David Spedding
1999–2004	Sir Richard Dearlove

The indefatigable Dick White, a veteran of MI5 service in World War II, is the only person to have been head of both MI5 and MI6, serving a total of 15 years as head of major intelligence services.

Michelson, Alice

East German COURIER for the KGB who was exchanged, along with three other Soviet Bloc AGENTS for 25 persons described as "helpful" to the United States.

She was arrested in New York in Oct. 1984 as she was boarding a flight to Czechoslovakia. Hidden in a cigarette pack were tapes of classified material given to her by a U.S. Army sergeant claiming to be working for the KGB. In June 1985, before she went on trial, she was exchanged in the SPY SWAP.

Microdot

The photographic reduction of writing or other material to facilitate transfer from one location to another without detection. The Germans are generally given credit for inventing the microdot. However, the French used microdots during the siege of Paris by the Prussians in 1870. Microdots at that time were 70 millimeters in size and contained 300,000 characters; microdots were sent across enemy lines by BALLOONS and PIGEON POST.

ALEXANDER FOOTE, a Soviet AGENT, wrote in his *Handbook for Spies* (1949) that the Soviet intelligence services had used microdots before World War II. Even if the Germans did not invent microdots, they made important contributions to the development of microdot technology and used microdots aggressively before and during World War II.

The United States learned of microdots through DUSKO POPOV, a DOUBLE AGENT who came to the United States in 1941. Although the British were controlling Popov and advised J. EDGAR HOOVER, director of the FBI, of his activities, Hoover directed that Popov leave the United States. After the war, Hoover wrote that Popov was a German AGENT who had "revealed" the German microdot equipment to the FBI. The British also used microdots during the war.

Because the preparation of microdots requires special photographic equipment, which would be suspect unless the spy had appropriate cover as a professional photographer or was an established amateur photographer, microphotography is usually confined to headquarters-to-agent communication. One microdot device used by the Germans was a six-foot-long optical bench weighing 4,200 pounds and employing handmade emulsion on glass sheets. Another model fit into a satchel and used high-resolution emulsion and thin film backing.

Microphotography also includes the use of positive-type film (as opposed to negative-type film); a bleaching of the image prior to dispatch occurs so that the "dot" appears as a clear piece of cellophane or thin plastic. This product of microphotography, referred to as a "mikrat," was extensively developed by the Germans during World

War II. Modern mikrats measure 1 mm by 1 mm and were probably employed by the Soviet intelligence services.

In the late 1950s the KGB was reportedly training agents to produce microdots by using a 35-mm reflex camera with the document to be photographed laid on a flat table. The agent would then clamp the camera to a chair (or any object that could hold the camera steady) and take the picture. After development, the negative would be placed between two glass slides to hold it flat; a piece of ordinary cellophane was then used to make it light-sensitive with specially prepared chemicals provided by the Soviets. The agent would then put a piece of white paper on the flat surface, clamping a small microdot camera over the paper.

The Soviets also used a microdot camera in the form of a small brass tube, about 1½ inches long with lenses at both ends. Exactly 35 inches above the bottom end of the microdot camera, a glass plate was mounted with the negative and a three-power hand magnifying glass held above the glass plate. Above that a 100-watt, clear glass electric light shone through the magnifying glass and then the negative and microdot camera. The agent raised or lowered the glass until he could focus the negative on the tiniest possible spot on a piece of white paper. He then marked the spot with an *x*, turned off the light, and, after about three minutes, took the cellophane out and developed it. After the cellophane was developed, he looked for a black dot about the size of a period. Using a razor blade, he then cut out the spot (microdot).

The agent made a slit 1/16-inch deep in one edge of a postcard, picked up the microdot with tweezers, and slipped it into the slot. He sealed the slot with a paste made from flour and water (because other pastes contain bone marrow that shows up under ultraviolet light).

Midas

First U.S. early warning SATELLITE, designed to detect the launching of long-range ballistic missiles. Conceived in the 1950s—before the Soviet orbiting of the first Sputnik in 1957—the project was designated MIDAS, an acronym for Missile Defense Alarm System. It was one of the early satellite efforts proposed by the U.S. Air Force. (See SAMOS.)

MIDAS was fitted with infrared scanners. Eight satellites, equally spaced in two orbital rings, were to provide complete coverage of missile launch sites in the Soviet Union. The eight satellites would be needed to maintain continuous SURVEILLANCE (rather than RECONNAISSANCE) of the sites.

The first MIDAS test vehicle was launched from Cape Canaveral, Fla., on Feb. 26, 1960. The launch initially went well, but when the Agena A satellite separated from the Atlas D booster there was an explosion. The second MIDAS launch on May 24, 1960, went almost perfectly. The Agena A sensor package—with 3,246 pounds of infrared sensor and data-link equipment—entered an orbit from 292 to 322 miles above the Earth.

Although fitted with batteries for a 28-day flight, the data link failed after 16 orbits.

Additional tests followed. There were problems: too many false alarms and too little reliability. In 1961 the MIDAS program was changed from a development effort to a test program, given the designation Program 461. The program seemed doomed until a MIDAS was launched on April 9, 1962—a year before the original MIDAS plan had envisioned an operational system.

The MIDAS went into an orbit 1,749 to 2,102 miles high; the satellite sensors operated for six weeks. During that time it successfully detected the launching of nine U.S. ballistic missiles. Although there would be more failures, the April 9 satellite had demonstrated the validity of the concept, especially since it detected the solid-propellant Minuteman and Polaris missile launches, which had smaller infrared signatures at launch than did larger, liquid-propellant missiles.

Despite additional successes, development of MIDAS halted in Nov. 1963 because of the need to detect submarine-launched missiles and the smaller, intermediate-range ballistic missiles. When flight-testing of modified satellites began in June 1966, there were again problems, and by the end of the year the follow-on MIDAS program was canceled.

In its place the United States initiated Program 949, a larger satellite that could be placed in a geosynchronous orbit 23,500 miles above the earth. This meant that only a few satellites, orbiting at the same speed as the earth, would be relatively stationary and hence would provide continuous surveillance of Soviet missile launch sites.

The first Program 949 launch occurred on Aug. 6, 1968. It entered a near-geosynchronous orbit of 19,686 to 24,769 miles above the earth. This and follow-up launches were intended primarily to watch the ocean-operating areas of Soviet ballistic missile submarines, which were of increasing concern to U.S. defense planners. (Land-based radars in Greenland, Alaska, and Canada were positioned to detect Soviet ballistic missiles during their early, boost phase trajectory.)

More Program 949 launches followed, some completely successful, some less so. While a final launch on Dec. 1972 was a good one, the whole program was looked at as a development effort, paving the way for the definitive U.S. early warning satellite—the Program 647.

The first Program 647 launch on Nov. 6, 1970, was only a partial success, as a geosynchronous orbit was not achieved. This was a 2,500-pound satellite with four 23-foot solar panels for recharging the batteries, allowing essentially unlimited endurance.

The second Program 647 launch on May 5, 1971, reached a perfect orbit. The flight time for a ballistic missile launched from the Soviet Union toward the United States would have a flight time of some 30 minutes. The Program 647 satellite could detect the launch and give essentially instantaneous warning; after six minutes it could provide sufficient data to determine the trajectory and, hence, target of the missile.

The satellite surveillance system was now operational. Its success led to an unprecedented amount of detail being made available to the public in 1973–1974, at which time the program was renamed the Defense Support Program (DSP). By the mid-1970s three DSP satellites were in geosynchronous orbit, two over the Western Hemisphere and one over the Eastern Hemisphere, providing continuous coverage of Soviet and Chinese launch sites. DSP satellites remain aloft today.

In addition to fixed ground receiving stations in the United States and at Alice Springs in Australia, several mobile ground receiving stations were developed. Subsequently, the Air Force's flying command posts (E-4 Looking Glass) and Airborne Warning And Control System (E-3 AWACS) aircraft were fitted with DSP receivers, providing a high degree of survivability for U.S. nuclear retaliation decision makers.

While designed to detect ballistic missile launches, the infrared detectors in these satellites can also detect some turbojet aircraft using afterburners for acceleration, especially when over water. However, this capability is rarely discussed by U.S. officials in public forums.

Midway

The "turning point" of World War II in the Pacific. The Battle of Midway ended with an inferior U.S. naval force decisively defeating a Japanese fleet attempting to capture Midway Island in the Hawaiian Islands and force the U.S. fleet into a decisive battle. The American victory at Midway was possible because U.S. Navy CRYPTOLOGISTS were able to read the Japanese naval CODE. (See NAVY COMMUNICATIONS INTELLIGENCE.)

Japanese strategy called for the capture of Midway and the western Aleutian Islands to create a Japanese defense line from Kiska in the Aleutians through Midway, Wake, the Marshall Islands and the Gilbert Islands, then west to Port Moresby and the Dutch East Indies. The capture of Midway would also be a response to the April 1942 bomber raid on Japan led by Lt. Col. James (Jimmy) Doolittle, would deprive the United States of a forward base for submarines, and would serve as a stepping stone for the capture of Hawaii.

U.S. Navy cryptologists were able to determine that a major Japanese operation was forthcoming but could not identify the target. Several Japanese CODE NAMES for places were being used. One of the U.S. Navy cryptologists, Comdr. W. J. HOLMES, suggested having the U.S. commander on Midway send a message to Pearl Harbor that the island's water-distilling unit had broken down, using a low-grade code that the Japanese could probably decipher. A short time later the cryptologists read a coded Japanese message stating that said there was a shortage of water on AF. Thus the Americans learned that the target was Midway, AF having been previously identified as the target of the Japanese operation.

The Japanese committed almost every available warship to the Midway-Aleutians assault, including eight of Japan's 10 aircraft carriers. U.S. Navy codebreakers had been piecing together a relatively accurate picture of this plan. Over the objections of some staff officers, who were skeptical about the codebreakers' analysis, the U.S. Pacific area commander, Adm. Chester W. Nimitz, decided to send his only three aircraft carriers against the Japanese forces led by Adm. ISOROKU YAMAMOTO. The Japanese were taken by surprise and, in the ensuing battle on June 4–5, 1942, four Japanese carriers and a Japanese cruiser were sunk by U.S. carrier dive bombers; another cruiser was severely damaged. All 250 planes on the carriers were lost, along with many of their trained pilots and maintenance crews. U.S. losses were one aircraft carrier and a destroyer.

This was the first decisive defeat suffered by the Japanese Navy since 1592. The battle also marked the zenith of Japanese expansion in the Pacific.

Also see Capt. JOSEPH J. ROCHEFORT.

Mielke, Erich

(b. 1907 d. 2000)

Head of East Germany's secret police, the Stasi (MFS) from 1957 to the fall of the BERLIN Wall in 1989.

Born in Berlin, Mielke became a member of the Communist Party in 1925 and fled Nazi Germany in the 1930s. In the Soviet Union he attended the elite International Lenin School in Moscow. He served in the Soviet-organized International Brigade that fought in the Spanish Civil War. After World War II he helped to organize police forces in Soviet-occupied eastern Germany and when East Germany was founded in 1950 he became deputy chief of state security, taking over the Stasi in 1957.

After German reunification, investigators opened a safe in Mielke's ornate office and found evidence showing that in Aug. 1931, as a member of a communist paramilitary unit, he killed two policemen during a riot in Berlin. Put on trial in the new united Germany, he was sentenced in 1993 to six years in prison. He was released after two years on humanitarian grounds. He died in a nursing home.

He was not prosecuted for running the Stasi or for the deaths of people shot at the Berlin Wall.

Mikhaylov, Gen. of the Army Vladlen Mikhaylovich

(b. 1925)

Chief of the GRU, Soviet MILITARY INTELLIGENCE, from 1987 to 1991. He had no background in military intelligence and no experience with foreign activities before becoming chief of the GRU.

Mikhaylov entered the Soviet Army in 1942 and became an officer upon completion of military school two years later. He served initially in the Far East, completed the prestigious Frunze Military Academy (war college) in 1954, and went on to command an Army division. He was chief of staff of the Turkistan Military District prior to becoming chief of the GRU.

Mikrat

The product of microphotography, as used in MICRODOTS.

Military Intelligence

(MI)

(1) Designation scheme for British intelligence/security activities (see MI); (2) The end product of the collection, processing, production, and dissemination of information related to foreign military forces (see INTELLIGENCE CYCLE). Military intelligence is usually concerned with foreign ground forces and is distinct from NAVAL INTELLIGENCE and, by some interpretations, air intelligence.

Also see ARMY INTELLIGENCE, ARMY INTELLIGENCE AND SECURITY COMMAND.

Military Intelligence Division

SEE ARMY INTELLIGENCE, U.S.

Miller, Richard

(b. 1937)

First FBI agent ever convicted of spying for the Soviet Union.

Miller, an overweight (250 pounds), inefficient, and sloppy agent, joined the FBI in 1964 but rarely acted like an FBI agent. In 1982 he was transferred from the local FBI office in Riverside, Calif., to the Los Angeles field office and assigned to the COUNTERINTELLIGENCE division, at that time a safer place to keep him under supervision than divisions concerned with domestic crimes. His record was poor. He peddled Amway products out of his FBI car, used his badge to cadge candy from a 7-11 store, and sold FBI information to a private investigator.

He once lost his gun and his credentials. One night, when he locked up the Los Angeles field office, he left the key in the lock. It was still there the next morning. Miller's reputation, as he himself put it, "wasn't very good, to say the least." Yet, Miller usually received an "excellent" rating—as did about 90 percent of all agents.

He was constantly behind on paperwork. A former colleague described him as "lunchy," meaning "a guy that's unkempt, disheveled. Looks like he's got bread crumbs and soup spots on his shirt and tie." His own lawyer said of him, "He was certainly no Efrem Zimbalist, Jr., and he was, in fact, much closer to an overweight Inspector Clouseau."

The father of eight children, Miller was always scrambling for money. He lived alone during the week in Lynwood, a Los Angeles suburb, and on weekends drove more than 100 miles to northern San Diego County, where he and his wife tried to run an avocado ranch that produced more debt than fruit.

The FBI physical standard for an agent of Miller's height—5 feet, 10 inches—was a maximum of 193 pounds. When Miller's weight reached 250 pounds, he was suspended for two weeks and told to lose his excess pounds. A few weeks after this low point in his career, a beautiful 34-year-old Soviet émigrée, SVETLANA OGOROD-NIKOV, asked him if he wanted to become a spy.

One day in Aug. 1984, FBI agents, who were keeping the Soviet Consulate in San Francisco under SURVEIL-LANCE, observed a woman getting out of a car later traced to the FBI field office in Los Angeles. She was Svetlana Ogorodnikov. The FBI surveillance team assumed that an agent from the Los Angeles office was on a case that took him to the consulate.

What they did not know at the time was that when Ogorodnikov went into the consulate she had in her hands Miller's badge and credentials to prove that the man in the car parked outside was indeed an FBI agent. She also had a copy of an FBI manual on the collection of intelligence. Miller had copied the manual on the Los Angeles field office's photocopying machine. The FBI later described the 24-page classified manual as a guide that could give the Soviets "a detailed picture of FBI and U.S. intelligence activities, techniques and requirements."

The consulate was kept under continuous surveillance because it was a Soviet spy nest. The FBI had once even tried to dig a tunnel under it. The burrowing had been detected, and so the counterintelligence agents had to be satisfied with conventional surveillance techniques—tapping phones, following Soviets believed to be KGB officers, and photographing people who entered and left the consulate, which was known as KGB West. Miller could not have picked a better place in North America to be seen by FBI spy hunters.

When Miller became a counterintelligence agent in 1982, Svetlana Ogorodnikov was the responsibility of an FBI agent, John E. Hunt, assigned to watch on the large Soviet émigré community in West Hollywood. Hunt met with her many times, once to accompany her to the office of a physician. Hunt said Ogorodmkov was being examined for "a rare blood disease." She later said that Hunt took her to the physician for an abortion and strongly implied that he was the father, apparently not knowing that the agent had had a vasectomy in 1960. When he retired in 1984, Ogorodnikov was handed over to Miller.

Ogorodnikov was believed to be a KGB "contact agent," who spotted potential recruits for KGB officers under diplomatic COVER. The field office watched her because she was not an ordinary Russian émigrée. She and her husband, Nikolay Ogorodnikov, had immigrated to the United States in 1973. Other émigrés called them pro-Soviet informers working for the KGB. She boasted of her connections with the Soviet Consulate and, unlike other émigrés, was allowed to travel back and forth to the Soviet Union.

After the first rendezvous observed by the FBI agents in San Francisco, she and Miller had what the FBI called "numerous personal meetings." They became lovers. Svetlana said she tried to resist Miller's sexual advances and submitted only "because he scared me." Claiming to be a KGB major, she promised $65,000 in gold and money—and a $675 Burberry trenchcoat—if he would spy for the KGB. The FBI stepped up its surveillance and began building a case in an operation given the CODE NAME "Whipworm."

She asked Miller to learn the whereabouts of KGB Maj. STANISLAV LEVCHENKO, who had defected, and Victor Belenko, a Soviet pilot who defected in a MiG-25 he flew to Japan in 1976. They had been condemned to death in absentia in the Soviet Union and presumably would be targets for KGB assassins. Miller did not provide the information.

In Sept. 1984, as the FBI was about to close in, Miller told his superior that for months he had been working on his own to penetrate the KGB by becoming a DOUBLE AGENT. He said that he had hoped to trick Svetlana—and the KGB—into thinking that he was a traitor as part of his plan. He said he also wanted to "prove to myself and to the rest of the FBI that I wasn't the klutz that everybody thought I was."

After a marathon interrogation that spanned several days, FBI agents arrested Miller. In a search of his apartment they found secret and confidential documents. The Ogorodmkovs were also arrested, and a search of their apartment produced such standard TRADECRAFT tools as ONE-TIME PADS, SECRET WRITING material, and photographic equipment for concealing material in MICRODOTS.

Svetlana and Nikolay interrupted their trial by pleading guilty in a deal that sentenced Svetlana to 18 years and Nikolay to eight years. She agreed to testify against Miller, who was charged with conspiracy to commit espionage and passing classified documents. Miller's defense attorneys virtually conceded the FBI case against their client, claiming, however, that he had merely bumbled while trying to carry out his self-appointed mission as a KGB MOLE for the FBI. The jury could not agree on his guilt, and the judge declared a mistrial in Nov. 1985.

In a second trial three months later, Svetlana testified—as a defense witness. She now insisted that Miller was innocent and that she had made a plea bargain to save herself from a life sentence. Under cross-examination, prosecutors revealed that she had confessed secretly to the judge at her interrupted trial. This time the jury found Miller guilty of six counts of espionage. He was sentenced to two life terms plus 50 years and fined $60,000.

In May 1994, Miller was released from prison following the reduction of his sentence to 13 years by a federal court judge.

Minaret

Highly classified, COMPARTMENTED program of the NSA to intercept communications from foreigners to foreign nationals or American citizens in the United States suspected of involvement with civil disturbances, especially regarding opposition to the Vietnam War. The July 1, 1969, charter for Minaret—itself a TOP SECRET word—called for the monitoring of "communications concerning individuals or organizations, involved in civil disturbances, antiwar movements/demonstrations and Military deserters involved in the antiwar movements. . . ."

Also see DOMESTIC INTELLIGENCE and Operation SHAMROCK.

Mincemeat

Ingenious British DECEPTION operation during World War II to make the German High Command believe that the Allies would invade the Balkans in mid-1943 instead of Sicily, the real objective. The operation called for making the Germans believe that they had, by accident, intercepted highly confidential documents that foretold Allied war plans. If successful, the Germans would divert troops to the Balkans at the cost of defending Sicily.

British NAVAL INTELLIGENCE took the corpse of a man who had recently died in England and preserved his body in dry ice. They quickly developed a persona for Major Martin of the Royal Marines: William Martin, a captain and acting major, born in Cardiff, Wales, in 1907, and assigned to Headquarters, Combined Operations.

The corpse was outfitted in a Marine officer's uniform, complete with service ribbons, identity disks and papers, theater ticket stubs, pound notes, loose change, a statement from his club for lodging in London, and so on. Most important, chained to him was a locked briefcase with official documents and a personal letter from one senior Allied officer to another. The letter and papers indicated that Major Martin was en route by aircraft from England to Allied headquarters in North Africa.

Major Martin was then placed in a sealed steel canister and taken on board the British SUBMARINE SERAPH, which sailed to a position off of Huelva on the coast of Spain. There, early in the morning of April 30, Lt. N. L. A. (Bill) Jewell, the submarine's commanding officer, and his officers, sworn to secrecy, opened the canister on the deck of the surfaced submarine. (The crew was told they were deploying a secret weather reporting device.) Major Martin was fitted with a life jacket and, after a final check of the body and its outfit, the 39th Psalm was read and the body gently pushed into the sea where the tide would bring it ashore.

The body, washing toward the shore, was found by a fisherman on April 30, and German operatives in Spain quickly learned of it. While local British officials, who also learned of the body, demanded its return, the briefcase was carefully opened by the Germans and photographed, the papers returned, and then given to British diplomats by Spanish officials. The photographs were rushed to BERLIN for analysis by German intelligence. Major Martin's death was mentioned in the next British casualty list and a month later published in *The Times* to further support the ruse. (It had previously been announced that several British officers had died when their aircraft was lost at sea en route to Gibraltar.)

When Major Martin's body and possessions were finally turned over to British officials and the briefcase examined, it was found that the papers had been read and carefully refolded and resealed—obviously by the Germans. The British Chiefs of Staff wired to Prime Minister Winston Churchill, then in the United States: "Mincemeat Swallowed Whole." Churchill's Chief of Staff, Gen.

Hastings L. Ismay, later wrote: "The operation succeeded beyond our wildest dreams. To have spread-eagled the German defensive effort right across Europe, even to the extent of sending German vessels away from Sicily itself, was a remarkable achievement."

"Major Martin" was laid to rest in the graveyard at Huelva. His real name was not revealed until 2003, when he was finally identified as Glyndwr Michael, who committed suicide in a warehouse in London. He was 34 years old.

The main instigator of the operation was EWEN MONTAGU, a lawyer who served in British naval intelligence during the war and afterwards became the Judge Advocate of the Fleet. He received the Military Order of the British Empire for conceiving Operation Mincemeat. Montagu's book about the operation, *The Man Who Never Was* (1953), was later made into a movie (1956) starring Clifton Webb.

Ming

CODE WORD used by British Special Operations Executive (SOE) for Germans and Germany.

Ministerstvo Gosudarstvennoy Bezopasnosti

[MGB]

SEE NKVD

Ministry of State Security

SEE MSS

Mintkenbaugh, Sgt. James A.

U.S. Army sergeant recruited by another soldier-spy, Sgt. ROBERT LEE JOHNSON, to spy for the Soviets in West Germany in the 1950s. Mintkenbaugh was a HOMOSEXUAL "and this fact," says a government report on the case, "interested the KGB handlers since the homosexual frequently is shunned by society and made to feel like a social outcast. Such a personality may seek to retaliate against a society that has placed him in this unenviable position."

The KGB assigned Mintkenbaugh to spot other American homosexuals and sent him to Moscow for training. There he was ordered to marry a Soviet woman recruited by the KGB and travel to Canada to get birth certificates of Canadians who had died soon after birth or in childhood. Mintkenbaugh was also told to go to work as a real estate salesman in Washington so that he could get personal information on military people and government employees looking for homes.

The elaborate KGB scheme ended before Mintkenbaugh could get started. In 1965 Johnson gave himself up and implicated Mintkenbaugh. Both men were tried, convicted, and sentenced to prison for 25 years.

Mir

Soviet manned orbiting laboratory, employed for scientific research as well as military activities, including RECONNAISSANCE. The *Mir* was placed in orbit on Feb. 19, 1986, succeeding the SALYUT series, the world's first space stations. On March 15 a spacecraft successfully docked with *Mir* to transfer two cosmonauts, who occupied the space station for 125 days.

The basic *Mir* —Russian for "peace"—was essentially a control and living complex with actual experiments and other activities taking place in specially outfitted modules that connected to the *Mir* .

In a report, *The Soviet Space Challenge* (1987), the U.S. Department of Defense predicted that "*Mir* will be used to conduct military experiments. Many of these experiments will use visual observations, cameras, radars, spectrometers, and multi-spectral electro-optical sensors—devices that could support, among other things, ASAT [Anti-satellite] and ballistic missile defense system development."

Compared with the Salyut 7, the last of the Salyut series space stations placed in orbit in 1982, the *Mir* had six docking ports for spacecraft (four more than the earlier craft), enhanced solar energy and power systems, greater computer capability, and individual "cabins" for crew members. The *Mir* 's solar panels provide nearly 10 kilowatts of power for housekeeping and research projects.

Mir was regularly supplied by spacecraft, with *Mir* 's crews being rotated on a regular basis, although the station was briefly left empty after a three-man crew returned to Earth in April 1989. Soviet officials cited a technical problem with new modules that were being prepared to mate with the space station as the reason for the delay.

The Russians carried aloft a Japanese journalist and, subsequently, French astronauts to spend time aboard the *Mir*. U.S. astronaut Norman E. Thagard, also launched in a Russian spacecraft, spent 115 days aboard the *Mir* in 1995. He was the first American to fly in a Russian spacecraft and established a record for an American in space.

In Nov. 1995 the U.S. space shuttle *Atlantis* docked with the *Mir* for three days to install a special docking port to *Mir* and for brief crew visits. On March 28, 1996, the *Atlantis* again docked with the *Mir* and U.S. astronaut Shannon W. Lucid transferred to the space station for a five-month stay on the Russian craft, the first such orbital transfer. (When the *Atlantis* returned to Earth on March 31 it marked the first time a U.S. shuttle flight had landed with fewer crewmen aboard than when launched.)

Mir crews established several records for time in space. On Dec. 27, 1991, cosmonaut Yuri Romanenko returned to Earth after 326 days in space, and on March 22, 1995, cosmonaut Valeri V. Polyakov broke even that record by spending almost 438 days—22 months—in orbit aboard *Mir* ! (The most time spent in *Mir* was achieved by cosmonaut Sergei Avdeyev, who logged just over 747 days in three flights.) More than 100 men and women from 15 countries had lived and worked aboard in teams of two to six as *Mir* carried out military and civilian projects for 15 years.

Slowly, the condition of the craft deteriorated. It was damaged by an onboard fire and by the collision of an unmanned Progress supply ship, and suffered breakdowns of machinery that could not be properly maintained or replaced because of the financial chaos after the demise of the Soviet Union in 1991. Because of technical and funding problems, *Mir* was abandoned from Aug. 27, 1999, to Feb. 20, 2000. The last crew of two cosmonauts departed on April 6, 2000, after six weeks on board. Unoccupied, *Mir* continued in orbit.

Subsequently, the lower house of the Russian parliament (Duma) passed a resolution proposing that *Mir* be used as a main element of a global monitoring system that would allow the world's countries a reliable defense against large-scale environmental and technological calamities, including those caused by terrorist acts and war. But there was no money available, and the Russian Aviation and Space Agency began preparations for the demise of *Mir* . A government spokesman said that what funding was available was needed for the Russian commitment to the International Space Station.

Using the engines of a Progress cargo ship docked to the abandoned station, Russian mission control pointed *Mir* toward Earth and the space station began a fiery reentry into the Earth's atmosphere. Wreckage that survived the reentry fell into the Pacific Ocean. The splashdown occurred about 9 A.M. Moscow time on March 23, 2001. When it fell to Earth, *Mir* and all of its appendages weighed about 138 tons.

Mira, Sgt. Francisco DeA.

A noncommissioned officer in the U.S. Air Force, Mira was assigned to the 601st Tactical Control Group in West Germany when he became the TARGET of a security investigation in 1983. He admitted to passing films of classified documents to a terrorist group, which in turn passed them to the Soviets. He was convicted by a court-martial and under a plea bargain received a seven-year prison term and dishonorable discharge.

Mitchell, Bernon F.

(b. 1929)

Cryptologist for the NSA who, with WILLIAM MARTIN, defected to the Soviet Union in 1960.

After high school Mitchell attended the California Institute of Technology for a year and a half. A C+ student, he enlisted in the Navy and after cryptologic training was assigned to the NAVAL SECURITY GROUP radio intercept station in Kamiseya, Japan. There he met and befriended Martin. When his Navy enlistment ended in 1954, Mitchell enrolled at Stanford University to complete his college degree in mathematics. He maintained

his friendship with Martin, and both began working at the NSA on July 8, 1957. Mitchell was hired despite having confessed during his interviews and POLYGRAPH tests that he had conducted sexual experiments with chickens and dogs when he was between the ages of 13 and 19.

Soon disillusioned by the NSA's activities, he and Martin flew to Cuba and met with Soviet diplomats in Dec. 1959. Subsequently, they took leave together in June 1960, first going to Mexico City, and the next day to Cuba, where they boarded a Soviet cargo ship. (See Martin entry for details of their defection and news conference after arrival in Moscow.)

Following their defection it was revealed that Martin and Mitchell were HOMOSEXUAL lovers.

By 1979 Mitchell had become disillusioned with the Soviet Union. He asked a U.S. State Department official if he could return to the United States as an immigrant or even as a tourist. His requests were rejected.

Mitrokhin, Nikitich

(b. 1922)

Archivist at KGB headquarters who defected to the West with detailed notes on some 300,000 classified documents.

Born in central Russia, he became an INTELLIGENCE OFFICER in 1948. Mitrokhin worked for almost 30 years, from 1956 until his retirement in 1984, in the foreign intelligence archives of the KGB. When the KGB's First Chief Directorate (foreign operations) moved to its new headquarters at Yasenevo, a suburb of Moscow, in June 1972, Mitrokhin was cited for his success in transferring the archives and his "irreproachable service to the state security authorities."

After making contact with British intelligence (MI6), Mitrokhin was EXFILTRATED from Russia in 1992 and given sanctuary—and a new identity—in the West. He brought with him six cases of handwritten notes that he had created describing roughly 300,000 documents in the KGB archives.

Based on his notes and personal knowledge of KGB records and personalities, he coauthored *The Sword and the Shield: The Mitrokhin Archive and the Secret History of the KGB* (1999) with Cambridge University historian CHRISTOPHER ANDREW. The book notes:

> When the German magazine *Focus* reported in December 1996 that a former KGB officer had defected to Britain with the names of hundreds of Russian spies, Tatyana Samolis, spokeswoman for the SVR, instantly ridiculed the whole story as "absolute nonsense." "Hundreds of people! That just doesn't happen!" she declared. "Any defector could get the name of one, two, perhaps three agents— but not hundreds!"

Mitrokhin did just that. In March 2002 he released a 178-page paper describing the KGB's DECEPTION, assassination, and sabotage operations in Afghanistan from

1978 to 1983. Mitrokhin had written the paper in secrecy while still in the USSR.

MKULTRA

Highly secret CIA research project into the possible use of LSD and other mind-altering drugs to produce the perfect AGENT—someone whose brain was under the control of a CASE OFFICER.

MKULTRA spanned the tenure of ALLEN W. DULLES as the DIRECTOR OF CENTRAL INTELLIGENCE (DCI) (1953–1961). It was proposed in April 1953 by RICHARD HELMS, a future DCI working in the CIA's clandestine service (then called the Directorate of Operations). He told Dulles that the CIA needed "to develop a capability in the covert use of biological and chemical materials" and "the production of various physiological conditions which could support present or future clandestine operations." If this could be accomplished, he said, the CIA would gain "a thorough knowledge of the enemy's theoretical potential, thus enabling us to defend ourselves against a foe who might be as restrained in the use of these techniques as we are."

Trying to explain later why the CIA would enter into such strange science, Helms said that a case officer or "clandestine operator" is trained to believe that "you can't count on the honesty of your agent to do exactly what you want, or to report accurately unless you own him body and soul." The soul, or at least the will, was the target of many MKULTRA experiments. One involving LSD resulted in a bizarre death.

The modern idea of mind-altering drugs can be traced to 1949, when the communist Hungarian government put Josef Cardinal Mindszenty on trial for treason. The cardinal, his eyes glazed, confessed in court. The CIA sent officers to Europe to discover what had been done to make the cardinal apparently controllable by his accusers. If the Soviets were manipulating people's minds, then the CIA wanted to know how it was done. The CIA was also interested in "truth serum" and in drugs that might induce amnesia.

The agency's Technical Services Staff (TSS), which produced TRADECRAFT gadgets such as miniature cameras and electronic BUGS, had a chemical division that studied poisons and disabling drugs. In the early 1950s Dr. SIDNEY GOTTLIEB, at that time director of the chemical division, suggested that the agency study the use of a powerful new hallucinogenic drug, LSD (lysergic acid diethylamide). After Dulles approved the Helms proposal, it was given the CODE NAME MKULTRA, the MK indicating it was a TSS project and the ULTRA being a randomly chosen cryptonym that had nothing to with the wartime ULTRA. Earlier, the project had been code-named Bluebird and Artichoke.

Although other drugs were studied, the emphasis was on LSD, an incredibly potent drug that was, by weight, a million times stronger than hashish. The studies, funded through CUT-OUTS ostensibly unconnected with the CIA, were done by such prestigious organizations as Columbia University and Mt. Sinai Hospital in New York, a National Institute of Mental Health research center, and the University of Illinois Medical School. One group of experimental subjects at the federal drug hospital in Lexington, Ky., was kept on LSD for 77 straight days.

Gottlieb's most notorious experiment began at a lodge in western Maryland, where he was meeting in Nov. 1953 with scientists from the U.S. Army's chemical and biological warfare facility at Fort Detrick, near Frederick, Md. Under a separate program, code-named MKNAOMI, Detrick developed poisons and counter-measures to KGB poisons. (See GEORGI MARKOV.) Among the chemicals developed at Detrick was the lethal shellfish toxin that FRANCIS GARY POWERS would later carry on his ill-fated U-2 spyplane mission over the Soviet Union in 1960.

One of the Detrick scientists was Dr. Frank Olson. While he and several others were sitting around the lodge on Nov. 19, 1953, Gottlieb spiked their drinks with LSD. Olson became agitated, moody, depressed, and was diagnosed as needing psychiatric attention. Gottlieb sent him, in the company of two colleagues, to a New York City psychiatrist. They returned to Maryland, but when Olson's condition worsened, they returned to New York and checked into a 10th-floor room in the Statler Hotel. Early on the morning of Nov. 27, Olson hurled himself through the window, plunging to his death. A forensic pathologist who reviewed Olson's death in 1994 said it was unlikely he committed suicide. Other experiments were carried out in SAFE HOUSES in New York City and San Francisco between 1953 and 1966. Prostitutes, lured to the safe houses, were served spiked cocktails while CIA officers photographed and recorded their reactions. Besides LSD, MKULTRA scientists tested psychedelic mushrooms, mescaline, amphetamines, and marijuana. Illegal drugs were obtained through cooperation of the U.S. Bureau of Narcotics.

Information about MKULTRA was tightly guarded. As a CIA audit of the program said, "Precautions must be taken not only to protect operations from exposure to enemy forces but also to conceal these activities from the American public in general. The knowledge that the Agency is engaging in unethical and illicit activities would have serious repercussions in political and diplomatic circles."

MKULTRA was partially revealed by the Rockefeller Commission, which had been appointed by President Ford to investigate alleged CIA abuses. Helms had ordered the destruction of documents about the project. But JAMES SCHLESINGER, who succeeded Helms as DCI, had directed aides to produce a list of illegal or questionable CIA activities, and some MKULTRA material had been included (see FAMILY JEWELS). When DCI WILLIAM E. COLBY turned the material over to the commission, it discovered the Olson case but did not name him. Not until the publication of the commission report in June 1975 did Olson's widow, recognizing the circumstances of the anonymous victim's fate, discover what had happened to her husband. (Congress later passed a bill paying $750,000 in compensation to the Olson family.)

When the CHURCH COMMITTEE examined what could be learned about MKULTRA, it concluded:

> From its beginning in the early 1950s until its termination in 1963, the program of surreptitious administration of LSD to unwitting non-volunteer human subjects demonstrates a failure of the CIA's leadership to pay adequate attention to the rights of individuals and to provide effective guidance to CIA employees. Though it was known that the testing was dangerous, the lives of subjects were placed in jeopardy and their rights were ignored.

The next act of disclosure came in 1979, when JOHN MARKS wrote *The Search for the "Manchurian Candidate,"* using the title of a 1962 film (based on a novel of the same name by Richard Condon) that popularized the idea of "brainwashing." (In the film, the Manchurian candidate was an American prisoner of war who had been programmed in a Manchurian prison camp to kill a presidential candidate years later. See MOVIES.) Many American prisoners taken during the Korean War tried to explain why they had made propaganda statements by saying they had been brainwashed by their Korean and Chinese captors. The idea that mind control was a possibility inspired the MKULTRA experiments.

Marks based his book on 16,000 pages of documents discovered in 1977 by members of the Carter administration while examining old, secret budget expenditures of the CIA. Working through the new FREEDOM OF INFORMATION ACT, he obtained the documents and used them as the basis for the book, augmented by interviews with people familiar with the project.

Mlad

SEE THEODORE A. HALL

Moby Dick

CODE NAME for one of the first strategic SURVEILLANCE projects of the U.S. Navy and CIA, using camera-carrying, unmanned BALLOONS launched from Western Europe to drift over the Soviet Union and take photographs.

Also see GENETRIX.

Modin, Yuri Ivanovich

(b. 1922)

Soviet INTELLIGENCE OFFICER who served as HANDLER for members of the CAMBRIDGE SPY RING.

Born in a small town in rural Russia, he was the son of a soldier who had fought on the Bolshevik side during the Russian Civil War (1917–1920). His father's assignments took young Yuri to many parts of the Soviet Union. In 1940 he entered a naval college in Leningrad (now St. Petersburg) to study engineering. When Germany invaded the Soviet Union in June 1941, he took up arms to fight the advancing Germans until the school and students were moved to the interior in 1942.

That year he became involved with Soviet intelligence—the NKVD—when a chef at the school stole some butter and was arrested and shot by the NKVD. Modin, who had testified in the case against the chef, was subsequently recruited into the NKVD, being sent first to Moscow to further his English-language studies, and in Dec. 1943 being assigned as a translator at NKVD headquarters at the LUBYANKA. From March 1944 until 1947 he translated the flow of documents and other intelligence sent to Moscow by the Cambridge spies, without knowing their identities.

Then, in late June 1947, Modin was sent to London, accompanied by his wife and young daughter. He was to be the assistant RESIDENT, working with Soviet AGENTS in Britain. (Modin had briefly visited London after World War II with a Soviet youth delegation.) Under the COVER of a press officer, he met regularly with ANTHONY BLUNT, GUY BURGESS, and JOHN CAIRNCROSS as well as other agents, all without detection by British COUNTERINTELLIGENCE. In 1951 he helped Burgess and DONALD MACLEAN escape to the Soviet Union.

Modin was reassigned to Moscow in May 1953, but was sent back to London a year later to help solve the problems of Cambridge spy HAROLD (KIM) PHILBY and again in 1955 to help set up the visit of Nikita Khrushchev to Britain. Modin remained in Britain until 1958 carrying out intelligence work.

But further visits became impossible when Blunt, undergoing lengthy interrogations by British counterintelligence (MI5), identified Modin as his handler. He continued his intelligence work for the KGB, including several visits to India. His final assignment was lecturing at the Andropov Institute in Moscow, a KGB SPY SCHOOL.

In Moscow he befriended the Cambridge spies who had sought sanctuary there and helped Philby write his autobiographical *My Silent War* (1968). Modin's own memoirs were published in 1994 under the title *My Five Cambridge Friends*. Modin concludes his book with an appraisal of the Cambridge spies:

> They weren't simply Communists or fellow travellers; they saw themselves as true revolutionaries, ready to sacrifice other people as well as themselves for the cause. Nor can they be faulted on account of their trust in [Josef] Stalin: the same error was made by an entire generation of honest men and women all over the world.
>
> In hindsight, it is clear that they were naive but in the 1930s, that was the way it was.
>
> When I think of them now, I see them as Don Quixote figures who spent their lives tilting at windmills, while history was inexorably destroying their ideal. Scorning the other illusions of humanity—power, wealth, love, ambition, serenity and glory—they chose to follow the greatest illusion of all, which is politics. They swore an oath of loyalty to the revolution. They did not break faith.

Mogarrebi, Maj. Gen. Ahmed

(b. 1920 d. 1977)

Senior Iranian officer executed by firing squad on Dec. 25, 1977, after being convicted by a military court of spying for the Soviet Union. Mogarrebi, age 57 at the time, admitted to having spied for nine years, passing information to the Soviets about Iran's purchases of aircraft and other military equipment from the United States.

Mogul

An early Cold War proposal to detect Soviet nuclear test explosions by sending BALLOONS from Western Europe over the Soviet Union carrying seismic detectors.

MOL

SEE MANNED ORBITING LABORATORY

Mole

A high-level AGENT who is hidden within an enemy's government or military or intelligence organization in the expectation that he or she will provide extremely valuable information. The most important Soviet moles were the members of the CAMBRIDGE SPY RING, who penetrated the British government, ALDRICH H. AMES in the U.S. CIA, and ROBERT HANSSEN of the FBI.

The West's most important mole in the Soviet government is believed to have been Col. OLEG PENKOVSKY. But there may have been another significant asset: The Russian moles revealed by Ames included at least one general in MILITARY INTELLIGENCE (GRU).

Molody, Col. Conon Trofimovich

SEE GORDON LONSDALE

Momentum

CIA program to train native Hmong (Meo) troops in Laos to fight communist insurgents in the 1960s. The headquarters for this secret army of several thousand was at Long Tieng. The Hmong troops and units of the regular Laotian Army also were used by U.S. officials to pin down North Vietnamese units, preventing them from entering South Vietnam.

Although the U.S. Military Assistance Advisory Group (MAAG) had been withdrawn from Laos under the Geneva accords of 1962, the United States had continued to maintain a significant covert presence, working closely with the Hmong troops.

Monarchist Association of Central Russia

SEE THE TRUST

Mongoose

Secret operation, ordered by President Kennedy, to get rid of Cuban leader Fidel Castro. Mongoose was born of the frustration and humiliation that followed the disastrous Bay of Pigs invasion of Cuba in April 1961 (see CUBA).

"We were hysterical about Castro," Secretary of Defense Robert S. McNamara later said. RAY CLINE, the Deputy Director for Intelligence of the CIA at the time, recalled that President Kennedy and his brother, Attorney General Robert Kennedy, believed "they had been booby-trapped at the Bay of Pigs, and it became a constant preoccupation, almost an obsession, to right the record somehow." Robert Kennedy said that to oust Castro "no time, money, effort or manpower is to be spared."

No peacetime COVERT ACTION has ever had such high-level control. Instead of allowing the CIA to handle Mongoose, the agency was given only part of the operation. Control was from the White House, under the SPECIAL GROUP (AUGMENTED) (SGA). Chaired by Gen. Maxwell D. Taylor, Kennedy's military adviser, the SGA included McNamara, Attorney General Robert Kennedy, Secretary of State Dean Rusk, JOHN MCCONE, the DIRECTOR OF CENTRAL INTELLIGENCE, national security adviser McGeorge Bundy, Under Secretary of State Alexis Johnson, Deputy Secretary of Defense Roswell Gilpatric, and Gen. Lyman L. Lemnitzer, Chairman of the Joint Chiefs of Staff. The SGA would meet 42 times between Jan. and Oct. 1962.

Brig. Gen. EDWARD LANSDALE, a Kennedy favorite because of his tough-talking and knowledge of guerrilla warfare, was chief of operations for Mongoose. In Feb. 1962 Lansdale conceived a six-part operational plan to "help the people of Cuba overthrow the Communist regime from within Cuba and institute a new government with which the United States can live in peace." Lansdale's plan called for starting a revolution in Cuba in July 1962, beginning guerrilla actions in Aug.–Sept. 1962, and touching off "open revolt and overthrow" in Oct. 1962, while simultaneously establishing a new government.

Lansdale envisioned sabotage and economic warfare against Cuba. And he asked for an extraordinary commitment—open use of U.S. military forces. The SGA, approving Lansdale's plan, conceded that "final success" would "require decisive U.S. interventions"—a major shortfall in the Bay of Pigs disaster. In July, seeing his timetable slipping and sensing that SGA was cooling on Mongoose, Lansdale suggested alternative actions that ranged from simply treating Cuba as a Soviet Bloc country to staging a "provocation" and overthrowing Castro "by U.S. military force." While the SGA pondered the next act in Mongoose, reports began coming in about a sudden increase in Soviet shipping to Cuba. This was the prelude to the CUBAN MISSILE CRISIS.

On Aug. 1 the CIA produced a NATIONAL INTELLIGENCE ESTIMATE on Cuba reporting that Cuba's armed services were strong enough to quell an insurrection and repel any invasion "short of direct U.S. military intervention in strength." The estimate did not respond to the sharp increase in Soviet ship traffic. A supplementary report on Aug. 22 said Cuban forces were being considerably strengthened. The CIA reports dampened SGA interest in Mongoose.

Simultaneously the CIA was planning the assassination of Castro, but this was not part of Mongoose. On Aug. 10, during an SGA meeting, McNamara, unaware of the CIA assassination planning, suggested that the SGA might want to consider simply killing Castro. McCone protested, as did Edward R. Murrow, the director of the U.S. Information Agency. Such talk did not belong in the White House, they said. But two days after that meeting Lansdale requested that WILLIAM HARVEY, the CIA officer running the agency's part of Mongoose, submit anti-Castro plans, "including liquidation of leaders."

Operation Mongoose was known to the Soviets by July 1962, according to Soviet Lt. Gen. Anatoli I. Gribvov, who oversaw operation ANADYR, the shipment of Soviet missiles to Cuba. "We had known about it and about other activities that made the likelihood of an invasion seem very real to Khrushchev and others in 1962," Gribvov wrote in *Operation ANADYR* (1994), which he authored with U.S. Army Gen. William Y. Smith, who served on Taylor's staff at the White House during Mongoose and the missile crisis. Smith, looking back at Mongoose, wrote that the SGA "never allowed consideration of the use of U.S. military force to proceed beyond the planning stage." Several times, he wrote, the SGA "backed away from making a firm commitment to use military force in Cuba."

On Aug. 23 President Kennedy, going back to Lansdale's July report, called for a review of his recommendations, with an emphasis on one that called for exerting "all possible diplomatic economic, psychological, and other pressures to overthrow the Castro-Communist regime without overt employment of U.S. military."

Kennedy also called for moves that would "deliberately seek to provoke a full-scale revolt against Castro that might require U.S. intervention to succeed."

American interests in Cuba were now on two tracks: Mongoose; and the growing crisis over stepped-up Soviet military aid to Castro. Robert Kennedy focused on Mongoose, berating McCone and the CIA "with lack of action in the sabotage field." The CIA share of Mongoose, known as Task Force W, was 600 CASE OFFICERS, and 3,000 contract AGENTS, the CIA's largest single clandestine program. Harvey, a legendary, cantankerous CIA officer, was running Task Force W out of Miami. He did manage to get agent teams into Cuba and to commit some acts of sabotage—"We want boom-and-bang on the island," Lansdale said—but Harvey's agents reported that the possibility of a general rising was slim. Robert Kennedy himself went to Miami to see why Mongoose was moving so slowly. He and Harvey had words, which did not do much for Harvey's subsequent career.

In early Oct. 1962, Mongoose and the Cuban missile crisis planning collided in the White House. As the mis-

sile crisis brought the United States and the Soviet Union to the brink of nuclear war, Robert Kennedy told McCone to stop all covert operations in Cuba. McCone passed the order to Harvey, who, correctly, saw a difference between operations and agents. Believing that TACTICAL INTELLIGENCE might be needed, he sent in an agent team on Oct. 21, the day before President Kennedy announced a naval blockade around Cuba. When Kennedy learned that Harvey had not stopped operations, Harvey was removed as head of Task Force W.

On Oct. 16, in the midst of the missile crisis, Robert Kennedy asked RICHARD HELMS, the CIA Deputy Director for Plans (clandestine activities), what percentage of Cubans "would fight for the regime" if the U.S. invaded Cuba. At that point, with high-level planners contemplating a military end to the crisis, Mongoose died.

Montagu, Capt. Ewen Edward Samuel

(b. 1901 d. 1985)

British judge, writer, and INTELLIGENCE OFFICER. Montagu served as a machine gun instructor at a U.S. naval air station in World War I. He attended Trinity College, Cambridge, and Harvard University, being called to the bar in 1924.

During World War II, Montagu served in the NAVAL INTELLIGENCE Division of the Admiralty, where he conceived Operation MINCEMEAT, one of the major hoaxes played on German intelligence during the war. From 1945 to 1973 he held the position of Judge Advocate of the Fleet.

He wrote *The Man Who Never Was* (1953) (about Operation Mincemeat, *The Archer-Shee Case* (1974), and *Beyond Top Secret* (1977).

Montes, Ana Belen

(b. 1958)

Analyst for the U.S. DEFENSE INTELLIGENCE AGENCY (DIA) who spied for Cuba. During her long career as a spy she blew the cover of at least four U.S. AGENTS in Cuba. Their fate has not been revealed. She is the highest-level Cuban spy yet discovered.

Born on a U.S. military base in West Germany, she earned a degree in foreign affairs from the University of Virginia and a master's degree at Johns Hopkins University School of Advanced International Studies. She began working for the DIA in 1985—the year that she also began working for the Cuban Intelligence Service.

As the leading DIA analyst on Cuba, she was a key contributor, and possibly the principal writer, of a 1998 Pentagon report that said Cuba posed no military threat to the United States. Montes kept in touch with her Cuban HANDLERS through encrypted radio messages.

The FBI arrested her 10 days after the Sept. 11, 2001, terrorist attacks on the United States. The timing of the arrest indicated that the FBI, after keeping her under SURVEILLANCE to learn more about Cuban espionage activity, decided to seize her in case her continued spying would aid terrorist groups. She had access to highly classified DIA information beyond Cuba.

In Oct. 2002 she was sentenced to prison for 25 years as part of a plea in which she agreed to brief the FBI about her spying activities.

Also see CUBA and MARIANO FAGET.

Moore, Edwin G., II

Disgruntled former CIA officer who tried to sell information to the Soviets.

On the night of Dec. 21, 1976, Moore threw several documents over the fence at an apartment building housing Soviet embassy families in Washington, D.C. A Soviet security guard, thinking the package was a bomb, called the U.S. Executive Protection Service, thus becoming the first known Soviet ever to assist in the arrest of a would-be American spy. U.S. Army explosives experts discovered that the package contained not a bomb but several CIA documents accompanied by an offer of "penetration into the headquarters operations of the CIA." A note asked for $200,000, to be left at a drop site in the Washington suburb of Bethesda, Md.

The FBI followed the directions in the note, left a dummy package at the site, and hid agents nearby. A man across the street from the drop, raking the leaves on his lawn, furtively looked around, put down his rake, and picked up the package. He was Moore.

Moore had not revealed anything to the Soviets, but his arrest was to reveal more about the lax security practices at the CIA. Moore had been employed from 1952 to 1963, primarily in map making and logistics studies. He had been fired from the CIA after having been arrested for arson. Acquitted on that charge, he appealed for reinstatement and was rehired in 1967.

Moore retired in 1973 because of a medical disability caused by a heart ailment. "His career," said a later CIA report, "had been marked by marginal work performance, chronic work frustrations, and a general reputation of being miscast in an intelligence agency." In his home FBI agents found classified CIA directories listing names, addresses, and phone numbers of CIA employees. Among the hundreds of documents was material dated *after 1973*, indicating that he had had contact with people at the CIA after his retirement.

Moore was convicted on two counts of espionage and three counts of unlawful possession of classified documents. Sentenced to 15 years in prison in May 1977, he was paroled in 1979.

Moore, Michael R.

U.S. Marine, absent without leave, who was planning to contact the Soviet Embassy in Manila in 1984 when his intentions were somehow discovered by U.S. intelligence officials. Confronted with the information, he was given a convenience-of-the-government discharge.

Moravec, Brig. Gen. Frantisek

(b. 1895 d. 1966)

Leading Czech INTELLIGENCE OFFICER. In World War I he fought on several Allied fronts as a member of the Czech "foreign legion." After the war he remained in the Army, entering the intelligence field in 1934 when, as a lieutenant colonel, he was assigned to the General Staff as head of espionage and COUNTERINTELLIGENCE. These were important to the Czech republic because of the threat from Germany and the 3.5 million Germans living in Czechoslovakia's Sudetenland.

In 1936 Moravec began intelligence exchanges with the Soviets and the following year was made head of Czech intelligence. In this period he had several successes against Germany, including the acquisition of PAUL THUMMEL as a spy.

When Germany took over Czechoslovakia on March 14, 1939, Moravec and his staff fled to Britain, where he worked for the Czech government in exile as well as with British MILITARY INTELLIGENCE. He played a major role in planning the assassination of REINHARD HEYDRICH in Czechoslovakia. He was awarded the U.S. Legion of Merit and Order of the British Empire for his services to Allied intelligence in World War II.

Moravec became deputy chief of the Czech General Staff while in Britain, but because of Soviet opposition he was dismissed in 1945. With the war in Europe over, he became a division commander in the Czech Army. When the communists seized power in Czechoslovakia in Feb. 1948 he was forced to flee to the United States, where he remained until his death.

His autobiography, *Master of Spies,* was published in 1975.

Morison, Samuel Loring

(b. 1944)

U.S. Navy intelligence analyst who gave SATELLITE photographs of a Soviet shipyard to a British news magazine. He was the only government employee ever convicted of leaking classified information to the media. (See LEAK.)

Grandson of the distinguished naval and maritime historian Samuel Eliot Morison, Morison served briefly as an officer in the Navy during the Vietnam War; he then worked as a civilian employee for the Navy's history office before becoming an analyst at the NAVAL INTELLIGENCE SUPPORT CENTER (NISC) in 1976. A short time later he became the part-time Washington representative for *Jane's Fighting Ships*, a British reference annual containing unclassified information about all the world's navies. His work for *Jane's* was done with approval of his Navy superiors, although the conflict of interest was apparent, since Morison held a TOP SECRET clearance and certain COMPARTMENTED clearances.

Morison had committed several previous security violations. For example, he sold a used copy of *Jane's Fighting Ships* to a civilian who found several classified documents stuck in the book and called the FBI about the violation. Morison visited the Norfolk naval base and used his NISC identification to get on the base and take ship photos for *Jane's*. When stopped by base security officials, he claimed, falsely, that he was taking the photos for NISC. Nothing substantial happened as a result of these incidents.

Then, in 1984, Morison stole from a colleague's desk a set of three SECRET satellite photographs that showed a nuclear-propelled aircraft carrier under construction at a Black Sea shipyard. He snipped the upper-left corner containing the "secret" label off each photo and sent them to *Jane's Defence Weekly*, a news magazine published by the Jane's organization.

He was arrested on Oct. 1, 1984, for stealing and giving away the satellite photographs. Morison denied any knowledge of the photos, but when *Jane's* returned the photos to the Navy, one of them was found to bear Morison's thumbprint. An FBI search of Morison's home turned up other classified documents he had taken from NISC.

Morison was tried for espionage as a lesson to leakers of information. Morison was indicted under a section of the 1917 ESPIONAGE ACT that prohibits people with lawful access to U.S. military documents from disclosing them to an unauthorized person. He was the first person in U.S. history actually to be tried under the statute. Daniel Ellsberg and Anthony Russo, who had given the PENTAGON PAPERS on the background of the Vietnam War to the press, had been charged under the law. But a federal judge had dismissed the case against them because of government misconduct in the WATERGATE era. The dismissal was not based on any deficiency in the espionage law.

Morison was found guilty in Oct. 1985 and sentenced to a two-year prison term. He was paroled after seven months in prison. President Bill Clinton pardoned him in 2001, ignoring protests from the CIA, whose officials believed that the pardon was a bad precedent.

Morros, Boris

(b. 1891, d. 1963)

Hollywood film producer who first spied for the Soviet Union and then became a DOUBLE AGENT for the FBI.

Russian-born Morros volunteered in 1934 to aid the Soviet espionage effort, installing an AGENT in the BERLIN office of the Paramount film company and indicating to his HANDLERS that he would aid them in injecting Soviet propaganda into Hollywood films. But his films were more "B" than red. His films included *The Flying Deuces* (1939), an Oliver and Hardy comedy, and *Second Chorus* (1940), with Fred Astaire and Paulette Goddard.

As a double agent for the FBI, he handed in names of American communist sympathizers—names that showed up in VENONA transcripts. He greatly expanded his double-agent role in a book, *My Ten Years as a Counterspy* (1959), which was made into a movie, *Man on a String*

(1960), starring Ernest Borgnine as a film version of Morros.

Mortati, Tommaso

Former U.S. Army paratrooper arrested in 1989 in Vincenza, Italy, as a member of the CLYDE LEE CONRAD spy ring, which passed secrets to Hungarian and Czechoslovakian AGENTS in the 1980s.

Mortati, born in Italy, immigrated to the United States and became a U.S. citizen. After his discharge from the Army in 1987, he lived in Italy; his American wife worked at a U.S. Army base in Vincenza. His arrest followed that of his recruiter, ZOLTON SZABO. Mortati said he had been recruited into the ring in 1981 and sent to spy training in Budapest for two weeks.

He continued working for the Hungarians while in the Army in Italy, receiving $500 a month in addition to payments for information, based on its importance. Italy's military secret service was informed about Mortati's activities by German and Austrian COUNTERINTELLIGENCE officials. The Italians searched Mortati's home and found a hidden two-way radio, which he used to transmit his reports. Up until the time of his arrest, he had received $500 a month from the Hungarian Intelligence Service. He admitted that in 1984 and 1985 he had attempted to bribe Italian Army officers for information. He was convicted in an Italian court, given a 20-month suspended sentence, and released.

Moscow Rules

British term for intricate signs and countersigns used to indicate a clandestine meeting or DEAD DROP. If appropriate, the signs signify that neither party is being followed. Such signs can also be used to alleviate the need for a face-to-face encounter.

The signs and countersigns can be chalk marks on trees or lampposts, or a carefully discarded bottle or metal can of a certain kind. The latter must be in a location where it will not normally be moved or picked up, and must be clean, so that an animal will not be attracted by an odor and move it. (See TRADECRAFT.)

Unofficially, Moscow Rules have made their way into popular belief and include "Assume nothing. Everyone is potentially under opposition control. Don't look back, you are never completely alone. Don't harass the opposition."

Mosquito

Versatile World War II aircraft that served extensively in the photo-RECONNAISSANCE role.

Flights by Mosquito PR.IV aircraft over the German research installation at Peenemünde on the Baltic from April to June 1943 led to the discovery of the V-2 rocket program. (See CONSTANCE BABINGTON-SMITH.)

Some PR models were flown by the U.S. Eighth Air

Force with the designation F-8. British Mosquitos and American-piloted F-8s kept all of Western Europe under daily SURVEILLANCE in 1943–1945. More than 3,000 photo and meteorological sorties were flown in 1943 by these "recce" aircraft.

The ultimate Mosquito reconnaissance variants were the PR.34 and PR.35. (The early models of British aircraft had Roman-numerical designations; later models used Arabic numbers.) The PR.34 model, which first flew in Dec. 1944, initially had a range of 2,500 miles; a bomb-bay modification, for the carrying of additional fuel, increased the range to 3,500 miles. The PR.35 was a night-flying photo plane that used flash bombs. One oblique and four vertical cameras were fitted in these aircraft. RAF Mosquitos became the first aircraft to use radar cameras that could penetrate clouds and darkness.

The Mosquito continued in British service in the PR role until late 1955, when it was finally replaced by the CANBERRA. In late 1948 a Mosquito PR aircraft made several overflights of Israeli territory at about 30,000 feet with impunity. However, on Dec. 1, 1948, a newly arrived Israeli P-51 Mustang took off and intercepted the Mosquito; although the Mustang's guns jammed after firing a few rounds, the Mosquito was hit and crashed into the Mediterranean with no survivors. Mosquitos transferred to Israel flew photo missions over Egypt during the 1956 Suez campaign and ranged as far as Tripoli to collect intelligence.

Mosquitos were invariably known as "Mossies" to their crews.

Mosquito, Operation

Plan suggested to President Reagan in 1981 by Count ALEXANDRE DE MARENCHES, French intelligence chief, to subvert Soviet troops in Afghanistan with DISINFORMATION and drugs that had been seized from the U.S. Drug Enforcement Agency. The drugs would be sold to the troops by Pakistanis and Afghans in French employ. As Marenches told it, Reagan endorsed the idea, but it was abandoned when WILLIAM J. CASEY, the DIRECTOR OF CENTRAL INTELLIGENCE, could not guarantee that the COVERT ACTION would remain covert.

Mossad

Israeli intelligence agency.

Although ISRAEL has several intelligence agencies, the term Mossad—short for Ha Mossad Le modi'm UleTafkidim Meyuhadim ("the Institute for Intelligence and Special Tasks")—is invariably used when speaking of the Jewish state's intelligence activities. While Mossad has suffered many failures and at times embarrassed Israel, more often it has had stunning successes, many of which have never been publicly revealed.

The Mossad evolved from the Political Department of the Israeli Foreign Ministry. Established shortly after the creation of the state of Israel on May 14, 1948, the Political Department was given responsibility for collecting intelligence outside Israel. The first director was Latvian-born Boris Guriel, who served in the British Army in World War II and was captured by the Germans. During the period before Israeli independence he worked for Shai, the intelligence arm of the underground Haganah force.

The Political Department's primary functions were to plant AGENTS—Israeli or native—in Arab countries and establish working relations with Western intelligence services. Political Department officers served under COVER in Israeli embassies throughout Western Europe.

But because of a conflict of personalities within the Political Department, differing individual priorities, and lack of knowledge of the SECRET WORLD, Prime Minister David Ben-Gurion finally stepped in and demanded a reorganization of Israeli intelligence. On April 1, 1951, the Mossad was established. Responsible directly to the Prime Minister's office, it was created in the mold of the U.S. rather than the British. (The British Secret Intelligence service [MI6] came under the Foreign Office).

Originally the Mossad was named Ha Mossad Leteum ("the Institute for Coordination"), a truly ambiguous title. Not until 1963 was it renamed the Institute for Intelligence and Special Tasks.

The agency's brief was to collect intelligence overseas. Any overseas "operations" at that time were to be carried out by the Army's Unit 131. Army intelligence (AMAN) and the Mossad had joint oversight of Unit 131. The first head of the Mossad was REUVEN SHILOAH, a founder of Shai with extensive service in the Haganah as well as experience as an agent in Arab countries and, during World War II, behind German lines for the British.

Shiloah's tenure was brief, but he was able to establish certain standards and beliefs within the agency, although its operations—and handling of funds—were relatively sloppy. From the outset, the Mossad was hampered by incompetence and traitors. The first was DAVID MAGEN. Sent into Egypt to operate a NETWORK of informers, he made illicit contact with Egyptian INTELLIGENCE OFFICERS. Another Israeli intelligence officer sent into Egypt, AVRAHANI DAR, botched his assignment horribly in what became known as the Lavon affair.

But Mossad triumphs in this period included acquiring a copy of Nikita Khrushchev's secret speech before the 20th Communist Party Congress in Moscow on Feb. 25, 1956, in which he denounced the late dictator Josef Stalin. A copy was provided to the U.S. CIA before that agency could acquire it from any other source. (After the fall of the Soviet Union, some Western intelligence sources speculated that the leaking of the speech was a combined Mossad-KGB operation. As the theory goes, Khrushchev wanted the speech known but politically could not simply release it; so he had the KGB do it, with Mossad assistance.)

Another Mossad success was WOLFGANG LOTZ, who operated in Egypt with great skill from 1959 to 1964, when he was found out, tortured, and imprisoned. Still another highly successful Mossad agent was ELIAHU COHEN, who infiltrated the highest levels of Syrian government and society before being uncovered.

The first head of the Mossad, Shiloah, injured in a car accident and suffering from the political infighting, stepped down in Sept. 1952, having served only 18 months. His successor was the ambitious ISSER HAREL, whose 11-year tenure as head of the Mossad would be the longest of any director. Harel came from the position of director of the SHIN BET, the only person to head both of those intelligence agencies. Also, on Ben-Gurion's orders, Harel was designated the Memuneh "the one in charge" of all Israeli intelligence activities, reporting directly to Ben-Gurion on both international and domestic security matters.

Under Harel the Mossad sought out former Nazis hiding in Europe and South America to bring them to trial. Mossad's greatest triumph in this field was the capture of Adolf Eichmann, the Nazi functionary who officiated over the killing of millions of Jews during the Holocaust. The joint Mossad–Shin Bet operation plucked Eichmann from his refuge in Argentina.

Also under Harel's direction, Mossad agents infiltrated Egyptian and West German intelligence agencies, using terrorist tactics to stop German scientists from working for Egypt. But Ben-Gurion wanted to strengthen Israeli–West German relations and turned against Harel. He reprimanded him for his campaign against the scientists, losing confidence in the man he had dubbed Memuneh. Harel resigned from government service in March 1963. (No one since has held such a senior position in Israeli intelligence.)

In Harel's place as head of the Mossad, Ben-Gurion appointed MEIR AMIT, the head of Aman. Significantly, before that appointment in 1962, Amit had never served in the intelligence field. He had made major contributions to Aman when, without warning, on March 26, 1963, Ben-Gurion called Amit to his office, having sent a plane to fetch him back from an inspection of military units near the Dead Sea. He was to take over the Mossad immediately.

Amit sought to change the Mossad into a modern intelligence organization focusing on what he considered to be its major task: the collection of military and political data on the Arab states. He regarded the Mossad as an information-gathering body that would henceforth eschew what he viewed as "show-off operations," which he felt were a waste of resources. Influenced by the economic and business courses he had taken in the United States, Amit wished to imitate the American corporate mentality and style of management. In this period the Mossad and Aman together sought out the intelligence that made the Six Day War (1967) one of the greatest military triumphs in Israeli history.

But six years later Israeli intelligence apparently failed to predict either the Egyptian crossing of the Suez Canal at the start of the Yom Kippur War or the effectiveness of Egyptian forces once they entered the Sinai. The AGRANAT COMMISSION placed blame for the intelligence failure on the chief of MILITARY INTELLIGENCE, Maj. Gen. Eliahu Zeira, and three other intelligence officers. Zvi Zamir, successor to Meir Amit as head of the Mossad, stepped down in 1974. (The Agranat Commis-

sion also laid blame on the chief of staff of the Israeli armed forces and the commander of the Southern Command. It cleared Prime Minister Golda Meir and Minister of Defense Moshe Dayan of "direct responsibility" for the disaster. Nevertheless, Meir and Dayan resigned after the report was issued.)

The commission also recommended changes in the organization of the Israeli intelligence community. The Mossad and a small research department of the Foreign Ministry would have an increased role in intelligence assessments, thus ending Aman's control of intelligence evaluation. Stung by the failures on the eve of the Yom Kippur War (and Aman was blamed for subsequent battle failures as well), the Israeli intelligence community adopted new methods and practices.

INTELLIGENCE WITHOUT WAR

Among the more spectacular nonwar intelligence successes were having an advanced MiG-21 fighter flown to Israel in 1963 by an Iraqi DEFECTOR while providing safe passage out of Iraq for his family; collecting some 200,000 technical documents on the Mirage aircraft from Swiss engineer ALFRED FRALENKNECHT; hijacking a shipload of 200 tons of uranium in a set-up deal for use in Israeli's atomic bomb program; making raids into downtown Beirut to assassinate leaders of Arab radical groups; and carrying out "hits" on other individuals in other Arab states.

The year 1976 brought possibly the greatest triumph of the Mossad—the Israeli raid on the airport at Entebbe, Uganda, known as Operation Thunderbolt. Palestinian terrorists had hijacked an Air France airliner and flown it into Entebbe, where they were holding 97 passengers and some of the crew (although all of the crew had been allowed to leave). Under Yitzhak Hofi, the Mossad interviewed released passengers, sought out data on the airport (originally built with Israeli help), and compiled dossiers on Ugandan President Idi Amin's movements, bodyguards, and even his personal automobile.

Then, on the night of July 3–4, the most spectacular hostage rescue in history was carried out, some 2,000 miles from Israel. Excellent intelligence, military planning, and performance by the Army–Air Force strike team rescued all but four hostages; Israeli loss was one officer, the commander of the strike force. (Six terrorists and 20 Ugandan soldiers were killed.)

Throughout this period, the Mossad also concentrated on obtaining intelligence about Arab weapons and electronics capabilities. The more advanced Arab weapons came from the Soviet Union, and the Mossad managed to obtain examples of many advanced systems—from Arab countries as well as elsewhere—much of which was shared with U.S. intelligence agencies.

Mossad's collection of intelligence on foreign TARGETS has often been highly successful, even when those targets were thought to be beyond Israeli's military striking power. For example, the target folders for the precision air strike on Palestine Liberation Army headquarters in Tunis—1,500 miles from Israel—and the air strike on

Iraq's nuclear reactor a decade before the Gulf War of 1991 demonstrated the excellence of Mossad intelligence collection.

Mossad's efforts, however, have not been infallible; assassins have occasionally killed the wrong people. And during the Persian Gulf war of 1991, the Mossad appears to have been unable to accurately predict certain Iraqi actions and capabilities, especially the threat from modified Scud missiles that would be fired against Israel. In 1990 the U.S. government estimated that the Mossad had a staff of between 1,500 and 2,000.

Mossad cooperation with U.S. intelligence agencies—approved and unapproved—has been considerable, up to acting as the go-between in handling weapons for the IRAN-CONTRA AFFAIR. But, for a long time after the discovery of JONATHAN POLLARD's spying for Israel, relations cooled between U.S. and Israeli intelligence agencies. Reportedly, prior to the Sept. 11, 2001, terrorist attacks on the United States, Mossad relayed warnings through other nations' agencies because of fears that a direct warning from Mossad would not receive serious attention.

MOSSAD DIRECTORS

The directors of the Mossad are listed below. Isser Harel is the only person to have served as a director of both the Shin Bet (1948–1952) and the Mossad; Meir Amit is the only person to have served as head of Aman (1962–1963) and the Mossad.

1951–1952	Reuven Shiloah
1952–1963	Isser Harel
1963–1968	Meir Amit
1968–1974	Zvi Zamir
1974–1982	Yitzhak Hofi
1982–1989	Nahum Admoni
1989–1996	Shabtai Shavit
1996–1998	Danny Yatom
1998–2001	Ephraim Halevy
2002–	Meir Dagan

Most Secret

Highest British security CLASSIFICATION; it is the equivalent of TOP SECRET in the United States.

Movies

Unlike spy novels (see LITERARY SPIES), spy movies usually do not rely on an air of authenticity for their entertainment value. The reader of a good spy novel usually gains insights by learning what is going on in the minds of spies and their pursuers. But in a movie, the slogging realities of espionage and counterespionage usually escape the camera. Most directors and producers opt for suspense and capers, and even special effects, rather than subtleties and true TRADECRAFT. Most spy movies are more accurately called spy thrillers, an espionage version of cops-and-robbers or cowboys-and-Indians.

James Grady, whose novel *Six Days of the Condor* (1974) was made into *Three Days of the Condor* (1975), assessed "spy-fi" films in 1985.

> Moviemakers love heroes and villains, clean endings, clear positions about right and wrong, and the endemic problem of moral ambivalence is often the reason they avoid accurately portraying spies. . . . Trying to sell the public a story that delves into the messy blood and guts of politics is risky business at the box office, so most spy movies are actually glorified and unrealistic global-cop films.

The spy film is a recognized genre. The authoritative Microsoft *Cinemania 95* compact disc movie directory lists 364 movies in the spy genre since 1928, when Germany's Fritz Lang used BERLIN as the backdrop for the first great spy movie, *Spies*. In it, the most villainous spy was made up to look like V. I. Lenin. Espionage during World War I got the romantic treatment in Britain in 1939, with *The Spy in Black*, in which a German AGENT, played by Conrad Veidt, has a love affair with a British agent, played by Valerie Hobson.

Espionage fascinated Hollywood producers in the pre–World War II era. A 1931 movie about MATA HARI starred Greta Garbo and focused on the romance of espionage. Most spy movies of that time, however, simply showed U.S. or British spies as the good guys, clad in suits and ties but still Wild West marshals; the bad guys were usually from fictitious or unnamed countries. Jitters about Hitler's Germany inspired many prewar spy movies. Alfred Hitchcock dominated that genre, beginning with *The Man Who Knew Too Much* in 1934, in which Leslie Banks plays an innocent who stumbles into espionage and whose child is kidnapped to keep him silent. The villain is Peter Lorre.

Hitchcock followed up with his 1935 classic *The Thirty-Nine Steps*, saying at the time, "I am out to give the public good, healthy, mental shake-ups. Civilization has become so screening and sheltering that we cannot experience sufficient thrills at first hand. Therefore, to prevent our becoming sluggish and jellified, we have to experience them artificially." This time, Robert Donat played the Briton who stumbles into a plot. Madeleine Carroll costarred. This spy thriller was based on JOHN BUCHAN's 1915 novel of the same name.

Sabotage (1936), another Hitchcock spy thriller, starred Sylvia Sidney, Oscar Homolka, and John Loder. Hitchcock picked Madeleine Carroll again for his 1936 spy movie *The Secret Agent*, which also starred John Gielgud and Peter Lorre. The movie, based on JOSEPH CONRAD's *The Secret Agent*, was retitled A *Woman Alone* in the United States. In the 1940 chase movie *Murder in the Air*, future President Ronald Reagan, playing Secret Service agent Brass Bancroft, caught a spy trying to steal a death ray (a popular fictional weapon that presaged Reagan's own "Star Wars" project).

John P. Marquand's Mr. Moto, the polite Japanese gentleman who specialized in saving innocents from spies and other malefactors, appeared in the 1930s, flourishing briefly as a series in Hollywood (with Peter Lorre as Mr. Moto). Mr. Moto, a victim of anti-Japanese prejudice, vanished with the advent of World War II.

Wartime U.S. spy thrillers included *Five Graves to Cairo,* a Billy Wilder film with Franchot Tone in Akim Tamiroff's oasis hotel trying to get secret information from General Erwin Rommel, played by Erich von Stroheim. In *The House on 92nd Street,* told in documentary style, the FBI tracks down Nazi spies who are after atomic bomb secrets.

During the war, movie spies were despicable Japanese and fiendish Nazis and, in American movies, the spy catchers were astute, courageous FBI agents. Few war movies focused on espionage, which was still an arcane subject for most action-seeking moviegoers. In *Across the Pacific* Humphrey Bogart, Mary Astor, and Sydney Greenstreet conspire in a Japanese effort to destroy the Panama Canal. In a 1943 movie, *Flight for Freedom,* Rosalind Russell plays a fictional spying aviatrix obviously modeled on AMELIA EARHART, popularizing the persistent belief that she was spying on Japanese naval bases when she was lost in the Pacific on her around-the-world flight in 1937.

The Mask of Dimitrios, based on a novel by ERIC AMBLER, links Peter Lorre, Sydney Greenstreet, and Zachary Scott in Middle East intrigue. *March of Time* documentaries, popular in the 1930s and 1940s, inspired the storytelling style of *13 Rue Madeleine,* which takes place during World War II. OFFICE OF STRATEGIC SERVICES (OSS) agent James Cagney slips into occupied France to outwit the GESTAPO and complete the mission of a slain agent. He is committing an inexcusable blunder, for any INTELLEGENCE OFFICER who knows the identity of his agents does not go behind enemy lines. But movie espionage rarely resembles real espionage.

Hollywood's wartime movie output included escapist films, including a spy comedy, *They Got Me Covered,* with Bob Hope and Dorothy Lamour chasing down Nazi spies in Washington. Another Hope spy spoof, *My Favorite Spy,* teamed him with Hedy Lamarr.

After the war, wartime spies still inspired moviemakers. In *Notorious* Hitchcock again used espionage as an excuse for thrills and suspense, with secret agent Cary Grant and anti-Nazi Ingrid Bergman intriguing to smash Claude Rains's Nazi spy ring in Argentina. Ben Hecht's script sets the story in South America shortly after World War II.

Among the better movies based on real wartime events were *Five Fingers,* with James Mason playing CICERO, a valet for a British diplomat and a spy for Germany, and *The Man Who Never Was,* based on Operation MINCEMEAT, in which Clifton Webb conceives the planting of a hoax corpse in a DECEPTION plan tied to the invasion of Sicily. In another wartime film, *The Quiller Memorandum,* George Segal plays Quiller, an agent assigned to break up a neo-Nazi organization in Berlin. Alec Guinness plays his chief. The script is by Harold Pinter, based on the novel by Adam Hall. Nazis were also the villains of a World War II–era thriller *Eye of the Needle,* in which master Nazi spy Donald Sutherland tries to

get secrets about D-DAY to Germany. The film was based on Ken Follet's novel of the same title.

Hollywood again turned to wartime Nazis for *Where Eagles Dare,* an impossible mission for Richard Burton and Clint Eastwood: They are ineptly disguised as Nazi officers in a caper involving a D-Day deception plot. The movie is distinguished by having absolutely no relationship to reality, and it perverts history by having German agents infiltrate the highest councils of Allied intelligence.

The Cold War gave the movies a new set of enemies: brutal Soviets and the nefarious KGB. A rare treatment of realistic espionage and counterespionage appeared in the 1948 film *The Iron Curtain,* in which Dana Andrews plays IGOR GOUZENKO, who defected from the Soviet Embassy in Ottawa and helped crack the ATOMIC SPY RING. East-West Cold War confrontation in VIENNA became the shadowy setting for *The Third Man,* in which spies are in the background and black marketeer Harry Lime (Orson Welles) is the hunted man. The screenplay was by GRAHAM GREENE, who noted that he used the term THIRD MAN before it became a label for HAROLD (KIM) PHILBY. Many believe that Greene, who knew Philby, based the Harry Lime character on Philby.

The Spy Who Came In from the Cold (1965), based on the novel by JOHN LE CARRÉ, took espionage as seriously as the book did. Richard Burton plays Alec Leamas, a burned-out British agent who, posing as a disgraced and dismissed officer, enters East Germany to destroy a Red spymaster.

The Manchurian Candidate (1962) popularized the idea of sinister communist "brainwashing," with Laurence Harvey playing a brainwashed Korean War veteran who has been programmed into a presidential assassin by Soviet and Chinese intelligence operatives. Frank Sinatra, from Harvey's old squad, has flashbacks to the brainwashing and moves to crack the plot, which is being run by Angela Lansbury. (For real attempts at brainwashing, see MKULTRA.)

Michael Caine became the screen's busiest spy actor in the 1960s, playing LEN DEIGHTON's soft-spoken Harry Palmer in *The Ipcress File.* Palmer gets involved in the defection of a high Soviet intelligence official (Oscar Homolka) in Deighton's *Funeral in Berlin.* High-speed but unrealistic espionage fueled *The Billion-Dollar Brain.* In 1987 Caine returned to espionage in *The Fourth Protocol,* a movie version of Frederick Forsyth's novel of the same name. In movies, agents are inevitably ignored by their superiors, and in *The Fourth Protocol* no one listens to Caine when he says a Soviet agent is sneaking components for nuclear weapons into Britain.

During the Cold War, as in World War II, movie spies were often not trained agents but innocent bystanders who had stumbled into a conspiracy. Beautiful women inevitably complicated life for the accidental spies. Hitchcock remade *The Man Who Knew Too Much* in 1955, with James Stewart and Doris Day stumbling into conspiracy as the time shifted from pre–World War II to the Cold War. In this, as in earlier Hitchcock movies, espionage is secondary to suspense. Hitchcock movies do not tell a spy story; they tell a thriller story. *(The Thirty Nine Steps* was remade in 1978, by director Don Sharp, and the cast included Robert Powell, Eric Porter, and John Mills.)

In *North by Northwest*, still another classic Hitchcock thriller, foreign spies pursue Cary Grant, an innocent American mistaken for a spy, while Eva Marie Saint provides a stunning performance as a DOUBLE AGENT. Hitchcock becomes somewhat more realistic with *Topaz*, in which French and U.S. intelligence officers team up to find a double agent; the realism comes from Leon Uris's novel *Topaz*, which was based on a real espionage scandal (see SAPPHIRE). Another movie successfully adapted from a novel was *Three Days of the Condor*, in which Robert Redford plays CIA researcher Joe Turner, who becomes a target of both good guys and bad guys.

In *Hopscotch*, Walter Matthau is also a CIA officer on the run, but the movie plays the pursuit for laughs rather than suspense. So does *The Tall Blond Man with One Black Shoe*, a 1972 French film in which an innocent violinist is mistaken for a spy. Hollywood remade it under the same title in 1990. AIR AMERICA, an airline in Southeast Asia run by the CIA, was the subject of a daredevils-in-action movie, the very well-done *Air America*, released in 1990, starring Mel Gibson and Robert Downey, Jr.

The epitome of the cinema's Cold War spy was IAN FLEMING's JAMES BOND [F]. Bond, who could at times be believable in the pages of a book, was incredible on the screen. Stunts, gadgets, and hairbreadth escapes were the standard plot ingredients. Readers of the Bond books hardly recognized their hero when he went Hollywood.

The Bond novels began with *Casino Royale* in 1953. Under the same title, a star-filled movie (Peter Sellers, Ursula Andress, David Niven, Orson Welles, Woody Allen, Charles Boyer) came out in 1967. The film was conceived and produced as a spoof of spy movies. The plot— to the extent that there was one—had something to do with the British government recalling Sir James Bond to crush an effort by his nephew to take over the world with clones of world leaders. David Niven plays James Bond; Woody Allen is his contemptuous nephew, "Jimmy Bond"; Joanna Pettet is the glamorous spy Mata Bond; and Orson Welles is the SMERSH villain Le Chiffre. Sellers plays baccarat expert Evelyn Tremble, recruited as a British agent to challenge Le Chiffre to a game. The film was a debacle, mainly because of Sellers' demands for artistic license in shooting the film, the ridiculous plot, the inane sexual innuendoes, and the conflicting personalities of the stars. The success of the Bond series inspired many lower-grade spoofs, including *Our Man Flint, Matt Helm, That Man,* and the Austin Powers movies.

The real James Bond film series began with Sean Connery playing the suave daredevil who makes love to beautiful women and fights mad villains who are trying, in various ways, to conquer the world. Connery becomes AGENT 007 in *Dr. No* (book 1958, film 1963), with Ursula Andress helping him fight a fiend in the West Indies who is threatening the world. In *From Russia, with Love* (book 1957, film 1963) Connery outwits Soviet agent

Robert Shaw, and in *Goldfinger* (book 1959, film 1964), Connery stops Gert Frobe, who wants to steal the gold from Fort Knox, with the aid of his bowler-tossing henchman Oddjob (Harold Sakata). Pussy Galore, an expert in the martial arts, is played by Honor Blackman, who had played a spy in the TELEVISION series *The Avengers*.

Connery remained in the Bond role in four more Bond films: *Thunderball* (book based on a screen treatment by Fleming and others, 1961; film 1965), which pits Bond against S.P.E.C.T.R.E., a murderous Soviet agency; *You Only Live Twice* (book 1964, film 1967); *Diamonds Are Forever* (book 1956, film 1971), and *Never Say Never Again* (1983), essentially a remake of *Thunderball*.

In *On Her Majesty's Secret Service* (book 1963, film 1969), the role of Bond remained the same but the actor changed, with fashion model George Lazenby playing Agent 007. Roger Moore took over the role in *Live and Let Die* (book 1954, film 1973). Moore continued playing Bond in *The Spy Who Loved Me* (book, with Vivienne Michel, 1962; film 1977); *The Man with the Golden Gun* (book 1965, film 1974); *Moonraker* (book 1955, film 1979); *For Your Eyes Only* (book 1960, film 1981); *Octopussy* (book 1965, film 1983); and *A View to a Kill* (1985).

The 16th Bond movie, *License to Kill* (1989), was the first whose title was not taken from a James Bond story by Ian Fleming. It did take parts from Fleming works, including the novella *The Hildebrand Rarity* (*Playboy*, March 1960). Timothy Dalton returned as James Bond in this film, the first Bond movie to receive an R rating for excessive violence. *Goldeneye* (named after Ian Fleming's Jamaica retreat) came out in 1995, with Bond played by Pierce Brosnan and "M" played by a woman, Dame Judi Dench. This is a double takeoff on reality. The head of MI5 is traditionally known by a single letter, in reality "C." And when the movie was released, MI5 was headed by a woman, STELLA RIMINGTON.

Connery returned to espionage service when he appeared in *The Russia House*, a slow-moving movie version of le Carré's novel of the same name (book 1989, film 1990). By 2003, there had been 20 Bond films and there was talk that the 21st would be the last. For the British, Bond is an enduring hero. British soldiers in the Iraq war in 2003 called their mission Operation James and used CODE NAMES based on James Bond movies, including Goldfinger, Blofeld, and Connery.

A forecast of the problems in undoing Cold War espionage and sabotage was depicted in *Telefon*, produced in 1977, starring Charles Bronson as a KGB officer secretly sent to America to destroy the ingenious network of Soviet SLEEPERS who had been sent into the United States, hypnotized so that a Robert Frost poem said over the telephone would activate them to leave their home or business and blow up civilian and military installations. Years later, a KGB renegade threatens to activate the network, and destroys a couple of targets just to prove he can do it. Lee Remick plays a KGB agent sent to help Bronson and then kill him.

A new series of spy spoofs arrived in the 1990s featuring "Austin Powers: International Man of Mystery." Powers, a lecherous agent totally lacking the suavity of James Bond, is played by Mike Myers, who said he was inspired by the spy films he had seen in his youth.

With the end of the Cold War and the start of the war on terrorism, the spy movie and the action movie merged until it was difficult to tell one from the other.

Mr. Bull

SEE ALLEN DULLES

MSS

Ministry of State Security, principal Chinese agency for intelligence collection and COUNTERINTELLIGENCE.

Raised from bureau to ministry status in 1983, the MSS was modeled after the KGB, at least for domestic SURVEILLANCE, and dominates the complex Chinese intelligence apparatus. The reason for establishing the MSS, said a Chinese statement in July 1982, was to combat foreign espionage agencies.

"Since China adopted the policy of opening to the outside world," the statement said, "intelligence agencies or secret services of some foreign countries have stepped up their activities to obtain China's state secrets and sent special agents into China for subversive and destructive purposes."

Western intelligence agencies had scarce and unreliable information about the MSS until 1985, when Yu Zhensan, the former director of the Foreign Affairs Bureau of the MSS, defected. Yu Zhensan probably exposed LARRY WU-TAI CHIN, a longtime CIA employee arrested for espionage in 1985. According to Western intelligence sources, MSS maintains intelligence operations in more than 170 cities in nearly 50 countries through its Foreign Affairs Bureau. It also has major operations in Taiwan, Hong Kong, and Macao. The MSS supervises the surveillance of foreigners, especially journalists.

The MSS is organized into 12 bureaus, including one for DOMESTIC INTELLIGENCE. Others are given geographic responsibilities or devoted to gathering electronic, scientific, and technological intelligence. One of the bureaus uses as its COVER the Institute of Contemporary International Relations. The institute publishes a classified journal, *Contemporary International Relations*, which has a limited circulation among senior Communist Party officials. The MSS also trains employees at the Beijing College of International Relations and Institute of Cadre Management in Suzhou.

The MSS reach beyond China includes the pursuit of Chinese dissidents into other countries and providing cover for Chinese diplomats and AGENTS planted among the 15,000 Chinese students who arrive in the United States each year, and the thousands of Chinese who travel as business representatives or members of scientific, academic, and cultural delegations. The MSS was also behind an effort, launched in 1995, to influence U.S.

policy by making illegal contributions to political campaigns.

A congressional report issued in May 1999 said that "Chinese spies had stolen secrets on seven of the United States' most advanced thermonuclear weapons, giving them nuclear design information 'on a par with our own.' " But the report added that the espionage revelation largely came from documents provided by a WALK-IN not fully trusted by U.S. intelligence analysts. They believed that the walk-in had been under the control of the MSS and might have been proffering fake documents for reasons not publicly disclosed.

Mueller, Airman 1st Class Gustav

U.S. Air Force enlisted man who wanted to spy. In 1949, while attending an intelligence school in Oberammergau, West Germany, Mueller was arrested for attempting to sell classified information to what he took to be Soviet INTELLIGENCE OFFICERS. In fact, he was dealing with U.S. COUNTERINTELLIGENCE agents.

Mueller was possibly the first U.S. serviceman to be tried for betraying secrets after World War II. He was sentenced to five years in prison and a dishonorable discharge.

Mueller, Robert S., III

(b. 1944)

Ninth director of the FBI, who headed the bureau as the United States began its war on terrorism.

Mueller became director on Sept. 4, 2001, five days before the attack on the World Trade Center and the Pentagon changed FBI priority from crime-fighting and spy-catching to hunting down terrorists. He replaced LOUIS FREEH, who had retired rather than complete his term in 2003.

Mueller, who served briefly as acting deputy attorney general, was endorsed by Attorney General John Ashcroft, who convinced President George W. Bush to put the FBI under closer control of the Department of Justice.

Mueller stepped into an agency already reeling from the arrest and conviction of FBI agent ROBERT HANSSEN for espionage. Then came a barrage of criticism about the failure of the FBI and the CIA to warn of al Qaeda targeting of America. Mueller reacted by beginning a massive overhaul of the FBI, transferring more than 500 agents from criminal investigations to TERRORIST INTELLIGENCE. New guidelines allowed agents to keep houses of worship under SURVEILLANCE and to develop leads in situations where there is no indication of criminal activity.

Mueller also pledged closer cooperation with the CIA, a perennial vow from FBI directors. As an indicator of cooperation, CIA analysts were assigned to FBI headquarters in Washington and FBI officials were sent to the CIA's counterterrorism center in LANGLEY, Va. He and GEORGE TENET, DIRECTOR OF CENTRAL INTELLIGENCE, work well together. But Tenet had a much closer relationship with President Bush, meeting nearly every day with Bush in the White House.

Mueller placed protection from terrorist attack at the top of the FBI's list of priorities, followed by traditional counter-espionage operations and protection against COMPUTER ESPIONAGE. He established the FBI's Office of Intelligence, shifted more resources to counterterrorism, and expanded recruitment efforts to hire linguists and analysts.

Mueller graduated from Princeton in 1966 and earned a master's degree in international relations at New York University in 1967. He then joined the Marine Corps, leading a rifle platoon of the 3rd Marine Division in Vietnam. After three years in the Marines, Mueller went to the University of Virginia Law School. Following graduation, he worked for three years in a San Francisco law firm and then began his government career, serving in U.S. Attorney's offices in San Francisco and Boston, where he entered a law firm.

In 1989 he came to Washington as an assistant to Attorney General Richard L. Thornburgh, and later became chief of the Justice Department's Criminal Division. He directed major prosecutions, including the conviction of Panamanian dictator Manuel Noriega and mobster John Gotti. In 1995 he became senior litigator in the Homicide Section of the District of Columbia's U. S. Attorney's Office. Three years later he returned to San Francisco as U.S. Attorney.

When President Bush took office in 2001, Mueller came to Washington, served his brief stint under Ashcroft, and then was selected for the FBI post.

Muggeridge, Malcolm

(b. 1903 d. 1990)

British writer and INTELLIGENCE OFFICER. Muggeridge spent much of World War II as an intelligence specialist in the Field Security Police. He once ran a security check on Gen. Sir Edmund Ironside, Chief of the British Imperial General Staff. Ironside, who had fascist leanings, was relieved of his position in 1940. Muggeridge was an official witness at the *in camera* trial of TYLER KENT, an American diplomat charged with security violations, and ANNA WOLKOFF, a Russian fascist. In 1941 he was assigned to MI6. Among his coworkers was HAROLD (KIM) PHILBY.

Muggeridge, renowned as a satirist and cynical observer of British life, was more amused than awed by what he saw as an intelligence officer. "Secrecy," he wrote, "is as essential to Intelligence as vestments and incense to a mass, or darkness to a spiritual seance, and must at all costs be maintained, quite irrespective of whether or not it serves any purpose."

In Mozambique, Muggeridge's first duty station, he arranged the arrest of a merchant captain whose ship was to rendezvous with a U-boat to pass on supplies. The U-boat, Muggeridge later wrote, was captured. He also served in Algeria, Italy, and France, where after liberation, he had to convince French intelligence authorities that some apparent collaborators had actually been British AGENTS using their friendship with Germans as COVER for their espionage activities.

Muggeridge was also involved in determining the status of P. G. Wodehouse, the British novelist who wrote humorously about the upper class. Wodehouse, interned in Vichy France and later taken to Germany, was accused of collaboration because of his radio broadcasts from BERLIN. While Wodehouse did not write any spy novels, his writings influenced German intelligence officers, who took Wodehouse's comedy seriously. Agents being sent to England were told that Wodehouse's hilarious putdowns of the aristocracy were accurate and authentic.

Also see DOUBLE-CROSS SYSTEM.

Murphy, Seaman Michael R.

Crewman aboard the U.S. strategic missile submarine *James Polk* who called the Soviet mission to the UNITED NATIONS in June 1981 and offered to make what was later officially described as "a deal that would be beneficial to both the Soviets and himself." He called the mission three times and his calls were apparently recorded by U.S. COUNTERINTELLIGENCE officials. Murphy admitted the calls. Investigation showed that Murphy, who had a SECRET clearance, had not given any information to the Soviets. He was honorably discharged from the Navy in Aug. 1981.

Museums

Several intelligence agencies and services have established museums. The most significant are those of the CIA in LANGLEY, Va.; the National Cryptologic Museum of the NSA and NATIONAL VIGILANCE PARK at FORT MEADE, Md.; the British Intelligence Corps Museum at Templar Barracks, Ashford, Kent; the KGB museum in the LUBYANKA building in Moscow. There is also a Military Intelligence Museum at Fort Huachuca, Ariz., site of the U.S. Army's military intelligence school. That museum, the NSA museum, and the British Intelligence Corps Museum are open to the public, but a "virtual tour" is available on the CIA Web site, *www.cia.gov*.

An organization of private citizens, many with intelligence and CRYPTANALYSIS experience, established a museum at BLETCHLEY PARK, the British World War II codebreaking center. Portions of the Buckinghamshire estate, including some of the war-built huts with replicas of wartime equipment, are open to the public.

The CIA headquarters complex in Langley has a small exhibit area with a few significant artifacts; it is not open to the public.

The Imperial War Museum in London and the Smithsonian Institution's Museum of American History in Washington, D.C., have mounted major exhibits on codebreaking. The only major private museum devoted to intelligence is the INTERNATIONAL SPY MUSEUM in Washington.

Music Box

Soviet slang for a clandestine radio.

Musician

Soviet slang for a radio operator.

Mutt and Jeff

Norwegians trained to be saboteurs by the ABWEHR and delivered to England by seaplane and rubber dinghy. They gave themselves up to local police, were TURNED, and made DOUBLE AGENTS as part of the DOUBLE-CROSS SYSTEM. John Moe was given the CODE NAME Mutt and Tor Glad the code name Jeff, after the comic strip and a Cockney rhyming slang for "deaf."

To convince Germans of Mutt and Jeff's success as saboteurs, Double-Cross officers set up fake acts of sabotage, including the damaging of a power station—complete with explosion and newspaper publicity. So impressed was the Abwehr that Mutt and Jeff's HANDLERS sent them equipment and cash in four parachute drops, all of which were detected. As usual, the cash went toward financing the Double-Cross System.

Double-Cross officers used radio messages from Mutt and Jeff to give the Germans information about plans for an Allied invasion of Normandy. This was part of FORTITUDE, a DECEPTION operation designed to keep Germans from learning the time and place of D-DAY.

Concerns about Tor Glad's loyalty led to his being detained (although his radio continued to send false information). After the war, he returned to Norway, where he was arrested for working for the Germans. The charge was subsequently dropped.

MVD

SEE NKVD

Mystic (M-17)

Soviet high-flying RECONNAISSANCE aircraft, similar in many respects to the U.S. U-2 spyplane. Development of the aircraft was completed in the late 1970s, and the first flight, in May 1982, occurred 27 years after the first flight of the U-2!

Designed by the Molniya (Myasischev) design bureau, the Mystic was intended specifically for strategic reconnaissance. In addition to 5,500 pounds of cameras and other military reconnaissance equipment, the aircraft has also been employed in scientific research (as have modified U-2 aircraft).

The aircraft is essentially a powered glider with a wide wingspan (132 feet) and a twin-boom tail configuration. The wing has special lift devices fitted to the trailing edges of its wings, increasing aerodynamic efficiency. The aircraft has two turbofan (jet) engines, providing a maximum speed of about 466 mph, with an operating altitude of 70,000 feet.

Endurance of the Mystic is listed in the Russian press as 1½ hours; if true, it is far less than the U-2's 9½ hours. The M-55 variant of the Mystic is slightly smaller (wingspan of 123 feet) and carries 3,000 pounds of mission equipment, but its flight endurance is rated at 6½ hours. The aircraft is flown by a single crewman. In a series of special tests in 1990, the aircraft bettered 25 world altitude-related flight records.

Mystic is the Western CODE NAME for the aircraft; the Soviet name was Stratosfera, with the design bureau designation M-17.

N-2

Designation of intelligence staff of a U.S. Navy organization.

NACIC

SEE NATIONAL COUNTERINTELLIGENCE CENTER

Nah, Vu Ngoc

(b. 1928 d. 2002)

Communist North Vietnam AGENT who was an adviser to two South Vietnamese presidents. A senior communist officer, he was an adviser to President Ngo Dinh Diem until Diem's assassination in Nov. 1963. Nha continued working for Diem's successor, Nguyen Van Thieu.

Nha had a small bedroom next to Thieu's quarters. "The president and I discussed not only matters of national importance, but also talked over his family's affairs," Nah said in an interview in 2001. "Some things were known only by him and me. He even gave me the key to his room."

CIA officials unmasked Nha, who was put on trial for espionage in 1969 and was sentenced to life imprisonment. He was freed in 1973 in a prisoner exchange and was promoted to major general in 1975, when the Vietnam War ended.

Nakano

Japanese Army's intelligence school in operation from 1938 to 1945. It was the only SPY SCHOOL to be operated by Imperial Japan.

The school, originally established in Kudan, a Tokyo neighborhood, was moved to the Nakano District in northwestern Tokyo in April 1939 to train Army personnel in commando operations, espionage, propaganda, sabotage, and subversion in addition to intelligence collection. Through the end of World War II the school and an adjunct facility at Futamata, opened in Sept. 1944, trained about 2,500 men.

Former CIA analyst Stephen C. Mercado, in his valuable history of the school entitled *Nakano* (2002), wrote about a typical student at the school, Motoshige Yanagawa:

> Issued a serge black suit, Yanagawa shed his military uniform and the grew his hair to civilian length. In the school compound, he studied the tricks of the intelligence trade. He practiced the art of disguise. . . . He also learned the basics of code breaking and encryption. Then there were the techniques of secret communications, such as how to use invisible ink. His instructors also introduced him to such tools as a camera attached to a man's waistband and operated by a vest button, and a camera disguised as a cigarette lighter. . . . The Nakano School also taught Yanagawa how to handle explosives, incendiaries, and time bombs. For a quieter means of assault that promised results no less lethal, the school taught Yanagawa how to handle bacteria. Some microbes released from an instrument resembling a fountain pen into an occupied town's well could incapacitate or kill the enemy.

(During the war Yanagawa started his own version of a spy school near Jakarta in the Dutch East Indies, training Indonesians to work for the Japanese; after the war some used their training to fight against the Dutch and reached senior positions in the Indonesian government.)

Nakano students—who used pseudonyms while at school—also learned how to ride horseback, swim long distances, and drive all types of vehicles, including tanks. But there was also instruction in "theory"—readings of the contemporary German strategist Erich Ludendorff and the ancient Chinese strategist SUN TZU.

Graduates of Nakano served throughout the Japanese empire during World War II in a variety of roles, from commandos to staff intelligence officers. A few worked under the COVER of consular officials in neutral countries (including India before Britain went to war in the Far East in Dec. 1941). There were, however, too few graduates to remedy the generally poor performance of the Japanese Army in the intelligence field.

After the war Nakano school graduates served in various roles in support of U.S. military operations in the Far East, some working for Gen. Douglas MacArthur's G-2 staff in postwar Tokyo.

Napoleon Solo [f]

Star of the 1960s American TELEVISION spy series *The Man from U.N.C.L.E.* Robert Vaughn was the smooth, sophisticated, and always successful Napoleon Solo; David McCallum played Illya Kuryakin, his faithful Russian sidekick.

Narodnyy Komisariat Gosudarstvennoy Bezopasnosti

NKGB; SEE NKVD

Narodnyy Komisariat Vnutrennikh Del

SEE NKVD

Nashi

The Russian word for "ours," nashi is slang used by the KGB to indicate a KGB-controlled AGENT or collaborator. The word has been corrupted in Western usage as "nash" for a person belonging to one's own side.

Nassiri, Nematollah

Head of the Iranian Intelligence and Security Service (SAVAK). Nassiri was well known in the West through his contacts with Western intelligence services. SAVAK was the beneficiary of expertise from the CIA, the British Secret Service (MI6), and the MOSSAD. In 1953, the shah, Muhammad Reza Pahlavi, was restored to his throne by a CIA-engineered coup against Muhammad Mossadegh (see KERMIT ROOSEVELT). Nassiri, a colonel in the shah's bodyguard, helped in the coup and was subsequently made chief of *SAVAK*. The secret police was ruthless in its pursuit of real and imagined enemies of the shah.

When the shah was overthrown in 1979, Muslim revolutionaries, led by the Ayatollah Khomeini, arrested Nassiri and 19 other senior officers, accusing them of "treason, mass murder, and torture." Nassiri was condemned to death by an extraordinary Islamic revolutionary court and executed by firing squad in Feb. 1979.

Although Khomeini abolished *SAVAK* and destroyed its records, he set up a new secret police as ruthless as its predecessor.

National Air Intelligence Center

Primary U.S. Department of Defense producer of foreign aerospace intelligence. Operating out of Wright-Patterson Air Force Base, in Ohio, the center analyzes data on foreign aerospace forces and weapons systems to determine capabilities, vulnerabilities, and intentions. Center analysts have also been involved in supporting American weapons treaty negotiations and verification.

National Agency Check

Background investigation for a U.S. SECURITY CLEARANCE. Conducted by the FBI, it includes a fingerprint check, check of Department of Defense central index, and a limited additional investigation of the person's past.

National Counterintelligence Center

(NACIC)

Coordinating organization for guiding all U.S. COUNTERINTELLIGENCE activities at the national level. The NACIC was established in 1994 by the NATIONAL SECURITY COUNCIL (NSC) through a Presidential Decision Directive.

The center is controlled by the National Counterintelligence Policy Board under the NSC. The center is staffed with men and women from the FBI, CIA, NSA, DIA, and the Departments of Defense and State. Among the NACIC's missions is the countering of INDUSTRIAL ESPIONAGE. The NACIC Threat Assessment Office compiles, from intelligence sources and open literature, the clandestine targeting of U.S. industry and technology by foreign powers or their intelligence services.

The center provides the NSC with analyses of threats to emerging or existing U.S. technologies, or to business executives at home or overseas. It also assesses the effect on U.S. interests of foreign ownership, technology transfers, and joint ventures.

The NACIC produces reports on industrial espionage to selected corporations and works to "enhance the relationship" between the INTELLIGENCE COMMUNITY and U.S. private industry.

National Foreign Intelligence Board

(NFIB)

Successor to the UNITED STATES INTELLIGENCE BOARD, the board acts as an advisory council to the DIRECTOR OF CENTRAL INTELLIGENCE (DCI).

The NFIB was created by President Jimmy Carter, who gave it a mission different from that of the United States Intelligence Board, which had been involved directly in the production of NATIONAL INTELLIGENCE ESTIMATES (NIEs). The NFIB was to have an advisory role. This was expanded and defined by President Ronald Reagan and his DCI, WILLIAM J. CASEY. In March 1981 Casey directed that the NFIB would produce, review, and coordinate national foreign intelligence; exchange intelligence among agencies in the INTELLIGENCE COMMUNITY; protect intelligence sources and methods; and respond to matters brought to it by the DCL. As constituted by Casey, the NFIB was chaired by the DCI with the deputy director of the CIA being its vice chairman. Other members were the director of the NSA, director of the DEFENSE INTELLIGENCE AGENCY, director of the State Department's BUREAU OF INTELLIGENCE AND RESEARCH, the assistant director of the FBI, intelligence representatives from the Department of Energy and the Treasury Department, and representatives of "National Intelligence Council Reconaissance programs," which undoubtedly meant the NATIONAL RECONNAISSANCE OFFICE, whose name at that time could not be publicly disclosed.

The NFIB reviews NIEs to confirm that they reflect the consensus of the intelligence community. The board also draws up intelligence priorities and is the collective authority for determining the dispensing of intelligence to allies. Information required for the actions or decisions at the highest level of government. One of the needs of NATIONAL INTELLIGENCE is foreknowledge, so emphasis is usually placed on ways of finding indicators about an event that has just taken place or is about to take place.

National intelligence, as defined by U.S. intelligence specialists, is distinguished by two features: It is intended to serve in the formulation of national security policy; and its content, transcending the information of a single agency, represents the consensus of the intelligence community. It is usually presented by the DCI to the president or to the NATIONAL SECURITY COUNCIL.

Also see STRATEGIC INTELLIGENCE.

National Geographic Society

Organization inspired by patriotism to aid the FBI and CIA during the Cold War and the OFFICE OF STRATEGIC SERVICES (OSS) during World War II. The society is the largest nonprofit scientific and educational institution in the world. Founded in 1889, the society published the first issue of the *National Geographic* magazine later that year. Subsequently, the society sponsored exploration and research expeditions, published books and maps as well as other magazines, and, more recently, has sponsored extensive television specials.

The most secret project involving the society and the CIA began in 1964, soon after China exploded its first nuclear device at a test site in a remote area in western China. The idea came from Gen. Curtis LeMay, U.S. Air Force chief of staff and member of the society's board of trustees, and Barry Bishop, *National Geographic* magazine staff member who in 1963 was on the team that became the first Americans to reach the summit of Mount Everest.

In *Spies in the Himalayas: Secret Missions and Perilous Climbs* (2003), M. S. Kohli and Kenneth Conboy reveal details of the complex operation. Bishop was to lead a team that would climb 25,645-foot Nanda Devi in India and, under the cover of a mountaineering expedition, place a device for electronically monitoring Chinese nuclear tests. The device was powered by a generator called SNAP (Systems for Nuclear Auxiliary Power), which contained 2.1 pounds of plutonium 238. Bishop was unable to join the SNAP-bearing team. But he aided the project as a consultant.

The team got to a point near the summit but was driven back by a storm. When a team led by Kohli got to the spot the next year, he could not find the device. Similar clandestine efforts continued until SATELLITES took over the monitoring task. Reports persist that the SNAP device was never found.

The *National Geographic* magazine itself became a spy tool in the 1980s. CIA technicians, using a laser beam, etched MICRODOT messages into pages of an individual copy of the magazine being sent to an AGENT. How long the CIA operation went on has never been made public. The KGB revealed the microdot message only in a copy of the Feb. 1983 issue of the magazine. Under strong magnification can be read what appears to be directions to a DEAD DROP: "Wait ten minutes only" and possibly a face-to-face meeting: "Our representative will say. . . ."

The National Geographic Society apparently had no knowledge of the CIA's doctoring of the magazine. It was given to Col. VLADIMIR VASILYEV, an officer of the GRU (Soviet MILITARY INTELLIGENCE) who had been recruited in Budapest by the CIA. The magazine seems to have been found when Vasilyev was arrested by the KGB in 1986. A copy of the doctored magazine is in the KGB MUSEUM in Moscow.

During World War II, National Geographic opened its files to the U.S. armed services, which needed information on little-known places, particularly in the Pacific. Among the information seekers were undoubtedly OSS researchers. And, National Geographic maps were used extensively in the map room of the White House during the war.

Through some Cold War years, society officials allowed FBI agents to use a room in the oldest Geographic buildings for SURVEILLANCE of the Soviet Embassy across the street. From a window in that office agents photographed people going into and out of the embassy (among them JOHN WALKER and RONALD PELTON). Cleaning crews were told to stay out of the room; a plaque on the door identified the office as "The Mid-Atlantic Research Committee." Later, the FBI moved next door, to a building, owned by the American Federation of Labor, which offered a better view of the embassy.

National Geospatial Intelligence Agency

SEE NATIONAL IMAGERY AND MAPPING AGENCY

National Imagery and Mapping Agency

(NIMA)

Intelligence and combat-support agency that provides what it calls "geospatial intelligence" to other components of the INTELLIGENCE COMMUNITY, and to military forces.

NIMA was established in 1996 by the National Imagery and Mapping Agency Act, which folded into NIMA the former Defense Mapping Agency, the Central Imagery Office, and the Defense Dissemination Program Office. NIMA also took over the functions of the Defense Airborne Reconnaissance Office and the NATIONAL PHOTOGRAPHIC INTERPRETATION CENTER.

The NIMA also took over the imagery exploitation of the NATIONAL RECONNAISSANCE OFFICE, along with the dissemination and processing of that imagery.

On Nov. 24, 2003, the NIMA was renamed the National Geospatial Intelligence Agency (NGA). Retired Air Force Lt. Gen. James R. Clapper, Jr., the head of NIMA at the time, said that the name change was "a more accurate portrayal of what NGA really does," and that it did not reflect a change in capabilities.

The headquarters of NIMA/NGA is in Bethesda, Md.

National Industrial Security Program

Program established by the Department of Defense for government contractors that prescribes the requirements, restrictions, CLASSIFICATIONS, and other safeguards necessary to prevent the unauthorized disclosure of classified information. The program was established by an Executive Order of Jan. 6, 1993. It is applicable to contractors of all executive branch agencies.

The requirements and regulations are spelled out in the program's *Operating Manual;* until 1995 it was called the *Industrial Security Manual for Safeguarding Classified Information.* Informally, security officers call it the "bible."

The Defense Security Service administers the NISP.

National Intelligence

Information required for the actions or decisions at the highest level of government. Among the needs of national intelligence is foreknowledge, so emphasis is usually placed on ways of finding indicators about an event that has just taken place or is about to take place.

National intelligence, as defined by U.S. intelligence specialists, is distinguished by two features: It is intended to serve in the formulation of national security policy; its content, transcending the information of a single agency, represents the consensus of the INTELLIGENCE COMMUNITY. In the United States, it is usually presented by the DIRECTOR OF CENTRAL INTELLIGENCE to the president and to the NATIONAL SECURITY COUNCIL.

Also see STRATEGIC INTELLIGENCE.

National Intelligence Authority

(NIA)

Precursor to the CIA. The NIA was created by an executive memorandum signed by President Truman on Jan. 22, 1946. Its purpose was the coordination of U.S. foreign intelligence activities. Truman designated as the members of the NIA Secretary of State James F. Byrnes, Secretary of War Robert V. Patterson, Secretary of the Navy James V. Forrestal, and, as the President's personal representative, Adm. William D. Leahy, the de facto chairman of the Joint Chiefs of Staff. The NIA members were directed to assign personnel from the State, War, and Navy departments to the CENTRAL INTELLIGENCE GROUP (CIG), which was headed by the DIRECTOR OF CENTRAL INTELLIGENCE. The NIA and the CIG lasted for 20 months. When the CIA was founded, on Sept. 20, 1947, it inherited all the people and records of the CIG.

National Intelligence Council

(NIC)

INTELLIGENCE COMMUNITY's center for mid-term and long-term strategic thinking. The council, an organization within the CIA, produces NATIONAL INTELLIGENCE ESTIMATES (NIEs).

The council—managed by a chairman, a vice chairman for evaluations, and a vice chairman for estimates—consists of National Intelligence Officers (NIOs), experienced analysts (often not from the CIA) who are specifically responsible for analyses that respond to the needs of CONSUMERS. NIOs are usually specialists in certain geographical areas, such as the Middle East, or subjects, such as TERRORIST INTELLIGENCE, nuclear proliferation, or weapons of mass destruction. The NIOs also work closely with policymakers and serve as personal staff officers and senior advisers to the DIRECTOR OF CENTRAL INTELLIGENCE in their specialties.

National Intelligence Estimate

(NIE)

Evaluations of national security concerns, usually regarding a specific country, prepared by the CIA's NATIONAL INTELLIGENCE COUNCIL. Typically an NIE is presented by the DIRECTOR OF CENTRAL INTELLIGENCE to the NATIONAL SECURITY COUNCIL. NIEs on specific subjects (such as a worldwide assessment of ballistic missile forces) have also been prepared at the request of the Senate Select Committee on Intelligence.

In 1950 the CIA set up the OFFICE OF NATIONAL ESTIMATES (ONE), a special group for developing NIEs. The office consisted of a staff, which gathered and summarized information for the NIEs, and a BOARD OF NATIONAL ESTIMATES (BNE), whose members—distinguished former military officers, State Department experts, academics—defined the framework of the NIEs and then oversaw their drafting.

The staff and board had virtually unlimited access to the most sensitive data. Although an NIE is the responsibility of the CIA, it is usually produced in collaboration with other members of the INTELLIGENCE COMMUNITY and, if necessary, will draw upon civilian experts.

From 1952 to 1967 the head of the ONE and chairman of the BNE was Sherman Kent, a former professor of history at Yale and the author of *Strategic Intelligence for American World Policy* (1949).

Kent tried to balance the language of NIEs between the "poets," who wanted to convince with words and phrases, and the "mathematicians," who wanted words like *probably* and *possibly* to have a precise meaning. Kent expressed the problem this way: "If you write to give no more than just the general idea or general feel you may get through with great success. Per contra, if you break your heart in an endeavor to make yourself fully and precisely understood, you may not."

Under Kent, NIE producers worked out a chart giving a mathematical rating to what an NIE meant when it used words and phrases like "almost certain" or "almost certainly not." Some people proposed that the chart be put on the inside back cover of every NIE:

```
100%  . . . . . . . . . . . . . . . . . . . certainty
93%, give or take about 6%  . . . almost certain
75%, give or take about 12%  . . probable
50%, give or take about 10%  . . chances about even
30%, give or take about 10%  . . probably not
7%, give or take about 5%  . . . . almost certainly not
0%  . . . . . . . . . . . . . . . . . . . . . impossibility
```

In 1993 the CIA's CENTER FOR THE STUDY OF INTELLIGENCE began publishing declassified NIEs on the Soviet Union prepared by Kent's BNE from 1950 through 1959. In Dec. 1957, for example, an NIE examined the issue of Soviet compliance with a two-year moratorium on nuclear testing. NIEs started with the conclusion and then went to the information on which the conclusion was based. This particular NIE concluded:

> We believe that, if the USSR agrees to a moratorium on nuclear tests, its initial policy will be to abide by the terms of the moratorium. We believe this because the Soviet leaders not only would not wish to follow a violation but because they probably would hope that the effect of the moratorium would give them political and strategic advantages . . . We conclude that the Soviet leaders would almost certainly regard the political consequences of getting caught red-handed as unacceptable, except in extraordinary circumstances. . . .

Under Kent, the ONE produced scholarly, often academic NIEs that eventually went out of style. The ONE was sharply criticized by Henry Kissinger, President Nixon's national security adviser, who complained about having to labor through "'Talmudic' documents to find their real meaning." Kissinger started having the National Security Council write estimates for him; those estimates tended to agree with him more than the ones produced by the ONE.

The ONE was abolished in 1973 by WILLIAM E. COLBY, the DIRECTOR OF CENTRAL INTELLIGENCE. But Colby continued to have NIEs produced by National Intelligence Officers. Aided by experts in and out of the CIA, the NIOs produced estimates that often differed considerably from the ONE PRODUCT.

With the end of what Kent often called the "bipolar world" of U.S.-Soviet tension, NIEs no longer had a tight focus on a potential nuclear enemy. Other countries, other issues, particularly TERRORIST INTELLIGENCE, preoccupy the NIOs of a new generation. The NIEs they are writing, according to CIA critics, are journalistic rather than scholarly, and often politically tuned to current administration policy.

National Maritime Intelligence Center

(NMIC)

Massive headquarters for U.S. Navy, Marine Corps, and Coast Guard intelligence activities, located in Suitland, Md., a suburb of Washington, D.C.

Dedicated on Oct. 20, 1993, the center was designed during the Cold War to consolidate a number of NAVAL INTELLIGENCE activities scattered around the Washington area. The building, with 660,000 square feet of floor space, is located on the large Suitland Federal Center site. Designed for some 2,000 technical and support personnel, it is inundated with computers and secure meeting spaces (see SENSITIVE COMPARTMENTED INFORMATION FACILITY), has a 350-seat auditorium as well as high-tech conference rooms, PHOTOGRAPHIC INTERPRETATION equipment, and other facilities.

National Photographic Interpretation Center

(NPIC)

U.S. intelligence agency charged with interpretation of photography from OVERHEAD sources, RECONNAISSANCE aircraft, and SATELLITES. It is referred to as *N-pic*.

NPIC became part of the NATIONAL IMAGERY AND MAPPING AGENCY when that organization was created in 1996. NPIC formerly was managed within the CIA Directorate of Science and Technology (DS&T). NPIC is still a joint CIA/Defense Department center whose product goes to the CIA and Pentagon to be incorporated into all-source intelligence reports. NPIC reportedly employs about 1,200 image interpreters and archivists.

In the mid-1950s, while the U-2 spyplane and CORONA photo satellites were under development, the CIA began assembling a staff of PHOTOGRAPHIC INTERPRETATION specialists who would handle their film. Arthur C. Lundahl was given the task of organizing the operation, including the selection and recruiting of people.

The CIA's photographic division was initially known by the CODE NAME HT/AUTOMAT. Lundahl adopted

HT/AUTOMAT based on the initials of the security officer (Henry Thomas) and Lundahl's view that the division was an "automat" where—like the restaurant chain—intelligence CONSUMERS could come and pick up whatever interpreted photography that they needed.

A nondescript office building at Fifth and K Streets Northwest in Washington, D.C., a crime-ridden area, was selected to house the expanded division. The three lower floors were used by an automobile firm and a real estate office. In *Eyeball to Eyeball* (1990), photo interpretation specialist Dino A. Brugioni described the first home of NPIC: "The building was not air-conditioned, and there were heating problems in winter."

The first U-2 OVERFLIGHT of the Soviet Union occurred on July 4, 1956. After studying many hundreds of feet of "practice film," the photo specialists at last had real photographs of the secrets of the Soviet Union. On Aug. 19, 1960, an Air Force plane snatched the first film canister to be ejected from a CORONA satellite carrying photos of the Soviet Union. And in response to Cuba's commencement of special relations with Moscow, on Oct. 27, 1960, a U-2 overflew the island for the first time, bringing another area under intensive overhead photography.

The division became increasingly involved with supporting national leaders. On Jan. 18, 1961, a few days before he left the White House, President Dwight D. Eisenhower signed NATIONAL SECURITY COUNCIL Intelligence Directive No. 8, which formally established the NPIC under CIA administration. Earlier, Eisenhower had personally approved the U-2 and Corona programs.

When his successor, John F. Kennedy, learned of the shabby NPIC accommodations, he ordered better space to be found for this most useful activity. Accordingly, on Jan. 1, 1963, the center moved to more spacious offices in Building 213 at First and M Streets Southwest, part of the Washington Navy Yard complex. (It remains there today.)

As U.S. interest in Cuba increased because of Soviet arms shipments, photography from P2V NEPTUNE Navy patrol aircraft was also sent to the center. Lundahl, wrote Brugioni, "asked that the crates and containers be carefully analyzed and measured using photogrametric means. He labeled the science of measuring, identifying, and cataloguing the crates and their contents *cratology.*"

The NPIC level of effort increased many times over during the CUBAN MISSILE CRISIS of 1962, although both the Air Force's Strategic Air Command and Navy photointerpretation centers were also employed to support that crisis. (See F-101 VOODOO, F8U CRUSADER.)

Those photographs were described in briefings to President Kennedy and his top advisers by Lundahl at the White House almost daily during Oct. 1962. Several top officials went to the Navy Yard to talk personally with the interpreters.

When Kennedy decided to confront the Soviets with having placed ballistic missiles in Cuba, NPIC-produced photos were carried by U.S. briefers to several Western capitals. And as contingency plans were made for either precision strikes on the island or an invasion, the top U.S. military commanders used NPIC photos and maps for their planning.

But, wrote Brugioni, there was a moment of humor in the crisis, thanks to one NPIC photo:

> President Kennedy detested military jargon—particularly the reporting of MRBM [Medium-Range Ballistic Missile] positions as "occupied" (with launchers) and "unoccupied." A low-flying reconnaissance plane happened to photograph a soldier using an open three-hole latrine. When the photo was shown to the president as one "occupied," he laughed and asked why he didn't have this primer earlier.

Subsequently, with the increase in U.S. participation in the Vietnam conflict, aircraft photography was again at the forefront of White House briefings. But Secretary of Defense Robert S. McNamara used NPIC-produced photography only to support his views. Lundahl never gave a briefing to President Johnson as he had to Kennedy. Brugioni recalled,

> Observation of the heavily bombed and cratered roads on high-altitude photography created the impression of a successful military operation, but on low-level photography, large numbers of [North] Vietnamese soldiers could be seen pushing bicycles laden with supplies, weaving their way around the heavily cratered areas. NPIC briefing boards showing the Vietnamese resupplying their forces . . . were never shown to the president, we were told. Although Secretary [of State Dean] Rusk was aware of the unfavorable intelligence, Rusk was reluctant to challenge the aggressive McNamara, fearing a State-Defense split.

Aircraft and satellite photography—as interpreted by NPIC—were factors in U.S. policy and military decisions in Vietnam and in subsequent U.S. conflicts and crises.

National Reconnaissance Office

(NRO)

U.S. agency responsible for strategic space-borne RECONNAISSANCE and SURVEILLANCE. An agency of the Department of Defense, the NRO designs, builds, and operates the nation's reconnaissance SATELLITES.

The NRO was so secret that its existence was not officially confirmed until 1992. The veil of secrecy was lifted again in Feb. 1995, when the NRO declassified 800,000 CORONA satellite images and transferred them to the National Archives. Then, in Dec. 1996, the NRO announced for the first time, in advance, the launch of a reconnaissance satellite. In 2002 NRO, which already had an Internet site, even opened a site for children.

Created on Aug. 25, 1960, to coordinate OVERHEAD reconnaissance by satellites and U-2 spyplanes, the NRO became an agency that spends far more funds than either the CIA or the NSA. The NRO was seen as settling disputes between the CIA and the Air Force, which had competing interests both in the use of satellites and what the satellites discovered. The Air Force wanted to find National Reconnaissance Office evidence to support its position that the Soviets were pursuing a policy of continual arms buildup that had to be matched by ever-growing appropriations for the Air Force. The CIA believed that satellite intelligence would provide objective evidence of the size of the Soviet armory.

The NRO is responsible for the design, development, and procurement of all U.S. reconnaissance satellites, and for their management once they are in orbit. The agency also provides INTELLIGENCE AND WARNING derived from satellite intelligence, monitors arms control agreements, keeps military operations and exercises under surveillance from space, monitors natural disasters, and at times provides satellite support for environmental issues. Among the satellites managed by the NRO are the FERRETS for SIGNALS INTELLIGENCE and satellites providing specialized communications.

The agency is part of the Department of Defense but is co-managed by the DIRECTOR OF CENTRAL INTELLIGENCE (DCI). It operates the 30-odd U.S. military satellite control stations around the world. These are never publicly designated as NRO facilities. The NRO lost some of its responsibilities in 1996 with the creation of the NATIONAL IMAGERY AND MAPPING AGENCY, which took over the imagery exploitation of the NRO, along with its dissemination and processing capabilities.

The DCI's Committee on Imagery Requirements and Exploitation (COMIREX) tells the NRO what is needed. In 1992 COMIREX became part of a new Central Imagery Office, an interagency center that handles the distribution of overhead intelligence to customers. ("Exploitation" is the INTELLIGENCE COMMUNITY's word for extracting information from NRO products.)

Since 1991 there has also been a DCI Environmental Task Force, consisting of about 50 scientists and governmental and private specialists. All have the necessary SECURITY CLEARANCES for examining NRO products, which they use for environmental research into such phenomena as volcanic eruptions and forest fires.

The NRO was conceived at a meeting in Aug. 1960 between President Eisenhower and an ad hoc group that he had appointed to study how to handle the new intelligence dimension promised by the Corona satellite and the developing SAMOS (Satellite and Missile Observation Satellite). Among those who met with Eisenhower were John H. Rubel, deputy director of research and engineering for the Department of Defense; Dr. George B. Kistiakowsky, Eisenhower's science adviser; and Dr. Joseph Charyk, Undersecretary of the Air Force.

The Air Force had been competing with the CIA for control of satellite intelligence and had opposed the CIA's control of the U-2 program. Now that the CIA had pioneered overhead reconnaissance with the U-2, the Air

Force feared that the Corona program would also be placed under CIA control.

Eisenhower was politically harmed when the Soviet Union shot down a U-2 on May 1, 1960 (see FRANCIS GARY POWERS). Three months later, when contemplating what to do about space reconnaissance, Eisenhower was still smarting from how the CIA had handled the U-2 incident. He decided that the satellite programs would have civilian-military oversight. From that decision came what was publicly known as the Office of Missile and Satellite Systems (OMSS), within the Office of the Secretary of the Air Force. The OMSS—later the Office of Space Systems—was the cover for the NRO. The first director was Charyk, who also continued as Under secretary of the Air Force. Insiders said he wore two hats, a white Air Force hat and a black one—referring to the NRO's status as a BLACK, or undisclosed, program. The first U.S. reconnaissance satellite orbited on Jan. 31, 1961.

The NRO quickly established itself as a valuable agency for delivering dramatic intelligence results, for example, evidence that dispelled the "missile gap" theory by showing that the Soviets had fewer missiles than had been reported and photographs of huge projects for building underground bunkers for Soviet leaders—confirming their belief in the likelihood of nuclear war. The NRO was also crucial in reaching arms control agreements with the Soviets, for it could manage the monitoring of satellites to produce verification.

Martin C. Faga, as Assistant Secretary of the Air Force for Space, was the last person to direct the NRO while its name was officially secret. His own career illustrates the dual nature of the NRO, for he had previously worked for the CIA. "It's fair to say that satellite reconnaissance has been a part of every security event of the last 30 years," Faga said, "whether it's preparing SAC [Strategic Air Command] for its bombing and missile missions, or assisting tactical units in the field, or keeping the president, secretary of Defense, national security adviser, and others informed. . . ."

The NRO grew in secrecy to a powerful, almost financially independent agency. Because of the deep secrecy that shrouded the NRO, its budget escaped congressional scrutiny, although criticism arose over its penchant for "gold-plated" technology. Estimates of the annual budget range from $5 billion to $7 billion. Also contributing to oversight problems has been the NRO's dual control.

The NRO is staffed by an estimated 4,000 employees of the Department of Defense, the CIA, and members of the armed services, most of them in the Air Force. Interpretation of satellite images is the responsibility of the CIA's NATIONAL PHOTOGRAPHIC INTERPRETATION CENTER, not the NRO. Although the NRO has had jurisdiction over some reconnaissance AIRCRAFT, beginning in June 1994 those tasks were handled by the Defense Airborne Reconnaissance Office (DARO), which managed the development and acquisition of all airborne reconnaissance by both manned and unmanned aerial vehicles, their sensors, data links, data relays, and ground stations. In

1996, the functions of DARO were taken over by the NA-
TIONAL IMAGERY AND MAPPING AGENCY. This administrative tangle has generated confusion and criticism. After
the Persian Gulf War of 1991, military planners complained that intelligence had been delivered too slowly,
singling out the NRO. The NRO responded by saying it
was working on "demand-pull architecture" that would
allow the planner of a combat mission to push a button
and bring onto the screen of a monitor specific information, such as photographs of buildings in a city where
peacekeeping forces had been trapped. The planner
would be able to bring up data on up-to-date intelligence
information that is as near as possible to real time.

Meanwhile, in 1990 the NRO bought almost 14
more acres than was needed for its planned four-build-
ing, $304 million office complex near Dulles Interna-
tional Airport, in Virginia, about 20 miles west of
Washington, D.C. The agency intended to use the extra
land for two additional buildings that it would sell or
lease to contractors it regularly deals with. All of this was
done without informing the Department of Defense or
the DCI.

Revelations about the plans were uncovered by congressional investigators, who were reacting to reports
that the NRO had failed to reveal the cost of its new
headquarters to Congress. The investigators further
found that the cost of the headquarters was 30 percent
higher than was deemed necessary for the NRO's 2,190
employees and nearly 1,000 on-site contractor personnel.

JOHN M. DEUTCH, who became DCI in May 1995,
was in office only a month when congressional investigators told him that the NRO had accumulated almost $4
billion in surplus funds without telling its supervisor
agencies about the unspent funds. (This amount exceeds
the annual operating budget of the State Department.)
Much of the money was believed to have been allocated
for the launching of replacement satellites. They did not
need to be replaced, but the NRO kept the money as
what a congressional investigator called "a pot of gold."
But as members of the Senate Select Intelligence Committee stated, "The NRO's top managers themselves had
no idea" how much was unspent. A later audit by the
NRO's new financial officer put the surplus at $4 billion.

Deutch and Secretary of Defense William Perry fired
Jeffrey K. Harris, NRO director and Assistant Secretary
of the Air Force for Space, and his deputy, Jimmie D.
Hill. The firings were seen as a prelude to the creation of
the new NATIONAL IMAGERY AND MAPPING AGENCY, which
would remain in the Department of Defense and be part
of the Intelligence Community. Incorporated into the
new agency would be the Defense Mapping Agency, the
Central Imagery Office, the National Photographic Interpretation Center, imagery analysis personnel from the
DEFENSE INTELLIGENCE AGENCY, and at least some parts of
DARO.

National Security Agency

SEE NSA

National Security Archive

A non-governmental, non-profit repository for declassified U.S. documents obtained through the FREEDOM OF
INFORMATION ACT (FOIA). The world's largest non-governmental library of declassified documents, the archive
is housed in the George Washington University's Gelman
Library in Washington, D.C.

The archive—(not to be confused with the National
Security Agency (NSA)—also serves as a research institute
on international affairs and provides legal aid in cases involving public access to government information. Archive
lawsuits under FOIA forced the U.S. government to release
previously secret documents ranging from the Kennedy-
Khrushchev letters during the CUBAN MISSILE CRISIS to the
diaries of Oliver North during the IRAN-CONTRA AFFAIR.

Archive funds, supporting a yearly budget of about
$1.8 million, come principally from publication revenues
and from private philanthropists, such as the Carnegie
Corporation, the John D. and Catherine T. MacArthur
Foundation, and the Ford Foundation. The archive re-
ceives no government funding.

The archive was founded in 1985 by journalists and
scholars who had obtained documentation from the U.S.
government under the FOIA and sought a centralized
repository for the materials. These holdings by 2004 included more than 2 million pages of material.

National Security Council

Agency established by the U.S. National Security Act of
July 26, 1947, to advise the President with respect to the
integration of domestic, foreign, and military policies relating to national security. The body acts on behalf of the
President to provide guidance and direction for the conduct of all foreign intelligence and COUNTERINTELLIGENCE
activities. As the senior policymaking body in the executive branch with respect to national security, the NSC is
also the ultimate CONSUMER of national intelligence efforts.

The statutory members of the NSC are the President,
Vice President, Secretary of State, and Secretary of Defense. The NSC is supported by a staff headed by the Assistant to the President for National Security Affairs,
generally known as the National Security Adviser.

National Security Information

Information determined by a U.S. government agency to
require protection against unauthorized disclosure. The
CLASSIFICATIONS of TOP SECRET, SECRET, and CONFIDENTIAL
are used to designate such information.

Also referred to as "classified information."

National Technical Means

U.S. term for the use of AIRCRAFT photography, SATELLITE
photography, the seafloor SOUND SURVEILLANCE SYSTEM,

and other means of RECONNAISSANCE to provide arms control verification.

In *Deep Black* (1986) William E. Burrows wrote that National Technical Means ". . . are deemed to be so important in the arms control process that interfering with them is specifically prohibited by each treaty. Finally, the [National Technical Means] systems act as a kind of alarm that is supposed to go off when any of many indicators signaling a possible attack against the United States or any of its allies is observed."

National Vigilance Park

Memorial at NSA in FORT MEADE, Md., dedicated to the "achievements and sacrifices" of military personnel who died in incidents relating to aerial RECONNAISSANCE. When the park was dedicated in 1997, NSA said that 152 cryptologists had lost their lives during World War II and the Cold War, including 64 engaged in aerial reconnaissance. Later, park officials raised this number to "over 200 'silent warriors' of the Air Force Security Service, NAVAL SECURITY GROUP and ARMY SECURITY AGENCY who perished flying Cold War reconnaissance missions in slow, mostly unarmed aircraft."

The park is adjacent to the National Cryptographic Museum (see MUSEUMS). The centerpiece of the park is a C-130 Hercules aircraft refurbished to resemble the EC-130A that was downed over Soviet Armenia on Sept. 2, 1958, by Soviet MiG-17 fighters. All 17 Americans died in the crash. The aircraft carried six flight crew members from the 7406th Support Squadron and 11 members of the Air Force Security Service attached to Detachment 1 of the 6911th Radio Group Mobile.

Also at the memorial is an Army RU-8D SIGNALS INTELLIGENCE aircraft. That plane honors eight men from the 371st Radio Research Company killed when two UH-1H Huey helicopters were shot down in Vietnam, and five soldiers from the 138th Radio Research Company who died when their fixed-wing JU-21A aircraft was shot down.

Surrounding the aircraft are 19 trees, symbolizing the types of reconnaissance aircraft lost during the Cold War—12 Air Force, four Navy, and three Army.

SEE AIRCRAFT SHOT DOWN.

NATO

SEE NORTH ATLANTIC TREATY ORGANIZATION

Naval Criminal Investigation Service

(NCIS)

U.S. Navy agency responsible for investigative and COUNTERINTELLIGENCE activities.

The NCIS had been the Naval Investigative Service (NIS) until Dec. 1992, when the Navy decided that a name change would somehow help the battered reputation of the NIS. The investigative service had been se-

verely criticized in the 1980s for its handling of espionage cases and again in 1992 for its failure to dig into sexual harassment charges stemming from a wild naval aviators' convention known as Tailhook.

In 1987, the NIS, as it was then known, became the prime investigative organization in the sensational spy case involving U.S. Marine guards at the U.S. Embassy in Moscow. Although the FBI is the lead agency for U.S. espionage cases, the NIS was called in because the Marines came under Navy jurisdiction. (See CLAYTON J. LONETREE.)

The service was also heavily criticized during 1985 for its failure to detect an international smuggling ring that stole sensitive F-14 Tomcat aircraft parts from the aircraft carrier *Kitty Hawk* and sold them to Iran; and the Walker spy ring, which had been operating within the Navy since 1968. (See JOHN A. WALKER.) During World War I a rapidly expanded OFFICE OF NAVAL INTELLIGENCE (ONI) began to employ professional investigators to collect information about the capabilities of foreign military organizations and possible subversion. ONI at that time became deeply involved in counterintelligence and security of Navy facilities. ONI retained responsibility for these missions through the Naval Investigative Service until the establishment of a separate Naval Investigative Service Command in 1985.

The NCIS has some 2,300 employees, about half of them civilian special agents.

Naval Intelligence

Body of intelligence dealing with naval and maritime activities, especially the technical aspects of ships and other weapons of potential enemies, and the means of developing and producing ships and weapons. See DIRECTOR OF NAVAL INTELLIGENCE, NAVAL INTELLIGENCE, U.S., OFFICE OF NAVAL INTELLIGENCE.

Naval Intelligence, U.S.

The nation's longest-surviving intelligence service, U.S. Naval Intelligence traces its origins to the establishment of the OFFICE OF NAVAL INTELLIGENCE (ONI) in 1882.

While ONI has always served as the intelligence staff for the Secretary of the Navy and Chief of Naval Operations, with the fleets having their own intelligence staffs, late in World War II the ONI also became responsible for OPERATIONAL INTELLIGENCE, a function previously assigned to the operating fleets.

Navy INTELLIGENCE OFFICERS also serve on the fleet staffs and man FLEET INTELLIGENCE CENTERS. Several separate naval intelligence agencies or subcommands were created during World War II. The most prominent was the Naval Photographic Interpretation Center (NAVPIC), created in 1941 to train and support fleet photographers.

During the Cold War a number of specialized commands were organized within naval intelligence. Initially these came under the Office of Naval Intelligence; however, in 1967 the NAVAL INTELLIGENCE COMMAND was established as part of a general Navy reorganization to reduce Navy headquarters personnel and to establish unified direction and oversight for the increasing number of intelligence subcommands.

A hallmark of the Cold War era was the major increase in SCIENTIFIC AND TECHNICAL (S&T) INTELLIGENCE, which led to creation of the Naval Scientific and Technical Intelligence Center (NAVSTIC) in 1960. In an effort to develop a parallel organization structure, in 1964 NAVPIC was redesignated the Naval Reconnaissance and Technical Support Center (NRTSC). NAVSTIC was located at the Naval Observatory in Washington, D.C.; beginning in 1967 its offices were moved to the Washington suburb of Suitland, Md., to collocate NAVSTIC and NRTSC. As part of a limited consolidation, these and other subcommands were placed under the Naval Intelligence Command, formed in 1967, under a rear admiral who also served as a deputy DIRECTOR OF NAVAL INTELLIGENCE.

With NAVSTIC and NRTSC both handling SATELLITE photography and related intelligence, the two agencies were combined in 1972 into the Naval Intelligence Support Center. The center soon established a reputation as the premier S&T center within the Department of Defense. (In 1988 it was renamed the Naval Technical Intelligence Center, or NTIC.)

Meanwhile, the operational intelligence activities of ONI—known as the Special Intelligence Section—were renamed the Navy Field Operational Intelligence Office (NFOIO) in 1957 and moved to FORT MEADE, Md., location of the NSA. By 1970, as Soviet at-sea operations were increasing dramatically, NFOIO was directed to establish a current intelligence section, called the Navy Ocean Surveillance Intelligence Center (NOSIC), at Suitland.

The continued concern over Soviet naval operations led the Navy to combine NFOIO and NOSIC into the Naval Operational Intelligence Center (NAVOPINTCEN) in 1981, located at Suitland and at the Baltimore-Washington International Airport. This center, keeping track of all Soviet naval-related activities, was charged with providing INDICATIONS AND WARNING, current operational intelligence, and in-depth analysis.

Meanwhile, TASK FORCE (TF) 168 was established in 1969 to manage intelligence collection and improve support to fleet intelligence activities. Over the years TF 168 evolved into the intelligence collection arm of Naval Intelligence, with personnel being assigned throughout the world.

In 1964 the Naval Intelligence Processing System Support Activity was set up in Alexandria, Va., to support the increasing use of computers aboard ship and throughout the naval intelligence community. Later the activity was assigned responsibility for worldwide intelligence telecommunications. While some of the activity was at Suitland to support other naval intelligence work, in 1979 the entire command was moved there. In 1985 the activity was given responsibility for data-processing security throughout the Navy. Inevitably, in 1988 it was renamed Naval Intelligence Automation Center to reflect more accurately the greater scope of its mission, and in

1990 the name was changed again, to Naval Intelligence Activity.

With indications that the Cold War was coming to an end, in the late 1980s the Director of Naval Intelligence, Rear Adm. Edward D. (Ted) Sheafer, took a major step toward consolidating intelligence activities. In Oct. 1991—on the eve of the breakup of the Soviet Union—NTIC, NAVOPINTCEN, TF 168, and portions of the oft-renamed Naval Intelligence Activity were merged into the new NATIONAL MARITIME INTELLIGENCE CENTER at Suitland.

In Jan. 1993, those portions of the intelligence community remaining outside the Naval Maritime Intelligence Center were combined with the center and placed directly under the Office of Naval Intelligence. Subsequently, Marine Corps and Coast Guard intelligence staffs were shifted to the National Maritime Intelligence Center. Then, in 2002, with the absorption of the U.S. Coast Guard into the new DEPARTMENT OF HOMELAND SECURITY, the small Coast Guard intelligence became part of that department's intelligence organization.

Beyond the multitude of naval intelligence organizations listed here, beginning with the start of the Cold War the Navy has maintained a large number of Naval Reserve intelligence units. The men and women in these units have, individually and as units, worked on a variety of projects. Individuals have also augmented fleet and intelligence center staffs during crises and wars.

Also see NAVAL CRIMINAL INVESTIGATIVE SERVICE.

Naval Intelligence Command

(NIC)

U.S. Navy command that provides support to the OFFICE OF NAVAL INTELLIGENCE (ONI). NIC was established on July 1, 1967, as part of a general Navy reorganization to reduce the number of Navy headquarters personnel and to establish unified direction and oversight for the increasing number of subcommands already subordinate to ONI.

The commander of NIC is usually a rear admiral who is "double-hatted" as a deputy DIRECTOR OF NAVAL INTELLIGENCE. When originally established, NIC was located in an office building in suburban Alexandria, Va. In 1979 it was transferred to the Federal Center in Suitland, Md., also a suburb of Washington, D.C. And in late 1993 it was moved into the new NATIONAL MARITIME INTELLIGENCE CENTER.

Naval Investigative Service

SEE NAVAL CRIMINAL INVESTIGATIVE SERVICE

Naval Security Group

(NSG)

U.S. Navy designation for NAVY COMMUNICATIONS INTELLIGENCE activities. The term was adopted on July 1,

1968, for both the headquarters activity (at the NAVAL SECURITY STATION in Washington, D.C.), and the various communications intercepts groups, both ashore and afloat, around the world.

Naval Security Station

First site of the headquarters of the DEPARTMENT OF HOMELAND SECURITY. Soon after its creation in 2002, Homeland Security moved into the facility, located at Massachusetts and Nebraska Avenues in northwest Washington, D.C. It had been the site of U.S. NAVY COMMUNICATIONS INTELLIGENCE headquarters from 1943 to 1995. The facility was formerly the Mount Vernon College for Women. The government took it over in late 1942, and the COMMUNICATIONS SECURITY GROUP occupied the former campus in early 1943.

The Naval Security Station remained at the Washington location until Nov. 1995, when the command was moved to FORT MEADE, Md., site of the NSA.

Also see NAVAL SECURITY GROUP.

Nave, Capt. Eric

(b. 1899 d. 1993)

Leading Australian-British naval CRYPTOGRAPHER who helped break Japanese CODES during World War II. Nave made a highly disputed claim that the British government had full knowledge of the Japanese JN-25 code (see JN-SERIES CIPHERS) on the eve of the PEARL HARBOR ATTACK of Dec. 7, 1941, but refused to tell the Americans of the impending strike.

Born in Australia, Nave entered the Royal Australian Navy and, required to learn a foreign language to pass the sub-lieutenant examinations, chose Japanese. As part of his language training he lived for two years in a small Japanese village.

Beginning in 1925 Nave was assigned to the Royal Navy to help in Japanese radio TRAFFIC ANALYSIS. He achieved his first major success on the occasion of the death of Emperor Yoshihito in 1926, when he compared the public broadcasts of official statements with coded versions of the same message being sent to Japanese embassies and naval commands abroad. A year later, he was able to develop the most comprehensive list of Japanese naval call signs then available in the West.

His accomplishments led to his being brought to England in 1927 for assignment to the GOVERNMENT CODE AND CYPHER SCHOOL (GC&CS). He helped to set up the GC&CS Japanese section and became the section head. When the Australian Navy requested his return, he was formally transferred to the Royal Navy in 1930.

In 1939, as the political situation in the Far East deteriorated, he was sent to Hong Kong to attempt to break the newly introduced JN-25 Japanese naval code. In his book *Betrayal at Pearl Harbor: How Churchill Lured Roosevelt into War* (1991), Nave claimed that the British codebreaking successes led to full knowledge of the planned Japanese strike against Pearl Harbor. But, he wrote, the British government failed to pass this on to U.S. commands. Nave's claim has not been corroborated by any responsible British or U.S. source.

Nave retired from the Royal Navy in 1947 and returned to Australia, where he helped to set up the AUSTRALIAN SECURITY AND INTELLIGENCE ORGANIZATION (ASIO). He served with the ASIO for 12 years, retiring in 1959 as its deputy director.

Navy Communications Intelligence

U.S. Navy COMMUNICATIONS INTELLIGENCE (COMINT) activities began in World War I when the Cryptologic Bureau was established, primarily to develop CODES and CIPHERS for naval use but also to break foreign communications. The Navy used elaborate systems at the peace conference in Paris in 1919 to encode messages for President Wilson and the State Department.

However, the Army's codebreaking staff, headed by HERBERT O. YARDLEY, was readily able to solve the Navy's systems. At the same time, the Navy codebreakers were having considerable difficulty in their own efforts. When the OFFICE OF NAVAL INTELLIGENCE learned of the efficacy of Yardley's efforts, the Cryptologic Bureau was closed down in July 1918.

Navy COMINT efforts against the Japanese Navy began in 1924 with the establishment of a COMINT organization within the Office of Naval Communications with the COVER designation of Research Desk. The unit was given the Navy code OP-20-G, with OP indicating the Office of the Chief of Naval Operations, 20 indicating Navy communications, and G the seventh unit within that office. (NAVAL INTELLIGENCE was OP-16 at the time.) Subsequently, the Research Desk was renamed the Communications Security Group.

The initial staff of the COMINT unit consisted of Lt. LAURANCE F. SAFFORD and four civilians. They were housed in the Main Navy Building, a "temporary" World War I–era structure on the Washington Mall. The staff's first task was to solve Japanese diplomatic codes because those messages were readily available. At the time there was no collaboration between Army and Navy codebreaking activities; indeed, the Army denied that its codebreaking BLACK CHAMBER even existed. Efforts to intercept the Japanese Navy's radio communications began in Oct. 1927, when a COMINT unit under Lt. Comdr. ELLIS M. ZACHARIAS, then the Asiatic Fleet's INTELLIGENCE OFFICER, on the U.S. cruiser *Marblehead*, monitored communications of a Japanese naval exercise. Other Navy ships periodically embarked a COMINT team—referred to as Fleet Radio Units (FRU)—so that trained radiomen could copy down the Kata Kana Morse code used by the Japanese for later analysis.

At the same time it established the COMINT unit, the Navy began setting up radio intercept stations. The first was in Peking (now Beijing), China, in 1925, manned by U.S. Marines. Subsequent intercept stations were set up in Shanghai; Heeia (on the eastern coast of Oahu, Hawaii); Guam; the Philippines; Bar Harbor, Maine; and Washington, D.C. In addition to the main Navy

COMINT staff in Washington (station NEGAT), COMINT units, for studying Japanese communications and working on DECRYPTING messages, were set up at Olongapo in the Philippines in 1932 (station CAST) and at PEARL HARBOR on Oahu in 1936 (station HYPO); these were set up to support the Asiatic and Pacific Fleet commanders, respectively. (The Hypo station was moved to the fortress island of Corregidor in Sept. 1941 following the construction of an extensive, underground, bombproof complex.) These three COMINT units were staffed by the ON-THE-ROOF GANG of Navy and Marine personnel.

The Navy COMINT attempts to break into Japanese communications were greatly helped when, in 1920, the Navy financed the first of a series of BLACK BAG JOBS against the Japanese Consulate in New York City by the Office of Naval Intelligence (ONI), FBI, and New York City police. At the consulate the "crooks" were able to pick the lock on the office and open a safe that contained a Japanese naval code book. The book was carefully photographed and replaced without the Japanese knowing they had been burgled. The book was appropriately mined by the COMINT unit.

Although a 1923 break-in attempt failed because the Japanese safe could not be opened, apparently in 1926 and again in 1927 the ONI-FBI returned to the New York consulate to successfully photograph revisions to the code books, and did so still again in Sept. 1929, when break-ins occurred during five consecutive nights at the office of the Japanese inspector of naval matériel in New York, all without detection. (More black bag jobs were reportedly made in 1938 or 1939.) The information gained from the 1920s break-ins led to the compilation of a Japanese code book that was bound in red buckram, from which the Japanese code acquired its American color-code designation RED.

The COMINT unit was able to provide Navy leaders with details of Japanese plans and operations, including the major exercise of 1930 and the trials of the rebuilt battleship *Nagato* in 1936, which demonstrated that the Japanese had significantly increased the warship's speed.

At the end of 1930 the Japanese changed their codes, going to a machine-generated Red code. (Significantly, no Japanese radio communication of the period referred to the attack on Pearl Harbor.)

The Japanese Navy again introduced a new fleet code on June 1, 1939. This was soon penetrated by the Navy COMINT unit. But it was changed again on Dec. 1, 1941, and was not recaptured until two weeks later, after the PEARL HARBOR ATTACK, when the Navy COMINT unit on Corregidor determined that the same code was in use, but with new keys. This was the third or fourth series of keys used with the same code, simplifying U.S. decryption.

While the fleet was employing book codes, the Japanese naval ATTACHÉS were using machine-generated codes, which the COMINT unit could read. In 1931 the COMINT unit was given permission to provide the Army's newly established SIGNAL INTELLIGENCE SERVICE with copies of all the code keys it had recovered. This occurred despite the Army's refusal even to acknowledge to

the Navy the existence of its own codebreaking Operation—the Black Chamber. After this, the Army worked primarily to break into the Japanese diplomatic code, while the Navy concentrated on naval codes and ciphers. However, during the winter of 1940–1941 the increased interest in Japanese diplomatic codes caused the Navy to join the Army in that work. The first machine that could break into the diplomatic code—called PURPLE—was built in 1940 at the Washington Navy Yard; the first complete Japanese message text was deciphered in the fall of the following year. The Army and Navy handled the deciphering and distribution of these messages jointly.

The Navy COMINT unit grew steadily, reinforced with a large number of reservists called to active duty in June 1941. By Dec. 7, 1941, the COMINT organization had 730 men and women—75 Navy officers, 645 enlisted personnel, and 10 civilians. Most were in Washington, with 186 at Pearl Harbor and 78 on Corregidor, plus 26 in transit to the Philippines (diverted to Australia after the war began).

Among the civilians was Mrs. AGNES MEYER DRISCOLL, about whom Rear Adm. EDWIN T. LAYTON, the Pacific Fleet's INTELLIGENCE OFFICER during the war, wrote in *And I Was There* (1985):

> In the navy she was without peer as a cryptanalyst. Some of her pupils . . . were more able mathematicians but she had taught cryptanalysis to all of them, and none ever questioned her superb talent and determination in breaking codes and ciphers. She understood machines and how to apply them. In 1937 she would share the fifteen-thousand-dollar prize granted by the Senate for her contribution to developing a cipher machine with Lieutenant Commander William F. Gresham.

After the war began the organization grew rapidly, and in early 1943 the Communications Security Group was moved to a former women's college at Nebraska and Massachusetts Avenues in northwest Washington. (See NAVAL SECURITY STATION.)

Meanwhile, the Japanese Navy continued to use the same codes, which the U.S. Navy was able to penetrate until a major code change occurred on June 1, 1942. The ability to read those codes and determine Japanese plans in advance made possible the U.S. successes at the battles of Coral Sea in early May 1942 and MIDWAY in early June 1942.

By this time the Navy had placed Radio Intelligence Units (RIU) on board the flagships of most task forces in the Pacific. The men of the RIUs intercepted Japanese radio transmissions and advised their admirals of Japanese tactical plans and intentions, as well as relaying material back to the FLEET RADIO UNIT PACIFIC (FRUPAQ) at Pearl Harbor. Dr. Ronald H. Spector, in *Listening to the Enemy* (1988), cites a FRUPAC report:

> Operating conditions for RI Units at sea were often difficult, and were increased greatly by the obvious

necessity for security. . . . One rather subtle problem was that of building the Admiral's confidence in his RI Unit. In many situations in which things were happening fast, the Admiral had to take the information of his RIU at face value, without explanation of its sources, and had to have confidence in his unit in order to take the necessary immediate action. For that reason, as often as possible, RI officers remained with one Admiral during the Admiral's whole tour at sea.

For much of the war the standard shipboard RIU was one officer and four operators—an extremely heavy work schedule for the unit, especially in combat, with almost continuous enemy transmissions to monitor.

Navy COMINT was especially important in SUBMARINE operations in the Pacific. To quote a report in *Listening to the Enemy,* "Without Communications Intelligence submarine operations would unquestionably have been far more difficult and costly because of the vast areas which had to be covered and the attainment of the ultimate objectives would have been greatly delayed." One of the first successes of COMINT in the war came in on Jan. 27, 1942, when Japanese radio intercepts were used to guide the U.S. submarine *Gudgeon* to intercept and sink the Japanese submarine *I-73* some 240 nautical miles west of Midway. The large Japanese craft went down with her entire crew of some 70 men, the first Japanese warship to be sunk by a U.S. submarine.

The U.S. Navy's codebreaking efforts were also used to support Army operations, as the Army's Signal Intelligence Service was not able to break into Japanese Army codes on a large scale until 1944. The Navy's codebreaking enabled the Army to tell when ships were bringing reinforcements by sea or when the Japanese fleet was providing aerial or ship support for ground operations.

During the war the Navy's COMINT efforts were able to penetrate all Japanese naval codes and ciphers except for the Flag Officer's Cipher—a slow, cumbersome, and complex cipher, which the Japanese stopped using early in the war.

By the end of the war Navy COMINT had 8,454 men and women assigned—1,499 officers, 6,908 enlisted men and women, and 47 civilians.

Since World War II, the Navy has continued to operate a network of COMINT stations ashore, as well as shipboard COMINT activities. Known since 1968 by the euphemism NAVAL SECURITY GROUP, these efforts first operated under the aegis of the ARMED FORCES SECURITY AGENCY and then the NSA.

Need to Know

A determination made by the holder of classified material that a prospective recipient has a requirement for access to or possession of the material. Holding a SECURITY CLEARANCE at a certain level does not automatically give a person access to all material at that classification.

Also see COMPARTMENTED.

Negat

CODE NAME for U.S. Navy CRYPTANALYSIS station at Navy Department headquarters in Washington, D.C., from the late 1930s through World War II. The station was part of the OP-20-G staff (NAVY COMMUNICATIONS INTELLIGENCE). Negat was located in the temporary buildings on Constitution Avenue built during World War I. It was moved after the war to the NAVAL SECURITY STATION at Massachusetts and Nebraska Avenues in northwest Washington, the campus of what had been the Mount Vernon College for Women.

Negat was the phonetic word for the letter *N* in military communications at the time.

Negative Intelligence

Intelligence known to have been COMPROMISED or known to have been acquired by an enemy but rendered useless to the enemy by COUNTERINTELLIGENCE activities.

Neighbors

Soviet slang for the KGB that is used by other Soviet intelligence activities. The term reportedly originated with the Soviet Foreign Ministry, which was physically located closer to the KGB headquarters (which became the "close" neighbors) and farther from the GRU headquarters (which became the "far" or "distant" neighbors).

Nesbitt, Frank A.

Former U.S. Air Force and Marine Corps communications officer who delivered unauthorized information to the KGB. Nesbitt served in the Air Force from 1963 to 1966, and in the Marine Corps from 1969 to 1979.

In Aug. 1989, while sightseeing in Sucre, Bolivia, he befriended a group of Russian ballet dancers. He met a Soviet official who put him in touch with the KGB representative at the Soviet Embassy in La Paz. From there, according to Nesbitt, he flew to Moscow and stayed 11 days in a SAFE HOUSE where he wrote from memory 32 pages of information on U.S. military communications. However, he became disillusioned when Soviet officials refused his request for citizenship and work.

He then traveled to Guatemala and contacted U.S. officials. They accompanied him to Washington, D.C., where he met with FBI officials and was arrested. He offered his services as a DOUBLE AGENT to the FBI, claiming that he had given no useful information to the Soviets.

Nesbitt was indicted on Nov. 8, 1989, of conspiring to pass sensitive national security information to the Soviet Union. He initially pleaded not guilty; on Feb. 1, 1990, he changed his plea to guilty in a plea agreement and was sentenced to 10 years in a psychiatric treatment facility at a federal prison. His lawyer had said that Nesbitt had "wanted to have some excitement in his life."

Net Assessment Group

Organization set up within the NATIONAL SECURITY COUNCIL under President Nixon in 1971 as part of a reorganization of the INTELLIGENCE COMMUNITY. The group was to review intelligence PRODUCTS and use them to make a net assessment. Usually, this would consist of comparisons between the military forces and capabilities of the United States and those of the Soviet Union.

The group was formed on Dec. 6, 1971, in response to the Blue Ribbon Panel created by President Nixon to recommend reorganization in the Department of Defense. The Director of Net Assessment reports to the Secretary of Defense.

Network

A group of AGENTS or ILLEGALS that has a common leader or HANDLER. A network may contain several CELLS to prevent the detection or COMPROMISE of one or more members from being able to identify all members of the network.

Neumann, Franz

(b. 1900 d. 1954)

OFFICE OF STRATEGIC SERVICES (OSS) officer who spied for the Soviets.

German-born Neumann fled Nazi Germany and entered the United States from England, where he graduated from the London School of Economics. He was an economist in the OSS German Section. He told his HANDLERS that he would pass to them "all the data coming through his hands," including U.S. ambassadors' and OSS officers' reports. This included the information the United States obtained on the July 1944 attempt to assassinate Adolf Hitler. After the war, he worked for the chief U.S. prosecutor at the Nuremberg war crimes trials. His CODE NAME was "Ruff."

NFIB

SEE NATIONAL FOREIGN INTELLIGENCE BOARD

NIA

SEE NATIONAL INTELLIGENCE AUTHORITY

NIC

SEE NAVAL INTELLIGENCE COMMAND

Nicholson, Maj. Arthur D.

U.S. Army officer fatally shot by a Soviet sentry while taking photographs in a restricted zone in East Germany. Nicholson, part of a U.S. liaison unit observing Soviet and Warsaw Pact military forces, was photographing Soviet military equipment when he shot on March 24, 1985.

The Soviets claimed that Nicholson, although an authorized military observer, was in a restricted military zone and was not supposed to be taking photographs.

Army Sgt. Jesse Schatz, who had accompanied Nicholson, said that the major had entered a building in a military facility and had taken photographs in the building. But Schatz said that Nicholson was outside the restricted area when the sentry shot him. Nearly an hour passed before Nicholson, who lay dying, was given medical attention.

Nicholson, Harold J.

(b. 1950)

CIA INTELLIGENCE OFFICER who confessed in March 1997 to spying for Russia. Nicholson, who had access to highly sensitive data, was the highest-ranking CIA official ever convicted of espionage. He was sentenced to 23 years and seven months in prison after pleading guilty in a plea bargain. The U.S. government thus avoided a trial and he avoided the possibility that if found guilty he would be sentenced to life in prison.

Nicholson, who sold SECRET documents to Russian officials at four meetings overseas, told investigators that he had received $300,000, although prosecutors said they could only prove that he had received about $200,000.

The information that he supplied included the identities and overseas assignments of CIA officers, one of whom was about to be posted to Moscow. "The passing of such information placed those officers' lives, as well as the lives of their foreign contacts, in danger," according to LOUIS FREEH, director of the FBI.

Nicholson, a 16-year veteran of the agency, was branch chief in the CIA's Counter-Terrorism Center when the FBI arrested him at Dulles International Airport, near Washington, D.C., on Nov. 16, 1996. He was about to leave the country for an alleged rendezvous in Switzerland with his Russian HANDLER. He was carrying 10 rolls of film containing images of classified CIA documents and a computer disk with a Russian program for encrypting messages.

The FBI had been investigating him for more than a year following his failure to pass a routine POLYGRAPH examination. According to the FBI, the polygraph indicated that he had lied about "unauthorized contacts with foreign intelligence services." Investigating, the FBI "uncovered a pattern of foreign travel followed by unexplained financial transactions." For example, in June 1994, while he was deputy chief of station in Malaysia, he had authorized meetings with Russian INTELLIGENCE OFFICERS, apparently in what his chief thought was a recruitment attempt. Shortly after this meeting, the FBI discovered, Nicholson had wired $12,000 to a U.S. savings account.

As the FBI investigation tightened on him, the FBI secretly installed a surveillance camera in Nicholson's CIA office. The camera recorded him as he took classified documents out of a safe, got on his hands and knees under his desk, and photographed the documents. Nicholson told investigators that he had started spying in

June 1994, a short time after fellow CIA officer ALDRICH AMES was caught spying for Russia. Nicholson, knowing that the Russians would need a replacement for Ames, nominated himself for the role.

To counteract criticism about persistent lack of cooperation between the CIA and FBI—even after the Ames case—JOHN M. DEUTCH, DIRECTOR OF CENTRAL INTELLIGENCE (DCI), appeared at a joint news conference with Freeh. "The arrest of Nicholson," Deutch said, "is the direct result of an unprecedented level of cooperation between the CIA and the FBI. We are now able to demonstrate quite conclusively that the post-Ames reforms work as designed. Clearly the post-Ames analysis and detection mechanisms the CIA and FBI put in place succeeded in the identification of Nicholson and his alleged espionage activities on behalf of the Russian intelligence service." But the arrest of Nicholson, so quickly after the Ames case, helped to propel Deutch out of his DCI post.

In the agreement that was part of the plea bargain, Nicholson not only forfeited all of his espionage earnings but also any possible future profits from sale of his story for books or movies. Nicholson admitted to a single charge, conspiracy to commit espionage. Two other counts, espionage and attempted espionage, were dropped. When he was sentenced, Nicholson said, "I have lost everything that was ever dear and important to me, everything that was ever of value." He told the sentencing federal judge that he had decided to earn money as a spy out of love for his three children. He said he had let his children down by spending so much time overseas and by failing to keep his marriage together. His successful CIA career "was blotted out by my actions for which I stand before you now."

The son of an Air Force officer, Nicholson graduated from Oregon State University and entered the Army as a 2nd lieutenant in 1973. He left the Army as a captain with intelligence experience and in 1980 he joined the CIA. Working on the clandestine side of the CIA, he was an undercover officer in Manila, Bangkok, and Bucharest, where in 1990 he was the CIA station chief. In 1992, when he was transferred to Malaysia, his wife sued for divorce and a court battle began over custody of their three children.

As his tour was ending in Malaysia, he made his deal to spy for Russia. In 1994 he was assigned to train CIA recruits at CAMP PEARY. He sold their identities to Russian HANDLERS in trips overseas, thus destroying their careers as clandestine officers. On his last visit to Singapore, FBI agents photographed him entering a car with Russian diplomatic plates. A short time later he deposited $20,000 and gave his son $12,000 for a car.

Nicholson used the CODE NAME "Nevil R. Strachey" when communicating with the Russians.

Nicolai, Col. Walther

(b. 1873 d. 1934)

Chief of the German MILITARY INTELLIGENCE service (Geheime Nachrichtendienst des Heeres), Section IIIb of the General Staff of the Field Army, from 1913 to 1921.

After attending a church school and joining the cadet corps, Nicolai entered the Army as a 2nd lieutenant. Following three years at the staff college, in 1904 he was appointed to the General Staff.

In July 1906 he became the first INTELLIGENCE OFFICER to be assigned to the I Army Corps at Konigsberg. He immediately concentrated on establishing a NETWORK of spies in the Russian frontier area. His efforts were highly successful. Nicolai subsequently became head of the Russian section of the military intelligence service, which was part of the headquarters of the German Field Army, and in 1913 he became the head of military intelligence, concerned with intelligence collection on both the French and Russian fronts.

Intelligence historian DAVID KAHN, in *Hitler's Spies* (1978), described Nicolai as "an energetic, blondish general staff officer of medium height, in his mid-thirties . . . He ran the spy agency exactly as he would lead a regiment in the field, for he was a Prussian officer, who did his duty wherever he was assigned."

His organization ran hundreds of AGENTS in enemy and neutral countries, and coordinated reports from other commands for the German General Staff. His best-known spy was MATA HARI—who provided no real intelligence to him. His most successful spy was Baron Schulga—known as Agent 17—who provided vital information on French Army movements as troops mobilized in Aug. 1914. He was able to send reports to Nicolai every two days, his COURIERS taking just 48 hours to cross from France through neutral Switzerland to Germany. In failing health (he was 73 when the war began), Schulga went to Germany in March 1916 and retired.

In 1915 Nicolai established an internal intelligence service, with informers in German industrial firms, various institutions, and even private groups. The effort was initiated to collect information about foreign countries, but as conditions inside Germany became unsettled, Nicolai discovered information of value about the homeland as well.

Nicolai's agents and operations achieved few successes; according to Kahn he suffered from three major failures:

1. He undertook no espionage in the United States until several months after the American declaration of war in April 1917.
2. He failed to collect ECONOMIC INTELLIGENCE on his enemies, an increasingly important factor in warfare.
3. He failed to learn in advance and advise the German High Command of an important new weapon appearing on the battlefield: the tank.

Six days after the armistice on Nov. 11, 1918, Nicolai's Section IIIb disbanded and he was transferred to the General Staff in BERLIN. There he established a small intelligence section that survived until the rebuilding of the German Army in the 1930s, when it evolved into FOREIGN ARMIES WEST.

Also see Vice Adm. WILHELM CANARIS, RICHARD HENTSCH.

NIE

SEE NATIONAL INTELLIGENCE ESTIMATE

Nightmover

SEE ALDRICH H. AMES

Nikitin, Capt. 1st Rank Alexandr K.

(b. 1952)

Retired Russian naval officer arrested on Feb. 6, 1996, by the Russian Federal Security Service (FSK) on charges of espionage. He was later convicted of espionage and divulging state secrets and served 10 months in prison before an appeals court acquitted him. In Sept. 2000 the Presidium of the Russian Supreme Court dismissed an attempt to reverse the acquittal.

At the time of his arrest, Nikitin was employed as a consultant by Bellona, a Norwegian environmental group studying the problems of hazardous nuclear material originating from Russian submarines. In 1995 the Russian government gave Bellona documents and computer records related to nuclear materials. Subsequently, the documents and records were taken back by the government, but were returned to Bellona in the fall of 1995. Bellona officials decried the temporary seizure, claiming it was harassment. However, an FSK official claimed that Bellona and other foreign environmental organizations were working beyond their charters.

Nikitin was arrested for giving state secrets to Bellona in the form of classified documents. He is believed to be the first Russian to be arrested for espionage related to an environmental group.

Reportedly, all Norwegian parliamentarians wrote to the Russian government on Nikitin's behalf, and on Feb. 18, 1996, the Norwegian daily newspaper *Dagblader* stated, "If Nikitin is convicted, it will be a catastrophe for the significant environmental work done so far in Russia."

That same month, U.S. Vice President Albert Gore met in Washington, D.C., with Russian President Boris Yeltsin's environmental adviser, Alexei Yablokov, to express American concern over the proceedings against Nikitin. Nitikin was held in prison for 10 months prior to being released pending trial. Amnesty International named him Russia's first prisoner of conscience since Andrei Sakharov.

Nisei

The Japanese term for "second generation," which has entered the English language, is used to label people born in the United States to immigrant Japanese parents (they are therefore U.S. citizens). More than 6,000 Nisei men served with U.S. military headquarters and intelligence units as translators and interpreters in the Pacific areas during World War II. (Many others served in Army combat units in the European theater.)

Beginning in the spring of 1941, before American entry into World War II, several Japanese-Americans in the U.S. Army received Japanese-language training. Many, despite their ancestry, had no practical knowledge of the language. They received language training at the Presidio in San Francisco, Calif., until all Japanese Americans were forcibly evacuated from the West Coast in 1942. The language school then moved to Camp Savage and, in Aug. 1944, to Fort Snelling, both near Minneapolis, Minn. The first class of 45 students graduated from the six-month program in May 1942. Some students also attended a one-year Japanese course at University of Michigan.

On Feb. 19, 1942, President Roosevelt issued an executive order that led to the detention of nearly 120,000 men, women, and children on the West Coast who were of Japanese descent. About two-thirds of them were citizens (Nisei), and more than one-fourth of them were children under 15. The Nisei were soon allowed to enlist in the U.S. Army. (In all, more than 17,000 Japanese-Americans served in the U.S. Army during World War II.)

Almost all of the 6,000 men given Japanese language training were U.S. Army enlisted men, and a few were made Army warrant officers. However, they were regularly assigned to Navy and Marine units to support intelligence activities, and some served in the China-Burma-India theater. (In addition, the U.S. Army had approximately 700 non-Japanese Americans trained in the Japanese language; the Navy used only non-Japanese Americans in this role.)

Most Nisei were employed to translate captured documents and interpret for prisoner of war interrogations; some served with Army COUNTERINTELLIGENCE units; and a very few were employed directly in MAGIC and ULTRA codebreaking efforts. Some were parachuted behind Japanese lines with Army RECONNAISSANCE units to assess the enemy situation.

One Nisei, Richard M. Sakakida, was among 15 trained by the FBI in 1941 for counterintelligence work. Then an Army master sergeant, Sakakida entered Manila as an anti-American, draft-dodging seaman. With this COVER he collected information on Philippine firms that might have associations with the Japanese. When war erupted in Dec. 1941, he donned his uniform and served as an Army translator. Captured by the Japanese when U.S. forces in the Philippines surrendered on May 6, 1942, he underwent interrogation and torture, all the time claiming that he was in the Army against his will. His story was believed, and he was released on Feb. 11, 1943, to be employed by the Japanese as an interpreter.

Sakakida was subsequently able to help engineer a prison escape. Although able to join a Philippine guerrilla group, he was not reunited with U.S. troops until Sept. 25, 1945. After the war Sakakida left the Army, entered the Air Force, and retired in 1975 with the rank of lieutenant colonel.

NKGB

SEE NKVD

NKVD

Narodnyy Komisariat Vnutrennikh Del (People's Commissariat for Internal Affairs), the "secret police" of Soviet dictator Josef Stalin. The NKVD and its immediate successors—the MVD, NKGB, and MGB—were responsible for both state security/espionage and internal security/repression from 1934 until 1953.

The terror and repression of the CHEKA—born of the Russian Revolution of 1917—and the replacement GPU and OGPU pale in comparison with the methods of the NKVD, in many respects history's premier apparatus for internal security and repression. However, the NKVD was also Stalin's foreign intelligence and security ORGAN, responsible for ferreting out secrets from the West and destroying enemies of the state who had fled to the West. The NKVD grew to a monstrous size—embracing not only traditional security and espionage roles but also internal and border troop formations, as well as the administrators of numerous institutions, including the vast *Gulag*, the constellation of prison camps that spread across the Soviet state.

The establishment of the NKVD was apparently linked to Stalin's decision to murder Sergei Kirov, a leading Russian revolutionary who in 1934 was head of the Leningrad Communist Party, the most powerful entity within the Soviet party organization. On July 10, 1934, the existing security/espionage organ, the OGPU, was subsumed into the new All-Union NKVD. GENRIKH YAGODA, already a veteran perpetrator of state terror, was named head of the new agency. British political writer-historian Robert Conquest observed in *The Great Terror: Stalin's Purges of the Thirties* (1968):

> The new body was to be efficiently deployed over the following years. Its increasingly privileged and powerful officers were to make its emblem—a serpent being struck down by a sword—prevail everywhere against the hammer and sickle of Party membership. From Politburo members down, no one was to be exempt from their attentions. They themselves were to remain under the careful control of the supreme political authority, Stalin.

On the afternoon of Dec. 1, 1934, in Leningrad, Sergei Kirov was walking through the darkened hallway of Communist Party headquarters, en route to a meeting. His ever-present personal bodyguard was not present when a young assassin shot him in the back. The murder had obviously been arranged by Yagoda, as Stalin saw no way to solve his complex political problems other than to kill his chief rival and then, seeking to blame those behind the killing, eliminate all potential opponents.

Yagoda's NKVD immediately conducted investigations and made arrests. The murderer and 116 others were convicted of conspiracy and were executed by the NKVD. Meanwhile, Yagoda built, reshaped, and honed the NKVD. Known as "bluecaps" for their hats and collar tabs, the NKVD officers were becoming the elite of the new Soviet society. Conquest observed:

> They were among the most highly regarded of the new *priviligentsia* which was arising from Stalin's anti-egalitarian policies. New and more ostentatious uniforms came in. At the same time, NKVD officers were expected to learn the social graces. Many of them married smart and good-looking wives from the old educated classes, the type who gravitate to power and money in whatever form, and who, moreover, gained immunity from the otherwise unfortunate results of their social origins. NKVD children attended special schools. Junior posts often went to the sons of high officials.

For himself, Yagoda took the grandiose title of General Commissar of State Security (equivalent to the rank of Marshal of the Soviet Union) and designed a suitably ornate uniform. But the man who created this apparatus did not live to see its fruition. NIKOLAI YEZHOV, head of the Party Control Commission that handled NKVD matters for the Communist Party, increasingly took over NKVD direction. Yagoda was dismissed from all his positions on Sept. 30, 1936, and Yezhov took charge. Yezhov formally denounced Yagoda at a meeting of senior NKVD officers at the LUBYANKA headquarters on March 18, 1937. Yagoda was executed after a show trial the following year, and throughout the Soviet Union senior NKVD officers were arrested, day and night, at home or in the office (and often while in their car en route between them). Some committed suicide—a pistol to the temple or a plunge through an open window, hoping to spare their families from retribution. In all, more than 3,000 of Yagoda's subordinates are said to have died in 1937.

THE GREAT TERROR

Meanwhile, the "great terror" began: The first major victims were the leaders of the Army—potential opponents of Stalin. On June 11, 1937, it was announced that eight of the most senior officers of the Red Army had been arrested and charged with treason. The following day they were executed. Another senior officer, also implicated in the conspiracy, committed suicide. More officers followed to THE CELLAR of LUBYANKA, and to the execution yard at the NKVD building at 11 Dzerzhinsky Street, and to execution cells in the massive Lefortovo prison, and in a score of other NKVD offices across the country. Three of the Red Army's five marshals were thus murdered, as were 14 of 16 senior army commanders, 60 of 67 corps commanders, 136 of the 199 division commanders, 221 of the 397 brigade commanders, and thousands of other officers.

The Navy was not immune, despite the Communist Party having taken personal control of that service after the bloody Kronshtadt revolt of 1921. All eight "flagmen" (admirals) were executed, as were thousands of lesser officers. (In Aug. 1938 M. P. Frinovsky, a former deputy head of the NKVD, was appointed commissar for the Navy; he was nominally head of the Navy until March 1939.) Throughout the country, the NKVD was arresting, and courts were trying, local political and party leaders. Also taken off the streets and from their beds were authors, poets, scientists, artists, engineers, and teachers. No one was immune from the "black marias," the arrest vans driven by bluecaps.

Soon, however, Stalin appeared to be tiring of the purge, realizing perhaps that he could not allow it to go further without fatally disrupting Soviet society, industry, and the military. Yezhov's power was waning. There were reports of interrogations getting out of hand, with Yezhov personally shooting some senior military officers. He was dismissed from his NKVD position on Dec. 8, 1938, remaining briefly in a lesser government position. In early 1939 he disappeared. There was no trial or ritual denunciation, as there had been for his predecessor.

His successor was LAVRENTY BERIA, who would become Stalin's most trusted lieutenant—if the term "trusted" could be associated with Stalin. The reign of terror was completed under Beria. INTELLIGENCE OFFICERS serving abroad—NKVD and GRU (MILITARY INTELLIGENCE)—were recalled to be "tried" and executed. Those who did not return tried to flee to the West; some succeeded. Others were killed by assassination teams sent to track them down. One political TARGET was Leon Trotsky, an "old Bolshevik" who had opposed Stalin's taking control of the government in the 1920s. Living in exile in Mexico, he was murdered by an NKVD assassin in 1940. A year later NKVD assassins executed the first senior Soviet intelligence officer to have defected, Maj. Gen. WALTER KRIVITSKY, who was found dead in a Capitol Hill hotel in Washington, D.C.

Not all "traitors" were executed. The prison camps—the Gulag—were being fed masses of men and women. There were true criminals, political prisoners, and those caught up in the quotas of the great terror. Despite a tremendously high death rate due to hard labor, scanty rations, brutal guards, and Siberian winters, there were an estimated 8 million Soviet prisoners in Gulag camps before the Soviet Union entered World War II in June 1941. (By some estimates, another million were in prisons.)

In the camps the men and women prisoners worked 10 hours a day, or 12, or 16. They built dams and canals (see GENRIKH YAGODA); they laid hundreds of miles of railroad track; they logged (women were formally forbidden from logging in 1951); they dug for gold—and later for uranium. They were not paid, and they were fed starvation rations, all chronicled in Aleksandr I. Solzhenitsyn's two-volume *The Gulag Archipelago* (1973, 1975).

Beyond the Gulag camps and the prisons, the NKVD operated other internment facilities. The scientific research center on the outskirts of Moscow—vividly described in Solzhenitsyn's *The First Circle* (1968)—was staffed by prisoners. There were also aircraft design bureaus operated by the NKVD and staffed by prisoners. Engineers and designers continued their work while incarcerated in "internal prison," sometimes under sentence of death. Many imprisoned aircraft designers served their internment at State Aviation Factory (GAZ) No. 39 in Moscow; others were at design bureaus (KB) while under detention; prisoner-designer Vladimir Petlyakov headed KB No. 100, Vladimir Myasishchev directed KB No. 102, and Andrei Tupolev was at KB No. 103.

Tupolev, the doyen of Soviet aircraft designers, had traveled to the United States and Germany in 1936 to study aircraft designs—with government approval. In 1938 he was arrested and charged with "sabotage." Imprisoned, he continued to design aircraft: "I did spend five years in jail. I am the only aircraft designer in the world who designed a four-engine bomber under house arrest," he told a journalist. (He was released in 1943.)

The NKVD also operated a submarine design bureau. The only submarine known to have emerged from that KB was the *M-400*, designed by B. L. Bzhezinsky in 1939. The 65½-foot, high-speed, combination submarine-submersible torpedo boat was launched in July 1941. Her hull was damaged by German artillery fire during the siege of Leningrad and construction was suspended in 1942; she was never finished.

FOREIGN ESPIONAGE

This obsession with internal security/repression did not deter the NKVD from overseas espionage activities. Most Western countries were targets, but the most sought-after secrets were in Britain and the United States; Britain had been viewed as an enemy since the Russian Civil War, while the United States had technology and manufacturing methods that Stalin coveted (see ARCOS AFFAIR, CPUSA).

The NKVD also established one of the most effective espionage NETWORKS of all time, the CAMBRIDGE SPY RING. For more than a decade these men spied out the secrets of Britain and the United States, some holding high positions in the British Foreign Office, MI5, and MI6. When Cambridge spy JOHN CAIRNCROSS reported that the British were involved in atomic research related to the development of a super weapon, it was the signal for Beria to tell his AGENTS in Britain, Canada, and the United States to establish an ATOMIC SPY RING and seek out the secrets of the atom.

When Germany attacked the Soviet Union in June 1941, Stalin suddenly found himself allied with Britain and the United States. This led to an increase in Soviet diplomatic, trade, and military delegations to both countries, as well as an increase in the number of NKVD and GRU LEGAL operatives.

Meanwhile, the massive troop units built up within the NKVD were increasingly committed to fighting for the Soviet homeland against *external* enemies. NKVD divisions, corps, and armies fought the Germans on the Eastern Front. Equally important, NKVD units operated behind Soviet lines in critical areas, ensuring that troops did not retreat. NKVD's special ranks were changed to military ranks in 1943, as Stalin sought to integrate his hated secret police into the military establishment.

A more specialized NKVD military police unit was required to meet wartime contingencies, and in 1941 Beria created SMERSH ("Death to Spies") as an agency of the NKVD under Commissioner of State Security 3rd Rank Vasili Chernyshov. From April 14, 1943, to March 16, 1946,. Smersh functioned as a separate agency directly under the State Committee of Defense, headed by Stalin. This marked the first and possibly only time that Soviet military COUNTERINTELLIGENCE came under the military establishment (albeit in the persona of Stalin) and not under the security organs. Significantly, Smersh officers had supremacy over standard NKVD forces.

During this period of independence from the NKVD, Smersh was commanded by Beria's deputy and protégé, Col. Gen. VIKTOR ABAKUMOV, the First Deputy Commissar for State Security. There was also a Navy section of Smersh. Meanwhile, NKVD combat units fought, often with distinction, in the battles of Moscow, Stalingrad, Leningrad, and the North Caucasus. (NKVD internal troops did not fight in battles; they were needed for COUNTERESPIONAGE duties, and perhaps 250,000 continued to guard the Gulag camps and other prisons, and the special NKVD trains that shuttled prisoners around the country.)

The NKVD was also responsible for one of the most noteworthy of the innumerable heinous crimes of World War II: the KATYN MASSACRE. The Soviets had captured about 200,000 Polish troops in late 1939 as the Soviet Union joined Nazi Germany in assaulting Poland. About 15,000 of the prisoners—including 8,700 officers—were never seen again. They were murdered by the NKVD.

Among the many other activities of the secret police during the war was management of the Soviet atomic bomb project. As Stalin learned details of the American-British efforts, he placed various aspects of Soviet atomic bomb development—as well as atomic espionage—under Beria.

REORGANIZATIONS

In 1941 Stalin reorganized the security organs. From Dec. 1938 to Feb. 1941, Beria had served as both commissar for internal affairs (NKVD) and head of the main Administration of State Security (GUGB), a subordinate agency of the NKVD.

For a brief period, from Feb. to July 1941, Stalin separated these two organs, creating a People's Commissariat of State Security (NKGB) under VSEVOLOD MERKULOV for state security-espionage while leaving the NKVD, responsible for internal security, under Beria. Merkulov was a member of Beria's "Georgian Mafia," so called because he, like Beria and many other Beria cronies, came from Soviet Georgia.

U.S. intelligence analyst John J. Dziak observed in *Chekisty: A History of the KGB* (1988), "These par-

ticular organizational changes . . . were never fully explained but they may have had something to do with digesting captive lands and peoples"—Estonia, Latvia, Lithuania, portions of Poland, and the extraction of Bessarabia and northern Bukovina from Romania. "Arrests, deportations, executions, and prison camps increased, demanding reorganized and expanded security forces."

However, wrote Dziak, "The shock of the German invasion propelled a fusion in July 1941 and the two organs were united once again as the NKVD under Beria." This arrangement lasted until April 14, 1943.

Again Stalin reorganized, establishing the NKGB—again under Merkulov—and the NKVD under Beria. Dziak wrote, "the victory at Stalingrad and associated Soviet advances offered the prospect of reconquered lands and populations. Hence, the 1943 NKGB-NKVD separation once again."

This arrangement lasted until March 16, 1946. At that time Smersh was merged into the new Ministry of State Security (MGB), becoming the Third Chief Directorate, responsible for military counterespionage. Merkulov became head of the MGB. Simultaneously, the NKVD—responsible for internal security—was elevated to the status of Ministry of Internal Affairs (MVD).

In this period Stalin also created the KI, or Committee of Information, to carry out the foreign intelligence and clandestine operations previously performed by the MGB. The KI was under the Council of Ministers, an awkward and, in practice, unworkable arrangement. There were too many overlaps and shortfalls in the KI's charter, and a year later, the GRU withdrew its foreign operations from the KI and returned several functions to the MGB. The KI was left with only foreign political and ECONOMIC INTELLIGENCE. These, too, were returned to the MGB in 1951, marking the end of the agency.

This MGB-MVD setup lasted for the rest of Stalin's life. The day after he died on March 5, 1953, Beria, at that moment the strongest of Stalin's potential successors, presided over another merger of the state security and internal security organs—under the rubric MVD, headed, of course, by Lavrenty Beria. (The massive reorganization had obviously been planned earlier.)

Beria shared power with others as the Soviet Union attempted to recover from the death of Stalin, who had ruled for almost three decades. But there could be no question that he envisioned himself becoming the first head of a state security agency to become chief of state. That vision ended in June 1953 when Beria was arrested and, a few months later, executed.

With his arrest, the NKVD and its successor agencies came to an end. Col. Gen. SERGEI KRUGLOV, a veteran NKVD and Smersh officer, took over the "super" MVD while the nation's political leaders sorted out and reorganized the complex institutions of Stalin's legacy.

The KGB (Committee for State Security) was established in March 1954 to undertake all state security and foreign intelligence operations (other than those assigned to the GRU). The MVD was reassigned to internal security functions, remaining the MVD.

CHIEFS OF THE NKVD-NKGB-MGB-MVD

The chiefs of these organs were:

NKVD

July 1934–Sept. 1936	Genrikh Yagoda (previously head of OGPU)
Sept. 1936–Dec. 1938	Nikolay Yezhov
Dec. 1938–Feb. 1941	Lavrenty Beria
July 1941–1946	Lavrenty Beria

NKGB (Narodnyy Komisariat Gosudarstvennoy Bezopasnosti)

Feb. 1941–July 1941	Vsevolod Merkulov
Apr. 1943–Mar. 1946	Vsevolod Merkulov

MGB (Ministerstvo Gosudarstvennoy Bezopasnosti)

Mar. 1946–Oct. 1946	Vsevolod Merkulov
Oct. 1946–Aug. 1951	Viktor Abakumov
Aug. 1951–Dec. 1951	Sergei Ogoltsov
Dec. 1951–Mar. 1953	SEMYON IGNATYEV

MVD (Ministerstvo Vnutrennikh Del)

1946–June 1953	Lavrenty Beria
Mar. 1953–Mar. 1954	Sergei Kruglov

NM-1

A technology demonstration aircraft developed by the Soviet Union for strategic RECONNAISSANCE.

Referred to as recativnyi strategicheskyi razvyedchik (strategic reconnaissance aircraft), the spyplane was to fly at more than 1,850 mph (Mach 2.8) at altitudes of about 100,000 feet. It would be fitted with high-speed cameras and, as they became available, other sensors.

The design was entrusted to Pavel V. Tsybin at the Flight Research Institute rather than to a traditional aircraft design bureau. Tsybin selected a radical design with a long, circular-section fuselage and relatively short wings with a large area provided by a trapezoidal platform, with wingtip jet engine pods. Propulsion was probably to derive from ramjets. The design was somewhat akin to CLARENCE (KELLY) JOHNSON's CL-282 and CL-400 designs, which evolved from the F-104 Starfighter.

The complexity of the design led the decision to build a slower technology-demonstration aircraft—designated NM-1—before proceeding with the full-scale, Mach 2.8 aircraft. This aircraft was flown in 1959–1960. It was found to have poor low-speed handling as well as other potential problems.

Data from the NM-1 flight tests and difficulties in development of the engines for the definitive aircraft led to cancellation of this ambitious project by 1960.

NMIC

SEE NATIONAL MARITIME INTELLIGENCE CENTER

NOC

SEE NON-OFFICIAL COVER

NOFORN

Derived from "no foreign," a U.S. security restriction that prevents CLASSIFIED documents or other material from being shown or transferred to a foreign citizen regardless of his or her SECURITY CLEARANCE.

Nolan, Brig. Gen. Dennis

(b. 1872 d. 1956)

U.S. Army officer whose efforts raised the status of MILITARY INTELLIGENCE before and during World War I.

Nolan graduated from the U.S. Military Academy in 1896 and served in the Spanish-American War. Later he was stationed in the Philippines, where the U.S. Army put down an armed revolt by Filipinos against U.S. occupation of the islands.

Assigned to the War Department's General Staff as a captain, Nolan worked closely with Capt. RALPH H. VAN DEMAN, a pioneer in ARMY INTELLIGENCE (U.S.). When the United States entered World War I in April 1917, Maj. Gen. John Pershing, commander of the American Expeditionary Force (AEF), chose Nolan to be his G-2, ordering him to develop an intelligence operation tailored to the war that the AEF was to fight.

Nolan set up an elaborate intelligence NETWORK, with officers specially trained for intelligence in every battalion and COUNTERINTELLIGENCE units in neutral countries to gather POLITICAL INTELLIGENCE as well as MILITARY INTELLIGENCE. To track down German spies behind the lines in France, Nolan set up the Corps of Intelligence Police, a rowdy crew of French-speaking sergeants who included a murderer and a deserter from the French Foreign Legion.

Nolan ingratiated himself with his British counterparts. The chief of British general headquarters intelligence called him "clear-headed, and very penetrating in his criticisms and questions. He is the exact opposite of the usual British conception of the American." The British shared their counterintelligence reports, some of which were ordinarily shown only to the Prime Minister and Foreign Secretary. Nolan also became a friend of Maj. STEWART G. MENZIES, a future Director-General of the British Secret Intelligence Service (MI6).

Nolan was promoted to brigadier general during the war; afterward he was returned to his permanent grade of major. His one-star rank was restored when he became director of the Army's Military Intelligence Division in Sept. 1920. At that time the Army engaged in DOMESTIC INTELLIGENCE aimed at finding communists—popularly called Reds—plotting to overthrow the U.S. government. Popular opinion turned against the use of soldiers for internal intelligence, and Nolan ended the practice.

NONCONTRACT

Derived from "non contractor," a U.S. security restriction to prevent CLASSIFIED documents or other material from being shown or transferred to commercial contractors regardless of their SECURITY CLASSIFICATION.

The restriction was abolished in 1995 because it was found to add little to the security of national defense programs.

Non-Official Cover

(NOC)

Term used by the CIA for CASE OFFICERS who operate overseas outside the usual diplomatic COVER. Most case officers work out of U.S. embassies, protected by a diplomatic cover. An individual caught working as an INTELLIGENCE OFFICER is usually declared persona non grata (referred to as "being PNG'd") and ordered to leave the host country. NOCs do not have that privilege, and so their work can be more dangerous.

When ROBERT M. GATES was DIRECTOR OF CENTRAL INTELLIGENCE he increased the number of NOCs, despite fears that this would place an added personnel and financial burden on the CIA. NOCs are denied the protection and the secure communications of an embassy. They work under a cover that is usually a legitimate or seemingly legitimate business.

NOCs usually operate outside of the UNITED STATES COUNTRY TEAM, the U.S. personnel in a country, including CIA officers, who are under the authority of the U.S. ambassador. NOCs may be involved in clandestine activities that are unknown to the ambassador.

NORCANUKUS

Security restriction that permits classified documents or other material to be shown or transferred to persons with the appropriate SECURITY CLEARANCE from Norway, Canada, the United Kingdom, and United States.

Nordpol (NORTH POLE)

German ABWEHR operation against the Dutch underground network set up by the British Special Operations Executive (SOE) during World War II.

In March 1941 the Germans forced a captured SOE radio operator to transmit messages to Britain in a code that the Germans had obtained. The operator omitted certain words that served as a warning that the sender was under enemy control; the receiver in Britain was not supposed to acknowledge the message if it did not contain those words. To emphasize his predicament, the captured operator also got the word captured into the message. Nevertheless, the operator acknowledged the message—leading the operator to believe that the British knew he was captured but wanted him to continue contacting Britain.

The Germans thus penetrated the Dutch operation and became aware of the time and place of arrivals from Britain, suggesting targets for sabotage and getting thousands of guns, containers of ammunition and explosives, and even food and currency.

For more than two years the GESTAPO or Abwehr captured AGENTS sent in by SOE and MI6 by parachute or by small boat. Eventually, Nordpol operatives were running 17 transmitters in Holland, sending thousands of false messages to the SOE and MI6. The Nordpol operation spread to Belgium and France, where more agents were captured.

Nordpol officers, knowing that the SOE dealt mostly with sabotage, invented acts of sabotage and kept running the captured SOE agents. But because it was more difficult to fake results from captured SIS agents seeking intelligence, they were usually executed immediately. In Sept. 1944, when the captured agents were no longer of any use to Nordpol, 47 of them were executed.

The SOE remained ignorant of Nordpol until about May 1943, when agents who escaped from the Germans were able to send messages to Britain. Two who managed to make it to Spain and then to Britain were imprisoned for giving aid to the enemy. Later in 1943, when other escaped agents told what had happened, the British released the original two and began to understand what had really occurred.

North Atlantic Treaty Organization

(NATO)

A major TARGET for espionage by Soviet intelligence during the Cold War, now a source for assets in the worldwide quest for TERRORIST INTELLIGENCE. NATO's efforts in the West's war on terrorism was enhanced in 2003 when seven former Soviet bloc nations—Bulgaria, Estonia, Latvia, Lithuania, Romania, Slovakia, and Slovenia—entered NATO. In 1999, Hungary, Poland, and the Czech Republic had also entered NATO.

After the Sept. 11, 2001, attacks on the World Trade Center and the Pentagon, NATO invoked Article V of its 1949 founding treaty, which pledges that an attack on any member of the alliance shall be considered an attack on all. Thus, NATO joined the war on terrorism. Although the new members add only limited military strength to NATO, they bring with them new intelligence resources that will aid in ferreting out terrorist threats.

NATO was founded early in the Cold War, soon after the Soviet Union blockaded BERLIN in 1948. By the time the Soviets ended the blockade in May 1949, nine World War II Allies—Belgium, Britain, Canada, Denmark, France, Luxembourg, the Netherlands, Norway, and the United States—had joined with Italy, a former Axis enemy, and two nations neutral in the war, Portugal and Iceland, to form NATO. The NATO nations set up three principal military commands (with two permanently under American officers and one under a British officer) and pledged that an attack on any one of them would constitute an attack on all of them. Turkey and Greece joined NATO in 1952.

When a rearmed West Germany joined NATO in 1955, the Soviet Union hastily organized the Warsaw Treaty Organization—consisting of the Soviet Union, Albania, Bulgaria, Czechoslovakia, East Germany, Hungary, Poland, and Romania. The intelligence services of each of these Eastern Bloc nations contributed to the unrelenting Soviet intelligence campaign. Several times the Soviets were successful in achieving a major intelligence objective: PENETRATION of NATO.

Western intelligence officials believe that penetration may have occurred very early. British Spy DONALD MACLEAN's position in the British Foreign Office in the late 1940s enabled him to provide his Soviet HANDLERS with details of U.S.-British thinking on the founding of NATO. An official U.S. appraisal of Maclean's work said: "In the fields of US/UK/Canada planning on atomic energy, US/UK postwar planning and policy in Europe, all information up to the date of [Maclean's] defection undoubtedly reached Soviet hands . . ." (Maclean defected in 1951.)

JOHN CAIRNCROSS, like Maclean a member of the CAMBRIDGE SPY RING, also revealed early secrets about NATO. YURI MODIN, an NKVD officer who handled members of the Cambridge ring, wrote that in fall 1948 Cairncross was working in the British Ministry of Defence on NATO plans when Modin asked him for information on the possible placing of nuclear weapons in West Germany. "A month later, I had in my possession every detail of NATO's plans for nuclear arms in Germany," Modin wrote in *My Five Cambridge Friends* (1994). "From the start," Modin said, "we knew what the American bases in Turkey, Norway, Iceland and Italy had cost to set up, the value of Britain's contribution of equipment, how many civilians were employed, who provided the food and who maintained the bases at what price. We also knew the nature of the weapons involved, how much they were worth and which country had supplied them."

The East German secret police, the Stasi (see MFS), was especially skilled at penetrating NATO. Handsome male Stasi AGENTS—dubbed "Romeos" by Western intelligence officials—targeted both West German agencies and NATO offices specifically to seduce secretaries and obtain secrets through SEX. Among the seduced spies was a German woman employed at NATO headquarters in Brussels. MARKUS WOLF, chief of the Stasi through most of the Cold War, boasted of placing agents in high councils of NATO. Some may never have been found.

HUGH GEORGE HAMBLETON, a NATO economist, spied for the Soviet Union for years. His espionage may have been revealed by ANATOLY GOLITSYN, a KGB officer who defected to the West in Dec. 1961. Golitsin told Western debriefers that a steady stream of NATO intelligence came to the Soviets from agents who were working at NATO.

Rear Adm. Hermann Luedke, chief of the logistics department of Supreme Headquarters Allied Powers Europe, was suspected of being the highest-ranking Soviet spy in NATO. Knowing he was under suspicion, he killed himself in 1968. Two other officers and a civil servant subsequently committed suicide, but any connection between them and Luedke was not made public at the time.

Probably the most valuable Soviet spy was REINER RUPP, who, together with his wife, provided the East Germans and, through them, the Soviet Union, with copies of an estimated 10,000 NATO documents. Their espionage, said a German prosecutor, "could have lost NATO a war."

Also valuable was U.S. Army Sgt. CLYDE LEE CONRAD, who ran a NATO spy ring that sold secrets of nuclear missiles and troop strength. Conrad, who served in Europe for ten years, in the late 1970s was in charge of maintaining classified documents at an Army base near Bad Kreuzbach, West Germany. The ring included at least two members of the Hungarian intelligence service. Reportedly, one of the Hungarians had also received payment from the CIA for what turned out to be fake documents.

Conrad recruited Sgt. RODERICK JAMES RAMSAY and Staff Sgt. JEFFREY S. RONDEAU, who continued the espionage into the 1980s, passing NATO defense plans to Czechoslovakian and Hungarian INTELLIGENCE OFFICERS. (As intelligence officers for NATO nations, Czechoslovakian and Hungarian intelligence officers are now *aiding* NATO.) Ramsay, a document custodian, was said to have sold intelligence about the use of tactical nuclear weapons and military communications. The Hungarian service, like other Soviet-trained Eastern Bloc agencies, shared its intelligence successes with the Soviets.

U.S. Army Warrant Officer JOSEPH G. HELMICH, JR., a crypto-material custodian stationed in Paris in the early 1960s, decided to pay off his debts by becoming a WALK-IN: He walked into the Soviet Embassy in Paris and offered to sell secrets about U.S. and NATO communications.

The Soviet spy ring CODE-NAMED SAPPHIRE was headquartered in France, but its tentacles reached into NATO. Among the Sapphire spies was Georges Piques, a NATO press secretary, who was seen by French SURVEILLANCE operatives passing material to a Soviet HANDLER. Piques claimed at his trial that he passed diplomatic and military information to the Soviets for the sake of easing international tension. He said that his handlers had shown him a letter from Soviet leader Nikita Khrushchev saying that he had been guided during the Berlin crisis of 1961 by NATO documents provided by Piques.

Nosenko, Yuri Ivanovich

(b. 1927)

Soviet DEFECTOR who became a prisoner of the CIA when his disclosures about the KGB polarized U.S. intelligence officials. Nosenko, a KGB officer under COVER as a member of a disarmament conference in Geneva, approached the CIA in 1963 and offered to become a DOUBLE AGENT. But he changed his mind, becoming a defector in Jan. 1964.

Nosenko, who spoke fairly good English, began his espionage career in 1945 in the GRU, Soviet MILITARY INTELLIGENCE, analyzing SIGNALS INTELLIGENCE from U.S. military communications in Asia. In 1953 he transferred to the KGB to work in foreign intelligence. He occasionally attempted to recruit American tourists in Moscow. In 1957, under cover of a Ministry of Culture official traveling with a Soviet athletic team, he visited Britain and got his first view of Western living standards. The visit may have contributed his decision to defect.

In 1959, as a KGB officer assigned to keep watch on foreigners, he became the case officer of Lee Harvey Oswald, a former U.S. Marine who had renounced his American citizenship and was living in the Soviet Union.

When Nosenko defected in 1964, he claimed to be a KGB lieutenant colonel when he was only a captain. This was one of his fabrications that raised suspicions in the CIA. The agency's chief COUNTERINTELLIGENCE officer, JAMES JESUS ANGLETON, believed that Nosenko was a DISINFORMATION agent whose mission was to confuse those investigating the assassination of President Kennedy. Nosenko claimed that he had been given the task of checking the KGB files of Oswald in Nov. 1963 following Oswald's arrest for the assassination of Kennedy. Nosenko said that he had found no current connection between Oswald and the KGB.

But doubt was cast on Nosenko because ANATOLY GOLITSYN, an earlier defector, had predicted that the KGB would send other defectors who would deny Golitsyn's claims—the chief one being that a MOLE CODE-NAMED Sasha had penetrated deep into the CIA. Golitsyn had said that Viktor Kovshuk, a high-ranking KGB officer, had been sent to Washington in 1957 specifically to "activate" Sasha, touching off a mole hunt by Angleton.

Nosenko said he had not heard of Sasha but knew of an agent code-named Andrei. He turned out to be a U.S. serviceman who had worked in the motor pool of the U.S. Embassy in Moscow, and who admitted to meeting Koshuk in 1957.

Angleton's mole hunters saw the revelation of "Andrei" as the kind of trick that Golitsyn had predicted. They relentlessly questioned Nosenko, trying in vain to get him to confess that he was not a defector but an agent sent to impersonate a defector. He was placed in a small room in solitary confinement, deprived of sleep, half-starved, and repeatedly interrogated. Another reason he was given such harsh treatment was to replicate the conditions under which the KGB kept Frederick Barghoorn, a Yale professor of political science seized by the KGB outside the Metropole Hotel in Moscow in 1963. The CIA believed that Nosenko had chosen Barghoorn as a hostage to exchange for a Soviet spy arrested in New York. But Barghoorn was held for two weeks; Nosenko was held in CAMP PEARY, the CIA's training center near Warrenton, Va., until 1968—four years.

When WILLIAM COLBY became director of the CIA in 1973, he ended the mole hunt, ordered back pay for Nosenko, and appointed him a consultant in COUNTERINTELLIGENCE.

Notional Agent

Fictitious or nonexistent secret AGENT, usually used for a source of fabricated information or cited in describing the means by which such information was obtained.

Also see DOUBLE-CROSS SYSTEM and GARBO.

Notional Mole

Fictitious MOLE, invented by an enemy intelligence agency to sow confusion in the TARGETED opposition agency. The concept of a notional mole was suggested by critics of JAMES JESUS ANGLETON, who as CIA chief of COUNTERINTELLIGENCE devoted immense resources to tracking down a mole who may have not existed at that time. (ALRICH H. AMES, the CIA mole discovered in 1994, did not begin his spying until 1985, a decade after Angleton's retirement.)

NPIC

SEE NATIONAL PHOTOGRAPHIC INTERPRETATION CENTER

NRO

SEE NATIONAL RECONNAISSANCE OFFICE

NSA

(NATIONAL SECURITY AGENCY)

The National Security Agency is the principal U.S. SIGNALS INTELLIGENCE (SIGINT) organization. The highly secret NSA intercepts radio communications, telephone calls, and computer modem and fax machine transmissions, as well as signals emanating from radar and missile guidance systems. NSA is also responsible for developing and protecting U.S. government CODES.

After the Sept. 11, 2001, attacks on the World Trade Center and the Pentagon, NSA and the CIA were sharply criticized by Congress and editorial writers for their failure to alert the nation to the terrorist threat. (See TERRORIST INTELLIGENCE.) Ironically, NSA had only shortly before unveiled a new goal: "Information dominance for America." Air Force Lt. Gen. Kenneth A. Minihan, who had become director in 1996, said that in the new century "techno-terrorists" would be a major NSA TARGET.

Minihan's successor, Air Force Lt. Gen. Michael V. Hayden, inherited the mandate, but on his watch the United States was the target. Responding to critics, he told Congress that the agency had known of a terrorist planning meeting in 2000 of al Qaida leaders in Kuala Lumpur and had "shared this information" with the INTELLIGENCE COMMUNITY. He also said that just prior to the attacks "NSA did obtain two pieces of information suggesting that individuals with terrorist connections believed something significant would happen on September 11th" and that "throughout the summer of 2001 we had more than 30 warnings that something was imminent."

But, maintaining that NSA's basic PRODUCT, SIGINT, is raw material that needs interpretation, he indicated that lawmakers looking for an intelligence breakdown should go elsewhere than NSA, where, he said, "The volume, variety and velocity of human communications make our mission more difficult each day."

He pointed out that NSA had "downsized about

one-third of its manpower and about the same proportion of its budget in the decade of the 1990s. That is the same decade when packetized communications (the e-communications we have all become familiar with) surpassed traditional communications. That is the same decade when mobile cell phones increased from 16 million to 741 million." In the words of NSA's SIGINT director, Maureen Baginski, the agency has to transform itself, becoming "hunters rather than gatherers."

NSA's Central Security Service (CSS) is responsible for U.S. CRYPTANALYSIS and CRYPTOSECURITY. The CSS has two missions: cracking other nations' CODES and providing Information Systems Security (INFOSEC) for official U.S. communications with encryption. INFOSEC expertise extends from protecting White House communications to safeguarding tactical military communications.

The director of NSA is also chief of the CSS and controls the signals intelligence activities of the military services. Both NSA and the CSS are under the Department of Defense, even though the agencies are part of the intelligence community and thus also under the DIRECTOR OF CENTRAL INTELLIGENCE (DCI).

NSA also monitors communications and signals emitted by the space vehicles and missile testing of other nations. The NSA National SIGINT Center provides "instant" intelligence. During crises, the center flashes messages code-named "Critic" to the White House Situation Room.

NSA headquarters are at FORT MEADE, Md., about midway between Washington, D.C., and Baltimore, Md. From there NSA controls a global eavesdropping network that uses SATELLITE, AIRCRAFT, ship, and ground intercept stations to provide the U.S. government with intelligence from virtually any place on earth. "There is not a single event that the U.S. worries about in a foreign policy or foreign military context that NSA does not make a very direct contribution to," Vice Adm. John M. McConnell, NSA director, said in 1995. It was a rare public assessment from NSA, whose initials are also said to mean "No Such Agency" or "Never Say Anything." (By convention, the agency is usually referred to as "NSA", not "the NSA".)

NSA plucks from the air a staggering amount of communications. By NSA estimates, the U.S. Library of Congress holds about 1 quadrillion bits of information. "With the technology that's on the drawing boards now," McConnell said, "we will fill up the Library of Congress about every three hours. That's the kind of volume we're having to deal with in a global context."

LOUIS W. TORDELLA, longtime deputy director of NSA, told the Baltimore Sun in 1995, "I think it's fair to say that the demands on the agency approach infinity. Everybody wants to know everything about everything."

But new technology is frustrating NSA's classic interception techniques, which are based on 20th-century technology—tapping into old-fashioned copper telephone wiring and listening into long-distance calls transmitted by satellites. Most international calls—about 180 billion minutes a year—depend not on satellites but on fiber-optic landlines and transoceanic lines. Wireless cell phones are much more difficult to tap than conventional phones.

ORIGINS

NSA evolved from the U.S. Army's SIGNAL INTELLIGENCE SERVICE and the ARMED FORCES SECURITY AGENCY (AFSA). Reacting to complaints of low-quality STRATEGIC INTELLIGENCE in the Korean War, a presidential committee urged the creation of a COMMUNICATIONS INTELLIGENCE (COMINT) agency subordinate to the Secretary of Defense. Meanwhile, the AFSA was secretly moving from ARLINGTON HALL, in a Virginia suburb of Washington, D.C., to Fort Meade.

President Truman's memorandum of Oct. 24, 1952, establishing the agency was itself TOP SECRET, with the added security of a CODE WORD. NSA's charter remains classified, except for a short excerpt, revealed in 1984 to show how the NSA was exempt from certain legal restrictions about the use of COMMUNICATIONS INTELLIGENCE (COMINT).

The CSS was established by presidential memorandum in 1972 to provide a unified cryptologic organization within the Department of Defense. Even less is known about CSS than about its parent agency. And deep within the CSS is an elite unit, the SPECIAL COLLECTION SERVICE (SCS), whose technicians eavesdrop on intelligence targets in hostile countries.

NSA has gone to extreme lengths to keep itself invisible. For years employees were ordered to say nothing more than "federal government" or "Department of Defense" in reply to questions about where they worked.

The first frank admission of NSA's work came from Moscow in Sept. 1960, when two agency cryptographers, WILLIAM H. MARTIN and BERNON F. MITCHELL, revealed their defection and held a news conference. They told of the U.S.-Britain codebreaking link and said that NSA routinely intercepted the communications of more than 40 nations, including not only the Soviet Union and Eastern Bloc countries but also such allies as Italy, Turkey, and France. Then in 1963, VICTOR N. HAMILTON, a research analyst in NSA's Near East section, appeared in Moscow and told the newspaper Izvestia that he and his colleagues were breaking the military and diplomatic CIPHERS and codes of numerous countries and were intercepting communications to the UNITED NATIONS.

The three traitors had disclosed the basic mission of NSA, but its desire for secrecy was still intense. Learning that an amateur cryptologist, DAVID KAHN, was writing a book on cryptography, NSA tried to stop publication and even placed his name on a WATCH LIST for intercepts. In 1966, when his publishers submitted the manuscript to the Department of Defense for review, they were told that publication "would not be in the national interest." After some squabbling over a few passages, the book, titled The Codebreakers, was published in 1967. (In more recent years NSA has welcomed Kahn, appointing him a visiting distinguished historian at the new NSA Center for Cryptologic History during 1995.)

The first detailed description of NSA appeared in

The Puzzle Palace (1982), by JAMES BAMFORD. The agency was not pleased with the book, but by then the FREEDOM OF INFORMATION ACT was enabling writers to obtain government documents that had previously (and sometimes arbitrarily) been denied. In a 1987 issue of NSA's monthly classified newsletter, Bamford and *New York Times* reporter Seymour Hersh were named in the same sentence with RONALD W. PELTON, an NSA analyst who sold secrets to the Soviet Union, as people who produced "a great deal of unwanted media exposure in recent years."

There is still not much in print about NSA. The Library of Congress catalog in 1995 listed only 12 books on the agency, and four of them were various editions of *The Puzzle Palace*. An indication of the amount of material now available about the NSA came with the CD release in 2003 of *21st Century Complete Guide to the National Security Agency*. Its contents, some 32,000 pages reproduced by recognition software, included information on NSA cryptology and history, including material from World War II and the Korean War.

The agency inherited 1940s intercepts of Soviet intelligence communications between the United States and Moscow. Those intercepts, given the U.S. code name VENONA, were historically rich, but NSA did not begin to release the Venona material until July 1995. By then, more than 60 million other NSA documents were in the process of declassification. As an indication of this new relative openness, the NSA's gateway to the public is the National Cryptologic MUSEUM, located in a former motel near NSA headquarters—and purchased to keep anyone from using it as a SURVEILLANCE outpost. (Also see NATIONAL VIGILIANCE PARK.)

THE WORLD OF NSA

The 650-acre NSA site at Fort Meade is the most visible component of a worldwide complex that includes ground stations in Sugar Grove, W. Va.; Yakima, Wash.; Anchorage, Alaska; and foreign countries, including Argentina, Australia, China, and New Zealand. Military cryptologic commands operate some NSA stations. During the Cold War the Navy provided spy ships (see *LIBERTY, PUEBLO)* as platforms for seagoing NSA listeners; U.S. Air Force and Navy aircraft also operated under NSA direction, sometimes along Soviet and Chinese border air space to stimulate their air defense systems to obtain ELECTRONIC INTELLIGENCE (ELINT) as well as COMINT. It was risky duty (see AIRCRAFT SHOT DOWN).

In space, NSA pulls down intercepts from two kinds of satellites: commercial satellites that relay telephone calls, fax messages, and computer modem transmissions; and ELINT satellites, designed to pick up two-way radio transmissions, microwave-relayed local telephone calls, and other electronic communications. During the second Gulf War in 2003, there were unconfirmed reports that NSA experts had succeeded in intercepting Iraqi cell phones and e-mails—an indication of NSA's growing ability to respond to 21st-century telecommunications.

The agency works in close cooperation with Britain's GOVERNMENT COMMUNICATIONS HEADQUARTERS, Canada's Communications Security Establishment, Australia's Defence Signals Directorate, and New Zealand's Government Communications Security Bureau in a global intelligence alliance known as the UKUSA Community (see UKUSA AGREEMENT). NSA has long maintained listening posts in Xinjiang Province in remote northwestern China, near what was the Soviet border, in close proximity to nuclear and missile testing sites.

At Fort Meade NSA operates a huge printing plant and a state-of-the-art factory to produce computer chips for its massive array of computers. The agency also runs the National Cryptologic School and procures all U.S. government secure communications devices. In 1993 NSA contracts in Maryland alone totaled over $700 million. The agency's annual budget is highly classified, but estimates hover around $3.5 *billion,* not including the intercept satellites paid for and operated by the NATIONAL RECONNAISSANCE OFFICE.

NSA codebreaking is concentrated at Fort Meade; the heart of the effort is a supercomputing facility staffed by one of the largest concentrations of mathematicians in the world. NSA employs some 20,000 people in Fort Meade and elsewhere in Maryland, making it the state's largest employer. Perhaps as many as 100,000 others—mostly military personnel—work for the agency around the world. Civilians who work for NSA live restricted lives. Lest they give secrets while under anesthesia, they must go to dentists and surgeons cleared by NSA's Security Office. Overseas visits are limited. Notification must be given if an employee or a relative marries a foreigner.

Although a Department of Defense agency, NSA's tasks are assigned by the DCI, operating under instructions from the NATIONAL SECURITY COUNCIL and advice from the NATIONAL FOREIGN INTELLIGENCE BOARD. The director of NSA—always a three-star admiral or general with an intelligence background—can offer services from a large menu.

In response to a request for a "watch" on a certain country, NSA can intercept local and long-distance telephone conversations, including those made from automobiles; messages to and from a country's capital to its embassies; messages from other countries referring to the targeted country; radio communications of the country's armed forces; background reports on what has been intercepted in previous weeks, months, or years; profiles of the country's leaders, based on what they have been saying on the telephone; specific or indirect references to words and phrases (such as nuclear or explosives) in various languages (see ECHELON).

An actual account of how NSA responds unfolded during investigations into the IRAN-CONTRA AFFAIR. Marine Lt. Col. Oliver L. North, the mastermind of the project, said that NSA arranged "some very specific, targeted intelligence collection that would give us, almost instantly, exactly what was happening very, very accurately." This included "detailed information on what these people [fellow conspirators in the selling of arms to Iran] were saying to each other, and the plans they were making."

While the agency is secretive about its accomplishments, over the years some have been revealed: conversations between Soviet leader Leonid Brezhnev and high-ranking officials, picked up from his limousine radio-telephones; Panamanian dictator Manuel Antonio Noriega talking to his mistress; information leading to the identity of Libyans involved in the bombing of Pan Am Flight 103 in 1988; telephone taps that pinpointed the location of Colombian drug lord Pablo Escobar, killed by Colombian security forces in Dec. 1993; and cell phone conversations during the Iraqi War in 2003.

NSA AND THE LAW

The FOREIGN INTELLIGENCE SURVEILLANCE ACT and other laws pertaining to NSA restrict its eavesdropping to foreign communication. The legislation has been interpreted to mean that one end of the communication can be in the United States—as long as the other end is in another country. The targeting of Americans is prohibited and, if any Americans' names are picked up in intercepts, the names must be deleted from transcripts and cannot be passed on to the CIA, FBI, or other government agencies. In such transcripts, a name is replaced with "U.S. person."

NSA regulations on carrying out the law are TOP SECRET. But this much is publicly known: If NSA or the FBI believes that a domestic intercept is vital to national security, the agency must obtain a warrant from the FOREIGN INTELLIGENCE SURVEILLANCE COURT (FISC). The court has never been known to refuse a request. By law, the court must annually tell Congress how many warrants are requested and approved, but details about the warrants remain secret. As many as 10,000 applications had been submitted from 1978 until May 2002. None was refused. Because terrorists are not considered "foreign agents" under FISC, a new set of criteria for surveillance was included in the USA PATRIOT ACT.

NSA does not need a warrant for monitoring foreign targets in the United States, such as the overseas communications of embassies. But it must get a warrant for a foreign target outside an embassy. When Haitian President Jean-Bertrand Aristide lived in Washington after being driven into exile in 1991, for example, the law would have required an FISC warrant to tap his phone and BUG his apartment, because he was in contact with Americans.

An example of what happens when an American is on the line came when Congressman Michael D. Barnes's calls to Nicaraguan officials were intercepted by NSA during the Reagan administration's efforts to topple the Nicaraguan government. "Reporters told me right wingers were circulating excerpts from phone conversa-

tions I'd had," Barnes told the *Baltimore Sun* for that newspaper's special report on NSA. Barnes said that WILLIAM J. CASEY, then DCI, showed him an NSA-intercepted cable from the Nicaraguan Embassy. The cable reported a meeting between embassy officials and a Barnes aide. Casey told Barnes he should fire the aide. Barnes said he did not object to being recorded. But he told the *Sun* that such incidents were a reminder of the potential for the abuse of NSA's eavesdropping capability.

The laws aimed at controlling NSA eavesdropping stemmed from 1975 congressional investigations of NSA domestic intelligence operations (see SHAMROCK). For 30 years, under secret agreements with telegraph companies, U.S. eavesdropping agencies got copies of international telegrams. An offshoot of the Shamrock operation, MINARET put about 1,600 Americans on a "watch list," automatically intercepting their international telephone calls or cables. Among those on the watch list were the Rev. Martin Luther King, Jr., and, for their active opposition to the Vietnam War, actress Jane Fonda, folk singer Joan Baez, and pediatrician Dr. Benjamin Spock. During the Shamrock operation NSA produced files on 75,000 Americans.

Since the end of the Cold War, NSA, like other intelligence agencies, has sought a new mission by providing ELINT about terrorists and drug traffickers. The agency also wants to make sure that it can keep on intercepting. Beginning with a campaign during the first Bush administration, both NSA and the FBI have been urging the installation of a "clipper chip" in telephones and computers to make it easier for the government to eavesdrop on encrypted communications. Computer and telecommunications firms oppose the idea, as do privacy advocates. But Microsoft Corp., reportedly at NSA's behest, designed its Windows programs so that encryption would be difficult.

As NSA entered the 21st century, international communications expanded tremendously in size and complexity. There were about 18 million Internet users in 1995; by 2000 there were 120 million, and their ranks grow prodigiously every day. By some estimates, more than 5 million e-mails are transmitted each minute, and each hour there are 35 million voice communications by land-line phones and cell phones, transmitted through cables and via satellites. Fiber-optic cables run under roads and oceans throughout the world, and this kind of cable is extremely difficult to tap. CIA officials joke that the best agents they can have in place nowadays are backhoe operators who know where to rip out fiber-optic cables.

NSA DIRECTORS

The two directors of the Armed Forces Security Agency are usually included among NSA directors because they were involved in the transition of the interception-code-breaking agency from an armed forces entity to a national one partly outside the military chain of command. They are Rear Adm. Earl E. Stone, July 1949–July 1951, and Maj. Gen. Ralph J. Canine, July 1951–Nov. 1952, when NSA was founded.

The subsequent directors were:

Nov. 1952–Nov. 1956	Lt. Gen. Ralph J. Canine, USA
Nov. 1956–Nov. 1960	Lt. Gen. John A. Samford, USAF
Nov. 1960–June 1962	Vice Adm. Laurence H. Frost, USN
July 1962–May 1965	Lt. Gen. Gordon A. Blake, USAF
June 1965–July 1969	Lt. Gen. Marshall S. Carter, USA
Aug. 1969–July 1972	Vice Adm. Noel A. M. Gayler, USN
Aug. 1972–Aug. 1973	Lt. Gen. Samuel C. Phillips, USAF
Aug. 1973–July 1977	Lt. Gen. Lew Allen, Jr., USAF
July 1977–Mar. 1981	Vice Adm. BOBBY RAY INMAN, USN
April 1981–April 1985	Lt. Gen. Lincoln D. Faurer, USAF
May 1985–July 1988	Lt. Gen. WILLIAM E. ODOM, USA
Aug. 1988–April 1992	Vice Adm. WILLIAM O. STUDEMAN, USN
May 1992–Feb. 1996	Vice Adm. John M. McConnell, USN
Mar. 1996–Feb. 1999	Lt. Gen. Kenneth A. Minihan, USAF
Mar. 1999-	Lt. Gen. Michael V. Hayden, USAF

NSC

SEE NATIONAL SECURITY COUNCIL

NSG

SEE NAVAL SECURITY GROUP

Nuclear Intelligence

(NUCINT)

Intelligence derived from the collection and analysis of radiation and other effects resulting from radioactive sources. These sources include nuclear and thermonuclear detonations, as well as beta emissions from nuclear weapons.

The first major NUCINT operation occurred on Sept. 3, 1949, when a U.S. Air Force B-29 SUPERFORTRESS RECONNAISSANCE aircraft flying from Japan to Alaska detected the first signs of a Soviet nuclear test. The Air Force had been directed on Sept. 16, 1947, to establish and operate a reconnaissance system to determine the time and place of all large explosions that might occur anywhere in the world, and to do so in a manner that would absolutely determine whether they were of nuclear origin.

Nugget

British term for the "bait" to be offered to a potential foreign DEFECTOR—money, political asylum, SEX, or a career opportunity in the West.

Nursemaid

Russian term for the security service (previously KGB) officer who accompanies delegations on trips to the West to prevent anyone from becoming a DEFECTOR. Such nursemaids (*nyanki* in Russian) are especially vigilant because if a member of the delegation defects, the security officer is vulnerable to imprisonment--or, in some cases in the past—execution for his failure.

OB

SEE ORDER OF BATTLE

Ob'edinyonnoye Gosudarstvennoye Politicheskoye Upravleniye

(OGPU)
SEE CHEKA

Odessa

Secret organization of former German SS officers that became a major TARGET of Western intelligence agencies. The main function of Odessa, founded after World War II, was the arranging of escapes of SS officers wanted for war crimes. The name Odessa is a German acronym from Organization der Entlassene SS Angehürige (Organization for the Release of Former SS Members). The Odessa had agents throughout Germany who, through an underground known as Die Spinne (the Spider) arranged for ex-SS officers to escape or elude Allied hunters.

U.S. and Israeli intelligence officials believe that Odessa engineered the escape to South America of Adolf Eichmann, the SS "expert" on Jews; Josef Mengele, the SS physician who performed heinous experiments on inmates of Auschwitz; and other, lesser-known SS officers. Existence of the organization became known to Allied occupation officers immediately after the war. One of the founders was believed to be OTTO SKORZENY, the daring German special operations commander.

SS officers reportedly smuggled huge sums out of Germany to finance the escapes. Fleeing SS men were provided with false identities and passage out of Germany at the end of the war. One major terminal of the Odessa escape route, according to Israeli intelligence, was Buenos Aires, Argentina.

The organization gained popular notoriety after publication of Frederick Forsyth's suspense novel *The Odessa File* (1972), subsequently made into a 1974 movie starring Jon Voight, Maria Schell, and Maximilian Schell.

Odom, Lt. Gen. William E.

(b. 1932)

Outspoken director of the NSA from May 1985 to July 1988. He was known as a hard-liner with the nickname "Zbig's superhawk" when he was military assistant to President Carter's national security adviser, Zbigniew Brzezinski.

A 1950 graduate of the Military Academy, Odom later earned a master's degree (1962) and doctorate (1970) in political science from Columbia University. He also specialized in the Russian language in Army schools, took parachute and ranger training, and attended the Army Command and General Staff College.

His assignments included the U.S. military liaison mission to Soviet forces in Germany in 1964–1966 and a spell as assistant Army ATTACHÉ in Moscow in 1972–1974. In Vietnam he worked in pacification programs in 1970–1971. He also held several teaching assignments at the Military Academy in West Point, N.Y.

When Brzezinski became President Carter's national security adviser in Jan. 1977, he named Odom as his military assistant; the two had met at Columbia University. In that role Odom was involved in planning responses to the Soviet invasion of Afghanistan, the capture of the U.S. Embassy in Tehran, and the holding of Americans as hostages.

Early in 1981 he left the NATIONAL SECURITY COUNCIL and in Nov. 1981 became the Army's Assistant Chief of Staff (Intelligence). While in that position he was promoted to major general in 1982 and to lieutenant general in 1984.

Odom became head of NSA in May 1985. A year later, concerned about the attention that would attend the planned trial of Soviet spy RONALD PELTON, a former communications specialist at NSA, Odom called for press censorship. He feared that intelligence collection methods would be revealed and proposed a public warning to the news media to restrict their reporting of the case. He also wanted the warning to include a threat of prosecution for reporters who ignored the advice. (Of course, the Soviets already knew any secrets that Pelton could reveal in an open trial.) The warning was issued, but without any threat of prosecution.

Odom also criticized officials of the Reagan administration for leaking sensitive information to the news media, saying that the administration was responsible for far more leaks to the press than Congress: "There's leaking from Congress . . . there's more leaking in the administration because it's bigger. I'm stuck with the consequences of it."

He continued, in a meeting with military reporters on Sept. 2, 1987, "Leaks have damaged the [communications intelligence] system more in the past three to four years than in a long, long time." His bottom line: "Just deadly losses." SEE LEAK

Odom left NSA and retired from the Army on Aug. 1, 1988. He became an adjunct professor at Yale and a senior fellow at the Hudson Institute. He is the author of *Fixing Intelligence* (2003).

Ofek

The first Israeli SATELLITE. The *Ofek* (Hebrew for "horizon") was developed to provide SURVEILLANCE of Arab missile and other weapon developments and deployments. The satellite effort—given the CODE NAME Precious Stone—was an outgrowth of the 1973 Yom Kippur War, in which Israel suffered a major surprise attack when the Egyptians crossed the Suez Canal. Subsequently, Egyptian tactics in the Sinai battles were very costly to the Israelis (see ISRAEL, AGRANAT COMMISSION).

Maj. Gen. MEIR AMIT, a former head of AMAN, Israeli MILITARY INTELLIGENCE, and the MOSSAD, and subsequently head of the General Satellite Corp., explained the need for Israel to have a spy satellite: "If you are fed from the crumbs of others according to their whims, this is very inconvenient and very difficult. If you have your own, independent capability, you climb one level higher."

The first *Ofek* satellite was launched from the Negev Desert on Sept. 1988. Carried aloft by a three-stage, Israeli-produced *Shavit* ("comet") rocket, the satellite weighed 155 pounds. An experimental vehicle, the *Ofek*-1 entered an orbit 250 to 1,150 miles above the Earth. The *Ofek*-2 satellite was lifted into orbit on April 3, 1990. With a similar orbit, this 160-pound vehicle has

been described as the progenitor of a camera-carrying satellite. Both the *Ofek*-1 and *Ofek*-2 decayed out of orbit after about four months. *Ofek*-3 burned up in space after five years. The latest in the series, *Ofek*-5, was launched in May 2002.

Office of National Estimates

(ONE)

CIA unit that produced NATIONAL INTELLIGENCE ESTIMATES (NIEs), seen by their creators as the ultimate intelligence PRODUCT.

The guiding genius of the ONE was Sherman Kent, whose career traces the modern evolution of U.S. intelligence. Before the U.S. entry into World War II, Kent joined the research and analysis branch of the COORDINATOR OF INFORMATION, the precursor of the wartime OFFICE OF STRATEGIC SERVICES (OSS). In Jan. 1943 he became the chief of OSS research and analysis for Europe and Africa. After the war and the abolition of the OSS, Kent worked briefly in the State Department's BUREAU OF RESEARCH AND INTELLIGENCE. In 1950 he joined the CIA, becoming deputy to William L. Langer, a peacetime diplomatic historian and Kent's wartime boss. Langer was the first chief of the newly created ONE.

The ONE replaced the Office of Reports and Estimates (ORE), which had been a focal point of criticism since the founding of the CIA in 1947. (Originally called the Office of Research and Evaluation, the ORE changed its name, but not its initials, after the State Department complained that it had the mission of research and evaluation.) In 1949 the NATIONAL SECURITY COUNCIL ordered a reorganization of the CIA. Rear Adm. ROSCOE HILLENKOETTER, the DIRECTOR OF CENTRAL INTELLIGENCE (DCI), at first resisted, but he was forced to comply in 1950 after the CIA—specifically, its analytical arm, the ORE—failed to foresee North Korea's invasion of South Korea.

Hillenkoetter's successor as DCI, Army Lt. Gen. WALTER BEDELL SMITH, abolished the ORE and created the ONE and the BOARD OF NATIONAL ESTIMATES (BNE), which was to provide independent intelligence analysis. Smith remembered Langer and Kent from World War II and brought them in to redesign the CIA's analysis system around the ONE. Smith wanted the ONE to become "the heart of the Central Intelligence Agency and of the national intelligence machinery."

Langer went back to Harvard in Jan. 1952 and Kent, a Yale man, took over the ONE. He was head of the ONE and chairman of the BNE from 1952 to his retirement in 1967. Kent "is a larger than life figure," wrote J. Kenneth McDonald, chief of the CIA history staff, in 1994. His tenure "was a major formative influence on the way that the Central Intelligence Agency and Intelligence Community prepare and present National Intelligence Estimates."

Kent often sounded like a haughty academician lecturing to undergraduates. "Let things be such that if our policy-making master is to disregard our knowledge and wisdom, he will never do so because our work was inaccurate, incomplete, or patently biased. Let him disregard us only when he must pay greater heed to someone else. And let him be uncomfortable—thoroughly uncomfortable—about his decision to heed this other," Kent wrote in a classified retrospect essay in 1968. He and his ONE had an "aura of Olympian detachment," CIA historian Donald P. Steury wrote in 1994 in an introduction to a collection of declassified Kent essays on NIEs. At some point, Steury added, the ONE "crossed the line between scholarly objectivity and intellectual arrogance."

In 1962, when the Soviet Union decided to put nuclear missiles into Cuba, Kent's vaunted NIEs concluded that it would not happen. A special NIE issued in Sept. 1962 said that the placing of missiles in Cuba "would be incompatible with Soviet practice to date and with Soviet policy as we presently estimate it." DCI JOHN A. MCCONE, relying on instinct, nevertheless ordered U-2 spyplane flights over Cuba and got evidence showing the Soviets were doing just what the NIE had said they would not do.

The ONE was on the path to oblivion when Kent retired in 1967. Henry Kissinger, President Nixon's National Security Adviser, did not like the product. The board was abolished in 1973 with the appointment of 12 National Intelligence Officers within the CIA who would provide specialized areas of expertise. The UNITED STATES INTELLIGENCE BOARD largely continues the functions of the Board of National Estimates.

Office of Naval Intelligence

(ONI)

First agency in American history established to collect information on the military affairs of foreign governments. It was founded on March 23, 1882, "to collect and record such naval information as may be useful to the [Navy] Department in wartime as well as in peace." The first Chief INTELLIGENCE OFFICER, Lt. THEODORUS B. M. MASON, held the post from June 1882 to April 1885. (The position was changed to DIRECTOR OF NAVAL INTELLIGENCE in 1911.)

By the time the United States entered World War I in April 1917, ONI had become responsible for the protection of naval ships and installations against espionage, sabotage, and subversion. Until the 1920s the ONI was also responsible for Navy information and historical activities. The two latter functions subsequently became independent Navy offices.

Late in World War II ONI also became responsible for OPERATIONAL INTELLIGENCE, a function previously assigned to the operating fleets. Naval intelligence was considered a staff function within the Office of the Chief of Naval Operations until late 1992. It originally had the organization code OP-16 (OP for Office of the Chief of Naval Operations, 16 indicating naval intelligence); this was later changed to OP-92. In the major Navy headquarters reorganization of 1992, ONI became N-2, a major staff office, bringing it more closely into alignment with the position of the intelligence organizations of the Joint Chiefs of Staff, unified commands, and the other military services.

Also see NAVAL INTELLIGENCE, U.S.

Office of Strategic Services

(OSS)

World War II–era U.S. intelligence and sabotage agency. President Roosevelt created the Office of Strategic Services on June 13, 1942. Placed under the jurisdiction of the Joint Chiefs of Staff, the OSS replaced the Office of COORDINATOR OF INFORMATION, a quasi-intelligence organization. Roosevelt named WILLIAM J. DONOVAN, who had been coordinator of information, director of the new intelligence agency.

Donovan, who had recently visited London and been extensively briefed by the British intelligence services, roughly modeled the OSS on the Special Operations Executive (SOE). The SOE operated raiding groups and supported resistance and guerrilla activities in German-occupied countries.

The OSS was manned by both military personnel assigned from the services and civilians. Donovan recruited a great variety of Americans: university professors, such as Arthur M. Schlesinger, Jr.; lawyers, including future Supreme Court justice Arthur Goldberg; and advertising men, journalists, and writers (including Gene Fodor, originator of the Fodor Guides); filmmakers (John Ford); and economists (for such matters as analysis of German war production in terms of good air-raid targets). David K. E. Bruce, director of OSS European operations, went on to become U.S. ambassador to France (1949–1952), West Germany (1957–1958), and the United Kingdom (1961–1969)—the only person to hold three major U.S. ambassadorships.

Cookbook author Julia Child served in the OSS in Washington, D.C., and later in China. Child recalls that the outfit was called "Oh! So Secret!" Others, because of the notables in the OSS ranks, said it meant "Oh, So Social." Both labels were appropriate; Donovan was a graduate of Columbia University and its law school (Franklin D. Roosevelt was a classmate), and his agency was both secret and filled with men and women listed in the social registers.

The first overseas operations of the OSS were in Europe and North Africa. Donovan's "theater headquarters" in London were established at 72 Grosvenor Street, near the American Embassy. Under a formal agreement with British intelligence officials, the OSS did not launch independent missions from Britain. In the beginning, OSS strength lay in North Africa, where it had gathered intelligence in advance of the American-British landings in Nov. 1942. The first of many OSS forays into Europe originated from North Africa, where OSS officials had recruited two AGENTS who set up an intelligence NETWORK in German-occupied southern France. When U.S. and British forces invaded southern Italy in 1943, OSS agents preceded them.

Later, the OSS generated joint missions with the British. To aid French Resistance units, JEDBURGH teams of three persons—an American, a Briton, and a Free French soldier—were dropped into France. The Jedburghs were dropped after the Normandy invasion, as were OSS Operational Groups, known as Donovan's "private army." These units of four officers and about 30 men, all of whom spoke at least passable French, worked behind the lines and often engaged in fire fights with German troops.

As the Allied armies advanced across Europe, OSS agents were parachuted into Germany, equipped with small radios (see JOAN ELEANOR). By the end of the war the OSS had placed nearly 200 agents in Germany; many were German prisoners of war who were given fake identification papers and specific assignments, for example, to locate V-1 "buzz" bomb launch sites and find out the effects of air raids on BERLIN.

Learning the scope of SOE operations in landing agents from small naval craft, Donovan sought his own navy, which he established on Dec. 3, 1943. He acquired several submarine chasers and motor torpedo boats, which he employed to ferry and supply agents, and to pick up captured material. Movie star Sterling Hayden, a captain in the Marine Corps, commanded an OSS flotilla of 14 sailing craft that ran supplies through the German blockade to Yugoslav partisans. (Hayden later served with the OSS in Germany, winning the Silver Star.)

Donovan himself went ashore on the Normandy beaches on June 7, 1944, the day after the D-DAY landings. He looked around and departed. Donovan also flew into an advanced base in Burma, 150 miles behind Japanese lines—the only time he was behind enemy lines.

The OSS developed independent operations in neutral countries, with operatives in Lisbon, Stockholm, Madrid, Istanbul, and Bern. ALLEN W. DULLES, head of OSS operations in Switzerland, established contacts with anti-Hitler Germans and worked on surrender overtures.

The OSS was organized into five divisions:

SI (Secret Intelligence): intelligence collection and espionage. (Originally referred to as SI/B after the initial of its division chief, David K. E. Bruce.)

SO (Secret Operations): sabotage, subversion, and guerrilla activities. (Originally referred to as SO/G after the initial of its division chief, M. Preston Goodfellow.)

R&A (Research and Analysis, known as the "Chairborne Division"): analyses of various conventional and secret operations, such as determining the effect of Allied bombing on German-occupied Europe.

MO (Morale Operations): BLACK PROPAGANDA efforts, such as operating fake German radio stations from Britain, ostensibly manned by (nonexistent) anti-Nazi groups.

X-2 (COUNTERINTELLIGENCE): for protecting U.S. intelligence activities. X-2 was intended to neutralize the German "stay-behind" networks that were working behind advancing Allied lines in Italy and France. It was set up by James R. Murphy, a lawyer who had worked with Donovan in the Department of Justice, and George K. Bowden, a tax law specialist. Also in

X-2 was JAMES JESUS ANGLETON, destined to become one of the nation's premier spy hunters.

Counterintelligence officers did not detect several Soviet agents in the OSS. VENONA decrypts of Soviet intelligence message showed that several OSS officers were recruited by American communists in the general campaign to find spies for the Soviets. (See CPUSA.) Testifying before a congressional committee in March 1945, Donovan said, "No man was taken in with my knowledge who was a communist." But the presence of probable communists, particularly Spanish Civil War veterans, was widely known. What was unknown was that some of them were Soviet agents. (See FRANZ NEUMANN, DUNCAN LEE, and MAURICE HALPERIN.)

OSS agents operated in the China-Burma-India area, often in collaboration with British forces. In China the OSS Detachment 202 developed plans for entering Japanese-controlled Indochina to garner intelligence. The proposal was approved—as was the suggestion to provide assistance to groups opposing the Japanese.

The last French troops under arms had evacuated Indochina in the spring of 1945, seeking refuge in China. In early June 1945, 25 French officers and about 100 Vietnamese colonial troops were assigned to the OSS. They were to be provided with U.S. arms and equipment and infiltrated back into Indochina. Most of their operations were unsuccessful because the Vietnamese refused to help the French. Indeed, at least one French-U.S. patrol was led into an ambush by the local communist forces, the Viet Minh.

At least one U.S. officer met with Ho Chi Minh, the Viet Minh leader, to discuss operations against the Japanese. Ho made it clear that the French would not be welcomed back. But the American was, and for two months he trained Viet Minh for attacks against Japanese lines of communications.

(Some American arms were provided to the Viet Minh; they would be a small fraction of those used in their war with the French that began in 1946.)

The major result of the OSS–Viet Minh cooperation was the rescue of several U.S. Army and Navy fliers shot down over the area. The prestige of the Viet Minh therefore increased, but the French began to distrust the Americans. In Aug. 1945 a small OSS force entered southern Indochina, but the war ended before any operations were initiated.

THE OPPOSITION

The OSS did not operate in either the Pacific Ocean Areas, which were under Adm. Chester W. Nimitz, or the Southwest Pacific Area, under Gen. Douglas MacArthur. Nimitz's theater initially consisted of jungle islands and barren coal atolls, where OSS operatives would have been useless. The Australian–New Zealand COASTWATCHERS operated on many jungle islands in both Pacific theaters, performing OSS-type RECONNAISSANCE.

In MacArthur's theater the OSS was not welcome. MacArthur felt that his own ALLIED INTELLIGENCE BUREAU provided the best capability for gathering intelligence, supporting Philippine resistance, and carrying out other activities in his theater. Further, the OSS came too late and offered him too little—and it was run by Donovan, someone outside MacArthur's control.

Many senior Army and Navy INTELLIGENCE OFFICERS also opposed the OSS, which, they felt, was invading their areas of responsibility and, at times, taking their best people. For example, although the Army and Navy had large networks of listening stations to intercept enemy communications, the OSS began establishing its own listening posts (see FBQ CORPORATION); two were set up in 1942, but the joint Chiefs shifted them to the Army SIGNAL INTELLIGENCE SERVICE.

Another enemy of Donovan was J. EDGAR HOOVER, director of the FBI. He, too, had plans for expanding his COUNTERESPIONAGE activities overseas and saw the OSS as a rival. While unable to stop Donovan, he was able to convince President Roosevelt that his agents should represent U.S. intelligence interests in South America during the war, and the OSS was excluded from the area.

Donovan also sought to establish ties, and possibly exchanges, with the NKVD, the principal Soviet intelligence service. He went to Moscow in Dec. 1943 in an effort to set up this relationship. There was an OSS-NKVD agreement for liaison over their respective operations in areas of interest to both countries. An NKVD liaison officer was to be sent to Washington.

This effort was stopped by the Joint Chiefs, with some advice to do so from Hoover. On Feb. 15, 1944, Hoover wrote to the Attorney General: "I think that the establishment of a recognized unit of the NKVD in the United States will be a serious threat to the internal security of the country. In addition, I do not think there is any real purpose or justification for the establishment of such an agency here." In fact, as was later discovered (see VENONA), Soviet intelligence did infiltrate the OSS, but the PENETRATION did not produce any significant results.

THE END OF A SERVICE

As the war was ending, Donovan proposed to President Roosevelt a postwar intelligence agency based on the OSS. Roosevelt died on April 12, 1945, before he took action on the matter. His successor, President Truman, was too busy to look into the issue and had some dislike for Donovan. The OSS was officially abolished by President Truman's Executive Order of Oct. 1, 1945; it ceased to exist on Jan. 12, 1946, when Donovan stepped down.

When the OSS was abolished, many of the 1,362 employees of Research and Analysis and the Presentation Branch (which prepared maps and other briefing documents) were transferred to the State Department as the Interim Research and Intelligence Service; many of the other 9,028 people in the OSS were assigned to the War Department's newly created Strategic Service Unit (SSU). Brig. Gen. John Magruder, who had been Donovan's

deputy, was named director of the SSU. Magruder retired in early 1946 and was succeeded by his executive officer, Lt. Col. William W. Quinn, who had coordinated OSS intelligence for the U.S. Seventh Army.

One of Quinn's first moves was the appointment of Angleton as director of counterintelligence in Italy. There Angleton met several Jews who would play important roles in Israeli intelligence after Israel was established in 1948. (See REUVEN SHILOAH.)

When Truman signed his 1945 order abolishing the OSS, he did note that the United States needed "a comprehensive and coordinated foreign intelligence program." But knowing that Nimitz and MacArthur had made no use of the OSS, and fearing Donovan's proposed highly centralized intelligence establishment, he moved on his own track toward a postwar intelligence community. But much of the OSS was to reemerge in Truman's July 1947 establishment of the CIA.

Among the future DIRECTORS OF CENTRAL INTELLIGENCE would be four veterans of the OSS: Allen Dulles, WILLIAM COLBY, RICHARD HELMS, and WILLIAM CASEY.

Official Secrets Act

British law passed in 1889 to enable the government to withhold information on official activities, regardless of subject or importance, by claiming that the information was secret. A new act passed in 1911 permitted individuals to be prosecuted for publishing information prejudical to the safety of the state. The act was amended in 1920, 1939, and 1989. Juries in several high-profile cases have acquitted persons charged with peacetime violation of the act.

Also see GEORGE BLAKE, D NOTICE, TYLER G. KENT, LITERARY SPIES, PETER WRIGHT.

Off-line System

CIPHER machine not connected to any other system; it produces an enciphered tape that can be delivered by hand or by mail or transmitted by another machine.

Oggins, Isaiah H.

(b. ? d. 1946)

American prisoner identified by Russian President Boris Yeltsin in Sept. 1992 as an American who had been arrested and executed for espionage in the Soviet Union.

Oggins was arrested on espionage charges in 1939 and sent to a Soviet prison. He was to have been freed after World War II when VIKTOR ABAKUMOV, head of the MGB (see NKVD, SMERSH), advised Soviet dictator Josef Stalin that the American should be "liquidated." He was executed in 1946.

Russian official Dmitri Volkogonov said in 1992 that the case was "a tragedy . . . worthy of Shakespeare," and that Oggins was not a spy.

Ogorodnik, Alexsandr D.

(b. ? d. 1977)

Spy for the CIA in the Global Affairs Department of the Soviet Ministry of Foreign Affairs in the 1970s. He is believed to be the first major U.S. AGENT placed in a senior Moscow position since Col. OLEG PENKOVSKY.

JOHN BARRON, author of *KGB Today* (1983), wrote that Ogorodnik approached the CIA in 1974, while he was serving in the Soviet foreign service in Canada. He passed on "hundreds" of classified documents to the CIA until he was caught photographing some of them in 1977. His CASE OFFICER, MARTHA PETERSON, was caught around the same time.

After admitting his guilt he was given a confession to sign. He asked for his favorite pen, which contained a CIA L PILL, supplied at his request sometime before. He bit off the tip of the pen, swallowed the pill, and died instantly. Reportedly, after that the KGB stripped and thoroughly searched suspected spies.

His CODE NAME was TRIGON.

Ogorodnikova, Maj. (?) Svetlana

(b. 1951)

Soviet KGB agent arrested in the United States in 1984 in a plot to obtain classified documents from her lover, FBI agent RICHARD MILLER. She later pleaded guilty to espionage charges, as did her husband, Nikolay.

Nikolay, a Ukrainian Jew born Nikolay Wolfson, fought in World War II beginning at age 11 and was captured by the Germans. Released, he became a street tough and, after four burglaries, was sent to prison for 14 years. When he got out of prison in 1968, he married Svetlana. In 1970 they were given permission to emigrate to Israel with their young son.

But in VIENNA they appeared to change their minds, going instead to the United States as political refugees. They settled in West Hollywood. Svetlana distributed Soviet magazines, worked off and on as a day nurse, and boasted of her connections with the Soviet Consulate. She also carried out the suspiciously improbable feat of traveling back and forth to the Soviet Union. Nikolay worked as a meat packer. Their son, Matvei, spent his summers at a Communist Party youth camp on the Black Sea and his parents talked of sending him to a military school in the Soviet Union.

Svetlana had come to the attention of the FBI in 1982 when agent John E. Hunt asked her to become an informer on the Russian community in the area. She tantalized the FBI by sometimes giving bits of information about pro-Soviet activity among the émigrés. The FBI field office kept track of her because, whatever she was, she obviously was not like the ordinary Russian émigrés. An attractive, slim, dark-eyed blonde, she soon became involved in a romantic relationship with Hunt. FBI records show that Hunt had 55 meetings with Svetlana in 1982 and 1983. One of these meetings consisted of a visit to a Los Angeles physician. Hunt said that the purpose of the visit was to have Svetlana examined for "a rare blood disease." Svetlana said that Hunt took her to the physician for an abortion. She strongly implied that Hunt was the father, apparently not knowing that the agent had had a vasectomy in 1960. (Hunt, at age 52, retired from the FBI in 1984.)

In 1984 Miller was assigned to work with Svetlana. He, too, was soon involved with her. He recalled an Aug. 1984 drive on a Los Angeles freeway:

> Oh, for me it was extraordinary. . . . I had never drunk before in my life. She had brought some margaritas and cognac. That cognac is the awfullest tasting stuff in the world. I thought-I thought, 'Man, this is my chance to be worldly,' and I was gonna just take the opportunity. And we were driving up I-5, just singing songs, and having a great old time throwing bottles out the window. I tried to stop her from throwing the bottles out the window.

The trip ended at the Soviet Consulate in San Francisco. Miller, a 47-year-old agent with an incredibly bad record for much of his 20 years in the bureau, apparently forgot that he himself would be under surveillance by FBI agents when he visited the Soviet Consulate. Soon after the boozy trip up I-5, the FBI learned, apparently through an informer, that Miller and Svetlana were having an affair. The FBI began tracking the pair, videotaping Miller's meetings with Svetlana, tapping phone calls, quietly checking Miller's case load, and simultaneously building a case against Svetlana, who was believed to be working for the KGB.

Svetlana said she tried to resist Miller's sexual advances and submitted only "because he scared me." Miller said in response, "Let's put it this way. I was more inclined toward lovemaking than she was."

She also claimed that she was a KGB major and she promised Miller $65,000 in gold and money if he would spy for the KGB. She introduced her husband to him as "Wolfson," the KGB treasurer for the operation. Miller may not have known that Wolfson actually was Svetlana's husband.

Miller was given specific tasks: to learn the whereabouts of KGB Maj. STANISLAV LEVCHENKO, a DEFECTOR, and to locate Victor Belenko, a Soviet pilot who had flown a MiG-25 to the West in 1976. Both of them had been condemned to death in absentia in the Soviet Union and presumably would be targets for KGB assassins.

On Sept. 27, 1984, Miller told his immediate superior, P. Bryce Christensen, the head of the office's COUNTERESPIONAGE squad, that for months he had been working on his own to penetrate the KGB by becoming a DOUBLE AGENT. He claimed that he had revealed his association with Svetlana because he wanted FBI help in arranging a trip to VIENNA with her. The FBI believed that he had somehow discovered that he was under FBI surveillance.

Miller and the Ogorodnikovs were arrested on the night of Oct 3. Brought to trial with Miller, Svetlana and Nikolay pleaded guilty to espionage in a deal that resulted in an 18-year sentence for Svetlana and an eight-year sentence for Nikolay. (They sent their son back to the Soviet Union.) During plea-bargain negotiations, Svetlana agreed to testify at Miller's trial. But she told confusing, often contradictory stories about her involvement with Miller and failed a POLYGRAPH test.

After three months the judge in Miller's case declared a mistrial in Nov. 1985. It was the first U.S. government espionage trial in history not to have ended in a conviction. Miller was found guilty in a second trial.

Nikolay was released from prison in Jan. 1990, having served five years of his sentence. He became a hotel bus driver and won a Los Angeles Police Department commendation for capturing a gunman trying to hijack his bus. But in Oct. 1991 he was arrested as the Immigration and Naturalization Service tried to have him deported.

Svetlana, released after serving half her 18-year sentence, fought attempts to deport her from the United States and then moved to Mexico. She illegally reentered the United States in 1999 and settled with a new husband on a ranch in Fallbrook, Calif., where, incredibly, another encounter with the FBI began.

The FBI, which had the ranch under surveillance as part of an investigation of the murder of an American in Mexico, used Svetlana to covertly tape conversations with the owner of the ranch, Kimberly Bailey. Svetlana also set up a meeting between Bailey and an FBI agent posing as a hitman who agreed to kill persons associated with the kidnapping and murder of Bailey's lover. In a subsequent trial, Svetlana's testimony helped convict Bailey, who, in Aug. 2002 was sentenced to life imprisonment for kidnapping; the jury did not convict her of murder because of insufficient evidence. After the trial, Svetlana dropped out of sight.

OGPU

SEE CHEKA

OIC

SEE OPERATIONAL INTELLIGENCE CENTRE

Okhrana

Russian secret apparatus during the czarist era. Russian secret police operatives can be traced back even beyond the era of Peter the Great (czar from 1672 to 1725), the founder of "modern" Russia. The term Okhrana, which dates from about 1881, was used to identify the political police—specialists trained to investigate political crimes, in some cases crimes set up by Okhrana agents to provoke arrests.

A Prussian, Wilhelm Stieber, helped to reorganize the existing Russian Secret Service into the Department of State Protection, subsequently called Okhrannoye Odyelyenye, or Okhrana. Although Czar Alexander I could not trust Stieber, a foreigner, to be involved in state secu-

rity, he paid Stieber well for his services, especially for his advice on organizing an external spy system to track down subversives who had left Russia and were plotting against the monarchy from abroad. (Alexander was killed in St. Petersburg in 1881 by a bomb thrown by a revolutionary.)

The Okhrana had its own secret CODES and communications systems, independent of the Interior and Foreign Ministries and military establishments, a large force of investigators, and numerous paid AGENTS to keep watch on potentially subversive societies. A principal tactic of the Okhrana was infiltration of the numerous subversive groups in Russia.

However, as British intelligence historian RICHARD DEACON wrote in *A History of the Russian Secret Service* (1972):

> The revolutionary societies were quick to detect any lack of diligence by the Okhrana and equally swift in combating the watchfulness of the Okhrana by ruses of their own. The leaders of these secret societies kept their true identities hidden far better than did the Okhrana agents more often than not. Their true names were hidden not only from the Okhrana but from their own rank and file, using nicknames or code-names.

Among the numerous agents and DOUBLE AGENTS who served the Okhrana was a secret revolutionary named Josef Vissarionvich Dzhugashvili. He later changed his name to Stalin.

Foreign intelligence collection by Okhrana was virtually nil except for SURVEILLANCE of Russians living abroad who might have been a threat to the czarist regime; the only foreign office of the Okhrana was located in the Russian Embassy in Paris. That the Okhrana was ineffective in collecting intelligence on potential enemies of Russia was evidenced in part by the catastrophic Russian military failures in the 1904–1905 war with Japan and in World War I.

For thirty-six years the Okhrana was active; it was feared, but was relatively ineffective when "enemies of the state" harassed and then, in 1917, overthrew the Romanov dynasty.

See OPRICHNINA and ROMAN MALINOVSKY.

Oldfield, Sir Maurice

(b. 1915 d. 1981)

Highly successful Director-General of the British Secret Intelligence Service (MI6) from 1973 to 1978.

Oldfield was the son of a tenant farmer and the first head of MI6 to come from such a background. After graduating from Manchester University in 1937, he entered the Army in 1941, joining the South Staffordshire Regiment. He subsequently transferred to Military Intelligence Corps, where as a corporal in field security he was automatically commissioned as a full lieutenant on April 13, 1943. He was sent to the Middle East, where

British intelligence sought to halt German espionage inroads into the area.

At the end of 1946 Oldfield was a major with the temporary rank of lieutenant colonel and several decorations for his wartime service. At that point he began to work for MI6, mostly at the London headquarters known as BROADWAY. His first overseas duty for MI6 was on the staff of the British commissioner-general for Southeast Asia from 1950 to 1953, and he was in Singapore again from 1955 to 1958.

Oldfield was station chief in Washington, D.C., from 1960 to 1964, as new reports surfaced that the British intelligence services were infiltrated by Soviet MOLES. (See CAMBRIDGE SPY RING.) Returning to London for the next decade, Oldfield was named Director-General of MI6 in 1973.

On Oct. 13, 1975, the Provisional wing of the Irish Republican Army attempted to kill Oldfield by leaving a 30-pound bomb wedged between the railings and the windowsill of Locket's Restaurant in London. Oldfield lived in the same building and was at home that evening. The bomb was defused by explosives experts about three minutes before it was due to explode.

He remained Director-General until Oct. 2, 1979. Upon his retirement, Prime Minister Margaret Thatcher appointed him coordinator of British security and intelligence in Northern Ireland.

In March 1980 he admitted to being a HOMOSEXUAL and at the end of May asked the Prime Minister to relieve him of his post because of ill health. He was considered to have been highly successful as head of MI6, especially in forging strong relationships with the U.S., French, and Israeli intelligence services.

In *Who's Who in Espionage* (1984), Ronald Payne and Christopher Dobson described Oldfield as "a bespectacled man with chubby face, a cheerful manner and a lively sense of humour, he was tough, though opposed to violence. Indeed, it is unlikely that he had any experience of the rough stuff of espionage."

There were stories—which were inaccurate—that Oldfield was the model for the JOHN LE CARRÉ [P] character GEORGE SMILEY [F].

ONE

SEE OFFICE OF NATIONAL ESTIMATES

One-Time Pad

An unbreakable CIPHER when used properly. Used improperly by the Soviet NKVD during World War II, it opened up much of the story of Soviet espionage efforts against the United States.

The one-time pad contains thousands of groups, usually of five digits. Each group represents a single word or a phrase. Then, to ensure security, the person using the pad next transposes or converts the numbers of his enciphered message to another set of digits by using a specific, but randomly chosen page of the pad (i.e, double or

SUPERENCIPHER process). The key to the pages and lines used on the pad would precede the encrypted message.

The one-time pad takes various forms, from a thick booklet the size of a postage stamp to a scroll about the size of a cigarette butt. The important feature is that the pad must be small, so that it can be easily concealed. The booklets can be very thick, several hundred pages, and sometimes in two colors, to distinguish enciphering and deciphering sections. The "printing" is often a form of reduced photography.

Further, the "paper" of the one-time pad can be made of cellulose nitrate or some other highly flammable material that enables its rapid destruction. During World War II the U.S. OFFICE OF STRATEGIC SERVICES and the British Special Air Service employed "pads" printed on silk handkerchiefs, printed with 600 cipher groups.

In theory there are but two copies of a specific one-time pad: one for the AGENT or diplomat, and one for the official with whom the agent or diplomat communicates.

CRYPTOGRAPHY historian DAVID KAHN cites 1918 as the year one-time pad ciphers were invented. In 1930 the Soviet Union began to employ the one-time pad for messages from its overseas diplomatic and intelligence officials, and subsequently agents, making their communications invulnerable to deciphering. The one-time pads were to be used only once.

The U.S. Army's SIGNAL INTELLIGENCE SERVICE and successor agencies were able to intercept, but not decrypt, messages sent by Soviet officials in New York to Moscow beginning in 1939. Not until Feb. 1, 1943, did the Army begin a major effort to decipher these messages under the VENONA program. During World War II the cryptographic material production office of the NKVD apparently reused some of the pages from one-time pads, and these were used by Soviet LEGALS and ILLEGALS in the United States in their communications with Moscow.

Because of the duplication of one-time pad pages, the Army obtained some minor decrypts of messages in 1943. The situation was more favorable for the codebreakers in 1944, even more so in 1945. Finally, in the summer of 1946 major breakthroughs were made, opening up the wartime spying efforts of the Soviet Union against the United States.

One-time pads continued in use into the Cold War era. Cuban revolutionary Che Guevara was carrying sheets of a one-time pad cipher when he was killed in Bolivia in 1967.

See ATOMIC SPY RING.

ONI

SEE OFFICE OF NAVAL INTELLIGENCE

On-the-Roof Gang

Slang for U.S. Navy and Marine personnel trained for radio TRAFFIC ANALYSIS and CRYPTANALYSIS prior to World War II. The term was derived from the steel-reinforced concrete blockhouse on the roof of the sixth wing of the

Main Navy Building on Constitution Avenue in Washington, D.C., where classes were held.

The training program began in 1928, when specially selected Navy and Marine radiomen were assigned to a three-month course in radio intercept, as well as training in the Kata Kana Morse code used by the Japanese.

The first class, with seven students, convened in Oct. 1928. In total, 25 classes were conducted through 1941, each with four to eight students. A total of 176 men attended the classes.

On the eve of World War II, members of the On-the-Roof Gang were assigned to Navy radio intercept and cryptanalysis teams in the Philippines, Guam, Hawaii, Shanghai, Bainbridge Island near Seattle, and Washington, D.C. Seventy of these personnel were evacuated from station CAST in the Philippines before the islands were overrun by the Japanese in early 1942. Seven were captured by the Japanese when Guam was taken in Dec. 1941, although the Japanese never learned of their activities. (Those in Shanghai were evacuated before the war began.)

During the war these men carried out a variety of naval activities, listening to Japanese radio communications and taking down Morse code messages. They were often able to identify specific Japanese radiomen by their use of the Morse code key and could thus identify specific ships and commands sending messages, an invaluable asset in traffic analysis.

Several of the gang were commissioned, and two reached the rank of Navy captain. These personnel were also called "roofers."

Oleksy, Jozef

Polish Prime Minister forced to resign on Jan. 24, 1996, after a military prosecutor launched a formal probe into allegations that he had spied for the Soviet Union. The investigation also looked into allegations that two former Soviet diplomats in Poland were spies.

Prosecutor Slawomir Gorzkiewicz announced he had decided to undertake an investigation after reports that Oleksy—at the time Interior Minister—passed information to Soviet intelligence. Oleksy denied the allegations by outgoing Interior Minister Andrzej Milczanowski that he had spied for Moscow from the time he was a provincial communist official in the 1980s until 1995, when he was speaker of democratic Poland's parliament.

Oleksy admitted to having had social contact with the two Soviet diplomats who later proved to be senior KGB officers but denied giving them information. Oleksy and his political party claimed that the spy allegations had been cooked up by Polish security AGENTS on behalf of an opposition embittered over former President Lech Walesa's Nov. 1995 election defeat by Oleksy's fellow ex-Communist Aleksandr Kwasniewski. Walesa applauded the prosecutor's decision to investigate Oleksy.

Oleksy had become Prime Minister 11 months earlier, the seventh prime minister in the six years since the collapse of communism in Poland.

On-Line System

A CRYPTOSYSTEM that is connected directly to a radio or telephone so that encryption and transmission are virtually simultaneous.

OP-20-G

SEE NAVY COMMUNICATIONS INTELLIGENCE

Open Code

A CRYPTOGRAPHIC system that employs an external text that has a real meaning, used in an attempt to disguise the hidden meaning.

Open Skies

Treaty signed in March 1992 between the United States, Russia, Great Britain, and France and a number of former republics of the Soviet Union to permit RECONNAISSANCE aircraft to conduct OVERFLIGHTS of their territory to photograph military installations. Subsequently, other members of the NORTH ATLANTIC TREATY ORGANIZATION and former Warsaw Pact members joined the Open Skies agreement. The treaty, signed by 42 participating nations, entered into force on Jan. 1, 2002.

The Open Skies concept can be traced to a proposal made by President Eisenhower at the summit meeting in Geneva with Soviet leader Nikita Khrushchev in July 1955. That proposal, inspired by a young Harvard political scientist named Henry Kissinger (later U.S. Secretary of State), was to have been a reciprocal program permitting U.S. and Soviet reconnaissance aircraft to overfly each other's territory as well as exchange blueprints and plans for fixed military installations. The British and French representatives at the meeting immediately supported Eisenhower's proposal.

Khrushchev scornfully dismissed the proposal as a U.S. attempt at sanctioned aerial espionage. Eisenhower, in his *Mandate for Change* (1963), recalled Khrushchev's saying that "the idea was nothing more than a bald espionage plot against the USSR. . . ." The Soviet leader did not even mention it in his account of the Geneva meeting in his memoirs, *Khrushchev Remembers* (1970).

That proposal, rejected by the Soviet Union, was subsequently used by the U.S. government in part as a rationale for the U-2 spyplane overflights of the Soviet Union and the employment of SATELLITES to spy on the Soviet Union. The current overflight treaty began with talks between representatives of the United States and the Soviet Union in 1989. It permits unarmed aircraft to fly over the entire territory of the participating nations.

The U.S. Air Force carries out the U.S. inspections, flying OC-135 reconnaissance aircraft, adapted from the C-135 STRATOTANKER. The aircraft carries a flight crew, relief crew (because of the distance of the flights), and foreign representatives. The first of several OC-135 aircraft became operational in late 1993. (See RIVET JOINT.)

The plane employed by Russia for Open Skies reconnaissance is the Tupolev Tu-154M, a large tri-jet aircraft similar to the Boeing 727. Fitted with synthetic-aperture radar, the modified Tu-154M-ON *(otkrytoye nebo*: open skies) entered service in 1999. As a prelude to the Russian overflights of the United States, in June 1995 a Tu-154 fitted with an aerial camera and infrared sensors, commanded by a former East German Air Force pilot, carried out a training mission over the United States.

Open Source

Intelligence derived from sources available to the public, especially from the news media. In the late 1980s the abbreviation-obsessed U.S. INTELLIGENCE COMMUNITY began using the acronym OSINT for Open Source Intelligence.

British historian A.J.P. Taylor once said that 90 percent of the information produced by intelligence agencies can be found in public sources. Sherman Kent, chief of the OFFICE OF NATIONAL ESTIMATES in the CIA, increased that to 95 percent for U.S. information because of the openness of U.S. society.

Open Source Intelligence

SEE OPEN SOURCE

Operational Intelligence

(OPINTEL)

Intelligence employed in planning operations within regional theaters or areas of operations. The term *operational intelligence* was used by the U.S. Navy through the 1980s for the intelligence provided to naval operating forces. Intelligence at this level is now considered to be TACTICAL INTELLIGENCE.

The U.S. focal point for such intelligence is the Operational Intelligence Watch (OIW), operating at the Cheyenne Mountain Operations Center, describes itself as "the nation's warning center for worldwide threats from space, missile, and strategic air activity, as well as geopolitical unrest that could affect North America and U.S. forces abroad."

Operational Intelligence Centre

British Admiralty activity in World War II to "collect, co-ordinate, analyse, and disseminate information from every possible source which could throw light on the intentions and movements of German maritime forces, naval, air, and mercantile." It was the key to British use of ULTRA decrypts and other forms of intelligence that were applied to the Battle of the Atlantic from 1939 to 1945, the worldwide campaign against German U-boats.

By 1936 British NAVAL INTELLIGENCE was no longer responsible for CRYPTANALYSIS, that responsibility having been transferred to the GOVERNMENT CODE AND CYPHER

SCHOOL. In June 1937 the DIRECTOR OF NAVAL INTELLIGENCE, Rear Adm. J. A. G. Troup, chose Paymaster Lt. Comdr. NORMAN DENNING to organize an intelligence center of the type that ROOM 40 had become at the end of World War I.

Denning began with one clerical assistant in a section named the Operational Intelligence Centre, which became the coordinating center for all information related to the war at sea from any source and had total responsibility for analysis and evaluation. The OIC was authorized in 1938 to disseminate its findings within the Navy. This was a major change in procedure from that of Room 40 in World War I.

Patrick Beesly, a key member of the OIC, wrote in *Very Special Intelligence* (1977):

> no maritime operation, whether it was something on the scale of Operation Neptune (the invasion of France) or the landing of an agent in Brittany, a commando raid in Norway or an attack on a German convoy off the Low Countries, ever took place without preliminary and detailed consultation between its planners and some member of the staff of O.I.C. The painstaking analysis of the German U-boat building programme, the reconstruction from the original small fragment of the German Naval [map] grid and then the solution of the transpositions which the U-Boat Command sought to disguise references to it, the selection of the best areas for Bomber Command's four-year minelaying campaign: all this required continuous and often laborious work without which little else would have been clear or effective operational action possible.

Operational Security

(OPSEC)

Actions to prevent unauthorized disclosure of information concerning planned, ongoing, or completed operations.

Also see COMMUNICATIONS SECURITY.

Operations Security

Similar to OPERATIONAL SECURITY; in the communications area, operations security can include the process of denying adversaries information about friendly capabilities and intentions by identifying, controlling, and protecting possible indications about the planning and execution of military operations and other activities.

Also see COMMUNICATIONS SECURITY.

Operative

Another term for AGENT.

OPINTEL

SEE OPERATIONAL INTELLIGENCE

Oprichnina

Police force established by Russia's Ivan the Terrible in 1565. Designed to suppress internal enemies, the Oprichnina was a distant predecessor of the later CHEKA, NKVD, and KGB.

Ivan the Terrible, the first grand duke of Muscovy to be crowned czar, established the Oprichnina as a force of 6,000 cavalrymen, dressed in black, riding black horses, their saddles carrying the symbol of a dog's head and broom to symbolize their mission: to sniff out and sweep away traitors to the state. The term *oprichnina* could be translated as "outriders," indicating that they were outside or above the law.

The Oprichnina was responsible for many atrocities during its seven-year reign of terror. Indeed, the entire city of Novgorod, one of the oldest in Russia, was laid to waste by the Oprichnina during a five-week massacre in 1570. Novgorod, the second city of Russia at the time, was suspected by Ivan the Terrible of collaborating with the enemy state of Lithuania. Tens of thousands were killed in the city.

Members of the Oprichnina received grants of land, their territory eventually comprising about one-half the territory of Muscovy. The force was abolished in about 1572.

OPSEC

SEE OPERATIONAL SECURITY

ORCON

CODE WORD used during the Carter administration to indicate material denied to contractors. Derived from the term *originator controlled*, the material could not be made available to any individual or agency without the approval of the originator.

Also see NON-CONTRACT.

Orczy, Baroness Emmuska

(b. 1865 d. 1947)

Creator of the SCARLET PIMPERNEL, one of the most popular fictional spies of her era.

Hungarian-born, she came to London with her family at age 15. There she learned English, the language in which she did all of her writing. First published in 1905, *The Scarlet Pimpernel* was the story of a British nobleman regarded as a fop but in reality the leader of the League of the Scarlet Pimpernel, a band of young Englishmen pledged to rescue the innocent aristocratic victims of the Reign of Terror in Paris during the French Revolution.

She used the novel's hero, Sir Percy Blakeney, in a dozen other novels, foremost among them *The Elusive Pimpernel* (1908) and *The Way of the Scarlet Pimpernel* (1933). She also wrote several detective novels and plays. *The Scarlet Pimpernel* was made into a movie in 1935

and 1982, a Broadway musical in 1997, and BBC-TV films that aired in 1998 and 2000.

Order of Battle

Intelligence describing the identity, strength, command structure, and disposition of enemy military forces. Variations of the term in U.S. usage include Electronic Order of Battle (EOB) and, previously, Soviet Order of Battle (SOB).

Organ

Russian-Soviet term for state security organizations such as the CHEKA, NKVD, or KGB.

Oriental Goddess

Machine at BLETCHLEY PARK that worked out settings for the BOMBES so that they could process settings for breaking into the CIPHERS generated by ENIGMA machines.

Orlov, Maj. Alexandr Mikhailovich

(b. 1895 d. 1973)

Senior Soviet INTELLIGENCE OFFICER in the 1920s and 1930s who became a fugitive in the United States to escape the Stalinist purges. He was one of the highest-ranking Soviet intelligence officials ever to defect to the West.

Orlov was born Leiba Lazarevich Feldbin, the son of a Jewish businessman, in the Belorussian town of Bobruysk. He abandoned his religion as he embraced communism. He served in the Red Army during the Russian Revolution, Civil War, and Russo-Polish War, commanding guerrilla units and working in Army COUNTERINTELLIGENCE. His efforts led to his being called to the attention of the Russian intelligence chief FELIKS DZHERZHINSKY.

From 1921 to 1923 Orlov completed law school at the University of Moscow and then served as an assistant prosecutor. In this role he worked with the state security ORGANS. In 1924 he returned to full-time intelligence work with the OGPU. Late in 1925 he was made a brigade commander of frontier troops in Transcaucasia, the move being made because of his earlier experience in guerrilla warfare. Some 11,000 troops under his command policed the Soviet borders with Persia (Iran) and Turkey.

In mid-1926 Orlov began his foreign intelligence work with an assignment as the OGPU RESIDENT in Paris. He continued to serve abroad and from 1933 was an ILLEGAL in several European cities. In 1932 he made a covert trip to the United States, using a Soviet passport in the name Lev Leonidovich Nikolayev. He fraudulently acquired a U.S. passport in the name of William Goldin, supposedly an Austrian-born immigrant to the United States.

Orlov went to Britain in July 1934 to become resident in London, directing Soviet intelligence activities there. He used his American COVER to start a refrigerator sales firm that served as a front for his espionage activities, including running the CAMBRIDGE SPY RING. In Oct. 1935 a chance meeting in London with an old acquaintance who recognized Orlov forced him to return quickly to Moscow. There he monitored Soviet spy operations abroad and was responsible for directing the intelligence and counterintelligence faculty of the Central Military School in Moscow, where NKVD personnel were trained.

From 1935 he held the rank of major in State Security (the equivalent of one-star military rank). That same year his book *Tactics and Strategy of Intelligence and Counter-Intelligence* was published for use by Soviet intelligence schools, establishing him as a dominant authority in the field.

In Sept. 1936 he went to Madrid as the NKVD resident in Republican Spain during the Spanish Civil War (1936 to 1939). Reportedly, on the eve of his departure, a young NKVD operator with whom he was having a love affair, Galina Voitova, shot herself in front of the LUBYANKA because Orlov had left her and refused to divorce his wife.

Soviet MOLE HAROLD (KIM) PHILBY, using the cover of a British journalist while in Spain, called Orlov "a man of action." In his book *My Silent War* (1969), Philby wrote: "He was energetic—I would even say a desperately energetic character. For instance he liked to always go about armed—probably as the result of his desperate energy and extravagantly romantic attitude towards his profession." At times Orlov even carried a submachine gun concealed under his trenchcoat, the traditional garb of spies of that era.

As NKVD resident in Spain, Orlov was charged with both intelligence collection and counterintelligence for Soviet forces in Spain as well as supervision of the flow of Soviet arms to the front and the Republican forces fighting Gen. Francisco Franco. Orlov also began building a secret police force under NKVD control within areas of Spain held by the Republicans; Orlov's mechanism for this was the Servicio de Investigación Militar, which he established and supervised. An Orlov-established SPY SCHOOL in Spain trained numerous future spies, among them American MORRIS COHEN. Orlov was the senior Soviet official in Spain during this period.

Recalled to Moscow in July 1938, Orlov balked, fearing that he would be executed; Josef Stalin was killing early Bolsheviks as well as Soviet officials who had served overseas. Orlov fled from Spain that month with $30,000 from the station safe and traveled via Canada to the United States, bringing his wife and 14-year-old daughter. (Already ill, the girl died shortly after their arrival in the United States.) Orlov used the American passport that he had acquired during his 1932 visit.

In the United States, Orlov and his wife lived almost entirely on those funds until the publication of his book in 1953 (see below). Reportedly, Orlov blackmailed Stalin by threatening to expose the Soviet Spy NETWORK in the West if attempts were made to assassinate him.

In a letter to the head of the NKVD, Orlov explained his flight:

My sole purpose now is to survive to bring up my child until she comes of age. Always remember that I am no traitor to my Party or my country. No one and nothing will ever make me betray the cause of the proletariat and of Soviet power. I did not want to leave my country any more than a fish wants to leave water, but the delinquent activity of criminal people has cast me up like a fish on ice.

I have not only been deprived of my mother country, but the right to live and breathe the same air as the Soviet people. If you leave me alone, I will never embark on anything harmful to the Party or the Soviet Union.

Orlov lived as a fugitive in the United States from 1938 until 1953, his presence in the country unknown to American officials. He revealed himself in 1953—the year in which Stalin died—in a series of articles in *Life* magazine and through his book *The Secret History of Stalin's Crimes* (1952). Orlov published additional books on Stalin's crimes and another on Soviet intelligence, *A Handbook of Intelligence and Guerrilla Warfare* (1962), based on the textbook he had written for use by the NKVD and Soviet military schools.

Playing a game with the U.S. intelligence services, Orlov told half-truths, even before congressional investigating committees. He continued to shield the identity of Soviet intelligence AGENTS in the West, never revealing a single agent's name during his 45 years in the United States. KGB officials met secretly with Orlov twice after his defection, in 1969 and 1971.

Many of the Soviet intelligence files on Orlov were published in the book *Deadly Illusions* (1993) by JOHN COSTELLO and former KGB officer Oleg Tsarev.

Orlov's CODE NAME within the Soviet intelligence system was Schwed ("Swede"); he mainly used the name Igor Konstantinovich Berg after he fled to the United States.

Ōshima, Gen. Hiroshi

(b. 1886 d. 1975)

Japanese ambassador to Nazi Germany during World War II who unwittingly provided the Allies with invaluable COMMUNICATIONS INTELLIGENCE. Oshima "was our main basis of information regarding Hitler's intentions in Europe," wrote Gen. George C. Marshall, the U.S. Army Chief of Staff, during the war.

Oshima was the son of a prominent Japanese family, his father having served as War Minister from 1916 to 1918. Following his graduation from military academy in 1905, Oshima had a successful Army career.

In 1934 he became Japanese military ATTACHÉ in BERLIN, with the rank of colonel. He spoke almost perfect German and was soon befriended by the influential Joachim von Ribbentrop. At the time, Adolf Hitler ostensibly used the Foreign Ministry for his foreign relations. In reality, Hitler fostered what became known as Dienststelle Ribbentrop (Ribbentrop Bureau), a competitive foreign office operated by the ambitious champagne

Gen. Hiroshi Ōshima with Adolf Hitler in Berlin in 1939; Foreign Minister Joachim von Ribbentrop stands between them. Ōshima's secret communications with Tokyo were decrypted by the Allies and provided invaluable information on Germany during World War II. (NATIONAL ARCHIVES)

salesman. (The bureau, which had more than 300 employees, was abolished when Hitler appointed Ribbentrop Foreign Minister in 1938.)

Under Ribbentrop's guidance, Oshima met privately with Hitler in the fall of 1935. With the support of the Nazi leadership and the Japanese Army General Staff, Oshima progressed rapidly while in Berlin, attaining the rank of lieutenant general, he was appointed ambassador to Berlin in 1938.

In late 1939 he was recalled to Japan, returning via the United States. Following requests from Germany for his return, Oshima returned to Berlin in early 1941. Until the end of the war in Europe, he dedicated his efforts to close relations between Germany and Japan, including military cooperation in the Indian Ocean area. American journalist William L. Shirer wrote that Oshima "often impressed this observer as more Nazi than the Nazis."

His close relationship with Hitler and Ribbentrop gave him unequaled access for a foreigner to German war plans and national policy. He made visits to the Russian Front and the German coastal defenses in France (the Atlantic Wall), and he met periodically with Hitler. All information that he gathered he duly reported by radio to Tokyo in the PURPLE diplomatic CODE—and thus almost simultaneously to American codebreakers.

The U.S. intercept effort and the MAGIC decoding effort garnered virtually all of Oshima's communications with Tokyo: approximately 75 during the 11 months of 1941, some 100 in 1942, 400 in 1943, 600 in 1944, and about 300 during the just over four months of 1945 that Germany was at war. For example, one Purple intercept decoded on Jan. 19, 1942, told how Ribbentrop had agreed to supply daily intelligence reports to Oshima, which he would send on to Tokyo. He warned that "any leakage of these reports due to our fault would be of grave consequence, so all handling of these reports should be strictly secret."

While some of his predictions were wrong—Oshima predicted that Britain would capitulate to Germany before the end of 1941—his reporting of the Nazi leadership's plans and policies and his factual data were invaluable to the Allies. For example, on June 6, 1941, he advised Tokyo that Germany would invade the Soviet Union on June 22 (see BARBAROSSA).

As the war progressed and Germany began to retreat, Oshima never lost his confidence in eventual German victory. Finally, on April 14, 1945, Oshima was forced to abandon Berlin. He and most of the remaining Japanese diplomatic staff traveled to the mountain resort of Bad Gastein. Less than a month later Germany surrendered and Oshima and his staff were taken into custody. They were brought to the United States by ship, arriving on July 11. After interrogation and internment in a resort hotel in Pennsylvania, Oshima was returned to Japan.

Back home, he briefly enjoyed freedom in his devastated country. But on Dec. 16, 1945, he was arrested and charged as a war criminal. After a delayed trial, he was found guilty of conspiring against peace by an Allied tribunal in Nov. 1948. His sentence was life imprisonment.

He was paroled in late 1955 and granted clemency less than three years later. Oshima died in 1975, not knowing that he had provided the Allies with invaluable intelligence during the war.

OSS

SEE OFFICE OF STRATEGIC SERVICES

Oster, Generalmajor Hans

(b. 1888 d. 1945)

Extremely anti-Nazi chief of staff of the ABWEHR, Germany's intelligence agency. He was hanged for his part in the abortive July 1944 plot to assassinate Adolf Hitler.

The son of a Protestant churchman, Oster fought in World War I as a General Staff officer and then joined the Reichswehr, the small army Germany was allowed under the Versailles Treaty that followed World War I.

From 1933 on he served in the War Ministry; as a colonel he became head of the Second Department of the

Abwehr, which dealt with administration and financial matters and kept the lists of German intelligence AGENTS.

In *The Abwehr* (1984) historian Lauran Paine observed that Oster had "a high sense of honour, abhorred corruption, was contemptuous of politicians and, when Nazi excesses became not isolated instances but a deliberate part of government policy . . . often, and not very prudently, denounced them." Paine continued, "He was a serious man, observant, practical, and realistic."

As war approached in Europe in 1939, Oster became chief of staff to Vice Adm. WILHELM CANARIS, head of the Abwehr. Concerned about German war preparations, he passed information to the Allies on German intentions to invade Norway and Denmark. Later he sought to protect Jews in occupied countries through various Abwehr operations.

Following a search of Abwehr offices by the GESTAPO that revealed planned meetings with the Vatican concerning possible negotiations to end the war, Canaris dismissed Oster from the Abwehr on April 15, 1943. Canaris told his staff to have no further contact with Oster, who was henceforth assigned to the reserves and, although allowed to wear his uniform, remained under virtual house arrest at his BERLIN and Dresden homes.

Under close watch by the Gestapo at the time of the bomb plot against Hitler on July 20, 1944, Oster was arrested the following day and imprisoned (as was Canaris). He was hanged on April 9—a month before the war ended—at Flossenburg concentration camp. Canaris was hanged the same day.

Other Work

Russian slang for espionage activities of INTELLIGENCE OFFICERS working under the COVER of staff at the UNITED NATIONS.

Ott, Airman 1st Class Bruce

U.S. airman arrested at Beale Air Force Base in California in Jan. 1986 for attempting to sell material on the SR-71 BLACKBIRD spyplane to two FBI agents posing as Soviet INTELLIGENCE OFFICERS. He had called the Soviet Consulate in San Francisco—known to the FBI as "KGB West"—with an offer to sell secrets.

The FBI intercepted the call and set up a phony meeting. Ott told a man he believed to be a Soviet AGENT that he wanted to be a long-term MOLE and hoped to shape his Air Force career to serve the KGB. He gave the disguised FBI agent a copy of the recall roster for the 1st Strategic RECONNAISSANCE Squadron and a handwritten list of promised secret documents that he could deliver. Ott wanted to be paid $600 immediately—to get back his repossessed car.

At a subsequent meeting, after Ott handed over other documents, he said that he wanted a total of $165,000 for the secrets he would deliver. The FBI gave him $400, and after he accepted the money they added a pair of handcuffs.

When arrested, Ott began babbling: "Thanks for catching me before this got out of hand . . . You caught me red-handed . . . I'm going to be a model prisoner. How much time do you think I'll get?" He was court-martialed and sentenced to 25 years in prison.

Ovakim, Maj. Gen. Gaik Badalovich

(b. 1898 d. ?)

NKVD RESIDENT in New York City in the 1930s. Ovakim arrived in the United States in 1933 and operated under COVER of the AMTORG commercial organization.

Educated as an engineer, Ovakim specialized in INDUSTRIAL ESPIONAGE. In *The FBI-KGB War* (1986), FBI agent ROBERT J. LAMPHERE and coauthor Tom Shachtman wrote: "He was often referred to as 'the wily Armenian,' and it was a measure of his slipperiness that it was never completely clear whether or not he really was an Armenian." Ovakim was small, standing five feet, seven inches tall and weighing 165 pounds.

According to Lamphere and Shachtman, his espionage recruits were scattered across the United States and into Mexico and Canada. He was responsible for recruiting JULIUS ROSENBERG and his wife, Ethel, into the ATOMIC SPY RING in 1938 (at that time the Soviets were interested in non-atomic secrets to which Julius Rosenberg had access). He also met with and passed on orders for the assassination of Leon Trotsky in Mexico to Ramón Mercader. (The act, carried out on Aug. 20, 1940, resulted in Trotsky's death from his wound on the following day.)

In May 1941 the FBI arrested Ovakim and charged him with being a foreign business representative who had not registered as such with the Department of Justice. In jail, Ovakim claimed diplomatic immunity and said that he was merely a purchasing agent for weapons who, for political reasons, had been unable to negotiate any major transactions. The Soviet Embassy paid his bail of $25,000 for his release.

Several of his AGENTS had been identified, and the FBI hoped to bring him to trial. However, since a half dozen Americans were being detained in the Soviet Union, an agreement was reached in which Ovakim was allowed to leave the United States in late July 1941. (Of the six Americans, three never reached the United States; before they could depart, Germany invaded the Soviet Union and two fell into German hands; the third was kept in a Soviet prison.)

Arriving back at NKVD headquarters in Moscow, Ovakim was head of the American desk when, in 1944, he approved a cable sent to the United States that permitted HARRY GOLD, an NKVD COURIER, to meet with DAVID GREENGLASS, a soldier working at the atomic bomb laboratory in Los Alamos, New Mex. Gold was from one espionage CELL and Greenglass from another being run by the NKVD. The implications of this breach in TRADECRAFT were significant, and Ovakim was demoted.

He was dismissed from the KGB (successor to the NKVD) in about 1956, after the death of spy chief

LAVENTRY BERIA and Nikita Khrushchev's denunciation of the excesses of the late dictator Josef Stalin.

Overflight

Mission by a spyplane—carrying cameras or SIGNALS INTELLIGENCE equipment or both—over an enemy country, usually to collect STRATEGIC INTELLIGENCE. Such flights are distinct from TACTICAL INTELLIGENCE collection, which involve flights over enemy forces. Also see UNMANNED AERIAL VEHICLES.

The term *overflight* came into use in the Cold War; the first Western overflights of the Soviet Union were made in 1952 by U.S. B-47 STRATOJET and British CANBERRA reconnaissance aircraft, the latter at the request of the U.S. government.

Overhead

The use of AIRCRAFT and SATELLITES to provide photographs and other intelligence about TARGET countries.

William E. Burrows wrote in *Deep Black* (1986):

"Overhead reconnaissance and surveillance mechanisms and those who operate them are charged with three basic responsibilities. They are supposed to discover and keep track of every military and economic development throughout the world that can [have an] impact in one degree or another upon the United States and its allies."

Also see NATIONAL TECHNICAL MEANS.

Overlord

SEE D-DAY

Overt Intelligence

Information collected openly from public or open sources such as newspapers, magazines, radio, and television. Also called OPEN SOURCE intelligence.

Owen, William James

Believed to be the only member of the House of Commons to be charged in the 20th century with betraying secret information of potential use to an enemy. A Labour "backbencher," he was charged with violating the OFFICIAL SECRETS ACT on Jan. 23, 1970, following a convoluted effort by Eastern Bloc intelligence agencies to subvert him.

Elected to Parliament in 1954 and appointed to the Defence Estimates Committee in Feb. 1960, he was persuaded to work for improved British relations with East Germany. In 1964 he became director of a tourist agency, Berolina Travel. In that position he visited East Germany several times and made a trip to the Soviet Union. He was befriended by a Czech commercial ATTACHÉ, Robert Husak. Subsequently, the Czech government paid him £2,300, entertained him, and gave him presents.

In return, Husak sought information about Owen's fellow members of Parliament, seeking those who would be vulnerable to blackmail. Owen also had access to classified information, but it is not clear if any was passed on to foreign INTELLIGENCE OFFICERS.

He was arrested in Jan. 1970 and resigned from the House of Commons that April. Owen was tried and acquitted, with the court directing him to pay £2,000 toward legal costs. After being acquitted, Owens revealed his dealings with Czech intelligence.

He was given the CODE NAME Lee by Czech intelligence.

Oxcart

SEE A-12 OXCART

Ozaki, Hozomi

(b. 1901 d. 1944)

Japanese author, journalist, and spy for the Soviet Union. Ozaki was the principal Japanese confederate of Soviet spy RICHARD SORGE.

Born in Tokyo but raised on Formosa (now Taiwan), where his father was a newspaper editor, Ozaki attended Tokyo Imperial University, graduating in 1925. The following year he joined the staff of the Tokyo newspaper *Asahi Shimbun*. He moved to the *Osaka Asahi* in 1927, and in 1929 became a correspondent in Shanghai, where he met Soviet spy Richard Sorge in 1930. He kept in contact with Sorge when the Soviet—under the COVER of a German journalist—went to Japan in 1933.

Ozaki was one of Japan's principal representatives to the Institute of Pacific Relations Conclave held at Yosemite National Park, in California, in 1936. A year later he was appointed a member of a high-level, policy-planning "brain trust" that advised the Prime Minister. He was thus in a key position to pass on high-level secrets to Sorge, motivated by his belief that the Japanese form of government had to be overthrown for the good of the country.

He was arrested on Oct. 14, 1941, tried for treason in 1943, and sentenced to death. He was executed by hanging, with Sorge, on Nov. 7, 1944.

P2V Neptune (P-2)

Principal U.S. Navy land-based anti-submarine/RECON-NAISSANCE aircraft for two decades after World War II. The Neptune was flown extensively on reconnaissance flights off the Pacific coasts of China and the Soviet Union, with several being attacked by hostile fighters.

The Neptune was useful for patrols along the Soviet and Chinese peripheries because of its long endurance and reliability. Flown by U.S. Navy patrol squadrons from 1947 until the early 1970s, the plane was also flown by several other nations. During the Vietnam War the Navy flew 24 modified Neptunes over land areas in an effort to monitor electronic SURVEILLANCE devices dropped along Viet Cong supply trails (designated AP-2 and OP-2) and four others for night attacks on supply lines (AP-2). The Army used some Neptunes as specialized ELECTRONIC INTELLIGENCE (ELINT) platforms in Vietnam (RP-2E), while the Air Force, too, flew seven aircraft in an electronic role (RB-69).

Although Neptunes were not converted to specialized ELINT aircraft, as were the A3D SKYWARRIOR and P-3 ORION, they were fitted with some "black boxes" for ELINT collection, and made extensive use of hand-held cameras for reconnaissance.

Four Neptunes were shot down from 1951 to 1955, three by Soviet fighters and one by Chinese interceptors. Other Neptunes were "buzzed" and chased. (See AIRCRAFT SHOT DOWN.)

The Lockheed-developed Neptune was fitted with twin reciprocating engines, supplemented in later models by two turbojet engines in pods that could give them a "burst" speed for closing with submarine contacts. The Neptune had an internal bomb bay for depth bombs and torpedoes, and could carry rockets under the wing for at-tacking surfaced submarines. (Twelve early P2V-3C Neptunes were fitted to carry atomic bombs and could be launched from aircraft carriers for strikes against land targets; they had to be loaded aboard the carriers by crane!) Early Neptunes had various combinations of 20 mm cannon and .50-caliber machine guns for self-defense. There were usually eight men in the crew.

The XP2V-1 made its first flight on May 17, 1945. The following year, a P2V-1 named *Truculent Turtle*, stripped for long-distance flight, established a record nonrefueled flight of 11,236 miles in 55 hours, 17 minutes. (The record was broken in 1962 by an Air Force B-52H strategic bomber that flew 11,377 miles without refueling.) The normal range for the P2V-5 variant, built in the greatest numbers, was 3,200 miles; top speed was 353 mph.

A total of 1,099 P2Vs were produced by Lockheed from 1945 through 1962; 89 additional aircraft (P-2J) were produced in Japan by Kawasaki.

The P2V designation was changed to P-2 in 1962.

P3V Orion (P-3)

Principal U.S. Navy anti-submarine/maritime RECON-NAISSANCE aircraft since the mid-1960s. In addition to being flown in those roles by the U.S. Navy, the Orion flies for 11 other navies and air forces. The U.S. Navy flies 12 extensively modified EP-3 aircraft in the ELECTRONIC INTELLIGENCE (ELINT) role.

Succeeding the P2V NEPTUNE as the Navy's primary land-based patrol aircraft, the Orion first flew operationally during the CUBAN MISSILE CRISIS of Oct. 1962 to monitor Soviet and Eastern Bloc merchant ships en route to Cuba. During the Vietnam War several squadrons served in Operation Market Time, which monitored communist junk and sampan traffic. It was not unusual for the aircraft to come under small-arms fire from communist guerrillas during these missions, many of which were flown at night. In the late 1990s and early 21st century, the Orion's mission evolved to include SURVEILLANCE of what the military calls the battlespace at sea or over land, instantly providing information to ground troops, especially U.S. Marines.

The Lockheed-developed aircraft was adapted from the L-188 Electra airliner. It is powered by four turboprop engines, has an internal bomb bay for depth bombs, torpedoes, and mines, and can carry additional weapons—including antiship missiles—on wing pylons. No defensive guns are fitted to the aircraft, which normally has a crew of 10. Sensors include radar, magnetic anomaly detection, infrared, and droppable sonar buoys.

The ELINT-configured EP-3 aircraft have direction finders, radar signal analyzers, and various communication intercept and recording systems in place of anti-submarine equipment.

The P-3C variant currently in U.S. Navy service has a maximum speed of 473 mph and a mission radius of 1,550 miles with 13 hours on station. (The aircraft is not fitted for in-flight refueling.)

During the Cold War the EP-3 Orions flew reconnaissance flights along the periphery of the Soviet Union, China, and other TARGET countries, carefully remaining beyond the 12-mile territorial limit. Periodically the Orions were "buzzed" by foreign aircraft. This practice became particularly prevalent off the coast of China in the late 1990s and, on March 31, 2001, a pair of Chinese J-8 jet fighters approached an EP-3E off Hainan Island.

Suddenly, one fighter veered into the EP-3E. Heavily damaged, the fighter fell into the sea, killing its pilot. The EP-3E, also heavily damaged, turned toward Hainan Island. While the Navy cryptologists hastily destroyed equipment and recordings, the pilots fought to control the aircraft and were able to bring it down at a Chinese airfield.

The 24 U.S. Navy personnel (21 men and three women) were detained—but well treated—by the Chinese. Their aircraft was searched, but not ransacked. After 11 days the crew was released and flown to U.S. territory in a chartered airliner. After lengthy negotiations, the United States was allowed to send 40 technicians to Hainan to partially disassemble the aircraft, which was then flown out in two Russian cargo planes, as the Chinese refused permission for U.S. military aircraft to land on Hainan. The EP-3E was rehabilitated and returned to Navy service.

The first flight of a modified Electra airframe took place on Aug. 19, 1958, and the first YP3V-1 on Nov. 25, 1959. Orions began joining the fleet in Aug. 1962. A total of 551 Orions were delivered to the U.S. Navy in addition to foreign deliveries; more than 100 additional aircraft were built in Japan (which also flies the EP-3 ELINT variant).

The Orion's designation was changed from P3V to P-3 in 1962.

Also see VQ SQUADRONS.

P4M-1Q Mercator

U.S. Navy land-based maritime RECONNAISSANCE/anti-submarine aircraft that was employed almost exclusively in the ELECTRONICS INTELLIGENCE (ELINT) role. At least two were attacked by Soviet and Chinese fighters while on ELINT flights off the Asian coast; one was lost with all 16 crewmen on board.

The aircraft, developed by the Glenn L. Martin Co., was one of several attempts in the 1940s to combine piston and jet engines in a single aircraft to provide maximum range with high speed. While the P4M lost out to the P2V NEPTUNE for the maritime patrol role, it was employed in the ELINT role from 1951 to 1960.

The P4M-1 entered service with a single patrol squadron in 1950, but the decision was made to complete and convert most of the 21 Mercators to the P4M-1Q ELINT configuration. The first ELINT aircraft flew that year, and the aircraft took over from older naval aircraft flying spy missions along the periphery of the Soviet Union and China (see PB4Y-2 PRIVATEER).

The specialized ELECTRONIC COUNTERMEASURES (VQ) Squadron 1 was established at Iwakuni, Japan, on June 1, 1955, flying P4M-1Q aircraft; VQ-2 was established on Sept. 1, 1955, at Port Lyautey, Morocco, with the P4M-IQ. (See VQ SQUADRONS.)

Periodically, Soviet and Chinese fighters would "buzz" the aircraft as they flew off the coast, just outside the 12-mile limit, monitoring radar and communications transmissions. On Aug. 22, 1956, a P4M-1Q was shot down over the Shengszu Islands, 37 miles off the coast of China, while on a night mission. All 16 men on board were killed; several bodies were found by U.S. search aircraft. On June 16, 1959, another P4M-1Q was attacked by Soviet fighters over the Sea of Japan, 85 miles east of Wonsan, North Korea. The damaged plane returned to Niho Air Base in Japan. The plane's tail gunner was seriously wounded.

The P4M-1Q was withdrawn from the VQ role in 1960.

The aircraft had two piston engines and two jet engines housed in combination nacelles on each wing. The aircraft had a streamlined shape and was rated at 410 mph (with both piston and jet engines) with a range of 2,265 miles at a slower cruising speed. In the ELINT role no bombs or torpedoes could be carried, but the planes had four 20 mm cannon and two .50-caliber machine guns for protection. The crew numbered 13.

The prototype XP4M-1 first flew on Sept. 20, 1946. All 21 production aircraft were delivered in 1950.

Padding

Additional words added to the beginning and end of a CODE message to confuse enemy decryption efforts in the event of interception. The padding should not relate directly to the context of the message.

An example of incorrect padding that *did* relate to the text and hence create confusion occurred on Oct. 25, 1944, during the naval battle for Leyte Gulf. A message sent by Adm. Chester W. Nimitz, the theater commander, to Adm. William F. Halsey, the Third Fleet commander, read: "TURKEY TROTS TO WATER GG [addressee] WHERE IS RPT [repeat] WHERE IS TASK FORCE 34 RR [end] THE WORLD WONDERS." "Turkey trots to water" and "the world wonders" were both padding; however, because Halsey believed that the latter phrase related to the message, he took it as a rebuke from Nimitz and dispatched Task Force 34 on a fruitless chase of Japanese surface ships.

PAG

Device developed by the German Air Force in World War II for parachuting AGENTS behind enemy lines. The PAG—short for Persönen-Abwurf-Gerät (personnel drop device)—was a metal-and-wood canister that could hold three agents strapped in a rigid, horizontal position and their equipment. While the pod was mounted under a wing, the agents could communicate with the pilot of the carrying aircraft by a telephone connection.

In his book *KG 200: The True Story* (1979), Luftwaffe pilot P. W. Stahl wrote:

> The use of the PAG simplified an operation in several ways. For one thing, it was possible to fix the landing point more accurately than when agents would leave the aircraft separately with their own individual parachutes: on the ground, especially, and especially in a "blind" terrain, they now did not have to search for each other. Secondly, all their additional equipment was on the spot. But the main reason that led to the development and operational use of these streamlined containers was to lessen the danger of injuries during parachute jumps at night in an unknown area.

The only drawback, Stahl continued, was the problem of disposing of the canister, which was some 12 feet long.

Also see KG 200.

Painvin, Capt. Georges

Leading Allied cryptologist of World War I, who was able to break the German ADFGX CIPHER. Painvin, originally trained as a paleontologist, was head of the French Cipher Bureau on March 5, 1918, when the ADFGX cipher was first intercepted by the French Army.

For the next three and a half months Painvin and his colleagues struggled with the cipher. The bureau's ability to eventually read German communications in the ADFGX cipher enabled the Allies to defeat a German assault in June 1918, saving Paris.

The effort was physically exhausting for Painvin. He lost 33 pounds during the spring of 1918, working entire days without leaving his desk. He then spent six months in the hospital recovering from the effort.

In 1919, when American codebreaker HERBERT O. YARDLEY arrived in France, Painvin entertained him, but Yardley was never given access to the secrets of the Cipher Bureau. Painvin left the Army after the war, had a

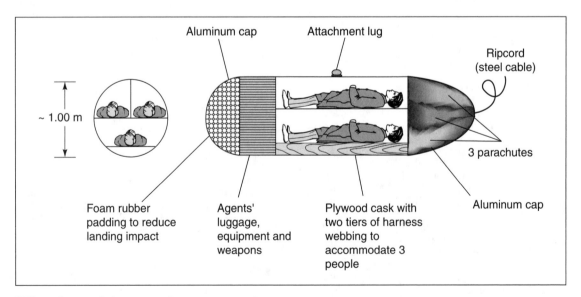

PAG parachute capsule. (COURTESY JANE'S PUBLISHING CO., LTD.)

very successful business career, and served as president of the Chamber of Commerce of Paris. Yet, he wrote, that cipher breakthroughs left "an indelible mark on my spirit, and remain for me one of the brightest and most outstanding memories of my existence."

The story of how Painvin broke into the ADFGX cipher was not revealed until 1966.

Paisley, John A.

(b. 1923 d. 1978)

Former CIA official who mysteriously disappeared. A body identified as Paisley's was found floating in Chesapeake Bay on Oct. 1978, a bullet wound in his head and 38 pounds of scuba-diving belt weights around his body.

At the time of his disappearance, the CIA described him as a relatively low-ranking employee who had retired in 1974. In fact, he had been deputy director of the CIA's Office of Strategic Research. Unofficial sources said that he helped plan the U-2 spyplane and the SAMOS and the KH-11 spy SATELLITE systems. (See KEYHOLE.) He also reportedly was a CIA liaison officer between the White House and the agency at the time of WATERGATE. (This led to speculation that he was "Deep Throat," the anonymous source of the Watergate information obtained by *Washington Post* reporters Carl Bernstein and Bob Woodward. Both denied that Paisley was Deep Throat.)

Paisley had an eventful career, but the CIA would not officially describe his assignments. Reportedly he worked with the NSA when the highly classified spy satellites were developed. He was also the agency liaison to the B TEAM, which evaluated the CIA in 1976, and is believed to have been involved in the complex intelligence operations that led to the death of NICHOLAS G. SHADRIN and the interrogation of YURI NOSENKO, a controversial Soviet DEFECTOR.

Paisley, who still worked for the CIA as a contractor, sailed his 31-foot sloop *Brillig* out of his dock at Solomons, Md., on Sept. 24, 1978. The next day the sloop was found aground near Point Lookout, Md., at the mouth of the Potomac River, 78 miles southeast of Washington, D.C. Investigators, including CIA security officers, found a briefcase containing a CIA report that Paisley was working on, a suitcase containing radio equipment, telegraph keys, and a single, hollow-core 9-mm bullet. No gun was found and there were no traces of blood.

On Oct. 1 a decomposing body with a bullet hole behind the left ear floated to the surface about 15 miles north of Point Lookout; the body had not sunk because internal gases overcame the weight of the scuba belts. The body was identified as Paisley's by dental records.

A life insurance company held up payment of $100,000 to his widow because of reports that the body was not Paisley's. Six months after his death, however, the money was paid to Mrs. Paisley, from whom Paisley had been estranged. The FBI also identified his body and said his death was a suicide. But a lawyer hired by Mrs. Paisley to investigate the death said, "Jumping off a boat with a gun

in hand, pulling the trigger while in the water, is, to be charitable about the matter, a weird way to commit suicide."

Rumors persisted that Paisley, who was fluent in Russian, had been spying for the Soviets and was murdered. The Senate Intelligence Committee investigated the death and in April 1980 reported that it had uncovered "no information which would detract from [his] record of outstanding performance in faithful service to his country." The committee did not release the full report, which dealt with the question of whether Paisley killed himself or was murdered.

Panay

U.S. gunboat that was carrying considerable SECRET material when she was sunk by Japanese bombers in 1937. Much of the secret intelligence related to Japanese military activities in China.

The *Panay* was one of several shallow-draft river gunboats built in the 1920s to protect American interests in China. She was to patrol the Yangtze River against pirates and warlords interfering with commercial shipping. The *Panay*, 191 feet long with a standard displacement of 474 tons, was armed with two 3-inch guns and several machine guns. Often the *Panay* would provide armed guards for Western craft traveling the river. After the Japanese invaded China in Nov. 1937 the U.S. river gunboats evacuated most of the American Embassy staff from the capital of Nanking (now Nanjing). The *Panay* remained to take off the last Americans when the situation in Nanking became untenable.

On Dec. 11, 1937, the last Americans from the embassy came on board the *Panay*, as did several journalists and a few foreigners. Also on board were a Japanese bombsight and several classified Japanese documents, as well as the ship's own CODE material. She moved upriver to avoid becoming involved in the fighting around the capital. The senior Japanese naval commander in Shanghai was informed of this movement, a precaution taken to avoid accidental attacks by Japanese forces.

On Dec. 12 Japanese naval aircraft were ordered by the Army commander in the area to attack "any and all ships" in the Yangtze above Nanking. Knowing of the presence of the *Panay* and the merchant ships, the Navy command questioned the order. Still, at 1:27 that afternoon nine Japanese naval bombers began attacking the *Panay*. The weather was good, visibility was clear, and the ship had two large American flags spread out on her awnings for aircraft recognition.

The aerial bombardment continued until the ship sank in shallow water at 3:54 p.m. Three U.S. sailors and an Italian on the ship were killed, and 43 other Navy men and five civilians were wounded. Shortly *before* the ship sank, Japanese officers came on board to search the ship, apparently seeking classified material that had not been jettisoned by the crew.

A formal protest was immediately lodged with the Japanese government. The Japanese accepted responsibility, although they claimed that the attack was unintentional. The Japanese government paid an indemnity of $2.2 million in April 1938, officially ending the incident.

The U.S. OFFICE OF NAVAL INTELLIGENCE held an urgent conference to determine what classified material might have been compromised in the *Panay*'s loss, and it was later revealed that the ship's officers had not destroyed all classified papers on board.

(On the same day as the *Panay* was sunk, two American merchant ships were attacked and Japanese Army artillery shelled the British gunboat *Ladybird* and took her into custody.)

Panfilov, Maj. Gen. Aleksei Pavlovich

(b. ? d. 1942)

Chief of the GRU, Soviet MILITARY INTELLIGENCE, from October 1941 to July 1942. As a colonel he had commanded the 2nd Mechanized Brigade in the successful 1938 campaign against the Japanese at Lake Khasan on the Soviet-Manchurian border.

He was executed during a purge in 1942. Little is known in the West about his career.

Pâques, Georges

SEE TOPAZ

Parol

Russian intelligence term for "password."

Party Piece

Highly successful British Security Service (MI5) break-in (BLACK BAG JOB) operation against the Communist Party of Great Britain in 1955. A telephone tap on a Mayfair apartment in London, where the party membership files were known to be kept, revealed when the apartment would be empty and a latchkey left under the doormat.

MI5 operatives quickly went to the apartment and made a wax impression of the key. Then, when the occupants were away for the weekend, operatives entered the apartment, picked the locks on file cabinets, carted away their contents to be photographed, and then carefully set them back in place.

The files—numbering 55,000 items—revealed the complete membership of the Party, recruitment techniques, and other details.

Patriot Act

SEE USA PATRIOT ACT

Pavement Artist

Intelligence slang for an operative skilled at tail or stakeout work.

PB4Y-2 Privateer

U.S. Navy maritime patrol aircraft flown extensively in an ELECTRONIC INTELLIGENCE (ELINT) role at the beginning of the Cold War. A PB4Y-2 on an ELINT mission off the coast of Latvia was attacked by Soviet fighters over the Baltic Sea on April 8, 1950, the first U.S. spyplane known to have been shot down by the Soviets. That plane had a crew of 10, none of whom survived, although there were reports of some being captured by the Soviets. The plane was unarmed.

The PB4Y-2 was a version of the B-24 Liberator heavy bomber, extensively modified for maritime patrol and anti-submarine operations. The Privateer was distinguished by its tall tail fin, which replaced the familiar twin-tail configuration of the B-24. The PB4Y-2 also had a seven-foot fuselage extension forward of the wing. It was a four-engine, high-wing aircraft with distinctive gun turret "blisters" on the after fuselage. It was normally heavily armed, with 12 .50-caliber machine guns. The internal weapons bay could hold 8,000 pounds of bombs. When modified for the ELINT role, most or all of the guns were removed.

The Privateer had a maximum speed of 237 mph and a maximum range of 2,800 miles. The aircraft's crew normally numbered 11.

The prototype PB4Y-2, one of three B-24D bombers converted by Convair into the PB4Y-2 configuration, flew on Sept. 20, 1943. Deliveries to the fleet began in March 1944 and continued through Oct. 1945, when 736 newly built Privateers were delivered to the Navy, a few of them flown by the Marine Corps. A transport version was also produced as the RY-3, of which 46 went to the U.S. Navy and 27 to Britain. After the war the Coast Guard flew the Privateer as the P4Y-2G and several were transferred to the French Navy for the war in Indochina.

Pearl Harbor Attack

The Japanese surprise attack on the U.S. Pacific Fleet at Pearl Harbor on Dec. 7, 1941, was a military catastrophe for both the Americans and Japanese. The air strike—Americans called it a "sneak" attack—killed 2,390 Americans, and wounded 1,178. (These figures, compiled by the National Park Service in 2001, differ from the previously accepted casualty total of 2,403 killed and 1,104 wounded.) The U.S. Pacific Fleet was crippled, and 75 percent of the aircraft on the airfields around Pearl Harbor were destroyed. The Japanese lost only 27 carrier-based aircraft plus five midget submarines. The planes, however, did not attack the dry docks or fuel storage tanks. If these had been destroyed, the U.S. Pacific Fleet would have had to shift its base to the West Coast, seriously delaying U.S. offensive actions in the Pacific.

The attack was the most serious American intelligence failure in the 20th century. But it also demonstrated the limitations of Japanese STRATEGIC INTELLIGENCE, for no warning had been given to Japanese political leaders that such an attack would unify Americans against Japan and cause them to demand the destruction of the Japanese Empire.

Almost immediately, U.S. investigations began into what went wrong in the months, weeks, and hours before the attack. U.S. intelligence organizations had provided a great deal of information that could have alerted political and military leaders to an impending attack on Pearl Harbor. But the intelligence did not add up to a warning of specific Japanese intentions. The story of ignored intelligence began in Aug. 1941, when DUSKO POPOV, a German spy who had become a DOUBLE AGENT for British intelligence, arrived in New York City from neutral Portugal. He carried a German espionage aid: MICRODOTS, which reduced a page of information to the size of the period ending this sentence. One of the microdots listed instructions from German intelligence, acting on a request from Japan: Go to Hawaii and get information on "Naval Strong Point Pearl Harbor."

British intelligence officials revealed Popov's mission to the FBI, which obtained a copy of the microdot. J. EDGAR HOOVER, director of the FBI, dismissed Popov as a "Balkan playboy" and refused to let him go to Hawaii. Hoover thus ignored the intelligence potential of the Pearl Harbor microdot.

The incident became an enduring example of how uncoordinated and unsophisticated U.S. intelligence was on the eve of America's entry into the war. But at the same time U.S. CRYPTANALYSIS was superb. A military cryptologist team under WILLIAM F. FRIEDMAN had already broken the Japanese PURPLE CODE in an operation known as MAGIC. In Nov. 1941 Japanese special envoys Kichisaburo Nomura and Saburo Kurusu arrived in Washington, D.C., to negotiate an easing of tension between Japan and the United States. Because of penetrations into Japanese diplomatic CODES, senior U.S. officials could read communications between the envoys and Tokyo.

Acting upon Magic intercepts of Japanese messages, on Nov. 27, the Navy Department sent Adm. Husband E. Kimmel, the fleet commander at Pearl Harbor, a message begining, "This dispatch is to be considered a war warning." The dispatch said that "an aggressive move by Japan is expected within the next few days." Also on Nov. 27, the War Department sent the Army commander in Hawaii, Lt. Gen. Walter Short, a similar dispatch warning "hostile action possible at any moment. If hostility cannot, repeat cannot, be avoided the United States desires that Japan commit the first overt act."

Kimmel, not wishing to arouse Hawaii's civilian population, did not raise the fleet's readiness status. Short, in charge of Hawaiian defenses, reacted to his warning by taking precautions against sabotage. This response stemmed from the belief that Hawaii's Japanese and Japanese-Americans could not be trusted and in war would turn against the United States. (The Army particularly subscribed to the fear of sabotage by people of Japanese heritage. In the mid-1930s Lt. Col. George S. Patton, Jr., then chief of ARMY INTELLIGENCE in Hawaii, drew up a plan to seize 128 leaders of Hawaii's Japanese community and hold them as hostages in the event of a U.S.-Japanese war.)

Short, following Army doctrine in response to a threat of sabotage, massed aircraft in wingtip-to-wingtip aggregations to make them easier to guard. Short's move hastened the planes' destruction when Japanese planes struck at the airfields around Pearl Harbor.

Eleven days after the Dec. 7 attack, President Roosevelt appointed a board of inquiry, known as the Roberts Commission for its chairman, Supreme Court justice Owen J. Roberts. The commission concluded its closed-door investigation on Jan. 23, 1942, and declared that Kimmel and Short had failed to exhibit the qualities expected of high command. Already relieved of their duties, they were given no new assignments, and soon retired.

The next six investigations, under Army or Navy auspices, were also secretly conducted. Not until the war ended could concern about military security give way to a resolve to air the facts about the Pearl Harbor disaster publicly. A joint congressional investigation began on Nov. 15, 1945, and continued through six months of hearings that produced 15,000 pages of testimony.

Both the majority and minority reports issued in July 1946 again put the primary blame on Kimmel and Short. This time the reasons for the conclusion were specific: The admiral and general had failed to heed the warnings sent to them from Washington; they had failed to alert their forces properly; they had not coordinated what defenses they did mount; they had not employed their personnel and equipment as well as they should have in anticipating the attack or in defending against it. The committee concluded that Kimmel and Short had made "errors of judgment" and were not guilty of "dereliction of duty."

The congressional investigation did not end the questions about Pearl Harbor. In 1945 U.S. codebreaking was still not fully revealed; many Magic intercepts would not be declassified for decades. In 1945, with many careers not yet ended, the bickering between military intelligence bureaucracies continued to obscure what was known by whom—and when it was known.

The Navy had set up a network of radio interception stations to monitor Japanese military communications (see NAVY COMMUNICATIONS INTELLIGENCE). Communications between Tokyo and the Japanese Consulate in Hawaii were considered low priority because they contained so many messages that were entirely commercial. One such message, sent to the consulate on Sept. 24, 1941, should have received more attention. It divided Pearl Harbor into five sectors and requested that the location of warships be indicated on a grid of the harbor. In later investigations, this became known as the "bomb plot" message; plot meant "grid," not "conspiracy," but the true definition was lost in the quest for conspiracy. Unknown to U.S. codebreakers, it was addressed to TAKEO YOSHIKAWA, a Japanese Navy spy working under COVER as a vice consul. (Similar requests for "grids" of military harbours were sent to Japanese diplomats in several countries.)

Distribution of decrypted Japanese messages was irregular. Many were routinely available in the U.S. Asiatic Fleet and to senior people in Washington, but not at the Pacific Fleet headquarters at Pearl Harbor.

Looming over all the investigations and conspiracy

theories was a general misunderstanding of just what "warnings" had gone to the military commanders at Pearl Harbor. As Roberta Wohlstetter, in her lucid and penetrating book *Pearl Harbor: Warning and Decision* (1962), pointed out, "There is a difference . . . between having a signal available somewhere in the heap of irrelevancies, and perceiving it as a warning; and there is also a difference between perceiving it as a warning, and acting or getting action on it. The distinctions, simple as they are, illuminate the obscurity shrouding this moment in history."

The Nov. 27 warnings to Kimmel and Short had been preceded by other warnings going back to at least April. But warnings about war were not warnings about an attack on Pearl Harbor. Neither in Washington nor in Pearl Harbor was there unqualified expectation of an attack at Pearl Harbor.

Kimmel and Short were denied access to the intelligence community's highly secret decryptions of intercepted Japanese diplomatic messages, although many were paraphrased and sent to Pearl Harbor "informally." The intelligence bureaucracies wanted to hold tightly the secrets their codebreaking unveiled. Magic was guarded so zealously that few people ever saw an original message. The war warnings might have been better understood by Kimmel and Short if they had seen the diplomatic messages. But it does not seem likely that higher-grade intelligence would have changed their perceptions of how to respond.

One specific intercepted Tokyo-Washington message said that if Japan-U.S. relations were "in danger," Tokyo would broadcast on feigned weather broadcasts the words "east wind rain." Conspiracy theorists contend that the words were broadcast on Dec. 5, but, mysteriously, the "warning" was not given to Kimmel and Short. In fact, according to the congressional report, Wohlstetter's research, and other studies, there is no evidence that such a message was actually transmitted.

The Pearl Harbor attack cast a long shadow over future U.S. intelligence activities. After World War II, when the U.S. armed forces' focus was on the Soviet Union, strategists worried about a "Pearl Harbor attack," usually referred to as "a bolt from the blue." This fear and the need to integrate fully all available intelligence was a key factor in President Truman's decision in 1947 to create the CIA. Similarly, President Eisenhower cited fear of a "nuclear Pearl Harbor" as the reason for developing the U-2 spy place.

The RAND Corp., created by the newly established U.S. Air Force to analyze strategic concepts, developed surprise-attack scenarios. In the late 1950s Roberta Wohlstetter, then a RAND consultant, began writing her book about the Pearl Harbor attack. All her sources were unclassified, most of them being the 39 volumes of congressional hearings published in 1946. According to the terms of her SECURITY CLEARANCE, she had to submit her manuscript to the Department of Defense for review.

From there it went to NSA, which classified it and ordered all copies of the manuscript destroyed. When she asked why, the answer was that she did not have sufficient clearance to be told.

By way of possible explanation, she later said, "If something is written about codes, they [NSA] get uptight." Another possibility, she said, was that her conclusion—leaders were hampered by too much information, too much "noise"—did not coincide with one Pentagon official's belief in the theory that President Roosevelt had known about the Japanese attack in advance and had allowed the Japanese to strike. "So he sent the manuscript to the agency where they classify everything," she said. Not until the Kennedy administration brought a new leadership into the Pentagon in Jan. 1961 was the book cleared for publication.

When *Pearl Harbor: Warning and Decision* finally appeared, it received stellar reviews. It remains a classic examination of the Pearl Harbor attack—as well as a primer on how, even in the best of intelligence worlds, things can go wrong. "We have to accept the fact of uncertainty and learn to live with it," Wohlstetter concluded. "No magic, in code or otherwise, will provide certainty. Our plans must work without it."

Similarly, historian DAVID KAHN has written, "No intelligence, analyzed or unanalyzed, existed that would have let America's commanders and President Roosevelt know in advance about the attack."

Pelton, Ronald W.

Former NSA intelligence analyst who sold the Soviet Union his incredibly detailed recollections of what he had learned during 14 years at the U.S. electronic espionage agency.

Pelton attended Indiana University, where he took a one-year Russian-language course. He joined the U.S. Air Force in 1960 and was sent to Pakistan, where he was assigned to a SIGNALS INTELLIGENCE activity, eavesdropping on Soviet communications. After being discharged in 1964, he worked for a time as a television repairman and then went to work at the NSA in 1965.

Pelton's capture and conviction as a spy brought to its conclusion a tantalizing case that began when an FBI telephone tap picked up a call to the Soviet Embassy in Washington, D.C., on Jan. 14, 1980. The caller told a Soviet diplomat, "I come from—I, I, I am in, with the United States Government."

"Ah, huh, United States Government. . . . Maybe you can visit," the diplomat said.

The caller agreed to go to the embassy the next night "so that it will be dark when I come in."

But at 2:32 P.M. on Jan. 15, the caller phoned the embassy and said he would be there in two minutes. The FBI had expected more warning. "We saw him go in, saw his back side, and we could not identify his exit," FBI director WILLIAM H. WEBSTER said later.

The tape of the calls was filed away, and nothing more on the case developed until Aug. 1985, when VITALY YURCHENKO, a KGB officer, defected to the United

States. He redefected three months later, but among the bits of information he gave was a remark about having met a former NSA employee in Washington, D.C., in 1980. When FBI agents interviewed Yurchenko, they learned that the man had red hair. Starting with a list of about 500 names, FBI agents found a few suspects. The trail led them to Pelton when NSA employees identified his voice on the 1980 tape.

Pelton had worked as an intelligence analyst for NSA for 14 years by 1979. He had piled up so many debts that he was forced to declare bankruptcy. Knowing that this could endanger his SECURITY CLEARANCE for SPECIAL COMPARTMENTED INFORMATION relating to signals intelligence, he resigned. A few months later he dialed the Soviet Embassy and became a WALK-IN.

He showed Yurchenko proof of his former NSA employment and demonstrated what coworkers at NSA called a photographic memory, an ability to summon up bits of information from many sources and produce a mosaic of intelligence. Pelton was the author of an NSA eavesdropping encyclopedia that listed some 60 Soviet signals that the agency's listening posts regularly intercepted, analyzed, and decrypted.

Yurchenko accepted Pelton as a genuine walk-in and listened to his major disclosure: The United States was using SUBMARINES to tap an underwater communications cable in the Sea of Okhotsk between Soviet installations on the Kamchatka Peninsula and the Soviet eastern coast. The project was code-named IVY BELLS.

A bearded Pelton had entered the embassy through the front door. Yurchenko had him shave off his beard. Dressed in bulky work clothes, Pelton slipped out of a side door with a group of Soviet employees. The group entered the van that regularly shuttled workers between the embassy and an apartment complex used as a Soviet residence.

On Oct. 15 the FBI got permission from the FOREIGN INTELLIGENCE SURVEILLANCE COURT for electronic SURVEILLANCE. Agents tapped Pelton's business phone and the phone on his girlfriend's apartment in the Georgetown section of Washington, and put a BUG in the apartment and an electronic tracking device on Pelton's car. No incriminating information turned up on the taps. The FBI now had only a voice on a tape and a recollection from a Soviet defector who redefected.

The FBI now tried to make Pelton incriminate himself. On Nov. 24, Pelton agreed to talk to FBI agents David Faulkner and Dudley Hodgson, who played for him the tape of the 1980 conversations with someone at the Soviet Embassy. Thinking that the FBI wanted him to become a DOUBLE AGENT, he cautiously talked about cooperating. Pelton said he had gone to VIENNA in April 1985, but the person he was supposed to meet had not appeared. Quite casually Hodgson asked how much money was involved. Caught off guard, Pelton replied that he could not remember whether the amount was $30,000 or $35,000 in addition to about $5,000 in expense money.

Pelton rattled on about his meetings in Vienna, say-

ing that he spent as long as eight hours a day, three or four days at time, writing answers to written questions about the NSA.

Arrested on the basis of what he told the FBI agents, Pelton was indicted for espionage and put on trial. Ironically, he had to agree, for the good of the country, not to reveal in court the secrets he was accused of selling to the Soviet Union. He agreed not to use any of the NSA CODE NAMES for the projects he had worked on, sold to the Soviets, or discussed with the FBI. He could look at the FBI report that recounted his conversation with Faulkner and Hodgson. The report itself was classified.

Although there was no evidence other than the conversation with the agents, a jury found him guilty in June 1986. The judge, saying that Pelton's sellout had done

Ronald Pelton. (FEDERAL BUREAU OF INVESTIGATION)

"inestimable damage," sentenced him to three concurrent life sentences.

Penetration

The recruitment of AGENTS from within, or the planting of agents or monitoring devices (BUGS) within a TARGET organization to gain access to its secrets or to influence its activities.

Penkovsky, Col. Oleg

(b. 1919 d. 1963)

GRU officer who, as a DEFECTOR IN PLACE, passed secrets to the United States and Britain from April 1961 until Aug. 1962. Information he supplied during the CUBAN MISSILE CRISIS helped President Kennedy assess Soviet intentions and capability.

The son of a czarist army officer who had fought the Bolsheviks in the Russian Civil War (1917–1920), Penkovsky attended an artillery school, was commissioned as an officer in the Red Army in 1939, and fought briefly in Jan. 1940 during the Soviet war against Finland. After the German invasion of June 1941, he was stationed in Moscow as a political officer with some intelligence duties. He volunteered for combat and served in anti-tank units in the 1944–1945 campaigns against the Germans. Immediately after the war he married a general's daughter. In 1948 Penkovsky graduated from the two-year course at the Frunze Military Academy (war college), where he learned English, and was then sent to the Military Diplomatic Academy to study STRATEGIC INTELLIGENCE.

In 1955 he went to Turkey as assistant military ATTACHÉ. Angry about his treatment by a superior, he anonymously reported him to Turkish intelligence. This was a mild foreshadowing of what he would later do as a spy for the West. Again posted to Moscow, in 1958–1959 he was sent to the Dzerzhinsky Military Academy for a course on rockets and missiles. Penkovsky hoped to return to a combat unit, but was kept in the GRU and was scheduled for attaché assignment in India. But his father's anti-Bolshevik past still haunted his career, and he was not sent. Penkovsky's defection was fueled by resentment over the way he was being treated.

Penkovsky's attempts to make contact with Western intelligence agencies were frustrating. One night in Aug. 1960, he handed a letter to two American tourists in Moscow and asked them to get it to the U.S. Embassy. "I have at my disposal very important materials on many subjects of exceptionally great interest and importance to your government," the letter said. "I wish to pass these materials to you immediately. . . ." Although he did not sign the letter, he provided enough clues for CIA analysts to identify him as Penkovsky, who had made friends with an American officer when both were military attachés in Turkey.

The CIA tried unsuccessfully to make contact, through a nervous, inexperienced INTELLIGENCE OFFICER operating under thin diplomatic COVER at the U.S. Embassy in Moscow. Penkovsky then approached British and Canadian businessmen in Moscow. Penkovsky's GRU assignment was liaison between Western businessmen and the State Committee for the Coordination of Scientific Research Work. In the ranks of both the businessmen and the Soviets were intelligence officers trying to exploit East-West contacts, which were then rare. Penkovsky by this time was a full colonel working under cover on the committee.

The British Secret Intelligence Service (MI6) had learned of Penkovsky's approach to a British businessman who had an informal relationship with MI6. Officials in both MI6 and the CIA were split over whether Penkovsky was an AGENT PROVOCATEUR. Complicating matters was the fact that the CAMBRIDGE SPY RING had deeply penetrated the British intelligence establishment; HAROLD (KIM) PHILBY was suspected by some American and British officials and could give away a defector in place.

Although the Americans still distrusted British security, they also did not want to use the U.S. Embassy in Moscow as an outpost for running Penkovsky; the State Department did not countenance elaborate intelligence operations. RICHARD HELMS, the CIA's director of clandestine operations, decided that the CIA and MI6 should try to run Penkovsky jointly. Meanwhile, Penkovsky had given GREVILLE M. WYNNE, a British businessman, a packet that Wynne delivered to the British Embassy, and a letter that Wynne carried when he flew out of Moscow in April 1961.

A few days later, Penkovsky arrived in London as head of a delegation from the Soviet research committee. A complex system was set up for running Penkovsky: a CIA-MI6 team, operating out of London, would run Penkovsky; Wynne, acting as a COURIER between London and Moscow, would be the CUT-OUT to MI6. In the first CIA-MI6 debriefing, Penkovsky suggested that Soviet leader Nikita Khrushchev might soon send missiles to CUBA, which had just successfully repulsed an American-sponsored invasion. His reports on specific Soviet weapons and military matters—code-named IRONBARK—astonished his debriefers.

His CIA-MI6 HANDLERS stroked his ego, photographing him in the uniforms of the U.S. Army and the British Army with the insignia of colonel.

Penkovsky had long lists of gifts that he wanted for himself, his wife and children, and influential friends, from ballpoint pens and watchbands to 60-year-old cognac and a ladies' gold watch. "I consider, as your Soldier, that my place during these troubled times is on the *front line*," he said in a letter to ALLEN W. DULLES, the DIRECTOR OF CENTRAL INTELLIGENCE (DCI). "I must remain on this front line in order to be your eyes and ears . . ."

The intelligence services initially obtained information from him by exhaustive debriefing sessions on his trips leading the committee delegation to London and Paris. In Moscow, exchanges of material took place in parks and doorways, where he met Janet Anne Chisholm, wife of Roderick Chisholm, an MI6 officer under cover at the British Embassy. The mother of three children, she had been an MI6 secretary before she married. Her children and her visits with them to a park were her cover. There were also exchanges between a CIA officer under cover in the U.S. Embassy. Penkovsky's handlers gave him a camera, rolls of film, and instructions; he gave them exposed rolls of films and documents he had hand-copied.

He produced so much material that the CIA set up a team of 20 translators and analysts to handle it; MI6 had 10 officers working on the documents Penkovsky photographed. The CIA gave President Kennedy information from Penkovsky, believing that he was providing the thoughts and plans of Soviet military and political leaders.

His CIA-edited memoirs also provided the public with details of the infighting of Soviet intelligence agencies. Telling how he reported on the incompetence of his GRU superior when he was stationed in Turkey, Penkovsky wrote:

> To straighten out this matter, I sent a cable to Moscow through the channels of our other intelligence organization in Turkey, the rezidentura (Soviet term for station in a foreign country) of the KGB. When GRU headquarters discovered this, I was recalled, accused of writing a report about my chief and sending it through channels of our bitter rival—the interservice jealousy between the GRU and the KGB runs through most Soviet intelligence activities.
>
> The matter did not end with my recall. The disagreement was finally reported to Khrushchev, who keeps a close watch on intelligence activities. Khrushchev gave orders to have the matter thoroughly investigated . . . I was spoken to rather sternly for not having treated my superiors with proper respect; at the same time, I was told that my action itself in alerting Moscow was correct.

(His superior was dismissed from the GRU and "punished" by the Communist Party. He became a department head at the Institute for Oriental Studies.)

In the summer of 1961, Penkovsky sent word that Soviet leader Nikita Khrushchev was planning to declare a separate peace with East Germany, setting off a crisis over divided BERLIN. Penkovsky was right, although Khrushchev did not carry out the threat. The spy also provided photographs of documents describing Soviet missiles and showing that Khrushchev's boasts of missile production had been exaggerated.

The "missile gap" was not what most Americans thought: There were far more U.S. missiles than Soviet ones. The CIA's BOARD OF NATIONAL ESTIMATES in the fall of 1961 lowered the number of nuclear missiles, using Penkovsky's information and photographs from a new source of intelligence, SATELLITES.

When the Cuban missile crisis erupted in the fall of 1962, U-2 spyplanes flying over Cuba photographed suspected missile sites. Analysts checked the photos against manuals on SS-4 medium-range missiles provided by Penkovsky, giving to President Kennedy "unmistakable evidence" of missiles in Cuba when he made his brink-of-war speech to the nation on Oct. 22.

The CIA was so convinced of Penkovsky's high-level access that he was given specific instructions on how to signal if he knew that the Soviet government "intends to go to war." He had set up a DEAD DROP for important exchanges in the foyer of a Moscow building (see TRADECRAFT). On Nov. 2, 1961, a CIA officer at the U.S. Embassy received a telephone signal—a "silent call" that an urgent message had been left at the dead drop. When the officer was reaching for the drop, he was seized by four KGB officers and arrested.

The officer, protected by diplomatic immunity, was expelled. Wynne was arrested in Budapest on Nov. 2 and turned over to KGB officers who flew him to Moscow and jailed him in the LUBYANKA. Penkovsky had been arrested on Oct. 22, unknown to Western intelligence.

At a show trial in May 1963, Penkovsky's espionage was fully revealed, as was Wynne's courier work. Penkovsky was sentenced to death, Wynne to three years in prison and five in a labor camp. Penkovsky's execution was announced on May 17, 1963. In April 1964 Wynne was exchanged in a SPY SWAP for GORDON LONSDALE and Peter and Helen Kroger (see MORRIS COHEN).

After Penkovsky's death, the CIA decided to make some of his revelations public in a BLACK PROPAGANDA operation that would reveal Soviet intentions but not reveal that the CIA was the source. PETER DERIABIN, a KGB COUNTERINTELLIGENCE officer who had defected in 1954, had become a CIA consultant. Deriabin, who had once worked for Penkovsky's father-in-law, edited the transcripts of Penkovsky's taped debriefings in London and Paris. A CIA-censored version of the transcripts was given to Frank Gibney, a former *Life* magazine writer and *Newsweek* editor. Gibney, who had collaborated with Deriabin on *The Secret World* (1959), was writing speeches for President Johnson in the summer of 1964 when he got the sanitized transcripts.

Given assurances by a NATIONAL SECURITY COUNCIL aide that the book was "in the national interest," Doubleday published *The Penkovsky Papers* (1965), a bestseller, with editions published in Britain, France, Germany, Korea, Japan, and Sweden. Deriabin was credited as the translator, but the CIA provenance was not acknowledged. In a preface to a 1982 edition of the book Gibney revealed its CIA origins.

The subjects addressed by Penkovsky ranged far and wide; in *The Penkovsky Papers* his "edited" commentary included the "missile gap":

> Khrushchev often boasts about the Soviet missiles or spreads all kind of propaganda about them. Often a new-model missile is still only in the testing stage—in fact, the tests may have proved unsuccessful—but there he is, already screaming to the entire world about his "achievements" in new types of Soviet weapons. The idea of Khrushchev and the Presidium of the Central Committee is to demonstrate somehow Soviet supremacy in the nuclear

field by any possible means: by launching new *sput-niks,* by nuclear explosions, etc.

On the Soviet system the Penkovsky account declares:

I am joining the ranks of those who are actively fighting against our rotten, two-faced regime, known by the name of Dictatorship of the Proletariat or Soviet Power. Yes, it is a dictatorship, not of the Proletariat, but of a small group of persons. It deceives my countrymen while they, being innocent, give their lives for this dictatorship, without knowing the entire truth. And they will probably never learn it, unless I or people like myself tell them the truth. . . . I am joining the ranks of a new army, the true people's army. I know that I am not alone; we are many. But we are still afraid of each other and we act only as individuals.

Penkovsky spoke to debriefers for some 140 hours, producing about 1,200 pages of transcripts. He delivered 111 rolls of film. A CIA assessment said that this was "the most productive classic clandestine operation ever

Col. Oleg Penkovsky. (CENTRAL INTELLIGENCE AGENCY)

conducted by CIA or MI6 against the Soviet target." Other evaluations were less enthusiastic. JAMES JESUS ANGLETON, the CIA counterintelligence chief, called Penkovsky "an anarchist and a crank who for some obscure reason is trying to get us into a war with Russia." Penkovsky had suggested, in his initial meeting with the CIA-MI6 team, that the West hide tactical atomic bombs in certain places in Moscow and, if a war started, detonate them to wipe out key Soviet officials. There was also speculation about the authenticity of Penkovsky's defection. But any doubt about the Soviet view of his espionage was dispelled when IVAN SEROV, head of the GRU, was demoted to major general and fired; he reportedly killed himself. Some 300 GRU and KGB officers and military officers were recalled, and a purge reached down as far as officers in artillery and rocket units. Author JOHN LE CARRÈ, often cynical about intelligence accomplishments, gave this assessment: "The information which Penkovsky provided and Wynne purveyed led, there is little doubt, to the greatest moral defeat suffered by either side in the cold war: Khrushchev's decision to withdraw his rockets from Cuba."

Responsibility for the betrayal of Penkovsky has never been publicly acknowledged by Western intelligence officials.

At the time Penkovsky was nearing exposure there were at least two Soviet spies operating in Britain: JOHN VASSALL and FRANK BOSSARD. While there is no evidence that they had direct knowledge of the Penkovsky case, they could have picked up a rumor and could have reported the sudden series of CIA-MI6 meetings in London.

As Deriabin and Jerrold L. Schecter point out in *The Spy Who Saved the World* (1992), still another Soviet spy in British intelligence, GEORGE BLAKE, may have provided the Soviets with the key years before. Blake had served with Charles R. Chisholm in Berlin and would have told the Soviets that he was an MI6 intelligence officer.

The KGB put both Chisholm and his wife under surveillance as soon as Chisholm was posted to the British Embassy in Moscow. A Soviet counterintelligence officer, quoted anonymously in the book, said, "Twice, at the end of 1961 and in 1962 [Soviet] Counterintelligence saw Mrs. Chisholm, while walking, stop to enter the entrances of apartment houses. Soon they saw a stranger nearby who appeared to be very nervous and trying to discover if there was surveillance of him . . . That stranger was Penkovsky." The officer then showed a videotape of Chisholm-Penkovsky meetings. The KGB had suspected Penkovsky for months before his arrest, but for reasons still unknown he was allowed to continue spying for the West.

The CIA gave Penkovsky the CODE NAME Hero; to MI6 he was Yoga.

Pentagon Papers

More than 4,000 pages of official documents that detail the start of U.S. involvement in the Vietnam War (see

VIETNAM). The "papers" were excerpts from an official, 7,000-page study that included many TOP SECRET and SECRET documents. A photocopied version of the study had been given to *The New York Times* by Daniel Ellsberg, a former Department of Defense official. *(The Washington Post* later also obtained a copy of the study.)

Ellsberg had transferred from the Pentagon to the State Department to become an adviser at the U.S. Embassy in Saigon during the Johnson administration. In Vietnam he worked for EDWARD G. LANSDALE, a CIA officer who considered Ellsberg a supporter of the war. In 1969, he returned to the RAND Corp., which did secret work for the Department of Defense. Ellsberg, a hawk who had become disillusioned over the war, was indicted for espionage and conspiracy, as was fellow RAND worker Anthony Russo. The charges were later dismissed by a federal judge because of government misconduct.

The Pentagon Papers covered American involvement in Vietnam from the early 1940s to March 1968. Considerable material on U.S. intelligence operations in Southeast Asia is included in the papers. The papers are based on an 18-month Department of Defense effort, including access to CIA and State Department files, to document the history of U.S. involvement in Vietnam. The study was initiated by Secretary of Defense Robert S. McNamara in June 1967.

When *The New York Times* began publishing the papers on June 13, 1971, President Nixon initially did not object to their publication, as they mostly reflected actions undertaken by earlier, Democratic administrations. He later said that he had not read the story. (Also on the front page of the *Times* that day was a wedding picture of Nixon and his daughter Tricia in the Rose Garden.) On Monday evening, however, Attorney General John Mitchell warned the *Times* to stop publishing the papers, and on Tuesday, June 15, the government got a restraining order against the *Times*. Nixon's national security adviser, Henry Kissinger, had persuaded Nixon to oppose the revelation of past U.S. diplomatic secrets because of the impact such an act would have on future American relations with foreign nations.

When the government succeeded in delaying newspaper publication, Sen. Mike Gravel convened a special meeting of his Subcommittee on Public Buildings and Grounds on the night of June 29, 1971, and entered the papers—all 4,100 pages—into the official record of the subcommittee. This act placed them in the public domain. Subsequently the *Post, Times,* and other newspapers continued publishing excerpts from the Pentagon Papers. They were later commercially published in book form in four volumes. Gravel wrote in his introduction to the volumes:

No one who reads this study can fail to conclude that, had the true facts been made known earlier, the war would long ago have ended, and the needless deaths of hundreds of thousands of Americans and Vietnamese would have been averted. This is

the great lesson of the Pentagon Papers. No greater argument against unchecked secrecy in government can be found in the annals of American history.

The Pentagon Papers tell of the purposeful withholding and distortion of facts. There are no military secrets to be found here, only an appalling litany of faulty premises and questionable objectives, built one upon the other over the course of four administrations, and perpetuated today by a fifth administration.

The Pentagon Papers show that U.S. administrations, beginning in the last quarter of the 20th century, created a new culture, a national security culture, protected from the influences of American life by the shield of secrecy.

Peppermint

CODE NAME for U.S. and British response to the fears that Germany could employ radiation poisoning to oppose Allied troops coming ashore on the Normandy beaches on D-Day (June 6, 1944). There was fear that the Germans would use radioactive materials, poison gas, or even toxins to repel the assault troops. Gen. Omar N. Bradley would write in his autobiography, *A Soldier's Story* (1951), "even a light sprinkling of persistent gas on Omaha Beach could have cost us our footing there."

U.S. and British chemical warfare specialists and specially trained medical personnel—known as "peppermint soldiers"—came ashore on D-Day carrying 1,500 unexposed film packets, 11 radiation meters, and a Geiger counter. They found no indications of radiation poisoning and, accordingly, no protective measures were taken—although such measures would have had no practical value. (The assault troops at Normandy carried syringes to inoculate themselves in the event that the Germans used biological weapons.)

Also see ALSOS MISSION.

Perforated Sheet

Piece of paper with about 1,000 holes cut according to a predetermined pattern, used to work out settings for the ENIGMA CIPHER machine prior to the development of the BOMBA and BOMBE calculating machines.

Peri, Michael A.

Former U.S. Army ELECTRONIC INTELLIGENCE specialist who in 1989 pleaded guilty to committing espionage while he was stationed in West Germany as an intelligence specialist in the 11th Armored Cavalry Regiment of the U.S. Army's V Corps. Authorities said that Peri defected to East Germany with classified computer equipment and then returned less than a month later.

"I really didn't have a plan," Peri said at a hearing on the charges. "My primary reason was to leave behind all the frustrations and problems at work. Everything had been wrong. I wasn't enjoying myself. I wanted to start over somewhere else."

Peri was sentenced to 30 years in prison.

Perkins, Master Sgt. Walter T.

U.S. Air Force intelligence specialist who was arrested in 1971 on his way to deliver TOP SECRET air defense plans to a KGB officer in Mexico.

Perkins was stationed at the Air Defense Weapons Center at Tyndall Air Force Base, in Florida, when he made the offer. His contact with the Soviets was detected by U.S. COUNTERINTELLIGENCE officials.

Perkins said he had thought that he could swap secret documents for American prisoners of war in North Vietnam. In a prosecution conducted by the Air Force, he was sentenced to three years in prison.

Petersen, Joseph S., Jr.

(b. 1914)

NSA codebreaker who provided documents to the Netherlands.

A graduate of Loyola University with a master's degree in science from St. Louis University, Petersen spent most of World War II as an Army specialist in CRYPTANALYSIS under WILLIAM F. FRIEDMAN, working on Japanese diplomatic CODES. He became friendly with Col. J. A. Verkuyl, a Dutch liaison officer who was also a cryptologist.

After the war Petersen joined the ARMY SECURITY AGENCY (which became the NSA in 1952) and sent Verkuyl concepts about cryptology that Petersen thought might be helpful to Dutch government cryptologists. He also sent information on how U.S. codebreakers had penetrated Dutch codes and CIPHERS. NSA security learned of Petersen's correspondence with the Dutch, and on Oct. 1, 1954, he was fired. Eight days later he was arrested—the first person to be charged with violating a new federal statute protecting COMMUNICATIONS INTELLIGENCE.

Petersen pleaded guilty to violating the statute, thus keeping sensitive cryptologic information from being aired in a trial. Sentenced to seven years in prison, he was released on parole in 1958.

Peterson, Martha

CASE OFFICER for the CIA arrested by the KGB in 1977 while she was serving under diplomatic COVER in Moscow.

Peterson, listed as a vice consul in the U.S. Embassy in Moscow, was caught servicing a DEAD DROP used by ALEKSANDR D. OGORODNIK (who had been discovered and apparently used the drop while under KGB SURVEILLANCE). When Peterson was arrested the United States, following diplomatic custom, did not acknowledge her

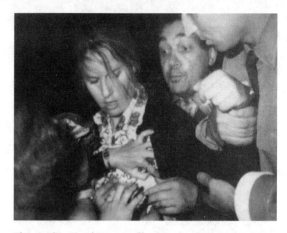

The apprehension of CIA case officer Martha Peterson in Moscow in 1977 by KGB officers who were "playing rough" according to U.S. officials. She was servicing a "dead drop" when arrested. The day after her arrest she was expelled from the Soviet Union, another move in the chess game of espionage. (KGB MUSEUM)

guilt but did acquiesce in her expulsion the day after her arrest.

CIA officials privately expressed outrage at the rough way in which KGB interrogators had handled Peterson. "She was not shown the usual courtesy expected by an intelligence officer," a retired CIA officer recalled. "They roughed her up—not injuring her, but playing rough." CIA debriefers later speculated that Peterson, whose husband also worked at the embassy, had embarrassed the KGB embassy watchers, who had not spotted her as an intelligence officer. When they belatedly did so, they took out their anger and frustration on her. "Unlike many intelligence officers," the retired CIA man said, "she had been 'living her cover' closely, working as a consular official, mostly on visa applications. People figured that the KGB had not spotted her as an INTELLIGENCE OFFICER for a long while, and someone was mad as hell."

The Soviet newspaper *Izvestia,* in a long report on Peterson, said that her dead drop was a crevice in a bridge over the Moscow River near the Luzhniki sports stadium. KGB officers—including one on a towering construction crane—had kept her under SURVEILLANCE from the time she left the embassy until she reached the bridge. She was accused of depositing gold, Russian currency, and cameras. Accompanying the story was a photograph showing her with a U.S. Embassy official at a table spread with the objects said to have been found in the dead drop. The newspaper also claimed that she had left ampoules of poison to be used by one of her agents to kill a Soviet citizen who was impeding CIA espionage. In fact, Ogorodnik already had a CIA L PILL, concealed in a fountain pen. While under questioning, he killed himself by biting off the tip of the pen and swallowing the pill.

The pen had been supplied at Ogorodnik's request sometime before.

Petrie, Sir David

(b. 1879 d. 1961)

Director-General of the British Security Service (MI5) during most of World War II.

Petrie began his career in the Indian Police, becoming assistant director of criminal intelligence. He was director of the Indian Intelligence Bureau from 1924 to 1931. Although his intelligence experience was confined to India, in 1940 Prime Minister Winston Churchill chose him to succeed Maj. Gen. Sir VERNON KELL, the founder and first head of MI5. Churchill had an unfounded belief that Britain was infested with saboteurs and subversives known collectively as the FIFTH COLUMN.

Churchill fired Kell after MI5 failed to find fifth columnists. The firing was triggered by an explosion of a gunpowder factory in Waltham Abbey in Jan. 1940. The explosion was later judged to be an accident, not an act of sabotage. When he was appointed, Petrie was given a three-tier commission—2nd lieutenant, acting colonel, and local brigadier—in the Army Intelligence Corps.

Petrie recruited intellectuals, eccentrics, and a motley crew of wartime operatives who performed brilliantly.

Under him, the DOUBLE-CROSS SYSTEM was developed—a scheme that TURNED German AGENTS, who sent a stream of false intelligence to the ABWEHR, German MILITARY INTELLIGENCE, while under MI5 control.

Petrie reorganized MI5 and brought in technical expertise. He also established a closer liaison with the Secret Intelligence Service (MI6.). He served until April 1946.

Petrov, Vladimir M.

A senior KGB officer who defected in Australia in April 1954. Under questioning by the Australian INTELLIGENCE OFFICERS, he gave details about the 1951 escape of British DEFECTORS DONALD MACLEAN and GUY BURGESS.

Petrov said a THIRD MAN was involved, and British newspapers seized on the term, eventually pinning the label on HAROLD (KIM) PHILBY.

Petrov joined Soviet intelligence (OGPU) in 1933 as a CIPHER clerk. During World War II he was stationed at the Soviet Embassy in Stockholm, Sweden, and in 1951 he was assigned to the Soviet Embassy in Canberra, Australia.

After the execution of LAVRENTY BERIA in Dec. 1953, Petrov had been implicated in Beria's plot to seize control of the Soviet government following the death of Soviet dictator Josef Stalin. When Petrov was recalled to Moscow, he defected while in Sydney. He exposed the Soviet espionage NETWORK in Australia, as well as details about Soviet CRYPTOLOGY.

PFIAB

SEE PRESIDENT'S FOREIGN INTELLIGENCE ADVISORY BOARD

Phelippes, Thomas

CIPHER and CODE expert in the employment of Sir FRANCIS WALSINGHAM, who ran an extensive intelligence organization for Queen Elizabeth I.

England's first great cryptologist, as early as 1538 Phelippes was in Paris working for Walsingham, corresponding with Walsingham's spies, and breaking into secret communications that were sent to him. He created secure ciphers and codes for English AGENTS and broke those of state enemies, including those used by supporters of Mary Stuart (Queen of Scots). He was skilled in solving ciphers originally written in French, Italian, Latin, and—to a limited extent—in Spanish as well as English.

The only known physical description of Phelippes was written by Mary Stuart; she described him as having blonde hair and a beard, and being "of low stature, slender every way, eated in the face with small pocks, of short sight, thirty years of age by appearance."

Ironically, it was probably Phelippes' work that brought about the death of Mary Stuart. Walsingharn, through his spies and interception of Mary Stuart's mail, was able to learn of a plot to assassinate Queen Elizabeth. But Walsingham lacked the names of the six young men who were to kill the queen. A letter sent by Mary Stuart on July 17, 1586, to one of her former pages, ANTHONY BABINGTON, was intercepted by Walsingham and found to contain an enciphered message.

Walsingham apparently had Phelippes add a postscript before it was resealed and sent on to Babington. The postscript—in the same cipher—asked for "the names and qualities of the six gentlemen which are to accomplish the designment."

Walsingham, however, decided to arrest Babington before he could respond. Babington and the six young men fled but were caught and condemned to death within a month. The letters that Phelippes had deciphered were used to convict Mary Stuart, who was convicted of high treason. She was beheaded on Feb. 8, 1587. American historian DAVID KAHN wrote in *The Codebreakers* (1968):

> There seems little doubt that [Mary Stuart] would have died before her time, the politics of the day being what they were. But there seems equally little doubt that cryptology hastened her unnatural end.

Philby, Harold A. R. (Kim)

(b. 1912 d. 1988)

Master Soviet spy who served as a longtime MOLE in British intelligence, betraying his country, his class, and countless victims of Cold War operations that he divulged. The THIRD MAN in the CAMBRIDGE SPY RING, he met two other members—GUY BURGESS and DONALD MACLEAN—at Cambridge in the 1930s. (See also ANTHONY BLUNT and JOHN CAIRNCROSS.)

He was the son of Harry St. John Philby, an explorer and adventurer who went to India as assistant commissioner in the Punjab and married there in 1910; his best man was Lt. Bernard Montgomery, who later became one of the most famous British generals of World War II (For a time in that war, St. John Philby, an avowed fascist, would be interned as a potential enemy of Britain.)

During World War I and before Iraq became a country, the ancient land was still known as Mesopotamia. British MILITARY INTELLIGENCE sent St. John Philby into "Mespot," as the British called it, to pit the tribesmen of King Ibn Saud of Saudi Arabia against tribes that favored the Turks. He succeeded brilliantly, becoming a confidant of King Ibn Saud. He was considered an "honorable correspondent," one of a number of upper-class Britons who provided information, or even went on missions, for Britain's MI6.

The Philbys' first child, Harold Adrian Russell Philby, was born in India. He was nicknamed KIM, after Rudyard Kipling's young spy hero. Philby attended his father's school, Westminster, and in 1929 went to Trinity College, Cambridge, to read history before taking the civil service examination. At Cambridge he was recruited by Soviet intelligence. "I was given the assignment to infiltrate COUNTERESPIONAGE however long it took," he later wrote. ". . . How, where, and when I became a member of the Soviet intelligence service is a matter for myself and my comrades."

He left Cambridge in 1933 and went to VIENNA, where on Feb. 24, 1934, he married Alice ("Litzi") Friedman, a communist being hunted down by the police. His wife's friend, EDITH TUDOR HART, a Soviet TALENT SPOTTER, saw him as a potential spy. By marrying Philby, Litzi received a British passport. At the time, Philby was portraying himself as an anticommunist and a supporter of General Francisco Franco in the Spanish Civil War. But he had made many friends among the communists and socialists in Vienna.

After a stint of writing for a liberal monthly, Philby continued his journalistic career by covering the Spanish Civil War for *The Times* of London. He was with the Nationalist forces of Franco and presented himself publicly as pro-fascist. He left Spain in 1939 and separated from Litzi because he was developing a new right-wing image and could not have a communist wife.

Philby claimed that after Spain he was again recruited for espionage work—this time by MI6. But according to British intelligence sources, Philby applied to get into MI6 and was aided by his father, who contacted "C," traditionally anonymous head of the Secret Intelligence Service (Sir STEWART MENZIES at the time). Despite the security problems that his marriage might cause, Philby was accepted into the intelligence service. In Sept. 1941 he was offered an executive post in Section V, the counterespionage part of SIS, "the heart of the secret world," as he described it.

Taking command of the Iberian subsection of Section V, he worked closely during the war with the SPECIAL OPERATIONS EXECUTIVE (SOE), which ran resistance groups and guerrilla activities in German-occupied countries. Among his agents were MALCOLM MUGGERIDGE and GRAHAM GREENE. Philby's performance in directing operations in Spain, Portugal, North Africa, and Italy won him high praise. Menzies took a liking to him. Fellow officers speculated that he might someday become "C."

In Oct. 1944 he was assigned to head a new part of SIS, Section IX, which would seek out communist penetration AGENTS. His appointment, Philby later wrote, "by anyone's standards was a grotesque mistake to make." In 18 months Philby expanded the one-man, one-room section into department that filled a whole floor and employed more than 30.

Philby came perilously close to being unmasked in Aug. 1945, when KONSTANTIN VOLKOV, an INTELLIGENCE OFFICER for the NKVD became a DEFECTOR. Volkov, whose COVER was vice consul at the Soviet Consulate in Istanbul, contacted his opposite number at the British Consulate and offered information on Soviet moles in the British government. He said two were in the Foreign Office and one was head of a COUNTERINTELLIGENCE agency in London. He warned that neither his information nor his offer to defect should be cabled to London because the Soviets had broken the British diplomatic CODES (which was not true).

Volkov's claim about moles was sent to London by diplomatic pouch and arrived a week later at MI6, reaching the desk of Philby—who realized that he was one of the moles that Volkov was to name. "I stared at the papers rather longer than necessary to compose my thoughts," Philby later wrote in his self-serving memoir, *My Silent War* (1968). Through a combination of luck and conniving, Philby managed to replace another intelligence officer who was to have gone to Istanbul. By the time Philby got to Istanbul, Volkov had vanished and was never heard of again. Apparently, Philby had contacted his Soviet HANDLER in London to pass on the information about Volkov's defection, dooming the would-be defector to execution.

Philby had better control of the situation when another defection occurred in Sept. 1945. IGOR GOUZENKO, a CIPHER clerk at the Soviet Embassy in Ottawa, defected and began telling Canadian intelligence officials what he knew. While Gouzenko was being debriefed in Canada, the MI6 officer attending the briefing sent his daily reports to Philby, who was able to pass what Gouzenko was telling the Soviets. Although Gouzenko's information led to the exposure of Col. NIKOLAI ZABOTIN, ALLAN NUNN MAY, and others, Philby escaped exposure.

In 1945 Philby received the Order of the British Empire for his wartime intelligence work. He had been nominated by Menzies. On the way back from Buckingham Palace after the investiture, Philby remarked to his companion, JAMES JESUS ANGLETON of the CIA, "What this country needs is a good stiff dose of socialism." As Angleton later recounted, he was stunned by the remark and filed it away.

In 1946, Philby married Aileen Furse, whom he had met in 1940 and with whom he had been living for some time. She had worked at BLETCHLEY PARK. They had three children while they lived together, and Aileen was pregnant when they married. (To marry, Philby had to be divorced from Litzi Friedman. MI5 tracked her down to East BERLIN, where she was living with a Soviet agent; she herself had spied for the Soviets while she lived in Britain. Knowledge of Litzi's background did not affect Philby's security clearance.)

At the end of 1946 Philby was posted to Istanbul as MI6 chief there to get field experience. During his two years in Turkey he sent some agents into Soviet Turkestan, to their doom. While in Istanbul, he was asked by his Soviet handler about an FBI investigation involving the British Embassy in Washington. This was an oblique reference to what had been triggered by an operation code-named VENONA, to break Soviet coded messages intercepted some time before. Decryption had indicated that a Soviet spy was working in the British Embassy.

After two years in Istanbul, Philby was sent to Washington, D.C., as MI6 liaison officer to the CIA and the FBI, one of the most sensitive postings in British intelligence. This, he later wrote, was "the era" of a spy roster he named—ALGER HISS, JUDITH COPLON, KLAUS FUCHS, HARRY GOLD, DAVID GREENGLASS, "and the brave" JULIUS [and ETHEL] ROSENBERG. Philby was also liaison officer to Canadian intelligence, enabling him to keep track of the ongoing investigations prompted by Gouzenko's disclosures.

Prior to his departure for Washington in 1949 Philby was briefed by Sir MAURICE OLDFIELD, who now had Philby's old job as head of Section IX. Oldfield told Philby about the Venona operation and also about the ATOMIC SPY RING investigation.

In Washington he was given relatively unencumbered access to U.S. intelligence agencies (but not U.S. MILITARY INTELLIGENCE, which was shared with the British through another channel). Philby became a particular confidant of Angleton, who by then was head of the CIA's Office of Strategic Operations. The two men met weekly to exchange secrets over lunch at Harvey's restaurant in Washington (a place also favored, coincidentally, by J. EDGAR HOOVER). "Our close association was, I am sure, inspired by genuine friendliness on both sides," Philby later wrote. "Our discussions ranged over the whole world. . . . Who gained most from this complex game I cannot say. But I had one big advantage. I knew what he was doing for the CIA, and he knew what I was doing for SIS. But the real nature of my interest was something he did not know."

Earlier in his career, Angleton had served with the OFFICE OF STRATEGIC SERVICES (OSS) in Rome. There he had met Teddy Kollek, who was conducting Rome-to-Palestine missions for what would become Israeli intelligence. Kollek had been in Vienna in 1934, when Philby married Litzi Friedman, and may have witnessed the wedding. Kollek, who subsequently became mayor of Jerusalem, visited Washington in 1949 and almost certainly met with his old friend Angleton. Years later, this led to speculation that Kollek told Angleton about Philby's communist connections in the 1930s, alerting Angleton to the possibility that Philby was a DOUBLE AGENT. Under this theory, Angleton made use of Philby while Philby was thinking he was making use of Angleton. But American intelligence authorities of the era strongly deny this possibility.

MEREDITH GARDNER, a U.S. codebreaker, also had contact with Philby in his role as liaison officer. Gardner, the key man in the Verona codebreaking, showed Philby some of the decrypted material and said that the suspected mole was in the British Foreign Office. Philby realized that Donald Maclean would soon be exposed and warned the KGB.

He also cabled the SIS in London, reminding officials that two Soviet defectors—Volkov and WALTER KRIVITSKY—had hinted that a high-ranking Foreign Office official from a good family had been a Soviet agent since the 1930s. This reminder would almost certainly intensify suspicions about Maclean. But Philby coolly reasoned that, after Maclean escaped, security officials would look back at Philby's warning and believe that he had not collaborated with Maclean.

Burgess and Maclean escaped to the Soviet Union in May 1951. (For details, see DONALD MACLEAN entry.) Philby immediately came under suspicion by both his own colleagues and U.S. intelligence. He drove to a desolate spot in Virginia and buried the camera, tripod, and other paraphernalia he had used to copy documents. Philby, now feeling "clean as a whistle," braced for the crisis, which he believed he could wriggle out of because British and American intelligence officials would hesitate to move against him without high-level orders from their superiors.

Angleton, however, was suspicious enough of Philby to convince WALTER BEDELL SMITH, DIRECTOR OF CENTRAL INTELLIGENCE, to ask the SIS to recall Philby because he was no longer acceptable to the CIA. Hoover agreed with Smith—a rare happening. Philby returned to London while Aileen, pregnant with their fifth child, remained in Washington.

In London, security officials seized Philby's passport and questioned him about his friendship with Burgess. Asked about Maclean, Philby said he did not know him and had in fact only met him twice since Cambridge. Despite these disavowals, he was dismissed in July, given £2,000 in severance pay, and promised £2,000 more in monthly payments over the next three years.

His passport was returned, and with the help of "C" (Adm. Sir HUGH SINCLAIR), Philby got a job as a correspondent in the Middle East for The *Observer* and *The Economist,* despite the fact that British newspapers were hinting that defector VLADIMIR M. PETROV, talking about the Burgess-Maclean escape, had named Philby as "the third man"—a phrase that would reverberate for years.

On Oct. 25, 1955, a member of Parliament asked Prime Minister Anthony Eden about Philby's role as the "third man." Foreign Secretary Harold Macmillan, who succeeded Eden as Prime Minister, publicly cleared Philby in the parliamentary debate that followed.

Philby had been a highly effective Soviet ASSET. While he was in Washington, for example, he learned of Anglo-American attempts to overthrow the communist government in Albania by sending in hundreds of guerrillas, first in an amphibious landing, then by parachute. The Soviets passed Philby's information on to the Albanians, who killed nearly all of the guerrillas. The rest were imprisoned. None escaped.

When Philby, seemingly cleared, went off to Beirut as a correspondent, his employers were not told that his work would be cover for reemployment by MI6. Incredibly, he went back to work as an AGENT, for the KGB also made contact with him in Beirut. (According to his handler, most of Philby's reports were valuable political observations rather than intelligence tidbits.) When Nicholas Elliott, an old friend from MI6, was appointed head of station in Beirut, Philby became one of his trusted agents as well!

In Beirut, Philby was reunited with his father.

Harold (Kim) Philby. (UPI/BETTMAN)

Philby's wife and five children remained in England, where on Dec. 11, 1957, Aileen died of heart problems complicated by tuberculosis. Philby had been carrying on an affair with Eleanor Brewer, wife of Sam Pope Brewer, *The New York Times* correspondent in Beirut. She divorced Brewer, married Philby in London in Jan. 1959, and returned to Beirut with him and his children.

In Dec. 1961 the net again closed around Philby. ANATOLY GOLITSYN, a KGB officer, defected to the CIA, which shared his disclosures with British intelligence officers. When they debriefed Golitsyn in the summer of 1962, they became convinced that Philby was a spy. In 1961 a turncoat British intelligence officer, GEORGE BLAKE, had been sentenced to 42 years for spying, and Philby could assume that a similar fate awaited him if he tried to make a deal.

Sometime late in 1962, MI6 decided it had enough evidence to confront Philby and possibly wring a confession from him. Nicholas Elliott, then in London, volunteered to carry out the mission. At the confrontation in Jan. 1963, Elliott told Philby, "I'm offering you a lifeline, Kim. Immunity from prosecution if you co-operate." Philby returned next day with a two-page typewritten confession that was largely fraudulent. For three days Elliott recorded more admissions, then returned to London, wondering if Philby would commit suicide.

But Philby escaped. KGB operatives in Beirut smuggled him aboard an Odessa-bound Soviet freighter. The Soviet government waited until July 3, 1963, to announce that he had been made a citizen of the Soviet Union and was living in Moscow. Later Philby became the first holder of the Order of the British Empire to be awarded the Order of the Red Banner. He worked for the KGB and, according to some Soviet reports, played a role in the rise to power of KGB chief YURI ANDROPOV. He also spent time writing *My Silent War.*

Eleanor Philby joined her husband in Moscow in Sept. 1963. In 1964, after returning from a visit to the United States, she discovered that Philby was carrying on an affair with Maclean's wife, Melinda. In May 1965 Eleanor returned to the United States. She wrote *The Spy I Loved* (1968) shortly before she died.

Melinda left Philby in 1966 and eventually returned to the United States. Through GEORGE BLAKE, a fellow British spy, Philby met a beautiful Russian woman, Rufina Ivanova, who was about 20 years his junior. They were married in Moscow in Dec. 1971.

In March 1988, in an interview with *The Sunday Times* of London, he said, "Although life here has its difficulties, I feel I belong and I never want to live anywhere else. It's my country and I served it more than 50 years. I want to be buried here. I want to rest where my work has been." Two months later, on May 11, he died of heart disease. He was buried in Kuntsevo military cemetery in Moscow, with the honors of a KGB general. Rufina Philby later wrote, with co-authors, a memoir, *The Private Life of Kim Philby: The Moscow Years* (2001), in which she says Philby did "an occasional job for the KGB" in Moscow; she provides no details.

In a clever work of fiction, *The Blue List* (1989),

British spy writer NIGEL WEST weaves a tale that Philby was actually a TRIPLE AGENT, in fact working for Britain against the Soviet intelligence services. But, in *The Crown Jewels* (1999), a nonfiction book written with ex-KGB officer, West devotes 50 pages of the book to samples of Philby's output preserved in KGB achives. The archives, West wrote, show that Philby was "an incisive, driven intellect dedicated to giving the Russians as comprehensive a picture as possible of how Britain's secret warriors conducted their business."

In 1990 the Soviet government issued a POSTAGE STAMP honoring Philby as part of a series of KGB heroes.

Phoenix

U.S. operation, run from 1967 to 1971, to identify and destroy the communist apparatus in South VIETNAM. Phoenix was a combined effort of the CIA, the U.S. Army, the Special Branch of the South Vietnamese Police, and South Vietnam's Central Intelligence Organization. But the CIA dominated through the U.S. aspect of the program, called ICEX (Intelligence Coordination and Exploitation).

ICEX was to collect information on what was called the "Vietcong infrastructure" and to "neutralize" it. Robert W. Komer, a CIA INTELLIGENCE OFFICER ran that effort, which he renamed Phoenix. His deputy, who in 1968 took over Phoenix, was WILLIAM E. COLBY who in 1973 became DIRECTOR OF CENTRAL INTELLIGENCE. (In Vietnam his COVER was director of Civil Operations and Rural Development Support for the Agency for International Development.)

According to the CIA, in the period 1968–1971 Operation Phoenix granted amnesty to 17,000 suspected communists; 28,000 were captured and 20,587 killed. Most of those killed died in military combat operations, their deaths being "credited" to Phoenix. The rest were killed by police or other security forces.

Colby always denied that Phoenix was involved in assassination, John Prados wrote in *Lost Crusader* (2003), adding, "Ultimately, the record should show that Phoenix was not an assassination program per se. . . . But what Phoenix *did* do, which its former czar consistently refused to acknowledge, was to elicit, indeed demand, lawlessness on the part of the Saigon regime and its American advisers."

Photographic Intelligence

(PHOTINT)

Intelligence based on conventional photography. In modern times PHOTINT is a subset of IMAGERY INTELLIGENCE.

PHOTINT had its beginnings as an important intelligence activity in World War I, especially when the photographs were taken from an AIRCRAFT. In World War II aerial photography reached greater levels of significance, with photography from SUBMARINES also gaining prominence. German-made cameras were the best available.

Indeed, during photo missions by the U.S. submarine *Nautilus* in the Pacific during World War II the Navy found that cameras built expressly for taking pictures through submarine periscopes were not as good as the hand-held German Primarflex. Because it was impossible for the U.S. Navy to purchase the Primarflex during the war, officials advertised in photography magazines for donations. As a result, ten Primarflex cameras were contributed to the Navy for use on photo missions.

In the post–World War II era photography has remained as important for intelligence services as have ELECTRONIC INTELLIGENCE and other specialized means of gathering information. The Cold War accelerated the development of wide-angle, high-speed cameras that could be effectively used from high-flying aircraft such as the CANBERRA, B-36, U-2, A-12 OXCART, SR-71 BLACKHAWK, BEAR, and MYSTIC.

Subsequently, advanced cameras were adopted for spy SATELLITES, beginning with the U.S. CORONA and the Soviet ZENIT.

Photographic Interpretation

The extraction of intelligence from photography of TARGET areas. Photography can be taken by AIRCRAFT, SATELLITES, SUBMARINES, UNMANNED AERIAL VEHICLES, surface ships, and by people on the ground.

The Official World War II Guide to the Army Air Forces, published by the U.S. Army in 1944, provided a useful description, although limited in scope to aerial photography:

> Photographic intelligence is derived from the interpretation of aerial photographs taken primarily by reconnaissance aircraft, and secondarily by cameras on bombing aircraft during bombing missions. Highly trained photo-interpreters analyze the photographs to prepare factual reports on damage assessment, industry, transportation, airfield activity, ground and coast defenses, camouflage, dummys and decoys, communications, ground force activities, shipping and ship building. Most important information is obtained by comparison of recent photographs with previously obtained photographs of the same area. Great advances have been made in the field of aerial photography in its military application through the development of various types of cameras for specialized jobs including high attitude, low altitude, high-speed, infra-red, mapping, color and night photography.

Not mentioned—for security reasons—was the beginning of radar photography, the image of radar "pictures" of areas of specific interest. The 1944 publication also stated: "Photographic reconnaissance contributes the largest portion of intelligence upon which military decisions can be based." The authors of *The Official World War II Guide to the Army Air Forces* had no knowledge of the Allied codebreaking efforts (i.e., MAGIC-ULTRA).

See NATIONAL PHOTOGRAPHIC INTERPRETATION CENTER and NATIONAL IMAGERY AND MAPPING AGENCY.

Pianist

Intelligence slang for a clandestine radio operator.

Piano

Intelligence slang for a clandestine radio.

Pickering, Jeffery L.

U.S. Navy enlisted man who admitted sending a five-page secret document to the Soviet Embassy in Washington, D.C., in 1983, apparently hoping to become a spy. When he was arrested by the FBI, he had a plastic addressograph card imprinted with the embassy's address. At the time he was stationed at the Naval Regional Medical Clinic in Seattle, Wash. He was sentenced to five years at hard labor and given a bad conduct discharge.

Pied Piper

U.S. Air Force classified competition for commercial firms held in 1955 to generate design studies for a SATELLITE RECONNAISSANCE system. This effort—to some extent a continuation of Project FEEDBACK—was a milestone in the development of U.S. spy satellites.

Pig

Russian intelligence term for a traitor.

Pigeon Post

Pigeons, with their unerring homing instincts, have been used to carry messages—often communications from spies—since Biblical times. Pigeons carried news of Olympic victories to Greeks absent from the games. The sultan of Baghdad set up a pigeon post in 1150 to link outposts in his empire.

During the siege of Paris in 1870–1871, Parisians sent out crates of pigeons in BALLOONS to friendly forces outside of the city. The pigeons flew back with messages over Prussian siege lines. One pigeon could carry numerous dispatches reduced by microphotography to MICRODOTS. Early in the 20th century Julius Neubronner, a German photographer, strapped 2½-ounce cameras on pigeons and sent them aloft to demonstrate their reconnaissance potential; an automatic timer clicked the shutter every 30 seconds.

During World War I a pigeon post linked Allied trenches. Balloons used in RECONNAISSANCE went aloft with pigeons that were dispatched to wing messages to the ground. The British Army's Field Intelligence Department used carrier pigeons for communications. A heroic pigeon, Cher Ami, carried messages that saved the American "lost battalion." Although wounded, Cher Ami flew 25 miles in 25 minutes. He was awarded the French Croix de Guerre with Palm. When he died, a taxidermist preserved him, and he was later presented to the Smithsonian Institution in Washington, D.C.

British MI5 agents drew up lists of lofts used by German-trained homing pigeons in Belgium, West Holland, and the Balkans. British intelligence documents show that at least two German pigeons were captured. An INTELLIGENCE OFFICER said in a report, "Both birds are now prisoners of war working hard at breeding English pigeons." The pigeon project was thought to be inspired by

A carrier pigeon being released from the port in a British tank in northern France in 1918. Pigeon post was used through World War II, but was superseded by radio communications, which are faster and more reliable. (IMPERIAL WAR MUSEUM)

SS chief HEINRICH HIMMLER, known by British intelligence to be a dedicated pigeon fancier.

French Resistance networks passed on bits of information to England in capsules borne by homing pigeons that the Royal Air Force had delivered in parachuted cages. Germans, aware of the winged spies, used marksmen and falcons to bring them down.

In World War II British troops that had just captured an Italian town sent back word via a pigeon named GI Joe. The message arrived just in time, for an air strike was about to be launched on the town. GI Joe received the Dickin Medal, awarded by the Royal Society for the Prevention of Cruelty to Animals. Another Dickin Medal went to a pigeon called Mercury for flying 480 miles over the North Sea to carry a message to Britain from a Danish resistance group.

In the 1950s, Israeli Army reconnaissance units, looking for Arab military installations in desert areas, equipped pigeons with electronic tracking devices. The birds were held until they were hungry, then sent off. The assumption was that the only food would be around an Arab camp. Tracking the pigeons electronically, the Israelis could secretly map likely sites for Arab facilities.

The U.S. Army pigeon service, which started during the Indian Wars of the 1870s, ended in 1957, when the last Army pigeons were distributed to zoos and pigeon hobbyists.

Pike Committee

U.S. House committee that in 1975 investigated charges of CIA and NSA abuses. The committee took its name from Representative Otis Pike (Democrat, New York). Testimony before the committee revealed some NSA activities publicly for the first time.

Prior to hearings of Aug. 1975, the committee requested the NSA "charter" that set forth the scope of the agency's power to intercept communications. The charter was actually an intelligence directive of the NATIONAL SECURITY COUNCIL issued in 1952, when NSA was secretly established. The charter had never been revealed.

The Pentagon official who represented NSA at the hearing appeared without the directive. Pike was outraged. "It seems incredible to me," he said, "that we are asked to appropriate large amounts of money for that agency which employs large numbers of people without being provided a copy of the piece of paper by which the agency is authorized." The committee voted unanimously to subpoena the directive. However, NSA and Justice Department officials managed to keep the directive from being made public (and except for a short section, it remained unrevealed).

WILLIAM E. COLBY, the DIRECTOR OF CENTRAL INTELLIGENCE, told the committee that NSA eavesdroped on "communications that go abroad from the United States or are abroad." Colby admitted that the communications of some Americans were picked up because their words "cannot be separated from the traffic that is being monitored." Colby then asked that any further discussion take place behind closed doors in executive session. Air Force Lt. Gen. LEW ALLEN, JR., the first NSA director ever to testify publicly, read a statement outlining the NSA's work—and then requested that questions of him also be asked in executive session.

Intelligence officials in both the CIA and NSA later complained about LEAKS from the committee. Pike's conduct of the hearings was often sharply partisan and criticized by Republicans. The result was disagreement on what should go into a final committee report. Much of the Pike Committee's work was overshadowed by the more extensive and better-organized CHURCH COMMITTEE.

The Pike Committee's report, issued in 1976, mentioned, for example, a "U.S. Navy submarine reconnaissance program often operating within unfriendly waters." This was IVY BELLS, a TOP SECRET Navy operation for tapping a Soviet seafloor communications cable. (It was not revealed until 1986, during the trial of RONALD PELTON, a former NSA analyst who had sold secrets—including Ivy Bells—to the Soviets.)

Pincher, Chapman

British author who wrote a book speculating that Sir ROGER HOLLIS, former Director-General of the British Security Service (MI5), had been a Soviet MOLE.

In 1976 Pincher, a well-known British defense writer, was planning to write a book based on former Prime Minister Harold Wilson's claims that the British Security Service had plotted to overthrow Wilson. After that book did not develop, Pincher wrote *Their Trade Is Treachery* (1981). The book was a sensation because of the charge against Hollis, who had headed MI5 from 1956 to 1965; he died in 1973. Pincher also believed that Hollis pushed through the clearances of KLAUS FUCHS, who was a Soviet spy.

Prime Minister Margaret Thatcher, in a statement in Parliament, denied that Hollis had been a Soviet mole, "although it was impossible to prove the negative." Meanwhile, the furor about Hollis continued.

One of Pincher's sources had been former MI5 officer PETER WRIGHT. (Some U.S. intelligence sources speculated that CIA COUNTERINTELLIGENCE chief JAMES JESUS ANGLETON had also "pointed Pincher toward the story.") Pincher found what he believed were more details and wrote *Too Secret Too Long* (1984), which furthered speculation about Hollis. Wright, who was in retirement in Tasmania, Australia, subsequently wrote *Spycatcher* (1987), which the British government tried to suppress. Wright made similar charges against Hollis.

Baron Victor Rothschild, a scientist, industrialist, and one-time MI5 officer, paid for Wright to travel to England to meet with Pincher. Rothschild's role in setting up the meeting inspired media theories that he was controlling information in the hope of spiking rumors that he had served the Soviets. On Dec. 3, 1986, in a letter to the *Daily Telegraph*, Rothschild demanded that the Director-General of MI5 "state publicly that it has unequivocal, repeat unequivocal, evidence that I am not, and never have been, a Soviet agent." Two days later Thatcher stated, "I am advised that we have no evidence that he was ever a Soviet agent." The question still bore that ambiguous answer when Rothschild died in 1990 at the age of 80.

Pinkerton, Allan

(b. 1819 d. 1884)

Private detective who during the American Civil War ran a MILITARY INTELLIGENCE service that produced very poor intelligence.

Pinkerton was born in Glasgow, Scotland, the son of a police sergeant Glasgow policeman who had been crippled in a riot. Apprenticed to a cooper but sensing a better future in the United States, he emigrated when he was 23, settling first in Chicago, and then setting up a cooper's shop in a nearby town in Kent County. After capturing a gang of counterfeiters, he was appointed a deputy sheriff, first in Kent County and then in Cook County, with headquarters in Chicago. He joined the newly organized police force there and became a detective, resigning in 1850 to found the Pinkerton National Detective Agency.

The agency's specialty was tracking and capturing railroad bandits. In 1860 a war over slavery was looming, and railroads were a potential target of sabotage. That year several of the Southern states seceded from the Union. Maryland, a border state, was still in the Union, but secessionists in Maryland were plotting to sabotage the railroads. The Philadelphia, Wilmington & Baltimore Railroad asked Pinkerton to send agents to Baltimore to thwart the saboteurs.

Pinkerton's success in protecting the railroads led to his being hired to guard President-elect Abraham Lincoln as he traveled to Washington, D.C., for his inauguration. Pinkerton and his detectives, learning of an assassination plot, arranged a night train for a secret trip that would carry Lincoln through Maryland to Washington.

Soon after the Civil War began in April 1861, Pinkerton was asked by Maj. Gen. George B. McClellan, then commander of the Union Army's Ohio Department, to establish an intelligence NETWORK. Under the COVER name Maj. E. J. Allen, Pinkerton traveled in the South, taking the measure of the political and military climate. When McClellan took command of the Army of the Potomac in the summer of 1861, Pinkerton accompanied him to Washington, where he set up a COUNTERINTELLIGENCE operation against Confederate AGENTS.

McClellan, lacking a formal military intelligence service, relied on Pinkerton and his detectives, whose investigative experience had been limited to railroad bandits and safe crackers. Some historians attribute McClellan's hesitancy in battle to a consistent exaggeration of Confederate strength, misinformation that can be traced to Pinkerton and his men. In July 1862, for example, Pinkerton estimated that Confederate Gen. Robert E. Lee had more than 200,000 men in his Army of Virginia. Mc-

Clellan's quartermaster general, basing his figure on a systematic study of Southern newspapers, estimated that Lee's forces totaled 60,000 to 105,000 men. Lee actually had fewer than 90,000 men.

At the battle of ANTIETAM in Sept. 1862, McClellan had a two-to-one superiority over Lee's forces and, through a Confederate security leak, a copy of Lee's plan for the invasion of Maryland. But McClellan relied on Pinkerton's poor intelligence reports and failed to exploit the Union's advantages.

Pinkerton claimed that his men gathered solid intelligence by such methods as interviewing Confederate deserters and counting Confederate campfires. But he invariably overestimated, sometimes by more than 100 percent. One of his most effective operations involved the interrogation of runaway slaves, many of whom he induced to TURN, sending them back into the South to collect TACTICAL INTELLIGENCE. (See BLACK INTELLIGENCE.)

His counterintelligence record in Washington was slightly better, for his men did apprehend several Confederate spies. But he released the skilled BELLE BOYD after personally interrogating her.

When Lincoln fired McClellan for his "slows," Pinkerton lost his patron and shifted from conducting battlefield intelligence to investigating profiteering businessmen. With his departure, a BUREAU OF INFORMATION

Allan Pinkerton with President Lincoln at Antietam, 1862. (LIBRARY OF CONGRESS/MATHEW BRADY)

was established under Col. GEORGE H. SHARPE. (Also see LAFAYETTE BAKER.)

After the war, Pinkerton resumed operation of his detective agency, which had begun to spread nationwide. The "Pinkertons" became especially known for their work as strikebreakers as well as private detectives.

Pinkroot I

SEE *PUEBLO*.

Pinnacle

Message series used by U.S. military forces to warn of foreign contact or interference. Pinnacle messages were sent by the *PUEBLO*, a U.S. INTELLIGENCE COLLECTION SHIP at the time of her capture by North Korean forces on Jan. 23, 1968.

Pitts, Earl Edwin

(b. 1953)

One of three FBI agents convicted of espionage. (The others were RICHARD MILLER and ROBERT P. HANSSEN.)

Pitts was arrested on Dec. 19, 1996, after a 16-month "sting" operation that involved his wife, Mary, a former FBI employee. The arrest rocked the U.S. INTELLIGENCE COMMUNITY, already in shock over the treachery of ALDRICH H. AMES and HAROLD J. NICHOLSON, both trusted CIA INTELLIGENCE OFFICERS. Nicholson's arrest had come a month before the arrest of Pitts. At first Pitts pleaded not guilty and appeared ready to stand trial. But, faced with what prosecutors said were 5,700 items of evidence, he agreed to a plea bargain that spared the government a trial and spared him the life sentence that a trial could have produced.

On Feb. 28, 1997, he pleaded guilty to spying for the Soviet Union and Russia. When the federal judge asked him why he became a spy, Pitts said, "I gave in to an unreasoning anger." Knowing that Pitts had earned thousands of dollars for his treachery, the judge said, "You never mentioned simple greed," and sentenced him to 27 years in prison.

Pitts, during an interview at the federal prison in Ashland, Kentucky, said that in June 1997 he had told FBI investigators that he was suspicious of ROBERT P. HANSSEN, who was arrested as a spy in Feb. 2001.

One piece of evidence was a computer disk found in Pitts's home. On it was a letter that Pitts had written on Feb. 25, 1990, to his KGB HANDLERS, explaining how difficult it was for him to make contact. At that time he was working in the FBI's records management office at Washington headquarters. He suggested DEAD DROP meetings for March through Dec. 1990. "For drop operations," he wrote, "I will pack my materials in milk cartons, with packing around the materials. The materials you will receive at the drops will be primarily film."

Other pieces of evidence came from the sting operation. To make it credible, the FBI allowed Pitts to provide TOP SECRET material to the agents posing as Russians. If the case against Pitts had gone to trial, the CLASSIFIED INFORMATION PROCEDURE ACT (CIPA) would have been invoked. The act sets down procedures for the introduction of classified material in trials. When Pitts pleaded guilty, one of his attorneys was undergoing a security clearance in anticipation of a CIPA-governed trial.

Pitts started spying for the Soviets in July 1987, while working on Squad 19 at the FBI office in New York. The squad's assignment was the SURVEILLANCE and recruitment of Soviet officials at the UNITED NATIONS.

He was in a position to provide invaluable information to the Soviets—and do tremendous damage to the FBI. He had access to the case files of a key FBI unit, the Soviet Espionage Squad, which trolled the United Nations for spies and potential DEFECTORS IN PLACE. Two of the squad's most famous cases were code-named TOP HAT and FEDORA.

Members of the squad worked undercover, coming in contact with Soviets while posing as business executives and even as waiters in restaurants near the United Nations. Pitts could tell his handlers about FBI surveillance techniques that the Soviets could then counter. Pitts' meetings with Soviets would not alert his fellow FBI agents because meeting and recruiting Soviets was his mission. Pitts began his betrayal by offering himself to Rollan Dzheikiya, a Soviet official at the UN. Dzheikiya set up a meeting between Pitts and the man who would be his KGB handler, Aleksandr Karpov. The place of the meeting was the main branch of the New York Public Library, on Fifth Avenue.

The FBI began a counterespionage investigation of Pitts in 1995 after Dzheikiya informed on him. Dzheikiya had retired from the Soviet foreign service and was working in New York for a Moscow-based trade firm. In order to get a green card quickly, he contacted the FBI and revealed that Pitts had started selling secrets to the KGB about six months after he was assigned to New York. (Pitts later said that he had offered his services because he needed money to live in expensive New York City.)

In a damage assessment of Pitts's betrayal, the FBI said he had access to "recruitment of Russian intelligence officers, DOUBLE AGENT operations, operations targeting Russian intelligence officers, the identities of U.S. spies, methods of recruiting DEFECTORS, and SURVEILLANCE schedules." The FBI said that no one was killed as a result of Pitts' treachery.

After serving in New York from Jan. 1987 to Aug. 1989, Pitts was assigned, at his request, to the Washington headquarters of the FBI. There he had access to virtually every file held by the agency, and from 1991 he supervised personnel security investigations at headquarters. Between 1989 and 1992 he made at least nine trips to New York City to supply information to his handlers. After each trip he made deposits in one or more of the eight bank and credit union accounts kept jointly by Pitts and his wife, Mary, who worked as a clerk for the FBI.

Following the collapse of the Soviet Union in 1991, Pitts continued to spy for Russia through the successor to the KGB, the SVR. He went dormant as a spy in 1992 when he was transferred to the FBI's legal counsel division, a poor location for espionage. By then he had earned at least $224,000 and had another $100,000 waiting for him in Russia if he decided to use an elaborate plan for an escape to Moscow.

The FBI sting involved a FALSE FLAG operation in which FBI agents posing as Russian intelligence officers reactivated him as a spy. During the sting, he made 22 deliveries of classified FBI documents to men he believed to be Russian spymasters. The fake Russians paid him $65,000, with every delivery and transaction being filmed.

The operation had begun on Aug. 26, 1995, when Rollan Dzheikiya showed up at Pitts's Virginia home and said he wanted to see Pitts. Mrs. Pitts became suspicious and in a later search of her husband's home office, found classified documents. She contacted the FBI, unaware that Dzheikiya had launched the sting operation, Pitts was already under surveillance, and their telephone tapped, under a secret warrant from the FOREIGN INTELLIGENCE SURVEILLANCE COURT. Pitts, meanwhile, had been transferred from FBI headquarters to the FBI Academy at Quantico, Va., where he would have less access to sensitive information and would be easier to observe.

The FBI wiretappers picked up a telephone call to a neighbor in which Mrs. Pitts told of going to the FBI with her suspicions. "I probably shouldn't have gone, shouldn't have gone to the Bureau, and it will probably mean the end of my marriage either way it goes," she said. "If he is on the up and up and he finds out that I went behind his back, we're finished." Told of the sting, she cooperated with the FBI.

Pitts had entered the FBI in 1983, after graduating from the University of Missouri Law School in Kansas City. He previously had served in the Army for five years as a fulfillment of his Reserve Officer Training Corps requirements at Central Missouri State University. He reached the rank of captain.

Plain Text

Original message in ordinary language—before being encoded or enciphered, or after being decoded or deciphered.

Plame, Valerie

CIA covert operative whose identity was revealed in 2003, creating a political uproar. Her name was printed on July 14, 2003, in the syndicated column of Robert Novak eight days after her husband, retired Ambassador Joseph C. Wilson IV, had written a *New York Times* article revealing that he had gone to Niger to investigate a report that Iraq had tried to buy "yellowcake" uranium from that country. Wilson found no such deal and charged that "some of the intelligence related to Iraq's nuclear program was twisted to exaggerate the Iraqi threat."

According to Novak, "Two senior administration officials told me Wilson's wife suggested sending him to Niger." Novak went on to say that Plame was a CIA operative who specialized in weapons of mass destruction (WMD). Infuriated, Wilson accused the Bush administration of setting up the LEAK—and thus ruining his wife's career—as retaliation for his criticism of the administration. The incident touched off investigations into the leaking of her name. CIA sources described her as being under NON-OFFICIAL COVER, posing as a private consultant on WMD. The deliberate identifying of covert operatives is a crime under the Intelligence Identities Protection Act of 1982.

Plausible Denial

Originally a way to arrange, coordinate, and conduct U.S. COVERT ACTION so as to "plausibly" permit official denial of U.S. involvement, sponsorship, or support. Later this concept evolved into a way for high officials and their subordinates to communicate without saying anything incriminating. In cautiously discussing possible covert action, they would not use precise language and thus would not reveal authorization and involvement. If they did say or write anything, under the doctrine of plausible deniability, their words would not be embarrassing or politically damaging if publicly revealed.

When a U-2 spyplane was shot down over the Soviet Union, for example, President Eisenhower had plausible deniability in the form of a COVER story that it was an unarmed plane on a weather-monitoring mission. That plausibility evaporated, however, when the Soviets revealed that the pilot, GARY POWERS, was alive and had confessed that he was a spy.

The words *plausible deniability* themselves are never used. A wordy nondefinition came in testimony in 1975 before the CHURCH COMMITTEE, which, among other issues, was investigating assassination plans fomented by the CIA. RICHARD M. BISSELL, JR., chief of CIA clandestine operations, was explaining how ALLEN W. DULLES, DIRECTOR OF CENTRAL INTELLIGENCE, had to brief President Eisenhower and President Kennedy on assassination plans: Dulles would indicate "the general objective of the operation that was contemplated, to make that sufficiently clear so that the president . . . could have ordered the termination of the operation, but to give the president just as little information about it as possible, beyond an understanding of its general purpose. Such an approach would have had as its purpose to leave him in the position to deny knowledge of the operation if it should surface."

Playback

To provide false information to an enemy while drawing out accurate information by impersonating a captured spy or by turning a spy, usually through radio transmissions. See DOUBLE-CROSS SYSTEM.

Playfair Cipher

Famous CIPHER of the 19th century, invented by Sir Charles Wheatstone, a British scientist and inventor whose achievements included the development of an electric telegraph before the invention of one by Samuel Morse in the United States.

Wheatstone's cipher was adopted by his friend and fellow scientist Baron Playfair who, in Jan. 1854, demonstrated it for Prince Albert, husband of Queen Victoria, and future Prime Minister Lord Palmerston. They were impressed by the cipher—which soon became known by Playfair's name, although he never claimed to have invented it.

Playfair is a block cipher that uses a key word followed by the remaining letters of the alphabet. If the key word is *COMPUTER* the block would look thus:

```
C  O  M  P  U
T  E  R  A  B
D  F  G  H  IJ
K  L  N  Q  S
V  W  X  Y  Z
```

The PLAIN TEXT is then enciphered with pairs of letters or digraphics. Pairs in the same row or column are replaced with the letters to their right; pairs not in the same row are replaced by the letter below them; and in pairs that are not in the same row or column, each letter is replaced by the letter that lies in its own row and stands in the column occupied by the other plain-text letter in the digraphic. Double letters have an X inserted between them (to avoid someone's reading the enciphered text and realizing that there is a double-letter word).

Thus, with the key word *COMPUTER*, the plaintext word *ATTACK* would have the letters paired, with an X between the double letters and another added at the end to given it an even number of letters. It becomes AT XT AC KX and would be enciphered as follows:

```
AT = BE
XT = RV
AC = TP
KX = NV
Or  E
B RV TP NV
```

The Playfair cipher was relatively easy to learn, remember, and use.

Wheatstone and Playfair explained the cipher to the Under Secretary of the Foreign Office. When the Under Secretary protested that it was too complicated, Wheatstone volunteered to show that three out of four boys at the nearby elementary school could be taught to use the cipher in 15 minutes. "That is very possible," said the Under Secretary, "but you could never teach it to ATTACHÉS."

But the cipher was employed by the Foreign Office and was used by British military forces in the Boer War and afterwards. Once learned, it was simple to use and difficult to break. For example, the digraphic minimizes the possibility of using letter frequency as a CRIB (for example, *e* being the most frequently used letter in the Eng-lish alphabet), while the insertion of an X between double letters further reduces the probability of cribs.

Wheatstone also invented a form of CIPHER DISK.

Plumbat

MOSSAD and LAKAM operation in 1968 to steal material for Israeli nuclear weapons production.

Plumbers

Special investigations unit established in 1971 by the Committee to Re-elect the President (Richard M. Nixon). The unit was to stop security LEAKS (hence the nickname) and to carry out clandestine intelligence collection and sabotage against the Democratic Party.

The Plumbers, who reported to John Ehrlichman, chief of staff to President Nixon, consisted of E. HOWARD HUNT, G. Gordon Liddy, David Young (assistant to National Security Adviser Henry Kissinger), and presidential assistant Egil (Bud) Krogh, Jr., who later became Undersecretary of Transportation.

The Plumbers supervised two BLACK BAG JOBS: the burglary of Daniel Ellsberg's psychiatrist's office in 1971 and the WATERGATE break-in of 1972. Ellsberg had infuriated Nixon by stealing and leaking the PENTAGON PAPERS, secret documents on the Vietnam War.

Poacher

Slang used by British INTELLIGENCE OFFICERS for a BIRD WATCHER (spy) who is in the field or operating area.

Poe, Edgar Allan

(b. 1809 d. 1849)

American novelist and poet who was an expert on CIPHERS. In this field he had considerable influence on the development of CRYPTOSYSTEMS by the British SECRET SERVICE. After studying the history of ciphers, from 1840 onward Poe wrote extensively on the subject in popular magazines and incorporated a cipher as a central plot element in his story *The Gold Bug* (1843).

Polgar, Thomas C.

CIA station chief in Saigon during the final stage of the Vietnam War.

As a young man in the 1930s, Polgar, a Hungarian Jew, fled to the United States. During World War II, the U.S. Army, impressed by his language ability, assigned him to the OFFICE OF STRATEGIC SERVICES (OSS), which trained him in Britain and dropped him behind German lines. After the war, he became one of the many OSS veterans who joined the new CIA. He served in BERLIN, where the CIA had a large Cold War station.

He served in VIENNA in the 1960 and later headed

the CIA station in Buenos Aires, where he ended an airliner hijacking by delivering drugged Coke to the hijackers.

Polgar was already a legend in the CIA Directorate for Plans (clandestine services) when he was made chief of station in Saigon in 1972 under COVER of special assistant to the ambassador. He had never been in Asia before.

Describing him in *Decent Interval* (1977), FRANK SNEPP, a former CIA INTELLIGENCE OFFICER in Vietnam, wrote:

> Because of his accent and his past Polgar always considered himself an outsider in the CIA's ivy-covered bureaucracy, and as an outsider he felt obliged continually to demonstrate his knowledge and astuteness.... His personal insecurities no doubt helped to shape his relationships with the Vietnamese.... For in dealing with Saigon's high and mighty, Polgar tended to suspend critical judgment, accepting what they told him even when he knew it to be self-serving.

By the time Polgar took over the CIA establishment in Vietnam, the war had reached its final stage, although U.S. policymakers were not publicly admitting it. Whatever influence the CIA had on the war was fading as President Nixon and Secretary of State Henry Kissinger were seeking ways toward a negotiated end to the war.

Polgar was on one of the last helicopters out of Saigon when the U.S. Embassy was evacuated in April 1975.

Polgar came out of retirement in 1987 to join the committee staff for the U.S. Senate Select Committee that investigated the IRAN-CONTRA AFFAIR. Polgar pressed unsuccessfully for a deeper congressional investigation of CIA involvement in Iran-Contra. In May 1991, when President GEORGE H. W. BUSH nominated ROBERT M. GATES as DIRECTOR OF CENTRAL INTELLIGENCE, Polgar used characteristically blunt language in an article in *The Washington Post*: "Gates acted as if he was in a complete fog or was interested primarily in keeping the truth from being aired in public or, indeed, from reaching Congress."

Political Intelligence

Information related to a nation or a group's internal political situation that could be of assistance to an opponent. Political intelligence was often a TARGET of U.S. intelligence activities in Southeast Asia in the 1960s. (See DOMESTIC INTELLIGENCE and VIETNAM.)

Pollard, Jonathan Jay

(b. 1943)

U.S. NAVAL INTELLIGENCE analyst who spied for Israel against the United States. By his own admission he passed to his Israeli HANDLERS more than 800 classified publications and more than 1,000 cables. The documents he provided would fill a space six by six by ten feet.

Pollard was educated at Stanford University and graduated in 1976. He enrolled in graduate school at the Fletcher School of Law and Diplomacy at Tufts University in 1977, but left without a degree in 1979. At Stanford he had told friends how he had fled Czechoslovakia in 1968 when it was revealed that his father worked for the CIA in Prague. These were lies, as were his boasts about connections at that time with the Israeli intelligence services.

Pollard, who once sent himself a telegram addressed to "Colonel" Pollard, entered false job and education information on his application for government employment, but no one caught him. He became a civilian intelligence analyst for the Navy in Sept. 1979. Following the standard BACKGROUND INVESTIGATION, he was given a SECURITY CLEARANCE for TOP SECRET, plus access to SENSITIVE COMPARTMENTED INFORMATION (SCI).

Soon after Pollard went to work for the Navy at the Naval Intelligence Support Center in Suitland, Md., near Washington, D.C., he made contact with a military ATTACHÉ at the South African Embassy in Washington. U.S. COUNTERINTELLIGENCE officials, learning of this contact, notified the Navy. Pollard lost his special clearances but was not fired. (If Pollard had handed over secrets to South Africa, they would have rapidly found their way to the KGB, because a high-level Soviet MOLE, Commo. DIETER FELIX GERHARDT of the South African Navy, was spying for the KGB at that time.)

In June 1984 Pollard was assigned as an analyst in the NAVAL CRIMINAL INVESTIGATIVE SERVICE, then called the Naval Investigative Service (NIS), and his special clearances were restored. He was placed in a new, high-priority unit, the Anti-Terrorism Alert Center in the NIS Threat Analysis Division of Naval Intelligence, with access to such sensitive material as SATELLITE photographs and reports of CIA AGENTS.

He went far beyond the bounds of his job, showing classified material to an Australian naval officer and to a supporter of the *mujahedeen* freedom fighters in Afghanistan. At least three of his social acquaintances received classified information from him in what authorities believe was an attempt by Pollard to set up a private information service.

At about this time he went to New York City and met an Israeli officer who identified himself as "Avi." He was Col Aviem (Avi) Sella, an Israeli Air Force officer and intelligence operative, in the latter role under COVER of a graduate student at New York University. Sella asked Pollard for a "sample" of the kind of information he could provide to Israel, assuring him that he would be paid for his services. A few days later the two men met in Washington, and Pollard handed Stella detailed information on the places in Iraq where chemical warfare weapons were manufactured.

Using standard TRADECRAFT, Sella, as the recruitment officer, handed Pollard off to his CASE OFFICER, Yosef (Yossi) Yagur, whose cover was consul for scientific affairs at the Israeli Consulate in New York. Yagur and

Pollard met in Paris with RAFAEL (RAFI) EITAN, a veteran Israeli intelligence official who ran the Israeli Defense Ministry's Liaison Bureau for Scientific Affairs, known as LAKAM.

While the men met in a Paris SAFE HOUSE, Pollard's fiancée, Anne Henderson, was taken to a jewelry store and told to pick out an engagement ring. She selected a $10,000 diamond and sapphire ring, which Sella later purchased and gave to Pollard for presentation to Henderson. The Israelis said that she should tell friends that the engagement ring was a gift from Pollard's "Uncle Joe Fisher."

As Pollard was about to leave Paris, Sella gave him between $10,000 and $12,000 in cash—Pollard would later say he forgot the exact amount—to pay for a grand tour of the Riviera, Italy, Switzerland, and Germany. Sella also promised Pollard a $1,500 monthly salary for his espionage efforts.

Back in the United States, Pollard quickly fell into an espionage routine. Under the loose security rules that governed the naval intelligence complex at Suitland, Pollard could make computerized searches on virtually any subject. One of his major sources for the theft of secrets was the DEFENSE INTELLIGENCE AGENCY, whose computerized data banks contained MILITARY INTELLIGENCE on nations throughout the world.

About three times a week Pollard would gather up the computer printouts, satellite photographs, and secret documents, put them in his briefcase, and walk out of the Suitland complex without having his briefcase searched. He would drive to a place where he could not be observed—such as in his car in a car wash—and transfer the documents from his regular briefcase to a suitcase that he reserved for his Friday or Saturday deliveries to the Washington apartments where Israelis copied the documents, which he would return on Monday. In Israel, a special team of analysts evaluated and distributed the Pollard material.

In the spring of 1985 Pollard's monthly (undeclared) spy pay was raised to $2,500 a month, and he was invited to take an all-expenses-paid European honeymoon. He and Anne Henderson were married in Venice and traveled to Zurich in a $700 private compartment on the Orient Express. From there they went to Israel.

While in Israel, the Pollards were entertained by Israeli intelligence officials, who gave them, as a parting gift, more than $10,000 in cash to cover their honeymoon expenses. A couple of months later, at a meeting with Pollard in Washington, Yagur showed Pollard an Israeli passport with Pollard's photograph and the identity of an Israeli citizen named Danny Cohen. Yagur also gave Pollard a Swiss bank account number and mentioned that $30,000 had already been deposited. A grateful Israel, Yagur said, would add $30,000 to that account every year for the next 10 years. After that, Pollard would presumably move to Israel as Danny Cohen.

Anne Henderson Pollard quit her public relations job at the National Rifle Association and approached a New York public relations firm that had been looking for a way to represent China. Among the items Pollard then brought home were five secret studies on diplomats in the Chinese Embassy and consulates. His wife made a brilliant presentation for the public relations job.

Alerted to Pollard's massive requests for data, Comdr. Jerry Agee, Pollard's commanding officer, ordered "especially close scrutiny" of Pollard's work habits and computer runs. On Nov. 8, 1985, he discovered that Pollard had obtained a printout of SCI information on Middle East subjects. A surreptitious check of Pollard's work space showed that the information was not there; he had therefore taken sensitive material out of the building without proper authorization. Agee called the NIS security office and the FBI.

On Monday, Nov. 18, Pollard, carrying a package containing 60 classified documents—20 of them TOP SECRET—was stopped outside the Navy facility and brought back to his office for questioning by FBI and NIS agents. After a series of desperate attempts to throw off the investigators and to get help from his handlers, on Thursday morning, the Pollards drove to the Israeli Embassy, followed by FBI agents.

The Israelis refused to give Pollard political asylum and, as he left the grounds of the embassy, he was arrested. Anne Henderson Pollard was arrested the next day.

Revelations about Israeli espionage in the United States threatened a breakdown in relations between the two countries. An Israeli government spokesman immediately branded the espionage a "rogue" operation, "an unauthorized deviation" from Israeli's "policy of not conducting any espionage activity whatsoever in the United States, or activities against the United States."

But it soon became obvious that this was a long-term, highly organized intelligence operation. Assessing the damage, Secretary of Defense Caspar Weinberger said, "It is difficult for me . . . to conceive of a greater harm to national security." He said that "substantial and irrevocable damage has been done to this nation," including the selling of data "intentionally reserved by the United States for its own use, because to disclose it, to anyone or any nation, would cause the greatest harm to our national security."

David Geneson, one of the two assistant U.S. attorneys who prosecuted Pollard, later said that much of the intelligence Pollard supplied "was unusable to the Israelis except as bargaining chips and leverage against the United States and other countries' interests." This is the closest anyone publicly came to acknowledging what intelligence officials said privately: Some of the information possibly found its way to the Soviet Union, most likely through one of the Soviet MOLES in the Israeli government. Further, the material that Pollard supplied included intelligence on U.S. agents or at least key contacts in the Arab world—men who could be TURNED by the Israelis—as well as information on codebreaking efforts by NSA.

Revelations about a technical collection system are "much like the loss of a network of agents," a government damage assessment said. The identity of U.S. agents, another report said, "could be inferred by a reasonably competent intelligence analyst."

Pollard had also allowed his handlers to copy his identification credentials, making it possible for them to equip other agents with the means to enter government facilities.

Pollard pleaded guilty to espionage charges and was sentenced to prison for life. His wife pleaded guilty to unauthorized possession of government property and to being an accessory to the possession of military documents by her husband. She was not charged with espionage. Sentenced to five years in prison, she constantly complained about her treatment. In a television interview she compared her experience to "what Auschwitz [death camp] must have been like 47 years ago in terms of medical treatment, in terms of abuse . . ." She was released in April 1990 after serving 37 months and divorced Pollard soon thereafter.

Pollard became a celebrity in Israel and the hero of an international campaign to release him. Seventy members of the Knesset (Israeli parliament) presented a petition to President Reagan in 1988, asking for a presidential pardon for Pollard and his wife. Pollard's champions compare his plight to that of Capt. ALFRED DREYFUS because Dreyfus was a Jew, as is Pollard. Dreyfus, however, was not a spy, whereas Pollard was a confessed spy. Pollard's cause is vociferously carried on by his second wife, Esther, who married him at his prison and then began an unremitting campaign to free him, saying she was "Jonathan's voice in the outside world," She and other Pollard supporters in the United States and Israel continually plead for a presidential pardon.

In 1993 Secretary of Defense Les Aspin revealed that Pollard had tried 14 times to disclose classified information in intercepted letters written from his prison cell. Aspin's revelation came less than a month after Israeli Prime Minister Yitzhak Rabin appealed to President Clinton to free Pollard. Clinton said he could only consider clemency recommendations from the Justice Department, and none had been presented. Previously, Prime Minister Yitzhak Shamir had made a similar appeal to President George H. W. Bush, who turned down the request. In 1996, following Rabin's assassination, his successor, Shimon Peres, on a visit to Washington, probably made a similar confidential appeal. In 1998 the Israeli government formally acknowledged that Pollard was its spy. He has been granted Israeli citizenship and has asked for payment for his services as an agent.

During Mideast peace talks in 1998, Israeli officials later said, they had reached an agreement with President Clinton to have Pollard released as part of an exchange of Israeli and Palestinian Liberation Organization prisoners. GEORGE TENET, DIRECTOR OF CENTRAL INTELLIGENCE, warning that the release of Pollard would incense the INTELLIGENCE COMMUNITY, reportedly threatened to resign if Clinton pardoned Pollard.

Pollard's lawyers periodically filed appeals to have him released from prison, usually claiming that he had a "deal" with the U.S. prosecutor, which was broken by his being given a life sentence. In Sept. 2003, Pollard himself was in court in Washington, D.C., as his lawyers argued that not only had the government violated the agreement, but his trial counsel was incompetent in failing to object to the violations and in failing to appeal the sentence. The latter objection came almost 16 years after his sentencing.

An editorial in *The Washington Post* after Pollard's appearance in court quoted a 1992 court statement by Judge Laurence H. Silberman and Ruth Bader Ginsburg—both on the D.C. Circuit Court at the time:

> [Pollard] has never denied that he is guilty of the crimes for which he was imprisoned. Nor is there any allegation that his guilty plea was induced by the promise of a specific sentence that he subsequently did not receive. Under such circumstances, it cannot be said that justice completely miscarried.

Pope, Capt. Edmond S.

(b. 1946)

Retired U.S. Navy INTELLIGENCE OFFICER convicted of stealing Russian state secrets.

Pope was sentenced by a Russian court to 20 years of hard labor in Dec. 2000, but a week later he was pardoned by President VLADIMIR PUTIN on humanitarian grounds because Pope had cancer.

Pope was the first American put on trial for espionage in Moscow since 1960, when U-2 pilot FRANCIS GARY POWERS was convicted of spying.

Pope was arrested in March 1999 by the FSB (Federal Security Service) for illegally obtaining secret designs for a Russian Shkval torpedo, the word's fastest with a speed of almost 200 knots. Pope insisted that he was interested in the torpedo's technology for commercial reasons. Knowledge of its existence was widespread.

In his book *Torpedoed* (2002), written with Tom Shachtman, Pope said that the timing of his arrest—two days after the election of Putin—was no coincidence. "If Putin and his backers wanted to send a signal to the Russian peoples that Russia would no longer be pushed around by the United States and would resist being relegated to a second-order power," Pope wrote, "there was no better signal than to arrest and charge with espionage an American businessman and former Naval intelligence officer."

Polyakov, Lt. Gen. Dimitri Fedorovich

(b. ? d. 1986)

Soviet GRU (MILITARY INTELLIGENCE) officer who was a DEFECTOR IN PLACE for the United States for 18 years. He is believed to have been the highest-ranking GRU officer ever to spy for the West.

Polyakov was a GRU colonel under COVER as a member of the Soviet mission to the UNITED NATIONS in Nov. 1961 when he told an American working for the FBI that he wanted to meet the commanding general of the U.S. First Army, headquartered on Governor's Island, off Manhattan. The commanding general invited Polyakov to a cocktail party, where he asked to be put in touch with the FBI. At a second party Polyakov was introduced to an FBI agent who said he was a CIA official.

The FBI began running Polyakov with the CODE NAME TOP HAT in Jan. 1962. Polyakov had trained many Soviet ILLEGALS in the United States and was in charge of all illegals at the time he became a defector in place. Among the illegals he exposed were KAARLO TUOMI and ALEKSANDR SOKOLOV. Through Polyakov the FBI is also believed to have discovered the espionage of U.S. Navy yeoman NELSON C. DRUMMOND, U.S. Army officer WILLIAM H. WHALEN, and U.S. Army enlisted men HERBERT W. BOECKENHAUPT and JACK E. DUNLAP. He is also credited with exposing the British spy FRANK BOSSARD.

Polyakov seemed inspired to spy because of his hatred of the Soviet system; he accepted gifts from the FBI but did not take money. When Polyakov was sent to Moscow in May 1962, he became the ASSET of the CIA. The FBI tried to keep in touch with him by running advertisements in the personal columns of *The New York Times* addressed to Donald F., using a simple CODE to direct him to DEAD DROPS in Moscow.

In Nov. 1965 Polyakov was posted to Rangoon, Burma, as a military ATTACHÉ. There he met the FBI agent who had recruited him and explained their meetings to his superiors as an attempt to recruit the American. He continued to supply information through assignments in Moscow and in India in 1973, the latter as a military attaché.

David Wise wrote in *Nightmover* (1995), Polyakov's "access to top-secret information was even greater; over the years, Polyakov provided extremely valuable political-military information, including data on Soviet strategic missiles, antitank missiles, nuclear strategy, chemical and biological warfare, crop diseases, and civil defense." U.S. intelligence sources say that the CIA created a small communications device for Polyakov that could encrypt and transmit nearly 50 pages of typed information. The data was picked up by a special receiver at the American Embassy in Moscow.

Polyakov was one of the many U.S. AGENTS betrayed by CIA COUNTERINTELLIGENCE officer ALDRICH H. AMES. Arrested by the KGB sometime after Ames began his spying, Polyakov was executed in 1986.

Without naming Polyakov, in Jan. 1990 the newspaper *Pravda* carried a report about a spy named "Donald," a Soviet official who had been in "a very important position." In describing Donald, *Pravda* seemed to trace Polyakov's career, but with some variations. *Pravda* reported, for instance, that Donald had recently been captured and sentenced to death; U.S. intelligence officials contend that he was executed in 1986. "Having access to many state secrets," *Pravda* said, "Donald was trading in everything the U.S. intelligence services were interested in." *Pravda* did not list the state secrets.

JAMES JESUS ANGLETON, CIA counterintelligence chief, believed that Top Hat and FEDORA, another FBI-recruited spy, were both DOUBLE AGENTS. Angleton insisted that Top Hat and Fedora were Soviet agents whose mission was the discrediting of a *real* Soviet defector, ANATOLY GOLITSYN. Angleton's unproven theory was that the Soviets desperately wanted to discredit Golitsyn because he had revealed that a MOLE had penetrated the CIA. In the 1980s WILLIAM J. CASEY, the DIRECTOR OF CENTRAL INTELLIGENCE, ordered his own investigation and concluded that Top Hat was legitimate.

Casey's critics, however, continued to insist that Top Hat was a double agent whose false information included data indicating that Soviet nuclear missiles were far more accurate than they really were. This supposedly led to U.S.-Soviet missile limitation agreements based on false information.

Pravda observed that Donald had approached FBI agents in New York in 1961 and that the FBI had communicated with him through personal ads in *The New York Times* addressed to MOODY-Donald F. "Uncle Charles and Sister Clara are OK," said the ads, which appeared in the *Times* for 10 consecutive days in 1964.

When Donald was caught, *Pravda* reported that he said, "I was accustomed to balancing on a knife edge and did not imagine any other life for myself. I felt in my spine the KGB was after me, but my own analysis of my actions erased my concerns."

U.S. intelligence officials believed that *Pravda*'s story on Donald was inspired by a desire to build up the sagging image of the KGB. According to the story, the KGB had found about 30 spies like Donald since the mid-1980s; many were betrayed by Ames.

Polygraph

Device used for attempting to determine whether a person is lying. The "lie detector," as it is often called, has been widely employed in COUNTERESPIONAGE work. Employees of the CIA, for example, regularly submit to FLUTTER—being questioned with a polygraph strapped on.

A polygraph typically measures a person's breathing, blood pressure, pulse rate, and palm perspiration. These measurements are indicated by a stylus that passes along graph paper. A steady line theoretically indicates calmness (and truth) when a question is asked; a wildly moving line in response to a question indicates stress (and, possibly, lying).

In recent years there has been a growing suspicion that the polygraph produces dubious results. Polygraphs did not intimidate such celebrated spies as U.S. Navy Chief Warrant Officer JOHN A. WALKER and CIA COUNTERINTELLIGENCE officer ALDRICH H. AMES. Walker boasted of beating the polygraph, and Ames twice passed polygraph tests. Ames said he was following instructions given to him by his Soviet HANDLERS. Psychiatrists say that spies are usually so adept at duplicity that their lies cannot be detected by a machine. Yet, in a report made in 2002, the National Research Council (NRC) of the National Academies urged that research be stepped up for improvement of lie-detection techniques; at the same time the NRC said that that there was not yet any alternative technique that outperformed the polygraph.

R. JAMES WOOLSEY refused to take a polygraph test when he became DIRECTOR OF CENTRAL INTELLIGENCE. Similarly, Secretary of State George P. Shultz threatened to resign if forced to take a polygraph test. He strongly opposed the imposition of polygraph tests by Congress in the 1988 Department of State authorization act. (In 1985 Congress passed a bill directing the Secretary of Defense to use polygraphs on anyone, including civilians and contractors, who handled classified and highly sensitive compartmented information. The Department of Defense Polygraph Institute was established to produce polygraph operators, officially described as graduates in "forensic psychophysiology.")

President Reagan allowed Shultz to administer the polygraph program at his own discretion. Shultz established regulations allowing employees generally to refuse to take a polygraph test. And if an employee failed a test, no unfavorable action could be taken without the approval of the Secretary of State.

U.S. courts have consistently ruled against polygraph evidence, mostly because polygraphs are not backed by sufficient scientific endorsement. In 2003, for example, a report by the National Research Council, commissioned by the Energy Department, said that while polygraphs may be effective in criminal investigations, when used as an employment tool, "available evidence indicates that polygraph testing as currently used has extremely serious limitations . . . if the intent is both to identify security risks and protect valued employees." The report looked at a hypothetical testing of a population of 10,000. If there were 10 spies in that population, the report said, 1,606 loyal employees would fail a test that was sensitive enough to identify eight of the spies.

In the INTELLIGENCE COMMUNITY, however, security officials have just as consistently upheld its use. In a 1987 study of 20,000 FBI polygraph interrogations, AGENTS who used the information said that less than 1 percent of the results had been wrong.

Many CIA officials became doubtful about the efficacy of the lie detector after learning from a defector that polygraph-approved Cuban AGENTS had been TURNED and were being run as DOUBLE AGENTS by Cuban counterintelligence officers. (See CUBA.)

Pontecorvo, Bruno

(b. 1913 d. 1993)

Italian physicist suspected of spying for the Soviet Union. A colleague of Soviet spy KLAUS FUCHS, Pontecorvo defected to the Soviet Union in Oct. 1950, during a European trip from which he had been expected to return to England.

Educated at Pisa University and Rome University, where he received a doctorate with honors in physics in 1934, after graduation he did laboratory work under Professors Edoardo Amaldi and Enrico Fermi. In 1936 he went to Paris on a fellowship to do research under Frédéric Joliot-Curie, a communist. In Paris he met Marianne Nordbloom, a Swede, whom he married in 1940, and when France fell to German conquest that year, they fled to the United States.

In 1943 Pontecorvo was invited to join the Anglo-Canadian atomic research team at Chalk River in Ontario, Canada, where he remained for six years. He is suspected of having spied during this period, but nothing has ever been proved against him. Nor was he identified in documents given to the Canadian authorities by IGOR GOUZENKO, the Soviet CIPHER clerk who helped expose the Soviet ATOMIC SPY RING. Gouzenko's information did lead to the conviction of another Chalk River physicist, ALAN NUNN MAY, as a spy.

In 1948 Pontecorvo became a naturalized British subject and was given a complete SECURITY CLEARANCE despite the fact that questions had been raised about connections he and family members had with the Communist Party in Italy. In Jan. 1949 he left Canada to become principal scientific officer at Harwell, Britain's atomic research center. In Jan. 1950, just before Klaus Fuchs was arrested, the station head and security officer at Harwell learned that Pontecorvo and his wife were communists, or at least communist sympathizers. Pontecorvo denied this, although he did admit that some members of his family were communists.

Because he was thought to be a potential security risk at Harwell, he was offered a position at Liverpool University, where he would not have access to secret information. He accepted the post and agreed to begin work in Jan. 1951.

But in Oct. 1950 Pontecorvo failed to return to Harwell from a vacation in Europe with his wife and three sons. Nothing more was known publicly about Pontecorvo until he held a press conference on March 5, 1955, in Moscow. He said that he had become a Soviet citizen in 1952 and worked in the Institute of Nuclear Physics of the Soviet Academy of Sciences, which later became the International Center of Research in the Use of Atomic Energy. In 1963 he was awarded the Order of Lenin for "great services in physics" and was elected a full member of the Soviet Academy of Sciences.

In 1980 a U.S. Treasury Department official said that Pontecorvo had a credit of $14,250 at the U.S. Treasury as royalty on a U.S. patent, which he shared with Fermi and three other physicists for a process that produces radioisotopes.

Ponting, Clive

Former assistant secretary at the British Ministry of Defence, tried in 1985 under the OFFICIAL SECRETS ACT for having provided a member of Parliament with classified documents concerning the sinking of the Argentine cruiser *Belgrano* by a British submarine during the 1982 Falklands conflict. He was acquitted by a jury despite major efforts by the government of Prime Minister Margaret Thatcher to convict him.

Popov, Dusko

(b. 1912 d. 1982)

Voluntary DOUBLE AGENT working for the British who came to the then-neutral United States in 1941 to form a bogus spy ring for the Germans.

Popov was a Yugoslav business promoter when the German ABWEHR recruited him. He informed the British, and when his Abwehr HANDLERS sent him to Britain in Dec. 1940, the TWENTY COMMITTEE, which handled double agents, gave him the British CODE NAME Tricycle, reportedly because of his proclivity for having two female sexual partners at a time. The Germans had code-named him Ivan. The intelligence he gave the Germans included false information about the size of the British armed forces.

In June 1941 the Abwehr ordered Popov to go to the United States and set up an espionage ring. At the request of Germany's Japanese allies, he also was to obtain specific information about Pearl Harbor and go to Hawaii to make sketches of military facilities there. The instructions were concealed in MICRODOTS on a fake telegram that Popov carried.

The British informed the FBI of Popov's double status before he arrived in the United States by Pan American Clipper from Lisbon on Aug. 12, 1941. But J. EDGAR HOOVER, the director of the FBI, believing that Popov *was* a German spy who had duped the British, refused to allow him to go to Hawaii.

Popov gave the FBI both its first examples of the German microdot process and a list of questions that German intelligence officers wanted answered about the United States. Many of the questions pertained to Pearl Harbor, which the FBI ignored, failing to see the possible significance of the German interest in Pearl Harbor.

Popov had arrived in the United States with a Yugoslav passport and $70,000. He rented a Park Avenue penthouse and began making the rounds of New York City nightclubs. The FBI put him under SURVEILLANCE and planted BUGS in his apartment. "Why, if I bend over to smell a bowl of flowers," Popov complained, "I scratch my nose on a microphone." He insisted that to convince his German handlers that his mission to the United States was not in vain, he needed information that would look like the authentic gleanings of a German spy.

The British Twenty Committee produced that kind of information. But Hoover dredged up little for Popov. Among the 1,421 pages of heavily sanitized pages in Popov's FBI dossier are secret FBI memos showing that the material given to Popov included back copies of the *Infantry Journal* and Army press releases. The OFFICE OF NAVAL INTELLIGENCE was "unable to furnish any specific information which would be suitable for counterespionage data," an FBI memo said.

The FBI operated a clandestine radio on his behalf but did not allow him to work as a double agent. He returned to Britain in July 1943 and did valuable double-dealing against the Germans until the invasion of Normandy in June 1944.

"I knew Dusko Popov well during the war, when he risked and achieved so much for the Allied cause," British INTELLIGENCE OFFICER EWEN MONTAGU wrote. "He could, in some respects, have been an IAN FLEMING hero—one of the bravest and gayest of men, possessing immense charm and personal magnetism."

Popov, Lt. Col. Pyotr

(b. ? d. 1958)

Soviet GRU (MILITARY INTELLIGENCE) officer who spied for the CIA as a DEFECTOR IN PLACE from 1953 to 1958.

On Jan. 1, 1953, Popov approached an American diplomat in VIENNA and handed him a message asking for a meeting. Popov provided the CIA with some of its earliest detailed information on the structure of the post-World War II GRU. He also provided information on Soviet intelligence operations in Austria and Yugoslavia.

He went to Moscow, possibly on leave, in 1954 and was then assigned to BERLIN, where he again provided valuable information, including plans for sending an ILLEGAL to the United States. Alerted, the FBI put the illegal under SURVEILLANCE soon after her arrival. Sensing that she had been BLOWN, she returned to Moscow.

Popov was ordered back to Moscow in 1958. There he was TURNED by the KGB and told to reveal his CIA connections. Popov arranged a meeting with Russell Langelle, a CIA INTELLIGENCE OFFICER under diplomatic COVER in the U.S. Embassy. During the meeting Popov managed to get across the fact that he had been turned. But it was too late. The two men were arrested. Langelle was expelled and Popov was executed, reportedly by being thrown alive into a furnace, with several GRU officers as witnesses.

The FBI's zealous surveillance was at first blamed for Popov's exposure. But there were later indications that Popov might have been betrayed to the KGB by GEORGE BLAKE, an officer of the British Secret Intelligence Service (MI6) who was a Soviet MOLE.

Portland Case

The media label for the arrest and conviction of five Soviet spies who obtained secrets from the Admiralty Underwater Weapons Establishment at Portland, England, in the 1950s.

Breakup of the ring began when the U.S. CIA received a series of letters signed "Sniper" from a Polish INTELLIGENCE OFFICER (who later defected and was identified as MICHAL GOLIENEWSKI.) Sniper claimed that the Soviets had a spy in the British Admiralty. The CIA passed the information to the British Security Service (MI5). Finding no likely suspects in the Admiralty, MI5 focused on the Portland naval facility.

The MI5 investigation trail led to HARRY HOUGHTON, a clerk at Portland who had previously worked for the naval ATTACHÉ in the British Embassy in Warsaw.

SURVEILLANCE of Houghton showed that he met regularly with a man later identified by his espionage pseudonym, GORDON LONSDALE. Houghton's girlfriend, Ethel (Bunny) Gee, also worked at the Navy facility and was placed under SURVEILLANCE.

Lonsdale was trailed to a house occupied by Peter Kroger and his wife Helen (also espionage pseudonyms; see MORRIS COHEN). In Jan. 1961, detectives of the SPECIAL BRANCH arrested Houghton, Gee, and Lonsdale as they met for a transfer of documents; the Krogers were also arrested.

The Portland Case, as it was called in the press, ended in March 1961 with the Old Bailey trial of all five on espionage charges. Their sentences: Houghton and Gee, 15 years each; Lonsdale, 25 years; the Krogers, 20 years each. Two security investigations were later made. The first criticized the Admiralty and lauded MI5. The second was more critical of MI5 for failing to discover the espionage without the aid of a DEFECTOR.

Positive Intelligence

Information that has been interpreted and can be used in intelligence reports.

Positive Vetting

British term for a SECURITY CHECK of prospective or already hired INTELLIGENCE OFFICERS, especially in the Security Service (MI5) and the Secret Intelligence Service (MI6). The lack of positive vetting was often cited as dangerous by critics, who argued that some of the MOLES in British services would have been turned away had their backgrounds been investigated more rigorously. (See CAMBRIDGE SPY RING.)

"Vetting" literally means getting a sick animal examined by a veterinarian; it has evolved into a term meaning "to test or scrutinize."

Postage Stamps

Historically, governments have been reluctant to honor their spies—successful or unsuccessful. However, several have been honored by postage stamps. Probably the first was NATHAN HALE, an inept but courageous and revered spy of the American Revolution. The U.S. Post Office issued a half-cent stamp honoring Hale in 1922 as part of a series commemorating famous Americans; among the others in the series were GEORGE WASHINGTON—an outstanding spymaster—as well as such historic figures as Lincoln, BENJAMIN FRANKLIN, Theodore Roosevelt, and U. S. Grant.

No additional "spy stamps" are recorded for the next four decades. In 1960, Romania issued a stamp honoring DANIEL DEFOE, a great literary figure who was a collector of DOMESTIC INTELLIGENCE in Britain.

The Soviet Union—always known for big achievements—produced no less than six spy stamps: First came RICHARD SORGE in 1960, a four-kopek stamp honoring

the man who successfully spied against the Japanese for eight years before he was caught and executed. In 1990 the Soviet government issued a set of five beautifully executed, five-kopek stamps honoring the following spies and spymasters:

> Hero of the Soviet Union Col. S. A. Vaupshasov (1899–1976), who in 1920–1924 was engaged in underground work in Belorussia against the Whites and Poles, and in 1937–1939 was operating in Spain; he remained active in intelligence work until 1953.
>
> Col. RUDOLF ABEL (1903–1971), who ran the ATOMIC SPY RING in the United States from 1948 to 1957.
>
> HAROLD (KIM) PHILBY (1912–1988), one a member of the highly successful CAMBRIDGE SPY RING, who spied out British and American secrets for the Soviet intelligence services in London and Washington, D.C. (The other members of the ring have not been similarly honored.)
>
> Hero of the Soviet Union I. D. Kudrya (1912–1942), who took part in numerous sabotage operations against the Germans in the Ukraine during 1941–1942; he was captured and killed by the Germans.
>
> Col. Conon Molody (1922–1970), a veteran of World War II and later an officer in the KGB, known in the West as GORDON LONSDALE.

The East German government, in 1964, issued a set of six stamps honoring Germans who fought Nazism in World War II, among them members of the RED ORCHESTRA. (MILDRED FISH HARNACK and her husband, Arvid, martyrs to the anti-Nazi effort, were honored by a 40-pfennig stamp; all six stamps, in addition to their face value, had a small surcharge added to help build a national memorial to victims of the Nazis.)

Postage stamps have themselves been used in espionage. On occasion secret messages in the form of MICRODOTS have been hidden under postage stamps. JULIUS ROSENBERG and his wife, Ethel, members of the atomic spy ring, are said to have used this method of communication.

There are allegations that in World War I a German spy at the British naval base at Invergordon, Scotland, used postage stamps themselves as a CODE. Three Peruvian stamps, for example, were said to indicate that three light cruisers were in the base. But such stories were more the fancy of spy novelists at the time than actual foreign AGENTS.

Warnings to be on the lookout for spies have been used on postage stamps in Cuba since 1943: The five-stamp issue included a five-centavo stamp with a man having a mask being pulled away from his face and the caption "Unmask the Fifth Columnists."

A stamp has also honored a nonspy—indirectly. In 1931 Canada issued a $1 stamp showing Mt. Edith Cavell in Alberta, named in honor of EDITH CAVELL, who was executed by the Germans in World War I. Although charged with helping Allied prisoners, she is often thought of as having committed espionage.

In 1996, the U.S. Postal Service issued a stamp honoring Swedish diplomat RAOUL WALLENBERG for saving

Spies on postage stamps. From top left: S.A. Vaupshasov, R.I. Abel, Kim Philby, I.D. Kudrya; from bottom left: K.T. Molody, Nathan Hale, Richard Sorge. Canadian Edith Cavell and Swede Raoul Wallenberg, both executed as spies, also were honored by postage stamps.

Hungarian Jews from the Holocaust. He was also a spy for the U.S. OFFICE OF SPECIAL SERVICES (OSS).

Potential Agent

Individual who is being developed or is under consideration for becoming an AGENT by an intelligence service.

Powers, Francis Gary

(b. 1929 d. 1977)

Pilot of the U.S. U-2 spyplane shot down over Sverdlovsk in the Soviet Union by an SA-2 missile on May 1, 1960.

Powers graduated from Milligan College in Tennessee in 1950 and joined the U.S. Air Force, training as a fighter pilot. In 1956, when he was a captain, he transferred to the U-2 program run by the CIA. The CIA had recently begun flying spyplanes over the Soviet Union from bases in Pakistan and Norway. The COVER story for the U-2 pilots was that they were working for the National Aeronautics and Space Administration (NASA).

After training in Nevada, Powers was sent to the U-2 base at Incirlik, Turkey, from where he flew missions along the Turkish-Soviet border. In 1960 he was ordered to Pakistan and briefed for his first flight across the Soviet Union. On May 1, 1960—May Day, a major Soviet holiday—he took off from Peshawar, Pakistan. He was to land in Bödo, Norway, a 3,788-mile flight, with 2,919 miles over the Soviet Union.

Among the sites the CIA hoped to photograph were those showing what progress the Soviets were making in the development of intercontinental ballistic missiles. A previous OVERFLIGHT, on April 5, had shown construction of a launch complex at Tyura Tam. President Eisenhower had authorized a second flight over the same area but had set May 1 as the absolute end of any U-2 flights for a while. Eisenhower, Prime Minister Harold Macmillan of Britain, French President Charles de Gaulle, and Soviet Premier Nikita Khrushchev had a summit meeting scheduled in Paris on May 16, to be followed by an unprecedented trip by Eisenhower to Moscow. He did not want any incidents spoiling those events.

Powers later claimed that he had been assured that at his altitude (over 70,000 feet) no Soviet aircraft or missile could intercept his U-2. Over Sverdlovsk, he was hit by a missile. He ejected and parachuted to the ground, where people held him until police arrived.

When the plane failed to reach Norway, CIA officials feared trouble, which was confirmed by radio intercepts showing that the Soviets had tried to intercept a plane over their territory. The CIA, assuming that Powers was dead, sent out a COVER story by having the Air Force announce that an American weather plane flying for NASA out of Turkey, which had been making "upper air studies," was overdue and presumed missing.

On May 5 Khrushchev announced the shooting down of the plane in a fiery speech and denounced "American aggressive circles" for trying to stop the summit conference with this provocative act. The United States stuck to its weather story, adding that it was possible that the pilot could have been unconscious because of a failure in the aircraft's oxygen system and that the plane, on automatic pilot, could thus accidentally have violated Soviet air space.

On May 6, Khrushchev made another speech, revealing that the pilot of the plane was "quite alive and kicking! We did this quite deliberately, because if we had given out the whole story, the Americans would have thought up still another fable."

In Washington ALLEN W. DULLES, the DIRECTOR OF CENTRAL INTELLIGENCE, offered to resign, but his offer was turned down. Eisenhower ultimately accepted responsibility for using "every possible means" to protect the United States "against surprise attack."

Khrushchev did go to Paris, but he refused to take part in summit talks unless Eisenhower apologized; he did not. Eisenhower's trip to Moscow was canceled.

Meanwhile, in Moscow the Soviets prepared for a major show trial for Powers. The CIA briefed Sam Jaffe, the CBS reporter assigned to the trial. According to Michael R. Beschloss in his *Mayday: Eisenhower, Khrushchev and the U-2 Affair* (1986), Jaffe "was given data on Soviet espionage for rebuttal if Khrushchev de-

CIA pilot Francis Gary Powers models the high-altitude, partial pressure suit worn by U-2 pilots. The U-2 shown here has a fake serial number on the tail fin, a ploy often used in official photographs of the spyplane because their actual serials could indicate how many were produced. (LOCKHEED)

nounced the U-2. In his reportage Jaffe should refer to Powers not as a spy pilot but as a reconnaissance pilot." Jaffe accompanied Powers's wife, Barbara, on the flight to Moscow. He later said that she told him she hated Powers, but she maintained a public attitude of support.

Powers, tried and convicted of spying in a public trial, was sentenced to 10 years in prison. On Feb. 10, 1962, he was traded for Soviet spy RUDOLF ABEL, who was in prison in the United States.

Despite much criticism for "surviving" the loss of his U-2, Powers was decorated by the CIA and personally lauded by Dulles. He became a test pilot for Lockheed Aircraft Corp. Unknown to him, the CIA was paying his salary. When he found this out, he quit Lockheed. He later became a helicopter traffic reporter. On Aug. 1, 1977, he died in a helicopter crash while reporting on traffic over Los Angeles.

Prairie Schooner

Highly classifed U.S. Navy undersea intelligence collection program in the 1970s.

Precious Stone

SEE *OFEK*

Predator

U.S. UNMANNED AERIAL VEHICLE (UAV) developed as a medium-altitude RECONNAISSANCE aircraft. The Predator is believed to be the first UAV to launch weapons in combat and to be used in support of counter-terrorist operations.

Built by General Atomics Aeronautical Systems of San Diego, Calif., for the U.S. Air Force, the Predator was given the designation RQ-1, indicating reconnaissance (R) and unmanned vehicle (Q); this was later changed to MQ-1, for multi-purpose when armed with Hellfire air-to-surface missiles. The basic Predator drone is $26\frac{2}{3}$ feet long with a wingspan of $48\frac{1}{2}$ feet, and weighs more than 2,000 pounds. It has a turbojet engine with a cruise speed of about 65 mph. With a loiter time of up to 40 hours and a maximum ceiling of 25,000 feet, the UAV was initially fitted with television cameras to provide real-time imagery to ground commanders or to operation centers via relay links to SATELLITES or other UAVs. Subsequently other sensors were fitted.

The Predator first flew in June 1994 and entered service with the U.S. Air Force the following year. The UAV undertook its first operational missions in the Yugoslav conflict from July to October 1995, operating out of Gjader in Albania. During that first deployment Predators flew 128 sorties and 850 flight hours over Bosnia. In 1996 and again in 1998 Predators were deployed to Taszar, Hungary. Britain, France, and Germany also used

UAVs for reconnaissance and artillery spotting in the Yugoslav conflict.

Beginning in Jan. 1999 Predators were flown from Kuwait on reconnaissance flights over Iraq. Subsequently, when U.S. forces began operations against the Taliban and al Qaeda in Afghanistan in Oct. 2002, Predators were used from the outset to support SPECIAL OPERATIONS FORCES as well as regular U.S. combat units, some working with personnel from the CIA's Special Activities Division.

Based on earlier Air Force tests, Predators were armed with Hellfire anti-tank missiles during the Afghan conflict and on several occasions were used to attack suspected enemy vehicles. In what was reported to be a CIA operation, a Predator launched a Hellfire missile to blow up five or six suspected Taliban officials as they traveled along a desert highway in northwest Yemen in Nov. 2002.

Also in 2002 the Air Force began tests of the Predator's ability to launch Stinger air-to-air missiles against airborne targets. That combination was first used later in the year against Iraqi aircraft during operations in the "no-fly" zones over Iraq, reportedly without scoring any "kills."

The Predator has also demonstrated the ability to carry and launch a smaller UAV, called the Finder, to assess whether areas have been contaminated by chemical, biological or nuclear agents.

The U.S. Air Force has begun procurement of the more capable Predator B UAV, able to fly higher and to carry more sensors or six Hellfire missiles (the original Predators can carry two missiles).

Preobrazhensky Office

Organization established by Czar Peter I in 1697 to suppress internal enemies. The Preobrazhensky was a distant predecessor of the later CHEKA, NKVD, and KGB. There was no "political police" establishment in Russia between the OPRICHNINA, abolished in 1572, and the Preobrazhensky.

The new office was originally set up to administer two regiments, the Preobrazhensky and Semyonovsky Guards, which had been established by a young Peter to develop new tactics. But the responsibilities of the Preobrazhensky Office rapidly expanded. It was assigned control of the tobacco trade, and the office undertook the investigation and prosecution of political offenders. It was given jurisdiction over all crimes—especially treason—"by word or deed."

In its investigative role the office could investigate and question any citizen of Russia, regardless of rank or station. The office itself was small—a chief and a few clerks and assistants. However, they could use the elite Preobrazhensky and Semyonovsky Guards to make arrests and detain people. Later, *boyars* (nobles) were seconded to the office to assist in "investigations," which included questioning under torture or the threat of its use. A man or woman found guilty of a crime against the state could be sentenced by the office, unless the czar himself wished to make that decision.

The Preobrazhensky Office itself soon established torture chambers. There the office "examined" 1,714 of the Streltsy, Russia's first professional soldiers, who had attempted a revolt in 1698. They were hideously tortured over a period of about six weeks. Most were then executed, by public hanging or beheading. Peter himself reportedly sometimes wielded the axe. Peter reduced the sentences of some 500 soldiers under 20 years of age; they were branded and mutilated; and some were exiled.

When Peter established St. Petersburg as his capital in 1705, the Preobrazhensky Office remained in the former capital of Moscow. Perhaps Peter felt the older city housed the potential opponents to his rule, as St. Petersburg was a new city that he had created.

The Preobrazhensky Office survived for some 30 years. It handled several thousand cases—including that of the czar's half-sister, who was imprisoned. The office was abolished in 1729, four years after Peter's death.

The head of the Preobrazhensky Office was Prince Theodore Romodanovsky. A boyhood friend of the czar, Romodanovsky was described by biographer Robert K. Massie in *Peter the Great* (1981):

A savage, brutal man, totally devoted to Peter . . . [he] dealt mercilessly with any suggestion of treason or rebellion. Through a network of pervasive eavesdropping and denunciation, followed by torture and execution, Romodanovsky and the Secret Office did their grim work well: Even under extreme oppression from tax collectors and labor conscriptors, cases of treason "by word and deed" never threatened the throne.

Often honored by Peter, Romodanovsky served as governor of Moscow and chief of police, and was given the rank of admiral. Romodanovsky ruled the Preobrazhensky Office until his death in 1717, when his son Prince Ivan succeeded him. The younger Romodanovsky sought retirement in 1729, a key factor in the ending of the highly efficient Preobrazhensky Office.

The name *Preobrazhensky* comes from the village of Preobrazhenskoe near Moscow, where Peter and his young friends—including Romodanovsky—"played" soldier and Peter began his self-education. The word means "transfiguration."

President's Daily Brief

(PDB)

CIA report prepared for the President and presented each day in a blue leather binder. The PDB is essentially the basis for timely presidential knowledge of information developed by the INTELLIGENCE COMMUNITY during the previous 24 hours. Little is known publicly about the circulation of the PDB, whose existence was classified until the early 1990s. A rare glimpse at the binder (without, of course, any contents) was provided by the CIA to an exhibit in 2000 at the Ronald Reagan Presidential Library and Museum in Simi Valley, Calif.

President's Foreign Intelligence Advisory Board (PFIAB)

Influential INTELLIGENCE OVERSIGHT panel of the U.S. Executive Branch. The Board reviews the performance of all government agencies engaged in the collection, evaluation, or production of intelligence or in the execution of intelligence policy. It also assesses the adequacy of management, personnel, and organization of intelligence agencies.

The President's Foreign Intelligence Advisory Board (PFIAB, pronounced "piff-ee-ab") was established by President Eisenhower on Feb. 6, 1956, as the President's Board of Consultants on Foreign Intelligence Activities. The members were distinguished citizens with experience in business, international relations, and intelligence.

In 1961 the board was revitalized and its charter broadened by President Kennedy, who probably used the group more than any other president. Chaired by JAMES R. KILLIAN from 1956 to 1963, the board met an average of once a week after Kennedy entered the White House, with the President often attending. He considered it the most useful of all his advisory boards. It submitted 170 formal recommendations to him, out of which he approved 125, rejected only 2, and deferred action on the others.

President Johnson continued the board, renaming it the PFIAB. President Nixon reorganized it in 1969, specifically giving it responsibility for "a continuous review and assessment" not only of foreign intelligence but of all operations undertaken by the CIA, as well as other agencies and services in the INTELLIGENCE COMMUNITY. This charge essentially remained unchanged through successive administrations.

President Carter abolished the PFIAB in May 1977 because of its support for COVERT ACTION and his belief that he was receiving sufficient advice on intelligence matters from the NATIONAL SECURITY COUNCIL.

It was reinstated by President Reagan on Oct. 20, 1981, with 19 "distinguished citizens" from outside the government appointed to the body. Addressing the Reagan era in his book *Veil: The Secret Wars of the CIA 1981–1987* (1987), reporter BOB WOODWARD described the PFIAB members as "a high-powered nonpartisan community of elders to whom the White House owed a favor."

Members of the PFIAB have included WILLIAM J. CASEY, a future DIRECTOR OF CENTRAL INTELLIGENCE; Edward Teller, Nobel Prize–winning "father of the H-bomb"; Clark Clifford, a future Secretary of Defense; Gen. Maxwell Taylor, former Chairman of the Joint Chiefs of Staff; EDWIN H. LAND of Polaroid fame and pioneer in SATELLITE camera development; former Texas governor and Secretary of the Navy John Connally; former ambassador Clare Booth Luce; Nelson A. Rockefeller; and future presidential candidate H. Ross Perot.

The members of PFIAB serve without compensation at the pleasure of the President. One member of the PFIAB is also chairman of the three-member Intelligence Oversight Board.

PFIAB CHAIRMEN

The chairman of the board have been:

1956–1963	Dr. James R. Killian
1963–1968	Clark H. Clifford
1968–1970	Gen. Maxwell D. Taylor, USA (Ret.)
1970–1976	Adm. George W. Anderson, USN (Ret.)
1976–1977	Leo Cheme
1982–1990	Ambassador Anne L. Armstrong
1990–1991	Sen. John G. Tower
1991–1993	Adm. BOBBY RAY INMAN, USN (Ret.)(acting)
1993–1994	Adm. William J. Crowe, Jr., USN (Ret)
1995	Rep. Les Aspin
1996	Sen. Warren B. Rudman (acting)
1997–	Rep. Thomas S. Foley
2001	Sen. Warren B. Rudman
2001–	Lt. Gen. Brent Scowcroft, USAF (Ret.)

Primakov, Yevgeny Maksimovich

(b. 1929)

Russia's first post-Soviet spymaster. Primakov was one of only two members of Soviet President Mikhail Gorbachev's security council to oppose the attempted coup against him in Aug. 1991. Subsequently, Russian President Boris Yeltsin appointed Primakov to head the Soviet security-intelligence apparatus, the KGB. He remained head of the agency after the demise of the Soviet Union and establishment of the SVR, the Russian Foreign Intelligence Service.

Primakov graduated from the Moscow University's Institute of Oriental Studies in 1953, after which he studied at Moscow State University, earning a Ph.D. in economics in 1969.

From 1953 to 1962 he was a radio and television correspondent, becoming editor and then chief editor of radio broadcasting, and subsequently for the main editorial board of the state committee for radio and television. He joined the staff of the newspaper *Pravda* in 1962, specializing in Asia, Africa, and the Middle East. In 1977 he left *Pravda* to become a deputy director at the Institute of World Economics and International Relations. Two years later he was named director of the Institute of Oriental Studies, a post he held until 1985, when he was named director of the Institute of World Economy and International Relations.

He became a candidate member of the Communist Party's Central Committee in 1987, and that same year he was elected a deputy to the Supreme Soviet. Mikhail Gorbachev used him as a personal envoy in the Middle East prior to naming him head of the KGB in Aug. 1991. He was the first non-intelligence-specialist to be appointed to head the principal Soviet intelligence ORGAN in the more than 70 years since the CHEKA was established. In a virtually unprecedented public statement two days after being nominated for the KGB post, Primakov told a news conference that he was in favor of greater glasnost, or "openness," in the intelligence business. Describing modern intelligence activities, he said:

> If you think that spies are people in gray coats, skulking around street corners, listening to people's conversations and welding iron bars, then my appointment is unnatural. We must use analytical methods, synthesize information. This is scientific work.

Primakov succeeded to head the SVR in Dec. 1991. He directed Russian foreign intelligence activities through the difficult transition from the Soviet Union to the Russian Federation.

On Jan. 10, 1996, Yeltsin nominated Primakov to be Russia's Foreign Minister. Prior to becoming head of the KGB he had traveled extensively throughout the world, including three trips to the United States in 1987–1990. In 1998 Yeltsin chose Primakov as a candidate for prime minister. In May 1999, when he refused to remove communists from the government, Yeltsin fired Primakov.

Prime, Geoffrey A.

(b. 1938)

British cryptologist at the GOVERNMENT COMMUNICATIONS HEADQUARTERS (GCHQ) who spied for the Soviet Union.

Prime studied the Russian language while he was in the Royal Air Force and served as a sergeant in a unit that intercepted Warsaw Pact military communications. He was still in the RAF when he was recruited by the KGB. After leaving the RAF in Sept. 1968, he worked for almost eight years in London as a transcriber for a commercial firm, maintaining contact with the KGB via shortwave radio.

In March 1976 he went to work at GCHQ in Cheltenham, where he translated Soviet communications intercepted by the British. He was assigned to the extremely secret J Division, which focused on the interception of the most sensitive Soviet communications, much of which was shared with the United States. He was appointed head of the J Division in Nov. 1976.

Prime quit GCHQ in Sept. 1977 and began driving a taxi in Cheltenham, saying he had left the government because of marital problems. He kept numerous classified documents, which he turned over to the KGB—for payment—in 1980.

A solitary, meticulous man, Prime had two secret lives: He was a spy and he was a pedophile, whose victims were girls 10 to 15 years old. He kept a record of his sexual depravity on index cards. A police investigation into sexual attacks on young girls around Cheltenham led to his arrest on sexual assault charges in 1982. After his arrest his wife revealed that he was a spy.

A search of his apartment yielded a hoard of 2,287

index cards on his victims—as well as a CODE pad and instructions on the use of MICRODOTS. He had access to what was described in court as "information of the utmost secrecy"—at least from 1968 to 1977. In 1982 he was convicted of espionage and sentenced to 35 years in prison; he also received a sentence of three years for sexual assault. He was released on parole in March 2001.

His Soviet CODE NAME was Rowlands.

Principal Agent

An AGENT who, under the direction of an INTELLIGENCE OFFICER, is responsible for the activities of other agents; a surrogate HANDLER.

Product

In intelligence terms, the final result of intelligence analysis that is prepared for the customer or user; it may be in oral, written, or graphic form.

Profumo Affair

Espionage and SEX scandal that precipitated the resignation of British Prime Minister Harold Macmillan.

The complex affair originated with artist-osteopath Stephen Ward, a player in British society, and his two protégées, teenage prostitutes Christine Keeler and Mandy Rice-Davies. Keeler engaged in sex with both Secretary of State for War John D. Profumo and the Soviet assistant naval ATTACHÉ, Capt. 3rd Rank YEVGENY IVANOV.

Soon after his arrival in London in March 1960, Ivanov was introduced to Ward socially, and the two became close fiends. At the time Keeler and Rice-Davies, teenage semi-nude dancers, were living with Ward, who was apparently having sexual relations with Rice-Davies, but not with Keeler. Ivanov met Keeler in the spring of 1961; his autobiographical *The Naked Spy* (1992) provided graphic descriptions of Keeler:

> There was some magic in Christine . . . . another girl from the provinces, simple and naive . . . . a dangerous creature, sly and treacherous. Her eyes told me that: they shone with passion, sensuality and cunning. Like a small furry animal, she was graceful and enchanting, but she was also a predator.

Ward quickly included Ivanov in his social circle, where the Soviet official met Lord Astor, Winston Churchill, Prince Philip, international oil magnate Paul Getty, and Profumo. Ivanov, an experienced INTELLIGENCE OFFICER of the GRU, was able to purloin documents—some secret—and socially interrogate many of Ward's friends.

Profumo was of particular interest to Ivanov. After entering Parliament in 1940, at the age of 24, he served in the Army during World War II and rose to the rank of

brigadier by 1945. He became a successful businessman, regained his seat in Parliament in 1950, and married actress Valerie Hobson. He held several positions in the Tory government of Harold Macmillan, who became Prime Minister in 1957, with Profumo becoming Secretary of State for War in 1960.

Profumo met Keeler on July 9, 1961. She had been swimming nude at Ward's country cottage, adjacent to Lord Astor's Cliveden estate in Berkshire, where Profumo was attending a party. The following day, despite the presence of his wife, Profumo flirted with Keeler. That night Ivanov drove Keeler to Ward's apartment in London, and she and Ivanov became sexually involved.

Three days later Ward told a contact at the British Security Service (MI5) that Ivanov had asked him specific questions about U.S. plans to put nuclear missiles into West Germany. Sir ROGER HOLLIS, Director-General of MI5, should have reported this to the Foreign Office, which has the power to expel any diplomat who attempts to breach the OFFICIAL SECRETS ACT. Hollis failed to do this. His questionable judgment about the Profumo affair later added weight to suspicions that he himself was a Soviet MOLE.

Ivanov wrote that he became interested in Keeler because he could see there was "obviously something going on" between her and Profumo. But, wrote Ivanov, "She was a half literate lass only good for showing her legs. Was I going to get her to ask [Profumo] about atomic secrets?" But Ivanov slept with her anyway. (Ivanov was married; his wife was a CODE clerk at the Soviet Embassy in London.)

Subsequently, Keeler began sleeping with Profumo.

Meanwhile, the Security Service warned Profumo about Ivanov and his close relationship with Ward. Although Profumo did not know at the time about Ivanov's relationship with Keeler, he decided to break off the relationship with her late in 1961.

Nearly a year later Keeler became involved with two West Indians; one was arrested after he fought with the other over her. The incident came to the attention of the press, which learned of Ward's relationship with Keeler. She revealed her relationships with Profumo and Ivanov in a story she sold to the *Sunday Pictorial* in late 1962. Ivanov quickly departed for Moscow.

Profumo denied everything and tried to have the news stories suppressed. Questions were asked in Parliament, and on March 22, 1963, Profumo formally denied having indulged in any improprieties with Keeler. Meanwhile, Ward was charged with living off the earnings of prostitutes. In an effort to save himself, Ward sent a letter to Macmillan stating that Profumo had lied to the House of Commons. With details of the Ivanov-Keeler link known, the press raised the issue of security LEAKS to the Soviets.

Writing to Macmillan on June 4, 1963, Profumo resigned from the government, admitting that he had lied.

But the press continued to headline the scandal until, in Oct. 1963, Prime Minister Macmillan resigned. A government report published at the time concluded that the connections between Profumo, Ward, Keeler, and Ivanov had not damaged British security—although Ivanov was to claim differently.

Meanwhile, Ward was brought to trial in the Old Bailey on July 22. On July 30 he took an overdose of sleeping pills. Although he was unconscious, the trial continued and he was found guilty of living off the immoral earnings of prostitution. He died without regaining consciousness.

Keeler was tried, convicted of perjury, and sent to prison. (Mandy Rice-Davies became a cabaret singer and opened a string of successful nightclubs.)

Profumo left politics and dedicated his life to charities. In 1975 Queen Elizabeth II rewarded him for his work with one of the country's highest honors, Commander of the British Empire.

Keeler, in the ghost-written *The Truth at Last* (2000), insisted that she may have cavorted as a bare-breasted nightclub dancer, but she had never been a prostitute, a role, she said, that the British establishment had invented to smear her.

Program 1010

TRW Corp. project to develop a fifth-generation imaging SATELLITE, given the CODE NAME KH-X and then the KEYHOLE-series designation 11; it was subsequently given the BYEMAN name KENNAN.

Proprietary Company

Term used by the CIA to designate ostensibly private, commercial entities capable of doing business, which are in fact established and controlled by intelligence services; the affiliation with the intelligence organization is usually secret. See AIR AMERICA.

Proskyov, Lt. Gen. of Aviation Ivan Iosifovich

(b. ? d. 1940)

Soviet fighter pilot and INTELLIGENCE OFFICER who served as chief of the GRU, Soviet MILITARY INTELLIGENCE, in 1939–1940.

Proskyov combined the roles of pilot and intelligence officer as a Soviet military adviser in Spain in 1937–1938. He participated in air battles and shot down several Nationalist aircraft in that conflict. At the same time he carried out a series of first-class recruitments among the internationalists from several countries who were participating in the conflict on the Republican side. Given the rank of brigade commander, Proskyov was awarded the Hero of the Soviet Union in 1937, the country's highest decoration.

Upon his return from Spain, Proskyov became chief of the GRU, a post he occupied from April 1939 until July 1940. He openly spoke against the Soviet pact with Germany (signed in Aug. 1939), which set the stage for Hitler's invasion of Poland and the start of World War II

in Europe. He was arrested on July 4, 1940, and shot the following day without trial.

Protective Intelligence

Information sought specifically to help protect a person believed to be in danger of assassination. The U.S. SECRET SERVICE developed the concept, beginning with a study of imprisoned assassins and would-be assassins. Researchers believed that learning about "similarities of characteristics, thoughts, or behaviors among past assassins" would help law enforcement officials better identify persons who might pose a threat to public figures, according to the Secret Service report on the research study.

The subjects of the research study were 83 people who had attacked or approached to attack prominent public officials or celebrities in the United States from 1949 to 1996. As an outgrowth of its protective intelligence program, the Secret Service created the National Threat Assessment Center (NTAC) in Washington, D.C., to provide guidance to law enforcement organizations called upon to investigate or prevent what the Secret Service calls "targeted violence."

In a protective intelligence investigation, said the Secret Service report, law enforcement officials seek a "prediction of violence," meaning that, "given certain circumstances or conditions, a specified risk exists that a particular subject will act violently toward a particular target."

Provocation

Activity intended to cause an individual, organization, intelligence service, or government to take actions that can cause damage to itself. A provocation AGENT (or AGENT PROVOCATEUR) provides false information as part of a provocation operation.

Psalm

U.S. special information-handling channel for classified material related to the presence of Soviet ballistic missiles in Cuba. This included material provided by Col. OLEG PENKOVSKY.

Psychic Intelligence

Information supposedly obtained by paranormal means, through extrasensory perception (ESP) or the use of psychic powers. The U.S. DEFENSE INTELLIGENCE AGENCY (DIA) spent an estimated $20 million on attempts to obtain psychic intelligence for more than a decade. The project, given the CODE NAME Stargate, started in the 1980s and continued until 1995, when officials, closing down the program, admitted the employment of psychics (known as "remote viewers") by the DIA and other intelligence agencies.

The Pentagon venture into the paranormal was apparently inspired by Soviet attempts at psychic intelligence gathering. Extensive disclosure of the Soviet experiments came in 1970 with the publication in the United States of the book *Psychic Discoveries Behind the Iron Curtain*. The authors, Sheila Ostrander and Lynn Schroeder, said that they had interviewed many prominent Soviet scientists who had been working on parapsychology and ESP for many years.

In an experiment that later intrigued U.S. Navy researchers, the Soviets placed baby rabbits in a submerged submarine, inserting electrodes into the brain of the mother rabbit and keeping her in a laboratory on shore. At the exact moment an experimenter killed a baby rabbit in the submarine, the mother's brain reacted. "There was communication," a Soviet scientist reported. "And our instruments clearly registered these moments of ESP."

The Soviet work seems to have begun soon after a French publication reported that the U.S. Navy had been testing ship-to-shore telepathy, using the *Nautilus*, the world's first nuclear-propelled submarine. Ostrander and Schroeder quoted Dr. Leonid L. Vasiliev, a Soviet physiologist, as saying, "We carried out extensive and, until now, completely unreported investigations on ESP under the Stalin regime! Today the American Navy is testing telepathy on their atomic submarines. . . . We must again plunge into the exploration of this vital field." Vasiliev wrote widely on parapsychology.

Pentagon officials became interested in *Psychic Discoveries Behind the Iron Curtain* soon after it was published, but whether that book led to the DIA program is not known. *The Washington Post* revealed in Nov. 1995 that Stargate psychics had been employed at FORT MEADE, Md., the site of NSA. Stargate was quietly ended around mid-1995, shortly after the CIA took it over and had it evaluated by outside consultants. On the basis of their negative report, the CIA leadership decided that no more funds should be spent on the program. If it had not been for unnamed senators, intelligence sources said, the psychic program would have been ended long before intelligence officials shut it down.

Some DIA officials believed that in at least 19 cases the "remote viewers" produced successful results. In one of the cited cases, in Sept. 1979 the NATIONAL SECURITY COUNCIL asked about a Soviet submarine under construction. A remote viewer predicted that a very large submarine with 18 to 20 missile launch tubes and a "large flat area" aft would be launched in 100 days. Two submarines with missile tubes (but with fewer missile tubes than predicted) were sighted in 120 days.

One of the remote viewers was Joseph McMoneagle, a U.S. Army warrant officer who was assigned to Stargate (then code-named Grillflame) in 1978. He said that the information he and other remote viewers supplied was always used to supplement intelligence from more conventional sources. Requests for psychic intelligence, he said, came from the CIA, NSA, the Joint Chiefs of Staff, the Drug Enforcement Agency, Secret Service, the Customs Bureau, and the Coast Guard.

Pueblo

U.S. Navy INTELLIGENCE COLLECTION SHIP boarded and captured by North Korean forces on Jan. 23, 1968, some 12 miles off the coast of Wonsan. The *Pueblo* was converted from an Army coastal cargo ship in 1966–1967 specifically for the collection of ELECTRONIC INTELLIGENCE (ELINT), being redesignated AGER 2. Although operated by the Navy, the ship was under the operational control of the NSA, which provided the technicians who served on board.

During 1968 the *Pueblo* was to participate in Operation ICHTHYIC with the USS *Banner* to conduct intelligence surveillance off the coasts of North Korea and Soviet Siberia. By the start of 1968 the *Banner* had successfully completed 16 intelligence collection missions. The *Pueblo*—on her first mission, code-named *Pinkroot I*—steamed out of Sasebo, Japan, on the morning of Jan. 11, 1968, heading northeast through the Tsushima Strait toward the Sea of Japan. On board the 176-foot Navy ship were 83 men: six officers, 73 enlisted men, two enlisted Marines who were Korean linguists, and two civilian Navy oceanographers. The ship was armed with two .50-caliber machine guns and with small arms.

The *Pueblo* was to spy on naval activities off North Korean ports, record samples of electronic signals off the North Korean coast, and keep any Soviet naval ships in the area under electronic SURVEILLANCE.

At 11:50 A.M. on Jan. 23 the *Pueblo* was steaming 15.8 nautical miles off the port of Wonsan when a North Korean SO-1 patrol ship was detected approaching. The ship "outgunned" the *Pueblo*, whose machine guns were under canvas covers that were frozen and in exposed positions. Four Korean torpedo boats soon appeared, and at 1:27 P.M. the first shots were fired.

Beginning at 12:55, the *Pueblo* had radioed U.S. commanders in Japan that she was being threatened. But no defensive action was taken by U.S. forces in Japan or South Korea—or by Commander LLOYD M. BUCHER, commanding officer of the *Pueblo*. Although some of his officers had earlier expressed concern about the approach of the North Korean craft, Bucher did not order the destruction of the classified documents and equipment until after the SO-1 had begun firing at his ship with a 57-mm cannon.

Bucher later wrote in the U.S. Naval Institute *Proceedings*:

Soon it became apparent that further flight was impossible, without a slaughter of the crew and the possible loss of all classified material. I thought to buy time by coming to a stop. During the firing the classified material destruction was not properly progressing. I had hoped that this above all else could be accomplished before we were all killed or the ship was seized or whatever was to happen. I desperately hoped that U.S. forces would appear on the scene, and I had communications from Kamiseya [Japan] indicating that "help was on the way." Two North Korean MiGs were now flying over us and firing rockets ineffectively. We had to depend on the promised help if the ship was to ever have a chance of breaking clear of the situation.

The ship's 28 intelligence specialists had neither the facilities nor the training necessary for anything but haphazard attempts at destroying the cryptographic equipment and key list materials. On board were 50 concussion grenades (which had been designed not to destroy documents but to be dropped in the water as a defense against hostile swimmers); a few fire axes; some sledgehammers; and two antiquated paper shredders, each of which would take 15 minutes to destroy a stack of paper eight inches high.

At 2:05 the *Pueblo* radioed: "DESTROYING ALL KEYLISTS AND AS MUCH ELEC EQUIP [electronic equipment] AS POSSIBLE . . ." At 2:18, mention was made of some cryptographic machines: "WE HAVE THE KW-7 AND SOME CARDS IN THE [KWR] 37 AND [KG-]14 TO SMASH. I THINK THAT JUST ABOUT IT." And, at 2:30, "DESTRUCTION OF PUBS [PUBLICATIONS] HAVE BEEN INEFFECTIVE. SUSPECT SEVERAL WILL BE COMPROMISED." At 2:32 P.M. the *Pueblo* was boarded by North Korean troops. The *Pueblo* stopped transmitting.

Of the more than 400 classified documents in the ship, an unknown number had been destroyed and some of the electronic intercept, communications, and cryptographic gear had been smashed. Many documents had not been destroyed. Some *Pueblo* sailors later recalled seeing one or two canvas mattress covers stuffed with secret documents that were to be weighted and dropped over the side still on board. Scores of classified documents littered the ship's passageways. Also surviving were some diagrams and manuals for repairing the gear. No one in the crew could later remember seeing those documents burned or thrown overboard.

Once captured, the *Pueblo* entered Wonsan under her own power. Soviet and Chinese intelligence specialists were climbing through the *Pueblo* within days of her being brought into port. The 83 Americans were quickly taken ashore, some wounded by the spurt of North Korean gunfire. One sailor soon died. The survivors were

The U.S. intelligence collection ship Pueblo *at sea during her brief career as a spy ship. Operating off the coast of North Korea, she was sent into "harm's way" without adequate contingency plans should she be attacked. Boarded at sea in 1968, she provided a bounty of intelligence material to her captors.* (U.S. NAVY)

interrogated, beaten, and forced to write confessions. They were released 11 months later after the United States apologized and admitted that the ship was in North Korean waters.

As President Johnson grappled with the war-threatening crisis that followed the seizure of the *Pueblo*, the possible compromising of enciphering equipment got little notice. CIPHER machines were low priority for an outraged President who was talking in private about the possible use of a nuclear weapon against North Korea. And for the Navy, the excruciating humiliation over the loss of a ship far transcended the loss of battered cryptographic equipment and outdated key lists.

A Navy court of inquiry held after Comdr. Bucher's release recommended a court-martial, but the Secretary of the Navy stayed any legal action against him. He retired from the Navy in 1973.

The *Pueblo*, which had become a Korean tourist attraction, remained moored in Wonsan harbor until Oct. 1999, when Korean sailors took her around the southern tip of South Korea to an anchorage near Pyongyang. In Oct. 2002, the ship was moved again, this time to Nampo, to coincide with the arrival of an American envoy; North Korean dictator Kim Jong Il had planned to return the ship to the United States as a goodwill gesture to President George W. Bush. But worsening relations between the two countries has indefinitely delayed the *Pueblo*'s return.

Pugh, Seaman Apprentice Ernest C.

U.S. Navy sailor who attempted to become a DEFECTOR. Pugh, who was stationed at the Defense Language School in Monterey, Calif., walked into the Soviet Consulate in San Francisco in Aug. 1982 and tried to defect. The Naval Investigative Service (NIS) reported that Pugh had requested political asylum in the Soviet Union prior to enlisting in the Navy. "Pugh had an affinity for the Soviet Union, and it became apparent during the investigation that the Soviets intended to use Pugh for espionage purposes," the NIS said. Diagnosed as having a personality disorder, he was given a convenience-of-the-government discharge.

Purple

U.S. CODE machine used to decipher Japanese diplomatic codes. The American machine functioned on the same principle as the Japanese *97-shiki O-bun Injiki*, or Alphabetical Typewriter 97 (the number derived from when it was invented—the Japanese year 2597 [1937]). The Japanese machine represented a radical departure from the German ENIGMA and other electrical encoding machines because it used a battery of six-level, 25-point switches with a plugboard to establish the key; Enigma and other encoding machines were based on the use of multiple rotors.

The Japanese machine was invented by Capt. Risaburo Itō of the Japanese Navy, and it was first used in Tokyo in Feb. 1939. (Itō had earlier translated HERBERT O. YARDLEY's *The American Black Chamber* [1931] into Japanese.) By Dec. 1941 the alphabetical typewriter was in use by the Japanese Foreign Ministry, Naval Intelligence, and 13 embassies.

The American Purple was largely the result of efforts by America's leading codebreaker, WILLIAM F. FRIEDMAN. He, his colleagues at the Army's SIGNAL INTELLIGENCE SERVICE—especially Frank B. Rowlett—and Navy specialists built the first Purple device in 1940 at the Washington Navy Yard after more than a year of intense efforts. The first complete Japanese message text was deciphered in the fall of the following year. (Friedman referred to his staff as "magicians," apparently the origin of the term MAGIC that was used for Purple-derived intelligence.)

Rear Adm. EDWIN T. LAYTON, the senior INTELLIGENCE OFFICER of the U.S. Pacific Fleet, later wrote in *"And I Was There"* (1985), "By the second week in September [1940] the current keys to the Purple cipher had been recovered and the rat's nest of wiring and chattering relays housed in a makeshift black wooden box finally rewarded the months of ingenious labor by producing the first decrypts of Tokyo's most secret diplomatic messages."

Eight Purple machines were produced in the United States by Dec. 1941. Two were used at the War Department and two at the Navy Department in Washington by the service intelligence departments; one was sent to the Philippines, to be operated by a Navy team (station CAST); and three were transferred to British codebreakers at BLETCHLEY PARK, the first of those being sent to Britain in the spring of 1941 on board the battleship *King George V*, along with four Americans to work with British codebreakers. (One of the three machines that went to Britain had apparently been originally intended for the intelligence staff at U.S. naval headquarters at Pearl Harbor.)

Beyond the Purple machine, the Army-Navy codebreakers had to determine the key, which the Japanese changed every day. This key was not only "recovered" on a regular basis, but a system of "predicted keys" was developed whereby older keys could be reused after undergoing manipulations.

In Washington the Army and Navy shared the Purple cryptologic and distribution efforts, the Army processing messages with an even date and the Navy those with an odd date, with a complete sharing of results. (Later, the Navy took odd months and the Army even months.) This combined intercept and cryptologic process produced some 7,000 decrypted and translated diplomatic messages in the six months before the PEARL HARBOR ATTACK by Japan on Dec. 7, 1941, an average of about 300 messages per week. The most important ones were carried by military officers to a small group of senior officials in Washington: President Roosevelt; the Secretaries of State, War, and the Navy; the Chief of Staff of the Army; the Chief of Naval Operations, and a few senior INTELLIGENCE OFFICERS of each service. Fourteen copies of each decrypted message were typed—12 for distribution (to be returned for destruction after reading) and two for Army and Navy files.

In the Philippines the radio intercepts made at Fort McKinley (near Manila) were forwarded to Washington and to the Navy decrypt team on Corregidor. The intercepts were passed to the two senior U.S. commanders in the Philippines, Gen. Douglas MacArthur and Adm. Thomas C. Hart.

No models of the original alphabetical typewriter are known to exist; only rough drawings survive. In defeat, the Japanese had destroyed all of them, except that some components were found buried in BERLIN by the Japanese embassy staff. (See HIROSHI OSHIMA.)

Purple was the name assigned by the U.S. Navy to the alphabetical-typewriter-produced Japanese codes; an earlier code was designated "red" because of the color of the notebook binder used by the Navy. (See RED BOOK.)

Also see RUDOLPH J. FABIAN, LAURENCE L. SAFFORD.

Putin, Vladimir

(b. 1952)

President of Russia and former KGB officer.

Most of Putin's career was spent in the KGB, first in the external intelligence department in East Germany. The assumption is he helped the regime track down anti-communists. But few details about his work are known in the West.

Born in St. Petersburg (then Leningrad), he graduated from law school in 1975 and is believed to have been selected for the KGB at that time. After attending the Intelligence Academy, he was reportedly assigned the task of recruiting foreign AGENTS. He then went to Germany, working there until 1989 when he returned to Leningrad (which in 1991, after a citywide referendum, would be again St. Petersburg.) Officially, he held "a high academic post" at Leningrad State University and in 1990 entered politics as an assistant to the mayor of Leningrad.

But he remained connected to the KGB, probably selecting officer candidates from the ranks of university students, and, according to some intelligence sources, he became one of the behind-the-scenes architects of the guerrilla war with Chechnya. That continuing struggle began after the Soviet Union collapsed and Russia, split into 15 independent republics, began building a democratic system.

Putin became first deputy of the mayor of St. Petersburg in 1994, helped to develop a political party called Our Home is Russia, and completed his doctorate in economics, with an emphasis on market theory. During the same period, he also headed the city emergency committee and monitored the activities of the law enforcement agencies.

In Aug. 1996, Putin transferred to Moscow to work under President Boris Yeltsin as deputy property manager. He was made the deputy chief of staff to Yeltsin in March 1997 and was looked upon as Yeltsin's successor. The following May he became first deputy chief of the presidential staff in charge of Russian regions and territories.

In July 1998, he was appointed director of the Russian Federal Security Service (FSB), which had been established in 1991 by Yeltsin to replace the KGB. In March 1999, Putin became secretary of the Russian Security Council while keeping his post of FSB director.

On Dec. 31, 1999, Yeltsin resigned and Putin replaced him, winning the post in March 2000 by receiving nearly 53 percent of the popular vote. One of his first moves was the strengthening of security services to root out official corruption.

Sergei Kovalev, a former lawmaker who served as Yeltsin's human rights chief, predicted in Feb. 2000 that Putin would use his KGB experience to shape "an authoritarian-police regime that will preserve the formal characteristics of democracy . . . However, life will not be sweet for Russia's fledgling civil society."

Puzzle Palace

Term generally used for the Pentagon Building, located in Arlington, Va., just outside Washington, D.C. It has been the headquarters for the Department of Defense and military services since 1942. However, author JAMES BAMFORD used the term for his book *The Puzzle Palace* (1982), the revealing and definitive public discussion of NSA.

Pyramider

U.S. secret communications SATELLITE study, details of which were sold to the Soviet Union by American spies CHRISTOPHER BOYCE and ANDREW D. LEE

In an unusual twist, VICTOR L. MARCHETTI, a former CIA officer, testified at Boyce's trial that such a satellite communications system had been planned in the 1960s. The CIA, said Marchetti, had also considered using the proposed satellite to transmit intentionally confusing data that could be intercepted by the Soviets so "the Russians would go bananas trying to figure out what it [the message] meant, when it actually meant nothing." Marchetti had been subpoenaed by Boyce's lawyers to establish that the Pyramider was not a viable project and should not have been classified TOP SECRET.

(Under cross-examination, Marchetti conceded that the project he had seen was in a preliminary stage when he left the CIA in 1969, and was not as capable and complex as the satellite envisioned in the later TRW study.)

Boyce, working on CIA satellite projects while employed by the TRW firm, had access to the Pyramider project, which was intended to provide the means for U.S. AGENTS in hostile areas to have two-way communication with CIA headquarters in LANGLEY, Va. The satellite could also collect intelligence from secretly emplaced sensors that could be planned on hostile territory by agents, or dropped from aircraft.

According to testimony during Boyce's trial, the Pyramider system would consist of three geosynchronous satellites that would provide a direct link to the CIA. A total of 3,500 communications and data channels would be available through the system, which would also be used as a backup communications link for non-covert radio traffic among U.S. embassies and to CIA headquarters.

The Pyramider had been initiated with a TRW study in 1973. Although the project never went beyond the study stage, its revelation to Soviet intelligence revealed U.S. technical capabilities in the satellite field, requirements for communicating with agents, and other information.

After the arrest of Boyce and Lee in Jan. 1977, a copy of the study that Lee had attempted to pass to his contacts at the Soviet Embassy in Mexico City was allegedly recovered by FBI agents.

The Pyramider satellite was to weigh an estimated 1,900 pounds. Two ground receiving stations were envisioned in the TRW study, one at CIA headquarters and one on Guam.

Q

SEE CHARLES FRASER-SMITH and ANTONIO J. MENDEZ

Q Clearance

U.S. SECURITY CLEARANCE given by the Department of Energy (DOE, formerly Atomic Energy Commission) to DOE employees, personnel of other government agencies, and contractors. A "Q" clearance is valid for access to RESTRICTED DATA and national security information at the SECRET and TOP SECRET levels, primarily concerning nuclear matters.

"Q" clearance is necessary for access to nuclear weapon material.

Also see L CLEARANCE.

Queen Anne's Gate

A small house at 16–18 Queen Anne's Gate, across from St. James's Park in London, which the intelligence branch of the British Army occupied from 1884 to 1901.

The house at 21 Queen Anne's Gate served as the office and official residence of the first chief of the (Secret Intelligence Service), MI6 Capt. MANSFIELD CUMMING, or "C," from 1909 until his death in 1923. He built a secret passageway between his office and the MI6 headquarters at BROADWAY.

Cumming's successors—also known as "C"—remained at Queen Anne's Gate until 1966, when MI6 moved to the modern CENTURY HOUSE, south of the Thames River at the Victoria Embankment.

Quicksilver

CODE NAME for the complex DECEPTION operation mounted to convince the Germans that the main D-DAY in France would be at Pas de Calais. (See FIRST U.S. ARMY GROUP.)

Rabbani, Ali Naghi

(b. 1920)

Iranian official in the Education Ministry who spied for the Soviet Union for 30 years.

Rabbani was arrested by INTELLIGENCE OFFICERS of the SAVAK, the Iranian secret police, as he was on his way to meet Evgeni Venediktov, his KGB CASE OFFICER, in May 1977.

Rabbani had been recruited by Soviet intelligence in the 1940s, when the Soviet Union was menacing Iran, then under the rule of Shah Muhammad Reza Pahlavi. The Soviets, supported by the anti-Shah party called the *Tudeb* (masses), occupied much of northern Iran. Although he did not learn valuable intelligence information at his education post, Rabbani had influential friends and passed items of POLITICAL INTELLIGENCE to the Soviets.

Tried and sentenced to death, Rabbani received a reprieve from the Shah, who indefinitely postponed Rabbani's execution in return for his giving the Savak information on Soviet intelligence activities in Iran.

Raborn, Vice Adm. William F., Jr.

(b. 1905 d. 1990)

U.S. DIRECTOR OF CENTRAL INTELLIGENCE (DCI) from April 28, 1965, to June 30, 1966, one of the shortest tenures for a DCI.

"Red" Raborn, as he was known since midshipman days, graduated from the Naval Academy in 1928. A naval aviator and ordnance specialist who served afloat and ashore, Raborn directed the Navy's Special Projects Office from 1955 to 1962, managing the Polaris submarine-launched missile program from its inception in Dec. 1955. Adm. Arleigh A. Burke, Chief of Naval Operations, said he chose Raborn "because he has the driving ability, he's got a lot of energy, he's full of enthusiasm, and he can persuade people. He can get things done." He did. The first Polaris missile was test-fired from the submarine *George Washington* on July 18, 1960, several years ahead of the original schedule.

Raborn's swift development of the Polaris missile was based on the PERT system—Program Evaluation and Review Technique. It became a model for managing large, complex projects in and out of government.

As a vice admiral, he served as Deputy Chief of Naval Operations for development from 1962 to 1963. He worked in private industry before and after his service as DCI.

President Johnson appointed Raborn, a fellow Texan, as DCI, to the surprise and chagrin of high-ranking officials of the CIA, who had wanted a professional INTELLIGENCE OFFICER from their own ranks. He had no previous intelligence experience when he became DCI—and according to CIA veterans of that era, it showed. Ronald Kessler, evaluating Raborn in *Inside the CIA* (1992), wrote that when President Johnson intervened in the Dominican Republic in 1965, "Raborn decided that he could best contribute by rushing every piece of paper received by the CIA to the president." RICHARD M. HELMS, then Deputy DCI, intervened, preventing raw, unevaluated material from getting to Johnson. "I never worked for a nicer guy who was more out of his element," said Walter N. Elder, who was Raborn's executive assistant. "I thought President Johnson did him a disservice by naming him DCI."

Radar Intelligence

(RADINT)

Intelligence derived from radar, in modern times a subset of IMAGERY INTELLIGENCE.

Radar Ocean Reconnaissance Satellite

(RORSAT)

World's first SATELLITE for oceanic RECONNAISSANCE, developed and deployed by the Soviet Union.

Known to Western intelligence as RORSAT, the satellites began undergoing testing for ocean reconnaissance in late 1967. Operational RORSAT satellites began going into orbit in 1974. The Soviets employed two types of satellites for seeking Western warships on the high seas: ELECTRONIC INTELLIGENCE (ELINT) Ocean Reconnaissance Satellite (EORSAT) vehicles, and RORSATs.

The ELINT, or FERRET, satellites detect and "lock on" to electronic signals emanating from ships, indicating their location and possibly, from the kind of radar signals, information on the type of ship; they cue in radar satellites to "look at" suspected ship TARGETS. The ferret satellites became operational about 1970. Weighing almost 18,400 pounds, they were initially placed in orbits 266 to 269 miles above the earth. Later versions had higher orbits. These satellites were orbited in pairs to provide more accurate "fixes" on possible targets. Each pair of EORSATs was usually coordinated with a single RORSAT.

The RORSAT vehicles use active radar to detect ships, normally orbiting at heights of some 540 to 590 miles above the earth. Their radar requires considerable electrical power, which is provided by a small nuclear reactor. The reactor section weighs about one ton and carries some 110 pounds of enriched uranium (U-235) to produce up to 10 kilowatts of power for some 90 to 120 days in space. The early RORSAT satellites were 45 feet long and weighed 10,000 pounds.

Later RORSAT satellites could send target data to missile-armed aircraft, surface ships, and submarines, as well as to ground stations.

When the service life of these Cosmos-series RORSATs is completed, the section carrying the radioactive fuel is detached and boosted into a higher orbit—more than 550 miles. There it circles the earth for more than 500 years and cause no danger when it does come down and burn up in the atmosphere.

However, the RORSAT Cosmos 954 malfunctioned and the reactor plunged into the atmosphere in Jan. 1978, scattering radioactive uranium fuel particles over Canada. After the loss of Cosmos 954, the Soviets redesigned the RORSAT to prevent another reactor and its fuel from falling to earth. In an ingenious plan, if the satellite has a malfunction, or when the mission is over, the small radioactive fuel rods are ejected out to decay as they reenter the atmosphere. The empty reactor core remains radioactive, but it is heavily shielded. The ROR-

SAT emergency scheme worked on Jan. 23, 1983, when the malfunctioning Cosmos 1402 reactor, having ejected its fuel rods, crashed into the Indian Ocean. (This satellite weighed only 6,600 pounds.)

Beginning in 1986, the Soviets carried out an unprecedented research and development program in ocean reconnaissance efforts. Both RORSATs and EORSATs were improved, exhibiting variations in orbital planes, periods, and inclinations. Improvements have yielded more reliable satellite operations of longer endurance over wider search areas, providing more accurate target data for air- and sea-launched antiship cruise missiles, probably as well as land-launched ballistic missiles emplyed against naval targets.

The threat posed by these satellites to Western naval forces was revealed in early statements about the proposed U.S. Anti-Satellite (ASAT) program. In 1979 a U.S. Department of Defense official stated, "The principal motivation for our ASAT program is to put us in a position to negate Soviet satellites that control Soviet weapon systems that could attack our fleet."

Subsequently, the Soviets developed radar satellites that sought to detect submarines operating underwater. The Soviets conducted radar tests of submarine detection with their SALYUT VII manned space laboratory, launched in 1982. (Periodically provided with replacement crews, the Salyut 7 remained in orbit until early 1991.)

The Cosmos 1500 oceanographic and earth resources satellite, launched on Sept. 28, 1983, carried Synthetic Aperture Radar (SAR). The space-based SAR could detect or measure sea-surface winds, surface effects of naturally occurring internal waves, surface oil slicks, and ice. It could process and transmit real-time radar images to more than 500 Soviet ships, military and civilian, as well as to ground stations.

Cosmos 1500 appeared to be the harbinger of SAR satellites that could detect submarines. The potential of satellite detection of submarines was also realized by U.S. officials, although such interest was rarely discussed in public. However, in 1985 the U.S. Chief of Naval Operations, Adm. James Watkins, said that scientific observations from an American space shuttle (orbital) flight the year before had perhaps revealed some submarine locations. A Navy oceanographer on the flight "found some fantastically important new phenomology [sic] that will be vital to us in trying to understand the ocean depths," the admiral explained. While not releasing details of the observations, which were called "incredibly important to us," a Navy spokesman implied that "internal waves," left by a submarine's underwater transit, were involved.

By 1988 Soviet officials stated that space reconnaissance "is accomplishing many missions, including the detection of submerged submarines," and that radars deployed on aircraft and satellites were being used to "detect the wakes of submarines." These statements, the latter by the head of Soviet naval intelligence, apparently referred to satellites that had already been deployed.

A 1993 article in the Russian General Staff magazine Voennaia mysl discussing future satellites declared: "All-weather space reconnaissance and other types of space support will allow detecting the course and speed of movement of combat systems and surface and subsurface [submarine] naval platforms at any time of day with high probability, and providing high-precision weapons systems with targeting data in practically real time."

The United States never developed a similar space-based ocean reconnaissance system.

Radio Fingerprinting

Method used to determine the identity of a radio transmitter sending Morse transmissions. Different types of radios produce a distinctive "signature" when they transmit.

TINA was the British term during World War II for the study of the characteristics of individual radio operators. TINA equipment could make a recording of an operator's Morse code technique for comparison with subsequent transmissions. This was supposed to be especially helpful in espionage activities to determine if an AGENT had been captured and someone else was transmitting with his or her identification.

TINA was not always successful in that role, in part because an individual's transmission technique could vary. However, TINA was able to distinguish radio operators aboard German ships and submarines, sometimes aiding in the identification of specific types and even of individual ships.

Radio Free Europe

U.S. propaganda operation, ostensibly financed through fund-drive appeals and other volunteer public contributions. Actually, Radio Free Europe (RFE) operated on funds provided by the CIA. RFE was established in 1948 by a highly secret NATIONAL SECURITY COUNCIL directive authorizing U.S.-sponsored propaganda activities.

RFE aimed foreign-language broadcasts at East European communist nations. A similar propaganda facility, Radio Liberty, was aimed at the Soviet Union.

The propaganda was factually based and designed to give people behind the Iron Curtain a Western viewpoint. But in Oct. 1956, when Hungarians began rising against their communist government, RFE took up their cause, in what the CIA psychological warfare director later called encouragement without incitement. RFE did, however, relay rebel broadcasts, giving them wider impact—and an implication of U.S. assistance.

The Soviet Union sent in troops and tanks to put down the Hungarian revolt. In two weeks of fighting, some 7,000 Hungarians were killed. The government of West Germany, site of RFE transmitters, demanded to know how much the broadcasts had inflamed the rebels. Secretary of State John Foster Dulles had been preaching a doctrine of "liberating the captive nations," and the Germans, as did many others, wondered whether his brother, ALLEN W. DULLES, the DIRECTOR OF CENTRAL INTELLIGENCE, had been actively trying to carry out the doctrine.

After 1956, the CIA kept a tighter rein on the rhetoric of RFE and Radio Liberty (which was almost continually jammed by the Soviets). Although the two radio operations were given open government funding in 1973, their CIA origins were not revealed until 1975, when the Rockefeller Commission report on CIA activities was published.

Both Radio Free Europe and Radio Liberty continued to operate after the end of the Cold War, broadcasting in more than 25 languages. Both also have supplemented their broadcasts with Web pages.

Rado, Alexander

SEE LUCY SPY RING

Rafter

One of the major electronic security operations of the Cold War era. Undertaken by the British Security Service (MI5) from 1958 onward, the electronics security effort was able to determine that from within the Soviet Embassy in London the KGB was keeping track of British communications related to COUNTERINTELLIGENCE activities, such as trailing KGB officers in cars. MI5 personnel could then correlate Soviet tracking efforts with their own activities, leading to more effective SURVEILLANCE of suspected Soviet AGENTS.

Also see PETER WRIGHT.

Rainbow

Program to reduce the radar signature of U-2 spyplanes. When the U-2s were developed in the mid-1950s, it was expected that they would be able to fly over the Soviet Union for two to four years before they were effectively detected and tracked by Soviet radar.

The very first flight of a U-2 over the Soviet Union, on July 4, 1956, and all subsequent flights were in fact detected by radar. When CLARENCE (KELLY) JOHNSON, designer of the U-2, learned of the detections, he initiated a program—given the CODE NAME Rainbow—to reduce the U-2's radar signature or, to use a later term, enhance their "stealth."

One scheme, dubbed Trapeze, called for long bamboo poles to be fitted to both wings, parallel to the fuselage. Wires would then be fitted over the poles as well as the wings and be rigged with other wires fitted with beads that were to "trap" and reduce the returns from radar pulses.

Another proposal, given the name Wallpaper, called for anechoic materials to be glued to the fuselage and wings of the aircraft in order to absorb radar pulses. Aircraft with this covering—called "dirty birds"—overheated and suffered hydraulic problems. One aircraft crashed during the 1956–1957 tests of this concept. The pilot was killed.

In place of such modifications, the decision was reached to develop the SR-71 BLACKBIRD as a successor to the U-2.

Rainbow Warrior

Ship owned by the environmental organization Greenpeace that was blown up by French intelligence operatives in Auckland Harbor, New Zealand, on July 10, 1985. One man drowned as the ship sank. Eleven crew members and visitors survived.

The ship was sunk by time bombs that divers had attached to the hull. Berthed at a commercial pier, the *Rainbow Warrior* was to have sailed as the mother ship to four yachts that were about to picket the coral atoll of Moruroa in French Polynesia, where France was to conduct underground nuclear tests. Greenpeace directors had dispatched the ship as part of a demonstration against the "nuclearization" of the Pacific Ocean.

The sinking of the ship was the work of the DGSE, the French external security service. Some details of the plot remain murky, but there seems little doubt that the originator was Minister of Defense Charles Hernu, who believed that Greenpeace was under Soviet influence. Officials of the French nuclear-testing program, fearing Greenpeace sabotage of the scheduled test, asked, through channels, for intelligence on Greenpeace and SURVEILLANCE of the *Rainbow Warrior*. Hernu apparently then alerted Adm. PIERRE LACOSTE, chief of the DGSE, and authorized him to set up an operation called K Cell.

French Army Lt. Christine-Huguette Cabon of DGSE was a MOLE inside Greenpeace, which she had infiltrated in New Zealand. Cabon had been in *Le Cadre Spécial*, a French SPECIAL OPERATIONS FORCES unit similar to the British Special Air Service. Injured in a parachute accident in 1982, she was transferred to DGSE. From New Zealand she sent back exaggerated reports of Greenpeace plans to sabotage the test.

With Cabon in place, DGSE sent two frogmen from a base in Corsica to Auckland. They arrived in Auckland harbor by yacht, and on the night of July 10 attached two time bombs to the hull of the ship, went ashore, and hid their equipment. This was supposed to be picked up and disposed of by two other DGSE agents, Maj. Alain Mafart and Capt. Dominique Prieur, who carried Swiss passports identifying them as Alain and Sophie Turenge.

The first bomb exploded around midnight, sending all 12 persons on the ship hurrying ashore, according to plan. But before the second, larger bomb went off, Fernando Pereira, a Greenpeace photographer, returned to the ship to get some equipment, according to the definitive account of the incident in *Sink the Rainbow* (1986) by John Dyson. Pereira, 33, was killed.

Two days later, police arrested a man and woman who had been seen around the docks on the night of July 9–10 by a watchman who had jotted down the license number of their rented car. The couple, claiming to be Alain and Sophie Turenge on their honeymoon, were quickly unmasked as French AGENTS and charged with murder and arson. "Sophie" carried a notebook with telephone numbers that included those of DGSE.

When the media broke the story, DGSE attempted a DISINFORMATION campaign, claiming that the photographer had been a KGB agent and that a sinister plot had been launched to embarrass France. But the cover-up failed, and, in the tumult that resulted, Lacoste and Hernu were forced to resign.

Maj. Mafart and Capt. Prieur pleaded guilty to involuntary manslaughter to spare the French government the embarrassment of a trial. In Nov. 1985 they were sentenced to 10 years in prison. After the French government agreed to pay the victim's family 2.3 million francs and to reimburse Greenpeace for the loss of *Rainbow Warrior*, Mafart and Prieur, as part of the agreement, were released from prison in New Zealand but kept on Hao Atoll, site of a French military base, 500 miles east of Tahiti.

Mafart, claiming to be in need of medical attention, was transported to France in Dec. 1987. Prieur's husband was sent to Hao, reputedly under orders to impregnate Capt. Prieur. She did become pregnant, and in May 1988 she was transported to France. New Zealand, incensed at the flagrant breach of the agreement, took the matter to a UNITED NATIONS tribunal, which ruled that France had acted in bad faith and should pay $2 million in compensation.

In 1995, Maj. Gen. Jean-Claude Lesquer, who had commanded the unit that sank the *Rainbow Warrior*, was awarded the Grand Officer of the Legion of Honor, France's second-highest military honor.

Ramsay, Roderick James

Former U.S. Army sergeant convicted for passing defense plans of the NORTH ATLANTIC TREATY ORGANIZATION to Czechoslovakian and Hungarian INTELLIGENCE OFFICERS. In 1994 he was sentenced to 18 years in prison.

Ramsay was recruited by CLYDE LEE CONRAD, another former U.S. Army sergeant who was convicted of treason in a West German court.

The FBI said that Ramsay, who held a TOP SECRET clearance, had been an assistant document custodian of the plans section of the 8th Infantry Division in Bad Kreuznach, West Germany. Ramsay was said to have received $20,000 for selling secrets that included information about military communications and the use of tactical nuclear weapons. Ramsay initially used a 35-mm camera to photograph classified documents and later began using a video camera because it was more efficient.

Apparently Ramsay's alleged involvement with Conrad emerged from the investigation and trial of Conrad. When Ramsay was arrested, FBI Director WILLIAM S. SESSIONS said that the investigation was one of the "most complicated foreign counterintelligence investigations ever conducted by the FBI." Two years after Ramsay was arrested, the FBI arrested another soldier, Staff Sgt. JEFFREY S. RONDEAU and later arrested former U.S. soldier KELLY THERESE WARREN.

Ratfucking

Term used by insiders to describe political infiltration of Democratic Party activities by Nixon supporters in the

1972 election campaign; this infiltration was spearheaded by the PLUMBERS.

Also see HUSTON PLAN.

Ratkai, Stephen

Canadian arrested in 1989 for trying to get SECRET information on how a U.S. Navy base in Newfoundland tracked Soviet submarines. Ratkai was videotaped by the ROYAL CANADIAN MOUNTED POLICE (RCMP) while offering an advance payment of $40,000 to a U.S. Navy officer working undercover in a joint operation involving the RCMP, the U.S. Naval Investigative Service (now the NAVAL CRIMINAL INVESTIGATIVE SERVICE), and the Canadian Security Intelligence Service.

The officer acting as an AGENT, Lt. Donna Geiger, was an administrative officer at the U.S. naval facility at Argentia, Newfoundland. Ratkai asked her to get him information. He also asked for personal information, including her astrological sign and her husband's hobbies.

Ratkai pleaded guilty to espionage in a Canadian court in Feb. 1989 and the following month was sentenced to two concurrent nine-year prison terms.

Intelligence officials believed that others were implicated with Ratkai, but there were no further arrests.

Raven

Slang for a male AGENT employed to seduce males or females to engage in espionage.

Razvedka

Razvedyvatelnoye Upravlenie is the Russian term for both RECONNAISSANCE and INTELLIGENCE. It forms the basis of the organizational names GRU and RU.

Razvedyvatelnoye Upravlenie

SEE RU

RD

SEE RESTRICTED DATA

Reconnaissance

Operation to obtain information about enemy activity or resources or meteorological, hydrographic, or geographic information for a particular area.

Also see SURVEILLANCE.

Rectal Concealment Device

Container smuggled by an AGENT in his rectum for various purposes. The container may carry a message or tools. A device on display at the INTERNATIONAL SPY MU-

Rectal concealment devices, such as this one containing a variety of tools, have been in use since ancient times. (COURTESY OF INTERNATIONAL SPY MUSEUM)

SEUM contains a knife and lock picks for use in case of capture.

Red Book

CODE NAME given to Japanese SUPERENCIPHER broken by U.S. NAVY COMMUNICATIONS INTELLIGENCE cryptographers.

The original "book" was a series of surreptious photographs taken during BLACK BAG JOBS, or break-ins, at the Japanese Consulate in New York City. "The operation required more than one visit," wrote Rear Adm. EDWIN T. LAYTON, in *"And I Was There"* (1985). "It was slow going with the cameras of that day to photograph the voluminous code book of the Japanese fleet." The FBI had told the OFFICE OF NAVAL INTELLIGENCE (ONI) that a Japanese naval officer was using the COVER of vice consul.

An ONI COUNTERESPIONAGE squad picked the locks on the consul's office door, opened the safe, and photographed the book page by page. Photographs of the pages were given to Dr. Emerson J. Haworth and his wife, Japanese linguists who often translated for the ONI. The Haworths translated the book into English, a task that took nearly four years. That material was then updated with photographs taken during other break-ins at the consulate in 1926 and 1927.

The translated, retyped material was put into two volumes, which were bound in red buckram. That was the origin of the names Red Book and Red Code.

The ONI passed the two-volume Red Book to the Navy's code and signal section, where the task of deciphering the Red Book was given to AGNES MEYER DRISCOLL, a cryptographer who, like master codebreaker WILLIAM F. FRIEDMAN, had been trained at Riverbank Laboratories. She cracked the Red Book code and, in the course of her work, trained a new young Navy officer, Lt. LAURENCE L. SAFFORD, who would become a leading advocate of machine cryptology.

Redl, Col. Alfred

(b. 1864 d. 1913)

A senior Austrian INTELLIGENCE OFFICER—and a Russian spy.

One of 14 children of a poor Austrian railway official, Redl at age 14 was able to enter the Lemberg Cadet School; after graduation he entered the Austrian Army.

Despite his low origins, he was recognized as a bright officer, astute in languages, with a talent for organization. He rose to the rank of colonel and from 1900 served as head of the Kundschaftsstelle, the Austrian espionage and COUNTERESPIONAGE service.

The Russians learned of Redl's HOMOSEXUAL preference and—supplying young men as well as money—blackmailed him. Redl revealed to the Russians the identities of Austrian spies in Russia, the Austrian CODES, and the Austro-Hungarian mobilization plans.

Austrian officials in 1913 intercepted envelopes containing money and addressed to a postal box in VIENNA. When Redl went to the post office to collect them, he was found out. The Austrian government sought to keep his treason a secret. (Lack of publicity would not only save embarrassment, but it could permit the Austrian Army to make changes in war plans without the Russians' knowledge.) Confronted by fellow officers, who had orders to kill Redl if he did not take his own life, Redl shot himself. His final note read: "Levity and passion have destroyed me. Pray for me. I pay with my life for my sins."

Among the documents Redl gave the Russians was an Austrian plan for war against Serbia, which the Russians showed to the Serbians. After the assassination of Archduke Franz Ferdinand in June 1914, Austria did go to war. But because the Serbians knew the Austrian plans, they were able to repulse the stronger Austrian forces. As a result, Russia and other powers in both European alliances responded. World War I had begun.

Also see Gen. MAXIMILIAN RONGE.

Red Orchestra

German name for an anti-Nazi, Soviet-directed resistance and espionage NETWORK centered in Germany during World War II.

The ring, which was Soviet intelligence's chief source of information from German-occupied Europe, consisted of several independent CELLS originally established by the GRU, Soviet MILITARY INTELLIGENCE. Its members penetrated key political and military offices, including the German Ministries of Aviation and Economics, the High Command of the Armed Forces, and the ABWEHR, Germany's MILITARY INTELLIGENCE agency. One member of the ring was an officer attached to the German Air Force's General Staff; another worked in the CIPHER section of the Army Chief of Staff.

Like most spy organizations of the war, the Red Orchestra produced more legends than valuable intelligence. Enhancing the legends was postwar Soviet propaganda that raised the Red Orchestra to Olympian height. There is no doubt that members of the network produced important intelligence, such as German aviation strength and Army movements on the Eastern Front. But military records fail to back up claims that the ring gave the Red Army intelligence that cost the German Army 200,000 casualties. Nor do documents confirm Nazi claims that intelligence from the Red Orchestra led to the German defeat at Stalingrad.

The story of the Red Orchestra is a human tragedy, for many of its members were youthful idealists, Germans who hated Adolf Hitler. The fact that they were Germans betraying the Fatherland inspired a frenzy of blood vengeance when they were caught. They were tortured and hideously executed, many by decapitation. They left a mixed legacy—despised by many West Germans for betraying Germany, officially lionized by communist East Germany because they had helped the Soviet Union.

Members included an American, MILDRED FISH HARNACK, originally of Milwaukee, Wis., who had met a German economist, Arvid Harnack, at the University of Wisconsin. They were married and she joined him when he returned to Germany in 1929. Harnack became a senior counselor in the Ministry of Economics and in 1937 joined the Nazi Party; by then he was a secret communist and may have had a connection with Soviet intelligence.

When Hitler rose to power, Arvid and Mildred Harnack became the nucleus of a left-wing resistance group, one of the origins of the orchestra. They helped Jews escape Germany and passed ECONOMIC INTELLIGENCE to the U.S. and Soviet embassies in BERLIN. When the European War began in Sept. 1939, they and their comrades organized sabotage in German factories and published an underground newspaper.

The espionage was conducted by cells in Germany and in conquered Belgium, France, and the Netherlands. Some accounts add to the orchestra the LUCY SPY RING, a Soviet network centered in Switzerland, and cells in Spain and Yugoslavia. But the core of the orchestra was in Germany, where, before the war, Soviet intelligence had established cells among communists. The CASE OFFICERS for those prewar spies were Leopold Trepper and Anatoli Gurevich, who used Soviet-trained radio operators.

Associated with the operations run by Trepper and Gurevich were URSULA KUCZYNSKI, who later aided KLAUS FUCHS, and Alexander Rado, key man in the Lucy ring. Gurevich, a GRU officer CODE-NAMED Kent, ran the Belgian cell out of Brussels. Trepper, the RESIDENT, or director, was code-named Otto. He was said to have been appointed head of Soviet espionage in Europe after the defection of WALTER KRIVITSKY in 1937.

Orchestra was used by the Abwehr as a generic term for an espionage network. (There was also an Ardennes Orchestra and a Maritime Orchestra.) Carrying on the musical metaphor, the leader of a network was called a "conductor," a spy's shortwave transmitter was a PIANO, and a radio operator was a PIANIST. "Red" indicated the orchestra's sympathies, for the first transmitter discovered by the Abwehr was sending messages to the Soviet

Union, not Britain. (Soviet intelligence used "piano" and "pianist" in the same way. The Soviet name for the ring was *Krasney Kapel*, "Red Choir.")

On June 26, 1941, four days after Germany invaded the Soviet Union, an Abwehr radio direction finder in Berlin discovered a secret radio transmitter operating in contact with Moscow, possibly from Belgium. Three members of the ring were arrested, but Trepper was released because the Germans accepted his credentials as a businessman from France. Trepper ("the Grand Chef," Abwehr called him) was able to warn several others.

More arrests followed in July 1942. About 85 suspects were rounded up in Hamburg, along with another 118 in Berlin. Of the first wave of AGENTS arrested, two killed themselves in custody, eight were hanged, and 41 were beheaded, among them Mildred Fish Harnack. Her last words, recorded by a prison chaplain, were, "And I have loved Germany so much." (In 1964 the East German government issued commemorative POSTAGE STAMPS honoring her and others for their work.)

From Aug. to Oct. 1942, the Germans "played back" captured agents who had, under torture, turned against their orchestra comrades. A special GESTAPO task force—Sonderkommando Rote Kapelle (Red Orchestra)—was assigned to the case.

A CIA study of the Red Orchestra says that its information would have been even better used by the Soviets had it not been for Josef Stalin's distrust of anything of German origin. The Red Orchestra, for example, had reportedly warned the Soviet Union of the planned German invasion in June 1941, but Stalin dismissed the warning.

The CIA study traced the Red Orchestra to Soviet networks in Europe as early as 1930. During the war the network extended beyond Germany, into Belgium, Holland, France, Switzerland, and Italy. "Several connections," the CIA study says, "were found in England, Scandinavia, Eastern Europe, the United States, and elsewhere."

Trepper was captured and was TURNED. He went back into the underground world and tried to continue to send information to Moscow. He survived the war.

In 1969 the Order of the Red Banner was posthumously awarded to several members of the Red Orchestra.

Redoubled Agent

DOUBLE AGENT whose dual role has been discovered by the service on which he is spying and who is used, wittingly or unwittingly and voluntarily or under duress, to serve the latter service against the former service.

Red Sox–Red Cap

SEE FRANK G. WISNER

Reenciphered Codes

SEE SUPERENCIPHER

Regan, Brian Patrick

(b. 1962)

Former U.S. Air Force intelligence analyst convicted of attempted espionage.

In a trial that ended in Feb. 2003, Regan was found guilty of attempting to sell classified documents to China and Iraq. He was sentenced to life imprisonment without parole. As part of a plea bargain, the government promised not to prosecute Regan's wife, Anette, and allowed her to keep part of his military pension. They had four children.

Regan, who served in the Air Force for 20 years, worked for TRW, a defense contractor, at the NATIONAL RECONNAISSANCE OFFICE (NRO), which manages U.S. spy SATELLITES. TRW is a frequent espionage TARGET. (See PETER LEE and CHRISTOPHER BOYCE.)

Regan was 38 years old when arrested in Aug. 2001 as he was about to board a commercial flight to Switzerland. He carried information with the coded coordinates of Iraqi and Chinese missile sites, along with addresses of the Chinese and Iraqi embassies in Switzerland and Austria. He had accused of writing to Iraq and Libya offering to sell U.S. secrets for $13 million.

Regan, who owed nearly $117,000 on his credit cards, had written directly to Saddam Hussein, saying that he would be "putting my self [*sic*] and family at great risk. If I am caught I will be enprisioned [*sic*] for the rest of my life, if not executed for this deed."

Reilly, Sidney

(b. 1874? d. 1925?)

British adventurer who spied, usually for Britain, during and after the turbulence of the Russian Revolution of 1917.

As befits a master spy, his true origin is not known. He told many versions of his ancestry and embellished details of his work as a spy. But there is no doubt that he was a hidden player in history and lived an incredible life, even allowing for exaggeration. Admirers have called him the greatest spy who ever lived.

He is believed to have been born in Russia, near Odessa, as Sigmund Rosenblum, the son of a Russian woman of Polish descent and a Jewish physician from VIENNA. His mother, however, was married at the time to another man, a Russian Army colonel who was well known in the court of the czar. (Reilly sometimes gave his birth year as 1874 and sometimes as 1877.)

According to one of the many versions of his early life, he left Russia for Brazil after learning of his illegitimate birth. While there, he claimed, he saved the lives of either two or three British officers, and they rewarded him with a British passport, which he used to reach England. In 1898, when he married a widow named Margaret Thomas, he gave his name as Rosenblum. A year later he took the name Sidney Reilly, and he kept it. He spoke English and Russian fluently and claimed to have mastered five other languages.

The story of his life—recounted in numerous books, articles, and a TELEVISION series starring Sam Neill—is full of contradictions and fanciful claims. Andrew Cook, for example, writes in *On His Majesty's Secret Service—Sidney Reilly ST1* (2002) that Reilly made Margaret Thomas a widow by poisoning her husband and that his exploits inspired IAN FLEMING to create a modern (but less ambiguous) AGENT named JAMES BOND [F].

Adept at disguises and living under COVER, Reilly zigzagged through 30-odd years of spying, mostly for Britain, covering his tracks or having them covered by someone else. Michael Kettle's *Sidney Reilly* (1983), a well-documented biography of the master spy, says Reilly's LEGEND was undoubtedly created with the aid of British intelligence to give him a false persona. The legend puts Reilly in India at the start of the 20th century, graduating from a college there, and working as a railway engineer in India. "It was this alibi," Kettle wrote, "which Reilly gave whenever the situation required it."

Reilly seems to have been recruited when he was in London by the British Secret Intelligence Service (MI6) and given the CODE NAME ST1. He reportedly produced intelligence on anti-czarist Polish and Russian refugees who lived in London's East End. He may have formally begun his espionage career during the Boer War of 1899–1902, when, pretending to be German, he sought intelligence on how the Netherlands was getting aid to the Boers. According to another story he learned welding in England and then slipped into Germany, taking a job at a Krupp factory to learn the German arms industry. Some reports have him at a German shipyard to steal plans for new German warships.

Shortly before the Russo-Japanese War (1904–1905) he went to Port Arthur (now Lüshun), a major Russian naval base in the Far East. Although he worked as a merchant in Port Arthur, there is little doubt that he was reporting to MI6 on the growing tension between Japan and Russia. Some accounts claim he played a major role in the Japanese surprise attack on Port Arthur. He returned to Britain when the war began, entered the Royal School of Mines, and in 1905 went on to Trinity College, Cambridge, staying there at least two years.

Now knowledgeable about petroleum exploration, and with the veneer of a Cambridge-educated English gentleman, he went to Persia. Britain and Russia had claims there as part of the GREAT GAME for control of Central Asia. Reilly supposedly led British oil explorers to a rich field that had been eyed by French oil interests. By then Reilly was probably based in St. Petersburg, a partner in a Russian armaments firm. He also became the Russian agent for a German shipbuilder bidding to restore the Russian Fleet, all but destroyed in the war with Japan. Reilly simultaneously helped the Germans get large contracts and kept the British Admiralty informed about German warship designs. He was also pocketing large commissions, building a good-sized fortune.

At the outbreak of World War I, Reilly was in New York City working as an arms agent for Russia. There he was joined by Nadine Massino, a Russian woman who fell in love with Reilly in St. Petersburg and divorced her husband, an official in the Ministry of Marine, to marry Reilly. He bigamously married her in New York.

Learning that Reilly was in New York, Capt. MANSFIELD CUMMING, head of MI6, told his AGENTS in the United States, Col. Norman Thwaites and Sir WILLIAM WISEMAN, to keep in touch with Reilly. Thwaites and Wiseman were under cover as part of the British Purchasing Commission. In 1916, possibly on the advice of Wiseman, Reilly left Nadine in New York and went to Canada, where he enlisted in the Royal Flying Corps.

Back in Britain, he agreed to enter Germany as a British spy. What he did in Germany during World War I depends upon what embellished Reilly story is told: One version is that he was flown into Germany and infiltrated the German General Staff. Another is that he passed through the German lines, obtained invaluable intelligence, and returned through the British lines.

British officials desperately tried to keep Russia in the war against Germany as political and social unrest swept the country in 1917. After this policy failed, British intelligence tried to rally anti-Bolsheviks to overthrow the Red revolutionaries and get the nation back in the war.

The man first picked for the job was Capt. GEORGE HILL. When he got entangled in a Romanian operation, MI6 sent in Reilly, who arrived in Moscow in May 1918. In July the Bolsheviks massacred the czar and his family at Ekaterinburg. In Aug. 1918, an anti-Bolshevik shot and grievously wounded revolutionary leader V. I. Lenin. Reilly undoubtedly was involved in the latter plot.

Reilly posed as Comrade Relinsky of the CHEKA, the Bolshevik secret police. Once, at the opera and believing he was about to be arrested, he tore incriminating papers into tiny pieces and swallowed the most dangerous ones while stuffing others into the lining of the sofa cushions.

Reilly later claimed that he had 60,000 Russian and Latvian soldiers ready to fight the Bolsheviks. He had even formed a shadow cabinet and was concocting a counterrevolution that could have changed history. Whatever he had and whatever it was that he really did, there was enough suspicion for the Cheka to charge that Reilly and the British diplomat ROBERT BRUCE LOCKHART were concocting a British plot. Lockhart, although fascinated by Reilly, did not fully trust him. "He was a Jew with, I imagine, no British blood in his veins," Lockhart later wrote. "He was a man cast in the Napoleonic mould. Napoleon was his hero in life and at one time he possessed one of the finest collections of Napoleana in the world." (Reilly later sold the collection to raise money for a counterrevolution against the Bolsheviks.)

Reilly drew Lockhart into the fringes of the anti-Bolshevik plan, but in the Bolshevik press it was described as the "Lockhart Plot." The Bolsheviks charged that the British planned to murder Lenin and another leader, Leon Trotsky, and set up a military dictatorship under White Russians. Lockhart, who later said he had nothing to do with a plot, managed to get out of Russia. Another British diplomat was killed. Meanwhile, an Allied force arrived in Archangel in a futile attempt to put down the Bolsheviks. "I had been within an ace of becoming master of Russia," Reilly later wrote.

Reilly was supposed to report back to MI6, but he vanished as the Bolsheviks went on a murderous rampage, killing an estimated 8,000 suspected enemies. Reilly and Hill managed to escape. (According to one story, they made their way across the Baltic Sea into Sweden and then over to Scotland. In another version, Reilly escaped on his own via a tug to Reval, a German city on the Baltic, and then to Helsinki. Whatever really happened, he did receive Britain's Military Cross for his exploits.)

After the war, Reilly became an adviser to Capt. Cumming, who sent him to the Paris Peace Conference to observe the White Russians and Bolsheviks. Cumming later described Reilly as "a man of indomitable courage, a genius as an agent but a sinister man I could never bring myself wholly to trust."

Reilly continued to urge Britain to support a "democratic" anti-Bolshevik group forming among White Russian émigrés in Paris. Their leader, Boris Savinkov, had been the Minister of War in the cabinet of Aleksandr Feodorovich Kerensky, prime minister of the provisional government that had first emerged after the resignation of the Czar in March 1917. Kerensky, overthrown by the Bolsheviks in Nov. 1917, had fled to Paris. Savinkov, aided by MI6 funds, was seen as the potential leader of 250,000 White Russians who had fled their native land during and after the revolution.

Reilly insisted that the Bolsheviks—"the arch-enemy of the human race" and "monsters of crime and perversion"—could be overcome. "The anti-Bolshevik movement all over Russia is proceeding with unprecedented vigour and is rapidly reaching a culminating point," he wrote in a report to the Foreign Office in Aug. 1921. "[V]arious leaders, of whom the most important is Boris Savinkov, are rapidly moving into a General Rising." Reilly predicted that the rising would come in the following month.

The rising never came, and MI6 began wondering about Reilly's reports. Intelligence officials, comparing his reports with Soviet cables intercepted and decrypted by the GOVERNMENT CODE AND CYPHER SCHOOL, realized that he was frequently not passing on reliable information. He was placed under SURVEILLANCE, at times because of suspicions that he was working either for the White Russians or as a DOUBLE AGENT for the Cheka.

In March 1921 the British government signed a trade agreement with the Soviet regime in what was to be a prelude to formal diplomatic recognition. (See ARCOS AFFAIR.) Reilly, frustrated by British indifference to his warnings about the Reds, became involved in the ZINOVIEV LETTER controversy. In 1924 he arranged to have a letter—supposedly from Grigori Zinoviev, the President of the Comintern, to the British Communist Party—delivered to the Foreign Office, making sure its contents were known to the press. Ramsay MacDonald, Britain's first Labour prime minister, kept the letter secret, but he was discredited when the *Daily Mail* published its contents. The letter's publication contributed to the Labour government's defeat in the next general election.

Reilly, rapidly losing his influence in government

and intelligence circles, corresponded with Winston Churchill and other politicians. He became well known in London, particularly after his marriage to Pepita Bobadilla, an actress. She soon fell into the espionage way of life, carrying a gun and sending telegrams in CIPHER.

Soviet intelligence officials had created a DISINFORMATION organization known as THE TRUST that purported to be anti-Bolshevik. So believable was the information put out by the Trust that Savinkov believed it; in Aug. 1924 he was lured to Moscow, where he was arrested and condemned to death. But, Reilly was told, the Trust was so powerful that it had intervened and Savinkov was pardoned.

In Feb. 1925, when Reilly was in New York City, an MI6 officer wrote to him about the Trust. Reilly, still believing that a counterrevolution could overthrow the Bolsheviks, contemplated asking for financial help from Henry Ford and Winston Churchill.

Reilly, seeking to meet leaders of the Trust, got help from the MI6 officer, who was also a victim of the organization's disinformation. He put Reilly in touch with a European representative of the Trust. In Sept. 1925 Reilly went to Helsinki and then to Viborg, on the Soviet-Finnish frontier. There he met a double agent, who was being run by MI6 but actually worked for the Cheka. He

Sidney Reilly.

told Reilly that only by going to Moscow could he meet the Trust's leaders.

In a letter to Pepita on Sept. 25, Reilly wrote, "I cannot imagine any circumstances under which the Bolshies could tumble to my identity—provided *nothing* is done from your side." He crossed into the Soviet Union that night, using a passport bearing the name Sternberg, and was never again seen outside the Soviet Union.

Reilly was executed, although the exact time and circumstances are still not yet known in the West. The Soviet press announced that on the night of Sept. 28 four "smugglers" had attempted to cross the Finnish-Soviet border and that two had been killed, one taken prisoner, and one mortally wounded. Reilly was not named. In June 1927 the Soviet government said that Reilly had been arrested "in the summer of 1925" while trying to enter the Soviet Union from Finland. Undoubtedly he was intensely interrogated about British intelligence for weeks or months before he was executed.

"For my part I sincerely believe that he is still alive," his wife wrote in a foreword to *Britain's Master Spy* (1933), but her belief was based on hope, not evidence.

Ilya Dzhirkvelov, a KGB INTELLIGENCE OFFICER who became a DEFECTOR in 1980, said he had seen Reilly's file, which showed he had died in the LUBYANKA.

Remotely Piloted Vehicles

(RPV)

SEE UNMANNED AERIAL VEHICLES (UAV).

Rennie, Sir John Ogilvy

(b. 1914 d. 1981)

Chief of the British Secret Intelligence Service (MI6) from 1968 to 1974.

Rennie was a career diplomat whose appointment was engineered to tighten Foreign Office control over MI6.

Educated at Wellington and Oxford, Rennie originally planned to be a painter. He served in the United States and Argentina during World War II, working for the British Information Service. After the war he was posted to the Foreign Office, eventually becoming Under Secretary of State.

At the time of his appointment to MI6 he had headed the Foreign Office's information research department, the peacetime version of what had been the wartime psychological warfare unit. That was the closest he had come to gaining intelligence experience.

Rennie served inconspicuously as "C" until his identity was exposed by publicity surrounding the arrest of his son on narcotics charges.

Resident

Russian term (also *rezident* or resident director) for the head of an espionage NETWORK.

To the Soviets, an ideal resident is someone who is not of Russian nationality or under diplomatic COVER, but a trusted INTELLIGENCE OFFICER who could run a network in one country while living in another.

Leopold Trepper, resident of the RED ORCHESTRA in Germany during World War II, was a Pole living in Brussels and posing as a Belgian businessman. Sandor Rado, resident of the LUCY SPY RING, another World War II Soviet network targeting Germany, was a Hungarian living in Switzerland.

RUDOLF ABEL, Soviet resident in the United States during the Cold War, was an officer in the GRU, Soviet MILITARY INTELLIGENCE. Although Russian-born, he adopted a convincing American identity.

Residentura

Russian term for an espionage office or staff in another country, under the direction of the RESIDENT.

Restricted

Former U.S. security CLASSIFICATION for information, the unauthorized disclosure of which could be expected to result in damage to national security. Established after World War II, "restricted" was the lowest U.S. security classification. It was followed, in ascending order, by CONFIDENTIAL, SECRET, and TOP SECRET.

"Restricted" is no longer used by the United States.

Restricted Data

U.S. CLASSIFICATION for information related to atomic energy. In accordance with the Atomic Energy Act of 1954, all atomic energy information is classified unless a positive action is taken to make it otherwise. This procedure is the opposite of that used elsewhere by the executive branch of the U.S. government (such as the Department of Defense and Department of State), which states that information is classified only when specifically noted.

The concept of "Restricted Data" is known as BORN CLASSIFIED.

No organization other than the Department of Energy (formerly Atomic Energy Commission) can classify atomic energy information, and once it is classified, no other agency can declassify it.

Resurs-F

Soviet third-generation RECONNAISSANCE SATELLITE, an extensive refinement of the earlier ZENIT satellites.

The first satellite in this series, the *Resurs-F1*, was launched on May 25, 1989. Weighing almost 14,000 pounds, it deployed two "subsatellites." The main satellite orbited 158 to 170 miles above the earth. It reentered—probably to return film and other data—on June 17, 1989.

The Resurs-F1 program apparently ended in 1993.

Rezun, Col. Vladimir Bogdanovich

SEE VIKTOR SUVOROV

Rhodes, Sgt. Roy A.

U.S. Army enlisted man who spied for the Soviets while he worked at the U.S. Embassy in Moscow in the 1950s. Discovery of his spying emerged from the defection in 1957 of Lt. Col. Reino Hayhanen of the NKVD, who for a short time was a CUTOUT for RUDOLF ABEL, a Soviet spy stationed in New York City.

Hayhanen defected in Paris en route to Moscow and was taken to New York City by the CIA. Turned over to the FBI, Hayhanen led FBI agents to Abel. When Abel was arrested and his photography studio searched, the FBI found a microfilm that Hayhanen could link to Rhodes, who had served in the embassy motor pool. Rhodes admitted spying.

Rhodes and Hayhanen were key witnesses at the espionage trial of Abel, who was convicted.

Rhodes was sentenced to five years at hard labor.

Rhyolite

U.S. SATELLITE used to intercept microwave point-to-point communications within the Soviet Union and China, that is, COMMUNICATIONS INTELLIGENCE (COMINT). In addition, Rhyolite was employed to collect TELEMETRY INTELLIGENCE (TELINT) from Soviet and Chinese ballistic missile tests.

Rhyolite had a geosynchronous orbit 22,300 miles above the earth. It was fitted with a massive antenna whose narrow, high-gain beam could be aligned to capture even faint microwave signals. The satellite was large—described as being half the size of a railroad freight car—with the "dish" antenna extending while in orbit to 70 feet in diameter. The COMINT/TELINT data was transmitted to ground stations in Australia, Britain, and the United States for analysis by GOVERNMENT COMMUNICATIONS HEADQUARTERS and NSA.

Reportedly, Rhyolite satellites could pick up major communication relay systems in the TARGET countries, as well as calls made from car phones by Soviet government officials both to the Kremlin, and to their mistresses.

Developed and produced by the TRW Corp., the first Rhyolite satellite was placed in orbit by an Atlas Agena-D booster on Mar. 6, 1973. (At least one experimental Rhyolite satellite was orbited as early as 1970.) An additional Rhyolite satellite was placed in orbit in 1977 and another in 1978; there may have been later launches before the system was replaced by the CHALET satellite (first launched in 1978).

Details of the Rhyolite project were sold to Soviet intelligence by GEOFFREY PRIME in Britain and by CHRISTOPHER BOYCE and ANDREW LEE in the United States. After the 1977 arrest and trial of Boyce and Lee, Rhyolite was renamed Aquacade.

Rice-Davies, Mandi

SEE PROFUMO AFFAIR

Richardson, Sgt. Daniel W.

U.S. Army enlisted man who passed military documents to an FBI agent who was posing as a Soviet spy.

Richardson, a career soldier who had been in the Army for 19 years, was targeted by the FBI after he attempted to contact a representative of the Soviet Union, apparently by calling the Soviet Embassy in Washington, D.C. Richardson was stationed at the Aberdeen Proving Ground, in Aberdeen, Md., a center for research and testing of military weapons and munitions.

After he made his supposed contact, he met with an FBI agent posing as a Soviet INTELLIGENCE OFFICER and offered to hand over documents. He was arrested in Jan. 1988 and later court-martialed on several charges, principally for selling unclassified pages from a military manual and a circuit board from an M1 tank. (Espionage laws prohibit conveying to a foreign power any material, classified or unclassified.) Richardson was sentenced to 10 years in prison, reduction in rank, forfeiture of $300 a month for 120 months, and a bad conduct discharge.

Richelieu, Cardinal de Armand Jean

(b. 1585 d. 1642)

Diplomat, royal adviser, and spymaster to King Louis XIII. Richelieu began his dual career in 1616 when, at the prompting of Marie de Médicis, mother of the king, Bishop Richelieu entered the court and was appointed secretary of foreign affairs. He became one of the most powerful men in Europe, largely because he ran the most effective and extensive spy network of his time.

Richelieu also had a personal need for spies because so many people were plotting against him. His first fall came barely a year after he became secretary, when a plot to lessen the influence of Marie de Médicis extended to the worldly bishop. By spinning a counterplot he returned to power in 1621, shortly before he was made a cardinal by the pope. In 1624 he became chief minister to the king.

Richelieu's chief AGENT was an aristocratic Capuchin friar, Franqois Leclerc du Tremblay, who was also in the Royal court. Tremblay, known as Richelieu's "gray eminence," held a fanatic belief that Catholic France should fight to restore Catholicism in the Protestant states of Europe. He and Richelieu set in motion an intricate plan to curb Catholic Austria so that France could dominate the anti-Protestant crusade. To do this, paradoxically, they secretly had to oppose the Holy Roman Emperor, Ferdinand II.

Tremblay went undercover to the German states, urging them not to support the emperor in what would become the Thirty Years' War. Although Richelieu supported the rise of Catholicism, he and his agents arranged for King Gustavus Adolphus of Sweden, a Protestant, to invade the empire.

Richelieu made VIENNA one of his espionage centers, giving the city a reputation for intrigue that continued into the 20th century.

Richelson, Dr. Jeffrey T.

(b. 1949)

A leading writer on U.S. spy SATELLITE programs and other intelligence activities. Richelson, who holds an M.A. and Ph.D. in political science from the University of Rochester, revealed much of the heretofore secret U.S. intelligence collection efforts in his book *America's Secret Eyes in Space: The Keyhole Satellite Program* (1990). He has also written extensively on general U.S. and Soviet intelligence subjects in books and articles, among the most useful being *The U.S. Intelligence Community* (1985), *Foreign Intelligence Organizations* (1988), and *The Wizards of Langley* (2002), the first definitive study of the CIA's Directorate of Science and Technology.

In addition to teaching at the university level, Richelson is a senior fellow at the NATIONAL SECURITY ARCHIVE in Washington, D.C.

Rideal, Sir Eric Keightley

(b. 1890 d. 1974)

British scientist who worked on the atomic bomb project and posthumously was accused of spying for the Soviet Union. Rideal, who was gassed while serving in the Royal Engineers in World War I, was a Fellow of the Royal Society. A member of the science faculty at Cambridge University, he was a key member of the British team that worked on the atomic bomb.

ALLAN NUNN MAY, another member of the British team, was tried and convicted of passing information about the atomic bomb project to the USSR. In a taped deathbed account of his espionage, May said that another scientist was involved. He did not name Rideal, but newly released Soviet intelligence files mention a scientist, carelessly code-named "Eric," who supplied atomic data. The British Security Service (MI5) had long suspected Rideal, who, like May and other Soviet MOLES, had attended Cambridge, a breeding ground for spies. (See CAMBRIDGE SPY RING.)

Rimington, Dame Stella

(b. 1935)

Former Director-General of the British Security Service (MI5), and the first woman to head a major nation's intelligence service. She was appointed in Dec. 1991, when MI5's role was uncertain because of the end of the Cold War. She focused on TERRORIST INTELLIGENCE, drug traf-

ficking, and international crime, over the protests of Britain's police agencies, which questioned MI5's jurisdiction in non-espionage matters. She stepped down in 1996.

Born Stella Whitehouse, the daughter of an engineer, she attended a convent school in Cumbria, in northwest England, and then went to a grammar school in Nottinghamshire, leaving with A levels in English, history, and Latin. After studying English at Edinburgh University, she trained as an archivist in Liverpool.

In 1963 she married a civil servant, John Rimington. They moved to Delhi, where he worked for the British High Commission. There, at a crossroads in her life, "quite by chance" she was recruited into MI5.

Little is known of her secret life from then until the 1970s, when she is believed to have worked both in London and in Northern Ireland gathering intelligence on the Irish Republican Army (IRA). "She had a very calm approach and was a very good organizer and administrator," an intelligence source told a London newspaper. "Like most people at a senior level in that field, she could absorb information very quickly and slot it into a larger picture."

Speaking at her former grammar school about her early MI5 career, she said:

> In those days, women were treated as second-class citizens in MI5. But all that has changed. Women are working alongside men in Northern Ireland or investigating Middle East terrorists . . . It is no good me pretending that for a woman it is easy getting to the top. It is very hard work, particularly if you are a mother. You have to work hard if you want to beat the men.

Immediately after taking over MI5, she made the service's principal target the terrorists of the IRA. And she became a target herself. When several suspected IRA terrorists were arrested in London in March 1993, among the documents seized was the address of a house where her elder daughter had lived.

Security officials worried that their Director-General was herself a potential terrorist victim, for she had taken few steps to protect herself. A London newspaper was able to get information on her credit cards from a computer data bank. She did her own shopping, and for a time her telephone number and address were publicly known. At the urging of other government officials, she improved her personal security.

Rimington, unlike her anonymous predecessors, began her tenure as a well-publicized Director-General. British newspapers vied with each other to publish the most glamorous photographs of her enjoying posh parties, champagne glass in hand, or lunching with Queen Elizabeth. She also lunched with members of Parliament and newspaper editors. The publicity was part of a program to "demystify the security services," observers said.

Soon after she was appointed, the Security Service—M15's formal name—published an unprecedented booklet that cautiously described the organization. Rimington, in an introduction to the booklet, said it was being published to "dispose of some of the more fanciful allegations surrounding" the work of MI5. She also provided a post office box number for the use of "members of the public who believe that they may have useful information."

After retirement, she wrote in *The Times* about her experiences. At a dinner one night, she said,

> I found myself sitting at the same table as the Ambassador of a former Warsaw Pact country. I could see that he was anxious to unburden himself of something. Halfway through the first course he suddenly announced to the rest of the table: "She knows the names of all my mistresses." The other guests, including Members of Parliament, looked around uneasily. And what did I know about them? From that point on they were very polite, but distant.

In 1996 she was made a Dame Commander of the Bath. Rimington subsequently published her memoirs, *Open Secret* (2001), which included a description of her tenure as head of MI5. A review by David Rose in *The Observer* noted:

> Written, as she states, without reference to letters, diaries or official documents, the content of her book has been selected and weeded twice: first by her own memory, and then by the Whitehall censors.
>
> The result of this second filter is a work bereft of even the most innocuous revelation, which makes few additions to public knowledge about MI5's activities against terrorists, subversives or foreign spies in the 27 years of Rimington's career. This could have been a gripping insider's account of the Cold War's victorious climax, followed by Rimington's strategic assessment of the perilous threats to Western civilisation created since its end. Instead, we get dull reiterations of MI5's legal parameters, padded with quotations from published manuals and Ministers' statements to the House of Commons.

Indeed, Rimington's account ignores several key issues, such as her reorganization of those components of MI5 that handled TERRORIST INTELLIGENCE and related matters.

In her biography she does call for reform of the OFFICIAL SECRETS ACT. Roger Bingham, of the pressure group Liberty, said that Rimington was right to challenge the Act, which he said was "long overdue" for reform. In an interview with *The Guardian*, Rimington said it should be made easier for former members of intelligence agencies to write about their work, and called for an independent review body to vet publications. She also revealed that MI5 tried to stop her publishing her book but said she never intended to betray secrets or embarrass the service.

Ring of Five

KGB slang for members of the CAMBRIDGE SPY RING, as reported by ANATOLI GOLITSYN, a senior KGB officer who defected to the West in Dec. 1961.

Also see SIR ROGER HOLLIS.

Ritter, Maj. Nikolaus

(b. 1897 d. ?)

INTELLIGENCE OFFICER for the ABWEHR, the German MILITARY INTELLIGENCE service, who developed AGENTS in the United States and Britain.

Ritter had one major success: In 1937 he obtained for Germany the plans for the U.S. Norden bombsight (see HERMAN LANG). This was the Abwehr's greatest coup in the United States. For the rest of his career, however, Ritter was a dismally ineffective spymaster.

After completing his university education in Cologne in 1924, Ritter became a textile salesman. In 1927 he managed sales from a New York City office.

Ten years later he returned to Germany, where he joined the Abwehr. For his first assignment he was put in charge of the Abwehr section in Hamburg, dealing with aviation intelligence for the German Air Force. Sent back to the United States in 1937 to recruit agents, he was introduced to Herman Lang, who worked in the plant producing the bombsight.

Ritter, using the CODE NAME Dr. Rantzau, also recruited WILLIAM SEBOLD, an American visiting his relatives in Germany. After attending a SPY SCHOOL in Germany, Sebold went back to the United States and became a DOUBLE AGENT, passing on enough information to the FBI to destroy Ritter's DUQUESNE SPY RING. Two other Ritter spies, WILLIAM COLEPAUGH and ERICH GIMPEL, were quickly caught after arriving by SUBMARINE.

One of the first British agents Ritter recruited was Arthur Owens, code-named Johnny, a Welsh engineer who sold Ritter information about Royal Air Force equipment. Ritter did not know that Owens was also the earliest double agent run by Britain's DOUBLE-CROSS SYSTEM. Johnny's British code name was Snow. As far as Ritter knew, Johnny was a valuable agent with about a dozen subagents. They were imaginary.

When Britain went to war against Germany in Sept. 1939, Owens was briefly jailed. Representatives of the TWENTY COMMITTEE, which ran the DOUBLE-CROSS SYSTEM, brought Owens' Ritter-supplied radio set and, from his cell in Wandsworth Prison, Snow launched the phenomenally successful British scheme to TURN Ritter's agents.

Ritter spent the war unaware that his agents were actually working for the British.

His autobiography, *Deckname Dr. Rantzau*, was published in Germany in 1972.

Rivet Joint

Major U.S. Air Force program during the Cold War to employ converted C-135 STRATOTANKER aircraft in the

ELECTRONIC INTELLIGENCE (ELINT) role. Designated RC-135, these highly specialized aircraft were also employed in SURVEILLANCE operations against Third World countries in addition to the Soviet Union.

Variations of the Rivet Joint program included Rivet Amber, a single RC-135B fitted with a large side-looking radar (that plane was lost over the Bering Sea in 1969 as a result of a structural failure). This prototype was followed by several similar RC-135V ELINT/radar aircraft. The Israeli Air Force converted at least one Boeing 707 (the basis of the C-135) to a similar ELINT/radar configuration.

In 2003 the U.S. Air Force operated 21 RC-135s in Rivet Joint configurations.

Robin

British CODE NAME for the first CANBERRA high-altitude RECONNAISSANCE flight over Soviet territory. The 1953 flight from Geilberstadt, West Germany, was over Kapstan Yar, a Soviet missile test site set up in 1951. The Soviets unsuccessfully tried to intercept the aircraft with jet fighters.

Rochefort, Capt. Joseph J.

(b. 1898 d. 1976)

Head of HYPO, the U.S. Navy CRYPTANALYSIS station located at Pearl Harbor, Hawaii, in the crucial months just before and after Japan's PEARL HARBOR ATTACK on Dec. 7, 1941.

A graduate of the University of California, Rochefort enlisted in the Navy during World War I. In 1919 he was commissioned an ensign and, after two years as an executive officer on board a destroyer, he became the officer in charge of the cryptographic section of NAVY COMMUNICATIONS INTELLIGENCE in Washington, D.C., succeeding Lt. Comdr. LAURANCE L. SAFFORD. "I've often said it is not necessary to be crazy to be a cryptanalyst," he said years later, "but it always helps."

Rochefort learned codebreaking skills from Safford and AGNES MEYER DRISCOLL. Driscoll was renowned for having achieved the first breakthrough in the Japanese CODE known as the RED BOOK.

After spending three years in Japan learning the Japanese language, he began alternating duty at sea with intelligence work ashore. When he was assistant operations and INTELLIGENCE OFFICER on the staff of the Pacific Fleet commander in the 1930s, Adm. Joseph M. Reeves called Rochefort "one of the most outstanding officers of his rank" whose "judgment and ability are truly remarkable"—especially for a non–Naval Academy graduate, he added. (Rochefort's lack of a Naval Academy ring would haunt his career.)

Rochefort reported to the underground headquarters of the Pearl Harbor codebreakers—the "dungeon," they called it—in June 1941. Rochefort named the unit the Combat Intelligence Unit as a COVER for the codebreaking. (It was later designated FLEET RADIO UNIT PA-

CIFIC.) He played a key role in deciphering and analyzing Japanese codes, which led directly to the overwhelming U.S. victory at MIDWAY in June 1942. Rochefort had predicted a Japanese attack on Midway; Navy intelligence officers in Washington believed that the attack would come two weeks later at Johnston Island or even the West Coast of the United States.

The U.S. commander in the Pacific, Adm. Chester W. Nimitz, accepted Rochefort's prediction, based on intercepts of Japanese messages. Immediately after the battle, Nimitz welcomed Rochefort to a staff meeting by saying, "This officer deserves a major share of the credit for the victory at Midway." Nimitz recommended Rochefort for the Distinguished Service Medal for his brilliant work. But officers in Washington denied the award. Rochefort was summarily relieved of his codebreaking post in Oct. 1942 and reassigned to a minor, noncombat command.

"Communications Intelligence fell in a no-man's-land between the Communications Division and the Intelligence Division of the Navy Department, subject to the pressures, jealousies, and petty politics of both divisions," W. J. HOLMES, an INTELLIGENCE OFFICER who served with Rochefort, wrote in *Double-Edged Secrets* (1979). "The only probable explanation of what happened to Rochefort is that he became the victim of a Navy Department internal political coup."

After the war, Nimitz wrote to the Navy Department on Rochefort's behalf. The publication of *"And I Was There"* (1985), by Rear Adm. EDWIN T. LAYTON, Nimitz's chief intelligence officer, resurrected the injustice. In 1986, through the efforts of Secretary of the Navy John Lehman, the Distinguished Service Medal was awarded posthumously to Rochefort, with President Reagan personally presenting it to his family in a White House ceremony.

Roessler, Rudolf

(b. 1897 d. 1958)

Anti-Nazi German who was a key member of the LUCY SPY RING.

Roessler served in the German Army during World War I, but unlike many veterans in tumultuous postwar Germany, he was anti-Nazi. After a time in BERLIN, where he wrote anti-Nazi articles and worked for a theater organization, he and his wife moved to Lucerne, Switzerland. There he managed a small publishing house and became a one-man intelligence operation.

Roessler had connections in the German Army who supplied him with intelligence, including a forecast of the German invasion of the Soviet Union, with the exact date, June 22, 1941, and the ORDER OF BATTLE.

In *The Craft of Intelligence* (1963), ALLEN W. DULLES, who was the European representative of the OFFICE OF STRATEGIC SERVICES in Bern at the time, wrote, "By means which have not been ascertained to this day, Roessler in Switzerland was able to get intelligence from the German High Command in Berlin on a continuous basis, often less than twenty-four hours after its daily decision."

While serving the Soviet Union, Roessler was also earning immunity from arrest as a spy by providing Swiss intelligence with information about German intentions toward Switzerland. The Swiss were particularly concerned about what appeared to be a massing of German troops near the Swiss-German border in July 1940. Through his German Army sources, he learned that the troop movements had nothing to do with an attack on Switzerland.

The threat lingered, however, and he continued to watch the Germans for the Swiss until the Swiss arrested him and members of the Lucy ring in May 1944, possibly to protect them from German SD officers who were hunting for them. Roessler and the others were released in Sept. 1944.

Roessler remained in Switzerland after the war, except for at least one mysterious visit to West Germany in the 1950s, when he was arrested on a vague charge of espionage. He was tried, convicted, and sentenced to prison for one year. He died in poverty in Switzerland, and an anonymous donor paid for his funeral.

Roger

U.S. State Department communications circuit used exclusively for communications relating to the CIA.

Roman, Howard

Real or possibly "working name" of the CIA CASE OFFICER who handled Col. MICHAL GOLIENEWSKI, a Polish INTELLIGENCE OFFICER. His defection to the West in Dec. 1960 provided information that led to the arrest of GEORGE BLAKE, a KGB spy in the British Secret Intelligence Service (MI6), and HARRY HOUGHTON, a civilian employee of the Portland naval base.

Rondeau, Staff Sgt. Jeffrey S.

U.S. Army enlisted man who pleaded guilty to conspiring to sell classified documents pertaining to the NORTH ATLANTIC TREATY ORGANIZATION to Czechoslovakian and Hungarian INTELLIGENCE OFFICERS. Rondeau was arrested in 1992, along with JAMES R. RAMSAY. They were accused of working with CLYDE LEE CONRAD, another former U.S. Army sergeant, who was convicted of treason in a West German court. In 1991 Ramsay, also a former Army sergeant stationed in Germany, was sentenced to 36 years in prison by a U.S. court for his involvement in the ring. As a recognition signal, Ramsay reportedly gave Rondeau a torn dollar bill to use when dealing with other members of the ring.

Ramsay was sentenced in 1994 to 18 years in prison.

Ronge, Gen. Maximilian

Director of the Austrian Army's intelligence service, the Kundschaftsstelle, during World War I.

Ronge caught ALFRED REDL, an Austrian INTELLIGENCE OFFICER who was a DOUBLE AGENT for Russia. Redl was working in the Kundschaftsstelle when he started spying for the Russians, giving them material that included Austrian war plans. After Austrian officials learned that Russia had the plans, Ronge was assigned to find the Austrian spy. To help him and keep him in his post, the Russians had given Redl the identities of minor AGENTS for him to seemingly discover. Impressed by his performance, Redl's superiors promoted him to director of the Kundschaftsstelle. In 1912 he was made chief of staff of an army corps in Hungary, then part of the Austro-Hungarian Empire.

Ronge, Redl's successor as head of the intelligence service, developed one of Redl's projects: interception of mail. In 1913 a cooperative German intelligence chief sent Ronge two envelopes from Germany addressed to a "Nikon Nizetas" at a general post office address in VIENNA. When the envelopes were not picked up, the German intelligence officer sent them to Ronge to investigate.

On discovering that the envelopes contained money and the addresses of agents in France and Switzerland, Ronge had them delivered to the Vienna post office, which he kept under SURVEILLANCE. Two more envelopes arrived and were found to contain apparent references to espionage from a Russian intelligence officer.

One day a man arrived to pick up the mail. It was Redl. Later, confronted by his fellow officers, Redl shot himself.

Roof

That part of an AGENT's LEGEND that he uses openly. Also see ON-THE-ROOF GANG.

Roofers

SEE ON-THE-ROOF-GANG

Rook

SEE ROBERT S. LIPKA

Room, The

Secret American society founded in 1927 by group of wealthy New Yorkers who had MILITARY INTELLIGENCE backgrounds or who felt intelligence work had a romantic interest. Its principal founders included VINCENT ASTOR and KERMIT ROOSEVELT. Other powerful men in the Room included banker Winthrop W. Aldrich and Foreign Service officer David K. E. Bruce. Others who joined were two future U.S. intelligence chiefs: WILLIAM DONOVAN and ALLEN W. DULLES. The Room, writes James Srodes in *Allen Dulles, Master of Spies* (1999), "also established the precedent for leaders of corporate America to provide the government with COVER and subsidized operations—through transportation, finance, and propaganda—which Washington could not undertake alone."

When World War II began in Europe in Sept. 1939, The Room changed its name to The Club, and it took a more active role in providing intelligence directly to President Roosevelt.

Room 40

Location and name of the Royal Navy's codebreaking operation during World War I. The Navy started its codebreaking efforts when war began in Aug. 1914, and British radio stations—naval and civilian—began picking up coded German communications. The DIRECTOR OF NAVAL INTELLIGENCE, Rear Adm. H. F. Oliver, recognized the potential of these messages and asked the director of naval education, Sir ALFRED EWING, to see if he could exploit them.

Ewing grabbed at the opportunity and rapidly assembled a staff to attack the German CODES: His first recruits were faculty members, particularly German instructors, at the Royal Naval Colleges of Dartmouth and Osborne, who were on their summer leave at the time. Among them was ALASTAIR DENNISTON, a German master at Osborne. (Later, Ewing recruited professors from Cambridge, seeking mostly classicists and linguists.)

Initially this staff, working in Ewing's cramped office, sorted and filed the intercepts, learning to distinguish German military messages from naval ones and to identify some of the transmitting radio stations. But they were unable to break into the German codes.

The situation changed dramatically on Oct. 13, 1914, when a code book taken from the grounded and blown-up German cruiser MAGDENBURG was delivered to the Admiralty. The book contained hundreds of pages of columns with five-digit and three-letter groups, which were substituted for German words in communications. But even with this windfall, the codebreakers were unable to break into the messages until another windfall arrived at the Admiralty: a code book seized from a German merchant ship off Melbourne, Australia. It held the second key needed to break into German naval communications, a guide to the SUPERENCIPHER process. By early Nov. 1914 the Ewing-Dermiston effort had broken into the German Navy's most secret communications.

(The German Admiralty conducted several reviews of its communications security during the war. German authorities learned that "the encipherment key to the codebook [was] not destroyed with certainty" when the *Magdenburg* was lost. In Aug. 1915 the Germans actually captured the Russian naval officer who had recovered the *Magdenburg's* code books; he confirmed the find. Even then the German Admiralty refused to believe that there could be serious consequences from this loss.)

The success of the initial British team meant that more CRYPTANALYSIS specialists were needed, and Room 40 in the Old Admiralty Building in Whitehall was assigned to them. From that point onward, Room 40 became a euphemism for Royal Navy codebreaking.

The codebreakers were further aided a month later when a British trawler pulled in a code book jettisoned by the German torpedo boat *S-119*. Throughout the war more German code books and enciphering keys were recovered, usually from U-boats sunk in shallow waters.

Room 40's efforts were expanded in time to include the deciphering of almost every message the German authorities sent to their surface ships, submarines, and merchant ships, as well as to their consulates and embassies. The Germans periodically changed the superencipher key, but the basic code book remained in service—and vulnerable to British codebreakers. In the course of the war about 20,000 German messages were deciphered in Room 40, some of vital importance. For example, the codebreakers learned in advance of the German battle fleet sortie in late May 1916 that led to the historic Battle of Jutland, the largest engagement between the British and German fleets in World War I. Unfortunately, the original question asked of Room 40 led to a correct, but misleading, response, because the British were unable to close the trap that Room 40 helped to set.

Still other windfalls came to Room 40 through neutral Sweden and the United States. The seafloor cables used for diplomatic traffic between Europe and the Western Hemisphere passed through British waters. The Germans continued to use cables for diplomatic communications during the war, passing through neutral Sweden. But the British were effectively able to tap into these cables and read the enemy's diplomatic mail (as well as that of the United States). As a result of this capability, they intercepted a telegram from the German Foreign Ministry to the ambassador to Mexico on Jan. 16, 1917, foretelling the German resumption of unrestricted U-boat attacks in the Atlantic and an effort to involve Mexico in the war. The interception of that message, called the ZIMMERMANN TELEGRAM, had major implications for America's entry into World War I in April 1917.

Until May 1917, the Room 40 codebreakers were kept separate from other aspects of Admiralty intelligence and operations. Consequently, Room 40 intelligence was disseminated to a small group of senior officers who lacked experience and, in some cases, even the broad knowledge of operations to make full use of the material.

As a result of a change, instead of sending raw decrypts to the Admiralty's Operations Division, Room 40 provided appreciations or reports that contained estimates of German intentions, as well as all relevant facts related to the decrypts of radio intercepts. This improved the usefulness of Room 40's efforts (and paved the way for the 1937 establishment of the Admiralty's OPERATIONAL INTELLIGENCE CENTRE).

Throughout the war British intercept stations plucked German radio messages from the air or took them off cables and forwarded them, still in code, to the Admiralty. After their receipt, they were sent by pneumatic tube to Room 40, where at times the rapid arrival of the cylinders sounded like machine-gun fire. Scores of intercepted messages arrived every day; from Oct. 1914 until Feb. 1919, the codebreakers in Room 40 were able to read some 15,000 secret German communications (as well as some American and neutral messages). This effort was invaluable in the vital campaign against the U-boats, as well as on the diplomatic and, to a lesser degree, the military front.

The German Navy learned of Room 40 when Adm. of the Fleet Sir John Fisher, First Sea Lord during the war, wrote in his *Memories* (1919):

> The development of the wireless has been such that you can get the direction of one who speaks and go for him; so the German daren't open his mouth. But if he does, of course, the message is in cypher; and it's the elucidation of that cypher which is one of the crowning glories of the Admiralty work in the late war. In my time they never failed once in that elucidation.

In 1923 the *World Crisis* series by Winston Churchill, the former First Lord of the Admiralty during the early part of the war, revealed the manner in which the signal books and ciphers were obtained from the sunken cruiser *Magdenburg*. Churchill told how the Royal Navy had made use of German decrypts: "The German fleet command, whose radio messages were intercepted by the English, played so to speak with open cards against the British command."

Thus warned, the German Navy's leadership took action to ensure that such an advantage would not accrue to an enemy in the future. The German Navy shifted from the use of code books to machine-generated ciphers (see ENIGMA) and established its own cryptanalysis organization, the highly successful B-DIENST.

After the war Room 40 evolved into the GOVERNMENT CODE AND CYPHER SCHOOL.

Roosevelt, Kermit

(b. 1916 d. 2000)

CIA official who planned and led the plot to overthrow the left-wing government of Iranian Prime Minister Mohammed Mossadegh in 1953.

Roosevelt had started his intelligence career as an amateur: He was a member of the THE ROOM, a secret society of wealthy Americans, founded by VINCENT ASTOR and Roosevelt in 1927. The Room's members informally gathered intelligence and passed it to high government officials. By the 1930s The Room's CONSUMERS included President Franklin D. Roosevelt.

Kermit Roosevelt, grandson of President Theodore Roosevelt, was teaching history at Harvard when America entered World War II. He joined the OFFICE OF STRATEGIC SERVICES (OSS) and served in the Middle East.

Roosevelt became an expert on this region, where in postwar years the CIA developed ASSETS and kept its operatives, including Roosevelt, under various COVERS.

In 1951, after nationalist groups had gained control of the Iranian parliament, the young Shah, Muhammad

Reza Pahlavi, reluctantly appointed Mossadegh Prime Minister. When Mossadegh nationalized Iran's oil, he triggered an international crisis, not only about the oil but also about a possible Soviet takeover of Iran.

In July 1953 Roosevelt met with the Shah, who approved of a joint British MI6-CIA plan CODE-NAMED AJAX. H. Norman Schwarzkopf, former head of the New Jersey State Police famed for his work in the 1932 Lindbergh kidnap case (and father of the U.S. commander in the Persian Gulf War of 1991), had commanded the imperial Iranian guard during World War II. Roosevelt convinced him to return to Iran and aid in the operation by keeping the troops on the Shah's side in the forthcoming coup.

In Aug. 1953 the Shah announced that he had removed Mossadegh and replaced him with Gen. Fazollah Zahedi. Mossadegh refused to step down, more rioting erupted, the Shah left Iran, and the coup began. Under Roosevelt's management, loyalist troops suppressed anti-Shah rioters and protected CIA-paid pro-Shah marchers. Zahedi led a force against Mossadegh, driving him into hiding and taking over as the Prime Minister. The Shah returned, the Western oil companies got new contracts, and the United States granted Iran $45 million in economic aid.

Roosevelt, secretly awarded the National Security Medal, was hailed as a hero who had proved that the CIA could manage a coup. His success led the CIA down the path toward more coups—even though Roosevelt warned the agency not to pursue such operations unless they were absolutely necessary for national security.

Roosevelt resigned from the CIA after rejecting a chance to lead a coup against Col. Gamal Abdel Nasser of Egypt. "Foster [Secretary of State Dulles] became too demanding," Roosevelt told James Srodes in *Allen Dulles, Master of Spies* (1999). "He had the idea that I could solve almost anything, anywhere."

Operation Ajax was the highlight of Roosevelt's career, which coincided with the tenure of ALLEN W. DULLES, the DIRECTOR OF CENTRAL INTELLIGENCE from 1953 to 1961.

(Another grandson of President Theodore Roosevelt, Archibald Roosevelt, also served in the CIA, mostly under cover as an employee of the Voice of America.)

RORSAT

RADAR OCEAN RECONNAISSANCE SATELLITE; SEE SATELLITES

Rose, Fred

(b. 1907 d. ?)

Member of the Canadian spy network revealed by IGOR GOUZENKO in 1946. Rose, as a member of the National Research Council, passed secrets about atomic research to the Soviet Union. When he was arrested in 1946 he had recently been elected a member of the Canadian House of Commons.

Born in Poland of Russian Jewish parents named

Rosenberg, he immigrated to Canada with his family in 1920. He did not become a Canadian citizen until his father died in 1926, because he had been classified a minor on his father's passport. He changed his name to Rose and joined the Canadian Communist Party in 1927. Imprisoned for sedition in 1931–1932, he was interned in 1942 because he was a communist. He was released the following year after falsely promising not to participate in illegal organizations or the Communist Party.

He was convicted of spying by a court in Quebec in June 1946 and sentenced to six years. He automatically lost his seat in Parliament.

Rosenberg, Julius

(b. 1918 d. 1953)

American who was a key member of the international ATOMIC SPY RING that gave secrets about the U.S. atomic bomb project to the Soviet Union. Rosenberg's wife, Ethel, was also a member of the ring.

The children of Jewish immigrants from Russia, the Rosenbergs were both born and raised in New York City. Julius graduated from City College of New York as an electrical engineer. Ethel, who had a beautiful operatic voice, was a high school graduate. She was three years older than Julius.

The Rosenbergs were exposed as Soviet spies after the arrest, confession, and conviction of British physicist KLAUS FUCHS in 1949. The U.S.-British-Canadian investigation of Fuchs was aided by TOP SECRET intelligence—intercepted, decrypted copies of cables between Soviet intelligence AGENTS in the United States and Moscow. The project, CODE-NAMED VENONA, was so secret that nothing about it could be released, lest the Soviets realize that their cable traffic had been compromised.

It was evidence provided by Fuchs, rather than the Venona material, that led the FBI to HARRY GOLD, who had been his COURIER. Arrested on May 22, 1950, on es-

pionage charges, Gold confessed to U.S. officials and revealed DAVID GREENGLASS and MORTON SOBELL as other spies at the atomic laboratory in LOS ALAMOS.

Greenglass and his wife, Ruth, both members of the American Communist Party (see CPUSA), implicated David's sister, Ethel Rosenberg, and her husband, Julius, who were also communists. Sobell and Julius Rosenberg were friends.

The Rosenbergs, like many American communists of the time, faithfully followed a twisting Communist Party line, which called for U.S. neutrality at the beginning of World War II and U.S. assistance for the Soviets after Germany attacked the Soviet Union in June 1941. In 1940 Julius began work as a civilian for the U.S. Signal Corps; he was fired in 1945 because of his pro-Soviet views. By then he was living the triple life of ordinary American, avowed party member, and underground AGENT for the Soviet Union. He was the leader of a CELL of engineers who during and after the war worked in defense plants and on military bases and stole what they could.

GAIK OVAKIMIAN, the NKVD RESIDENT in New York City in the 1930s, recruited the Rosenbergs, as well as other spies. Ovakimian was under COVER of AMTORG, the Soviet purchasing organization that was actually a large-scale espionage operation. The Rosenbergs were initially not in a cell devoted to getting atomic secrets; they were drawn into the atomic ring when Gold and Greenglass, in separate cells, worked together in a breach of TRADE-CRAFT. David Greenglass told the FBI that soon after he was assigned to Los Alamos, N. Mex., in 1944, Ethel and Julius persuaded him to spy for the Soviet Union.

Several Americans spying for the Soviets slipped out of the country after Fuchs and Gold were arrested. Among them were MORRIS COHEN and his wife, Lona, who were agents under RUDOLF ABEL, then the New York resident.

In June 1950 Rosenberg obtained passport photos for himself and his family. But it was too late. The FBI arrested him on espionage charges on July 17 and took Ethel into custody on Aug. 11. Their two sons, Michael, 7, and Robert, 3, were put in the care of Ethel Rosenberg's mother.

In March 1951 the Rosenbergs, along with Sobell and Greenglass, went on trial in New York City before Judge Irving Kaufman. The Department of Justice recommended that Julius Rosenberg be executed and that Ethel Rosenberg be sentenced to 30 years in prison. Kaufman linked the Rosenbergs' espionage to the Korean War, which had begun less than a month before Julius Rosenberg's arrest, declaring that by helping the Soviets to get the atomic bomb much earlier than they would have on their own, the couple had set in motion the events leading to the war and had "undoubtedly . . . altered the course of history to the disadvantage of our country." He sentenced them both to death.

The sentences shocked the world. Sympathizers—ranging from liberals to hard-line communists—rallied to have the sentences set aside. However, after more than 20 appeals over more than two years, the Rosenbergs

Julius and Ethel Rosenberg with Martin Sobell (left). (NATIONAL ARCHIVES)

were both executed in the electric chair in Sing Sing Prison, in Ossining, N.Y., on June 19, 1953. Ethel was the first woman to be executed in the United States for a federal offense since Mary Surratt was hanged in 1865 for her role in the plot to assassinate President Lincoln. Julius and Ethel Rosenberg were the only American traitors ever to be executed during what was technically peacetime.

In the years that followed, doubts grew over the Rosenbergs' guilt. Their sons, who had been adopted and had taken their adoptive parents' name, as adults began their own campaign, claiming that evidence of their parents' innocence had been suppressed. But evidence that has emerged in recent years has confirmed the Rosenbergs' guilt.

Former Soviet leader Nikita Khrushchev, in *Khrushchev Remembers: The Glasnost Tapes* (1990), recalled how Soviet dictator Josef Stalin had praised the Rosenbergs. "I was part of Stalin's circle when he mentioned the Rosenbergs with warmth," Khrushchev said. "I cannot specifically say what kind of help they gave us, but I heard from both Stalin and [Vlachyslav M.] Molotov, then Minister of Foreign Affairs, that the Rosenbergs provided very significant help in accelerating the production of our atomic bomb."

In 1995, NSA released Venona transcripts showing that Soviet INTELLIGENCE OFFICERS who were running the atomic ring in 1944 referred to Julius Rosenberg by the CODE NAMES Antenna and Liberal. A cable noted that Ethel Rosenberg knew "about her husband's work," and, although she "does not work, " she was " a devoted person."

The Rosenberg's HANDLER for much of the 1940s, ALEXANDR FEKLISOV wrote of his pleasant relationship and approximately 50 meetings with Julius in *The Man Behind the Rosenbergs* (2001).

Rosenblum, Sigmund

SEE SIDNEY REILLY

Rositzke, Harry

(b. 1911 d. 2002)

CIA intelligence officer who ran covert operations against the Soviet Union and Eastern Europe from 1949 to 1954.

Rositzke was a linguist specializing in Anglo-Saxon languages when he joined the OFFICE OF STRATEGIC SERVICES (OSS) during World War II. He continued his intelligence career in the CIA. Working out of Munich, he became chief of COVERT OPERATIONS against the Soviet Union and Eastern Europe. As CIA station chief in New Delhi from 1957 to 1962, he worked against the Soviets and handled espionage in Tibet aimed against the Chinese. From 1962 until his retirement in 1970, he recruited Soviet and Warsaw Bloc diplomats. In *The CIA's Secret Operations: Espionage, Counterespionage, and Covert Action* (1977), he revealed some details of early

Cold War operations, including the parachuting of Ukrainian AGENTS into their homeland to operate against the Soviet regime.

Rote Kappelle

SEE RED ORCHESTRA

Rotor

EDWARD H. HEBERN developed the first CIPHER machine to make use of rotors to provide random encipherment.

The famed ENIGMA cipher machine contained interchangeable wheels or rotors and several plug connectors. The rotors—which could be replaced—were the key to the almost innumerable permutations that were available to encipher a message. The rotor settings could be rapidly changed—up to several times per day—to further complicate codebreaking efforts.

The early Enigma machines had three rotors, increased to four and five in later machines used during World War II. In addition, extra rotors could be provided for substitutions. The U.S. SIGABA also worked on the rotor principle.

Rowlands

SEE GEOFFREY PRIME

Royal Mitre

SEE RICHARD C. SMITH

Royal Canadian Mounted Police
(RCMP)

Canadian agency—popularly known as the Mounties—responsible for COUNTERINTELLIGENCE until the creation

The rotor "basket" of the U.S. Sigaba encryption machine showing ten rotors in place; two additional rotors and a counter are lying next to the machine. Multiple rotors provided ciphers that were virtually impossible to break without "cribs." (NATIONAL SECURITY AGENCY)

of the Canadian Security Intelligence Service (CSIS) in 1984. But the RCMP still is involved in TERRORIST INTELLIGENCE, maintaining a National Security Tip Line aimed at gathering citizens' leads on terrorists.

There has always been more to the Mounties than officers in scarlet tunics and broad-brimmed hats chasing outlaws in Canada's back woods areas. As a national police organization, the RCMP was charged with investigating acts of subversion against Canada. The role of plainclothes Mounties was always veiled in secrecy. When the Yukon gold rush began in 1896, some Canadian government officials wondered if the parade of miners and camp followers was really a U.S. plot to get Americans into Canada and annex part of it. Canada sent AGENTS—presumably Mounties in disguise—into the United States to hunt for a conspiracy. There was none.

Prior to World War II, Canada's intelligence activities were vested in the Army and Navy. Then COMMUNICATIONS INTELLIGENCE and CRYPTOGRAPHY entered Canada via HERBERT O. YARDLEY, who had run the U.S. codebreaking BLACK CHAMBER. In 1941 Yardley established in Canada the Examination Unit of the National Research Council. During the war Canadian intercept stations worked closely with their U.S. and British counterparts, tracking and transcribing German and Japanese communications.

The RCMP's major intelligence role during World War II was to aid Canadian WILLIAM STEPHENSON, head of the BRITISH SECURITY CO-ORDINATION (BSC), the COVER for North American operations of the Secret Intelligence Service (MI6). The RCMP provided security for Stephenson and aided him in setting up and maintaining Station M, a highly secret base on the north shore of Lake Ontario. There the BSC ran a laboratory for forging documents and mail. Certain letters mailed by German AGENTS in North America to ACCOMMODATION ADDRESSES in neutral Spain and Portugal were intercepted and sent to Station M, where they were doctored to thwart or compromise the agents. (See also CAMP X.)

The most famous RCMP case came in Sept. 1945 when IGOR GOUZENKO, a CIPHER clerk at the Soviet Embassy in Ottawa, defected with his pregnant wife and their child. Gouzenko provided information showing that the Soviets were running an extensive spy NETWORK in North America. Hunted by NKVD men from the embassy, Gouzenko went into hiding, guarded by the RCMP. When his wife went to the hospital to have their baby, she posed as the wife of a Polish farmer; a Mountie, posing as her husband and speaking broken English, accompanied her. Stephenson subsequently sent the baby girl a layette.

The RCMP, meanwhile, publicly staged a manhunt for Gouzenko to deceive the Soviets into believing that Gouzenko was still at large. Then, in Feb. 1946, Mounties began a series of arrests that led to 20 spy trials in Canada and the breakup of the U.S.-British-Canadian ATOMIC SPY RING. (See FRED ROSE.)

After that mammoth espionage investigation, the RCMP was reorganized so that a unit, modeled on Scotland Yard's SPECIAL BRANCH, handled counterintelligence

and countersubversion. The government rejected a proposal for the creation of a National Bureau of Investigation, similar to the CIA.

Canadian counterintelligence operations were relatively rare, considering the number of Soviet intelligence OPERATIVES in the country. During the 1961–1962 debriefings of Col. OLEG PENKOVSKY, a Soviet DEFECTOR IN PLACE, he said that the GRU, Soviet MILITARY INTELLIGENCE, considered Canada "a happy hunting ground for intelligence collection." After Penkovsky's execution in 1963, the CIA decided to allow transcripts of his debriefings to be published, without public CIA sponsorship. In deference to Canadian sensibilities, the CIA removed the remark about Canada from the transcripts that were the basis for the best-seller *The Penkovsky Papers* (1965).

The RCMP did outwit the KGB in 1978 when Igor Vartanian, a KGB officer under cover as the Soviet Embassy's first secretary for sports and cultural affairs, attempted to recruit a Mountie. The Mountie reported the approach and was told to become a DOUBLE AGENT. He strung Vartanian along by passing "carefully screened non-sensitive information or completely fabricated material," according to a Canadian government report on the scam. When the RCMP had enough evidence, the Canadian government expelled Vartanian and 10 other KGB officers under diplomatic cover and told two on leave in the Soviet Union that they should stay there.

Civil rights violations during internal security investigations in the 1970s—mail tampering, unauthorized wiretaps, BLACK BAG JOBS—led to the establishment of a special government commission on RCMP illegal activities. In 1981 the commission recommended that intelligence responsibilities be taken away from the RCMP and given to a separate security service. Politicians and the RCMP resisted the idea until 1984, when legislation created the Canadian Security Intelligence Service (CSIS).

The CSIS was chartered to collect intelligence with the purpose of preventing "threats to the security of Canada," including espionage, sabotage, and "foreign-influenced activities." The CSIS allows the use of "intrusive" SURVEILLANCE, including wiretaps and surreptitious searches of citizens whose activities are "intended ultimately to lead to the destruction by violence of the constitutionally established system of government in Canada."

Like the CIA and MI6, the CSIS does not have law enforcement powers. When the CSIS wants someone arrested, it must turn to a special unit of the RCMP.

RPV

REMOTELY PILOTED VEHICLES; SEE UNMANNED AERIAL VEHICLE (UAV)

RS-70 Valkyrie

RECONNAISSANCE and strike aircraft proposed by the U.S. Air Force as a means of saving the B-70 Valkyrie, a supersonic, high-altitude strategic bomber. The B-70 was essentially stillborn because of the high procurement and maintenance costs for such a large and complex aircraft. Also, the plane's flight conditions were very poor except at its designed maximum speed of Mach 3 at 70,000 feet, and the Soviet Union had been building up high-altitude bomber defenses.

Development of the B-70 began in late 1954 when Gen. Curtis LeMay, Commander-in-Chief of the U.S. Strategic Air Command, requested the development of a successor to the B-52 bomber with as high a speed as possible. North American Aviation was awarded a contract for the aircraft's development in Dec. 1957. The design evolved rapidly.

In Nov. 1959, during a meeting to discuss defense programs, President Eisenhower told the Air Force Chief of Staff that "the B-70 left him cold in terms of making military sense." The president also noted that if the B-70 were allowed to reach the production stage, it would not be available for eight or 10 years, by which time missiles would be the primary strategic retaliatory weapon. On Dec. 29, 1959, the Air Force reluctantly made the decision to procure only a single prototype XB-70 for technology development. However, the B-70 program underwent resuscitation a few months later as the 1960 presidential campaign rekindled interest in strategic weapons. In Aug. 1960 the Eisenhower administration increased the program to 13 prototype and test aircraft, moving the B-70 toward production.

The program continued after President Kennedy entered the White House in Jan. 1961. The first XB-70 had still not flown when, later that year, the Air Force redesignated the aircraft as a Reconnaissance Strike Bomber (RSB-70 and, subsequently, RS-70). Under the RS-70 concept, 60 aircraft would be procured to carry out reconnaissance of enemy targets during a nuclear missile attack and, if required, attack them immediately with air-to-surface missiles. (Desperate to keep the B-70 effort alive, the Air Force also looked into the possibility of employing the B-70 as a *transport* aircraft.)

Even within the Air Force, however, there were serious questions about proceeding with the B-70. The penultimate blow came in April 1961, when Secretary of Defense Robert S. McNamara directed that the program be reduced back to prototypes without weapon systems.

The B-70 was the heaviest aircraft ever to fly when the first prototype took to the air on Sept. 21, 1964; the second aircraft flew in 1965. The latter aircraft achieved a sustained speed of Mach 3 for 32 minutes.

The second aircraft was destroyed in a mid-air collision with an F-104 fighter during a "photo shoot" on June 8, 1966, and the flight test program was halted. Thus ended a most ambitious reconnaissance aircraft. (The first XB-70 was transferred to the National Aeronautics and Space Administration and flew until Feb. 4, 1969.)

Also see NM-1.

RSHA

Reichssicherheitshauptamt (Reich Central Security Office), the main Nazi secret police organization. The RSHA, as it was known for its German initials, was established in 1939 to unite all German police security organizations, including the GESTAPO and the SD. The chief of the RSHA was REINHARD HEYDRICH. When he was assassinated in June 1942 by British-trained Czech AGENTS, he was succeeded by ERNST KALTENBRUNNER.

Office III supervised the action groups' (Einsatzgruppen) task forces, whose innocuous label hid their sinister purpose: They were extermination units that killed 2 million men, women, and children in occupied countries, usually by shooting them and throwing their bodies into mass graves.

Office VI of the RSHA supervised activities against Jews and was headed by Adolf Eichmann.

RU

Razvedyvatel'noe Upravlenie or RU, the intelligence directorate of a Soviet-Russian military formation.

Ruff

U.S. CODE WORD for reports and evaluations based on photography from the CORONA series of SATELLITES.

Rupee

British CODE WORD for COUNTERINTELLIGENCE material provided by Soviet Col. OLEG PENKOVSKY. See ARNIKA.

Rupp, Reiner

(b. 1945)

Employee of the NORTH ATLANTIC TREATY ORGANIZATION (NATO) who spied for East Germany from 1977 to 1989. He and his wife provided the East Germans—and, through them, the Soviet Union—with copies of an estimated 10,000 documents. Their espionage, said a German prosecutor, "could have lost NATO a war."

Rupp, born in West Germany, was recruited into the MFS (Stasi), the East German intelligence agency, in 1968, while a student. He was told to continue his studies and await further instructions. In 1970, while in Brussels, he met British-born Ann-Christian Bowen. A secretary at the Ministry of Defence in London, in 1968 she had been posted to Brussels with the British military mission to NATO. At that time, the Stasi was targeting secretaries in NATO and West German political and military offices. The Stasi called its handsome male AGENTS "Romeos," but Rupp claimed to have genuine feelings for the British secretary.

They fell in love, and Rupp told her that the Stasi had recruited him. By then, she had endorsed his anti-American and anti–Vietnam War sentiments. She also accepted his espionage activities and accompanied him to East BERLIN for training, where she, too, agreed to spy. They were married in 1972.

She smuggled NATO documents out of headquarters

in her handbag; some of the documents were stamped COSMIC, the highest NATO secrecy classification. At home Rupp photographed them with a camera supplied by the Stasi, and she brought them back the next day. He received instructions in CODE on a radio also supplied by the Stasi. To their HANDLERS, he was Topaz and she was Turquoise.

In 1977 Rupp began working in NATO's international economics division; he, too, began bringing home documents to photograph. Ann-Christian Rupp continued to spy until 1980, when the first of their three children was born. She later said that she had become disillusioned with communism and somehow felt that motherhood and espionage did not mix. The couple's Stasi handlers accepted her decision. Rupp continued spying, but, as Ann-Christian later said, "We had constant discussions and I was nagging him to stop."

Rupp began having doubts, ironically because he could see in the documents he was copying that NATO plans were defensive; after the Soviet invasion of Afghanistan in 1979, it was his turn to be disillusioned. He told his wife that he had stopped spying, but he was lying. Money may have had something to do with his decision. The Stasi was paying him about $1,500 a month, and even as the Berlin Wall was coming down, he kept spying.

After reunification of the two Germanys in Oct. 1990, Ann-Christian read that Western intelligence officials, sifting through Stasi files, were searching for a spy with the CODE NAME Topaz. With the aid of an informer, German COUNTERINTELLIGENCE finally tracked down Rupp and arrested him and his wife in July 1993 when they traveled to Germany to visit his relatives.

"I did wrong, and I'm prepared to pay for it," Rupp said in Nov. 1994, when he was convicted of treason and sentenced to 12 years in prison. Ann-Christian received a 22-month suspended sentence.

Russia-USSR

For centuries Russian rulers—whether czars, commissars, or modern communist leaders—have used an all-powerful secret police to find and punish internal enemies. The roots of the KGB and its post-Cold War successors can be found in the domestic police and spy apparatus of Russian czars, beginning with the black-clad cavalrymen of the OPRICHNINA, created by Ivan the Terrible in 1565. Russians were spared an organized secret police from the abolition of the Oprichnina in 1572 until 1697, when Czar Peter I—Russia's first "modern" ruler—established the PREOBRAZHENSKY OFFICE, which could question and torture any Russian citizen, regardless of rank or station.

Beginning late in the 19th century, the czar's secret police ORGAN was the OKHRANA, whose OPERATIVES included specialists trained to investigate political crimes, including some set up by the Okhrana to frame subversives. In 1887 the secret police executed Aleksandr Ulyanov, the son of a school inspector, for plotting to assassinate the czar. Aleksandr's brother later went into exile and—taking the name Vladimir Ilyich Lenin—would one day avenge his brother's death.

There was virtually no foreign intelligence collection under the czars, as evidenced in part by the catastrophic Russian military failures in the 1904–1905 war with Japan. Nor was the Okhrana an effective COUNTERINTELLIGENCE agency against the foreign AGENTS in Russia. When Russia was rebuilding its shattered navy after the Russo-Japanese War, SIDNEY REILLY, a sometime British AGENT, operated freely in the capital of St. Petersburg, simultaneously helping German firms obtain large contracts and informing the British Admiralty about German warship designs.

Anti-czarist movements, fanning popular disgust over the conduct of the war against Japan, launched the Revolution of 1905, which was ruthlessly put down by troops.

Russia's entry into World War I revived the revolutionary movement. Riots, sparked by food shortages and antiwar sentiments, challenged the government and the Okhrana. Facing defeat in the field and rioting at home, Czar Nicholas II was forced to abdicate in the spring of 1917, and for a brief time, Russia had a form of democratic parliamentary government.

But this situation was unacceptable to Lenin and his Bolshevik Party, which sparked a revolution against the fledgling parliamentary government. This time, revolution could not be put down. Lenin called for Russian withdrawal from the war and urged "all power to the soviets"—the workers' and soldiers' councils that would form the provisional government.

In Oct. 1917, the Bolsheviks seized Petrograd (as St. Petersburg had been renamed in 1914), and soon took Moscow and other cities as well. As czarist generals and armies resisted, the revolution catapulted the nation into civil war, with the Reds demanding a dictatorship of the proletariat and their opponents calling for a return to the Romanov monarchy. These so-called White Russians soon found foreign allies.

The British, desperate to keep Russia in the war against Germany, used Reilly and other agents to find some way to overthrow the Reds. Reilly and a British diplomat-spy, BRUCE LOCKHART, were implicated in a plot that went awry. When Lenin was shot and grievously wounded, the act was blamed, perhaps rightly, on the British, who were trying to thwart the Bolsheviks. Reilly claimed to have 60,000 anti-Bolsheviks ready to do Britain's bidding. In this climate of plotting and intrigue, Lenin created the CHEKA—a police organization to combat counterrevolutionaries and to punish "spies, traitors, plotters, bandits, speculators, profiteers, counterfeiters, arsonists, hooligans, agitators, saboteurs, class enemies, and other parasites."

Cheka "press gangs" rounded up thousands of men and women to work on fortifications and other projects during the fighting against the Germans before the Bolshevik capitulation. Later, the Cheka impressed workers for other labor projects, some for use against the White Russian and Allied forces during the Russian Civil War, which lasted into 1920.

To head the Cheka, Lenin chose FELIKS DZERZHINSKY, a political agitator from a Polish noble family who had once been imprisoned by the Okhrana. He commanded the Bolshevik headquarters during the revolution and took charge of guarding Lenin and other party leaders.

"We stand for organized terror," Dzerzhinsky said of the Cheka. "Terror is an absolute necessity during time of revolution. . . . The Cheka is obliged to defend the revolution and conquer the enemy even if its sword does by chance sometimes fall upon the heads of the innocent."

The Cheka quickly grew strong and ruthless, leading the massacre of "enemies of the people." The Foreign Department of the Cheka sought counterrevolutionaries beyond Russian borders, especially the large numbers of former White officers and officials, as well as active White Russian political émigrés who fled to BERLIN and Paris. One of the Cheka's most successful operations was THE TRUST, an organization ostensibly run by monarchists. Lured back to Russia in the belief that the Trust would restore the czar, many Russians died or were imprisoned.

By 1925, the Cheka (later named GPU—the General Political Administration—and then OGPU—Unified State Political Administration) had by some estimates executed more than 250,000 enemies of the Bolshevik leadership and imprisoned 1,300,000 people. They and thousands of others were being exiled to the first Soviet prison camps in Siberia and other remote areas.

Renaming the Cheka the GPU marked the start of a series of name changes for the state security apparatus, which, regardless of its official name, was also always called the ORGAN:

	State Security	Combined	Internal Security
1917–1922	—	Cheka	—
1922–1923	—	GPU	—
1923–1934	—	OGPU	—
1934–1941	—	NKVD	—
1941	NKGB	—	NKVD
1941–1943	—	NKVD	—
1943–1946	NKGB	—	NKVD
1946–1953*	MGB	—	MVD
1953	—	MVD	—
1954–1960	KGB	—	MVD
1960–1966	—	KGB	—
1966–1968	KGB	—	MOOP
1968–1992	KGB	—	MVD

In 1947–1951 the KI handled certain aspects of foreign intelligence.

Regardless of name, from Cheka to KGB, the purpose of these organs was the same: to protect Soviet leaders from all enemies, foreign and domestic. The Soviet leader who made most murderous use of them was Josef Stalin, who in 1924 had emerged from the power struggle to succeed Lenin. To stay in power, especially in his first few years as dictator, he used the organs as his personal killing machine. One of his key managers of terror was GENRIKH G. YAGODA, a pharmacist. He may have used his professional skill to kill Lenin, who, after being severely wounded in the assassination attempt, died in 1924 after a series of heart attacks.

During the 1920s and 1930s, through the Communist International (later known as Comintern), Soviet intelligence services ran espionage operations in various countries, recruiting agents from the nations' communist parties. When Stalin disbanded the Comintern in 1943, the NKVD sent instructions to its residents on how to continue espionage operations. This message, intercepted and eventually decrypted by the U.S. VENONA project, showed beyond doubt the NKVD's connection to national communist parties, particularly those in England and the United States. (See CPUSA.)

THE PURGES BEGIN

On Dec. 1, 1934, Sergey Kirov, a founder of the Bolshevik Revolution, was assassinated by a former CHEKIST. This was the opening shot in the series of massive purges initiated by Stalin. Yagoda, as head of what was then the NKVD, took charge of the investigation of Kirov's assassination and initiated the flood of arrests that followed.

NIKOLAY YEZHOV, a former Red Army political commissar, was appointed NKVD chief in Sept. 1936 and continued the purges with increased fervor, extending the murder wave from political leaders to the military.

Yezhov lasted until 1938. Known as the "bloodthirsty dwarf," he condemned so many people that jails and prison camps filled to overflowing and the NKVD strained its resources to the breaking point.

Three of the five marshals of the Soviet Union were executed for helping "enemies" or engaging in counterrevolutionary activities. Scores of senior Army and Navy officers and thousands of lesser officers were arrested and executed. Three thousand senior NKVD officials were denounced as former czarist police spies, thieves, and embezzlers, and then executed. Purges also decimated the ranks of the GRU, the Soviet MILITARY INTELLIGENCE service.

Yezhov's successor was LAVRENTY BERIA, who had been head of the secret police in Stalin's native Georgia. Soon after his appointment, Beria became the first chief of the secret police to become a candidate (nonvoting) member of the ruling Politburo. At the time there were ten full, voting members, including Stalin and the newly appointed Nikita Khrushchev.

Beria was infamous as a policeman and as a rapist. He regularly picked up young girls on the street and took them to his office, where he forced them to commit sodomy and then raped them. Increasing SURVEILLANCE in foreign countries of the few remaining old Bolsheviks, Beria targeted Leon Trotsky, who had been Stalin's rival to succeed Lenin. Assassins dispatched by Beria killed Trotsky in Mexico in Aug. 1940.

Beria sent his predecessor Yezhov (who had once planned to arrest Beria) to a psychiatric institute, where soon afterwards he was found hanging from a window bar. Beria's NKVD executioners killed survivors of the

Yagoda-era NKVD leadership, as well as many from the Yezhov period. Some killed themselves.

Soviet intelligence was especially ravaged. Agents working outside the Soviet Union were recalled to Moscow, where they were arrested and shot. Among those who unwittingly traveled home to their deaths was YAN BERZIN, an early director of Soviet military intelligence. Many others who refused the recall were tracked down and killed. WALTER KRIVITSKY, NKVD RESIDENT in the Netherlands, fled to the United States, where assassins found him. An NKVD resident in Turkey hid in Belgium and was killed. The chief of intelligence in the Far East succeeded in reaching safety in Manchuria, where he defected to the Japanese Kwantung Army. ALEKSANDR ORLOV, recalled while serving the NKVD in the Spanish Civil War, chose exile in the United States.

Karl Ramm, a friend of master spy RICHARD SORGE, returned from Shanghai to his death. Sorge reportedly refused to return and performed brilliantly in Japan, where the Japanese later arrested him for espionage and executed him. The purges continued until Germany invaded the Soviet Union on June 22, 1941. (See BARBAROSSA.)

WORLD WAR II

When war began, Beria became one of Stalin's most important lieutenants. Internally, his secret police took on increased responsibilities—both to protect the Kremlin leadership and to ensure the loyalty of the armies fighting the Germans. Externally, Beria broadened foreign intelligence gathering. He assigned NKVD operatives to Soviet diplomatic delegations in Britain, Canada, and the United States.

A Soviet purchasing commission was established in the United States to speed the transfer of arms to the Soviet Union. Like an older, still functioning purchasing unit, AMTORG, the wartime commission grew to more than 1,000 employees and became a collection point for stolen military and industrial secrets.

Beria's most valuable work involved stealing secrets for the Soviet effort to build an atomic bomb. Beria was eventually given management of the Soviet internal research and development program, while as an international spymaster, he managed the ATOMIC SPY RING in the United States, Canada, and Britain.

Early in the war the NKVD was responsible for internal security in the Soviet Union, as well as for ensuring the loyalty of the Army. A new COUNTERESPIONAGE organization was formed: SMERSH, an abbreviation of the words *smert shpionam,* meaning "death to spies." Smersh meant terror to all soldiers who even thought for a moment of defection or not giving their utmost for the motherland. Among the NKVD officials who served in Smersh and went on to senior positions in Soviet intelligence was Col. Gen. IVAN SEROV, who transferred to the NKVD after surviving the purges of the GRU. Serov liquidated anti-Soviet inhabitants of Estonia, Latvia, and Lithuania and was personally involved in the KATYN MASSACRE.

Stalin did not trust his capitalist allies, and the feeling was mutual. U.S. and British leaders so distrusted Stalin that details of D-DAY were kept from him. Some Allied officials wanted no information whatsoever passed to Stalin. But under a compromise, British and U.S. military missions in Moscow were told to inform Stalin about the date but not the place of the invasion. He was told that the landings would be around June 1, 1944. (However, soon after the Normandy landings, Gen. Dwight D. Eisenhower, the Allied commander in Western Europe, asked Stalin to have the Red Army go on the offensive to help relieve German pressure on his invasion beaches.)

The Soviet Union used espionage and DISINFORMATION persistently during the war. Besides the atomic bomb spies, two British INTELLIGENCE OFFICERS, HAROLD (KIM) PHILBY and JOHN CAIRNCROSS, also passed on information to the Soviets. Meanwhile, Soviet disinformation and propaganda specialists gave little publicity to U.S. aid, consistently diminished U.S. combat victories, and even attributed the liberation of Paris to the Red Army and French communist partisans.

Soviet intelligence organs ran several brilliant operations that supplied intelligence from the German High Command (see LUCY SPY RING and RED ORCHESTRA). But Stalin usually suspected or ignored the high-grade intelligence he was getting. Several military deception operations were also successful (see MAX and SCHERHORN).

After the war, Beria directed atomic bomb development, while continuing to run the state security and intelligence organs. Beria regarded himself as Stalin's heir and secretly prepared himself for the role by placing his men in key places. On the night of March 1, 1953, Beria met alone with Stalin at the dictator's dacha at Kuntsevo. A short time later, Stalin suffered a stroke. He died on March 5.

Beria began making moves to take over the government while joining Stalin's other heirs in the collective leadership. He was able to have Georgi Malenkov, whom he could influence, join him and Nikita Khrushchev in a ruling troika. Perhaps Beria joined forces—temporarily—believing that the country was not yet ready for another dictator from Georgia. Meanwhile, liberation forces stirred in Soviet satellites in Eastern Europe, particularly in Hungary.

Beria consolidated his police powers under a super-MVD organ, but on June 26 he was seized at the Kremlin and secretly tried. Just as secretly, he was executed on Dec. 23, 1953.

Col. Gen. Serov, deputy chief of military intelligence (GRU) and one of the conspirators, became chairman of the newly established KGB, whose emblem proclaimed its role—sword and shield of the Soviet Union. Serov and YURI ANDROPOV, the Soviet ambassador to Hungary, in 1956 deceived the rebellious Hungarian leaders by first leading them on and then capturing, torturing, and executing them. In Dec. 1958 Serov became chief of the GRU and presided over unbridled corruption. This turned into a boon for Western intelligence agencies, as GRU officers, fed up with the corruption, became DEFECTORS IN PLACE, providing valuable intelligence.

THE SPY WAR

When World War II ended in Aug. 1945, Soviet intelligence had new areas in which to operate, for the war bestowed upon the Soviet Union vast tracts of land and large populations taken from Germany, Romania, Czechoslovakia, and Japan. Before the war, the Soviet Union was the largest country in the world, covering one-seventh of the earth's surface. After the war, Soviet-controlled territory covered one-sixth of the planet's land area.

In the 1920s, when the Soviet Union did not yet have diplomatic relations with the United States, Amtorg, a so-called purchasing agency, served as Moscow's eyes and ears in America. That organization was the beginning of an espionage NETWORK that would take root and flourish in the coming decades. When the United States recognized the Soviet regime in Nov. 1933, Maxim Litvinov, the commissar for foreign affairs, cynically agreed to end what were diplomatically called communist propaganda activities in the United States. A former spymaster in Britain, Litvinov of course was lying. He knew that Soviet espionage efforts had an ambitious goal: PENETRATION of the U.S. government, with the aid of American communists. (See ELIZABETH BENTLEY, WHITTAKER CHAMBERS, and JUDITH COPLON.)

Soviet espionage against the West continued unabated during World War II, but U.S. officials did not realize its dimensions until just after the war ended, when IGOR S. GOUZENKO, a CIPHER clerk in the Soviet Embassy in Ottawa, Canada, defected. Gouzenko provided the first revelations about the atomic spy ring, which involved British scientists KLAUS FUCHS and ALAN NUNN MAY, along with JULIUS ROSENBERG and other American traitors.

Soviet intelligence used three methods of operating in the United States and Britain. First, members of the Communist Party, particularly in the United States (CPUSA) and Britain, were drawn to spy for the Soviet Union for idealistic reasons (see AMERASIA CASE and CAMBRIDGE SPY RING). Second, Soviets worked as LEGALS—diplomats under COVER, or GRU and KGB officers in trade missions or acting as correspondents for the Soviet news agency Tass. The third source of espionage was ILLEGALS, Soviet citizens trained in SPY SCHOOLS to adopt new identities and live in the United States (see RUDOLF ABEL and RUDOLPH HERRMANN) or in Britain (see GORDON LONSDALE and MORRIS COHEN).

The GRU had run highly successful espionage operations against Germany during the war (see LUCY SPY RING, RED ORCHESTRA, and RICHARD SORGE). After the war Soviet intelligence activities grew rapidly in Europe, setting up new branches in the Soviet occupation zone. Soviets established spy agencies and trained local OPERATIVES throughout the zone, which encompassed eastern Germany (later to be named the German Democratic Republic), Poland, Czechoslovakia, eastern Austria, Hungary, Romania, and Bulgaria.

Subverting democratic governments and installing Moscow-approved surrogates, the Soviet Union transformed all but Austria into satellites and, with the addition of Albania, welded them into what was known in Cold War terms as the Eastern Bloc, arrayed against the West. East confronted West at one particular flash point: Berlin, divided into East Berlin and West Berlin, teeming with spies and MOLES. Under the four-power zone system, Berlin was watched by four intelligence systems, with the United States, Britain, and France aligned against the Soviet Union.

The first crisis came in June 1948 when the Soviets, hoping to force the Western powers to abandon the city, cut off all air, land, and river traffic, besieging more than 2 million residents of Berlin. The Allies—as the Americans, British, and French still called themselves—stood firm. An airlift of Allied aircraft brought food, medical supplies, and even coal into the city, and the crisis gradually eased.

East and West also faced off in VIENNA, the longtime spy center of Europe, where the four-power system continued until occupation forces withdrew from Austria in 1955. But it was Berlin that became the setting for real crisis—and for fictional espionage, dramatized by JOHN LE CARRÉ in *The Spy Who Came In from the Cold* (1965). (See MOVIES and LITERARY SPIES.)

The creation of the NORTH ATLANTIC TREATY ORGANIZATION (NATO) gave Soviet intelligence a new TARGET, and over the years a number of NATO spies were unmasked. A lesser-known, non-NATO target was Sweden, where the GRU was especially active, because of its location and ease of penetration. Swedish Air Force Col. STIG WENNERSTROM was a GRU agent for 15 years. According to a 1984 study, the KGB and GRU at that time had 80 officers in Sweden, along with 160 intelligence officers from Czechoslovakia, East Germany, Hungary, Poland, and Romania. This did not include "tourist" and "cultural" exchange groups.

The KGB and GRU had close, if not controlling, ties to Eastern Bloc intelligence services. Agents of East Germany's MFS (Stasi) worked in tandem with Soviet counterparts. The same was true in Bulgaria, which developed a reputation for WET AFFAIRS. (See GEORGI MARKOV.)

Mehmet Ali Agca, a Turk who shot Pope John Paul II in May 1981 in a well-organized assassination plot, implicated the Bulgarian secret police. VICTOR SHEYMOV, a KGB DEFECTOR in 1990, linked the plot to the KGB. A Soviet spokesman branded the story a lie, pointing out that Sheymov, who defected in 1980, was not proferred by the CIA as a witness to Italian authorities investigating the assassination attempt.

KHRUSHCHEV'S COLD WAR

Nikita Khrushchev, who had approved and supported Stalin's purges in the Ukraine, emerged from the power struggle after Stalin's death as first secretary of the party. In Feb. 1956, in a secret speech at the 20th Party Congress, he was strong enough to challenge Stalin's memory, denouncing the dictator for his crimes and for fostering "a cult of personality." (The MOSSAD, Israel's foreign intelligence agency, managed to get a copy of

Khrushchev's speech and promptly passed it to the CIA. But there are some indications that the KGB was in on the LEAK because Khrushchev wanted the West to know about the speech.)

While Khrushchev reduced Soviet conventional military forces, he emphasized the development of nuclear weapons, first to be delivered against the West by jet bombers and then by long-range ballistic missiles. With an "iron curtain" closing off most accurate sources of information about Soviet technology and military developments, first President Truman and then Eisenhower authorized limited OVERFLIGHTS of the Soviet Union by U.S. planes (some flown by British crews); some British CANBERRAS also flew these missions. Eisenhower approved the development of the U-2 high-altitude spyplane and SATELLITES to determine the dimensions of Soviet weapons programs. From 1956 to 1960, U-2s overflew the Soviet Union, followed by RECONNAISSANCE satellites.

Khrushchev, preaching "peaceful coexistence" but threatening, "We will bury you," triggered crises that twice took the United States and Soviet Union to the brink of nuclear war. On both occasions, Western intelligence failed to forecast the Soviet moves.

In June 1961 Khrushchev declared that he would turn East Berlin over to East Germany, cutting West Berlin off from the West. President Kennedy called up 250,000 military reservists and activated several mothballed Navy ships. The immediate crisis eased. Then, in August, with Western leaders getting no advance warning from intelligence sources, the Soviets and East Germans began swiftly erecting a wall and other barriers along the length of Germany's East-West border.

In fall 1962, again without detection on the part of Western intelligence agencies, Khrushchev began to emplace ballistic missiles with nuclear warheads in Cuba, provoking the CUBAN MISSILE CRISIS. Although U.S. intelligence agencies had initially failed, they rallied in the crisis. U-2 spyplanes and then low-flying F8U CRUSADER and F-101 VOODOO photo planes obtained definitive photographic evidence of the missile emplacements.

Also valuable was the intelligence on missiles being provided by Col. OLEG PENKOVSKY, a GRU defector in place.

After a confrontation that threatened a nuclear exchange (with the U.S. intelligence services not realizing that nuclear warheads were already ashore in Cuba), Khrushchev backed down and the missiles were withdrawn. His retreat weakened his hold on the Kremlin and he fell from power in Oct. 1964. Under Leonid Brezhnev, detente with the West alternated with a hard line—the invasion of Czechoslovakia in 1968, the invasion of Afghanistan in 1979. In the SECRET WORLD the work of spies went on, but the work was slowly evolving.

Soviet legals under diplomatic or commercial cover concentrated on getting industrial and technical secrets, such as tank armor and submarine detection systems. No longer was the Soviet Union interested in infiltrating the U.S. government or recruiting ideological agents. The Soviets got offers of secrets from WALK-INS, many of them U.S. servicemen, who offered secrets for cash.

Soviet spies sometimes worked in the heart of the capitalist world. In 1961 the Soviets founded an engineering company in France run by a naturalized Frenchman. The company did French defense work for 14 years before French intelligence discovered that it was a front for getting information about NATO's early warning network and French military and commercial aircraft technology. In 1965 France expelled the manager of Aeroflot in Paris for stealing secrets of the Concorde, the joint Anglo-French supersonic aircraft. Soviet agents manipulated corporate executives to get what the Soviet Union needed. The Japanese Toshiba Corp. and Kongsberg Vaapenfabrik, a state-controlled Norwegian firm, worked together, under Soviet persuasion, to sell a Leningrad (St. Petersburg) shipyard the expertise for manufacturing advanced propellers for submarines.

Soviet diplomatic delegations became so infested with spies that the tit-for-tat expulsion of diplomats became routine. When OLEG GORDIEVSKY, the senior KGB officer at the Soviet Embassy in London, defected in Sept. 1985, he gave the British Security Service (MI5) a list of names; Britain immediately expelled 25 Soviet diplomats, charging them with espionage. The Soviets retaliated by expelling 25 Britons, including correspondents and businessmen, from the Soviet Union. Between 1970 and 1985, Britain expelled 144 Soviets under diplomatic cover. In contrast, the United States expelled only six Soviet intelligence officers. The large difference was attributed to the fact that in the United States the FBI preferred to keep Soviet agents under SURVEILLANCE in order to identify their American contacts.

Brezhnev died, after a long illness, in Nov. 1982. He was succeeded by YURI ANDROPOV, former head of the KGB. (Andropov shares with GEORGE H. W. BUSH and CHAIM HERZOG the rare distinction of becoming a head of state after being the head of a major intelligence agency.) Slick KGB propagandists portrayed Andropov as a sophisticated statesman, ignoring his role as a ruthless suppressor of the Hungarian and Czech uprisings. Ailing through his short reign, he was succeeded by an even sicker Konstantin Chernenko, whose death in March 1985 brought a new-style Soviet leader, Mikhail Gorbachev.

GLASNOST SPYING

Through this series of rapid leadership changes, the Soviet intelligence apparatus remained intact. The arrest in Aug. 1986 of American correspondent NICHOLAS S. DANILOFF was a classic KGB frame-up, staged in retaliation for the FBI arrest of GENNADI ZAKHAROV, a Soviet intelligence officer under cover at the UNITED NATIONS, a spy nest for Soviet legals.

After the Daniloff-Zakharov incident was settled, Gorbachev, who was campaigning to reform the Soviet government through glasnost (open criticism) and perestroika (restructuring or economic reform), met with President Reagan in Reykjavik, Iceland. As the two leaders began a cautious relationship, the spy war went on.

Within the U.S. INTELLIGENCE COMMUNITY, 1985 was labeled the YEAR OF THE SPY, following the public disclosure of more than 20 major spy cases, most of them walk-ins. The Reagan administration expelled 55 Soviet diplomats for spying.

One of Gorbachev's most powerful supporters was Gen. VIKTOR CHEBRIKOV, head of the KGB and unconvinced about glasnost or perestroika. When the Chernobyl nuclear power plant exploded in April 1986, the KGB tried to keep the world's worst nuclear reactor accident a state secret. Not until fallout reached Scandinavia was the world alerted. Wide swaths of the Belarus and Ukraine republics were contaminated by radioactivity. Government reaction was slow and initially ineffective.

While Gorbachev was seeking stronger economic ties with the West, Chebrikov attacked the West for infiltrating the glasnost atmosphere, saying that "our political, military, and economic interests have suffered damage." After Chebrikov's outburst, the newspaper *Izvestia* interviewed a cartographer who said that the KGB had long ago ordered the falsification of maps. On maps "almost everything was changed—roads and rivers were moved, city districts were tilted," he said. Fake maps seem silly in an age of SATELLITES, but they symbolized the KGB's rigid style. In Oct. 1988 Gorbachev removed Chebrikov.

Chebrikov's successor was VLADIMIR KRYUCHOV, who watched with suspicion and dread as Gorbachev created a full-time parliament, proclaimed multi-candidate elections, began the withdrawal of Soviet troops from Eastern Europe and Afghanistan, and stood by as communist regimes fell, along with the Berlin Wall. In Aug. 1991 Kryuchov and other hard-liners attempted to overthrow Gorbachev. Thousands of Russians took to the streets, defying tanks to protest the attempted coup. Boris Yeltsin, a critic of Gorbachev's slow reforms, had been elected president of the Russian Republic in June in the first popular election in Russian history. Standing on a tank in a Moscow street in Aug. 1991, he became the symbol of defiance and emerged as a hero. To him would belong the future of Russia, for after Dec. 1991 there no longer was a Soviet Union.

As head of the new Russian Federation, Yeltsin abolished the KGB, replacing it with the SVR, Foreign Intelligence Service, and FSK, Federal Security Service, and setting up agencies for presidential and communications security. The SVR, which reported directly to Yeltsin, publicly warned that a new kind of spy war had begun. The SVR charged that Western intelligence agencies were using bribes and payoffs to obtain state secrets. In May 1996 Russia expelled four British diplomats after charging that Britain was running a spy ring out of the British Embassy. Britain responded by expelling four Russian diplomats.

As a sign of new openness, in Jan. 1993, the SVR published what was hailed as the first report ever made public by a Russian intelligence organization. It was entitled "New Challenge After the Cold War: Proliferation of Weapons of Mass Destruction." Based on OPEN SOURCES, it had a propaganda angle, for it urged the nuclear powers to cut their existing nuclear weapons stocks and to control fissionable materials.

Western intelligence agencies, analyzing the SVR, decided that it had too little money to spy abroad. But the GRU, funded through the military services, still had funds available, and its overseas NETWORK of legal ATTACHÉS continued to seek out Western secrets.

By the mid-1990s the poor economic situation in Russia, the lengthy civil war in Chechnya, frustration over crime, and other factors had led to a growth in reactionary forces in the Russian parliament and on the political scene in general. In this environment, the role and powers of the SVR and FSK intelligence services were ominously being strengthened.

During the summer of 1996, the internal turmoil in Russia led to serious challenges to Yeltsin's reelection as President. After the presidential election on June 16, 1996, Yeltsin faced a runoff contest with Gennady Zyuganov, the Communist Party candidate. In the interval before the July 3 runoff vote, Yeltsin ousted several hardliners from his leadership. Most were senior Defense and Army officials; also fired were Mikhail Barsukov, head of the FSK, and Aleksander Korzhakov, the head of the Presidential Security Service (SBP), previously part of the KGB.

Barsukov's career was in the Kremlin's guard unit; he had been appointed commander of the Kremlin guards in Dec. 1991, was a staunch supporter of Korzhakov, and became head of the FSK in 1995. He has been described as strict, taciturn, and unpopular with his peers and subordinates.

Korzhakov's career was also in the Kremlin guard, and he was assigned as head of presidential security in 1993. Korzhakov was described as the second most powerful man in Russia, a close friend and tennis partner of Yeltsin.

ROBERT GATES, the U.S. DIRECTOR OF CENTRAL INTELLIGENCE, visited Moscow and St. Petersburg in Oct. 1992 and established working contacts developed between the first deputy heads of the CIA and SVR. In Jan. 1992 a SVR delegation visited the United States, meeting with members of Congress, journalists, and academics. R. JAMES WOOLSEY, Gates' successor, visited Moscow and St. Petersburg in Aug. 1993, but cut short his visit to fly to Tbilisi after the CIA station chief in Georgia was murdered.

The arrest of CIA INTELLIGENCE OFFICER ALDRICH H. AMES in Feb. 1994 produced another visit—this time a journey by angry CIA officials who flew to Moscow to find out why Russia was still engaged in Cold War–style espionage. But the Russians were fuming, too, for Ames had told his handlers that the CIA was running agents in Russia.

In April 1995, the FSK was reorganized into the Russian Federal Security Service (FSB).

On July 2, 1996, Yeltsin signed a decree to merge the Federal Protection Service (FSO) and the Presidential Security Service (SBP)—the new agency to be called the State Protection Service (GSO). He placed the new GSO under Lt. Gen. Yuri Krapivin. The reorganization, coupled with the June firings and the ascendancy of Alexander Ivanovich Lebed, an outspoken lieutenant general of airborne troops, as Yeltsin's top security adviser, brought a new, centralized direction to Russian internal security activities. (Lebed had ranked third in the June 16 election, garnering 14.5 percent of the vote; Yeltsin had 35 percent and Zyuganov captured 32 percent of the vote.)

Yeltsin won reelection in July 1996. He was succeeded on Dec. 31, 1999, by VLADIMIR PUTIN, an ex-KGB officer who had been head of the FSB. Putin strengthened the FSB by giving it control of border guards and a communications SURVEILLANCE agency known as FAPSI. Putin has also sharply increased Russian espionage activities in Europe and North America, according to *Jane's Intelligence Digest*, which also says that intelligence officers are stepping up their efforts to recruit members of Russian émigré communities.

Lt. Col. Alexander Litvinenko, a former FSB officer granted political asylum in the United Kingdom, says that if an émigré refuses to cooperate, "the intelligence officer then threatens the would-be recruit with legal prosecution in Russia, and if the person continues to refuse, the charges are fabricated."

RYAN

A major Soviet intelligence collection effort aimed at determining if the United States was preparing a surprise nuclear strike against the USSR. It was the largest Soviet peacetime intelligence operation ever undertaken.

Reacting to President Ronald Reagan entering the White House in Jan. 1981 and to the U.S. plans for the deployment of new theater nuclear missiles to Europe (Pershing and Tomahawk), Soviet leader Leonid Brezhnev and KGB Chairman YURI ANDROPOV made a joint appearance before a closed session of senior KGB officers in May 1981.

Brezhnev took the podium first and briefed the assembled INTELLIGENCE OFFICERS on his concerns about U.S. policy under Reagan. Andropov then asserted that the United States was making preparations for a surprise nuclear attack on the USSR. The KGB and the GRU, Soviet MILITARY INTELLIGENCE, he declared, would join forces to mount a new intelligence collection effort to monitor indications and to provide early warning of U.S. war preparations. The effort was given the code-name RYAN—an acronym from the Russian Raketno-Yadernoye Napadenie ("nuclear missile attack").

Then, in an Aug.-Sept. 1981 naval exercise, an armada of 83 U.S., British, Canadian, and Norwegian ships, led by the nuclear-propelled aircraft carrier *Dwight D. Eisenhower*, managed to transit from the Atlantic into the Norwegian Sea undetected by Soviet forces, using a variety of carefully crafted and previously rehearsed concealment and DECEPTION measures. A combination of passive measures (maintaining radio silence and operating under emissions control conditions) and active measures (radar-jamming and transmission of false radar signals) turned the allied force into something resembling a stealth fleet, which even managed to elude a Soviet low-orbit, active-radar SATELLITE launched specifically to locate it. The exercise—with the *Eisenhower* carrying nuclear-capable strike aircraft—was of great concern to the Soviet leadership.

In March 1982 the senior KGB officer in charge of coordinating requirements at the agency's headquarters was sent to Washington to oversee collection of indications-and-warning intelligence. Further, RYAN intelligence was placed in the daily briefing books for members of the *Politburo*.

On Feb. 17, 1983, KGB headquarters notified all senior officers in foreign embassies that RYAN had "acquired an especial degree of urgency" and was "now of particularly grave importance," according to CHRISTOPHER ANDREW and OLEG GORDIEVSKY's *Instructions from the Center: Top Secret Files on KGB Foreign Operations 1975–1985* (1991). The KGB residents received new orders instructing them to organize a "continual watch" using their entire operational staffs. Soviet concerns were raised another notch on March 23, when President Reagan announced his plan for a national missile defense system—promptly dubbed "Star Wars" by the press after the science fiction films of director George Lucas. Four days after the president's announcement—and in direct response—Andropov lashed out. Having succeeded to head the Soviet leadership upon Brezhnev's death in Nov. 1982, the career KGB officer accused the United States of preparing a first-strike attack on the Soviet Union and asserted that President Reagan was "inventing new plans on how to unleash a nuclear war in the best way, with the hope of winning it," according to the Soviet newspaper *Pravda* on March 27, 1983.

Some 40 ships of the U.S. Pacific Fleet conducted a similar exercise in April–May 1983 with a high degree of stealth. Those ships came within 450 miles of the Kamchatka Peninsula and Petropavlovsk, the major Soviet missile submarine base of the Pacific Fleet. The U.S. carriers *Midway* and *Enterprise* both had nuclear strike aircraft embarked.

Finally, in Nov. 1983 a NORTH ATLANTIC TREATY ORGANIZATION command post exercise called Able Archer included a practice drill that took NATO forces through a large-scale simulated release of nuclear weapons. In response, on Nov. 8 or 9, KGB headquarters sent a flash cable to West European operatives advising them—incorrectly—that U.S. forces in Europe had gone on alert and that troops at some bases were being mobilized. The cable speculated that the (nonexistent) alert might have been ordered in response to the then-recent bomb attack on the U.S. Marine barracks in Beirut that had killed more than 200 Americans, or was related to impending U.S. Army maneuvers, or was the beginning of a countdown to a surprise nuclear attack. Recipients were asked to confirm the U.S. alert and evaluate these hypotheses. Soon, in the tense atmosphere generated by the crises and rhetoric of the past few months, some KGB officials concluded that American forces had been placed on alert—and might even have begun the countdown to war.

A short time later the alert dissipated, in part because of President Reagan reducing his rhetoric against the USSR in light of indications that the Soviets were reacting to U.S. stimuli. Also contributing to the resolution of the threat was the death of Andropov in Feb. 1984.

President Reagan said in his memoirs—without reference to British intelligence reports or Able Archer—that in late 1983 he was surprised to learn that "many people at the top of the Soviet hierarchy were genuinely afraid of America and Americans," and "many Soviet officials feared us not only as adversaries but as potential aggressors who might hurl nuclear weapons at them in a first strike," according to Don Oberdorfer in *From the Cold War to a New Era: The United States and the Soviet Union, 1983–1990* (1991).

Moreover, Andrew and Gordievsky wrote in *KGB: The Inside Story of Its Foreign Operations from Lenin to Gorbachev* (1991) that,

> The world did not quite reach the edge of the nuclear abyss during Operation RYAN. But during Able Archer 83 it had, without realizing it, come frighteningly close—certainly closer than at any time since the Cuban missile crisis of 1962.

Significantly, while the Soviet Union had gone to a high state of strategic forces alert in 1983, the United States had not.

2nd Signal Service Battalion

U.S. Army unit that provided personnel for signal intercept stations around the world during World War II.

The battalion was originally activated on Jan. 1, 1939, as the 2nd Signal Service Company, under the Army's Chief Signal Officer. It was assigned several officers and 101 enlisted men. Prior to that the Army's SIGNAL INTELLIGENCE SERVICE (SIS) had been dependent for radio intercepts on Signal Corps units at Fort Monmouth, N.J.; Fort Sam Houston, Texas; the Presidio, San Francisco, Calif.; Fort Shafter, Oahu, Hawaii; Fort McKinley in the Philippines; and Quarry Heights in the Panama Canal Zone.

The formation of the company placed all SIS intercept operations under centralized control. Initially, the 2nd Signal Service Company headquarters was at Fort Monmouth, but in Nov. 1939 it was moved to Washington, D.C., to be collocated with SIS. With war beginning in Europe, SIS operations were expanded, but there was a continued shortfall of men as the Army was growing rapidly and highly trained radio personnel were in short supply. For example, when Japan launched the PEARL HARBOR ATTACK on Dec. 7, 1941, the Company's detachment in the Philippines was authorized 24 enlisted men; it had but 16.

When the United States went to war, the SIS had 45 officers assigned and the 2nd Company had 177 enlisted men—44 officers and 28 enlisted in Washington, and 1 officer and 149 enlisted with detachments elsewhere, including an intercept school detachment at Fort Monmouth. (There were also 109 civilians assigned to SIS.)

By the spring of 1942 there were 15 Army intercept detachments (the one in the Philippines had been evacuated to Australia) with more than 700 personnel. In April 1942 the company became the 2nd Signal Service Battalion. In July 1942 SIS and the battalion's headquarters moved to ARLINGTON HALL in Arlington, Va., a suburb of Washington, although the headquarters constituted little more than a military personnel section for the enlisted men (and later women) of the Army's intercept service.

Detachments were sent to Army listening posts throughout the world to intercept German and Japanese communications and to monitor U.S. military communications to ensure that they maintained COMMUNICATIONS SECURITY procedures. There was also a school detachment, which was moved from Fort Monmouth to Vint Hill Farms, Va., in Oct. 1942.

The SIS and 2nd Battalion were essentially unified on Nov. 19, 1942, when Col. Frank W. Bullock, who had been head of SIS since the previous April, assumed command of the battalion as well. (He was actually "triple-hatted," also being the commanding officer, Arlington Hall Station.)

Recruiting qualified personnel was a continuing problem. For example, by early 1943, of the 521 enlisted men sent to the Vint Hill Farms intercept station in Virginia, 28 were found to be illiterate and hence unacceptable for communications intercept work. Soon enlisted women (WACs) were being assigned to the battalion—11 female officers and 800 enlisted were initially requested.

There were major morale problems among the enlisted men assigned to Arlington Hall. Many had the same assignments as SIS and 2nd Battalion officers and SIS civilians, who were being paid considerably more money. "There was, in fact, so it seemed, no correlation between the rank a worker held and his accomplishments," read the official battalion history. "Naturally, many enlisted men felt that they were being treated unfairly. Efforts were made to solve this problem but without complete success. One solution was, of course, to send outstanding [enlisted] men to Officer Candidate

School, but the quota was small." In addition, although it was difficult to give enlisted men direct commissions, 58 enlisted Japanese linguists were made 2nd lieutenants.

When the war ended in Aug. 1945, the 2nd Battalion maintained intercept detachments at several locations within the United States and on Guam, as well as in Asmara (Eritrea), New Delhi, Alaska, and Hawaii. Under battalion control were 792 officers, 2,704 enlisted men, and 1,214 enlisted women—at more than 4,700, the largest "battalion" in the Army; the head of the intercept service and battalion was a brigadier general. (These numbers do not include 5,661 civilians employed by Army communications intelligence at the end of the war and 17,000 officers and enlisted men engaged in SIGNAL INTELLIGENCE activities under theater commanders.)

S

SEE SECRET

S-2

Intelligence staff of a U.S. Army brigade, regiment, and battalion. The designation G-2 is used at the division and higher levels of Army organizations. S-2 may also refer to an INTELLIGENCE OFFICER for a U.S. Army unit.

Also see G-2 and J-2.

Sackett, Nathaniel

(b. 1737 d. 1805)

INTELLIGENCE OFFICER personally recruited by Gen. GEORGE WASHINGTON during the American Revolutionary War.

Sackett started out as a COUNTERINTELLIGENCE specialist, serving on the New York Committee for Detecting and Defeating Conspiracies, which unmasked British spies and COURIERS. In Feb. 1777, Gen. Washington asked him to set up a NETWORK in the New York area to obtain "the earliest and best Intelligence of the designs of the enemy." Washington paid him $50 a month (the equivalent of almost $1,000 today), and gave him $500 for the recruitment of other agents (about $8,274 today).

Sackett left little information about his network. In one of his operations, he sent an AGENT into an "English Neighborhood" and told him to get a license to sell poultry. This COVER let him move freely from the city to the country, where Sackett probably set up a system for getting the poultry seller's bits of information.

Safe House

Innocent-looking house maintained by an intelligence service for conducting clandestine or covert activities, such as the interrogation or hiding of a DEFECTOR.

JOHN LE CARRÉ [p], in his best-selling novel *Tinker, Tailor, Soldier Spy* (1974), wrote of the thoughts of Peter Guillam as he entered a safe house:

Safe houses I have known, thought Guillam, looking round the gloomy flat. He could write of them the way a commercial traveller could write about hotels: from your five-star hall of mirrors in Belgravia, with Wedgwood pilasters and gilded oak leaves, to this two-room scalp-hunters' shakedown in Lexham Gardens, smelling of dust and drains, with a three-foot fire extinguisher in the pitch-dark hall. Over the fireplace, cavaliers drinking out of pewter. On the nest of tables, sea-shells for ashtrays; and in the grey kitchen, anonymous instructions to "Be Sure and Turn Off the Gas Both Cocks" . . . He pressed the button and heard the clunk of the electric lock echoing in the stairwell. He opened the front door but left the chain till he was sure Toby was alone.

Le Carré continued:

There was tea on a tray: Guillam had prepared it, two cups. To safe houses belongs a certain standard of catering. Either you are pretending that you live there or that you are adept anywhere; or simply that you think of everything. In the trade, naturalness is an art, Guillam decided.

Safford, Capt. Laurance F.

(b. 1893 d. 1973)

Pioneer in U.S. Navy CRYPTANALYSIS and founder of the Navy's codebreaking organization.

Capt. Laurance Safford. (NATIONAL SECURITY AGENCY)

A 1916 graduate of the U.S. Naval Academy, Safford served at sea and in 1924 established the Navy's COMMUNICATIONS INTELLIGENCE (COMINT) unit to monitor Japanese naval communications. Located within the Office of Naval Communications with the COVER designation of Research Desk, the unit was given the Navy code OP-20-G, with OP indicating the Office of the Chief of Naval Operations, 20 indicating Navy communications, and G the seventh unit within that office. Subsequently, the Research Desk was renamed the Communications Security Group. The initial staff of the COMINT unit consisted of Lt. Safford and four civilians. Their first task was to solve Japanese diplomatic codes because those messages were readily available.

After again serving at sea from 1925 to 1929, Safford returned to cryptologic duties for three more years before going back to sea. He took command of OP-20-G in 1936 and remained in cryptology work for the remainder of his Navy career. From 1949 to 1951 he was special assistant to the Director of the ARMED FORCES SECURITY AGENCY, after which he retired from active service.

In 1958 Congress awarded Safford $100,000 for his wartime inventions in lieu of patents.

SAINT

Planned, but never developed, the U.S. SATELLITE Inspector (SAINT) that was to inspect Soviet satellites to determine their purpose and whether they were carrying weapons.

The SAINT program was approved for development in mid-1960. It was initially planned to have a television camera and radar; later models might have infrared, X ray, and radiation sensors to determine more particulars of the TARGET satellite. The SAINT satellites were to be launched into orbit and, using their own propulsion system once in orbit, maneuver to within about 50 feet of target satellites. The information derived from the SAINT's sensors would be sent by data link to a ground station.

Some Air Force proponents of SAINT hoped that later models would also be fitted with a kill mechanism.

It was canceled in Dec. 1962 for lack of funds and conceptual shortcomings. And neither the Eisenhower nor Kennedy administrations showed any interest in placing weapons in space by arming such an inspection system.

Salon Kitty

German SD establishment in which, according to German spy chief WALTER SCHELLENBERG, "important visitors from other countries could be 'entertained' in a discreet atmosphere and . . . offered seductive feminine companionship. In such an atmosphere the most rigid diplomat might be induced to unbend and reveal useful information."

Salon Kitty was set up in a large house in a fashionable district of BERLIN. It is described in *The Schellenberg Memoirs* (1956):

> Double walls were built for the incorporation of microphones, These were connected by automatic transmission to tape recorders which would record every word spoken throughout the house. Three of our department's technical experts, bound by oath, were put in charge of this apparatus. The ostensible owner of the house was provided with the necessary domestic and catering staff for the establishment to be able to offer the best service, food, and drink.

The women of the establishment were recruited from "the most highly qualified and cultivated ladies of the *demimonde*." And, according to Schellenberg, "quite a few ladies from the upper crust of German society were only too willing to serve their country in this manner."

The salon was highly successful in garnering secrets from its clients, mostly foreign diplomats. Occasionally the salon was visited by Nazi leaders, particularly REINHARD HEYDRICH, when, of course, the microphones were turned off.

Salyut

Soviet manned orbiting laboratory, employed for scientific research as well as military activities, including RECONNAISSANCE. The *Salyut 1* was placed in orbit on April 19, 1971, the world's first space station. On June 7, a spacecraft successfully docked with *Salyut 1* and transferred three crewmen who operated the laboratory until June 29.

(After departing the space station, the three cosmonauts died of asphyxiation during reentry when a hatch was jarred open. Space suits were not even carried on the mission; they would be on all future flights to Salyut space stations. Because of the need to provide space suits, crews being shuttled to the spacecraft were reduced from three to two for the next decade.)

While the *Salyut 1* remained in orbit less than six months, it was followed by similar manned space stations, the last—*Salyut 7*—being placed in orbit on April 19, 1982. The giant, 21-ton spacecraft had an orbit 294 miles above the earth. It remained in orbit until early 1991.

The Salyuts were almost continuously occupied, as spacecraft ferried men and supplies to the orbiting stations. The laboratory commander is believed always to have been a military officer, although civilians did serve as accompanying flight engineers. These laboratories enabled the Soviet Union to accumulate several times more manned space flight time than did the United States. Soviet officials stated that cosmonauts in these space stations used visual observations, cameras, spectrometers, and multispectral electro-optical sensors in their observations of Earth. The U.S. government publication *The Soviet Space Challenge* (1987) stated that these observations have "applications for reconnaissance and targeting."

Based on known experiments, the Salyut laboratories Nos. 1, 2, 3, and 5 are generally considered to have been military operations, while Nos. 4, 6, and 7 were civilian operations, although there was obvious overlap. For example, the Soviets conducted radar tests of submarine detection from *Salyut 7*.

The word *Salyut* means "salute," a tribute to the first manned space flight by Yuri Gagarin, which occurred 10 years before the launch of *Salyut 1*.

The Salyut space stations were succeeded by the MIR series, first orbited in 1986. A similar MANNED ORBITING LABORATORY planned by the United States was not fully developed and deployed.

Sam

CODE NAME of a British mission to Moscow in Aug.–Sept. 1941 to form a link between the British intelligence services and the Soviet NKVD.

The British delegation to Moscow was from the SOE (Special Operations Executive), led by Brig. GEORGE HILL, a former Secret Intelligence Service (MI6) officer. Investigative reporter CHAPMAN PINCHER, in his *Too Secret Too Long* (1984) wrote: "The selection of Hill was extraordinary because the Soviets knew that he had been involved with another spy, Sidney Reilly, in an abortive effort to assassinate members of the Bolshevik Committee after the Russian Revolution." (See SIDNEY REILLY.)

The Sam mission was able to obtain Soviet agreement for full collaboration in subversion and propaganda in all countries outside the Soviet Union and British Commonwealth. As a result of this agreement, an NKVD officer was officially assigned to London, while the British military mission to Moscow provided a conduit for intelligence. However, the British gained little as a result of the Sam mission and the ensuing agreements. Indeed, the British government complained that not even TECHNICAL INTELLIGENCE about captured German weapons was being provided. However, the SOE liaison in Moscow was allowed some contact with Russians and was occasionally permitted to visit areas where other British officers were not welcome.

In contrast, the British provided the Soviets with significant assistance, including intelligence derived from ULTRA, although the source was not *officially* revealed. But JOHN CAIRNCROSS and other Soviet spies in Britain were already revealing Ultra to the Soviets, along with other intelligence that the British considered too sensitive to pass to Moscow.

The NKVD also proposed that the British make parachute drops of NKVD AGENTS into German-held territory to make contact with Soviet prisoners and other groups in Western Europe. The British agreed, and several NKVD agents were brought into Britain by SUBMARINE, given some training, and dropped into occupied Europe.

Meanwhile, other Soviet agents were hard at work in Britain stealing secrets. See CAMBRIDGE SPY RING.

SAMOS

The SATELLITE and Missile Observation System (SAMOS), a U.S. Air Force RECONNAISSANCE satellite.

Unlike the CORONA photographic satellite, which returned film canisters to earth, SAMOS was designed with on-board film processing; the resulting pictures were line-scanned and then relayed to a ground station via a television-type downlink.

SAMOS—like Corona—was derived from the Weapon System (WS) 117L project and the PIED PIPER competition among commercial firms for a reconnaissance satellite. The satellite was initially named Sentry and, subsequently, SAMOS.

The Air Force was able to fund development of SAMOS at the same time as the CIA was developing Corona because there was major congressional support for satellite programs in the late 1950s, a time of concern over the so-called missile gap between the United States and Soviet Union. However, the SAMOS downlink technology was not sufficiently mature. In later satellites the film would, as in Corona, be ejected from the satellite and its parachute snatched in flight by special recovery aircraft.

In addition to funding questions, the issue of control of SAMOS was a major concern at the time. Whereas Corona was a CIA project, the Air Force initially considered SAMOS its own. Several senior government officials, however, believed that reconnaissance satellites were national assets and not the "property" of individual armed services. The SAMOS situation was largely resolved on Aug. 25, 1960, when the highly classified NATIONAL RECONNAISSANCE OFFICE (NRO) was established. Hidden within the Air Force staff in the Pentagon, the NRO was a Department of Defense agency but part of the INTELLIGENCE COMMUNITY and thus under direction of the DIRECTOR OF CENTRAL INTELLIGENCE (that is, the head of the CIA).

The Air Force provided most of the support for the NRO. When SAMOS was moved under the NRO, Air Force headquarters, which provided the COVER for the NRO, could thus exercise a high degree of management over the project. But the project was outside the standard Air Force chain of command and, significantly, Gen. Curtis LeMay, head of the Strategic Air Command, was not involved in control of the satellite.

The first attempted launch of a SAMOS satellite on Oct. 11, 1960, failed when a power cable linking the launch tower to the Agena booster rocket did not separate, ripping out a piece of the satellite. The *SAMOS 2* launch on Jan. 31, 1961, was successful. It was able to transmit photos down to a U.S. ground station for nearly a month. It required several months to analyze the pictures, which were of poor quality, compared to the Corona film. The satellite weighed 4,190 pounds and had orbited 295 to 346 miles above the Earth.

By the time of the first successful SAMOS launch, the Corona satellites had been delivering useful photography for more than five months.

The next two attempts to launch SAMOS satellites also failed. Then came a string of successes, interspersed with only a few failures. Of 31 attempts through Nov. 27, 1963, all but five were successful. However, wrote WILLIAM E. BURROWS in *Deep Black* (1986):

> Resolution was another matter, though. Some observers have noted that resolution progressed from twenty feet [the size of a ground object that could be observed] to about five as the program advanced. Others, including the CIA's Herbert Scoville, Jr., have asserted that SAMOS never really yielded useful pictures.

Still, SAMOS data was used by President Kennedy in his deliberations during the CUBAN MISSILE CRISIS of 1962.

Although the SAMOS satellites were not given a KEYHOLE designation, the basic SAMOS camera system was used in the unsuccessful LANYARD program as the KH-6.

Sanitize

To delete specific material or revise a report or other document to prevent the identification of intelligence sources and collection methods. Sometimes, sanitizing goes beyond its protective boundaries, blacking out on declassified documents anything that might prove to be embarrassing if made public.

"Sanitizing" techniques are themselves secret. But the CIA gave a rare look at the process in a declassified 1977 critique that said: "sanitization, which is inherently difficult and time-consuming, is made even more so by the lack of precise, up-to-date guidance." As an example, the critique singled out the practice of sanitizers who "'play it safe,' and without regard to any specific criteria, quickly cut out everything that looks sensitive."

Sansom, Odette

(b. 1913 d. 1995)

World War II AGENT for British SOE who was captured and tortured by the GESTAPO. She was the first woman ever awarded the George Cross.

Born in France, she married an Englishman, Roy Sansom, in 1931 and was living in England in 1940 when she volunteered for Britain's First Aid Nursing Yeomanry. She soon was picked by SOE to work with the French Resistance. Her CODE NAME was Lise.

In Nov. 1942 she was landed by boat in the south of France and joined a Resistance network that was betrayed through the varied treacheries of MATHILDE CARRÉ.

Odette Sansom and another SOE operative, Capt. Peter Churchill, were captured by the Gestapo (as all Nazi intelligence organizations in France were called). By convincing the Germans that she and Churchill were married and that she was responsible for their presence in France, she saved him from a firing squad. He would survive his imprisonment by falsely claiming to be Prime Minister Winston Churchill's nephew.

In 14 harrowing interrogations—she was burned with a hot iron and had her toenails pulled out—she refused to identify two agents hunted by the Gestapo.

Odette Sansom and Churchill were married in 1947 after her husband's death. She later divorced Churchill and married another SOE veteran, Geoffrey Hallowes.

Sapphire

CODE NAME for a Soviet spy ring said to have operated within SDECE, the French intelligence agency. The report came in Dec. 1961 from ANATOLY GOLITSYN, a KGB AGENT who defected to the U.S. CIA.

The Sapphire MOLES, Golitsyn said, had penetrated the government of Charles de Gaulle, the military headquarters of the NORTH ATLANTIC TREATY ORGANIZATION (NATO) in Paris, and SDECE itself. At the recommendation of CIA COUNTERINTELLIGENCE chief JAMES JESUS ANGLETON, President Kennedy wrote to de Gaulle, telling him of the revelation. The CIA station chief in Paris handed the letter to de Gaulle personally.

De Gaulle, suspecting a CIA-engineered plot against him, reacted by ordering the SDECE to break off relations with the CIA. When Angleton saw no French reaction to the Sapphire accusations, he ordered a BLACK BAG JOB (a surreptitious entry) into the French Embassy in Washington to get CODE books so that he could read diplomatic traffic and see exactly what the French were doing. When the break-in was discovered, the SDECE station chief in Washington was recalled.

The Sapphire case formed the plot of the novel *Topaz* (1967) by Leon Uris, which was later made into a film (see MOVIES). The book was so authentic that some observers believed that the CIA had fed Uris the information. A French INTELLIGENCE OFFICER successfully sued Uris and the film company. Uris made his legal experiences the subject of another book, *QB VII* (1970).

Among the Sapphire spies was Georges Piques, a NATO press secretary whom French SURVEILLANCE operatives had seen passing material to a Soviet HANDLER. He gave diplomatic and military secrets to the Soviets to ease international tension, Piques claimed at his trial. He said that his handlers had shown him a letter from Soviet leader Nikita Khrushchev saying that he had been guided during the BERLIN crisis of 1961 by NATO documents that Piques had provided. He was sentenced to life, later reduced to 20 years, for treason.

VENONA intercepts showed that André Labarthe, a scientist in the French Air Ministry, was a Soviet agent in the 1940s. French intelligence believed that he had recruited Piques in Algiers in 1944.

Sasha

SEE SERGE KARLOW, YURI NOSENKO

Satellites

Probably the most important source of strategic intelligence and, to some degree, tactical intelligence and technical intelligence since the early 1960s. Describing the significance of photographic satellites, President Johnson, in March 1967, declared:

> I wouldn't want to be quoted on this, but we've spent $34 or $40 billion dollars on the space program. And if nothing else had come out of it except the knowledge we've gained from space photography, it would be worth ten times what the whole program has cost. Because tonight we know how many missiles the enemy has and, it turned out, our guesses were way off. We were doing things we didn't need to do. We were building things we didn't need to build. We were harboring fears we didn't need to harbor.

The earliest known efforts to investigate the collection of information from space occurred in 1946–1947 when former German V-2 missiles, which were being test-launched by the U.S. Army, were fitted with a small camera. The camera, provided with a heater to protect it from high-altitude cold and a parachute to return it to earth, took photos from a peak altitude of just over 100 miles. (When the V-2 missile supply was exhausted in 1947, cameras were fitted to high-altitude research BAL-LOONS to continue testing, although they were limited to an altitude of little more than 100,000 feet. The balloon concept was later employed in a strategic RECONNAIS-SANCE role over the Soviet Union.)

The first major step toward U.S. development of reconnaissance satellites came from a 1954 recommendation of the RAND Corp. that the Air Force pursue such craft. Later that year—unknown to Rand and known to very few in the Air Force—President Eisenhower gave the CIA approval to develop the U-2 spyplane for OVERHEAD reconnaissance of the Soviet Union.

President Eisenhower's support for the U-2—and subsequently for satellites—originated from his concern over the Soviet developments of strategic nuclear weapons that could threaten the United States with a nuclear version of the PEARL HARBOR ATTACK. In 1954 Eisenhower had asked JAMES R. KILLIAN, president of the Massachusetts Institute of Technology, to chair a panel to look into the potential of long-range, strategic missile developments. Some 50 distinguished scientists and engineers from academia, laboratories, and the government were assembled to look into various aspects of strategic offensive weapons, strategic defense, and strategic intelligence technologies. EDWIN H. LAND of Polaroid fame chaired a subpanel on intelligence.

The panel's 1955, highly classified report began: "We *must* find ways to increase the number of hard facts upon which our intelligence estimates are based, to provide better strategic warning, to minimize surprise in the kind of attack, and to reduce the danger of gross overestimation or gross under-estimation of the threat."

The panel urged development of the U-2, which would become operational in 1956 and was expected to have a useful life of only two years because of Soviet air-defense developments. A satellite was considered a promising follow-on project. Eisenhower embraced the panel's recommendations and established a continuing relationship with Killian, who served as his science adviser, and Land, who would have considerable influence on U.S. spyplane and satellite development.

In 1956 the U.S. Air Force initiated the project Weapon System (WS) 117L to develop a series of reconnaissance satellites. U.S. concern over Soviet bomber development in the mid-1950s led to an increased interest in satellites, with President Eisenhower approving the CORONA photographic satellite, to be developed by the CIA, and the SAMOS, to relay television pictures taken from film, for development by the Air Force.

Even as those projects were being given the green light, in Jan. 1956 the Soviet government approved the high-priority development of a reconnaissance satellite, the ZENIT. Despite the openness of American society, Soviet military and political leaders believed that much of the U.S. defense buildup was hidden.

Both nations conducted research into missile development, with both countries building on the knowledge of German scientists and material taken at the end of World War II. Still, the West was shocked when, on Aug. 3, 1957, an R-7 intercontinental ballistic missile rocketed several thousand miles from its launch pad to hit the earth in Soviet Siberia. In guarded words, the Soviet news agency, Tass, announced that a "super-long distance intercontinental multi-stage ballistic rocket flew at an . . . unprecedented altitude . . . and landed in the target area." (Not for another 16 months would a U.S. Atlas intercontinental missile be tested over its full range.) Then, three months later, on Oct. 4, an R-7 rocket booster placed the world's first satellite in orbit, the *Sputnik 1*. Although it weighed only 184 pounds, the satellite was 166 pounds heavier than the first U.S. satellite, which would not be placed into orbit for another three months. Larger Soviet satellites followed, accelerating U.S. concern over Soviet weapons accomplishments and giving rise to the "missile gap" controversy, as well as demands for better intelligence.

The world's first "spy" satellite was apparently the U.S. Navy's GRAB—for Galactic Radiation And Background experiment. The first GRAB satellite was launched on June 22, 1960—two months before the first successful Corona mission was launched. GRAB had an unclassified mission as it carried a publicly announced experiment to measure solar radiation (hence its name). But GRAB's primary purpose, not revealed until June 1998, was ELECTRONIC INTELLIGENCE (ELINT) collection: to record emissions from radars within the USSR, which it did successfully for more than two years.

The first successful U.S. Corona satellite photographic mission took place in Aug. 1960. That one mission provided more photographic coverage of the Soviet Union than all 23 successful U-2 spyplane flights over the Soviet Union. The satellite had exposed 3,000 feet of film showing 1.6 million square miles of territory.

Also in Aug. 1960 the rivalry between the Air Force and CIA for control of satellite programs—and hence the most important strategic intelligence available—was resolved with the creation of the highly secret NATIONAL RECONNAISSANCE OFFICE within the Department of Defense. The Air Force's SAMOS satellite flew its first successful mission in Jan. 1961, but the quality of its photography—sent to earth via a television-type datalink—was poor in contrast to the photos that Corona parachuted back to earth. The Corona photographic satellite would soon carry "piggyback" ELINT packages.

The first successful *Zenit* Soviet flight—given the mission designation *Cosmos 7*—was flown in July 1962.

More advanced photographic and ELINT satellites would follow those pioneers in space intelligence. And more specialized intelligence satellites would follow: The U.S. MIDAS and its follow-up DSP satellites provided early warning of ballistic missiles launches—and had some capability to detect high-performance aircraft. The Soviet RADAR OCEAN RECONNAISSANCE SATELLITE (RORSAT) would be the first satellite deployed for ocean reconnaissance. Teamed with the ELINT Ocean Reconnaissance Satellite (EORSAT) vehicles, the nuclear-powered RORSAT would detect Western warships on the high seas.

The concept of putting man in space for intelligence collection as well as for research purposes was also proposed in both the United States and Soviet Union. But the U.S. MANNED ORBITING LABORATORY was aborted in 1969 because of delays and budget limitations. The Soviet SALYUT series and the follow-up MIR "space stations" supported a variety of military programs, including intelligence collection. The combination RORSAT/EORSAT satellites and, possibly, the Salyut/Mir operations may also have contributed to Soviet anti-submarine warfare through the detection of submerged submarines.

The belated U.S. space shuttle program has produced some intelligence collection, albeit intermittent, of much shorter duration, and undoubtedly at greater cost. Further, the openness of the shuttle program has limited its military role except as a satellite-launching vehicle. The shuttle also introduced a severe limitation on U.S. satellites. The shuttle was sold to Congress and the public on the basis of being a more efficient method of placing satellites in orbit and servicing them. But it is more difficult to launch a shuttle to put a satellite into orbit than simply to fire one aloft on a rocket booster; after the *Challenger* disaster on Jan. 28, 1986, further shuttle flights were grounded until Sept. 1988. (There was another lengthy grounding following the *Columbia* disaster on Feb. 1, 2003.)

An attempt to launch a classified U.S. satellite on April 18, 1986, with a rocket booster failed. Not until Sept. 5, 1986, was another U.S. military satellite placed in orbit. In contrast, the Soviets retained the rocket booster as the means of orbiting satellites, allowing them considerably more flexibility. During crises and conflicts the Soviets have been able to orbit more reconnaissance satellites rapidly, as they did during the Argentine-British war over the Falklands in 1982, and the Persian Gulf War in 1991.

In the late 1980s another aspect of satellite intelligence came to the fore when the French SPOT satellite,

first orbited in Nov. 1986, was employed to produce photography for commercial sale. Heretofore, relatively little satellite photography had reached the public, and none from satellites with the fine resolution of SPOT's cameras had done so. Indeed, U.S. spy satellite photography could not even be used in the Secretary of Defense's publication *Soviet Military Power*, published from 1981 onward as the official view of the Soviet military threat. (Later issues did use purchased SPOT photography.)

A few satellite photos did reach the public. SAMUEL L. MORISON gave copies of classified satellite photos of a Soviet shipyard to the magazine *Jane's Defence Weekly,* and Air Force Lt. Gen. Lawrence A. Skantze compromised security when he used satellite photos to show new Soviet fighter aircraft to garner support for new U.S. Air Force aircraft.

The availability of SPOT photography and the end of the Cold War in 1991 brought new pressure on the U.S. government to make high-resolution photography available. In 1993 R. JAMES WOOLSEY, the DIRECTOR OF CENTRAL INTELLIGENCE (DCI), told Congress that the government would end its blanket opposition to the sale of "remote sensing" images able to spot objects on the ground as small as 3¼ feet (one meter).

The U.S. government had previously feared that release of satellite photos would reveal how the satellites worked. But it was obvious that the Soviets knew how reconnaissance satellites worked, both from their own experience and from espionage. WILLIAM P. KAMPILES, a CIA employee, in 1978 sold the Soviets the KH-11 manual for only $3,000, providing technical data on the latest U.S. spy satellite (see KEYHOLE). Adm. STANSFIELD TURNER, DCI at the time, later wrote, "The CIA's security procedures were surprisingly lax." Telling about the Kampiles case in *Secrecy and Democracy* (1985), Turner related, "When we learned that one was missing, we also found we could not account for thirteen others!" It was not known how many of those KH-11 manuals had found their way into Soviet hands.

Nonintelligence satellites have also been developed and orbited for warning of ballistic missile launches, communications, navigation, mapping, monitoring earth resources, weather reconnaissance, research, and attacking enemy satellites. The release of SPOT photography and the subsequent U.S. sale of satellite photos—which American firms believed to be a $1 *billion* business—provided the opportunity for more accurate maps, better environmental and crop predictions, more accurate news coverage, and other benefits.

However, the intelligence collection satellites must be considered in a separate, transcending category. JEFFREY RICHELSON, in his comprehensive *America's Secret Eyes in Space* (1990), wrote:

> On the one hand, the photo-reconnaissance satellite has been a partner to the atomic and nuclear weapons whose use could devastate the civilized world. Both the United States and the Soviet Union have relied on their reconnaissance satellites to locate and identify targets to be attacked in the event

of war. At the same time, those satellites have played a significant role in preventing the occurrence of war and permitting arms limitation agreements. In the first year of their operation, the Corona satellites helped dispel America's fear of Soviet strategic superiority that had haunted many Americans since the launch of Sputnik.

Since then, knowledge has largely prevailed over fear in assessing foreign military capabilities, at least on the part of those individuals and agencies with access to satellite intelligence. And the arms limitation agreements of the past, present, and future would not be possible without such devices to verify compliance.

Further, beyond the United States and Soviet Union, several other nations have launched intelligence collection satellites. Two of the more recent entries into the spy satellite field have been Israel and Japan. Israel, which launched its OFEK 1, a combination photo and ELINT satellite, on Sept. 19, 1988, is concerned with military and technical intelligence TARGETS in neighboring Arab countries. Additional satellites of the series have since been launched; *Ofek 3,* launched in 1995, has ultraviolet and other imaging sensors.

Japan, which had earlier sent aloft scientific research satellites, orbited its first pair of multi-purpose Information Gathering Satellites (IGS) on March 28, 2003. Launched from the same booster, one IGS has optical

sensors and the other radar. Japan is particularly concerned with North Korean missile developments.

Of course, other countries that cannot afford to develop and orbit their spy satellites can purchase at least photographic images from commercial satellite firms.

Also see FEEDBACK.

Sattler, James Frederick

(b. 1938)

MOLE for the East German intelligence service in the United States. Born in New York City, Sattler attended the University of California at Berkeley and later studied in East and West Germany and in Poland. Fluent in German, he traveled frequently to Europe, teaching, doing research, and attending international conferences, for a time working for the Atlantic Institute for Foreign Affairs in Paris.

In the early 1970s Sattler began working in Washington, D.C., as a foreign policy analyst for the Atlantic Council of the United States, a foreign policy organization that focused on the political and military problems of the NORTH ATLANTIC TREATY ORGANIZATION. At times U.S. government officials used the council as a sounding board for potential plans.

Sometime about 1973, Sattler was unmasked as a spy by an East German INTELLIGENCE OFFICER who had

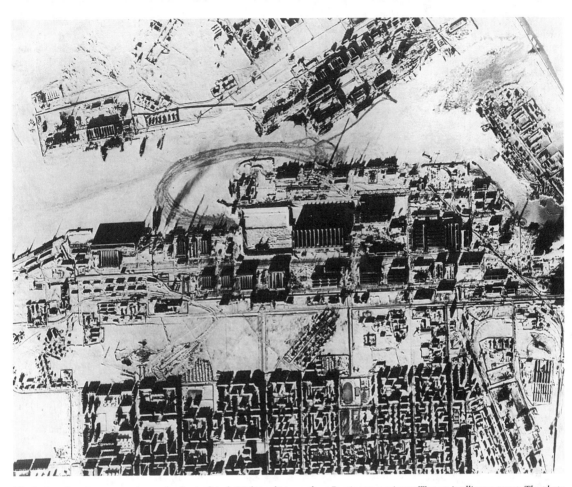

The Soviet submarine construction yard at Severodvinsk (Molotovsk) in northern Russia was a primary Western intelligence target. The photo at left was taken in Aug. 1941 by a German reconnaissance aircraft; that at right on Feb. 10, 1969, from a higher altitude, by a Corona spy satellite. (CENTRAL INTELLIGENCE AGENCY)

defected to West Germany and had named several AGENTS, including Sattler, whose information had been supplied to the KGB.

Sattler had been recruited in 1967, some six years before his activities were revealed. On learning that the defector had named Sattler, the FBI asked Secretary of the Navy John Lehman, who knew Sattler, to ask him if he would be interested in becoming a DOUBLE AGENT. After admitting his espionage activities to Lehman, Sattler fled to Mexico, where he tried in vain to get help from the Soviet Embassy.

Sattler then briefly returned to Washington, where the Department of Justice, using a little-known federal law, ordered him to register as a spy. On March 23, 1974, Sattler filled out Form GA-1, issued by the Department of Justice's Internal Security Section. Sattler checked *Yes* to this question: *Do you have knowledge of the espionage, counterespionage or sabotage tactics of a foreign government or foreign political party?* He then provided a description of his life as a spy:

Since 1967, I have transmitted to my principals in Berlin, GDR, information and documents which I have received from the North Atlantic Treaty Organization and from individuals in institutions and government agencies in the Federal Government of Germany, United States, Great Britain, Canada, and France.

I photographed a portion of this information with a microdisc camera and placed the microdiscs in packages which I mailed to West Germany which I know were subsequently received by my principals in Berlin, GDR. Other documents and information I photographed with a Minox camera and personally carried the film to my principals in Berlin or handed them to a courier. The microdisc camera was given to me by my principal.

Sattler admitted receiving approximately $15,000 for his services as well as an "honor decoration" issued by the Ministry for State Security of East Germany.

U.S. COUNTERESPIONAGE agents then reportedly TURNED Sattler long enough to track his communications system, which ran from Washington to Canada to West Germany to East Germany and, finally, to Moscow.

Sattler disappeared shortly after he signed the statement admitting that he was a spy. Lehman believed that had Sattler not been discovered, by the 1980s he "could have been anything. . . . An Assistant Secretary of Defense—or maybe State—by now."

Satyr

British program to uncover the mysteries of the highly sophisticated microphone found in the Great Seal of the United States that hung above the ambassador's desk in the U.S. Embassy in Moscow. Planted by the Soviets and discovered by the United States in 1952, the BUG had apparently revealed many American secrets to Soviet intelligence.

The bug was revealed by SWEEPERS making a routine check of the ambassador's office prior to a visit by the U.S. Secretary of State. But U.S. technicians were unable to comprehend the workings of the device. The microphone was activated and powered from a distant location, using microwave beams.

Accordingly, it was taken to Britain, where electronics specialist PETER WRIGHT examined the device and was able to discern its secrets. But it took him 18 months—in an effort given the CODE NAME Satyr—to produce a British prototype of the device for use in British COUNTERESPIONAGE activities.

Savak

Iranian secret police and intelligence agency that ended with the Islamic revolution that culminated in Shah Muhammad Reza Pahlavi's flight out of the country on Jan. 16, 1979.

Savak is a contraction of the Farsi words *Sazamane Etelaat va Amniate Kechvar* (Security and Intelligence Organization). Long feared and hated, the Savak institutionalized the Shah's personal opposition to any political challengers while he modernized the country. The agency, whose principal mission was the eradication of threats to the Shah, arrested, tortured, and murdered thousands of opponents to the Shah's regime.

While the U.S. CIA maintained a major station in Iran, with a complement estimated at 50 to 75 personnel, the CIA did not conduct espionage activities against Iran. Rather, it relied on the Savak for information on internal matters, which contributed to the failure of the CIA to predict the overthrow of the Shah's government.

An indication of the close CIA-Savak cooperation can be seen in a secret memorandum to the U.S. ambassador, dated June 2, 1974, referring to a CIA report on the "Soviet intelligence presence in Iran." The report said there were 67 "identified" Soviet INTELLIGENCE OFFICERS in Tehran, including three in the Soviet Hospital and one in the Aeroflot office. Besides those officers, the CIA report said, there were probably more, including "young officers serving their first familiarization tours in Iran which is a traditional assignment post of Soviet intelligence apprentices." Copies of the report were given to the Savak and the Shah.

The CIA's major presence in Iran began in 1953, when KERMIT ROOSEVELT and fewer than 30 American, British, and Iranian AGENTS mounted an operation that brought down the government of the leftist government of Mohammed Mossadegh. The Savak was established in 1956 with the help of the CIA and Israel's MOSSAD.

The Shah permitted the CIA to operate freely in Iran to conduct intelligence collection against the Soviet Union. Also in Iran was a major NSA electronic listening post, as well as a massive U.S. military staff to help the Iranian armed forces employ new air, ground, and naval weapons. All of these U.S. activities, however, were monitored by the Savak and its army of informers.

As unrest with the Shah's regime grew at home and abroad in the 1970s, the Savak undertook some operations in the United States against dissident students. Savak agents in the United States, operating with the knowledge of the CIA and FBI, monitored the estimated 30,000 Iranian students attending U.S. colleges and universities. The head of the U.S. Savak operation used diplomatic COVER while a member of the of Iranian Mission to the UNITED NATIONS.

At the end of its existence, the Savak had an estimated 5,000 officers and employees, supported by many thousands of informers. When Islamic fundamentalists took over the country, the Savak's headquarters in Tehran was attacked and the agency's files looted. Gen. Nematollah Nassiri, the third and last head of the Savak, was shot at his headquarters, along with some 60 members of the Savak.

In Feb. 1979 the Islamic assembly approved a bill abolishing the Savak and establishing a National Intelligence Center, without police powers.

Also see ALI NAGHI RABBANI.

SBP

The Russian Presidential Security Service. Formerly the Ninth Chief Directorate of the KGB, the SBP was established as an independent government agency on Dec. 17, 1993.

In addition to providing security for top Russian officials and the guard force for the Kremlin, the SBP supervises top-level government communications and executive aircraft (formerly the 235th Air Squadron), operates and protects underground command centers, maintains the special underground train system that connects key government facilities in the Moscow area, and protects other "strategic facilities."

The head of the SBP from 1993 to June 1996 was Maj. Gen. Aleksandr V. Korzhakov, formerly with the KGB's Ninth Chief Directorate. He was fired following an incident in which SBP officers apprehended two campaign advisers to Yeltsin as they left a government building carrying $538,000 in cash.

Yeltsin replaced Korzhakov with his personal bodyguard, Anatoliy Kuznetsov.

Also see RUSSIA-USSR.

Scalp Hunter

British slang for INTELLIGENCE OFFICERS who specialize in defections and in differentiating genuine DEFECTORS from fakes and plants. They help to identify potential defectors and, if necessary, arrange for intimidation or entrapment.

Scarbeck, Irwin C.

American Foreign Service Officer who passed secrets to Eastern European communist nations. He was second secretary at the U.S. Embassy in Warsaw in 1960 when he fell in love with a 22-year-old Polish girl. In a classic blackmail operation, hostile INTELLIGENCE OFFICERS photographed him with the girl and threatened to expose him—a married man with four children—unless he handed over U.S. secrets. Resisting that demand, he did provide classified political documents. Tried and convicted, he was sentenced to 30 years. In 1963 the sentence was reduced to 10 years.

Scarlet Pimpernel

Fictional spy in the adventure novel *The Scarlet Pimpernel* by Hungarian-born English author Baroness EMMUSKA ORCZY. First published in 1905, the novel tells the story of the leader of the League of the Scarlet Pimpernel, a band of young Englishmen pledged to rescue the innocent aristocratic victims of the Reign of Terror that followed the French Revolution. The novel's hero—Sir Percy Blakeney—outwits his French revolutionary opponents through his courage and ingenious disguises, identifying himself in his secret rescue missions by a signet ring with the image of a scarlet pimpernel blossom.

The story was made into a classic film in 1935 and a TV movie in 1982. The 1935 film starred Leslie Howard, Merle Oberon, and Raymond Massey. Howard played the Englishman who led a double life, saving innocent victims of the French Revolution while pretending to be a foppish, poetry-spouting gentleman back home in England.

Schellenberg, Brigadeführer Walter

(b. 1910 d. 1952)

German intelligence official and, after the dissolution of the ABWEHR in 1944, head of the foreign operations of the unified German intelligence service.

Schellenberg's intelligence career began in 1933 with the SS, initially working in COUNTERINTELLIGENCE. In June 1941 he became head of Department IV, or foreign intelligence, of the RSHA, with the rank of SS Brigadeführer.

(He was the youngest general in the SS at the time.) Schellenberg personally directed and participated in the VENLO INCIDENT, the attempt to kidnap the Duke of Windsor from Portugal (Operation VALLI), the RICHARD SORGE case, the CICERO operation, and the attempt to "sell" Jews and other concentration camp inmates as the end of the war neared. From mid-1944 Schellenberg took over the duties of the Abwehr, the German military intelligence organization.

Describing Schellenberg, intelligence historian DAVID KAHN wrote in *Hitler's Spies* (1978) that he "was a boyish, charming SS brigadier, who looked well in his black SS uniform with silver trim . . . . his brains, his flair, and his loyalty" had gained him Department IV at the age of 31. Hugh Trevor-Roper was highly critical of Schellenberg in *The Last Days of Hitler* (1947): "Among the universally parochial minds of the SS, Schellenberg . . . enjoyed an undeserved reputation . . . . he was in fact a very trivial character."

Schellenberg was a confidant of HEINRICH HIMMLER and REINHARD HEYDRICH, who was his immediate superior, and he had regular contact with Adolf Hitler. After Heydrich's assassination, Schellenberg was considered as a candidate for head of the RSHA, but he was rejected as too young and too unorthodox, at least from a Nazi perspective. When ERNST KALTENBRUNNER was named head of the RSHA, Schellenberg was given direct access to Himmler, although nominally he was Kaltenbrunner's subordinate.

As World War II neared its climax in Europe, Schellenberg attempted to influence Himmler, urging him to begin negotiations with neutral representatives to arrange a surrender to the Western allies; Schellenberg hoped that Himmler would succeed Hitler as head of the German state. He also worked toward the protection and release of concentration camp inmates. He was dismissed as chief of Department IV by Kaltenbrunner on April 30, 1945, as Himmler was vilified by Hitler because of his efforts to negotiate with the West. Schellenberg then joined the government of Grand Adm. Karl Dönitz, who had succeeded Hitler that night. When the war ended a week later, Schellenberg was in Sweden attempting to negotiate a German surrender.

At the Nuremberg war crimes trials Schellenberg was acquitted of all but two charges—being a member of the SS and SD, which the international tribunal declared to be criminal organizations, and executing Russian prisoners without trial. But the court considered Schellenberg's belated efforts to aid concentration camp prisoners as mitigation and he was sentenced to six years' imprisonment. Shortly after his release in June 1951 he completed *The Schellenberg Memoirs*; he died less than a year later of liver disease.

Scherbius, Arthur

(b. 1878 d. 1929)

German inventor of the ENIGMA machine, the first practical mechanical device for ENCIPHERING messages. He based the machine on ROTORS that changed position every time a letter key was depressed to provide a different, randomly selected letter substitute. Intended for commercial use, its formal name was the "Glow-lamp Ciphering and Deciphering Machine Enigma." The machine was first exhibited in 1923 but did not meet with immediate success.

BORIS HAGELIN took over the machine, making improvements. Scherbius went bankrupt and died before the machine entered mass production in the late 1920s for the Swedish and German armed forces.

Scherhorn

Soviet DECEPTION operation in World War II in which the German armed forces were tricked into believing that 2,500 of their troops were trapped behind Soviet lines at the Berezina River.

Oberstleutnant (lieutenant colonel) Heinrich Scherhorn was the alleged commander of the trapped troops who, on Aug. 19, 1944, made radio contact with the German High Command detailing the unit's plight. From that date until Scherhorn's last message on April 4, 1945, the German armed forces and SS expended considerable effort—men, aircraft, and equipment—in efforts to rescue the troops. There are reports that two SS groups were sent in to help effect a rescue of the Scherhorn group, and that OTTO SKORZENY, who had rescued Benito Mussolini, was planning to mount an operation to save Scherhorn in March 1945.

So appealing and heroic were the radio messages from Scherhorn that Adolf Hitler promoted the group commander to oberst (colonel) and awarded him the Knight's Cross. All the officers mentioned in the radio messages were also promoted! In reality, Scherhorn and some 200 of his men had been captured by the Soviets during the Belorussian offensive in the summer of 1944. Scherhorn began sending messages under Soviet guidance.

Like Operation MAX, Scherhorn's activities demonstrated the Soviet expertise in such deception.

Schlesinger, James R.

(b. 1929)

Briefly the U.S. DIRECTOR OF CENTRAL INTELLIGENCE (DCI), from Feb. 1973 to July 1973, after which he served as Secretary of Defense until Nov. 1975 and as Secretary of Energy from Aug. 1977 to Aug. 1979.

An economist and expert in energy and national security matters, Schlesinger had earned his B.A., M.A., and Ph.D. in economics from Harvard University. He was subsequently a consultant to the Federal Reserve Board of Governors and professor at the University of Virginia before becoming director of strategic studies at the RAND Corp. from 1963 to 1969.

Entering government, Schlesinger served as assistant and acting director of the Bureau of the Budget (later changed to the Office of Management and Budget) from 1969 to 1971. While there he drew up a plan to revamp the INTELLIGENCE COMMUNITY. He was chairman of the Atomic Energy Commission from 1971 to 1973, when President Nixon appointed him DCI. Nixon, who never liked or trusted the CIA, had fired Schlesinger's predecessor, RICHARD HELMS, for not being more helpful to him in the WATERGATE affair.

Schlesinger was directed to remake the CIA. He did so by authorizing compilation of the FAMILY JEWELS list (although WILLIAM E. COLBY presented them to Congress) and firing more than 1,000 CIA personnel (out of an estimated 15,000), invoking a "20 years and you're out" edict. He seemed uncomfortable at the CIA, and Nixon sent him to the Defense Department.

Among Schlesinger's earliest moves at the Pentagon was to direct an extensive analysis of U.S. and Soviet strategic weapons development, seeking to understand how and why the two superpowers developed their nuclear arsenals. He also oversaw the final withdrawal of U.S. military forces from Vietnam.

Schlesinger's tenure at the Defense Department ended abruptly as part of the so-called Halloween massacre, the critics' term for the executive branch reorganization in early Nov. 1975, when President Ford not only fired Schlesinger but also fired Colby as DCI and replaced him with GEORGE H. W. BUSH. Schlesinger declined an appointment as chairman of the Export-Import Bank but was later named Secretary of Energy. After he left that Cabinet post, he continued to serve in governmental and private organizations. A member of the Defense Policy Board, he was also chairman of the board of the MITRE Corp., a major defense and intelligence company.

Schluga, Baron August

(b. 1841 d. 1917)

Spy who served Prussia and Germany from 1866 to World War I.

Born in Hungary, in what was then the Austro-Hungarian Empire, Schluga studied at the Polytechnical Institute in VIENNA and joined the Austrian Army. He fought bravely at the battle of Magenta in the Italian War of 1859 and was destined for a General Staff post. But he resigned to become part of the Austrian landed gentry.

Posing as a journalist, he managed to get into Austrian Army headquarters in 1866 while Helmuth Count von Moltke, chief of the Prussian General Staff, was preparing for war against Austria. Schluga brought Moltke the Austrian ORDER OF BATTLE, immeasurably helping Moltke defeat the Austrians.

Schluga, operating out of Paris, served Moltke again prior to the Franco-Prussian War (1870–1871). By then designated AGENT 17, he delivered intelligence to the military ATTACHÉ in the Prussian Embassy in Paris. His spymasters did not even know where he lived, let alone how he got his information. Once more his intelligence helped to produce a Prussian victory.

From 1870 to 1914 Agent 17 was a SLEEPER, never activated by his German superiors (Prussia had now been absorbed into the imperial Germany). His spymaster was Maj. WALTHER NICOLAI, who headed the General Staff's intelligence bureau, known as III b. Nicolai got a trickle of intelligence from Schluga in the years of peace. Then, just before World War I began, Schluga passed to Germany the plan for the major deployments scheduled on the fifth day of French mobilization. Some military historians rank this intelligence as the greatest coup ever achieved by a spy in an enemy country.

German commanders failed to exploit the intelligence, however—a frequent phenomenon in espionage history. Schluga, 73 and in ill health, slipped into Germany after the war began. After a rest, he returned to Paris in May 1915 and regularly sent intelligence messages via COURIERS to Switzerland.

Schluga's stream of intelligence was almost too good, historian DAVID KAHN wrote in *Hitler's Spies* (1978). Schluga "whether consciously or not, repeatedly emphasized French weaknesses in character and in government." This reinforced the belief of Erich von Falkenhayn, chief of the General Staff of the German field army, that the French lacked the "will and ability to attack. Consequently, in the summer of 1915 he discounted clear indications of a threatening offensive. . . . But finally the authoritative tone of the heavy [Allied] guns overruled the spy. Falkenhayn moved to repel the Allied advance."

Schluga, the dean of German spies, kept his sources and methods secret even from his superiors. He sent his final report in March 1916 and then made his way to Germany, where he died a year later.

Schmidt, Hans-Thilo

(b. 1888 d. 1943)

The German who gave the Allies the keys to the German ENIGMA CIPHER machine. Historian DAVID KAHN called him "the spy who most affected the Second World War." The secrets he provided enabled the Poles to break the Enigma ciphers, knowledge they then shared with the French and British.

Schmidt was born in BERLIN, son of a baroness and a professor at the Charlotten School. It is unknown whether or not the younger Schmidt served in World War I. After the war he owned a chemical factory, which failed in the inflation-ridden Germany of the 1920s. His brother, Rudolf Schmidt, a professional soldier, was second in charge of the Signal Corps unit that handled cryptology for the Army and Ministry of Defense—the Chiffrierstelle.

Thus, Schmidt was able to obtain a position as a civilian clerk who, according to Kahn's *Kahn on Codes* (1983), "distributed cipher material and supervised its destruction when it went out of force." He remained with the Chiffrierstelle after his brother left in Oct. 1929. Just over a year before Adolf Hitler came to power in Germany, on Dec. 1, 1931, Schmidt joined the Nazi Party.

Sometime between then and Oct. 1932, still in the Chiffrierstelle, Schmidt offered to sell Enigma secrets to the French. Sources vary as to exactly when the first documents were passed to Capt. GUSTAVE BERTRAND, head of the decoding staff of French intelligence. Bertrand immediately shared the documents with the Poles, who had the best codebreaking effort in Europe at the time, and the British. The Poles record having documents in hand on Dec. 7, 1931, although most sources cite a 1932 handover of material as the first. (The British made no use of the material at the time.)

The material from Schmidt was invaluable, according to Kahn:

> His reason was money. A weakling, a hedonist, a dissipate, he wanted the money for his women [he was married] and high living. But perhaps there was also an unacknowledged motive for his treason. His father had attained the highest nongovernmental status a civilian could get. His mother was a noblewoman. His brother was rising in the army, Germany's most prestigious institution. He himself was a failure. Perhaps he wanted to revenge himself on his family by doing something that would undermine the society that had conferred so much upon them and that, if discovered, would destroy them.

In 1934 Schmidt transferred to the newly established Forschungsamt—Research Office—an intercept and codebreaking activity. From there he continued his treason, providing valuable cryptographic material to Bertrand. Given the CODE NAME Asché, he met with the French 19 times during the seven years of his treason, mostly in Switzerland but also in other places (including, in Aug. 1938, Paris, where he was wined and dined by the French).

Schmidt passed to the French—and, through Bertrand, to the Poles and British—not only information on the Enigma machine but also reports of German codebreaking successes against the French and other countries. His espionage continued until war enveloped Europe in Sept. 1939. He continued his work at the Forschungsamt until Nov. 1942. At that time the Germans took into custody a man named Lemoine, a former German who had become a French citizen and worked with French intelligence. To save himself, he revealed Schmidt, among others.

The GESTAPO then arrested Schmidt. He was executed in July 1943. (His brother, a highly successful general specializing in armored warfare, was relieved of his command and ousted from the Army.)

Schoof, Petty Officer 3rd Class Charles Edward

U.S. sailor found guilty of conspiring to commit espionage. He was arrested in Dec. 1989 on board the tank landing ship *Fairfax County,* along with Petty Officer 3rd Class John Joseph Haeger.

Schoof called the Soviet Embassy in Washington, D.C., offering information on radar, communications, and electronic countermeasures. Schoof asked the embassy to send someone to pick up the documents, which Haeger, who knew the combination, was to take from the ship's document safe. The two sailors apparently did not know that Norfolk, Va., where the ship was stationed, was beyond the travel zone allowed Soviet diplomats. Nor did they realize that the FBI and NSA routinely tapped embassy phones.

In April 1990 Schoof was sentenced to 25 years in prison and Haeger to 19 years. Under a 1987 revision of federal parole guidelines, they were expected to serve virtually all of their sentences.

Schulmeister, Karl

(b. 1770 d. 1853)

Spymaster for Napoléon Bonaparte, who called him "the emperor of spies." Born in Alsace, the son of a Lutheran clergyman, he spoke French, German, and Hungarian. He also had a talent for disguise.

Schulmeister was a SECRET AGENT by 1804. The following year he became a full-scale spy for Napoléon. France was at war with Austria, and Schulmeister was sent to VIENNA in disguise in 1805 to spy out enemy movements. In the guise of a Hungarian nobleman he became a member of the staff of Austrian Gen. Karl Mack and provided false information on the French Army. This information supposedly led to Mack's defeat by Napoléon at Ulm in Oct. 1805.

Schulmeister, however, is known to have received money from both France and Austria. Exposed and arrested, he was rescued when the French occupied Vienna, where he became commissioner of police.

He also sent spies for Napoléon against the Prussians and Russians, reportedly placing one of his AGENTS in the headquarters of Czar Alexander I. He continued to serve Napoléon until 1809, when Napoléon married the Austrian Archduchess Marie Louise. Austrian anger over Schulmeister's brutality in Austria forced Napoléon to retire him. Schulmeister expected a major decoration for his services, but Napoléon reputedly told him, "Gold is the only suitable reward for spies."

Schulmeister rejoined Napoléon after his escape from Elba.

When the Austrians invaded Alsace in 1814, they took care to destroy Schulmeister's estates there. Following the French defeat at Waterloo in 1815, Schulmeister was one of the first of Napoléon's supporters to be arrested. He saved himself by paying a huge ransom. He never regained his wealth, and lived out the rest of his life in Alsace.

Schwartz, Lt. Comdr. Michael

U.S. Navy officer accused of providing secrets to the Saudi Arabian government.

Schwartz was investigated for illegally disclosing the classified information while he was assigned to the U.S. military training mission in Saudi Arabia between Nov. 1992 and Sept. 1994. He was specifically charged with mishandling classified documents, making a false statement, and espionage. After a date was set for a general court-martial, Schwartz requested a separation from the Navy in lieu of going to trial.

He was allowed to leave the Navy in Dec. 1995 with an "other than honorable" discharge.

SCI

SEE SENSITIVE COMPARTMENTED INFORMATION

Scientific Liaison Bureau

SEE LAKAM

Scientific and Technical (S&T) Intelligence

Information or intelligence relating to foreign scientific or technical research and development. These include developments in basic and applied research, scientific and technical characteristics, capabilities, and limitations related to foreign military systems, weapons, and other matèriel as well as industrial and manufacturing aspects of weapons development.

"The effort to obtain early warning of the adoption of new weapons and methods by potential or actual enemies" is the definition used by British scientist R. V. Jones, who was involved in the anticipation of German technical developments during World War II.

In his superb book *The Wizard War* (1978), Jones outlined how a fundamentally new weapon proceeds:

(1) general scientific research of an academic or commercial nature
(2) someone in close touch with a military service, and who is aware of service requirements, thinks of an application of the results of academic research
(3) ad hoc research and small-scale trials are performed in a service laboratory
(4) large-scale trials are undertaken
(5) the new weapon is adopted by the service

Dr. Jones pointed out that the first stage is generally public, and common knowledge to all progressive countries. The later stages are more difficult to observe, and "the only method of dealing with [them] is by direct espionage, or the observations of indiscretions by research personnel . . ."

He then observed that information leaks out in five ways:

(1) accidental indiscretions, including deciphered message, of which there are always a large number, and if these are pieced together a valuable impression may be gained
(2) indiscretions encouraged by alcohol and/or mistresses (SEX)

(3) information that cannot be kept secret and yet can give useful information to an enemy (for instance, HIGH-FREQUENCY DIRECTION FINDING of radio transmissions, loss of equipment in combat)

(4) direct observation by AGENTS—"Such a method is difficult and hazardous, and comparatively little is obtained; its value is large."

(5) information obtained from disaffected nationals (DEFECTORS)—"Frequently this is unreliable and must always be checked."

Jones was head of Scientific Intelligence on the British Air Staff and scientific adviser to the Secret Intelligence Service MI6 from 1939 to 1946.

SCIF

SEE SENSITIVE COMPARTMENTED INFORMATION FACILITY

Scranage, Sharon

A clerk for the U.S. CIA in Ghana from May 1983 to May 1984, charged in July 1985 with espionage and LEAKING secrets to the government of Ghana. After her return to the United States, Scranage admitted to the FBI that she had given her former Ghanaian lover, Michael Soussoudis, the names of CIA employees and informants in Ghana.

Soussoudis, a first cousin of the leader of Ghana, Jerry Rawlings, was arrested on July 10 during a visit to the United States. He was charged with espionage and sentenced to a 20-year prison term on Nov. 25. His sentence was suspended immediately on condition that he leave the country within 24 hours. In effect he was exchanged by American authorities for the release from jail in Ghana of eight men who allegedly worked for the CIA.

In Nov. 1985 Scranage was sentenced to five years in prison. This sentence was reduced to two years in April 1986, allowing her to be released after serving 18 months.

Scytale

Earliest known device for CRYPTOLOGY. Invented by the Spartans, it consisted of letters written on a strip of cloth or leather in an apparently random manner, with the coded message hidden by superfluous letters. It revealed a message when wrapped around a rod or staff of a specific size.

SD

Sicherheitsdienst (German security service), the intelligence collection and espionage section of the SS. As described by SS chief HEINRICH HIMMLER, the SD's task was to "discover the enemies of the National Socialist concept." Through a vast network of informers and AGENTS throughout Germany and conquered Europe, the SD worked closely with the GESTAPO to seek out and destroy Germany's political and ethnic enemies.

SD thugs also carried out the Nacht und Nebel Erlass (Night and Fog Decree), which Hitler issued in Dec. 1941 as a way of preventing the creation of martyrs by public execution. Under this operation, citizens of occupied countries were taken to Germany secretly to "vanish without leaving a trace." The decree stated "no information [could] be given as to their whereabouts or their fate." The Germans had a word for what happened to the tens of thousands of victims: They were *vernebelt*, "transformed into mist."

The Nuremberg International Military Tribunal that tried German war criminals after the war accused the SD, as well as the SS and Gestapo, of "the persecution and extermination of the Jews, brutalities and killings in concentration camps, excesses in the administration of occupied countries, the administration of the slave labor program and the mistreatment and murder of prisoners-of-war."

Also see REINHARD HEYDRICH.

SDECE

Service de Documentation Extérieure et de Contreespionnage (External Documentation and Counterespionage), the French intelligence agency that became a powerful, uninhibited organization both inside and outside France.

The SDECE was founded as a replacement for the DGER, an intelligence service fostered by Gen. Charles de Gaulle. When he resigned as interim President of France in Jan. 1946, the SDECE emerged as the replacement for the DGER. At the same time, Gaullist ANDRÉ DEWAVRIN was replaced by Henri Ribière, a socialist and confidant of the Secretary of the Interior.

Officially, the DGER was merely renamed. In reality, the change was drastic, for the DGER had been an internal security agency, notorious for tapping phones and opening the mail of people under SURVEILLANCE by the government. The new charter for the SDECE forbade it to operate inside France, giving it only the mission to "seek, outside national boundaries, all information and documents which might inform the government." The SDECE was officially under the Ministry of Defense, but in reality it was controlled by the President through an adviser.

The SDECE was known as *la piscine,* "the swimming pool," because its Paris headquarters was near a public swimming pool. The SDECE had a COUNTERINTELLIGENCE section devoted to protecting itself and other French intelligence agencies from MOLES. The SDECE was strictly prohibited from launching counterintelligence operations in France, except for those it conducted toward foreign embassies. Any domestic security operations, said its charter, "will rest with a special division of the Department of the Interior." As was usual in France, the power of one intelligence agency was curbed by giving power to another agency.

In Indochina immediately after World War II, the SDECE tried to create a local resistance organization, modeled on the French Resistance of World War II. Working at first with Nationalist China's CENTRAL INVESTIGATIONS AND STATISTICS BUREAU, the SDECE ferreted out suspected communists and tried to organize a French-style underground in the jungles of Indochina. Later, when the communists took over China in 1949, Nationalist Chinese officers fled to Indochina and worked for the SDECE. The attempts at producing an anticommunist underground failed to keep the Vietminh from driving the French out of Indochina.

In Indochina, as in Algeria, the SDECE had an intelligence rival, the DEUXIÈME BUREAU, the French MILITARY INTELLIGENCE organization. In France, the SDECE frequently clashed with the SÛRETÉ GÉNÉRALE, the police criminal investigation organization that, unlike the SDECE, had the power to arrest.

In Sept. 1949 Sûreté investigators uncovered a complex plot involving the Army chief of staff and another general who, for political reasons, had given secret documents to an SDECE informer. He in turn had given them to the *Vietminh*. The story was quashed, but the Paris correspondent of *Time* magazine learned of it. French intelligence wire-tappers intercepted the dispatch to *Time* magazine in New York City, and the French government asked the U.S. State Department to stop publication, creating a new crisis in U.S.-French relations only months after the founding of the NORTH ATLANTIC TREATY ORGANIZATION (NATO).

The "scandal of the generals" hurt the Army and the SDECE. But the SDECE's little-known CRYPTOGRAPHIC division maintained a high reputation for having broken several Soviet codes, providing the Counterintelligence Division with a steady stream of intelligence.

The SDECE Action Service trained Army volunteers as saboteurs to parachute into enemy territory in Indochina. By the 1950s the SDECE had its own airport at Persan-Baumont near Paris. From here a number of exiles from communist-controlled Eastern Europe were flown and then parachuted into their homelands to act as AGENTS for NATO intelligence services. But because of the PENETRATION of the SDECE by Soviet-trained French communists, security forces in the drop zones were alerted, and none of the agents was ever heard from again.

An innocuously named Geographic Division collected political, military, and economic information on TARGETS selected on the basis of questionnaires the SDECE sent to government departments. The requests could range from a request to get information on U.S. aerospace companies to one asking for a plan to get rid of Libyan dictator Muammar al-Qaddafi.

The SDECE had a reputation for bizarre operations, such as removing fuel from Soviet aircraft that landed in France to analyze it for antifreeze ingredients. SDECE operatives were also implicated in anesthetizing Soviet COURIERS traveling on the Orient Express; the operatives then rifled through the documents the couriers were carrying. Through a liaison between the SDECE and the CIA, in 1952 France gave a posthumous Legion of Honor medal to Joseph Kennedy, Jr., to help then-Sen. John F. Kennedy win French-American votes in Massachusetts. The little favor arranged by the SDECE would pay off when Kennedy became President.

As France became embroiled in wars against insurgents in Indochina and North Africa, the SDECE expanded its intelligence role to encompass BLACK BAG JOBS, kidnapping, and murder. The "era of political assassinations," as a French INTELLIGENCE OFFICER described it, began in 1958, during a profound crisis stemming from the war in Algeria between the French Army and Algerian insurgents. The parliament made de Gaulle prime minister and gave him the power to rule by decree for six months.

His new power extended to the SDECE, whose Action Service got its orders from the de Gaulle administration. Assassins hired and trained by the SDECE were supposedly members of a terrorist group called the Red Hand. They assassinated an Algerian politician in a drive-by shooting and killed an arms dealer by blowing up his Mercedes. Both murders occurred in West Germany, and there was speculation that Gen. REINHARD GEHLEN, the head of BND, the West German intelligence agency, was allowing the SDECE to operate with immunity in his country.

"Dozens of assassinations were carried out," P. L. Thyraud de Vosjoli wrote in a 1970 autobiography, whose title, LAMIA, was his operational CODE NAME. "Besides the use of guns or knives, more sophisticated methods had been perfected. Carbon dioxide [air] guns ejecting small syringes had been purchased in the United States—but the SDECE people substituted the tranquilizing drug with a lethal poison. The victim showed all the symptoms of having suffered from a heart attack." Victims included arms dealers, intellectuals, French supporters of Algerian nationalism, and leaders of liberation movements in French territories in Africa.

Between 1956 and 1961 hijackers recruited by the SDECE boarded six ships and seized their cargoes, allegedly bound for Algerian rebels. Another ship was blown up in Hamburg Harbor with a French naval mine. The Swiss attorney general committed suicide in March 1957 after word leaked that he had helped the SDECE by giving agents transcripts of telephone taps and other Swiss intelligence data. In Algeria, Deuxième Bureau officers with military units ordered the killing of suspected insurgents and the burning of villages deemed to house anti-French sympathizers.

The SDECE plotted to kill Ahmed Ben Bella, a veteran of the French Army in World War II who had become a leader of the Algerian insurgents. After failing to kill him, the intelligence agency tried another scheme to silence him. In Oct. 1956 an aircraft carrying Ben Bella to an Arab League meeting in Tunis was diverted to Algiers, where French soldiers boarded the aircraft and kidnapped Bella, keeping him in prison until the French-Algerian conflict ended.

Under a new constitution giving additional powers to the presidency, de Gaulle was elected President in 1959. The war dragged on, and SDECE assassinations continued. In 1961, when de Gaulle decided to end the Algerian civil war by granting Algeria independence, conspiratorial Army officers threatened to take over the French government.

Teams of assassins, including Vietnamese recruited by SDECE veterans of Indochina, were sent to Algeria to terrorize or kill opponents of Gaullist policy. To get rid of the assassins, called *les spéciaux,* Gaullist officials in Jan. 1961 ordered the blowing up of the headquarters of the assassins in Algeria. The incident, like many French intelligence operations, was leaked to the newspapers.

The SDECE's reputation for murderous "actions" reverberated throughout the French-Algerian conflict, which ended in 1962 after seven years of fighting, in which some 100,000 Algerians and 10,000 French soldiers were killed. With the end of the colonial wars, SDECE officers concentrated on counterintelligence in France. But the internal security of the SDECE came into question in Dec. 1961 when a KGB defector claimed that the Soviets had deeply penetrated the agency. (See SAPPHIRE.)

The already blemished SDECE became enmeshed in another scandal in Oct. 1965, when Mehdi Ben Barka, a left-wing Moroccan political leader, disappeared from a Paris street. Two SDECE agents picked up Ben Barka and handed him over to the Moroccans for torture and questioning. Although Ben Barka's body was never found, he is assumed to have been killed and his body smuggled out of France.

In 1970, in an attempt to clean up the SDECE, de Gaulle's successor, Georges Pompidou, appointed Count ALEXANDRE DE MARENCHES head of the agency. When Marenches took over the SDECE, he said, "Some agents were running drugs and guns; others were engaged in kidnapping, murder, and the settling of the most bloody scores." With the end of de Gaulle's tenure, cooperation sharply increased between the SDECE and the CIA. In 1975, for example, the two services worked with Zaire officials to get arms to the National Front for the Liberation of Angola.

Linked to the SDECE since the 1950s had been the Service d'Action Civique (SAC), an organization of about 8,000 de Gaulle followers who broke up anti–de Gaulle meetings and in general acted as a "dirty tricks" arm for the SDECE. Marenches concentrated on cleaning out SAC connections in the agency. He got rid of about half of the SDECE's 1,000 employees and modernized its collection and analysis procedures.

When socialist François Mitterrand was elected President in 1981, he replaced Marenches with Pierre Marion, former head of Air France and an aerospace company. French newspapers reported that the hard-line right-wing leaders of the SDECE refused to hang up portraits of Mitterrand. With Marion's appointment came a change in name. The SDECE became the DGSE, Direction Générale de la Sécurité Extérieure (General Directorate of External Security).

Sebold, William G.

(b. 1902 d. 1956)

German-American who became a DOUBLE AGENT for the United States.

German-born, Sebold served in the German Army during World War I and arrived in the United States in 1922 aboard a merchant ship. He jumped ship in Galveston, Texas, changed his name from Wilhelm G. Debowski to William G. Sebold, and eventually became a naturalized American citizen. He traveled to California and found work at the Consolidated Aircraft Corp. in San Diego. In 1939, when Sebold went to Germany to visit his family, he quit his job, but his place of employment was still on his passport, and it was spotted by German intelligence.

Maj. NIKOLAUS A. RITTER, the ABWEHR officer in charge of espionage against the United States and Britain, recruited Sebold as a spy, using as BIOGRAPHIC LEVERAGE his police record as a petty smuggler. If his criminal record and an illegal entry were exposed, he would certainly be deported from the United States. He was also well aware that if he refused, he would endanger his mother, brothers, and sister in Germany.

Sebold began his espionage career in a SPY SCHOOL in Hamburg. A boarding house served as a "training barracks," where only English was spoken. He learned to operate a radio transmitter, got a new U.S. passport as "Harry Sawyer," and the names and addresses of four German AGENTS in New York. He was to radio their intelligence to Hamburg, using the CODE NAME Tramp, or arrange for it to be placed on MICRODOTS and mailed to ACCOMMODATION ADDRESSES in Shanghai, Portugal, and Brazil. His contacts included Frederick Duquesne, the leader of a spy NETWORK, and HERMAN LANG, who worked for the Norden Co., which manufactured the TOP SECRET Norden bombsight.

William G. Sebold (left) with one of his agents in his office, set up by the FBI specifically to photographic surveillance of his meetings. The clock and calendar were carefully placed to document the meetings with German spies. (FEDERAL BUREAU OF INVESTIGATION)

Before leaving Germany, Sebold went to the U.S. consulate in Cologne and reported what had happened. He agreed to become a double agent. The FBI paid him $50 a week and had him set up an office. The walls were painted white for better photography by a hidden camera, and a wall clock and calendar were placed so as to be in scenes filmed by the camera.

Following German instructions, but secretly aided by the FBI, Sebold set up a shortwave radio on Long Island and, beginning in May 1940, transmitted to Germany almost every day. Then, in Jan. 1942, less than a month after the PEARL HARBOR ATTACK and America's entry into World War II, the FBI struck, rounding up 33 German spies. (See DUQUESNE SPY RING.)

Second Bureau

SEE DEUXIÈME BUREAU

Second Story

U.S. Air Force effort in 1958 to obtain CIA funding for the development of RECONAISSANCE SATELLITES. The CIA subsequently took over the project, which was given the name CORONA.

Secret

U.S. security CLASSIFICATION for national security information, the unauthorized disclosure of which could be expected to result in serious damage to national security, such as a disruption of international relations or the impairment of the effectiveness of a program or policy of vital importance. This is the second-highest U.S. security classification. The other U.S. security classifications are CONFIDENTIAL and TOP SECRET.

Secret Agent

Person acting clandestinely as a spy or saboteur; also called an undercover agent. "Secret Agent Man" was a popular British TELEVISION series.

Secret Intelligence Service

SEE MI6 (SIS)

Secret Office

English government office from the late 1600s until 1847 for the interception of domestic and foreign mails. The formal establishment of the office was a result of the government's need for better intelligence, beginning with the Commonwealth period (that is, the rule of Oliver Cromwell, 1649–1658) onward.

The organization, attached to the Post Office, subsequently became known as the Secret Office and was headed by the Foreign Secretary. The mail intercept effort was given legal status under various acts of Parliament that enabled the Secretaries of State to issue warrants to the Postmaster General to open and examine letters for communications that could do damage to the state.

The Secret Office was staffed for most of its life by the BODE FAMILY, which was brought to England from Hanover in 1732 to work in the office with the agreement that their children would enjoy the patronage of the government. The Bode family provided most of the Secret Office staff until its abolishment. When the senior Bode retired in 1784, he was succeeded by Anthony Todd, who retained Bode's three sons in the office. When Todd retired in 1791 or 1792, he was succeeded by his nephew, Mr. Madison; and his successor in 1799 was William Bode.

Periodically government officials would direct the Special Office to pay special attention to mails to or from certain individuals. The intelligence gleaned from the mails was, at times, brought directly to the attention of the throne. For example, a letter from the Earl of Holderness to Todd on June 18, 1757, stated: "I have laid before His Majesty your letter of last night, with its enclosure, and the King commended this fresh instance of your constant diligence and attention to His service."

In 1844 the office became the subject of a parliamentary inquiry after revelations of the interception of letters to and from Giuseppe Mazzini, an Italian nationalist living in England. Mazzini supposedly placed small seeds in his letters and determined that has mail had been opened when they were missing upon arrival. He persuaded Thomas Duncombe, a radical member of Parliament, to call the matter to the attention of Parliament.

An inquiry and debate followed, with William Bode, head of the Secret Office, giving testimony to both the House of Commons and and the House of Lords. The practice of intercepting mail by general warrant as opposed to an express warrant was condemned.

The office was abolished by Lord Palmerston, the Secretary of State for Foreign Affairs, on Jan. 1, 1847. The staff was pensioned off, followed by numerous appeals of this injustice done to the Bode and Todd families. Subsequently, additional payments were made.

Also see JOHN WALLIS, JOHN WILKINS, and EDWARD WILLES.

Secrets Act

SEE OFFICIAL SECRETS ACT

Secret Service

Generic term for a nation's intelligence service.

An English secret service dates back to 1573, when Sir FRANCIS WALSINGHAM established an intelligence organization for Queen Elizabeth I (see MI6).

In the United States the Secret Service is not an intelligence organization, the service having been established by Congress in 1865 as an agency of the Department of the Treasury to fight counterfeiting of U.S. currency.

After the assassination of President McKinley in 1901, the Secret Service was given the additional duty of protecting the U.S. President and, subsequently, other U.S. government officials and former presidents. Those roles and other activities relating to the illegal use or handling of currency remain the mission of the Secret Service.

The Secret Service became a component of the Department of HOMELAND SECURITY when that department was established in 2003.

There is a myth that there was a U.S. Secret Service with intelligence responsibilities, especially during the American Civil War. The fiction exists in part because detective ALLAN PINKERTON, in his memoir *Spy of the Rebellion* (1888), called himself the chief of the United States Secret Service; LAFAYETTE C. BAKER did the same, calling his memoir *The History of the United States Secret Service* (1867).

Secret Service Bureau

First modern British intelligence organization, established in 1909 under the War Office.

In 1910 the bureau's Foreign Section was placed under the aegis of the Admiralty, while the Home Section remained under the War Office. The first head of the Secret Service Bureau was Navy Capt. Sir MANSFIELD CUMMING.

By the end of World War I the Foreign Section had been moved to the Foreign Office and was known as the Secret Intelligence Service (SIS) with the designation of MI6, for MILITARY INTELLIGENCE department No. 6.

(Cumming served as head of MI6 from 1910 until his death in 1923.)

The Home Section of the Secret Service Bureau evolved into the Security Service, with the designation MI5.

Secret World

Term for the espionage or spy "business." Bruce Page and his colleagues wrote in *The Philby Conspiracy* (1969):

The trouble is that a man can hold almost any theory he cares to about the secret world, and defend it against large quantities of hostile evidence by the simple expedient of retreating behind further and further screens of postulated inward mystery. Secret services have in common with freemasons and *mafiosi* that they inhabit an intellectual twilight—a kind of ambiguous gloom in which it is hard to distinguish with certainty between the menacing and the merely ludicrous. In such circumstances the human affinity for myth and legend easily gets out of control.

Secret Writing

A spy's classic method of communication. Secret writing is probably as old as writing itself. Ovid (born in 43 B.C.) advised in his *Art of Love* that a love letter "escapes the eye when written in new milk; touch it with [charcoal] dust and you will read." Although now overshadowed by radio and other modern communication techniques, secret writing endures.

The CIA once gave recruited AGENTS or a WALK-IN a "secret writing carbon," apparently ordinary writing paper, impregnated with a chemical. A secret writer put the CIA paper on top of another piece of paper and, using a pen, pencil, or typewriter, wrote on the CIA paper. The writing was invisibly transferred to the second piece of paper. CIA INTELLIGENCE OFFICERS handling agents or walk-ins were instructed:

(a) have him print his address in his homeland where he can receive mail and then have him address an envelope to *himself;*
(b) establish an SW [secret writing] indicator (name or phrase);
(c) issue and explain carefully scorch or waterdeveloped SW system and explain that a letter with further instructions in SW will be mailed to him from inside his country. . . .

The instructions, compromised in the 1970s and presumably changed since, said the walk-in would be sent "secret messages" on the back of innocent-looking letters mailed by the CIA. The messages could be developed by soaking the letter in water or over heat. "If a gas stove is to be used," the instructions said, "it is suggested that a clean frying pan be placed over the open flame. . . ."

The simplest secret writing uses organic inks: milk, vinegar, lemon juice, even human urine. These inks dry invisibly and can be developed by applying heat. Espionage agencies have produced many inks made of chemicals that could be developed only by a specific chemical.

During World War II the British Secret Intelligence Service (MI6), under the COVER of the BRITISH SECURITY CO-ORDINATION had established a highly secret mail-interception operation in Bermuda—opening, checking, sometimes tampering with the letter inside, and then resealing the envelope. There, at other censorship stations, letters were checked for several kinds of invisible ink. A multi-brush device was run down the suspected page, each brush dipped in different chemical-detection fluid. For a time Germans thwarted such detection by splitting a sheet of paper, writing the secret message in invisible ink on the inside of one of the split sides, and then restoring the paper. Thus, no chemicals appeared on the outside of the paper. For reading, the paper is split again; it is easier the second time.

The idea of invisible ink had been around for a long time. Write using lemon juice as ink, for instance, and the writing will be invisible. Heat the paper and the writing will appear, looking like words written in brown ink. Another technique: Conceal a message within a hard-boiled egg by writing on the shell with ink made of alum and vinegar; the message will penetrate the porous shell and leave the message on the white of the egg.

During the American Revolutionary War, British agents used two types. One could be made visible by holding the paper over the flame of a candle; the other could be read by applying a common chemical. Maj. JOHN ANDRÉ, the chief British intelligence officer in New York (and BENEDICT ARNOLD'S HANDLER) told his agents to put an *F* in the corner of letters containing invisible ink needing fire to read and *A* for those needing acid.

GEORGE WASHINGTON, in his role as spymaster during the Revolutionary War, urged his agents to use invisible ink not only because it would make "communications less exposed to detection" but would also "relieve the fears" of agents carrying the innocent-looking messages.

Washington gave exact instructions on how an agent should use invisible ink: "[H]e should occasionally write his information on the blank leaves of a pamphlet . . . a common pocket book, or on the blank leaves at each end of registers, almanacs, or any publication or book of small value." He also told his agents that a "much better way" is to write a letter "with some mixture of family matters" and the secret message, which would be invisible, "between the lines and on the remaining part of the sheet."

Washington wanted an ink that was more complicated than heat-and-see ink; he sought an ink that could not be read merely by heating the paper or by coating it with an ordinary chemical. And he got what he wanted, from an unexpected source: Sir James Jay, a British doctor who lived in London and dabbled in chemistry.

James Jay, who had been knighted by King George III, was the brother of a leading Patriot, John Jay, who worked on COUNTERINTELLIGENCE cases during the Revolution. (He would later become Chief Justice of the Supreme Court.)

James Jay's invisible ink did not become visible by heating. As he described it, his ink "would elude the generally known means of detection, and yet could be rendered visible by a suitable counterpart." Jay's invisible ink consisted of two chemicals. An agent used one chemical to write an invisible message. To read the message, the reader had to brush a second chemical on the paper; that chemical made the message visible. The two-bottle system gave Washington the secure form of writing that he wanted.

Invisible ink was invaluable in Washington's day, when he and his agents needed only short messages to exchange information. But, as DAVID KAHN points out in *The Codebreakers* (1967), "The chief difficulty with secret inks was their inability to handle the great volume of information that spies had to transmit in a modern war." This problem led to increasing use of MICRODOTS.

Sécurité Militaire

SEE DST

Security Check

Term for BACKGROUND INVESTIGATION, the process that determines whether a person or firm should have access to classified information (a SECURITY CLEARANCE).

Security Clearance

Access given to military personnel, government employees, and contractor personnel to work with classified information in the performance of their assignments.

In the United States, the Department of Defense has three levels of clearance. From least to most restricted access, they are CONFIDENTIAL, SECRET, and TOP SECRET. The clearance RESTRICTED DATA is given by the Department of Energy (formerly Atomic Energy Commission).

The classification FOR OFFICIAL USE ONLY is *not* a security classification, although many in the U.S. government do not realize this.

In a report to the President in 2001, the SECURITY POLICY ADVISORY BOARD said that there were some 350,000 initial background investigations and 162,000 re-investigations "in the system," with more than 300,000 other investigations yet to submitted.

See CLASSIFICATION.

Security Policy Advisory Board

Organization set up by presidential direction in 1994 to serve as an independent and non-governmental advisory body on U.S. security policy, which was then undergoing a post–Cold War analysis at the highest level of government. The board's members are appointed by the President for terms of up to three years. At the same time a Security Policy Board, chaired by the DIRECTOR OF CENTRAL INTELLIGENCE, was established to develop policies for handling future intelligence missions, including TERRORIST INTELLIGENCE.

Security Risk

Person whom authorities consider likely to undertake actions that could threaten the security of a country. The term became popular in the United States during the 1950s because of the anticommunist antics of Sen. Joseph McCarthy.

On Feb. 9, 1950, McCarthy told a West Virginia audience, "I have here in my hand a list of 205 . . . a list of names that were made known to the Secretary of State as being members of the Communist Party and who nevertheless are still working and shaping policy in the State Department."

Although McCarthy later changed the number to 57, his accusation rocked the government, ushering in the era of "McCarthyism"—government and congressional investigations of persons presumed to be communists or subversives. When his hunt reached the U.S. Army, his credibility evaporated. The Senate passed a resolution of censure against him in Dec. 1954 for conduct "contrary to Senate traditions." The censure effectively ended his political career. Not one communist in government was identified through the extensive McCarthy-dominated investigations. (But names of that era reappear again in the intercepts of Soviet espionage messages. See VENONA.)

But throughout the United States, people who had been heard criticizing the government, or had been found reading a book or magazine article about the Soviet Union, or had refused to sign loyalty pledges were called "security risks."

Security Service

SEE MI5

Select Committees

SEE UNITED STATES

Semichastny, Vladimir Yefimovich

(b. 1924)

Head of the KGB from Nov. 1961 to April 1967.

Semichastny, like his mentor and predecessor, ALEKSANDR SHELEPIN, was involved in a number of embarrassing incidents involving the KGB. For example, he sanctioned the arrest of Professor Frederick Barghoorn of Yale University when he was visiting Moscow in Oct. 1963. Semichastny hoped that by charging Barghoorn as a spy he could induce the United States to release IGOR IVANOV, arrested by the FBI that month for espionage.

Barghoorn was a personal friend of President Kennedy and was not involved in any illegal activities, as was forcefully stated by Kennedy at a press conference. The Soviets were humiliated and quickly released Barghoorn. (Ivanov was allowed to leave the United States in 1971.)

Subsequently, Semichastny participated in the ouster of Soviet leader Nikita Khrushchev in Oct. 1964, an act that undoubtedly led to his being retained by the new Soviet leadership. There are some indications that Leonid Brezhnev, who led the coup against Khrushchev, wanted to assassinate him, but Semichastny refused to allow KGB participation.

During his tenure Semichastny attempted to create a new public image of the KGB, permitting an article to appear in the newspaper *Izvestia* that included an interview with "a senior KGB officer" (himself); in the article he stated "many young Party and Komsomol [youth League] workers have joined the KGB and none of the people who, during the time of the personality cult [of Josef Stalin], took part in the repressions against innocent Soviet people is now in the Service." More articles and books on the security ORGANS appeared, and Soviet spies became heroes in print—RUDOLF ABEL, GORDON LONSDALE, HAROLD (KIM) PHILBY, and RICHARD SORGE.

Brezhnev finally replaced Semichastny on May 18, 1967, as part of a Kremlin power shuffle. YURI ANDROPOV, the new chief of the KGB, had the task of rebuilding the image and effectiveness of the service.

Senior

U.S. Air Force CODE NAME prefix for classified electronic projects; also used for some other classified programs (such as SENIOR BOWL).

Senior projects included: Senior Spear, a COMMUNICATIONS INTELLIGENCE (COMINT) system for U-2 aircraft; Senior Stretch, a COMINT system for the U-2; Senior scout, a SIGNALS INTELLIGENCE (SIGINT) system for the C-130H Hercules aircraft; Senior Hunter, a system for supporting EC-130E aircraft fitted for psychological warfare broadcasts; and Senior Warrior, a U.S. marine Corps version of the Senior Scout SIGINT system.

Senior Bowl

CODE NAME for the mating of modified B-52 strategic bombers with the D-21 unmanned RECONNAISSANCE aircraft. The two aircraft were mated for four spy missions over China, none of which was successful.

Sensitive

Information or material that requires a high degree of security protection.

Sensitive Compartmented Information

(SCI)

Intelligence that requires special controls for restricted handling within COMPARTMENTED channels. This intelligence is available only to persons with a NEED TO KNOW, regardless of the level of SECURITY CLEARANCE that they hold. This material also requires special storage facilities. Early SCI intelligence was related to COMMUNICATIONS INTELLIGENCE.

SCI is sometimes mistakenly used as representing Special Compartmented Intelligence.

Sensitive Compartmented Information Facility

(SCIF)

U.S. term for a facility—a room or larger working space—that is especially constructed for handling TOP SECRET and SENSITIVE COMPARTMENTED INFORMATION. The room's walls, floor, and ceiling have special materials to prevent BUGS from being placed on adjacent structures to monitor conversations or equipment in the room. Special telephone and power lines defeat wiretaps. A SCIF has no windows and is equipped with other special security features.

Seraph

British SUBMARINE that carried out a number of intelligence and special operations during World War II, one under the nominal command of an American officer. The *Seraph,* completed in June 1942, went on her first operation in support of the planned North African invasion when, during the last two weeks of Sept. 1942, the submarine carried out a periscope RECONNAISSANCE of the

Algerian coast. This was the *Seraph's* first combat mission, under the command of Lt. N. L. A. (Bill) Jewell.

After this mission the *Seraph* returned to Gibraltar where, instead of being given orders to operate against the German and Italian forces in the Mediterranean, the submarine was assigned to Operation Flagpole: carrying Gen. Dwight D. Eisenhower's deputy, Lt. Gen. Mark Clark, to North Africa for secret negotiations with Vichy French officers. Loaded with folding canoes, submachine guns, walkie-talkie radios, and other supplies, the submarine embarked Clark, two other Army generals, U.S. Navy Capt. Jerauld Wright, several other officers, and three British commandos. (Wright subsequently reached the rank of full admiral.)

With this party on board, the *Seraph* sailed to the Algerian coast. There the collapsible canoes were launched to carry Clark and his party ashore on the night of Oct. 20. His meeting helped to reduce French opposition to the landings (although the French were not told that troop ships were already at sea and that the landings would commence within a few days).

After some problems and delays, the *Seraph* finally came to within 300 yards of the beach on the morning of Oct. 23 to embark her passengers. Because of the importance of returning them to Eisenhower's headquarters at Gibraltar as soon as possible, the Americans were transferred at sea to a PBY Catalina flying boat. A few days later Lt. Jewell received orders to sail to the coast of southern France to secretly take aboard Gen. Henri Honoré Giraud. The general was to be asked to allow the Anglo-American troops into North Africa to gain support for the Allies from the French colonies. But Giraud would not travel in a British submarine, so strong were the anti-British feelings among Frenchmen at the time. Capt. Wright embarked in the *Seraph* as nominal commanding officer of the submarine, which was temporarily transferred to the U.S. Navy. Lt. Jewell remained on board to actually direct operations (Wright not being a submariner).

The Giraud party was picked up from the town of Le Lavendou by the *Seraph* on the night of Nov. 5–6 and transferred at sea to a PBY for the flight to Gibraltar.

The *Seraph* finally sailed on her first war patrol in the Mediterranean on Nov. 24, 1942. She was soon called upon to join other submarines in carrying U.S. and British commandos for reconnaissance operations in the Mediterranean. In Dec. 1942 the *Seraph* torpedoed and damaged an Italian merchant ship, which was sunk later in the day by British surface ships. That same month she rammed and damaged an Italian submarine.

In early 1943 the *Seraph* sailed for England and a needed refit. In April she set out again for the Mediterranean, still under command of Lt. Jewell. In addition to her normal crew, packed in dry ice was the unidentified body of a dead man dressed as a Royal Marine officer, with a briefcase handcuffed to his coat that contained several secret documents. On the morning of April 30 the *Seraph* surfaced off the coast of Spain and the body, with a life jacket, was lowered over the side in Operation MINCEMEAT.

During the remainder of 1943 the *Seraph* operated against German and Italian forces in the Mediterranean and attacked several convoys, but her only kills were a few barges and other small craft destroyed by gunfire. For the rest of the war the *Seraph* operated in the eastern Atlantic and Norwegian Sea, and served as a guide ship for the D-DAY landings on June 6, 1944.

The Seraph remained in active service into the 1960s. When the submarine was scrapped in 1965, parts of her conning tower were preserved as a memorial at the Citadel campus in Charleston, S.C. (Clark was a graduate of the Citadel and its president from 1954 to 1965).

Sgt. Crest [p]

Pseudonym for a U.S. Air Force enlisted man assigned to the 40th Tactical Fighter Group in Italy. He was stopped and arrested in Dec. 1976 while attempting to enter West Germany from East Germany. Subsequent investigation revealed that Crest had been involved in black market operations and had dealings with Hungarian intelligence officials. However, because of lack of evidence he was not prosecuted but was administratively discharged from the Air Force. His case was given a pseudonym.

Serov, Col. Gen. Ivan Alexandrovich

(b. 1905 d. 1962)

Soviet Army officer, NKVD officer, chairman of the KGB from 1954 to 1958, and chief of the GRU, Soviet MILITARY INTELLIGENCE, from 1958 to 1962. Having survived the bloody purges of the Stalin era despite his involvement with state security organs, Serov was forced to retire from his GRU position in 1962 because of his close ties to Col. OLEG PENKOVSKY, a major spy for the West. Serov was considered a brutal, albeit "not enthusiastic," executioner.

Originally a military intelligence officer, at the time of the GRU purges in the late 1930s he managed not only to survive but also to transfer to the NKVD. According to some reports, on June 12, 1937, he executed Marshal of the Soviet Union Mikhail Tukhachevski, the first major victim of Stalin's purges of the military establishment, and other leading figures of the Red Army. (Some sources put his assignment to the NKVD in 1938.)

Beginning in 1940 Serov was continually engaged in the suppression and murder of enemies of the Soviet state. He distinguished himself in the pursuit and liquidation of the anti-Soviet groups in Estonia, Latvia, and Lithuania in 1940 and again in 1944–1947, and he was personally involved in the murder of Polish officers in the KATYN MASSACRE. He was deputy chief of SMERSH in 1941, a deputy to LAVRENTY BERIA from 1943 to 1945, and the deputy chief of Smersh in Soviet-occupied Germany in 1945.

After World War II he served in the NKVD and then became deputy chief of GRU. As deputy chief of the GRU, Serov was one of the conspirators against Beria after Stalin's death in 1953. After the fall of Beria that June, Serov became deputy head of the MVD (formerly NKVD) and the following year the chairman of the newly established KGB. Together with Ambassador YURI ANDROPOV, he seized the leaders of the Hungarian revolution of 1956 by deceit and took part in their torture and execution, earning him the nickname the "hangman of Hungary."

In Dec. 1958 Serov became chief of the GRU. As a former NKVD and Smersh official he had many enemies in the Army and GRU. Under his leadership, corruption in the GRU flourished; those years were also the most unproductive in the history of the GRU. It was the only period of the Soviet regime when GRU officers voluntarily made contact with Western services and gave them considerably more valuable information than they took from them.

In 1962, because of the defection of Penkovsky to the West, Serov was demoted to the rank of major general and stripped of his decorations. He died a short time later.

Nikita Khrushchev, who removed Serov from his post as chairman of the KGB to the less influential position of chief of the GRU, wrote in *Khrushchev Remembers* (1970) that the subsequent dismissal of Serov in 1962 was because he was "careless." According to Khrushchev, Serov "was an honest, uncorruptible, reliable comrade despite his mistakes. I respected and trusted him. He was a simple person, simple to the point of being naive."

The Service

The nickname of KGB officers for their own service.

Service de Renseignements

SEE SR

Services, Press and Broadcasting Committee

SEE D-NOTICE

Sessions, Judge William S.

(b. 1930)

Director of the FBI from Nov. 1987 until he was fired by President Clinton on July 19, 1993, for ethics violations.

A former U.S. attorney and Justice Department official, Sessions spent 13 years as a federal judge in Texas, where he gained a reputation for being a stern but fair-minded jurist. He received national attention when he presided over the trial of several men charged in the 1979 assassination of federal judge John H. Wood.

Sessions' appointment by President Reagan for a ten-year term as director of the FBI was easily confirmed by Congress. His support in Congress was enhanced when, early in his tenure, he censured six FBI employees for mishandling an investigation into a group that opposed the Reagan administration's policy in Central America. Sessions, who liked being referred to as "Judge Sessions," resisted internal FBI pressure to appeal a court finding that the FBI engaged in a pattern of discrimination against Hispanic agents.

His congressional backing was strongest among liberal Democrats, who applauded what The *New York Times* called "his mild displays of independence" from the Reagan administration.

During his tenure the FBI was heavily involved in investigations of the terrorist bombing of Pan Am Flight 103 in 1988, the Ill Wind investigations into bribery and fraud in the Pentagon, and cases growing out of the savings and loan scandals.

By 1992, however, charges were being made that Sessions had evaded paying taxes and was refusing to cooperate with an investigation of a home mortgage loan. Following an investigation by the Justice Department's internal ethics office, in Jan. 1993 Attorney General William P. Barr sent Sessions a strongly worded letter ordering him to pay income taxes on benefits that he had not disclosed and to reimburse the FBI almost $10,000 for the cost of a security fence around his home. Barr also chastised Sessions for violating regulations on the use of his official limousine and FBI aircraft.

Within the FBI he was being criticized for his handling of administrative matters and for allowing his wife to influence his official decisions. Sessions fought in vain to hold on to the FBI position, and in July 1993 he left office. In Dec. 1999 the Texas attorney general appointed Sessions state chair of Texas Exile, a state initiative aimed at reducing gun crime.

Seven Doors

U.S. intelligence operation aimed at recruiting a Soviet believed to be an INTELLIGENCE OFFICER and turning him or her into a DEFECTOR IN PLACE.

The operation was contemplated in Teheran, Iran, in 1976, when Americans and Soviets frequently tried such recruitment attempts on each other. The approach, "a controlled social relationship operation," was to be made by an American, untrained in intelligence but run by U.S. intelligence officers.

Scattered references to the operation appear in documents seized and circulated by Iranian militants who took over the U.S. Embassy in Teheran in 1979. The documents did not reveal the outcome of the attempt, but they did provide insights into the paperwork behind such an operation, which was run by the U.S. Air Force Office of Special Investigations.

The Air Force officer assigned to the operation had to sign an agreement that he would voluntarily undergo a POLYGRAPH examination, that he would live under a pseudonym during the operation, and that his wife would be debriefed. She would be "assessed for potential in fulfilling an operational role directed toward the respective targets' wives, when and if such a situation warrants . . ." The commanding officer's wife, who was to be involved, was eventually ruled out.

Each step of the planned recruitment was accompanied by memos, whose subjects ranged from events at cocktail parties to decisions that kept extending the start of the operation. Documents about Seven Doors begin to appear in Aug. 1976; the operation was still going on in March 1978, but the Soviet officer had still not been approached.

Sex

Real and fictional, a part of espionage since biblical times. Joshua's two spies, sent "to spy secretly . . . view the land, even Jericho" (Joshua 1:2) hid at the home of the harlot Rahab. (See BIBLICAL SPIES.)

From then to the present, sex has been used both to garner secrets from the unsuspecting and to blackmail people into revealing secrets. A complex espionage case involving romance surfaced in 2003 with the arrest of KATRINA LEUNG, who, while living the life of a California socialite, was secretly an AGENT for the FBI—and, officials charged, a lover of her FBI HANDLER. She was accused of being a DOUBLE AGENT who allegedly worked for China while appearing to be an agent providing information about China to her handlers. FBI officials said that she had had a 20-year affair with former agent James J. Smith, who was also arrested. Officials also said that she had also been the lover of her previous handler.

The most celebrated example of sex in espionage—that of exotic dancer and femme fatale MATA HARI—was built almost completely on myth. She was not an effective spy, but rather naive and easily duped by her friends and foes alike.

But Mata Hari's image, false as it was, persisted. The proliferation of World War II–era posters warning against German and Japanese spies, emblazoned with such slogans as "Loose Lips Sink Ships," more often had a rendering of a seductive blonde than caricatures of Adolf Hitler or Emperor Hirohito.

This is not to say that all TARGETS were men. VERA GERHARDSEN, wife of the Norwegian prime minister, was allegedly seduced by a young KGB officer in Moscow. He was then posted to Oslo to continue the liaison with her—and to garner secrets about Norwegian defenses and the NORTH ATLANTIC TREATY ORGANIZATION.

American-born MILDRED FISH HARNACK, heroine of the RED ORCHESTRA anti-Nazi espionage and resistance NETWORK of World War II, slept with an ABWEHR officer at the request of her husband, another Red Orchestra member. After determining that she had obtained information from the Abwehr officer, a GESTAPO officer reported that it was "incomprehensible" to him "how a woman in bed with her lover could put to him questions bearing no actual relationship to what was happening at the moment, unless she did so with treasonable intent." Both she and the officer were found guilty of treason and executed.

The principal targets of espionage-related sex have overwhelmingly been men who knew secrets. In the PROFUMO AFFAIR of the early 1960s, a teenage prostitute simultaneously romanced a Soviet naval INTELLIGENCE OFFICER, Capt. 3rd Rank YEVGENY IVANOV, and the British secretary of state for war, John D. Profumo. The complex relationship eventually caused the resignation of prime minister Harold Macmillan.

In another cold war love affair, the first known compromise of a U.S. Marine on embassy guard duty occurred in Moscow when a Soviet SWALLOW seduced him into providing information to her "uncle," a KGB officer (see Cpl. CLAYTON LONETREE). Another KGB match involved RICHARD MILLER, an FBI agent in California, who fell victim to the charms of a KGB officer, SVETLANA OGORODNIKOVA.

The Soviets were not the only side to employ sex in espionage during the Cold War. In Operation Deep Root in 1968, the ROYAL CANADIAN MOUNTED POLICE managed to obtain a photograph showing the wife of a Soviet diplomat having sex with a Canadian. The Canadians then tried to force the woman to reveal secrets. She refused and promptly departed for Moscow.

In another diplomatic love affair during the same year, the KGB tried to blackmail the British ambassador to Moscow with photographs showing him engaged in sexual acts with a Russian maid who worked in the ambassador's residence. He reported the blackmail attempt to the Foreign Office, which had him discreetly questioned by the British Security Service (MI5). The intelligence officers were shocked, not at his indiscretion but at the fact that the KGB had apparently been able to enter and photograph inside the residence. After a quiet investigation, the ambassador admitted that the events had taken place outside the residence. He had been set up in at least one room equipped with a camera.

Some kinds of sex and espionage do not mix. GEOFFREY PRIME, a British CIPHER expert who was selling secrets to the Soviets, also molested young girls. When arrested for the sex crimes, his wife revealed to authorities that he was also a Soviet spy.

During World War II the U.S. OFFICE OF STRATEGIC SERVICES (OSS) parachuted female AGENTS into German-held territory. However, some male OSS agents protested, fearing that they would crack and divulge secrets if the team was captured and the female agent was tortured. Two decades later ALLEN W. DULLES, an OSS veteran and the U.S. DIRECTOR OF CENTRAL INTELLIGENCE (DCI) wrote in *The Craft of Intelligence* (1963):

> Women in CIA undergo much the same training as men and can qualify for the same jobs, except that overseas assignments for women are more limited. One reason for this is the ingrained prejudice in many countries of the world against women as "managers" of men—in their jobs, that is. An agent brought up in this tradition may not feel comfortable taking orders from a woman, and we cannot change his mind for him in this regard.

Unreported by Dulles was the fact that while he was running an OSS network in Switzerland, one of his AGENTS, MARY BANCROFT, was his mistress. He also did not report (possibly because he did not know) the existence of persistent prejudice against women within the CIA. That situation continued for at least another three decades. In 1995 the CIA agreed to pay more than 250 female CASE OFFICERS back salaries totaling nearly $1 million and making 25 retroactive promotions as part of a settlement to head off a gender-based discrimination suit. In addition, 15 women who had transferred out of case officer assignments were allowed to return to their former roles. (One woman who was a case officer, MARTHA PETERSON, was arrested by the KGB in 1977 while she was serving under diplomatic COVER in Moscow. CIA officers said privately that the KGB did not show her the normal courtesy afforded intelligence officers, probably because they resented working against a well-trained woman.)

The class action suit by female case officers against the CIA had begun in Dec. 1992. Realistic negotiations did not begin until Sept. 1993, however, with then DCI R. JAMES WOOLSEY becoming personally involved. By 1999, according to Nora Slatkin, executive director of the CIA, the agency had reversed the males-only story. During the previous year, she said, "roughly a third of the people appointed to the top 64 command positions in the CIA were women—overall, women now hold a quarter of these positions."

Dulles ruled against the use of women to ensnare men in CIA operations. Whether this tactic was ever employed after his tenure is a question that remains unanswered.

See HOMOSEXUALS, HONEY TRAP, RAVEN, ROMEO, and SWALLOW.

Sexpionage

Term coined by British journalist David Lewis in his book by that name, published in 1976. He claimed that the first recorded use of SEX in espionage occurred in the tenth century B.C., when Delilah used her charms to destroy Samson. (See BIBLICAL SPIES.) The present authors, however, find little in the realm of espionage in this act: Samson was an enemy; Delilah simply captured and, with the help of a barber, disarmed him, while he was asleep.

SGA

SEE SPECIAL GROUP (AUGMENTED)

Shadrin, Nicholas George

(b. 1928 d. 1975)

Soviet naval officer who defected to the United States. The FBI subsequently forced him to become a DOUBLE AGENT, and as a result he was captured by the KGB and killed.

Born Nikolai Fedorovich Artamonov, he attended the Frunze Higher Naval School (academy), graduating in 1949, and served in the Soviet Navy. In 1955 he became the youngest commanding officer of a destroyer, with the rank of captain 3rd rank.

While his ship was in Gdansk, Poland, to train Indonesian sailors in 1959, he and his Polish girlfriend defected to Sweden, crossing the Baltic Sea by small boat on the night of June 7–8. (He left a wife in the Soviet Union, from whom he was later divorced, and married the woman with whom he escaped from Poland.)

After asking for political sanctuary, he went to the United States and, taking the name Shadrin, performed low-classification work for the U.S. DEFENSE INTELLIGENCE AGENCY. In Sept. 1960, immediately prior to the visit by Nikita Khrushchev to the United States, Shadrin testified before the House Un-American Activities Committee. He attacked the Soviet political system and gave the committee details of the Soviet espionage system.

Shadrin and his wife subsequently became American citizens. In 1972 he received his doctorate in international affairs from the George Washington University in Washington, D.C., his thesis being an in-depth evaluation of the Soviet Navy.

Although Shadrin had been tried in absentia in the Soviet Union and sentenced to death, he was contacted by the KGB in 1966 and, at the direction of the FBI, became a double agent. It was while on a trip to VIENNA in this role that he was abducted by KGB agents on Dec. 20, 1975. According to Soviet defector VITALY YURCHENKO (1985), Shadrin was fatally chloroformed by accident while struggling with his captors in the back of an automobile in Vienna. He was to have been protected by the U.S. CIA while in Vienna, but the CIA officers bungled the operation.

Shai

Intelligence service of the Haganah (Defense), the underground Jewish army in Palestine prior to the establishment of the state of ISRAEL on 14 May 1948. The Haganah, established in 1920, sought to protect Jewish settlements and interests against both the Arabs and the British, who controlled Palestine through an international mandate until the establishment of the Jewish state. (Many members of the Haganah served in the Jewish Brigade of the British Army in World War II, while others carried out clandestine missions for the British in countries allied with Germany).

An intelligence branch called Shai, for Sherut Yediot (Information Service), was established within the Haganab in 1934. Shai-provided intelligence soon became vital as the Haganah sought to counter Arab attacks on Jewish settlements, assist the illegal immigration of Jews to Palestine during and after World War II, and, on the eve of Israeli independence, counter the British efforts to leave the Arabs in key military positions when the British withdrew. Shai established its AGENTS in the British police force and among customs officials, postal workers, and telephone operators as it sought to gain information about British plans and operations.

Shai had a major success in 1946 when it broadcast over its clandestine radio station the contents of the British "black book" with data on members of the Jewish underground. The commanding officer of the British Army in Palestine reportedly described Shai as "a perfect intelligence system." Shai was abolished in July 1948 when AMAN, the military intelligence service, and SHIN BET, the domestic secret service, were established.

See ISRAEL.

Shalin, Col. Gen. Mikhail Alekseevich

Chief of the GRU, Soviet MILITARY INTELLIGENCE, from 1951 to 1956 and again from Nov. 1957 to Dec. 1958.

Little is known of his career and activities despite his several years of service in this post. Col. OLEG PENKOVSKY, who spied for the West, in his autobiographic *The Penkovsky Papers* (1965), called Shalin "a good, experienced intelligence officer . . . working in intelligence since the war."

Shamrock

Probably the most ambitious DOMESTIC INTELLIGENCE operation undertaken by the U.S. armed forces. Shamrock was a continuation of the World War II operation to intercept overseas cable traffic to detect foreign intelligence communications.

In late 1945, with the war over, Brig. Gen. W. Preston Corderman, chief of the ARMY SECURITY AGENCY (ASA), knew how difficult it would be to continue and improve the Army's expertise in CRYPTOGRAPHY without having access to foreign cables. According to historian JAMES BAMFORD in *The Puzzle Palace* (1982), "He felt it was of the utmost importance to establish, in some way, a very secret, very intimate arrangement with the three major cable companies in order to have access to the all important telegrams."

ASA soon made arrangements with Western Union Telegraph Co., ITT Communications, and RCA Communications to have access to all overseas cables to and from foreign embassies and consulates—as well as all such communications by private American citizens and commercial firms. The operation began with Army personnel (in civilian clothes) picking up from the cable firms the daily tapes of cables; this system was later changed to provide hard copies of each and every overseas telegram that the firms handled.

The heads of the cable firms, however, were apprehensive about the illegality of handing over the telegrams to the Army. They sought assurances from the Secretary of Defense, then the Attorney General, and even the President that they would not be subject to federal prosecution. Secretary of Defense James V. Forrestal did meet with firm's top executives on Dec. 16, 1947, to assure them—in the name of President Truman—that the intercept effort "constituted a matter of great importance to national security."

Subsequently, members of Forrestal's staff met secretly with key members of Congress to discuss legislative relief for the clandestine intercept operation. But when it appeared that there would be a formal bill and appropriate hearings, that avenue was quickly closed off.

Operation Shamrock continued under the aegis of the ARMED FORCES SECURITY AGENCY when it was secretly founded in 1949, and subsequently under the NSA when it was established in 1952.

A CIA report on Shamrock, made public in 2000, revealed details about the operation: "During the 1950s, paper tape had been the medium of choice. Holes were punched in the paper tape and then scanned to create an electronic transmission. Every day, an NSA courier would pick up the reels of punched paper tape that were left over and take them back to FORT MEADE [NSA headquarters]. In the early 1960s, the companies switched to magnetic tape." The companies wanted the reels returned, so in 1966 LOUIS W. TORTELLA, deputy director of NSA, found, with the help of the CIA, rental office space in New York City "so that NSA could duplicate the magnetic tapes there." This lasted until 1973, "when CIA pulled out of the arrangement because of concerns raised by its lawyers. NSA then arranged for its own office space in Manhattan. Tordella recalled that "years would sometimes go by without his hearing anything about Shamrock. It just ran on, he said, without a great deal of attention from anyone."

NSA computers would race through the tapes, seeking out preprogrammed names, addresses, words, or even phrases, and in a fraction of a second reproduce the full text of the telegram. Such WATCH LISTS of names and addresses would include all communist embassies and legations, as well as persons suspected of having communist sympathies; the words and phrases could include "blueprint," "atomic bomb," or any other term that might lead to a foreign or domestic intelligence operation.

(During this period the FBI was similarly being passed copies of international cables from the various cable offices in Washington, D.C.)

When Robert F. Kennedy became Attorney General in 1961 he distributed a watch list of racketeers to various government agencies, among them NSA. This effort undoubtedly contributed to Kennedy's successes in prosecuting major crime figures. Kennedy also provided NSA with a watch list of U.S. citizens and business firms that had dealings with Castro's CUBA. Here, too, U.S. law enforcement agencies began benefiting directly from Shamrock.

The peak of Army-NSA domestic spying began in 1967, however, when Maj. Gen. William P. Yarborough, the Army's ASSISTANT CHIEF OF STAFF (INTELLIGENCE), sent a message to NSA director Marshall Carter, requesting that NSA provide information about possible foreign influence on the civil disturbances in the United States related to the Vietnam War. This NSA operation was given the CODE NAME MINARET and included overseas telephone calls as well as cables. An NSA director would later state that from 1967 to 1973 NSA monitored the overseas telephone calls and cables of as many as 1,650 American citizens and U.S. organizations as well as those of almost 6,000 foreign nationals and groups.

Even this domestic intelligence effort would be expanded. After the assassination of civil rights leader Martin Luther King, Jr., his suspected killer, James Earl Ray, and his family were added to the NSA cable watch list. Subsequently, drug trafficking and suspected drug handlers were included in the eavesdropping effort.

Under the Nixon administration there were efforts to expand NSA involvement in domestic intelligence even further. (See HUSTON PLAN.)

Operation Shamrock and its offshoots came to an end in 1975. In the early 1970s congressional investigating committees began looking into domestic spying by the CIA, an effort that soon extended to NSA. (See CHURCH COMMITTEE and PIKE COMMITTEE.) It seemed only a matter of time before Congress or the press would reveal the full dimensions of the 30-year-old NSA efforts. Accordingly, on May 12, 1975, NSA director LEW ALLEN, JR., wrote a memorandum that ended what Senate Intelligence Committee chairman Frank Church had called "probably the largest government interception program affecting Americans ever undertaken."

Shark

Name assigned by the British GOVERNMENT CODE AND CYPHER SCHOOL to the German ENIGMA CIPHER machines fitted with a fourth ROTOR. These machines were introduced by the German Navy on Feb. 1, 1942. This was one of the most significant events in German cryptology in World War II, as it deprived the Allies of their ability to read U-boat communications.

The four-rotor Enigmas, designated M4 by the Germans, replaced three-rotor machines. The fourth rotor, however, remained in a single position for the encryption of a message, while the three other rotors could change position with each letter. The four-rotor machines were used by the Navy only in U-boats.

In Oct. 1942 the submarine *U-559* was attacked and damaged by British destroyers off the coast of Egypt, near El Alamein. The stricken U-boat had surfaced and been abandoned by her crew. An officer and a sailor from the destroyer *Petard* jumped into the water and swam to the submarine, followed by a 15-year-old canteen assistant. The first two entered the U-boat and were able to hand up to the boy the four-rotor Enigma machine, charts, and signal books before the submarine sank—with the two of them trapped inside.

The Enigma machine from the *U-559* was sent to the British codebreakers at BLETCHLEY PARK. With the help of the *U-559*'s treasure trove, Bletchley Park codebreakers were able to use U-boat weather broadcasts as a CRIB to break into the four-rotor ciphers. Success against Shark was achieved on Dec. 13, 1942.

However, not all Shark keys could be recovered. For example, no settings were recovered for a ten-day period in Jan. 1943, and none was broken from Feb. 10 to 17.

Still, most keys were recovered, usually in less than 24 hours, making them invaluable for Allied antisubmarine operations.

Sharpe, Maj. Gen. George H.

(b. 1828 d. 1900)

Senior Union Army INTELLIGENCE OFFICER during the U.S. Civil War. Sharpe was the only intelligence officer of the Army of the Potomac, the principal Union fighting force. Information he gathered helped lead to the defeat of Gen. Robert E. Lee at the crucial battle of Gettysburg in July 1863.

A lawyer who had served with the U.S. diplomatic corps, Sharpe was commissioned as a captain in the New York State Militia on May 11, 1861. He was mustered out three months later to be commissioned a colonel in the 120th Regiment of New York Volunteers.

In early 1863 he was named head of the BUREAU OF INFORMATION of the Army of the Potomac. He held that position until the end of the war in 1865, processing the large amount of information that spies and deserters brought out from the Confederate lines. He was awarded the brevet rank of brigadier general in Dec. 1864, and for war service was subsequently promoted to major general.

In 1867, Secretary of State William H. Seward sent Sharpe to Europe in futile search of plotters in the assassination of President Lincoln. He later served as an envoy in Latin America and held several public offices in New York.

Sheep Dipping

U.S. intelligence term for camouflaging or disguising the true identity of equipment or individuals, especially used in reference to military equipment or services—including personnel—assigned to clandestine intelligence activities, generally under the direction of a nonmilitary sponsor.

Shelepin, Aleksandr Nikolayevich

(b. 1918)

Head of the KGB from Dec. 1958 to Nov. 1961.

A history and literature major while studying at the Moscow Institute of Philosophy and Literature, Shelepin was a guerrilla leader during World War II, becoming a senior official of the Communist Youth League (*Komsomol*) in 1943, and head of the *Komsomol* from 1952 to 1958. He accompanied Nikita Khrushchev on the Soviet leader's trip to China in 1954.

Shelepin then became the second head of the KGB, the intelligence-security ORGAN established after the death of Soviet dictator Josef Stalin. Khrushchev appointed Shelepin in part because of several major KGB defections in the 1950s during the tenure of IVAN SEROV as head of the KGB. Shelepin attempted to return state security to its position of importance during the Stalinist era. He demoted or fired many KGB officers, replacing them with officials from Communist Party organizations and, especially, from the *Komsomol.*

He left the KGB and was promoted to the Central Committee secretariat in Nov. 1961, where it is believed he still exercised control over the KGB, which was taken over by his protégé VLADIMIR SEMICHASTNY. Shelepin became a First Deputy Prime Minister in 1962. He was a principal player in the coup against Khrushchev in Oct. 1962, obviously influencing the KGB to support the conspirators.

Shelepin probably expected to become First Secretary and de facto head of the government when Khrushchev was overthrown. Aleksandr Solzhenitsyn suggested that Shelepin had been the choice of the surviving Stalinists in the government, who asked what "had been the point of overthrowing Khrushchev if not to revert to Stalinism?"

Rather, Shelepin's reward was to be made a full member of the ruling Presidium (Politburo) in Nov. 1964—by a significant margin its youngest member. But he still held ambitions of becoming the "first among equals." His colleagues on the Presidium watched him carefully, seeking to halt his ambitions. He survived in that body until 1975, when he rapidly fell from power.

Shevchenko, Arkady Nikolayevich

(b. 1930 d. 1998)

The most senior Soviet diplomat to defect to the West. Shevchenko was an Under Secretary-General of the UNITED NATIONS when he defected on April 6, 1978. For the previous two and a half years in that position he had provided U.S. intelligence with secret information and documents about the Soviet Union.

Born in a Ukrainian coal-mining town, he was the son of a medical family—his father a physician, his mother a nurse. His father was given a commission in the Red Army's medical corps.

In 1949 Shevchenko entered the Moscow State Institute of International Relations, which trained future Soviet diplomats. He graduated in 1954 and, after returning for graduate studies, in 1956 joined the Foreign Ministry to begin a promising diplomatic career.

His first visit to the United States was for a conference in 1958. He subsequently served in New York in the 1960s and became Under Secretary-General for Political and Security Council Affairs in early 1973.

As he rose in the Soviet hierarchy he became more and more disillusioned with the leadership. In his memoirs *Breaking with Moscow* (1985), Shevchenko wrote:

> I sat at a table with [Leonid] Brezhnev, [Andrei]] Gromyko, and other members of the Politburo, and I learned a great deal about the men who were the masters of the Soviet Union. I saw how easily they called vice virtue, and just as easily reversed the words again. How their hypocrisy and corruption had penetrated the smallest aspects of their lives, how isolated they were from the population they ruled.

> Gromyko, for example, had not set foot in the streets of Moscow for almost forty years. Almost all the others were no different. In the gilded, stale, and silent Kremlin corridors a museum has been ensconced, a museum of ideas, visible but fossilized as a fly in amber. Those who have made their careers preserving these relics have tried to force the Soviet people to believe in a social system based on utopian myth. . . .

> The Kremlin was the last place on earth where one might expect directness, honesty, and openness.

In 1974 Shevchenko approached U.S. officials and revealed that he wished to defect to the United States. After being persuaded to remain at the United Nations and to provide intelligence on Soviet matters, he was given the U.S. CODE NAME Andy.

Finally, believing that the Soviet government was becoming suspicious of him, on a Friday evening, while ostensibly driving to the Soviet diplomatic country home on Long Island, N.Y., he defected. His wife and daughter did not go with him. (He remarried in 1978.)

Sheymov, Maj. Victor Ivanovich

(b. 1946)

DEFECTOR from the Eighth Chief Directorate of the KGB, a specialist in SIGNALS INTELLIGENCE and COMMUNICATIONS SECURITY.

Sheymov graduated from the Moscow State Technical University in 1969 with a degree in engineering, having specialized in missile and spacecraft designs. He then worked on space warfare at a scientific research institute of the Ministry of Defense.

In 1971 he entered the KGB, being assigned to the Eighth Chief Directorate and, subsequently, the First Chief Directorate (foreign intelligence), where he monitored cable traffic from KGB residences around the world. Sheymov returned to the Eighth Chief Directorate in 1976 to work in the highly sensitive area of CIPHER communications.

Disillusioned with the Soviet system, Sheymov contacted the U.S. officials in Moscow and in 1980 the CIA arranged for him to escape from Moscow, along with his wife and daughter.

The story of Sheymov's KGB career is told in his autobiographic *Tower of Secrets* (1993). Responding to reports that the KGB was involved in the May 1981 assassination attempt on Pope Paul II, Sheymov said he had seen a telegram, signed by YURI ANDROPOV, which said: "Obtain all information possible about how to get close to the Pope." Sheymov gave the hidden message: explained: "Everyone knew what it meant. It meant they wanted to assassinate the Pope."

Shi Pei Pu

SEE BERNARD BOURSICOT

Shiloah, Reuven

(b. 1909 d. 1959)

First director of the Israeli MOSSAD and in many respects the "father" of modern Israeli intelligence services.

Born Reuven Zaslanski in Jerusalem, Shiloah came from an Orthodox Jewish family. He was a short man, and behind his glasses his blue-gray eyes focused a penetrating stare on the person to whom he was speaking.

During World War II, Shiloah, a founder of SHAI, the Haganah's intelligence arm, went behind German lines on missions for the British. He also worked with the U.S. OFFICE OF STRATEGIC SERVICES (OSS) in Washington, D.C., Cairo, and Istanbul. Among the Americans he dealt with was JAMES JESUS ANGLETON of the X-2, the COUNTERINTELLIGENCE section of the OSS. Shiloah developed a close relationship with Angleton, who would later head counterintelligence for the CIA.

In 1949 Shiloah was named chairman of Israel's Coordinating Committee of the Intelligence Services in an attempt by the government to oversee and coordinate the several Israeli intelligence services. (Shiloah would head that body until March 1953.) But problems continued (see AMAN). There were no clear lines of responsibility, and there were personality conflicts within the intelligence community. Finally, Prime Minister David Ben-Gurion stepped in and demanded a reorganization of Israeli intelligence. On April 1, 1951—when the state was three years old—the Mossad was established. It was tasked with overseas intelligence collection and was to be responsible directly to the Prime Minister's Office.

Shiloah's tenure as head of the Mossad was brief, but he was able to establish certain standards and beliefs within the agency, although its operations—and handling of funds—were relatively sloppy.

The continued controversy among Israeli intelligence leaders, along with injuries from an automobile accident in mid-1952, led Shiloah to step down in Sept. 1952 as head of the Mossad. A year later he was sent to Washington as Minister Plenipotentiary at the Israeli Embassy.

Discussing Shiloah's tenure as head of the Mossad in *Israel's Secret Wars* (1991), Ian Black and Benny Morris wrote: "Friends as well rivals explained that he had never suited the job; they defined him as an 'ideas man' rather than an organization man immured in the brass tacks of clandestine operations." Problems with the Baghdad NETWORK and the SHIN BET, among others, "had simply worn him down."

Shimshon

Intelligence and sabotage unit within the Palmach, the commando wing of the underground Jewish army in Palestine during the British mandatory period. Shimshon teams carried out operations against the Arabs from 1943 until the founding of the state of Israel on May 14, 1948. The Shimshon unit continued within the Israeli Army until 1950.

Shin Bet

Israel's internal security force. Its duties include the protection of the El Al national airline, Israeli government buildings and embassies, defense industries, scientific installations, and industrial plants deemed vital for national security. Among Shin Bet's ASSETS are fluent Arabic speakers, who can pass as Palestinians and operate freely on the West Bank.

Shin and *bet* are the names of the first two Hebrew letters of the term Sherut Habitachon Haklah (General Security Service). Shin Bet has had numerous publicized failures; its successes, unlike those of the MOSSAD, have rarely been publicized.

Shin Bet was established on June 30, 1948, six weeks after Israeli independence. Commanded by ISSER HAREL, initially it was part of the Israel Defense Forces, which provided support, pay, and military ranks for Shin Bet's few personnel. (Harel was made a lieutenant colonel.) Harel believed that Shin Bet should be a civilian organization, and in early 1950 it was placed directly under the Ministry of Defense.

Still "lost" within the budget and policy disputes of the ministry, Harel continued to press Prime Minister David Ben-Gurion—a close friend—to establish an autonomous agency. This was done later in 1950, with Shin Bet reporting directly to the prime minister.

Meanwhile, with the disgrace and fall of ISER BE'ERI in 1949, Harel additionally became head of AMAN, Israeli MILITARY INTELLIGENCE. At Ben-Gurion's direction, he was named MEMUNEH, "the one in charge" of all Israeli intelligence activities. Harel held on to the Shin Bet job until 1952, when his deputy, Isi Dorot, took command for a year. Subsequently the directors of the Mossad and Shin Bet were separate positions.

Internal security in Israel for most of the country's history stemmed from concern about the large Arab population—some 18 percent in late 1948, declining to smaller fractions as the Jewish population increased by immigration as well as births. The Arab threat was twofold: First, there was the possibility of espionage on behalf of the surrounding Arab states, which not only fought major wars with Israel but also sent in saboteurs and terrorists; second, there was the possibility of domestic sedition. In time, with limited recognition by Arab states, beginning with Egypt in 1979, the internal threat from terrorist organizations increased, especially the Islamic Jihad, Hamas, and Hezbollah. These groups fought against any agreements with the Israelis. (The situation was exacerbated much later when accommodations were finally reached granting Palestinians limited control of the West Bank and Gaza—the so-called occupied territories.)

This concern with the Arab population tended to preoccupy Shin Bet. But there was also PENETRATION by non-Arab countries—friends as well as foes. Shortly after he arrived in Israel in 1948, WOLFF GOLDSTEIN was sending information back to the Soviet NKVD and, subsequently, the KGB. Later SHIMON LEVINSON also spied for the Soviets. Both men reached senior positions in the Israeli government and did considerable damage before being discovered. Several lesser Soviet AGENTS were also tracked down. And YOSSI AMIT spied for the United States, Israel's key ally.

As Soviet policy shifted from supporting Israel to becoming the principal arms supplier of Arab states, Shin Bet expanded its interests to provide coverage of Soviet and Eastern Bloc diplomats in Israel.

However, Shin Bet's emphasis continues to be Arab affairs. The agency's Arab Affairs Department maintains an index of Arab terrorists and Shin Bet units, working with Amarn, use undercover detachments, known as Mist'aravim, to combat potential terrorist organizations and the military wing of Hamas.

Avraham Ahituv resigned as director of Shin Bet in Dec. 1980 in the midst of a political controversy surrounding assassination attempts against three Arab mayors of West Bank towns in June 1980. The mayor of Nablus lost both legs in the bombings, and the mayor of Ramallah lost a foot.

Shin Bet officials attempted to cover up the April 12, 1984, beating deaths of two Arab bus hijackers near Gaza. The Arabs were captured when Army troops stormed a bus held by the hijackers; two other terrorists had been killed in the attack, which also cost the life of an Israeli woman soldier who was a passenger on the bus. Shin Bet director Avraham Shalom tendered his resignation in July 1986 in the aftermath of revelations that the two hijackers were alive when led away by Shin Bet officers, who at the time reported that they had been killed in the assault on the bus. (Shalom and three operatives were given a full pardon by President CHAIM HERZOG in June 1986, although the four men had not yet been charged or convicted of a crime in connection with the murders. Herzog—twice head of military intelligence—issued a blanket pardon to avoid further damage to security. Subsequently, seven other members of the Shin Bet were pardoned for their roles in the incident.)

A year later Shin Bet was involved in more controversies: In May 1987 the Israeli Supreme Court ruled that the agency had used illegal interrogation methods and had given false testimony in the espionage case of Army Lt. Izat Nafsu, a member of the Circassian minority. The soldier, who was freed after seven and a half years in prison for allegedly selling secrets and stolen weapons to Palestinian guerrillas, had been framed by Shin Bet.

Shin Bet officers had presented false testimony to the military tribunal that had tried Nafsu. A judicial commission set up to investigate the methods and practices of Shin Bet reported in 1987 that for the previous 17 years Shin Bet interrogators had routinely lied in court about their interrogation methods. The commission also said that they had regularly used physical and psychological mistreatment to obtain confessions.

Before the end of 1987 it was revealed that three Shin Bet officers had been suspended for allegedly trying to cover up the circumstances of the death in prison of a 23-year-old Palestinian being interrogated in 1987. Yosef Harmelin resigned as Shin Bet director the following

year. In Dec. 1987 concern over internal security increased with the start of the Palestinian uprising known as the Intifada. Young Arabs began rioting in the West Bank and Gaza—stoning Israeli security forces, smashing the windows of Arab shopkeepers who remained open during strike hours, and generally running amok. The Israeli answer was force—tear gas, beatings, rubber bullets, and at times real bullets as Shin Bet and police opened fire with real guns against young boys armed with stones.

The uprising created a new, younger generation of militant Palestinian leadership; a sense of self-reliance; and an ability on the part of the local Palestinians to transcend religious, political, economic, and social differences to form a common front against Israeli control of the area. The first intifada—which lasted until 1990—was superimposed over the existing Arab "threats" to Israel.

Still another internal security threat came to the fore in 1993, when secret talks between Israel and the Palestine Liberation Organization (PLO) were revealed. Portions of the West Bank and Gaza would eventually be turned over to a PLO authority. There was immediate Israeli right-wing opposition to such moves. But Shin Bet was slow in recognizing the extent of this opposition. Israelis living in the occupied territories, a minute number of settlers, soon became violent in their opposition. Attacks on Arabs—including one by a lone gunman on Muslims at prayer in a mosque—brought a new reality to the issue of internal security.

Shin Bet failed to prevent the assassination of Prime Minister Yitzhak Rabin on Nov. 4, 1995. The thought of a Jew killing another Jew for "political" reasons was apparently so abhorrent that the agency had not fully investigated reports of a possible attempt on the prime minister's life.

The murder, which was captured on a home video, clearly showed the ease with which the assassin had approached his target. Karmi Gilon, director of Shin Bet, took full responsibility for the failure to protect Rabin. His successor, Rear Adm. AMI AYALON, had just stepped down as head of the Israeli Navy. He was the first Shin Bet director to be named publicly at the time of his appointment, an obvious move to help restore public confidence in the security service. In Mar. 2000 Prime Minister Ehud Barak replaced Ayalon with Avraham Deichter, who had served Barak in an army commando unit that Barak once headed.

In Mar. 2001 the launching of the hard-line administration of Prime Minister Ariel Sharon signaled a new round of Israeli-Palestinian conflict and a new flaring of intifida. Then, in June 2001, cast in an unprecedented role, GEORGE TENET, the U.S. DIRECTOR OF CENTRAL INTELLIGENCE, journeyed to Israel to bring together senior Israeli and Palestinian security officials to establish a U.S.-brokered truce, which ultimately failed. When violence flared again—punctuated by Palestinian suicide bombers' massacres—Shin Bet provided the Israeli military with precise information for retaliatory strikes against suspected intifada leaders.

DIRECTORS OF SHIN BET

The directors of Shin Bet are listed below; note that Yosef Harmelin twice headed the agency; Isser Harel is the only person to have served as a director of both Shin Bet and the Mossad.

1948–1952	Isser Harel
1952–1953	Isi Dorot
1953–1963	Amos Manor
1964–1974	Yosef Harmelin
1974–1981	Avraham Ahituv
1981–1986	Avraham Shalom
1986–1988	Yosef Harmelin
1988–1994	Jacob Peri
1995–1996	Karmi Gilon
1996–2000	Ami Ayalon
2000–	Avraham Deichter

Shoe

Russian slang for a passport.

Shoemaker

Russian slang for a forger. See COBBLER

Shopped

British intelligence term meaning assassinated or murdered.

Shopworn Goods

Information offered by a DEFECTOR or would-be defector that is so dated or unrelated to intelligence needs as to be worthless to the country or intelligence service to which it is being offered.

Shtemyenko, Gen. of the Army Sergei Matveyevich

(b. 1907 d. 1976)

Senior Soviet staff officer and twice chief of the GRU, Soviet MILITARY INTELLIGENCE, from 1946–1948 and 1956–1957. GRU Col. OLEG PENKOVSKY wrote in *The Penkovsky Papers* (1965) that he "worked very hard and introduced many wise reforms" to the GRU, and "He was good chief, mainly because of his administrative abilities but was disliked by the generals of the General Staff."

Of peasant origins, Shtemyenko entered the Red Army in 1926 and served mostly in artillery and armored units until assigned to the General Staff in Sept. 1939. In May 1943 he was named head of the Operations Directorate of the General Staff and thus became a high-level planner of Soviet military operations and a principal assistant to Josef Stalin.

He served as chief of the GRU from April 1946 until Nov. 1948, when he was appointed chief of the General Staff and promoted to General of the Army. In the June 1952 controversy between Stalin and the Politburo he sided with Stalin but was nevertheless removed from his post, demoted to lieutenant general, and assigned to command the Volga Military District, away from Moscow. In 1956 he was recalled to Moscow by Marshal of the Soviet Union Georgi Zhukov, reinstated as a General of the Army, and reappointed chief of the GRU. With the ouster of Zhukov in Oct. 1957, Shtemyenko was again dismissed and again demoted to lieutenant general. However, in June 1962 he was made commander-in-chief of Ground Forces (head of the Army). In 1968 he was promoted—for the third time—to General of the Army and appointed a First Deputy Minister of Defense and Chief of Staff of the Warsaw Pact Forces; he held those positions at the time of his death.

Shtemyenko's career was feverish as well as resilient. His name was put forward three times for the rank of Marshal of the Soviet Union, the first time at the age of 41, but he never received the honor. He is considered by some observers to have been the most energetic, erudite, and merciless of all GRU chiefs.

Shtemyenko authored two major military histories, *The Soviet General Staff at War* (1981) and *The Last Six Months* [of World War II] (1973), both of which went through several revised editions.

SI

SEE SPECIAL INTELLIGENCE

Siblings

(1) The term for another intelligence service of the same country; (2) At one time the term used in the CIA for the DEFENSE INTELLIGENCE AGENCY.

Sigaba

Principal U.S. CIPHER machine for higher-classification encryptions during World War II. Also called ECM (Electrical Enciphering Machine). The Sigaba is believed to have been the only cipher machine used in the war that was never compromised by any nation.

Development of Sigaba began in 1935 as a joint Army-Navy project; it entered service in 1938. The U.S. Army designation was M134-C, the Navy CSP-888.

Like the ENIGMA encryption machine, the Sigaba employed ROTORS—10 replaceable wheels; up to four rotors could turn with each letter selection, compared to one in the Enigma, and the rotors could reverse direction (unlike the Enigma rotors, which could turn in only one direction). The Sigaba was designed as an ON-LINE SYSTEM, meaning that it was connected directly to a radio or telephone so that encryption and transmission would be simultaneous. However, it was not used in that manner; instead, it produced an enciphered tape that could then be transmitted by radio.

In addition to being used by the U.S. Army, Army Air Forces, Navy, and Marine Corps, U.S. SPECIAL LIAISON UNITS (SLUs) employed the Sigaba, as did British SLUs in the China-Burma-India Theater.

There was never any serious attempt by the Germans or Japanese to break into the Sigaba ciphers. The Germans called it the "American Big Machine." Only one is known to have been lost: In Feb. 1945 a U.S. Army truck was stolen by French Resistance fighters. The thieves, wanting the truck and not its contents, dumped the safe-like container with the Sigaba and M138 backup converter into a nearby lake and fled. The machine was recovered.

Sigaba was in use by U.S. military forces into the 1960s. Despite the fact that it has been out of service for three decades, little information on the Sigaba was available until NSA began releasing long-classified documents in 1995. As a result, cryptologist John J. G. Savard was able to produce a thorough description of Sigaba's inner workings on his Web site.

See home.ecn.ab.ca/~jsavard/crypto/ro0205.htm.

SIGINT

SEE SIGNALS INTELLIGENCE

Signal Intelligence Service

(SIS)

U.S. Army organization established on Apr. 24, 1930, to consolidate all Army activities engaged in cryptology under the Signal Corps. The SIS was responsible for producing the Army's own CODES and CIPHER devices and for efforts to DECRYPT the communications of potential enemies. Previously, Army cryptologic functions had been carried out by the War Department's MILITARY INTELLIGENCE

The U.S. Sigaba machine is the only cipher machine produced by any nation that is not known to have been compromised. Here paired Sigaba machines are in use at Arlington Hall Station. The rotor "basket" drops into the top of the machine. (NATIONAL SECURITY AGENCY)

DIVISION through a clandestine effort headed by HERBERT O. YARDLEY and funded with State Department support. That effort had been halted in 1929 by then Secretary of State Henry Stimson, who believed and reputedly remarked later, "Gentlemen do not read each other's mail."

The first chief of SIS was WILLIAM F. FRIEDMAN, who created a small and extremely talented staff: four junior CRYPTANALYSTS and one cryptanalyst-clerk. An Army officer was placed in charge of SIS in 1935, with Friedman continuing as the guiding force of the organization.

In addition to its cryptologic activities, SIS published a series of influential studies on cryptology and developed machine ciphers for secure Army communications. The greatest pre–World War II accomplishment of SIS was breaking the machine cipher employed by the Japanese Foreign Ministry, the so-called PURPLE cipher. Through purely cryptanalytic methods, Friedman and his colleagues, working closely with the Navy, were able to produce an analog of this machine and read Japanese communications as quickly—or even more so—than the intended recipients. The decrypts of Purple messages were initially called MAGIC.

When war erupted, SIS rapidly expanded. At the time of Pearl Harbor SIS had 45 Army officers, 177 enlisted men, and 109 civilians—a total of 331. Most of the enlisted men and one officer were with field units; the remainder were in Washington.

In June 1942 the growing SIS moved from its World War I–era temporary buildings on the Washington Mall to ARLINGTON HALL in nearby Virginia. That same month personnel from the Army's 2ND SIGNAL SERVICE BATTALION–the intercept arm of SIS–began operations at Vint Hill Farms in Warrenton, Va., a major radio intercept station "feeding" Arlington Hall. (Prior to the war the Army had seven fixed radio intercept stations; 10 more were established during the war. See below.)

SIS was renamed the Signal Intelligence Service Division in 1942 and, subsequently, Signal Security Division, Signal Security Branch, Signal Security Division, Signal Security Service, and, from, July 1, 1943, through Sept. 14, 1945, the Signal Security Agency (SSA).

In June 1942 the agency was given exclusive responsibility for exploiting foreign diplomatic communications, a mission previously shared with the Navy. While SIS achieved an outstanding triumph breaking into Purple, breaking into Japanese military codes was much more difficult, because the Japanese Army employed REENCIPHERED CODES and not a code machine. Not until Apr. 1943 was the agency able to make a single entry into a Japanese Army system. The first usable intelligence was not derived until June 1943 and not until 1944 were Japanese Army communications read on a continuous basis.

Similar frustration was encountered in the Army's work on German military systems, which the British at BLETCHLEY PARK were also working on. The official and excellent *U.S. Army Signals Intelligence in World War II* (1993), edited by James L. Gilbert and John P. Finnegan, notes that the lack of British cooperation "—justified by the British on grounds of security and economy of effort—became even more grating when the Army became aware that the British were willing to share high-level COMINT [COMMUNICATIONS INTELLIGENCE] with the U.S. Navy to meet the operational needs of fighting the U-boat war."

The U.S. Army's success against Japanese military codes led to belated full collaboration by the British at Bletchley Park. (With this collaboration high-level COMINT became known as ULTRA within the U.S. Army and Navy, as it was within the British services.)

In addition to the vast increase in Army radio-intercept units that served in every theater, the Army also supported the Army Air Forces' establishment of radio intercept squadrons to support numbered air forces, which began in 1944. But problems continued throughout the war. To quote Gilbert and Finnegan,

> the Army's strategic and tactical signals intelligence assets were still not coordinated properly. Tactical COMINT units were trained by the Army Ground Forces, not SSA [Signal Security Agency], and they functioned under the direction of theater and numbered air force commanders, not SSA, despite the fact that this division of labor did not reflect the reality that the communications intelligence process was a seamless web.

At this time coordination between the Army and Navy was poor, despite their fine pre–Pearl Harbor cooperation in the handling of Purple and the setting up of an Army-Navy Communications Intelligence Coordinating Committee in early 1944.

Finally, at the end of the war the new head of Army intelligence, Maj. Gen. CLAYTON BISSELL, spurred better cooperation with the Navy. At his direction, on Sept. 15, 1945—13 days after the end of the war—the ARMY SECURITY AGENCY was established to control "all signals intelligence and security establishments, units, and personnel" and to function directly under the MILITARY INTELLIGENCE DIVISION (G-2).

By the end of the war SIS had undergone a 30-fold increase: On Aug. 14, 1945, it numbered 792 officers, 2,704 enlisted men, 1,214 enlisted women, and 5,661 civilians—a total of 10,371. Most were at Arlington Hall. In addition, there were 17,000 Army personnel engaged in signal intelligence activities under theater and other major commanders. This buildup was hampered by some ridiculous Civil Service and Army regulations, as well as the Secretary of the Army's decree that no officer under age 28 could be in Washington after Jan. 31, 1942, regardless of expertise or experience that might be of value to intelligence activities!

SIS operated 17 fixed radio intercept stations during the war; in addition, there were hundreds of mobile Army intercept stations with Army units in the field.

Established before the war:

Corozal, Panama Canal Zone
Fort Hancock, N.J.
Fort Hunt, Va.
Fort McKinley, near Manila, Philippines

Fort Sam Houston, Texas
Fort Scott, Presidio of San Francisco, Calif.
Fort Shafter, Hawaii

Established during the war:

Amchitka, Aleutian Islands
Asmara, Eritrea
Bellmore, Long Island, N.Y.
Fairbanks, Alaska
Guam
Indian Creek Station, Miami Beach, Fla.
New Delhi, India
Petaluma, Calif.
Tarzana, Calif.
Warrenton, Va.

These stations used secure codes to forward their intercepts to SIS in Washington, D.C., and later to Arlington Hall.

In the Philippines in 1941 the Army intercepts, taken by the Army's 2nd Signal Service Company, were also delivered to the Navy unit on Corregidor—Station CAST—which had a Purple machine for the decryption of Japanese diplomatic communications. Those were passed to the two senior U.S. commanders in the Philippines, Gen. Douglas MacArthur and Adm. Thomas C. Hart. Fort McKinley was lost when Manila was abandoned in late Dec. 1942, although some intercepts were still made from Corregidor before the intelligence personnel were evacuated from the island in early 1942. (Corregidor fell to the Japanese on May 6, 1942.)

The Guam intercept station was established after Marines retook the island in mid-1944. The stations at Bellmore and Tarzana, originally established by the OFFICE OF STRATEGIC SERVICES (OSS), were taken over by SSA and used to monitor U.S. radio communications for security purposes.

Codebreaking is as much pencil and paper as machines. These women of the U.S. Army's Signal Intelligence Service are working at Arlington Hall, site of the SIS and its successor agencies from June 1942 until the late 1980s. (NATIONAL SECURITY AGENCY)

The Army also received a large number of intercepts from the Navy's intercept stations at Bainbridge Island, Wash., and Bar Harbor, Maine. The SSA was renamed the ARMY SECURITY AGENCY (ASA) on Sept. 15, 1945, and merged with ARMY INTELLIGENCE (G-2) in 1977 to form the ARMY INTELLIGENCE AND SECURITY COMMAND (INSCOM).

Also see NAVY COMMUNICATIONS INTELLIGENCE.

Signals Intelligence

(SIGINT)

Intelligence derived from combinations of COMMUNICATIONS INTELLIGENCE (COMINT) and ELECTRONICS INTELLIGENCE (ELINT).

Silicon Valley

Area near Sunnyvale–Palo Alto–San Jose, Calif., built up from the 1960s onward, possessing the highest concentration of high-technology industry in the United States. Primarily known for computer-related technologies, the area has become a major TARGET for foreign intelligence agencies and INDUSTRIAL ESPIONAGE activities.

In the early 1980s Silicon Valley was the ninth-largest manufacturing center in the United States, producing one-third of the semiconductors and related devices, one-quarter of the guided missiles and space vehicles, and almost one-sixth of the electronic computing equipment made in the United States. Also located in Silicon Valley were the Moffett Naval Air Station, a major anti-submarine warfare center (now operated largely by the National Aeronautics and Space Administration); an Air Force SATELLITE tracking and servicing center at Sunnyvale; and a major Lockheed Missile and Space Co. facility.

Although the collapse of dot-coms in the 1990s put Silicon Valley into a slump, espionage continued unabated. In 2002 and 2003 U.S. officials cracked down on Chinese natives accused of shipping equipment to China or stealing trade secrets. Events in the early 21st century appeared to have changed little since 1992, when FBI agents, noting the foreign intelligence penetration of the Valley, told *Forbes* magazine:

> An estimated 10% of all Silicon Valley engineers are Chinese ethnics. The vast majority are loyal employees. But [China] has learned how to elicit information from some. Mainland Chinese, visiting as students or on exchange programs, act as "spotters," compiling lists of Chinese ethnics working at U.S. firms. Some are invited to come to China and visit with relatives still living on the mainland—all at no cost.

The agents also emphasized French efforts at INDUSTRIAL ESPIONAGE against U.S. firms in the area—a PENETRATION that also continued into the 21st century.

Sillitoe, Sir Percy

(b. 1888 d. 1962)

Director-General of the British Security Service (MI5) from 1946 to 1953.

Sillitoe began his intelligence career when he joined the South African police force in 1908. He subsequently served with the Northern Rhodesian police from 1911 until 1923, when he went to Britain and continued his police work. In 1929 he set up the country's first forensic science laboratory. During World War II, as chief constable of the coastal county of Kent, he worked closely with MILITARY INTELLIGENCE.

In April 1946 he was appointed head of MI5. His tenure was marked by the operation of a large number of Soviet spies within the British government and even the intelligence services. Only one spy was discovered by MI5 during his time in office: William M. Marshall. An MI5 WATCHER observing a Soviet diplomat saw him speaking to Marshall, a radio operator in the British Foreign Office, who had recently returned from duty as a CIPHER clerk in the British Embassy in Moscow.

Sillitoe retired after eight years in MI5. He then went to work for the De Beers firm in South Africa, tracking down diamond smugglers.

Silver

SEE VIENNA

Sinclair, Adm. Sir Hugh

(b. 1873 d. 1939)

Director-General of the British Secret Intelligence Service (MI6) from June 1923 to Nov. 1939. Sinclair succeeded Sir MANSFIELD CUMMING, the founding head of MI6, who held that position from 1909 to 1923.

A career naval officer, Sinclair had joined the Royal Navy in 1886. After shipboard and shore assignments, including command of the battleship *Hibernia*, he served during World War I as deputy DIRECTOR OF NAVAL INTELLIGENCE under Rear Adm. REGINALD (BLINKER) HALL. He succeeded Hall in that position from 1919 to 1921, having been promoted to rear admiral. He was serving as head of the submarine service when he was named to the MI6 position.

As Director-General of MI6 he was concerned both with the threat of political infiltration from the Soviet Union and of rearmament by Germany. His efforts were often frustrated because of the very limited funding made available to him by the Foreign Office.

As the war approached, he began to make preparations for MI6 to carry out sabotage and guerrilla operations as well as espionage against Germany. On Nov. 4, 1939, two months after World War II began in Europe, Sinclair died in office.

Sinclair, Maj. Gen. Sir John

(b. 1897 d. 1977)

Director-General of the British Secret Intelligence Service (MI6) from 1953 to 1956.

He was known as "Sinbad" Sinclair because he served as a Navy midshipman after being educated at Winchester and the Royal Naval College, Dartmouth. He entered the Army in 1918 and following a year at the Royal Academy, Woolwich, he was commissioned in the Royal Artillery. In World War II he served as deputy director of military operations. Thus, he had little intelligence experience when he was appointed to MI6. His tenure was somewhat abbreviated because of the revelation that MI6 had employed retired Navy diver LIONEL CRABB to carry out a spy mission against the cruiser *Ordzhonikidze,* which had brought Soviet leaders Nikita Khrushchev and N. A. Bulganin to Britain in April 1956. When Crabb was killed and the spy mission publicly revealed, Prime Minister Anthony Eden fired the Foreign Office adviser to MI6 and then Sinclair. (An official inquiry had exonerated Sinclair of direct involvement in the Crabb operation.)

Singleton

Intelligence operations conducted by a single INTELLIGENCE OFFICER or AGENT. These operations include intelligence collection, servicing agents, and COURIER services.

SIS

(1) SIGNAL INTELLIGENCE SERVICE; (2) Secret Intelligence Service (MI6).

Skorzeny, Generalmajor Otto

(b. 1908 d. 1976)

SS officer who led several daring commando-style operations. Skorzeny began his spectacular career as a member of Leibstandarte-SS Adolf Hitler, the Führer's bodyguard regiment. He also fought as an SS officer in the campaigns in France and the Low Countries in 1940 and the subsequent German campaign in the Soviet Union.

Skorzeny studied British commando tactics and training, hoping to establish a similar special operations unit in the SS. He received little support until he successfully completed his first major mission: the release of Benito Mussolini after the Italian dictator was deposed and arrested in July 1943. Hitler personally selected Skorzeny for the mission, which was complicated by the fact that the Italian authorities kept moving Mussolini. Skorzeny, who organized an intensive intelligence effort to find him, remained a step behind him in the game of hide-and-seek with the dictator's Italian captors. Once, reconnoitering a hideout on an island off Sardinia, Skorzeny's plane was shot down by Allied aircraft.

Skorzeny finally learned that Mussolini was in a heavily guarded resort hotel in the Gran Sassos mountains north of Abruzzi. On Sept. 12, 1943, Skorzeny and an assault force flew to the high plateau in LZ gliders, landing on a 3,000-foot meadow next to the hotel. Cowing Mussolini's guards, Skorzeny entered the hotel, found the dazed dictator, told him that Hitler had sent him, and said, "You are free!" Skorzeny shoved Mussolini into a small Fi 156 Storch aircraft that could barely take off from the rock-strewn meadow and delivered him to VIENNA that night, completing what Skorzeny called an "impossible mission."

There were rumors that Skorzeny would attempt to kill Soviet dictator Josef Stalin at the conference in Tehran when he met with Prime Minister Winston Churchill and President Roosevelt in late 1943.

Following the July 20, 1944, assassination plot against Hitler, Skorzeny sped to the Ministry of War in Berlin and for a short while during the confusion virtually ran the German Army. He organized an SS battalion to help guard the ministry, found evidence of the plot, and rounded up many of the conspirators.

Skorzeny's next mission—given the CODE NAME Mickey Mouse—was inspired by Hitler's desire to keep Hungary in the Axis. In Sept. 1944 Adm. Miklós Horthy, the dictator of Hungary, had begun trying to negotiate a separate peace with the Soviet Union, whose troops were nearing Budapest. Skorzeny took a special force into Hungary and kidnapped Horthy's son Mikio, threatening to kill him if Horthy did not resign. Skorzeny also seized Horthy's citadel and ruled Hungary for a short time until a fascist puppet regime was installed.

When Germany launched the Ardennes offensive that triggered the Battle of the Bulge in Dec. 1944, Skorzeny once again showed his genius for special operations. In an operation code-named GREIF ("snatch"), he trained a force of English-speaking German soldiers, dressed them in American uniforms, and, with captured U.S. vehicles, sent them behind American lines to raise havoc.

Skorzeny's ersatz GIs cut communications wires, changed road signs, and gave confusing, GI-to-GI information to U.S. soldiers stunned by the sudden German attack. At the headquarters of the Supreme Headquarters Allied Expeditionary Forces at Versailles, just outside Paris, extra security was thrown around Gen. Dwight D. Eisenhower because of planted rumors that a Skorzeny-led assassination squad had targeted Eisenhower. American forces captured many of the disguised GIs and summarily executed them as spies.

Skorzeny was captured by U.S. forces in Austria in May 1945. An American war crimes tribunal accused him of illegal warfare in the Battle of the Bulge. He was acquitted after a British officer testified that British and U.S. special forces had used similar irregular tactics.

German authorities arrested him and placed him in an internment camp in Darmstadt. He escaped in July 1948, assumed a new identity, and helped to found ODESSA, a secret West German organization of former SS officers. According to Skorzeny-inspired accounts, Odessa and its escape network, Die Spinne (the spider), helped get hundreds of SS officers out of Germany. Odessa-aided escapees reportedly included the infamous Adolf Eichmann.

Skorzeny settled in Spain, started an export-import business as a cover for Die Spinne activities, and helped to maintain the escape network that got SS officers to safety in sympathetic countries in the Middle East and South America. In 1959 Skorzeny, who had access to caches of SS loot, bought a country estate in Ireland and began raising horses. He died in Madrid.

Skunk Works

Slang for Lockheed Aircraft Corporation's design bureau at Burbank, Calif., founded in 1943 by CLARENCE L. (KELLY) JOHNSON. The bureau—the existence of which was long kept a secret—was established initially to build the P-80 Shooting Star, America's first jet-propelled combat aircraft. Subsequently the bureau designed and built the highly secret U-2, A-12 OXCART, and SR-71 BLACKBIRD spyplanes.

Other aircraft produced by the Skunk Works include the U.S. Air Force's F-117A "stealth" strike aircraft. The bureau also developed the Navy's *Sea Shadow,* a stealth research ship.

The name Skunk Works was chosen because of its proximity to a foul-smelling chemical plant, akin to the skunk works of Al Capp's newspaper comic strip "L'il Abner."

The heads of the Skunk Works were:

1943–1975	Clarence (Kelly) Johnson
1975–1991	Benjamin Rich
1991–1993	Sherman Mullen
1993–	Jack Warden

Also see CL-282 and CL-400.

Skylark

CODE NAME for planned flights of U.S. A-12 OXCART spyplanes over Cuba. Operation Skylark called for "emergency" operational readiness for overflights beginning on Nov. 5, 1964, one year before the A-12 actually became operational.

A CIA detachment began training for the Cuban flights, which would be undertaken on two weeks' notice. However, the U-2 RECONNAISSANCE aircraft continued to make the Cuban OVERFLIGHTS, the A-12 being reserved for more critical requirements.

Slammer

U.S. project for obtaining firsthand information from Americans in prison for espionage. The videotaped interviews by U.S. INTELLIGENCE OFFICERS were conducted to gain insights into the motives and attitudes of U.S. spies.

A second project, made in 1993 and called "Son of Slammer," was aimed at perpetrators of COMPUTER ESPIONAGE.

Air Force security-education officers were still using the projects in 2003 because the instructors believed that the studies were still valuable and that their major findings still prevailed: (1) No offender entered a position of trust with the intent to betray; (2) they were highly manipulative, dominant, self-serving, easily influenced, lacked self-esteem, were immature, and had an inability to cope; (3) large number were substance abusers; (4) and their decision to betray was based in part on their belief that their coworkers would not turn them in. The study also showed that they had antisocial personalities.

The SECURITY POLICY ADVISORY BOARD in 1997 urged that a Slammer database be established to create among senior officials a "clearer understanding of the dynamics of espionage and an incorporation of that enhanced understanding into government and industry security programs."

Although the Slammer interviews remain classified, excerpts from them have been leaked. Imprisoned spies who were interviewed include MICHAEL WALKER, whose father, JOHN A. WALKER, JR., recruited him. Michael Walker was a U.S. sailor when he was arrested. He told his interviewer that when he was copying documents in the classified spaces of a U.S. Navy warship, the other sailors "saw what I was doing but never took any notice. There were a couple of times when it got kind of close, but I was good at lying."

JEFFREY CARNEY, a U.S. Air Force communications specialist who spied for the Soviets, said that he had no trouble "putting my nose in books where I didn't belong . . . talking to people, gathering information from conversations. It was actually very obvious. Somebody should have noticed."

Journalist Jeff Stein, who has seen portions of the Slammer report, wrote in *The New York Times* that the authors of the report discovered that "behavioral changes are often associated with acts of espionage. Heavy drinking, drug dependence, signs of depression or stress, extramarital affairs and divorce could be warning signs of a security problem. The authors believe that if co-workers and bosses could be educated to intervene with a troubled employee early on, damaging espionage might be prevented."

Slavens, Brian E.

U.S. Marine Corps deserter who in 1982 called the Soviet Embassy in Washington, D.C., and offered to sell military information to the Soviet Union. His telephone call was intercepted by the FBI. He was arrested, convicted on espionage charges, and sentenced to two years at hard labor.

Sleeper

A spy in a TARGET area who does not engage in espionage until he or she is activated at a future time.

The 1992 British TELEVISION drama series *Sleeper* told of two Soviet sleepers sent to Britain in the 1960s. But when ultimately contacted by THE CENTER in Moscow and ordered back because the Cold War has ended, they have made new lives for themselves—one is married with children, and the other has become a successful financial account executive. Neither man wants to return to Russia. The drama raised the question about what exactly did happen to the Soviet sleepers planted in the United States and Britain during the Cold War. At least two post–Cold War sleepers have reportedly been found in Canada.

Canada deported the two alleged sleeper spies in 1996—then in 2002 learned that they had married their Canadian lovers and were trying to return to Canada. According to *Covert Entry* (2002), by Andrew Mitrovica, a Canadian investigative journalist, since their deportation, Yelena Olshevskaya and Dmitry Olshevsky married Canadians and went to the Canadian Embassy in Moscow to inquire about new Canadian citizenship.

The sleepers had taken the identities of two Canadian infants who had died more than 30 years ago. A Soviet spy using the name GORDON ARNOLD LONSDALE used a similar technique. Like "Lonsdale," the two latter-day sleepers were said to be planning to move to the United States, where they would spy for Russia, probably engaging in INDUSTRIAL ESPIONAGE. The ROYAL CANADIAN MOUNTED POLICE and the Canadian Security Intelligence Service (CSIS) discovered the sleepers. To learn more, Mitrovica wrote, the CSIS planned to have an INTELLIGENCE OFFICER WOO, and possibly seduce, Olshevskaya. But she had already found a new lover—as had her husband.

SLU

SEE SPECIAL LIAISON UNIT

Smedley, Agnes

(b. 1894 d. 1950)

An American, long involved in intrigue and espionage, who played a key role in the Far East Soviet spy ring headed by RICHARD SORGE.

An idealist from an early age, in New York City in 1918 Smedley became involved with an Indian revolutionary movement financed by the German government as a means of damaging Britain, then at war with Germany, by undermining British imperial rule in India. Smedley was arrested for violating the U.S. neutrality laws, but she was not brought to trial and was soon released. This incident and others aroused in her a strong hatred for the United States and, by extension, the West. Although she had sexual relations with men (and was briefly married at age 18), she generally dressed in a mannish style. Later, in communist-held territory of China, she wore the uniform of the Red Army.

She was in BERLIN in the 1920s and became active in the communist movement while earning a living as a writer. She taught at the University of Berlin and founded the city's first birth control clinic. She visited Moscow in 1921 to attend a meeting of Indian revolutionaries. In 1928 she went to China via Moscow and by then had become a well-known character in the ranks of international communism.

While in the Far East she was a correspondent for the German newspaper *Frankfurter Zeitung* (and later the *Manchester Guardian*), working out of Shanghai. Although she did not speak Chinese and knew little about the country or the people, she immediately began writing "authoritatively" about China in both articles and books. Her articles revealed little of China, but much of her prejudices and attitudes.

With her strong communist sympathies, she befriended Sorge, who worked for the GRU, Soviet MILITARY INTELLIGENCE. He used her apartment for clandestine radio transmissions, and she introduced Sorge to her friend OZAKI HOZUMI, who would become his principal Japanese collaborator.

Hozumi was her first recruit for Sorge's spy ring. Sorge would write: "The only person in China upon whom I knew that I could depend was Agnes Smedley, of whom I had first heard in Europe. I solicited her aid in establishing my group in China and particularly in selecting Chinese co-workers." Sorge generally remained in the background until Smedley had identified and begun to develop a candidate for his espionage ring.

Others in her Shanghai circle included URSULA KUCZYNSKI, another top Soviet spy, and ROGER HOLLIS, a future head of the British Security Service (MI5).

When Sorge moved from China to Japan in 1933, Smedley went to the Soviet Union for medical treatment. She then traveled through Europe and back to New York, returning to China in 1935. There she continued to send intelligence material to Moscow and continued her attempt to influence people with her idealistic and naive views of communism.

The British ambassador to China in the late 1930s, Sir Archibald Clark-Kerr (later Lord Inverchapel) considered her one of the "greatest women" on earth; he subsequently became British ambassador to the United States, and his views helped confuse the issue of American policy toward China after World War II. Similarly, Smedley became friends with Joseph Stilwell, later the commanding general of U.S. forces in Burma and China, and had some influence on his views of China; some said there was a great "mutual admiration" between the two Americans. Also influential was her book *Battle Hymn of China* (1943), which praised the communist forces in China and compared the Nationalist Kuomintang with the Nazi Party in Germany.

From 1941 onward she remained in the United States, writing and lecturing on China. After the war, Maj. Gen. CHARLES WILLOUGHBY, Gen. of the Army Douglas MacArthur's chief INTELLIGENCE OFFICER, exposed Smedley as a key member of the communist conspiracy in the Far East in an official report, completed in 1947 and released in Washington, D.C., two years later. Smedley wrote to President Truman asking him to force

MacArthur to apologize to her or to waive the general's immunity so that he could be sued for libel. The Department of the Army issued a retraction: "The [intelligence] division has no proof to back up the spy charges. The report was based on information from the Japanese police and should have said so. While there may be evidence in existence to substantiate the allegations, it is not in our hands."

Several journalists took up the cry for Smedley. And former Secretary of the Interior Harold L. Ickes wrote: "No one who knows Miss Smedley would ever suspect that this courageous and intelligent American citizen has stooped to be so low as to be a spy for any country—even for her own to which she is deeply attached . . ."

The House Un-American Activities Committee, reacting to rumors about her espionage, subpoenaed her, but she had left for England, where she died in 1950. She left her estate to Chu-The, former commander of the Chinese communist military forces, which were then fighting U.S. troops in Korea. When she died she was writing a biography of Chu-The. She requested that her body be cremated and the ashes "be laid to rest at any place designated by General Chu-The or his heirs." The ashes were buried in Peking (now Beijing), with honors, and several Chinese leaders were among the reported 800 people who attended the interment.

Willoughby repeated his charges against Smedley in his book *Shanghai Conspiracy* (1952). His extensive discussion of Smedley and her activities begins:

> The American, Miss Agnes Smedley, has been one of the most energetic workers for the Soviet cause in China for over twenty years. She was one of the early perpetrators, if not the originator, of the hoax that the Chinese Communists were not really Communists at all but were only local agrarian revolutionists innocent of any Soviet connections. This concocted tale has had enormous effect in molding American opinion on China, both private and official.

Smersh

Soviet intelligence organization with broad activities in field of counterespionage, personally organized and named by Soviet dictator Josef Stalin. The name is an abbreviation of the Russian words *smert' shpionam,* meaning "death to spies."

Smersh was charged with tracking down traitors and deserters behind the front lines, shooting retreating soldiers, and arresting men who escaped from German captivity; in addition to the Soviet Army, Navy, and Air Force, Smersh had jurisdiction over the NKVD military forces and institutions. Smersh also supervised a network of informers within the armed forces and helped to direct partisan operations behind German lines.

COUNTERINTELLIGENCE activities within the armed forces were carried out by the Osobye Otdely (Special Departments) of the NKVD prior to the establishment of Smersh. Smersh was created in 1941 by LAVRENTY BERIA

as an agency of the NKVD under Commissioner of State Security 3rd Rank Vasili Vasilevich Chernyshov. From April 14, 1943, to March 16, 1946, Smersh functioned as a separate agency directly under the State Committee of Defense headed by Stalin. During this period of independence from the NKVD, Smersh was commanded by Beria's deputy and protégé Col. Gen. V. S. ABAKUMOV, the First Deputy Commissar for State Security. At the same time, apparently under Abakumov's overall direction, Petr Andreevich Gladkov became head of the Smersh naval component (1943–1946); Chernyshov, with the rank of colonel general, remained a deputy head of Smersh into 1946, after which he became Deputy Minister of the newly established MGB.

The principal directorates or administrations of Smersh were:

> *First Administration:* Provide representatives at all levels of Soviet military units down to the battalion and company level to observe officer and enlisted personnel, and monitor informers.
> *Second Administration:* Conduct operations (including support of partisans, military police–type activities), carry out liaison with the NKVD and NKGB, and provide special security troops to protect headquarters and senior officers (on the average a company to each army and a battalion to each front).
> *Third Administration:* Receive, maintain, and disseminate intelligence related to Smersh activities.
> *Fourth Administration:* Carry out investigations of military personnel suspected of anti-Soviet activity and of civilians in areas of military activity.
> *Fifth Administration:* Provide tribunals of three Smersh officers (a troika) to try suspects.

Smersh had a cadre of personnel transferred from NKVD, thus ensuring continuity and expertise in pursuing death to spies. All men and women in Smersh, from senior officers to clerks, secretaries, and typists, held officer rank.

Smersh officers were assigned to all higher-level field headquarters, with Smersh detachments operating at subordinate levels. Former Smersh officer A. I. Romanov [p] wrote in his autobiographical *Nights Are Longest There* (1972) that even Marshal of the Soviet Union Georgi Zhukov, in some respects the highest-ranking Soviet officer in the war, "as a high-ranking non-*chekist*, had been completely surrounded by *Chekist* generals. . . . The higher a man's rank and the stronger his apparent power, the more he was kept under surveillance by the security services." Lt. Gen. A. I. Vadis was Zhukov's chief of Smersh.

Among the many thousands of victims arrested by Smersh during and immediately after the war was artillery officer and writer Aleksandr Solzhenitsyn.

Late in the war Smersh teams entered Germany behind advancing Soviet troops to seek out Nazi officials. In early May 1945, Lt. Col. Ivan I. Klimenko, commander of the Smersh unit with the 79th Rifle Corps (3rd Shock Army) brought his men into the Reich Chancellery garden, the site of the Führerbunker, Hitler's underground headquarters. Klimenko—through the astute observations of another soldier, Ivan Churakov—found and took possession of the charred bodies of Adolf and Eva Hitler, as well as those of Josef and Magda Goebbels and their six children, who had been murdered by their mother. Smersh officials took charge of the interrogations and investigation (including autopsies) to ensure that the actual remains of Hitler had been found and not those of a double.

In *The Gulag Archipelago* (1973), novelist-historian Aleksandr Solzhenitsyn told of the authority of a

> State Security representative in the army—a SMERSH man, and a mere lieutenant; but the portly old colonel, the commander of the unit, stands up when you enter the room and tries to flatter you, to play up to you. He doesn't even have a drink with his chief of staff without inviting you to join them. The fact that you have only two tiny stars on your shoulder boards doesn't mean a thing; it is even amusing. After all, your stars have a very different weight and are measured on a totally different scale from those of ordinary officers. (On special assignments you are sometimes even authorized to wear major's insignia, for example, which is a sort of incognito, a convention.) You have a power over all the people in that military unit, or factory, or district, incomparably greater than that of the military commander, or factory director, or secretary of the district Communist Party.

Smersh's functions were taken over by the newly established MGB in 1946, becoming the Third Chief Directorate (counterintelligence) of that ministry.

One-time British intelligence officer IAN FLEMING later used an organization known as Smersh as the "bad guys" in some of his JAMES BOND novels.

Also see GRU.

Smith, Richard C.

(b. 1924)

Former enlisted man in the U.S. ARMY INTELLIGENCE AND SECURITY COMMAND (INSCOM) arrested for espionage, tried, and acquitted.

From 1973 to 1980, while attached to INSCOM, Smith worked on the U.S. DOUBLE AGENT program Royal Mitre, developing cover stories for them. He left the Army in 1980 and started a video production company in his home state of Utah. He had learned Japanese while in the Army, and in June 1981 he went to Tokyo as a representative of several American firms looking for Japanese investors.

Smith was arrested in April 1984 on charges of accepting $11,000 from a Soviet agent in payment for the identities of six U.S. double agents. Smith admitted taking the money but said that he had done so as part of a plot set up by the CIA to infiltrate the KGB with double agents.

After his arrest Smith told the FBI that in Tokyo two men approached him and identified themselves as CIA employees. Aware of his background, they asked him to help in a plan to penetrate the KGB through Tokyo. (Two years before, KGB Maj. STANISLAV LEVCHENKO had defected from the KGB RESIDENTURA in Tokyo and told the CIA about Soviet espionage activities in Japan.)

Smith said that the CIA operatives had instructed him to pose as an American businessman who, broke and dying of cancer, was willing to sell anything—including secrets he possessed—so that he could provide his widow and four children with a legacy. In fact, Smith did have four children and his video business was bankrupt by the time he carried out the plot by meeting with a KGB officer in Tokyo in 1982 and 1983.

After not hearing back from the CIA operatives, Smith told the FBI what he had done. After 10 months of questioning Smith intermittently, the FBI finally decided not to believe him. He was arrested and then indicted for espionage, largely on the basis of his own story.

The trial called for the use of the CLASSIFIED INFORMATION PROCEDURES ACT, which protects security information by allowing a judge to decide on ways to keep secrets out of trials. Smith, who said that the CIA had left him out in the cold, wanted classified documents for his defense that would prove his story. When the trial judge ruled that Smith could use certain classified information, the Department of Justice appealed to the Fourth U.S. Circuit Court of Appeals, which narrowed the amount of information that would be made available to Smith. The appellate court's ruling included footnotes that could not be made public because they contained classified information.

When Smith went on trial in April 1986, the judge ordered the government to produce a witness to clarify the CIA's involvement with Smith. The witness said that the CIA had no record of the men Smith allegedly met in Tokyo. But the jury believed Smith and acquitted him.

Smith, Gen. Walter Bedell

(b. 1895 d. 1961)

DIRECTOR OF CENTRAL INTELLIGENCE (DCI) from Oct. 1950 to Feb. 1953. Smith had served in World War II as chief of staff to Gen. of the Army Dwight D. Eisenhower, the Supreme Allied Commander in Europe.

Inevitably nicknamed "Beetle," Smith had a high school education when he entered the Indiana National Guard in 1910. He served as an infantry soldier in France with the 4th Division during World War I. Subsequently commissioned in 1917, he served as an INTELLIGENCE OFFICER and attended all major Army schools and colleges, returning to the Infantry School as an instructor. As a junior officer he was reassigned from the Army to the Bureau of the Budget for four and a half years, and also served as executive vice chairman of the board that completed the disposal of surplus World War I materials.

Smith quickly gained a reputation for harmoniously handling intricate and differing views of military and civilian leaders.

At the time of America's entry into World War II he was a brigadier general and the secretary of the Army's General Staff, a key position for an up-and-coming officer. Smith was appointed chief of staff to Lt. Gen. Eisenhower in Sept. 1942 as Eisenhower was planning the U.S.-British invasion of French North Africa. He remained with Eisenhower throughout the war, rising to the rank of lieutenant general. As Eisenhower's chief of staff he negotiated the Italian surrender in Sept. 1943 and the German surrender in May 1945. Eisenhower called Smith "the general manager of the war."

Eisenhower, in *Mandate for Change: 1952–1956* (1963), wrote of a conversation he had with British Prime Minister Winston Churchill:

> he expressed his admiration of the way Bedell Smith, my brilliant Chief of Staff in World War II, and I used to work together. He said that he had been in my headquarters on a day when Bedell was carrying on a heated argument with me, I not only allowed him to argue; I urged him to continue. The Prime Minister thought the incident a quite notable clash of views and men. But then, he said, I made a decision which settled the proposition and, to his amazement, Bedell's instant reaction was exactly as if he had got his own way—which he had not.

In 1946 Smith was in the process of taking over the operations division of the General Staff when he was appointed ambassador to the Soviet Union. He retained his military status and served in that position until March 1949.

He then became Commanding General of the First Army, with headquarters in New York City. Smith held that assignment only a few months. He was appointed DCI in Oct. 1950 by President Truman after the failure of U.S. intelligence to predict the North Korean assault on South Korea in June 1950. On July 1, 1951, while serving as DCI, Smith was promoted to full general.

HAROLD (KIM) PHILBY, a Soviet MOLE in British intelligence, wrote of Smith in *My Silent War* (1968):

> He had a cold, fishy eye and a precision-tool brain. At my first meeting with him, I had taken a document of twenty-odd paragraphs on Anglo-American war plans. . . . He had flipped over the pages casually and tossed it aside, then engaged me in close discussion of the subjects involved, referring from memory to the numbered paragraphs. I kept pace only because I had spent a whole morning learning the document by heart.

(Philby invariably and incorrectly called him "Bedell-Smith.")

Smith departed the CIA and retired from active duty in early 1953, when President Eisenhower appointed him Under Secretary of State, a position he held until 1954.

He wrote *Eisenhower's Six Great Decisions* (1956) and *My Three Years in Moscow* (1949), among other books.

Smudger

Intelligence slang for a photographer.

Snepp, Frank W.

CIA officer who, after two tours of duty in Southeast Asia, protested U.S. policy failures in the Vietnam War.

After earning a master's degree from Columbia University in 1965, majoring in Elizabethan literature, Snepp entered the CIA, apparently to avoid being drafted during the Vietnam War. Initially he was assigned as an analyst specializing in NORTH ATLANTIC TREATY ORGANIZATION affairs.

Some of Snepp's colleagues played a practical joke on him by volunteering him for assignment to the CIA station in Vietnam. Although he sought to avoid the assignment, he was warned that his refusal to go would jeopardize his career in the agency. He served in Vietnam from 1969 to 1971, preparing estimates and briefings as well as handling interrogations and informants.

He returned to CIA headquarters at LANGLEY, Va., where he served on the Vietnam Task Force, but was reportedly removed from that team for "political reasons." Snepp returned to Vietnam in 1972 for a second tour, as the senior analyst for the Saigon CIA post's indications analysis branch. He served there until the evacuation of the U.S. Embassy in April 1975.

Snepp was then sent to Thailand, where he debriefed journalists and refugees escaping from the communist takeover of South Vietnam. In Aug. 1975 he was recalled to CIA headquarters to be promoted and receive an award for his "analytical acuity" during the final weeks of the war.

Three weeks later Snepp resigned after futile attempts to develop an objective "after-action" report on the CIA's activities in Vietnam. Determined to produce an accurate record of CIA failures in Vietnam, he wrote *Decent Interval*, published in 1977 with the subtitle *An Insider's Account of Saigon's Indecent End Told by the CIA's Chief Strategy Analyst in Vietnam*. He was particularly critical of Secretary of State Henry Kissinger's highly secretive "virtuoso performance" in negotiating "peace" with the North Vietnamese. His 580-page tome also criticized Ambassador Graham Martin and other U.S. as well as Vietnamese officials.

The CIA argued that Snepp had violated his secrecy agreement with the agency and sued for the profits from the book. In 1980 the suit reached the Supreme Court, which decided in favor of the CIA. Snepp was forced to relinquish $140,000 in royalties from the book. He recounted his legal battle with the CIA in *Irreparable Harm* (1999)

Snepp was also required to submit his novel *Convergence of Interest* to the CIA for approval in 1980. The novel was about alleged CIA involvement in the assassination of President Kennedy. The CIA found no legal problems with what Snepp said in the novel except the use of the real name of a CIA officer, which Snepp had used along with the real identities of others. But when the agency asked him to delete the name of the man in question, Snepp countered that it had been taken from another book on the Kennedy assassination, *Legend: The Secret World of Lee Harvey Oswald* (1978) by Edward Jay Epstein. Snepp also said the AGENT had been named in other books, one written by a CIA agent and approved by the agency. After being advised of the prior publication of the name, the CIA withdrew its opposition, noting that the agent in question had "retired under cover." In the end, however, Snepp did use a pseudonym for the agent.

Snow, Operation

Reported Soviet intelligence operation in the summer of 1941 to force the U.S. government to take a hard line with Japan to evoke a Japanese-U.S. war. Such a conflict would divert Japanese attention from the USSR, which faced a crisis with Germany. (The crisis erupted into war with the German invasion of June 22, 1941; see BARBAROSSA.)

A key player in the Soviet effort was HARRY DEXTER WHITE, a Soviet AGENT OF INFLUENCE and an Assistant Secretary of Treasury. Herbert Romerstein and Eric Breindel in *The Venona Secrets* (2000) also named LAUCHLIN CURRIE, another Soviet AGENT, who touted his government colleagues with the claim that the U.S. State Department was going to sell China "down the river" if an ultimatum was not issued to Japan to stop aggression in China.

Former Soviet INTELLIGENCE OFFICER Vitali Pavlov revealed the first details of the operation in his Russian-language *Operatsia Sneg* [Operation Snow] (1966).

Sobell, Morton

(b. 1917)

Longtime friend of JULIUS ROSENBERG, a member of the ATOMIC SPY RING in New York City, and a co-defendant in the trial of Rosenberg and his wife, Ethel.

Sobell, like Julius and Ethel, was the son of Russian-Jewish immigrants to the United States. Classmates at City College of New York, Sobell and Rosenberg remained close friends after college. Beyond his undergraduate work, Sobell received an M.S. in electrical engineering from the University of Michigan.

He first came to the attention of U.S. COUNTERINTELLIGENCE officials in Jan. 1941, when he and Max Elitcher, both employees of the Navy Department, used Sobell's car to take people to and from an antidraft rally sponsored by the American Peace Mobilization Committee, an organization known to include many communists. Sobell soon left the Navy Department, going to work for a commercial firm, Reeves Instruments, but Elitcher continued to work for the Navy during World War II.

The FBI apparently next came across Sobell in 1948 when Elitcher and his wife, believing that they were under FBI SURVEILLANCE, went to the Sobell home in Queens, N.Y., on July 30 to spend the night. They were confident they had shaken the tail, but Sobell was furious and concerned. He told the visitors that he had some material for the Rosenbergs that was "too good to throw away," yet too dangerous to be kept in the house.

Sobell and Elitcher then drove into Manhattan and parked in a deserted waterfront area. Max waited in the car while Sobell walked to the nearby Rosenberg apartment carrying a can of 35mm film.

Nothing more happened to Sobell until July 1950 when Julius Rosenberg was arrested. Sobell and his family fled to Mexico. The FBI discovered the family at an apartment in Mexico City, but Morton was away, visiting Veracruz and Tampico in an attempt to find a freighter on which the family could travel to Eastern Europe without proper travel documents. He returned to his apartment on Aug. 16, and that evening Mexican security police arrested him as an undesirable alien.

On Aug. 18 Sobell was turned over to the FBI at the U.S.-Mexican border; the rest of his family was set free on the U.S. side. Although Sobell claimed that he and his family were on vacation in Mexico, documents found in his Mexican apartment revealed his plans to flee the country.

Sobell went on trial with the Rosenbergs and DAVID GREENGLASS in March 1951. Convicted, he was given a 30-year sentence. Several years later a further link was established when Reino Hayhanen, an assistant of RUDOLF ABEL, a Soviet ILLEGAL in New York City, defected to the West rather than return to the Soviet Union. Hayhanen revealed that in 1955 he had been sent to dig up a cache of $5,000 to give to Helen Sobell to cover legal costs. He did dig up the money, but kept it himself.

Helen Sobell was not accused in the spy ring case. But in *The FBI-KGB War* (1986), FBI agent ROBERT J. LAMPHERE and Tom Shachtman wrote: "The idea that Mrs. Sobell could be involved with the Soviets was debunked by Rosenberg case critics at the time, but was later confirmed by a fortuitous find of microfilm in an old wallet of Abel."

Sobell was initially sent to the penitentiary on Alcatraz Island in San Francisco Bay. He was subsequently transferred to the federal prison at Atlanta, Ga., where Abel was incarcerated. The two men became regular chess players, their games ending only when Abel was exchanged for U-2 pilot FRANCIS GARY POWERS in 1962.

Sobell, who was released from prison in Jan. 1969, always professed his innocence. NSA and FBI officials linked Sobell's name to CODE NAMES in VENONA intercepts of Soviet intelligence messages. But he still persisted in denying that he had ever spied. Sobell's wife, Helen, also claimed he was innocent and worked continually for his release. They were divorced in 1980. She died in 2002.

SOE

Special Operations Executive created by the British government on July 16, 1940, to undertake sabotage, subversion, and the formation of secret military forces in

German-occupied countries of Europe. It was a de facto intelligence-gathering agency in those occupied areas.

The SOE was strongly supported by Prime Minister Winston Churchill, who wanted a special force to "set Europe ablaze." The SOE was formed from three separate organizations already in existence in the summer of 1940: MI R of the War Office; Section D (sabotage) of MI6; and EH (Electra House), a propaganda group within the Foreign Office.

A highly secret agency, the SOE was placed under the COVER of the Ministry of Economic Warfare, which provided a useful location for handling information about enemy industry and other sabotage targets. Thus the Minister of Economic Warfare, Dr. Hugh Dalton, became de facto head of the SOE. Initially SOE was organized into three major sections: S01 dealt with propaganda, S02 with operations, and S03 with planning. After a year only S02 remained, becoming the basis for the SOE.

SOE operations were conducted in France, the Netherlands, Scandinavia, the Balkans, the Middle East, Africa, and the Far East. In Europe especially, as well as in some other areas, the SOE worked with the U.S. OFFICE OF STRATEGIC SERVICES (OSS). There was rivalry between the SOE and OSS in the Balkans, North Africa, and even France despite agreements between the two agencies on their respective areas of operations and responsibilities. The SOE was also plagued by petty jealousies and rivalry with MI6, which caused each agency to withhold information from the other, sometimes to the detriment (and death) of AGENTS in the field.

Probably the most disastrous SOE operation was in Holland, where the Germans found an attaché case abandoned by an MI6 agent that contained the names and addresses of all his Dutch associates. With this information and SOE's failure to follow radio-security procedures or to recognize warning signals from captured Dutch agents, the Germans succeeded in forcing Dutch operatives to work for them. As a result they captured the entire SOE underground network in Holland, seizing 51 SOE agents, nine MI6 agents, and one—Beatrix Terwindt—from MI9, the British office in charge of escape and evasion from German-controlled areas. Terwindt survived concentration camps; 47 of the others were shot. (See NORDPOL.)

Documents made public in 1998 showed that in 1944 the SOE seriously planned to assassinate Adolf Hitler, an idea that produced many plans and much debate. Plots included poisoning his milk or apple juice, blowing up his train, or having a sniper kill him on his morning walk at Berchtesgaden, his mountain retreat. The debate over the assassination dragged on until Hitler settled the matter himself by committing suicide in his Berlin bunker on April 30, 1945.

The SOE attempted to work with Soviet forces, and SOE planning for operations in the Soviet Union began in late 1940 in anticipation of a German invasion. After the German assault took place in June 1941, a British SOE mission to Moscow in Sept. 1941 established a mutual formal liaison with the NKVD stipulating that neither agency would conduct subversive operations in each other's territory (including the British Commonwealth and mandated territories). The British were to parachute Soviet agents into Europe in a series of operations. (See MAMBA). But the NKVD provided little help in carrying out a plan to suborn Russians who had been forced to serve in the German Army and had been recaptured by the Soviets. The SOE went ahead with these operations in Europe without Soviet approval, using Russians who were recaptured by British forces.

Soviet hostility toward the SOE (as well as the OSS) intensified from 1944 onward because of perceived SOE inefficiency as well as Soviet suspicion of SOE activities in areas considered within the Soviet sphere of influence. There were, however, several examples of successful cooperation between the SOE and NKVD, especially in Afghanistan and Yugoslavia.

Assessing the SOE's contribution to the war, historian M. R. D. Foot wrote in SOE (1984,) that SOE "did divert enemy attention away from the main fighting fronts towards their own rear areas. Hitler himself is said at one time to have spent—it might be fairer to say, to have wasted—about an hour every midday (considering the last twenty-four hours' ABWEHR and SD reports on suspected SOE activities." And, he added, "By its examples, it has enriched the human stock of brave and noble ways to behave."

At the end of the war the SOE developed extensive plans to participate in the soon-to-be-called Cold War, but the agency was disbanded in early 1946. SOE strength peaked at about 13,000 men and women, both military and civilian. The SOE had three operational heads:

Aug. 1940–May 1942	Sir Frank Nelson
May. 1942–Sept. 1943	Sir Charles Hambro
Sept. 1943–Jan. 1946	Maj.-Gen. Sir Colin Gubbins

Also see VERA ATKINS.

SOG

SEE SPECIAL OPERATIONS GROUP

Sokolov, Aleksandr

(b. 1919)

Soviet spy who was deported, along with his wife, from the United States in Oct. 1964.

Sokolov and his wife were charged with conspiring to commit espionage in the United States from 1957 to 1963 by attempting to collect intelligence on U.S. missile sites, nuclear weapons, and other military activities. They pleaded not guilty to the charges. The U.S. government decided not to prosecute because of concerns that SENSITIVE information would be made public in a trial.

One of the principal witnesses against the Sokolovs was KAARLO RUDOLPH TUOMI, a DOUBLE AGENT working for the FBI.

Sokolov, a Soviet citizen, asked to be deported to Czechoslovakia rather than to the Soviet Union. The U.S. government acceded to his request.

Solo

CODE NAME for a longtime COUNTERINTELLIGENCE operation conducted by the FBI against the U.S. Communist Party. (See CPUSA.)

From the mid-1950s until about 1977 two brothers, Jack and Morris Childs, were trusted members of the U.S. Communist Party, carrying cash from Moscow to the United States to finance the party, meeting Soviet leaders Nikita Khrushchev and Leonid Brezhnev, and conveying their Cold War attitudes toward the United States. At the same time, the Childs brothers were informers for the FBI.

Ukrainian-born Morris Childs joined the American Communist Party in 1921 and was sent to the Lenin School in Moscow for training as an AGENT in the espionage underground that Soviet intelligence was running in the United States. In 1932 Morris's younger brother, Jack, became the business manager of the Young Communist League and was also sent to Moscow for training. Later Morris became the Moscow correspondent for *The Daily Worker,* the newspaper published by the U.S. Communist Party.

After a hiatus during the 1940s, in 1954 Morris Childs returned to the communist underground. One of his duties was getting money from Moscow to U.S. communists. From about that time, however, Morris and Jack Childs were working for the FBI.

The brothers reported to the FBI that Stanley Levison, a close adviser to civil rights leader Dr. Martin Luther King, Jr., was a communist. Armed with this information, ,J. EDGAR HOOVER, director of the FBI, began his campaign to discredit King and privately spread the word to U.S. officials that King had communist ties.

The first authoritative information on the Solo operation came in *The FBI and Martin Luther King Jr.: From 'Solo' to Memphis* (1981) by historian David J. Garrow. More details came in *Operation Solo* (1996) by JOHN BARRON, an author well connected to FBI sources. Barron said that Morris Childs had a close relationship with YURI ANDROPOV, then head of the KGB and later the head of the Soviet Union. Barron also said that the brothers were sent on missions to Cuban leader Fidel Castro and China's Mao Zedong.

Morris Childs reported that he had witnessed meetings about the widening split between the Soviet Union and the People's Republic of China. By getting such inside information through Solo, U.S. officials had more knowledge about the Soviet-China breach than historians had previously believed.

Sombolay, Specialist 4th Class Albert T.

U.S. soldier convicted of espionage and aiding the enemy by passing information to Iraqis and Jordanians to support the "Arab cause."

Born in Zaire, Africa, Sombolay became a U.S. citizen in 1978 and enlisted in the U.S. Army in 1985. In Dec. 1990, while assigned to the 8th Infantry Division in Baumholder, Germany, he contacted the Iraqi and Jordanian embassies. (Iraq had invaded Kuwait in Aug. 1990 and Operation Desert Shield, prelude to the full-scale Gulf War, had begun.)

Sombolay passed information on U.S. troop readiness to the Jordanian Embassy in Brussels and promised to provide videotapes of U.S. weapons and plans. More information, he said, would be delivered when his unit was deployed to Saudi Arabia. He made a similar offer to the Iraqi Embassy in Bonn, Germany, but got no response.

On Dec. 29, his unit was deployed as part of Desert Shield, but he remained in Germany and kept trying to contact Iraqis. He also handed over to a Jordanian AGENT a chemical-warfare suit, boots, and gloves, along with decontamination gear.

ARMY INTELLIGENCE learned of his activities in ways not disclosed. In July 1991 he pleaded guilty to espionage and aiding the enemy before a military judge in Baumholder, West Germany. He was sentenced to confinement at hard labor for 34 years.

Sonia

SEE URSULA KUCZYNSKI

Sorge, Richard

(b. 1895 d. 1944)

Highly successful Soviet spy whose reports from Japan permitted the shift of major Soviet military forces from the Far East to help stop the German advances of 1941–1942.

Born in Russia to a German father and Russian mother, Sorge received a doctorate in political science from the University of Hamburg. He served in the German Army in World War I and was wounded three times. Sorge became a communist in 1920 and began working for the GRU in Germany in the late 1920s with the COVER of a teacher. After serving in Moscow from 1924 to 1927, he was sent to Scandinavia (1927), the United States (1928), Britain (1929), and Shanghai (1930). There he met another Soviet spy, URSULA KUCZYNSKI.

Under the cover of a correspondent for a German magazine, Sorge then served as a Soviet spy in Japan from Sept. 1933 until his arrest in Oct. 1941. As the Tokyo correspondent of the *Frankfurter Zeitung,* Germany's most respected newspaper, and two other German publications, he infiltrated the German Embassy in Tokyo, the Japanese General Staff, and even the imperial family to collect valuable military and POLITICAL INTELLIGENCE. He also sought to persuade the Japanese to avoid war with the Soviet Union.

He was able to inform the Soviets in 1941 that the Japanese planned to move south (toward the Dutch Indies and French Indochina). With this knowledge, Soviets were able to shift military forces from the Far East to the German front confident that the Japanese would not launch an attack to support the German invasion of European Russia.

Sorge's principal Japanese collaborator was HOZUMI OZAKI, an adviser to the Japanese premier, who gained information using his access to classified information on military and government policies. Ozaki said that he had become a traitor to save Japan, which "had to be reconstructed as a socialist state." He saw himself helping Sorge to prevent Japan from attacking and destroying the Soviet Union. (Ozaki was raised and educated in Taiwan. He learned English at special schools and turned to Marxism in 1923 to find out more about politics, social problems, and minorities. AGNES SMEDLEY had introduced Ozaki to Sorge in Shanghai in 1930.)

The Sorge spy ring was discovered by accident as Japanese COUNTERESPIONAGE efforts focused on locating communists were led to Sorge although he had a strong anti-Soviet reputation. Both Sorge and Ozaki were arrested on Oct. 16, 1941, tried, and hanged on Nov. 7, 1944. Sorge was posthumously given the Hero of the Soviet Union award and was honored by a Soviet POSTAGE STAMP.

Sorge used the cover names Johnson in China and Ramsey in Japan.

SORM

INTERNET SURVEILLANCE operation used in by the Russian Federal Security Service (FSB).

SORM (Sistema Operativno-Rozysknykh Meropriyatii, or System of Ensuring Investigative Activity) began in 1995 when the government gave the FSB the right to monitor telecommunications. The Internet was added in 1998 by SORM-2, whose regulations called for Internet service providers to install, at their own expense, a special device that could track credit card transactions and e-mail messages. The device also allowed a Web site to be monitored without the user's knowledge. The service providers send the retrieved data directly to the FSB.

President VLADIMIR PUTIN authorized the use of SORM not only by the FSB but also by seven other federal security agencies, including the tax police and interior ministry police. Officially, the FSB and other agencies would need a warrant to read any of the Internet material. But human-rights critics do not believe that the eavesdroppers would be that scrupulous.

Russian government officials compared SORM to the U.S. NSA eavesdropping system known as ECHELON. But Jim Dempsey, senior counsel at the Center for Democracy and Technology in Washington, D.C., disagreed. "Echelon and its allied systems in the UK, Canada, Australia and New Zealand," he said, "take the technology as it finds it—that is, Echelon is not coercive. It does not rely upon government-mandated surveillance features being built into telecom systems. With SORM-2, Russia is going farther than any other democratic country in controlling the design of private-sector communications systems for surveillance purposes."

SOSS

SEE SOVIET OCEAN SURVEILLANCE SYSTEM

SOSUS

SEE SOUND SURVEILLANCE SYSTEM

Souers, Rear Adm. William H.

(b. 1892 d. 1973)

First U.S. DIRECTOR OF CENTRAL INTELLIGENCE (DCI), appointed on Jan. 23, 1946, the day after President Truman signed the presidential directive establishing the CENTRAL INTELLIGENCE GROUP. Souers was DCI only until June 1946.

Souers, a 1914 graduate of Miami University of Ohio, had a successful career in mortgages, securities, and investments. In April 1929 he was appointed a lieutenant commander in the Naval Reserve and remained on inactive status as an INTELLIGENCE OFFICER until 1940. He was then called to active duty and assigned to the district intelligence office at Great Lakes, Ill. He had other intelligence assignments at the naval district headquarters in Charleston, S.C., and San Juan, P.R.

In July 1944 Souers reported to the Office of the Chief of Naval Operations in Washington, D.C., as assistant chief of NAVAL INTELLIGENCE in charge of plans. Souers was promoted to rear admiral in 1945. During this period he also served as representative of the Secretary of the Navy on the government committee studying the formation of a central intelligence organization.

Truman, with great interest, personally reviewed the proposals for a central intelligence service. "My inclination was to favor the plan worked out by the Army and the Navy, with the aid of Adm. Souers, and I was ready to put it into effect," he wrote in his memoir *Years of Trial and Hope: 1946–1952* (1956).

Although Souers wished to return to his business career, Truman persuaded him not to, recalling, "I assured him that as soon as the Army, Navy, and State Departments would agree upon a candidate acceptable to me I would release him." The CENTRAL INTELLIGENCE GROUP—immediate predecessor of the CIA—came into being on Jan. 22, 1946. Souers was formally appointed the following day, and two days later Truman invited Souers to the White House to present him with his "badges of office"—a black cloak and wooden dagger. (See CLOAK AND DAGGER.)

Souers supervised the establishment of the Central Intelligence Group, with the President and his chief of staff, Fleet Adm. William D. Leahy, taking a personal interest in the new service.

After five months as DCI, Souers briefly returned to private life. However, at the request of the newly established Atomic Energy Commission he conducted an extensive survey of intelligence requirements for the commission. In Sept. 1947 President Truman appointed Souers the first executive secretary of the new NATIONAL SECURITY COUNCIL, a position he held until Jan. 1950. Upon leaving the council he became a special consultant to the President on national security matters while returning to his business career. He retired from the Naval Reserve on Jan. 1, 1953. Souers continued to be involved in national security matters; speaking out during the communist-hunting McCarthy era, he warned that the Subversives Control Act and the wave of anticommunism sweeping the country contained "the seeds of danger." Souers said that unconstrained and indiscriminate anticommunist activities could be as dangerous to American liberties as anything the communists could do.

Sound Surveillance System

(SOSUS)

U.S. seafloor acoustic detection system for detecting SUBMARINES. During much of the Cold War the U.S. Navy operated SOSUS arrays in various parts of the Atlantic and Pacific, as well as across the Strait of Gibraltar and off the North Cape (north of Norway). SOSUS is used to detect transiting submarines and, in wartime, would be used to direct Allied air, surface, and submarine forces to underwater targets. However, the SOSUS arrays are vulnerable to active and passive (jamming) attacks by hostile naval and, possibly, merchant forces.

During World War II the U.S., British, and Soviet navies installed limited-capability acoustic arrays on the ocean floor in shallow waters, especially near harbors. Immediately after the war the U.S. Navy began a major development program of deep-ocean arrays. By 1948 arrays were being tested at sea, and by 1951 the first SOSUS arrays were being implanted at sea. Also termed Project Caesar, the first set of operational hydrophones was installed at Sandy Hook, N.J., south of Manhattan, followed in 1952 by a deep-water (1,200-foot) installation off Eleuthera, in the Bahamas. That year the Chief of Naval Operations directed the establishment of six arrays in the western Atlantic, all to be ready by the end of 1956. The first arrays in the Pacific were operational in 1958. Installations in other areas followed, especially the Norwegian Sea area. (The locations of U.S. SOSUS arrays were eventually identified in Soviet magazines.)

Initially a number of Naval Facilities (NAVFACs) were established as the shore terminals for SOSUS; these were located along both U.S. coasts and in the Caribbean, Iceland, and Japan as well as at other overseas locations. Subsequently, the seafloor hydrophones have been replaced, and the NAVFACs in the United States and Caribbean have been consolidated as more capable arrays and computers have been developed.

The SOSUS system and surface ships fitted with the Surveillance Towed-Array Surveillance System (SURTASS) are linked with the so-called Integrated Undersea Surveillance System (IUSS). Acoustic data from the NAVFACs

and Regional Evaluation Centers (REQ are provided through the Ocean Surveillance Information System (OSIS) to the Atlantic, Pacific, and European area Fleet Command Centers (FCC) and to the Naval Ocean Surveillance Information Center (NOSIC), in Suitland, Md., near Washington, D.C., as well as to national command centers.

Published sources cite SOSUS detection ranges of "hundreds" of miles. An improved SOSUS-type system known as the Fixed Distributed System (FDS) is under development. This system is intended to detect quiet, deep-running Russian submarines. A shallow-water FDS variant is being developed, with greater emphasis on fiber optics than SOSUS-type systems, and possible integration of nonacoustic sensors.

The Advanced Deployable System (ADS) is also being developed. ADS is intended to provide an undersea surveillance system to detect diesel-electric submarines operating in shallow waters, observe mine-laying activity, and track surface contacts. The system will operate directly with tactical forces (ships and aircraft). During a crisis or conflict ADS is to be deployed within 10 days to the operational area.

In the late 1960s then Secretary of Defense Robert S. McNamara first publicly acknowledged the existence of SOSUS.

The Soviet Navy had employed limited seafloor acoustic systems to detect submarines since World War II, when hydrophones were planted near harbor entrances and across bays to detect German U-boats. The Soviets deployed a modern acoustic detection system with planar arrays in the Pacific near the Soviet landmass where surveillance of a broad area is desired. This project was called Cluster Lance by the NORTH ATLANTIC TREATY ORGANIZATION. The Soviets may also have deployed barrier arrays at points of ingress and egress from their strategic missile submarine operating areas in the Barents, Greenland, and Kara Seas, placed in or near trenches at choke points along the polar archipelago. These arrays were to serve as choke point "trip wires" to detect Western attack submarines and were not for long-range surveillance (as is the U.S. SOSUS system). However, the lack of fixed, long-range acoustic systems has forced the Soviets to rely largely on ship and aircraft acoustic detection for open-ocean search. (SATELLITES may also be used for submarine detection.)

When the Cold War ended, some SOSUS hydrophone arrays in both the Atlantic and Pacific were shut down. The North Pacific SOSUS was used by biologists for listening to marine mammals' low-frequency vocalizations.

Souther, Glenn M.

(b. 1957 d. 1989)

U.S. Navy enlisted man who spied for the Soviet Union. Souther, a Navy photographer with a TOP SECRET clearance, had access, according to the Soviets, to "the most secure and valuable documents disclosing plans of the U.S. Navy's operations in a nuclear war . . ."

Souther enlisted in the Navy in 1976 and later said he had begun spying for the Soviets in 1980. He was a WALK-IN: He went to the Soviet Embassy in Rome and offered to become a spy. In 1982 his estranged Italian-born wife told an agent of the NAVAL CRIMINAL INVESTIGATIVE SERVICE (then NIS) that she believed her husband was a Soviet spy. The NIS agent dismissed her report as the ravings of a vengeful woman with a marital problem.

Souther's active duty in the Navy ended in 1982, but he remained in the reserve. His weekend-a-month reserve service was in the public affairs office of the Naval Air Station in Norfolk, Va. There he attended Old Dominion University, majoring in Russian. In 1983 the DEFENSE INVESTIGATIVE SERVICE began a background investigation of Souther to upgrade his security clearance to top secret. In Dec. 1984, soon after getting the new clearance, he began working in the FLEET INTELLIGENCE CENTER EUROPE AND ATLANTIC, where he gained access to SENSITIVE COMPARTMENTED INFORMATION, PHOTOGRAPHIC INTELLIGENCE, and SIGNALS INTELLIGENCE.

In 1985, after the arrest of Navy Warrant Officer JOHN WALKER, a naval officer who had married Souther's ex-wife again reported suspicions about Souther. But NIS officials decided that, since Souther was a civilian, the investigation should be handled by the FBI. The FBI office in Norfolk, which had orchestrated the arrest of Walker, filed away the Souther report for eight months.

On May 21, 1986, two FBI agents asked Souther whether he had had any contact with any hostile intelligence service. He said he had not. On June 9 he flew to Rome and vanished. On July 17 the Soviet newspaper *Izvestia* reported that he was in Moscow and had been granted political asylum. Two days later he appeared on Soviet television and announced his decision to change his life. He did not admit that he had been a spy.

On June 27, 1989, the Red Army paper *Krasnaya zvezda* reported that Mikhail Yevgenyevich Orlov, a 32-year-old Soviet intelligence officer, had died. The obituary, which lauded Orlov for "working for a better future for all mankind," referred to Orlov by another name: Glenn Michael Souther.

The Russian use of a different name for Souther prompted speculation in Western intelligence circles that he had been a longtime plant—a Soviet citizen posing as an American. Some officials had suspected that the Soviets sometimes selected children or teenagers to become spies in the United States, raising them in a KGB facility that simulated a U.S. community. But VLADIMIR KRYUCHKOV, chief of the KGB, later said at a news conference in Moscow that Souther was an American recruited while he was in the Navy. Kryuchkov also said Souther killed himself because "his nervous system could not stand the pressure" of his dual life. He supposedly asked to be buried in a KGB uniform—he was a KGB major. The ceremony, with full military honors, was conducted at Novokuntsevskoye Cemetery, near Moscow, where HAROLD (KIM) PHILBY, the British spy, was buried. Souther left a Russian wife and an 18-month-old daughter.

Soviet Ocean Surveillance System

(SOSS)

A worldwide SURVEILLANCE system established by the Soviet Union during the 1960s to keep track of Western warships, especially U.S. aircraft carriers—and eventually submarines. The Soviet Ocean Surveillance System was the principal means of keeping track of Soviet and foreign naval and air forces. It was fed by a variety of surveillance and RECONNAISSANCE activities, among them the Navy's operating forces (aircraft, surface ships, and submarines) and specialized intelligence collection activities.

The principal contributors to SOSS were aircraft, radio intercepts, SATELLITES, surface ships, submarines, and spies—AGENTS of both the KGB and GRU. The Soviet space stations of the SALYUT and MIR programs may also have had an input to the SOSS. The aircraft were primarily the long-range BEAR-D, which flew from bases in the Soviet Union and, beginning in 1970, also from Cuba, with some flights stopping at Conakry, before crossing the Atlantic to Cuba.

In addition to naval ships, SOSS used information obtained from the state-owned and centrally controlled merchant and fishing fleets, and especially from the large Soviet research fleets. The last consisted of ships and aircraft engaged in academic oceanographic and polar research, which supports the nation's civilian and military space and atmospheric research programs.

The information collected by the various components of SOSS was correlated at command centers in the four fleet headquarters—Northern (Arctic), Baltic, Pacific, and Black Sea—and at naval headquarters in Moscow. These centers had hardened, highly survivable communication facilities with alternative facilities ready to serve as a backup, ensuring the rapid intake of intelligence data and the rapid outflow of directions to fleet and tactical commanders. Although Soviet tactics were highly dependent upon communications, after the outbreak of hostilities it was possible that Soviet forces would be less dependent than Western naval forces on command direction because of the Soviets' relatively rigid doctrine and tactics.

In addition to these fixed facilities, several cruisers and several submarine tenders were fitted with command and control systems to process and employ the products of SOSS.

Some portions of SOSS have survived the end of the Cold War, especially satellite reconnaissance systems.

Also see RADAR OCEAN RECONNAISSANCE SATELLITE.

Soviet Union

SEE RUSSIA-USSR

Spann, (Johnny) Michael

(b. 1969 d. 2001)

CIA officer who was the first American known to be killed in combat against Taliban forces in Afghanistan.

Spann, a member of the CIA's elite SPECIAL ACTIVITIES DIVISION, was questioning Taliban prisoners at a prison fortress in Mazar-i Sharif on Nov. 25, 2001, when an uprising began. The prisoners, who had smuggled guns and grenades into the prison, attacked soldiers of the Northern Alliance and their American allies. Spann and another CIA officer began firing and tried to fight their way out of the prison. The other officer escaped but Spann was fatally wounded. The men were able to alert outside forces. The prison battle raged for three days.

Spann, who had previously served as an officer in the U.S. Marine Corps, joined the CIA in 1999 and had been in Afghanistan for six weeks.

Special Access Program

U.S. intelligence term for a program established to control access and distribution and to provide protection for particularly SENSITIVE information that requires controls beyond that required for CONFIDENTIAL, SECRET, or TOP SECRET material.

There are strict restrictions on who can authorize a special access program.

Special Activities Division

CIA paramilitary organization primarily designed for work in TERRORIST INTELLIGENCE.

The unit's existence became known in the fall of 2001, when U.S. SPECIAL OPERATIONS FORCES arrived in Afghanistan to hunt down al Qaeda leaders and aid the Northern Alliance against the troops of the ruling Taliban. The CIA paramilitary teams, working with the Special Operations Forces and the Afghans, provided intelligence for U.S. air strikes. Among their weapons was the PREDATOR, an unmanned surveillance aircraft that the Air Force and CIA armed with Hellfire missiles. (See UNMANNED AERIAL VEHICLES.)

MICHAEL SPANN, the first American known to be killed in combat in Afghanistan, is believed to have been a member of Special Activities Division (SAD) team. Like other team members, he was heavily armed but did not wear a uniform with insignia. SAD operatives fight in small teams—typically, six men with military training and knowledge of foreign languages.

The Predator that killed al Qaeda leaders in Yemen in Nov. 2002 was probably operated by a SAD team.

Specialist

FBI term for an employee trained for SURVEILLANCE operations. Specialists are not FBI agents, whose law-enforcement status gives them the power to arrest. Typically, specialists tail suspects, or "persons of interest," videotaping them in some operations. Their work is similar to that of British WATCHERS.

Special Branch

Scotland Yard department that conducts police work for British intelligence agencies, especially MI5. Members of the Special Branch carry out SURVEILLANCE, arrest suspects, and testify at their trials. MI5 does not have arrest powers and, to keep its officers' identities secret, rarely allows them to testify at trial. As a police agency, the Special Branch also protects foreign dignitaries and, in cooperation with MI5, watches for would-be terrorists and assassins.

Special Collection Service

Elite, highly secret U.S. ELECTRONIC INTELLIGENCE group that conducts eavesdropping operations in hostile countries. Members of the group, which includes specialists from the NSA, usually serve under diplomatic COVER, setting up highly sensitive electronic equipment in the U.S. Embassy or theoretically safe buildings in the TARGET country. The service is controlled by the NSA, which provides the equipment and backup personnel. CIA experts are also often assigned to the service.

"It's the black-bag, breaking-and-entering, Mission Impossible–type agency," says John Pike, an intelligence analyst.

In a typical operation, a Special Collection Service team uses highly sensitive equipment to listen in on communications, including conversations, emanating from a specific TARGET, which could be a government office or a terrorist headquarters. The work is so sensitive that very little is known about the unit. Even the training site is highly classified. There is no public record of the unit's achievements, but it is highly regarded in the U.S. INTELLIGENCE COMMUNITY.

Special Compartmented Intelligence

SEE SENSITIVE COMPARTMENTED INFORMATION

Special Group (Augmented)

(SGA)

White House committee that ran a U.S. campaign to overthrow Cuban leader Fidel Castro.

In Nov. 1961 President Kennedy approved a COVERT ACTION sabotage and subversion project with the CODE NAME MONGOOSE and created a cabinet-level committee, known as the Special Group (Augmented), to control the project.

Never before had a covert action project had such high-level control. The White House group included Secretary of Defense Robert S. McNamara; U.S. Attorney General Robert Kennedy, the President's brother; Secretary of State Dean Rusk; and Gen. Maxwell D. Taylor, the President's military adviser, who was chairman. Also in the SGA were JOHN A. MCCONE, newly named DIRECTOR OF CENTRAL INTELLIGENCE; McGeorge Bundy, the national security adviser; Under Secretary of State U. Alexis Johnson; Deputy Secretary of Defense Roswell Gilpatric; and Gen. Lyman L. Lemnitzer, Chairman of the Joint Chiefs of Staff. The SGA secretary was Tom Parrott, a CIA officer who occasionally fed what he knew back to that agency.

The operational director of Mongoose was Maj. Gen. EDWARD LANSDALE, an expert on insurgency, who reported to the SGA. Mongoose activities centered on Miami and were code-named Task Force W, under WILLIAM K. HARVEY, a CIA veteran.

The SGA was to meet 42 times from when was it was formed until Oct. 1962, when the CUBAN MISSILE CRISIS abruptly ended Operation Mongoose. At an SGA meeting in Dean Rusk's office on Aug. 10, the Kennedy administration's most secret plan—the assassination of Castro—came up when McNamara raised the idea as a possibility, not knowing that such a plan was already in existence. He was admonished by Edward R. Murrow, the director of the U.S. Information Agency, who had been invited to the meeting. McCone later phoned McNamara and told him that such talk was not appropriate.

Information about this meeting—and about the SGA and Mongoose—emerged from the CHURCH COMMITTEE investigation into CIA abuses of power.

Special Intelligence

(SI)

U.S. COMPARTMENTED intelligence, primarily dealing with SIGNALS INTELLIGENCE.

Special Liaison Unit

(SLU)

U.S. and British units established during World War II at major forward commands to provide special handling of ULTRA and, subsequently, MAGIC decrypts.

The SLUs were conceived by Group Capt. F. W. WINTERBOTHAM. He explained in *The Ultra Secret* (1974):

I pointed out that there would have to be very strict rules as to the number of people who could know the existence of this information and perhaps, on a more delicate footing, rules for those in receipt of the information, to ensure that they did not take any action which would either arouse enemy suspicions or confirm his fears that the Allied commander had any pre-knowledge of his plans. This one, I knew, was a hard one to put over to a commander-in-chief. In some circumstances it might be very tempting to make a quick but tell-tale *coup*.

The head of the individual SLU had authority from the highest U.S. and British military commanders to enforce this policy. The SLU officer was personally responsible for delivering an Ultra/Magic message to the senior commander or a specific individual on his staff designated to receive it. After the message was read it was taken back by the SLU officer and destroyed.

The SLUs communicated with BLETCHLEY PARK in England, with ARLINGTON HALL outside Washington, D.C., and with various NAVY COMMUNICATIONS INTELLIGENCE facilities, using ONE-TIME PADS and the U.S. SIGABA and British TYPEX machines. These cipher transmissions were never "read" by the Germans or Japanese, with the possible exception of some minor Typex transmissions.

The SLUs were so efficient that Prime Minister Winston Churchill began using them for his own communications when maximum secrecy was useful, such as in discussions of personalities. Similarly, in Dec. 1944, when there were serious disagreements between Gen. of the Army Dwight D. Eisenhower and Field Marshal Bernard L. Montgomery, the SLU communications link was used to transmit Eisenhower's personal message to Churchill stating that Eisenhower was prepared to tell his boss, Gen. of the Army George C. Marshall, that it was either "him or Montgomery."

Winterbotham had responsibility for establishing and monitoring the SLUs through the Allied operational areas.

Special Operations Executive

SEE SOE

Special Operations Forces

(SOF)

Term used for military units that are trained for clandestine entry into an area to carry out acts of sabotage, intelligence collection, and other "unconventional" missions. Special Operations Forces personnel usually undergo rigorous physical training and are expected to "live off the land" in certain situations. They can be introduced into a hostile area by helicopter, parachute from conventional aircraft, small boats, or SUBMARINES.

In the United States each service has its own Special Forces personnel: Green Berets and Delta Team (Army), the latter especially trained for hostage rescue; SEALs (Navy), for Sea-Air-Land operations; and Special Operations Command (Air Force). Those units were mostly established during the Vietnam War, in large part at the impetus of President John F. Kennedy. There is an increasing interest in SOF units by officials concerned with terrorist attacks. (See TERRORIST INTELLIGENCE.)

U.S. Special Forces joined with CIA teams in covert operations during the Vietnam War and for anti-drug operations in Colombia. The U.S. invasion of Afghanistan in 2001 was led by Special Forces units and armed CIA operatives. One of the early U.S. casualties was CIA paramilitary officer (JOHNNY) MICHAEL SPANN, who was killed on Nov. 25, 2001, while interrogating prisoners during a firefight that broke out a prison fortress in Mazar-i Sharif. See SPECIAL ACTIVITIES DIVISION.

The British Special Air Service (Army) and Special Boat Service (Royal Marines) are among the most renowned SOF units. Formed in World War II, those clandestine units served throughout the Cold War in British territories around the world, especially in Northern Ireland in a secret war against the Irish Republican Army (IRA). In a dramatic and televised assault on Iranian Embassy in London on May 5, 1980, an SAS force ended a siege, killing five Iranian gunmen and capturing a sixth; 19 hostages were freed but one died and two were injured in the cross fire. Also highly publicized was the role of the SAS and SBS in the Falklands War in 1982. Reportedly, an SAS team was landed in Argentina by helicopter to report on aircraft operations, while an SBS team was put into the frozen wastelands of South Georgia by helicopter.

U.S. and probably British special forces were inserted into Iraq before conventional forces attacked in the Gulf Wars of 1991 and 2003, and into Afghanistan in 2001.

Under the Soviet regimen the USSR organized a large SPETSNAZ (an abbreviation for Chasti Spetsial'nogo Naznacheniya) special operations force that included air, naval, and ground components. Unlike Western special forces, the Spetsnz organization is controlled by MILITARY INTELLIGENCE (GRU). While details of Spetsnaz operations during the Cold War are sketchy, a Spetsnaz storming of a Moscow theatre in Oct. 2002 was seen on television around the world. After pumping a vast amount of incapacitating gas through the theater's ventilation system, about 200 Spetsnaz soldiers, masked and heavily armed, entered the theater, where they shot and killed about 50 Chechens holding hostages. The gas killed more than 100 spectators.

Many other nations also have Special Forces. Most of those units now have the role of hostage rescue and counter-terrorist operations as well as intelligence collection and "smash and grab" roles.

Special Reporting Facility

(SRF)

Euphemism for CIA personnel reporting to Department of State activities. They are usually INTELLIGENCE OFFICERS operating under COVER at U.S. embassies.

Special Security Officer

Individual in a U.S. government or commercial organization who manages the handling of documents and other materials of a SPECIAL ACCESS PROGRAM. He or she is also responsible for the SENSITIVE COMPARTMENTED INFORMATION FACILITY.

Special Tasks

Russian intelligence term for assassinations, kidnappings, murders, and sabotage operations. An NKVD group was organized specifically for carrying out special tasks about 1936 by NIKOLAY YEZHOV; similarly, on July 5,

1941, an NKVD Administration for Special Tasks was set up for espionage operations against Germany and its allies.

See PAVEL SUDOPLATOV.

S.P.E.C.T.R.E.

The Special Executor for Counter-Intelligence, Terrorism, Revenge, and Extortion, a huge, multinational criminal organization found in several JAMES BOND [F] spy novels and MOVIES.

Conceived by IAN FLEMING, S.P.E.C.T.R.E. originally stood for Special Executive for Terrorism, Revolution, and Espionage. It would be the COVER for Bond's villains—former SMERSH, GESTAPO, Mafia, and Black Tong of Peking AGENTS, and, later, members of the Baader-Meinhof gang. The organization first appeared in *Dr. No* (1958).

With headquarters in Paris, S.P.E.C.T.R.E. also had a sun-drenched island for training its operatives (actually at Pinewood Studios in England).

Speculatores

Intelligence collection officials established in the Roman legions at the time of Gaius Julius Caesar (100–44 B.C.). Each legion of 1,000 men was assigned ten speculators.

The establishment of the speculatores was the first known instance of intelligence personnel appearing in a military staff organization. By the time of Caesar the art of war had progressed sufficiently for military commanders to be able to differentiate between intelligence and operational functions.

Spetsnaz

Abbreviation for Chasti Spetsial'nogo Naznacheniya, Soviet-Russian special forces that are similar to the U.S. SPECIAL OPERATIONS FORCES. Spetsnaz special warfare forces are controlled by the Main Intelligence Directorate (GRU) of the Russian General Staff. But the Soviet KGB had responsibility for the planning and operations of those groups in peacetime, a responsibility passed to the FSK, the Russian Federal Security Service.

The term Spetsnaz was used during World War II to designate NKVD-NKGB-GRU special units that operated behind the German lines. Their activities included intelligence collection (including the capture of prisoners), attacks on German transportation and supply lines, assassination of collaborators, the spread of propaganda to local populations, and support for partisan units.

Spetsnaz forces conduct reconnaissance and special warfare missions in "peacetime" as well as in war. Peacetime operations, such as the assassination of Afghanistan's president in Dec. 1979, were under the direction of the KGB.

By the late 1980s several Spetsnaz brigades of approximately 1,000 men were assigned to each of the four groups of forces in Europe, as well as to several of the major military districts. A naval Spetsnaz brigade was assigned to each of the four Soviet fleets. The naval brigades had combat swimmers as well as parachutists. Their training included parachuting, scuba diving, demolition, sabotage, SURVEILLANCE, and TARGET selection, as well as languages.

According to GRU defector VIKTOR SUVOROV there were 20 Spetsnaz brigades plus 41 separate companies. Thus, total strength of Spetsnaz forces in the 1980s could have been on the order of 30,000 troops within the Soviet armed forces (which at the time had almost 5 million men and women in the five military services).

Spetsnaz troops are trained and equipped to carry out a number of sensitive missions, among them clandestine RECONNAISSANCE, sabotage or destruction of targets behind enemy lines, and assassination.

See SPECIAL OPERATIONS FORCES.

Spitfire

The outstanding British fighter aircraft of World War II, which was produced in several photo-RECONNAISSANCE (PR) variants. The Spitfire, or "Spit," was an effective, superb flying machine.

The aircraft's combat debut occurred on Oct. 16, 1939, when Spitfire fighters shot down two German bombers over the Firth of Forth; these were the first German aircraft to be shot down over Britain since 1918. The first photo-reconnaissance sortie was flown the following month, on Nov. 18, by a converted Spitfire I from a base in France over the German city of Aachen. Specialized Spitfire PR aircraft, subsequently widely flown in the war, were fitted with two oblique cameras in the wings. The Spitfire's speed made it an excellent unarmed photo aircraft; several PR variants were used for both low-level and high-level reconnaissance. The Fighter-Reconnaissance (FR) variants retained a gun armament.

The Spit was the most widely used Royal Air Force (RAF) fighter during World War II; small numbers were also flown by the U.S. Army Air Forces and U.S. Navy, as well as by several other nations.

The Spitfire began as a private venture, and the prototype "eight-gun fighter," as it was known, flew on March 5, 1936. Production was approved in June 1936, and deliveries to RAF Fighter Command began in June 1938. Altogether, 20,351 Spitfires were built through Oct. 1947, including many hundreds of reconnaissance aircraft; 2,408 similar naval Seafires were built for carrier operation.

Relatively few Spitfire reconnaissance aircraft were lost during the war. But Israeli anti-aircraft guns and fighters shot down four armed reconnaissance Spitfires within a few minutes in 1948 (some of the kills being made by Israeli "Spits"). See AIRCRAFT SHOT DOWN.

The Spitfire was a particularly clean design, with a Rolls-Royce in-line engine and a small air intake under the fuselage. The elliptical wingtips and pointed tail fin were particularly distinctive. The aircraft went through a large number of improvements and modifications during the war.

The Spitfire was a single-seat aircraft. Maximum speed for the Spitfire I was 362 mph at altitude; combat range with 15 minutes in combat was 395 miles; maximum range was 575 miles. The later PR models had considerably more range than contemporary fighter models.

Sponsor

Slang for an organization or intelligence service that finances, controls, or itself carries out an operation.

Spook

Used as a noun for a person or as an adjective to describe equipment, operations, or agencies involved in intelligence activity that is usually intelligence collection.

SPOT

French commercial SATELLITE that provides intelligence-quality photographs. SPOT—for Système Probatoire d'Observation de la Terre—was first launched from Guinea aboard an Arianne rocket booster on Feb. 22, 1986. Orbiting some 515 miles above the earth, the *SPOT 1* satellite weighed 4,000 pounds and carried two cameras. Between the 1986 launch of *SPOT 1* and mid-2002, more than 7.5 million images of the Earth had been acquired.

Previously, the only photographic satellite images that were readily available to the public—and hence other countries—were from the U.S. Landsat program, whose satellites first orbited in 1972. But SPOT photos were superior and for sale at a nominal price. Further, for a price, the SPOT Image Corp. would direct the satellite to photograph specific TARGETS.

William E. Burrows wrote in *Deep Black (1986)*:

> SPOT's implications are profound because it blurs the distinction between civilian and military observation from space in direct proportion to the clarity of its imagery. The satellite's potential for intelligence officials have already begun tasking it for that purpose and will continue to do so until France's own military intelligence satellite, Helios, is launched. . . .

SPOT photography has been used by the news media and, beginning in the late 1980s, by the U.S. Department of Defense for use in the unclassified publication *Soviet Military Power*. Defense officials were reluctant to publish U.S. satellite images during the Cold War.

In May 2002 the NATIONAL IMAGERY AND MAPPING AGENCY (NIMA) signed an "Imagery for Citizens" contract that permitted NIMA to release Controlled Image Base (CIB) products, derived from approximately 5,500 SPOT 10-meter panchromatic images, to the public. A 10-meter resolution indicates the maximum size of an object visible in the imagery.

The Imagery for Citizens program, started in 1998 under NIMA management, provides public and educational access to vast archives of government imagery and geographic information, including some that were previously classified.

Spotter

SEE TALENT SPOTTER

Spy Dust

Harmless powder the KGB used in the 1980s in an effort to keep track of Western diplomats and MILITARY ATTACHÉS. Several chemicals, including nitrophenyl pentadien (NPPD) and luminol, were used against specific Westerners. When the use of spy dust was discovered, the U.S. ambassador to the Soviet Union, Arthur A. Hartman, told reporters in Moscow on Feb. 14, 1986, "We want to make clear to the Soviet authorities that active measures against Americans in Moscow are not acceptable." He added, "It's unacceptable to subject Americans to any outside substance."

The previous year U.S. officials discovered that the Soviets were placing NPPD on door handles and in cars to trace the movements of U.S. officials. The Soviet government rejected the charge. (No ill effects were detected from the substances.)

Spy Schools

Institutions where intelligence services train their AGENTS and INTELLIGENCE OFFICERS. Sometimes internal staff and analysts are also sent to such schools.

Formal spy schools—or at least extensive classroom sessions—appear to have been first established early in the 20th century. Dr. Armgaard Karl Graves, in *The Secrets of the German War Office* (1914), tells of his acceptance into the German Secret Service in 1903 and describes his five months of training before he was to be dispatched to Port Arthur in the Far East:

> During those five months I was kept at a steady grind of schooling in certain things. Day after day, week after week, I was grounded in subjects that were essential to efficient Secret Service work.
>
> Broadly, they could be divided into four classes—topography, trigonometry, naval construction and drawing. . . . A Secret Service agent sent out to investigate and report on the condition, situation, and armament of a fort like Verdun in France must be able to make correct estimates of distances, height, angles, conditions of the ground, etc. This can only be done by a man of the correct scientific training.

Beyond these formal classes in BERLIN, Graves visited the museum of the German General Staff and armament works and shipyards in Kiel and Wilhelmshafen. "There I was taught every detail of the mechanics of naval construction and I was not pronounced equipped until I

could talk intelligently about every unassembled part of a gun, torpedo tube, or mine."

By World War II there were two major espionage schools operated by Germany's RSHA, one in The Hague and one in Belgrade (see A-SCHULE). Several lesser spy schools were operated by the ABWEHR, German MILITARY INTELLIGENCE, and SD. There were at least a score of these, and they usually trained spies for specific missions in specific geographic areas. These were clustered in Berlin, Hamburg, Königsberg, Stettin, Stuttgart, and VIENNA. Following the invasion of the Soviet Union in June 1941, the Germans set up nine schools in occupied Soviet territory—with a capacity of 10,000 spies and saboteurs. Most of the students were Soviet soldiers who had agreed to work against the Stalinist regime.

Describing one of the schools for training agents to operate against the West in *Hitler's Spies* (1978), DAVID KAHN wrote:

> Agents studied Morse code, radio construction and repair, cipher systems, invisible ink, microdots, spotting and shaking shadows, and recognizing aircraft types. Instruction was nearly always individual. [Compared to large classes for agents going to the Russian Front.] So time-consuming and costly was this training that only about 200 young men attended the Hamburg school throughout the entire war.

The Russian intelligence-security services established specialized intelligence schools early in the Soviet era, both for agents being sent overseas and for internal security personnel. Former Soviet NKVD officer A. I. Romanov [p], in his memoirs *Nights Are the Longest There* (1972), wrote of attending a state security school in the Moscow suburb of Babushkin in 1942. There were, he recalled, four "special subjects" taught at the school. No. 1 was political affairs:

> During the whole of my time at the NKVD school I don't recall a single occasion when the political affairs period lasted for more than ten or fifteen minutes . . . . what was the point of wasting time, which was short anyway, on long talks about success in the fields of the collective farms or the factories, or even about the splendour of Marxism-Leninism, when in all the special subject lessons we were taught hard facts about the essential nature of both the Soviet State and communism, about difficulties and mistakes and plans for the future, in any case without any dull, long-winded routine propaganda.

Another subject was the organization and activities of foreign intelligence services. This had two parts: first, Germany and its allies; second, the intelligence services of Britain and the United States. There also was operational work—the TRADECRAFT of intelligence and espionage.

Romanov pointed out that at this school, during wartime, the instructors "left the school immediately the lesson was over. I am sure that they had other duties. Perhaps these other duties were their main job or perhaps they just went to other identical schools and taught the same lessons there. Sometimes they would simply miss a lesson and be replaced by another instructor."

The state security ORGANS—namely, NKVD, MVD, KGB, and their successors—have operated several spy schools to train Soviet and Eastern European intelligence and security officers. The training facility at Pushkin, near Moscow, is known to have been used extensively to train Arab terrorists.

The Military-Diplomatic Academy in Moscow is the senior postgraduate institution for intelligence officers. Most of its graduates go to the GRU (MILITARY INTELLIGENCE) but some go to the other state security organs. Col. OLEG PENKOVSKY, a 1953 graduate of the school, reported that in the early 1960s the KGB took between 30 and 40 percent of the graduates of the Military-Diplomatic Academy.

Senior schools operated by the KGB during the Cold War were the Andropov Institute (Moscow), Mossovet Higher Border Command School (Moscow), Dzerzhinsky Higher Border Command School (Alma-Ata), and Voroshilov Higher Border Military Political School (Bolitsino).

The MVD—responsible for internal police forces—operated a separate school system. In 1992 the MVD's Dzerzhinsky Higher Military Command School in Saratov became the Russian Academy of Security under the FSB (Federal Security Service).

The GRU has long operated a large education system. The principal school is the Military-Diplomatic Academy, but GRU officers also study at intelligence faculties at the Training Center of ILLEGALS, Frunze Military Academy, Naval Academy, Military Signals Academy, Military Institute of Foreign Languages, Cherepovetski Higher Military Engineering School for Communications, Higher Naval School of Radio Electronics, SPETSNAZ Faculty of the Ryazan Higher Airborne School, Kiev Higher Military Command School, and Kharkov Higher Military Aviation and Engineering School. (Following the breakup of the Soviet Union in Dec. 1991, some of these schools were outside the new Russian Federation.) In addition, GRU agents are trained in various aspects of spy tradecraft at specialized schools.

In *The Man Behind the Rosenbergs* (2001), spymaster ALEXANDER FEKLISOV recalls his year-long stay at a school an hour from Moscow, where he took courses in tradecraft: "Making contact, recruitment and management of sources of information(countless ways of discovering whether we were under surveillance and, when necessary, how to break a 'tail.')"

The first major American spy school system was established by the OFFICE OF STRATEGIC SERVICES (OSS) in Britain to support operations in Europe during World War II. These were established in conjunction with the British Special Operations Executive (SOE). Like German and British wartime spy schools, they were generally short-term classes, tailored to specific missions in specific geographic areas. There was also a school in Canada on the north shore of Lake Ontario, secretly operated by BRITISH SECURITY CO-ORDINATION. Known as CAMP X, it drew Canadian, British, and American agents to train for operations in Europe.

The major U.S. intelligence agencies operate formal school programs. The CIA trains its intelligence officers at CAMP PEARY, Va., and the FBI at the academy located near the sprawling Marine Corps Base in Quantico, Va. Both agencies use a variety of military schools for specialized training for their agents, including the Department of Defense–operated POLYGRAPH school at Fort Jackson, S.C. The FBI Academy, of course, emphasizes criminal law and other law enforcement studies, placing special stress on weapons training. This aspect of FBI training was reinvigorated after the Waco and Ruby Ridge incidents and because of the growing concern over the number of heavily armed private militias in the United States. Since the attacks on the World Trade Center and the Pentagon on Sept. 11, 2001, both the FBI and the CIA have added studies related to TERRORIST INTELLIGENCE. But little is known publicly about the specifics of these studies.

U.S. ARMY INTELLIGENCE long trained its intelligence personnel at FORT HOLABIRD in Baltimore, Md. (invariably called The Bird); that school has moved to Fort Huachuca, Ariz. The Army, Navy, and Air Force offer specialized intelligence curricula at their respective war colleges and postgraduate schools. The primary U.S. graduate-level intelligence institution is the JOINT MILITARY INTELLIGENCE COLLEGE, located at Bolling Air Force Base in Washington, D.C. (formerly the Defense Intelligence College, renamed in May 1993). A highly specialized school for an NSA elite unit, the SPECIAL COLLECTION SERVICE is so secret that even its location is classified.

All U.S. military services and intelligence agencies make use of the Defense Language School in Monterey, Calif., to train agents and ATTACHÈS in foreign languages.

Also see NAKANO.

Spy Shops

Commercial stores that sell high-tech BUGS and SURVEILLANCE equipment, marketed as "personal protection devices." Much of the equipment is the kind to which heretofore only major intelligence agencies had access. The largest store chains in this field include the Spy Factory, Inc., and Counter Spy Shops. The firms have stores throughout the Western world as well as in Moscow and in Sofia, Bulgaria. Spyzone Online offers Internet purchasers "all your online espionage needs, regarding security, surveillance, counter surveillance and countermeasure equipment."

A vast variety of microphones and cameras disguised as clocks, briefcases, and even food are for sale, as are devices to ascertain if one's office, home, or telephone is bugged. Also available are night-vision goggles, night cameras, invisible inks, and even a "truth phone" that can allegedly detect if a caller is lying. A new market opened up in 2003 when a company brought out a line of "spy toys" aimed at kids.

The federal government cracked down on one chain, Spy Factory, closing down 11 U.S. stores after company officers pleaded guilty to smuggling and selling illegal wiretap devices. The company sold transmitters—hidden in calculators, electrical plugs, and ballpoint pens—that had been slipped into the country illegally from Japan. Only law enforcement officers could legally purchase the devices.

Spy Swaps

The exchanging of AGENTS and INTELLIGENCE OFFICERS who have been caught and imprisoned by an enemy country. During the Cold War many East-West swaps in BERLIN were arranged by WOLFGANG VOGEL.

Possibly the most famous swap was the exchange of U-2 spyplane pilot FRANCIS GARY POWERS for convicted Soviet spy RUDOLF ABEL in Berlin on Feb. 10, 1962. Another major swap was the exchange of British go-between GREVILLE WYNNE and Soviet spy GORDON LONSDALE at another East-West crossing point near Spandau in West Berlin, on April 22, 1964. (Wynne was the go-between for U.S. and British intelligence services and Soviet Col. OLEG PENKOVSKY.

Sometimes "hostages" are exchanged for spies. For example, Briton Gerald Brooke, an idealistic young man involved with an anticommunist émigré organization, had volunteered to carry forbidden pamphlets into the Soviet Union. He was arrested for smuggling documents. But the Soviet government later announced that he would be tried for espionage and would likely face 15 years in prison. He had already served four years in a Soviet prison. He was neither a spy nor an employee of the British intelligence services.

In exchange for Brooke, the British released PETER KROGER and his wife Helen, highly effective spies who had worked in the United States as well as Britain. Brooke was flown from the Soviet Union to London (on a Soviet aircraft) on July 23, 1969. In the complex spy swap two other British citizens, who had been sentenced to lesser prison terms for alleged drug smuggling, were allowed to leave the Soviet Union, and three other British citizens—three men and a woman—were allowed to enter the Soviet Union, marry their sweethearts, and leave with them.

In return, on Oct. 24, 1968, the Krogers were flown to Warsaw, Poland. They had served almost eight years in British prisons. They flew first class, the Polish Embassy having paid for their tickets.

See BENJAMIN CHURCH.

Squillacotte, Marie

(b. 1958)

Department of Defense lawyer convicted in Oct. 1998 of passing secrets to communist East Germany. Also arrested with her in Oct. 1997 for were her husband, Kurt Stand, and a friend, James Clark. She was sentenced in

1999 to 21 years in prison and Stand to 17 years. Clark, who pleaded guilty and testified for the government, was given a 12-year sentence.

In 2001 the U.S. Supreme Court declined to review the case. Squillacotte's lawyer had claimed that she had been entrapped by a sting operation in which an FBI agent posed as a South African seeking U.S. secrets.

Stand, born in 1955, was the son of a German immigrant who introduced his son to the Stasi, East Germany's spy agency (see MFS). As a youngster, he attended a summer youth camp in East Germany. Stand was a representative of an international organization of food industry unions and a member of the board of the Democratic Socialists of America, known as anticommunist radicals.

Clark, who worked for the East Germans from 1976 until the fall of the Berlin Wall in 1989, sent his HANDLERS classified documents he had obtained from friends in the State Department. He described himself as "an activist in the international socialist movement." He said that he spied "entirely for ideological reasons."

Clark, born in 1948, was a paralegal for the Army from 1988 to 1996. He quit, he is quoted as saying, because he was afraid he would lose his SECURITY CLEARANCE on account of his activities in Germany. According to the FBI, Clark learned Morse code and secret photography in East Germany. He is said to have photographed classified CIA and State Department documents, sewn the film into doll's clothes, and mailed the package to Germany. He started working for a private security firm after he left the army.

After marrying in 1980, Squillacote and Stand moved to Washington, where she attended law school at Catholic University. Following graduation in 1983, she became a lawyer for the National Labor Relations Board, where her father had worked. In 1980 she got a fellowship at the House Armed Services Committee. This led to a job in the Pentagon, and in 1992 she began working in the Office of the Undersecretary for Acquisition Reform.

The couple's two children—Karl and Rosa—were said to have been named after Karl Liebknecht and Rosa Luxemburg, founders of the German Communist Party.

The espionage case began when FBI agent Katharine Alleman, assigned to check Stasi files in BERLIN for U.S. spies, found documents identifying Clark as a spy recruited in 1976; Stand as a spy recruited in 1973 when he was a student in Wisconsin; and Squillacote as a spy recruited in 1981.

Stasi documents, which described the men as "ideological" recruits, also showed payment of $17,500 to Clark, who had the CODE NAME Jack, and $24,650 to Stand, code-named Junior.

The three met at the University of Wisconsin at Milwaukee in the mid-1970s. Clark and Stand were members of the Young Workers Liberation League, the student arm of the U.S. Communist Party (CPUSA).

After learning about the American names in the Stasi files, the FBI received authority from the FOREIGN INTELLIGENCE SURVEILLANCE COURT to tap the suspects' phones, put BUGS in their homes, and conduct secret searches. According to the affidavit, the searchers of Clark's condo found a shortwave radio, 3,500 German marks, and records of periodic calls to Berlin. In Squillacote's computer the FBI found a letter she had written to Ronnie Kasrils, South Africa's deputy minister of defense and a Communist Party leader.

In Aug. 1996 she received a reply—written by an FBI agent. He suggested a meeting in New York City in October. Talking to a man she assumed was a potential South African spymaster, she told of her past work for East Germany. "I've violated Federal 18 lots and lots," she allegedly said. (Title 18 of the federal code includes laws concerning espionage against the United States.)

As recorded by the wired FBI agent, she said, "Between myself and my husband, we go back in this work to 1981. And I'm kinda proud of it." The agent said she gave him a classified memo signed by Secretary of Defense William Perry; he gave her $1,000. At a second meeting in Jan. 1997, the FBI alleged, she handed over four documents classified secret.

The FBI scammed Clark by setting up a meeting between him and an agent who said he was a friend of Harry, a Stasi HANDLER Clark knew by that code name. FBI sources said Harry—real name Lothar Ziemer—had offered to work for the agency, but for some reason his offer was refused.

FBI agents listening to the bugs overheard Clark muttering to himself: "Closing right in . . . They're going to give me a lie detector test . . . An easy mark. An easy mark I am. . . . Gonna say you're a spy. . . ."

SR

Service de Reseignements (Information Service), a branch of the French DEUXIÈME BUREAU (DB).

After France's defeat by Germany in 1870 the SR was established by the French Army to gather MILITARY INTELLIGENCE on German troops occupying Alsace-Lorraine. Like the DB, the SR suffered from the aftermath of the Dreyfus affair, in which Capt. ALFRED DREYFUS was framed for espionage by French INTELLIGENCE OFFICERS. In 1899, as a direct result of the scandal, the SR was abolished as a separate agency; its functions were divided between the military's DB and the SÛRETÉ GÉNÉRALE, a civilian police organization.

The section under the DB coordinated foreign intelligence, COUNTERINTELLIGENCE, telephone tapping, and, through a division known as the central registry, gathered intelligence from sources outside the SR. In World War I the Service de Renseignements Aériens was created to handle the PRODUCT of aerial RECONNAISSANCE.

The SR, through AGENTS and sharp analysis, determined some aspects of the strategy that the German Army would use in its opening offensive in World War I. Modern historians, however, question claims that the agency had obtained the actual German war plan from a mysterious German general in 1904.

After World War I, the SR dealt primarily with counterintelligence, relying on telephone taps, agents, and analysis of OPEN SOURCE intelligence on foreign armies and arms industries. Under the DB, the SR eventually resumed an important role in the complex world of French intelligence.

In 1936 the SR regained its independence, although it was still theoretically controlled by the DB. Its responsibilities included both counterintelligence and the gathering of intelligence, with Germany being the prime TARGET. The SR also had sections that gathered and analyzed foreign weapon and aviation development. SR listening posts intercepted radio communications from Germany, Italy, Spain, and elsewhere in Europe.

The SR-DB intelligence apparatus was generally credited with producing a credible stream of intelligence about Germany. But as its officers later bitterly complained, France's military and political leadership failed to make use of the intelligence.

When Germany overran France in May 1940, the SR continued to exist in unoccupied France—that part of the country that was governed by the pro-Nazi Vichy regime. Tainted by its service in Vichy, the SR was viewed with suspicion by Gen. Charles de Gaulle and his followers. As head of the Free French movement in Britain, de Gaulle formed his own intelligence agency, the BCRA, the Bureau Central de Renseignements et d'Action (Central Bureau for Information and Action).

After the Anglo-American invasion of North Africa in Nov. 1942, de Gaulle forced the BCRA and the SR to merge, with the SR becoming the technical division of a new agency, the DGSS.

SR-71 Blackbird

Strategic RECONNAISSANCE aircraft developed as the successor to the U-2 spyplane, the SR-71 remains the world's fastest and highest-flying operational aircraft.

A Mach 3 photo-electronic aircraft, the SR-71 was a development of the A-12 OXCART developed by the Lockheed SKUNK WORKS as the successor to that firm's U-2 spyplane. Whereas the U-2 had been designed for high altitude and had a relatively slow speed (Mach 0.7), the SR-71 was fast, flying at some 2,000 mph (Mach 3) at altitudes of 85,000 feet and, because it produced a smaller radar "signature," was less vulnerable to interception. Its cameras were able to sweep more than 100,000 square miles of the earth each hour.

Fabricated of titanium, the SR-71 has an unconventional design with a long, tapering fuselage of very small cross-section blending into a delta wing with rounded wingtips. The forward part of the fuselage is flattened and has sharp chines along each side. A turbojet engine nacelle is blended into the middle of each wing and each nacelle supports a low tail fin, canted slightly inward. Skin temperatures on the fuselage rise considerably during high-altitude, high-speed flight and the fuselage stretches 11 inches. The immense amount of fuel needed for high-speed flight fills most of the fuselage and acts as a heat sink. (Although the plane is unarmed, there were proposals to fit a pod under it for carrying a nuclear weapon.) The aircraft can be refueled in flight. It is flown by a crew of two.

The initial contract with Lockheed called for four aircraft. Three were completed as YF-12A fighter prototypes (See A-12 OXCART). The fourth became the first SR-71, which flew for the first time on Dec. 22, 1964. The plane was to have been designated RS-71, but President Johnson inadvertently transposed the letters during his announcement of the plane's existence. (RS would have indicated Reconnaissance-Strike, a logical follow-up to the RS-70 VALKYRIE.)

The SR-71 variant became operational in Jan. 1966 with the U.S. Air Force's 9th Strategic Reconnaissance Wing. In addition to flying from U.S. bases, SR-71s regularly operated from Kadena Air Base, Okinawa, and Mildenhall Royal Air Base in Britain.

They flew many missions over China; an SR-71 photographed China's first H-bomb explosion in 1967. The SR-71's were first used over North Vietnam in 1968. The aircraft subsequently flew reconnaissance missions over Cuba, Libya, Nicaragua, the Middle East, and the Persian Gulf area. In Sept. 1974 an SR-71 flew from New York to London in 1 hour, 54 minutes at an average speed of 1,894 mph (Mach 2.8). In July 1976, an SR-71 set the absolute world speed record of 2,193 mph (Mach 3.31) over a straight course; in addition, a closed-circuit record was set at 2,092 mph (Mach 3.17).

The "final" SR-71 flight was on March 6, 1990. The SR-71 was to be retired in a cost-cutting action, while its predecessor, the U-2, continued to fly strategic reconnaissance missions.

The SR-71 Blackbird was developed as successor to the highly successful U-2 spyplane. Both were products of the Lockheed Skunk Works, as was the SR-71's progenitor, the A-12 Oxcart. The SR-71—a Mach 3 aircraft—was very expensive to maintain and fly, compared to the U-2. (U.S. AIR FORCE)

In 1995, however, Congress provided funds to reactivate two SR-71 aircraft to provide a limited Mach 3 reconnaissance capability, but the plane was not returned to operational service.

Although the actual numbers built are still classified, probably 28 aircraft were produced. Just under 20 aircraft were in the inventory in 1990 when the SR-71 was retired, of which only eight or nine were operational at any one time because of the aircraft's high maintenance requirements. (The Pentagon had announced the loss of eight SR-71s in accidents through 1970. Unlike the U-2s, none was lost to hostile fire.)

Since the SR-71 tooling was destroyed after the production run, no more could be built. According to designer CLARENCE (KELLY) JOHNSON, then-Secretary of Defense Robert S. McNamara specifically ordered the destruction so that SR-71 variants would not compete for funding with the McDonnell Douglas F-15 Eagle and other combat aircraft.

SRF

SEE SPECIAL REPORTING FACILITY

SS

Adolf Hitler's elite personal guard, which became a political police and intelligence force that symbolized Nazi terrorism and slaughter. The Schutzstaffel (Protection Detachment), abbreviated as SS, was created in the early 1920s as a small unit to serve as a bodyguard for Nazi leaders. The SS, with only 280 members, was a tiny but well-disciplined unit under the 60,000-strong SA or "brown shirts," the thuggish Nazi paramilitary organization.

The SS began to grow in 1929 when Hitler appointed HEINRICH HIMMLER as Reichsführer SS. Himmler, an ambitious and fanatic disciple of Hitler, saw a major role for the SS as a mystic brotherhood to enforce and perpetuate Nazi ideology. Known as the "black shirts," with skull-and-crossbones insignia on their black tunics, the force attracted a more elite-minded German than the street-fighting SA.

By 1930 Himmler had recruited an SS force of more than 3,000 men, each a paragon of Nazi standards for racial purity, for SS men were expected to show an Aryan ancestry going back to the 18th century. Candidates' pedigrees were examined by the Race and Settlement Office, headed by Richard-Walther Darré, a pig breeder who was the author of the "blood and soil" theory that claimed European civilization was the work of racially pure Germans. The office also investigated the prospective brides of SS members.

The SS motto was "Believe! Obey! Fight!" The SS men, who fancied themselves modern Teutonic knights, usually fought by slaughtering unarmed foes. Soon after the invasion of Poland in Sept. 1939, SS units launched their first reign of terror in a conquered land—what the SS called the "housekeeping of Jews, intelligentsia, clergy, and the nobility."

When Germany invaded the Soviet Union in June 1941, the SS was given the task of annihilating the Soviet Jews and "Bolshevik agitators." To do this, the SS set up action groups (Einsatzgruppen) to follow the German Army's advances into the Soviet Union. Einsatzkommando detachments rounded up civilians, mostly Jews, and shot them down in massive slaughters. More than 2 million Jews were murdered by these SS units, according to war crimes testimony.

Separate from the Einsatzkommandos, the SS also formed an elite combat force, the Waffen SS. In 1934, Hitler had assured the nation's military leaders that they were to be the "sole bearer of arms" in Germany's external affairs. However, the "heavy" SS police units were soon wearing Army uniforms (except on ceremonial occasions), had a military organization, and were provided with heavy weapons.

When the war began, there were some 20,000 SS in military units. Hitler's need for elite combat forces led to the rapid growth of the Waffen SS; by the end of 1944 the Waffen SS had some 600,000 troops, with seven Panzer (armored) divisions and numerous lesser units; SS commanders directed several corps and armies. The SS units were larger and more heavily armed than conventional Army units. The Waffen SS was both a producer and CONSUMER of TACTICAL INTELLIGENCE.

These units fought on virtually every European battlefield. Although their activities were far removed from the police and internal suppression of other SS forces, the Waffen SS was considered by the Allies to be equally guilty of criminal behavior.

In Germany and the conquered lands, the vast network of concentration and death camps was guarded and—with the GESTAPO—operated by the SS. Thus, the SS was directly responsible for the privation, torture, and deaths of millions of Europeans—Jews and Christians, Germans and foreigners.

The Nuremberg International Military Tribunal that tried German war criminals after the war declared the SS and Gestapo organizations guilty of war crimes. The tribunal declared that, except for some clerical and low-level members, every individual member of the SS was a war criminal guilty of planning and carrying out crimes against humanity.

Also see SD.

SSO

SEE SPECIAL SECURITY OFFICER

S&T

SEE SCIENTIFIC AND TECHNICAL INTELLIGENCE

Stashinsky, Bogdan

(b. 1931)

KGB assassin who was trained to use poison dust on his victims.

A Ukrainian, Stashinsky had been working for Soviet intelligence ORGANS since the age of 19 when, in 1957, he was given the assignment of murdering Lev Reber, a Ukrainian nationalist leader living in West Germany.

Stashinsky was to use a special pistol loaded with a capsule of prussic acid and fire the pistol into Rebet's face. The capsule would be crushed and the acid expelled. Inhaling the prussic acid would poison the victim and trigger a fatal heart attack. Stashinsky was provided with an antidote that he was to take immediately before attacking Rebet.

On Oct. 12, 1957, he ambushed and killed Rebet.

Next Stashinsky was assigned to murder Stefan Bandera, another exiled Ukrainian leader. This time he was provided with a double-barreled pistol, to spray the poisoned acid in the face of Bandera's bodyguard as well as the principal target.

Stashinsky lost his nerve. He reported to his superiors that circumstances prevented him from carrying out the assignment. He was told to try again and did so on Oct. 15, 1959. (No bodyguard was with Bandera.)

In Dec. 1959, Stashinsky was awarded the Order of the Red Banner for his successes. And he was given a new assignment: to kill Raoslav Stetskow, who had been Prime Minister of the Ukrainian Republic in 1941 and was also living in West Germany.

About this time Stashinsky married an East German woman, who was horrified to find out her new husband's profession. Feeling remorse, guilt, and fear, he and his wife defected to U.S. officials in BERLIN on Aug. 12, 1961. Stashinsky was placed on trial and confessed his "successes"; he was sentenced to eight years in prison but was secretly released at the end of 1966 and taken to the United States. Nothing is publicly known about his life since then.

Stasi

SEE MFS

Station X

SEE BLETCHLEY PARK

Stepashin, Lt. Gen. Sergey Vadimovich

(b. 1952)

Senior Russian INTELLIGENCE OFFICER of the post-Soviet era.

Born in Port Arthur (Lu-shun), People's Republic of China, Stepasshin was a 1973 graduate of the Higher Political School of the Internal Affairs Ministry (MVD) in Leningrad. Stepashin also studied for a doctorate in history at the Military-Political Academy. His thesis was "Party Direction of Fire Fighting Formations."

He served in the MVD troops and taught at the Leningrad Ministry of Internal Affairs Institute. In 1990 he became deputy chief of the Political Department at the Higher Political School, combining his political duties with lecturing at the school.

From 1990 to 1993 he was an elected deputy of the Russian Federation's Supreme Soviet, representing the left-of-center cooperation faction of the Army Reform Group. From 1991 to 1993, the period in which the Soviet Union was dismantled, he was chairman of the Supreme Soviet's Defense and Security Committee. He also headed a state commission investigating activities of the KGB and state security apparatus. During this tumultuous period, in Aug. 1991, he quit the Communist Party.

Following the review of KGB activities, in 1991 the FSK, the Russian Federal Security Service, was established and Stepashin was appointed deputy general director of the new agency. That same year the Russian Security Ministry (MB) was created, and Stepashin additionally became a deputy minister.

In Sept. 1991 he was promoted from colonel to major general; a year later, he was promoted to lieutenant general.

For nine months he combined his duties at the MB with his work in the Supreme Soviet. In Sept. 1992 he attempted to resign from the Supreme Soviet, but that body voted to request that President Boris Yeltsin relieve him of his duties in the security services instead so that he could carry out his duties in the Supreme Soviet. (The MB was abolished in 1993.)

In March 1994 President Yeltsin appointed Stepashin to the Russian Federation's Security Council and named him head of the FSK and also director of the Federal COUNTERINTELLIGENCE Service. His other posts under Yeltsin were director of the Administrative Department of the Government Administration, the Minister of Justice and the Minister of the Interior of the Russian Federation consecutively.

On April 27, 1999, he was appointed deputy prime minister in the government of YEVGENY MAKSIMOVICH PRIMAKOV. Then, on May 12, 1999, Yeltsin fired Primakov's entire government and appointed Stepashin acting prime minister. That government lasted 82 days, until it was dismissed by Yeltsin. On April 19, 2000, the Duma made Stepashin chairman of the Accounts Chamber of the Russian Federation for six years.

Stephenson, Sir William

(b. 1896 d. 1989)

Director of BRITISH SECURITY CO-ORDINATION (BSC) in the United States during World War II. He was the British spymaster in the United States.

Canadian-born, Stephenson served in the Royal Canadian Engineers in World War I. After being gassed on the Western Front in 1915 he was invalided out to England. Following his recovery he transferred to the Royal Flying Corps and as a fighter pilot was credited with shooting down 26 German aircraft before he was himself shot down and taken prisoner. He escaped and

returned to British lines, providing detailed observations on what he had seen in Germany.

After the war Stephenson became a boxer, earning the world amateur lightweight champion title. He then became involved in commercial radio development and other interests, among them aviation. In 1934 he won the King's Cup air race in an aircraft that he had designed and built in one of his factories. During the 1930s he also developed an interest in intelligence while visiting German industrial concerns. He provided information to the British Secret Intelligence Service (MI6) and to Winston Churchill to support the latter's drive for British rearmament.

In May 1940 Churchill, newly appointed prime minister, named Stephenson his personal representative to President Roosevelt and assigned him to establish BSC in the United States. Stephenson also represented the Security Service (MI6) and SOE (Special Operations Executive) in the United States, and acted as the British liaison to the FBI and OFFICE OF STRATEGIC SERVICES (CSS). His nominal COVER when the office was established was that of British passport control officer.

He met some opposition in the United States in 1940–1941 because of American isolationism, although his efforts were supported by Roosevelt and J. EDGAR HOOVER, director of the FBI, and WILLIAM DONOVAN of the OSS. Later, the relationship between Hoover and Stephenson cooled, causing some difficulties. (See DUSKO POPOV.)

Stephenson was knighted after the war.

At the start of the Cold War he was involved in the case of IGOR GOUZENKO, a Soviet CIPHER officer who defected to the West.

Stephenson's exploits were chronicled in *A Man Called Intrepid* (1976) and *Intrepid's Last Case* (1983), both by William Stevenson, and *The Quiet Canadian* (1962), retitled *Room 3603* in the United States, by H. MONTGOMERY HYDE. Stephenson was often referred to as Intrepid.

Sterilize

To remove from material to be used in clandestine operations any marks or components that could identify it as originating with the sponsoring organization or nation.

Steve Brody

U.S. Navy plan to use F2H-2P Banshee photo-RECONNAISSANCE aircraft to overfly prospective nuclear targets in the Soviet Union. In 1951–1952 the lack of aerial photography of the Caucasus, Crimea, and Ukraine areas led Navy INTELLIGENCE OFFICERS in the U.S. Sixth Fleet in the Mediterranean to plan an aerial mission over those areas.

The Sixth Fleet's aircraft carriers were assigned the mission of striking targets in those areas with nuclear weapons. According to Capt. William C. Chapman, then the fleet's air intelligence officer, "The only photography we or anyone on our side had was World War II German stuff. . . . Most of it was made in winter, and all I ever saw of it was mostly white, crisscrossed maybe here and there by railroad tracks."

Addressing the fleet's nuclear strike mission, Chapman continued, "The probability of an AJ Savage hitting a Soviet target was almost nil; lack of photographic intelligence was the first hurdle. . . ."

At least four F2H-2P photo planes were to be launched from a carrier operating south of Salonika in the Aegean Sea. The mission would have required the F2H-2P aircraft to fly about four hours over the Soviet Union to obtain the needed coverage. The proposal for the highly sensitive photo mission was hand-carried to Washington, D.C., in May 1952. It would require President Truman's personal approval. But Secretary of Defense Robert Lovett refused to take the proposal to the White House and the operation was aborted.

(Steve Brody was a New York saloonkeeper who, in 1886, jumped off the Brooklyn Bridge to win a wager. "To pull a Brody" instantly became a term for doing a dangerous stunt.)

Steve Canyon

Clandestine U.S. Air Force program to provide pilots for air control of strikes against communist forces in Laos during the Vietnam War. From 1967 to 1973, the USAF officers were SHEEP DIPPED to the CIA, which controlled air operations in Laos. (The country was theoretically neutral, so the United States could not openly maintain military forces there. See AIR AMERICA.) Steve Canyon was a popular American comic strip created by Milton Coniff. The character was so popular with the USAF that it fashioned a personnel file on him.

Stevens, Maj. H. R.

British Secret Intelligence Service (MI6) officer who, with Capt. S. PAYNE BEST, was lured into a meeting with German intelligence AGENTS and captured at Venlo on the Dutch frontier on Nov. 9, 1939. (See VENLO INCIDENT.) The two were interned by the Germans for the duration of the war.

At the time of the incident Stevens had the COVER of British passport control officer at The Hague in the Netherlands. However, the Germans knew his true identity. He and Best believed that they were meeting with representatives of an anti-Hitler movement in the German armed forces.

The postwar investigation into German knowledge of MI6 showed that, while Stevens gave up more information than Best, a third MI6 officer, CHARLES (DICKIE) ELLIS, who remained in the secret service until the 1950s, had also been a prewar source of information.

Stieber, Wilhelm

(b. 1818 d. 1882)

Prussian who revolutionized intelligence activities in Europe in the 19th century.

After studying for the Lutheran ministry, Stieber changed his mind and became a lawyer. Between 1845 and 1850 he built up a successful law practice, while also working as an informer and spy. He specialized in criminal cases and knew in advance what evidence would be produced against his clients in court because he was also editor of the police periodical. In spite of the scandal that ensued when this was revealed, King Frederick William remained a supporter of Stieber and appointed him commissioner of police. He was called "the spymaster" and "the king of sleuth-hounds."

When William I became ruler of Prussia, Stieber was dismissed. He changed allegiance, between 1858 and 1863 working for the czar of Russia and helping to organize the czar's secret police service. Stieber traced Russian political activists after they had left Russia. He continued to spy for Prussia while working for Russia, and on behalf of Count von Bismarck of Prussia he also traveled to Austria to spy.

Largely because of the information he collected, Prussia easily defeated Austria in 1866. Afterwards he spent 18 months in France establishing an espionage NETWORK. On behalf of the Prussian government he also organized the Central Information Bureau and set up his own news organization and recruited spies in railroads and hotels. He also bought newspapers in neighboring countries and published pro-German propaganda.

Stigga, Oskar Ansovich

(b. 1894 d. 1938)

Senior officer in the GRU, Soviet MILITARY INTELLIGENCE.

Born in Latvia, he served as a soldier in World War I. After the Bolshevik revolution he became a communist and an officer in the Red Latvian Riflemen, who suppressed counterrevolutionaries and served as V. I. Lenin's bodyguard. (The Latvians strongly supported the Bolsheviks during this period because of the German occupation of Latvia; they were thus mercenaries of the Bolsheviks.)

When the GRU was formed in Oct. 1918, Stigga became a deputy chief and served as an ILLEGAL in Latvia, Lithuania, and Poland. The following year he was chief of intelligence on the Western Front and in Aug. 1920 became a deputy chief of the GRU. He continued to travel extensively to establish intelligence NETWORKS. Like other overseas GRU officials, he was recalled to Moscow in 1938 and executed.

Stockade

British Security Service (MI5) operation from 1960 to 1963 to break into French high-grade CIPHERS.

The operation, supervised by PETER WRIGHT, was carried out by placing a radio frequency BUG, or tap, on specific telephone cables that carried communications to and from the French Embassy. The taps ran to an MI5 operations room set up in the nearby Hyde Park Hotel.

According to Wright in his book *Spycatcher* (1987):

For nearly three years, between 1960 and 1963, MI5 and GCHQ [GOVERNMENT COMMUNICATIONS HEADQUARTERS] read the French high-grade cipher coming in and out of the French Embassy in London. Every move made by the French during our abortive attempt to enter the Common Market was monitored. The intelligence was avidly devoured by the Foreign Office, and verbatim copies of [President Charles] De Gaulle's cables were regularly passed to the Foreign Secretary in the red box.

Stockwell, John

(b. 1937)

Former CIA officer who strongly criticized the agency in books and lectures.

Born in Africa, Stockwell served for several years in the U.S. Marine Corps, rising to the rank of major, before joining the CIA in 1964. He had several assignments in Africa and served in South Vietnam in 1973–1975.

Upon his return to the United States in 1975 he was named to command the Angolan TASK FORCE (2) that was planning covert U.S. arms support and potentially military operations in that former Portuguese colony. At the time Angola was racked by bloody civil war. The principal American interest was to stop the Soviets and Chinese from gaining influence in the area.

Disillusioned with U.S. policy in that conflict, Stockwell resigned from the CIA in 1976 and went public, writing books and giving lectures attacking the agency as well as U.S. policies in the Third World. His books were *In Search of Enemies: A CIA Story* (1978); an exposé of CIA activities in Africa, and *The Praetorian Guard: The U.S. Role in the New World Order* (1990). The latter was a scathing attack on the foreign policies of the administrations of Presidents Reagan and George H.W. Bush. Stockwell is also a founding member of ARDIS—the Association for Responsible Dissent—an organization of former CIA and government officials who are openly critical of the CIA's activities.

Straight, Michael W.

(b. 1916 d. 2004)

American writer-editor who was recruited into the CAMBRIDGE SPY RING by ANTHONY BLUNT.

Straight belonged to a wealthy, Anglophile American family. His brother, who flew for the Royal Air Force in World War II, became a British subject. His mother, the widow of an American investment banker, lived in England, as Michael had since the age of 10.

In 1934, after a year at the London School of Economics, he entered Trinity College, Cambridge, and was made a member of a secret society called the Apostles. Blunt was also a member. Straight also became a member of the communist cell at Cambridge, joining other future members of the Cambridge spy ring. Straight was recruited as an AGENT for international communism (the

Comintern) by Blunt in Feb. 1937, while he was mourning the death of poet John Cornford, a communist friend who had gone off to fight on the Republican side in the Spanish Civil War.

Blunt, suggesting that Straight could best remember his friend by working for the Comintern, at first urged him to return to the United States after Cambridge and become a banker "to provide appraisals of Wall Street's plans to dominate the world economy." That idea was later withdrawn, and Straight was told to await contact in the United States. Straight believed that Blunt was acting for GUY BURGESS, another Apostle who would become a spy for the Soviet Union.

Straight duly went to the United States and used family connections with President Roosevelt to become a volunteer worker in the State Department and later in the Department of the Interior, where he wrote speeches for Roosevelt and cabinet members. Around this time he met a Soviet INTELLIGENCE OFFICER who identified himself as "Michael Green" and said he had been contacted by Straight's friends at Cambridge.

Straight later maintained that he gave the Soviets "nothing save for reports of my own opinions." At the time, penetration of the U.S. government was a prime objective of Soviet intelligence. Straight's Soviet HANDLERS feared that he would be exposed if he became involved with another Soviet spy in the State Department, ALGER HISS. The two men met, but no relationship developed, probably because Hiss had been instructed to avoid Straight. (See WHITTAKER CHAMBERS and VENONA.) Straight's handler was told that Straight "is a big agent in perspective, and burning him is not our intention."

Straight became an influential liberal voice in the United States as editor and publisher of the *New Republic,* a magazine founded by his parents. He also wrote three novels and other books. From 1969 to 1977 he was the deputy chairman of the National Endowment for the Arts.

As Straight wrote in his memoirs, *After Long Silence* (1983), he and his wife were living in Washington, D.C., in 1940 when Burgess visited them. Straight later told his wife that Burgess and Blunt were Soviet agents. She then informed her analyst, Dr. Jennie Welderhall, who in 1948 confessed to Mrs. Straight that she had passed the information on to her husband, a British Embassy official. "I was greatly relieved, unwilling as I was then to act as an informer," Straight wrote.

Then, in March 1951, Straight was "surprised and shocked" to see Burgess in the British Embassy and swore he would turn him in unless he left the Foreign Office. Straight was afraid that Burgess could be costing American lives in the Korean War. Burgess was soon on his way to warn DONALD MACLEAN, another Cambridge spy, that British and U.S. COUNTERINTELLIGENCE was closing in on them. Straight's encounter with Burgess seems to have had nothing to do with the decision; the warning had come from HAROLD (KIM) PHILBY.

In June 1963 Straight was in line to become chairman of the Advisory Council on the Arts, a new federal agency being created by President Kennedy. Concerned that a

SECURITY CHECK by the FBI might expose his communist past, he went to Arthur Schlesinger, a distinguished historian and adviser to the President, who arranged an FBI interview for Straight. He finally told the FBI about Blunt; Burgess had long since been identified as a spy.

The FBI passed the information on to Arthur Martin, head of D1, the British Security Service (MI5) unit that dealt with Soviet espionage in Britain. Martin had been trying to extract a confession from Blunt, who was art advisor to Queen Elizabeth. Straight's information gave Martin what he wanted. Straight later wrote that Blunt had told him he was relieved that Straight had turned him in.

Strategic Intelligence

Intelligence employed in the formulation of policy and military plans at the national and international levels.

Historians Edward Luttwak and Dan Horowitz, in *The Israeli Army* (1975), describe strategic intelligence as "warning of the enemy *intention* to attack, and 'tactical' warning, i.e., the detection of actual physical preparations for an attack."

Stringer

A low-level AGENT who lives or works near an intelligence TARGET and who passes along significant information when it comes to his attention. A stringer's reporting may be regular, periodic, or infrequent, depending upon the nature of the target and his or her access to it.

Such agents generally receive little specialized training. They may be paid a small stipend on a regular basis, with a bonus for special reporting.

Strip Cipher

The use of long strips of letters that can be arranged in different orders for letter substitution to create a CIPHER. The strip cipher used by the U.S. Army and Navy in World War II (designated M-138 and CSP-642, respectively) was used for very low-grade ciphers. It consisted of up to 30 interchangeable strips.

The Japanese broke into the U.S. Consulate in Kobe in late 1937 and photographed the M-138 strip cipher. They subsequently captured the strip cipher, apparently on several occasions, beginning with the fall of Wake Island in Dec. 1941; but they could never solve the cipher on a regular basis.

Strong, Maj. Gen. Kenneth W. D.

(b. 1900 d. 1982)

Head of intelligence for Gen. Dwight D. Eisenhower, the Supreme Allied Commander in Europe during World War II.

Born in Scotland, Gen. Strong graduated from the British military academy at Sandhurst. Before the war,

Strong served as assistant British military ATTACHÉ in BERLIN, and for the first year and a half of the war headed the German section in the War Office. In 1942–1943 he was head of intelligence for the British Home Forces.

After the U.S. military debacle at Kasserine Pass in Tunisia in Feb. 1943, Lt. Gen. Eisenhower asked the British government to replace his then head of intelligence, Brig. Eric Mockler-Ferryman, with another British officer "who has a broader insight into German mentality and method." Eisenhower added, "In his successor, I now look for a little more inquisitiveness and greater attention to checking and cross-checking reports from various sources." The British proposed Strong, then a brigadier.

The two men got on well. In *Intelligence at the Top* (1968), Strong wrote that Eisenhower

> had an immense talent for listening to oral explanations and distilling their essence. I was also to discover that the best way to deal with him was to be completely frank, no matter what national considerations or other controversial factors were involved in any issue. . . . Most people in high places have too much to read. . . . Only on a few occasions, when it was essential that something should appear on the record, did I produce a written Intelligence appreciation for Eisenhower.

Eisenhower sent Strong with his chief of staff, Brig. Gen. WALTER BEDELL SMITH, to Lisbon in Aug. 1943 to secretly arrange with Italian representatives for the surrender of Italy.

At the height of the Allied campaign in Europe, Strong had more than a thousand men and women on his staff. He finished the war as a major general. Strong objected to activities of the U.S. OFFICE OF STRATEGIC SERVICES in the European area because he disliked the idea of a secretly funded, largely civilian organization involved in military operations in wartime.

Strong became the first Director-General of Intelligence in Britain's Ministry of Defence in 1964; under his direction the military intelligence staffs of the three British armed services were combined into a defense intelligence staff. (His deputy was Vice Adm. NORMAN DENNING.) Strong retired in 1966.

Studeman, Vice Adm. William O.

(b. 1940)

The Deputy DIRECTOR OF CENTRAL INTELLIGENCE (DCI) from April 1992 to Aug. 1995, and the acting DCI in early 1993, Studeman was only the second U.S. Navy INTELLIGENCE OFFICER to attain four-star rank. (See Adm. BOBBY RAY INMAN.)

A 1962 graduate of the University of the South in Tennessee, Studeman was commissioned in the Navy the following year and attended flight officer school. Studeman subsequently served in a number of intelligence assignments during his career, both ashore and afloat. He also attended the Naval War College and earned a master's degree from George Washington University.

In 1980 he became executive assistant to the Vice Chief of Naval Operations, and in 1984 he was promoted to Commodore as the director of the Navy's Long-Range Planning Group. In Sept. 1985, he became DIRECTOR OF NAVAL INTELLIGENCE, after which, in Aug. 1988, as a vice admiral, he became Director of NSA. He held the NSA position until being named Deputy DCI in 1992. In early 1993 he served as acting DCI pending the appointment of R. JAMES WOOLSEY to the post.

He retired from the Navy when he left the Deputy DCI position on Oct. 1, 1995.

Studies and Observation Group

(SOG)

U.S. Army HUMAN INTELLIGENCE (HUMINT) collection organization in the Vietnam War. Part of the Military Assistance Command (MAC), Vietnam, SOG (also known as MACSOG) had its headquarters on Pasteur Avenue in Saigon. The innocuously named Studies and Observation Group inserted intelligence teams deep into enemy territory by land, parachute, helicopters, and PT boats.

Founded in Jan. 1964, SOG was given this mission: "to execute an intensified program of harassment, diversion, political pressure, capture of prisoners, physical destruction, acquisition of intelligence, generation of propaganda, and diversion of resources against North Vietnam."

SOG was an elite joint-service organization directly controlled by the U.S. Commander-in-Chief Pacific Command. It worked closely with a South Vietnamese counterpart organization. Ethnic Chinese from South Vietnam were often members of SOG patrols into Vietcong territory.

The CIA was also involved in SOG. One of SOG's best-known operatives was WILLIAM BUCKLEY, a CIA officer who was kidnapped in Beirut in 1984 and later murdered. In posthumous accounts of Buckley's career, SOG is linked to Operation Phoenix, the highly secret program for assassinating Vietcong leaders.

SOG received a belated Presidential Unit Citation in 2001 "for extraordinary heroism, great combat achievement and unwavering fidelity while executing unheralded top secret missions deep behind enemy lines across Southeast Asia." The citation told of SOG teams penetrating "the enemy's most dangerous redoubts in the jungled Laotian wilderness and the sanctuaries of eastern Cambodia. Pursued by human trackers and even bloodhounds, these small teams out-maneuvered, out-fought and out-ran their numerically superior foe to uncover key enemy facilities, rescue downed pilots, plant wiretaps, mines and electronic sensors, capture valuable enemy prisoners, ambush convoys, discover and assess targets for B-52 strikes, and inflict casualties all out of proportion to their own losses."

Also see VIETNAM.

Sturgeon

SEE FISH

Submarines

Submarines have an inherent intelligence collection capability because of the covert nature of their operations. Beginning early in the 20th century, submarines entered hostile areas and collected intelligence by landing personnel on a beach or by periscope observation. The first submarine periscope photos are believed to have been taken by the British submarine *E-11*. She transited the dangerous Turkish Straits and Sea of Marmara and photographed Constantinople through a periscope with a box camera on Dec. 13, 1915.

During World War II several nations made extensive use of submarines for RECONNAISSANCE and espionage activities, with the Japanese also launching floatplanes from their submarines for reconnaissance. Japanese submarine-launched aircraft flew such missions 34 times from Nov. 1941 to Nov. 1942. They overflew such areas as Pearl Harbor; Melbourne and Sydney, Australia; Auckland and Wellington, New Zealand; Amchitka and Kiska, in the Aleutian Islands; Diégo Suarez, Madagascar; and the Oregon coast.

In 1942 German U-boats landed sabotage teams of four men each on the U.S. Atlantic coast, at Long Island (New York) and Florida. A two-man team also landed by U-boat at Frenchman Bay in Maine in 1944. All of the teams were quickly captured by U.S. officials, principally because some of the saboteurs decided to contact the U.S. government after they arrived. (See FBI.)

Submarines were particularly useful for general surveillance, especially in straits and other areas where enemy ships passed on a regular basis. Periscope photography was a valuable source of intelligence regarding hostile coasts. Such photography was particularly important for planning amphibious landings, as the periscope's low-lying perspective was similar to that of the coxswain of a landing craft approaching the beach. The U.S. submarine *Nautilus,* pioneering American submarine photography, was fitted with brackets to mount a camera on a periscope; a darkroom was provided to process film on board to allow any unsatisfactory photographs to be retaken, and the crew included an enlisted photographer. Thus fitted, in Sept. 1943 the *Nautilus* carried out periscope reconnaissance of Tarawa and Makin in the Gilbert Islands in preparation for the Nov. 1943 U.S. landings on those atolls. On Nov. 19, one day before the assault, the *Nautilus* again entered the Tarawa lagoon. The atoll had been under air attack for five days and a surface bombardment was in progress. The *Nautilus* found that heavy log walls built on the beaches were so far undamaged, as were the coastal guns, some of which were firing at the *Nautilus*. This information was radioed to the task force commander along with estimates of the height of the surf at the beaches.

More submarine reconnaissance missions followed during the war in the Pacific. A pre-invasion submarine reconnaissance mission involved taking up to 2,000 photographs of the target area. In addition to photo-reconnaissance, the submarine *Burrfish* put a landing party on the beaches of Palau and Yap islands in July 1944 to obtain beach intelligence.

In the eastern Atlantic and Mediterranean the British submarine SERAPH was involved in intelligence DECEPTION operations as well as other "special ops." (See MINCEMEAT.)

Since World War II submarines have been employed for ELECTRONIC INTELLIGENCE (ELINT) and ACOUSTIC INTELLIGENCE (ACINT) collection. British and U.S. submarines undertook operations of this kind in Soviet coastal waters, beginning in the 1950s. These submarines operated on a regular basis off major Soviet naval ports in Arctic and Pacific areas. The submarine *Totem* undertook the first British operation off the Kola Peninsula in 1954.

The start date of similar U.S. operations remains classified, but the *Gudgeon* apparently operated close in to Vladivostok in July 1957 and was heavily harassed by Soviet destroyers that forced her to the surface. Some of those U.S. "penetration" missions were given the CODE NAME HOLY STONE.

During the 1970s, in a program known as IVY BELLS, the U.S. submarines *Halibut* and, subsequently, *Parche* were employed to install recording devices for tapping into an underwater communications cable at a depth of some 400 feet in the Sea of Okhotsk, between Soviet bases on the Kamchatka Peninsula and the Soviet Far Eastern coast. This operation was revealed to the Soviets in Jan. 1980 by the U.S. traitor RONALD PELTON. The Soviets quickly shut down the American operation. (One of the seized seafloor recording devices is now on display in the KGB MUSEUM in Moscow.) The *Halibut* also towed a deep-sea camera rig during clandestine searches to find a sunken Soviet ballistic missile submarine in the Pacific. Once located by the cameras, the Soviet submarine was partially recovered by the salvage ship *HUGHES GLOMAR EXPLORER* in a secret operation given the code name JENNIFER. (When the salvage operation was revealed some Soviet officials blamed the loss on a collision with a U.S. submarine that was trailing the Soviet craft to collect ACINT.)

U.S. submarines also carried out intelligence collection missions against China, North Korea, North Vietnam, Libya, Cuba, and other countries during the Cold War era.

The U.S. Navy's passionate campaign to keep submarine espionage during the Cold War a secret partially ended with the publication of *Blind Man's Bluff* (1999), by journalists Sherry Sontag and Christopher Drew. The best-seller gave details of several secret submarine missions and was an excellent read despite containing a large number of factual errors.

Three other notable books also revealed secrets of submarine operations during the Cold War: Dr. Roger C. Dunham, a former nuclear reactor operator in the *Halibut*, told of the search for the sunken Soviet submarine in *Spy Sub* (1996); Lee Vyborny, an original crew member of the small nuclear submarine *NR-1*, and author Don Davis, told of that remarkable craft in *Dark Waters* (2003); and journalist Jim Ring's account of British submarine operations in the Cold War, *We Come Unseen* (2001), evoked much concern by British authorities.

U.S. and British secret operations have continued beyond the Cold War. Two U.S. nuclear submarines were spying on Russian naval exercises in the Barents Sea on Aug. 12, 2003, when the nuclear missile submarine *Kursk* suffered an internal explosion and sank with all 118 men on board. (Initially the Russian Navy leadership blamed her loss on a collision with a U.S. submarine!)

Soviet submarines have been similarly employed in espionage activities. One older diesel-electric submarine of the Whiskey class ran aground in Swedish waters near a sensitive military installation in Nov. 1981, while on an apparent espionage-training operation. Swedish officials had long accused the Soviet government of sending submarines into their territorial waters, even producing photographs showing the tracks of a bottom-crawling midget submarine. But no such craft existed in the Soviet Navy and the seafloor marks were eventually identified as having been made by fishing gear.

The U.S. Holy Stone operations led to several collisions between U.S. and Soviet submarines. Neither navy lost an undersea craft in these incidents, but several submarines were damaged. Those undersea encounters occurred in Soviet coastal waters as well as in international waters.

Some Soviet reports claim that such underwater collisions occurred because they are trailing U.S. submarines in an attempt to garner ACINT and other information. This was the reason given by the Soviets for the loss of a diesel-electric submarine in the North Pacific in 1968 (see above) and of a nuclear-propelled Yankee missile submarine off Bermuda in 1986. Available evidence indicates that both submarines were lost because of operational problems. Both submarines carried nuclear-armed ballistic missiles.

Sucking Dry

Russian term for debriefing an AGENT after he or she returns from a mission.

Sudoplatov, Pavel Anatolievich

(b. 1907 d. 1995)

Soviet assassin and spymaster.

Born to a Ukrainian father and Russian mother, Sudoplatov ran away from home in 1920 to join the Red Army and fight in the Russian Civil War. He joined a CHEKA battalion and, because he could read and write, became a telephone operator and CIPHER clerk.

During the 1920s and 1930s he held a succession of posts in the state intelligence ORGAN, mostly operating against Ukrainian nationalists. He married in 1928. His wife, Emma, was also in Soviet intelligence.

In 1935 he was sent to Finland and then to Germany to work under COVER, infiltrating the Ukrainian nationalist movement headquartered in BERLIN and working with the Nazi Party. He was accepted by the exiles and visited Ukrainian supporters in VIENNA and Paris, where his wife, working as a COURIER for the NKVD, met him. Sudoplatov continually reported on overseas enemies of the Soviet state. "My successful journey to Western Europe changed my status in the intelligence community. My mission was reported to Stalin. . . . Later, I was awarded the Order of the Red Banner and received it from President M. I. Kalinin," Sudoplatov wrote in his autobiographical SPECIAL TASKS (1994). In 1937–1938 he traveled to the West as a courier on a cargo ship under cover as a radio operator. During that period he met with Soviet dictator Josef Stalin. Sudoplatov wrote in *Special Tasks:*

> I was thirty years old and still could not control my emotions. I was overwhelmed and could not believe that the leader of the country would meet with a rank-and-file case officer. When Stalin shook my hand I could not collect myself to report to him succinctly. Stalin smiled and said: "Young man, don't be so excited. Report the essential facts. We have only twenty minutes."

He soon met again with Stalin as the assassinations of Ukrainian nationalists—at home and abroad—were plotted. Sudoplatov personally assassinated Yevhen Konovalets in Rotterdam in May 1938, presenting the Ukrainian nationalist leader with a box of chocolates that soon exploded, killing him. Fleeing Rotterdam, Sudoplatov ended up in Spain, where for several weeks he acted as a Polish volunteer in a guerrilla group run by the NKVD, attached to the Republican forces. Back in Moscow, Sudoplatov was charged with planning the assassination of Leon Trotsky, a political opponent of Stalin. Trotsky was subsequently murdered in Mexico by Ramón Mercader, an NKVD officer. (The attempt was made on Aug. 20, 1940; Trotsky died of his wounds the following day.)

During this period Sudoplatov survived Stalin's purges of the NKVD, all the more remarkable because of his extensive visits to Western Europe.

On July 5, 1941, shortly after Germany invaded the Soviet Union, Sudoplatov was appointed director of the Administration for Special Tasks—responsible for espionage operations against Germany and its allies. His organization grew rapidly to some 20,000 men and women, including 2,000 non-Soviets. In Oct. 1941, his organization was redesignated as Independent Department Two of the NKVD, and Sudoplatov began reporting directly to NKVD commissar LAVRENTY BERIA. He was also promoted to commissar of state security 3rd grade, the equivalent of lieutenant general in the Red Army.

Describing the operations he commanded, Sudoplatov wrote in *Special Tasks:*

> During the course of the war, we placed 212 guerrilla detachments and units comprising 7,316 men to the rear of the enemy. We trained a thousand officers and technicians in sabotage for the Red Army. We also sent 3,500 civilian saboteurs and agents. The [NKVD] parachutists' unit dropped an additional 3,000 guerrillas behind enemy lines.

Informed by DONALD MACLEAN and other sources of the U.S.-British atomic bomb project, in 1942 Stalin established a special committee on atomic energy, headed by Beria, to coordinate the efforts of Soviet scientists and research activities dealing with atomic issues. Sudoplatov was attached to the committee as its director of intelligence. In July 1943 the foreign intelligence and security services of the NKVD were reorganized as a separate commissariat, the NKGB. Sudoplatov was assigned to the NKGB to head Department "S," which would supervise all atomic espionage operations of the GRU as well as the NKGB.

Thus, Sudoplatov coordinated all intelligence from the ATOMIC SPY RING as well as other Soviet espionage efforts in the United States, Canada, and Britain. His memoirs detail these activities, naming not only the better-known atomic spies but also J. Robert Oppenheimer, the technical head of the U.S. atomic bomb (Manhattan) project, Enrico Fermi, Niels Bohr, and other distinguished scientists.

Such accusations are clearly false. Quite possibly Soviet spies KLAUS FUCHS, BRUNO PONTECORVO, and others openly obtained information from Oppenheimer (given the Soviet CODE NAME Star) and Fermi in the course of their work on the atomic bomb; by identifying these scientists as their sources, the true spies may have led Sudoplatov to consider the others de facto Soviet AGENTS.

After the war Sudoplatov continued as a senior intelligence officer, working directly with Stalin as well as Beria. Stalin died in March 1953 and Beria became one of three men who took control of the Soviet state. On June 26, Beria and several of his deputies were arrested. Sudoplatov's name was often heard in the interrogations of Beria, who was executed on Dec. 23, 1953.

After being questioned, Sudoplatov himself was arrested on Aug. 21. Although steadfastly claiming that he was not a conspirator with Beria, and that all of his actions during more than three decades in state security organs had been "legal" within the Soviet state, in 1958—five years after his arrest—he was sentenced to 15 years in prison.

Released in 1968, Sudoplatov immediately began a campaign to have the charges against him overturned and his pension reinstated. In 1992 he was "rehabilitated."

Special Tasks was written in collaboration with his son, Anatoli, and veteran writers on Soviet affairs Jerrold L. and Leona P. Schecter.

Sugita, Col. Ichiji

Senior Japanese Army INTELLIGENCE OFFICER who participated in major campaigns and surrenders in World War II.

A 1925 graduate of the Japanese Military Academy, he was commissioned as a 2nd lieutenant in infantry. After standard assignments, in Jan. 1937 he became an assistant military ATTACHÉ in the United States and in Sept. 1938 was sent to Britain. In early 1939 he was assigned to the General Staff in Tokyo. He was the only member of the Army General Staff with specialized intelligence training.

In Nov. 1941, a month before the PEARL HARBOR ATTACK and U.S. entry into World War II, Sugita, as a lieutenant colonel, was assigned as intelligence officer to the 25th Army for the Japanese campaign against Malaya and Singapore. During that campaign Sugita was badly injured in a motorcycle accident. Despite severe pain, he continued to perform his duties, and in Feb. 1942 he helped to negotiate and translate the surrender of Lt. Gen. A. E. Percival, commander of the British Commonwealth forces defending Singapore.

Sugita subsequently served on Guadalcanal, where he endured the ordeal and privation of that jungle campaign. He planned the evacuation of 13,000 troops from the island in Japan's first land defeat of the war. Returning to staff duties in Tokyo, he also flew to Southeast Asia to observe the ill-fated Japanese assault on Imphal, India.

When Japan surrendered to the Allies on board the U.S. battleship *Missouri* on Sept. 2, 1945, in Tokyo Bay, Sugita was a member of the Japanese delegation. Across the surrender table he saw Gen. Percival, recently released from a Japanese prison camp, whom he had escorted to another surrender table three years earlier. (At the time of the surrender on the *Missouri* Sugita was assigned as secretary to the Prime Minister.)

Imprisoned after the war, he was released in May 1947. Sugita subsequently joined the Japanese Ground Self-Defense Force (Army). He became Chief of Staff in March 1960, holding that position until March 1962.

Sukhomlinov, Gen. Vladimir

(b. 1844? d. 1926)

The Imperial Russian minister of war from 1908 to Jan. 1914, whose stupidity and greed prevented the Russian Army from having the weapons it needed when World War I broke out in Aug. 1914. After the war he was tried for treason.

A dashing cavalry officer in the 1877 war against the Turks, he believed "that military knowledge acquired in that campaign was the permanent truth," wrote Barbara Tuchman in her classic *The Guns of August* (1962). The Russian foreign minister, wrote Tuchman, said of Sukhomlinov, "It was very difficult to make him work but to get him to tell the truth was well-nigh impossible." But he was charming and toadied to the Czar and Czarina, while despising and interfering with the Grand Duke Nicholas, commander of the armies in the field and a most competent military leader.

Sukhomlinov—fat, indulgent, greedy, and a crook—took a voluptuous wife 32 years his junior (his fourth) while serving as the war minister. An Austrian crony of Sukhomlinov, who supplied evidence for his wife's divorce and was often in Sukhomlinov's home as an intimate, undoubtedly had access to the papers that the minister brought home. The Austrian, Altschiller, was his country's chief AGENT in Russia. Sukhomlinov also defended subordinates who were obviously providing the Germans with intelligence of various kinds.

Finally forced to step down as minister of war in 1914 because of his incompetence, he remained in Russia during the first three years of World War I. But in Aug. 1917, with the Czar gone and the country in crisis, he was arrested and brought to trial on the charge of treason as well as lesser crimes. He was acquitted of treason but found guilty of abuse of power and "inactivity," and sentenced to hard labor for life.

A few months later he was liberated as the Bolsheviks took control of parts of the country and he made his way to BERLIN.

Sukhomlinov subsequently wrote his memoirs, which he dedicated to the deposed Kaiser, who had led Germany to war with Russia.

Sunset

British CODE NAME for highly classified material based on ENIGMA decrypts prepared by the NAVAL INTELLIGENCE Department of the Admiralty and sent to the Admiralty delegation in Washington, D.C., during World War II. When Prime Minister Winston Churchill was at the Casablanca Conference with President Roosevelt in Jan. 1943, there was no SPECIAL LIAISON UNIT available to pass him ULTRA material; accordingly, Sunset "telegrams" were provided to him.

Suntan

CODE NAME for the proposed Lockheed CL-400 spyplane, intended as a successor to the U-2 aircraft. It was never built.

Sun-tzu

(b. circa 510 B.C.)

Early fourth century B.C. Chinese general with a keen sense of the value of intelligence. Sun-tzu wrote the classic *Ping-fa* (The Art of War). The earliest known textbook on war and espionage, it is still required reading in both Eastern and Western military services.

A native of the Ch'i state at the mouth of the Yellow River, Sun-tzu spent most of his life as a general for the adjacent state of Wu and at times was the commander of Wu's armies.

Sun-tzu wrote, "A hundred ounces of silver spent for information may save ten thousand spent on war," and "If you know the enemy and know yourself, you need not fear a hundred battles. If you know yourself and not the enemy, for every victory you will suffer a defeat. If you know neither yourself nor the enemy, you are a fool and will meet defeat in every battle."

Sun-tzu wrote that there were five classes of spies: (1) local inhabitants; (2) government officials of the enemy who could be persuaded to keep their positions but to change their loyalty; (3) enemy spies who could be persuaded to change sides, providing information about the enemy and also possibly sending back false information; (4) spies who perform acts of espionage against the enemy for the purpose of deception; these are sacrificed to give the enemy false information (i.e., they will be executed by the enemy); and (5) spies sent behind enemy lines who survive the operation and return with information.

In *Ping-fa* he wrote:

As living spies we must recruit men who are intelligent but appear to be stupid; who seem to be dull but are strong in heart; men who are agile, vigorous, hardy, and brave; well-versed in lowly matters and able to endure hunger, cold, filth, and humiliation.

Superencipher

Process of "super" encoding to increase security of communications. For example, if the word *battleship* is encoded in a four-letter code as VTMG, under the process of superenciphering each letter would have a substitute letter for actual transmission. For example, V might become B, T becomes E, M becomes R, and G becomes P, with the word battleship being transmitted as BERP.

Sûreté Generale

French police agency whose duties include DOMESTIC INTELLIGENCE.

The Sûreté can be traced back to Napoleonic times. In 1804 Napoléon's prefect of police, Joseph Fouché, established the Sûreté, or secret police, within the Ministry of General Police. The powerful agency ran a spy network that ranged beyond France, informing Napoléon about his political enemies, both internal and external. Much of the Sûreté's intelligence came from the old French tradition of surreptitious mail opening (see BLACK CHAMBER and FRANCE).

After the fall of Napoléon and the establishment of the French Republic, the Sûreté continued to focus on serving the government by gathering political intelligence. Besides keeping opposition politicians and political movements under SURVEILLANCE, Sûreté operatives kept watch over German AGENTS who had infiltrated French businesses and journals.

By the end of the 19th century the Sûreté had expanded into a COUNTERINTELLIGENCE agency, under the Interior Ministry, with a few agents in major European cities, such as BERLIN, Geneva, and St. Petersburg. Sûreté officials sometimes countenanced cooperation with the OKHRANA, the secret police of Czar Alexander III, especially after France and Russia formed an alliance in 1894. But when the Okhrana operated openly in France, intimidating and achieving the deportation of Russian dissidents, French radicals agitated against the Sûreté. To French liberals, the Sûreté became a lasting symbol of political repression.

With the rise of communism, the Sûreté fanned the Red Scare sweeping Europe, finding Bolsheviks in all strata of French society and often fighting the SR in uncoordinated battles against communist subversion. In the 1920s the French Communist Party incited workers to espionage to aid the Red Army and world communism. INTELLIGENCE OFFICERS in the Soviet Embassy distributed questionnaires that specified what intelligence Communist Party members were expected to get. The Soviets were particularly interested in getting spies into French arms and aircraft factories.

The questionnaires turned public opinion in favor of the Sûreté, which arrested a member of the French Communist Party's central committee and his girlfriend. They subsequently fled to the Soviet Union.

The Sûreté has remained essentially a police agency, with military-based intelligence agencies, such as the SDECE, doing the spying for France. The Sûreté has sometimes found itself caught up in intelligence controversies; its agents, for example, participated in the 1965 kidnapping of Mehdi Ben Barka, a left-wing Moroccan political leader. But mostly, the Sûreté has been analogous to Britain's SPECIAL BRANCH of Scotland Yard—the police who do the trailing and arresting of spies.

Surreptitious Entry

SEE BLACK BAG JOB

Surveillance

The systematic observation of a specific area—including space, air, surface, and underwater—or of a specific person, by various means of intelligence collection.

Although surveillance techniques vary little from one nation's intelligence agencies to the next, the British and the Soviets for a while in the 1940s were both reading from the same set of instructions. ANTHONY BLUNT, while working for the British Security Service (MI5), was for a time the officer in charge of the WATCHERS, the women and men who carried out surveillance of foreign agents and spy suspects. Blunt gave each one his weekly task and knew the details of each case. He reportedly analyzed surveillance techniques, recommending changes. Blunt was a Soviet MOLE in MI5, so he then passed everything about British surveillance on to the Soviets. As a result, Soviet AGENTS could elude British watchers. How long this went on is not known.

Suvorov, Viktor [p]

Former GRU Col. Vladimir Bogdanovich Rezun, who defected to the British in VIENNA in 1979.

Rezun was commissioned as an officer after attending the Kharkov Guards Tank Command School and subsequently served in armored units of the Soviet ground forces. His unit participated in the 1968 invasion of Czechoslovakia, at which time he came to the attention of the head of intelligence of the assaulting army and was assigned to MILITARY INTELLIGENCE. He underwent SPETSNAZ training in 1969 and, after attending the prestigious Frunze Military Academy in Leningrad, was assigned to GRU headquarters in Moscow.

He served as an assistant military ATTACHÉ in VIENNA from 1975 to 1979 while carrying out intelligence activities. He was reportedly being sought by GRU officers when he defected. Settling in Britain, Rezun wrote several books under the pseudonym Viktor Suvorov while in the West: *The Liberators: My Life in the Soviet Army* (1981), *Inside the Soviet Army* (1982), *Inside Soviet Military Intelligence* (1984), *Inside the Aquarium: The Making of a Top Soviet Spy* (1986), *Spetsnaz: The Inside Story of the Soviet Special Forces* (1987), *Cleansing: Why Did Stalin Decapitate His Army?* (1999), and *Suicide: Why Did Hitler Attack the Soviet Union?* (2000).

(Aleksandr Suvorov, whose surname Rezun adopted as a pseudonym, was Russia's greatest general of the 18th century.)

SVR

The Russian Foreign Intelligence Service. The SVR was established in Dec. 1991 by Russian President Boris Yeltsin as one of the successor agencies to the KGB. The SVR was subordinate to the short-lived Ministry of Security (MB).

The SVR took over the foreign intelligence functions of the KGB, with the COUNTERINTELLIGENCE activities being transferred to the newly created FSK. (Similarly, the presidential security functions and related activities previously carried out by the KGB were transferred to the new agency.)

The first director of the SVR was YEVGENY PRIMAKOV, appointed to head the KGB in Oct. 1991 following the abortive coup against Mikhail Gorbachev. He remained in charge of the KGB and the successor SVR until Jan. 9, 1996, when Yeltsin named him Russia's foreign minister and later prime minister. (The organization is sometimes referred to as SVRR.)

Vyacheslav Ivanovich Trubnikov, whose specialty was India and Pakistan, succeeded Primakov in 1996.

About 15,000 people are said to work for the SVR. Its operational directorates include Internal Security, TECHNICAL INTELLIGENCE, Illegal Networks, Non-proliferation of Weapons of Mass Destruction, ECONOMIC INTELLIGENCE, and a single directorate devoted to Organized Crime, Terrorism, and Drug Trafficking.

Swallow

Russian term for a female AGENT, especially one used in HONEY TRAP situations where SEX is used to obtain information, or to create a situation where a TARGET can be blackmailed at a later time.

Sweeper

Term for electronic technician who examines, or "sweeps," an office or facility to determine if electronic BUGS have been planted.

Szabo, Sgt. 1st Class Zoltan

U.S. soldier who launched a long-lived spy ring within the U.S. Army in Germany.

Szabo introduced, Sgt. 1st Class CLYDE LEE CONRAD to Hungarian INTELLIGENCE OFFICERS in 1975. Conrad became the master spy of the ring. Szabo, convicted of espionage in 1989, received only a 10-month suspended sentence after assisting in the investigation that led to Conrad and the smashing of the ring by a long and complex FBI-Army intelligence investigation.

12 Intelligence and Security Company

Part of the Intelligence Corps formed by the British Army in Northern Ireland in 1942. The Intelligence Corps was a key element in British COVERT ACTION against the terrorism of the Provisional Wing of the Irish Republican Army and the Irish National Liberation Army. (See 14 INTELLIGENCE COMPANY.)

30th Assault Unit

British multi-service combat unit in World War II that collected TECHNICAL INTELLIGENCE on German forces during amphibious landings. The unit, organized in part by IAN FLEMING, creator of JAMES BOND [f], first saw action in the Anglo-American North Africa landings in Nov. 1942.

The unit, also known as No. 30 Commando, came ashore with the first wave of Allied landing forces to seize enemy documents and equipment before they could be destroyed or lost. The unit subsequently participated in operations in Sicily, Italy, and elsewhere in the Mediterranean, capturing valuable documents as well as CIPHER, radio, and radar equipment, and weapons. In Sicily the unit captured a complete set of Italian Air Force ciphers for homing beacons, enabling Allied planes to fly to targets in northern Italy guided by Italian navigation beacons.

The British had learned that in 1941 the Germans had a similar intelligence commando unit that had entered Athens with the first German troops and seized important documents from the abandoned British headquarters there. Other, similar German units were known to exist.

The 30th Assault Unit returned to Britain in late 1943 to prepare for the Normandy landings in 1944. However, the British 15th Army Group requested the return of the Army component of the unit to Italy for operations there. Thus, only the naval component participated in the D-DAY landings. At Normandy the 30th Assault Unit landed with the 47th Royal Marine Commando to help capture and collect technical intelligence at a German coastal radar station.

T-10

CODE NAME assigned by the FBI to actor Ronald Reagan in the 1950s when he was an informer during the communist scare period.

The earliest FBI record on Reagan was dated Nov. 18, 1943, when Reagan told of "nearly coming to blows" at a party when an unidentified German sympathizer made anti-Semitic remarks. Reagan was then in the U.S. Army, assigned to the Army Air Forces motion picture unit at Camp Roach in Culver City, Calif. His name appears again in 1946 during an FBI investigation of the Hollywood Independent Citizens' Committee of Arts, Sciences and Professions, which the FBI considered a "communist front." Reagan quit the committee, he told the FBI, after its members voted down a resolution condemning communism as well as fascism.

Reagan, as president of the Screen Actors Guild, testified before the House Un-American Activities Committee in Oct. 1947, when the committee was looking for communists in the entertainment business. Reagan and his wife at the time, actress Jane Wyman, told of cliques in the guild that "follow the party line."

Reagan subsequently became governor of California and, in 1981, the 40th President of the United States.

Tactical Air Reconnaissance Pod System

SEE TARPS

Tactical Intelligence

Intelligence for planning and conducting tactical operations at the force or unit level. It focuses on an enemy's capabilities, immediate intentions, and the environment.

The U.S. Navy used the term OPERATIONAL INTELLIGENCE through the 1980s to refer to tactical intelligence provided to naval operating forces.

Military history is full of examples of tactical intelligence being ignored by commanders who did not accept it because it interfered with plans or clashed with assumptions about the enemy's intentions.

Days before the German offensive in the Ardennes in Dec. 1944—the Battle of the Bulge—U.S. outposts facing the Germans reported hearing vehicles moving along the front. Other U.S. soldiers reported seeing German troops in clean uniforms, indicating that they had recently moved to the front. These small bits of information, added to others coming in at a higher level, could have led Allied commanders to the realization that the Germans were about to launch a major offensive. But the importance of this tactical information was only seen afterwards, in the postmortems following the stunning German surprise.

Sometimes, tactical intelligence is heeded. In March 1945, when Germans were destroying or defending all bridges across the Rhine, advance units of the U.S. 9th Armored Division at the edge of the town of Remagen, Germany, discovered that the Ludendorff Railway Bridge was still intact. They reported the discovery, and as the intelligence went up the hierarchy of command, the Americans took the bridge. (The Germans attempted to blow it up, but the bridge did not collapse.) When the news reached Gen. Dwight D. Eisenhower, the Supreme Allied Commander, he changed his battle plans and ordered all available troops to head for Remagen, speeding the advance of American troops into Germany.

Also see STRATEGIC INTELLIGENCE.

Tactical Exploitation of National Capabilities (TENCAP)

U.S. military program that seeks to integrate national RECONNAISSANCE capabilities into the tactical decision-making process. National systems are designed to support STRATEGIC INTELLIGENCE requirements. TENCAP was intended to leverage the national technology to provide downlinking of these strategic systems to tactical levels to speed up the tactical decision-making process. Those capabilities include NATIONAL TECHNICAL MEANS, primarily SATELLITES and reconnaissance AIRCRAFT.

In 1973 the Army took the lead within the Department of Defense by establishing a program to execute the Army's tactical exploitation of national capabilities, serve as the unique technical and fiscal interface with the national program offices, and manage the TENCAP hardware acquisition.

That approach was so successful that Congress in 1977 ordered all military services to establish TENCAP programs based on the Army's model. Within the Army ground processing terminals initially were developed for use at corps and higher headquarters. Technology and applications have evolved so that certain systems could then be employed at division level and below. National data combined with data from other sources provides an accurate and current picture of the enemy and the terrain during planning and execution, enhancing the INTELLIGENCE PREPARATION OF THE BATTLEFIELD (IPB).

The Army TENCAP program remains the largest and most successful of the individual services programs, in part because the other services have invested only limited resources (people and funding) in the effort.

Tai Li, Lt. Gen.

(b. ? d. 1946)

Chief of intelligence for Chiang Kai-shek's Nationalist Chinese government during World War II. Tai Li was the organizer and chief of the BUREAU OF INVESTIGATION AND STATISTICS, the intelligence arm of the National Military Council of Nationalist China from 1932 to 1946.

He was a member of Chiang's military police in the 1920s, rising to captain by 1927. His career is lost in the murk of COVER stories and COUNTERINTELLIGENCE, for he probably did some highly secret infiltration of China's communist organizations. He was said to have so buried his past that he burned the records of his early life and killed people who knew him as a teenager.

People called him "the butcher," whispering tales of the torture and executions he seems to have gleefully supervised. Richard Deacon in *The Chinese Secret Service* (1974) quotes a description of one of Tai Li's techniques: "He lined up some locomotives on a siding, got the fireboxes red hot, opened their doors, tied down the whistles to shut out the screams, and one after another threw his living victims into the fiery furnaces." He was said to have burned alive thousands of labor leaders, intellectuals, and students—all viewed by him as Chiang's enemies.

Tai Li believed that alcohol and women were "weapons" that he could wield to control men he targeted. He forbade his officers and servants to marry, saying that inevitably marriage meant that two people, rather than one, knew a secret.

When Western nations went to war against Japan in 1941, Tai Li cooperated with China's new allies, organizing guerrilla units and intelligence nets. From 1942 to 1945 he was also director of the Sino-American Cooperative Organization (SACO), which had up to 3,000 U.S. military personnel in China for weather reporting, combat, and intelligence activities. Through SACO, Tai Li learned the names of AGENTS working for the U.S. OFFICE OF STRATEGIC SERVICES.

"It was the boast of the organization," an American wrote, "that there was not a single village in China in which there was not a Tai Li spy to report on subversive activities. By terrorizing a man's family it was easy to keep the man in line." Tai Li and his men also assassinated an unknown number of people who had nothing to do with fighting Japan. Many of the assassins, it was said, used silencer-equipped pistols supplied by Americans.

Tai Li held the rank of lieutenant general at the time of his death in an airplane crash on March 17, 1946, near Pangchow. Officially, the plane hit a mountain during bad weather. Rumors persisted that he was killed by his enemies.

Talent Keyhole

U.S. classification for OVERHEAD/SATELLITE photography. Talent Keyhole and SPECIAL INTELLIGENCE classifications concern data that are the product of SIGNALS INTELLIGENCE collection or OVERHEAD RECONNAISSANCE, or a combination of both.

Talent Spotter

Person who alerts an INTELLIGENCE OFFICER to someone who is a potential AGENT or DOUBLE AGENT. The intelligence officer will then gather background information on the proposed agent and will make an approach. The spotter need not be a full-fledged agent and is more likely to be a bartender or bank teller who is being paid, often through a CUTOUT, for the names of likely prospects. The talent spotter may also be told, in a FALSE FLAG ploy, that the talent seeker is a friendly nation or commercial firm.

Tallmadge, Maj. Benjamin

(b. 1754 d. 1835)

INTELLIGENCE OFFICER for Gen. GEORGE WASHINGTON during the American Revolution. Tallmadge's greatest accomplishment was the establishment of the CULPER RING, which provided Washington with vital intelligence.

Washington's appointment of Tallmadge as a spymaster in 1778 resulted from the general's disappointment over the failure of the NATHAN HALE spy mission in 1776; Hale had been discovered and was executed.

Tallmadge was instrumental in unmasking Maj. Gen. BENEDICT ARNOLD as a traitor. Arnold had ordered Tallmadge to aid "John Anderson," to whom Arnold had given a pass to go through American lines. When troops detained Anderson and found he carried documents about the garrison at West Point, Tallmadge shrewdly connected the man (who was a British officer Maj. JOHN ANDRÉ) with Arnold. Tallmadge wanted to have Arnold held for interrogation by Washington, but he did not have the authority to do so. André was held and later executed; Arnold escaped.

In ciphers that Tallmadge devised for his AGENTS, he was 721.

Target

Person, agency, facility, area, or country against which intelligence operations are directed.

Target of Opportunity

Person, agency, facility, or area that becomes available as a target for intelligence operations without prior planning.

TARPS (TACTICAL AIR RECONNAISSANCE POD SYSTEM)

Each of the Navy's 11 aircraft carriers had one squadron with about 14 F-14 Tomcat fighters, three of which are wired to carry the TARPS pod. The TARPS is fitted with a digital imaging and datalink to provide near real-time imagery to commanders ashore and aboard ship. (Early versions of TARPS, first introduced in the early 1980s, had reconnaissance imagery that had to be downloaded after the aircraft returned to the carrier.)

The F-14/TARPS, however, flown by non-specialized reconnaissance pilots, does not provide the quality or quantity of tactical reconnaissance that was possible with some earlier carrier-based AIRCRAFT. That shortfall was keenly felt during Operation Desert Storm in the Persian Gulf in 1991. According to the U.S. Director of Naval Intelligence at the time, Rear Adm. Thomas A. Brooks, the TARPS "was totally inadequate" in providing sufficient and timely bomb damage assessment during Operation Desert Storm.

TARPS replaced specialized reconnaissance aircraft based on the A3J VIGILANTE, F4H PHANTOM, and F8U CRUSADER.

When the F-14 is retired in about 2010, the carrier-based reconnaissance role is expected to be taken over by a specialized variant of the F/A-18 Hornet as well as UNMANNED AERIAL VEHICLES.

The TARPS pod is 17 feet long and weighs 1,850 pounds. It is fitted under the F-14's fuselage; missiles can be carried in addition to the pod. The pod initially had a two-position (vertical and forward oblique) KS-87 frame camera, a KA-99 low-altitude panoramic camera, and an AN/AAD-5 imaging infrared sensor. Subsequently, digitizers have been used to send reconnaissance imagery via datalink from the TARPS to recipients in soft copy in near-real time. Each image displays the latitude and longitude of the location photographed.

Task Force (1)

COVER designation for U.S. Navy intelligence operations. "task force" is normally used for a seagoing operation involving ships and other naval forces. In the case of Task Force 96, the U.S. Navy command organization to coordinate activities of INTELLIGENCE COLLECTION SHIPS in the Far East in the late 1960s, actual ships were involved. Task Force 96, operating under the Commander U.S. Naval Forces Japan, was assigned the spy ships *Banner* and *PUEBLO*.

But "task force," in its intelligence usage, came to mean an intelligence-gathering organization when the OFFICE OF NAVAL, INTELLIGENCE (ONI) ordered its intelligence-gathering unit, the Naval Field Operations Support Group (NFOSG), to establish "a worldwide intelligence collection organization while preserving nonintelligence attributability of collection operations."

Because the existence of NFOSG was publicly known, naval intelligence officials wanted a way to provide individual cover for NFOSG activities so that if a single operation was BLOWN, NFOSG's role as a cover organization would not be. The cover selected was "task force," a standard Navy name for an operational unit.

"Should the unit's initial task force designation—157—be compromised in any way it would be simply replaced by another one of the numbers. While the Task Force 157 designation was not intended to replace the NFOSG designation as the organization's real name . . . the NFOSG designation fell into disuse over time," wrote intelligence historian JEFFREY T. RICHELSON.

Task Force (2)

CIA groups established to respond to international crises, especially where paramilitary activities are involved. These task forces are generally composed of 25 to 100 persons, including analysts, military specialists, and intelligence officers.

As examples, in the 1960s the CIA established a Congo TF and a Cuban TF. The former was changed to a branch within the CIA because of the long duration of the crisis in that area. In the 1970s the CIA established a short-lived Libyan TF, a Portugese TF to respond to the political crisis in that country, and an Angolan TF in response to the civil war and Soviet–Cuban influence in the former Portugese colony.

Task Force 20

U.S. Army unit that participated in the Iraqi conflict of 2003, primarily seeking reported chemical, biological, and nuclear weapons (i.e., Weapons of Mass Destruction). The covert unit was comprised primarily of Army SPECIAL OPERATIONS FORCES.

Although unable to locate the sought-for weapons, the unit was able to capture several wanted Iraqi leaders as well as Palestinian guerrilla leader Mohammed Abbas. (The task force did locate a cache of land mines that apparently were designed for the dispersal of chemicals.)

Task Force 20 was also used to rescue PFC Jessica Lynch, a soldier captured by Iraqi forces during the conflict. With other U.S. forces, TF 20 rescued Lynch from a hospital behind Iraqi lines.

Task Force 157

During the 1970s Task Force 157 (TF 157) was involved in a variety of intelligence missions, ranging from monitoring ports to providing a TOP SECRET communications channel used to arrange the 1971 clandestine trip to China of Henry A. Kissinger, President Nixon's national security adviser. (See WEATHER.)

The task force had about 75 contract AGENTS, including EDWIN P. WILSON, a former CIA officer who was later convicted of selling arms to Libya.

The task force's official cover was the Naval Administrative Services Command, ostensibly a Navy unit for supporting naval personnel in remote areas; TF 157's unofficial cover was an international maritime consulting firm, Pierce Morgan Associates. The firm was located in the same Alexandria, Va., building as the Administrative Services Command. TF 157 had about 25 field offices throughout the world and ran at least 10 PROPRIETARY COMPANIES in the United States and other countries.

The unit was so secret that its existence was itself secret, as was the fact that the Navy had a program for gathering HUMAN INTELLIGENCE (HUMINT). In testimony before the Senate Appropriations Committee in 1973, however, Vice Adm. W. D. Gaddis, Deputy Chief of Naval Operations for Logistics, revealed the existence of HUMINT by saying that the "Navy's human intelligence collection program is expanding operations in sensitive areas." He was referring to TF 157.

Sometimes through newspaper advertisements, the unit recruited civilians who worked as CASE OFFICERS, running agents and operations at the field offices. In Germany, for instance, they got leads to retired veterans of the German Navy, who might work as agents by intercepting mail between East and West Germany.

One operation involved the creation of a spy , ostensibly for the Iranian Navy. Wilson, using a proprietary cover, bought a trawler and sold it to Iran for $500,000. The ship was to sail near Soviet ships and monitor their electronic emissions. But there were few such TARGETS in the Persian Gulf—and the ship was not seaworthy.

One of the unit's missions was to monitor of nuclear weapons being shipped by the Soviets. Ships were checked at such narrow passages—"choke points"—as the Straits of Gibraltar and the Bosporus by "civilian" yachts carrying Navy technicians and nuclear detection equipment. (See CLUSTER SERIES.)

The unit also provided data on Soviet weapons for the Strategic Arms Limitation Talks (SALT) negotiations. And, TF 157 ferried agents from Taiwan to mainland China, where they installed electronic monitoring equipment; those operations ceased after Nixon's historic visit to China in 1972. In Vietnam, TF 157 provided information about Haiphong Harbor, aiding in the 1972 mining of the harbor by U.S. naval aircraft. In Oct. 1973, the task force reported detecting nuclear weapons being shipped to Egypt during the Yom Kippur War against Israel, although the detections were not conclusive.

Investigation into purchasing practices of the task force led to discoveries of dealings between contract agents like Wilson and firms selling equipment and supplies to TF 157. In Oct. 1974, about the time of these discoveries, then-Capt. BOBBY RAY INMAN became DIRECTOR OF NAVAL INTELLIGENCE. He was under Pentagon orders to cut back intelligence spending, and TF 157 was one of the possible budget-slashing sites. After a futile attempt to have it taken over by the CIA or the DEFENSE INTELLI-GENCE AGENCY, in July 1976 Inman abolished TF 157, effective Sept. 30, 1977.

"Case officers were told to destroy all records of employment by the Navy . . ." according to historian Richelson. "They were to deny that the task force ever existed."

But the existence of TF 157 became known in May 1977 when BOB WOODWARD of *The Washington Post*, who had been working on a story about Wilson, heard of the task force.

Task Force 168

As TF 157 was being abolished, its assets and projects were distributed within the INTELLIGENCE COMMUNITY. Some of the TF 157 activities were assigned to Task Force 168, which provided TACTICAL INTELLIGENCE and TECHNICAL INTELLIGENCE to fleet commanders.

TF 168 had itself been created by the NAVAL INTELLIGENCE COMMAND (NIC) in 1969 to evade NIC staff cuts. In 1977 it inherited from TF 157 the Navy Scientific and Technical Element, Far East, and two intelligence units stationed in Munich, Germany, primarily to interrogate refugees and defectors for information valuable to ONI.

Also see GOLDFINGER.

Tavrin

SEE ZEPPELIN

Taylor, Brig. Gen. Telford

(b. 1908 d. 1998)

U.S. Army officer who worked at BLETCHLEY PARK, the British ULTRA codebreaking establishment, during World War II. He later became the U.S. chief prosecutor on the international military tribunal at Nuremberg that tried Nazis for war crimes.

As a colonel at Bletchley Park, Taylor was responsible for distributing Ultra material to the principal U.S. Army and Army Air Forces headquarters in Europe. (See SPECIAL LIAISON UNIT.)

As the war was ending in Europe, U.S. Supreme Court Justice Robert H. Jackson, who had been appointed chief prosecutor at the war crimes trial, asked that Taylor be assigned to the prosecution staff. Taylor succeeded Jackson as chief prosecutor, presiding over 12 trials of Nazis and military leaders tried by civilian tribunals in 1946–1949.

Taylor wrote *The Anatomy of the Nuremberg Trials* (1992); several books about World War II, including *The Breaking Wave: World War II in the Summer of 1940* (1957), regarded as one of the best analyses of the Battle of Britain; and *The Grand Inquest: The Story of Congressional Investigations* (1955).

Team B

SEE B TEAM

Technical Intelligence

(TECHINT)

Intelligence derived from foreign sources related to technical equipment and capabilities. During World War II the British and German armies established specialized units that accompanied or followed the lead assault units to seize technical material. (See 30TH ASSAULT UNIT.) The U.S. Army organized the ALSOS MISSION to seize enemy material related to atomic bomb development.

During the Cold War technical intelligence included the gathering of intelligence through computers (see COMPUTER ESPIONAGE), electronic sensors, SATELLITES, and overhead photography. Technical intelligence is often so dependent upon technology that its users assume they need little or no HUMAN INTELLIGENCE. In intelligence agencies throughout the world there are frequent debates over the relative value of the two collection methods.

Also see SCIENTIFIC INTELLIGENCE and ALSOS MISSION.

Telekrypton

Secure transatlantic radio communications system used by the U.S. OFFICE OF STRATEGIC SERVICES during World War II.

Telemetry Intelligence

(TELINT)

TECHNICAL INTELLIGENCE derived from the interception, processing, and analysis of foreign telemetry.

Telemetry intelligence began with the space race between the United States and the Soviet Union, when the United States wanted to monitor the telemetry being broadcast during Soviet space launches. Initially aircraft with electronic sensors were used to fly at a high altitude near test facilities during these Soviet launches, intercepting and recording the electronic telemetry for later analysis. Three B-47 STRATOJET bombers, stationed at Incirlik Air Force Base in Turkey and designated EB-47E(TT), were fitted with a crew capsule in the bomb bay that carried a pair of electronic warfare officers. An external fairing carrying sensor antennas was fitted to each side of the nose. For Soviet launches out of Kasputin Yar, missions were flown over the Black Sea; for launches out of Tyuratam, the aircraft flew over northeastern Iran. The flights were carried out from 1958 until about 1967. Air Force RC-135 RIVET JOINT aircraft also tracked Russian and Chinese missile launches in the Pacific. (See C-135 STRATOTANKER.)

The U.S. Navy has operated the missile tracking ship *Observation Island* in the Pacific since 1981 to monitor missile launches; the ship is part of the Cobra Judy program.

Knowing that telemetry can be intercepted, missiles can transmit falsified data, warns the U.S. Air Force intelligence-targeting guide on telemetry intelligence.

Television

Real-life espionage reached American television screens in the early 1950s when congressional investigations of communism went before the cameras. Viewers did not realize that what they saw on screen was the product of executive sessions that they could not see because of closed-door rules.

Then in 2003 came new revelations, produced by the release of transcripts of the executive sessions of the Sen. Joseph McCarthy's Senate Permanent Subcommittee on Investigations of the Committee on Government Operations—the McCarthy hearings of the 1950s. (Investigative records of the Senate are sealed for 50 years.) The release of the five volumes of the hearings marked the largest such opening of documents related to the McCarthy hearings.

The archives showed that McCarthy, a Wisconsin Republican and the source of the word *McCarthyism* to describe smear attacks, interrogated witnesses in a kind of audition before deciding whether to put them before the TV cameras. The released transcripts show that he ignored witnesses who would not enhance his TV image or help him in his thesis of treason and communist plots.

"Anybody who stood up to McCarthy in closed session, and did so articulately, tended not to get called up into the public session," said Senate Associate Historian Donald Richiee. "McCarthy was only interested in the people he could browbeat publicly."

The television images of the 1950s, which introduced millions of Americans to allegations of espionage in their own country, soon became familiar: Senators or House members on a podium, witnesses with right hand raised to swear they were telling the truth, and glaring klieg lights. The spies were few, but viewers did get insights into TRADECRAFT from undercover AGENTS for the FBI. In 1954 McCarthy, searching for communist spies in the U.S. Army, drew one of the largest audiences in television's short history. When McCarthy faded away, the televising of Congress did not. The search for spies in congressional hearing rooms continued into the 1960s; but not until the days of the PLUMBERS and WATERGATE were large audience again lured to the screen for intelligence revelations.

One of the FBI undercover agents who appeared before Congress, Herbert A. Philbrick, led audiences from the real SECRET WORLD of espionage to the television world where fact gives way to fiction. Philbrick, who rose high in the U.S. Communist Party, wrote a popular book, *I Led Three Lives* (1952), which was made into a television series of the same name. In a fairly close approximation of how the FBI infiltrated the U.S. Communist Party, actor Richard Carlson played Philbrick, whose three lives were undercover agent, MOLE inside the Communist Party, and ordinary American who did not let people know about his two secret lives. (See CPUSA.)

Like the makers of MOVIES, television producers have been drawn to espionage as a source of drama since the medium's earliest days. Such real spies as JOHN WALKER and ROBERT HANSSEN did become the stuff of TV dramas.

But, given the narrow boundaries of television, spy dramas almost always became even more improbable and absurd than spy movies. Some producers took the easy—and humorous—way out by simply making the exploits of spies laughable. The ridiculous doings of MAXWELL SMART [f] in *Get Smart* are a fine example of a television series making the secret world funny.

In a television series, realism about espionage has been as rare as social realism in situation comedies. One early show of the 1950s, made by Hollywood film producers, was *A Man Called X*. Promotion material implied that the latter was based on real cases involving the CIA, then a shadowy government entity about which little was known.

The United States Information Agency (USIA) founded the Voice of America as a collection of government-controlled radio stations that spread pro-American information around the world. When Third World countries began television broadcasting in the 1950s, the USIA went into that medium, supplying free film to countries with newly acquired television. USIA-prepared films also went into foreign editions of some U.S. newsreels through a program with the CODE NAME Kingfish. The CIA provided subsidies to Fox Movietone and Hearst-MGM in return for their inserting the USIA films.

American television added this real-world information to its own staples: adventure series about cowboys and Indians or cops and robbers. Writing about this period in *Tube of Plenty* (1990), radio and television historian Erik Barnouw said, "A deluge of spy fiction, latching onto a timely topic, provided the rationale [for actual U.S. COVERT ACTION], and got Americans used to the idea. On television it was *The Man from U.N.C.L.E., The Girl from U.N.C.L.E., Get Smart, I Spy, The Man Who Never Was, Mission Impossible,* and others—some amiable, some witty, some melodramatic." *Mission Impossible* became one of the most successful of all U.S. television series about spies. The message—that nothing is impossible for practitioners of U.S. covert action—was a reflection of what was perceived as the truth in Third World countries that imported the show. To prevent complaints from those countries, the producers accommodated American diplomats by sending the missions to fictional countries.

The places were vaguely Third World or Soviet-like, with signs that were foreign-looking but readable: Alarilm, Ddnjer, Elevaten, Entrat Verbaten. Villains with sinister accents got what they deserved: trickery, betrayal, sometimes death (at the hands of their fellow countrymen, not Americans).

Built into the show's opening was what, in real life, would come to be known as the government's PLAUSIBLE DENIAL: "As always," the anonymous voice on the tape told the leader of the Impossible Missions Force (IMF), "should you or any of your IMF be caught or killed, the Secretary will disavow any knowledge of your actions. This tape will self-destruct in five seconds. . . . Good luck."

Jim Phelps (Peter Graves) was the leader of the IMF after the first season. The other members of the IMF were Barney Collier (Greg Morris), a skilled black technician who invented gadgets that functioned at the edge of plausibility; Cinnamon Carter (Barbara Bain), a woman irresistible to duped villains; Rollin Hand (Martin Landau), a master of disguise; and muscular Willy Armitage (Peter Lupus), who usually simply carried things or impersonated the villains' uniformed guards. Other actors in the IMF at various times included Leonard Nimoy and Ann Warren. In the United States the series ran from Sept. 1966 until April 1973 on CBS and was brought back, on ABC, in 1988 and 1989. In 1996 *Mission Impossible* reappeared as an even more implausible movie starring Tom Cruise.

Get Smart, a leading prime-time television series in the 1960s, was a spoof on modern intelligence, American style. The lead bumbler was Maxwell Smart, played by Don Adams. Agent 99 (Barbara Feldon) helped to keep him out of worse trouble. The signature prop was Maxwell Smart's telephone-in-a-shoe, and his favorite phrase as he botched an operation was, "Oops, sorry about that!" Maxwell Smart worked for an agency known only as "Control," whose director (Edward Platt) was known only as "the Chief." The global enemy was K.A.O.S., whose only purpose seemed to be to provide weekly capers for Control. (For a real spy shoe, see MAXWELL SMART).

Sharing prime time in that era were two other "spy-fi" hits. *I Spy* featured Robert Culp and television's first black hero, Bill Cosby, as agents with a sports COVER: Culp was touring tennis player Kelly Robinson, and Cosby played his trainer Alexander Scott. (In the real world, the KGB often used traveling athletic groups as cover.) The show featured many episodes in which Culp and Cosby helped Asians and Africans resist communist inroads into their societies. The CIA reputedly arranged for the export of *I Spy* to developing countries to impress people with the CIA's power and benevolence.

In *The Man from U.N.C.L.E.,* debonair Robert Vaughn played NAPOLEON SOLO, a cool, sophisticated agent working for the United Network Command for Law and Enforcement, an international organization that, like the real UNITED NATIONS, was a spy nest. Aiding Solo was Russian Illya Kuryakin (David McCallum). Alexander Waverly (Leo G. Carroll) headed the agency.

The short-lived spinoff *The Girl from U.N.C.L.E.* (1966–1967) starred Stefanie Powers as agent April Dancer. In *Scarecrow and Mrs. King,* a later romantic comedy-espionage thriller, Kate Jackson played Mrs. Amanda King, a divorced suburban mother who accidentally became involved with Scarecrow, the CODE NAME for Lee Stetson (Bruce Boxleitner), who worked for a U.S. intelligence agency.

The FBI, starring Efrem Zimbalist, Jr., as Inspector Erskine, began a long run on ABC in 1965. The FBI seal appeared on the screen to stamp every show with the approval of J. EDGAR HOOVER, director of the FBI. All scripts had to be approved by the FBI, and only actors cleared by the FBI could play agents. Although Hoover often boasted of FBI COUNTERINTELLIGENCE prowess, the television agents chased more robbers than they did spies. In

the 1990s came *The X-Files,* supposedly named for bizarre, unsolved cases in FBI files. A show very much not approved by the FBI, it dealt with extraterrestrial agents, leaving the terrestrial ones to the real FBI.

Spy TV at the beginning of the 21st century veered between fantasy and realism. In *She Spies,* three beautiful crooks are removed from prison and told they will remain free as long as they are willing to serve as agents for a secret government agency in adventures that focused on their bodies rather than on espionage. *The Agency,* filmed with the cooperation of the CIA, did provide realistic glances at operations; *24 Hours* also focused on the inner workings of an agency, the gimmick being that the 24 hours spanned an entire TV season.

The CIA in 2000 paid homage to TV spies by putting on an exhibit in its MUSEUM (which is closed to the public). Included in the exhibit were such fictional spy gadgets as Maxwell Smart's shoe phone, Patrick Macnee's bowler hat and Diana Rigg's leather pants from the *The Avengers.* There also were guns and a silver pen communicator from *The Man from U.N.C.L.E.*

BRITISH SPY-FI

The British added to the spy-fi genre with characters and storylines inspired by JAMES BOND, including *Secret Agent Man, The Saint,* and *The Avengers,* a spoof of MI5. *The Saint,* based on books by Leslie Charteris dating back to the 1920s, was adapted for British television in 1962; Roger Moore, who would later be cast as James Bond, portrayed Simon Templar, alias the Saint. Although a detective who solved crimes, the Saint occasionally ventured into espionage.

Secret Agent Man starred Patrick McGoohan as a hard-working, low-key British secret service operative, usually working in the Third World in this intriguing series. The highly successful theme song, "Secret Agent Man," was sung by Johnny Rivers. McGoohan went from spoof to surrealism in the somewhat bizarre television series *The Prisoner,* in which he played an INTELLIGENCE OFFICER who tries to resign, only to be kidnapped to a strange place where veterans of espionage must live out their lives lest they reveal secrets. He continually comes tantalizingly close to escaping. The setting for *The Prisoner* was the unique "village" of Portmeirion in Wales.

Each episode of *The Avengers,* which began in 1962, opened with the statement, "Extraordinary crimes against the state have to be avenged by agents extraordinary"—a variation on Bond's "license to kill." The main characters were John Steed (played by Patrick Macnee) and a female assistant. The most successful of several who played the latter part was the talented actress Diana Rigg. She replaced Cathy Gale, played by Honor Blackman, and was named Emma Peel, supposedly from a note suggesting that Gale's successor have "man appeal." Realism was scarce in this amusing, long-running series. (Dame Diana Rigg went on to become a leading star of the British stage and the hostess for the very popular *Mystery!* series on American public television.)

Unlike television series, individual British espionage dramas showed a respect for the secret world, especially as limned by the master of espionage fiction, JOHN LE CARRÉ, *Tinker, Tailor, Soldier, Spy* (1979) and *Smiley's People* (1982), both presented in several episodes and taken from his books of the same title, were outstanding. Sir Alec Guinness played such a convincing GEORGE SMILEY [f] in both television adaptations that Le Carré later said Guinness "took the character away from me" and "I defected from him."

Another great British espionage saga adapted for television was *Reilly: Ace of Spies,* based on the incredible adventures of SIDNEY REILLY, who has been called the greatest spy of modern times. The 12-episode series, shown in America on public broadcasting stations in 1985, starred Australian actor Sam Neill as Reilly. The story captured the mood of the early 20th century and the character of Reilly, a man who knew he was a legend in his time.

The Sandbaggers, first shown in 20 episodes from 1978 to 1980, focused on an elite covert action branch of British intelligence. Much of the action involved the head of the Sandbaggers, Neil Burnside (Roy Marsden), battling his superiors. They constantly left him short of resources, and seemed more interested in pleasing the prime minister than in winning the Cold War, which Burnside and his Sandbaggers seemed to fight on their own. As an import on American public television, it gathered enough of a cult following to produce a fan club and a site on the INTERNET.

The end of the Cold War essentially ended the spy-fi genre both in Britain and the United States. An epilogue came in 1992 with the three-part drama *Sleeper,* which focused on two Soviet SLEEPERS who had been sent to Britain in the 1960s. As the Cold War ended, they were contacted. But they had made new lives for themselves and neither wanted to return to Russia.

TELINT

SEE TELEMETRY INTELLIGENCE

Tempest

CODE NAME for investigations and studies of acoustic or electric communications. Tempest guards "compromising emanations"—unintentional intelligence-bearing signals that, if intercepted and analyzed, would disclose classified information. Although Tempest refers to both acoustic and electric communications, most Tempest security measures deal with electrical signals, such as those transmitted by computer keyboards and electric typewriters.

Also see COMPUTER ESPIONAGE.

TENCAP

SEE TACTICAL EXPLOITATION OF NATIONAL CAPABILITIES

Tenet, George J.

(b. 1953)

DIRECTOR OF CENTRAL INTELLIGENCE (DCI), nominated by President Clinton on March 19, 1997, and confirmed by the Senate on July 10, 1997. The President had originally proposed his national security adviser, Anthony Lake, for the position. But Lake withdrew his name when it became clear that his confirmation was in doubt because several Senators were critical of the way he ran the 150-member NATIONAL SECURITY COUNCIL (NSC) staff; they questioned Lake's ability to manage the CIA and its 80,000 employees as well as the rest of the U.S. INTELLIGENCE COMMUNITY.

Tenet, the fifth DCI in six years, had served as Deputy Director of Central Intelligence (DDCI) since July 1995 and as acting Director during the stormy interregnum between DCI JOHN M. DEUTCH and the expected arrival of Lake. (Deutch resigned in Dec. 1996.)

As a CIA veteran, Tenet restored the confidence of the CIA's Directorate of Operations, the clandestine service that had been mired in a bitter feud with Deutch since he fired two senior officers in the wake of CIA abuses in overt operations in Guatemala. (Deutch had also publicly criticized unnamed officers of the clandestine service as arrogant and ineffective.)

Deutch and Tenet had a good working relationship, but Deutch never let his subordinate forget who was in charge. When Tenet sprouted a thick black beard, Deutch started calling him "Carlos," after the terrorist known as Carlos the Jackal. Finally, Deutch ordered him to shave off the beard. "George is a tremendously loyal and devoted public servant," Deutch said of his deputy. "I really realized how devoted a deputy he was in an extremely important meeting with important foreign dignitaries. He cleared the room to tell me I needed to zip up my fly."

Tenet's first action as DCI was to establish the basic mission of the post-Cold War CIA

to pursue the hardest targets that threaten American interests around the world. . . . At the end of the day, this is an espionage organization. It must generate information that is unique and makes a contribution against each of those targets, otherwise we don't know why were are here. We no longer are in search of a mission. We know what the mission is, we know what the targets are.

In one of his first appointments as DCI, he called Jack G. Downing out of retirement to run the Directorate of Operations. Tenet described Downing as "legendary in the directorate in terms of his stature and what he expects of people." A Marine veteran of Vietnam, a former chief of station in Moscow, and a linguist fluent in Chinese and Russian, Downing had retired after Deutch passed him over for promotion.

Tenet was born in New York City, the son of Greek immigrants. He began his government career at 29 when he joined the staff of Sen. John Heinz (Republican of Pennsylvania). In 1985 he went on the staff of the Senate Intelligence Committee, which oversees the U.S. intelligence community. Four years later he became staff director. At the beginning of President Clinton's second term in 1997, Tenet became senior director for intelligence programs at the NSC, working under Lake. When Deutch became DCI, he selected Tenet as his deputy.

During his time as deputy, Tenet took over staff operations in Deutch's absence and worked behind the scenes to improve the CIA's relationships with Congress and the FBI. He was expected to hone these skills as he took over a CIA still struggling to emerge from the Cold War.

In the wake of the Sept. 11, 2001, attacks, Tenet became one of President George W. Bush's most trusted advisers. Tenet met almost daily in the Oval Office with the President to give a one-on-one briefing, focusing on TERRORIST INTELLIGENCE. As national security adviser Condoleezza Rice put it, President Bush "begins his day on the war on terrorism." When a dispute erupted over intelligence prior to the Iraqi War, he took the blame and became a steady supporter of administration policies on the war.

In a 2003 assessment of what he must watch and analyze, Tenet spoke of "challenges such as the world's vast stretches of ungoverned areas—lawless zones, veritable 'no man's lands' like some areas along the Afghan-Pakistani border—where extremist movements find shelter and can win the breathing space to grow."

Ter Braak, Jan Wilhelm

The only known German spy to enter Britain during World War II and escape being captured or TURNED by the DOUBLE CROSS SYSTEM. However, he accomplished nothing for his spymasters during the five months that he was free in Britain.

He was about 27 years old, and his real identity and nationality have never been established. He came down by parachute at Haversham in Berkshire, near Cambridge, probably on Nov. 3, 1940, with papers in the name of Ter Braak, a Dutchman. He took lodgings in Cambridge, claiming to have been evacuated at Dunkirk in the summer of 1940. He said he was working for a Dutch newspaper in London. His identity papers were poor forgeries, and there was some suspicion about him; but there were no follow-up investigations.

He made many day trips, some to observe military airfields, but there is no evidence that he actually reported anything back to Germany. When his radio set was found, it had not been used.

Finally, his money ran out. On April 1, 1941, his body was found in an air raid shelter in Cambridge. He had shot himself in the temple.

(Two other men claimed to have parachuted into Britain during the war, evaded capture, and returned to Germany; there is no corroborating evidence for their claims.)

Terminated with Extreme Prejudice

Expression denoting the execution of an AGENT or an INTELLIGENCE OFFICER by his or her agency. *Terminated* thus has the dual meaning of cessation of employment and life. The phrase does not apply to the execution or assassination of non-intelligence personnel.

Terpil, Frank E.

SEE EDWIN P. WILSON

Terrorist Intelligence

Information collected about organizations or individuals planning acts of violence against TARGETS, usually civilian, to further political or social goals. In the United States, this type of intelligence took on the highest national priorities after the terrorist attacks against the World Trade Center and Pentagon on Sept. 11, 2001.

Those acts caused U.S. intelligence agencies to shift massive resources to counter-terrorist operations. The United States thus joined a group of nations that had been fighting terrorist activities for many years, such as the British government's campaign against the Irish Republican Army (IRA), the Israeli campaign against the Hamas terrorists, the Italian government against the Red Brigade, the Russian government against the Chechen rebels, and the Philippine government against guerrillas believed to be associated with al Qaeda, the group responsible for the Sept. 11 attacks. The broad nature of terrorist activities has led a high level of international cooperation in both the exchange of terrorist intelligence and the prosecution of suspected terrorists.

Speaking of the broad reach of al Qaeda, GEORGE TENET, the DIRECTOR OF CENTRAL INTELLIGENCE, said, "The network is extensive and adaptable. It will take years of determined effort to unravel this and other terrorist networks and stamp them out." He particularly cited the group's sophisticated biological weapons capability.

The complexities of terrorist intelligence was illustrated by the way the CIA handled a meeting of al Qaeda leaders in Malaysia in 1999. After monitoring the meeting, the CIA learned that two of the men had entered the United States. But the CIA is not a domestic intelligence organization, and not until Aug. 2001 did the CIA ask that the men be put on the U.S. government watch lists that would bar them from entry into the United States. The two men were among the terrorists who took part in the attacks on Sept. 11, 2001.

Congressional demands for improved monitoring of terrorists led to suggestions for a new agency devoted to terrorism intelligence. The FBI and CIA successfully lobbied against that proposal. But the new Department of Homeland Security (see HOMELAND SECURITY) did inaugurate the Terrorist Threat Integration Center that encompassed elements of the FBI's Counterterrorism Division, the CIA's Counterterrorist Center, and Department of Defense activities. Homeland Security officials said the center would "fuse and analyze all source information related to terrorism" and "close the 'seam' between analysis of foreign and domestic intelligence on terrorism."

Theremin, Leon

(b. 1896 d. 1993)

Russian inventor who produced BUGS, including the listening device hidden in the Great Seal of the U.S. Embassy in Moscow and exposed in 1960 at the United Nations by Henry Cabot Lodge.

Theremin came to the United States after the Russian Revolution of 1917. He invented and patented in 1929 an electronic musical instrument that bears his name. In 1938 Soviet intelligence officers snatched him from his New York City apartment and took him to the Soviet Union. In a labor camp there he built covert listening devices, better known as bugs. His most famous product was the one found in the Great Seal that had been presented to the embassy in 1952.

That bug had no internal power and thus no wires. A van parked near the embassy beamed an ultra-high frequency signal that was reflected from the bug, which was modulated by sound waves from conversations striking the bug's diaphragm.

Theremin's strange musical instrument made weird-sounding music for such science-fiction movies as *The Day the Earth Stood Still*. The Theremin was also discovered by musical groups, including Led Zeppelin.

Third Man

Label used by the British press to refer to the person who was involved in setting up the escape to the Soviet Union of British spies DONALD MACLEAN and GUY BURGESS. Eventually, the label was accurately pinned on HAROLD (KIM) PHILBY. (See CAMBRIDGE SPY RING.) Later came the labels FOURTH MAN and FIFTH MAN.

After the exposure of Philby, author GRAHAM GREENE, himself a former INTELLIGENCE OFFICER under Philby, pointed out that the first use of "third man" was by Greene in *The Third Man,* a great 1950 suspense MOVIE whose plot centered on the man in the title role in postwar VIENNA. The film's plot revolved around black market racketeering, not espionage.

Thompson, Harry T.

Former U.S. Navy yeoman who, while unemployed at San Pedro, Calif., spied for the Japanese against the United States in 1934–1935. Thompson's HANDLER was Toshio Miyazaki, a Japanese Navy officer who was in the United States ostensibly to study English.

Thompson sold engineering, gunnery, and tactical information about the Pacific Fleet. He was arrested by the FBI, tried and convicted of espionage, and sentenced to 15 years in prison.

Thompson, Airman 2nd Class Robert G.

U.S. Air Force clerk convicted in 1965 of passing secrets to the Soviet Union and sentenced to 30 years for espionage. He confessed to giving hundreds of photographs of classified documents to his Soviet HANDLERS while he was stationed in BERLIN. He was a participant in one of the most intricate three-way SPY SWAPS in history.

In May 1978 Thompson was taken from his U.S. prison cell to Berlin, where he was exchanged for Alan van Norman, an American student who had been sentenced to a two-and-a-half-year prison term for attempting to smuggle an East German family into West Germany. Norman had been held for three months when the swap took place.

According to Air Force records, Thompson was born in Detroit, Mich. When he was exchanged, at age 43, he said that he had been born in Leipzig of a Russian father and a German mother. He also said that he would spy again for the Soviets if given the chance. He then crossed into East Germany (where Leipzig was then located) and disappeared.

Also involved in the exchange was Miron Marcus, an Israeli who had been held in Mozambique since Sept. 1976, when bad weather forced his private plane to land while it was en route to South Africa. Mozambican troops fired on the plane when it landed, wounding Marcus and killing his brother-in-law.

Marcus insisted that he was on business when his plane was forced to land. But Western intelligence sources said that he might have been attempting to gather information about Soviet and Cuban activities in Mozambique for Israeli and perhaps U.S. intelligence agencies.

The intricate three-way deal had been arranged by WOLFGANG VOGEL, who had negotiated the 1962 spy swap of FRANCIS GARY POWERS, a U-2 pilot shot down over the Soviet Union, and RUDOLF IVANOVICH ABEL, an NKVD agent who had spied in the United States.

Thomson, Sir Basil

(b. 1861 d. 1939)

Assistant commissioner of the SPECIAL BRANCH (Criminal Investigation Department) of the Metropolitan Police (Scotland Yard) from 1913 to 1921.

Educated at Eton and Oxford, Thomson, the son of a bishop, became a prison warden, shifting to law enforcement in 1913 when he was appointed head of the Special Branch. When World War I began in 1914, Thomson's Special Branch had a staff of 70; by the end of the war it numbered 700. He was responsible for the arrest of several German spies. He also interrogated MATA HARI, who was suspected of spying for the Germans when she was in England, on her way to Holland.

Under Thomson the Special Branch established its lasting relationship with MI5, the British COUNTERINTELLIGENCE agency, which did not (and does not) have the power of arrest. The Special Branch also handled SURVEILLANCE and assignment for MI5.

After the war, during the "Red scare" that swept Britain, Thomson sought out communists and radicals. He resigned in 1921 amid growing criticism of the failure of intelligence agencies to halt the terrorism of the Irish Republican Army. Hope for his return was dashed in 1925 when he was arrested in Hyde Park for "fondling" a prostitute. He tried to explain that he was doing secret work and claimed that the communists had set up his arrest.

Thorpe, Amy Elizabeth

(b. 1910 d. 1963)

American-born AGENT who worked for MI6 and the OFFICE OF STRATEGIC SERVICES (OSS) during World War II. She operated under the CODE NAME Cynthia.

The daughter of a U.S. Marine Corps officer who retired and became a lawyer, Amy Elizabeth Thorpe grew up in the high society of prewar Washington. It was there that she met and in 1937 married Arthur Pack, commercial secretary at the British Embassy.

When Pack was posted to Warsaw, Poland, Thorpe assisted MI6, reportedly becoming the lover of the private assistant to the Polish foreign minister, thus obtaining access to SENSITIVE diplomatic information. She is said to have shown "great bravery" in the Spanish Civil War, helping political refugees from both sides to escape. She then traveled to South America on behalf of MI6.

During Pack's tenure at the British Embassy in Warsaw in 1938, she eavesdropped on a diplomatic conversation and passed on what she had heard to the embassy passport control officer, who was an MI6 INTELLIGENCE OFFICER under diplomatic COVER. He enlisted her as an agent, asking her to make friends with Polish officials and continue her eavesdropping. She is reputed to have heard talk about a Polish codebreaking device known as ENIGMA.

In the summer of 1940 Thorpe went to the United States, where she worked for the office of BRITISH SECURITY COORDINATION (BSC). Thorpe then became romantically involved with the Italian naval ATTACHÉ and later claimed to have acquired an Italian CIPHER. By then she had separated from Pack.

After Germany conquered France and set up the puppet Vichy regime, she was assigned to penetrate the Vichy Embassy in Washington, D.C. Claiming to be a sympathetic journalist, she called the press attaché, Charles Brousse, and asked to interview the ambassador. She gleaned some information from this talk, met with Brousse again—and began a romance. After she admitted to her lover that she worked for British intelligence, he began providing him embassy secrets.

When the United States entered the war, she began to work for the OSS and MI6 simultaneously. In June 1942, to get naval code books from the Vichy Embassy, she ran a BLACK BAG JOB that involved a safecracker supplied by the British. The code books were photographed in a room in a nearby hotel.

As a result of her operation, Allied strategists were able to read Vichy message traffic concerning the disposition of the French fleet in North Africa prior to the Allied invasion in Nov. 1942.

Generally credited with being a highly successful agent, she inspired varying recollections. BSC operative H. MONTGOMERY HYDE wrote in *Room 3603* (1963), "She had no obvious sexual allure. She was neither beautiful nor even pretty in the conventional sense." But William Stevenson, in his biography of BSC head WILLIAM STEPHENSON, *A Man Called Intrepid* (1976), wrote that Thorpe was the "most exotic of lady spies . . . a striking girl . . . a slender yet voluptuous figure." Both writers did agree that she had green eyes. Stevenson cites BSC papers:

> She had a keen incisive brain and was an accurate reporter. She was extremely courageous, often asking to run risks we could not allow. She was paid little more than her living expenses although her value to Britain and ultimately to her native America is incalculable. Her cover name of Cynthia was known to perhaps three persons at most.

Pack and Thorpe divorced, and Pack committed suicide in 1945. Brousse and Thorpe married, and lived in a medieval castle in France. Thorpe died of mouth cancer in 1963, and Brousse was electrocuted by an electric blanket a decade later. Her account of her espionage career, *Cynthia*, was published in 1966.

Thümmel, Paul

British DOUBLE AGENT in the German ABWEHR. An agent of the Abwehr since 1934, he served in Dresden and Prague before the outbreak of World War II, and then in the Balkans and Turkey. Thümmel, a confidant of Abwehr chief WILHELM CANARIS, was a conduit for anti-Hitler forces in Germany, passing secret documents to the British officials through local anti-Nazi groups.

Thümmel originally worked for Maj. FRANTISEK MORAVEC, head of the Czech Military Intelligence Service, who gave him the CODE NAME A54. With his access to both the Abwehr and SD, the Nazi security service, Thümmel produced remarkably fine and timely intelligence. He predicted the German occupation of Czechoslovakia in March 1939, enabling the British to get Moravec and his family out of the country. He provided the Allies with a nearly perfect ORDER OF BATTLE on the Luftwaffe early in the war.

Following the conquest of Czechoslovakia, Thümmel could pass on his intelligence only through the Czech resistance movement. Arrested by the GESTAPO in Feb. 1942 and court-martialed, he managed to win his release by claiming that he had been trying to infiltrate the Czech movement.

He had supplied British intelligence so well that Sir STEWART G. MENZIES, head of MI6, said, "When A24 reports, armies march." After his arrest and release, the British decided to EXFILTRATE him with a rescue attempt code-named Anthropoid. The effort failed, and again he was arrested by the Germans. This time he was imprisoned for treason and was executed in April 1945.

His Czech code name was Franta. His aliases included Dr. Holm and René.

Thurloe, John

(b. 1616 d. 1668)

Secretary of State and intelligence chief for Oliver Cromwell. Thurloe operated an effective intelligence organization in England and on the European continent. His espionage and intelligence service operated against the Restoration efforts of Charles Stuart.

Previously a lawyer in Sussex, Thurloe was financially supported by Cromwell, who ruled England from 1649 to 1658, for most of the Commonwealth period. Thurloe built the most efficient intelligence organization in Europe. He directed intelligence activities through his official position of Postmaster General. He subsequently (and at times simultaneously) held the posts of Secretary of State, Home Secretary, Chief of Police, Foreign Secretary, War Secretary, and Counsellor of State. His intelligence organization included a network of AGENTS in European capitals and in England as well as a massive mail intercept operation (see JOHN WALLIS).

Thurloe survived Cromwell, and served as Secretary of State in the succeeding administration of the Lord Protector's son Richard (1658–1659). Thurloe was arrested for high treason on May 15, 1660. Subsequently released, he spent the last eight years of his life writing papers on foreign policy. He compiled seven volumes of correspondence, which constitute an invaluable primary source of information for the Cromwell period.

Tiedge, Hans Joachim (b. 1937)

West German COUNTERINTELLIGENCE officer who defected to East Germany in Aug. 1985.

Tiedge, a senior officer of West Germany's BFV counterintelligence agency, was a specialist in East German espionage. He had served in West German intelligence since 1966.

Colleagues described him as despondent, alcoholic, deeply in debt, and unable to deal with life. His wife, Ute, had died in July 1982 in a fall at the family home in Cologne. His daughters were involved with drugs. (His wife's death had been ruled an accident at the time. After Tiedge's defection, the Cologne prosecutor's office initiated an inconclusive homicide investigation into her death.)

Despondent as he may have been, Tiedge was professional enough to give the East Germans information that would guarantee him a welcome. He betrayed at least two AGENTS working for BfV in East Germany and warned at least three East German agents to flee West Germany. But he apparently could not save MARGARETE HOEKE, a secretary in the office of West German president Richard von Weizsacker. Almost at the same time that Tiedge defected she was arrested on espionage charges.

Timokhin, Col. Gen. Yevgeniy Leonidovich

Chief of the GRU, Soviet MILITARY INTELLIGENCE, in 1991–1992. Prior to his appointment to the GRU, Timokhm was deputy chief of the main staff of the Soviet Air Defense Forces. He was one of the few officers from outside the security ORGANS or Soviet Ground Forces to head the GRU.

TINA

SEE RADIO FINGERPRINTING

Tisler, Frantisek

CIPHER clerk in the Czech Embassy in Washington, D.C., who was a DEFECTOR IN PLACE for the FBI in the 1950s.

Tisler, on home leave in the summer of 1957, got drunk with an old friend, also on leave. The friend, a military ATTACHÉ at the Czech Embassy in London, told Tisler that he was running an AGENT who was working on a guided missile project for the Royal Air Force. Tisler passed this information to his FBI HANDLER and. J. EDGAR HOOVER, director of the FBI, had it passed to the British Security Service (MI5). The British tracked the tip down to Brian F. Linney, an electronics engineer for a company doing defense work. Linney pleaded guilty to violating the OFFICIAL SECRETS ACT and was sentenced to 14 years in prison.

The FBI gave Tisler bits of information that he passed on to Prague, where intelligence officials were so impressed that they gave him a promotion—and a post in Prague. The FBI, upset about losing such a good ASSET, exposed Tisler's successor as a spy, forcing his recall. Tisler was then reassigned to Washington for a year before being posted back to Prague again. At that point, he and the FBI decided to end his espionage career. One night he passed the files from his office out the window to FBI agents and at dawn left the embassy for a life in the United States under a new identity.

TK

SEE TALENT KEYHOLE

Tkachenko, Aleksey G.

Soviet diplomat in Washington, D.C., who was the point of contact for JOHN WALKER at the time of Walker's arrest for espionage on May 19, 1985.

Tkachenko, ostensibly the third secretary at the Soviet Embassy, was supposed to have serviced the Walker DEAD DROP that night in Poolesville, Md. FBI agents, who had staked out the drop site, saw Tkachenko drive by in a car registered to the embassy; his wife and a child were in the car to give the appearance of a family evening drive. Walker had dropped a 7-Up can at a prearranged spot to signal that he had placed the material at the drop, near a specified tree. On seeing the signal, Tkachenko was to proceed to the drop, pick up the bag, and leave Walker a packet of cash.

But an FBI agent picked up the can as evidence and Tkachenko, not seeing it, had driven away. Walker, not knowing the drop had been aborted, left a garbage bag full of classified documents. FBI agents recovered the bag and arrested Walker when he returned to his nearby motel.

Tkachenko, his wife, and two daughters left the United States on May 23. Their departure was so sudden that, reportedly, they left half-cooked hamburgers on the stove in their apartment.

Also see TRADECRAFT.

Tobias, Radioman 3rd Class Michael T.

U.S. Navy sailor who offered to sell classified documents to the Soviet Union. In Aug. 1984 Tobias, who served on the tank landing ship *Peoria,* told a U.S. SECRET SERVICE agent in San Diego, Calif., that he would sell classified documents for $1,000. Previously, he said, an unidentified "foreign power" had offered him $100,000 for the key cards for U.S. cryptographic machines. Tobias had taken the key cards from the ship instead of shredding them, as called for in security regulations. Tobias had been seen near the Soviet Consulate in San Francisco the night before.

Tobias had conspired with his brother and two others to extort the money by telling the Secret Service that they had the cards and would give them back for cash. In the course of their scheme two of the 12 key cards disappeared and were not recovered. Tobias was arrested as he prepared to leave the country.

In Nov. 1985 Tobias was found guilty of attempting to extort money with threats, compromising classified information, and stealing government property. He was sentenced to 20 years imprisonment.

Tokumu Han

"Special section"—for cryptology—of the Imperial Japanese Navy's Naval General Staff.

The section, established in the early 1920s, had some early success against Chinese CODES and the U.S. State Department's gray code. In 1937, a Tokumu Han officer, aided by a locksmith and accompanied by a photographer, broke into the U.S. Consulate in Kobe and photographed the U.S. brown code (used by the State Department and the Navy). The Japanese also photographed the M-138 CIPHER device. However, the break-in did not produce any breakthroughs for Tokumu Han.

By World War II the section had grown from a few officers to a large enterprise that included radio intercept stations and several thousand naval personnel and civilians. Among the workers were NISEI women who had learned English in the United States and returned to Japan. They were used to translate open conversations on radio telephones.

Tokumo Han "failed almost completely in extracting usable information from American messages," David Kahn wrote in *The Codebreakers* (1967). "They did not even attempt to solve medium- and high-echelon messages, couched in cryptosystems far beyond their ability. They concentrated instead on three simpler cryptosystems of the lowest level of command. Even with these, they achieved only limited success."

Much of the Japanese SIGNAL INTELLIGENCE effort was devoted to TRAFFIC ANALYSIS. But the analysis did not produce significant results.

Tokyo Rose

U.S. servicemen's name for female Japanese propaganda broadcasters in World War II. Provided with DISINFORMATION by their Japanese superiors, several English-speaking women gave the impression of having secret information, giving their American and British listeners the impression that Japanese intelligence was better than it really was.

Japanese radio propaganda during World War II operated under the direction of the War Information Bureau. All English-speaking workers were screened by the KEMPEI TAI and the Special Security Police. One of them was Iva Ikuko Toguri d'Aquino, a Japanese-American born in Los Angeles and a graduate of the University of California at Los Angeles. When Japan staged the PEARL HARBOR ATTACK on Dec. 7, 1941, she was visiting a relative in Japan. She, along with others, made the broadcasts under duress, it was later claimed.

The first went on the air as "Ann," short for *an*nouncer. She later became "Orphan Annie—your favorite enemy." The propaganda broadcasters usually relied on information picked up from U.S. commercial radio stations. American newscasts were searched for information, particularly disasters, that could be passed on by the broadcasters. Between records of dance bands and light classical music, the women—all eventually called Tokyo Rose—offered servicemen bogus casualty figures, some mentioning specific U.S. military units; tales of infidelity by wives and sweethearts back home; and prophetic reports of upcoming operations.

After the war the U.S. government identified Tokyo Rose as d'Aquino, even though others had done what she had done. (The U.S. Office of War Information said that government monitors, listening 24 hours a day to Japanese broadcasts, never heard the words "Tokyo Rose.")

Returned to the United States, she was tried in 1949 for treason and undermining U.S. troop morale. At her trial she insisted that she had been forced to make the broadcasts. She said she was one of at least 20 "Tokyo Roses." Acquitted of treason but convicted of the lesser charge, she served 10 years in prison. President Ford formally pardoned her in 1977.

Tolkachev, Adolf G.

Soviet aviation specialist who provided classified material to the U.S. government.

Soviet aviation specialist Adolf Tolkatchev is carried off by KGB officers at his arrest in 1985 for spying for the United States. Former CIA officer Edward Howard had exposed Tolkatchev, who was executed. Information from Aldrich Ames confirmed Howard's disclosure. Both CIA officers revealed Russians working for the United States; several were executed. (KGB MUSEUM)

Tolkachev, who worked at a Soviet aerospace research institute in Moscow, was arrested by the KGB in June 1985 after being exposed by former CIA officer ED-WARD L. HOWARD. The Soviet Union announced on Oct. 22, 1986, that Tolkachev had been executed.

Tolkachev had been spying for the United States since the late 1970s. He provided plans, specifications, and test results on existing and planned Soviet aircraft and missiles. American journalist BOB WOODWARD wrote in *Veil: The Secret Wars of the CIA, 1981–1987* (1987) that Tolkachev "also opened a window into the future—the research, development, and new generations of weapons, particularly on new radar-defeating 'stealth' technology. Estimates were that his intelligence was worth billions of dollars."

Howard had been briefed about Tolkachev and was supposed to take over as his CASE OFFICER upon his arrival in Moscow. Tolkachev's case officer, Paul M. Stombaugh, Jr., was detained by the KGB on June 13, 1985, as he was about to meet with Tolkachev. On that same day, in Washington, D.C., ALDRICH W. AMES, a CIA officer turned Soviet MOLE, handed over to his Soviet HANDLER several pounds of CIA documents that included Tolkachev's name. Ames's information thus confirmed Howard's.

According to KGB documents obtained by the Cold War International History Project, Gen. VIKTOR M. CHEB-RIKOV, head of the KGB, told Soviet leader Mikail S. Gorbachev on Sept. 25, 1986, "Yesterday Tolkachev's sentence was implemented."

"American intelligence was very generous with him," Gorbachev remarked. "They found 2 million rubles [about $500,000] on him."

"This agent gave very important military-technical secrets to the enemy," Chebrikov said.

Tolkachev's CIA CODE NAME was "GTSPHERE."

Tompkins, Maj. Peter

U.S. Army officer who entered Rome in Jan. 1944 as an AGENT of the OFFICE OF STRATEGIC SERVICES (OSS), while the city was still occupied by German troops.

Tompkins formed a partisan band in Rome and received a stream of information about the city until it was liberated by the U.S. Fifth Army in June 1944. The intelligence he provided was never acted upon by U.S. forces because of command problems.

As the liberators were arriving and the Germans withdrawing, Tompkins, acting on his own, issued orders on OSS letterheads he had printed, ordering the Italian Army to guard all public utilities.

Tompkins' OSS CODE NAME in Rome was "Pietro."

Top Secret

(TS)

U.S. security CLASSIFICATION for national security information, the unauthorized disclosure of which could be expected to result in *exceptionally grave damage* to national security, such as war or a break in diplomatic relations. This is the highest U.S. security classification. The other U.S. security classifications are CONFIDENTIAL and SECRET.

Top Hat

SEE DIMITRI POLYAKOV

Topaz

SEE SAPPHIRE

Tortella, Louis W.

(b. 1911 d. 1996)

Deputy director of the NSA from 1958 to 1974.

Tortella began his codebreaking career in 1942, when, as a U.S. Navy lieutenant (junior grade), he was assigned to OP-20-G (see NAVY COMMUNICATIONS INTELLI-GENCE) to work on the German ENIGMA machine. He was on a team of mathematicians who planned, designed, and put into use the BOMBE, a machine used to decipher the Enigma keys. He was later sent to the OP-20-G radio intercept stations at Bainbridge Island, Wash., and Skaggs Island, Calif.

After the war, as a civilian, he joined the ARMED FORCES SECURITY AGENCY and devised policy for the creation of NSA in 1952, becoming its deputy director in 1958. Running daily NSA operations, he served under six military directors.

A pioneer in the use of machines to break codes, he brought more and more powerful computers into NSA. After his retirement he continued to advise the agency until a few months before his death.

Toubianski, Meir

Israeli accused of spying for the British.

A major in the British Army's Corps of Engineers during World War II, Toubianski became a captain in the Israeli Army after Israel became a nation on May 14, 1948. On June 30, 1948, the day that ISSER BE'ERI took charge of AMAN, Israel's MILITARY INTELLIGENCE agency, Be'eri accused Toubianski of treason and had him arrested. Convicted of spying for the British in what Be'eri called a "field court-martial," Toubianski was executed by an Army firing squad that same day.

The evidence against Toubianski was entirely circumstantial. Further, all of the officers on his court martial except Be'eri later claimed that they were merely interrogating the suspect, and did not know that they were imposing a death sentence. In 1949 he was posthumously judged innocent, his rank was restored, his remains were reinterred with full military honors, and his family was paid a compensation.

A military court in Dec. 1948 found Be'eri guilty of manslaughter in another case and he was dismissed from military service. Arrested again in 1949 for the execution of Toubianski, Be'eri was tried, found guilty, and sentenced to a token one-day prison term "in consideration of [his] loyal service. . . ."

Tourist

U.S. intelligence term during World War II for a team of AGENTS placed behind German lines.

Townsend, Robert

New York City businessman who was a member of the highly successful CULPER RING that spied for GEORGE WASHINGTON during the American Revolution. Washington, needing intelligence on British forces and intentions, ordered Maj. BENJAMIN TALLMADGE to set up an espionage net. Townsend was one of Tallmadge's recruits.

Because Townsend, a Quaker, had not spoken out about the Revolution, he easily assumed the role of a British sympathizer in New York in 1778 when Gen. Sir Henry Clinton, commander of British forces in America, occupied the city. Townsend even joined a Tory militia to preserve his COVER. His name was never used in messages, which used his CODE NAME, Culper Junior.

Townsend wrote his reports in coded SECRET WRITING, on the specific instructions of Washington, who told him that "he should occasionally write his information on the blank leaves of a pamphlet, on the first, second, and other pages of a common pocket book, or on the blank leaves at each end of registers, almanacks, or any new publication or book of small value." He also suggested interlining the secret writing in letters to friends.

Townsend wrote a gossip column for a Tory newspaper whose other contributors included Maj. JOHN ANDRÉ, an amateur poet. Townsend ran a coffee shop—another source of POLITICAL INTELLIGENCE with the owner of the newspaper, who almost certainly was also an American spy.

TR-1

SEE U-2

Tradecraft

Espionage techniques and tricks that substantiate the view of practitioners that their work is a skilled occupation or craft. The operational skills include tricks of SURVEILLANCE and running AGENTS. Tradecraft, mentioned frequently in the novels of JOHN LE CARRÉ [p], appears frequently in real cases. Practices are taught in training and are then handed down from one generation of AGENTS to another.

David W. Szady, a veteran FBI agent who specialized in COUNTERINTELLIGENCE, philosophized about why the classical ways are the best and the most reliable. "Dead drops here, face-to-face meets overseas. They are classical because they work," he said. "Radio is often a problem because of the chances of detection and the need to maintain the equipment, which is often miniaturized and delicate. In my experience, the classic ways work. . . . There are only three basic needs of an espionage operation: a way for the agent to get ahold of someone in an emergency, a way for the intelligence officer to get information from the agent, and a way to pay him."

The DEAD DROP, the BRUSH CONTACT—the ways to meet, to exchange, without seeing each other—these are the essential elements of tradecraft. Following are some examples of standard tradecraft:

- Switch off a car's interior lights so they do not come on when door is opened. This is useful for picking up or dropping off someone when the driver suspects the car is being followed.
- Thoroughly wash car, including interior, after a pickup or dropoff to remove telltale dirt, mud, or foliage that could identify the area where the car was driven.
- Before use, wash out cans, bottles, or jars to be used as caches or signals during a drop or pickup at a dead drop to keep wild animals from carrying them off.
- When boarding or leaving a subway, train, or bus, act nonchalantly, then jump in or out at the last moment to elude possible followers.

Here are some tradecraft examples from cases mentioned in entries in this book:

JAMES HARPER wrote a limerick on the back of a laundry list. His HANDLER tore it in half, gave one half back to Harper, and retained the other. When Harper appeared at an appointed time and place to meet a CUT-OUT, the cut-out identified himself by showing the other half of the laundry slip.

HARRY GOLD used one half of a Jell-O box top when he met DAVID GREENGLASS as proof that Gold was connected to JULIUS ROSENBERG in the ATOMIC SPY RING. When meeting KLAUS FUCHS, Gold carried a pair of gloves in one hand, along with a green-covered book. Fuchs was to carry a ball. Fuchs later was to meet his Soviet handler while carrying in one hand a book by Bennett Cerf with a yellow-and-green dust jacket and in the other hand five books tied with string.

JONATHAN JAY POLLARD was instructed to make a list of pay phones near his apartment. His Israeli HANDLER assigned a Hebrew letter to each one. The handler would call Pollard at home and mention a letter. Pollard would then go to the phone indicated by that letter and wait for the call.

JOHN WALKER got specific instructions for his dead drop, which was near a certain tree. He put his documents in a trash bag, along with cans and bottles that he had cleaned (see above). His drop site had to be within a 25-mile radius of the center of Washington, D.C., the area in which Soviet diplomats were allowed to travel without special permission. The safest place for a drop in the metropolis is a wooded area. It is hard to follow people in the woods, and the ordinary objects lying around there—discarded beer cans, other trash, rocks—can be drops.

NELSON C. DRUMMOND, on the first Saturday of the month, walked south on Seventh Avenue in New York City starting at 125th Street, carrying a black bag and wearing a cuff link, with a horsehead design in his lapel. A man would approach and ask, "Can you show me the way to the Savoy Ballroom?" He was to say, "Yes, I will show you the way." The meeting followed.

During his CIA training EDWARD HOWARD was taught to use a JACK IN THE BOX, or JIB, a snap-up dummy that someone under surveillance carries in a briefcase after getting into the passenger seat of a car. As soon as the car is temporarily out of sight of the surveillance car, the person in the passenger seat activates the JIB, opens the door, and leaps out. Those in the following car continue to see two figures in the car. Howard successfully escaped from FBI surveillance by making a JIB out of a coat hanger, sawn-off broom handle, his wife's wig holder, and a disguise wig, which he later claimed to have stolen during his CIA training. He put the baseball cap he had been wearing on the dummy and then jumped from the car while it was making a turn and momentarily his car was out of sight of the tailing FBI car.

Some of the most elaborate tradecraft ever to be made public came from the Moscow dead drop instructions that OLEG PENKOVSKY, a mole in the GRU, Soviet MILITARY INTELLIGENCE, gave to his CIA handlers:

In the entrance (foyer)—to the left upon entering therein a dial telephone, No. 28, is located. Opposite the hall is a steam heat radiator, painted in oil paint in a dark green color. The radiator is supported by a single metal hook, fastened into the wall. If one stands facing the radiator, then the metal hook will be to the right, at the level of one's hand hanging from the arm.

Between the wall, to which the hook is attached, and the radiator there is a space of two–three centimeters. For the dead drop, it is proposed to use

the hook and the space, open space, between the wall and the radiator.

While serving that dead drop, a CIA officer under diplomatic COVER in Moscow was captured by the KGB.

The CIA communicated with another GRU officer by slipping him a copy of the *National Geographic* magazine. On a black line in an advertisement on an inside page, CIA technicians using a laser had embedded a microscopic message, similar to a MICRODOT, giving instructions about a dead drop. The magazine is in the KGB MUSEUM in Moscow. The GRU officer was caught—betrayed by Howard and ALDRICH H. AMES.

Traffic Analysis

A form of SIGNALS INTELLIGENCE in which radio intercepts are studied to determine patterns. Even if interceptors are not able to read an enemy's code, they can draw inferences from such elements as the source of a signal, its length, and its regularity in terms of time and wavelength. Relays of the same message indicate connections between, say, army units that are all being given the same orders.

During World War II the Japanese, with virtually no prowess in codebreaking, often relied on traffic analysis to make intelligence estimates. A surge of U.S. traffic sometimes could be tracked, so that a sudden increase of transmissions from Hawaii directed toward the southwest Pacific could mean a move in that direction. Sudden radio silence usually indicated an impending action.

Aware that surges of traffic provided the enemy with an indicator of action, U.S. communications specialists added new disciplines to military traffic. PADDING was added to messages, so that the length—or brevity—of a message would not be an indicator. A more sophisticated method was the opposite of radio silence: a continual stream of number groups; most of them were meaningless, but buried in the stream were real messages.

Travis, Comdr. Edward

Director of BLETCHLEY PARK, the British codebreaking center, at the beginning of World War II.

The founding director of Bletchley Park (BP) was Comdr. ALASTAIR DENNISTON; Travis was the day-to-day manager.

A Royal Navy officer, Travis tried to run Bletchley Park like a ship. The staff of eccentric dons and undisciplined mathematicians, however, saw Travis as a tyrant. Some complained directly to Prime Minister Winston Churchill in Oct. 1941, saying, "We have done everything we possibly can through the normal channels." Well aware of the value of BP, Churchill tried to pacify the complainers by ordering an increase in its staff and resources.

Early in 1942 Denniston was replaced by Travis as director of BP, who also became director-general of BP's parent organization, the GOVERNMENT COMMUNICATIONS HEADQUARTERS (GCHQ). He was so dictatorial that people at BP called him "der Führer." But BP continued to be a phenomenally successful intelligence enterprise.

He retired as head of GCHQ in 1952.

Trebitsch, Ignatz Timotheus

(b. 1897 d. ?)

AGENT for German intelligence in Britain before and during World War I and then for a number of countries during a bizarre espionage career that took him from Hungary to China.

Born in Hungary, the son of Orthodox Jews, Trebitsch initially studied to become a rabbi at the Jewish Seminary in Hamburg. He left the seminary and went to England, where he abandoned the Jewish faith to become an Anglican. Trebitsch later returned to Hamburg to train for the Lutheran ministry. Then he moved again, to Canada.

In Canada he married a German woman and reverted to the Anglican Church. Returning to England in 1902, he became a curate, but resigned in late 1903 to travel extensively in Europe on behalf of British industrialists and politicians, from whom he took money for petroleum speculation. In 1910 he became a member of Parliament (changing his name to Trebitsch Lincoln). By then he was in the employ of German intelligence; he may have been working for Germany since 1902.

On the eve of World War I, Trebitsch went bankrupt and did not have the funds to stand for reelection. He offered his services to British NAVAL INTELLIGENCE, was rejected, and fell under suspicion. In early 1915 he fled to the United States, where, backed by funds from the German Consulate in New York City, he wrote anti-British articles.

The United States extradited him to Britain in 1916 on charges of fraud (not espionage). He was tried and given a three-year prison sentence. On his release he went first to Hungary and then to Germany, where he became involved in a right-wing conspiracy. Abandoning Germany, he turned to China, working there for a warlord who was being secretly supported by Britain.

By the early 1920s Trebitsch-Lincoln, as he was then known, was a Buddhist monk working for Chinese intelligence while possibly also working for the British, Germans, Dutch, and Japanese. Now known as Abbot Chao Kung, he played a role in getting former Chinese Emperor Pu Yi into the hands of Japanese military officials, who made Pu Yi the puppet emperor of Manchuria.

"Lincoln was always a modest asset to us even in his old age when we knew he was backing the Japanese. He had a complicated mind, but we probably understood it better than your Westerners," a former officer in the Chinese secret service told espionage writer RICHARD DEACON for his book *Kempei Tai* (1982).

At the beginning of World War II Abbot Chao Kung was said to be making German propaganda broadcasts from Tibet. He was reported dead in Oct. 1943, but another report, in May 1947, claimed that he was alive in India.

Treff

Russian slang for secret meeting. The word was probably derived from *treif*, the Yiddish word for "unclean," that is, nonkosher, food.

Treholt, Arne

Head of the press section of the Norwegian Foreign Ministry charged with supplying SECRET NORTH ATLANTIC TREATY ORGANIZATION (NATO) documents to the Soviet Union. OLEG GORDIEVSKY, British MOLE in the KGB, called Treholt one of the KGB's most important agents. Treholt also served as a state secretary in the Norwegian Ministry of Ocean Law.

In 1980, when he was a member of the Norwegian delegation to the UNITED NATIONS in New York, the FBI placed him under SURVEILLANCE. Treholt, was arrested in Jan. 1984 by Norwegian authorities while boarding a plane for VIENNA. He was alleged to have a suitcase full of NATO documents. About 6,000 more pages of NATO documents were said to have been found in his home. He was 42 years old when arrested.

According to testimony at his 11-week jury trial in Norway, he received more than $7,000 from Soviet HANDLERS.

He was found guilty and sentenced to 20 years in prison. He was released quietly, according to Norwegian sources, after serving less than 10 years.

Tricycle

SEE DUSKO POPOV

Trigon

CODE NAME for a Soviet citizen who was an AGENT for the CIA. The code name appeared in the U.S. press several times in the fall of 1980, when Republican members of Congress claimed that Trigon had been compromised by a NATIONAL SECURITY COUNCIL (NSC) official who had inadvertently leaked the existence of the agent to an Eastern European diplomat at a Washington party. The issue flared briefly as part of the presidential election campaign between Republican Ronald Reagan and the incumbent, Democratic President Jimmy Carter.

As recounted by more LEAKS from Republican sources, the NSC official's remark was reported by the diplomat in a cable that was intercepted and decoded by NSA. Carter administration sources said, however, that Trigon had been discovered at least two years before, tried in a Moscow court, and convicted. They said he had been exposed by his own expensive living on his espionage earnings.

Triple Agent

An AGENT who serves three intelligence services in an agent capacity but who, like a DOUBLE AGENT, wittingly or unwittingly withholds significant information from two services at the instigation of the third service.

Also see REDOUBLED AGENT.

Trithemius, Johannes

(b. 1462 d. 1516)

Fifteenth-century Benedictine monk in Germany who was one of the most revered figures in occult sciences. His scholarship earned him the accolade "Father of Bibliography."

A year and a half after his death his *Polygraphiae libri sex* (Six Books of Polygraphy) was published in Latin. Soon afterwards it was reprinted in French and German. Most of the massive volume consisted of columns of words printed in large Gothic type that Trithernius used in his systems of CRYPTOGRAPHY. The work also contained a square table, or tableau, that enabled enciphering through substitution. However, the abbot's most dramatic contribution to the development of codes was that each letter of the PLAIN TEXT was replaced by a word or phrase, so that the enciphered word read like an ordinary sentence.

The first four letters of Trithemius's alphabet could be translated as follows:

A	B	C	D
I hail thee	beautiful	lovely	we hasten
Mary	Pallas	Isis	Astarte
Filled	magnified	devoted	enthroned
of grace	of enticement	of knowledge	of charm
the Lord	a god	desire	felicity
with thee	at thy breast	in thy arms	in thy heart
thou art blest	thou art admired	thou art the shield	loved
of women	of the miserable	of all wise men	of lovers
fruit	work	delicacy	treasure
is blest	is eternal	is admirable	is adorable

Thus, through word substitution for letters, the plain text word *BAD* could be written as "beautiful Mary in thy heart," or "work of women [is] treasure." Trithemius produced 14 such alphabets, and the sender could choose any one of them, stating at the outset to the recipient which one he was employing for the specific message. Because the alphabet is similar for Latin, English, and French, a message (alphabet) in one language could be encoded in another language.

The major problem with the scheme was the large number of words needed to compose a message, which made the operation time-consuming.

Trithemius's book *Steganographio* (Covered Writing), written in 1499, was published in 1606.

Troung, David

SEE RONALD L. HUMPHREY

Trust, The

DECEPTION organization established by the Bolshevik regime in Russia during the revolution that began in Oct. 1917, ostensibly as an association to help overthrow the new Bolshevik government. The organization, formally the Monarchist Association of Central Russia, was established and run by the Bolshevik government under FELIKS DZERZHINSKY, in an effort to identify and control anti-Bolshevik efforts.

The Trust acted as a magnet for anti-Bolsheviks, who returned to Russia not knowing that they were being lured into a trap. Outside Russia, the Trust identified the sympathies of émigré groups, confused Western intelligence agencies, and distributed DISINFORMATION about the Bolsheviks.

France and other countries donated funds to the Trust in the belief that they were aiding the anti-Bolshevik Russians. There *was* an anti-Bolshevik movement, the Russian Combined Services Union (ROVS), formed first to foster anti-Bolshevik and then anti-Soviet activities. The Bolsheviks infiltrated the ROVS and kidnapped both its original leader, who died in their hands, and his successor, who was executed in the Soviet Union.

U.S. intelligence analyst John J. Dziak, in his excellent book *Chekisty: A History of the KGB* (1988), wrote that the Trust "utilized not only provocation to achieve its counterintelligence goals, but trafficked heavily in forged and other spurious documents and intelligence reports against the émigrés and Western intelligence services."

The Trust was abolished about 1924, in part because of its exposure by SIDNEY REILLY, who went into Russia on a guarantee by the Trust. At its peak the organization had about 5,000 operatives in and out of Russia.

TS

SEE TOP SECRET

Tsou, Douglas

Chinese-born former FBI employee who was indicted in 1988 for espionage following his admission that in 1986 he had written a letter to a representative of the government of Taiwan in which he revealed the identity of an INTELLIGENCE OFFICER of the People's Republic of China.

In his 1991 trial, the Chinese officer, stationed in Taiwan, had unsuccessfully approached the FBI with an offer to work as a DOUBLE AGENT. Although the information Tsou passed to a Taiwanese representative in Houston was SECRET, Tsou said he considered the information declassified because the offer was not accepted (for reasons not disclosed by the FBI).

Tsou, who had fled to Taiwan when the communists rose to power on the mainland in 1949, lived there for 20 years, then moved to the United States and became a naturalized U.S. citizen. He worked for the FBI from 1980 to 1986, first in San Francisco and later in Houston.

In Jan. 1992 he was sentenced to 10 years in prison.

Tsuji, Col. Masanobu

Japanese Army officer who after World War II subsequently embarked on a mysterious political-espionage career.

Commissioned in 1923, Tsuji was chief of operations and planning on the staff of the 25th Japanese Army in Malaya in Dec. 1941. He was the architect of a campaign that was highly successful although notorious for Japanese atrocities.

Tsuji, sought by Allied officials for war crimes after the war, said he was ordered "by the Japanese High Command to disappear and preserve himself for the reconstruction of Japan." He escaped to Thailand, spent some time in China and Indochina, returned to Japan when the Allies restored Japan's sovereignty in 1952, and was elected to the upper house of parliament. He later went to Vietnam as a correspondent for a Japanese newspaper and again disappeared.

Japanese sources said that Tsuji wrote to his family in April 1964 from Saigon saying he would be home by the end of the month. But he disappeared, and four months later Radio Beijing claimed that Tsuji had been killed by AGENTS of the CIA in Laos, a claim U.S. officials denied.

Tsuji wrote *Singapore: The Japanese Version*, first published in Japanese in 1950 and in English a decade later. This was both an account of the successful campaign that he planned as well as a tirade against the British and their Asian allies (although Tsuji was a great admirer of Winston Churchill). He also wrote *Guadalcanal* (1960). His subsequent *Japan's Greatest Victory: Britain's Worst Defeat* told how the Japanese believed that they were embarked upon a great mission as the saviors of all people of the Far East, to bring about an end to centuries of European aggression in Asia. Tsuji said that the Japanese campaigns so weakened the white minorities in the region that the nations of Asia subsequently were able to expel their American and European overlords.

In their *Soldiers of the Sun: The Rise and Fall of he Imperial Japanese Army* (1991), Meirion and Susie Harries wrote:

> Tsuji was an exceptionally intelligent staff officer with a flair for operational planning—talent vitiated by megalomaniac ambition, violent prejudices, and ruthless disregard for human life. In his own eyes he was an idealist prophet of Asian unity and an anticommunist crusader. He strides through the pages of his own numerous books as the architect of every successful stratagem, the hero of death-defying encounters—flying over enemy lines in tiny spotter planes, storming enemy dugouts in tanks—prescient, dynamic, and misunderstood.

Tuberville, Sir Thomas

English knight who served as a spy in the service of King Philip IV of France. In the Anglo-French War of 1293–1298 he attempted to incite Scots and Welsh against Edward I.

Tubman, Harriet

(b. 1821 d. 1913)

Ex-slave who became a spy for the Union during the American Civil War. Born to slave parents in Maryland, Tubman escaped to freedom in Pennsylvania around 1849 by following Polaris, the north star. During the 1850s she became a leading abolitionist and one of the conductors on the Underground Railroad, which brought other slaves, including her own parents, to freedom.

When the Civil War began, she volunteered, first as a Union Army cook, then as a nurse, and finally as a spy. She led Union raiding parties into Confederate territory in Maryland and Virginia.

In 1863 she organized a scouting service consisting of former slaves who could slip through Confederate lines and locate supply dumps. Black river pilots working for Tubman located Confederate "torpedoes," as river mines were called. After she did the RECONNAISSANCE for a raid up the Combahee River in South Carolina, a Confederate officer reported, "The enemy seems to have been well posted as to the character and capacity of our troops and their small chance of encountering opposition, and to have been well guided by persons thoroughly acquainted with the river and country."

After the war, she tried unsuccessfully to collect $1,800 in back pay. She finally got a pension in 1899 but only as the widow of a veteran. She settled in Auburn, N.Y., opened schools for freedmen in the South, and sponsored a home for poor blacks in Auburn. In acknowledgment of her work during the Civil War, she was buried with full military honors.

Tunnels

A frequent technique for gaining entry to intelligence TARGETS.

Intelligence services of many countries have used tunnels as a way to literally penetrate the opposition; in modern times the tunnels have been used for eavesdropping with the use of phone taps or BUGS. U.S. and British intelligence agencies used tunnels to gain access to Soviet communications on several occasions during the Cold War. The best known efforts were the BERLIN TUNNEL and one in VIENNA; in anticipation of a rich bounty of intelligence, they were given the CODE NAMES Gold and Silver, respectively.

In 2001 there were reports that a tunnel had been dug under the new Russian Embassy on Wisconsin Avenue in northwest Washington, D.C., to provide access to listening devices under the embassy. Disclosure of the tunnel was reportedly one of the secrets revealed by ROBERT HANSSEN, the FBI agent arrested and convicted of spying for the Soviets and, subsequently, for Russia.

The Russian Embassy, built in the 1970s and 1980s, was not fully occupied until 1991 because of a dispute between the United States and the Soviet Union over charges that each country was bugging the other's embassy.

In 1978 U.S. intelligence officials found that the Soviets were digging a tunnel under the U.S. Embassy in Moscow. That discovery, along with the discovery of hidden listening devices, led to a U.S. State Department decision to build a new embassy. But American security officials charged that Russian construction workers were under KGB control. After finding listening devices in the building, the dispute dragged on, and not until 2000 was the new U.S. Embassy occupied following considerable reconstruction. The Russians were then allowed to fully occupy their new building in Washington.

Tunny

SEE FISH

Turpitude

SEE ZEPPELIN (2)

Tuomi, Kaarlo Rudolph

Soviet MILITARY INTELLIGENCE OFFICER who became a DOUBLE AGENT, working for the United States.

Born in the United States, Tuomi was instilled with a love of communism at an early age by his Finnish stepfather. In 1933 his family moved from Michigan to the Soviet Union. Four years later the NKVD arrested his stepfather, who was never seen again.

After working as a lumberjack to support his mother, in 1939 Tuomi was drafted into the Red Army. Although trained for intelligence duty, he was assigned to the infantry when the Germans invaded the Soviet Union in June 1941. During the war he was decorated for bravery. After leaving the Army in 1946, he enrolled in the Teacher's Institute at Kirov. While there he married one of the daughters of the family with which he was a boarder. Late in 1949 the secret police (MGB) blackmailed Tuomi into working as an informer. After graduating from the institute, he remained—at the MGB's bidding—an English instructor. His career as a teacher-informer continued at other educational activities until 1957, when he was recruited by the KGB to serve as an ILLEGAL in the West.

He underwent specialized SPY SCHOOL training for three years. However, because of the deteriorating relations between the United States and Soviet Union at the time, Tuomi was being seconded to the GRU. He was sent to Western Europe in mid-1958 with the COVER of an American tourist to familiarize himself with Western society. He arrived in Canada in Dec. 1958 carrying the papers of a Finnish-American; once in Canada, he assumed to cover of an American businessman, Robert B. White of Chicago. On New Year's Eve he crossed into the United States by train.

After establishing his LEGEND in the United States, he made contact with his GRU HANDLER. Picked up by the FBI, who had him under observation since he had crossed the Canadian border, Tuomi was forced to admit his real identity to U.S. officials. He was turned into a double agent, working as a clerk at Tiffany's and later for a steamship firm while he remained in contact with the GRU and awaited specific assignments. Meanwhile, the FBI had access to all of his communications with the Soviet Union and learned much about contemporary GRU TRADECRAFT.

In June 1963, scheduled to return to the Soviet Union for a brief visit and then come back to the United States, he elected to remain in his native country, leaving his wife and children in the Soviet Union. He disappeared into the population, and not until 1971 did the FBI, in a *Reader's Digest* article, reveal his service as a double agent.

Turing, Alan

(b. 1912 d. 1954)

British mathematician and cryptologist at BLETCHLEY PARK during World War II who led the group that found a way to crack Germany's ENIGMA CIPHER machine.

Turing's maternal grandfather was known as the genius who saved India for Britain by inventing a fan that whisked and cooled the subcontinent's hot, humid air. Following in his grandfather's footsteps, in 1936, two years after graduating from Cambridge, Turing wrote a paper, "On Computable Numbers," forecasting the computer. His theoretical version, called the "universal Turing machine," could, he said, imitate any other machine.

Carrying this theory into reality, Turing and his colleagues at Bletchley Park were presented with an Enigma machine and told to build another machine that could fathom its machinations. The team created the BRONZE GODDESS, "a large copper-coloured cupboard"; it was a primitive computer that cracked its first codes in April 1940. This was the beginning of ULTRA, the epochal effort that gave the Allies the ability to read German codes. Later, when the Germans upgraded Enigma, Bletchley Park cryptologists, using Turing's theories, built the COLOSSUS, the first programmable digital computer.

Turing, a long-haired young man in "rumpled and dirty clothes," was a HOMOSEXUAL. When schoolboys were reported molested in a town near Bletchley Park early in 1944, Turing was transferred to a secret MI6 radio laboratory at Hanslope Park in Buckinghamshire. There he worked on a voice scrambler, while at Bletchley Park his colleagues produced the Colossus.

After the war, Turing's homosexuality made him a SECURITY RISK, in the opinion of intelligence officials. He died of cyanide poisoning (most likely a suicide) after being convicted in Manchester of being a practicing homosexual.

Andrew Hodges' biography *Alan Turing: The Enigma* (1983) was the basis for a play, *Breaking the Code,* by Hugh Whitemore, which opened in London in 1986 and later in New York. A television version appeared in 1997.

Turn

To transform an AGENT into a DOUBLE AGENT. This is usually done through coercion, as happened in Britain during World War II when the TWENTY COMMITTEE gave German agents the choice of being turned or being executed. Blackmail, often involving SEX, can also help accomplish a turning. Sometimes, however, an INTELLIGENCE OFFICER can persuade a hostile agent to turn for patriotic, altruistic, or monetary reasons.

Turner, Adm. Stansfield

(b. 1923)

Career U.S. naval officer who was DIRECTOR OF CENTRAL INTELLIGENCE from March 1977 to Jan. 1981.

A 1946 graduate of the Naval Academy, Turner served one year at sea and then attended Oxford University as a Rhodes Scholar, where he earned a master's degree in 1950. He subsequently served in various sea assignments, including command of several surface warships (a minesweeper, destroyer, and guided missile destroyer). Turner also served in the offices of the Chief of Naval Operations and the Assistant Secretary of Defense (Systems Analysis), and was executive assistant and naval aide to the Secretary of the Navy.

After attending Harvard Business School he was promoted to rear admiral in 1970. He subsequently commanded a carrier task group and then became head of the Navy's Systems Analysis Division. He became president of the Naval War College in 1972, serving for two years. He next became Commander, U.S. Second Fleet and NATO Striking Fleet in the Atlantic. In Sept. 1975 he became the NORTH ATLANTIC TREATY ORGANIZATION's Commander-in-Chief Allied Forces Southern Europe, with the rank of admiral.

When President Carter entered office in Jan. 1977, his lack of knowledge of intelligence matters and prospective DCIs led him to select his Naval Academy classmate—whom he barely knew—to serve as DCI. Turner was appointed DCI while on active duty. (He retired from active duty in Dec. 1978.)

As DCI, Turner began shifting the assets of the CIA, emphasizing intelligence gathered from SATELLITES and ELECTRONIC INTELLIGENCE over reliance on HUMAN INTELLIGENCE. He also drastically cut back on the agency's clandestine operations. He dismissed a number of veterans of the Directorate for Operations and forced nearly 150 more into early retirement. They were told of his decision in a letter that said, "It has been decided that your services are no longer needed."

Turner ran the CIA as an admiral would, giving orders and expecting them to be carried out. He did not like people drinking at lunch. In the Navy, an admiral's displeasure in this regard would have turned subordinates into lunchtime teetotalers; in the CIA it made him look like a moralistic martinet. His actions created lasting resentment, as did his tendency to second-guess analysts by adding his own views regardless of their validity.

Under Turner the CIA drew back its veil of secrecy a bit. He appointed an office of public affairs under a former Navy officer. To counteract anti-CIA attitudes on college campuses, Turner invited university presidents to the CIA for seminars.

After leaving the DCI post, Turner became a lecturer and writer, authoring *Secrecy and Democracy* (1985), an account of his four years as DCI. When he submitted the manuscript for review, CIA officals asked for more than 100 deletions. In a prefatory note, Turner implied that the censorship was aimed more at protecting the CIA than guarding secrets. In 1994, at a conference on intelligence, he sharply criticized the CIA for its failure to predict the toppling of the Shah of Iran or the collapse of the Soviet Union.

Twenty Committee

The group of British intelligence officials, including wartime amateurs, who held the key to the DOUBLE-CROSS SYSTEM, which transformed German spies into DOUBLE AGENTS. To German INTELLIGENCE OFFICERS, the double agents appeared to be operating successfully because they were transmitting back to Germany information that seemed to be valid.

The committee's name came from the pun produced by the Roman numeral XX and its double-cross purpose. It was also called the Double-Cross Committee and the XX Committee. The group provided tantalizing information—an ingenious mixture of real and fake secrets—that the TURNED agents transmitted to a completely deceived ABWEHR, the German intelligence agency that believed it was handling the agents.

The Twenty Committee focused much of the system on BODYGUARD, the overall DECEPTION plan for the Allied invasion of Europe. The plan was developed to help hide the real date, location, and details of D-DAY, the June 1944 Normandy landings. A nonexistent military force, the FIRST U.S. ARMY GROUP, was part of the deception.

The origin of the committee was the W-Board, which consisted of the commander in chief of Home Forces and the directors of military, naval, and air intelligence. The W-Board established a working committee, W-Section, and that became the Twenty Committee, which began meeting in Jan. 1941. Charged with handling COUNTERESPIONAGE against German agents in Great Britain, the committee soon assumed the task of developing deceptive information for the doubled agents.

The British Security Service, MI5, established a special section, B1(a), under. Lt. Col. T. A. Robertson, to find and handle German agents. Beginning in Oct. 1941, the Twenty Committee provided B1(a) with the deceptive information supplied to the agents. The chairman of the committee was Sir JOHN MASTERMAN, an Oxford don. The 14 members included Robertson; EWEN MONTAGU of NAVAL INTELLIGENCE; Col. John H. Bevan of the LONDON CONTROLLING STATION (for ULTRA); and representatives of the Supreme Headquarters Allied Expeditionary Forces and various other British intelligence agencies. Norman

Holmes Pearson, head of X-2, the counterintelligence branch of the OFFICE OF STRATEGIC SERVICES, was part of the committee but technically was not a member. Montagu conceived of another elaborate deception plan, MINCEMEAT, to throw off the Germans prior to the Allied invasion of Sicily.

Masterman attributed the near-perfect attendance record of the committee to the fact that he always provided tea accompanied by excellent buns.

Also see DUSKO POPOV.

Typex

The principal British CIPHER machine used for higher-classification encryptions during World War II.

Development of the Typex began with a 1926 interdepartmental committee established to examine the value of cipher machines to replace the BOOK CIPHERS then in use by all three British military services, as well as the Foreign Office, the Colonial Office, and the India Office. During this period the British purchased two ENIGMA machines for evaluation.

In Jan. 1935 the committee recommended that the Air Ministry procure three cipher machines of an improved Enigma type, referred to as Type X. The development and procurement of the machine—soon known as Typex—was successful, and by Sept. 1939, when war began in Europe, the War Office (Army) and Air Ministry (Royal Air Force) had adopted the machine for use with high-grade ciphers. The Royal Navy, however, decided against the Typex, remaining dependent upon cipher and code books. (Not until late 1943 did the Navy began adopting a cipher machine—the Combined Cypher Machine—used by the U.S., British, and Canadian Navies; it was based on the U.S. SIGABA machine.)

The Typex was a multi-rotor machine similar in principal to the Enigma. The Typex was considered fast, efficient, and secure. Although the British lost several Typex machines to the Germans at Dunkirk and in North Africa early in the war, the Germans undertook no serious effort to break into the Typex ciphers. (Similarly, there was no major German effort to solve ciphers produced by the Combined Cypher Machine.)

Operational units, the Army down to division headquarters, and all major ground commands of the Royal Air Force used the Typex, which was also used by all British SPECIAL LIAISON UNITS, except for those in the China-Burma-India Theater, which employed the U.S. Sigaba. A few U.S. military units used Typex.

U-2

The world's best-known spyplane. The U-2 is a U.S. photo and electronic RECONNAISSANCE aircraft that was developed specifically for intelligence collection over the Soviet Union. The aircraft was flown over the Soviet Union from July 1956 until May 1960. It was also flown over other TARGET areas, including China, Cuba, Egypt, Israel, Laos, and Vietnam. British pilots flew some of the flights over the USSR and several aircraft were transferred to Taiwan for flights over China. The U-2 has continued in front-line U.S. service into the 21st century, outlasting its planned successor, the SR-71 BLACKBIRD aircraft.

Work on the U-2 began about 1953 as a BLACK program sponsored by the CIA with RICHARD M. BISSELL as the program manager. CLARENCE (KELLY) JOHNSON, head of the Lockheed SKUNK WORKS, was the chief designer. President Eisenhower, who personally approved the production of 30 U-2 aircraft, supported the U-2 because of concern that Soviet strategic nuclear weapon developments could threaten the United States with a surprise attack in a nuclear version of the PEARL HARBOR ATTACK.

In 1954 Eisenhower had asked JAMES R. KILLIAN, president of the Massachusetts Institute of Technology, to chair a panel to look into the potential of long-range, strategic missile developments. Some 50 distinguished scientists and engineers from academia, laboratories, and the government were assembled to look into various aspects of strategic offensive weapons, strategic defense, and strategic intelligence technologies. EDWIN H. LAND of Polaroid fame chaired a subpanel on intelligence; the panel's highly classified report of Feb. 1955 began: "We *must* find ways to increase the number of hard facts upon which our intelligence estimates are based, to provide better strategic warning, to minimize surprise in the kind

of attack, and to reduce the danger of gross overestimation or gross under-estimation of the threat." The panel urged U-2 operations.

The U-2 was to fly over Soviet territory at altitudes above 60,000 feet. Essentially a powered glider, it had "such a unique configuration that there was little chance of its being mistaken for a bomber," according to Eisenhower's memoir *Waging Peace, 1956–1961* (1963). In addition to cameras, the early U-2s had a miniaturized ELECTRONIC INTELLIGENCE (ELINT) system, more advanced than any previously built, to collect Soviet radar signals. The reconnaissance systems were regularly updated; the U-2B of the early 1960s had a camera fitted with a 944.7-millimeter lens that could take 4,000 paired photos of a strip of earth 125 miles by 2,174 miles.

The U-2 flew for the first time on Aug. 1, 1955. The first U-2 OVERFLIGHT of the Soviet Union took place on July 4, 1956, with Moscow the primary target. The following year a U-2 was reported to have looked down on the first Soviet intercontinental missile on its launcher at Tyuratam, east of the Aral Sea.

The flights over the Soviet Union were piloted by civilian pilots under contract to the CIA, actually on loan or SHEEP DIPPED from the Air Force; the planes were initially assigned to the 1st, 2nd, and 3rd Weather Reconnaissance Squadrons (Provisional). The first flights over the USSR were flown from the Royal Air Force base at Lakenheath, England; then, because of political problems, the U-2s were based at Wiesbaden, near Frankfurt, in West Germany. Then, to get the U-2 bases closer to their targets, the "European" U-2s were based at Incirlik air base near Adana, Turkey, with some of their flights taking off from remote airfields in Pakistan. Similarly, Far Eastern operations were initially flown from the U.S. air base at Atsugi, Japan.

U-2s were assigned to the U.S. Air Force beginning in

June 1957 and from 1974 all strategic reconnaissance U-2s were assigned to the Air Force. The 9th Strategic Reconnaissance Wing at Beale Air Force, Calif., took over U-2 operations and continues to do so. From 1982 to 1991 the 17th Strategic Reconnaissance Wing was established at Alconbury Royal Air Force Base, England, for U-2 and operations in the European theater.

British pilots also trained to fly the U-2, and in 1958 President Eisenhower persuaded Prime Minister Harold Macmillan to have his pilots overfly the Soviet Union. The first of several British-piloted U-2 overflights was made on Aug. 24, 1958.

When the U-2 was built it was estimated that it would be able to fly safely over the Soviet Union for only two years before the Soviets would be able to detect it and shoot it down. But all 24 overflights of the Soviet Union between 1956 and 1960 were tracked by Soviet radar. On May 1, 1960, a U-2B flown by CIA pilot FRANCIS GARY POWERS was shot down by a Soviet SA-2 surface-to-air missile near the industrial center of Sverdlovsk in central Russia. Powers had taken off from Peshawar, Pakistan, and had intended to cross the Soviet Union and land in Bödo, Norway, in a 9½-hour flight covering 3,788 miles—of which 2,919 miles would be over the Soviet Union. Apparently several SA-2 missiles were fired by the air defense unit commanded by Maj. M. R. Voronov. The U-2 seems to have suffered an engine problem and as it lost altitude it was severely damaged by an SA-2 missile.

Powers's aircraft was fitted with a plastic explosive linked to a delayed timing switch that he was to initiate prior to ejecting from the aircraft. The explosive was intended to destroy the camera, *not* the aircraft. Powers was unable to initiate the destruct mechanism.

He parachuted from the aircraft and was captured immediately upon landing. The wreckage of his crashed aircraft was later placed on display in Gor'kiy Park in Moscow. Subsequently the wreckage was placed in a museum.

The Powers U-2 flight occurred 15 days before a scheduled summit conference of major world leaders in Paris. As a result of the U-2 incident, Premier Nikita Khrushchev demanded an apology at the conference from President Eisenhower, causing the collapse of the meeting and a worsening of American-Soviet relations. Following this incident U-2s were no longer flown over the Soviet Union, but they continued to be flown over other areas of interest to the United States.

U-2s were flown extensively over Cuba; the first flight, personally authorized by Eisenhower, was made on Oct. 27, 1960, by a CIA aircraft. On the night of Oct. 13–14, 1962, Air Force pilots began making the Cuba flights. The U-2s revealed the buildup of Soviet weapons on the Caribbean island, precipitating the CUBAN MISSILE CRISIS. On Oct. 27, 1962, a U-2 piloted by Air Force Maj. RUDOLF ANDERSON, JR., was shot down over Cuba by a Soviet SA-2 surface-to-air missile; Anderson was killed.

U-2 flights over China flown by Nationalist pilots from Taiwan began early in 1960. The first Taiwanese U-2 loss occurred in Sept. 1962, and China probably shot down a total of five Taiwanese U-2s during the 1960s. (The last flight over China was made in June 1974.) There was also one CIA-piloted mission that took off from the U.S. aircraft carrier *Ranger* in the mid-Pacific in May 1964. That U-2G successfully photographed the island of Mururoa, part of French Polynesia, to spy on French atomic bomb tests being conducted there.

Other unusual U-2 missions included spy flights over China made by U.S. pilots flying from India. In 1962, when following another Chinese-Indian clash the Delhi government turned to the West for military assistance (although continuing to procure arms from the Soviet Union). After lengthy negotiations, in early 1964 the Indian government agreed to the CIA using the Charbatia air base near Cuttack, on the eastern coast of India. A single U-2 made two or three U-2 overflights of China and Tibet, the first in May 1964 and probably the last one in Dec. 1964, shortly after the first Chinese nuclear test at Lop Nor. All flights were successful. Intelligence about Chinese military forces in the border region was shared with the Indian government in this highly secret operation.

And, on Jan. 27, 2000, an ER-2—a non-military U-2 variant—of the National Aeronautics and Space Administration (NASA) entered Russian air space with Russian government permission. The flights were part of a multinational ozone research project, taking off from Kiruna, Sweden. (NASA participation in the project also included a modified DC-8 transport and balloons carrying research instrumentation.)

Military U-2s were particularly active in the Middle East beginning with the Suez conflict of 1956. During the Gulf War of 1991 U-2s were flown in Saudi Arabian air space to provide real-time intelligence on Iraq (which was data-linked to ground stations). They subsequently monitored the "no fly zones" of Iraq, were briefly flown over Iraq under the aegis of the UNITED NATIONS to seek out illegal weapons, and again in the Gulf War of 2003 provided valuable intelligence.

Fifty-one aircraft of the U-2A/B/C series were built from 1955 to 1969. These aircraft were periodically modified and updated before the last was retired in 1989. Another six were produced from "spare parts" ordered to support those aircraft. Twelve larger, more capable U-2R models were manufactured in the late 1960s; they were fitted with advanced reconnaissance radar and a variety of electronic sensors as well as cameras. Then the TR-1 *Tactical Reconnaissance* version, similar to the U-2R, was developed to provide surveillance over European battlefields. From 1979 to 1989 the Air Force took delivery of 27 TR-1s and another eight similar U-2R variants while the NASA received two similar *Earth Resources* ER-1 models. (The TR-1s were redesignated U-2R in 1991.) NASA also flew several earlier U-2s.

Thus, a total of 106 U-2s were produced. In 2003 the U.S. Air Force still had 31 U-2s in its inventory.

At least two U-2R COMMUNICATIONS INTELLIGENCE (COMINT) aircraft were fitted with a large, airfoil-shaped radome on a short dorsal pylon to relay COMINT data by SATELLITE; several U-2s and two TR-

A U-2R cruises at high altitude. This enlarged variant has under its wings "slipper" tanks that contain fuel and sensors. U-2s continue to serve despite the advent of satellites and unmanned aerial vehicles. And, it has "outlived" its successor, the SR-71 Blackbird. (LOCKHEED)

High-flying U-2s were not immune. Soviet-built SA-2 Guideline missiles shot down seven U-2s from 1960 to 1967—one over the USSR, one over Cuba, and probably five over China. These are part of the remains of four of the spyplanes put on display at the Military Museum in Beijing in 1965.

1B models had a second position for pilot training. The Navy flew two U-2s with special radar to evaluate an ocean surveillance role, but that program was canceled. Several U-2s fitted with arresting hooks have flown from U.S. Navy aircraft carriers in addition to the one operational mission (see above).

The early U-2s had a single turbojet engine with a maximum speed of 430 mph; a more powerful engine increased this to 528 mph in the later U-2C, and the current U-2R has a top speed of 510 mph. The ceiling for the U-2 was originally some 60,000 feet (85,000 feet for the U-2C and 90,000 feet for the U-2R). The early U-2s had a range of 2,200 miles, extended to 3,000 miles in the U-2C, and 3,500 miles in the U-2R. A few U-2C aircraft were fitted for in-flight refueling to extend their range.

Also see RAINBOW.

UAV

SEE UNMANNED AERIAL VEHICLE

UKUSA Agreement

"Quite likely the most secret agreement ever entered into by the English-speaking world," is the way JAMES BAMFORD described the UKUSA Agreement in his seminal study *The Puzzle Palace* (1982).

UKUSA—the United Kingdom–United States of America Security Agreement—is the successor to the BRUSA AGREEMENT (British-U.S. Agreement) of 1943, which provided for the full exchange of SIGNALS INTELLIGENCE (SIGINT) and cooperation in the SIGINT effort between the two Allies. The UKUSA agreement of March 5, 1946, essentially combined the SIGINT efforts of Australia, Canada, and New Zealand as well as those of the United States and Great Britain. Each of the five nations had spheres of cryptologic coverage, some of which were shared; for example, Britain made use of its listening post in Hong Kong and the United States its listening posts in South Korea, Japan, and Taiwan to provide SIGINT coverage of mainland China. UKUSA member agencies include NSA, the United Kingdom's GOVERNMENT COMMUNICATIONS HEADQUARTERS (GCHQ), Canada's Communications Security Establishment (CSE), Australia's Defence Signals Directorate (DSD), and New Zealand's Government Communications Security Bureau (GCSB).

The UKUSA nations agreed to use standardized CODE WORDS, terminology, intercept-handling techniques, and security procedures. All rules and procedures were spelled out in a comprehensive document known as the International Regulations on SIGINT (IRSIG), although "international" in this context meant a highly classified procedure shared by only five nations.

The UKUSA agreement has survived political events that have divided the United States and Great Britain, albeit temporarily, such as differences over the Suez campaign of 1956. Still, periodic accusations have been made on both the British and U.S. sides that the other has cheated on the agreement. PETER WRIGHT, scientist at Britain's Security Service (MI5), in his *Spycatcher* (1987), wrote of learning that one WILLIAM K. HARVEY was establishing a Staff D section in the CIA: "If the Americans wanted to mount a cipher attack and did not wish to share the product with us, or if they wanted to operate against the UK, or a Commonwealth country, *as we were sure they were doing,* Staff D was the obvious place from which to do it." [Emphasis added]

In recent years, interest in UKUSA eavesdropping has shifted to ECHELON, the CODE NAME for a sophisticated system for plucking certain words out of communications relayed by commercial SATELLITES.

Ultan, Donald

Brooklyn-born employee of the U.S. Embassy in VIENNA who was a TARGET for Soviet intelligence because he was a CODE clerk—the highest priority for KGB and GRU efforts. In this complex and somewhat bizarre plan, which unfolded in the 1960s, a Soviet AGENT who was a naturalized citizen of a Western country invited a close friend of Ultan for a drink, thus enabling a "chance" meeting in a café with a semi-retired Belgian businessman who was, of course, a KGB officer.

This encounter in turn led to a meeting with Ultan. The KGB officer never appeared to be particularly interested in Ultan but instead scheduled more encounters with Ultan's friend. There followed many hours of friendly meetings in cafes and coffee houses, chess playing, and an occasional outing. Ultan, who was Jewish and, like most Belgians, fluent in French, began a pleasant association with the Belgian, who claimed also to be Jewish and to have relatives in Israel.

Only after five months did the KGB agent ask Ultan to provide code information for money. After a brief delay, Ultan went to the embassy security officer and revealed the KGB contact. The Soviet effort against Ultan was sophisticated and, in the words of a U.S. intelligence report on the incident, "well-planned."

Ultra

The generic term for COMMUNICATIONS INTELLIGENCE (COMINT) obtained by Britain and the United States during World War II. Ultra consisted of the CRYPTANALYSIS of all German radio communications employing the ENIGMA machine and Japanese military communications employing enciphering machines. However, deciphered Japanese diplomatic communications were known as MAGIC.

Early in World War II the British used a variety of CODE WORDS at various times for high-grade COMINT, among them Sidar, Swell, and Zymotic; they soon settled on Ultra, Pearl, and Thumb as the three code words for COMINT, in descending order of importance. With the BRUSA AGREEMENT of 1943 the U.S. codebreaking agencies adopted the British terminology, with Pearl and Thumb later replaced by the single code word Pinup.

Prior to 1941 the British circulated the decryptions

of German radio traffic under the code name BONIFACE, the implication being that the information was supplied by a SECRET AGENT. Subsequently, the classification Ultra SECRET was employed. Initially the precise use of the term was only as a security grading for outgoing signals and documents; the actual information itself was referred to as SPECIAL INTELLIGENCE or "Z" (see Z PRIORITIES).

Ultra had a key role in many Allied victories, the most important being the Battle of the Atlantic (Sept. 1939–May 1945), the longest "battle" and in several respects most vital and complex theater of World War II. The Atlantic was a vital route for Britain to bring in supplies to survive and for the United States to build up troops, aircraft, and other war matériel to take to the European theater of operations.

The Battle of the Atlantic was a close battle: "The only thing that ever really frightened me during the war was the U-boat peril," wrote Prime Minister Churchill. "I was even more anxious about this battle than I had been about the glorious air fight called the Battle of Britain." Both the German U-boat command and the Allies were heavily dependent upon CRYPTANALYSIS for their respective successes.

The German B-DIENST service was able to give the U-boat command precise information of the routing of Allied convoys during the early part of the war. The Allied codebreaking effort gave invaluable information on U-boat movements, in the end having more effect on the outcome of the battle. The distinguished German naval historian Jürgen Rohwer, who served in U-boats at the end of the war, concluded:

> If we have to place the many factors which decided the outcome of the Battle of the Atlantic in the order of precedence, we should place Ultra at the top, followed by the closing of the air-gap in the North Atlantic, the high-frequency direction-finding equipped escort and [anti-submarine] support groups, the introduction of decimeter radar, etc.

Dr. Rohwer believes that without the Ultra successes the Battle of the Atlantic would still have been won by the Allies, but that the turn in favor of the Allies would have occurred much later than the spring of 1943.

Umbra

Overall U.S. CODE WORD for the highest-grade SIGNALS INTELLIGENCE (SIGINT) derived from KEYHOLE series SATELLITES and possibly other sources. The code names Trine and Dinar were apparently used earlier for Cold War SIGINT.

These code words were also used by the British on their SIGINT material under the terms of the UKUSA AGREEMENT.

Umbrella Gun

SEE GEORGI MARKOV

U.N.C.L.E.

SEE TELEVISION

Undercover Agent

SEE SECRET AGENT

Under Secretary of Defense (Intelligence)

The senior intelligence position in the U.S. Department of Defense, established in March 2003 to control all of the department's intelligence activities and agencies, including the DEFENSE INTELLIGENCE AGENCY, NATIONAL RECONNAISSANCE OFFICE, NATIONAL MAPPING AND IMAGING AGENCY, and NSA. The secretary is also responsible for Defense Department liaison and coordination with the INTELLIGENCE COMMUNITY STAFF as well as the CIA and other non-Defense intelligence agencies and offices.

The first Under Secretary was Dr. Stephen A. Cambone.

United Kingdom

SEE ENGLAND–GREAT BRITAIN–UNITED KINGDOM

United Nations

Since its founding near the end of World War II, the United Nations (UN) has been a magnet for spies. While delegates from Allied countries were meeting in San Francisco in 1945 to create the UN, the United States was eavesdropping. Using what had become standard radio intercept and codebreaking techniques, American intelligence-monitoring organizations were picking up diplomatic messages between San Francisco and embassies in Washington and then relaying them to high-level officials in Washington as MAGIC diplomatic intercepts.

In the 1970s the CHURCH COMMITTEE revealed that the CIA had slipped a Russian-speaking, lip-reading expert in a press booth overlooking the Security Council chamber to monitor the lip movements of Russian delegates as they whispered to each other during debates at some of the open meetings of the Council.

Many of the diplomatic intercepts were kept secret until 1993, and even then the released documents were censored. The NSA, although finally admitting in 1993 that the United States had eavesdropped on some Allies, was still sensitive about certain intercepts of presumably friendly diplomats. Stephen Schlesinger, in a 1995 article in the scholarly *Cryptologia,* said that the intercepts enabled the United States to "write the UN Charter mostly according to its own blueprint."

Rumors of U.S. electronic eavesdropping swirled around UN corridors during the debates running up to the Iraqi War in 2003. A British newspaper quoted an alleged NSA memo on targeting UN delegates. U.S. public information officers declined to comment on the newspaper report. At that time, many delegates suspected that U.S. intelligence resources were used to monitor UN inspectors in Iraq to search for weapons of mass destruction. There was no credible proof of these suspicions.

The Soviet Union had been quick to see the UN as a potential hub of espionage. DONALD MACLEAN, a longtime Soviet MOLE in the British Foreign Office, was frequently involved in UN matters. In the spring of 1945 he argued strongly for the Soviet position on two key UN issues: the Soviet right of veto in the Security Council and UN membership for the Ukraine and Belorussian Republics, which in effect gave the Soviet Union three votes in the UN General Assembly.

In 1946 the Soviets, in a proposal aimed at the United States and Britain, introduced a resolution requiring each UN member to declare the number and location of its armed forces on the territories of other countries. To produce a response, Maclean worked with the director of the U.S. State Department's Office of Special Political Affairs, whose responsibilities included the UN. The director was ALGER HISS, who would later be accused of spying for the Soviets. (Still later, VENONA revelations confirmed the accusations.) The two men exchanged information on their respective nations' overseas troops. So Maclean was able to report to the Soviets that the United States had troops in 108 locations, including 52,590 in South Korea. That information was of particular interest in 1950 when the Korean War began.

From its inception to the end of the Cold War the UN and its subordinate agencies (especially those in Geneva and VIENNA) were among the favorite operating sites for Soviet intelligence gathering—and for the spy-hunting agents of the FBI. Conversely, EARL EDWIN PITTS, an FBI agent assigned to keep Soviet UN officials under SURVEILLANCE, was himself recruited by the Soviets in 1987 and was later arrested for and convicted of espionage.

The first known case involving an American and a UN spy came in March 1949 when JUDITH COPLON, a Justice Department employee, was arrested carrying documents she was about to hand over to Valentin Gubitchev, a Soviet assigned to the UN group planning the future UN building on the East River. (At that time the UN headquarters was at Lake Success, Long Island.) Gubitchev was sentenced to 15 years for espionage but was allowed to leave the country.

Until the mid-1950s the Soviets maintained tight restrictions on staffing UN positions, fearing that exposure to the West would inspire defections. Then, as former colonies in Africa and elsewhere became independent and sought UN membership, Soviet intelligence officials saw the possibility of using the UN as a rendezvous for Soviet INTELLIGENCE OFFICERS and Third World leaders. KGB officers also promoted "the connection between UN and Soviet front organizations, such as the World Peace Council," according to a 1985 report of the U.S. Senate Select Committee on Intelligence.

By obtaining positions in the International Atomic Energy Agency in Vienna, Soviet intelligence officers gained access to Western nuclear information. One of the

Soviets' earliest introductions to data-bank technology came in 1974, when a Soviet official attending a UN meeting in New York was shown the *New York Times* data-bank system. The following week the wife of the KGB RESIDENT in New York began using the UN's data bank to tap into the *Times* data bank, making the acquisition of OPEN SOURCE intelligence much easier.

ARKADY SHEVCHENKO, an Under Secretary-General of the UN, became the highest-ranking Soviet official to defect to the United States. Several other Soviet defectors from the UN helped the FBI to expose spies in the United States. One of the defectors was a Pole who led the FBI to WILLIAM H. BELL, a Hughes Aircraft Corp. employee who was later convicted of espionage.

In the halls of the UN, Shevchenko later wrote, it was easy to distinguish regular diplomats from KGB operatives:

> The first giveaway was money. The KGB . . . spent it much more generously than real diplomats. A Foreign Ministry employee would need to hoard the dollar portion of his salary for as much as a year or more before he could afford to buy a used American car. KGB agents had the cash to get one as soon as they arrived in New York. They also had money to entertain lavishly. A mid-level Mission or Secretariat staffer who is regularly seen treating non-Soviets to round after round of drinks is almost certainly using KGB funds . . .

(UN employees wryly referred to their Soviet colleagues' espionage as their "other work.")

The 1985 Senate report said, "Approximately one-fourth of the Soviets in the UN Secretariat are intelligence officers and many more are co-opted by the KGB or GRU. All Soviets in the Secretariat must respond to KGB requests for assistance." Another 200 UN employees came from Eastern Bloc nations that routinely contributed intelligence information to the Soviets.

In Feb. 1972, as U.S. and Soviet negotiators were working on the anti-ballistic missile treaty and SALT I strategic arms limitations agreement, FBI agents arrested Valery Markelov, a Soviet intelligence officer who worked under the cover of a translator at the UN. He was charged with obtaining classified documents about the F-14A Tomcat fighter from a Grumman engineer, who turned out to be a DOUBLE AGENT working for the FBI. (Three months later, as President Nixon was about to have a summit meeting with Brezhnev, the U.S. government quietly quashed the espionage indictment and Markelov, who had been out on bail, was allowed to return to the Soviet Union.)

In 1973, Anatoli Andreyev, an intelligence officer working as a UN librarian, met a civilian employee of the U.S. Department of Defense at a librarians' conference. For a year the two exchanged unclassified documents of "mutual" interest. Then Andreyev offered to help the American financially in exchange for specific classified documents. After a U.S. protest to the United Nations, the Soviet quietly left the United States.

An attempt by Soviet UN spies to recruit Lt. Comdr. ARTHUR LINDBERGH touched off a diplomatic incident in 1977. Similar approaches to members of the U.S. armed forces were tried by UN employees or officials from Soviet and Eastern Bloc countries. In one case the Soviet intelligence officer, a UN translator, was arrested but not tried. Even though he did not have diplomatic immunity, he was allowed to return to the Soviet Union in what many observers believed was a secret deal involving the release of a U.S. agent.

UN assignments permitted Soviets to travel to areas of the United States (and other countries) where Soviet citizens would normally not be allowed to go. But perhaps most dangerous from the West's viewpoint, senior Soviet officials in the United Nations had access to the personal files of all UN employees, permitting them to identify potential collaborators and blackmail victims.

When the Cold War ended, spying waned at the UN but did not disappear. The republics of the former Soviet Union were more interested in gaining membership and seeking aid than in continuing espionage.

United States

Spying is as American as GEORGE WASHINGTON and GEORGE H. W. BUSH, spymasters at two significant junctures in American history. Washington fostered MILITARY INTELLIGENCE that helped to win the American Revolution (1775–1783). Bush, as DIRECTOR OF CENTRAL INTELLIGENCE (DCI) and then as President, oversaw the CIA, a singularly American institution, for it works secretly in an open society.

Washington and Bush were not the only presidents to have direct involvement with intelligence and COVERT ACTION. Theodore Roosevelt, as Assistant Secretary of the Navy, on March 12, 1898, gave instructions to Lt. G. L. Dyer, the naval ATTACHÉ at the U.S. Embassy in Madrid, in CIPHER. "Abrolhando geoselenic abtruppen," began one message, ordering Dyer to inform the Navy about Spanish Navy ships that were sailing to Havana. The U.S. battleship *Maine* had been sunk in Havana Harbor on Feb. 15, and war with Spain was a month away.

For George Washington, intelligence was vital to victory in the Revolution. He sometimes acted like a CASE OFFICER, directly running AGENTS, giving specifics on the use of SECRET WRITING, telling an INTELLIGENCE OFFICER that he wanted "Intelligence of the Enemy's situation & numbers—what kind of Troops they are, and Guards they have—their strength and where posted." He also knew the absolute cardinal rule of espionage: "There can be scarcely any need of recommending the greatest Caution and secrecy in a Business so critical and dangerous."

The terms COVERT ACTION, psychological warfare, and special operations had not yet been coined. Washington, however, saw the need for irregular action against an enemy and in 1776 ordered Lt. Col. Thomas Knowlton, a hero of the Battle of Bunker Hill, to form a RECONNAISSANCE unit of volunteers able to gather intelligence "either by water or by land, by night or by day."

The unit became known as the Knowlton Rangers, the first official U.S. Army military intelligence organization.

In that same grim year of the Revolution a young officer, NATHAN HALE, volunteered to go behind British lines and spy. The mission failed and Hale died on a British gallows. With the Knowlton Rangers and the legendary heroism of Nathan Hale, the U.S. Army took its first steps toward establishing an intelligence service.

On Nov. 29, 1775, the Continental Congress created the first U.S. agency for collecting foreign intelligence—the COMMITTEE OF SECRET CORRESPONDENCE. The Congress declared that "the sole purpose" of the committee of was for "Corresponding with our friends in Great Britain, Ireland and other parts of the world." But the real, unstated purpose was the gathering of intelligence; the chairman, BENJAMIN FRANKLIN, shared with Washington a firm belief in the importance of this activity.

By 1777 Washington had set up an intelligence service, initiating direct correspondence with the patriotic Committees of Safety in each of the colonies, and bringing more structure to his use of spies. (See CULPER RING and Maj. BENJAMIN TALLMADGE.) John Jay, who would become the first Chief Justice of the Supreme Court, handled several COUNTERINTELLIGENCE operations.

As President, Washington guided the new nation through the shoals of democracy and confronted the first attempt at congressional oversight. In 1791 Congress established a committee to investigate a defeat suffered by an Army expedition against the Indians. Washington's cabinet recommended that the executive branch "ought to communicate such papers as the public good would permit & ought to refuse those the disclosure of which would injure the public." Washington decided to cooperate with Congress and presented the information, setting a precedent that would be cited in the 1970s when Congress began questioning CIA covert actions.

As the young United States of America grew westward beyond the Cumberland Mountains, the Army sent off expeditions—Lewis and Clark to the Northwest, Pike to Colorado—that were partly intelligence missions. Capt. Benjamin L. E. Bonneville, heading out on an expedition beyond the Rockies in 1832, was ordered to gather intelligence on the "warriors that may be in each tribe or nation that you meet with. . . ."

Military intelligence and NAVAL INTELLIGENCE played insignificant roles in the War of 1812. There was no Gen. Washington demanding intelligence. Spying was on the level of scouts, brave men sent out on reconnaissance missions.

During the American Civil War spies served on both sides, an easy enough undertaking because the people on both sides were Americans and the borders between North and South were difficult to discern and continually changing. The Confederacy used many women as agents. Among them were BELLE BOYD, who outwitted ALLAN PINKERTON, the Union's counterintelligence expert, and Rose Greenhow, a wealthy Washington party giver who picked up POLITICAL INTELLIGENCE from her guests and passed it on through one of the many NETWORKS the Confederates ran in Washington. (JOHN WILKES BOOTH, who assassinated President Lincoln, was an agent in one of these.) Escaped slave HARRIET TUBMAN and many other black Americans acted as spies during the war.

Neither the Union nor the Confederacy had a formal, top-level military intelligence service. Pinkerton, private detective turned spymaster, and his successor, LAFAYETTE C. BAKER, are often described as "intelligence chiefs" for the Union during the war. In fact, there was no such chief and there was no civilian-run intelligence organization working for the Union. But a military BUREAU OF INFORMATION was set up by Maj. Gen. GEORGE H. SHARPE.

After the war, the Army and Navy founded permanent intelligence offices. (See ARMY INTELLIGENCE, U.S., and NAVAL INTELLIGENCE, U.S.) In 1882 Secretary of State John Watson Foster (grandfather of ALLEN W. DULLES, future DIRECTOR OF CENTRAL INTELLIGENCE), posted military attachés to London, BERLIN, Paris, VIENNA, and St. Petersburg, ostensibly to gather books and publications "to give early notice of any new or important publications or inventions or improvements in arms."

From the Spanish-American War (1898) came the saga of the "message to Garcia," carried by a U.S. Army intelligence officer, Lt. Andrew S. Rowan, to Gen. Calixto García y Iñigues, the commander of the Cuban rebel army.

The ZIMMERMANN TELEGRAM, a complex foreign intelligence operation, helped to draw the United States into World War I. On Jan. 16, 1917, German Foreign Minister Arthur Zimmermann sent a telegram to the German ambassador to Mexico revealing plans for imminent unrestricted submarine warfare—and instructing the German ambassador to offer Mexico an alliance with Germany and promise that "Mexico is to reconquer the lost territory in Texas, New Mexico, and Arizona." The telegram was intercepted and decrypted by British naval intelligence (see ROOM 40) and was revealed to the United States to stoke U.S. rage against Germany. On April 2, 1917, when President Wilson asked Congress for a declaration of war, he cited the telegram as proof that Germany "means to act against our peace and security."

The British prowess in handling the Zimmermann telegram showed how superior and sophisticated were the intelligence capabilities of Britain compared with the limited resources of the United States. When the United States entered the war, the U.S. Army General Staff had a Military Information Division but no significant intelligence service. Largely through the efforts of a pioneering officer, Maj. RALPH H. VAN DEMAN, the American Expeditionary Force had a Military Intelligence Division. He also created the Army's Corps of Intelligence Police, an odd band of criminals, vagabonds, and ordinary soldiers who had nothing in common except that they could all speak French. Patrolling forward areas, they hunted spies and saboteurs.

Maj. Van Deman also launched the Army's first extensive DOMESTIC INTELLIGENCE campaign—soldiers joining with civilians to track down spies and draft dodgers on the home front. The campaign was a prelude to the postwar searches for "Reds" and subversives.

REDS AND SPIES

World War I brought an end to U.S. innocence about intelligence and subversion. Modern U.S. spy and counterspy organizations are outgrowths of ideas and organizations developed mainly during that war. In the hunt for Germany's spies and saboteurs, intelligence organizations sprang up in the State Department, the Army, the Navy, and the Justice Department. The legal basis for their work was the ESPIONAGE ACT of 1917, which made giving aid to a U.S. enemy unlawful. In 1918 the act was amended to prohibit speech or writing "intended to incite resistance to the United States or promote the cause of its enemies." This act, much amended, has remained the nation's basic espionage law. Its view of espionage as an ideological menace has also persisted.

The Sedition Act was passed in 1918, and in 1919 Supreme Court Justice Oliver Wendell Holmes, Jr., set forth guidelines for when a real or imagined need for national security can abridge the constitutional right of freedom of speech. In an opinion on an espionage case, Holmes said, "When a nation is at war, many things that might be said in times of peace are such a hindrance to its effort that their utterance will not be endured so long as men fight." Going beyond wartime, Holmes said that Congress has a right to put the nation above an individual when absolute freedom of speech would create "a clear and present danger." That phrase would ring down the years, echoing especially in the Cold War to explain away executive branch abuses of power.

Soon after the war, reacting to public panic toward "Red" threats of revolution reaching America from Russia, the Justice Department became the focal point for actions against suspected subversives and spies. The department's Bureau of Investigation (BOI) was the principal U.S. weapon against spies, though the bureau drew upon help from the OFFICE OF NAVAL INTELLIGENCE (ONI). The BOI went after Reds and aliens with a particular vengeance under its aggressive young director, J. EDGAR HOOVER, who continued his long reign as the BOI evolved into the FBI. Besides the real and imaginary home-grown Reds there was the Soviet variety. When the Bolsheviks seized power in Russia in 1917, the United States withheld recognition of the regime. In the 1920s the Soviet Union was represented by the American Trading Organization (AMTORG), one of whose founders was FELIKS DZERZHINSKY, director of the CHEKA, the Bolshevik secret police. Although the Amtorg did engage in the trade, it also engaged in espionage. Many Amtorg officials were Soviet intelligence officers seeking industrial and military secrets and recruiting Americans, especially members of the American Communist Party, as spies.

After U.S. recognition of the Soviet regime in 1933, Soviet military attachés joined their civilian comrades in trying to acquire U.S. secrets. Adm. William H. Standley, the U.S. Chief of Naval Operations, complained, "Russian attachés, military, naval, and commercial, picked up everything—copies of all technical and trade magazines and military and naval professional magazines, blueprints, and everything from nuts and bolts to washing machines, tractors, and combine harvesters." (Standley later served as U.S. ambassador to the Soviet Union from Feb. 1942 to Oct. 1943.)

Japan was also gathering intelligence, especially about the U.S. Fleet and its bases, as early as 1912, when the new battleship *Arkansas* arrived in Panama carrying President Taft for an inspection of the Canal Zone. An observant U.S. Navy officer looked warily at Japanese waiters, barbers, and fishermen who were seeking information. "We suspected that some of them were spies," he later reported, "but the general attitude was: 'So what!' "

Not of that attitude was John A. Gade, a New York banker and former U.S. naval attaché, who in 1929 approached the Navy's district intelligence officer in New York and discussed ideas about "some sort of a central Intelligence Agency" that would report directly to President Hoover. In his proposal he said that, compared with other countries, Americans "were amateurs where they were past masters." Gates suggested placing a "National Intelligence Service" in the State Department, with a "Chief Central Officer" at the "Central hub of the Wheel of Information."

The idea died, primarily because of opposition by military intelligence chiefs. Besides, neither Hoover nor his Secretary of State, Henry L. Stimson, had any interest in intelligence. The State Department had a Division of Foreign Intelligence; all it actually did was distribute, primarily to government officials and members of Congress, "items of any news value" culled from public foreign sources. The War Department had the BLACK CHAMBER, a codebreaking group organized in 1913 by HERBERT O. YARDLEY. It operated during World War I and was still busy when Stimson discovered it. He ceased funding it.

The Navy's ONI did little more than collect information on foreign navies and commercial fleets. The ONI did not evaluate the information it gathered, primarily from naval attachés, one of whom remembered being told that "reputation and career did not profit" from any ventures into "questionable activities." G-2, as U.S. Army Intelligence was generally known, mustered about 90 people in 1922; by 1929, there were only 74; and in 1936, the number dropped to a low of 66.

In May 1940, with the European War eight months old, the British Security Service (MI5) discovered that TYLER KENT, a CODE clerk in the U.S. Embassy in London, was smuggling copies of transatlantic conversations between President Roosevelt and Prime Minister Winston Churchill to a pro-German organization. When U.S. State Department officials heard of Kent's arrest, they first asked the Army's G-2 for help. When G-2 said it could not "guarantee service," the State Department turned to the FBI, until then thought of as the agency of G-men who tracked down gangsters, not spies. Before the FBI could get involved, the British had tried, convicted, and jailed Kent.

OSS TO CIA

Japan's PEARL HARBOR ATTACK on Dec. 7, 1941, revealed to U.S. political and military leaders the incredible shambles of U.S. intelligence—a collection of bickering, uncoordinated, understaffed agencies. Almost lost in the outrage over this intelligence failure was the fact that U.S. CRYPTOLOGY had already given the United States the ability to read some Japanese codes and would soon deliver the aptly named MAGIC—decrypted radio intercepts that would help to win the war. (See EDWIN T. LAYTON, LAURANCE SAFFORD, THEODORE S. WILKINSON, and WILLIAM F. FRIEDMAN.)

"It's a good thing that you got me started on this," President Roosevelt said to WILLIAM J. DONOVAN at 2 A.M. on Dec. 8, 1941. Roosevelt had founded the Office of CO-ORDINATOR OF INFORMATION (OCI), the executive branch's first intelligence organization independent of the armed services, in July 1941 and had appointed Donovan, a World War I hero, to head it. In June 1942 the OCI became the OFFICE OF STRATEGIC SERVICES (OSS) under Donovan.

The creation of the OSS gave the United States an agency that would engage in espionage and covert action throughout the world during World War II. The OSS gathered and evaluated intelligence while also running guerrilla and subversive operations against the enemy. This double mission of intelligence and covert action would form the pattern for the postwar spawn of the OSS, the CIA.

While the OSS often operated as a freewheeling outfit answerable only to Donovan, military leaders worked on ways to coordinate the intelligence agencies of the U.S. armed services. The result was the Joint Intelligence Committee, whose members included intelligence representatives from the Army, Navy, the State Department, the OSS, and the Foreign Economic Administration.

Rooted in the origin of the OSS was the idea that bright young graduates of Ivy League colleges could give an intellectual underpinning to a profession that traditionally had relied on the gleanings of humdrum military attachés. As Yale professor Robin W. Winks wrote in *Cloak & Gown* (1987):

> More than once a non-Yale, indeed non–Ivy League member of the Office of Strategic Services in World War II would find, at some remote outpost in south or southeast Asia, or in Africa, that both American and British intelligence officers, whether desk bound or spooks back from the field, would conclude a festive occasion by linking arms and singing the "Whiffenpoof Song."

The FBI's Hoover and senior military intelligence officers fought the OSS. While Donovan's people were able to carry out espionage and sabotage behind enemy lines in North Africa, Europe, and the China-Burma-India Theater, they were unsuited for the war in the Pacific. And in the Southwest Pacific theater (which came to include the Philippines), Gen. Douglas MacArthur already had his own espionage organization (see ALLIED INTELLIGENCE BUREAU). Hoover also resented what he perceived as intrusions of British intelligence (see BRITISH SECURITY COORDINATION, DUSKO POPOV, WILLIAM STEPHENSON).

Hoover staked out Latin America and the United States as FBI spy-hunting grounds, and the bureau rapidly demonstrated its new skills. (See WILLIAM COLEPAUGH, DUQUESNE SPY RING, ERICH GIMPEL, and WILLIAM G. SEBOLD.)

The FBI's Soviet espionage squad in New York City also kept a quiet watch on Soviet spies working from the spy nest that was the Soviet Consulate. Arrests of Soviet spies were rare because U.S. officials did not want to disturb a touchy wartime ally. One of the few Soviets arrested in the 1940s was GAIK OVAKIMIAN, who had been running spies in North America since the 1930s.

The extent of Soviet espionage was not realized until, just after the war ended, IGOR S. GOUZENKO, a code clerk in the Soviet Embassy in Ottawa, Canada, defected and provided material that revealed the existence of an ATOMIC SPY RING involving British scientists KLAUS FUCHS and ALAN NUNN MAY, along with JULIUS ROSENBERG and his wife, Ethel, and many other Americans.

In 1939 the U.S. Army SIGNAL INTELLIGENCE SERVICE (SIS) had begun collecting intercepted encrypted Soviet cables between the United States and Moscow. In a project code-named VENONA, the SIS in 1943 began trying to decrypt the messages. Not until the summer of 1946 was codebreaker MEREDITH GARDNER able to read portions of messages that had been sent between Soviet intelligence officers in New York and their superiors in Moscow. In Dec. 1946, he broke into another message sent to Moscow two years earlier. It contained a list of the leading scientists working on the U.S. atomic bomb. The Venona transcripts also revealed the extent to which the American Communist Party (see CPUSA) served as a source of agents for Soviet espionage activity in the United States. To keep the Soviets unaware of the code-breaking, the secrets of Venona were not released until 1995; some 3,000 messages have been released.

THE COLD WAR BEGINS

On Aug. 29, 1945, near Hamhung, Korea, Soviet fighters fired on and forced down an American B-29 SUPER-FORTRESS that was dropping supplies to Allied prisoners of war. World War II had been over for 15 days. Unknown to the crew of the B-29, the Cold War was beginning.

An "Iron Curtain," in Winston Churchill's memorable phrase, slammed down on Eastern Europe. To pierce that curtain, or at least peer behind it, the United States began to develop a massive intelligence apparatus. Donovan had seen the need and had urged President Truman to create, around the core of the OSS, a peacetime intelligence agency separate from the military services. Truman resisted the idea. When he abolished the OSS on Oct. 1, 1945, he gave the OSS Research and Analysis Branch to the State Department; OSS clandestine and counterintelligence resources became the Strategic Services Unit (SSU) in the War Department.

Bureaucratic infighting over intelligence management continued among the military services, the State Department, and the FBI. In Jan. 1946 Truman created

the CENTRAL INTELLIGENCE GROUP and made SIDNEY W. SOUERS, a fellow Missourian and Navy rear admiral, the first Director of Central Intelligence. There was not much to direct, but Souers's small staff produced a daily intelligence summary that Truman liked. It was a predecessor to the PRESIDENTIAL DAILY BRIEF, one of the CIA's foremost PRODUCTS.

A crisis in Turkey, a coup in Czechoslovakia, a civil war in Greece—all triggered by the Soviet Union—challenged the "Truman Doctrine," which pledged that the United States would support "free peoples who are resisting attempted subjugation." To fight the Cold War, on July 26, 1947, Truman signed the National Security Act, which established the NATIONAL SECURITY COUNCIL (NSC), the U.S. Air Force (which formerly had been part of the Army), and the Central Intelligence Agency.

Within a year covert action emerged as an instrument of U.S. policy. The NSC circulated among Truman's principal advisers a TOP SECRET directive authorizing "propaganda, economic warfare . . . sabotage . . . subversion against hostile states, including assistance to underground resistance movements. . . ." The covert action would be run by the OFFICE OF POLICY COORDINATION (OPC), administratively within the CIA but under State Department and Pentagon supervision. FRANK G. WISNER, an OSS veteran, began running covert operations from Albania to Korea, which, meanwhile, had become the battlefield of a real war.

The CIA failure to predict North Korea's invasion of South Korea in June 1950 led to a reorganization that included the production of NATIONAL INTELLIGENCE ESTIMATES (NIEs), which henceforth provided Truman and succeeding presidents with factual analyses. The NIEs came from the Directorate of Intelligence; the covert action came from the Directorate for Plans (later Operations) which absorbed the OPC.

Covert action threatened the traditional checks-and-balances mechanism between the executive and legislative branches of government. (Eventually, the third branch, the judicial, was also affected; see FOREIGN INTELLIGENCE SURVEILLANCE COURT.) The CIA offered the executive branch—primarily, the White House and the NSC—opportunities to act in such secrecy that Congress would not be able to fulfill its role of watchdog over the executive. Illegal wiretaps had been flourishing. The FBI, searching for spies and subversives, had tapped several thousand phones and installed more than 2,000 BUGS.

In the crusade against domestic communists—fueled by the Reds-in-government charges of Sen. Joseph McCarthy (Republican of Wisconsin)—civil liberties were often abused. The rationale of a "clear and present danger" reappeared. In 1948, the Department of Justice moved against the U.S. Communist Party under the Smith Act, which prohibited advocating the violent overthrow of the government. "There are today many communists in America," said Attorney General J. Howard McGrath in April 1949. "They are everywhere—in factories, offices, butcher stores, on street corners, in private businesses. And each carries in himself the germ of death for society."

The FBI arrested 145 Communist Party leaders. Many of the 109 convictions came from trials at which FBI informants, planted in the party, appeared as star government witnesses. The most successful FBI penetration of the party involved informers who met consistently with Soviet leaders in Moscow. (See SOLO.)

A Congressman introduced a bill to require the Librarian of Congress to list all the books in the library that might be regarded as subversive. Congressional hearings under the glare of television lights sought communists in universities, churches, and labor unions.

Actor Ronald Reagan—the FBI gave him the CODE NAME "T-10"—testified about communism in Hollywood. His appearance, which made him an anti-communist lecturer, put him on the road that led to the White House.

Entertainers who refused to answer questions, citing their rights under the Fifth Amendment to the Constitution, were condemned as "Fifth Amendment communists" and blacklisted from television and radio. Congressman Richard M. Nixon gained publicity for his pursuit of ALGER HISS, a former State Department official accused of espionage by WHITTAKER CHAMBERS.

Overseas, there seemed to be no bounds to what the lavishly funded CIA could do. (The agency's budgeted funds are hidden in the general accounts of other agencies and departments. Congress has also exempted the CIA from laws requiring disclosure of "functions, names, official titles, salaries or numbers of personnel.") CIA covert operators managed coups in Egypt (1952), Iran (1953), and Guatemala (1954). Through dummy foundations, the CIA secretly provided funds to a host of organizations, including the intellectual magazine *Encounter,* edited by the British poet Stephen Spender; the National Student Association, and the American Newspaper Guild, among others. To display the creativity and intellectual freedom of American artists, the CIA generously and secretly subsidized exhibitions of avantgarde artists Jackson Pollock, Robert Motherwell, Willem de Kooning, and Mark Rothko. The American public contributed to fund-raising campaigns for RADIO FREE EUROPE, which purported to be privately operated but was actually run by the CIA.

NSA, operating in deep secrecy, eavesdropped around the world. A DOMESTIC INTELLIGENCE program codenamed SHAMROCK monitored the overseas calls and cables of American citizens, U.S. organizations, and foreign nationals. CIA scientists, in a secret program codenamed MKULTRA, experimented with brainwashing and tested LSD and other hallucinogenic drugs on unwitting subjects.

Seeking intelligence about Soviet technology and military developments, first Truman and then Eisenhower authorized limited OVERFLIGHTS of the Soviet Union by American planes (some flown by British crews). The CIA, in a secret Lockheed facility called the SKUNK WORKS, developed the U-2 high-altitude spyplane. Soon afterward, work began on the U-2's successor, the SR-71 BLACKBIRD, which flew at three times the speed of sound (Mach 3), faster than any plane flying within the atmosphere. And realizing that counters to manned spy-

planes were inevitable, during the Eisenhower administration spy SATELLITES were also developed. Eisenhower felt that only with detailed OVERHEAD intelligence of the Soviet Union would the United States be safe from a "nuclear Pearl Harbor."

President Eisenhower accepted another clandestine plan: a CIA proposal to overthrow Cuban leader Fidel Castro by staging a commando-like raid with CIA-trained guerrillas drawn from the Cuban émigré community in Florida. By the time Eisenhower's successor, John F. Kennedy, took office, the CIA force had grown to some 1,400 men. The Bay of Pigs invasion, on April 17, 1961, was a disaster. (See CUBA.) Obsessed by Castro, Kennedy ordered MONGOOSE, a mammoth CIA operation aimed at bringing down the Cuban leader by sabotage—or, with Mafia help, by assassination.

The second year of the Kennedy administration brought the United States and Soviet Union close to a nuclear confrontation in the CUBAN MISSILE CRISIS. U.S. intelligence—high-flying U-2s and low-flying F8U CRUSADER and F-101 VOODOO photo planes—achieved great success in spying out the Soviet attempt to secretly emplace in Cuba missiles that could strike the United States. But U.S. intelligence failed to detect that nuclear warheads for the missiles were already in Cuba, or the extent of the Soviet buildup.

CONGRESS STEPS IN

From their founding, the CIA and NSA were exempt from the kind of public scrutiny given the Defense and State Departments. The entire INTELLIGENCE COMMUNITY—encompassing the DEFENSE INTELLIGENCE AGENCY, the NATIONAL RECONNAISSANCE OFFICE (NRO), the FBI, and other agencies—was immune from all but wink-and-a-nod oversight by Congress. One exception was the EASTLAND DOCUMENT, an assessment of damage to U.S. nuclear activities caused by Soviet spy DONALD MACLEAN, demanded by Sen. James Eastland, chairman of the Senate Internal Security Subcommittee.

However, disillusionment with the conduct of the Vietnam War (see PENTAGON PAPERS, VIETNAM) and the revelations of the WATERGATE scandal eventually turned the congressional spotlight on covert action. In 1974 the Hughes-Ryan Act, an amendment to the Foreign Assistance Act, called upon the President to report any covert actions to relevant congressional committees in a timely fashion. In 1976 President Ford endorsed the idea of a congressional oversight committee; he also, rather casually, issued a directive that outlawed assassination as an instrument of American policy.

More scrutiny came from the CHURCH COMMITTEE and the PIKE COMMITTEE, which aired the abuses of the CIA, the dark secrets known as the FAMILY JEWELS. Out of these hearings came the Senate Select Committee on Intelligence and the House Permanent Select Committee on Intelligence. The Intelligence Authorization Act of 1981 set up a special procedure for reporting covert actions: the CIA must notify the chairman and vice chairman of cognizant committees, along with the majority leaders of the Senate and House. The method of notification was called a "finding," later designated as a "presidential finding," which was to describe the action within a reasonable period of time after it had begun. Questions about what was "reasonable" often provoked controversy.

This procedure was violated by WILLIAM J. CASEY, DCI under President Reagan, who failed to notify the committees properly when covert operators mined harbors in Nicaragua in an attempt to support the Contras, insurgents trying to bring down the elected left-wing government of Nicaragua. Sen. Barry Goldwater (Republican of Arizona) wrote to Casey: "I've been trying to figure out how I can most easily tell you my feelings about the discovery of the President having approved mining some of the harbors of Central America. It gets down to one, little, simple phrase: I am pissed off!"

Congressional displeasure, so eloquently stated by Goldwater, led to further restrictions on the Reagan administration's use of CIA covert operations in Nicaragua. And these led to the IRAN-CONTRA AFFAIR.

The stock of U.S. intelligence had never been lower than it was in the 1980s. Besides Iran-Contra, there was the YEAR OF THE SPY, 1985, during which three major spy cases were uncovered, raising issues about the whole state of U.S. counterintelligence. By the end of the year 10 Americans were under arrest for espionage and an 11th was in Moscow, having eluded FBI surveillance. "Some of you may be wondering if the large number of spy arrests in recent weeks mean that we're looking harder or whether there are more spies to find," President Reagan said in Dec. 1985. "Well, I think the answer to both questions is yes."

Indeed, the large number of Soviet spies uncovered throughout the 1980s—in addition to JONATHAN POLLARD who sold secret documents to Israel—makes the title DECADE OF THE spy an apt description.

HUNTING FOR MISSIONS

The development of spy satellites, begun in the Eisenhower administration, made overhead verification of disarmament agreements possible. As each new disarmament talk seemed to lead to another, the Cold War began fading. First President Reagan and then former spymaster President Bush discovered they could do business with Soviet leader Mikhail Gorbachev. His withdrawal of troops from Afghanistan eased tensions (and ended a CIA arms-smuggling operation to the mujahedin rebels fighting the Soviets). By Oct. 1990, when the last sections of the Berlin Wall fell and the collapse of the Soviet Union loomed, the Cold War was over.

There would still be spies. The arrest in Feb. 1994 of CIA counterintelligence officer ALDRICH H. AMES showed that the spy war still went on. Ames, whose treachery cost the lives of at least ten U.S. agents, was a transitional traitor, who started spying for the Soviet Union and was spying for Russia when the FBI ended his career. The CIA discovered belatedly that he needed to earn much more than his government salary to buy a $40,000 red Jaguar

XJ6 and a $540,000 house. (In 1996 Congress passed legislation providing U.S. citizenship to the widows and children of Russian agents executed after Ames betrayed them.)

The Cold War had given U.S. (and Soviet) intelligence agencies a clear-cut purpose. The end of the Cold War meant the end of this purpose. The search for a new mission began. TERRORIST INTELLIGENCE, drug trafficking, INDUSTRIAL ESPIONAGE—they all appeared on the agenda. The CIA also ran a few traditional intelligence operations in support of U.S. and United Nations peacekeepers in Somalia, Haiti, and Bosnia.

The Senate Select Committee on Intelligence felt, however, that something more fundamental than a shift to new missions was necessary. The agency's handling of the Ames case "suggests the need for a fundamental change in the culture of the CIA," the committee said, and JOHN DEUTCH was appointed DCI to do the changing. He won a fiscal vote of confidence from Congress, which in 1996 increased intelligence spending by 6.3 percent, putting the intelligence budget in the neighborhood of $30 billion.

He talked of reorganization and a tightening of control over the entire intelligence community. But hanging over his plans was a question asked publicly by THOMAS POLAR, a retired CIA officer who had been station chief in Saigon at the end of the Vietnam War. "What," he asked, "is the clandestine service supposed to be doing these days?"

WAR ON TERROR

No one seemed to have a simple answer to that simple question. Then came the Sept. 11, 2001, attacks on the World Trade Center in New York and the Pentagon. President George W. Bush declared a war on global terrorism and that became the first—and nearly the only—mission for the U.S. intelligence community.

In the tumult that followed Sept 11, the intelligence community faced two challenges: how to explain accusations of an "intelligence failure" and how to focus on developing intelligence from a shadowy enemy operating out of many countries in many ways. Criticism of intelligence agencies faded from public view, although the search for blame continued inside the system.

The nominal enemy was al Qaeda, led by a fanatic leader named Osama bin Laden. NSA and the CIA mobilized all their resources to find bin Laden and crush al Qaeda. Small CIA paramilitary units, teamed up with SPECIAL OPERATIONS FORCES, entered Afghanistan to overthrow the Taliban regime, smash al Qaeda, and capture bin Laden. Britain also contributed special forces. Joining with anti-Taliban fighters, the coalition did succeed in bringing down the Taliban and gravely hurt al Qaeda. But bin Laden eluded his hunters and al Qaeda did not die. (See SPECIAL ACTIVITIES DIVISION.)

Back in Washington, the Bush administration and Congress responded to the Sept. 11 attacks by creating new government entities: HOMELAND SECURITY quickly evolved from White House office to cabinet department.

The USA PATRIOT ACT gave sweeping new powers to civilian intelligence in the war on terror, blurring the line between domestic and foreign intelligence operations.

When the focus shifted in 2003 from al Qaeda to Iraq, so did controversy about U.S. intelligence agencies, particularly the CIA. While supplying intelligence to the National Security Council and U.S. forces invading Iraq, critics attacked CIA analysts both for supplying intelligence that hewed to Bush administration policy and for tweaking intelligence so that it did *not* hew to policy.

Meanwhile, the Department of Defense was undergoing major reductions in numbers of personnel, and had several reorganizations, including the establishment of the NATIONAL MILITARY IMAGERY AGENCY and, in April 2003, the position of UNDER SECRETARY OF DEFENSE (INTELLIGENCE) (USD[I]). The latter is the most senior intelligence position ever provided within the Department of Defense, and has control over all defense intelligence activities, including the DEFENSE INTELLIGENCE AGENCY, NRO, and NSA. The USD(I) is also the department's principal liaison to the CIA. Further, in 2003, Secretary of Defense Donald H. Rumsfeld stated that future decisions in the Department related to intelligence would be based on four key issues:

> *Persistence:* The ability for long "dwell times," in all weather, all of the time (referred to as "24/7" in public relations).
> *Defeating enemy countermeasures:* Discerning the enemy's most critical information despite enemy efforts to protect that information.
> *Exquisiteness:* Discerning an enemy's most critical information, for instance, weapons of mass destruction, vulnerabilities in the capabilities that the enemy needs to survive.
> *Horizontal integration:* The need to break down the traditional "stovepipe" approaches and sharing information across the Intelligence Community, including non–Department of Defense agencies.

Rumsfeld created a special Pentagon intelligence unit. It had no name, at least publicly, and did not initiate intelligence. The reason for its existence was never openly revealed. Some CIA analysts said that its role was to sift through scraps of intelligence that supported Rumsfeld's theses (such as suspected links between Iraq and al Qaeda). "The analysts have gone to ground," said a retired CIA officer called up to work on Iraqi issues. After the war, DCI George J. Tenet ordered a review by retired CIA officers to see whether prewar intelligence assessments were confirmed by information discovered when U.S. forces took over Iraq.

Elsewhere, from the Golden Gate Bridge to the Brooklyn Bridge, Americans lived under color-coded warnings of possible terrorist biological, chemical, or nuclear attacks: green for a low risk of attack, blue for guarded, yellow for elevated, orange for high, and red for severe. The warnings were made and changed on the basis of intelligence that was disseminated on a NEED TO KNOW basis to national officials, state governors, and mayors, other local officials, and first responders. Ordinary citizens were advised to set aside a "safe room" and keep a stock of emergency items and enough food and water for three days.

One phrase of Homeland Security instructions conjured up intelligence analysts' nightmare: "While there is no way to predict what will happen. . . ."

United States Country Team

The concept that in a country represented by a U.S. ambassador, he or she is in charge. The CIA station chief, while reporting to the DIRECTOR OF CENTRAL INTELLIGENCE, is also supposedly under the ambassador. The only exceptions to the ambassador's authority are members of the military who are in the country and under the command of a U.S. area military commander.

President Kennedy issued a letter outlining the authority of the ambassadors in his administration, and this practice has continued. In these letters, however, there is inevitably an exemption for the CIA. The letter that President Clinton wrote, for example, stated, "You have the right to see all communications to or from mission elements, however transmitted, except those specifically exempted by law or executive decision." That final phrase is seen as a loophole for the CIA.

United States Intelligence Board

(USIB)

Successor to the BOARD OF NATIONAL ESTIMATES (BNE) as the overseer of NATIONAL INTELLIGENCE ESTIMATES within the CIA.

In 1973 WILLIAM E. COLBY, the DIRECTOR OF CENTRAL INTELLIGENCE, abolished the OFFICE OF NATIONAL ESTIMATES and the BNE, replacing that system with National Intelligence Officers (NIOs) who were responsible for specific regions or topics. The United States Intelligence Board was replaced three years later by the NATIONAL FOREIGN INTELLIGENCE BOARD.

The NIOs reported to the DCI through a deputy for national intelligence who was also the director of the National Foreign Assessment Center. Beginning in 1979 the NIOs were known collectively as the NATIONAL INTELLIGENCE COUNCIL.

Unmanned Aerial Vehicles

(UAV)

Unmanned aircraft used for RECONNAISSANCE and limited ground-attack operations.

Although unmanned aerial vehicles—originally called "drones" and then Remotely Piloted Vehicles (RPVs)—have been around since World War I, only in the 1960s, during the Vietnam War, were they used extensively as intelligence collection platforms. Their popular name in the Vietnam War was BUFFALO HUNTER. Since the 1980s these aircraft have been known in the U.S. military as Unmanned Aerial Vehicles (UAV).

Israel made the first significant post-Vietnam use of drones for intelligence in the 1980s, against the Syrians in Lebanon and the Bakka Valley. In 1982, when Israel forced Yasir Arafat and his Palestine Liberation Organization out of Beirut, an Israeli Mastiff UAV overflew a U.S. amphibious ship in the harbor and was undetected. The drone sent television pictures through a downlink to its control station in southern Lebanon. A year later a camera-carrying Mastiff spotted an unsuspecting U.S. Secretary of Defense Caspar Weinberger visiting Beirut. Again the UAV was not detected by U.S. forces. The television films from those incidents helped to inspire subsequent development of the U.S.-Israeli UAV called the Pioneer, the first widely used U.S. reconnaissance drone that was first procured by the U.S. Navy in 1985. The UAV carried a television camera as its primary sensor, relaying the real-time picture back to the operator aboard ship or on the ground.

(The U.S. Navy had, in the 1960s, operated several hundred ship-based drones called DASH—for Drone Anti-Submarine Helicopter. That aircraft was based on warships and, after a submarine was detected by shipboard sonar, the DASH would be dispatched to deliver a torpedo or nuclear depth charge on the target. The DASH, with a radius of about 50 miles from the launching ship, was also used by the battleship *New Jersey* for gunfire spotting during the ship's 1968 deployment to Vietnam.)

The Soviet Union, Britain, France, and Germany as well as other nations have also developed reconnaissance drones, but Israel and the United States are the leading manufacturers and users of those aircraft.

The United States used reconnaissance UAVs extensively in the Persian Gulf War of 1991. At the start of air operations in the 1991 conflict the U.S. Air Force and Navy launched target drones into Iraq to trick the Iraqis into turning on their radars so they could be attacked by U.S. radar-suppression aircraft. This technique was first used by the Israelis against Syrian air defenses.

In the 1991 conflict the Pioneers were flown by the U.S. Navy from battleships and by U.S. Army and Marine Corps from shore launchers. Some 40 Pioneers flew 552 sorties for a total mission duration time of 1,641 hours.

At least one Pioneer was airborne at all times during Operation Desert Storm, which was fought in Jan.–Feb. 1991. The drones were employed to adjust naval gunfire, assess battle damage, and conduct reconnaissance.

On Feb. 27, 1991, a Pioneer detected two Iraqi patrol boats off Faylaka Island and naval aircraft were called in to destroy the craft. Seeing the UAV and believing that they were about to be attacked, Iraqi soldiers on the island surrendered to the Pioneer! It was history's first known surrender of enemy troops to an unmanned vehicle.

Another Gulf War drone was the Pointer, a small, hand-launched UAV that resembles a model aircraft. The Pointer is carried in two backpacks, one for the 45-pound vehicle and the other for the 50-pound control unit. Several Pointers were deployed to Saudi Arabia with the U.S. Marines in 1991. The Pointer's sensor payload is a black-and-white television camera using an 8mm videocassette. It can be modified to carry a chemical agent detector. Flight endurance is more than one hour. For recovery the Pointer is directed into a deep stall.

The improved PREDATOR UAV was used in Bosnia beginning in 1994, to provide reconnaissance and SURVEILLANCE for peacekeeping forces, and in Afghanistan in 2001 and in the Iraqi War of 2003. In the latter conflicts, and in Yemen in 2003, the Predator UAV was operated by the CIA as well as the U.S. Air Force, and in Afghanistan and Yemen in 2003 Predators, believed to be operated by the CIA, fired missiles against ground targets. Another important U.S. UAV flown in that period was the GLOBAL HAWK, a very-long-range reconnaissance aircraft.

Following the terrorist attacks on the United States on Sept. 11, 2001, various government agencies have given consideration to using long-endurance UAVs, such as the Global Hawk, for domestic surveillance operations. Also, the military services are looking at a variety of combat UAVs—called UCAVs—for air-to-air and air-to-ground combat.

UAVs offer several advantages over manned aircraft. Obviously a pilot's life in not at risk, UAVs can under some circumstances be flown on one-way missions if the range or payload requirement cannot be matched by manned aircraft, and by most criteria UAVs are generally cheaper than equivalent manned aircraft.

Unmanned aerial vehicles are bringing a new dimension to warfare, including intelligence collection. The General Atomics Predator, developed by the Central Intelligence Agency, has been used by the CIA, U.S. Air Force, and U.S. Navy for reconnaissance and by the CIA for attacks against ground targets. It has retractable wheels and a small propeller fitted at the rear. (U.S. NAVY)

Unshlikht, Iosif Stanislavovich

(b. 1879 d. 1938)

Acting chief of the GRU, Soviet MILITARY INTELLIGENCE, in 1935 and possibly 1937 while YAN K. BERZIN was in the Far East carrying out a purge of NKVD officials and then in Spain supporting the Republican government in the Spanish Civil War and recruiting GRU AGENTS.

Born a Polish nobleman, Unshlikht was active in left-wing Polish politics and a leader of the October 1917 revolution in Russia. Immediately after the revolution he helped form the secret police, which soon became the CHEKA, founded by fellow Pole FELIKS DZERZHINSKY.

The largest and longest-range UAV now flying is the Northrop Grumman (Teledyne Ryan) Global Hawk. It has a wingspan of 116¼ feet and a length of 44 feet. The Global Hawk—possibly an eventual successor to the U-2—is fitted with several sensors. It has intercontinental range. (NORTHROP GRUMMAN)

In 1920 Unshlikht was a member of the short-lived Polish revolutionary government. From 1921 to 1923 he was a deputy chairman of the GPU, after which he became a deputy chief of the GRU. He traveled abroad regularly to organize agent activities in Germany, Lithuania, and Poland. In 1935, while Berzin was out of Moscow, Unshlikht acted as chief of the GRU. Subsequently, he was assigned as director of the main administration of the Red Air Force and was a candidate member of the Central Committee of the USSR.

He was arrested in the Stalinist purges and on July 29, 1939, he was shot—along with Berzin.

Unwitting Agent

An AGENT who furnishes information without knowing that the ultimate recipient is an intelligence service or without being aware of the true identity of the government involved. When arrested for espionage, JERRY WHITWORTH unsuccessfully claimed to be unwitting. He said he believed that JOHN WALKER was recruiting him to provide information for the reference book *Jane's Fighting Ships*.

Uritski, Corps Comdr. Solomon Petrovich

(b. 1895 d. 1937)

Chief of the GRU, Soviet MILITARY INTELLIGENCE, from April 1935 to June 1937.

Uritski was active in the October revolution and ensuing civil war and was a leader in the attacks against sailors in the Kronshtadt rebellion of 1921. Little is known of his subsequent career until he became head of the GRU. He was arrested and shot in 1937 during the Stalinist purges.

USA Patriot Act

Sweeping national-security law passed in the wake of the Sept. 11, 2001, attacks on the World Trade Center and the Pentagon. The name of the act is an acronym for "Uniting and Strengthening America by Providing Appropriate Tools Required to Intercept and Obstruct Terrorism."

The act broadly expands law enforcement's SURVEILLANCE and DOMESTIC INTELLIGENCE powers. The 342-page bill, signed into law by President George W. Bush on Oct. 26, 2001, amended 15 different federal statutes covering disparate issues that include surveillance of INTERNET use, money laundering, immigration, and ways to provide for the victims of terrorism.

The new law also extended the power of the FEDERAL INTELLIGENCE SURVEILLANCE COURT (FISC) to authorize clandestine SURVEILLANCE of suspects in terrorist cases. The number of judges of the FISC was increased from seven to eleven.

The law also allows the sharing of the information collected with "any Federal law enforcement, intelligence, protective, immigration, national defense, or national security official in order to assist the official receiving that information in the performance of his official duties."

Librarians interpreted new powers in the USA Patriot Act as a threat to long-standing privacy laws as the guidelines issued by the Department of Justice allowed the FBI to monitor library users and the books they read. The law was written so that it would expire in 2005 unless renewed by Congress.

USIB

SEE UNITED STATES INTELLIGENCE BOARD

V

Vanaman, Brig. Gen. Arthur W

(b. 1892 d. 1987)

U.S. Army Air Forces (AAF) officer with ACCESS to ULTRA intelligence who flew on a bomber mission over Europe and was shot down over Germany. So far as is known, he was the only U.S. officer with knowledge of Ultra who was captured by the Germans.

Vanaman enlisted as an Army pilot in 1917 and was commissioned in 1920. He held mostly air engineering assignments and, from July 1937 to June 1941, was assistant U.S. air ATTACHÉ in BERLIN. Vanaman then held senior positions in AAF matériel agencies and was promoted to brigadier general in March 1942. In May 1944 he was ordered to join the Eighth Air Force in England as assistant chief of staff for intelligence. On a mission over Germany on June 27, 1944, his plane was shot down, and he became a prisoner of war. However, the Germans did not grill him, and he was able to maintain the secrecy of Ultra.

On April 23, 1945, Vanaman was released by WALTER SCHELLENBERG to advise American officials that Allied prisoners of war needed supplies and that some German leaders wished a negotiated peace with the Western allies.

After the war he reverted to his permanent rank of colonel, but he was promoted to major general in 1948.

(A British officer with access to Ultra, Air Commo. Ronald Ivelaw-Chapman, was shot down over German-occupied France in May 1944; he bailed out of the crippled Lancaster bomber before it crashed and was initially rescued by the French Resistance but later captured by the GESTAPO. He, too, was able to keep Ultra a secret from his captors. A large number of Polish codebreakers with knowledge of the Allies' early success in breaking into ENIGMA codes were captured by the Germans in late 1939, but none is known to have revealed any secrets.)

Van Deman, Maj. Gen. Ralph H.

(b. 1865 d. 1952)

U.S. Army INTELLIGENCE OFFICER who is considered the father of modern American MILITARY INTELLIGENCE.

An 1889 graduate of Harvard University, he read law for one year and then began medical school. He was commissioned in the Army in 1891 and was able to finish medical school in 1893. However, he remained an infantry officer and attended the Infantry and Cavalry School at Ft. Leavenworth, Kan.

In 1898, Van Deman was assigned to the Army's Military Information Division, and served in Cuba for a year. He then served in the Military Information Section of the Philippines Department in 1901–1903, collecting intelligence against both the natives and the Japanese. While in the Philippines he discovered and stopped a plot to assassinate Gen. Arthur MacArthur (father of World War II's Gen. Douglas MacArthur).

Van Deman returned to Washington, D.C., to attend the Army War College. He was then sent to China in 1906 to conduct a secret RECONNAISSANCE in conjunction with Japanese interests there. Back in Washington in 1915, now a major, Van Deman was assigned to the War College Division, not to intelligence duties. No one was assigned to intelligence work at the time, so he read and filed military information reports from the U.S. Mexican campaign and from the European war. He began a system of summarizing the incoming information for distribution to interested staff sections.

After America's entry into World War I in April

1917, Van Deman was unable to persuade the Army Chief of Staff, Gen. Hugh Scott, that the Army should have an intelligence organization. Scott believed that the U.S. Army could just say to French and British intelligence, "Here we are now ready for service—we would be pleased if you hand over to us all the necessary information concerning the enemy which your intelligence services have obtained."

Within 48 hours of seeing the Secretary of War, Van Deman was made head of the new Military Intelligence (MI) Branch of the War College Division. It was called intelligence instead of information because the British were already using that term and the U.S. Army would be working with them.

Van Deman asked for and was given the authority to grant direct commissions to his subordinate officers. He asked major city police departments for some of their best people to work for him. By the end of the war, MI consisted of 282 officers and 1,100 civilians and controlled COUNTERINTELLIGENCE offices throughout the United States. In 1917 Van Deman commissioned HERBERT O. YARDLEY, a State Department CODE clerk and amateur cryptologist. Yardley was given the job of organizing MI8, the Cipher Bureau. The Cipher Bureau, which would have great success.

Van Deman retired from the Army in 1929.

During World War II he organized volunteers in the United States to help provide intelligence to the military services and FBI. After the war he spoke frequently about the menace of communism to the United States.

Vandenberg, Gen. Hoyt S.

(b. 1899 d. 1954)

The second DIRECTOR OF CENTRAL INTELLIGENCE (DCI), from June 1946 to April 1947, and subsequently the second Chief of Staff of the U.S. Air Force.

A 1923 graduate of the Military Academy and a fighter pilot, Vandenberg was Assistant Chief of Staff of the U.S. Army Air Forces when World War II began. He remained in staff work throughout the war, serving in North Africa in 1942–1943, and was deputy chief of the Air Staff from 1943 to 1946. In the latter position he also went to Moscow as the senior air member of the U.S. Military Mission to Moscow. In 1946 he became the ASSISTANT CHIEF OF STAFF (INTELLIGENCE), the G-2 on the Army's General Staff.

Vandenberg was hoping to command the independent U.S. Air Force that was expected to be created by President Truman. Instead the President appointed him DCI. The appointment was a shrewd choice for Truman, who needed political support for the creation of the Department of Defense, the Air Force, and the CIA. Vandenberg was a nephew of Sen. Arthur Vandenberg, a powerful Republican and president pro tem of the Senate.

As DCI, Vandenberg directed the CENTRAL INTELLIGENCE GROUP (CIG), a precursor to the CIA, which would be established in July 1947. Under Vandenberg the CIG gained some independence and was given authority to collect and analyze intelligence. Previously the CIG could only collect intelligence and was producing a daily and weekly summary of intelligence and operational cables for Truman. Vandenberg told the White House that the nation needed an independent central intelligence agency.

Vandenberg created the Office of Research and Evaluation, which was soon renamed the Office of Reports and Estimates at the insistence of the State Department, which did not want the office confused with its own BUREAU OF INTELLIGENCE AND RESEARCH. Vandenberg also acquired the remnants of the abolished OFFICE OF STRATEGIC SERVICES. This gave the CIG the right to collect clandestine foreign intelligence. To fulfill this new charter, Vandenberg asked for and got the right for the CIG to work in Latin America, which during World War II had been the exclusive domain of the FBI with respect to intelligence activities.

After the creation of the U.S. Air Force in Oct. 1947, Vandenberg was appointed Vice Chief of Staff of the new service with the rank of full general. He subsequently served as the second Chief of Staff of the Air Force, from May 1948 through June 1953.

Vanunu, Mordechai

(b. 1954)

Nuclear technician who revealed Israeli nuclear bomb secrets and was enticed—by SEX or the promise of sex—into returning to Israel, where he was arrested for espionage and treason.

Vanunu was the son of an Orthodox Jewish family that immigrated to Israel from Morocco. Although an outspoken leftist student at Ben-Gurion University in the Negev, he was hired as a technician at the highly classified nuclear research-production facility at Dimona in the Negev Desert. He worked at Dimona for nine years but was laid off in 1985. A short time later he left Israel, going first to Australia and then to England. He took with him a suitcase filled with TOP SECRET data. His attorney later claimed that Vanunu's goal was not to harm Israel but to warn Israelis of the nuclear threat. In London, Vanunu told The Sunday Times that Israel had stockpiled almost 200 nuclear weapons since the 1960s, far more than most experts had estimated.

In Sept. 1986, a few days before the Times story was to appear, Vanunu disappeared. He had been lured to Rome by a blonde woman he believed to be an American called Cindy. She was an AGENT of the MOSSAD. In Rome, reportedly, Vanunu was drugged, taken aboard a yacht, and returned to Israel in chains.

His seven-month trial on two counts of espionage and one count of treason was held in secret; the only words made public came from the court's 60-page verdict on March 25, 1988: "We decided the defendant is guilty on all three counts." The three-judge panel sentenced him to 18 years in prison—calculated from Oct. 7, 1986, the day he was brought back to Israel.

The prosecution had asked for a life sentence. The court could have imposed the death penalty, but no Israeli has been sentenced to death by a court. Anti-nuclear groups centered in Great Britain have made him a martyr to their cause and the object of a campaign aimed at getting him freed. He was released in April 2004.

Vascio, Staff Sgt. Giuseppe

U.S. Air Force photographic laboratory technician who was arrested in 1952 after trying to sell flight-test data on the new F-86E Sabre aircraft to North Korea. Vascio was then stationed in South Korea. A World War II hero, Vascio had twice earned the Distinguished Flying Cross. He was convicted of conspiracy to pass secrets to the enemy and sentenced to 20 years at hard labor and a dishonorable discharge.

Vassall, William John

(b. 1924 d. 1996)

British Admiralty clerk who spied for the Soviet Union. He was arrested on Sept. 12, 1962, confessed, was tried, and on Oct. 22, 1962, was sentenced to 18 years in prison. Vassall served 10 years of his sentence.

Investigation into Vassall's espionage began when ANATOLI GOLITSIN, a Soviet DEFECTOR, told his interrogators that a HOMOSEXUAL working in the Admiralty was a Soviet spy. MI5 operatives tracked down Vassall.

A clergyman's son, Vassall had a varied government career. He had been an assistant private secretary to the civilian Lord of the Admiralty and had served in the British Embassy in Moscow as a clerk to the naval ATTACHÉ. In Dec. 1956 he had been cleared "for access to classified atomic energy information and for regular and constant access to Top Secret defence information." Vassall reportedly had been blackmailed into spying when his homosexual proclivities were noted by Soviet INTELLIGENCE OFFICERS when he was stationed in Moscow.

During the war he had been a photographer in the Royal Air Force, and he put his photographic skills to work copying documents. A search of his rooms produced an Exakta camera and hidden rolls of film.

The slack security investigation of Vassall led to the creation of the Vassall Tribunal, which found that Vassall's free-spending habits should have aroused suspicions about him. The tribunal also said that Vassall's open homosexuality, which made him a prey to blackmail, also should have subjected him to closer scrutiny by security officers.

His HANDLER referred to him as "Vera."

Vasilyev, Col. Vladimir Mikhailovich

(b. ? d. 1986)

GRU officer who spied for the United States and was betrayed.

The CIA recruited Vasilyev in Budapest in either the late 1970s or early 1980s. He supplied his HANDLERS with reports on weapons and military plans until the KGB arrested and executed him in 1986. He provided information that led to the arrest of CLYDE LEE CONRAD, an American soldier who stole and sold NORTH ATLANTIC TREATY ORGANIZATION defense plans.

After Vasilyev's arrest and execution, the KGB revealed that the CIA had communicated with him through MICRODOT messages concealed in *National Geographic* magazine. (See NATIONAL GEOGRAPHIC SOCIETY.)

At first U.S. COUNTERINTELLIGENCE officials thought he had been betrayed by EDWARD LEE HOWARD, a CIA officer who had defected to the Soviet Union in 1985. But with the arrest of CIA officer ALDRICH AMES in 1994, officials speculated that, in order to protect Ames, the KGB had passed out DISINFORMATION linking Howard to Vasilyev.

His CIA CODE NAME was "Accord."

Vaupshasov, Col. S. A.

(b. 1899 d. 1976)

Soviet INTELLIGENCE OFFICER who in 1920–1924 was engaged in underground work in Belorussia, which was occupied by anti-Soviet Poles. After several intelligence assignments, in 1937–1939 he went to Spain, where he carried out intelligence operations behind the lines of the Nationalist forces during the Spanish Civil War.

During World War II he headed a major guerrilla unit that operated behind German lines in the Minsk region. After the war he continued in intelligence activities.

Vaupshasov was awarded the Hero of the Soviet Union and was honored by a Soviet POSTAGE STAMP issued in 1990.

Veil

Supposed CODE NAME for a DISINFORMATION program that the CIA is said to have planned against Muammar al Qaddafi, dictator of Libya. *Washington Post* reporter BOB WOODWARD said that he had seen memos about Veil and another similar plan, code-named Vector, and wrote a *Post* article about a "secret U.S. deception plan" in Oct. 1986.

President Reagan and his DIRECTOR OF CENTRAL INTELLIGENCE, WILLIAM J. CASEY, denied the existence of the program. Woodward used *Veil* as the title of his 1987 book on Casey and the CIA.

Vela

U.S. SATELLITE developed to detect nuclear explosions.

Three types of Vela satellites were deployed: Vela Hotel satellites, orbited in pairs to detect explosions on earth; Vela Sierra, to spot atmospheric and space detonations; and Vela Uniform, to pick up vibrations from underground and underwater explosions. The Vela Hotel satellites were "parked" some 60,000 miles above the earth—roughly one-fourth the distance to the moon.

The first U.S. detections of nuclear weapons from space were made by the *Explorer 4* satellite, which detected five U.S. high-altitude nuclear tests in 1958. The *Explorer 4*, launched on July 26, 1958, was a radiation research satellite. Additional tests of monitoring equipment were carried out with Discoverer series satellites.

On Oct. 17, 1963, the first pair of Vela Hotel satellites was placed in orbit. Each satellite—launched on the same Atlas-Agena D booster rocket—weighed 485 pounds. The gamma rays and neutron detectors in the satellites could detect a nuclear detonation as small as ten kilotons as far as 100 million miles from earth. The sensors could also measure solar flares, lightning, and radiation from sources other than nuclear explosion.

Vela launches continued, with improvements being made to their sensors. The last pair—*Vela 11* and *Vela 12*—was orbited on April 8, 1970. Subsequently, satellites of the DSP program (see MIDAS) were fitted with nuclear detectors.

The Vela satellites detected nuclear detonations by the Soviet Union and China as well as other countries. They also made highly useful observations of natural phenomena.

Vela is Spanish for "watchman."

(Prior to the Vela satellites, the principal means of detecting nuclear detonations outside the United States was by aircraft fitted to collect fallout from explosions. A modified B-29 SUPERFORTRESS collected radioactive material from the first Soviet nuclear detonation on Sept. 3, 1949, over the Sea of Japan. The bomb had been detonated in the Kazakh Desert on Aug. 25. Later, U-2 spyplanes were used in this role.)

Vendetta

SEE ZEPPELIN (2)

Venlo Incident

Kidnaping of two British INTELLIGENCE OFFICERS from MI6 by Nazi SD officer WALTER SCHELLENBERG.

On Nov. 8, 1939, Schellenberg, posing as a German Army officer in an anti-Hitler plot, lured Capt. S. PAYNE BEST and Maj. H. R. STEVENS to Venlo, a Dutch town near the German-Netherlands border, where Best and Stevens were to meet key members of the alleged conspiracy. As the two British officers waited for Schellenberg and other ostensible conspirators, a car crashed through the border checkpoint, Nazi gunmen firing at the Dutch border guards. The Nazis, disregarding Dutch neutrality, kidnapped the Britons and took them to Germany, where they were relentlessly interrogated by the GESTAPO.

The incident had widespread consequences. Adm. Sir HUGH SINCLAIR, director of MI6 (traditionally known as "C") lay dying as the events leading up to the kidnapping took place, and his deputy, Sir STEWART G. MENZIES was running MI6 and in direct charge of the British attempt to topple Hitler through high-ranking dissidents in the German Army. But the Nazis, aware of the plot, were

running their own hoax against the British, directed by Schellenberg.

Britain had been at war against Germany only since Sept. 3. Prime Minister Neville Chamberlain had staked great hopes on rapidly ending the war by dealing with the dissidents. The work of Best and Stevens was vital to Chamberlain's plan. Sinclair died on Nov. 4, and Menzies became acting "C." Chamberlain and other government officials were deciding whether to make Menzies "C" when the kidnapping debacle happened. Menzies was appointed, but under a cloud.

Meanwhile, Best and Stevens were giving up information (Stevens more than Best, apparently), wiping out much of the MI6 network in Europe. They had also identified Belgian and Dutch intelligence operatives. HEINRICH HIMMLER, head of the SS, used this information in a statement he made attempting to justify the German invasion of Belgium and Holland in May 1940. Germany also claimed that the British Secret Intelligence Service had plotted to kill Hitler. Schellenberg was given the Iron Cross First Class by Hitler himself for the kidnapping. The rising SD officer's success at Venlo led to his being selected to lead a plot to kidnap the Duke of Windsor, the former King Edward VIII, and put him on the throne of an England conquered by Germany. See WILLI.

Venona

CODE NAME for the U.S. codebreaking project that deciphered portions of the texts of Soviet intelligence messages between Moscow and other cities in the 1940s. Most messages concerned spy activities in the United States. Many names in the newspaper headlines of the 1940s—ELIZABETH BENTLEY, WHITTAKER CHAMBERS, KLAUS FUCHS, ALGER HISS, DONALD MACLEAN, and the ATOMIC SPY RING spies HARRY GOLD, DAVID GREENGLASS, JULIUS ROSENBERG and his wife, Ethel—appear in the messages. The decrypts show what U.S. COUNTERINTELLIGENCE officials knew about those cases at the time. But the messages could not be used publicly because officials could not reveal that U.S. codebreakers had penetrated major Soviet cryptographic systems.

The Venona operation was formally ended in 1980. But extensive information about it was not officially released until 1995. By 1997, about 3,000 messages had been released, most so secret that even President Truman had almost certainly not seen them. Documents indicate that he was aware of a secret codebreaking counterespionage operation but did not have knowledge of its details. He does not appear to have known that the operation had uncovered the extent to which Soviet intelligence ORGANS had PENETRATION of U.S. government agencies.

Venona's existence was revealed to the Soviets by a man who had actually worked on the intercepted cables—WILLIAM WEISBAND, a Russian-language linguist at the U.S. ARMY SECURITY AGENCY. He disclosed the Venona successes, supplementing the information provided to the Soviets by British spy HAROLD (KIM) PHILBY, British liaison officer to U.S. intelligence. The first leak had come in 1948 from Bentley, who, after breaking with a Soviet spy ring, told a federal grand jury that an aide to President Roosevelt had learned that American codebreakers had nearly cracked "the Russian secret code." That was the Venona project. Her remark indicated the extent of Soviet penetration. (The presidential aide was almost certainly LAUCHLIN CURRIE.)

Historian Allen Weinstein and former KGB officer Alexander Vassiliev had access to American communist files in Soviet intelligence archives; they used those files, along with Venona decrypts, in *The Haunted Wood: Soviet Espionage in America—The Stalin Era* (1999). They were able to show that it was Philby who first told Moscow that Elizabeth Bentley had defected to the FBI. Their research also showed that when WILLIAM DONOVAN, head of the OFFICE OF STRATEGIC SERVICES (OSS), was in Moscow in Dec. 1943, among the INTELLIGENCE OFFICERS he met with was "Gen. Alexander Ossipov." While telling the general about secret OSS operations, Donovan did not realize that the Russian actually was Maj. Gen. GAIK OVAKIMYAN, who had been the NKVD RESIDENT in New York City in the 1920s and had been arrested by the FBI in 1941, not as a spy but as an unregistered foreign businessman.

Donovan was seeking cooperation between the OSS and the NKVD, unaware that his close friend and key aide, Maj. DUNCAN LEE, was working for the NKVD. Donovan was so naive that Lee felt compelled tell the NKVD that Donovan was in earnest. Lee also reported that when Donovan heard that FBI Director J. EDGAR HOOVER was against the cooperation "he called Hoover a fool." Among other OSS officers working for the Soviets were MAURICE HALPERIN and FRANZ NEUMANN.

The decrypted messages were never exploited in real time, nor were all messages deciphered. Codebreakers in 1946, for example, were working on messages of 1944. Each time a decrypted message yielded a potential lead to tracking down a spy, the codebreaking agency turned the information over to the FBI and often to a liaison officer from British intelligence. The French intelligence agency DST was also given Venona material showing that Pierre Cot, Minister for Air in the 1930s, and André Labarthe, a scientist at the French Air Ministry, had been working for Soviet intelligence.

The Venona messages were full of CRYPTONYMS, some of which Western analysts could link to specific people. One of the most frustrating cryptonyms was "Mlad." Only when the NSA made the messages public, beginning in 1995, did U.S. officials tie Mlad to THEODORE A. HALL, a physicist who had worked on the atomic bomb project. Another cryptonym, "Ales," referred to a Soviet AGENT who had accompanied President Roosevelt to Yalta in Feb. 1945, when he conferred with Prime Minister Winston Churchill and Soviet dictator Josef Stalin. A cable said that Ales had been working for Soviet intelligence since 1935. From clues in this and other messages, officials identified Ales as Alger Hiss.

The messages link Moscow with AGENTS in the United States, Europe, Latin America, and Australia.

About 850 messages involve NKVD activities in San Francisco and Mexico City and the GRU, Soviet MILITARY INTELLIGENCE, in New York and Washington. The breadth of Soviet spying is astounding. One long message to NKVD chief LAVRENTY BERIA describes an operation to get Leon Trotsky's assassin out of a Mexican prison. Another tells about an agent's work for the wartime censor's office. Yet another claims that the Soviets can obtain formulas for colored motion picture processes from the head of the 20th Century-Fox film laboratory.

U.S. intelligence officials, in a 1997 summary of Venona, said that analyses of the messages identified 115 Americans as Soviet agents. Another 100 cryptonyms cloaked the identity of other American agents whom officials either could not or did not identify. So successful was the NKVD at recruiting Americans that, as one Venona message shows, a plan was formed, though not carried out, to recruit First Lady Eleanor Roosevelt. The idea was to get her together with the wife of VASSILI ZARUBIN, the NKVD RESIDENT in New York.

The Soviet agents were in the White House, on Senate committee staffs, in the U.S. Army, the Office of Strategic Services, the State Department, the Justice Department, the War Production Board, and the Treasury Department. (One message asked U.S. HANDLERS to stop placing agents in the Treasury Department because too many were already there.) Other agents worked for the Manhattan Project (see ATOMIC SPY RING), and were employed by defense factories. Others, like WHITTAKER CHAMBERS and MICHAEL STRAIGHT, were journalists.

New light was also shed on the activities of wealthy and influential Americans, such as Alfred K. Stern and his wife, MARTHA DODD, daughter of the former U.S. ambassador to Germany. Accused of being Soviet agents by an FBI informer, Stern and Dodd fled to Czechoslovakia in 1957 and at a press conference denied the accusation. Venona messages, however, reveal their connections with key spy ring members. Also found to be agents were Lauchlin Currie, an administrative aide and State Department liaison to Presidents Roosevelt and Truman, and HARRY DEXTER WHITE.

MEREDITH GARDNER, the cryptologist credited with breaking the codes of Venona, issued special reports recording what he was finding in the messages so that he could speedily alert U.S. intelligence officials. The subjects of the reports, released in 1997, included atomic spying, the code names of British Spy Donald Maclean, the espionage network of Julius Rosenberg, and the NKVD hunt for a DEFECTOR from the Soviet trade mission in Washington.

When the Venona messages became available to U.S. counterintelligence officials, they substantiated the statements of ex-communist Chambers, who had given the FBI details about Soviet espionage in the United States in the 1930s. Venona also produced background for the information given by IGOR GOUZENKO, a CODE clerk in the Soviet Embassy in Ottawa, Canada, who defected in 1945 and revealed the extent of Soviet spying, including information about the Atomic Spy Ring. Bentley, a veteran COURIER for the NKVD and sometime handler of agents, had gone to the FBI in 1945 and confessed her espionage, naming names. With Venona-supplied information, the FBI could confirm many of her statements.

The U.S. Army's SIGNAL INTELLIGENCE SERVICE (SIS) had been accumulating the intercepted Soviet messages since 1939 but had not tried to crack them. Gene Grabeel, a young SIS employee who had been teaching school only weeks before, began sorting the messages by diplomatic mission and by cryptographic system or subscriber. She found five systems. One seemed to involve trade and Lend-Lease, the sending of U.S. war matériel to Britain and the Soviet Union. Diplomats used a second system. The other three systems were used by Soviet intelligence services—the NKVD and GRU (military intelligence). The Venona project (initially code-named BRIDE) began in Feb. 1943, when the SIS (a forerunner of NSA) started working on encrypted Soviet diplomatic communications at ARLINGTON HALL in suburban Washington, D.C.

In Oct. 1943 Lt. Richard Hallock, an Army Signal Corps reserve officer who had been an archaeologist at the University of Chicago, made a small break into the trade-traffic cryptographic system, providing a tool for further progress on the other systems. In 1944 another cryptanalyst, Cecil Phillips, made a discovery that allowed a limited break into what later turned out to be the CIPHER system used by the NKVD. It would be nearly two more years before parts of any of these NKVD messages could be read, or even recognized as spy messages as opposed to routine diplomatic or trade communications.

The key breakthrough came in the summer of 1946, when Meredith Gardner, an SIS analyst, noted similarities in the pattern of several messages. The cryptographic system used by the NKVD involved a code book in which words and phrases were represented by numbers. These numbers were then further enciphered by a technique called additive—the addition of random number groups taken from a ONE-TIME PAD, consisting of pages of random numbers, copies of which were used by the sender and receiver of a message to add and remove an extra layer of encipherment. For example, if the first word in the message was *atomic* and the code book number group for the word was 3856, then 3856 was added to, say, 1349, the first group on the one-time pad. The addition used the Fibonacci, or "Chinese arithmetic" method, in which numbers greater than 9 were not carried forward. So in that message, *atomic* would become 4195.

HOW WAS IT DONE?

One-time pads used only once are unbreakable. But the Soviet cryptographic material manufacturing center had reprinted some one-time pads. Gardner saw the repetition in the midst of thousands of number groups. It was this repetition that gave U.S. codebreakers the breakthrough. The Soviet duplication of one-time pads was rare in 1942, increasing in 1943, and even more so in 1944. Thus, the code-breakers' success rate improved for those years.

To break into the system successfully, analysts first had to identify and strip off the layer of additive to attack the underlying code. Working with nothing more than their own brains, the U.S. cryptographers essentially broke into code books that they had never seen. Some 1942–1943 messages were not successfully attacked until 1953–1954, when a second major cryptanalytic breakthrough was made through pure analysis by Dr. Samuel P. Chew at NSA. After this breakthrough, a partially burned Soviet code book began to have a role.

During the last days of World War II in Europe, a MILITARY INTELLIGENCE team headed by Lt. Col. Paul Neff, acting under Arlington Hall's direction, obtained a photocopy of the code book from a German Foreign Office SIGNAL INTELLIGENCE archive in a castle in Saxony. The Nazis had acquired this code book—and others—from Finns who had taken them from the Soviet Consulate in Petsarno, Finland, on June 22, 1941. Officers in the consulate had managed to burn the code book only partially before the Finns seized the building. Neff's team got the code book back to U.S. lines only a day before Soviet occupation forces moved into the area. At about the same time, Lt. Oliver Kirby, also connected to Arlington Hall, recovered related cryptographic material in Schleswig, Germany. (Both Neff and Kirby later became senior civilian officials at the NSA.)

Meanwhile, Gardner had extracted a phrase from an NKVD message sent from New York to Moscow on Aug. 10, 1944. Later analysis showed that this message referred to clandestine activity in Latin America. On Dec. 13 Gardner managed to read a message about the U.S. presidential election campaign of 1944. Then, on Dec. 20, 1946, he broke into another 1944 message and hit pay dirt: a list of the leading scientists working on the U.S. atomic bomb project. In late April or early May 1947, Gardner read two messages, sent in Dec. 1944, showing that someone on the U.S. Army's General Staff was providing highly classified information to the Soviets. (The NSA, in releasing the Venona material in 1995, would only say, "These two messages are currently undergoing declassification review." Several cryptonyms were listed as "identity protected.")

Brig. Gen. Carter W. Clarke, the assistant U.S. Army G-2 and a key figure in the wartime MAGIC project, was stunned by what was emerging from the decrypts. He notified the FBI, which in Oct. 1948 assigned special agent ROBERT LAMPHERE to Venona. Later the British sent analysts to work on Venona. Later still, U.S. and British intelligence officials told Australian counterparts about decrypts of communications between Moscow and Canberra. (See below.)

Kim Philby, a Soviet MOLE in British intelligence assigned to Washington from 1949 to 1951, occasionally visited Arlington Hall, saw Venona decrypts, and regularly received summaries of U.S. progress in Venona. He undoubtedly reported the breakthrough to his Soviet handlers. From him and other sources, the Soviets knew that U.S. and British intelligence services were aware of their wartime ally's espionage.

In June 1945 Moscow warned that a "foreign intelligence service" was showing an interest in the movement of Soviet diplomatic mail and would attempt to "extract documents" from these courier shipments. Another security warning message in May 1947 ordered ambassadors, consuls, and their subordinates to discharge from their personal service immediately any foreigners they might have hired as "cooks, nursemaids, washerwomen, maids, etc."

PETER WRIGHT, an officer in the British Security Service (MI5), was shown Venona messages in the late 1950s. He realized that some of the cryptonyms could be an existing spy in MI5. One of the British spies identified by Venona was Cedric Belfrage, who worked from 1941 to 1943 for BRITISH SECURITY CO-ORDINATION, the wartime intelligence organization headquartered in New York City.

In *Spycatcher* (1987), Wright wrote, "I remember wondering, as I read the tantalizing decrypts, how on earth anyone at the top of MI5 had slept at night in the dozen years since they were first decrypted." (Wright, obviously, exposed the existence of Venona before it was officially revealed.) He wrote that the FLUENCY COMMITTEE used Venona material in its search for a mole in British intelligence, as did investigators probing the espionage of Sir ANTHONY BLUNT and the bona fides of ANATOLI GOLITSYN, a Soviet DEFECTOR.

Among the hundreds of cryptonyms were Antenna and Liberal, both later identified as names for Julius Rosenberg. One message mentioned that Liberal's wife was named Ethel.

Another said that Rosenberg (referred to as Liberal) was so busy with spying that his handlers were "afraid of putting Liberal out of action with overwork." In a message assessing Ethel Rosenberg, the NKVD says, "Sufficiently well developed politically. Knows about her husbands [sic] work. . . ." Other messages refer to the clandestine activities of Harry Gold, David and Ruth Greenglass, and Klaus Fuchs. Some cover names of people involved in the atomic spy ring remain publicly unidentified.

Venona messages show that Leonid Kvasnikov (cover name Anton), headed atomic bomb espionage in the United States. He, like the Rosenbergs (who came under his control) had many other high-tech espionage TARGETS, such as developments of U.S. jet aircraft, radar, and rockets. Also revealed were extensive contacts of Soviet intelligence with the U.S. Communist Party and the way the Soviet spy NETWORK operated under cover of consulates, the AMTORG trade mission, the Soviet news agency Tass, and Soviet inspectors in U.S. factories producing war matériel being sent to the Soviet armed forces.

About 260 messages between the GRU's London Residency and headquarters in Moscow in 1940–1941 cover a wide range of topics, including the establishment of at least three clandestine radio stations. One agent, code-named Baron, apparently reported information obtained from U.K. decryption of German ENIGMA traffic. There is also a reference to Klaus Fuchs. The GRU resident in London was probably Simon Kremer, who had

the cover assignment of private secretary to the military ATTACHÉ.

More than 200 messages were sent between Moscow and Australia from 1943 to 1948, mostly referring to agents inside government departments, including a possible mole in an intelligence service. (See AUSTRALIAN SECURITY AND INTELLIGENCE ORGANIZATION.)

The 200-odd Australian messages turned up ten spies. One of them, Ian Milner, defected to Czechoslovakia and entered that country's intelligence service. In 1954, VLADIMIR M. PETROV, a senior KGB official, defected in Australia, along with his wife, a code clerk. The agents he supposedly revealed were probably released by Australian officials who had seen Venona decrypts and used Petrov as a false conduit to throw off Soviet counterintelligence officers. Australian messages showed that agents there gave Allied STRATEGIC INTELLIGENCE to the Soviets, who let Japanese officials see them. The Soviet Union at that time, although a Western ally in the European War, maintained relations with Japan until the last week of the Pacific War.

Another set of some 450 messages concerns Soviet espionage in Sweden, which was neutral during World War II. One, sent to Moscow on April 13, 1942, mentions a German peace initiative involving banker Jakob Wallenberg, uncle of RAOUL WALLENBERG, a Swedish diplomat who did work for the OSS.

Most Venona messages pertained to the operation of agents and TRADECRAFT, including countermeasures against the FBI, meeting scenarios, and the photographing of documents. So much material was collected by Soviet spies that, beyond information sent by enciphered messages, photocopies of classified documents had to go to Moscow by diplomatic courier. In one message, New York informed THE CENTER in Moscow that it had 56 rolls of film from "Robert." Other messages describe the NKVD assessment and recruitment of American communists as spies.

Messages mention "Stanley" as an agent in British intelligence with a responsibility for Mexico; that agent was later found to be Philby. From a reference to "Hicks" as a man who sent more opinion than facts, mole hunters identified GUY BURGESS. Travels of "Johnson" coincided with those of Blunt. Venona also contained information about Soviet penetration of Charles de Gaulle's Free French movement, which would be the core of postwar French government.

"Albert" was ISKHAK AKHMEROV, a Soviet INTELLIGENCE OFFICER who did two U.S. tours of duty as an ILLEGAL. EARL BROWDER, whose cover name was "Rulevoj," also showed up in the decrypts.

The Venona achievement remained highly secret until 1995, except for Peter Wright's revelations and some other "leaks" that indicated the United States had special sources of intelligence. (Of course, the Soviet government knew about Venona from Philby, Weisband, and possibly other spies.)

In 1995 NSA began to release more than 1,200 Venona messages. They exposed the extent of Soviet espionage against the United States during the 1940s and

BRIDE

~~TOP SECRET~~

TO BE KEPT UNDER LOCK AND KEY :
NEVER TO BE REMOVED FROM THE OFFICE.

D045

USSR

▮▮▮▮▮▮

Ref No: s/NBF/T176

Issued: ▮▮ 2/4/1952

Copy No: 21

JOURNALISTS' VIEWS ON CANDIDATES FOR APPOINTMENTS TO BE MADE BY THE U.S. GOVERNMENT.

From: NEW YORK

To: MOSCOW

No: 1507   23 Oct. 1944

To VICTOR.

From a chat with ARSENIJ[i]
[69 groups unrecoverable]
[SW]ING[ii] assert[a] that HENDERSON[iii] will not be appointed to this post. Thomas REYNOLDS, a correspondent of the CHICAGO SUN who is on very friendly terms with CAPTAIN's [KAPITAN][iv] close adviser - ROZENMAN[v], said that HENDERSON[iii] will be given the post of economic [D adviser] with the Military administration of Occupied Germany. DURDLE-DEE [SHMEL'][vi] and SWING[ii] consider the most serious candidacy in 1944 is that for the head of the ARSENAL[vii]. They and correspondent HIGHTOWER [KHAJTAUER], who has connections with the BANK[viii], assert that so far the question has not been decided. Several correspondents have named General WEDEMEYER [VIDEMEJER] as commander of the occupation forces of the COUNTRY [STRANA][ix], however there is no possibility of checking the information. Apparently one [3 groups unrecovered] General CLARK, but at the instance of MURPHY [MERFI][x] his candidacy has been turned down because he is a Jew.

No. 844.   MAY [MAJ][xi]

23rd October

                    [T.N. and Comments overleaf]

Distribution

also revealed the important role that SIGNALS INTELLIGENCE and CRYPTOGRAPHY had played in U.S. counterintelligence.

(For code names found in Venona decrypts see Appendix A.)

Vertrauensmann

Literally, "a man of our confidence" or "confidential agent," a word that appears frequently in German diplomatic telegrams in World War II. To Anglo-American translators, the word often was given the meaning "SECRET AGENT."

Vetterlein, Kurt

German engineer who during World War II operated an intercept station that unscrambled and transcribed the scrambled trans-Atlantic telephone conversations between President Roosevelt and Prime Minister Winston Churchill.

In the 1930s Vetterlein was assigned by the Research Institute of the German Post Office (which ran Germany's telephone system) to work on ways to unscramble telephone calls. He knew the general technique used by the American Telephone & Telegraph Co. to scramble voices. The Germans had one of the AT&T machines, called the A-3.

Operating from a building on the Dutch coast, the interception unit—called simply the Research Post—picked up only the conversations of many high-ranking leaders. "The spectacular feat of tapping into the top-level Allied radio-telephone conversations produced no great results," DAVID KAHN wrote in *Hitler's Spies* (1978). "They did not give the Germans any extraordinary insight into Allied plans."

VIAT

South Vietnamese private air transport corporation used in the 1960s to conduct clandestine operations over North Vietnam. The airline was a PROPRIETARY COMPANY run by the CIA. VIAT often used pilots from AIR AMERICA, another CIA proprietary company.

Vienna

A center of international intrigue from the days of the Austro-Hungarian Empire to the Cold War.

A pleasant city for tourists, Vienna has also attracted spies and counterspies because of its location, straddling the realms of East and West in Europe. From here Russia and Germany spied on each other in imperial days. Neutral Austria does not look for spies; there is no COUNTERINTELLIGENCE agency to bother known INTELLIGENCE OFFICERS, as in Paris, London, Washington, and Tel Aviv.

The Soviets so preferred to stage meetings with their Western AGENTS in Vienna that the U.S. FBI called the routine the "Vienna procedure." ANATOLI GOLITSYN, a KGB officer who defected to the West in 1961, was stationed in Vienna from 1953 to 1955, keeping watch on Soviet émigrés. PETER DERIABIN, another KGB DEFECTOR, also had a tour in Vienna as a counterintelligence officer who arranged for ILLEGALS to remain in the city after the pullout of Soviet occupation troops in 1954.

After World War II Austria, like Germany, was divided into American, Soviet, British, and French occupation zones. Unlike BERLIN, which had been divided into four separate zones, Vienna was administered jointly. This was visibly demonstrated by the military police jeeps that patrolled the city carrying soldiers from each of the four occupying powers. Invisibly, the Western allies often teamed up to spy on the Soviets.

The MOVIE *The Third Man* (1950) captured perfectly the shadowy atmosphere of postwar Vienna. GRAHAM GREENE's screenplay focused on the black market rather than on espionage. But as a former INTELLIGENCE OFFICER himself, he knew that the city was a natural place for intrigue.

U.S. and British intelligence agencies, working against Soviet intelligence in Vienna, discovered that a telephone cable to Soviet headquarters ran underground near the boundary between the British and Soviet zones. In a project code-named Silver, they dug a TUNNEL and tapped a telephone junction box. The COVER for a tap, a shop that sold Harris tweed, had a basement listening post. As David Martin reported in *Wilderness of Mirrors* (1980), the shop became so popular that the intelligence services had to divert an unexpected amount of energy and talent to keep up the business.

In the 1950s Vienna began to fade in importance next to Berlin, a flashpoint of East-West crisis and a center of large spy stations. (It was also the site of another tunnel, code-named Gold; see BERLIN TUNNEL.) But because Vienna is the site of the international Atomic Energy Agency, it attracted Cold War spies. Soviets got positions there and at the UNITED NATIONS Industrial Development Organization to acquire technology and circumvent U.S. and Western restrictions on its transfer to the Soviet Union.

Diplomats under cover at the Soviet and U.S. embassies trolled diplomatic cocktail parties for recruits. The large CIA station included counterintelligence officers watching for American spies. There were many.

Navy radioman JOHN A. WALKER, JR., who spied for the Soviets, met with his HANDLER in Vienna 11 times during his espionage career. RONALD W. PELTON, who betrayed NSA secrets, went to Vienna twice to talk in a SAFE HOUSE. On his third trip, he later said, he walked around his meeting site—the gardens of the imperial summer palace, Schönbrunn—for about three days, but was not contacted. His handlers suspected that he might have been turned, so they left him out in the cold. JAMES HARPER, who had been supplying the Soviets with information about ballistic missiles, was also sent to Vienna.

Marine Sgt. CLAYTON J. LONETREE, recruited at the U.S. Embassy in Moscow, met a new handler when he was transferred to the U.S. Embassy in Vienna. Former

CIA officer EDWARD LEE HOWARD made at least one round trip between the United States and Vienna, probably for training, prior to his flight to Moscow as a fugitive. FELIX S. BLOCH was deputy chief of mission at the U.S. Embassy in Vienna when he was accused of spying. But his face-to-face was in Paris, where a French SURVEILLANCE team photographed him meeting with a Soviet intelligence officer.

It was also in Vienna that Soviet defector NICHOLAS SHADRIN disappeared while working as a DOUBLE AGENT for the FBI against the KGB. In fact, the CIA had failed to provide local protective coverage for him and he was abducted by the KGB and accidentally killed.

Vietnam

There are many names for war in Vietnam, a vast battlefield for intelligence operations through much of its modern history. The French called theirs "the war without fronts." Ho Chi Minh and his Vietminh used "the people's war." To Americans it would be an "unconventional war" for the "hearts and minds" of the Vietnamese. And within the American war there was a secret war conducted by the CIA and U.S. ARMY INTELLIGENCE.

The roots of the secret war went back to World War II, when, in the spring of 1945, operatives of the OFFICE OF STRATEGIC SERVICES (OSS) joined forces with Ho Chi Minh and his coalition communist nationalists, the Vietminh. They were fighting the Japanese, who had occupied portions of French Indochina—Vietnam, Cambodia, and Laos—since the fall of France in June 1940.

By taking Indochina, Japan cut off supplies reaching China via a railroad from the Indochinese port city of Haiphong. The Japanese had long allowed French garrisons to remain in Indochina; fearing an Allied invasion of the area, however, on March 9, 1945, they had attacked the garrisons. Surviving French troops and civilians, weak and ill equipped, began fighting their way through Japanese lines to China. Thousands were taken prisoner, 2,200 were killed, and about 3,000 reached China.

To the OSS, Ho Chi Minh was an ally against the Japanese. Thus OSS units, with support from French guerrillas, trained Vietminh units in commando warfare, parachuted arms and supplies to the Vietminh, and sent AGENTS behind Japanese lines to gather intelligence about Japanese forces. The Vietminh aided downed U.S. fliers and took part, along with French guerrillas and OSS operatives, in a commando raid on a Japanese division headquarters in June 1945. The raiders captured documents that gave Allied planners valuable intelligence on Japanese operations in Southeast Asia. When Japan surrendered in Aug. 1945, the OSS, still seeing the Vietminh as allies, joined them as they proclaimed the independence of Vietnam and marched into Hanoi.

In France, Gen. Charles de Gaulle, determined to regain Indochina and bitter about OSS aid to the Vietminh, sent troops into Saigon in Oct. 1945. The French DEUXIÈME BUREAU began reestablishing an intelligence NETWORK. But French intelligence provided only a last-minute warning of an attack on Hanoi and other garrison sites by the Vietminh under Vo Nguyen Giap on Dec. 19, 1946. Vietnam was again at war.

At first the French hunted down communists, with the help of Nationalist Chinese officers who had worked for Nationalist China's CENTRAL BUREAU OF INVESTIGATION AND STATISTICS. Then the French intelligence service SDECE developed the concept of "Vietnamese maquis," resistance groups modeled on the World War II maquis that fought the Germans with sabotage and espionage in occupied France. But resistance movements that worked in the urbanized society of France did not transfer well into the jungles and paddies of Indochina.

The French-sponsored native resistance groups were no match for the Vietminh, whose own intelligence teams, the Trinh Sat, consistently discovered French military plans. Another idea was the *Groupement de Commandoes Mixtes Aéroportés* (GCMA), airborne commando groups that tried to harass the Vietminh and gather intelligence. The GCMA units also fell victim to the Trinh Sat's knowledge of where and how to gather intelligence in their own land.

The war's end in July 1954 was foreshadowed by France's humiliation at Dien Bien Phu. The symbol of French defeat in Indochina, Dien Bien Phu fell on May 7, 1954, after a bloody, 56-day siege. Ten thousand French, North African, Foreign Legion, and loyal Vietnamese troops died at Dien Bien Phu; another 10,000 were taken prisoner by the Vietminh. In the peace talks that followed, the French agreed to a partitioning of Vietnam along the 17th parallel, with a communist North Vietnam under Ho Chi Minh and a Republic of South Vietnam under Ngo Dinh Diem in the south, with Saigon as its capital. This was to be a temporary measure pending nationwide elections in 1956.

Some 80,000 French troops remained in the Republic of Vietnam, to the displeasure of Diem, who was anti-French. "To the French secret services," wrote Douglas Porch in *The French Secret Services* (1995), "fell the task of enforcing French interests, a charge which they assumed with the self-interested conviction of a service, some of whose members had developed a cozy business relationship with the Binh Xuyen," a Vietnamese criminal organization with ties to the French underworld.

American EDWARD C. LANSDALE—an OSS veteran and CIA officer—intrigued against both the French and the communists. He once organized a South Vietnamese Army raid on the Binh Xuyen, which was provided with intelligence by the Deuxième Bureau. Lansdale launched what he called a counter-terrorist campaign against the French, targeting INTELLIGENCE OFFICERS. Before a serious breach occurred between the two countries' intelligence services, in May 1955 France withdrew all forces from Indochina, leaving it to the United States and Ho Chi Minh.

THE LONGEST WAR

By Jan. 1961, when President Kennedy took office, Ho Chi Minh controlled some 15,000 Viet Cong guerrillas in

South Vietnam. To turn back the communists, Kennedy put his faith in counterinsurgency units in the belief that they could do more to stabilize Indochina than conventional military forces. In May 1961, Kennedy sent 400 of the U.S. Army's Green Berets to Vietnam to "expand present operations in the field of intelligence, unconventional warfare, and political-psychological activities." Linked to the Green Berets was the growing CIA presence in Vietnam. In 1962 Kennedy gave the CIA responsibility for all paramilitary activities in Vietnam and, secretly, in Laos.

With each succeeding military escalation of the war there was an intelligence escalation. Intelligence in this war, however, was not like that of any war the United States had ever fought. Besides the usual MILITARY INTELLIGENCE units there was a civilian intelligence apparatus, at best paralleling the military and often competing with it.

In Aug. 1964, while U.S. Navy destroyers sailed in the Gulf of Tonkin off North Vietnam gathering ELECTRONIC INTELLIGENCE under an operation CODE-NAMED DESOTO, Operations Plan 34A was being run by the CIA. One aspect of Plan 34A called for hit-and-run attacks against North Vietnamese shore installations by high-speed craft manned by South Vietnamese or mercenaries hired by the CIA. When North Vietnam reacted to the raids by sending torpedo boats after the destroyers, the U.S. Congress, at President Johnson's request, responded with the Tonkin resolution. It authorized the use of U.S. forces to support Vietnam and became the legal basis for the Vietnam War.

Direct U.S. involvement in the war increased as a result. There was a buildup of U.S. troops in the south (peaking at 525,000); intensive air strikes were carried out against communist positions (real and suspected) in South Vietnam, as were periodic bombings of North Vietnam; and intensive naval and clandestine activities were undertaken. At the height of the war the CIA occupied three floors of the U.S. Embassy in Saigon and had about 700 employees in Vietnam under the broad COVER of Office of the Special Assistant to the Ambassador (OSA). The head of the OSA was WILLIAM E. COLBY, a future DIRECTOR OF CENTRAL INTELLIGENCE. Other CIA covers were the Combined Studies Detachment and the STUDIES AND OBSERVATION GROUP (SOG), a HUMAN INTELLIGENCE collection organization.

The SOG inserted intelligence teams into enemy territory by land, parachute, helicopters, and PT boats. Another CIA operation, also part of the 1961 Operations Plan 37-A, dropped teams of Vietnamese "covert agents" into North Vietnam. All of them were killed, captured, or turned into DOUBLE AGENTS who sent false radio messages that lured in more teams to their doom. North Vietnam's Ministry of Public Security had nearly perfect intelligence on exactly where the agents had landed.

When the CIA finally realized what was happening, the agency tried to stop the program. The Army took it over, and by 1968 about 500 would-be agents had been lost. Declassified postwar documents, obtained by former intelligence officer Sedwick Tourison for his book *Secret Army Secret War* (1995), show that nearly 400 were imprisoned for up to 27 years.

In Laos, the CIA secretly mounted its largest paramilitary operation: the building of L'Armée Clandestine, about 30,000 Meo tribesmen, other Laotians, and about 17,000 Thai mercenaries. The secret army of the secret war was supplied by the CIA's AIR AMERICA, a CIA PROPRIETARY COMPANY. (See CIVILIAN IRREGULAR DEFENSE GROUP.)

The CIA ran the Laos war from Thailand under cover of the 4802nd joint Liaison Detachment. To preserve the appearance that it was not an American war, no U.S. ground troops were committed, except for some Green Beret operations using cross-border teams in uniforms without U.S. insignia, carrying Chinese or Soviet weapons. They also operated in Cambodia.

News of the CIA army remained a secret until 1965, when U.S. newspapers published some details. The broad scope of the war in Laos, however, was not revealed officially until 1969, and even then many details were withheld. Even official Washington sometimes ignored the CIA war. "We often forget there is a significant—secondary—war going on in Laos," National Security Adviser Walt Rostow wrote to President Johnson in Aug. 1966.

An air of distrust hung heavy over U.S.–South Vietnam relations. U.S. intelligence officers were especially suspicious of their counterparts—and even more so of South Vietnamese politicians.

The handling of local agents could be complex. In one operation, a CIA officer worked with highland peasants along the Laos-Vietnam border. They were hunters, charcoal makers, and rattan gatherers who would not look suspicious around the Ho Chi Minh Trail complex in the border area. "They were our eyes and ears on the ground," he later wrote in a CIA publication. "Most of the agents were organized in small nets of a half-dozen under a principal agent who, in turn, was controlled by Vietnamese agent handler with an American case officer counterpart. The American case officer typically worked with two or three agent handlers."

Meanwhile, the communists were infiltrating the South Vietnamese government. The highest-ranking MOLE was Vu Ngoc Nha, an adviser first to President Diem, a devout Catholic killed in a 1963 coup, and then to President Nguyen Van Thieu. Nha posed as a Catholic recommended by church leaders. He was said to have advised Thieu to furlough soldiers for a few days during Tet (the lunar new year) in late Jan. 1968. It was then that the North Vietnamese struck with a widespread and morale-shattering attack that eventually led to the U.S. decision to quit the war. Hanoi officials revealed in 1988 that Nha had been a deep-PENETRATION agent.

The CIA's PHOENIX program was to have been the centerpiece of the CIA-orchestrated campaign to win the war by winning the hearts and minds of the Vietnamese. Phoenix ran under cover of the Civil Operations/Revolutionary Development Systems (CORDS) pacification program. In Phoenix offices throughout Vietnam hung a sign that summed up what realists thought of the program: "When you got 'em by the balls, their hearts and minds will follow."

Phoenix, ostensibly a campaign to destroy the Vietcong by capturing and prosecuting local leaders, became a murderous instrument in the hands of the South Vietnamese. The program was run first by Robert W. Komer, who later became President Johnson's special assistant for Vietnam, and then by Colby.

Komer later wrote that the United States was involved in two wars—one fought by the troops and the other by the Department of State, the Agency for International Development, the U.S. Information Agency, and the CIA. In his book *Bureaucracy at War* (1986), Komer wrote, "Though national intelligence estimates at the Washington level were generally realistic, what might be called tactical intelligence in the field was for long critically weak. . . . The kinds of intelligence most needed in Vietnam were simply alien to the standard institutional repertoires of most U.S. and GVN [Government of South Vietnam] intelligence services involved."

Gen. William C. Westmoreland, who commanded U.S. forces in Vietnam from 1964 to 1968, said in 1970, when he was U.S. Army Chief of Staff, "We were not exactly a giant without eyes, although that allusion has some validity." The search for ways to see the invisible enemy characterized some of the technology of the war.

AERIAL RECONNAISSANCE

Aerial RECONNAISSANCE was extensive (see A-12 OXCART, BUFFALO HUNTER, SR-71 BLACKBIRD, and U-2). But so were triple-canopy tropical forests that made photography difficult. Ingenious attempts were made to penetrate the forests with sensor technology. Project Igloo White targeted the 3,000-mile Ho Chi Minh Trail, the main supply line for the Viet Cong and North Vietnamese in South Vietnam. Aircraft dropped thousands of tiny, dart-shaped transmitters that buried themselves in the ground. Protruding from them were antennas that looked like jungle plants. Seismic sensors were to pick up the tramp of people or the vibrations of a passing truck. The transmitters, which would self-destruct if uprooted, were dropped at crossroads along the trail. Signals from the transmitters were picked up in Thailand, where a computer transformed the signals into patterns for intelligence analysts to interpret.

U.S. reconnaissance aircraft also ranged far and wide over potential intelligence TARGETS in North Vietnam. One set of targets of particular interest showed the prison camps in North Vietnam in which American fliers who had been shot down were being held. When intelligence discerned a POW camp at Son Tay, deep in the heart of Vietnam—23 miles from the center of Hanoi—a daring raid was planned. The CIA built a model of the Son Tay compound (code-named Barbara) and carefully planned a helicopter raid. It was carried out in Nov. 1970 with great skill. Despite a fierce firefight, the raiders escaped without a single serious casualty. But they also left without a single POW. There were no POWs. Intelligence had failed. (The CIA blamed the failure on the fact that

the agency had not been involved in the Army's planning for the raid.)

Interpretations of intelligence were not always granted a hearing in Washington. Sometimes the blind giant was also deaf. In Vietnam, as in many wars over many centuries, the generals and the politicians did not always listen to intelligence reports.

In July 1965, a joint study by the CIA and the DEFENSE INTELLIGENCE AGENCY (DIA) said that bombing North Vietnam had only a marginal effect on the North's ability to wage war. The CIA particularly said that the attacks would not lead to changes in communist policy. Another study, issued three weeks later by the CIA alone, reinforced its earlier evaluation. The military services and the DIA dissented. In 1966, after another study questioned the effects of bombing, the CIA issued still another estimate, which argued that the bombing had failed because of restrictive rules of engagement.

The CIA position shifted dramatically again in Aug. 1967, when DCI RICHARD MCG. HELMS gave President Johnson a personal evaluation of the bombing. Helms noted that since March 1967 there had been more than 10,000 bombing sorties a month against North Vietnam. But, he continued, "despite the increasing hardships, economic losses and mounting problems in management and logistics caused by the air war, Hanoi continues to meet its own needs and to support its aggression in South Vietnam. Essential military and economic traffic continues to move."

Three weeks later Helms followed up with a "sensitive" analysis from the CIA's OFFICE OF NATIONAL ESTIMATES prepared for Johnson alone. The paper looked at the "Implications of an Unfavorable Outcome in Vietnam" and concluded that the risks of a loss in Vietnam "are probably more limited and controllable than most previous arguments have indicated."

Even in the final scenes of the visible war on April 30, 1975—people rushing up a ladder to board a helicopter on the roof of a CIA outpost in Saigon (not the U.S. Embassy)—there was a feeling that the truth about the secret war would remain untold. FRANK SNEPP, a CIA analyst who was there at the end, wrote in his book *Decent Interval* (1977):

> The full impact of CIA losses and failures in Vietnam will probably never be known. There are too many unanswered questions. But based on what can be ascertained, it is not too much to say that in terms of squandered lives, blown secrets and the betrayal of agents, friends and collaborators, our handling of the evacuation was an institutional disgrace. Not since the abortive Bay of Pigs invasion of 1961 had the agency put so much on the line, and lost it through stupidity and mismanagement.

Vogel, Wolfgang

East German lawyer who specialized in setting up SPY SWAPS during the Cold War.

His first swap, in Feb. 1962 at the midpoint of

BERLIN's Glienicke Bridge over the Havel River, involved Col. RUDOLF ABEL, a Soviet ILLEGAL who had been arrested in New York City, and FRANCIS GARY POWERS, convicted of espionage and jailed by the Soviet Union after his U-2 spyplane was shot down.

Vogel also arranged for the release of GÜNTER GUILLAUME, who spied for the Stasi (MFS) while a member of Chancellor Willy Brandt's staff. West German officials at first refused to set Guillaume free from his 14-year sentence. But Vogel won out, as he usually did, trading Guillaume for eight captured West German, British, and American AGENTS.

His lesser-known dealings included brokering during the Cold War the secret release of 250,000 East Germans—dissidents, clergymen, union leaders, and other victims of the Stasi. West Germany secretly paid more than three *billion* marks in ransom to free these people. By some estimates, a physician cost as much as $100,000, with lesser fees for people of other trades and professions. Sometimes the secret payments were in kind: potash, coffee, rubber, bananas, or elevators.

In another complex swap, ROBERT G. THOMPSON, a U.S. Air Force clerk convicted of espionage, was freed from his U.S. prison and taken to East Germany in exchange for an American student held by East Germany and an Israeli held in Mozambique. Vogel also arranged for the release of Soviet dissident Anatoly Scharansky, who had been arrested in Moscow in 1977 on charges of spying for the West. Scharansky and three imprisoned Western agents crossed the Glienicke Bridge to West Berlin while MORRIS COHEN and his wife Lona, agents held by the West, crossed into East Berlin, along with three East German agents held by West Germany.

Vogel, who took a small fee for his transactions, described himself as "the middleman between the all-powerful and the powerless." While Germany was divided he was also the middleman between political leaders in East and West who could not be seen talking to each other directly. East Germany, in an extraordinary exception to Marxist rules, let Vogel maintain a private practice and become prosperous.

Vogel was arrested by German authorities and put on trial in Berlin, the once divided city that was the stage for his profitable dramas. In Jan. 1996 Vogel was convicted of extorting money from East German emigrants. Convicted of perjury, blackmail, and falsifying documents, he was fined $63,500 and given a two-year suspended sentence.

Voit, Capt. Ludwig

Founder of German COMMUNICATIONS INTELLIGENCE during World War I. In 1914 Voit set up a radio station with a CRYPTOGRAPHY section in General Headquarters and established intercept stations that could intercept Allied radio communications. The cryptographic section was the basis for the Per Z codebreaking effort of the 1930s and World War II. Per Z, attached to the Foreign Office, solved some of the codes of 34 countries.

Volkov, Konstantin

INTELLIGENCE OFFICER of the NKVD who became a DEFECTOR. Volkov used as his COVER the position of vice consul at the Soviet Consulate in Istanbul.

In Aug. 1945 he contacted his opposite number at the British Consulate and offered information on Soviet MOLES in the British government, saying that two were in the Foreign Office and one was head of a COUNTERINTELLIGENCE agency in London. He also warned that neither his information nor his offer to defect should be cabled to London, because the Soviets had broken the British diplomatic codes.

His claims about moles were sent to London by diplomatic pouch and thus arrived a week later at MI6, reaching the desk of HAROLD (KIM) PHILBY—who realized that he was one of the moles that Volkov was about to name. "I stared at the papers rather longer than necessary to compose my thoughts," Philby later wrote in his self-serving memoir, *My Silent War* (1968). By a combination of luck and conniving, Philby managed to take the place of another intelligence officer who was to have gone to Istanbul. By the time Philby got to Istanbul, Volkov had vanished and was never heard of again.

Years later, after Philby's espionage was revealed, British intelligence officials backtracked on the Volkov case and concluded that Philby had tipped off the Soviets, in effect signing Volkov's death warrant. They assumed he had been ordered back to Moscow and executed. In his memoir, Philby told of writing a report suggesting that the Soviets might have placed a BUG in Volkov's quarters or that he had confessed. As for the possibility that he had been betrayed by a British spy, that theory "was not worth including in my report."

von Bredow, Lt. Col. Ferdinand

Chief of the ABWEHR, Germany's MILITARY INTELLIGENCE organization, from 1930 to 1932.

Von Bredow, who had served in the Abwehr since its founding in 1921, reorganized the agency and recruited German arms dealers as AGENTS. When his friend Kurt von Schleicher became Defense Minister, he made von Bredow one of his key aides and appointed a naval officer, Rear Adm. Conrad Patzig, to replace him. Von Schleicher later became the last Chancellor of the Weimar Republic before Hitler came to power.

von Rintelen, Capt. Franz

(b. 1877 d. 1949)

German INTELLIGENCE OFFICER sent to the United States during World War I to commit acts of sabotage.

The son of an international banker, von Rintelen learned English at an early age. He entered the German Navy in 1903 and was serving in the naval High Command when war broke out in Aug. 1914.

Traveling on a Swiss passport made out to Emile V. Gache, von Rintelen entered the United States in March

1915 to direct German sabotage in the United States, which, although officially neutral, was supplying Britain, France, and Russia with arms. Von Rintelen supervised the mass production of cigar bombs." A cigar-size metal tube was divided into two compartments filled with acids and separated by a copper disk, which acted as a timing device. The tube was plugged with wax at either end. When the acids ate through the disk and mixed they produced an intense stream of flame that shot out of the tube.

The bombs were produced on board a German ship berthed in New York City. Von Rintelen hired Irish longshoremen with anti-British sympathies to slip the bombs into munitions loaded onto ships bound for Britain. The bombs were timed to burst into flame while the ships were in mid-Atlantic.

The boastful von Rintelen claimed that some ships blew up, while on others the fires were detected but the dousing of them damaged the munitions. Three of the fire-bombed ships, he later wrote, carried supplies that he had, through a CUT-OUT, sold to the Russians. So he had actually made money besides destroying the ships and their cargoes. There is no record of exactly how many ships his sabotage sank or damaged.

Von Rintelen also worked on schemes to get workers in munitions plants to go on strike. He was despised by Frank von Papen, the military ATTACHÉ at the German Embassy in Washington, D.C. Von Papen was in charge of German espionage and sabotage in the United States. Worried that von Rintelen's schemes would hurt other, more important operations, von Papen succeeded in having him recalled. British codebreakers intercepted messages concerning the recall, and in Aug. 1915, when von Rintelen, using his Swiss identity, arrived at Southampton on a Dutch ship, he was arrested and extradited to the United States. He was tried and convicted of fomenting strikes and sent to a federal penitentiary until the end of the war.

He wildly exaggerated his exploits in his memoir, *The Dark Invader* (1933), taking credit for fatally infecting horses and mules sent to the Allies from America. He also claimed to have had a hand in the Black Tom explosion in New York Harbor in July 1916, even though he was in prison at the time of the explosion.

Vortex

SEE CHALET

Vosjoli, Philippe de

SEE TOPAZ

VQ Squadrons

U.S. Navy fleet air RECONNAISSANCE squadrons that operate the Navy's ELECTRONIC INTELLIGENCE (ELINT) spyplanes. From the mid-1950s squadrons VQ-1 in the Far East and VQ-2 in the European-Mediterranean area carried out ELINT missions in support of TECHNICAL INTELLIGENCE collection requirements as well as providing TACTICAL INTELLIGENCE to fleet and area commanders.

Naval aircraft began flying electronic missions during World War II, employing a variety of land-based aircraft as well as flying boats. As the Cold War began, the Navy initiated flights around the Soviet periphery with modified PBM Mariner two-engine flying boats and land-based PB4Y-2 PRIVATEER four-engine bombers. These planes were assigned to regular Navy patrol squadrons (designated VP). The first U.S. AIRCRAFT SHOT DOWN in a Cold War spy flight was a PB4Y-2 from VP-26 based at Port Lyautey (now Kénitra), Morocco. (That aircraft, shot down off Latvia on April 8, 1950, had staged through Wiesbaden, West Germany, for the Baltic Sea mission and was to land in Copenhagen, Denmark, after the ELINT mission.)

The Navy recognized the need for dedicated ELINT squadrons, and VQ-1 was established as an ELECTRONIC COUNTERMEASURES (ECM) squadron at the naval air station at Iwakuni, Japan, on June 1, 1955. The unit initially flew the P4M-1Q MERCATOR aircraft; VQ-2 was established as an ECM squadron on Sept. 1, 1955, at Port Lyautey, first flying the P4M-1Q and A3D-1Q SKYWARRIOR aircraft. The latter aircraft could fly from land bases as well as aircraft carriers. The term ECM was intended as a COVER for the squadrons' true purpose.

The designation VQ was changed to fleet air reconnaissance squadron on Jan. 1, 1960. The squadrons continue in operation: VQ-1 is now based at Whidbey Island, Wash., and VQ-2 at Rota, Spain. Each squadron currently flies ELINT-configured EP-3E variants of the P-3 ORION patrol aircraft.

In June 1967 an ELINT-configured C-121 CONSTELLATION, with at least two Hebrew linguists on boad, intercepted Israeli communications concerning the attack on the U.S. intelligence ship *LIBERTY*. The aircraft, from VQ-2, recorded Israeli transmissions that convinced NSA officials that the attack was caused by mistaken identity.

An EP-3E Orion from VQ-1 collided with a Chinese fighter off Hainän Island on Apr. 1, 2001. The J-8 fighter crashed into the sea, its pilot killed. The heavily damaged EP-3E was able to land on Hainan. There were no injuries among its crew of 21 men and 3 women. They had destroyed some equipment and recordings before the plane landed. (The crew was released after 11 days and the aircraft was disassembled and flown to the United States for rehabilitation.)

In 1991 the Navy established two additional VQ squadrons to operate the ES-3A Viking ELINT aircraft from aircraft carriers. These were VQ-5 at Agana, Guam, and VQ-6 at Cecil Field, Fla. However, the ES-3A aircraft—which replaced the A3D Skywarriors aboard carriers—was short-lived. Because of budgetary limitations, the Navy decided to take the ES-3A aircraft out of service and VQ-5 and VQ-6 were disestablished in 1999. The last ES-3A had been delivered in 1995.

Walk-in

Someone who voluntarily offers to spy. An unheralded DEFECTOR, or a "dangle," a walk-in is a potential AGENT or MOLE who literally walks into an enemy embassy or intelligence agency without prior contact or RECRUITMENT.

During the DECADE OF THE SPY the term was especially applied to Americans who walked into Soviet embassies or other offices and preferred secret information. They included civilians and uniformed men from the Army, Navy, Marines, Air Force, major defense contractors, CIA, NSA, and FBI.

From the 1960s through the 1980s Soviet intelligence achieved major successes not by the recruitment of spies but by walk-ins. Walk-ins who "volunteer information for sale," said a 1986 report by the U.S. Senate Select Committee on Intelligence, are "the most dangerous agents of all," accounting for "the greatest losses of the most highly classified information."

Walker, Lt. Cmdr. Arthur J.

(b. 1934)

Retired U.S. Navy officer recruited as a spy by his brother, retired Chief Warrant Officer JOHN A. WALKER, JR.

Arthur Walker enlisted in the Navy in 1953 and became a sonarman first class on submarines. He was commissioned an ensign and remained in the submarine force. In 1968 he began teaching anti-submarine warfare at the Atlantic Fleet Tactical School in Norfolk, Va., remaining there until his retirement in 1973 as a lieutenant commander.

He then set up a business installing or upgrading car radios. After the business failed, Arthur went to work for the VSE Co., a military contracting concern that provided engineering services to the Navy. John recruited Arthur as a spy, and in Sept. 1980, Arthur began giving John classified material that he handled at VSE.

After arresting John Walker on May 20, 1985, the FBI linked his brother to spying. While Arthur was being interviewed by the FBI, he waived his right to remain silent and gave a confession.

According to the charges, Arthur had given his younger brother "documents, files, photographs, booklets, and defense plans relating to U.S. naval forces," knowing that John was passing them on to the Soviet Union. Other documents included a report on equipment failures aboard Navy amphibious ships and a damage-control manual from the command ship *Blue Ridge*.

During his trial in Norfolk his wife, Rita, testified that after John was arrested, Arthur, in a confessional mood, had told her that in the late 1960s and early 1970s he had had an affair with John's wife, Barbara. At the trial the government prosecutor said that Arthur might have been spying for Walker while he was on active duty, but this accusation was not developed further.

Arthur's defense rested without calling any witnesses. He was convicted and sentenced to three life terms and fined $250,000.

Walker, Chief Warrant Officer John A., Jr.

(b. 1937)

Retired Navy warrant officer arrested in 1985 on espionage charges that he operated a spy ring that included his son, MICHAEL WALKER, and brother, Lt. Comdr. ARTHUR J. WALKER as well as Senior Chief Radioman JERRY A. WHITWORTH, all of whom had served in the U.S.

John A. Walker, at the time of his arrest in 1985—wearing his toupee.
(FEDERAL BUREAU OF INVESTIGATION)

Navy. The Walker case was probably the largest and most damaging spy episode in the history of the U.S. Navy.

Walker, who held a "top secret-cryptographic" clearance, was a WALK-IN at the Soviet Embassy in Washington, D.C., probably in 1967 while he was assigned to the Submarine Training Center in Charleston, S.C., where he bought a bar and restaurant. (This is the contention of his wife, Barbara, who later reported his espionage to the FBI. Walker told the FBI that he had begun spying earlier while he was watch officer and message center officer on the staff of Submarine Force, Atlantic Fleet in Norfolk, Va.)

Walker enlisted in the Navy in 1955 and became a communications specialist. His assignments included duty in two nuclear-propelled strategic missile submarines from 1962 to 1966. After his assignments in Charleston and Norfolk, he became assistant director of the radioman's school at the Naval Training Center in San Diego. It was there that he met Whitworth, a senior chief radioman who held the same cryptographic clearances as Walker.

Walker retired from the Navy, but not from spying, in 1976. Whitworth and later Walker's son, Michael, and brother, Arthur, supplied him with classified documents. After leaving the Navy he operated two commercial firms in Norfolk—a general detective agency called Confidential Reports, Inc. and a firm for detecting BUGS, Electronic Counter-Spy, Inc.

Walker met with Soviet agents in VIENNA, Hong Kong, and the Philippines as well as in the United States. He is believed to have been awarded a high rank in the Soviet armed forces.

John Walker's daughter, Laura Walker Snyder, was in the Army when he attempted to involve her in the spy ring

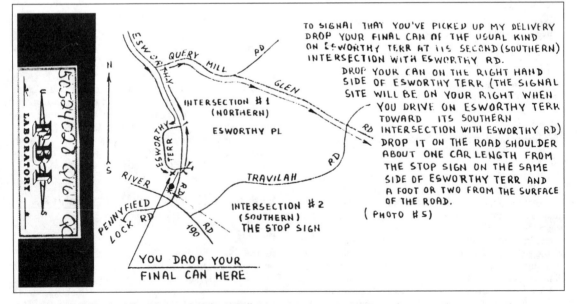

Directions prepared by the KGB with a map for John A. Walker. (FEDERAL BUREAU OF INVESTIGATION)

too, but without success. Laura recalled that her father urged her to abort her pregnancy so that she could stay in the Army and become a spy. "He told me I was stupid for quitting [the Army], that I had no hope for the future, that I would never amount to anything. I was an idiot."

Walker took a peculiar pride in his espionage work. "No member of the organization or prospective members has any of the classic problems that plague so many in this business," he once wrote to the Soviets in his best executive manner. "We have no drug problems, alcoholic problems, homosexuality. All are psychologically well-adjusted and mature. And the organization could launder funds."

The FBI was informed of John Walker's spying activities in Nov. 1984 by Walker's former wife, Barbara, urged on by Laura. Barbara had been aware of his spying for some time and had accompanied him when he serviced DEAD DROPS to leave classified material and pick up his payments. After years of estrangement and drunken arguments, they had divorced in 1976. She had twice informed the FBI of his spying, but the first time her drunken ramblings had been ignored.

The FBI watched John Walker from late 1984 and arrested him on May 20, 1985, after he left 129 classified documents (stolen by his son on the aircraft carrier *Nimitz*) at a dead drop in Poolsville, Md. Soviet Vice Consul ALEKSEY TKACHENKO, who was sighted near the drop site, left the United States on May 23.

On the eve of his trial, in Oct. 1985, John Walker and his son, Michael, agreed to plead guilty to espionage and to assist the government in the case against Jerry Whitworth. Walker was sentenced to life imprisonment and his son to 25 years in prison.

John Walker repeatedly failed POLYGRAPH tests administered by government interrogators during debriefing sessions. The questioners were particularly dissatisfied with his answers about the origin and dimensions of his spy ring.

By the time Walker was arrested for espionage in 1985, U.S. intelligence officials estimated that the Soviet Union had received and decoded more than 1 million messages through the CRYPTOMATERIAL that Walker had supplied. "The Soviets gained access to weapons and sensor data and naval tactics, terrorist threats and surface, submarine and airborne training, readiness, and tactics," said Secretary of Defense Caspar W. Weinberger in assessing the Walker-Whitworth damage. "We now have clear signals of dramatic Soviet gains in all areas of naval warfare, which must now be interpreted in the light of the Walker conspiracy."

John Walker's nickname, derived from his initials, was "Jaws."

Walker, Yeoman 3rd Class Michael

(b. 1962)

U.S. Navy sailor recruited by his father, JOHN A. WALKER, to spy for the Soviet Union.

Michael remembered his first acquaintance with family espionage in an incident with his drunken mother. "[She] came up to my room—it was about midnight—dragged me downstairs into the living room, started screaming and yelling at me"; in the midst of that diatribe, she shouted, "Your father is a spy!" Michael, then about 13 years old, told her he did not believe her.

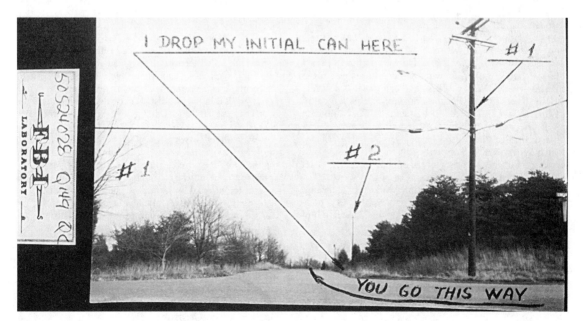

Directions prepared by the KGB on a photograph of a drop location for John A. Walker. (FEDERAL BUREAU OF INVESTIGATION)

Sometime later, when he was in high school, he and his father would often go to a neighborhood bar together. Michael could see that his father was wealthy. He owned a couple of boats, an airplane, and was a lavish spender, especially around young women. After a few drinks, John Walker would say that some day he would tell Mike about how he made his money. Michael had suspicions, but, he claimed later, he did not then know that his father was a spy.

At the urging of his father, who wanted Michael to become a spy, Michael joined the Navy in Dec. 1982. His first assignment after boot camp was as a yeoman striker—a plain seaman striking for advancement in a specialty—aboard the aircraft carrier *America*. When he came back from his maiden cruise in July 1983, he took leave and went ashore to visit his father, with whom he had been living when he enlisted. They went to his father's den one night, and Michael began talking about his job on the *America*.

"At first I made reference that I was handling classified information. I was giving my Dad a rundown of the job I had, and he was interested," Michael later recalled. "Then, a few weeks later, he approached me and said, 'Well, I can pay you if you deliver classified information to me from your work space. . . . You want to make the money, there's a lot of it out there to be made.' " He told Michael that he could make "anywhere from a thousand dollars a week to five thousand dollars a month."

In Oct. 1983 Michael, by then engaged to be married, was living on the naval air station in Virginia Beach, Va. One night as he went on liberty, he stuck a classified document under his uniform shirt and took his first stolen secret to his father. "Well, he was pleased," Michael recalled. "He was happy that I actually had the guts to do it. He didn't say a whole lot. He thumbed through the document, and he said this was good, and that's about it." Later, they went up to John Walker's second-floor workroom, where Walker showed his son how to use a Minox camera. They also talked about the fact that Michael's mother knew his father was a spy. Walker told his son: "She is a problem and can put us away."

In Dec. 1983 Michael married Rachel Allen, a cashier at a bar his father frequented. The following month he was transferred to the carrier *Nimitz*. He reported first to the ship's special services department, which supervised recreational activities aboard ship and arranged for liberty trips ashore. In Sept. 1984, Michael was assigned to the operations office of the *Nimitz*.

When FBI agents arrested John Walker in Maryland on May 20, 1985, he had just left at a DEAD DROP a plastic garbage bag full of classified documents passed to him by Michael.

Michael's spying was uncovered during the FBI investigation of John Walker prior to his arrest. The FBI advised Navy authorities in extreme secrecy, fearing that Michael might have shipmates who were also spying.

On May 20 Michael Walker was placed under guard on board the *Nimitz* and questioned by NAVY CRIMINAL INVESTIGATION SERVICE agents while the carrier was at anchor in Haifa, Israel. The agents found 15 pounds of classified material hidden on the ship by Michael. He confessed to spying. Taken off the ship, he was flown to Andrews Air Force Base outside of Washington, where FBI agents arrested him.

Under a 1985 plea bargain that John Walker arranged, in exchange for John Walker's cooperation with federal authorities, Michael was given a 25-year sentence.

In Feb. 2000 Michael Walker was released and placed on probation for the rest of his sentence.

Walking the Cat

U.S. intelligence term for going back to the beginning of an operation or the performance of an AGENT and continuing forward to the present time. This procedure is used when an agent or operation is BLOWN, to determine whether something happened that led to the disaster.

Wallenberg, Raoul

(b. 1910 d. 1947?)

Swedish diplomat credited with saving some 20,000 Hungarian Jews by his bold and courageous work in Nazi-held areas. He was also a spy for the U.S. OFFICE OF STRATEGIC SERVICES (OSS).

A member of a prominent Swedish family, Wallenberg earned a degree in architecture from the University of Michigan. In July 1944, he went to Budapest under the auspices of the International Red Cross on a mission to save the Jews being sent to the death camp at Auschwitz. Appointed an official of the Swedish legation in Budapest, he rescued Jews on their way to the extermination camp, gave them protective papers, rented buildings, and housed thousands of Jews.

When Germans once tried to seize Jews from Wallenberg's protected area, he rushed outside and shouted, "This is Swedish territory. . . . If you want to take them, you will have to shoot me first." He plucked Jews out of death marches and removed them from ghettos, saving about 20,000 in his Swedish "territory" and aiding in the protection of 70,000 confined Jews who survived until liberation.

Wallenberg was supported by advice and funds from the U.S. War Refugees Board. But he was also working for the OSS. Reportedly, President Roosevelt personally approved Wallenberg's humanitarian mission and his spying activities. The latter was periodically suspected after his disappearance, but documents released by the CIA are more positive. CIA historian Kevin Ruffner has stated that on the basis of these documents "it is a reasonable conclusion that Raoul Wallenberg was of benefit to American intelligence."

At Washington's behest, Wallenberg was assigned to the Swedish legation in Budapest. It was, according to *U.S. News & World Report,* an effort to counter U.S. pressure for Sweden—neutral in the war—to stop shipping iron ore to Germany.

On Jan. 16, 1945, during fierce fighting for Bu-

The United States issued a postage stamp in 1997 honoring Swedish diplomat Raoul Wallenberg, who saved the lives of thousands of Hungarian Jews during World War II. Not mentioned in the publicity surrounding the stamp was the fact that Wallenberg also worked for the U.S. Office of Strategic Services.

dapest, Soviet troops liberated Wallenberg's facilities and the area around it. But Soviet officials apparently believed that Wallenberg was an American spy—and how they would have such information is a matter of some conjecture. The Soviets would not aid him in getting the Jews to freedom. On Jan. 17, he went with a Soviet officer and his driver to Soviet military headquarters at Debrecen, about 120 miles east of Budapest. He was not seen again and was assumed to have been arrested.

Postwar efforts to trace him led to reports of his being seen in various Soviet prisons. In 1957 the Soviet government, in response to international interest in Wallenberg, said that he had died in Moscow's LUBYANKA prison on July 17, 1947, of "a heart attack." But he was reportedly seen after that date within the Soviet prison system, notably at the Vladimir prison some 120 miles northeast of Moscow. Among those who saw him were German prisoners of war who were subsequently repatriated.

The Soviets said his arrest and imprisonment were a "tragic mistake." In Oct. 1989, Soviet authorities gave Wallenberg's family some of his personal belongings—passport, money, calendar book, and a permit to carry a pistol—but no personal papers.

In 1997 the U.S. Postal Service issued a POSTAL STAMP honoring Wallenberg with the single word *humanitarian*. After NATHAN HALE, Wallenberg is only the second known spy to be honored by a U.S. stamp.

Wallis, Dr. John

(b. 1616 d. 1703)

English clergyman, mathematician, and Oxford University professor who served as a cryptographer for JOHN THURLOE during the regime of Oliver Cromwell (1649–1658). Wallis directed the highly efficient deciphering organization of the English SECRET SERVICE under Thurloe. The system was used to seek out secret messages in vast amounts of correspondence from Royalists

and their sympathizers intercepted by the government (Thurloe was postmaster general).

When Charles II came to the throne in 1660, he sought out Wallis to continue his cryptologic efforts. Wallis eventually became chaplain to the king. When William III (William of Orange) came to the throne in 1689, he asked Wallis to train a young man as a successor, so impressed was the monarch with Wallis's skills. When Wallace died, his grandson, 20-year-old William Blencowe, carried on his efforts. Blencowe was the first English cryptographer to be given the title "Decypherer" and to receive a regular stipend for his services. (He committed suicide in 1712.)

Wallis was considered by many scholars as the most influential English mathematician before Sir Isaac Newton. He was the author of *Essay on the Art of Decyphering* in addition to several works on mathematics.

Walsingham, Sir Francis

(b. circa 1532 d. 1590)

The architect of an extensive intelligence organization in Elizabethan England aimed mainly against Catholics. He was Secretary of State and adviser to Queen Elizabeth I from 1573 until his death.

Walsingham, a fervent Protestant, was educated at King's College, Cambridge. He initially became involved in intelligence while secretary to the English ambassador to France. When Elizabeth became queen he returned to England. After coming to her attention he was appointed ambassador to France in 1570; he returned to England in 1573 to become Principal Secretary and a member of the Privy Council, and established the secret service in London in 1573.

Walsingham, whose motto was "Knowledge is never too dear," began developing an extensive, highly competent foreign intelligence organization. His efforts marked the first national and comprehensive English intelligence organization. He also established an elaborate CIPHER operation, as a result of his own fascination with CODES.

His AGENTS operated in France, Germany, Italy, the Low Countries, Spain, and Turkey, with some being ensconced in foreign courts. This spy network was financed mostly from Walsingham's private fortune. Many of his people were recruited from Cambridge and Oxford universities.

Walsingham's numerous intelligence successes included deriving intimate knowledge of the Spanish plans for the Armada being sent against England. His interception of letters from Mary Stuart (Queen of Scots) to conspirators led to her trial and execution in 1587, which Walsingham enthusiastically endorsed.

His ardent Protestantism led to frequent disagreements with the queen over her failure to enthusiastically promote the Protestant cause. Queen Elizabeth affectionately referred to Walsingham as "my Moor" because of his dark complexion and good looks. But she rewarded him poorly despite his loyal service and successes. He died in poverty and debt.

Walsingham's daughter Lady Sidney was involved in his espionage operations.

Also see CHRISTOPHER MARLOWE.

Walton [p]

U.S. Army and Air Force enlisted man who provided information to the GRU while stationed in West Germany. "Walton," as he is known in U.S. Air Force intelligence records, served in the U.S. Army from 1961 to 1964 and enlisted in the U.S. Air Force several months later.

He was separated from the Air Force in 1972 at his own request, charging that he had been discriminated against because he was black. He was driving a taxi in Houston, Texas, when he was interviewed by the Air Force OFFICE OF SPECIAL INVESTIGATIONS in the 1970s. He was granted immunity from prosecution (and the protection of a pseudonym in the records) in return for giving a full account of his espionage activities.

Warning Notice Intelligence Sources or Methods

(WNINTL)

Former U.S. security category warning that a document contained information on intelligence sources or methods. The Cold War–era category was eliminated in late 1995 as the marking added little to security.

Warren, Kelly Therese

Former U.S. soldier convicted of passing sensitive information to Hungarian and Czechoslovakian AGENTS while a member of the CLYDE LEE CONRAD spy ring.

Warren was 31 at the time of her indictment in 1997. She had been a clerk in the headquarters of the 8th Infantry Division in Bad Kreuznach, Germany, from 1986 to 1988, handling war plans. She was the fifth member of the ring to be arrested and convicted for conspiring to commit espionage in a joint FBI–Army Intelligence investigation that lasted for more than 10 years. In Feb. 1999 she was sentenced to 25 years in prison.

When she was arrested in 1997 in Georgia, U.S. officials said she had been recruited by RODERICK JAMES RAMSAY. She earned $7,000, which she said she needed for paying off debts. Federal agents had suspected her involvement for almost 10 years.

Washington, Gen. George

(b. 1732 d. 1799)

Commander—and spymaster—of continental troops in the American Revolution.

Washington had a considerable interest in and aptitude for intelligence activities. "Washington was in fact the most important intelligence officer of the American Revolution, the chief American spy master. He recruited spies, instructed them in their treacherous craft, sent

them out, welcomed them back, and paid them off," wrote former CIA officer G. J. A. O'Toole in his comprehensive history *Honorable Treachery* (1991).

Washington had limited formal military or academic education. He gained much of his knowledge of RECONNAISSANCE and military operations as a surveyor and as a colonial officer serving with the British Army during the French and Indian War. His first military venture came on July 3, 1754, in the Allegheny Mountains, when his outnumbered troops, fighting in a heavy rain, lost a battle against a French force at a rudimentary fortification he called Fort Necessity. This defeat did not deter Washington, and he continued to serve the British and, between military duties, manage his estate at Mount Vernon, near Alexandria, Va.

When the colonies decided to fight for independence, Washington was offered command of all continental troops, which he accepted on July 3, 1775. He held that command through successes and defeats until the final British withdrawal from the colonies in early 1783.

His first known venture as a spymaster came on July 15, 1775, when he recorded the payment of $333\frac{1}{3}$ to an unidentified person "to go into the town of Boston; to establish a secret correspondence for the purpose of conveying intelligence of the Enemys movements and designs." Washington employed more spies during the course of the conflict, and he encouraged an awareness of the importance of intelligence in his subordinates: "As everything, in a manner, depends upon obtaining intelligence of the enemy's motions, I do most certainly entreat you and General [Henry] Clinton to exert yourselves to accomplish this most desirable end," he wrote to Gen. William Heath on Sept. 5, 1776.

By 1777 Washington had established an intelligence service, initiating direct correspondence with the patriotic Committees of Safety in each of the colonies and bringing more structure to his use of spies. This led to a series of spy networks in those areas occupied by British troops. And when the British entered a new area, "stay-behind" spies would wait to report their every movement to Washington.

In the summer of 1778 he ordered Maj. BENJAMIN TALLMADGE to establish a spy network in New York. Known as the CULPER RING, this network was one of the most successful of Washington's intelligence operations. While Tallmadge was the CASE OFFICER for the spy ring, Washington was directly involved in the operation. In a code used by the ring, he was Agent 711. The full text of the code was published in *George Washington, Spymaster* (2004). Later, when his forces were about to enter New York City, Washington directed Tallmadge to go into the city before the Continental Army to protect his agents from possible retaliation by the withdrawing British.

Washington also displayed astuteness in COUNTERESPIONAGE activities. When one of his officers sought to arrest a suspected British spy, Washington told the officer to befriend the man and invite him to dinner. Then, Washington proposed, he should give the British agent an opportunity to steal a document that would provide inflated figures of the strength of his army. Periodically Washington would use DECEPTION to mislead British commanders—such as keeping up camp fires and having sentries patrol an area long after his troops had departed.

Two future American leaders, John Jay (who would become the first Chief Justice) and Alexander Hamilton (the first Secretary of the Treasury) also were involved directly in Washington's intelligence activities. And in France, BENJAMIN FRANKLIN ran intelligence and counter-intelligence activities, along with COVERT OPERATIONS. Success in intelligence activities certainly contributed to the colonial victory over the British. With victory, Washington bade farewell to his troops in 1783, and with less fanfare—paid off his spies.

Washington served as first President of the United States from 1789 to 1797, turning down offers of a third term. When war with France threatened, on July 3, 1798, Washington accepted a commission as lieutenant general and Commander-in-Chief of the Army, a commission that he retained until his death.

Records survive to testify to Washington's astuteness in intelligence activities. And novelist JAMES FENIMORE COOPER wrote a most successful historical novel, *The Spy: A Tale of the Neutral Ground* (1821), based on the activities of one of Washington's spies.

Watchers

British Security Service (MI5) term for observers who follow Soviet-Russian diplomats and other embassy staff members around London and in other parts of Britain.

Watch List

Compilation of names of persons considered of interest to an intelligence service; with high-speed computers, words like "terrorist" and "nuclear weapon" could be included in watch lists.

Operation SHAMROCK by U.S. COMMUNICATIONS INTELLIGENCE agencies involved a massive watch list of Americans as well as foreign individuals and organizations.

Watergate

Apartment-hotel complex in northwest Washington, D.C. It was the location of Democratic National Committee headquarters, broken into by the Nixon administration's PLUMBERS (Special Investigation Unit) on the night of June 17, 1972, to plant bugging devices and photograph documents. The Watergate break-in led to the eventual exposure of President Nixon's illegal activities and his resignation.

The five Watergate burglars, all arrested and convicted, were James W. McCord Jr. (security coordinator for the Committee to Re-elect the President, former FBI agent, and former employee of the Office of Security of the CIA); Bernard L. Barker (realtor and former CIA employee, who had been involved in the 1962 Bay of Pigs invasion); Frank A. Sturgis (a soldier of fortune with CIA connections); Eugenio R. Martinez (part-time CIA informant); and Virgilio R. Gonzalez (locksmith).

The burglary was discovered by a security guard, who called the Washington police. The police investigation led to the implication of two other men: E. HOWARD HUNT and G. Gordon Liddy, who were also in the Plumbers. Hunt, a former CIA officer, had worked with Barker in CIA operations.

Although the CIA had no official knowledge of the break-in, the connections with the principals raised suspicions that this was a "rogue" operation set up with PLAUSIBLE DENIAL. None of the burglars was then working for the CIA, but McCord had retired from the agency in 1970 and Martinez, a CIA contract employee, was on the CIA payroll. Hunt had received technical help from the CIA when he broke into the office of Daniel Ellsberg's former psychiatrist after publication of the PENTAGON PAPERS, which Ellsberg had made public.

The men made no statements that linked them to the White House. When they felt they had been abandoned, McCord wrote a letter to the judge claiming that a White House cover-up was cloaking the real authority for the burglary. This launched the scandal that became known as Watergate.

Also see L. PATRICK GRAY, RICHARD M. HELMS.

Weather

CODE NAME for the TOP SECRET communications system of U.S. Navy TASK FORCE 157. It was used by Henry Kissinger, President Nixon's national security adviser, for arranging his secret trip to China in 1971. Kissinger, fearing leaks, wanted to bypass the White House and State Department communications systems.

Weather used an outdated NSA machine system to encrypt messages before they were handed off to the existing U.S. Navy communications system, where the encrypted messages were reencrypted. Thus, only TF 157 personnel at the transmitting and receiving end could read the doubly encrypted messages.

A TF 157 COURIER picked up Kissinger's message at the White House. Then a TF 157 officer encrypted it and had it transmitted to a TF 157 office at the U.S. Navy facility at Yokosuka, Japan, near Tokyo. The unit commander decrypted it and personally took it to the Chinese Trade Mission in Tokyo.

Kissinger also used the TF 157 system to communicate with U.S. delegates at a four-power conference on BERLIN.

Weber, Ruth

SEE URSULA KUCZYNSKI

Webster, Timothy

(b. 1822 d. 1862)

AGENT of ALLAN PINKERTON who spied for the Union during the Civil War and helped to thwart an attempt to assassinate president-elect Abraham Lincoln.

Born in Newhaven, England, Webster immigrated with his parents to the United States in 1830. After a stint as a New York City police officer, he went to work for Pinkerton. Before Lincoln's inauguration, Webster infiltrated a Maryland group of southern sympathizers planning to assassinate the president-elect and exposed the plot. He became so accepted in Maryland as a Confederate that another Pinkerton man arrested him as a spy—but when he learned of Webster's identity, arranged for his "escape."

In Richmond, capital of the Confederacy, Webster was hired as an AGENT by Confederate Secretary of War Judah Benjamin. Ordered to carry message to Confederate agents working in the North, he did so, after showing the messages first to his Union HANDLERS. His information led to the arrest of a Confederate spy working for the Union Army.

Webster, betrayed by two other Pinkerton agents who traded their information for their lives, was hanged in Richmond by the Confederates as a spy on April 29, 1862. He was the first American to meet such a fate since the British hanged NATHAN HALE in 1776.

In 1871 Pinkerton arranged for Webster's body to be transferred from Richmond to Northern soil, for burial in Onarga, Ill. There, too, was buried Webster's son, Timothy, Jr., who had been in the Union Army and died in a Confederate prison.

Webster, William H.

(b. 1924)

The only man to serve as both the Director of the FBI (from 1978 to 1987) and DIRECTOR OF CENTRAL INTELLIGENCE (DCI) (from 1987 to 1991). He resigned over the criticisms from members of the administration of President GEORGE H. W. BUSH and members of Congress at the intelligence failures during the U.S. invasion of Panama in 1989 and the CIA's failure to predict the Iraqi invasion of Kuwait in 1990.

Webster received his bachelor's degree from Amherst College and his law degree from Washington University Law School (St. Louis) in 1949. After practicing law in St. Louis, in 1960 he was named U.S. attorney for the Eastern District of Missouri. President Nixon appointed him to a federal judgeship in 1971.

Webster was not seeking the position when President Carter appointed him to head the FBI, a 10-year appointment. He saw his role as rebuilding the image of the FBI after the WATERGATE scandal and the autocratic policies of J. EDGAR HOOVER, who had died in office in 1972.

As director of the FBI, Webster suggested that the United States could help curb the espionage war with the Soviet Union by reducing the number of documents being classified; at the same time he proposed reducing the number of U.S. personnel with TOP SECRET clearances to help prevent espionage incidents. "People driving around with secret material stashed in their trunk, that leave them around their house or leave them on their desks at night, have an ambivalence . . . that preconditions them to be receptive to a money offer [from foreign INTELLIGENCE OFFICERS] when they need it," he said.

Webster also directed a more aggressive policy against spying. As he told a public gathering in Washington, D.C., "We had three convictions [for espionage] in 1984, which is a lot more than the previous year. And we've had over nine convictions this year [1985] so far. At the same time there were eight arrests in fiscal 1984, and there have been 14 so far this year on espionage charges."

Following the death of WILLIAM J. CASEY, Webster became DCI in May 1987 and vowed to restore the reputation of the CIA, which had been discredited by the IRAN-CONTRA AFFAIR. Before the end of the year he dismissed two CIA employees involved in Iran-Contra, demoted one, and issued letters of reprimand to four others.

Soon after he took over the CIA, Webster told a congressional committee that he had reorganized the agency to improve COUNTERINTELLIGENCE and to strengthen security at U.S. embassies around the world. (The CIA, however, would fail for six more years to detect ALDRICH AMES, who was spying for the Soviet Union, and would become a member of the CIA COUNTERINTELLIGENCE staff.)

Webster resigned as DCI on May 8, 1991, but at President Bush's request remained in office until Aug. 31, 1991.

Weichu, Zang

SEE HOU DESHENG

Weisband, William

(b. 1908 d. 1967)

U.S. ARMY SECURITY AGENCY linguist who, as an AGENT for Soviet intelligence, revealed VENONA, the secret U.S. program to intercept and decipher Soviet cables. His revelations, coupled to those of British spy HAROLD (KIM) PHILBY, put the Soviets on warning.

Weisband, born in Odessa (but claiming birth in Egypt to confuse potential COUNTERINTELLIGENCE probes), immigrated to the United States in the 1920s and became an American citizen in 1938. In 1942 he joined the U.S. Army Signals Security (as it was then known) and worked on SIGNALS INTELLIGENCE and communications security in North Africa and Italy. He later returned to ARLINGTON HALL and joined its Russian Section as a "linguist adviser" who spoke fluent Russian.

MEREDITH GARDNER, key Venona codebreaker, later recalled that Weisband "had watched him extract the list of Western atomic scientists" from a set of messages, according to an NSA report on Venona. A member of the American Communist Party, Weisband had been recruited by the Soviets in 1934 as part of a highly effective effort that essentially made the American Communist Party an auxiliary of Soviet espionage agencies. (See CPUSA.)

Counterintelligence officials believe that Weisband had been supplying the Soviets with codebreaking information from 1945, when he joined the Russian Section of the agency, until he was permanently "suspended" in 1950. He was never arrested for espionage.

According to the NSA report on Venona, Weisband's name surfaced in the spring of 1950, when the Korean War intensified efforts by U.S. intelligence agencies to learn more about Soviet spying. But by then the Soviets knew the United States was reading the old cables—and now the United States knew the Soviets knew.

As related by the NSA, CODE NAME Nick had been identified as Amadeo Sabatini, who had fought in Spain together with Soviet spy MORRIS COHEN. Grudgingly, it appears, Sabatini provided the FBI with enough information to unmask Jones Orin York (code name Needle), who, when questioned in April 1950, said that Weisband had been his HANDLER and had helped him buy a camera for photographing documents.

Weisband was "suspended" from his job "on suspicion of disloyalty" and later called before a federal grand jury investigating communist activity. He refused to appear and as a result, Weisband was convicted of contempt in Nov. 1950 and sentenced to one year in prison. He lived quietly in Virginia until he died of a heart attack in 1967.

NSA analysts believe that Weisband's earliest reports on codebreaking efforts "were probably sketchy and might not have provided clear warning to Moscow about the PENETRATION of the espionage messages. By 1947, Weisband "could have reported" that the "messages were being read.... Where Weisband had sketched the outlines of the cryptanalytic success, British liaison officer Kim Philby received actual translations and analyses on a regular basis after he arrived for duty in Washington in autumn 1949." This helped the Soviets "protect some of its agents and operations. Various accounts indicate that in October 1949 Moscow began advising American agents . . . to flee the country through Mexico."

Weisband's name did not appear in the NSA's original release of Venona transcripts because there was no definite reference to his name. But officials poring over the many Venona CRYPTONYMS found three messages mentioning *Zveno*, the Russian word for "link." By comparing dates associated with *Zveno* in the messages to Weisband's personnel records, officials were able to identifty Weisband as *Zveno*. His name became public through other sources and his significant involvement in the Venona saga was not confirmed by NSA until 2000.

Welch, Richard S.

(b. 1929 d. 1975)

CIA official in Athens, murdered on Dec. 23, 1975, after PHILIP AGEE, a former CIA AGENT, exposed Welch and called for CIA officials to be "neutralized." A career CIA operative, Welch became station chief in the Greek capital under the COVER of a State Department special assistant to the ambassador. However, his real position was fairly well known in Athens.

In 1975 Agee wrote in the anti-CIA magazine *Counter-Spy* that CIA agents should be identified and "neutralized." Another article in the same issue identified Welch as CIA station chief in Athens. Based on the *Counter-Spy* article, the *Athens News* in Nov. 1975 also identified Welch and gave his home address.

On Dec. 23 he was shot to death outside his home by three gunmen claiming to be part of a left-wing group called the Revolutionary Organization of November 17th. Welch's body was returned to the United States for burial in Arlington National Cemetery, in formal ceremonies attended by President Ford and a host of senior officials, including the DIRECTOR OF CENTRAL INTELLIGENCE, WILLIAM E. COLBY. A spokesman for *Counter-Spy* magazine quickly declared that "If anyone is to blame for Mr. Welch's death, it is the CIA. We don't want to see anyone shot."

Wennerstrom, Col. Stig

(b. 1906 d. ?)

Swedish Air Force officer who was a Soviet spy.

Wennerstrom entered the Swedish Navy in 1929 and applied for flight training the following year. After attending flying school, he learned Russian and was trained in intelligence. Promoted to captain in 1939, he was sent to Moscow that same year as the air ATTACHÉ in the Swedish Embassy. He subsequently became a defense staff air intelligence officer.

He was promoted to major in 1945 but was dissatisfied with his rate of promotion and what he perceived as a lack of appreciation of his work. After he had returned to Moscow in 1948 as a colonel, Wennerstrom's lamentations caught the attention of Soviet spy recruiters, who began a campaign to get him to work as an AGENT. Flattered and entertained at parties, Wennerstrom was told that he could win clandestine promotion in the GRU, the Soviet MILITARY INTELLIGENCE agency. He began spying in 1948, continuing as he moved through assignments in Sweden and for the NORTH ATLANTIC TREATY ORGANIZATION. He was an attaché in Washington, D.C., in 1952–1957.

In 1959, the U.S. ambassador in Bern, Switzerland, received a letter addressed to the director of the FBI. The letter was opened by the CIA head of station. The letter, signed "Sniper," said that someone in Poland was offering to spy for the United States. Sniper, offering some information, said that a Swedish Air Force officer who had served as an air attaché was a spy. The trail quickly led to Wennerstrom.

When Wennerstrom's espionage was revealed he was a senior official in the Swedish Ministry of Defense. Placed under SURVEILLANCE, he was seen contacting Soviets in Stockholm. He was then transferred to an innocuous post while the Swedish Security Police tapped his phone and built a case against him. The investigation led to his arrest on June 20, 1963, and the expulsion of two Soviet CASE OFFICERS. After confessing to 14 years of spying, he attempted suicide. He was tried and sentenced to hard labor for life.

His Soviet CODE NAME was "Eagle."

Wesson [p]

U.S. Air Force enlisted man who spied for the Soviets. "Wesson," born in England, served in the Air Force from 1957 to 1963, first as an aircraft radio operator and then as a weapons systems operator. An investigation into espionage activities in the Air Force led to his being interrogated. Investigators were convinced that he was a spy. Records about him use the pseudonym "Wesson." The disposition of his case is not publicly known.

West, Nigel [p]

(b. 1952)

Pseudonym of Rupert Allason, the leading writer of the Cold War era on the subject of British intelligence. His books are scrupulously researched and incorporate what he has called "guidance" by INTELLIGENCE OFFICERS.

He had been a member of the Metropolitan Police in London and became interested in intelligence when he researched a book on the subject. With Donald McCormick, he researched and co-authored a BBC documentary series, *Spy*, in 1980.

His books include *MI5: British Security Service Operations 1909–1945* (1981); *A Matter of Trust: MI5 1945–1972* (1982); *MI6: British Secret Intelligence Service Operations 1909–1945* (1983); *The Branch: A History of the Metropolitan Police Special Branch 1883–1983* (1983); *Unreliable Witness: Espionage Myths of the Second World War* (1984), published in the United States as *A Thread of Deceit: Espionage Myths of World War II*; *GCHQ: The Secret Wireless War 1900–86* (1986), published in the United States as *The SIGINT Secrets* (1988); *Mole Hunt: Searching for Soviet Spies in MI5* (1987); *Crown Jewels* (with Oleg Tsarev, 1998), and *VENONA: The Greatest Secret of the Cold War* (1999).

The manuscript for *A Matter of Trust* was stolen by a senior Security Service (MI5) officer in an attempt to stop its publication. At the time, another copy of the manuscript was carried to New York City for publication of the American edition of the book, entitled *The Circus: MI5 Operations 1945–1972* (1982). On Oct. 12, 1982, the British government asked for a court injunction to prevent publication because "the conduct of [intelligence] investigations and operations may be prejudiced and put at risk." The court granted the injunction and issued an order to the publisher. This was the first that the publisher or West knew of the injunction.

In the American edition of the book West said that after some discussions with intelligence officials "certain names would be deleted" because these were officers "who had all undertaken dangerous missions abroad and whose identification might compromise them." After these deletions were made, the book was published.

His book *The Secret War for the Falklands* (1997) revealed behind-the-scenes British intelligence activities and the SPECIAL OPERATIONS FORCES operations planned against Argentine airfields.

In *The Blue List* (1989), his first work of fiction, he weaves a tale that HAROLD (KIM) PHILBY was actually a DOUBLE AGENT working for Britain against the Soviet intelligence services. His novel *Cuban Bluff* (1991) fictionalized the CUBAN MISSILE CRISIS.

The son of a former Conservative Member of Parliament, he successfully ran for Parliament as a Conservative in 1987. After 10 years in Parliment representing Torbay, Allason was defeated in the Labour Party's landslide victory of May 1, 1997.

Westphal, Jürgen

High-ranking civilian employee of the West German Defense Ministry who was arrested on Dec. 11, 1986, on suspicion of spying for East Germany or possibly other communist countries. Westphal worked on a project to improve the efficiency of computer systems used by West Germany's military forces. He was apparently caught before he passed on information to his contacts, who had recruited him in Aug. 1986 in VIENNA.

Wet Affairs

Russian slang for intelligence operations involving a killing, "wet" being a reference to blood. Sometimes called "wet job."

U.S. intelligence analyst John J. Dziak, in *Chekisty: A History of the KGB* (1988), provides a list of Soviet state security organizations that carried out direct action or wet affairs:

Pre-1936	Foreign Department (INO) (CHEKA-GPU-OGPU)
1936–1941	Administration for Special Tasks (NKVD)
1941–1946	Fourth Directorate (Partisans)(NKGB)
1946–1953	Spets Byuro No. 1 (NKGB- MGB)
1953–1954	Ninth Section, First Chief Directorate (MVD)
1954–late 1960s	Department 13, First Chief Directorate (KGB)
late 1960s–early 1970s	Department V, First Chief Directorate (KGB)
early 1970s–1991	Department 8, Directorate S (Illegals), First Chief directorate (KGB)

Wet Squad

Slang for a Soviet-Russian group for carrying out murder or assassination operations.

Wet Work

Western slang for intelligence operations involving murder or assassination.

Whalen, Lt. Col. William H.

U.S. Army intelligence specialist arrested in 1966 for having spied for the Soviets for at least two years while he was in the Office of the Joint Chiefs of Staff. Whalen was charged with revealing "information pertaining to atomic weapons, missiles, military plans for the defense of Europe, information concerning the retaliation plans of the United States Strategic Air Command, and information pertaining to troop movements, documents, and writings relating to the national defense of the United States." Tried and convicted, he received a 15-year prison sentence.

Whalen is believed to have been unmasked by Maj. Gen. DIMITRI POLYAKOV, a Soviet GRU officer who spied for the United States for nearly 20 years.

White

(1) Slang for an unclassified or open (acknowledged) classified program; (2) someone who has not been identified as an intelligence operative.

White, Sir Dick (Goldsmith)

(b. 1906 d. 1993)

During a 32-year career in intelligence, White was the only person to serve as head of both the British Security Service (MI5) and the Secret Intelligence Service (MI6). He enjoyed a reputation as a thorough professional.

Educated at Bishop's Stortford College—where he held the record for running the mile—and Christ Church College, Oxford, he then attended the Universities of Michigan and California for two years, after which he briefly taught school. In 1936 he began his career in intelligence with MI5. His assignments included nine months in Germany before World War II. During the war he served in MILITARY INTELLIGENCE, rising to the rank of colonel. His assignments included being on the staff of Gen. Dwight D. Eisenhower, the Supreme Allied Commander in western Europe.

After the war he served in MI5, and was made head of B Division (COUNTERESPIONAGE) in 1946. He held that important position until he became Director-General in 1953. He was knighted in 1955.

Following the botched effort by MI6 to learn technical details about the Soviet cruiser *Ordzhonikidze*, at anchor in Portsmouth Harbor, using the aged diver LIONEL CRABB, White became Director-General of MI6. The move was made hastily, to chastise the intelligence service for having embarrassed the government by spying on the ship that brought Soviet leader Nikita Khrushchev to Britain.

White was the first non-career military or naval officer to head MI6. When he assumed his appointment he learned that the service had ignored his recommendations that HAROLD (KIM) PHILBY never be employed in intelligence work again. White, who had interrogated Philby in 1951, was certain he was a Soviet AGENT. Further, then-Prime Minister Harold Macmillan had several months earlier stated publicly that there was no evidence against Philby.

As more evidence became available, White sent Nicholas Elliott to Beirut to force a confession from Philby, who was working there as a journalist—thanks to MI6 recommendations. The operation was bungled, and Philby fled to the Soviet Union. Although stung by Philby's escape, White did believe that he had taken the proper approach in trying to bring Philby back to Britain.

Philby later proffered his opinion of White, as head of MI5's B Division, in *My Silent War* (1968):

> He was a nice and modest character, who would have been the first to admit that he lacked outstanding qualities. His most obvious fault was a tendency to agree with the last person he spoke to. With his usual good sense, he was content to delegate a lot of work to his subordinates, and to exercise his gifts for chairmanship with a view to keeping harmony in the division.... His capacity for avoiding departmental fights paid off in the outcome.

Still plagued by Soviet spies in the intelligence services, White was forced to support the FLUENCY COMMITTEE, set up to determine if ROGER HOLLIS, his successor as head of MI5, was a Soviet MOLE.

MI5 officer PETER WRIGHT described White in his *Spycatcher* (1987): "He was tall with lean, healthy features and a sharp eye. There was something of David Niven about him, the same perfect English manners, easy charm, and immaculate dress sense. Indeed, compared with his Board [of directors at MI5], he was positively raffish." Wright also offered a view of White's move from MI5 to MI6:

> The decision to appoint Dick White as Chief of MI6 was, I believe, one of the most important mistakes made in postwar British Intelligence history. There were few signs of it in the mid-1950s, but MI5, under his control, was taking the first faltering steps along the path of modernization. He knew the necessity for change, and yet had the reverence for tradition which would have enabled him to accomplish his objectives without disruption. He was, above all, a counterintelligence officer, almost certainly the greatest of the twentieth century, perfectly trained for the Director-General's chair. He knew the people, he knew the problems, and he had a vision of the sort of the effective counterespionage organization he wanted to create.

White retired from MI6 in 1968, becoming the intelligence and security officer for the Cabinet Office. He officially retired from that post in 1972, although he remained "on call" to the government.

White Cloud

U.S. Navy SATELLITE for ocean RECONNAISSANCE. The Navy–NATIONAL RECONNAISANCE OFFICE project called for groups of three of the FERRET satellites to be used to triangulate on hostile warships at sea employing ELECTRONIC INTELLIGENCE (ELINT) sensors.

The White Cloud system was not deployed. The Soviet Union did deploy an ELINT satellite system (see RADAR OCEAN RECONNAISSANCE SATELLITE).

White, Harry Dexter

(b. 1892 d. 1948)

U.S. Treasury Department official who was an AGENT for the Soviet Union.

His Soviet HANDLERS considered White an AGENT OF INFLUENCE, telling him, for example, to encourage American support for China, which could bring the United States into conflict with Japan. Such a conflict could remove the threat of Japan attacking the Soviet territory in the Far East.

White served in the U.S. Army in France during World War I. He did not begin serious academic studies until 1930, when he successively attended Columbia, Stanford, and Harvard Universities, earning a doctorate.

An influential Treasury Department policymaker during World War II, White was deeply involved in the creation of the International Monetary Fund (IMF) and the World Bank. VENONA decrypts of Soviet intelligence communications provided the FBI with information showing that during the 1945 conference in San Francisco on the founding of the UNITED NATIONS, White met with a Soviet INTELLIGENCE OFFICER and told him about U.S. negotiating positions on several issues.

An Assistant Secretary of the Treasury under Roosevelt, he stayed in government during the Truman administration, but in 1945 after two DEFECTORS—ELIZABETH BENTLEY and WHITTAKER CHAMBERS—named him as a Soviet AGENT, he became a political liability. Truman appointed him the U.S. executive director of the IMF. He resigned from the IMF in 1947. He died the following year of a heart attack.

His Soviet CODE NAMES, according to VENONA decrypts, were "Richard," "Lawyer," and "Reed."

Whitworth, Senior Chief Radioman Jerry

(b. 1939)

U.S. Navy communications specialist who provided classified information, including CRYPTOMATERIAL, to JOHN A. WALKER for transfer to the Soviet Union. During Whitworth's trial in March-April 1986 an FBI official stated that Whitworth's espionage damaged U.S. security even more than the atomic spying of Ethel and JULIUS ROSENBERG.

A graduate of Coalings Junior College, Whitworth served in the Navy from Sept. 1956 to Oct. 1983. He was a radio specialist, and during the later stages of his 26-year career Whitworth served in several highly sensitive positions; he worked with SATELLITE communications and various cryptographic systems on board several ships, including the aircraft carrier *Enterprise,* as well as at shore stations.

Although the FBI did not know it at the time, the first break in the Whitworth case came in May 1984 when a letter arrived at the FBI field office in San Francisco from someone who said he had been "involved in espionage for several years" and had "passed along top secret cryptographic keylists for military communications, tech manuals for same, intelligence messages, etc." The letter went on to say that he was part of a ring and that the FBI could contact him through an advertisement in *The Los Angeles Times* addressed to "RUS."

The RUS letters, as the FBI called them, continued, in reaction to the FBI advertisement. But finally RUS wrote in August to say, "I've done a lot of serious thinking and have pretty much come to the conclusion that it would be best to give up the idea of aiding in the termination of the espionage ring previously discussed."

When the FBI captured John Walker on May 20, agents found at the DEAD DROP a plastic garbage bag containing classified documents and three letters. One letter referred to "D," who apparently was a Walker spy who wanted to quit. Piecing together clues from that letter and others found in a search of Walker's home, the FBI decided that "D" resembled a former Navy radioman whose name, Jerry A. Whitworth, had turned up in the background investigation of Walker. A "Brenda" mentioned in one of Walker's letters had to be Brenda L. Reis, Whitworth's wife since 1976.

Two agents called on Whitworth in Davis, Calif. During the interview he left the room and could be seen pulling two sheets of paper from the printer next to his computer. When he allowed the agents to search his mobile home, one of them found what he had so ineptly hidden: the printout of a letter to Walker, written that day. The FBI did not immediately arrest Whitworth, although agents kept him under highly visible surveillance. He was allowed to surrender on his own on June 3. By then, the FBI was convinced that both "D" and RUS were Whitworth.

A grand jury indicted Whitworth for conspiring to commit espionage. He was also charged with the crime of espionage itself and with copying and taking a document in violation of another section of the Espionage Law of 1914. Five other counts concerned income tax law violations that essentially constituted failure to report his espionage earnings, which the government estimated to be at least $332,000. The counts were legally entwined, so that Whitworth had to be tried simultaneously for both spying and tax cheating.

John Walker, as part of his plea bargain to win clemency for his son, MICHAEL WALKER, was the key witness against Whitworth. Michael also testified against Whitworth, as did John Walker's ex-wife, Barbara Joy Crowley Walker, who turned Walker in; their daughter, Laura Walker Snyder, who said John Walker had tried to recruit her; and Lt. Comdr. ARTHUR WALKER, John Walker's brother.

Whitworth was sentenced to 365 years in prison and fined $410,000. Under a formula incorporated in the sentence, it would be 60 years before Whitworth could be paroled. The judge who sentenced him said he was "a man who represented the banality of evil . . . a zero at the bone. He believes in nothing. His life is devoted to determining the wind direction and how he can make a profit from the coming storm."

Wicher

(GALE)

Polish CODE NAME for the Poles' pioneer work in decrypting the German ENIGMA machine.

Wilderness of Mirrors

Expression to signify the confusion of the world of intelligence and espionage. JAMES JESUS ANGLETON, long-time head of COUNTERESPIONAGE for the CIA, is generally credited with coining the term, having written that the Wilderness of Mirrors "is that . . . myriad of stratagems, deceptions, artifices and all the other devices of disinformation which the Soviet bloc and its coordinated intelligence services use to confuse and split the West," thus producing "an ever-fluid landscape where fact and illusion merge. . . ."

The term was used by David C. Martin as the title for his book about Angleton—*Wilderness of Mirrors* (1980).

Wilkins, Bishop John

(b. 1614 d. 1672)

Bishop of Chester, England, who served as a cryptographer for JOHN THURLOE. He invented CIPHER systems and wrote a manual on the subject for Thudoe. His CODES were in wide use through the American Civil War.

Wilkins was a parliamentarian under Oliver Cromwell during the Commonwealth period following the execution of King Charles I in 1649, and he survived to serve King Charles II after the monarchy was restored in 1660.

Wilkins also produced many learned treatises on technical subjects. In his book *Mathematicall Magick*, he described the advantages of operating a "submerged vessel" on voyages through polar regions because of the safety of such a craft from the dangers of ice, cold, and severe weather conditions encountered by surface ships—undoubtedly the first person to write about submarine navigation in the Arctic.

Wilkinson, Maj. Gen. James

(b. 1757 d. 1825)

American Army officer who was an AGENT for Spain.

Wilkinson, who served with Maj. Gen. BENEDICT ARNOLD during the American Revolution, was promoted to brigadier general in the Continental Army in 1777. The following year he became secretary to the Board of War, but lost that post because he had been in a plot to remove Gen. GEORGE WASHINGTON as commander-in-chief of the Army. For the rest of his Army career Wilkinson continued to plot against his superiors.

After the Revolution, Wilkinson went to Kentucky, then part of Virginia, and became an agent for Spain, scheming to keep the region out of the United States. Kentucky became a state in 1792, but Wilkinson, still in the Army, continued his subversive work, serving Spain's efforts to annex western territory.

In 1796, Wilkinson became the commander-in-chief of the U.S. Army. He continued to work for Spain and even took an oath of allegiance to the King of Spain. In 1805, as governor of the Louisiana Territory, in addition to serving as commander-in-chief, he conspired with former Vice President Aaron Burr to create an empire in the West. He later betrayed Burr and became the principal witness against him when Burr was tried for treason (and acquitted).

Wilkinson survived a court-martial growing out of the Burr affair—and two more courts-martial following his disastrous leadership in the War of 1812. Promoted to major general in 1813, he was honorably discharged in 1815. He was seeking a Texas land grant when he died in Mexico City. It was said of him that he "never won a battle or lost a court of inquiry." Historian Frederick Jackson Turner called Wilkinson "the most consummate artist in treason that the nation ever possessed."

Wilkinson, Vice Adm. Theodore S.

(b. 1888 d. 1946)

U.S. DIRECTOR OF NAVAL INTELLIGENCE (DNI) at the time of the PEARL HARBOR ATTACK.

First in his class of 1909 at the Naval Academy, his subsequent assignments ashore and afloat included successive command of four destroyers (1920–1926) and, later, command of the battleship *Mississippi*. Historian Samuel Eliot Morison wrote that at the start of World War II Wilkinson "had one of the best brains in the armed forces."

As a rear admiral he became DNI in Oct. 1941. Under his direction, the MAGIC decrypts of Japanese diplomatic communications were distributed to senior officials in Washington, D.C. But Wilkinson and his staff were not allowed to evaluate, much less disseminate, the vast amount of Magic and other intelligence coming into his office. Rather, evaluating the material, predicting future Japanese fleet movements, and deciding who should see this information was the responsibility of the war plans officer, Rear Adm. Richmond Kelly Turner. Wilkinson, who had several trained Japanese-language officers on his staff—and language nuances were important in dealing with the Japanese—was "ordered not to develop enemy intentions."

Turner would hold all such information closely, dribbling out bits and pieces to those he felt should see them.

Thus, there was no overall picture within the U.S. Navy, let alone in Washington, of what the Japanese Fleet was doing. But, wrote Morison in *The Rising Sun in the Pacific 1931–April 1942* (1948), "as Admiral Wilkinson made the same underestimate of the enemy's capabilities and overestimate of his common sense as did everyone else, the result might have been the same if he had been made responsible."

With Turner controlling all intelligence, however, there was no opportunity for an overall analysis of the Japanese capabilities and potential actions.

Another point of debate has been that Wilkinson and Turner withheld the Magic diplomatic decrypts from the Navy and Army commanders at Pearl Harbor, although it is unlikely that they would have helped those commanders to be on the alert for a Japanese attack. However, some of the intelligence was paraphrased and unofficially passed to the NAVAL INTELLIGENCE staff at Pearl Harbor. (The U.S. Army and Navy commanders in the Philippines had access to the Japanese diplomatic CODE with their own PURPLE machine.)

The lack of a central U.S. analysis staff, coupled with the failure to permit Wilkinson to bring his keen mind and his highly qualified staff to address the issues, made it inevitable that the United States would be taken by surprise when the Japanese initiated hostilities in the Pacific.

Wilkinson left the DNI post in July 1942, going to the Pacific to command a battleship division before becoming involved in amphibious operations. For the remainder of World War II he commanded U.S. amphibious forces in several major assaults against Japanese-held islands.

He died in an automobile accident.

Willes, Bishop Edward

(b. 1694 d. 1773)

Eighteenth-century English cryptographer who succeeded JOHN WALLIS and his grandson William Blencowe as the leading codebreakers of their time, becoming England's "Decypherer."

Willes, like Wallis, was a clergyman. But Willes used his codebreaking services for the Crown to accelerate his advancement in the church, reaching the post of Bishop of Bath and Wells.

He was able to use his skills to decipher correspondence of Francis Atterbury, the Bishop of Rochester, to reveal his involvement in a conspiracy to restore the Stuarts to the throne. This effort threatened to force Willes to reveal some of his deciphering methods before the House of Lords. However, the Lords voted "that it is not consistent with the public safety to ask the Decypherers any questions, which may tend to discover the art or mystery of deciphering." (Atterbury was convicted and banished from England.)

Willes's eldest son succeeded him as Decypherer in 1742.

Willi

German CODE NAME for the operation to kidnap Britain's Duke of Windsor in July 1940 and take him from Portugal to Germany. The Nazis hoped to restore him to the British throne after the German conquest of Britain.

Edward, the son of George V, assumed the throne as Edward VIII in Jan. 1936 when his father died. But the new king was in love with an American divorcée, Wallis Warfield Simpson. Unable to marry her—the Church of England, of which the monarch was constitutional head, at that time forbade the remarriage of divorced persons—he stunned the world on Dec. 10, 1936, by abdicating.

The ex-king and Simpson married in France. As the Duke and Duchess of Windsor, in Oct. 1937 they toured Nazi Germany and met with Adolf Hitler, fanning speculation that they were pro-Nazi. The trip was paid for by the Nazi government, which believed that the duke was a potential ally.

When Britain went to war in Sept. 1939, the duke became liaison officer with the British Military Mission at French General Headquarters. He actually served as an AGENT for British MILITARY INTELLIGENCE, which wanted information on French defenses, particularly the Maginot Line. The duke, wrote Michael Bloch in *Operation Willi* (1981), "turned out to have a flair for his undercover job; and his five secret reports give a devastating picture of French unpreparedness. . . . Had these warnings been heeded in London, the course of the war might have been different; but they were ignored."

As German armies overran France, the Windsors made their way to neutral Spain, then to Portugal, where German diplomatic and intelligence officials plotted ways to keep the duke in Europe and perhaps get him into Germany. The intelligence officials included representatives of Dienststelle Ribbentrop, the private intelligence service run by German Foreign Minister Joachim von Ribbentrop. In Lisbon the duke received a telegram from Prime Minister Winston Churchill, ordering him back to Britain. Churchill pointed out that the duke was under military authority and would "create a serious situation"—an implication of court-martial—if he refused the order. (The duke had the temporary rank of major general.) Then came another telegram appointing the duke governor of the Bahamas, a small British possession in the Caribbean.

Working against time, the Germans sent WALTER SCHELLENBERG, a highly effective SS INTELLIGENCE OFFICER, to Portugal to handle the operation. The plan was to entice the Windsors over the border into Spain and keep them there to "protect" them from plots on their lives. When the duke declined to go to Spain and decided to sail to the Bahamas, Schellenberg later said, Hitler himself ordered that the ex-king be abducted. But Schellenberg, possibly deliberately, failed to carry out the abduction, and the duke sailed for Nassau on Aug. 1, 1940.

Willoughby, Maj. Gen. Charles A.

(b. 1892 d. 1972)

Chief INTELLIGENCE OFFICER (G-2) for Gen. of the Army Douglas MacArthur from 1941 to 1951. Willoughby was considered paranoid and vulnerable to emotional extremes by his peers; as a general officer he was often angry, screaming at subordinates, his abuses punctuated by the term ULTRA, much to the chagrin of other intelligence and communications officers.

Born Karl Weidenbach in Germany, Willoughby studied in Europe, majoring in philosophy and modern languages. After several visits, he moved to the United States in 1910 and became a U.S. citizen. He enlisted in the Army that same year and was able to complete college in 1914. (He later earned a master's degree at the University of Kansas and attended the Army Command and General Staff School and the Army War College.)

He received an Army commission in 1916. Seven months later, in June 1917, he was shipped to France with the 1st Division of the American Expeditionary Force. He soon transferred to Army aviation, where he was involved with aviation training. Returning to the United States in 1918, he was placed in charge of the first air mail service.

During the 1920s and 1930s he served in various Army posts in the United States and at U.S. embassies in South America. In 1940, as a colonel, he was ordered to the Philippines; and in July 1941, when Gen. MacArthur was called back into the U.S. Army to command U.S. Army Forces in the Far East, Willoughby became his ASSISTANT CHIEF OF STAFF FOR INTELLIGENCE.

When the Japanese advances in the Philippines forced MacArthur to flee from Corregidor, the fortress island in Manila Bay, by PT boat and aircraft to Australia, Willoughby was one of the staff officers who accompanied him on the breakout. Upon reaching Australia, Willoughby continued to serve as MacArthur's G-2. As G-2 for the Southwest Pacific Area, Willoughby exercised broad authority over a variety of intelligence activities, including the ALLIED INTELLIGENCE BUREAU, the Royal Australian Navy's COASTWATCHERS, the highly effective Allied Translator and Interpreter Section, and other units. However, BELL, the U.S. Navy's CRYPTANALYSIS station in Australia was under the control of the Chief of Naval Operations in Washington, D.C., not Willoughby.

Willoughby served MacArthur throughout the war and afterwards, when MacArthur became the Allied commander in Japan and then the commander of UNITED NATIONS forces in the Korean War. MacArthur was fired as commander of Allied forces in the Far East on Apr. 11, 1951. In May 1951 Willoughby departed Japan, returning to the United States for medical treatment.

Willoughby subsequently wrote *Shanghai Conspiracy* (1952), the story of the RICHARD SORGE spy ring in Japan, based on his report of "how Communists under the guise of idealism work with no scruples . . . how they operate and how they manipulate innocent liberals to give aid and comfort to the enemy." He also wrote a biography, *MacArthur: 1941–1951* (1954).

A most critical appraisal of Willoughby came from his opposite number in the Pacific. In *"And I Was There"* (1982), Rear Adm. EDWIN T. LAYTON, intelligence officer for the Pacific Fleet, and his collaborators wrote:

> Willoughby was flawed, as an intelligence officer, by the conviction that his avid reading of military history had made him an authority on strategy. Worse than that, he was jealous in his own domain and resented excessively the intrusion of others. MacArthur, aware of this quirk, nevertheless protected him—of all "the gang" he was the only one to serve his master without a break from 1941 to 1951—and was prone to accept his appreciations as gospel, particularly as Willoughby produced the intelligence estimates which were most likely to be palatable.

(The term "gang" referred to MacArthur's senior officers who were with him in the Philippines, particularly on Bataan, where U.S. forces were defeated by the Japanese in the first four months of 1942.)

Willsher, Kathleen

Member of Soviet spy network in Canada revealed by IGOR GOUZENKO.

A graduate of the London School of Economics, she worked for the British High Commission. Frustated by an arid personal life and a lack of rapid promotion, she was ripe for RECRUITMENT by Soviet intelligence. As a member of the Canadian Communist Party, she passed to other communists information she obtained from the commission's registry, of which she served as the assistant registrar.

She was arrested on Feb. 15, 1946, tried on May 3, and sentenced to three years in prison. Her Soviet CODE NAME was Ellie.

Wilmoth, James R.

SEE RUSSELL P. BROWN

Wilson, Edwin P.

Renegade CIA employee who supplied arms and explosives to Libyan leader Muammar al-Qaddafi.

After serving in the U.S. Marine Corps, Wilson joined the CIA Office of Security in 1951 and became a contract employee in 1955. He infiltrated the Seafarer's International Union and, while still a CIA contract employee, lobbied for the union. Sometime in the 1960s he founded a CIA PROPRIETARY company, Consultants International. About this time the line between his private and CIA dealings became hazy. Later investigation showed that he was authorizing procurement contracts and getting kickbacks from the contractors.

He drifted out of the CIA and into TASK FORCE 157 (TF 157), a highly secret U.S. Navy intelligence operation. Wilson apparently set up another proprietary company, but details about it are known only from unofficial sources. According to one report, he proposed a worldwide commodities firm that would simultaneously give TF 157 global access to ports and a profit that would finance TF 157 operations—after deductions for Wilson's salary and expenses.

Wilson's contacts included U.S. Air Force Col. Richard V. Secord, chief of the Air Force Military Advisory Group in Iran. Secord, a future major general, later played a role in the IRAN-CONTRA AFFAIR.

In Oct. 1975, as the DIRECTOR OF NAVAL INTELLIGENCE, BOBBY RAY INMAN, was contemplating the abolition of TF 157, the commander of the unit notified Wilson that his contract would end on April 30, 1976. Wilson, using a congressional contact, met with Inman and offered to set up another task force. The meeting accelerated Inman's decision to abolish TF 157.

Wilson was arrested in 1982 on the arms charge and was later convicted of plotting to murder government prosecutors who had brought him to trial. He was sentenced to a total of 57 years in prison.

In 2004 a federal judge dismissed an indictment against him, saying that the government prosecutors did not fully describe Wilson's ties to the CIA. Wilson, 75, was expected to be freed because the governement did not plan to retry him.

Window System Code

SEE PERFORATED SHEET

Winterbotham, Group Capt. Frederick William

(b. 1897 d. 1990)

Royal Air Force (RAF) officer in charge of the distribution of ULTRA intelligence to Allied commanders in the European-Mediterranean areas during World War II. His book *The Ultra Secret* (1974) was one of the earliest revelations of the great codebreaking success of the Allies. Although two earlier books had revealed the Ultra secret, Winterbotham's garnered worldwide headlines (see ENIGMA).

At the start of World War I he was a junior officer in the Royal Gloucester Hussars Yeomanry, a cavalry unit. In 1916 he was able to enter the Royal Flying Corps and flew in combat in France in April 1917. He was shot down in an aerial dogfight on July 13, 1917, and spent the next 18 months as a prisoner of war.

After the war he studied law at Christ Church College, Oxford, but after graduation in 1920 he went into farming and traveled. Winterbotham returned to Britain to become the RAF representative to the Secret Intelligence Service (MI6) in Dec. 1929 and visited Germany regularly from 1934 to 1938 to observe the buildup of the German Air Force. In 1934 he was able to meet personally with Adolf Hitler and other Nazi officials as well as with senior officers of the new Luftwaffe. (In 1938 the Germans learned that he worked for MI6 and he was warned not to return to Germany.)

In early 1939, Winterbotham established a SCIENTIFIC INTELLIGENCE unit in his air section of MI6 to begin monitoring advanced German weapons and electronics developments. This—and the fact that his offices were located in the same building as the GOVERNMENT CODE AND CYPHER SCHOOL—led to his involvement in British codebreaking.

Following the relocation of British codebreakers to BLETCHLEY PARK in Aug. 1939, parts of MI6 moved there the next month, including Winterbotham's staff.

In the spring of 1940, when British codebreakers at Bletchley Park began to decipher German radio messages, Winterbotham was given the responsibility for distributing those highly classified decrypts. He realized the need for a secure means of transmitting Ultra to the military staffs and to commanders in the field. Accordingly, he developed a scheme for SPECIAL LIAISON UNITS to handle Ultra intelligence and operate with the headquarters of major field commanders. They would use special radio circuits and virtually unbreakable ONE-TIME PADS. Winterbotham established rules that protected the Ultra secret from the Germans and, indeed, from the world for more than 20 years after the war.

He retired after the war, having been awarded a "modest" decoration for his services. In addition to *The Ultra Secret,* he wrote *The Nazi Connection* (1978), detailing his activities in Germany in the 1930s.

Wiseman, Sir William

(b. 1885 d. 1962)

British SECRET SERVICE BUREAU representative in the United States during World War I—an AGENT OF INFLUENCE.

A graduate of Cambridge University, where he was a champion boxer, Wiseman was descended from an old and distinguished naval family and held a baronetcy. He tried his hand as a journalist (rarely being published) and then wrote plays (which were never performed), after which he went to America and made his fortune in a variety of businesses in Canada and Mexico.

When World War I began in Aug. 1914 he returned to Britain to volunteer for the Army and was commissioned a captain in the Duke of Cornwall's Light Infantry. After being gassed in Flanders in 1915 he was returned to London where, after recuperating, he joined what was then MI1(c), the foreign section of the SECRET SERVICE BUREAU, the predecessor of MI6. Sent to the United States in early 1916, Wiseman reported on German attempts to sabotage U.S. munitions production for Britain, ran the British Purchasing Commission, and tried in every way possible to bring the United States into the war on Britain's side.

Wiseman also obtained financial backing—the then

considerable sum of $75,000—from the Wilson administration to send with a British AGENT he had selected to go to Russia in an attempt to help keep the Russians in the war against Germany. The agent was SOMERSET MAUGHAM. After the U.S. entered the war in April 1917, Wiseman made an effort to provide all intelligence possible to the United States.

Col. Edward M. House, President Wilson's principal adviser, told King George V that Wiseman was "one of the most efficient men of his age [he] had ever met." He met regularly with House, U.S. officials, and, on several occasions, President Wilson. Wiseman was also accepted as a member of the ROOM.

Wiseman's tenure in the United States was highly successful. Recalling that success, in May 1940 Prime Minister Winston Churchill appointed Sir WILLIAM STEPHENSON to head a similar organization, BRITISH SECURITY CO-ORDINATION, with headquarters in New York City.

Just a month before, the British consul general in San Francisco had informed the British Embassy in Washington, D.C., that he had been approached by an acquaintance who was also known to the German consul. The acquaintance wished to establish relations on a confidential basis with someone in the British government. Stephenson advised the FBI of the contact, which was monitoring the German consul's telephone calls. Stephenson, after discussions with FBI director J. EDGAR HOOVER, invited the retired Wiseman to make the contact.

Working with an intermediary, Wiseman and the German consul—who had been Adolf Hitler's commanding officer in World War I—met in San Francisco. The issue of negotiating with Hitler was quickly dismissed, and the discussion shifted to the possibility of reestablishing the monarchy in Germany with the help of the German Army! (The German Kaiser had abdicated in 1918.) Wiseman and the German consul talked on several occasions, with Wiseman gleaning considerable POLITICAL INTELLIGENCE as well as some strategic information from the meetings.

News of these discussions reached the U.S. State Department, and the contact was broken off because such political negotiations could violate the neutral status of the United States.

Wisner, Frank G.

(b. 1909 d. 1965)

The quintessential U.S. INTELLIGENCE OFFICER who served in the OFFICE OF STRATEGIC SERVICES (OSS) during World War II and the CIA during the Cold War.

A 1934 graduate of the University of Virginia Law School, Wisner joined a Wall Street law firm. When the United States entered World War II he was commissioned in the Navy. Assigned to the OSS, he worked in the SI (Secret Intelligence) branch. After the war Lt. Comdr. Wisner was one of the OSS officers who dealt with the GEHLEN ORGANIZATION and watched the Soviet takeover of Eastern Europe.

Wisner then returned to Wall Street, but his interest in foreign affairs led him to join the Department of State in 1947 as the assistant secretary for occupied countries.

In June 1948 the NATIONAL SECURITY COUNCIL established the Office of Policy Coordination (OPC) within the CIA to carry out a program of political, psychological, and economic warfare against the Soviet Union. Significantly, although the OPC would be funded by the CIA's unvouchered funds, it would not be under the control of the DIRECTOR OF CENTRAL INTELLIGENCE (DCI). Rather, the head of OPC would receive directions from a joint panel of the Departments of Defense and State. Secretary of State George C. Marshall chose Wisner to head the OPC.

"It was a haphazard system and the marvel is that it worked as well as it did . . ." wrote veteran U.S. intelligence executive RAY CLINE in *Secret Spies and Scholars* (1976).

The OPC grew rapidly. In his comprehensive history of U.S. intelligence, *Honorable Treachery* (1991), G. J. A. O'Toole wrote,

> Although brilliant and energetic, Frank Wisner was not a talented manager, and he found that the difficulties of administering a burgeoning government department were compounded by the very nature of covert action. There was little experience with such things in American government. All of the lessons had been learned in the wartime OSS, and chief among them was the precept that covert operations could not be managed through bureaucratic routine and strict lines of authority.

The OPC also suffered from being in competition with other parts of the CIA, especially the Office of Special Operations. When WALTER BEDELL SMITH became DCI in Oct. 1950 he decided to move OPC into the CIA. A new Plans Directorate—a COVER name—was set up to direct both the OPC and Office of Special Operations in carrying out covert operations, the change becoming effective in Oct. 1951. ALLEN W. DULLES was named head of the Plans Directorate; Wisner remained head of the OPC.

When the Korean War began in June 1950, Wisner's OPC established outposts in Japan to carry out operations in Korea, which was mostly overrun by communist forces. Even after the U.S. landing at Inchon in Sept. 1950, which led the massive Allied offensive, the OPC continued clandestine operations behind enemy lines.

In Aug. 1952 the OPC and Office of Special Operations were merged and Wisner was placed in charge (Dulles having been promoted to Deputy DCI). Wisner's deputy was RICHARD HELMS, a future DCI.

Wisner's operations now increased in scope and range as he sought to foment anti-Soviet movements in Eastern Europe. In 1956, when a revolt erupted in Hungary, Wisner wanted to have his AGENTS help the Hungarians and initiate uprisings elsewhere in Eastern Europe—a proposal that was designated Operation Red Sox–Red Cap. President Eisenhower said no to Wisner, and the Hungarian revolt was soon suppressed by the Red Army.

Wisner, who had been in VIENNA and then on the Hungarian border during the revolt and Soviet suppression of it, returned to the United States dejected. He soon turned his attention eastward, trying to foster an army coup against Sukarno, Indonesia's pro-Soviet leader. This effort also failed, further depressing Wisner, who was hospitalized for six months with nervous exhaustion and a case of severe hepatitis.

When he returned to duty, Dulles, the new DCI, sent him to London as CIA station chief. But his problems continued, and he resigned from the CIA in 1961. Four years later he committed suicide with a shotgun.

Witzke, Lt. Lothar

(b. 1896 d. ?)

The only German spy condemned to death in the United States during World War I. He was not executed.

Witzke was a naval cadet on the cruiser *Dresden* off South America when the ship was sunk; he was interned in Valparaiso, Chile. He managed to escape from internment and to reach San Francisco, where the German consul and spymaster Franz von Bopp recruited him as a spy and saboteur.

Witzke worked for a while with KURT JAHNKE, another German spy and saboteur. As a sabotage team they were implicated in a rash of munitions explosions prior to U.S. entry into the war in 1917.

Using the alias Pablo Waberski, Witze slipped into Mexico when Jahnke was there, late in 1917, running German AGENTS along the border. Paul Altendorf, a former Mexican Army officer who had been recruited by U.S. ARMY INTELLIGENCE, accompanied Witze to the United States. Drunk one night, Witze told Altendorf about acts of sabotage he and Jahnke had committed.

Altendorf managed to get word about Witze to an American consulate official. Witzke, who had entered the United States on a Russian passport as Paul Waberski, was placed under SURVEILLANCE by U.S. Army Intelligence. He was arrested in Arizona, and a search of his baggage produced a CODE book and CIPHER table, which were sent to Army cryptographers in Washington, D.C. When one of his papers was decrypted, it was shown to be a "strictly secret" introduction to German diplomats in Mexico describing him as a German SECRET AGENT whose "code telegrams" should be sent as official dispatches. Under questioning, Witze said, "I am very young to die, 22 years. But I have done my duty." He would not admit to having been a spy. Put on trial before a military commission at Fort Sam Houston, Texas, in Aug. 1918, he was convicted and sentenced to death. He was awaiting execution when the war ended on Nov. 11, 1918.

His sentence was commuted to life imprisonment, but he was released and deported to Germany in 1923. During his confinement he had been repeatedly questioned about the spectacular destruction of the huge munitions depot on Black Tom Island on the New Jersey side of New York Harbor on July 30, 1916. He had told Altendorf that he and Jahnke had almost drowned when the waves caused by the explosion nearly swamped their boat in the harbor.

In 1925, when U.S. officials were trying to fix blame for sabotage during the war, the German government responded with denials, including one from Witzke, who charged that he had confessed only when "[police] beat me on the head with rubber sticks until I broke down."

WNINTEL

SEE WARNING NOTICE—INTELLIGENCE SOURCES OR METHODS

Woikin, Emma

Member of the Soviet spy network in Canada revealed by IGOR GOUZENKO. She worked in the Canadian Department of External Affairs and passed on information to Col. NIKOLAI ZABOTIN, the military ATTACHÉ at the Soviet Embassy in Canada. Zabotin was director of Soviet espionage activities in Canada.

Woikin was arrested in 1946, tried, and convicted. She received a prison sentence of two and a half years.

Wold, Intelligence Spec. 3rd Class Hans Palmer

U.S. Navy enlisted man who was arrested in 1983 with a roll of film containing photographs of TOP SECRET documents. Absent without leave from his ship, the aircraft carrier *Ranger,* he was found in the Philippines by the NAVAL CRIMINAL INVESTIGATIVE SERVICE (NIS), who found the film. Because Wold was an intelligence specialist, he was rigorously questioned and admitted that he had photographed the RECONNAISSANCE information with the intent of selling it to the Soviet Union.

Court-martialed in Oct. 1983, he was convicted of "making photographs with intent or reason to believe information was to be used to the injury of the U.S. or the advantage of a foreign nation." He was sentenced to four years at hard labor.

Wolf, Markus

(b. 1923)

East German spymaster. Born in Germany, Wolf was the son of a Jewish physician, playwright, and communist. The family moved to Switzerland when Adolf Hitler came to power. The young Wolf then went to live in France and traveled to Moscow in 1934 to attend the Comintern's school for émigrés.

After World War II he returned to Germany to assist the Soviet government in establishing an East German regime in 1949. There Wolf worked first as a radio commentator and then in the East German diplomatic service, becoming the country's first chancellor when a mission was established in Moscow.

In 1958, Wolf became head of the Chief Administration, Intelligence (HVA), the foreign intelligence arm of the MFS, or Stasi. His principal efforts—and achievements—were placing spies in the West German government of Chancellor Willy Brandt; he succeeded, and when GÜNTER GUILLAUME was uncovered as an East German MOLE in 1974, Brandt was forced to resign.

Wolf retired in 1987 from the Stasi at his own request because of poor health.

When the two Germanys merged in 1990, Wolf was among several East German former intelligence officials who were tried for their previous activities and indiscretions. He was found guilty in 1993 and sentenced to six years in prison. However, the unified Germany's Constitutional Court ruled on May 23, 1995, that former Stasi officials could not be prosecuted for conducting Cold War espionage against the West. The 5-to-3 ruling effectively gave amnesty to Wolf and other East German former foreign intelligence officials.

In 1996 Wolf was refused entry to the United States to discuss a proposed spy book with a U.S. publisher. (He had already sold his life story to a Hollywood movie company.) But he was given a temporary visa to visit Israel, where intelligence officials welcomed him.

In 1997 Wolf again was put on trial, this time for three kidnappings: in 1955, of a translator working for U.S. authorities, who was released after she refused to spy; in 1959, of a friend of Brandt, released after refusing to denounce Brandt as a Nazi sympathizer; and in 1962, of an East German defector who spent 10 years in prison after his abduction. Wolf was found guilty and given a two-year suspended sentence.

In his memoirs, *Spy Chief in the Secret War* (1997), he said that two CIA INTELLIGENCE OFFICERS called on him shortly after the fall of the Berlin Wall and offered him a new identity in California in exchange for the names of his agents. The book was published in the United States as *Man Without a Face* (1997).

Wolf, Ronald C.

Former U.S. Air Force pilot who sold classified information to an FBI undercover agent posing as a Soviet INTELLIGENCE OFFICER.

Wolf, who served in the Air Force from 1974 to 1981, was arrested in May 1989 in Dallas, Texas. Trained as a Russian voice-processing specialist, he held a TOP SECRET clearance and flew RECONNAISANCE missions in the Far East.

He was discharged in 1981 "due to financial irresponsibility" and was unemployed when he was arrested. He pleaded guilty on espionage charges in Feb. 1990 and was sentenced to 10 years in prison.

Wolff, Jay Clyde

Former U.S. Navy enlisted man convicted of offering to sell classified documents dealing with shipboard weapons systems. He was arrested in Dec. 1984 in Gallup, N. Mex., in a classic FBI sting. Wolfe, 24, had met with an FBI undercover agent and offered to sell the documents for $5,000 to $6,000. He pleaded guilty to attempting to sell classified documents. In 28 June 1985 he was sentenced to five years in prison.

Wolkoff, Anna

(b. 1903 d. 1969)

Russian fascist who, early in World War II, was an accomplice of TYLER KENT, a CODE clerk at the U.S. Embassy in London. She was charged by the British with violating the OFFICIAL SECRETS ACT by getting from Kent "documents which might be useful to an enemy" and copying them "with intent to assist an enemy." She was also charged with trying to send a coded letter to WILLIAM JOYCE, the traitorous "Lord Haw Haw," who broadcast anti-Allied propaganda for the Nazis from BERLIN.

Wolkoff belonged to the Right Club, which was profascist and anti-Semitic. When Great Britain went to war against Germany in Sept. 1939, the Right Club supposedly disbanded, but it merely went underground and planned ways to aid Germany. Wolkoff, using a CUT-OUT at the Italian Embassy, sent information to Berlin, including suggestions for Joyce's propaganda broadcasts.

The daughter of the last naval ATTACHÉ in the Imperial Russian Embassy and a maid of honor to the czarina, she was under SURVEILLANCE as a suspected German spy when she met Kent. Her family operated the Russian Tea Room near the Natural History Museum in London, a rendezvous for White Russians.

She was arrested on the same day as Kent—May 20, 1940. A young boy watched wide-eyed as she was put into a police car. He would never forget that first brush with espionage. He was the future spy novelist LEN DEIGHTON.

Tried in camera in the Old Bailey, Wolkoff was sentenced to 10 years for attempting to assist the enemy. She was released in 1947.

Wood, Sgt. James D.

U.S. Air Force enlisted man who worked for the Air Force Office of Special Investigations. He was arrested in 1973 after FBI agents saw him meeting with a Soviet diplomat. The agents found hundreds of classified documents in a car Wood had rented.

Wood was caught as a result of FBI SURVEILLANCE of the diplomat Viktor A. Chernyshev, a first secretary at the Soviet Embassy in Washington, D.C.

Wood, who cooperated with the FBI, was given a dishonorable discharge and a two-year prison term.

Woodward, Bob

(b. 1943)

American journalist who, following the WATERGATE break-in, coauthored with Carl Bernstein the articles in

The Washington Post that led to the resignation of President Nixon. Woodward's later book *Veil: The Secret Wars of the CIA 1981–1987* (1987), chronicled the tenure of WILLIAM J. CASEY, President Reagan's DIRECTOR OF CENTRAL INTELLIGENCE (DCI).

Woodward attended Yale University, participating in the school's Naval Reserve Officer Training Corps (NROTC) program. Commissioned in the Navy in 1965, he served in a command ship and a cruiser, spending the last half of his five years on active duty in Navy communications at the Pentagon.

In 1971 he went to work for *The Washington Post.* With Bernstein, he broke the story that the Watergate break-in had been carried out by the White House. He and Bernstein chronicled the fall of Nixon in their books *All the President's Men* (1974) and *The Final Days* (1976). The former was made into the 1976 film *All the President's Men,* starring Dustin Hoffman as Bernstein and Robert Redford as Woodward.

Woodward's book *Veil* describes how Casey was given a free hand by President Reagan and was probably the most powerful DCI in the 40-plus years of the CIA's history. After the publication of *Veil,* Reagan denounced the book as "an awful lot of fiction about a man who was unable to communicate at all." Much of the controversy over the book centered on Woodward's description of a deathbed interview with Casey, which Casey's widow would later claim never took place. That interview, said Woodward, lasted four minutes, and Casey managed just 19 words.

But Reagan did admit to some of the revelations in the book. For example, he confirmed that he had signed a secret order authorizing counter-terrorist actions in Lebanon.

Woodward wrote the book while he was assistant managing editor of the *Post* for the investigative staff.

Woodward wrote two revealing, best-selling books on President George W. Bush's war on terrorism (Bush at War, 2002) and the war in Iraq (Plan of Attack, 2004).

Woolsey, R. James

(b. 1941)

U.S. DIRECTOR OF CENTRAL INTELLIGENCE (DCI) from Feb. 1993 to Jan. 1995. A longtime Washington insider, Woolsey tried to bring the CIA into the post–Cold War era.

A graduate of Stanford University and a Rhodes scholar with a master's degree from Oxford University in England, Woolsey later earned a law degree from Yale University. He served in the Army from 1968 to 1970, working on strategic arms limitation issues, and was on the staff of the NATIONAL SECURITY COUNCIL.

In 1970 Woolsey was appointed general counsel to the Senate Committee on Armed Services, where he served until 1973, when he entered private law practice. In 1978–1979 he served as Under Secretary of the Navy, after which he returned to private practice. During the 1980s he also participated with Soviet and NORTH ATLANTIC TREATY ORGANIZATION officials in talks on

weapon limitations. In 1989 he was appointed U.S. negotiator to the talks on the conventional forces in Europe, with the rank of ambassador. After the successful conclusion of an agreement with the Soviet Union, in July 1991 he once again returned to law practice.

President Clinton appointed Woolsey DCI as the Cold War was ending and the U.S. INTELLIGENCE COMMUNITY, as well as the CIA, required redirection and restructuring. At the time the agency was also under fire for discrimination against women in promotion and assignment policies, illegal actions in Guatemala, and the exposure in 1994 of ALDRICH H. AMES as a Soviet MOLE in the agency.

Woolsey served as DCI for just over two years; in Jan. 1995 he resigned as DCI following criticism for his failure to punish officials at the CIA who had had responsibility for supervising Ames.

World Wide Web

SEE INTERNET

Wright, Peter

(b. 1916 d. 1995)

Officer in the British Security Service (MI5) who, while in the service and afterward, charged that British security had been incompetent and that the British intelligence establishment was riddled with Soviet MOLES. His charges centered on the belief that ROGER HOLLIS, Director-General of MI5, was himself a Soviet AGENT.

After attending Oxford University, Wright, the son of a scientist, joined the Admiralty Research Laboratory at the start of World War II. After the war he worked as a Navy scientist with the Marconi Company, and in 1949 he was asked by MI5 to become an unpaid "external scientific adviser" on how military scientific resources could be used in COUNTERESPIONAGE activities. In 1952 a sophisticated listening device was discovered in a concealed cavity within the American great seal that hung over the desk of the ambassador in the U.S. Embassy in Moscow. The Soviet BUG was taken to Britain, where Wright was able to discover its secrets. (See SATYR.)

This success led to his being asked in 1955 to join MI5 as the first scientist employed by that service. He was primarily involved in electronic SURVEILLANCE—both defeating Soviet espionage efforts and planting British bugs in foreign embassies (see ENGULF).

In time Wright became involved in efforts to determine if Soviet moles existed within the British intelligence services, MI5 and MI6. Wright worked with the VENONA decrypts and, in collaboration with U.S. and Canadian intelligence services, sought to uncover new clues about Soviet espionage penetrations.

He came to believe that Hollis, who served as head of MI5 from 1956 to 1965, had worked for the Soviets. His charges led to the formation of the MI5-MI6 FLUENCY COMMITTEE, which he chaired.

Wright, who retired in Jan. 1976, revealed details of

his career in counterespionage—and his suspicions—in *Spycatcher* (1987). The British government sought to stop publication of the book, invoking the OFFICIAL SECRETS ACT. But Wright sidestepped that attempt by having the book first published in Australia.

Wu-tai Chin, Larry

SEE LARRY CHIN

Wychegerde, Mynheer (Jan)

Merchant, wheat broker, and 16th-century spy for England's minister-spymaster Sir FRANCIS WALSINGHAM. Born in northern Germany, Wychegerde was a naturalized citizen of Dixmude in West Flanders by the 1580s, when he carried out intelligence missions for Walsingham.

He provided the English with important intelligence of the activities of Spanish forces in the Low Countries while selling food to them.

Wynne, Greville M.

(b. 1919 d. 1990)

British businessman who served as the principal contact for U.S. and British intelligence with Col. OLEG PENKOVSKY, a Western spy in the GRU, Soviet MILITARY INTELLIGENCE.

Wynne was educated at Nottingham University and served during World War II as an officer in military intelligence. In 1950 he established his own business exporting heavy industrial equipment. He frequently traveled abroad and made several trips to the Soviet Union.

He met Penkovsky in Moscow in Dec. 1960 while attending a trade conference. Penkovsky asked Wynne to contact British intelligence on his behalf (having previously tried in vain to contact the CIA).

Wynne began acting as a go-between in April 1961, visiting Moscow and arranging for Penkovsky to be debriefed by the British Secret Intelligence Service (MI6) and the CIA during his visits to London and Paris.

By 1962, when it became evident that Penkovsky was in trouble, plans were made for Wynne to provide his escape to the West through a trade exhibition in Leningrad (St. Petersburg). Two trucks were specially fitted with machinery displays in which Penkovsky could hide. Wynne took the trucks to Budapest, Hungary, for a trade fair, planning to go on to Helsinki and then into the Soviet Union.

On Nov. 2, 1962, as Wynne left a party in Budapest, he was seized by KGB officers at gunpoint, pushed into a car, and driven off. Penkovsky had already been arrested on Oct. 22, 1962, unknown to British intelligence at the time. Wynne was flown to Moscow and spent the next six months in the LUBYANKA in filthy, harsh conditions, interspersed with periods of good treatment (even a visit from his wife) as the KGB sought to have him confess his complicity with Penkovsky.

Put on trial in Moscow with Penkovsky in May 1963, Wynne was found guilty of spying and sentenced to three years in prison and five more in a labor camp. He was treated particularly harshly in prison, as the Soviets were trying to force an exchange of convicted spies.

After serving less than a year of the sentence, Wynne became part of a SPY SWAP in BERLIN on April 22, 1964. He was exchanged for GORDON LONSDALE, convicted by the British as a Soviet spy.

Wynne's disjointed account of his own experiences and his relationship with Penkovsky was published in 1968 as *Contact on Gorky Street*.

X, Project

U.S. Army project from 1965 to the early 1980s to train foreign INTELLIGENCE OFFICERS, especially in Latin America. While few details of the project have been revealed, the manuals for the program taught foreign officers to spy on political opponents, infiltrate opposing political parties, kidnap rebels' family members, offer bounties for killed or captured insurgents, and employ blackmail tactics.

The manuals were used to train foreign officers in the United States as well as in their own countries. The contents of some of the manuals used in Project X were revealed in 1997. They were prepared by the Army Intelligence Center and School at FORT HOLABIRD, near Baltimore, Md., and then at Fort Huachucha, Ariz.

Project X was initiated in 1965 to train South Vietnamese and other Asian officers at the U.S. Army Pacific Intelligence School on Okinawa. Subsequently, Project X operated in Iran to train intelligence officers of the Shah's army prior to the Iranian revolution. The areas in which Project X efforts were employed expanded to Latin America and, possibly, other areas before Project X was reportedly closed down in the early 1980s. The U.S. Army still has a continuing program to train foreign intelligence officers.

X-2

The designation for the COUNTERESPIONAGE and COUNTERINTELLIGENCE division of the OFFICE OF STRATEGIC SERVICES (OSS) during World War II.

The branch was first headed by Hubert Will, a Chicago lawyer. Will's successor, Norman Holmes Pearson, in peacetime a Yale University English professor, had designated the unit as X-2, possibly to indicate its liaison with the British XX, or TWENTY COMMITTEE.

Pearson spent some time at BLETCHLEY PARK, the site of British ULTRA work, before setting up the X-2 liaison. He was acting chief of the London branch from July to Oct. 1943 and chief from Sept. 1944 to Jan. 1945. He also ran the Iberian–North African desk in London. Among Pearson's British colleagues was HAROLD (KIM) PHILBY, who monitored Iberian activities for MI6, the British Secret Intelligence Service. Pearson later recalled that he had been warned to be careful around Philby, who was later unmasked as a Soviet AGENT when he defected to Moscow in 1963.

By OSS accounts, X-2 aided in the apprehending of some 1,300 enemy agents. Pearson, in a classified history of the OSS, wrote that X-2 not only worked closely with the British but also received counterintelligence material from French, and Italian, Norwegian sources; he also said X-2 got cooperation from Belgian, Danish, Dutch, Swedish, and Turkish, services. At the end of the war X-2 had built up files on 300,000 persons.

X-2 had about 25 members when it was set up at the MI6 offices in London in June 1943. By the fall of 1944, X-2 had 500 men and women working out of 16 field stations throughout the world. Most X-2 workers had been lawyers and professors; Pearson said he preferred lawyers "because they had been trained to make up their minds on the evidence at hand, whereas professors prefer to meditate."

JAMES JESUS ANGLETON worked in X-2, as did a wide variety of people. A sampler, as reported by Robin W. Winks in *Cloak & Gown* (1987), yielded

a professional singer, a concert pianist, the former head of the English department in a school in

Peking, several socialites, young girls just out of high school . . . a woman flight instructor, the superintendent of a mattress factory, the son of the writer John P. Marquand, a Coca-Cola executive, a football coach, a bartender (from the Yale Club) . . . a beauty parlor operator . . . at least three men and two women of great wealth and three women who had not finished high school. . . .

Although the women were essentially as well educated as the men, Winks found, all were secretaries, translators, or filing clerks, except for one woman who was a decoder.

Poet John Hollander wrote a book-length poem, "Reflections on Espionage," in which Pearson appears as Puritan, his cover name in X-2.

XX

SEE DOUBLE-CROSS SYSTEM

XYZ Committee

One of the informal groups of people who traded information while working privately in the 1930s to prepare Britain for war. Other groups were called Focus and Electra. They were watched over by WILLIAM STEPHENSON, then an intelligence confidant of Winston Churchill, who was out of power at the time. Stephenson was later chief of the BRITISH SECURITY CO-ORDINATION network operating out of New York City.

Y Service

British signals-intercept agency of World War II era, officially known as the Composite Signals Organization (CSO). CSO was the cover name for the intercept service of the GOVERNMENT CODE AND CYPHER SCHOOL.

After the war the Secret Intelligence Service (MI6) established the "Y Section," which handled telephone taps of Soviets in Austria and BUGS in buildings occupied by Soviet missions in Britain and countries in Western Europe.

"Y" was also the British term for the intercept process.

Yaakov, Brig. Gen. Itzhak

(b. 1926)

Retired Israeli general charged with passing confidential information to "unauthorized individuals" with the intention of "compromising the security of the state."

Yaakov, an Israeli-American with dual citizenship, was arrested in May 2001, after he celebrated his 75th birthday at a party attended by what a newspaper called "a who's who of Israeli political and economic leaders."

Officials, while saying that the case did not involve espionage, accused him of divulging classified information obtained while he was in the Israeli Army 27 years before. He was held in a prison hospital because of his heart condition.

Born in Tel Aviv, he served in the Palmach, a paramilitary branch of the Haganah, the Jewish underground self-defense force before independence, and from 1955 to 1973 was in the Israeli military. He is believed to have worked on Israel's highly secret nuclear weapons development. After leaving the military, he became chief scientist for Israel's Trade Ministry and was widely regarded as the founder of Israel's technology industry.

He immigrated to the United States in the late 1970s and in 2000 retired as chairman of a company that develops computer data storage systems.

Yagoda, Genrikh Grigoryevich

(b. 1891 d. 1938)

Soviet intelligence official who was head of the OGPU in 1934 and of its successor intelligence security ORGAN, the NKVD, from 1934 to 1936. The son of Jewish Latvian peasants and a pharmacist by profession, Yagoda became head of the toxicological laboratory at the Kremlin. According to Thaddeus Wittlin's *Commissar* (1972), Yagoda was able to "speed up" V. I. Lenin's death after he was shot as well as "stopping forever Maxim Gorky's painful tubercular coughing," thus facilitating Josef Stalin's rise to uncontested leadership of the Soviet Union.

When VYACHESLAV MENZHINSKY was made head of the OGPU in 1926, Yagoda became his principal deputy, having already served as second deputy chairman since 1923 (see CHEKA). He also personally directed the building of the canal that joined the White Sea with the Baltic Sea. The canal, built from Nov. 1931 to Aug. 1933, used nearly 300,000 slave laborers, of whom approximately one-third died in the effort.

Aleksandr Solzhenitsyn wrote in *The Gulag Archipelago* (1975) of Yagoda's direction of the canal project:

> All administrations were to be renamed *staffs of battle sectors!* Fifty percent of the administrative staffs were to be thrown into construction work (would there be enough spades?). They were to

work in three shifts (the night was nearly polar)! They would be fed right on the canal site (with cold food)! For "tufta" [theft of socialist property] they would be put on trial.

In January [1933] came *the storm of the watershed!* All phalanxes, with their kitchens and property, were to be thrown into one single sector! There were not enough tents for everyone. They slept on the snow—never mind. *We'll manage!*

In April there was an incessant forty-eight-hour storm assault—hurrah! *Thirty thousand people did not sleep!*

Because of Menzhinsky's failing health and passive style of leadership, power within the OGPU passed to Yagoda, who took charge of the agency in 1934. The OGPU was assimilated into the reorganized NKVD on July 10, 1934, with Yagoda continuing as head of that agency. He soon took the grandiose title of General Commissar of State Security (equivalent to the rank of Marshal of the Soviet Union).

Soviet defector OLEG GORDIEVSKY and CHRISTOPHER ANDREW wrote in *KGB* (1990): "Yagoda became a classic example of a bureaucrat corrupted by excessive power, with a growing pretentiousness which matched his increasing brutality . . . . one of his officers found him absorbed in designing for himself a new full-dress uniform: white woollen tunic decorated with gold braid, a small gilt dagger of the kind once worn by Tsarist naval officers, light blue trousers and shoes of imported patent leather."

Stalin never fully trusted Yagoda—his investigations cleared some of Stalin's enemies, and he was obviously an opportunist rather than an ideologue. Another factor undoubtedly was Stalin's anti-Semitic views.

Yagoda was dismissed from all his positions in 1936 (along with his principal deputy, Georgi Prokofyev). He was denounced for being part of a counterrevolutionary conspiracy by his successor, NIKOLAI YEZHOV, on March 18, 1937, but was not arrested until April 3, 1937. Yagoda was accused of working for the czarist OKHRANA as well as the German secret service, and of being used by them to penetrate the Cheka. After a show trial he was executed the following year. Yagoda's wife and sister were sent to Gulag labor camps (and apparently survived).

Yakovlev, Anatoli

Soviet INTELLIGENCE OFFICER of the NKVD who was the HANDLER of HARRY GOLD, a COURIER for the ATOMIC SPY RING.

Gold, a U.S. soldier assigned to atomic bomb laboratory at LOS ALAMOS, N. Mex., was instructed by Yakovlev to make contact with DAVID GREENGLASS, another member of the ring. According to Gold, during a meeting in a New York City bar in 1945, Yakovlev gave him a piece of onionskin paper on which was typed "Greenglass" with an Albuquerque, N. Mex., address typed on it. He was told to go to that address and say, "I

come from Julius" (or, in another version, "I come from Ben"). The man who answered the apartment door in Albuquerque, near the Los Alamos laboratory, was Greenglass. In his testimony at the trial of JULIUS ROSENBERG and his wife, Ethel, Gold said that Greenglass give him documents that Yakovlev later called "extremely excellent and very valuable."

Gold also was a go-between of KLAUS FUCHS and Yakovlev. Gold also told U.S. officials following his arrest that his sources of intelligence on U.S. military programs lived in cities other than Philadelphia (Gold's home city) and that he paid money to those sources that he had in turn received from Yakovlev.

The last meeting between Gold and Yakovlev occurred on the night of Dec. 26, 1946, in New York City, where Gold was then working. At the meeting Yakovlev told Gold that he should begin to plan for a mission to Paris in March 1947. During the conversation Gold mentioned the name of his employer. Yakovlev became very excited. He told Gold that he had almost ruined 11 years of Soviet intelligence efforts by working for that individual because he had recently been investigated by the FBI. Yakovlev left hurriedly, stating that Gold would not see him in the United States again.

Yakovlev, who was working under COVER as the Soviet vice-consul in New York City, left the United States within the next few days. He had used the recognition name John.

Yamamoto, Adm. Isoroku

(b. 1884 d. 1943)

Commander-in-Chief of the Japanese Combined Fleet when World War II broke out in the Pacific, and key architect of Japan's successes at the start of the war. Yamamoto is believed to have been the highest-ranking victim of an intelligence-directed attack during the war.

Yamamoto, a participant in the 1921–1922 Washington Naval Conference and later naval ATTACHÉ in Washington, studied English at Harvard University. He was considered a progressive officer and a strong supporter of naval aviation, in the 1930s refining it as the Navy's principal shock weapon. He was the director of the aeronautical branch of the Navy Ministry and later became Vice Minister of the Navy, resisting the "total war" school of Japanese militarism. The Japanese Prime Minister appointed Yamamoto Commander-in-Chief of the Combined Fleet in Aug. 1939, in part to spare him from possible political assassination, a frequent fate of opponents to militarism.

Yamamoto commanded the fleet during the highly successful first six months of the war, after which the Navy suffered a major defeat in the Battle of MIDWAY in June 1942 and the Allies went on the offensive. In Jan. 1943 Yamamoto sought to shore up Japanese defenses in the Solomon Islands by staging a series of air raids on Allied forces. In the aftermath of these raids, which Yamamoto mistakenly believed to have been successful, he began a tour of forward bases.

On the afternoon of April 13 his staff transmitted a radio message to the bases involved in the tour. Three U.S. Navy intercept stations received the message simultaneously. U.S. Marine Lt. Col. Alva B. Lasswell at the FLEET RADIO UNIT PACIFIC (FRUPAC) at Pearl Harbor led in the DECRYPTION of the Yamamoto message, and on the morning of April 14 a preliminary translation was issued. A more complete translation soon followed:

> On 18 April CinC Combined Fleet will visit RYZ [Ballale], R—and RXP [Bruin] in accordance with the following schedule:
> 1. Depart RR [Rabaul] at 0600 in a medium attack plane escorted by 6 fighters. Arrive at RYZ at 0800. Proceed by minesweeper to R—arriving at 0840.
> 2. At each of the above places commander in chief will make a tour of inspection and at—he will visit the sick and wounded but current operations should continue.

The codes for three of the four locations were known to the U.S. Navy codebreakers (given above in brackets).

Adm. Chester W. Nimitz, the U.S. Commander-in-Chief Pacific Ocean Areas, was briefed on the message. The late naval historian and Japanese linguist Roger Pineau wrote:

> Historians have written that, because the assassination of so eminent a person might have political repercussions, [Admiral] Nimitz checked with Washington and received the go-ahead from Secretary of the Navy Knox and President Roosevelt. Nowhere, however, have I found a reliable source for this assertion. Naval archives, the national archives, and the FDR Library at Hyde Park [New York] revealed no record that Roosevelt's approval was requested, or, in fact, there was any communication on the subject between Washington and Nimitz.

Rather, Adm. Nimitz conferred with his subordinate commander in the Solomons area, Vice Adm. William F. Halsey, and they made the decision to kill Yamamoto. This was accomplished on April 18, 1943, by 18 U.S. Army Air Forces P-38 Lightning fighters flying from Guadalcanal. Yamamoto was killed in the P-38 attack. The Japanese did not suspect that their codes had been broken and that he had been assassinated.

Capt. Pineau observed in his article in *Naval Intelligence Professionals Quarterly* (April 1988): "The shootdown of Yamamoto was probably the most spectacular single event to result from the breaking of one message in communications intelligence."

Yardley, Herbert O.

(b. 1889 d. 1958)

Pioneer in American codebreaking who later "told all" in a book revealing secrets of the BLACK CHAMBER.

Yardley grew up in the Midwest. Highly popular in school, he learned telegraphy at an early age from his father, and his first job was as a railway telegrapher. He also learned at a young age to play poker, which became a lifelong passion. Yardley went to work as a telegrapher with the State Department in 1912 and showed a special interest in CIPHERS and CODES.

Cryptanalytic activities in the U.S. War Department began in June 1917, when Yardley was commissioned as a 1st lieutenant in the Army's MILITARY INTELLIGENCE Division. The United States had entered World War I in April 1917, and Yardley's section, originally two civilian employees in addition to himself, increased rapidly. When the war ended in Nov. 1918, his MI-8 section numbered 18 Army officers, 24 civilian cryptographers and cryptanalysts, and 109 typists and stenographers—a total of 151 men and women. There were six subsections in MI-8:

1. Code and cipher solution: performing these services for the War Department, Navy, State Department, and justice Department. These efforts made use of radio intercepts made by U.S. Army listening stations with the American Expeditionary Force (AEF) in Europe and intercepts from the large station established in late 1918 to intercept transatlantic communications at Houlton, Maine.
2. Code and cipher compilation: preparing these for U.S. forces to use.
3. Training: training MI-8 personnel plus men going abroad with the AEF to Europe and U.S. troops going to Siberia.
4. Secret inks: preparing invisible inks for U.S. forces and examining some 2,000 letters per week for signs of secret inks being used by spies. (See SECRET WRITING.)
5. Shorthand: studying various shorthand systems.
6. Communications: handling messages to and from U.S. military ATTACHÉS and INTELLIGENCE OFFICERS serving overseas.

Near the end of the war Yardley went to Europe to meet with AEF, British, and French cryptologists. After the war the Army's leadership initially believed that Yardley's codebreaking section should be continued and its existence kept highly secret. The section's appropriation for 1919 was $100,000 with $60,000 provided by the War Department and $40,000 by the State Department. In July of that year Yardley and his staff of some 50 men and women were ensconced in a private residence at 22 East 38th Street in New York City in an effort to hide their existence. At this time the organization took on the COVER name Code Compilation Company, but was officially called the Cipher Bureau. Unofficially it was referred to as the American BLACK CHAMBER.

A year later, however, Yardley's appropriation was cut to $50,000, of which the State Department again contributed $40,000 on the basis that Yardley's work was of interest primarily to U.S. foreign relations rather than to the Army, which was almost exclusively engaged in garrison and training responsibilities in the United States. Of considerable importance in this period was

Yardley's success in the summer of 1921 in breaking Japanese diplomatic codes, sent by commercial cable lines, used by the Japanese negotiators in Washington, D.C., for the conference on naval warship limitations and Pacific fortifications. American diplomats were provided with detailed information on the Japanese positions, enabling the United States to obtain favorable terms in the Washington Treaty of 1922.

The principal PRODUCT of the Cipher Bureau during this period was a "bulletin," issued every few days to a select few on the Army's General Staff and in State Department. It contained mostly political intelligence and was of less and less interest to the Army.

By 1929 the appropriation for Yardley's Cipher Bureau had declined to $25,000, enough to support Yardley and a staff of five persons—$9,375 was paid to Yardley, who by now had little interest in codebreaking. (The War Department provided $10,000 and the State Department $15,000 of the funds.) The Chamber's severely limited efforts were oriented mainly to reading Japanese diplomatic messages.

Then, in March 1929, Herbert Hoover was inaugurated as President and Henry L. Stimson became Secretary of State. In early May several translations of coded Japanese messages were placed on his desk. According to a report prepared by codebreaker WILLIAM F. FRIEDMAN, Stimson's reaction "was violent and his action drastic. Upon learning how the material was obtained, he characterized the activity as being highly unethical and declared that it would cease *immediately*, so far as the State Department was concerned. To put teeth into his decision he gave instructions that the necessary funds of the State Department would be withdrawn *at once*." Later Stimson reportedly explained his actions by saying, "Gentlemen do not read each other's mail."

The Army prevailed to have State Department funding continued until the end of June 1929, so that the New York offices could be closed down, the files sent to the War Department, and the employees given three months' severance pay. At the same time, the responsibilities for codebreaking were transferred from the Army's Military

Intelligence Division to the Chief Signal Officer (see SIGNAL INTELLIGENCE SERVICE).

Angry and frustrated, Yardley immediately began work on *The American Black Chamber,* which caused an uproar when it was published in 1931. The book revealed how the Cipher Bureau had broken the Japanese diplomatic code. It was a best-seller around the world, but especially in Japan. There a tremendous controversy erupted. The Foreign Ministry, embarrassed by the revelations, changed to cipher machines (see PURPLE).

Yardley also abridged the book for serialization in *The Saturday Evening Post,* America's leading magazine. Trading on the success of the book and series, he became a frequent lecturer and wrote more articles. He had kept some 5,000 intercept messages, which he gave to a collaborator to develop into a book. The manuscript was seized by the government, however, and in June 1933 Congress passed a law preventing the publication of any material that had been in any official diplomatic code.

Yardley also wrote two novels, *The Red Sun of Nippon* and *The Blonde Countess*; the latter was made into a popular film entitled *Rendezvous* (1935), starring William Powell, Cesar Romero, and Rosalind Russell.

In 1938 Yardley went to China at the invitation of Chiang Kai-shek to help in the war with Japan. For two years he worked for the Nationalist Chinese breaking Japanese tactical codes. He returned briefly to America before going to Canada in 1941 to establish a codebreaking agency for the government.

Back in Washington, he was involved in a variety of businesses, none having to do with codebreaking, and wrote another novel, *Crows Are Black Everywhere.* And in late 1957 he published *The Education of a Poker Player,* another highly successful book, still in print half a century later. A codebreaking historian described Yardley as follows: "Short, balding, witty, a marvelous raconteur, with what one acquaintance called 'a dynamo of concentrated intellectual power in his head' and a way of talking that expressed utter conviction, he exercised a strong attraction upon many of those who knew him."

Many codebreakers—his peers and successors—would never forgive him for revealing the Black Chamber's successes.

(Yardley's wife, Edna, worked for the Cipher Bureau in the 1920s and for the Army's Signal Intelligence Service in World War II.)

Year of the Spy

Three major U.S. spy cases were revealed in 1985: JOHN A. WALKER, JR., who sold cryptologic secrets to the Soviet Union; JONATHAN JAY POLLARD, who sold massive amounts of classified material to the Israelis; and RONALD PELTON, who revealed of some of the most sensitive activities of NSA to the Soviets.

Walker, a retired Navy warrant officer, had involved his older brother, retired Lt. Comdr. ARTHUR WALKER; his son, Yeoman 3rd Class MICHAEL WALKER; and his best friend, Chief Radioman JERRY WHITWORTH, in his espionage activities. All went to prison. Walker's wife, Bar-

Capt. Herbert O. Yardley in Paris in Feb. 1919. (NATIONAL ARCHIVES)

bara, knew of his spying and even helped him. No charges were brought against her.

Pollard was a civilian employee of U.S. NAVAL INTELLIGENCE. Subject to visions of grandeur, Pollard had his ego and bank accounts fed by the Israelis, for whom he stole every document he could lay his hands on. His wife, Anne Henderson Pollard, also went to prison for possession of classified material. She later divorced Pollard.

Pelton, who had a phenomenal memory, told the Soviets everything he remembered from his work at NSA, especially U.S. Navy SUBMARINES tapping into Soviet seafloor communications cables. He, too, is behind bars.

Also see DECADE OF THE SPY.

Yellow Fruit

CODE NAME for U.S. Army COUNTERINTELLIGENCE operation that led to investigations about the mismanagement of some $300 million in BLACK operations funds over a five-year period. Some critics of such operations saw Yellow Fruit as a precursor of IRAN-CONTRA.

The accounting of the funds was made difficult because they were "laundered" so that they would be untraceable to any U.S. source.

Investigations into the spending led to the courts-martial of three Army officers and a sergeant. In the most severe punishment, in Nov. 1986 Lt. Col. Dale E. Duncan was sentenced to 10 years in prison, fined $50,000, ordered to forfeit $3,350 a month in salary for 10 years, and dismissed from the service. He was convicted of diverting secret funds to his own use while running a PROPRIETARY COMPANY in connection with Yellow Fruit. Much of the testimony in the courts-martial of Duncan and the others was secret; details of the operation were not made public. Duncan served two and a half years, paid $20,000 of the fine, and forfeited $90,000 in pay. He was paroled in 1989.

A military court reversed the conviction, saying, "There appears to have been little guidance from higher echelons concerning the handling of funds within the cover intelligence community other than the concern of 'live your cover' and 'accomplish your mission.'" The court ruled that he had not been guilty of criminal misconduct.

The inquiry began in 1983 and included audits of secret funds handled by the Delta Force, an elite unit assigned to deal with terrorists and hostage rescue missions.

Also see ARMY INTELLIGENCE AND SECURITY COMMAND (INSCOM) and SPECIAL OPERATIONS FORCES.

Yezhov, Nikolai Ivanovich

(b. 1895 d. 1939)

Head of the NKVD from 1936 to 1938, a period that included most of the Stalinist purges or "great terror" that decimated the Red Army's leadership as well as the NKVD and other parts of Soviet society. This period was called *Yezhovchina* in Russian after him. Yezhov was the only ethnic Russian to serve as head of Russian-Soviet state security ORGANS from 1917 to 1953.

He was referred to as "the dwarf" and, after becoming head of the NKVD, "the bloodthirsty dwarf." Boyish-looking, he stood about five feet tall.

Yezhov joined the Communist Party in 1917 and held several provincial posts until he was discovered by Soviet dictator Josef Stalin. In 1934 he became a member of the Secretariat of the Central Committee, a key government agency, and head of the Party Control Commission. Within the Communist Party apparatus he was soon directing NKVD affairs. He was made the People's Commissar of Internal Affairs, the head of the NKVD, on Sept. 30, 1936. With him came some 300 followers into the ranks of the NKVD. The following year Yezhov was made a candidate member of the ruling Politburo.

On March 18, 1937, he denounced his predecessor, GENRIKH YAGODA, as a czarist police chief, embezzler, and thief. On April 3, 1937, Yagoda was arrested. Meanwhile, Yagoda's former deputies and department chiefs were informed that the Central Committee wanted them personally to investigate the political reliability of regional and local party officials throughout the country. They dutifully departed Moscow, but they never arrived at their destinations. At each train's first stop they were arrested by Yezhov's henchmen, driven back to Moscow by automobile, and imprisoned. Next followed the mass arrest and execution of Yagoda's followers—at least 3,000 NKVD officers who did not commit suicide. Yezhov also established "mobile squads" to assassinate communists living outside the Soviet Union. And he was responsible for purges in the Ukraine and of foreign communists living in the Soviet Union.

KGB defector Oleg Gordievsky would later tell of Yezhov in his book *KGB* (1990):

> He showed particular interest in the methods used to extract confessions from those prisoners who put up the most resistance, and would always ask the interrogators 'what, in their opinion, was the last straw that broke the prisoner's back'. Yezhov took personal pride in reducing one tough Old Bolshevik to tears by threatening his children. One of the NKVD interrogators who witnessed Yezhov's triumph said later, 'In my whole life I have never seen such a villain as Yezhov. He does it with pleasure.'

Soon, however, Stalin appeared to be tiring of the purge, realizing perhaps that he could not allow it to go further without fatally disrupting Soviet society, industry, and the military. Yezhov's power was waning. There were reports of interrogations getting out of hand and of his personally shooting some senior military officers. After being dismissed from his NKVD position on Dec. 8, 1938, he remained briefly People's Commissar of Water Transport (to which post he had been appointed earlier in the year).

By Feb. 1939 he had disappeared. There was no trial or ritual denunciation, as there had been for his predecessor. However, the town leaders of Yezhovo-Cherkessk quickly dropped the first half of its name after briefly renaming it for the NKVD chief. Yezhov's deputy, LAVRENTY BERIA, succeeded him as People's Commissar and head of the NKVD.

He is believed to have been executed on Stalin's orders in 1939, surviving his predecessor by only one year. American intelligence historian John J. Dziak wrote in *Chekisty: A History of the* KGB (1988): "His fate was never officially announced but rumors of his end ranged from execution, to suicide, to madness, to having been murdered by a fellow inmate. It is highly unlikely that Stalin would have kept him alive."

Yoshikawa, Takeo

Japanese spy in Hawaii before the Japanese PEARL HARBOR ATTACK. Yoshikawa, a 1933 graduate of the Japanese Naval Academy at Eta Jima, served briefly at sea and had begun flight training when, at the end of 1934, he was stricken with a severe stomach ailment. He was discharged from the Navy in 1936.

A year later he entered NAVAL INTELLIGENCE and was assigned to Navy Headquarters in Tokyo. While on intelligence duty he intercepted a short-wave radio broadcast in plain English from Australia announcing that 17 transports with Australian troops had cleared Freetown en route to England. He passed the information on to the German Embassy and received a personal letter of thanks from Adolf Hitler.

Yoshikawa was sent to Hawaii in April 1941 under the COVER of a vice consul with the name Morimura. He provided a stream of intelligence to Tokyo about the U.S. Fleet at Pearl Harbor. The Japanese Consulate in Oahu transmitted his reports in the PURPLE encryption system up to Dec. 7, 1941, to the Foreign Ministry in Tokyo, which passed them on to the Navy. Although he reported in detail on the disposition of American warships and other conditions at Pearl Harbor, he had no knowledge that an attack was actually planned. Also, although some 160,000 persons of Japanese ancestry lived in Hawaii at the time, Yoshikawa never used any in his espionage activities: "those men of influence and character who might have assisted me in my secret mission were unanimously uncooperative . . .," he later wrote in the U.S. Naval Institute *Proceedings* (Dec. 1960).

After the attack on Pearl Harbor, Yoshikawa was interned by U.S. authorities. As he had burned his CODE book and all other material that could identify him as a spy, American intelligence officials did not know for some time that he was the chief Japanese intelligence AGENT in Hawaii. He was thus repatriated to Japan with other diplomatic personnel in Aug. 1942. He worked in naval intelligence for the remainder of the war.

Yurchenko, Col. Vitaly

(b. 1936)

KGB officer who defected to the United States and redefected back to the Soviet Union.

He defected in Aug. 1985. Then, on a rainy Saturday night in November, he was sitting with CIA security officers at a restaurant in the Georgetown section of Washington, D.C., when he stood and said he wanted to leave.

"If I'm not back in 15 minutes," he said, "don't blame yourself." He then walked about a mile up Wisconsin Avenue and entered the Soviet compound. After spending the weekend in the compound, he appeared at the redefection news conference on Monday. He said that he had been kidnapped and drugged. CIA and FBI officials, who said he had defected and had been cooperative, denied his allegations. The CIA described Yurchenko as a 15-year veteran of the KGB, a general-designate who coordinated espionage "work against American citizens."

The son of a factory worker who died in World War II, Yurchenko went to military training school and entered the Soviet submarine service. He was commissioned as a Navy lieutenant and sent to Pacific Fleet headquarters in Vladivostok. His career in the KGB began in 1959 when he became a COUNTERINTELLIGENCE officer in the armed forces, remaining in that role through most of the 1960s.

In 1958 he married an engineer. The couple had a daughter in 1961 and adopted a son born in 1969.

Yurchenko had been well known to U.S. intelligence officials. As KGB security officer for the Soviet Embassy in Washington from 1975 to 1980, Yurchenko met regularly with FBI agents, whom he got to know in the course of their mutual business: protecting the Soviet Embassy in Washington. Yurchenko and his FBI colleagues met at Danker's, a restaurant on E Street in northwest Washington, near FBI headquarters. His favorite drink was scotch.

After his U.S. assignment he was posted to Moscow as chief counterintelligence officer for internal security. He also worked with DEFECTORS to the Soviet Union, including HAROLD (KIM) PHILBY and GEORGE BLAKE. In April 1985 he was made deputy chief of the First Department of the First Chief Directorate of the KGB, which supervised intelligence operations in North America. He was personally managing KGB officers in Montreal and Ottawa when he defected.

Yurchenko had been sent to Rome from Moscow and had been staying at the Soviet Embassy in Rome. Telling his colleagues there that he was going to the Vatican Museum, instead, he went to a pay phone across the street from the U.S. Embassy and called a CIA officer, who told him to enter the embassy immediately. On Aug. 1, 1985, Yurchenko walked into the U.S. Embassy in Rome and said that he wanted to defect. The CIA, rating him as the no. 5 man in the KGB, called him the most important defector in decades. An attempt was made to have him become a DEFECTOR IN PLACE, but Yurchenko said he wanted to defect to the United States.

The CIA station chief in Rome cabled CIA headquarters in LANGLEY, Va., to say that Yurchenko had given some information on two MOLES: a man CODENAMED Robert and an NSA employee. One of the first CIA officers to read the report was ALDRICH H. AMES, who was himself a mole. Ames later was one of the CIA debriefers of Yurchenko and reported back, through his KGB HANDLER, what Yurchenko was telling the CIA.

Information from Yurchenko led to the unmasking of RONALD PELTON, an NSA analyst who sold information to the Soviets. Yurchenko also alerted authorities to the spying of former CIA employee EDWARD LEE HOWARD and gave a plausible account of the mysterious death of NICHOLAS G. SHADRIN, a U.S. DOUBLE AGENT who died in 1975.

Some COUNTERINTELLIGENCE officials, in the wake of Ames's betrayal, believe that "Yurchenko may have been sent by the KGB to betray Howard and Pelton in order to protect a bigger player, Rick Ames," according to David Wise in *Nightmover* (1995). Ames was arrested in Feb. 1994.

Wise quotes Harry B. Brandon, an FBI counterintelligence officer, as saying, "Is it possible they [the KGB] doubted Ames and sent Yurchenko here as a test to see if Ames would report Yurchenko's debriefing? Once it was determined that Ames was reporting on Yurchenko's disclosures, they told Yurchenko to come home. . . . The Yurchenko thing is still extraordinarily puzzling."

"You could sit two people down with exactly the same set of facts, and they would come up with opposite conclusions: He was a DOUBLE AGENT; no, he was a defector who became depressed," said Sen. David L. Boren (Democrat of Okla.), a member of the Senate Select Committee on Intelligence. The depression they related to Yurchenko's love life. Reportedly, the CIA took him to Ottawa and arranged a meeting with a Soviet Embassy employee who had been his lover. But when she spurned him, he gave up the idea that he could settle down in the United States with her. His marriage was faltering and his son was troublesome.

Intelligence analysts wondered about the "escape." The CIA security officers (by some accounts, there was only one) did not call the FBI or the Washington police; apparently, no attempt was made to intercept him. And why take him to a restaurant a few blocks from the Soviet compound?

The day after his "redefection," Yurchenko went to the State Department and said he was returning freely; the CIA produced a psychologist, who interviewed Yurchenko and agreed that he was not being coerced. But if he were a traitor, was he not facing imprisonment, even death? Western intelligence officials are still perplexed. Those who believed it was an act say that Yurchenko gave up Pelton and Howard because they were no longer useful. Perhaps by tossing the CIA those names Yurchenko was protecting a more valuable ASSET. Analysts who came to that conclusion believe their theory was confirmed by arrest of CIA mole Ames, who he had not given up.

Yurchenko supervised the handling of cases in the United States and Canada. One such case involved Navy radioman JOHN A. WALKER. Yurchenko had to decide whether Walker had been compromised by the FBI before his arrest, meaning that Walker had possibly provided DISINFORMATION to his Soviet handlers. Yurchenko determined that Walker had not been compromised. In his talks with CIA and FBI debriefers Yurcherko described the Walker case as one of the most important in KGB history. Through the CRYPTOMATERIAL provided by Walker and his fellow spy, Navy radioman JERRY A. WHITWORTH, the KGB was able to decipher more than 1 million messages, Yurchenko said.

There were reports that he had been executed upon returning to the USSR, but in April 1986 he was interviewed on German television and said that he had been undergoing unspecified "medical treatment." In an interview with a Moscow newspaper in Aug. 1986, he said that the CIA had tried to get him to implicate the Soviet Union in the 1981 assassination attempt on Pope John Paul II.

Z

007

SEE JAMES BOND [F]

Zabotin, Col. Nikolai

(b. ? d. 1946)

Soviet GRU RESIDENT in Canada from 1943 to 1945. Zabotin arrived in Canada in the summer of 1943 with IGOR S. GOUZENKO, a CIPHER clerk who was his subordinate officer. He directed the GRU spy ring in Canada that was stealing atomic secrets, recruiting Dr. ALLAN NUNN MAY, a nuclear physicist, and others.

When Gouzenko defected to the Canadian government in Sept. 1945, he revealed Zabotin's espionage activities. Canadian officials planned his arrest, but he evaded the authorities, traveled to New York, and, in Dec. 1945, boarded the Soviet merchant ship *Alexandrov*.

Accounts differ as to Zabotin's fate. Some reports contend that he jumped to his death from the *Alexandrov* as he was returning to the Soviet Union. More likely, he died of "heart failure" four days after his arrival in Moscow in Jan. 1946.

His Soviet CODE NAME was Grant.

Zacharias, Rear Adm. Ellis M.

(b. 1890 d. 1961)

Well-known senior U.S. Navy INTELLIGENCE OFFICER during World War II—and a Cold War prophet. A 1912 graduate of the Naval Academy, Zacharias was sent to Japan from 1920 to 1924 to study Japanese language and politics. He then served as a cryptographer on the Navy's Asiatic Station from 1926 to 1931.

Following school and intelligence assignments as well as sea duty, Zacharias was intelligence officer for the 11th Naval District (San Diego) from 1938 to 1940. He claimed that he had warned Adm. Husband E. Kimmel, the U.S. Pacific Fleet commander, of the coming PEARL HARBOR ATTACK, but Kimmel later testified that he had no recollection of such a conversation.

Zacharias commanded the heavy cruiser *Salt Lake City* from 1940 to 1942, participating in several Pacific actions. He served as deputy head of naval intelligence in 1942–1943 and then returned to sea in command of the battleship *New Mexico,* again seeing combat in the Pacific. After serving as chief of staff of the 11th Naval District in 1944–1945, he directed the Navy's psychological warfare program against Japan, broadcasting messages to the Japanese urging their surrender.

Zacharias retired in 1946, having been promoted to rear admiral on the Retired List. After his autobiographical *Secret Missions* was published later that year, he lectured and wrote on international and defense issues. His book *Behind Closed Doors*, a history of the start of the Cold War, published in 1950, predicted that World War III between the United States and Soviet Union would be "likely to materialize some time between the summer of 1952 and the fall of 1956."

Zacharski, Marian

An agent of the Polish intelligence services who was convicted of spying in the United States. Zacharski was caught after he bought secrets from WILLIAM H. BELL, an employee of the Hughes Aircraft Corporation.

Zacharski arrived in California in 1976 as the West Coast branch manager for the Polish American Machinery Company (POLAMCC), a firm incorporated in the United States as the marketing arm for the Polish trade agency Metal Export. As a salesman, Zacharski sold industrial equipment to the California-based aerospace industry. He developed a friendship with his neighbor Bell, who was deeply in debt. Beginning with requests for unclassified documents, Zacharski eventually persuaded Bell to provide secret material, ostensibly paying him as a "consultant." Bell received about $110,000 in cash and gold coins worth about $60,000 until 1981, when he was arrested by the FBI.

Zacharski was exposed by a Pole assigned to the UNITED NATIONS who defected and informed the FBI about Polish intelligence activities in the United States. Zacharski was a stand-in for the KGB, the ultimate receiver of Bell's information.

Bell, who agreed to cooperate with the FBI, engaged Zacharski in an incriminating conversation while wearing an FBI listening device under his shirt. Zacharski was arrested for espionage and in Dec. 1981 was sentenced to life imprisonment. Bell received an eight-year sentence. In June 1985 Zacharski was exchanged in a SPY SWAP, along with three other Eastern Bloc spies, for 25 persons held by Eastern Bloc countries.

Zaharoff, Sir Boris

(b. 1850 d. 1936)

International armaments contractor who operated a large, highly effective INDUSTRIAL ESPIONAGE network in Europe. Born in Turkey, reportedly of a Russian father and Greek mother, Zaharoff was an agent of the Vickers shipbuilding and armaments firm and subsequently chairman of the Vickers-Maxim arms corporation. He was reputed to have had close relations with British intelligence services—including master spy SIDNEY REILLY and the British king.

Zaharoff was referred to as the "merchant of death" by contemporary newspapers. He was a gatherer and purveyor of INDUSTRIAL INTELLIGENCE.

Zakharov, Gennadi F.

Soviet employee of the UNITED NATIONS (UN) whose arrest for spying in 1986 produced the retaliatory arrest of an American journalist in Moscow, jeopardizing a proposed summit meeting between President Reagan and Soviet leader Mikhail Gorbachev.

Zakharov, a Soviet INTELLIGENCE OFFICER assigned to recruit potential AGENTS, arrived in New York from Moscow to assume his post as scientific affairs officer assigned to the Center for Science and Technology for Development, part of the UN secretariat. The actual working of an agent is usually handled by a LEGAL—a KGB or GRU officer operating under diplomatic COVER as a member of the Soviet mission to the UN. If legals are caught spying, they can be expelled but not arrested and put on trial for espionage.

SURVEILLANCE teams of the FBI noted that Zakharov spent considerable time on college campuses in the New York area. Several students he approached reported him

to the FBI, but for various reasons, none of them could be developed as DOUBLE AGENTS. Then, in April 1983, the FBI recruited one of Zakharov's recruits, Leakh N. Bhoge, a 25-year-old man from Guyana. The FBI gave him the CODE NAME Plumber; the KGB name for him was Birg.

Zakharov told Bhoge, who was majoring in computer science, that he was a scientific researcher at the UN and needed help in getting information on robotics and computer technology. As Bhoge's graduation neared in late 1984, Zakharov urged Bhoge to get a job working on artificial intelligence or robotics. The FBI arranged for Bhoge to get a job in a machine shop that manufactured precision parts for radar and military aircraft engines. The shop was owned by the father of an FBI agent.

In May 1986 Zakharov dictated an agreement, which Bhoge wrote down, signed, and handed to Zakharov, who paid him some money to seal the bargain. Under the agreement, Bhoge would work as a spy "for seven to ten years, and after that . . . the contract can be renewed or extended." Payment would depend upon the quantity of the information he provided to the Soviets. During his meetings with Zakharov, Bhoge was wired with an FBI electronic device that transmitted conversations to an FBI vehicle parked nearby.

The FBI, knowing that the State Department would oppose arresting Zakharov, asked for permission from the White House. The FBI argued that Zakharov, although a lightweight and not particularly dangerous spy, provided the United States with an opportunity to show its displeasure at the flagrant use of the UN for spying. The Reagan administration was still smarting from the YEAR OF THE SPY (1985), when several U.S. spies had been discovered. Permission for the arrest was granted.

On Aug. 23 two FBI agents, a man and a woman posing as a pair of joggers, arrested Zakharov as he talked to Bhoge on a subway platform in Queens, New York. The FBI charged that Zakharov was a KGB intelligence officer who had paid Bhoge $1,000 for three classified documents showing the design of U.S. Air Force jet engines. The FBI had provided the documents to Bhoge. A search of Zakharov's apartment turned up ONE-TIME PADS, chemicals for SECRET WRITING, and greeting cards with MICRODOTS, nearly invisible specks containing encoded information.

Exactly a week later, KGB agents arrested NICHOLAS S. DANILOFF, a correspondent for *U.S. News & World Report*, in Moscow and charged him with espionage. Zakharov was allowed to plead no contest in U.S. federal court and was released to fly to the Soviet Union at the same moment that Daniloff was released in Moscow. The Reagan administration said it was not a SPY SWAP because Daniloff was not a spy.

Zakharov, Marshal of the Soviet Union Matvei Vasilievich

(b. 1898 d. 1972)

Chief of the GRU, Soviet MILITARY INTELLIGENCE, from 1949 to 1952, and twice the Chief of the Soviet General Staff.

Although Zakharov was in Petrograd (St. Petersburg) during World War I, he avoided being conscripted into the Army. He came out actively against the war, and joined the Bolshevik-controlled Red Guard in April 1917. He was with the Bolsheviks who stormed the Winter Palace in Oct. 1917.

He then took part in the suppression of anti-Bolshevik forces, held positions in the Red Army, and attended the prestigious Frunze Military Academy. By Sept. 1935 he had command of a regiment—at age 37. He held that command briefly, and in 1936 was sent to the new General Staff Academy, which was to train "suitable candidates in the art of strategy and supreme command." Having survived the Stalinist purges of the 1930s, in July 1937 Zakharov became chief of staff of the Leningrad Military District and, from May 1938, a deputy chief of the General Staff.

When Germany invaded the Soviet Union in June 1941 he was a major general and chief of staff of the newly formed Ninth Army at Odessa. He dispersed his forces, and his Air Force probably took fewer losses than any other target of the initial German air attacks. Later he was given command of the prestigious Second Belorussian Front, taking part in the massive June 1944 offensive against Germany. After the war Zakharov became head of the General Staff Academy.

In Jan. 1949 he became chief of the GRU, which was expanding its operations in the quest for TECHNICAL INTELLIGENCE about new Western weapons. In June 1952 a political struggle broke out over convening the 19th Communist Party Congress. The Politburo insisted; Stalin objected. The chief of the General Staff and Zakharov supported Stalin and were dismissed from their posts. After Stalin's death in March 1953, Zakharov's fall continued, but in May 1953 he was appointed commander of the Leningrad Military District and was able to hold on to that post.

In Oct. 1957 a struggle broke out between the Politburo—led by Nikita Khrushchev—and Marshal Georgi Zhukov. In this affair Zakharov was fully on the side of the Politburo and for this he was immediately appointed commander-in-chief of the Group of Soviet Forces in Germany. In 1959 he was promoted to Marshal of the Soviet Union and in April 1960 was appointed Chief of the General Staff.

But in the change of Soviet political-military leadership after the Soviets backed down in the CUBAN MISSILE CRISIS, Zakharov was dismissed in 1963. He then took an active part in the conspiracy against Khrushchev, and after the successful coup d'état in Oct. 1964 he was reappointed Chief of the General Staff. He served until Sept. 1971, when illness caused him to step down. He died four months later.

Zamir, Zvi

(b. 1925)

Director of the Israeli MOSSAD from 1968 to 1974.

Zamir, a native of Poland, arrived in Palestine as an infant. He joined the Israeli Army soon after Israel became a nation in May 1948. He was a major general when he was named to succeed MEIR AMIT as director of the Mossad. Zamir had no intelligence background (except for a tour as a gentleman spy/military ATTACHÉ in Great Britain). But observers said Prime Minister Levi Eshkol appointed Zamir precisely because he had never become entangled in Israel's complex intelligence apparatus.

When Black September terrorists kidnapped 11 Israeli athletes at the Olympic Games in Munich in 1972, Zamir flew to Munich. But he failed to convince West German authorities to let an Israeli anti-terrorist team rescue the hostages, and the athletes were massacred. Zamir was then charged with avenging their deaths. Prime Minister Golda Meir created a secret vengeance committee that authorized the assassination of any Black September terrorists responsible, directly or indirectly, for the massacre.

Zamir named MIKE HARARI the chief of the vengeance team. Although a scandal and bungling attended the work of the assassins, Zarnir survived the uproar. He also escaped personal humiliation in the investigations over intelligence failures in the Yom Kippur War (1973). He retired honorably after completing a five-year term as Mossad director.

Zarubin, Maj. Gen. Vassili Mikhalovich

(b. 1894 d. 1974)

Senior NKVD RESIDENT in the United States during much of World War II.

Zarubin's work in the security-intelligence field apparently began in the Vladivostok area after the Russian Civil War. He became the head of the economic department of the regional security service involved with economic crimes. After about two years at Vladivostok he was moved to the Siberian city of Kharbin, where many White Russians had fled after the Bolshevik victory in the Civil War, and was involved with issues affecting China. He was cited for his efforts.

Subsequently, with his wife, Lisa, he worked as an INTELLIGENCE OFFICER in Finland, France, and then Germany, where he served from 1934 to 1937. Reportedly his duties included setting up espionage NETWORKS in those countries.

Back in the USSR, Zarubin survived the purges that decimated the Soviet intelligence community as well as other parts of the Soviet society. Early in 1941 he was again ordered to the Far East where he attempted to subvert German officials to the Soviet cause.

As the German armies were approaching Moscow and encircling Leningrad in fall 1941, Zarubin was ordered to the United States, with the specific order—apparently from Josef Stalin—to prevent Germany from making a separate peace with Western countries, which would free the entire German war machine to fight on the Eastern Front against the USSR.

Zarubin legally entered the United States at San Francisco on Dec. 25, 1941, en route to New York City.

Under the COVER of second secretary at the Soviet Embassy, for three years he served as the senior NKVD resident in the United States. (He replaced GIAK OVAKIM, who had been arrested by the FBI in May 1941.)

An anonymous letter sent to the FBI on Aug. 7, 1943—in Russian—stated,

> [Zarubin] personally deals with getting agents into and out of the U.S.A. illegally, organizes secret radio stations and manufactures forged documents. His closest assistants are:
> 1. His wife directs political intelligence here, has a vast network of agents in almost all ministries including the State Department. She sends false information to the NKVD and everything of value passes on to the Germans through a certain Boris MOROZ (HOLLYWOOD). Put her under observation and you will quickly uncover the whole of her network.

The letter went on to list eight other associates.

According to a 2003 article by Vladimir Konoplitsky in *Pravda*, "He made a very significant contribution to the development of relations between the USSR and the United States. To crown it all, he started fishing for nuclear secrets together with his wife Lisa."

Zarubin was the NKVD contact with EARL BROWDER, head of the CPUSA and a Soviet AGENT. Zarubin also handled an operation, code-named Achievement, that attempted to free the assassin of Leon Trotsky from a Mexican prison.

His highly successful career as an intelligence officer ended unexpectedly when the NKVD administration received a report from a Soviet AGENT in New York saying that Zarubin was allegedly connected with U.S. intelligence services. A six-month investigation found that the allegations were false. However, Zarubin, recalled to the USSR, departed the United States in Aug. 1944. He was not allowed to again leave the Soviet Union.

He continued to work in the security field until 1948. At age 54, with the rank of major general in the NKVD, he was retired, reportedly because of poor health. After his death—26 years later—he was awarded the Order of Lenin and a village in the Far East was named "Zarubino."

In the VENONA intercepts of Soviet intelligence communications his CODE NAME was Maxim; his wife was code-named Vardo. They were also known as Poppy and Mommy. Zarubin also operated under the alias Zublin, with the code name Maxin.

Zehe, Alfred

East German exchange professor arrested in the United States in 1983 for spying against U.S. Navy activities. After pleading guilty to eight counts of espionage, he was imprisoned but was exchanged on June 11, 1985, in a SPY SWAP between the United States and East Germany.

In a test of U.S. espionage laws, Zehe claimed that as an East German who received classified information in Mexico, he was immune from U.S. law. The court found that Congress intended espionage laws to apply to noncitizens whether or not the acts were committed in the United States, as long as U.S. secrets were involved.

Zelenograd

Russian city some 40 miles northwest of Moscow that in the late 1950s became the center for high-technology research, including computer development and specialized intelligence equipment. It thus became a high-priority target for Western espionage, and foreign visitors were not normally allowed in the city during the Soviet era.

The city, previously called Kryukovo, was renamed in the mid-1960s. The population of Zelenograd in the late 1980s—at the end of the Cold War—was 170,000, providing some 35,000 workers for 26 major scientific research institutes and factories in the city. With the end of the Soviet defense buildup there has been large-scale unemployment in the city; some 4,500 workers had left by early 1993. Efforts to partially convert to commercial electronics were started and numerous small electronics and computer firms were established.

Zelle, Margaretha

SEE MATA HARI

Zenit

The first Soviet photo SATELLITE. First placed in orbit two years after the first successful U.S. CORONA satellite, in some respects the Zenit was a more sophisticated satellite.

In the 1950s the Soviet Union, like the United States, feared the development of advanced strategic weapons by the competing superpower. The decision was made to develop a spy satellite in Jan. 1956. Seven months later, in Aug. 1956, the Experimental Design Bureau (OKB) No. 1 was established under rocket scientist Sergei Korolev specifically to design satellites.

The world's first satellite to enter earth orbit was *Sputnik 1*, launched on Oct. 4, 1957. The small, 184-pound satellite captured the world's headlines and imagination. Of significance to Western military analysts was the power of the rocket booster and the accuracy required to place the satellite in orbit. A month later, on Nov. 3, 1957, the Soviets launched another satellite, placing the then phenomenal payload of 1,120 pounds into earth orbit. On board *Sputnik 2* was the live dog Laika, instrumented to relay psychological data back to earth on the animal's reaction to weightlessness, radiation, and other environmental conditions. The satellite *Sputnik 3*, which was launched into orbit on May 15, 1958, weighed 2,926 pounds, a payload not matched by the United States for six years. The size of the payloads and the missiles needed to carry them were impressive, as they foreshadowed the potential for placing military payloads in orbit, especially RECONNAISSANCE systems.

The first reconnaissance satellite was named Zenit (Zenith) and was adapted from the Vostok manned spacecraft first launched on April 12, 1961, carrying cosmonaut Yuri Gagarin. The Kovalev design bureau designation for the Vostok spacecraft was 1K for the first manned spacecraft. The Zenit would be project 2K.

The satellite would weigh some 11,000 pounds (compared to 1,874 pounds for Corona); it would be fitted with four cameras—two high-resolution and two low-resolution, plus a limited SIGNALS INTELLIGENCE (SIGINT) or FERRET capability. The latter system would relay signals down to a ground station in the Soviet Union while the exposed film was parachuted back to Earth within the camera section. This system was more complex than Corona's single camera, which was expended in space and had no SIGINT capability.

The first attempt to launch a Zenit satellite, on Dec. 11, 1961, failed when the booster rocket's third stage malfunctioned. The Zenit satellite fell to earth in Siberia

and was never located. On the second Zenit flight, on March 16–19, 1962, the missile and recovery system functioned perfectly, but the satellite's orientation system malfunctioned. Thus, the camera did not photograph its intended TARGETS.

The third Zenit launch—a spycraft labeled *Cosmos 7*—on July 28, 1962, was a success. After an almost-four-day flight, the *Cosmos 7* returned a film packet to Soviet territory that contained useful earth photographs. Subsequently, the Zenit and its successor camera satellites provided Soviet intelligence specialists and military planners with details of Western defenses, just as the Corona and its successors were doing for Soviet targets. Like its U.S. counterpart, this first Soviet spy satellite was cloaked in secrecy. The U.S. satellites were given the cover of being Discoverer series research satellites. The Soviets followed suit, and it was apparently several years before the Western intelligence community realized the true nature of the Red spy satellites. The Zenit series spy

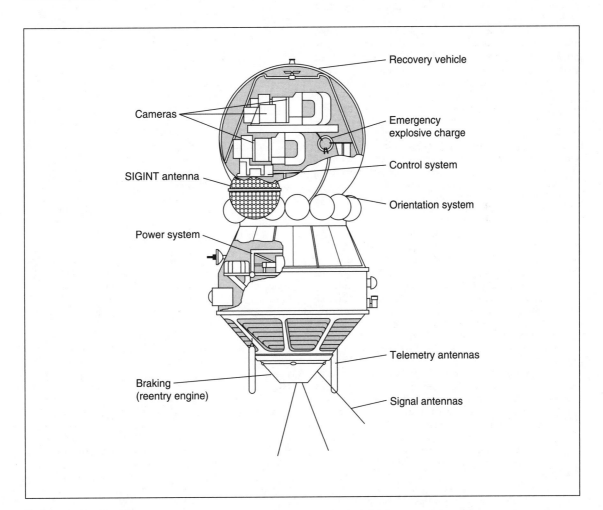

Zenit reconnaissance satellite.

satellites, like their American cousins, provided national leaders and military planners with key ingredients for their major decisions.

The follow-up RESURS-F and KOMETA satellites were refinements of the Vostok/Zenit series, with improved cameras. The SIGINT "piggyback" package was deleted from the later photoreconnaissance satellites and fitted in specialized vehicles (see RADAR OCEAN SURVEILLANCE SATELLITE). Fourth- and fifth-generation photo satellites have been developed and orbited. Flight times have also been lengthened. The basic Zenit satellites orbited for up to eight to 12 days; the *Kometa* and later satellites operated up to eight weeks.

Zeppelin, Operation (1)

Name for an elaborate German plan to assassinate Soviet dictator Josef Stalin in Moscow. The plan began in July 1944 when ERNST KALTENBRUNNER, head of the RSHA (Reich Central Security Office), asked the Air Force's KG 200, a unit that specialized in putting AGENTS behind enemy lines, if it could land a man within 60 miles of the Soviet capital of Moscow. At the time the German front lines were several hundred miles from Moscow.

A German transport plane was to make a clandestine flight to a landing in the countryside near Moscow. An assassin—a former Russian officer captured by the Germans who had demonstrated his loyalty—would be unloaded with a motorcycle and the weapons to assassinate Stalin as he drove through Moscow. His assassination team members had been thoroughly prepared, they were well armed and equipped for escape after the operation, and there was a hideaway waiting for them in Moscow. (Before the mission a woman was added to the hit team. She was also a former Russian officer. On the eve of the mission the two were married.)

Operation Zeppelin began with a German RECONNAISSANCE party being parachuted into the proposed landing area to ensure that the location was suitable. That team sent a radio signal that all was well. On the night of Sept. 5–6, 1944, the four-engine Ardo Ar 232B took off from an airfield in Latvia and headed toward the landing site, which was about 60 miles from Moscow, between Smolensk and the capital. The 370-mile flight was uneventful. However, as the plane was about to land in the early morning, it was met by Soviet anti-aircraft gunfire.

The advance team had been captured and forced to radio the "go" signal back to Germany; the radio checks had failed to detect that the team had been TURNED. The anti-aircraft guns had opened fire without authority from the Soviet forces setting a trap for the plane. (The Soviets did not know the plane's cargo or mission.)

The pilot quickly regained altitude and flew toward an alternative landing site, near Karmanovo, east of Smolensk. This secondary site seemed clear. The plane landed, but a wing hit a tree, tearing off an engine and starting a fire that would serve as a beacon for Soviet troops. Quickly, Maj. "Tavrin" and Sub-Lt. "Shilova"

got onto the motorcycle carried in the Ar 234B and sped off toward Moscow. The six crewmen of the smashed plane set off on foot toward the west. The fliers carried maps, Soviet money and cigarettes, and emergency provisions, but they could not speak Russian. And, of course, they wore German uniforms.

The assassins sped on through the night. When stopped by a sentry at a roadblock, they properly produced the necessary documents. But as former Luftwaffe pilot P. W. Stahl related in *KG 200: The True Story* (1979), the sentry was just about to return the documents and let the couple proceed when the major made a fateful remark: "Hurry up, will you please. We have been on our way all night!" The sentry hesitated. Until just a short while ago it had rained in streams—yet the clothing of the motorcyclists and their machine were remarkably dry. He raised the alarm, and that was the end of Operation Zeppelin.

Twenty-four hours after the crash, the Ar 234B crewmen sent a radio signal that they were attempting to escape on foot. They were never heard from again.

Zeppelin, Operation (2)

Major British DECEPTION operation during all of 1944 to convince the German High Command that the Allies planned significant additional operations in the Mediterranean area to draw German troops away from northwest Europe.

According to British historian Michael Howard in the strategic deception volume of *British Intelligence in the Second World War* (1990), "It had always been an intrinsic element of Allied planning for the invasion of north-west France, and indeed in German expectation of Allied plans, that German forces in the south of France should be pinned down by the threat or the reality of an attack on the French Mediterranean coast."

This concept fit perfectly with the views of Prime Minister Winston Churchill, who always sought the "soft underbelly" of the German empire (southern Europe) to avoid a possible ground stalemate in the European conflict, as occurred in World War I.

Zeppelin ploys were developed by "Force A," a staff that could call on various Mediterranean-area commands for support. The main thrust of Zeppelin was to make the Germans believe that Lt. Gen. George S. Patton's U.S. Seventh Army in Algiers would strike the French southern coast. But few troops were actually in North Africa, and this specific deception—given the CODE NAME Vendetta—consisted mainly of dummy tanks, stores, and landing craft being assembled, as well as fake exercises being conducted out of Oran. Also, passing British warships, including the aircraft carriers *Indomitable* and *Victorious* en route to the Far East, added to the realism of the exercises.

The deception was to continue through July, but the withdrawal of what forces were available for real assignments brought Vendetta to an end in late June, when rumor was passed that the attack had been postponed.

(In fact, U.S. and French troops did land in southern France on Aug. 13, 1944.)

German sources reveal that Vendetta was only a partial success.

Vendetta was complemented at the eastern end of the Mediterranean by Operation Turpitude, to make the Germans believe that the Allies intended landings on the mainland of Greece and the Balkan Peninsula, with a preliminary assault against the large island of Rhodes off the coast of Turkey. Again, dummy forces were established, for this hoax in Syria as well as in North Africa.

This effort continued until late June. Again, the deception had only limited success. The German High Command on June 8 issued a warning that "clear indications of imminent operations in the eastern Mediterranean demand quite exceptional vigilance."

Only one German division was moved out of the Mediterranean area following the U.S. D-DAY landings on June 6, 1944, and it did not arrive in the "critical period" of the landings. According to Howard's tome, " 'A' Force in fact may have fallen short of the ambitious goals it had set itself, but it had done all that had been expected of it by the [British-U.S.] Combined Chiefs of Staff."

Zimmermann Telegram

Intercepted message whose contents stunned the United States and became a key factor in the U.S. decision to enter World War I. On Jan. 16, 1917, German Foreign Minister Arthur Zimmermann sent a telegram to the German ambassador to Mexico revealing plans for imminent unrestricted submarine warfare. Zimmermann directed the ambassador to offer Mexico an alliance with Germany and promise "an understanding on our part that Mexico is to reconquer the lost territory in Texas, New Mexico, and Arizona."

British NAVAL INTELLIGENCE intercepted and decoded the telegram (see ROOM 40). Rear Adm. Sir REGINALD (BLINKER) HALL, director of British Naval Intelligence, immediately realized the strategic value of the telegram. If U.S. officials saw it, their outrage would undoubtedly ease American entry into the war. The Foreign Office wanted him to release it. But Hall did not want the Germans to discover that his cryptographers had cracked the high-level German diplomatic code. Knowing that Zimmermann had sent the telegram by several routes, Hall had an AGENT in Mexico City obtain a copy sent by a lower-level cipher.

The British showed the telegram to the American ambassador in London, who in turn transmitted it to the State Department in Washington. A shocked President Wilson arranged for the telegram to be released on March 1 by the Associated Press without information about how it had been intercepted and deciphered. American pacifists condemned it as a hoax perpetrated by the British. But its authenticity was confirmed by Zimmermann himself at a March 3 press conference.

When President Wilson asked Congress for a declaration of war on April 2, 1917, he cited the telegram as proof that Germany "means to act against our peace and security."

Zinoviev Letter

An alleged 1924 secret communication from Grigori Zinoviev, president of the Soviet Comintern, to the Communist Party of Great Britain. The letter, later revealed as a forgery, urged communist cells in the British Army and labor unions to get ready to start a revolution. The letter, published in British newspapers on Oct. 25, 1924, four days before a general election, helped to destroy Britain's first Labour Party government, under Ramsay MacDonald.

The Comintern, a Moscow-directed organization for fostering worldwide communism, was seen as a grave threat to Britain in the 1920s. Responding to the "Red Scare," the Secret Intelligence Service MI6 sought revolutionaries, especially in the ranks of the Labour Party and trade unions. The investigations turned up the letter, and MI6 did not say how it had been intercepted. The mod-

You never know who's listening!

CARELESS TALK COSTS LIVES

Spies can be anywhere: A World War II poster. (IMPERIAL WAR MUSEUM)

ern consensus is that the letter was forged by *British* plotters trying to bring down a Labour Party perceived as dangerous to the nation. Master spy SIDNEY REILLY was probably involved.

Intelligence documents released in 1997 indicate that the letter was an ingenious fake. British intelligence apparently had an ASSET that provided verbatim transcripts of Politburo sessions. Revolutionary plans were aired in those sessions. So the Zinoviev letter had what was probably genuine rhetoric but was nonetheless forged to advance a British-inspired plot. Speculation about the transcript supplied centered on Boris Bajanov, who had been Josef Stalin's private secretary and later became Politburo secretary. Bajanov fled Russia in 1928 and reportedly was settled in France, under official protection, in a move to dispel suspicion that he had been a British AGENT.

Britain's Labour government had established diplomatic ties with the Soviet Union and had been planning to sign a commercial treaty with Soviets. When the letter was published, a shocked MacDonald sent a protest to the Soviet government. But the damage was done. Labour suffered an enormous loss in the next election, and the Conservatives came back into power.

Ironically, Stalin soon eliminated both the Comintern and Zinoviev, who was falsely accused of working for foreign intelligence services. In a 1936 show trial, he was condemned to death and soon shot.

Z Priorities

Early British priority marking scheme for the distribution of ENIGMA decrypts in World War II. The decrypts were marked with from one to five Zs, with the higher number of Zs indicating the higher priority.

Zublin, Vassili

SEE VASSILI ZARUBIN

APPENDIX

VENONA CODE NAMES

The following code names have been identified in the Venona decryptions. Several additional names have been identified, but withheld from the public. Note that several individuals have multiple code names.

Abram	Jack Soble
Akim	Serge G. Luk'yanov
Albert	Iskhak Akhmerov
Alek	Allan Nunn May
Ales	Alger Hiss
Antenna	Julius Rosenberg
Anton	Leonid Kvasnikov
Arno	Harry Gold
Arsenal	U.S. War Department
Babylon	San Francisco
The bank	Department of State
Bear Cubs	U.S. Republican Party
Big House	Moscow Center
Bill of Exchange	Robert Oppenheimer
Boar	Winston Churchill
Boatswain	Vice President Henry Wallace
Boris	Aleksand P. Saprykin
Bumblebee	David Greenglass
Calibre	David Greenglass
Caliph	William C. Bullitt
Capitalist	Averell Harriman
Captain	President Roosevelt
Charles (Charl'z)	Klaus Fuchs
Clark	Igor Gouzenko
Clever Girl	Elizabeth Bentley
Country	United States
Countryside	Mexico
Czech	Robert Menaker
Decree	Lend-Lease
Deputy	Vice President Henry Wallace
Echo	(possibly) Bernard Schuster
Enormoz	Manhattan Project or A-bomb
Fellowcountryman	member of the U.S. Communist Party
Frost	Boris Morros
Gennadi	Giak Ovakimian
Gift	Grigori Kasparov
Good Girl	Elizabeth Bentley
Goose	Harry Gold
Hare	Maurice Halperin
Helmsman	Earl Browder
Hen-Harrier	Cordell Hull
Hicks	Guy Burgess
Homer	Donald Maclean
House	Moscow Center
Imperialist	Walter Lippmann
Intelligensia	J.B.S. Haldane
Island	Great Britain
Islanders	British
Izba	Office of Strategic Services
Izra	Donald Wheeler
Johnson	Anthony Blunt
Jurist	Harry Dexter White
Khata	Federal Bureau of Investigation
Kapitan	President Roosevelt
Karfagen	Washington, D.C.
Koch	Duncan C. Lee
Konspiratoria	tradecraft and operational security
Kulak	Thomas Dewey
Lawyer	Harry Dexter White
League	U.S. Government
Leslie	Lona Cohen
Liberal	Julius Rosenberg
Line	specific long-term task or operation, such as the Line for the atomic bomb
Link	William Weisband
Lotsman	Vice President Henry Wallace
Luka	Pavel P. Klarin
Maj	Stepan Apresyan

Codename	Identity
Marquis	Joseph Milton Bernstein
Maxim	Vassili M. Zarubin
Maxin	Vassili Zubilin
May	Stepan Apresyan
Mer	Iskhak Akhmerov
MI	(probably) Chile
Mim	Mikhail I. Mikhailov
Myrna	Elizabeth Bentley
Needle	Jones Orin York
Neighbors	how the NKVD referred to GRU and vice
Nick	Amadeo Sabatini
Ostrov	Great Britain
Page	Lauchlin B. Currie
Pair (The)	Nicholas and Maria Fisher
Pal	Nathan Silvermaster
Petr	Aleksandr P. Grachev
Petrov	Lavrenty Beria or Vsevolod Merkulov
Pilot	William Ullmann
Prince	Laurance Duggan
Probationers	Soviet agents
Radio Announcer	William Donovan
Ras	Charles de Gaulle
Relay	Morton Sobell (doubtful identification)
Rest	Klaus Fuchs
Richard	Harry Dexter White
Robert	Nathan Gregory
Rulevoj	Earl Browder
Ruppert	Franz L. Neumann
Serb	Morton Sobell (doubtful identification)
Sergej	Vladimir S. Pravdin
Sherwood	Laurance Duggan
Silvermaster	Nathan Gregory
Sima	Judith Coplon
Sound	Jacob Galos
Stanley	Harold (Kim) Philby
Stock	Mikhail Shalyapin
Technician	Fedor A. Nosov
Tourist	James Hill
Tyre	New York City
UCN/9	Cedric Belfrage
Vadim	Anatoli Gromov
Vardo	Elizabetha Zarubin
Viktor	P.M. Fitin
Vitaliy	Pavel Revizor
Vladislav	Nikolay G. Redin
Volkov	Andre Orlov
Wasp	Ruth Greenglass
Young	Theodore Alvin Hall
Zemlyak	member of the Commnist Party
Zveno	(possibly) William Weisband
Zvuk	Jacob Golos

RECOMMENDED READING

In many *Spy Book* entries we have mentioned or quoted from other books. Some, such as Joyce Wadler's book *Liaison* (1993) about Bernard Boursicot, apply only to the entry in which they are cited; others address a broad range of intelligence matters.

We recommend the following books to readers who wish to know more about the entries. We do not include any fictional works in this list; for those, see entry LITERARY SPIES. But, we do make one exception: *The Spy Who Came In from the Cold* (1963) by John le Carré, a book that captures better than any nonfictional work the atmosphere of the Cold War, especially in Berlin, and the dark, weary, deceitful, often grubby world of espionage.

AUTOBIOGRAPHIES AND BIOGRAPHIES

[Where necessary for clarity, the subject's name appears in brackets.]

Accoce, Pierre, and Quet, Pierre. *A Man Called Lucy, 1939–1945.* New York: Coward-McCann, 1966.

Allen, Thomas B. *George Washington, Spymaster: How the Americans Outspied the British and Won the Revolutionary War.* Washington, D.C.: National Geographic, 2004.

Blitzer, Wolf. *Territory of Lies.* New York: Harper & Row, 1989. [Jonathan Jay Pollard]

Borovik, Genrikh. *The Philby Files.* Boston: Little, Brown, 1994.

Boyle, Andrew. *The Fourth Man.* New York: Dial Press, 1979. [Sir Anthony Blunt]

Brissaud, André. *Canaris.* New York: Grosset & Dunlap, 1974.

Bucher, Lloyd M., and Rosovich, Mark. *Bucher: My Story.* Garden City, N.Y.: Doubleday, 1970.

Carter, Miranda. *Anthony Blunt: His Lives.* New York: Farrar, Straus and Giroux, 2001.

Cave Brown, Anthony. *The Last Hero: Wild Bill Donovan.* New York: Times Books, 1982.

———. *"C".* New York: Macmillan, 1987. [Sir Stewart Menzies]

Cecil, Robert. *A Divided Life.* New York: Morrow, 1988. [Donald Maclean]

Colby, William, and Forbath, Peter. *Honorable Men: My Life in the CIA.* New York: Simon & Schuster, 1978.

Currey, Cecil B. *Edward Lansdale: The Unquiet American.* Boston: Houghton Mifflin, 1988.

Deacon, Richard. *"C": A Biography of Sir Maurice Oldfield, Head of MI6.* London: Macdonald, 1984.

Feklislov, Alexander, and Kostin, Sergei. *The Man Behind the Rosenbergs.* New York: Enigma Books, 2001. Originally published in France under the title: *Confession d'un agent soviétique, 1999.*

Gazur, Edward. *Alexander Orlov: The FBI's KGB General.* New York: Carroll & Graf, 2002.

Gehlen, Reinhardt. *The Service.* New York: World Publishing, 1972.

Grose, Peter. *Gentleman Spy: The Life of Allen Dulles.* Boston: Houghton Mifflin, 1994.

Hart, John Limond. *The CIA's Russians.* Annapolis, Md.: Naval Institute Press, 2003.

Höhne, Heinz. *Canaris: Hitler's Master Spy.* Garden City, N.Y.: Doubleday, 1979.

Höhne, Heinz, and Zolling, Hermann. *The General Was a Spy.* New York: Coward, McCann & Geoghegan, 1972. [Reinhard Gehlen]

Hurt, Henry. *Shadrin: The Spy Who Never Came Back.* New York: Reader's Digest Press, 1981.

Hyde, H. Montgomery. *Room 3603.* New York: Farrar Straus, 1962. Entitled *The Quiet Canadian* in Great Britain. [William Stephenson]

Ivanov, Yevgeny, with Sokolov, Gennady. *The Naked Spy.* London: Blake, 1992. [Christine Keeler and friends]

James, Sir William. *The Eyes of the Navy.* London: Methuen, 1955. [Adm. Sir William Reginald Hall]

Kalugin, Oleg. *The First Directorate: My 32 Years in Intelligence and Espionage Against the West*. New York: St. Martin's Press, 1994.

Khrushchev, Nikita. *Khrushchev Remembers*. Boston: Little, Brown, 1970.

———. *Khrushchev Remembers: The Glasnost Tapes*. Boston: Little, Brown, 1990.

———. *Khrushchev Remembers: The Last Testament*. Boston: Little, Brown, 1974.

Knight, Amy. *Beria: Stalin's First Lieutenant*. Princeton, N.J.: Princeton University Press, 1993.

Krivitsky, W.G. *In Stalin's Secret Service: Memoirs of the First Soviet Master Spy to Defect*. New York: Enigma Books, 2000.

Layton, Edwin T. *"And I Was There."* New York: Morrow, 1985.

Levchenko, Stanislav. *On the Wrong Side*. Washington, D.C.: Pergamon-Brassey's, 1988.

Lockhart, Robert Bruce. *Memoirs of a British Agent*. London: Macmillan, 1974. Reprinted 1932 edition.

———. *Reilly: The First Man*. New York: Viking Press, 1987.

Marshall, Bruce. *The White Rabbit: The Secret Agent the Gestapo Could Not Crack*. London: Cassel & Co, 2001 [Forest Frederick Edward Yeo-Thomas]

Ostrovsky, Victor, and Hoy, Clair. *By Way of Deception: The Making and Unmaking of a Mossad Officer*. New York: St. Martin's Press, 1990.

Paine, Lauran. *The Abwehr*. London: Robert Hale, 1984. [Rear Adm. Wilhelm Canaris]

Penkovsky, Oleg. *The Penkovsky Papers*. Garden City, N.Y.: Doubleday, 1965.

Persico, Joseph E. *Casey*. New York: Viking, 1990.

Philby, H.A.R. *My Silent War*. New York: Grove Press, 1968. Recommended with reservations. Many people mentioned in this account of Philby's traitorous life have denied his version of events. The book was written under KGB auspices.

Philby, Rufina, with Peake, Hayden, and Lyubimov, Mikhail. *The Private Life of Kim Philby: The Moscow Years*. New York: Fromm International, 2000.

Powers, Thomas. *The Man Who Kept the Secrets: Richard Helms and the CIA*. New York: Knopf, 1979.

Prados, John. *Lost Crusader: The Secret Wars of CIA Director William Colby—The True Story of One of America's Most Controversial Spymasters*. New York: Oxford University Press, 2003.

Romanov, A.I. *Nights Are the Longest There: A Memoir of the Secret Security Service*. Boston: Little, Brown, 1972.

Schecter, Jerold L., and Deriabin, Peter S. *The Spy Who Saved the World*. New York: Charles Scribners, 1992. [Col. Oleg Penkovsky]

Schellenberg, Walter. *The Schellenberg Memoirs*. London: Andrew Deutsch, 1956.

Srodes, James. *Allen Dulles: Master of Spies*. Washington, D.C.: Regnery, 1999.

Stevenson, William. *A Man Called Intrepid*. New York: Harcourt Brace Jovanovich, 1976. [William Stephenson]

———. *Intrepid's Last Case*. New York: Ballantine, 1983. [William Stephenson]

Strong, Sir Kenneth W.D. *Intelligence at the Top*. Garden City, N.Y.: Doubleday, 1968.

Sudoplatov, Pavel Anatolievich. *Special Tasks*. Boston: Little, Brown, 1994.

Suvorov, Viktor. *Aquarium: The Career and Defection of a Soviet Military Spy*. London: Hamish Hamilton, 1985.

———. *The Liberators: My Life in the Soviet Army*. New York: Berkley, 1981.

Tanenhaus, Sam. *Whittaker Chambers: A Biography*. New York: Random House, 1997.

Theoharis, Athan G., and Cox, John Stuart. *The Boss: J. Edgar Hoover and the Great American Inquisition*. Philadelphia: Temple University Press, 1988.

Troy, Thomas F. *Donovan and the CIA: A History of the Establishment of the Central Intelligence Agency*. Frederick, Md.: University Publications of America, 1981.

Truman, Harry S. *Years of Trial and Hope: 1946–1952*, vol. 2 in *Memories*. Garden City, N.Y.: Doubleday, 1956.

West, Nigel (ed.). *The Faber Book of Espionage*. London: Faber and Faber, 1993. [British intelligence operatives.]

Williams, Robert Chadwell. *Klaus Fuchs: Atom Spy*. Cambridge: Harvard University Press, 1987.

Wolf, Markus. *Man Without a Face: The Autobiography of Communism's Greatest Spymaster*. New York: Times Books, 1997.

Wynne, Grenville. *Contact on Gorky Street*. New York: Antheneum, 1968.

BRITISH INTELLIGENCE

Babington-Smith, Constance. *Air Spy: The Story of Photo Intelligence in World War II*. New York: Harper & Brothers, 1957.

Beesly, Patrick. *Very Special Intelligence: The Story of the Admiralty's Operational Intelligence Centre 1939–1945*. London: Greenhill, 2000. Reprint of 1977 edition.

Deacon, Richard. *A History of the British Secret Service*. London: Frederick Muller, 1969.

Foot, M.R.D. *SOE: The Special Operations Executive 1940–1946*. London: Pimlico, 1999. Reprint of 1984 edition.

Hesketh, Roger. *FORTITUDE: The D-Day Deception Campaign*. Woodstock, N.Y.: Overlook Press, 2000.

Hinsley, F. Harry; Thomas, E.E.; Ranson, C.F.G.; and Knight, R.C. *British Intelligence in the Second World War* in 4 vols. London: Her Majesty's Stationery Office, 1979–1990.

Hyde, H. Montgomery. *Secret Intelligence Agent: British Espionage in America and the Creation of the OSS.* New York: St. Martin's Press, 1982.

Masterman, John Cecil. *The Double-Cross System in the War of 1939–45.* New Haven, Conn.: Yale University Press, 1972.

Montagu, Ewen Edward Samuel. *The Man Who Never Was.* Philadelphia: Lippincott, 1954.

———. *Beyond Top Secret Ultra.* New York: Coward, McCann, Geoghegan, 1978.

Modin, Yuri. *My Five Cambridge Friends.* London: Headline, 1994.

Page, Bruce, and Leitch, David, and Knightley, Phillip. *The Philby Conspiracy.* New York: Ballantine, 1981. Updated reprint of 1969 edition.

Pincher, Chapman. *Their Trade in Treachery.* London: Sidgwick and Jackson, 1981.

———. *Too Secret Too Long.* New York: St. Martin's Press, 1984.

Porter, Bernard. *Plots and Paranoia: A History of Political Espionage in Britain 1790–1988.* London: Routledge, 1989.

Ring, Jim. *We Came Unseen: The Untold Story of Britain's Cold War Submarines.* London: John Murray, 2001.

Sinclair, Andrew. *The Red and the Blue: Cambridge, Treason and Intelligence.* Boston: Little, Brown, 1986.

West, Nigel. *The Circus: MI5 Operations 1945–1972.* New York: Stein and Day, 1983. Published in England as *A Matter of Trust.* London: Weidenfeld and Nicolson, 1982.

———. *The Secret War for the Falklands: The SAS, MI6, and the War Whitehall Nearly Lost.* London: Little, Brown, 1997.

———. *GCHQ: The Secret Wireless War 1900–86.* London: Weidenfeld and Nicholson, 1986.

———. *MI5: British Security Service Operations 1909–1945.* London: The Bodley Head, 1981.

———. *MI5: The True Story of the Most Secret Counterespionage Organization in the World.* New York: Stein and Day, 1982.

———. *MI6: British Secret Intelligence Service Operations 1909–1945.* New York: Random House, 1983.

Winterbotham, F.W. *The Nazi Connection.* New York: Harper & Row, 1978.

Wright, Peter. *Spycatchers.* New York: Viking, 1987.

CRYPTOGRAPHY

Benson, Robert Louis, and Warner, Michael. *Venona: Soviet Espionage and the American Response 1939–1957.* Washington, D.C.: National Security Agency and Central Intelligence Agency, 1996.

Bamford, James. *The Puzzle Palace.* New York: Penguin, 1982.

Boyd, Carl. *Hitler's Japanese Confidant: General Oshima Hiroshi and Magic Intelligence, 1941–1945.* Lawrence, Kans.: University Press of Kansas, 1993.

Drea, Edward. *MacArthur's ULTRA.* Lawrence, Kans.: University Press of Kansas, 1992.

Gilbert, James L., and Finnegan, John P. (eds.) *U.S. Army Signals Intelligence of World War II.* Washington, D.C.: Government Printing Office, 1993.

Hinsley, F. Harry, and Stripp, Alan (eds.). *Code Breakers.* Oxford: Oxford University Press, 1993.

Kahn, David. *The Codebreakers.* London: Weidenfeld and Nicholson, 1967.

———. *Kahn on Codes.* New York: Macmillan, 1983.

———. *Seizing Enigma: The Race to Break the German U-boat Codes, 1939–1943.* Boston: Houghton, Mifflin, 1991.

Lewin, Ronald. *The American Magic.* New York: Farrar, Straus and Giroux, 1982.

———. *Ultra Goes to War.* New York: McGraw-Hill, 1978.

Prados, John. *Combined Fleet Decoded: The Secret History of American Intelligence and the Japanese Navy in World War II.* New York: Random House, 1995.

Spector, Ronald H. *Listening to the Enemy.* Wilmington, Del.: Scholarly Resources, 1988.

Winterbotham, F.W. *The Ultra Secret.* New York: Harper & Row, 1974.

Yardley, Herbert O. *The American Black Chamber.* Indianapolis: Bobbs-Merrill, 1931. Reprinted: New York: Ballantine, 1981.

FRENCH INTELLIGENCE

Marenches, Count Alexandre de, and Andelman, David A. *The Fourth World War: Diplomacy and Espionage in an Age of Terrorism.* New York: Morrow, 1992.

Porch, Douglas. *The French Secret Service.* New York: Farrar, Straus and Giroux, 1995.

Thyraud de Vosjoli, Philip. *Lamia.* Boston: Little, Brown, 1970.

ISRAELI INTELLIGENCE

Black, Ian, and Morris, Benny. *Israel's Secret Wars.* New York: Grove Weidenfeld, 1991.

Raviv, Dan, and Melman, Yossi. *Every Spy a Prince.* Boston: Houghton Mifflin, 1990.

RUSSIAN-SOVIET INTELLIGENCE

Andrew, Christopher, and Gordievsky, Oleg. *KGB: The Inside Story.* London: Hodder and Stoughton, 1990.

Barron, John. *KGB: The Secret World of Soviet Secret Agents.* New York: Reader's Digest Press, 1974.

———. *KGB Today: The Hidden Hand.* New York: Reader's Digest Press, 1983.

Central Intelligence Agency, The Rote Kapelle. *The Central Intelligence Agency's History of Soviet Intelligence and Espionage Networks in Western Europe, 1936–1945.* Washington, D.C.: University Press of America, 1979.

Costello, John. *Deadly Illusions.* New York: Crown, 1994.

———. *Mask of Treachery.* New York: Morrow, 1989.

Deacon, Richard. *A History of the Russian Secret Service.* London: Frederick Muller, 1972.

Dziak, John J. *Chekisty: A History of the KGB.* Lexington, Mass.: Lexington Books, 1988.

Glantz, David. *Soviet Military Intelligence in War.* London: Frank Cass, 1990.

Hingley, Ronald. *The Russian Secret Police.* New York: Simon & Schuster, 1970.

Perrault, Gilles. *The Red Orchestra.* New York: Schocken Books, 1969.

Richelson, Jeffrey T. *Sword and Shield: Soviet Intelligence and Security Apparatus.* Cambridge, Mass.: Ballinger, 1986.

Ruud, Charles A., and Stepanov, Sergei. *Fontanka 16: The Tsar's Secret Police.* Phoenix Mill (England): Sutton, 1999.

Schecter, Jerrold, and Schecter, Leona. *Scared Secrets: How Soviet Intelligence Operations Changed American History.* Dulles, Va.: Brassey's, 2002.

Shevchenko, Arkady. *Breaking With Moscow.* New York: Knopf, 1985.

Smith, Bradley F. *Sharing Secrets with Stalin: How the Allies Traded Intelligence, 1941–1945.* Lawrence: University Press of Kansas, 1996.

Solzhenitsyn, Aleksandr I. *The First Circle.* New York: Harper & Row, 1968.

———. *The Gulag Archipelago* in 3 vols. New York: Harper & Row, 1974–1978.

Suvorov, Viktor. *Inside the Soviet Army.* London: Hamish Hamilton, 1982.

———. *Inside Soviet Military Intelligence.* New York: Macmillan, 1984.

Weinstein, Allen, and Vassiliev, Alexander. *The Haunted Wood: Soviet Espionage in America— The Stalin Era.* New York: Modern Library, 2000.

West, Nigel, and Tsarev, Oleg. *The Crown Jewels: The British Secrets at the Heart of the KGB Archives.* New Haven, Conn.: Yale University Press, 1999.

U.S. INTELLIGENCE

Agee, Philip. *Inside the Company: CIA Diary.* New York: Stonehill, 1975.

Allen, Thomas B. *George Washington, Spymaster: How the Americans Outspied the British and Won the Revolutionary War.* Washington, D.C.: National Geographic, 2004.

Allen, Thomas B., and Polmar, Norman. *Merchants of Treason.* New York: Delacorte, 1988.

Andrew, Christopher. *For the President's Eyes Only: Secret Intelligence and the American Presidency from Washington to Bush.* New York: Harper-Collins, 1995.

Bakeless, John. *Turncoats, Traitors and Heroes.* Philadelphia: Lippincott, 1959.

Bamford, James. *Body of Secrets: Anatomy of the Ultra-Secret National Security Agency.* New York: Random House, 2001.

———. *The Puzzle Palace.* New York: Penguin, 1982.

Beschloss, Michael R. *Mayday: Eisenhower, Khrushchev, and the U-2 Affair.* New York: Harper & Row, 1986.

Breckinridge, Scott D. *The CIA and the U.S. Intelligence System.* Boulder, Colo.: Westview, 1986.

Brugioni, Dino A. *Eyeball to Eyeball: The Inside Story of the Cuban Missile Crisis.* New York: Random House, 1990.

Burleson, Clyde W. *The Jennifer Project.* Englewood Cliffs, N.J.: Prentice-Hall, 1977.

Cline, Dr. Ray S. *The CIA Under Reagan, Bush and Casey.* Washington, D.C.: Acropolis Books, 1981.

———. *Secrets Spies and Scholars: Blueprint of the Essential CIA.* Washington, D.C.: Acropolis Books, 1976.

Cohen, Sen. William S., and Mitchell, Sen. George J. *Men of Zeal.* New York: Viking, 1988.

Cristol, Judge A. Jay. *The Liberty Incident: The 1967 Israeli Attack on the U.S. Navy Spy Ship.* Dulles, Va.: Brassey's, 2002.

Deane, J. Allen, and Shellum, Brian G. (eds.). *At the Creation 1961–1965.* Washington, D.C.: Defense Intelligence Agency, 2002.(Documents related to the establishment of the Defense Intelligence Agency.)

Dorwart, Jeffrey M. *Conflict of Duty.* Annapolis, Md.: Naval Institute Press, 1983.

———. *The Office of Naval Intelligence [1865–1918].* Annapolis, Md.: Naval Institute Press, 1979.

Dunham, Roger C. *Spy Sub: A Top Secret Mission to the Bottom of the Pacific.* Annapolis, Md.: Naval Institute Press, 1996.

Garrow, David J. *FBI and Martin Luther King, Jr., From 'Solo' to Memphis.* New Haven, Conn.: Yale University Press, 2001. New and enlarged reprint of the original 1981 edition.

Gates, Robert M. *From the Shadows.* New York: Simon & Schuster, 1996.

Holmes, Wilfred Jay. *Double-Edged Secrets.* Annapolis, Md.: Naval Institute Press, 1979.

Jeffreys-Jones, Rhodri. *The CIA & American Democracy.* New Haven, Conn.: Yale University Press, 1989.

Kent, Sherman. *Strategic Intelligence of American World Policy.* Princeton: Princeton University Press, 1949.

Kessler, Ronald. *Inside the CIA.* New York: Pocket Books, 1992.

Klehr, Harvey, and Radosh, Ronald. *The Amerasia Spy Case: Prelude to McCarthyism.* Chapel Hill: University of North Carolina Press, 1996.

Lamphere, Robert J., and Shachtman, Thomas. *The FBI–KGB War: A Special Agent's Story.* New York: Random House, 1986.

Lindsey, Robert. *The Falcon and the Snowman.* New York: Pocket Books, 1979.

———. *The Flight of the Falcon.* New York: Pocket Books, 1983.

Maas, Peter. *Killer Spy: The Inside Story of the FBI's Pursuit and Capture of Aldrich Ames, America's Deadliest Spy.* New York: Warner Books, 1995.

Marchetti, Victor I., and Marks, John D. *The CIA and the Cult of Intelligence.* New York: Knopf, 1974.

Marks, John D. *The Search for the "Manchurian Candidate."* New York: Dell, 1988. Reprint of 1979 edition.

Martin, David. *Wilderness of Mirrors.* New York: Harper & Row, 1980.

O'Toole, G.J.A. *Honorable Treachery.* New York: Atlantic Monthly Press, 1991.

Petry, Mark. *Eclipse* New York: Morrow, 1992.

Polmar, Norman. *Spyplane: U-2 History Declassified.* St. Paul, Minn.: MBI Publishing, 2001.

Powers, Francis Gary, and Gentry, Curt. *Operation Overflight: A Memoir of the U-2 Incident.* Dulles, Va.: Brassey's 2004. Reprint of 1970 edition.

Richelson, Jeffrey T. *America's Secret Eye in Space: The U.S. Keyhole Spy Program.* New York: Harper & Row, 1990.

———. *The U.S. Intelligence Community.* Cambridge, Mass.: Ballinger, 1985

———. *The Wizards of Langley: Inside the CIA's Directorate of Science and Technology.* Boulder, Colo.: Westview Press, 2002.

Romerstein, Herbert, and Breindel, Eric. *The Verona Secrets: Exposing Soviet Espionage and America's Traitors.* Washington, D.C.: Regnery, 2000.

Snepp, Frank. *Decent Interval.* New York: Random House, 1977.

Sontag, Sherry, and Drew, Christopher. *Blind Man's Bluff: The Untold Story of American Submarine Espionage.* New York: Public Affairs, 1998.

Steury, Donald P. (ed.). *Sherman Kent and the Board of National Estimates: Collected Essays.* Washington, D.C.: Center for the Study of Intelligence, Central Intelligence Agency, 1994.

Taubman, Philip. *Secret Empire: Eisenhower, the CIA and the Hidden Story of America's Space Espionage.* New York: Simon & Schuster, 2003.

Tourison, Sedwick. *Secret Army War.* Annapolis, Md.: Naval Institute Press, 1995.

Turner, Stansfield. *Secrecy and Democracy: The CIA in Transition.* Boston: Houghton Mifflin, 1985.

Winks, Robin W. *Cloak & Gown: Scholars in the Secret War.* New York: Morrow, 1987.

Wise, David. *Nightmover.* New York: HarperCollins, 1995.

———. *Spy: The Inside Story of How the FBI's Robert Hanssen Betrayed America.* New York: Random House, 2002.

Wise, David, and Ross, Thomas B. *Molehunt: The Secret Search for Traitors That Shattered the CIA.* New York: HarperCollins, 1995.

———. *The U-2 Affair.* New York: Random House, 1962.

Wohlstetter, Roberta. *Pearl Harbor: Warning and Decision.* Palo Alto, Calif.: Stanford University Press, 1963.

Woodward, Bob. *Veil: The Secret Wars of the CIA 1981–1987.* New York: Simon & Schuster, 1987.

Zacharias, Ellis M. *Secret Missions: The Story of an Intelligence Officer.* Annapolis, Md.: Naval Institute Press, 2003. Reprint of 1946 edition.

GENERAL

Becket, Henry S.A. [pseud.]. *The Dictionary of Espionage: Spookspeak into English.* New York: Stein and Day, 1986.

Brook-Shepherd, Gordon. *The Storm Birds.* New York: Weidenfeld & Nicholson, 1989.

Burrows, William E. *Deep Black: The Startling Truth Behind America's Top-Secret Satellites.* New York: Random House, 1986.

Casey, William. *The Secret War Against Hitler.* Washington, D.C.: Regnery Gateway, 1988.

Cave Brown, Anthony. *Bodyguard of Lies.* New York: Bantam, 1975.

Deacon, Richard A. *History of the Chinese Secret Service.* London: Frederick Muller, 1974.

———. *Kempei Tai: The Japanese Secret Service Then and Now.* Rutland, Vt.: Charles E. Tuttle, 1990.

Deriabin, Peter, with Bigney, Frank. *The Secret World.* New York: Ballantine Books (new edition), 1982.

Dulles, Allen W. *The Craft of Intelligence.* New York: Harper & Row, 1963.

Eftimiades, Nicholas. *Chinese Intelligence Operations.* Annapolis, Md.: Naval Institute Press, 1994.

Gaddis, John Lewis. *Now We Know.* New York: Oxford University Press, 1997.

Kahn, David. Hitler's Spies: *German Military Intelligence in World War II.* New York: Macmillan, 1978.

Knightley, Phillip. *The Second Oldest Profession: Spies and Spying in the Twentieth Century.* New York: Norton, 1987.

Lindgren, David T. *Trust but Verify: Imagery Analysis in the Cold War.* Annapolis, Md.: Naval Institute Press, 2000.

Masters, Anthony. *Literary Agents.* Oxford: Basil Blackwell, 1987.

Mercado, Stephen C. *The Shadow Warriors of Nakano: A History of the Imperial Japanese Army's Elite Intelligence School.* Dulles, Va.: Brassey's, 2002.

Mobley, Richard A. *Flash Point North Korea: The Pueblo and EC-121 Crises.* Annapolis, Md.: Naval Institute Press, 2003.

Murphy, David, and Kondrashev, Sergei. *Battleground Berlin.* New Haven, Conn.: Yale University Press, 1997.

Persico, Joseph. *Piercing the Reich.* New York: Ballantine, 1979.

Richelson, Jeffrey T. *Foreign Intelligence Organizations.* Cambridge, Mass.: Ballinger, 1988.

Schecter, Jerrold, and Schecter, Leona. *Scared Secrets: How Soviet Intelligence Operations Changed American History.* Dulles, Va.: Brassey's, 2002.

Stoll, Clifford. *The Cuckoo's Egg.* New York: Doubleday, 1989.

Waller, John H. *The Unseen War in Europe.* New York: Random House, 1997.

West, Nigel. *Unreliable Witness: Espionage Myths of the Second World War.* London: Weidenfeld and Nicholson, 1984. [Published in the United States as *A Thread of Deceit: Espionage Myths of World War II*; New York: Random House, 1985.]

BIOGRAPHIES OF AUTHORS

NORMAN POLMAR has written or coauthored more than 30 books on military, aviation, and intelligence subjects, gaining him international renown. He is the author of several reference books published by the U.S. Naval Institute, and from 1967 to 1977 was the editor of the United States sections of *Jane's Fighting Ships*. He is a columnist for the Naval Institute *Proceedings* and *Naval History* magazines. A defense consultant, Mr. Polmar has been an adviser to several members of Congress, three Secretaries of the Navy, officials of the Department of Defense, foreign governments, and shipbuilding and aerospace firms. In 1977-1978 he held the DeWitt C. Ramsey history chair at the National Air and Space Museum in Washington, D.C.

THOMAS B. ALLEN's highly successful writing career has included the highly acclaimed *War Games* among the dozen books that he has written in addition to his seven collaborations with Norman Polmar. Previously the senior book editor of the National Geographic Society, and before that managing editor of Chilton Books, he has written numerous books for the *National Geographic Magazine*. His articles have appeared in newspapers and magazines throughout the world. Tom Allen has also led international "spy tours."

Both authors have traveled extensively in Russia, China, and Cuba as well as Western and Eastern Europe—the scenes for many of the entries in Spy Book. Both live in the Washington, D.C. area.